SYMBOL	DESCRIPTION
j	Sometimes used to represent subscripts in a double summation: $\sum_{j=1}^{m}\sum_{i=1}^{n} X_{ij} = (X_{11} + X_{21} + \cdots + X_{n1}) + (X_{12} + X_{22} + \cdots + X_{n2}) + (X_{1m} + X_{2m} + \cdots + X_{nm})$
L, L_1, L_2	Contrast used with analysis of variance
L(D)	Unit normal loss function
L_j	Lower limit of class interval
LCL	Lower control limit
$\log \hat{Y}(X)$	Logarithm to base 10 of $\hat{Y}(X)$; used in regression to find curve, $\hat{Y}(X) = ab^x$
λ (lambda)	Mean rate in a Poisson process
λ_A, λ_S	Mean arrival and service rates used in queuing applications
M	(1) Median of population (2) Monetary amount for calculating utility
MSA	Mean square (between columns) in a two-factor analysis of variance
$MSAB$	Interactions mean square; used in two-factor analysis of variance
MSB	Mean square (between rows) in a two-factor analysis of variance
$MSCOL$	Mean square (between columns) in an analysis of variance using a Latin square
MSE	(1) Error mean square; used to calculate the F statistic in analysis of variance (2) Mean squared error in exponential smoothing
MSR	Regression mean square
$MSROW$	Mean square (between rows) in an analysis of variance using a Latin square
$MSTR$	Mean square; used to calculate the F statistic: (1) (between columns) for the treatments in a one-factor analysis of variance (2) (between letters) in a three-factor analysis of variance using a Latin-square design
m	(1) Sample median (2) Number of variables used in multiple regresion and correlation analysis (3) Number of smoothing parameters in exponential smoothing
μ (mu)	Arithmetic mean of a population
μ_0	Value of the population mean assumed under the null hypothesis
μ_0, μ_1	Prior and posterior expected means
$\mu_1, \mu_2, \mu_3, \ldots$	Population means in analysis of variance
$\mu_{11}, \mu_{12}, \ldots$	Means of treatment combination populations; used in analysis of variance
$\mu_{\cdot 1}, \mu_{1\cdot}, \mu_{\cdot\cdot}$	Population means for factors or overall; used in analysis of variance
μ_b	Breakeven level for mean
μ_A, μ_B	Means of populations A and B, which are compared using two samples

SYMBOL	DESCRIPTION
$\mu_{Y \cdot X}$	Conditional mean for Y for a specified value of X; used in regression analysis, where $\mu_{Y \cdot X}$ represents the height of the true regression line
$\mu_{Y \cdot 12}$	Conditional mean for values of Y for specified values of X_1 and X_2; used in multiple regression analysis, where $\mu_{Y \cdot 12}$ represents the height of the true regression plane
N	Number of observations in a population
n	(1) Number of observations in a sample (2) Number of trials in a Bernoulli process
$n!$	n factorial, or the product $n \times (n-1) \times (n-2) \times \cdots \times 2 \times 1$
n_A, n_B	Sample sizes for two-sample tests comparing the parameters of two populations A and B
n_a, n_b	Number of observations of type a and type b obtained in a sample; applicable to the number-of-runs test
$O_1, O_2 \ldots$	Outcomes in a decision structure
P	(1) Proportion of sample observations having a particular characteristic (2) Proportion of successes from a Bernoulli process
$\Pr[A]$	Probability of event A
$\Pr[A\|B]$	Conditional probability of A given B
$\Pr[A \text{ and } B]$	Probability of the intersection of events A and B; event occurs only when both A and B occur (also called the joint probability)
$\Pr[A \text{ or } B]$	Probability of the union of A and B; occurs when either A or B occurs, or when both A and B occur
$\Pr[X = x]$	Probability that the random variable X assumes one of several particular values
$\Pr[X \leq x]$	Cumulative probability that X assumes any value less than or equal to X
P^*	Critical value for P
P_A, P_B	Proportions of observations having a particular characteristic for samples from populations A and B
P_C	Combined sample proportion; used to compare two population proportions
P_r^n	Number of permutations of r items taken from a collection of size n when different orders of selection are counted
$\bar{P}$	Combined sample proportion
p_n, p_0	Prices per unit of an item in year n and in base period 0; used to find index numbers
π (pi)	(1) Proportion of a population having a particular characteristic (2) Probability of a trial success in a Bernoulli process
π_0	Value of the population proportion assumed under the null hypothesis
$\pi_1, \pi_2, \pi_3, \ldots$	Values of population proportions in testing for equality of several population proportions

Statistics for Modern Business Decisions

SIXTH EDITION

Statistics for Modern Business Decisions

SIXTH EDITION

LAWRENCE L. LAPIN
San Jose State University

THE DRYDEN PRESS
Harcourt Brace Jovanovich College Publishers
Fort Worth Philadelphia San Diego New York Orlando Austin San Antonio
Toronto Montreal London Sydney Tokyo

Editor in Chief Robert A. Pawlik
Acquisitions Editor Scott Isenberg
Developmental Editor Millicent Treloar
Project Editor Jim Patterson
Production Manager Alison J. Howell
Designer Brian Salisbury
Permissions Editor Van Strength

Cover © M.C. Escher/Cordon Art—Baarn—Holland

Address for Editorial Correspondence
The Dryden Press, 301 Commerce Street, Suite 3700, Fort Worth, TX 76102

Address for Orders
The Dryden Press, 6277 Sea Harbor Drive, Orlando, FL 32887
1-800-782-4479, or 1-800-433-0001 (in Florida)

ISBN: 0-15-500004-7

Library of Congress Catalog Number: 92-70669

Printed in the United States of America

3 4 5 6 7 8 9 0 1 2   0 6 9   9 8 7 6 5 4 3 2 1

The Dryden Press
Harcourt Brace Jovanovich

THE DRYDEN PRESS SERIES IN MANAGEMENT SCIENCE AND QUANTITATIVE METHODS

Forgionne
Quantitative Management

Freed
Basic Business Statistics

Gaither
Production and Operations Management
Fifth Edition

Glaskowsky, Hudson, and Ivie
Business Logistics
Third Edition

Hamburg
Statistical Analysis For Decision Making
Fifth Edition

Ingram and Monks
Statistics for Business and Economics
Second Edition

Lapin
Statistics for Modern Business Decisions
Sixth Edition

Lapin
Quantitative Methods for Business Decisions with Cases
Fifth Edition

Lee
Introduction to Management Science
Second Edition

Mason, Lind, and Marchal
Statistics: An Introduction
Third Edition

Miller and Wichern
Intermediate Business Statistics

Weiers
Introduction to Business Statistics

Zikmund
Business Research Methods
Third Edition

THE HBJ COLLEGE OUTLINE SERIES

Lapin
Business Statistics

Pentico
Management Science

Rothenberg
Probability and Statistics

Tanis
Statistics I: Descriptive Statistics and Probability

Tanis
Statistics II: Estimation and Tests of Hypothesis

PREFACE

In writing this introductory statistics book for students of business and economics, my overriding goal has been to enliven statistics, to make it more interesting, relevant, and easier to learn. It is no secret that today's student too often finds statistics boring and irrelevant and more difficult than necessary. Reflecting the evolution of statistical methodology, a *new goal* has been incorporated into this *sixth edition* that gives proper coverage of *exploratory data analysis.* This topic, along with descriptive and inferential statistics, is treated as essential to everyone's understanding of statistics.

To illustrate that statistics is really interesting and relevant, this book treats it as essentially a decision-making tool and includes many modern concepts and applications. All topics are introduced by carefully chosen examples that illustrate more than technical mathematical concepts. The stage is set, the motivation is provided, and the rationale is given as each new concept is presented. Accordingly, the importance of inferences is highlighted when a statistics professor compares the effectiveness of a new textbook with the book she currently uses. Testing for the equality of several proportions, an ad agency wishes to determine whether there are any differences in terms of reader recall among three different kinds of magazine advertisements. The fact that sampling is just one source of potential error is emphasized by detailing some of the blunders committed in taking the U.S. Decennial Census. Many of the examples and exercises are clearly related to present-day issues, such as health, conservation, and the environment. Several examples of each major area of business and economics—such as accounting, marketing, finance, production, forecasting, and consumer behavior—serve to richly illustrate the applications of statistics.

A course in high school algebra is the only background required. And although this book should prove more accessible than most, the relevant nature of its presentation has not been achieved at the cost of avoiding reputedly difficult material. Probability, hypothesis testing, and other more difficult topics receive generous explanation, often from several viewpoints. The reader is encouraged to rely more on intuition than on rote memory; less than the customary emphasis is placed on the mechanical and computational aspects of statistics. Purely mathematical symbology has been minimized; for example, instead of the Boolean cup and bowl notation, the italicized *and* and *or* are used in describing probability concepts.

This sixth edition introduces several major improvements in presentation. The book's original character of being easy to use is enhanced by chapter opening lists titled "Before reading this chapter, make sure you understand" and "After reading this chapter, you will understand"; the former concisely itemizes prerequisite concepts that the reader should understand before reading; the latter poses major *questions* that the reader will want to answer while reading the chapter. The *answers* to the opening questions are given in the reformatted end-of-chapter *summary.* Most chapters have a "Real-Life Statistical Challenge" section, followed by questions, and a "Statistics in Practice" problem set, both of which feature *real data.* These new course enrichment features are more challenging and less rigidly structured than the regular exercises and complement end-of-chapter *cases.* Computer applications are more prominent, with expanded coverage given to *Minitab.*

The sixth edition is the most extensively revised ever. New examples illustrate key concepts. Stock buying decisions give added flavor to the concept of variance, which serves as a *measure of risk* as well as a measure of dispersion. An expanded section on sampling and random variables employs *repeated* sampling experiments to give credence to the central limit theorem. *More diagrams* are used. *More real data* serve to introduce concepts. For example, baseball superstar performance statistics are used, not only to add perspective for understanding basic regression and correlation concepts, but also to make statistics *more interesting and relevant.*

To facilitate these changes, some chapters have been revamped. An expanded Chapter 1, "About Statistics," includes coverage of the basic ideas of data analysis. The descriptive statistics in Chapter 2 includes many *more data display types.* Chapter 3, which presents statistical measures (mean, etc.), has been *streamlined* to facilitate data analysis as well as traditional statistics. Chapter 5 now has a shorter and dramatically *simplified probability* discussion that gives only the essentials. (No probability topics have been lost in the shuffle; the more difficult material has been relocated later in the book.) Time-series in Chapter 12 now includes *seasonal* exponential smoothing. A *model-building* segment has been added to multiple regression (Chapter 11), and a discussion of *stepwise multiple regression* procedures has been included.

The sixth edition has been reorganized by grouping the chapters into coherent parts.

Part I Basic Statistical Concepts
Part II Drawing Conclusions from Samples: Inferential Statistics
Part III Important Business Applications of Statistics
Part IV Further Topics in Inferential Statistics
Part V Probability Applications for Business Analysis
Part VI Decision Analysis

Parts I and II provide the key concepts for introductory courses. Part III houses the important business applications—time series, quality control, and index numbers—which now appear *earlier* in the book. Advanced inference topics are positioned in Part IV, facilitating the picking and choosing of course materials. To that end, further probability topics are now grouped into Part V, conveniently arranged so that instructors can separate probability material, making it easier to *customize* and *enrich* courses. The more challenging counting methods and Bayes' theorem are discussed here in the new Chapter 20. Chapter 21 covers subjective probability, a topic of broad interest whose relocation should make it more accessible. Chapter 22 presents further probability distributions, now separated from goodness-of-fit testing in Chapter 23. As in previous editions, decision theory appears at the back of the book, in Part VI, a convenient placement for the many instructors who use some of those topics in a second statistics course. This segment includes new material on Bayesian sampling with the mean (Chapter 28) and utility theory (Chapter 29). *Users of earlier editions will find a detailed synopsis of the book's major changes in the Instructor's Manual.*

Many new problems have been added, and a number of the original ones have been updated or modified. Most sections within chapters have their own problem sets, permitting the student to relate the questions easily to the concepts just covered. This arrangement also gives the instructor flexibility in picking topics within a chapter. All problems are graded, so that each set begins with easy exercises and increases in difficulty. As a further improvement, much of the statistical jargon and notation has been simplified. All of these changes should make the book easier to use and to teach from.

The book has been thoroughly class tested in a variety of circumstances and courses in many colleges and universities. The experience of hundreds of instructors has been drawn upon in writing this sixth edition.

The modern flavor of the book is enhanced by the expanded computer coverage. Great care has been taken not to tie this book too closely to any particular software or computer. It can still be used *without* computers, and all passages involving computers are primarily of an enrichment nature and are strictly *optional.* The exercises have been expanded to include *optional* computer problems having data sets too large to be reasonably solved by hand.

An examination of the table of contents reveals that there is much to choose from in this book. The chapters have been constructed to make it easy for the instructor to design a course to fit individual needs. Classical statistics has not been mixed with statistical decision theory—this book may be used with either emphasis. Many modern texts supplant classical statistics; both the old and the new are available here. Overall, the presentation is familiar except for the inclusion of several topics omitted from most texts. Chapter 15 considers two-sample inferences. Chapters 16, 17, and 18 discuss analysis of variance and chi-square applications. Chapter 17 includes several probability distributions—the hypergeometric, Poisson, exponential, and uniform. These may be conveniently omitted or incorporated in a course without loss of continuity. Chapter 19 contains some nonparametric statistics most useful for business applications. The Bayesian decision-making procedures of Chapters 24–29 emphasize decision trees; much of the symbology and terminology of decision theory is avoided to allow a simpler and more pragmatic presentation. The chapters on so-called Bayesian methods have been used primarily to extend statistics to areas where classical procedures have proved inadequate in analyzing decisions under uncertainty.

A glossary of statistical symbols is provided on the endpapers for easy reference. Abbreviated answers to all even-numbered exercises are included in the back of the book. Complete solutions to all exercises are available in the Instructor's Manual, and nearly 200 additional exercises and more than 600 examination questions and their solutions are available in a Testbook. The Instructor's Manual also provides teaching suggestions and hints on structuring courses. A *Study Guide* containing more than 200 solved problems is also available for student use as a workbook.

Also available to accompany this book is the *Guide to EasyStat,* a computer manual that incorporates a complete software package called *EasyStat,* all included on a diskette that comes inside every manual. *EasyStat* is a user-friendly program for any IBM PC-compatible system. The computer manual is keyed to the text and contains its own detailed examples and hundreds of problems. A special feature of *EasyStat* is a master data set comprising U.S. Decennial data for 1,000 urban employed homeowners. Students can select their own random samples from 14 different categories and analyze them separately. Class results can be pooled to illustrate concepts of sampling error.

The new end-of-chapter features, "Real-Life Statistical Challenge" and "Statistics in Practice," were written by my colleague, Jerome Burstein, of San Jose State University. I wish to thank Jerry for helping to make my book more relevant, interesting, and functional. I am greatly indebted to the many people who have assisted me in preparing this book. Special thanks go to Janet Anaya of San Jose State

University, who carefully checked the manuscript for accuracy. I also wish to thank my colleagues whose comments were invaluable in setting the tone and the reviewers of this edition: Raymond J. Ballard, East Texas State University; Roger Even Bove, West Chester University; Douglas P. Dotterweich, East Tennessee State University; Jim Knudsen, Creighton University; and Richard M. Smith, Bryant College.

Finally, thanks go to the book team at The Dryden Press: Scott Isenberg, acquisitions editor; Millicent Treloar, developmental editor; Jim Patterson, project editor; Alison J. Howell, production manager; and Brian Salisbury, designer.

I am deeply grateful to my students, who over many years of debugging the book helped identify the problems a reader might face.

Lawrence L. Lapin

CONTENTS

PART I

BASIC STATISTICAL CONCEPTS

CHAPTER 1

ABOUT STATISTICS

AFTER READING THIS CHAPTER, YOU WILL UNDERSTAND:

The meaning of "statistics."
The role of data in statistics.
Data classifications and the basic statistical building block.
The distinctions between the population and the sample.
The types of statistical data.
Two essential types of modern statistical methodology.

Statistics plays a major role in modern lives. It is impossible to read a newspaper or watch television news without encountering statistical information, such as the latest presidential approval percentage, the present month's annual inflation rate, the level of the Dow Jones Industrial Stock Index, or the drop in SAT scores. It is obvious that such statistics permeate the decision-making process. Presidents and other politicians make crucial policies based on the latest opinion poll results. The U.S. Federal Reserve System bases far-reaching monetary policy choices on trends in inflation, while important investors continually monitor their actions, which are anticipated by stock prices. SAT scores serve as a barometer for assessing the quality of public education, affecting not only daily policy but school board elections and local taxing decisions.

We are all affected by statistical information, and some truly informed people are immersed in statistics. Regardless of your chosen career path, your educational experience will be greatly enhanced by knowing how to look beyond everyday numbers and how to generate and report statistical information. Such knowledge will enable you to cope with the unavoidable potential for errors that underlie so much survey information. Through study of statistics you will become aware of the opportunity for statistical misapplications—ranging from unintentional bias to manipulation or fraud. You will also become familiar with the tremendous opportunities that a statistical approach can offer investigators and decision makers.

1-1 THE MEANING OF STATISTICS

Although the word "statistics" commonly brings to mind masses of numbers, graphs, and tables, these play a limited role in modern statistics, in which the focus is placed on *making decisions in the face of uncertainty.* This book describes some of the more useful methods and procedures that can be applied to numerical evidence to facilitate decision making in the face of uncertainty. Certain basic principles are explained within a theoretical framework to enable you to achieve a greater appreciation and understanding of how and why they work.

A concise statement summarizing the subject of this book is the

DEFINITION: **Statistics** is a body of methods and theory that is applied to numerical evidence when making decisions in the face of uncertainty.

This definition treats statistics as a separate academic field, just like physics, history, or biology. As a discipline, statistics has advanced rapidly during the twentieth century to become recognized as a branch of mathematics.

Partly due to the relative newness of statistics as a subject of study, the word *statistics* has acquired several meanings. In its earlier and most common usage, statistics means a collection of numerical facts or data. In sports, for example, batting averages, rushing yardage, and games won or lost are all statistics. Closing prices from the New York Stock Exchange, figures showing sources of income and expenditures for the federal budget, and distances between major cities are also statistics. Your reported income on last year's tax return is a statistic. Examples of this usage are the **vital statistics**—figures on births, deaths, marriages, and divorces—and the contents of publications listing population and economic data, such as the *Statistical Abstract of the United States.* The main distinction

STATISTICS AROUND US

From the Bushman to the Space Scientist

Everyone—from such remote people as the Bushman in Africa's Kalihari desert to space scientists who plan grand tours of the planets—uses statistics. A successful Bushman locates water in a manner that puzzles some geologists. He sucks through a reed stuck in the sand in what his experience tells him is a likely spot, as if he were drinking a thick milkshake from a straw. Sometimes no water is found, but often enough the Bushman does find a "drink hole." His very survival depends on his skill at locating drink holes—on using his experience to cope with uncertainty.

Similarly, scientists depend on experience to determine an optimal space-vehicle configuration that will withstand the rigors of an environment far more hostile than earth's atmosphere and that will survive long enough to fly past Jupiter and eventually to even more distant planets. If the communications system fails, the mission itself will be a failure. The system must be super-reliable—designed so that its chances for survival are high. Millions of hours of human experience can contribute to design decisions. Even so, there are no guarantees that the chosen design will function as intended. Again, decisions must be made in the face of uncertainty.

Both the Bushman's and the space scientist's mechanisms for making choices utilize limited experience, and in this respect they are not substantially different. The remaining element that makes their mechanisms statistical is that *both use numerical evidence.* To evaluate the reliability of communications equipment, components must be tested under stress to determine the number of hours they can function before failing. The scientist's evidence is numerical. But what about the Bushman's? He knows that one set of conditions favors the presence of water more than another. Every wet hole reinforces his knowledge of factors that are positive to water, and each dry hole strengthens his awareness of the negative factors. Thus, the Bushman's numerical evidence is the *frequency* of successful drink holes he finds under various prevailing conditions. Even though the presence of water is a qualitative factor, frequencies of occurrence are themselves numerical.

between our definition of statistics and this usage of the word is its form: singular versus plural. Statistics (singular) *is* a subject of study; statistics (plural) *are* numerical facts.

THE ROLE OF STATISTICS

Our definition of statistics is particularly appropriate for readers who are primarily interested in applications to business and economics, where there is a high incidence of decisions made under uncertainty. Business decisions involving both numerical data and uncertainty are encountered at all levels of business. Consider the following list:

The Decision Maker	The Decision	The Uncertainty
Manager	Whom to hire	Employee performance
Planner	Facility locations	Volume needed
CEO	Set policies for:	
	Pricing	Demands
	New products	Market shares
	Financing	Costs
Federal Reserve	Interest rate targets	Effect on:
		Inflation
		Employment
		Growth
Sales manager	Customer communication	Order size
Investor	Stock to buy	Rate of return

TYPES OF STATISTICS: DESCRIPTIVE, INFERENTIAL, AND EXPLORATORY

The emphasis on the decision-making aspects of statistics is a recent one. In its early years, the study of statistics consisted of methodology for summarizing or describing statistical data.

DESCRIPTIVE STATISTICS

This area is known as **descriptive statistics** because it is concerned with summary calculations and graphical displays, such as those in Figure 1-1. Descriptive statistics is often just a small part of two more sophisticated types of statistics: inferential and exploratory.

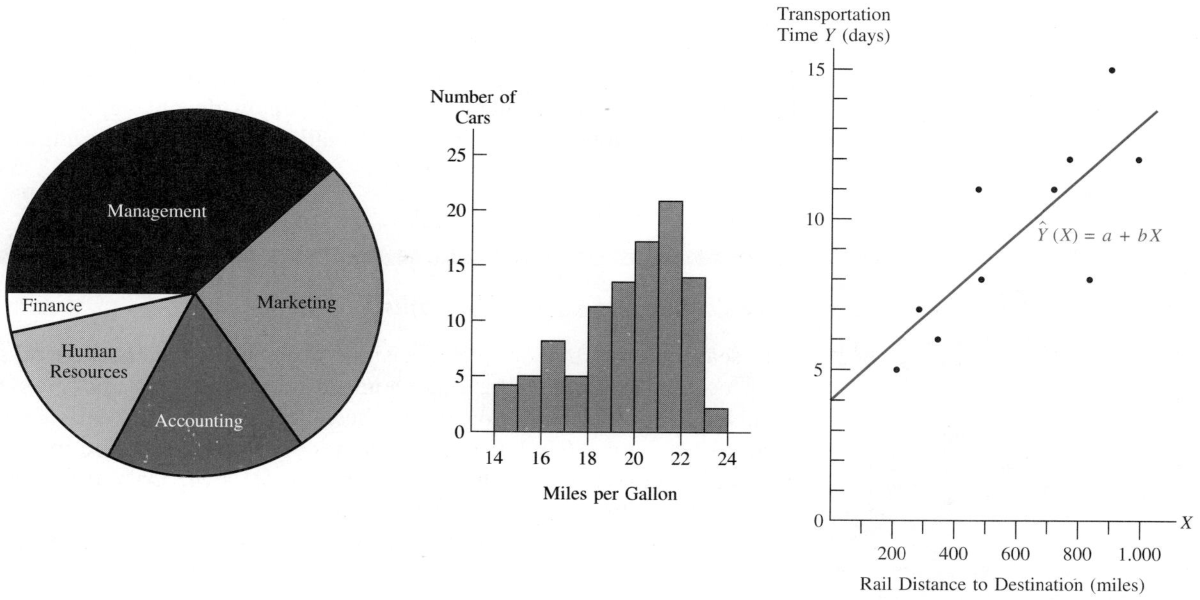

FIGURE 1-1 Graphical displays to describe statistical data.

Inferential Statistics

Descriptive statistics contrasts with the modern statistical approach in which generalizations are made about the whole (called the **population**) by investigating a portion (referred to as the **sample**). Thus, the average income of *all* families in the United States can be estimated from figures obtained from a *few hundred* families. Such a prediction or estimate is an example of an inference. The study of how inferences are made from numerical data is called **inferential statistics**.

Inferential statistics acknowledges the potential for error in making generalizations from a sample. This still does not guarantee that correct conclusions will be reached, since samples may deviate from the underlying population. Such discrepancies are called **sampling errors**. But sampling errors may be insignificant when sampling is done randomly. Statisticians use **probability** to assess the likelihood of making large sampling errors.

Inferential statistics acknowledges that the potential for error exists in making generalizations from a sample. Because of the important role it plays in statistical inference, we will discuss probability in Chapter 5, after we examine descriptive statistics for populations having *known* properties. This will prepare us for developing statistical inferences about populations whose characteristics are *unknown*. Our formal definition for the field of statistics applies to both its descriptive and its inferential forms. This book emphasizes inferential statistics because it can play such a dynamic role in decision making. But first we will focus on descriptive statistics in Chapters 2 and 3.

Exploratory Data Analysis

For many years statistical procedures have been classified primarily as either descriptive statistics or inferential statistics. The borders between those original statistical realms are becoming blurred, as a third major statistical area, **exploratory data analysis**, has evolved. This newer statistical methodology makes heavy use of descriptive statistics while extending statistical procedures beyond their traditional forms. Exploratory data analysis is not limited to circumstances that are conveniently explained by probability theory and need not, therefore, be based on convenient models that simply do not apply. Data analysis allows investigators the freedom to systematically utilize small samples and "ill-

STATISTICS AROUND US

Television Programming and Statistics

The seasonal controversy over decisions made by television networks to drop certain programs illustrates some of the principles and problems involved. The information on which these decisions are based is obtained from a sample of a few hundred TV viewers who are believed to be a representative microcosm of the viewing public at large. Only those shows indicated by the sample to be most popular are allowed to continue. Although articulate segments of the public complain that their tastes are not represented, the agency responsible for the collection of sample data has demonstrated that its audience is selected in accordance with accepted scientific sampling procedures.

behaved" data in reaching meaningful conclusions, even if the conclusions would not otherwise qualify within the known inferential framework.

Throughout this book opportunities will be explored for using exploratory statistics to complement traditional methods.

EXERCISES

1-1 For each of the following decisions, give an example of potential numerical data that might be helpful in making the choice.
(a) in which magazine to place an ad
(b) where to locate the pet food in a supermarket
(c) screening job applicants
(d) number of retail feet for gifts in a card shop

1-2 Consider the following numerical data. Suggest for each a decision situation where the data might be used in reaching a choice.
(a) batting averages of players on your favorite softball team
(b) earnings per share for companies in an industry
(c) average starting salaries for students in various majors
(d) examination scores from two statistics classes taught by different methods

1-3 From the first section of your favorite newspaper, identify four instances of numerical data which may be used for making a decision under uncertainty.
(a) List each item.
(b) Indicate for each example (1) the potential decision maker, (2) what choices might be considered, and (3) the uncertainties involved.

1-2 STATISTICAL DATA

A collection of data is referred to as a **data set**. To illustrate, consider the following daily temperatures (low, high) reported at 10 P.M. by a Channel 11 weather forecaster.

(52,73)	(47,81)	(55,79)	(57,75)	(46,80)
(56,64)	(54,73)	(52,77)	(53,72)	(49,69)

Each of the above temperature pairs applies to a single location. They are the elements of the data set referred to as **data points**.

A statistical evaluation usually involves one or more **variables**. In the above set the daily *high* temperature is one variable. A second variable is the daily *low* temperature. From those two, a third variable, the daily temperature *range*, may be determined.

CLASSIFICATIONS FOR DATA AND VARIABLES

Data sets involve two classes of data. **Quantitative data** involve numerical values. To illustrate, consider the data sets in Figure 1-2 representing the current payrolls of three Central City employers. Hourly rates of pay and the hours worked are quantitative data. Each employee record constitutes a data point, with the amounts and specific types varying among employers. The second class of

Ace Widgets

Name	Born	SS#	Class.	Hours	Rate	Exemps . . . .
.						
Adams, A.	10/65	521-48-0237	DB	42	11.25	02 . . .
.						
.						

DanDee Assemblers

SOC SEC	NAME	GRP	RATE	HRS	COM . . . .
	.				
471-22-1189	B. Johnson	H	8.50	37.5	25.50 . . .
	.				
	.				

Central City

Dept	Name	ID	Hrly	Hours . . .
	.			
Power	Smith T.	9258	11.35	46 . . .
	.			
	.			

FIGURE 1-2 Data sets for hourly worker payrolls of three Central City empployers.

data is **qualitative data**. The payroll data include employee department or classification and are examples of qualitative data, which is ordinarily categorical in nature.

A variable need not be limited to a single data set. Following the same designations as the respective data type, a variable may be either quantitative (hourly pay) or qualitative (sex, classification). Levels for quantitative variables are called **variates**. In the payroll data, the hourly earnings (dollars per hour) for the three persons listed are \$11.25, 8.50, and 11.35. The counterparts to level for a qualitative variable are **attributes** or **categories**. For those same persons, the employee classification (or group or department) variable lists attributes DB, H, and Power.

TYPES OF QUANTITATIVE DATA

Four types of quantitative data are encountered in statistical investigations.

1. **Nominal data** arise when numbers are used to represent categories or attributes. Such values often arise when information is coded for data processing. Thus, a university might designate majors by numbers, so that a 5 might apply to an accounting student, a 37 for finance, and a 51 for marketing. Such data should not be treated as numerical, since relative size has no meaning.

2. **Ordinal data** are often encountered when items are ranked by importance, strength, or severity. One example is provided by the Beaufort wind scale, which assigns numbers to wind forces at sea. A gentle breeze is rated at 3, a strong breeze at 6, and a strong gale at 9. The increasing severity of winds is reflected by the Beaufort numbers, so that 3 is less than 6, since gentle breezes are less forceful than strong ones, while 6 lies below 9 because strong breezes

are weaker than strong gales. Simple arithmetic operations are not meaningfully applied to ordinal data. Even though $6 - 3 = 3$ and $9 - 6 = 3$, it would be wrong to conclude that the increase in wind severity between a gentle and a strong breeze is identical to the change in force between a strong breeze and a strong gale.

3. **Interval data** provide ranking, and the arithmetic operations of addition and subtraction are meaningful. For example, each degree level on the Celsius temperature scale reflects that a constant amount of heat is necessary to raise the temperature of water one notch, regardless of the starting level. Thus, the same amount of heat is used to raise water from 30 to 40 as from 60 to 70, since $40 - 30 = 10$ and $70 - 60 = 10$ are the same differences. But 0, achieved at the freezing point of distilled water, is arbitrarily chosen. (The Fahrenheit scale has a zero defined differently.) Thus, 60 is not twice as hot as 30, and the ratio 60/30 has no meaning.
4. **Ratio data** allow for all basic arithmetic operations, including division and multiplication. Typical business data, such as revenue, cost, and profit fall into this group. Physical measurements and time increments are usually ratio data.

Most statistical procedures are based on arithmetic operations, limiting them to applications involving interval or ratio data. A limited class of statistical methods may be used with ordinal data. With nominal data, statistics is primarily concerned with counting frequencies of occurrence.

EXERCISES

1-4 Publications, such as *Business Week, Fortune,* and *Forbes,* contain data sets. Find an example of a data set. Then do the following.
(a) Identify the data points.
(b) Determine useful variables, indicating whether each is quantitative or qualitative. Identify for that data point the level or attribute for each variable found.

1-5 Give an example of each of the following data types.
(a) nominal (c) interval
(b) ordinal (d) ratio

1-6 Indicate for each of the following situations which of the four types of quantitative data applies.
(a) Survey questions that ask you to scale a product from 1 (extremely poor) to 10 (absolutely wonderful).
(b) ZIP codes used in sorting mail.
(c) Richter scale used to express earthquake energy.
(d) Supermarket checkout times.
(e) Daily high temperatures.

1-3 THE POPULATION AND THE SAMPLE

The basic element of statistics is an **observation**; it represents what we actually see. An observation may be a physical measurement (weight or height), an answer to a question (yes or no), or a classification (defective or nondefective). Observations relevant to a particular decision constitute a **population**. Stated more formally, we have the following

DEFINITION: A statistical **population** is the collection of all possible observations of one or more variables.

In most applications we will encounter, the population will ordinarily involve a single variable. But a population may be *multi-dimensional*. As with variables, populations may be quantitative, qualitative, or even both (when there is more than one dimension).

Note that a statistical population exists whether all, some, or none of the possible observations are actually made. It may be real (such as the height of 30-year-old males in Schenectady in June 1992) or hypothetical (such as the longevity of laboratory rats fed a special diet that is not yet widely used). Because it consists of all possible observations, a population is often referred to synonymously as a **universe**.

In contrast to the statistical population, which consists of all possible observations, the **sample** contains only some of the observations. We make the following

DEFINITION: A **sample** is a collection of observations representing only a portion of the population.

DISTINGUISHING BETWEEN THE DATA SET, POPULATION, AND SAMPLE

The statistical population and sample may encompass portions of several data sets. Figure 1-3 may be helpful in sorting things out. There we consider the population of hourly pay rates for all workers in the Central City area. Every payroll in town applies, so that numerous data sets are needed to define the population data. Although the individual data points involve other types of information, only the hourly pay from each applies to the population of interest. The number of elementary units in a population can involve fewer data points than the entire data set. That would be the case if an investigator were interested in wages of only a portion of the city workers—for instance, just the employees of the Power Department.

The population consists of all the possible observations that might be made. It exists whether or not those observations are actually made. (It may be too expensive to gather all of the population data.) The sample contains just a portion of the population observations. The levels of the variable are actually found for each sample observation.

Thus, the population is usually not totally *known* (but it will be precisely *defined*). Only the sample observations are actually made. The sample results are the basis for making generalizations about the population.

Statistical methodology is mainly concerned with evaluating sample information. Ordinarily, only a few randomly chosen observations are made, and the resulting sample then provides information for drawing conclusions about the population. A population can even exist in theory only, and only the sample observations would then be real. Such a grouping is called a **target population**. Testing situations give rise to target populations. For example, attitude toward a prototype package design might be determined only for a sample group, unless that design is later chosen for final product distribution.

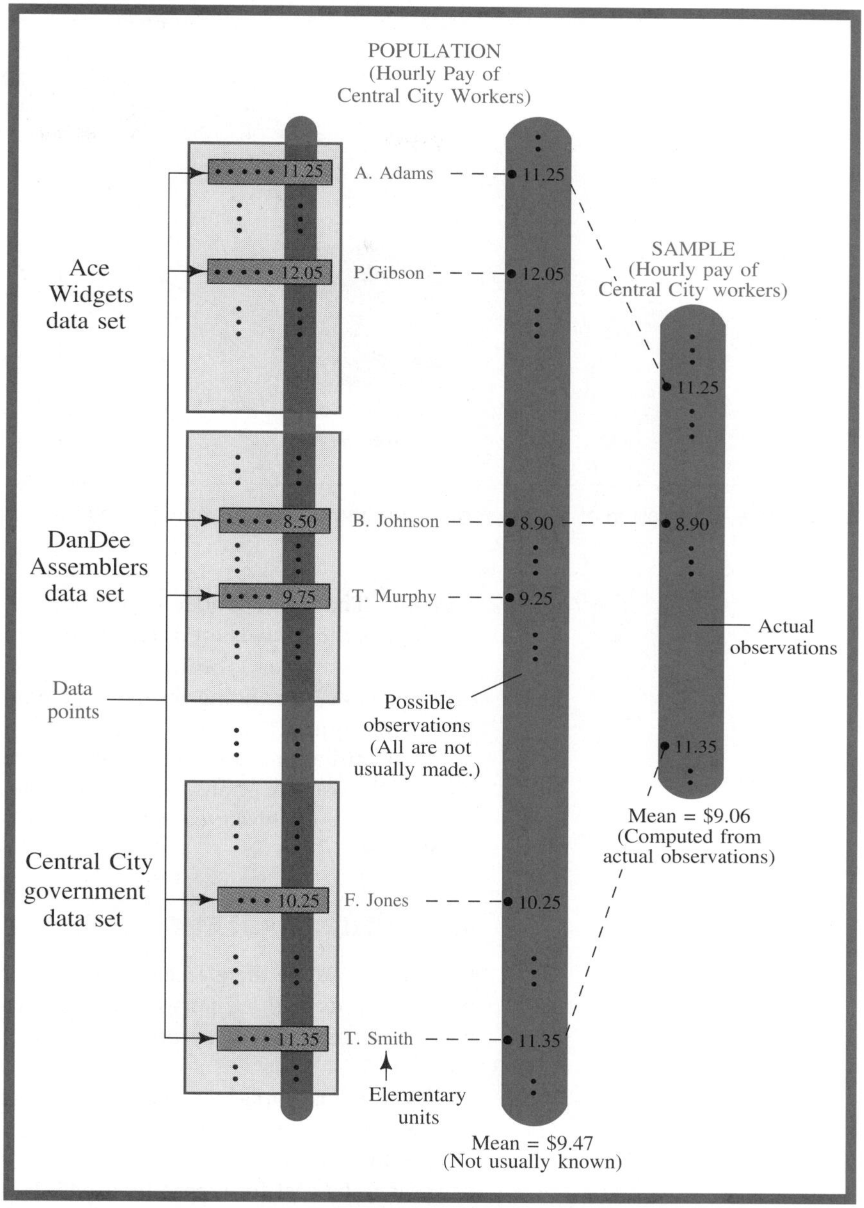

FIGURE 1-3 Relationship between data sets, the population, and the sample.

ELEMENTARY UNITS

A statistical population consists of **observations** of some characteristic of interest associated with the individuals concerned, *not* the individual items or persons themselves. Suppose that the state legislature needs to know the hourly wages of Central City workers in order to analyze proposed changes in labor laws. To find these, the employee records for all companies might be searched and the wages determined. Each number obtained constitutes an observation of the wage

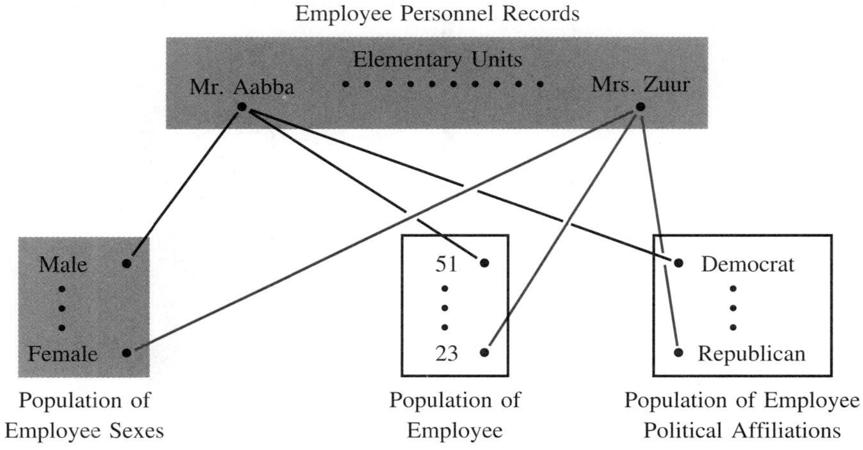

FIGURE 1-4 Illustration of how several different populations may be obtained from the same elementary units.

variable. The entire collection of numbers so obtained is the population; the employees themselves are referred to as the **elementary units** of the population.

A limitless variety of different populations may be obtained from the same elementary units, depending on the characteristic of interest. This principle is illustrated in Figure 1-4. Thus, a company could have different populations for political affiliation, sex, marital status, years of education, height, weight, eye color, job classifications, and years on present job, where each population is composed of observed characteristics of the same elementary units—the employees.

WORKING POPULATION AND THE FRAME

How do we define the elementary units of a population? The employer can define the employees as those persons on the payroll, so that the names of all employees may be obtained from payroll records. Such a source of elementary units is called a **frame**.

The frame is important in statistical studies because it helps to define the population. Suppose that a sample of voter preference toward candidates is taken to predict the outcome of an election. The sample should represent the population of votes to be cast for a specific office. In selecting the sample of voters, the only frame available to the opinion surveyor is the roll of registered voters. The elementary units listed in this frame may differ from those of the population, because some people who are registered will not vote. The votes that would be cast if all those who are registered voted constitute the **working population**, because its frame is the only one currently available. The sample must be drawn from this population.

QUALITATIVE AND QUANTITATIVE POPULATIONS

As with the variables used to define them, populations may be **quantitative** or **qualitative**. In our presentation of statistics, we will discuss these two kinds of populations separately but in parallel. Different methods are required to describe

TABLE 1-1 Illustration of Possible Observations for Various Quantitative and Qualitative Populations

Quantitative Population Observations

Elementary Unit	Characteristic of Interest	Unit of Measurement	Possible Variate
person	age	years	21.3 yr
microcircuit	defective solder joints	number	5
tire	remaining tread	millimeters	10 mm
account balance	amount	dollars	$5,233.46
employer	female employees	percent	35%
common stock	earnings per share	dollars	$3.49
operator	errors	proportion	.02
light bulb	lifetime	hours	581 hr
can of food	weight of contents	ounces	15.3 oz

Qualitative Population Observations

Elementary Unit	Characteristic of Interest	Possible Attributes
person	sex	male, female
security	type	bond, common stock, preferred stock
building	exterior materials	brick, wood, aluminum
employee	experience	applicable, not applicable
television	quality	defective, nondefective
firm	legal status	corporation, partnership, proprietorship
patient	condition	satisfactory, critical
student	residence	on-campus, off-campus

and summarize each type of population: Arithmetic operations can be performed on numbers, so that, for example, we can calculate the average height of a collection of 30-year-old men; other procedures must be employed to summarize a qualitative population.

We refer to a particular observation of a qualitative variable as an **attribute** or category. Thus, for the variable marital status we might observe any one of the following attributes: single, married, divorced, or widowed. An observation of a quantitative variable such as hourly wage will be a particular numerical value or **variate**, such as $8.40, 12.15, or 10.50. Table 1-1 presents examples of observations from various quantitative populations.

DEDUCTIVE AND INDUCTIVE STATISTICS

An important dichotomy underlies statistical reasoning. This concept is illustrated in Figure 1-5, in which two kinds of sampling situations with coins are presented.

Deductive Statistics

Deduction ascribes properties to the specific, starting with the general. For example, probability tells us that if a person is chosen by lottery from a group containing nine men and one woman, then the odds against picking the woman are 9 to 1. We deduce that in about 90 percent of such samples the person will be male. The use of probability to determine the chance of obtaining a particular kind of sample result is known as **deductive statistics**.

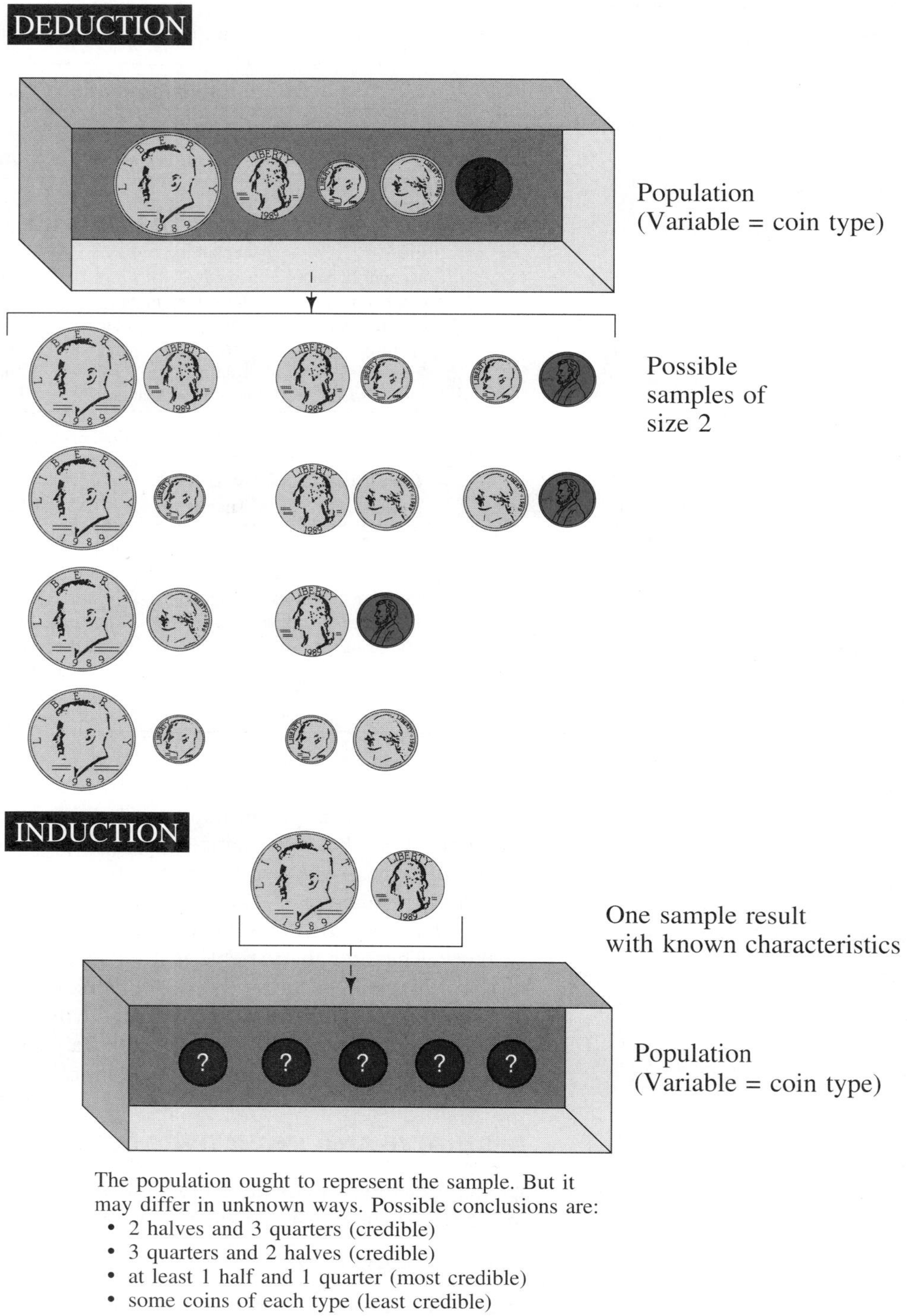
DEDUCTION
Population
(Variable = coin type)
Possible
samples of
size 2
INDUCTION
One sample result
with known characteristics
?
?
?
?
?
Population
(Variable = coin type)
The population ought to represent the sample. But it may differ in unknown ways. Possible conclusions are:
• 2 halves and 3 quarters (credible)
• 3 quarters and 2 halves (credible)
• at least 1 half and 1 quarter (most credible)
• some coins of each type (least credible)

FIGURE 1-5 Illustration of deduction and induction using coins.

Figure 1-5 shows how we may deduce what kinds of samples might be obtained when two coins are randomly selected from a box containing five coins. Ten equally likely sample outcomes are presented.

Inductive Statistics

In Chapters 5, 6, and 7 we will learn how to apply deductive techniques when we know everything regarding the population in advance and we are concerned with studying the characteristics of the possible samples that may arise from *known* populations. In much of the remainder of the book, we will reverse direction and use **inductive statistics**. Induction involves drawing general conclusions from the specific. In statistics this means that inferences about populations are drawn from samples. The sample is all that is known; we must determine uncertain characteristics of the population from the incomplete information available.

Figure 1-5 illustrates this principle when only the sample result is known and a conclusion must be drawn about the entire population of coins. The statistical challenge is to draw a meaningful conclusion that is also credible. Inductive and deductive statistics are completely complementary. We must study how samples are generated before we can learn to generalize from a sample. The role of deduction in statistical analysis is a limited one and the pragmatic aspects of statistics are largely inductive. But we cannot understand inductive statistics unless we first study deductive statistics.

STATISTICAL ERROR

Statistics is characterized partly as art and partly as science. It is an art because we must rely heavily on experience and judgment in choosing from the vast number of procedures available for analyzing sample information. But statistics embodies, to various degrees, all elements of the scientific method—most notably the element of **error**. Because statistics concerns uncertainty, there is always a chance of making erroneous inferences. Statistical procedures are available both to control and to measure the risks of reaching erroneous conclusions. To illustrate this point, consider television-viewer opinions.

Television networks use *sample* information to help make the hard choices about which programs to drop. Those who disagree with the network choices also base their arguments on a sample—the opinions of their own friends and acquaintances. The problem here is that such a sample is **biased** in favor of persons who have similar tastes, education, and social experience. The validity of opinion surveyors' claims is supported by a random selection from the public at large in which everyone has an equal chance of representation. As we will see in Chapter 8, the survey agency chooses a sample large enough to minimize the chance of error.

The survey agency cannot be legitimately criticized, unless it can be shown that its samples were not random and were therefore biased in favor of specific groups. Even when large samples are taken, bias can be introduced by statistical errors due to improper procedures. We will discuss some of the more serious sources of bias in Chapter 4.

EXERCISES

1-7 Consider a group of your friends. Comment on the suitability of using one person's GPA in attempting to make conclusions regarding the academic performance of the entire group.

1-8 For each of the following problem situations, (1) provide an example of an elementary unit; (2) provide an example of a characteristic of interest; and (3) state whether the population would be qualitative or quantitative.

(a) An aircraft manufacturer's investment plans will be affected by the fate of a congressional appropriation bill containing funds for a new fighter plane. The company wishes to conduct a survey to facilitate planning.

(b) A politician plans to study the voter response to pending legislation to determine her platform.

(c) The California Public Utilities Commission is seeking operating cost data that will help it establish new rates for the San Francisco-Los Angeles airline routes.

1-9 For each of the following situations, discuss whether the suggested frame would be suitable.

(a) An insurance company is using home-theft claims processed in the past year as its frame to determine the number of thefts from its policy holders of items valued below $50.

(b) A public health official uses doctors' records of persons diagnosed as suffering from flu as his frame to study the effects of a recent flu epidemic.

(c) A stock exchange official studying the investment attitudes of owners of listed securities uses the active accounts of member brokerage firms as her frame.

1-10 Fred Fox collects old Monopoly markers. He will select items at random from a box containing one each of the slipper, hat, dog, thimble, and car.

(a) A sample of two markers is selected. List the possibilities.

(b) Suppose that three markers are chosen. List the possibilities.

1-11 For each of the following situations, indicate whether deductive statistics or inductive statistics best categorizes the investigation.

(a) A listing is made of all the possible number outcomes from tossing a pair of dice.

(b) Ten randomly chosen students are tested in order to determine how well economics principles are understood by university students.

(c) A pharmaceutical researcher gives super doses of an experimental substance to rats in order to assess side effects.

SUMMARY

1. What is the meaning of "statistics?"

As an area of academic study, **statistics** is a body of methods and theory that is applied to numerical evidence when making decisions in the face of uncertainty. The topic may be subdivided into three main groups: **descriptive statistics** is concerned with summary calculations and graphical displays; **inferential statistics** involves drawing conclusions about a complete **population** by using the information contained in a **sample**; and the third area, **exploratory data analysis**, is the newest type of statistics. The word statistics has other meanings, most notably numerical facts.

2. What is the role of data in statistics?

Data are the central focus of modern statistics. Fundamental to any investigation is the **data set**, a grouping comprising one or more **data points**. A statistical investigation is concerned with one or more **variables**.

3. **How are data classified and what is the basic statistical building block?** Statistical data may be **quantitative** or **qualitative**. The basic building block is the **observation**, a measurement or classification of an **elementary unit**.

4. **What are the distinctions between the population and the sample?** Statistical investigations involve **populations** or **samples**. The population includes the totality of observations that *might* be made, while the sample is just that portion where observations are *actually* made. Population observations may never be completed, which is the case for the **target population** (e.g., the recovery times of patients who would have been treated by a drug never released). They might instead be part of a **working population**, having an accessible **frame** (source of elementary units) that does not coincide with the population of interest.

5. **What are the types of statistical data?** We ordinarily encounter quantitative observations that are **ratio data**, like distances, times, or monetary units, where all arithmetic operations may be meaningfully applied. But observations might involve **interval data**, like temperatures, where addition and subtraction are the only meaningful operations. **Ordinal data** convey size ranking only, while **nominal data** are arbitrarily chosen categorical numbers.

6. **What are two essential types of modern statistical methodology?** In developing methodology for or in explaining statistics, an important dichotomy is **deductive statistics** versus **inductive statistics**. Deductive statistics considers what types of samples might be generated from a population of *known* characteristics. Probability concepts are used for coping with the uncertainties involved. Inductive statistics is concerned with the process of making generalizations about the *unknown* population using known sample results. Inferential statistics is largely inductive. A key concern in drawing conclusions from samples is minimizing **error** and avoiding **bias**.

REAL-LIFE STATISTICAL CHALLENGE

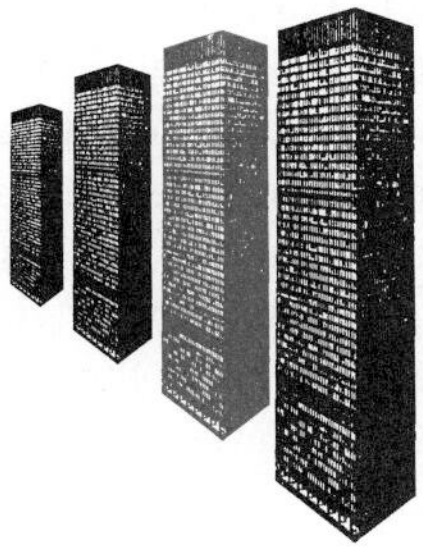

Collecting Data about the Homeless

In the 1990 Census of Population, government planners attempted to count the total number of homeless in the United States. Government and social agencies were unsure how many people were homeless or even how to go about counting them. Estimates ranged from 50,000 to over 3 million.

In the spring of 1990, the U.S. Bureau of the Census attempted to count all the homeless. Over 22,000 census takers visited over 11,000 shelters and 24,000 "preidentified street locations." A total of 178,282 people were found at overnight shelters and 49,793 at the street locations for a total of 228,075 individuals. Most groups, including the census takers themselves, believe this figure still underestimates the true number of homeless people. The results of their findings for selected cities are found in Table 1-2.

Aggregate data helps cities and nonprofit organizations know roughly how many homeless people exist in a given city. However, to truly assist individuals, much more information is needed.

REAL-LIFE STATISTICAL CHALLENGE

TABLE 1-2 Estimates of the Homeless Population in Selected U.S. Cities, 1990.

Rank	City	State	Number in Shelters	Number Visible on Street	Total
1	New York	NY	23,383	10,447	33,830
2	Los Angeles	CA	4,597	3,109	7,706
3	Chicago	IL	5,180	1,584	6,764
4	San Francisco	CA	4,003	1,566	5,569
5	San Diego	CA	2,846	2,101	4,947
6	Washington	DC	4,682	131	4,813
7	Philadelphia	PA	3,416	1,069	4,485
8	Newark	NJ	1,974	842	2,816
9	Seattle	WA	2,170	360	2,530
10	Atlanta	GA	2,431	60	2,491
11	Boston	MA	2,245	218	2,463
12	Houston	TX	1,780	151	1,931
13	Phoenix	AZ	1,710	276	1,986
14	Portland	OR	1,553	149	1,702
15	Sacramento	CA	1,287	265	1,552
16	Baltimore	MD	1,144	387	1,531
17	Dallas	TX	1,200	293	1,493
18	Denver	CO	1,169	100	1,269
19	Oklahoma City	OK	1,016	234	1,250
20	Minneapolis	MN	1,052	28	1,080
	Total		68,838	23,370	92,208

Sources: U.S. Bureau of the Census, 1991; and the *Universal Almanac 1992:* 215.

How to gather data about the homeless has usually been controversial. Advocates for the homeless disagree (at times quite vigorously) about which questions to ask people. Some data elements on a form may be used for aggregate statistical purposes; others address concerns of abuse—child, spousal, and substances (alcohol and drugs). Some of the data elements may be hard to gather, and in some cases completely forthright and honest answers require a degree of trust not easy to develop during the brief intake process[1].

The form shown in Figure 1-6 is used in Santa Clara County, California, to help process incoming homeless individuals in its Winter Shelter at the National Guard Armory in San Jose. Once collected, the data is transcribed onto magnetic cards (similar to an ATM card). Using this magnetic card system speeds up check-in on subsequent nights. The clients at this shelter are primarily single adults, although some adults with children also stay at the facility. Similar forms (but with different questions) are used for shelters targeted toward migrant farm workers, battered spouses, and single parents and couples with childern.

While the details requested on the form seem very intrusive, clients can decline to answer most of the questions with which they feel uncomfortable. The demographic details are summarized for reporting purposes, and the summary data is provided to funding groups such as county and state agencies and private foundations.

[1]Discussion drawn from Project SHARE Prototype, Jerome Burstein, Principal Investigator.

REAL-LIFE STATISTICAL CHALLENGE

Emergency Housing Consortium

91/92 Winter Shelter Intake Form

Reference Number: ____________ Date: ____________

First Name: ____________ Birthdate: ____________

Family Name: ____________ Veteran: ☐ Yes ☐ No

SSN: ____________ Discharge Date: ____________

Last City: ____________ Shelter: ____________

Last State: ______ Last Zip: ______ Intake by: ____________

Individuals

Adult Male: ____
Adult Female: ____
Child Male: ____
Child Female: ____
Total: ____

Ethnicity

White: ____
Black: ____
Hispanic: ____
Asian: ____
Native American: ____
Other Ethnic: ____
Unknown Ethnic: ____
Total: ____

Age

Under 5: ____
5 to 12: ____
13 to 17: ____
18 to 20: ____
21 to 30: ____
31 to 44: ____
45 to 59: ____
60 & Older: ____
Unknown: ____
Total: ____

Employment

Full Time: ____
Part Time: ____
Unemployed: ____
Training: ____

Benefits

AFDC: ____
GA: ____
SS: ____
SSI: ____
Veteran: ____
SDI: ____
Unemployment: ____

Parentics

Couple: ____
Female Parent: ____
Female Single: ____
Make Single: ____
Male Parent: ____
Two Parents: ____

Emergency Information

Name: ____________
Address: ____________
City: ____________
State: ____________
Phone: ____________

Income

None: ____
Below Very Low: ____
Very Low: ____
Low: ____
Moderate: ____

Personal/Medical

How long homeless? ____________
Date last employed? ____________
Skills: ____________
Disabled? ◯Yes ◯No
Sick Now? ◯Yes ◯No
Medical Problems? ____________
Allergic to? ____________
Taking Medicine? ◯Yes ◯No
What Medicine? ____________

FIGURE 1-6 Sample Intake Form.

Discussion Questions:

1. What difficulties might census takers have in locating the homeless in or near your community?
2. Refer to the form in Figure 1-6. Indicate examples of nominal, ordinal, interval, and ratio data. Which questions would you feel uncomfortable answering?

REVIEW EXERCISES

1-12 You are assisting the brand manager for a new household product to devise a marketing plan.

(a) List four questions for which numerical data might be helpful in making the choice.

(b) For each question in (a), provide (1) the source of data and (2) the type of data.

1-13 You have been asked to assist an accountant to prepare a detailed routine for auditing a chemical company. Suggest where you might find data for the following.

(a) Freight costs for shipments of various sizes.

(b) Number of orders of various quantities for chosen products.

(c) How salaries compare to similar jobs in other companies in the same industry.

1-14 Indicate for each of the following situations whether the type of statistics involved is primarily inductive or deductive.

(a) Assessing the chance that a particular ticket will win the lottery.

(b) A quality assurance manager rejects shipments of parts when more than 2 items in a sample of 25 are defective, since the evidence then strongly indicates that the shipment is of poor quality.

(c) A professor knows the exam scores of all 30 students in her class. She wants to know the possible levels of the average test score for five randomly selected students and how likely each possibility is.

(d) The government uses experimental results in deciding whether or not a new drug would have excessive side effects with all potential users.

1-15 For each of the following quantities, indicate whether the data would be classified as (1) nominal, (2) ordinal, (3) interval, or (4) ratio.

(a) movie ratings, 1 to 10	(e) employee payroll code numbers
(b) heights of men	(f) Richter earthquake intensity scale
(c) daily high temperatures	(g) task completion times
(d) football player jersey numbers	(h) GMAT test scores

1-16 For each of the following statistical investigations, identify a potential source of error and suggest how it might be remedied.

(a) As he shakes hands with potential voters, a congressional candidate asks how he or she will vote.

(b) A software company asks persons to evaluate EZ-Calc against competing packages. The questionnaire is on the backside of the EZ-Calc warranty registration card.

(c) A telephone survey firm makes calls only between 9 A.M. and 5 P.M. This minimizes overtime costs.

STATISTICS IN PRACTICE

1-17 How are statistics used where you work? If you do not have any work experience, ask a relative or friend how statistics are used at their workplace. What are the elementary units? Provide an example of the frame and the working population.

1-18 How are statistics used in a nonwork environment such as a social club or religious organization? You may want to ask a relative or friend how statistics are used at organizations they are familiar with. What are the elementary units? Provide an example of the frame and the working population.

1-19 *Collecting a master class data set.* A class project, create a list of class data using the following variables:

Case Number	Sex	Age	Height	Major	Favorite Food	State/Province or Country of Birth
1	F	26	57	Aviation	Pizza	Georgia
2	M	19	71	Accounting	Hamburgers	Mexico

To help organize the data and to facilitate future evaluations, assign each successive student a case number, starting with 1.

1-20 *Developing a data set.* List several types of data to gather from your classmates, along with the questions you would ask in eliciting the data. Include both qualitative or quantitative variables, and include among your quantitative variables at least one of each type: nominal, ordinal, interval, and ratio. Indicate for each of your variables which type it is. Indentify any questions that people might feel uncomfortable answering.

1-21 *Collecting a group's class data set.* Form small groups and compare your list, adding or deleting variables as needed, until you arrive at a group consensus regarding what data to collect. (Your instructor may suggest some ideas.) Then collect your group's data, getting one observation from each member of the entire class for every variable. Use as his or her case number the student's position on your group's list.

CHAPTER 2

DESCRIBING AND DISPLAYING STATISTICAL DATA

BEFORE READING THIS CHAPTER, MAKE SURE YOU UNDERSTAND:

The various meanings of "statistics."
The role of data and the distinction between quantitative and qualitative data.
The distinction between samples and populations.
The types of statistical data.
The dichotomy between deductive and inductive statistics.

AFTER READING THIS CHAPTER, YOU WILL UNDERSTAND:

How statistical data are organized in terms of frequency of occurrence.
What kinds of numerical and graphical displays are used for data.
How to compare data sets and make further summaries.
What common forms are taken by statistical data.
How to display data when two or more variables are present.
What special data displays may be useful for important statistical applications.

The arrangement and display of statistical data are important elements of descriptive statistics. Raw numbers alone do not provide any underlying pattern from which conclusions can be drawn. For example, we might believe that doctors generally have high incomes and that younger people usually earn less than older people. But even if we had access to all the tax returns on file with the Internal Revenue Service, without arranging, sifting and sorting the original income data, we would not be able to determine if doctors earn more than dentists, if some lawyers earn more than most doctors, or if greater experience in a particular occupation increases salary. Only by organizing the data can we gain information to use in career planning.

Such descriptive statistics sets the stage for everything else.

2-1 THE FREQUENCY DISTRIBUTION

FINDING A MEANINGFUL PATTERN FOR THE DATA

The ages of a sample of 100 statistics students are given in Table 2-1. If we wish to describe this sample, how should we proceed? The values in Table 2-1 have not been summarized or rearranged in a meaningful manner, so we refer to them as **raw data**. We might begin by grouping the ages in a meaningful way.

A convenient way to accomplish this is to group the ages into categories of two calendar years, beginning with age 18. Each age will then fall into one of the categories 18.0–under 20.0, 20.0–under 22.0, and so on. We refer to such groupings of values as **class intervals**. Now if we summarize the raw data simply by counting the number of ages in each class interval, we should be able to identify some properties of the sample.

First we list the class intervals in increasing sequence, as in the first column of Table 2-2. Then, reading down the list of raw data for each successive age, we place a tally mark beside the corresponding class interval and a check mark beside the number on the original list so that it will not be counted twice. When the tally is complete, we count the marks to determine the total number of observations in each class interval. The final result indicates the **frequency** with which ages occur in each class interval and is called a **frequency distribution**. In Table 2-2, we find that 10 of the 100 statistics students fall into the interval 18.0–under 20.0.

TABLE 2-1 Ages of a Sample of 100 Statistics Students

Age (years)									
20.9	33.4	18.7	24.2	22.1	18.9	21.9	20.5	21.9	37.3
57.2	25.3	24.6	29.0	26.3	19.1	48.7	23.5	23.1	28.6
21.3	22.4	22.3	20.0	30.3	31.7	34.3	28.5	36.1	32.6
33.7	19.6	18.7	24.3	27.1	20.7	22.2	19.2	26.5	27.4
22.8	51.3	44.4	22.9	20.6	32.8	27.3	23.5	23.8	22.4
18.1	23.9	20.8	41.5	20.4	21.3	19.3	24.2	22.3	23.1
22.9	21.3	29.7	25.6	33.7	24.2	24.5	21.2	21.5	25.8
21.5	21.5	27.0	19.9	29.2	25.3	26.4	22.7	27.9	22.0
23.3	28.1	24.8	19.6	23.7	26.3	30.1	29.7	24.8	24.7
23.5	22.9	26.0	25.2	23.6	21.0	30.9	21.7	28.3	22.1

TABLE 2-2 Frequency Distribution for Student Ages

Age	Tally	Number of Persons (class frequency)
18.0–under 20.0	𝍸 𝍸	10
20.0–under 22.0	𝍸 𝍸 𝍸 |||	18
22.0–under 24.0	𝍸 𝍸 𝍸 𝍸 |||	23
24.0–under 26.0	𝍸 𝍸 ||||	14
26.0–under 28.0	𝍸 𝍸	10
28.0–under 30.0	𝍸 |||	8
30.0–under 32.0	||||	4
32.0–under 34.0	𝍸	5
34.0–under 36.0			1
36.0–under 38.0	||	2
38.0–under 58.0	𝍸	5
	Total	100

The number 10 can be referred to as the **class frequency** for the first class interval.

Each class interval has two limits. For the first interval, the **lower class limit** is 18.0 and the **upper class limit** is "under 20.0." (We use the word *under* to distinguish this limit from 20.0 exactly, which serves as the lower limit of the second class interval.) No matter how precisely the raw data are measured, this designation prevents ambiguity in assigning an observation to a particular interval. For example, the age 19.99 years is represented by the first class, whereas 20.01 years would fall into the second class (20.0–under 22.0). The **width** of a class interval is found by subtracting its lower limit from the lower limit of the succeeding class interval. For example, the width of the first class interval is $20.0 - 18.0 = 2.0$. All intervals except the last class interval have the same width. As we will see, beginning and ending class intervals must sometimes be treated differently.

GRAPHICAL DISPLAYS: THE HISTOGRAM

A visual display can be a very useful starting point in describing a frequency distribution. Figure 2-1 graphically portrays the frequency distribution of student ages. Age is represented on the horizontal axis, which is divided into class intervals of two years in width. The classes are represented by bars of varying heights, corresponding to the class frequency (the number of observations in each interval). Thus, the vertical axis represents frequency. Such a graphical portrayal of a frequency distribution is called a **histogram**.

Since 23 of the ages are 22.0–under 24.0, the corresponding bar is of height 23. Only one person is between 34.0 and 36.0 years old, so the height of that bar is 1. Neighboring bars touch, emphasizing that age is a continuous scale.

Note that the highest class interval, 38.0–under 58.0, is 20 years wide—ten times as wide as the standard intervals. With only five ages falling between 38.0 and 58.0, there is, on the average, one-half an observation every two years in this interval. This bar therefore has a height of $\frac{1}{2}$. Treating the two-year width as a

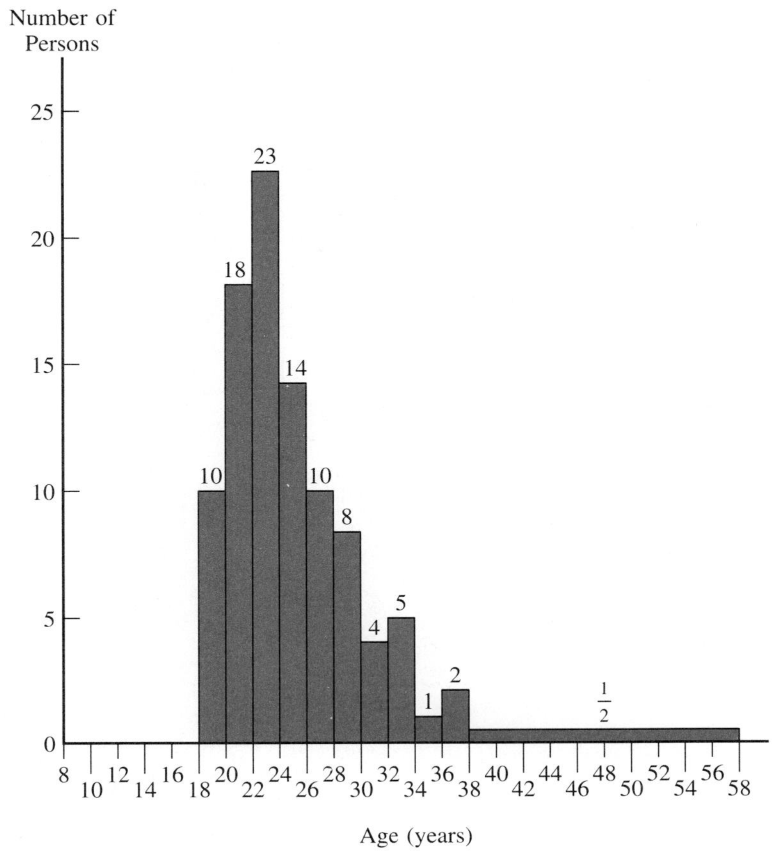

FIGURE 2-1 Histogram for the frequency distribution of student ages.

standard unit, *the area inside any bar* (its height times its width in standard units) *equals the number of observations in the corresponding class interval.* Thus, the area inside the first bar is $10 \times 1 = 10$, and the area inside the last bar is one-half the number of standard two-year class intervals, or $\frac{1}{2} \times 10 = 5$, which is the number of observations in that category.

GRAPHICAL DISPLAYS: THE FREQUENCY POLYGON

An alternative graphical portrayal of a frequency distribution is the **frequency polygon**, shown in Figure 2-2 for the same sample of student ages. In Figure 2-2, each class interval is represented by a dot positioned above its midpoint at a height equal to the class frequency. Each midpoint is typical of all values in the interval and is defined by the average of the interval's class limits. Thus, the midpoint of the first interval is $(18.0 + 20.0)/2 = 19.0$; the midpoint of the second interval is 21.0; and so on. The midpoint of the last interval is $(38.0 + 58.0)/2 = 48.0$. The dots are connected by line segments to make the graph more readable. To complete the frequency polygon, line segments are drawn from the first and last dots to the horizontal axis at points one-half the

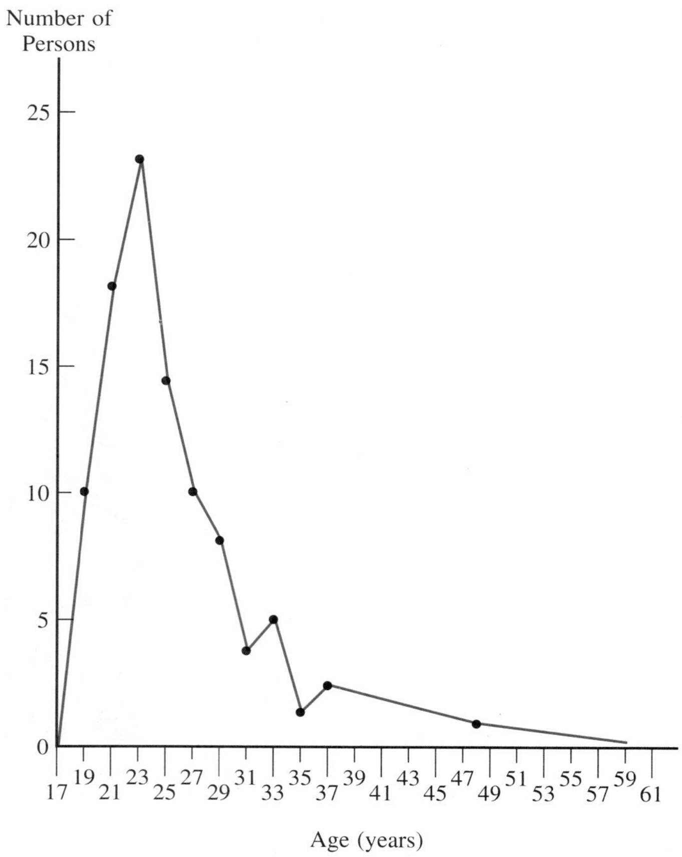

FIGURE 2-2 Frequency polygon for sample of student ages.

width of a standard class interval below the lowest and above the highest class intervals, respectively (in this case, touching the axis at 17 and 59).

DESCRIBING A POPULATION: THE FREQUENCY CURVE

A frequency distribution, similar to that found for student ages, may be constructed for any quantitative data set. In many statistical applications, the only data available are *sample* observations. The nature of the complete population remains *unknown*. The unobserved population values may be represented in a general sense by a **frequency curve**, like the one in Figure 2-3, which might apply to the original *population* of student ages. The basic shape of a population's frequency curve is usually suggested by the histogram or frequency polygon originally constructed from the sample data. Because populations are usually quite large in relation to the number of observations in a sample, the frequency curve would resemble a frequency polygon or a histogram with many class intervals of tiny widths. If these intervals were individually plotted, the entire collection of population data would present a less jagged graph than one obtained from the sample data alone, and this graph would be almost totally smooth (like the curve

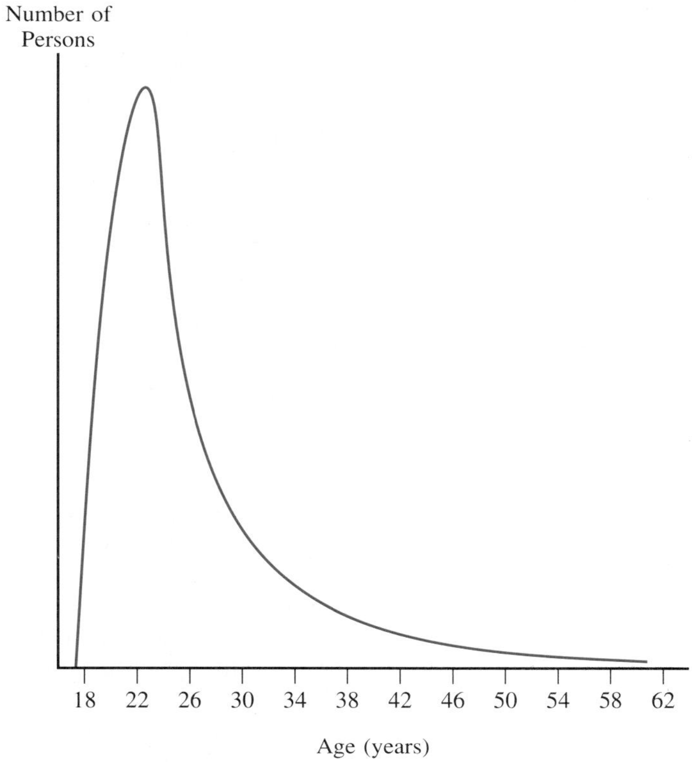

FIGURE 2-3 Suggested shape of a smoothed frequency curve for the entire population.

in Figure 2-3). Later in this chapter, we will examine some forms of the frequency distribution that are commonly encountered for populations.

DESCRIPTIVE ANALYSIS

We have managed to translate the confusion of our raw data on student ages into a pattern based on frequencies. The frequency distribution tells us two things: It shows how the observations cluster around a central value, and it illustrates the degree of dispersion or difference between observations.

We know that no student is younger than 18 and that ages below 28 are most typical. Of these, the most common age is somewhere between 22 and 24, which (from general information obtained from the registrar's office) we know to be higher than usual for the student who enters college right after high school and graduates at about age 22. The students in the sample are generally older, but we can rule out the possibility that they might be graduate students because of the substantial number of younger persons. It is possible that the population could be made up of night students and that the older persons work on their degrees on a part-time basis while holding full-time jobs.

The appropriateness of this conclusion may be substantiated by the incidence of persons over 30, who are most likely to have financial burdens and thus not be full-time students. Although predominantly young, the sample is peppered with

TABLE 2-3 Fuel Consumption Achieved by 100 Large-Sized Cars (raw data)

Fuel Consumption (mpg)									
19.0	20.8	22.0	22.7	20.0	18.9	16.6	16.8	20.8	14.7
15.1	21.8	21.1	21.5	21.1	15.5	19.3	15.1	20.6	16.8
18.2	20.5	15.3	16.2	16.3	22.8	22.7	21.9	22.5	17.1
19.1	21.6	19.0	18.3	18.6	22.1	17.5	22.9	21.7	18.7
21.9	20.2	14.5	14.1	22.9	20.2	17.3	22.6	19.3	21.7
21.5	22.6	18.7	19.2	22.8	21.6	21.7	20.5	22.7	20.4
18.8	15.1	16.5	20.5	19.1	17.4	19.7	19.2	16.4	21.9
14.3	19.2	19.7	17.1	21.4	21.9	21.7	19.2	23.9	19.6
20.9	18.5	20.2	18.2	20.2	22.4	20.4	21.6	21.3	22.4
20.5	18.1	20.7	21.3	16.9	20.3	23.9	18.8	21.1	21.9

persons approaching or exceeding the age of 40. Five students are relatively so much older that they have been put into a special group—the "over 38s." Their ages (41.5, 44.4, 48.7, 51.3, and 57.2) are spread so thinly along the age scale that it is more convenient to lump these more extreme ages into a single special category.

This descriptive analysis provides us with an image of the student sample that is not immediately available from the raw data. The entire description is based on frequencies of occurrence—the heart of all statistical analysis. As we will see in Chapter 5, frequency is the basis for probability theory and as such plays a fundamental role in all procedures of statistical inference.

CONSTRUCTING A FREQUENCY DISTRIBUTION: NUMBER AND WIDTH OF CLASS INTERVALS

A frequency distribution converts raw data into a meaningful pattern for statistical analysis. In doing this, detail must be sacrificed to insight.

The first step in constructing a frequency distribution is to specify the number of class intervals and their widths. No totally accepted rule tells us how many intervals are to be used. Between 5 and 20 class intervals are generally recommended, but the number is really a matter of personal judgment. When all intervals are to be the same width, the following rule gives the required

CLASS INTERVAL WIDTH

$$\text{Width} = \frac{\text{Largest value} - \text{Smallest value}}{\text{Number of class intervals}}$$

EXAMPLE: DESCRIBING FUEL CONSUMPTION DATA

Using the 100 observations of fuel consumption in miles per gallon (mpg) for the fleet of cars listed in Table 2-3, suppose we wish to construct five class intervals of equal width.

TABLE 2-4 Frequency Distribution for Fuel Consumption of 100 Cars Using Five Class Intervals

Miles per Gallon	Number of Cars
14.0–under 16.0	9
16.0–under 18.0	13
18.0–under 20.0	24
20.0–under 22.0	38
22.0–under 24.0	16
Total	100

SOLUTION: We find the required width by taking the difference between the largest and smallest values, 23.9 − 14.1 = 9.8, and dividing by 5 to obtain 1.96 mpg. To simplify our task, we can round off 1.96 to 2.0 for the width and 14.1 to 14.0 for the lower limit of our first class interval. The frequency distribution is provided in Table 2-4 and graphed in Figure 2-4(a).

Figure 2-4 also contains histograms for the same fuel consumption data using 10 class intervals (b) and 20 class intervals (c). Notice that the histogram profiles become progressively "lumpier" as the number of classes increases. Both the 5-interval and 10-interval graphs provide concise summaries of the data, but a pronounced "sawtooth" effect occurs with 20 intervals. The poorness of the 20-interval summary reflects the large number of intervals in relation to the size of the sample. One way to decide how many class intervals to use would be to try several—plot a histogram for each and select the one that provides the most logical explanation of the underlying population pattern. A large number of class intervals will provide more data, but too many will produce meaningless oscillations.

STEM-AND-LEAF PLOTS

As a preliminary step in constructing a frequency distribution, the data may be conveniently arranged in a **stem-and-leaf plot**. This display organizes the raw data in tabular form by locating each observation on a "tree." This is done by separating the values into **stem digits** and **leaf digits**.

To illustrate, consider again the fuel consumption (mpg) data in Table 2-3. On a blank piece of paper begin by listing the possible miles per gallon in whole numbers followed by a decimal point.

14. |
15. |
16. |
17. |
18. |
19. |
20. |
21. |
22. |
23. |

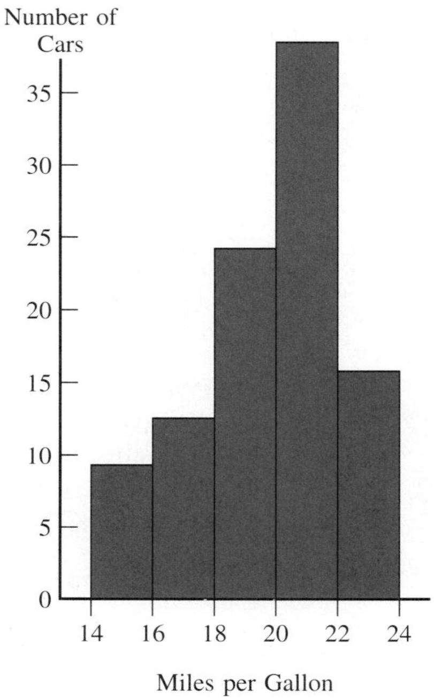

(a) 5 Class Intervals

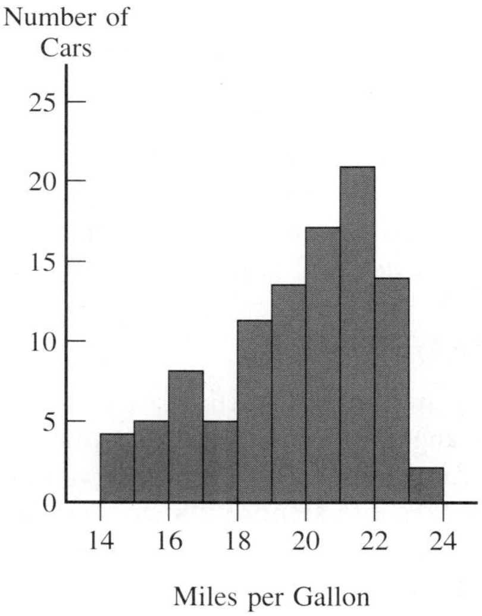

(b) 10 Class Intervals

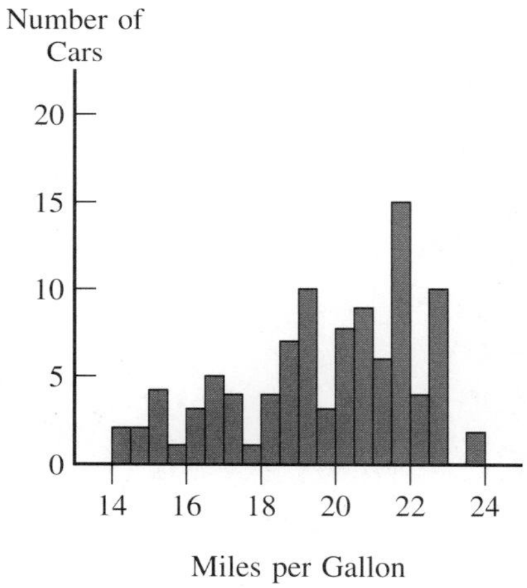

(c) 20 Class Intervals

FIGURE 2-4 Histograms for fuel consumption of 100 cars using three different sets of class intervals.

The list constitutes the *stems* of the plot. A vertical line is placed directly to the right of the listed entries to separate those quantities from the leaves. There will be one leaf for each observation of fuel consumption in Table 2-3. Consider the first three entries in column one: 19.0, 15.1, 18.2. Detaching the last digits, we get 0, 1, and 2. These digits determine the first three *leaves* on the plot and are placed directly after their respective stems. The following is a display of the plot at this stage of construction.

```
14. |
15. | 1 <———————— 15.1
16. |
17. |
18. | 2 <———————— 18.2
19. | 0 <———————— 19.0
20. |
21. |
22. |
23. |
```

The fourth entry in column one of Table 2-3 is 19.1 miles per gallon. This establishes the second leaf on the 19. stem.

```
19. | 0  1 <———————— 19.1
```

Proceeding down the successive columns, the remaining leaves are placed onto their respective stems. The completed stem-and-leaf plot is provided below.

```
                          Leaf
                      (last digit)
        14. | 3 5 1 7
        15. | 1 1 3 5 1
        16. | 5 2 3 9 6 8 4 8
        17. | 1 4 5 3 1
        18. | 2 8 5 1 7 3 2 6 9 8 7
Stem    19. | 0 1 2 0 7 2 1 3 7 2 2 3 6
        20. | 9 5 8 5 2 2 7 5 0 2 2 3 4 5 8 6 4
        21. | 9 5 8 6 1 5 3 1 4 6 9 7 7 9 6 7 3 1 7 9 9
        22. | 6 0 7 9 8 8 1 4 7 9 6 5 7 4
        23. | 9 9
```

A compelling advantage of the stem-and-leaf plot is that it contains essentially the same information as a histogram. (To see this, rotate the page counterclockwise 90 degrees. If you then add a frequency axis having one tick per leaf and highlight each leaf digit with a magic marker, you will have the histogram in Figure 2-4(a).) No information is lost, since the complete set of raw data is readily available, but in a more useful form. In Chapter 3 we will see how the stem-and-leaf plot enables us to compute more quickly certain summary data measures.

The stem-and-leaf plot can be cumbersome when the number of observations is large. (Imagine a stem with 105 leaves.) Also, the tree may not be very useful if the data range is wide and expressed to more than three significant figures. If this is the case, the potential stems could outnumber the leaves.

ACCOMMODATING EXTREME VALUES

Class intervals of equal width will facilitate comparisons between classes and provide simpler calculations of the more concise summary values to be discussed later in this chapter. But, as we noted about the distribution of the age data in Table 2-2, it is sometimes better to lump the extreme values into a single category.

This becomes quite evident during the construction of a frequency distribution for individual annual earnings. Most persons earn incomes of less than $50,000, and a few earn between $50,000 and $100,000. But the rare, extremely well-to-do have substantially higher incomes. A frequency distribution graph with equal intervals of income width of, say, $5,000 would be hard to draw and difficult to read. The resulting histogram would be analogous to a few mountain peaks (representing frequencies for the lower income levels) sitting to the left of many successively smaller anthills (representing the number of persons in each progressively rarer, higher income category). This difficulty can be avoided by grouping the higher incomes into a single class interval of, say, "$100,000 or more."

COMPUTER-ASSISTED CONSTRUCTION

Today we are fortunate to have statistical software packages widely available for personal computers and time-sharing operations. Such computing power greatly aids constructing frequency distributions and graphical displays. The greatest effort is data input. Once the sample data are in computer memory, an investigator can try various interval widths and numbers of class intervals, plotting on the terminal screen a histogram for each combination. The analyst can then print out for permanent use that frequency distribution judged to achieve the best balance between summarizing the data and preserving detail. Figure 2-5 shows such a histogram for the fuel consumption data in Table 2-3, constructed on an IBM PC using EasyStat.

QUALITATIVE FREQUENCY DISTRIBUTIONS

When the data are qualitative, each attribute is like a class interval. The following frequency distribution was obtained for the majors of 100 Beta Gamma Sigma members.

Major	Frequency
Accounting	17
Finance	4
Management	38
Marketing	27
Human Resources	14
Total	100

The data are summarized graphically in Figure 2-6. Each category is represented by a bar or spike. These do not touch, emphasizing that the attributes are qualitative categories. A similar graphical display, called a **bar chart**, could be constructed for the frequency distribution of a **discrete variable**, such as family size or the number of rooms at home, where only whole numbers or integers serve as the categories.

The Statistics Around Us box on page 34 shows how frequency of occurrence can reduce the confusion of raw data.

THE PIE CHART

A common graphical display of qualitative data is the **pie chart** shown in Figure 2-7 for the student majors described earlier. The pie chart is a highly intuitive

```
Interval                              Frequency
                                 ---------------------------------------
                                 0    10   20   30   40   50   60   70
     14.0 under 16.0        9    :*****
     16.0 under 18.0       13    :*******
     18.0 under 20.0       24    :************
     20.0 under 22.0       38    :*******************
     22.0 under 24.0       16    :********
     24.0 under 26.0        0    :
```

Note: Figure generated on an IBM PC using EasyStat.

FIGURE 2-5 Histogram for fuel consumption data.

display in which the size of each slice is proportional to the frequency of the category. Although some drafting skill is required to construct a proper pie chart by hand, many computer software packages will generate a finished pie chart from supplied categories and frequencies.

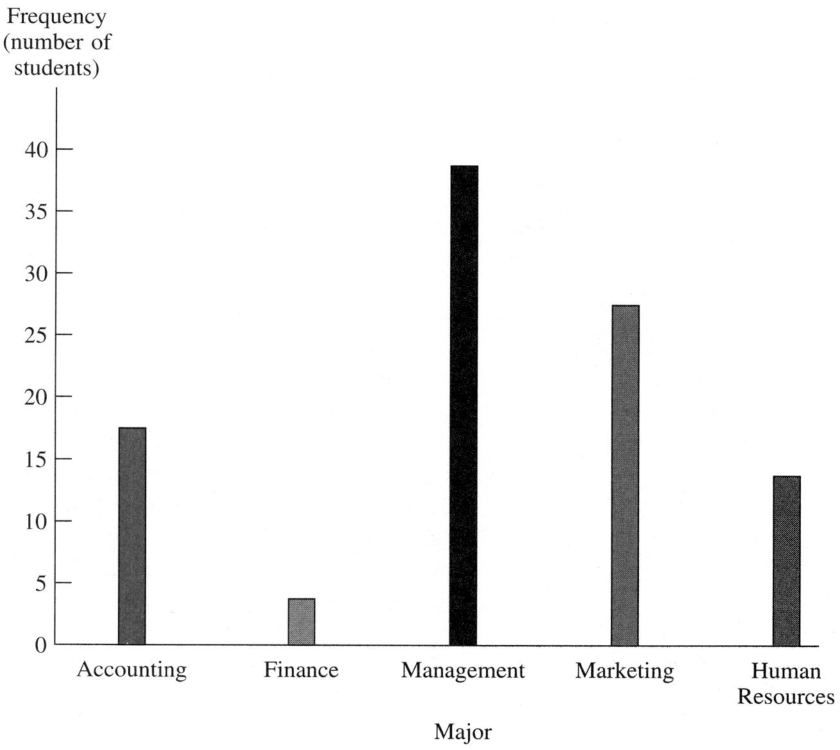

FIGURE 2-6 Bar chart for frequency distribution of Beta Gamma Sigma members' majors.

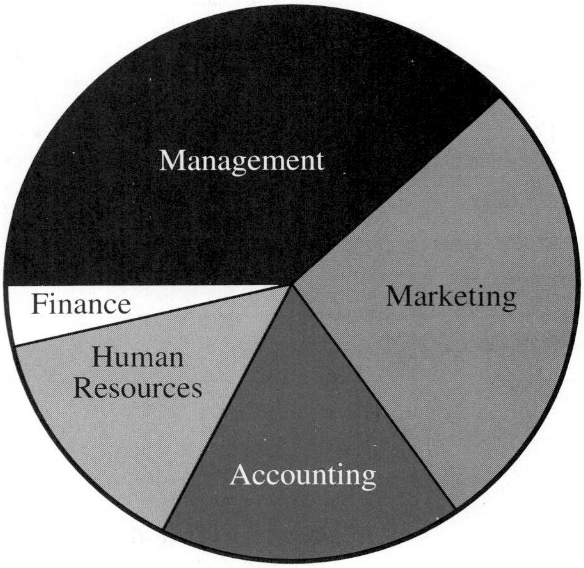

FIGURE 2-7 Pie chart for student majors.

STATISTICS AROUND US

Cryptanalysis

Cryptanalysis is the breaking of secret codes or ciphers. In its simplest form, a **cipher** is a message in which another alphabet has been substituted for the ordinary one. Consider the following message.

AOYNS	YIRXJ	AJRRS	OOYIR	YGDYP
MQQCY	CYMOQ	JAPQM	QDPQD	RMGMI
MGXPD	PDQMG	GRVPS	PQJRO	YMQYJ
OKYOA	OJHRJ	IASPD	JIHYM	IDIBA
SGGXM	OOMIB	YKISH	UYOPR	MIQYG
GSPMP	QJOXM	IKCYG	LSPRC	JJPYH
YQCJK	PMIKL	OJRYK	SOYPA	JOBYI
YOMGD	ZDIBM	UJSQL	JLSGM	QDJIP

To decipher this message, we must find the counterparts to the letters in the original message. The frequency distribution of letters in the cipher message is given in Table 2-5.

The letters occurring in ordinary English may be arranged in sequence of decreasing frequency.

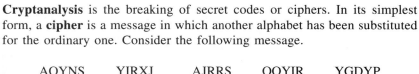

English letters	e	t	a	o	n	i	r	s	h	d	l	u	c	m	p	f	y	w	g	b	v	j	k	x	q	z
Frequency	26	18	16	16	14	13	13	12	12	8	7	6	6	6	4	4	4	3	3	3	2	1	1	1	$\frac{1}{2}$	$\frac{1}{2}$
	High									*Medium*												*Low*				

A similar arrangement of the ciphertext letters may be made.

Ciphertext	Y	M	J	P	O	I	Q	G	S	R	D	A	K	C	H	B	L	X	U	N	V	Z	E	F	T	W
Frequency	21	18	17	16	16	15	14	12	11	11	10	7	6	5	4	4	4	4	2	1	1	1	0	0	0	0

It would be highly unusual for this particular message to provide an identical match—letter for letter—strictly on the basis of frequency. But the frequencies can help us to find the more likely possibilities. By trial and error (for instance, substituting e for Y or M and t for one of the other high-frequency letters), portions of the original words can be found. This is a slow process at first, but as each letter is identified, it becomes easier to match the remaining ones.

The complete key for our message is

Ciphertext	M	U	R	K	Y	A	B	C	D	E	F	G	H	I	J	L	N	O	P	Q	S	T	V	W	X	Z
Original text	a	b	c	d	e	f	g	h	i	j	k	l	m	n	o	p	q	r	s	t	u	v	w	x	y	z

The cipher is constructed by using the word MURKY for the first five original text letters and listing the remaining ciphertext letters in alphabetical sequence. The text of the full message reads

> Frequency of occurrence lies at the heart of statistical analysis. It allows us to create order from confusion. Meaningfully arranged, numbers can tell us a story and help us choose methods and procedures for generalizing about populations.

TABLE 2-5 Frequency Distribution for Letters in the Cipher Message

Letter	Tally	Number of Letters	Letter	Tally	Number of Letters
A	𝍸 ||	7	N	|	1
B	||||	4	O	𝍸 𝍸 𝍸 |	16
C	𝍸	5	P	𝍸 𝍸 𝍸 |	16
D	𝍸 𝍸	10	Q	𝍸 𝍸 ||||	14
E		0	R	𝍸 𝍸 |	11
F		0	S	𝍸 𝍸 |	11
G	𝍸 𝍸 ||	12	T		0
H	||||	4	U	||	2
I	𝍸 𝍸 𝍸	15	V	|	1
J	𝍸 𝍸 𝍸 ||	17	W		0
K	𝍸 |	6	X	||||	4
L	||||	4	Y	𝍸 𝍸 𝍸 𝍸 |	21
M	𝍸 𝍸 𝍸 |||	18	Z	|	1
				Total	200

EXERCISES

2-1 For each of the following sample arrival times, determine the class interval widths for constructing frequency distributions.

Largest Value	Smallest Value	Number of Intervals
(a) 6.04 min	.54 min	11
(b) 2.50 hr	.10 hr	6
(c) 38 sec	3 sec	5
(d) 45 min	10 min	7

2-2 The following sample levels of precipitation (inches) have been obtained for selected U.S. cities during the month of April.

2.9	3.7	3.2	4.0	3.9	2.1	2.9	2.9	1.1
0.4	3.0	3.2	1.0	2.2	5.4	3.5	3.6	4.0
0.7	2.8	1.8	1.5	4.0	4.0	0.3	2.2	3.3
3.8	2.6	2.2	4.2	5.4	4.8	3.3	2.7	1.8
4.4	2.6	2.9	2.0	1.2	3.6	3.9	0.8	3.1
3.1	3.7	0.3	3.7	4.1	4.5	2.3	1.5	3.4
3.4	3.3	1.2	5.9	3.6	3.8	4.0	3.6	
5.0	3.4	2.6	3.3	5.8	0.6	2.9	2.4	
1.6	3.6	0.7	2.9	3.1	2.9	2.0	3.2	
1.2	1.8	3.6	2.7	3.4	2.9	0.5	2.4	

Source: *The World Almanac and Book of Facts,* 1988 edition, © Newspaper Enterprise Association, Inc., 1987, New York, NY: 181.

(a) Construct a stem-and-leaf plot.
(b) Construct a table for the frequency distribution that has intervals of width 1 inch. Use 0 as the lower limit of the first interval.
(c) Plot (1) a histogram and (2) a frequency polygon for the frequency distribution you constructed in (b).

2-3 Sample weekly sales receipts for McBurger franchises are provided below.

$ 3,145	$15,879	$ 6,914	$ 4,572	$11,374
12,764	9,061	8,245	10,563	8,164
6,395	8,758	17,270	10,755	10,465
7,415	9,637	9,361	11,606	7,836
13,517	7,645	9,757	9,537	23,957
8,020	8,346	12,848	8,438	6,347
21,333	9,280	7,538	7,414	11,707
9,144	7,424	25,639	10,274	4,683
5,089	6,904	9,182	12,193	12,472
8,494	6,032	16,012	9,282	3,331

(a) Construct a table for the frequency distribution that has six class intervals of equal width. Round the width to the nearest $1,000 and use $3,000 as the lower class limit of the first interval.
(b) Plot a histogram of the frequency distribution you constructed in (a).

2-4 Refer to the sales receipt data given in Exercise 2-3.

(a) Construct a table for the frequency distribution that has 12 class intervals of width \$2,000, with \$3,000 as the lower limit of the first interval.

(b) Plot a frequency polygon of the frequency distribution you constructed in (a).

(c) Do you think a more accurate data summary could be obtained by using a fewer or a greater number of class intervals? Discuss the reasons for your choice.

2-5 The following sample temperatures (°F) have been obtained for selected U.S. cities during the month of April.

47°	49°	51°	49°	60°	46°	50°	58°	46°
55	45	47	42	42	68	53	56	56
35	43	54	76	55	50	68	49	46
56	37	38	69	62	60	50	70	72
62	66	49	46	62	52	43	61	53
51	49	30	52	57	69	50	55	52
54	48	60	65	37	53	48	80	
63	51	69	68	63	18	59	38	
43	66	52	39	75	58	45	66	
49	47	46	55	45	60	46	49	

Source: *The World Almanac and Book of Facts,* 1988 edition, © Newspaper Enterprise Association, Inc., 1987, New York, NY: 181.

(a) Construct a stem-and-leaf plot.

(b) Construct a table for the frequency distribution that has intervals of width 10°. Use 10° as the lower limit of the first interval.

(c) Plot (1) a histogram and (2) a frequency polygon for the frequency distribution you constructed in (b).

2-6 The following heights (inches) have been obtained for the female staff at the *Daily Planet.*

62.4	63.7	65.1	64.8	66.2
64.4	63.9	60.5	64.8	64.8
61.2	59.7	62.8	63.4	61.4
63.8	63.3	63.0	58.9	65.6
62.1	63.6	61.3	62.7	61.3
58.8	63.1	64.3	63.7	62.5
60.3	64.8	63.6	65.0	61.7
67.2	60.9	64.7	64.9	59.9
66.3	61.1	63.7	62.7	61.7
63.2	60.8	65.4	62.5	64.9

(a) Construct a table for the sample frequency distribution that has ten class intervals of width 1 inch. Use 58 inches as the lower limit of the first interval.

(b) Plot a histogram of the frequency distribution you constructed in (a).

2-7 Second National Bank obtained the following frequency distribution of automatic teller transaction times. It has too many classes. Construct a table for the frequency distribution with half as many intervals, each twice as wide.

Class Interval (seconds)	Frequency	Class Interval (seconds)	Frequency
10–under 15	5	45–under 50	21
15–under 20	13	50–under 55	39
20–under 25	25	55–under 60	28
25–under 30	32	60–under 65	59
30–under 35	33	65–under 70	37
35–under 40	27	70–under 75	11
40–under 45	32	75–under 80	1

2-8 Using a separate category for each alphabetical character and treating upper- and lower-case letters as equal, construct a table for the frequency distribution of the first 200 letters of Abraham Lincoln's Gettysburg Address.

> Fourscore and seven years ago our fathers brought forth on this continent a new nation, conceived in liberty, and dedicated to the proposition that all men are created equal.
>
> Now we are engaged in a great civil war, testing whether that nation, or . . . .

Compare your distribution with the first one listed on page 35. Do you think that Lincoln used "ordinary" English? Explain.

2-9 Refer to the women's heights data given in Exercise 2-6.

(a) Construct a table for the frequency distribution that has five class intervals of width 2 inches. Use 58 inches as the lower limit of the first interval.

(b) Plot a histogram of the frequency distribution you constructed in (a).

2-10 Criticize each of the following designations for class intervals of monthly household electricity bills.

(a)	(b)	(c)
$10–15	$11–22	$10–under 15
15–20	21–32	16–under 20
20–25	31–42	21–under 25
etc.	etc.	etc.

2-11 A sample of 100 engineering students has been categorized by sex, marital status, and major. The number of persons in each category is summarized below.

Sex	Marital Status	Major	Number of Students
male	married	electrical	14
male	married	mechanical	16
male	married	civil	10
male	single	electrical	5
male	single	mechanical	19
male	single	civil	4
female	married	electrical	5

(continued on next page)

Sex	Marital Status	Major	Number of Students
female	married	mechanical	12
female	married	civil	0
female	single	electrical	5
female	single	mechanical	8
female	single	civil	2
		Total	100

Construct a table for the frequency distribution characterized by (a) sex, (b) marital status, and (c) major.

2-12 The following sample data have been obtained for the number of professional women employed (thousands) in the United States in 1986.

Profession	Number of Women
Engineering/Computer science	347
Health care	1,937
Education	2,833
Social/Legal	698
Arts/Athletics/Entertainment	901
All others	355

Source: Bureau of Labor Statistics.

Construct a bar chart.

2-13 Comment on the appropriateness of each of the following class interval widths for a frequency distribution of pay rates for a sample of 100 hourly workers in a metropolitan area.

(a) $.05 (b) $.25 (c) $.50 (d) $1.00 (e) $2.00

2-2 RELATIVE AND CUMULATIVE FREQUENCY DISTRIBUTIONS

Two useful extensions of the basic frequency distribution are the relative and the cumulative frequency distributions.

RELATIVE FREQUENCY DISTRIBUTIONS

A **relative frequency** is the ratio of the number of observations in a particular category to the total number of observations. Relative frequency may be determined for both quantitative and qualitative data and is a convenient basis for the comparison of similar groups of different size. For example, consider comparing family incomes in sparsely populated Nevada with those in California, the most populous state. It would not be very meaningful to say that only 6,000 families in Nevada have achieved a particular level of income and that 250,000 families in California receive the same income. But if we say that 1% of the families in Nevada and only .8% of the families in California have achieved this income level, we can make a realistic comparison between family incomes in the two states. We must compare the *proportions* (percentages)—not the total frequencies—of families who have achieved this income level in each state.

TABLE 2-6 Calculation of Relative Frequency Distribution for Age of Accounts Receivable

(1) Age (days)	(2) Number of Accounts (frequency)	(3) Relative Frequency
0–under 30	532	.330
30–under 60	317	.196
60–under 90	285	.176
90–under 120	176	.109
120–under 150	158	.098
150–under 180	147	.091
Totals	1,615	1.000

The relative frequencies are calculated by dividing the number of observations in each category by the total number of observations. Once the frequency distribution itself is obtained, the relative frequency computations are a matter of simple arithmetic. This is illustrated in Table 2-6 for each class interval of data on the age of department store accounts receivable (accounts 180 days or older are written off as uncollectible). The relative frequency of accounts less than 30 days

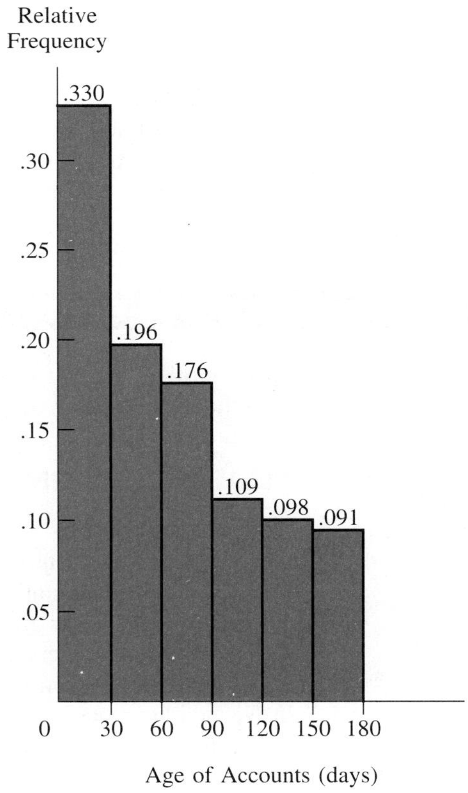

FIGURE 2-8 Relative frequency histogram for age of department store accounts receivable.

TABLE 2-7 Frequency Distributions for Students by Sex

Large University			Small College	
Sex	Frequency		Sex	Frequency
male	6,000		male	400
female	4,000		female	100
Totals	10,000			500

old (the class interval of 0–under 30) is 532/1,615 = .330, which means that 33% of all accounts are less than 30 days old. The other relative frequencies are also calculated by dividing the class frequency in column (2) by the total number of accounts.

The sum of all the relative frequencies must always be 1. Columns (1) and (3) constitute the **relative frequency distribution** for these data. The histogram for this distribution is shown in Figure 2-8. A histogram constructed using relative frequencies will have the same shape as one constructed using original tallies, or absolute frequencies. Only the scale on the vertical axis will change.

Analysis of relative frequencies can sometimes be useful when analysis of absolute frequencies is not. A department store's credit sales will fluctuate considerably over the seasons, but the same seasonal patterns will generally persist from year to year. If the credit worthiness of the store's customers remains about the same as it has been in the past, then the relative frequency distributions for the ages of accounts receivable obtained during the same calendar month in two successive years should not be noticeably different when growth is steady. A substantial difference in relative frequencies may be due to erratic growth or to a change in the quality of credit customers or in collection procedures. Absolute frequencies cannot isolate the effect of sales growth from the effect of changes in credit procedures.

Relative frequency may also be used to compare two qualitative populations. Table 2-7 shows the frequency distribution by sex of students on two campuses. The number of men competing for dates at the large university is 6,000, whereas the number at the small college is only 400. The relative frequency distributions are provided in Table 2-8. In terms of relative frequency, there is less competition at the university, where the proportion of men is smaller (.60 at the university versus .80 at the college).

TABLE 2-8 Relative Frequency Distributions for Students by Sex

Large University			Small College	
Sex	Relative Frequency		Sex	Relative Frequency
male	.60		male	.80
female	.40		female	.20
Totals	1.00			1.00

CUMULATIVE FREQUENCY DISTRIBUTIONS

A **cumulative frequency**, used only when the observations are numerical, is the sum of the frequencies for successively higher class intervals. For example, we might find that 8,439 men in a population of 10,000 are less than 6 feet tall; stated differently, 84.39% of the population is shorter than 6 feet. Cumulative frequencies can provide useful descriptions of a population, especially when they are expressed relatively as percentages or proportions. We can judge our chances of being accepted by a graduate school, for example, partly by the percentage of persons who obtained lower scores on the admissions examination. (Cumulative frequency is relative to some probability concepts we will encounter in Chapter 6.) The cumulative frequencies are determined by adding the frequency for each class interval to the frequencies for preceding intervals.

EXAMPLE: SALES OF TELEVISION SETS

Table 2-9 contains data from a sample of 100 annual sales figures for television sets sold by retail stores. We will construct cumulative frequencies for these data.

TABLE 2-9 Frequency Distribution for Unit Television Set Sales

(1) Units Sold	(2) Number of Stores (frequency)
100–under 200	0
200–under 300	5
300–under 400	39
400–under 500	31
500–under 600	16
600–under 700	6
700–under 800	3

SOLUTION: The cumulative frequency for sales under 300 units is found by adding the frequency of sales at or above 100 (but under 200) to the number of stores having sales at or above 200 (but under 300), or 0 + 5 = 5. The remaining cumulative frequencies are shown in Table 2-10.

TABLE 2-10 Calculation of Cumulative Frequencies for Unit Television Set Sales

(1) Units Sold	(2) Number of Stores (frequency)	(3) Cumulative Frequency
100–under 200	0	0
200–under 300	5	0 + 5 = 5
300–under 400	39	5 + 39 = 44
400–under 500	31	44 + 31 = 75
500–under 600	16	75 + 16 = 91
600–under 700	6	91 + 6 = 97
700–under 800	3	97 + 3 = 100

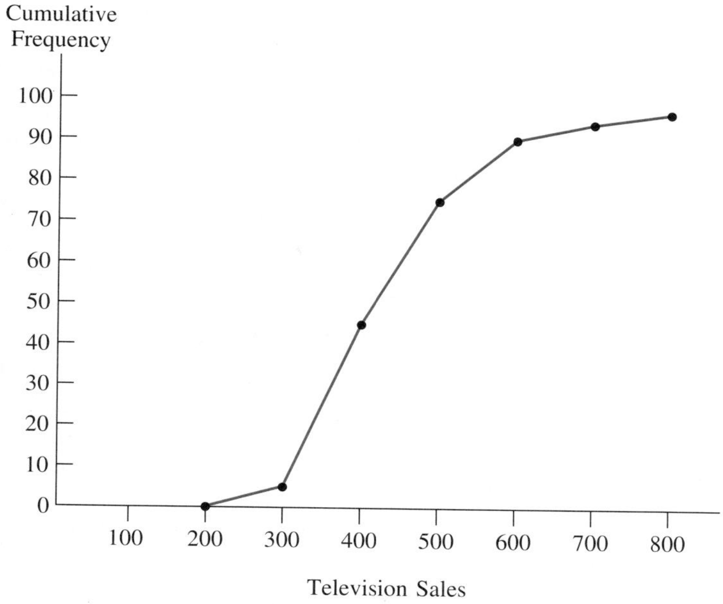

FIGURE 2-9 Ogive for cumulative frequency distribution of television sales.

The cumulative frequency for a class interval represents the total number of observations falling in or below that interval. In the preceding example, columns (1) and (3) of Table 2-10 constitute the **cumulative frequency distribution** for the television sales data. Likewise, **cumulative relative frequencies** are found by adding successive relative frequencies, and these results determine the **cumulative relative frequency distribution**. The largest cumulative relative frequency is 1.0.

Sometimes it is desirable to plot the cumulative relative frequency distribution in a graph, as shown in Figure 2-9. The ordinate (vertical height) of a plotted point represents the cumulative frequency for values less than the abscissa (the horizontal axis value). Such a curve is called an **ogive**.

EXERCISES

2-14 Refer to the fuel consumption data in Table 2-4.

(a) Construct a table for the relative frequency distribution.

(b) Construct a table for the cumulative frequency distribution.

2-15 Ingrid's Hallmark Shop obtained the following frequency distribution of times between arrivals of customers.

(a) Construct a table for the relative frequency distribution. Then plot a histogram for the distribution.

(b) Construct a table for the cumulative frequency distribution. Then plot an ogive for the distribution.

Time (minutes)	Number of Customers
0.0–under 3.0	210
3.0–under 6.0	130
6.0–under 9.0	75
9.0–under 12.0	40
12.0–under 15.0	20
15.0–under 18.0	15
18.0–under 21.0	10

2-16 The following is the frequency distribution of consecutive days absent during 1989 by Midget Motor employees.

Consecutive Days Absent	Number of Employees
0–under 5	3,100
5–under 10	810
10–under 15	510
15–under 20	320
20–under 25	120
25–under 30	30
30–under 60	110

(Employees absent a total of 60 or more consecutive days are reclassified as inactive. Each employee is counted just once, being placed in the category corresponding to his or her longest absence.)

(a) Construct a table for the relative frequency distribution.

(b) Construct a table for the cumulative *relative* frequency distribution.

(c) Plot an ogive using the data obtained in (b).

2-17 Copymat orders occasional spot checks of tardy and absent employees. A particular audit of payroll records resulted in the following sample frequency distributions.

	Number of Employees by Office				
	A	B	C	D	E
Tardy	60	60	10	56	2
Absent	60	30	20	24	15
On job and on time	1,080	510	270	720	233
Totals	1,200	600	300	800	250

(a) Determine the relative frequency distributions for each office.

(b) Using office *A* as a standard, which regions have an excessively high number of tardy employees?

(c) Compared to office *A*, which regions have an unusually large number of absent employees? Do you think that the managers of these regions are necessarily "softer" than the manager in region *A?* Explain.

2-18 The cumulative relative frequency distribution for the number of shares owned by each of the 1,000 shareholders of Kryptonite Corporation is provided below.

Number of Shares	Cumulative Proportion of Shareholders
0–under 5,000	0.36
5,000–under 10,000	0.63
10,000–under 15,000	0.81
15,000–under 20,000	0.90
20,000–under 25,000	0.97
25,000–under 30,000	1.00

(a) Construct a table for the relative frequency distribution.
(b) Determine the original frequency distribution using your answer to (a).
(c) Determine the cumulative frequency distribution using your answer to (b).

2-3 COMMON FORMS OF THE FREQUENCY DISTRIBUTION

Statistical methodology has been developed to analyze samples taken from populations having various general forms. By placing populations in various categories, we can increase our analytical powers considerably by using techniques that apply to all populations in the same **distribution family**. All quantitative populations have some form of distribution. Most populations can be classified into a few well-known distributions, although the mathematical equations describing them may be complex. The shape of the sample histogram usually indicates the form of the population distribution.

In the following figures, some of the more common general shapes of frequency curves appear beside representative sample histograms. Figure 2-10 represents the relative frequency distribution of the diameters of a production batch of 1-inch-thick steel reinforcing rods. Note that the histogram is fairly symmetrical about the interval .995–1.005 inches, with frequency dropping for the next higher and lower intervals. The histogram bars on the left and right become progressively shorter, tapering off at about .91 and 1.09 inches, respectively. The smoothed frequency curve beside the histogram is bell-shaped and belongs to a class of

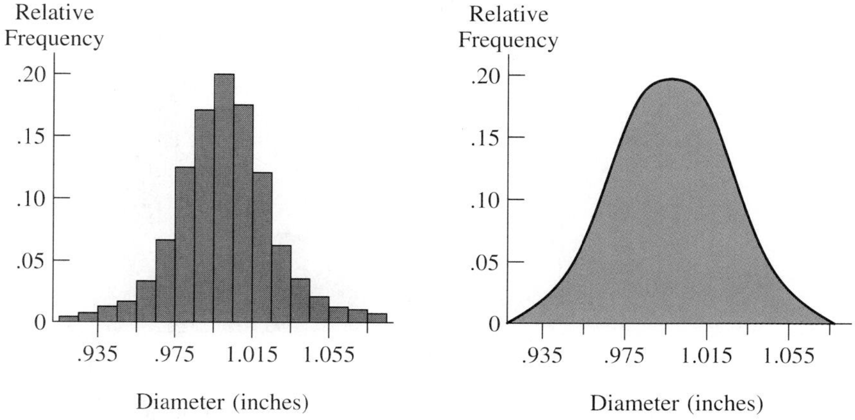

FIGURE 2-10 Sample histogram (left) and population frequency curve (right) for steel rod diameters.

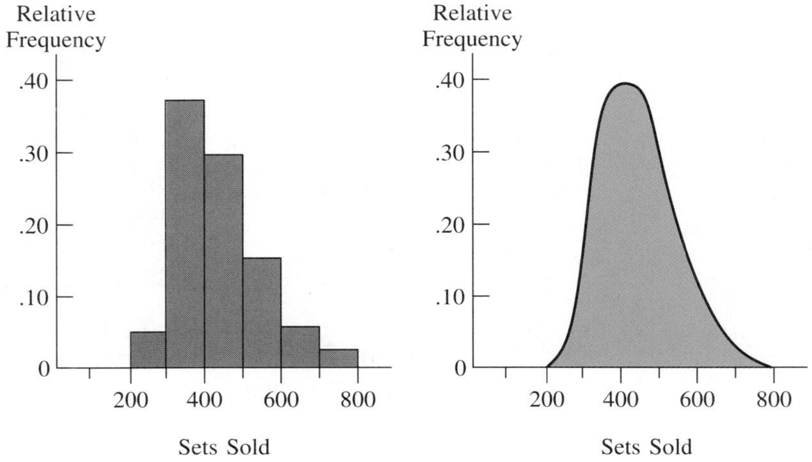

FIGURE 2-11 Sample histogram (left) and population frequency curve (right) for television sales.

populations having the **normal distribution**. We will have more to say about normal curves in Chapter 7. A large number of populations have frequency distributions in this category, including many physical measurements.

Figure 2-11 shows the histogram for the television sales data given in Table 2-9. Here the data are **skewed** to the right, because a few stores had sales levels that were quite high. Beside the histogram is a frequency curve in which the right "tail" is longer than the left. This general shape corresponds to a class of skewed distributions in which there are a few small observations and in which proportionately more large observations fall over a wide range of values.

Another type of skewed distribution is provided in Figure 2-12, where the fuel consumption frequency curve has a longer left tail. In this case, the smaller values are widely spread from 14 through 18 miles per gallon, and the rarer large values fall into the single class 23.0–under 24.0.

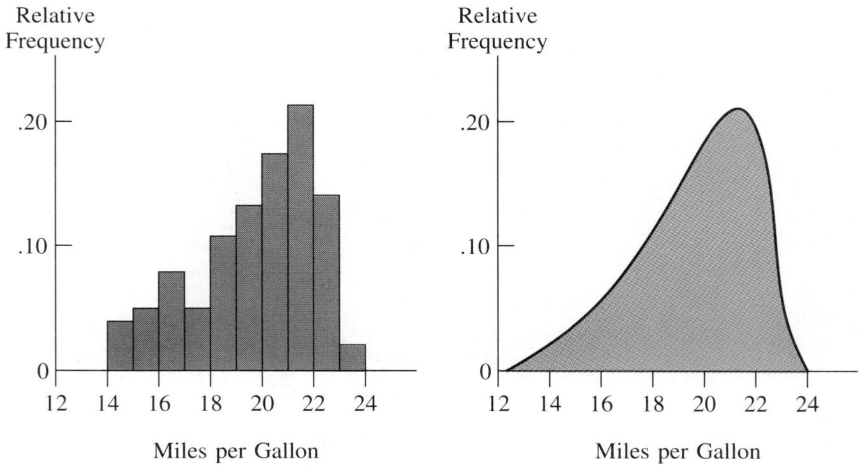

FIGURE 2-12 Sample histogram (left) and population frequency curve (right) for fuel consumption.

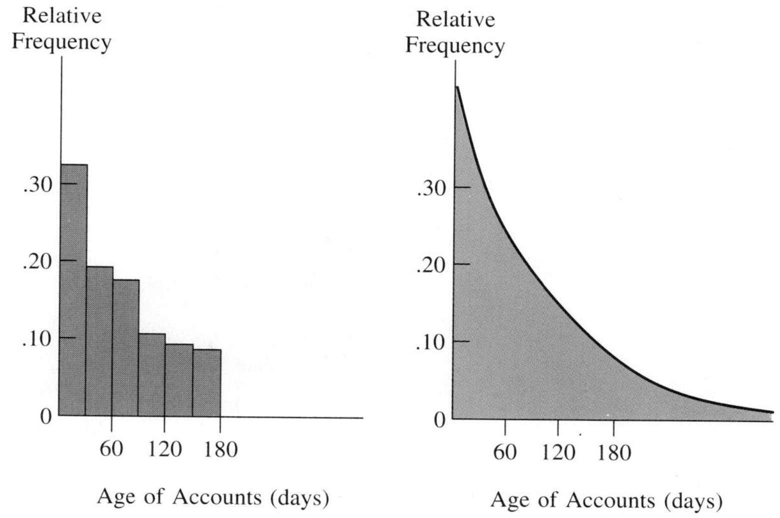

FIGURE 2-13 Sample histogram (left) and population frequency curve (right) for the age of department store accounts receivable.

The distribution given in Table 2-6 for the age of department store accounts receivable is plotted in Figure 2-13. Here, the smoothed frequency curve has the general shape of a reversed letter J. This type of distribution is sometimes called the **exponential distribution**. Such a frequency curve approximates a great many populations in which the observations involve items that exhibit changes in status over time. Exponential distributions have been used to characterize equipment lifetimes until failure. They are also used to describe the time between successive arrivals by cars at a toll booth or by patients in a hospital emergency room and are therefore useful in the analysis of waiting-line or queuing situations.

The left portion of Figure 2-14 is the histogram for the lengths of pieces of scrap roofing lumber from a construction job. Any piece shorter than 20 inches (the width between studs) cannot be used. Because the lumber arrives from the mill in various lengths, a piece of scrap is likely to be any length between 1 and 20 inches. (Scrap shorter than 1 inch is not counted.) The histogram is therefore approximated by a rectangle. Because no particular width is favored, such a population is a member of the **uniform distribution** family.

Later we will encounter other, less common shapes, and we will discuss how one particular shape—the bimodal—can help identify nonhomogeneous population influences. Classifying the various shapes of frequency distributions enables us to obtain better population descriptions and to be selective in choosing statistical techniques for analysis.

EXERCISES

2-19 For each of the following populations for the *ages* of persons, sketch an appropriate shape for the frequency distribution and explain the reasons for your choice.

(a) Science-fiction novel readers.
(b) Persons who do not work full-time.
(c) Persons who have false teeth.
(d) Children in a grammar school.

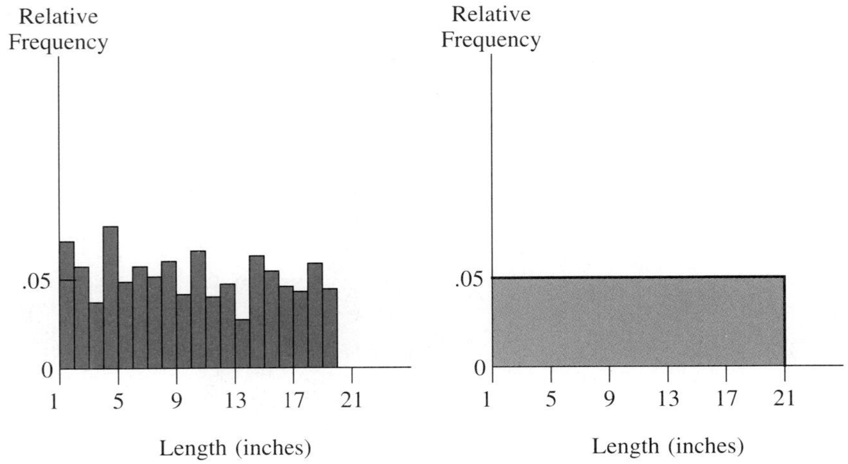

FIGURE 2-14 Sample histogram (left) and population frequency curve (right) for lengths of scrap pieces of lumber.

2-20 For each of the following populations, sketch an appropriate shape for the frequency distribution and explain the reasons for your choice.
(a) The times required by a pharmacist to fill new prescriptions.
(b) The last two digits in numbers assigned to telephones in a metropolitan area.
(c) The number of persons employed by manufacturing firms.
(d) The duration of stay of patients hospitalized with nonchronic diseases.

2-4 DISPLAYING DATA IN MULTIPLE DIMENSIONS

Statistical investigations may involve two or more variables, such as income, years of education, and age; production cost and quantity; or type of degree and salary. Statistical investigations attempt to uncover relationships between two or more variables, such as how income levels relate to different educational backgrounds and ages, or how degrees differ in salary level. A starting point is often a data display.

QUANTITATIVE DATA DISPLAYS—THE SCATTER DIAGRAM

Figure 2-15, generated on an IBM PC using Minitab®, shows a data display for two quantitative population variables. The **scatter diagram** relates total production cost to the production lot size. There is one asterisk for each sample production run. The asterisks are located at the coordinates for the observed cost and lot size for a particular sample run. (The "2"s indicate that two observations have nearly the same coordinates.) A visual inspection indicates that cost should increase with lot size. Chapter 10 shows how a line or a curve can be used to summarize that relationship.

QUALITATIVE DATA DISPLAYS—THE CROSS TABULATION

When both variables are qualitative, a two-dimensional counterpart to the scatter diagram may be used. Table 2-11 shows a **cross tabulation** for the sample of

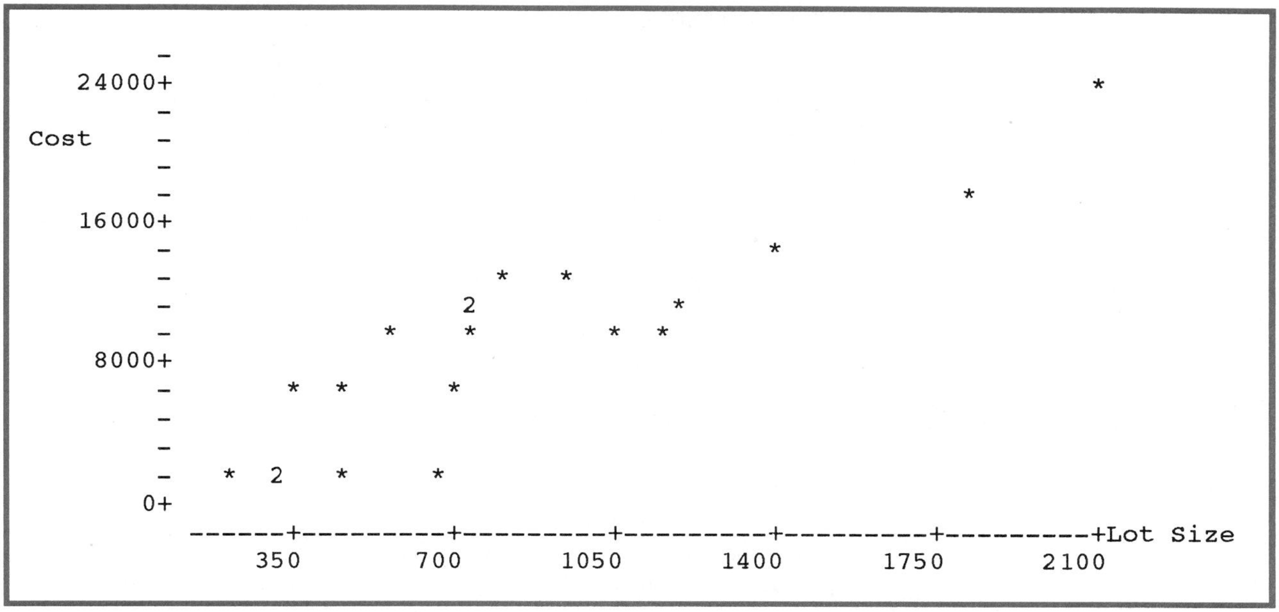

Note: Figure generated on an IBM PC using Minitab.©

FIGURE 2-15 Scatter diagram for total cost versus size of production run.

Beta Gamma Sigma members encountered earlier. Each member is counted into the total of a particular cell. There is one row for each major (5 levels) and one column for each sex (2 levels).

A cross tabulation is a logical starting point for evaluation of qualitative data. From a quick examination of Table 2-11, we can determine that the sexes are not evenly represented among the majors, even when we account for fewer female members. Chapter 16 shows how a similar cross tabulation with sample data might be used to test whether various occupational categories in an overall population have disproportionate representation of the sexes.

TABLE 2-11 Cross Tabulation for Beta Gamma Sigma Members

	Sex		
Major	**Male**	**Female**	**Total**
Accounting	8	9	17
Finance	3	1	4
Management	22	16	38
Marketing	16	11	27
Human Res.	9	5	14
Total	58	42	100

HIGHER DIMENSIONAL DATA

When there are three or more variables, it can be challenging to display the data graphically. The scatter diagram concept extends to any number of dimensions. In three dimensions, each data point would resemble marbles suspended in a room, one corner of which serves as the origin for two horizontal axes where the walls join the floor and one vertical axis where the two walls join. Chapter 11 describes how a *plane* may be found that summarizes the relationship between the variables. Higher dimensional relationships are not usually portrayed graphically. Instead, statistical procedures seek a mathematical expression to explain them.

EXERCISES

2-21 Refer to the student data given in Exercise 2-11. Construct a cross tabulation of marital status versus sex. What can you conclude regarding the tendency of each sex to be married?

2-22 Refer to the student data given in Exercise 2-11. Construct a cross tabulation of major versus marital status. What can you conclude regarding the tendency of students in the various majors to be married?

2-23 The following checkout times and purchase amounts were obtained by a student during one Saturday morning at a local supermarket.

Time	Purchase	Time	Purchase
2.5 min	$29.75	13.5 min	$136.05
1.0	11.15	9.0	68.50
7.6	42.14	2.1	9.14
8.5	94.07	3.4	25.23
4.6	33.01	5.7	53.18

Construct a scatter diagram using checkout time for the vertical axis and purchase amount for the horizontal axis.

2-24 The following sample data have been obtained for automobiles driven in the United States.

Year	Average Distance (miles)	Average Fuel Consumption (gallons)
1960	9,450	661
1965	9,390	667
1970	9,980	735
1975	9,630	712
1976	9,760	711
1978	10,050	715
1979	9,480	664
1980	9,140	603
1981	9,000	579
1982	9,530	587
1983	9,650	578
1984	9,790	553
1985	9,830	549

Source: Energy Information Administration, Annual Energy Review, 1986.

Construct a scatter diagram. Use average fuel consumption for the vertical axis and average distance for the horizontal axis.

2-25 Refer to your graph from Exercise 2-23. Use a straight-edge to draw a line that seems to fit the data points.
(a) According to your line, find the checkout time expected when the purchase is (1) \$20, and (2) \$70.
(b) The checkout time level where the line crosses the vertical axis represents the *fixed* component of time required for every transaction, regardless of purchase amount. What is this time?
(c) The *variable* component of checkout time is the slope of the line, in minutes per dollar of purchase. Compute this by dividing the difference between (2) and (1) from part (a) by \$50.
(d) Using only your answers from (b) and (c), compute the checkout time expected for a purchase of \$100.

2-5 SPECIAL DATA DISPLAYS

The histogram is an important display for quantitative data partly because it dovetails with mathematical concepts relating probability concepts to the sampling process. Alternative displays are sometimes used when the number of data points is small or when the purpose of the statistical investigation is to take an immediate action rather than make a generalization.

THE BOX PLOT

When the amount of data is limited, a clear pattern may not be distinguishable with a histogram or frequency polygon. Consider the results obtained by a production supervisor who wishes to calibrate the control mechanism for filling jars of instant coffee. A proper calibration should accomplish two things: (1) provide contents of jars close to 16 ounces and (2) yield little fluctuation in contents from jar to jar. Over a trial period, successive samples are taken, with adjustments made after each. The following data were obtained.

	Sample 1	*Sample 2*	*Sample 3*	*Sample 4*	*Sample 5*
	15.1	16.3	16.0	15.9	15.9
	16.5	15.8	15.8	16.2	16.1
	14.7	15.7	15.5	16.0	16.0
	15.5	16.7	16.2	16.1	16.1
	13.8	16.3	16.2	15.9	15.9
			Percentiles		
25th	14.25	15.75	15.65	15.9	15.9
50th	15.1	16.3	16.0	16.0	16.0
75th	16.0	16.5	16.2	16.15	16.1

Figure 2-16 shows a box plot for each sample. The borders of the box are positioned at the 25th and 75th percentiles, while the box is divided at the 50th percentile. Chapter 3 gives a detailed discussion of how to obtain these summary values. The line segment at the left of each box is a "whisker" extending to the minimum observed value for the respective sample, while the line for the right whisker stops at the maximum sample observation. Notice that the successive boxes become narrower and that the middle becomes closer to the desired 16 ounces.

Once the regulator valve is calibrated, only minor adjustments will be required for day-to-day operations. Another display is useful for this purpose.

THE CONTROL CHART

Each day the foreman in charge of instant-coffee filling takes a sample of jars. The mean values for 28 days are plotted in the **control chart** in Figure 2-17. On Day 11 and Day 18 the filling process was "out of control," and the regulator

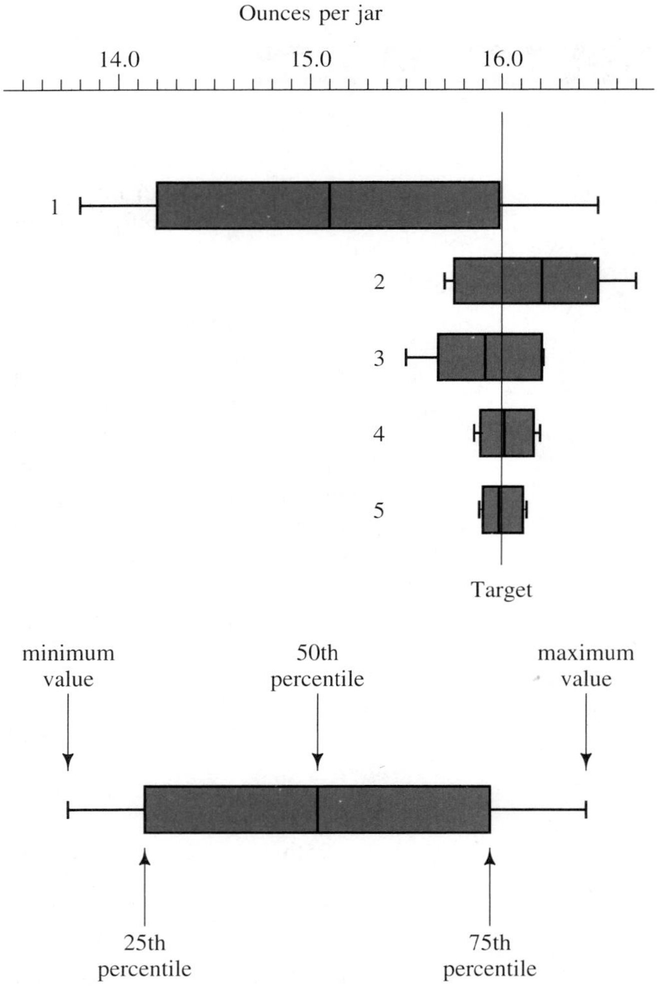

FIGURE 2-16 Box plots obtained from successive samples of instant coffee jar contents, made during calibration of regulator.

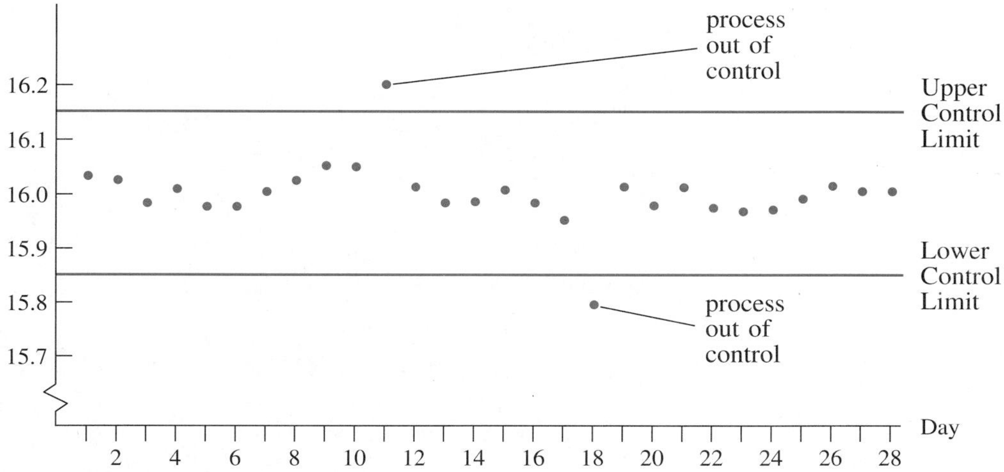

FIGURE 2-17 Control chart used to monitor process for filling instant coffee jars during production.

valve was then cleaned and readjusted. Chapter 13 describes how to find the limits for control charts. That is a procedure of **statistical quality control**.

THE TIME SERIES PLOT

Perhaps the most common data display in business applications is the **time series plot**, shown in Figure 2-18 for Ingrid's Hallmark Shop (an actual store). The sales for each month are plotted for the five-year period 1986–90. Notice the pronounced seasonal pattern reappearing every year, with maximum sales in December, followed by a dramatic January dropoff.

The time series plot is very similar to the control chart. But instead of locating points that are out of control, the time series plot is useful for identifying meaningful patterns. Chapter 12 describes in detail various statistical procedures for evaluating time series data. The ultimate objective of **time series analysis** is in **forecasting** the future levels of one or more variables.

EXERCISES

2-26 Construct a box plot for weekly closing prices of DanDee Assemblers shares.

Prices $18.50 19.85 19.25 18.25 17.75 16.50 17.25 17.25 18.25 19.00
Percentiles 25th–17.25 50th–18.25 75th–19.06

2-27 Construct a box plot for the number of daily orders generated by a telemarketer selling newspaper subscriptions.

Subscriptions 5 2 7 8 11 15 7 6 4 13
Fractiles 25th–4.75 50th–7 75th–11.5

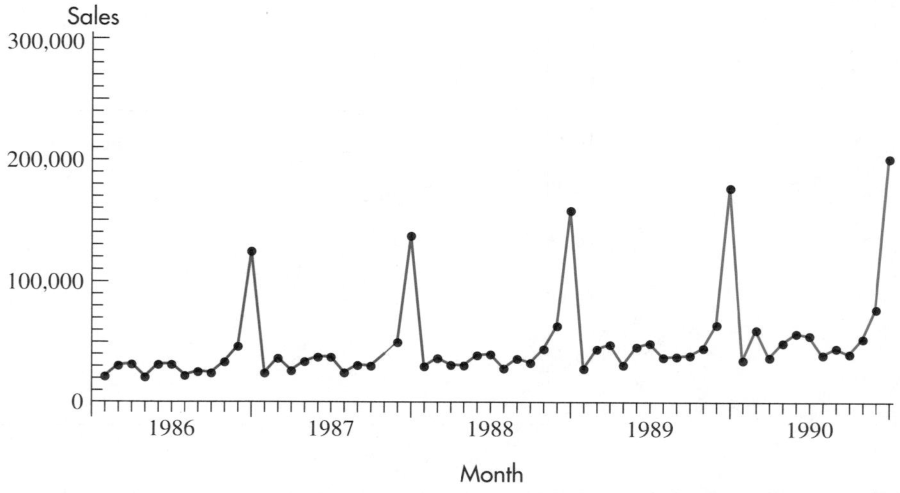

FIGURE 2-18 Monthly Sales by Ingrid's Hallmark shop.

2-28 The following data apply to the mean contents of five-pound cans of ground coffee.

Mean	5.1	4.8	5.5	5.6	5.3	5.6	5.1	4.9	4.6	4.9	5.0	5.0
Day	1	2	3	4	5	6	7	8	9	10	11	12

Plot these data on a control chart. Use 4.75 pounds as the lower limit and 5.25 pounds as the upper limit. On which days (if any) is the process out of control?

2-29 Consider the average driving distance for autos in Exercise 2-24.
(a) Plot the time series on a graph.
(b) What can you conclude regarding how average driving distance has changed over the 1960–1985 period?

2-30 Consider the average fuel consumption for autos in Exercise 2-24.
(a) Plot the time series on a graph.
(b) What can you conclude regarding how average fuel consumption has changed over the 1960–1985 period?

SUMMARY

1. **How are statistical data organized in terms of frequency of occurrence?**
A first step in organizing the **raw data** obtained from a statistical investigation is to establish the **frequency distribution**. All observations are classified by category or size. Numerical values are placed into **class intervals**. The number of observations in a particular group is the **class frequency**.

2. **What are the kinds of numerical and graphical displays of data?**
Two graphical displays are commonly obtained from sample data. One is the **histogram**, a chart having a bar for each class; each bar is as tall as the number of observations found for that group. A similar picture is provided by the **frequency polygon**, which is applicable only when the data are quantitative.

Another display is the **stem-and-leaf plot**, which maintains the raw data and arranges the numbers more conveniently. A **pie chart**, in which each slice is proportional to the category frequency, is a common display for qualitative data.

3. **How do we compare data sets and make further summaries?**
   Comparisons are best made using **relative frequencies** instead of the original tallies. A complete collection of these constitutes the **relative frequency distribution**. Another useful set of values applicable to quantitative observations are the **cumulative frequencies**. Even more helpful are the **cumulative relative frequencies**, which collectively provide a table called the **cumulative relative frequency distribution**.

4. **What are the common forms of statistical data?**
   Frequency distributions are not ordinarily known for populations, since a census is not usually taken. Nevertheless, the form of the underlying distribution may be known. Populations are often represented by familiar **frequency curves**, such as the bell-shaped **normal curve**.
   Several shapes for the histogram or frequency curve are important to statistics. In addition to the normal curve, important shapes include those **skewed** positively or negatively and representatives of distribution families, such as the **exponential distribution** or the **uniform distribution**.

5. **How may data be displayed when two or more variables are present?**
   Multidimensional data displays are important for assessing the relationships between variables. The **scatter diagram** exhibits quantitative data points in two-dimensional space, with one axis for each variable. A counterpart with qualitative data is the **cross tabulation**, with rows for the levels of one variable and columns for the levels of the other. Each data point is counted in a cell total, with one cell for each level combination of the two variables. Statistical procedures extend to higher dimensions, even when graphical displays may be impossible to construct.

6. **What are some of the special data displays that are useful for important statistical applications?**
   Special displays are encountered in statistical applications: the **box plot** is an alternative to the histogram when there are few data points; the **control chart** is useful in statistical quality control; and the **time series plot** is helpful in forecasting evaluations.

REAL-LIFE STATISTICAL CHALLENGE

Selling to the Personal Computer Marketplace.

The information age of the 1990s has brought a maturing of the personal computer market. Personal computer systems, consisting of a microcomputer, a printer, software or programs, and other accessories are a multibillion-dollar business. Sales in this market offer great rewards. Successful selling requires specific and accurate information to design a successful sales strategy. For example, in which newspapers or trade journals should a computer equipment company advertise?

REAL-LIFE STATISTICAL CHALLENGE

InfoWorld, a data-gathering division of IDG, keeps track of the sales of personal computers throughout the world. They provide advertisers and distributors with data concerning where people are buying their products. Table 2-12 shows the total sales by metropolitan statistical area (MSA) for the top ten personal computer markets in the United States. *InfoWorld* found that "as of 1991, there were 53,887,000 personal computers installed in the United States for a value of $92.2 billion."

Other data can be combined with the total sales data to help marketing strategists develop winning approaches. For example, adding census data to the original data in Table 2-12 allows us to learn more about each of these markets. Using population data for each MSA presented in Table 2-13 helps us determine the per capita (per person) dollar value we might expect to see in each community. The per capita values are shown, and the metropolitan areas have been reranked by these per capita figures.

These ten markets account only for about 24 percent of the total market. Table 2-14 summarizes the data for other MSAs.

Discussion Questions:

1. Calculate the cumulative relative frequency for the ten MSAs in Table 2-12.
2. What types of visual displays might provide understandable presentations for the data in Tables 2-13 and 2-14? Create the displays.

TABLE 2-12 Top Ten Computer Markets

Rank	Metropolitan Statistical Area	Installed Units	Percentage of U.S. Units	Value of Installed Base (000s)	Population	Per Capita Installed Base
1	Los Angeles-Long Beach, CA	2,137,643	4.0	$3,658,370	8,863,164	$413
2	New York, NY	2,110,269	3.9	3,611,522	8,546,846	423
3	Washington, DC-MD-VA	1,832,859	3.4	3,136,761	3,923,574	799
4	Chicago, IL	1,455,488	2.7	2,490,927	6,069,974	410
5	Boston, MA	1,222,103	2.3	2,091,511	2,870,669	729
6	Philadelphia, PA-NJ	1,203,674	2.2	2,059,972	4,856,881	424
7	Detroit, MI	834,817	1.5	1,428,709	4,382,299	326
8	San Jose, CA	825,387	1.5	1,412,570	1,497,577	943
9	Minneapolis-St Paul, MN-WI	756,412	1.4	1,294,526	2,464,124	525
10	Anaheim-Santa Ana, CA	733,941	1.4	1,256,069	2,410,556	521

Source: InfoWorld, an IDG company, "The Personal Computer Market by Metropolitan Statistical Areas, 1991."

TABLE 2-13 Top Ten Computer Markets Ranked by per capita Dollar Value

Rank	Metropolitan Statistical Area	Installed Units	Percentage of U.S. Units	Value of Installed Base (000s)	Population	Per Capita Installed Base
1	San Jose, CA	825,387	1.5	$1,412,570	1,497,577	$943
2	Washington, DC-MD-VA	1,832,859	3.4	3,136,761	3,923,574	799
3	Boston, MA	1,222,103	2.3	2,091,511	2,870,669	729
4	Minneapolis-St Paul, MN-WI	756,412	1.4	1,294,526	2,464,124	525
5	Anaheim-Santa Ana, CA	733,941	1.4	1,256,069	2,410,556	521
6	Philadelphia, PA-NJ	1,203,674	2.2	2,059,972	4,856,881	424
7	New York, NY	2,110,269	3.9	3,611,522	8,546,846	423
8	Los Angeles-Long Beach, CA	2,137,643	4.0	3,658,370	8,863,164	413
9	Chicago, IL	1,455,488	2.7	2,490,927	6,069,974	410
10	Detroit, MI	834,817	1.5	1,428,709	4,382,299	326

Sources: InfoWorld, an IDG company, "The Personal Computer Market by Metropolitan Statistical Areas, 1991" and U.S. Bureau of the Census, release 1991.

3. What other business factors (for example, local manufacturing or service industries) should we consider when we study this data?
4. Which other types of high-technology equipment (for example, mobile telephones and fax machines) might we expect to have similar patterns?

TABLE 2-14 Cumulative Totals for Top 150 Markets and the Remainder of the U.S. Markets

Metropolitan Statistical Areas (MSAs)	Installed Units	Percentage of U.S. Units	Value of Installed Base (000s)
Top 10	13,112,593	24.3	$22,440,937
Top 25	21,905,822	40.7	37,489,701
Top 50	29,086,856	54.0	49,779,347
Top 75	33,143,843	61.5	56,772,490
Top 100	36,009,714	66.8	61,627,151
Top 150	39,782,020	73.8	68,083,087
Remainder of U.S.:			
MSA 151-333	5,079,011	9.4	8,692,235
Not in MSAs	9,025,969	16.8	15,447,078
	14,104,980	26.2	24,139,313

REVIEW EXERCISES

2-31 A sample of MBA students has been selected. The students' ages have the following frequency distribution.

Age (years)	Number of Students
20–under 25	18
25–under 30	23
30–under 35	15
35–under 40	13
40–under 45	7
45–under 50	6
50–under 55	5
55–under 60	5
60–under 65	8
Total	100

Construct a table for the relative and cumulative frequency distributions.

2-32 Refer to the student data given in Exercise 2-11. Construct a cross tabulation of major versus sex. What can you conclude regarding the prevalence of each sex within the majors?

2-33 Sky King provided the following incomplete fuel consumption data for its delivery fleet.

Miles per Gallon	Number of Vans	Relative Frequency	Cumulative Frequency
6.0–under 8.0	—	—	—
8.0–under 10.0	23	—	29
10.0–under 12.0	—	.34	—
12.0–under 14.0	17	.17	—
14.0–under 16.0	—	—	92
16.0–under 18.0	—	—	—
Totals	100	1.00	

(a) Determine the missing values.
(b) Plot the cumulative frequency ogive for this population.

2-34 The following heights (inches) have been obtained for the male staff at the *Daily Planet*.

73.1	66.0	65.9	72.0	67.5
69.9	69.1	68.4	74.3	69.9
72.1	69.4	71.0	70.1	71.5
61.5	70.0	63.4	71.0	66.2
68.3	74.2	68.9	73.8	69.3
71.3	74.6	66.9	69.8	68.8
73.0	65.0	63.7	70.9	76.6
69.7	64.8	71.2	70.7	67.5
75.1	71.5	72.0	76.1	68.2
66.8	72.0	69.7	73.0	70.6

(a) Construct a table for the frequency distribution that has sixteen class intervals of width 1 inch. Use 61.5 inches as the lower limit of the first interval.
(b) Plot a histogram using your answer to (a).
(c) Add a column of relative frequencies to the table found in (a).
(d) Add a column of cumulative relative frequencies to the table found in (a).
(e) Plot the cumulative relative frequency ogive.
(f) What proportion of the sample lies (1) under 70.5″, (2) under 75.5″, and (3) under 66.5″ tall?

2-35 Hops Brewery has two divisions, one in the South and the other in the North. Separate frequency distributions for the hourly wages of workers in the South and North are provided below.

South		North	
Hourly Wage	**Number of Workers**	**Hourly Wage**	**Number of Workers**
$ 5–under 6	150	$ 5–under 6	0
6–under 7	300	6–under 7	0
7–under 8	150	7–under 8	0
8–under 9	100	8–under 9	0
9–under 10	50	9–under 10	50
10–under 11	50	10–under 11	150
11–under 12	50	11–under 12	150
12–under 13	50	12–under 13	200
13–under 14	50	13–under 14	100

(a) Plot frequency polygons for each division separately but on the same graph.
(b) Combine the South and North data into a single table for the all-company frequency distribution.
(c) Plot a frequency polygon using the data obtained in (b).
(d) Comparing the graphs in (a) to that in (c), which presentation do you think provides more meaningful managerial information? Explain.

2-36 A sample of 350 persons has been categorized by sex, marital status, and occupation. The number of persons in each category is summarized below.

Sex	Marital Status	Occupation	Number of Persons
male	married	blue collar	75
male	married	white collar	37
male	married	professional	12
male	single	blue collar	55
male	single	white collar	38
male	single	professional	3
female	married	blue collar	13
female	married	white collar	32
female	married	professional	2
female	single	blue collar	12
female	single	white collar	66
female	single	professional	5
		Total	350

Construct a table for the frequency distribution by (a) sex, (b) marital status, (c) occupation.

2-37 The following sample data have been obtained for the number of monthly trades in portfolios managed by Ponzi Trust Company.

17	25	32	41	43
31	28	27	39	36
25	19	21	28	26
30	32	26	27	34
21	24	20	25	31

(a) Construct a stem-and-leaf plot.
(b) Construct a table for the frequency distribution that has six class intervals of width 5 transactions. Use 15 transactions as the lower limit of the first interval.
(c) Determine the relative frequency for each class using your answer to (b).
(d) Determine the cumulative frequency distribution for each class using your answer to (b).

2-38 Refer to the sample data given in Exercise 2-36. Construct tables showing the following cross tabulations.
(a) sex versus marital status
(b) marital status versus occupation
(c) sex versus occupation

STATISTICS IN PRACTICE

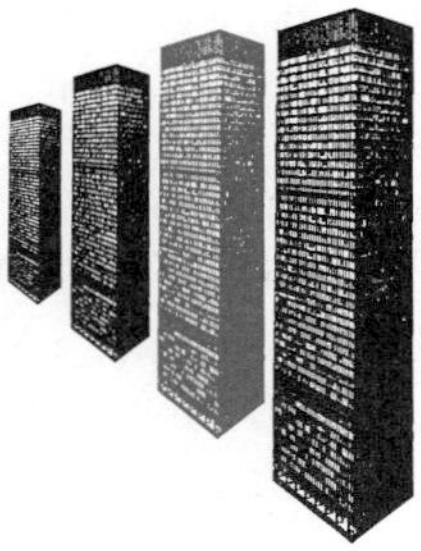

2-39 Use the master class data from Exercise 1-19.
(a) For the height data, find the frequency, cumulative frequency, relative frequency, and relative cumulative frequency distributions.
(b) Use the frequency distribution for heights and to construct a histogram.
(c) Separate the class by sex, compare the height distributions, and create a chart to illustrate your findings.
(d) For one nominal variable, create an appropriate visual display.
(e) Categorize the class data by place of birth. Create one category for the state, province or country where your school is located and one for all others. Create a cross tabulation using place of birth by major or favorite food.
(f) Use the student age variable in a grouped format, and compare against favorite food or state of birth.

2-40 Using your group class data list developed in Exercise 1-21, perform the following operations for describing and displaying statistical data.
(a) For one quantitative variable (having an interval scale) find the frequency, the cumulative frequency, relative frequency, and relative cumulative frequency distributions.
(b) Use the frequency distribution from part (a), to construct a histogram.
(c) Create an appropriate visual display for one qualitative variable.
(d) Create a cross tabulation with two nominal variables.

2-41 *The Last Cold War Olympics.* Consider the best way to organize the medal total data from the 1988 Summer Olympics presented in Table 2-15. With the merger of East and West Germany and the breakup of the Soviet Union, can the data be reorganized? Why or why not?

TABLE 2-15 Olympic Medals Earned at the 1988 Summer Games for the Top Six Countries

Country	Gold	Silver	Bronze	Total
USSR	55	31	46	132
East Germany	37	35	30	102
United States	36	31	27	94
West Germany	11	14	15	40
Bulgaria	10	12	13	35
South Korea	12	10	11	33
Others	76	104	95	275
Total	237	237	237	711

2-42 Table 2-16 shows the twenty most populous countries for the years 1991 and 2100.

(a) Can you meaningfully calculate the cumulative frequencies? Discuss.
(b) Calculate the cumulative relative frequencies for these two lists.
(c) In illustrating the populations for the *continents* listed, would there be any ambiguousities.

TABLE 2-16 World's Twenty Most Populous Countries: 1991 and 2100 Estimates

1991				2100			
Rank	**Country**	**Population**	**Continent**	**Rank**	**Country**	**Population**	**Continent**
1	China	1,151,300,000	Asia	1	India	1,631,800,000	Asia
2	India	859,200,000	Asia	2	China	1,571,400,000	Asia
3	United States	252,800,000	N. America	3	Nigeria	508,800,000	Africa
4	Indonesia	181,400,000	Asia	4	Indonesia	356,300,000	Asia
5	Brazil	153,300,000	S. America	5	Pakistan	315,800,000	Asia
6	Russia	147,400,000	Europe/Asia	6	United States	308,700,000	N. America
7	Japan	123,800,000	Asia	7	Bangladesh	297,100,000	Asia
8	Nigeria	122,500,000	Africa	8	Brazil	293,200,000	S. America
9	Pakistan	117,500,000	Asia	9	Mexico	195,500,000	N. America
10	Bangladesh	116,600,000	Asia	10	Russia	180,400,000	Europe/Asia
11	Mexico	85,700,000	N. America	11	Ethiopia	173,300,000	Africa
12	Germany	79,500,000	Europe	12	Vietnam	168,100,000	Asia
13	Vietnam	67,600,000	Asia	13	Iran	163,800,000	Asia
14	Philippines	62,300,000	Asia	14	Zaire	138,900,000	Africa
15	Thailand	58,800,000	Asia	15	Japan	127,900,000	Asia
16	Iran	58,600,000	Asia	16	Philippines	125,100,000	Asia
17	Turkey	58,500,000	Europe/Asia	17	Tanzania	119,600,000	Africa
18	Italy	57,700,000	Europe	18	Kenya	116,400,000	Africa
19	United Kingdom	57,500,000	Europe	19	Myanmar (Burma)	111,700,000	Asia
20	France	56,700,000	Europe	20	Egypt	110,500,000	Africa
	Total	3,868,700,000			Total	7,014,300,000	

Source: *1992 Information Please Almanac*

CASE Ingrid's Hallmark Shop I

Ingrid's Hallmark Shop, a 2,000 square foot card and gift shop, is located next to a large supermarket in a suburban town of nearly 20,000 residents. The stores are among others in a small strip center.

Ingrid has fine-tuned her business by adapting the type and mix of gifts to the needs of her clientele. She has learned, through experience, to drop slow selling items and to expand merchandise breadth and depth for the faster selling lines of goods. She can never be sure which items will do well, however, because of ever-changing tastes and trends. It is necessary for Ingrid to constantly try new things.

In deciding on specific gifts to order, Ingrid has developed a few guidelines. For example, she avoids bulky items, preferring small gifts of high value for their size. But, since Ingrid's customers typically choose gifts on impulse while shopping for Hallmark staples, there is a price threshold above which gifts move very slowly. Ingrid has learned to limit her gift buying to items with a retail price that falls in the fast-moving range.

Ingrid wants to improve her gift buying by taking a more active stance. She wants to be able to anticipate specific customer needs. Although she knows a great deal about individual customers, Ingrid needs to gain an overall perspective. To do this, a small marketing research firm has been retained to make a statistical evaluation of Ingrid's customers.

Using public domain data for the census tracts covering and contiguous to the town where Ingrid's Hallmark Shop is located, a sample of homeowners has been selected from Ingrid's market. Table 2-17 shows a partial listing of the sample data obtained. (There is one row for each sample customer.)

TABLE 2-17 Sample Data for Customers of Ingrid's Hallmark Shop

Age	Income	Home Value	Age	Income	Home Value
30	$17,005	$ 37,000	35	$25,110	$156,000
49	35,505	88,400	46	52,510	117,200
36	10,005	44,300	45	36,050	133,800
35	30,445	60,000	33	23,005	80,300
30	10,200	34,700	45	10,805	38,200
39	18,915	83,100	47	35,005	72,300
42	21,005	61,300	51	28,005	69,600
43	22,295	43,600	30	9,745	45,300
28	7,010	53,600	30	34,080	101,800
39	17,505	59,300	59	8,505	58,700
49	4,050	55,000	48	25,505	14,900
35	21,430	56,400	57	14,505	36,000
40	21,005	45,200	44	23,005	78,900
20	11,005	131,400	35	23,940	159,300
40	20,005	69,900	39	18,005	48,500
45	47,015	71,400	36	49,515	67,900
34	3,005	77,700	34	25,060	73,100
35	18,005	103,700	37	12,510	45,600
65	13,080	40,500	32	13,005	40,900
52	30,010	85,600	34	18,265	105,200

Questions

1. Comment on the appropriateness of using census tract data to help Ingrid formulate her strategy for buying gifts. Give any suggestions for improving the sample data in terms of (a) identifying the target populations, (b) choosing the sample customers, and (c) completing the observations.
2. Consider the ages of the sample customers.
   (a) Construct a stem-and-leaf plot.
   (b) In three sentences, describe the homeowners as a group.
   (c) Assuming that the sample is representative of all of Ingrid's customers, what type of gifts do you believe Ingrid might want to concentrate on when making her buying decisions? Explain.
3. Consider the incomes of the sample customers.
   (a) Determine a meaningful class interval width. Use the width to construct a table for the frequency distribution.
   (b) Plot (1) a histogram, (2) a frequency polygon, and (3) a cumulative frequency ogive using your answer to (a).
   (c) Based on the income profile suggested by the sample, suggest to Ingrid a few price points for gift items. Explain.
4. Consider the home values of the sample customers.
   (a) Recommend a display that would meaningfully summarize the data.
   (b) Prepare the display.
5. If a follow-up survey were taken, what sample data or information—other than age, income, and home value—do you think would be helpful? What arguments would you present to convince Ingrid to follow your recommendations?

CHAPTER 3

SUMMARY DESCRIPTIVE MEASURES

BEFORE READING THIS CHAPTER, MAKE SURE YOU UNDERSTAND:

The distinction between quantitative and qualitative data (Chapter 1).
The types of data displays and how to construct them (Chapter 2).
The common forms taken by statistical data (Chapter 2).

AFTER READING THIS CHAPTER, YOU WILL UNDERSTAND:

How to evaluate statistical data.
How to measure central tendency.
How to obtain and use percentiles and related measures.
How to measure central tendency.
How together the mean and the standard deviation provide added descriptive power.
How to summarize qualitative data.

We have seen how the frequency distribution arranges raw data into a meaningful pattern. Now we are ready to investigate further ways to summarize statistical data. Knowledge of the frequency distribution alone is not sufficient to answer many statistical questions. For example, in evaluating a new drug, researchers must establish whether it improves patient recovery. The new drug must be compared in some way with the drug in current use. Sample data can provide recovery times for the two treatments, but a direct comparison of histograms would be cumbersome. Instead, the **average** recovery times for the two drugs would more clearly establish whether the new treatment is better. If the new drug significantly speeds up the average patient's recovery, it should replace the old drug.

This chapter considers a variety of summary measures. Each is a number precisely measuring various properties of the observations. There are two major classes of summary numerical values for quantitative data. One measures **location**. Measures of location may be concerned with **central tendency**, a value around which the observations tend to cluster and which typifies their magnitude. The **arithmetic mean** is one of the more commonly used measures of central tendency. A second grouping of location is concerned with **position**. Not limited to the center, measures of position are placed according to frequency of occurrence. Another broad category of numbers provides measures of **dispersion** or **variability** among the observation values. These measures indicate how observed values differ from each other. Conceptually, the simplest of these is the **range**, which expresses the difference between the largest and smallest observations. A useful summary measure for qualitative data is the **proportion**, which indicates how frequently a particular attribute is observed.

Summary data measures are ordinarily computed from *sample* data, since all of the parent population is not usually observed. A computed summary measure is referred to as a **statistic** and conveys a property only for the data actually observed. Sample statistics, such as the arithmetic mean, have their counterparts in the population. The mean of all potential observations is a type of **population parameter**. Exact values for population parameters are not ordinarily computed, since observations are rarely made of the complete population.

3-1 THE ARITHMETIC MEAN

The arithmetic mean is the most commonly encountered and best understood of the measures of central tendency. Consider the cash balances (thousands of dollars) of five manufacturing firms: 101.3, 34.5, 17.6, 83.4, and 52.7. The mean 57.9 is calculated by adding these values and dividing the sum by the number of firms (5).

$$\frac{101.3 + 34.5 + 17.6 + 83.4 + 52.7}{5} = \frac{289.5}{5} = 57.9$$

SYMBOLIC EXPRESSIONS FOR CALCULATING THE ARITHMETIC MEAN

Since the arithmetic mean is calculated in the same way for any group of raw data, it is convenient to express this calculation symbolically. Because we may not yet know the value of a particular observation, we may also have to assign a special symbol to each observation. Traditionally, the letter X is used to represent an observed value. To distinguish each observation, we use the numbers 1, 2, 3, . . . as **subscripts**. Thus, X_1 represents the first observation value; X_2, the second; X_3, the third; and so on. The symbol X_1 is referred to as "X sub 1." Another advantage of expressing observation values symbolically is that algebraic expressions can be used to state precisely how each statistical measure is calculated, so that the same procedure can be applied to any set of data.

The mean is represented by the special symbol $\bar{X}$, called "X bar." To calculate the mean, we divide the sum of the values by the number of observations made, which is represented by the letter n. The following formula is used to calculate the

MEAN

$$\bar{X} = \frac{X_1 + X_2 + \cdots + X_n}{n}$$

In our previous illustration, the sample size was $n = 5$, and the observed values were $X_1 = 101.3$, $X_2 = 34.5$, $X_3 = 17.6$, $X_4 = 83.4$, and $X_5 = 52.7$.

Sometimes it is convenient to use an even more concise formula for the mean. Just as we use a plus sign (+) to add two quantities together, we can represent the sum of several values by a **summation sign**, which takes the form of $\sum$ (the uppercase Greek **sigma**). The mean can then be expressed as

$$\bar{X} = \frac{\sum X}{n}$$

THE POPULATION AND SAMPLE MEAN

If the five cash balances represent only a sample from a population of observations of all medium-sized companies in the nation, then the result of the calculation is a *sample* mean of 57.9 thousand dollars. If, instead, they are the entire set of observations for the population of cash balances at the foundries in Marlborough County, then 57.9 thousand dollars is the *population* mean.

The symbol $\bar{X}$ often represents a level for the sample mean, with n then denoting the **sample size**. A major application of statistics is using a sample to draw conclusions regarding the *unknown* population mean, which is traditionally represented by μ (the lowercase Greek **mu**). μ is the equivalent of "m," the first letter in mean. (Several other population parameters are also represented by Greek letters.) Generally, we do not compute μ directly, because the entire population is not usually observed. Ordinarily, the value of μ remains unknown; only $\bar{X}$ is calculated, and this value serves as an estimate of μ.

USING A COMPUTER TO CALCULATE THE MEAN

When the number of observations is large, it can be time consuming to calculate the mean by hand—even with the assistance of a calculator. Consider the sample

TABLE 3-1 Sample Temperatures (°F) for Selected Cities

Temperatures (°F)								
58	59	62	59	67	59	62	68	54
64	56	58	52	53	75	63	66	65
46	55	64	78	64	61	77	59	57
63	50	50	75	71	68	60	76	77
69	73	52	57	65	62	53	63	62
60	59	48	63	65	75	57	58	62
63	58	68	73	50	62	58	79	
70	61	75	74	71	36	67	50	
55	74	62	48	79	67	56	73	
57	57	58	65	55	68	55	55	

Source: *The World Almanac and Book of Facts,* 1988 edition, copyright © Newspaper Enterprise, Inc., 1987, New York, NY: 181.

temperature (°F) data in Table 3-1 obtained for selected U.S. cities during the month of May. These data were entered into an IBM PC using Minitab and double checked for accuracy. Most computer software allows for quick correction of any data input errors.

Figure 3-1 displays the printout generated on a computer using the temperature data. A variety of statistical measures are provided. The mean is computed by averaging the 86 temperatures. We find it to be $\bar{X} = 62.244$. (The other descriptive statistics will be explained later.)

DECISION MAKING WITH THE MEAN

The mean plays an important role in decision making. A product manager can use the mean cost per 1,000 readers as a guide in selecting magazines in which to place advertisements. A student might select his or her major based partly on the mean starting salaries of graduates in the respective fields. The following Statistics Around Us box on page 68 shows how useful the mean can be in production management.

```
MTB > describe c1

                N      MEAN    MEDIAN    TRMEAN     STDEV    SEMEAN
Temp.          86    62.244    62.000    62.333     8.598     0.927

              MIN       MAX        Q1        Q3
Temp.      36.000    79.000    57.000    68.000
```

Note: Figure generated on IBM using Minitab.

FIGURE 3-1 Computer printout for sample temperature data.

STATISTICS AROUND US

Deciding When to Adjust Bottle Filling Controls

The quality control manager for Astronic Tonics uses the arithmetic mean for deciding when to shut down production for equipment maintenance. She is establishing a policy that will tell workers when to adjust the filling controls for 6 oz bottles of mineral water.

Under ideal conditions, the population mean contents for all filled bottles should be exactly $\mu = 6$ oz. Unfortunately, over time the controls tend to drift, so that the true value for the population mean might be some smaller amount, like $\mu = 5.85$ or $\mu = 5.91$ oz. It might also be greater, so that population means like $\mu = 6.15$ or $\mu = 6.22$ oz are possible. In any of these cases, the filling process would be so far off target that the controls need to be adjusted. Unfortunately, it would be too expensive to precisely measure the contents of every bottle, and *the true value for μ at any time can never be known.*

Nevertheless, the process can be monitored by means of *samples.* Every fifteen minutes a sample of $n = 20$ bottles is removed from the production line, the content volume of each is precisely measured, and the sample mean contents $\bar{X}$ is then computed. The following **decision rule** is applied.

CONTINUE filling operations whenever 5.90 oz $\leq \bar{X} \leq$ 6.10 oz.

STOP and adjust control valves if $\bar{X} <$ 5.90 oz or if $\bar{X} >$ 6.10 oz.

In using the above rule, the manager knows that the computed $\bar{X}$ may be above or below the true level for μ. Thus, sometimes abnormally extreme sample results will give a "false" signal, and production will be stopped for unneeded adjustment. Conversely, $\bar{X}$ may fall within the "continue" range even after a large drift in μ has occurred, and serious overfilling or underfilling may go uncorrected for awhile. But her rule is chosen to achieve an acceptable balance between these two erroneous actions.

APPROXIMATING THE MEAN USING GROUPED DATA

Generally, the first step in analyzing or describing a collection of raw data is to construct a frequency distribution by arranging the raw data into groups or classes according to size. It is usually possible to obtain good approximations to the mean using only these summary data. These shortcut procedures may save time and effort. And, when published data have already been grouped and the raw data are unavailable, they might be the only way to find the summary values.

The grouped procedure for approximating $\bar{X}$ is shown in Table 3-2. There the frequency distribution for fuel consumption is provided.

Every class interval is represented by its midpoint. The first of these, 15, is found by averaging the limits of the first class interval: $(14.0 + 16.0)/2 = 15$. The remaining midpoints can then be easily found by adding one class interval width (here, 2 miles per gallon) to the preceding class midpoint. A **weighted average** is then computed by multiplying each midpoint by the relative frequency for its class. The following summarizes the procedure for computing the

MEAN USING GROUPED DATA

$$\bar{X} = \sum X(f/n)$$

TABLE 3-2 Calculation of the Mean Fuel Consumption Using Shortcut with Grouped Data

Fuel Consumption (miles per gallon)	Number of Cars f	Class Interval Midpoint X	Relative Frequency f/n	$X(f/n)$
14.0–under 16.0	9	15	.09	1.35
16.0–under 18.0	13	17	.13	2.21
18.0–under 20.0	24	19	.24	4.56
20.0–under 22.0	38	21	.38	7.98
22.0–under 24.0	16	23	.16	3.68
Totals	100		1.00	19.78

$$\bar{X} = \sum X(f/n) = 19.78$$

The successive class midpoints are represented by Xs and the class frequencies by fs. Each relative frequency f/n is computed by dividing the class frequency by the number of observations. The resulting approximate $\bar{X}$ gives weight to each class value in proportion to its relative frequency.

The value 19.78 found in Table 3-2 is only an *approximation* of the mean and can be expected to differ from the value calculated directly from the raw data. This is because all fuel consumptions in a particular class interval are represented by a single number. The raw fuel consumption data are provided in Table 2-3 (page 28). The arithmetic mean of these data, calculated without grouping, is 19.718 miles per gallon. This differs only slightly from the value calculated for $\bar{X}$ using the shortcut method. For practical purposes, the approximation is usually close enough.

Some statisticians prefer to use the following mathematically equivalent expression.

$$\bar{X} = \frac{\sum fX}{n}$$

Each fX term approximates the sum of all the values in the respective interval.

EXERCISES

3-1 The following numbers of new employees were hired by a sample of McBurger franchises during 1989.

14 6 12 19 2 35 5 4 3 7 5 8

Calculate the mean.

3-2 A data processing manager purchased remote terminal processing time to run special jobs at two different computer "utilities." She wishes to sign a long-term contract with the firm whose computer causes the least delay on the average. The numbers of minutes of delayed processing per week were obtained during trial periods with each firm and are provided below.

CompuQuick	210	15	47	93	104			
Dial-a-Pute	18	341	523	25	19	293	115	203

Assuming that trial experience is representative of future performance, which firm should receive the business? Substantiate your answer with appropriate calculations.

3-3 Refer to the Astronic Tonics bottle filling example (box on page 68). For each of the following sample results, (a) calculate the mean and (b) indicate whether the operations should be *continued* or *stopped* for adjustment of control valves.

(1) 8 A.M., July 5: 5.85, 5.95, 5.85, 5.75, 5.65
(2) 2 P.M., July 5: 6.05, 6.00, 6.10, 5.90, 5.95, 6.05, 6.05
(3) 1 A.M., July 6: 6.05, 5.80, 6.10, 5.90, 5.95, 6.05, 6.05
(4) 4 A.M., July 6: 6.05, 6.20, 6.15, 6.15, 6.00, 6.10

3-4 The following frequency distribution has been obtained for the lifetimes of TryHard batteries.

Lifetime (hours)	Number of Batteries
0.0–under 20.0	500
20.0–under 40.0	250
40.0–under 60.0	125
60.0–under 80.0	61
80.0–under 100.0	15
100.0–under 120.0	6

Calculate the mean.

3-5 The following frequency distribution has been obtained for the lifetimes of Whammo floppy disks.

Lifetime (hours)	Number of Disks
0.0–under 50.0	5
50.0–under 100.0	16
100.0–under 150.0	117
150.0–under 200.0	236
200.0–under 250.0	331
250.0–under 300.0	78
300.0–under 350.0	27
350.0–under 400.0	8

Calculate the mean.

3-6 The sales manager of Kleen Janitorial Supplies allows sales representatives to give special introductory prices to new customers. He wishes to weed out those salespersons who take undue advantage of specials, "milking" them of commissions and bringing in little new continuing business. Investigating the files for the past ten months, he has determined for each of the five sales representatives the following precentages of specials buyers who placed second orders.

Percentage of Specials Buyers Retained				
A	**B**	**C**	**D**	**E**
36	9	11	33	18
43	16	5	17	17
49	21	6	45	23
18	14	14	29	6
17	33	25	17	31
32	8	12	27	42
24	19	11	61	19
19	17	9	47	13
28	26	28	35	26
36	11	14	14	33

(a) Calculate the mean percentage of specials buyers retained for each salesperson.
(b) Using your answers to (a), calculate the mean percentage of such customers retained for the sales force as a whole.
(c) Assuming that the sales manager will take remedial action against those salespersons who produce lower than average retention, which salespersons should be singled out for milking specials?

3-7 Unified Airways provided the following distance data for domestic flights.

629	1076	1134	1082	704
639	956	887	901	1831
1150	1585	575	419	1209
814	869	978	928	823
730	859	745	1009	1095
746	554	757	924	1020
552	790	804	1188	974
1047	893	1653	746	1458
1087	2062	1110	625	902
1201	854	604	1390	530

Calculate the mean.

3-8 Consider the percentages of specials buyers retained by all salespersons in Exercise 3-6 as a single data set.
(a) Construct a table for the frequency distribution that has six class intervals of equal width. Use 5.0–under 15.0 as the first interval.
(b) Calculate the mean using the grouped data for the distribution in (a).
(c) Calculate the mean using the ungrouped data. By how much is this above or below your answer to (b)?

3-9 Refer to the domestic flight distances given in Exercise 3-7.
(a) Construct a table for the frequency distribution that has 17 class intervals of equal width. Use 400.0–under 500.0 miles as the first interval.

(b) Calculate the approximate level of the sample mean using your answer to (a).

(c) In Exercise 3-7 the sample mean of the ungrouped data was determined. By how much is your answer to (b) above or below the mean found in Exercise 3-7?

3-10 *Computer exercise.* Refer to the sample levels of precipitation given in Exercise 2-2. Calculate the mean.

3-11 *Computer exercise.* Refer to the sample temperatures given in Exercise 2-5. Calculate the mean.

3-2 THE MEDIAN AND THE MODE

THE MEDIAN

After the mean, the most common measure of central tendency is the **median**. Like the mean, the median provides a typical numerical value. The median, denoted by m, is the central observation when all the data are arranged in increasing sequence. For the heights 66, 68, 69, 73, and 74 inches, the median is $m =$ 69 inches, the central value. If a person 70 inches tall were added to the initial group, then the median would be obtained by averaging the two central values from 66, 68, 69, 70, 73, 74. Thus, the median would be $m = (69 + 70)/2 =$ 69.5 inches.

In general, *the median is the value above or below which lies an equal number of observations.* We find the median from the raw data by listing the observations in sequence from lowest to highest and then selecting the central value if there is an odd number of values or averaging the two central values if there is an even number of observations.

THE MEDIAN CONTRASTED WITH THE MEAN

In different senses, the arithmetic mean and the median are both averages. The mean is the arithmetic average of variates, and the median is the average of position. When we use the term **average**, we speak of the arithmetic mean.

A mean can be algebraically manipulated; the combined mean of two populations can be calculated from the individual means. Due to these convenient mathematical properties, many statistical techniques employing the mean have been developed. The median is not as well suited to mathematical operations. For example, the median of a combined population cannot be obtained from the separate component population medians. Fewer statistical techniques employ the median due to the mathematical difficulties associated with it.

On the other hand, the mean is influenced by extreme values to a much greater degree than the median. Consider the net worth levels of your close friends. Suppose that you meet one of the world's few billionaires and include him in your circle of friends. The addition of this person would distort the mean level of wealth so greatly that "on the average" all of your friends would be multimillionaires—hardly a meaningful summary. But the median would not be significantly influenced by the billionaire. The median is more democratic, giving each elementry unit only one "vote" in establishing the central location.

Generally, the median provides a better measure of central tendency than the mean when there are some extremely large or small observations.

THE MODE

A third measure that may be used to describe central tendency is the **mode**—the *most frequently occurring* value. Consider the simple illustration provided by the collection of five observations: 2, 3, 4, 4, and 7. The mode is 4, because 4 occurs most often.

The interpretation of the statistical mode is analogous to that of the fashion mode. A person dressing in the current style is "in the mode." But a current fashion can be a poor description of what most people are wearing, because a variety of styles is worn by the general public. In statistics, the mode only tells us which single value occurs most often; it may therefore represent a minority of the observations.

As a basis for decisions, the mode can be insidiously undemocratic. For example, most shoe stores stock only the most popular sizes, so the mode is their deciding parameter. One reason for this is that the turnover on unusual sizes is so low that they are unprofitable. When such sizes are stocked, there is ordinarily little choice of color or style (and what there is will usually be on the conservative side). A significant number of people who wear unpopular sizes find it difficult to buy shoes in stores and may have to resort to mail-order purchasing. Not being of modal size, they are forced to be hopelessly out of mode in the sense of fashion as well.

When the data are grouped into classes, the mode is represented by the midpoint of the interval having the greatest class frequency. We refer to this group as the **modal class**. When the frequency distribution is portrayed as a smoothed curve like the one in Figure 3-2, the mode corresponds to the possible observation value lying beneath the highest point on the frequency curve—the location of maximum clustering. The mode can therefore serve as a basis for comparing the typicalness of the other measures of central tendency. The modal class for the fuel consumption data in Table 3-2 is the class interval 20.0–under 22.0, and the sample mode is

$$\text{Mode} = \frac{20.0 + 22.0}{2} = 21.0$$

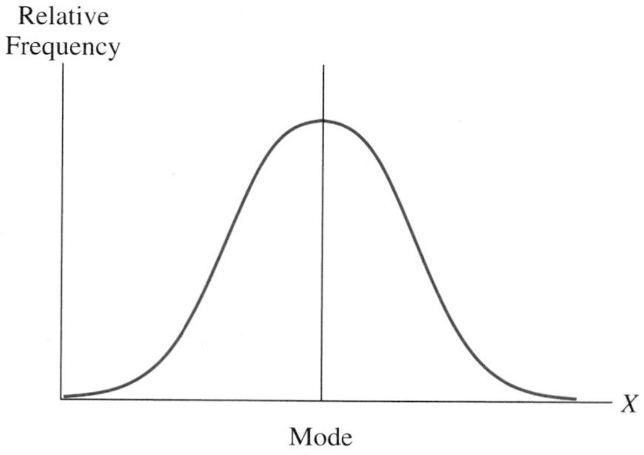

FIGURE 3-2 Illustration of the location of the mode.

FINDING THE MEDIAN AND MODE FROM A STEM-AND-LEAF PLOT

When the raw data are arranged in a stem-and-leaf plot, the median and mode can be found easily. The following stem-and-leaf plot was obtained using the temperatures given in Table 3-1.

Stem	Leaf
3	6
4	6 8 8
5	8 5 7 9 6 5 0 9 8 7 8 0 2 8 9 2 7 3 0 5 9 3 7 8 6 5 9 8 0 5 4 7
6	4 3 9 0 3 1 2 4 8 2 3 5 7 4 5 5 1 8 2 2 7 8 2 3 0 7 8 6 3 5 2 2
7	0 3 4 5 8 5 3 4 1 1 9 5 5 7 6 9 3 7

The plot must be further refined before the desired statistics can be found. By sorting the leaf digits on each stem in ascending order, an **ordered stem-and-leaf plot** is obtained. The ordered stem-and-leaf plot for the sample temperatures is constructed below.

Stem	Leaf
3	6
4	6 8 8
5	0 0 0 0 2 2 3 3 4 5 5 5 5 5 6 6 7 7 7 7 7 8 8 8 8 8 8 9 9 9 9 9
6	0 0 1 1 2 2 2 2 2 2 2 3 3 3 3 3 4 4 4 5 5 5 5 6 7 7 7 8 8 8 8 9
7	0 1 1 3 3 3 4 4 5 5 5 5 6 7 7 8 9 9

The median of the 86 observations is the average of the 43rd and 44th values (the boxed leaf digits).

$$m = \frac{62 + 62}{2} = 62$$

Figure 3-1, the computer printout, confirms the above value as the median.

Coincidentally, the mode is also 62, since the "6" stem has seven "2" digit leaves, the most frequently occurring of all the leaves on a single stem.

POSITIONAL COMPARISON OF MEASURES: SKEWED DISTRIBUTIONS

When a variable has a **symmetrical** frequency curve like the one in Figure 3-3(a), the mean, median, and mode coincide. When the distribution is not symmetrical, the mean and median will lie to the same side of the mode. The frequency curve in Figure 3-3(b) has a tail tapering off to the right. Such an asymmetrical frequency distribution is said to be *skewed to the right,* meaning that the data cluster around a relatively low value, although there are some extremely large observation values. In this case, the mean lies to the right of the mode, reflecting the influence of the larger values in raising the arithmetic average. The median, which is less sensitive to extremes, must lie to the left of the mean. A rightward skewed distribution will also have a mode that is smaller than the median. The median will therefore lie somewhere between the mode and the mean.

Because rightward skewed data will always have a median smaller than the mean, subtracting the median from the mean results in a positive difference. For

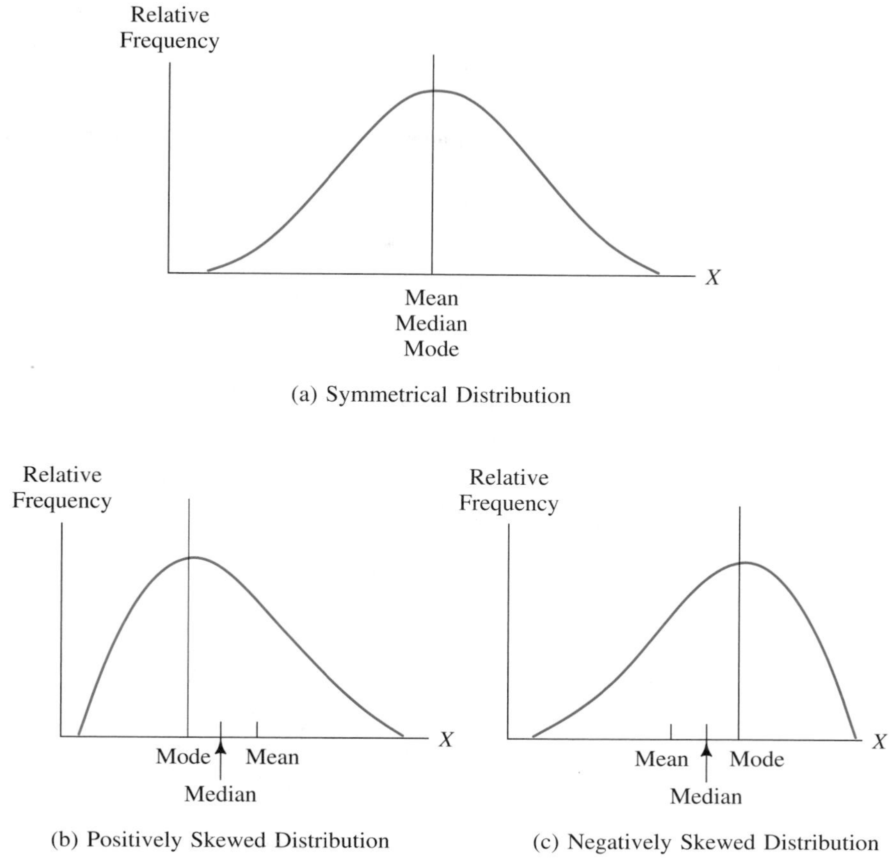

FIGURE 3-3 Positional comparison of center measures for symmetrical and skewed frequency distributions.

this reason, such a frequency distribution is said to be **positively skewed**. This expression also reflects the fact that the long tail of the distribution tapers off in a positive direction from the center of the distribution.

Generally, a variable having a lower limit but no theoretical upper boundary will exhibit a positively skewed distribution. This is true of the annual wages earned by construction workers in the United States. A lower limit is established by the legal minimum wage. Some blue-collar aristocrats, such as operating engineers (who drive heavy equipment), plumbers, electricians, and iron workers, earn more than many doctors when their overtime premiums are considered. In total numbers, however, the high earners are relatively sparse, creating a long, thin, rightward tail in the frequency curve. Economic data often have positively skewed frequency distributions.

Figure 3-3(c) shows a frequency curve that is *skewed to the left*—the direction toward which its long tail points. Because the extremes are relatively small values, the mean lies below the mode. Again, the median will lie somewhere in between the mean and the mode. Subtracting the median from the mean (a smaller value) results in a negative difference, so the frequency curve is said to be **negatively skewed**.

Negatively skewed distributions result when the observed values have an upper limit and no significant lower boundary. For example, the ages of viewers who watch a television program on which "old favorites" are played would be a negatively skewed population. Aimed at a predominantly middle-aged and elderly audience, with commercials touting denture deodorants, laxatives, and home health-care remedies, the show would not be that appealing to younger viewers. The few young people who might watch it would bring the mean viewing age below what would be considered typical, so that the *median* age would more truly represent a typical population value in this case.

The median is the most realistic measure of location for data having skewed distributions.

BIMODAL DISTRIBUTIONS

The mode has been defined as the most frequently occurring value. But if two or more values occur with equal or nearly equal frequency, then there are two or more modes. A variable that has two modes is said to have a **bimodal distribution**.

The presence of more than one mode has a special significance in statistical analysis: It indicates potential trouble. Comparing or drawing conclusions about bimodal populations can be dangerous because they usually arise when some nonhomogeneous factor is present. Figure 3-4(a) presents the frequency curve of heights of adult patients admitted to a large hospital during the past year. The curve is bimodal, with the two modes occuring at 5′3″ and 5′10″. In this case, the nonhomogeneous factor is sex: The two modes result from the fact that an equal number of male and female patients have been measured. It would be more meaningful to separate the population into male and female populations and analyze the two more homogeneous populations separately.

To illustrate the potential difficulty, suppose we wish to compare patient heights in the year before the new maternity ward opened to those in the current year. The proportion of female patients would be higher in the second year, so the overall mean height would be less. The patients would not have become shorter, as a cursory analysis might indicate. By separately comparing the two female populations, the mean heights would not noticeably change over the two-year period.

Figure 3-4(b) shows another distribution having a double-humped frequency curve. This curve represents the high school grade point average of students at a university. Humps in frequency occur at 2.8 and 3.5. Although the mode is 3.5, we would still classify this as a bimodal population, because a nonhomogeneous factor influences the grades of the high school students. A relatively small group of disadvantaged students is to be given remedial work. Although these remedial students are comparatively ill-prepared now, their *college* grade point averages are not expected to differ substantially from those of the other students.

EXERCISES

3-12 A sample audit of Gizmo Corporation records showed the following numbers of plant accidents per month.

0	1	3	4	5	2	2	6	7	2	0	1

Calculate the (a) mean, (b) median, and (c) mode.

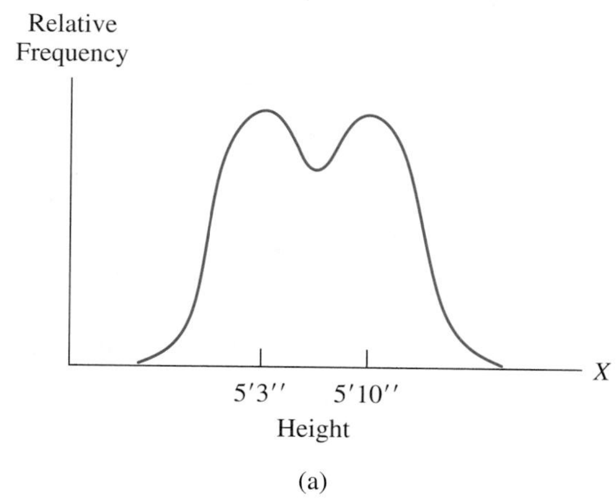

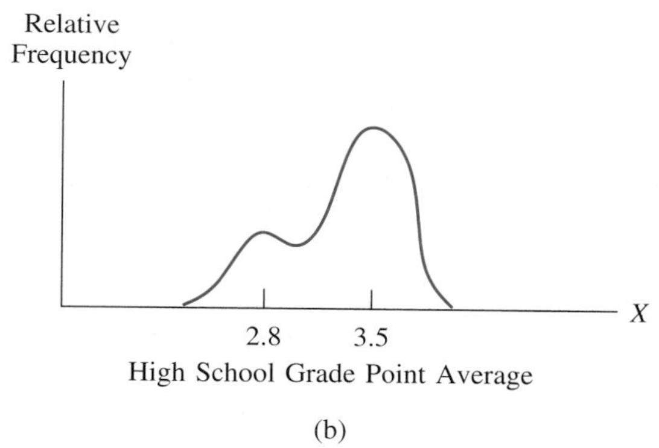

FIGURE 3-4 Illustrations of bimodal frequency distributions.

3-13 Unified Airways provided the following distances for foreign flights.

2139	2128	2507	2350	2311
2276	2161	2750	2002	1863
2427	2011	2677	2347	2188
2227	1927	2006	1921	3192
2129	3245	2084	2096	2079
2442	2050	2230	2097	2490
2076	2061	2595	1960	2980
1988	2111	1889	2324	1750
2255	2535	2654	2121	2272
1976	1974	2035	1990	2840

Calculate the median.

3-14 Sample family installment debts are provided below.

$2,032	$ 232	$ 493	$5,555
597	4,893	4,432	4,444
203	796	978	329
97	852	1,427	972

3,333	1,712	2,121	438
1,212	1,940	5,067	705
5,769	1,843	4,337	3,976
2,347	3,525	5,213	3,034
2,137	3,414	4,896	5,035
2,049	4,327	2,172	4,222

Calculate the median.

3-15 A statistics instructor gives four exams of equal weight. From the scores on these, she will determine a single central score value for each student. Suppose that she lets each student decide *in advance of the first test* whether his or her particular grade will be determined by a mean or by a median test score.

(a) Would you request the mean or the median? Why?

(b) For each of the following hypothetical sets of test scores, indicate whether the mean or the median would provide the greatest central value.

(1)	(2)	(3)	(4)
95	80	80	60
60	50	75	80
75	75	65	90
65	70	60	90

3-16 For each of the following situations, indicate a possible source of nonhomogeneity in the data, and discuss why the population should or should not be split to better serve the purposes of the statistical study.

(a) Six months ago, a new driver safety program was initiated by a state's highway patrol. For the past year, the governor's office has maintained records of the number of weekly accidents. A study is being made to evaluate highway construction standards.

(b) An appliance manufacturer wishes to make a powerful home vacuum cleaner. To be most effective, the cleaner must be heavier than the normal weight of such an appliance. A representative group of employees, including men and women, is used to obtain data on how much weight a person can carry up a flight of stairs without excessive fatigue. These data will be used to set a maximum vacuum cleaner weight.

(c) An automobile manufacturer has obtained data on the total worker-hours required to assemble each car at two identically equipped plants of the same size. Each plant produces the models of cars ordered by dealers in its geographical region. These data will be used to establish production standards for each car model.

3-17 Combine the Unified Airways data for domestic flight distances (Exercise 3-7) and foreign flight distances (Exercise 3-13).

(a) Construct a table for the frequency distribution that has successive class intervals of equal width. Use 400.0–under 500.0 miles as the first interval.

(b) Plot a histogram using your answer to (a).

(c) What common form does the shape of your histogram suggest? Do you think it is meaningful to combine the distance data for domestic and foreign flights?

3-18 *Computer exercise.* Refer to the sample levels of precipitation given in Exercise 2-2. Calculate the median.

3-19 *Computer exercise.* Refer to the sample temperatures given in Exercise 2-5. Calculate the median.

3-3 PERCENTILES, FRACTILES, AND QUARTILES

Another broad category of statistical measures expresses frequency information for quantitative populations. The most common is the **percentile**, which is that value below which a stated percentage of the observations lie. For example, an instructor might find that 32 out of 40 students earned less than 150 points on a final examination. The percentage of such scores is $(32/40) \times 100 = 80$, and 150 points is the 80th percentile. If 165 points is the 90th percentile, then 90% of the 40 test scores—($.90 \times 40 = 36$ of them)—fell below 165.

Another way of conveying the same information is in terms of the **fractile**, which is that point below which a stated fraction of the values lie. Thus, 150 points is the .80-fractile, while 165 is the .90-fractile.

Earlier in this chapter you encountered one percentile in another context. *The median is the same quantity as the 50th percentile or the .50-fractile.*

There are three special percentiles. These are the **quartiles**, which divide the data into four groups of equal size. The **first quartile** is the same as the 25th percentile and the .25-fractile. The **second quartile** is the 50th percentile, while the **third quartile** equals the 75th percentile. (There is no need for a "fourth" quartile.)

EXAMPLE: YOUR CLASS STANDING

When you graduate, your school might classify your relative percentile position in terms of your grade point average (GPA). The following data apply to a particular class having exactly 800 graduates.

GPA	Percentile
2.3	25
2.5	50
3.1	75
3.5	90
3.7	95
3.9	99

We will determine the quartiles.

SOLUTION: The first quartile is 2.3; 25% of the graduates, or $.25 \times 800 = 200$ students, earned a grade point average lower than 2.3. The second quartile is 2.5, the 50th percentile; $.50 \times 800 = 400$ students earned GPAs of less than 2.5. The third quartile (also the 75th percentile) is 3.1; $.75 \times 800 = 600$ students earned GPAs below 3.1. There are 200 GPAs in each of the following groups: below the first quartile (2.3); at or above the first quartile but below the second (2.5); at or above the second quartile but below the third (3.1); and at or above the third quartile.

Finding Percentiles from Ungrouped Data

When all raw data are available, the percentiles may be established by ranking the values from lowest to highest. For example, consider the ten sample completion times (seconds) for cash withdrawal transactions obtained from an automatic teller machine.

	$Q_{.10}$ 17.2	$Q_{.25}$ 21.25						$Q_{.75}$ 37.25		
Value	17	19	22	28	32	33	34	37	38	39
Position	1	2	3	4	5	6	7	8	9	10
	1.1 $d(n + 1)$	2.75 $d(n + 1)$						8.25 $d(n + 1)$		

The 10th percentile is any point above 17 seconds but not exceeding 19 seconds. We might use 17.5, 18.0, or 18.99 as the 10th percentile. The 20th percentile may be any point greater than 19 seconds but less than 22 seconds.

There is considerable leeway in selecting percentiles directly from raw data. To avoid ambiguity, we adopt the following procedure.

PROCEDURE FOR FINDING PERCENTILES FROM RAW DATA

1. **Sort the raw data in ascending order.** Denote X_1 as the first sorted value, X_2 as the second, and so on, up to X_n, with n being the total number of observations. The subscripts represent the *position* of the data value.
2. **Establish the decimal equivalent.** It is convenient to use the letter d to denote the decimal equivalent of the desired percentage point. This procedure is limited to $d \geq 1/n$ with the limitation that $d \leq (n - 1)/n$. Using that value as a subscript, we will denote Q_d as the corresponding percentile value to be found.
3. **Find the relative position of the desired percentile.** This may be expressed as

   $$d \times (n + 1)$$

   Then, let k be the *largest integer* such that

   $$k \leq d(n + 1)$$

   The desired percentile will lie between X_k and X_{k+1}.
4. **Calculate the percentile value.** The following expression applies.

   $$Q_d = X_k + [d(n + 1) - k](X_{k+1} - X_k)$$

We will illustrate the procedure using the $n = 10$ sample ATM service completion times. The 10th percentile is calculated using $d = .10$. The relative position of $Q_{.10}$ is

$$.10 \times (10 + 1) = 1.1$$

The largest integer not exceeding 1.1 is 1, so that using $k = 1$, we have

$$X_k = X_1 = 17 \quad \text{and} \quad X_{k+1} = X_2 = 19 \text{ seconds}$$

Using these values we calculate

$$\begin{aligned} Q_{.10} &= 17 + [.1(10 + 1) - 1](19 - 17) \\ &= 17.2 \text{ seconds} \end{aligned}$$

Now, consider the 25th percentile for the same data. Using $d = .25$, we calculate

$$.25 \times (10 + 1) = 2.75$$

so that $k = 2$, and $Q_{.25}$ will lie between positions 2 and 3. Using

$$X_k = X_2 = 19 \quad \text{and} \quad X_{k+1} = X_3 = 22 \text{ seconds}$$

we calculate

$$\begin{aligned} Q_{.25} &= 19 + [.25(10 + 1) - 2](22 - 19) \\ &= 21.25 \text{ seconds} \end{aligned}$$

It is easy to see that the 75th percentile involves $k = 8$ and, thus, lies between positions 8 and 9. Using the respective observation values, we obtain

$$\begin{aligned} Q_{.75} &= 37 + [.75(10 + 1) - 8](38 - 37) \\ &= 37.25 \text{ seconds} \end{aligned}$$

The median, the 50th percentile, lies between positions 5 and 6.

$$m = \text{Median} = Q_{.50} = 32 + [.50(10 + 1) - 5](33 - 32) = 32.50$$

We discovered earlier that it can be a time consuming task to sort a large set of raw data by hand. It may be easier to construct an ordered stem-and-leaf plot. Referring to the sample temperatures given in Section 3-1, we can use the following plot obtained earlier.

```
                                    Leaf
        3 | 6
          |                       21st        22nd
        4 | 6 8 8                     ↘      ↙
Stem    5 | 0 0 0 0 2 2 3 3 4 5 5 5 5 5 6 6 7 7 7 7 7 8 8 8 8 8 8 9 9 9 9 9
        6 | 0 0 1 1 2 2 2 2 2 2 2 3 3 3 3 3 4 4 4 5 5 5 5 6 7 7 7 8 8 8 8 9
        7 | 0 1 1 3 3 3 4 4 5 5 5 5 6 7 7 8 9 9                    ↗   ↖
                                     ↗ ↖                    65th       66th
                                82nd     83rd
```

We can count the positions for any of the $n = 86$ observations. The 95th percentile has relative position $.95(86 + 1) = 82.65$, so that with $k = 82$, $Q_{.95}$ lies above the 82nd observation by .65 times the distance between that point and the $(k + 1)$st $= 83$rd observation, at

$$\begin{aligned} Q_{.95} &= X_{82} + [82.65 - 82](X_{83} - X_{82}) \\ &= 77 + .65(77 - 77) = 77 \text{ degrees} \end{aligned}$$

The 25th percentile has relative position $.25(86 + 1) = 21.75$ and lies between the 21st and 22nd observations. Both equal 57 degrees, thus the desired percentile must be the same value, and $Q_{.25} = 57$. Likewise, the 75th percentile has relative position $.75(86 + 1) = 65.25$ and lies between the 65th and 66th observations. Both positions correspond to 68 degrees, and $Q_{.75} = 68$.

Finding Percentiles with a Computer

Once data have been entered into a computer, some of the percentiles can be provided. The computer printout in Figure 3-1 reports 57 as the first quartile and 68 as the third quartile. Other percentiles can be obtained by hand computations using either a stem-and-leaf plot or a frequency distribution constructed by the computer.

Finding Percentiles from Grouped Data

When the raw data are unavailable or have already been grouped into a frequency distribution, the procedure may be modified slightly to account for the missing details.

Instead of positioning individual observations, we position groups according to the *cumulative* frequencies for class intervals. We denote k as the greatest cumulative class frequency $\leq d(n + 1)$, and represent the *upper limit* of the corresponding interval as X_k. The next highest interval will have cumulative frequency h, and the upper limit will be designated as X_h. The following expression then is used to find the

PERCENTILE COMPUTED WITH GROUPED DATA

$$Q_d = X_k + [d(n + 1) - k]\left(\frac{X_h - X_k}{h - k}\right)$$

so that Q_d results from a simple linear interpolation between neighboring class limits.

(Should $d(n + 1)$ be smaller than the first cumulative class frequency, the percentile will lie within the first interval. Then $k = 0$ and for $X_k = X_0$ we use the lower limit of the first class interval. The class frequency of that same interval serves as the value for h, with X_h equal to the upper limit of the first interval. Should Q_d fall in the last class interval, h will equal the cumulative frequency for that interval and X_h will equal the upper limit.)

To illustrate, consider the following example.

EXAMPLE: FUEL CONSUMPTION DATA

The following fuel consumption data originally appeared in Table 3-2. The cumulative frequencies are listed below. We will find the 25th, 90th, and 50th percentiles.

Class Interval	Frequency	Cumulative Frequency
14.0–under 16.0	9	9
16.0–under 18.0	13	22
18.0–under 20.0	24	46
20.0–under 22.0	38	84
22.0–under 24.0	16	100
	$n = 100$	

SOLUTION: The 25th percentile has relative position .25(100 + 1) = 25.25. The greatest cumulative frequency not exceeding 25.25 is 22 for the second interval, so that $k = 22$, $Q_{.25}$ will fall in the subsequent (third) interval, the cumulative frequency of which is $h = 46$. This percentile is between the limits $X_{22} = 18.0$ and $X_{30} = 20.0$. We calculate

$$\begin{aligned} Q_{.25} &= 18.0 + [25.25 - 22]\left(\frac{20.0 - 18.0}{46 - 22}\right) \\ &= 18.27 \text{ mpg} \end{aligned}$$

The 90th percentile has relative postion .90(100 + 1) = 90.9, so that $k = 84$, $h = 100$, and

$$\begin{aligned} Q_{.90} &= X_{84} + [90.9 - 84]\left(\frac{X_{100} - X_{84}}{100 - 84}\right) \\ &= 22.0 + 6.9\left(\frac{24.0 - 22.0}{16}\right) \\ &= 22.86 \text{ mpg} \end{aligned}$$

The 50th percentile or *median* $Q_{.50}$ is located at position .50(100 + 1) = 50.5. Using $k = 46$ and $h = 84$, we have

$$\begin{aligned} m = \text{Median} = Q_{.50} &= 20.0 + [50.5 - 46]\left(\frac{22.0 - 20.0}{84 - 46}\right) \\ &= 20.24 \text{ mpg} \end{aligned}$$

Finding Percentiles Graphically

If the cumulative frequency distribution has already been plotted, percentiles may be read directly from the graph. This is fast and avoids the need for computation.

Figure 3-5 shows the cumulative frequency ogive for the fuel consumption data. The vertical axis now expresses cumulative *relative* frequencies. The 25th percentile is the horizontal coordinate of that point on the curve at height .25.

$$Q_{.25} = 18.3 \text{ mpg}$$

The value must agree with the computed value for $Q_{.25}$ (found earlier to be 18.27 mpg), but the graphical solution will ordinarily be less precise. Likewise, the 75th percentile is the horizontal coordinate of that point on the curve at height .75.

$$Q_{.75} = 21.6 \text{ mpg}$$

EXERCISES

3-20 The following numbers of accounting courses were taken by a sample of business students.

5	2	0	1	1	4	7	2	2	3
9	7	0	2	2	4	8	8	1	3

Determine the (a) 10th, (b) 25th, (c) 50th, (d) 75th, and (e) 90th percentiles.

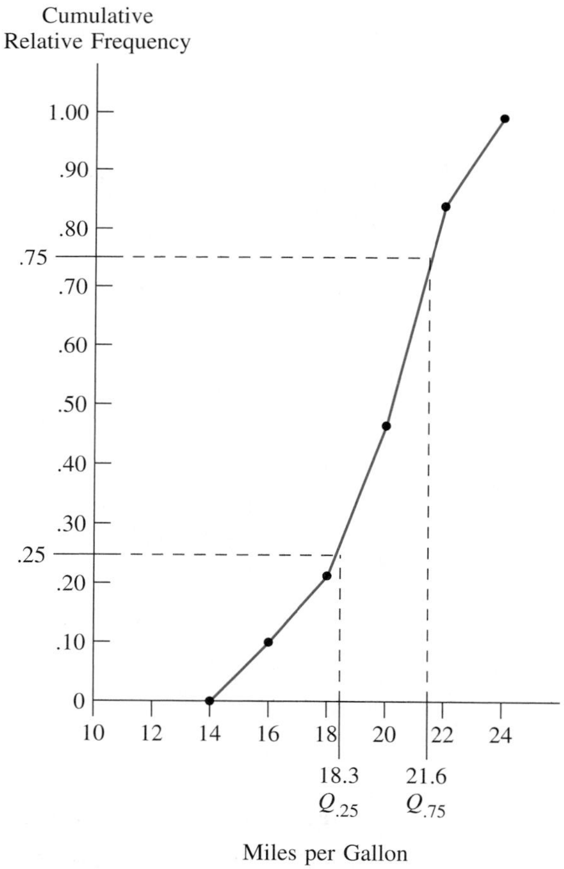

FIGURE 3-5 Fuel consumption percentiles (fractiles) read from the cumulative relative frequency ogive.

3-21 The following GMAT scores were obtained for a sample of Slippery Rock graduates.

588 462 718 725 664 395 382 455 510 584 602 644

Determine the (a) 10th, (b) 25th, (c) 50th, (d) 75th, and (e) 90th percentiles.

3-22 Refer to your answers to Exercise 2-2.
(a) Construct an ordered stem-and-leaf plot for the sample levels of precipitation.
(b) Determine the (1) 10th, (2) 25th, (3) 50th, (4) 75th, and (5) 90th percentiles.

3-23 Refer to your answers to Exercise 2-5.
(a) Construct an ordered stem-and-leaf plot for the sample temperatures.
(b) Determine the (1) 10th, (2) 25th, (3) 50th, (4) 75th, and (5) 90th percentiles.

3-24 The following cumulative frequency distribution has been obtained for the concentrations of pollutants found in air samples above Smogville.

Concentration (parts/million)	Cumulative Frequency
0–under 1	5
1–under 2	12
2–under 3	25
3–under 4	37
4–under 5	50
5–under 6	67
6–under 7	75
7–under 8	84
8–under 9	89
9–under 10	90
10–under 11	95
11–under 12	98
12–under 13	100

Determine the following values.
(a) .90 fractile (c) 1st quartile (e) median
(b) 37th percentile (d) 3rd quartile

3-25 Use the cumulative relative frequency distribution given in Exercise 2-18 for the number of shares of stock. Determine the following values.
(a) 36th percentile (c) .97 fractile
(b) .90 fractile (d) 81st percentile

3-26 The following cumulative relative frequency distribution has been obtained for the GMAT during a base period.

Test Score	Cumulative Relative Frequency
200–below 250	.01
250–below 300	.03
300–below 350	.09
350–below 400	.19

Test Score	Cumulative Relative Frequency
400–below 450	.36
450–below 500	.55
500–below 550	.74
550–below 600	.88
600–below 650	.96
650–below 700	.99
700–below 750	1.00

(a) On graph paper, plot the ogive.

(b) Assuming that intermediate values may be read to a good approximation from your graph, determine the .25, .50, and .75 fractiles.

3-4 MEASURING VARIABILITY

We have encountered several measures of central tendency, each of which provides a valuable summary of statistical data. Means or medians will often serve as the basis for comparing two or more populations. But other summary measures can be useful for making comparisons. Next in importance to central tendency are **measures of variability**, which express the extent to which observed values differ from each other.

Statistical terminology includes **dispersion** as a synonym for variability. The concepts are illustrated by the following pairs.

Lower Variability Observations	Higher Variability Observations
.75″ .84″ .63″ .79″ .72″ (diameters of hummingbird eggs)	6.4″ 7.1″ 8.2″ 7.5″ 6.8″ (diameters of ostrich eggs)
2.3 .5 2.0 3.2 1.8 2.8 1.6 (minutes waiting, McDonald's)	15 25 34 54 2 48 (minutes before seating, Le Bistro)
11.2 13.1 8.9 10.2 10.3 7.1 (earnings per share—oils)	55 33 − 62 108 226 49 − 28 (earnings per share—high tech.)
680 650 720 700 750 690 710 670 (GMAT scores, Harvard MBAs)	350 750 460 640 530 480 510 610 (GMAT scores, seniors)

A quick comparison of the raw data values on the left with those in the same row on the right easily establishes that the second set of values are more spread out, exhibiting greater variability. When observations are represented by frequency distributions, that sample or population having higher variability will involve either more class intervals or wider class widths.

IMPORTANCE OF VARIABILITY

The role of variability is illustrated in Figure 3-6, where the frequency curves for the net earnings of dairies and ranches are compared. Although both populations have the same medians, ranch earnings exhibit *greater variability* than dairy incomes. Although both forms of agriculture involve cattle and must meet comparable feed requirements, dairy farmers are blessed with stable milk prices (often

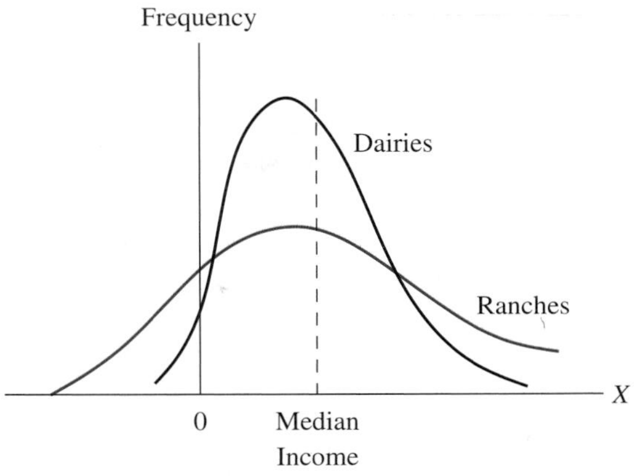

FIGURE 3-6 Frequency curves for the earnings of dairies and ranches.

due to regulation), whereas ranchers must sell their beef at the volatile market price. The greater variability in income makes ranching a riskier venture than owning a dairy, even though the earnings of both enterprises have identical central tendencies (equal medians). Here, statistical variability might help the new agricultural college graduate to choose between ranching or dairy farming.

Figure 3-7 shows the sample frequency distributions for the completion times of two chemical processes. Method B appears to be cheaper on the average. But method A would make planning easier because its completion times are less varied. If the final product is perishable or must be made to customer order, so that it can be stored in quantity for very long, then method A might be the superior

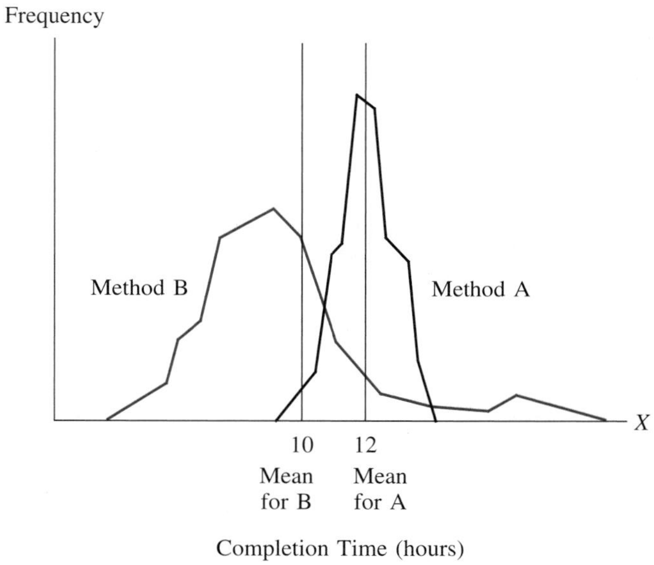

FIGURE 3-7 Frequency distributions for the completion times of two chemical processes.

method. *In a great many situations, reduction in variability is itself an improvement.*

Variability or dispersion may be measured in two basic ways: in terms of **distances** between particular observation values, or in terms of the **average deviations** of individual observations about the central value.

DISTANCE MEASURES OF DISPERSION

Distance measures of dispersion are popular when the only purpose is to describe a collection of data. The most common distance measure is the **range**, which is obtained by subtracting the smallest observation from the largest. For example, suppose that the five students in a college accounting honors program have the following IQs: 111, 118, 126, 137, 148. The range of these values is $148 - 111 = 37$. The figure 37 represents the total spread in these observations. The range provides a concise summary of the total variation in a sample or a population, but its major disadvantage as a useful measure is that it ignores all except the two most extreme observations. These two numbers may be untypical values, even among the higher and lower observations.

Other distance measures ignore the most extreme observations. These are **interfractile ranges**, which express the differences between two fractiles.

THE INTERQUARTILE RANGE

A useful measure of dispersion is the **interquartile range**. This range represents *the middle 50% of the observations.* It is computed by taking the difference between the third quartile ($Q_{.75}$) and the first quartile ($Q_{.25}$).

$$\text{Interquartile range} = Q_{.75} - Q_{.25}$$

To illustrate, consider, again, the ten sample ATM transaction times (seconds).

17 19 22 28 32 33 34 37 38 39

In Section 3-3, we obtained

$$Q_{.25} = 21.25 \qquad Q_{.50} = 32.50 \qquad Q_{.75} = 37.25$$

The interquartile range is

$$Q_{.75} - Q_{.25} = 37.25 - 21.25 = 16.00 \text{ seconds}$$

The interquartile range is always computed in the same way, regardless of whether the Qs are generated from raw data, from grouped data, with a computer, or from a graph. An ogive for family income is illustrated in Figure 3-8. The fractile values may be read from this graph. The first quartile is \$7,900 and the third quartile is \$18,100, so that the interquartile range is \$18,100 − \$7,900 = \$10,200.

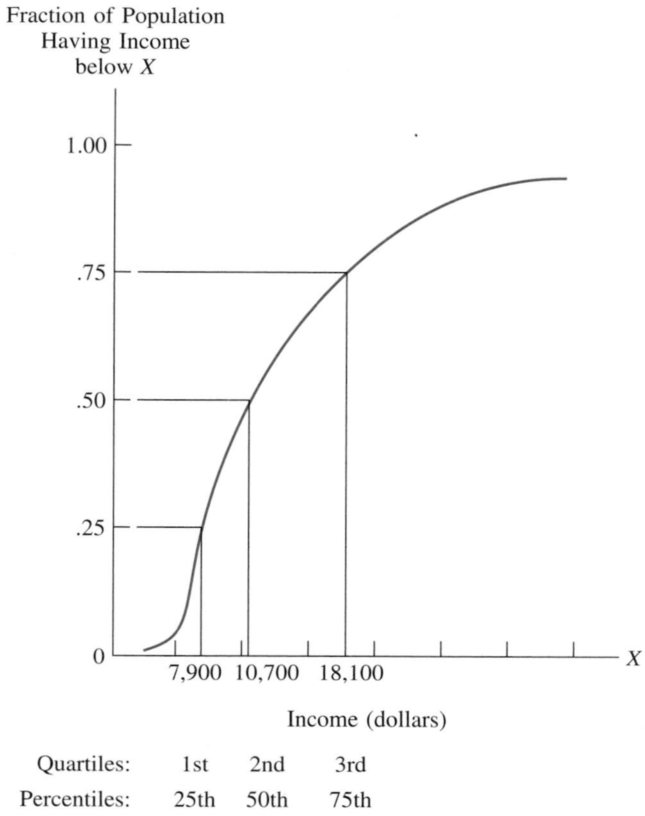

FIGURE 3-8 Cumulative relative frequency distribution for family income.

Other interfractile ranges, such as those representing the middle 90% or 99% of the observation values, may be used but seldom are.

STATISTICS AROUND US

Doctors' Incomes vs. Teachers' Salaries

The earnings of doctors in Kent County have a first quartile of $55,000 and a third quartile of $135,000, so that the interquartile range is

$$\$135{,}000 - 55{,}000 = \$80{,}000$$

The salaries of teachers in the same county have a first quartile of $13,500 and a third quartile of $22,000. The interquartile range is

$$\$22{,}000 - 13{,}500 = \$8{,}500$$

This means that the earnings of doctors are nearly 10 times as varied as teachers' salaries.

THE BOX PLOT AND QUARTILES

The range and interquartile range may be combined in a box plot. Figure 3-9 shows the box plot for the ATM transaction times. A line segment starts at the minimum observed level and ends at the maximum value. The box begins at the first quartile, ends at the third quartile, and is divided at the median. The overall length of the plot gives the range, while the length of the box provides the interquartile range.

Box plots can be useful when comparing data groups. Figure 3-10 shows box plots for successive samples of task completion times obtained from a worker undergoing training. Notice that as the worker gains mastery of the task, the task is completed faster and with less variability. This is demonstrated by progressively shorter plots and boxes.

MEASURES OF AVERAGE DEVIATION

The main disadvantage of the distance measures of dispersion is that they do not consider every observation. To include all observations, we can calculate how much each one deviates from the central value and then combine these deviations by averaging. The deviation most commonly considered is the difference between the observed value and the mean.

$$X - \bar{X}$$

Averaging the deviation values results in 0. For example, consider the five values 1, 2, 3, 4, and 5. Subtracting 3 (the mean) from each number, we obtain deviations of −2, −1, 0, 1, and 2. These add up to 0, so the average deviation is 0. We might avoid this difficulty by ignoring the minus signs. We could average the **absolute values** of each deviation (2, 1, 0, 1, and 2) and obtain the **mean absolute deviation** 1.2, which reflects every observation. But because it is mathematically diffcult to work with absolute values, two other measures of dispersion are more commonly used.

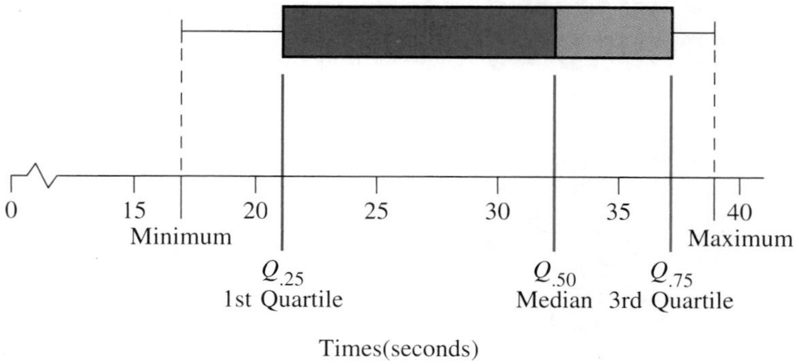

FIGURE 3-9 Box plot for sample ATM transaction times.

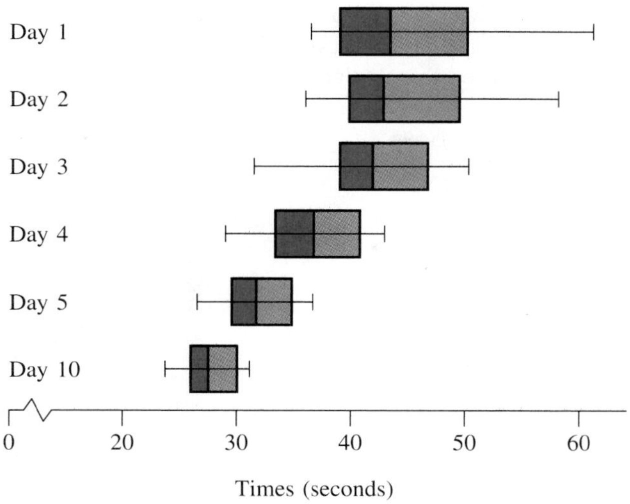

FIGURE 3-10 Successive sample box plots for task completion time by a trainee.

THE VARIANCE

The most important measure of variability is found by averaging the **squares** of the individual deviations; the resulting value is the **mean of the squared deviations**. Performing this calculation on the IQs for the five accounting students cited earlier, the mean value is

$$\bar{X} = \frac{111 + 118 + 126 + 137 + 148}{5} = 128$$

The deviations from the mean value are

$$\begin{aligned} 111 - 128 &= -17 \\ 118 - 128 &= -10 \\ 126 - 128 &= -2 \\ 137 - 128 &= 9 \\ 148 - 128 &= 20 \end{aligned}$$

and the mean of the squared deviations is

$$\frac{(-17)^2 + (-10)^2 + (-2)^2 + (9)^2 + (20)^2}{5 - 1} = \frac{289 + 100 + 4 + 81 + 400}{5 - 1}$$

$$= \frac{874}{4} = 218.5$$

The measure of variability obtained in this manner is referred to as the **variance**. In averaging the squared deviations, the divisor is reduced by one observation, so that the above calculation uses 5 − 1 = 4 instead of 5. (This is for technical reasons to be discussed in Chapter 8.) The following expression is used to calculate the

VARIANCE

$$s^2 = \frac{\sum (X - \bar{X})^2}{n - 1}$$

THE SAMPLE AND POPULATION VARIANCE

As with the mean, a distinction is made between the computed level for s^2, which when computed from sample data is called the **sample variance**, and the **population variance** (not ordinarily computed). The population variance is represented symbolically as σ. (The symbol σ is the lowercase Greek **sigma**, and σ^2 is called "sigma squared.")

Two practical difficulties are associated with the use of the variance. First, the variance is usually a very large number compared to the number of observations themselves. Thus, if the observations are largely in the thousands, the variance is often in the millions. Second, the variance is not expressed in the same units as the observations. In the previous example, the variance is 218.5 *squared* IQ points. This is because the deviations, measured in IQ points, have all been squared. The variance for heights, originally measured in feet, will therefore be expressed in square feet. The variance for fuel consumption will be in squared miles per gallon.

In spite of these difficulties, the mathematical properties of the variance make it extremely important in statistical theory. Furthermore, the difficulties may be overcome simply by working with the square root of the variance, called the **standard deviation.**

THE STANDARD DEVIATION

The square root of the variance in IQ levels is

$$\sqrt{218.5} = 14.78$$

which yields the standard deviation in IQ level. The standard deviation is expressed in the same units as the observations themselves; the value 14.78 is a point on the same numerical scale.

The **standard deviation** is represented by the letter s without its exponent 2. The following expression may be used to calculate the

STANDARD DEVIATION

$$s = \sqrt{\frac{\sum (X - \bar{X})^2}{n - 1}}$$

Note that both sides of the equation simply contain the square root of the expression for the variance. Both the variance and the standard deviation provide the same information; one can always be obtained from the other. The standard deviation is a practical descriptive measure of dispersion, whereas the variance is generally used in developing statistical theory.

The standard deviation is computed in Table 3-3 for a sample of $n = 5$ heights.

USING A COMPUTER TO CALCULATE THE STANDARD DEVIATION

When the number of observations is large, it can be an especially tedious task to compute s. By hand or using a calculator it may easily take an hour to find s and s^2 for the temperature data in Table 3-1. As with the statistical measures encountered earlier, software packages will compute the standard deviation automatically, reporting its value with the other summary statistics. The computer-generated output in Figure 3-1 provides $s = 8.598$ degrees as the standard deviation for the temperatures. (Although the variance is not listed, the value can be computed quickly by hand by squaring s.)

TABLE 3-3 Calculation of Standard Deviation for Heights

	Height (inches) X	Deviation $X - \bar{X}$	Squared Deviation $(X - \bar{X})^2$
	66	66 − 70 = − 4	16
	73	73 − 70 = 3	9
	68	68 − 70 = − 2	4
	69	69 − 70 = − 1	1
	74	74 − 70 = 4	16
Totals	350	0	46

$$\bar{X} = \frac{\sum X}{n} = \frac{350}{5} = 70 \text{ inches}$$

$$s = \sqrt{\frac{\sum (X - \bar{X})^2}{n - 1}} = \sqrt{\frac{46}{5 - 1}}$$

$$= \sqrt{\frac{46}{4}} = \sqrt{11.5} = 3.391 \text{ inches}$$

SHORTCUT CALCULATIONS FOR THE VARIANCE AND STANDARD DEVIATION

The standard deviation may be calculated from individual values with a mathematically equivalent equation that is usually simpler to use.

SHORTCUT CALCULATIONS

$$s^2 = \frac{\sum X^2 - n\bar{X}^2}{n-1} \quad \text{for variance}$$

$$s = \sqrt{\frac{\sum X^2 - n\bar{X}^2}{n-1}} \quad \text{for standard deviation}$$

The use of this formula for the standard deviation is illustrated in the following example. The shortcut procedure is recommended whenever s is computed by hand or with a calculator.

EXAMPLE: FIRST-YEAR EARNINGS OF MARKETING AND ACCOUNTING MAJORS
A university placement director collected sample data giving first-year earnings of marketing and accounting majors. The $n = 12$ marketing majors' earnings (in thousands of dollars) are:

18.5	12.0	17.0	22.5	31.4	10.2
25.6	19.2	17.6	17.3	22.2	13.3

The $n = 9$ accounting majors' earnings are:

18.5	20.1	19.4	17.3	21.0	20.5	20.2	19.0	18.6

SOLUTION: It is easiest to arrange the data in *columns*. The following apply for the marketing majors.

Earnings (thousands of dollars) X	Deviation $(X - \bar{X})$	Squared Deviation $(X - \bar{X})^2$
18.5	− .4	.16
12.0	− 6.9	47.61
17.0	− 1.9	3.61
22.5	3.6	12.96
31.4	12.5	156.25
10.2	− 8.7	75.69
25.6	6.7	44.89
19.2	.3	.09
17.6	− 1.3	1.69
17.3	− 1.6	2.56
22.2	3.3	10.89
13.3	− 5.6	31.36
226.8		387.76

The mean and standard deviation for marketing majors are

$$\bar{X} = \frac{\sum X}{n} = \frac{226.8}{12} = 18.9 \qquad s = \sqrt{\frac{\sum (X - \bar{X})^2}{n - 1}} = \sqrt{\frac{387.76}{12 - 1}} = 5.94$$

The following data and calculations apply for the accounting majors. (Here the standard deviation is computed using the shortcut expression.)

Earnings (thousands of dollars) X	X^2
18.5	342.25
20.1	404.01
19.4	376.36
17.3	299.29
21.0	441.00
20.5	420.25
20.2	408.04
19.0	361.00
18.6	345.96
174.6	3,398.16

The mean and standard deviation for accounting majors are

$$\bar{X} = \frac{\sum X}{n} = \frac{174.6}{9} = 19.4$$

$$s = \sqrt{\frac{\sum X^2 - n\bar{X}^2}{n - 1}} = \sqrt{\frac{3{,}398.16 - 9(19.4)^2}{9 - 1}} = 1.17$$

Notice that the sample earnings for the accounting majors involve the higher mean. However, the standard deviation of earnings for marketing majors is substantially greater, reflecting higher variability in that sample. (This might be explained by a substantial number of commission sales positions held by the persons in that sample group.)

Just as we calculated the mean from the frequency distribution in Section 3-1, we can use grouped data to calculate the variance and the standard deviation. We use the following procedure for the

GROUPED DATA CALCULATIONS

$$s^2 = \frac{\sum fX^2 - n\bar{X}^2}{n - 1} \quad \text{for variance}$$

$$s = \sqrt{\frac{\sum fX^2 - n\bar{X}^2}{n - 1}} \quad \text{for standard deviation}$$

The grouped data computations for the standard deviation are illustrated in Table 3-4, using the earlier fuel consumption data. We find that $s = 2.34$ miles per gallon.

As in the case of calculating the mean from grouped data, only an *approximate* value for the standard deviation can be obtained using this procedure. For most purposes, the approximate value is close enough to the true value that would be calculated directly from the raw data. In making the grouped data approximation, some statisticians prefer to use the following mathematically equivalent expressions

$$s^2 = \frac{\sum f(X - \bar{X})^2}{n - 1} \qquad s = \sqrt{\frac{\sum f(X - \bar{X})^2}{n - 1}}$$

A PRACTICAL USE FOR THE STANDARD DEVIATION

The standard deviation is a parameter that, when combined with statistical techniques, provides a great deal of information. When the population has a special frequency distribution called the normal curve, we can find the percentage of

TABLE 3-4 Calculation of Standard Deviation with Grouped Fuel Consumption Data

(1) Fuel Consumption (miles per gallon)	(2) Number of Cars f	(3) Class Interval Midpoint X	(4) $X(f/n)$	(5) X^2	(6) fX^2
14.0—under 16.0	9	15	1.35	225	2,025
16.0–under 18.0	13	17	2.21	289	3,757
18.0–under 20.0	24	19	4.56	361	8,664
20.0–under 22.0	38	21	7.98	441	16,758
22.0–under 24.0	16	23	3.68	529	8,464
Totals	100		19.78		39,668

$\bar{X} = \sum X(f/n) = 19.78$ miles per gallon

$$s = \sqrt{\frac{\sum fX^2 - n\bar{X}^2}{n - 1}} = \sqrt{\frac{39{,}668 - 100(19.78)^2}{99}}$$

$$= \sqrt{5.4865} = 2.34 \text{ miles per gallon}$$

observations falling within distances of one, two, or three standard deviations from the mean. About 68% of all observations lie within the region $\mu \pm 1\sigma$. For example, suppose a group of men have a mean height of $\mu = 5'9''$ and a standard deviation of $\sigma = 3''$. If these heights constitute a normal distribution, then 68% of all men will be between $\mu - \sigma = 5'6''$ and $\mu + \sigma = 6'0''$ tall. Furthermore, about 95.5% of the population will lie within $\mu \pm 2\sigma$, and 99.7% will fall within $\mu \pm 3\sigma$.

The normal curve is described mathematically in terms of only two parameters, μ and σ. Thus, for populations characterized by this curve, we can construct a close representation of the entire frequency distribution simply by knowing the mean and the standard deviation. We will discuss this more thoroughly in Chapter 7.

Chebyshev's Theorem

A theoretical result called Chebyshev's theorem, named for the mathematician who proposed it, indicates that the standard deviation plays a key role in any population.

CHEBYSHEV'S THEOREM: The proportion of observations falling within z standard deviations of the mean is at least $1 - 1/z^2$.

This theorem says that regardless of the characteristics of the population, the proportions in the second column hold.

Number of Standard Deviation Units z	Chebyshev's Minimum Proportion of Observations within $\mu \pm z\sigma$	Normal Distribution Approximate Proportion of Observations within $\mu \pm z\sigma$
1	$1 - 1/1^2 = 0$	.68
2	$1 - 1/2^2 = .75$	.955
3	$1 - 1/3^2 = .89$	.997
4	$1 - 1/4^2 = .9375$	.9999

Since Chebyshev's theorem applies for any population, it is too general to be of much practical use. Usually a more precise determination of how many observations lie within z standard deviations of the mean can be found when the form of a population's frequency distribution is known, as we have shown for the normal curve. The practical significance of Chebyshev's theorem is that it tells us that a great deal of information is imparted by the population standard deviation.

Finding the Proportion of Observations Falling Between Two Values

The above properties allow us to establish approximately how many observations fall between any two points, even when μ and σ are the only known population quantities. Any point X will lie at some distance above or below the mean μ. This distance may be expressed by the difference $X - \mu$ (a negative quantity when X is smaller than μ). When divided by σ, the separation distance may be converted into standard deviation units z.

$$z = \frac{X - \mu}{\sigma}$$

EXAMPLE: BANK TRANSACTION TIMES

Suppose that the time taken by a bank teller to cash a money order is on the average $\mu = 60$ seconds and that the standard deviation is $\sigma = 10$ seconds. What percentage of all money orders will take between 40 and 80 seconds to be cashed?

SOLUTION: The standard deviation distances separating the two limits are

$$z = \frac{40 - 60}{10} = -2 \quad \text{for } X = 40 \quad \text{and} \quad z = \frac{80 - 60}{10} = 2 \quad \text{for } X = 80$$

Chebyshev's theorem indicates that *at least* $1 - 1/z^2 = 1 - 1/2^2 = .75$, or 75%, of the transactions will take between $\mu \pm z\sigma$ seconds. Here the limits are $60 \pm 2\ (10)$ seconds, or from 40 to 80 seconds.

An even higher percentage would apply if the money-order transaction times were normally distributed. In that case, *approximately* 95.5% of all money orders would take somewhere between 40 and 80 seconds to cash. Chapter 7 shows how to find similar percentages for a variety of computed levels for z.

EXERCISES

3-27 The following earnings per share have been obtained for a sample of electronics stocks.

-2.01 .05 .23 .17 1.42 $-.53$ .12 .48 1.10 .24

(a) Calculate the mean.
(b) Calculate the (1) variance and (2) standard deviation.

3-28 The following price-earnings ratios were obtained for a sample of penny stocks.

25 16 50 19 42 37

Calculate the (a) variance and (b) standard deviation.

3-29 The following hourly unit sales of Iceburgers have been obtained for a sample of McBurger restaurants.

35 47 57 16 12 33 38

(a) Calculate the range.
(b) Calculate the (1) variance and (2) standard deviation.
(c) Determine the (1) .25, (2) .50, and (3) .75 fractiles.
(d) Calculate the interquartile range.
(e) Construct the box plot.

3-30 For each of the following decision situations, discuss why a central value may not be a wholly adequate summary measure by itself.

(a) The temperatures actually achieved in each room of a building with standard temperature control settings are being used to determine whether the system should be modified.

(b) Balancing an automobile assembly line requires that sufficient personnel and equipment be positioned at each work station so that no one station will be excessively idle. The task completion times at each station are being used to help determine how this may be done.

(c) To plan for facilities expansion, a hospital administator requires data on the convalescent times of surgical patients.

3-31 Refer to the TryHard battery lifetime data given in Exercise 3-4. Calculate the standard deviation.

3-32 *Computer exercise.* Refer to the Unified Airways domestic flight distance data given in Exercise 3-7. Calculate the (a) range, (b) variance, and (c) standard deviation.

3-33 The Unified Airways domestic flight distance data given in Exercise 3-7 provide a 75th percentile of 1,095 miles and 25th percentile of 746 miles. What is the interquartile range?

3-34 Refer to your answers to Exercise 3-26. Calculate the interquartile range.

3-35 Astronic Tonics replaces its spigots whenever the filling process becomes too erratic, based on the computed level of the standard deviation for the volume of ingredients. Whenever the computed value for s exceeds .08 oz, the spigots are replaced. For each of the samples in Exercise 3-3, (a) calculate the standard deviation, and (b) indicate whether the spigots should be replaced.

3-36 Refer to your answers to Exercise 3-22.
(a) Calculate the (1) range and (2) interquartile range.
(b) Construct a box plot.

3-37 Refer to your answers to Exercise 3-23.
(a) Calculate the (1) range and (2) interquartile range.
(b) Construct a box plot.

3-38 The following frequency distribution has been obtained for a sample of $n = 100$ student grade point averages (GPA).

GPA	Number of Students
0.0–under 1.0	1
1.0–under 2.0	7
2.0–under 3.0	58
3.0–under 4.0	34

Using grouped data calculations, calculate the (a) mean and (b) standard deviation.

3-39 Use Chebyshev's theorem to determine for each of the following non-normal populations the two points between which the percentage of values falling is (a) at least 75% of the population values, (b) at least 89%, and (c) at least 93.75%.

(1)	(2)	(3)	(4)
$\mu = 3''$	$\mu = \$100$	$\mu = 5$ min	$\mu = 75\%$
$\sigma = .15''$	$\sigma = \$5$	$\sigma = 1$ min	$\sigma = 10\%$

3-40 In describing the extent of quality control in her company, the president of

Gumby Rubber Company states that the mean weight of a particular tire is 40 pounds, with a standard deviation of 1 pound. She adds that about 68% of all tires weigh between 39 and 41 pounds, whereas almost all tires weigh between 37 and 43 pounds. State the assumptions on which these statements rest.

3-41 Dogpatch women's heights are normally distributed with $\mu = 5'5''$ and $\sigma = 2.2''$.
(a) Find the value of z such that percentages of the population falling within $\mu \pm z\sigma$ is (1) 68%, (2) 95.5%, (3) 99.7%, and (4) 99.99%.
(b) Determine in each case the two end points of the interval containing the specified percentage of the population values.

3-42 *Computer exercise.* Refer to the sample levels of precipitation given in Exercise 2-2. Calculate the (a) variance and (b) standard deviation.

3-43 *Computer exercise.* Refer to the sample temperatures given in Exercise 2-5. Calculate the (a) variance and (b) standard deviation.

3-5 THE PROPORTION

In describing a qualitative population, the key measure of interest is the **proportion** of observations that fall into a particular category. Like the measures we have already discussed, the population parameter is a separate entity from the sample statistic. The population parameter is referred to as the **population proportion** and is denoted by π (the lowercase Greek **pi**).* The analogous sample statistic is the **sample proportion**, which is represented by P. The following ratio is used to calculate the

PROPORTION

$$P = \frac{\text{Number of observations in category}}{n}$$

A proportion may assume various values between 0 and 1, according to the relative frequency with which the particular attribute occurs. Like the other population parameters, π is ordinarily unknown and may be estimated from the sample results. The statistical procedures for estimating π and P are analogous to those used to estimate a population mean from a sample. But the differences between these procedures are substantial enough to require parallel statistical development throughout this book.

The proportion is important in many kinds of statistical analysis. For example, it is often used as the basis for taking remedial action. An unusually high

*Statistics has its own special notation, and here π is not the 3.1416 used in geometry to express the ratio of the circumference to the diameter of a circle. Just as μ and σ, the Greek equivalents of m and s, are the first letters in the words *mean* and *standard deviation*, π, the Greek p, is the first letter in the word *proportion.*

proportion of sales returns will be singled out as a managerial problem. A machine that produces a large proportion of oversized or undersized items must be adjusted or repaired. The level of impurities in a drug might be expressed as a proportion; if this figure is too high, the drug cannot be used. In many elections for public office in the United States, the winner is the candidate who receives a plurality—that is, the person who receives the highest proportion of votes.

If a sample of $n = 500$ persons contains 200 men and 300 women, then the sample proportion of women is $P = 300/500 = .60$. If a machine has produced a sample of $n = 100$ parts, 5 of which are defective, then the sample proportion of defective parts would be $P = 5/100 = .05$. This same machine might actually produce defective items at a consistently higher rate than experienced in the sample, so that the population proportion of defective parts could be a different value, such as $\pi = .06$. The proportion may also be expressed as a percentage. Thus, 60% of the first sample are women, and 5% of the items in the second sample are defective.

The proportion is the only measure available for qualitative data. It indicates relatively how many observations fall into a particular category. (When the observations are attributes, such as male or female, central tendency or variability have no meaning.) The type of question answered by P or π is *how many* rather than *how big.*

Sometimes we may wish to express the proportion of observations having a collection of attributes. For example, the first list on page 35 presents the frequency distribution of the letters in a representative sample of 200 letters of ordinary English text. We may wish to find the proportion of vowels. We find that "a" occurs 16 times and that "e" occurs 26 times; the frequencies for "i," "o," and "u" are 13, 16, and 6, respectively. Thus, in 200 letters, vowels occur $16 + 26 + 13 + 16 + 6 = 77$ times. The proportion of vowels is therefore $P = 77/200 = .385$. These five letters, taken together, occur 38.5% of the time in the sample of ordinary English text.

The proportion is not limited to qualitative data. We may also use it to represent the relative frequency of a quantitative category. For example, the median is the .50 fractile; thus, the proportion of observations falling below the median is $P = .50$. Likewise, the proportion of items falling below the third quartile is $P = .75$.

EXERCISES

3-44 Refer to the personal debt data given in Exercise 3-14. Determine the proportion of families whose indebtedness lies below (a) \$1,000, (b) \$1,500, (c) \$3,000, and (d) \$5,000.

3-45 A Fair Employment Practices investigator wishes to identify discrimination against employees based on sex. The following data have been obtained for the number of men and women in management positions in five firms within the computer industry.

	Firm				
	A	B	C	D	E
Men	2,342	532	849	1,137	975
Women	156	115	57	145	139

Calculate the proportion of women managers in each firm. Assuming the investigator will study more thoroughly the firm with the lowest proportion of women managers, which firm would be selected?

3-46 In each of the following situations, discuss whether a mean, a proportion, or both would be an appropriate parameter on which to base decisions.

(a) A garment manufacturer wishes to ship dresses of the highest quality. Many things can cause a dress to be defective, including incorrect sizing, improper seams, creases, and missing stitches.

(b) The Federal Trade Commission requires that the weights of ingredients in packaged goods be indicated on the label. A soap manufacturer wishes to comply. Underweight production batches (populations) are reprocessed rather than shipped. For the sake of efficiency, a large number of packages (elementary units) are weighed simultaneously, and the weight of the packaging material is subtracted to obtain the weight of the ingredients.

(c) A drug maker is testing a new food supplement believed to reduce levels of anemia. The supplement is not expected to work on all patients, but when it does, the extent to which it will reduce anemia by increasing the red corpuscle count in the blood should be measurable.

3-47 MacroSoft rejects incoming shipments of floppy disks if the proportion of inspected items found to be defective exceeds .05. For each of the following four shipments, (a) determine the proportion of defectives found, and (b) state whether MacroSoft would accept or reject the shipment.

	Shipment			
	(1)	(2)	(3)	(4)
Items inspected	100	500	600	1,000
Items defective	7	25	10	39

SUMMARY

1. How are statistical data evaluated?

Statistical data are ordinarily evaluated in terms of **summary measures**. When applicable to all possible population observations, these are referred to as **population parameters**. Summary values, however, are usually computed from sample data only, and the resulting quantities are called **sample statistics**.

2. How is central tendency measured?

With quantitative data, the **computed mean** $\bar{X}$ is the common measure of **central tendency**. It can be used to estimate the value of the **population mean** μ, a parameter not usually computed. You compute the sample mean using the expression

$$\bar{X} = \frac{\sum X}{n}$$

or, for grouped data,

$$\bar{X} = \sum X(f/n)$$

There are also two other measures of central tendency. The **median** is the point dividing the data into two groups of equal size. The **mode** is the most frequently occurring value. All three measures of central tendency are helpful in describing frequency distributions, and the mode is important in explaining a **bimodal distribution**, which arises when nonhomogeneous units are observed.

3. **How are percentiles and related measures obtained and used?**
Quantitative data are sometimes summarized in terms of **percentiles** and **fractiles**. Such a number is the point below which a stated percentage or proportion of the observations lie. There are three special percentiles, called **quartiles**, which divide the observations into groups of successive size, each containing 25% of the data points. The **interquartile range** is the useful summary measure that encompasses the middle 50% of values; it equals the difference between the third and first quartiles.
One very useful data summary, the **box plot**, gives a visual display of the data extremes, the range and median, all the quartiles, and the interquartile range.

4. **How do we measure variability?**
In addition to identifying the center of a sample or a population, statisticians are concerned with measuring its **variability**, or the extent to which the observed values differ from one another. The simplest measure of variability is the **range**, which expresses the difference between the greatest and the smallest observation values. Since the range provides limited information, statisticians prefer to use the **variance** as the basic measure of variability. You find the variance by computing for each observation its **deviation** from the mean, then squaring those deviations and finding their average. You would not ordinarily compute the **population variance**, represented by the symbol σ^2. Instead, you will compute the variance, which is denoted by s^2, from the following.

$$s^2 = \frac{\sum (X - \bar{X})^2}{n - 1}$$

You will find it more convenient to work with the **standard deviation**, s or σ, obtained by taking the square root of the variance.

5. **How do the mean and standard deviation together provide added descriptive power?**
The population mean and standard deviation provide useful summaries of the underlying frequency distribution. For normally distributed populations, the values for μ and σ completely specify the characteristics of the frequency curve.

6. **How do we summarize qualitative data?**
Qualitative data are summarized by a single parameter, the **population proportion**, denoted by π. This quantity is estimated by the computed **proportion** P, which is equal to the number of observations having a particular characteristic divided by the number of observations.

REAL-LIFE STATISTICAL CHALLENGE

Selecting the Automobile of Your Dreams

What do you want in a car? What type of car do your classmates want to drive? What types of cars do businesses want for their fleets? Cars can be classified in a number of ways. Crash survivability, top speed, braking distance, and passenger comfort are just a few factors. For purposes of comparing automobiles in terms of their fuel efficiency, the U.S. Environmental Protection Agency separates cars by size. These sizes include: two-seater, minicompact, subcompact, compact, midsize, and large. In 1990, there were over two hundred models sold in the

TABLE 3-5 First Set of Car Data

Manufacturer	Model	Type	Transmission Type	Engine Displacement (liters)	Highway Mileage/ Gallon
Alfa-Romeo	Spider	Two-seater	M5	2.0	30
Buick	Reatta	Two-seater	L4	3.8	27
Cadillac	Allante	Two-seater	L4	4.5	22
Chevrolet	Corvette	Two-seater	L4	5.7	24
Chevrolet	Corvette	Two-seater	M6	5.7	25
Chrysler	TC/Maserati	Two-seater	M5	2.2	25
Chrysler	TC/Maserati	Two-seater	L4	3.0	24
Ferarri	Testarossa	Two-seater	M5	4.9	15
Honda	Civic CRX	Two-seater	L4	1.5	35
Honda	Civic CRX	Two-seater	M5	1.5	35
Honda	Civic CRX-HF	Two-seater	M5	1.5	52
Honda	Civic CRX	Two-seater	M5	1.6	33
Lamborghini	Countach	Two-seater	M5	5.2	10
Lotus	Lotus	Two-seater	M5	2.2	27
Maserati	Karif	Two-seater	M5	2.8	20
Maserati	Karif	Two-seater	L4	2.8	18
Maserati	Spyder	Two-seater	L4	2.8	18
Maserati	Spyder	Two-seater	M5	2.8	20
Mazda	RX-7	Two-seater	M5	1.3	24
Mazda	RX-7	Two-seater	L4	1.3	23
Mazda	Miata	Two-seater	M5	1.6	30
Mazda	RX-7	Two-seater	M5	1.3	25
Mercedes-Benz	500 SL	Two-seater	M5	5.0	21
Nissan	300ZX	Two-seater	M5	3.0	24
Nissan	300ZX	Two-seater	L4	3.0	24
Maserati	222E	Minicompact	L4	2.8	18
Maserati	222E	Minicompact	M5	2.8	20
Nissan	240SX	Minicompact	M5	2.4	27
Nissan	240SX	Minicompact	L4	2.4	25
Porsche	944-S2	Minicompact	M5	3.0	26
Porsche	911-FWD	Minicompact	M5	3.6	22
Porsche	928-S4	Minicompact	M5	5.0	19
Porsche	911-4/2	Minicompact	M5	3.6	24
Porsche	928-S4	Minicompact	A4	5.0	19
Volkswagen	Cabriolet	Minicompact	M5	1.8	32
Volkswagen	Cabriolet	Minicompact	A3	1.8	28

SOURCE: U.S. Environmental Protection Agency, 1989.

United States by a wide range of domestic and foreign manufacturers.

In the next chapter, we will review the complete list. Table 3-5 gives a shorter list made up of "sportier" vehicles. It shows the highway mileage data for 25 two-seaters and 11 minicompacts. The table shows the model, manufacturer, type of car, transmission type, engine displacement in liters, and miles per gallon in the highway test. The transmission type is either manual (M) or automatic (A or L) and can have different gear-box shift configurations (3, 4, 5, or 6 forward).

TABLE 3-6 Second Set of Car Data

Manufacturer	Model	Type	Trans-mission Type	Engine Displacement (liters)	Highway Mileage/ Gallon
Honda	Civic CRX-HF	Two-seater	M5	1.5	52
Honda	Civic CRX	Two-seater	M5	1.5	35
Honda	Civic CRX	Two-seater	M5	1.6	33
Volkswagen	Cabriolet	Minicompact	M5	1.8	32
Mazda	Miata	Two-seater	M5	1.6	30
Alfa-Romeo	Spider	Two-seater	M5	2.0	30
Lotus	Lotus	Two-seater	M5	2.2	27
Nissan	240SX	Minicompact	M5	2.4	27
Porsche	944-S2	Minicompact	M5	3.0	26
Mazda	RX-7	Two-seater	M5	1.3	25
Chrysler	TC/Maserati	Two-seater	M5	2.2	25
Chevrolet	Corvette	Two-seater	M6	5.7	25
Mazda	RX-7	Two-seater	M5	1.3	24
Nissan	300ZX	Two-seater	M5	3.0	24
Porsche	911-4/2	Minicompact	M5	3.6	24
Porsche	911-FWD	Minicompact	M5	3.6	22
Mercedes-Benz	500 SL	Two-seater	M5	5.0	21
Maserati	Spyder	Two-seater	M5	2.8	20
Maserati	222E	Minicompact	M5	2.8	20
Maserati	Karif	Two-seater	M5	2.8	20
Porsche	928-S4	Minicompact	M5	5.0	19
Ferarri	Testarossa	Two-seater	M5	4.9	15
Lamborghini	Countach	Two-seater	M5	5.2	10
Honda	Civic CRX	Two-seater	L4	1.5	35
Volkswagen	Cabriolet	Minicompact	A3	1.8	28
Buick	Reatta	Two-seater	L4	3.8	27
Nissan	240SX	Minicompact	L4	2.4	25
Chrysler	TC/Maserati	Two-seater	L4	3.0	24
Nissan	300ZX	Two-seater	L4	3.0	24
Chevrolet	Corvette	Two-seater	L4	5.7	24
Mazda	RX-7	Two-seater	L4	1.3	23
Cadillac	Allante	Two-seater	L4	4.5	22
Porsche	928-S4	Minicompact	A4	5.0	19
Maserati	222E	Minicompact	L4	2.8	18
Maserati	Spyder	Two-seater	L4	2.8	18
Maserati	Karif	Two-seater	L4	2.8	18

SOURCE: U.S. Environmental Protection Agency, 1989.

TABLE 3-7 First Comparison by Automobile Type—Means, Variances and Standard Deviations for Engine Displacement and Highway Mileage

		Engine Displacement (liters)			Highway Mileage (miles per gallon)		
Type	Number	$\bar{X}$	s^2	s	$\bar{X}$	s^2	s
Two-seater	25	2.92	2.15	1.47	25.24	64.86	8.05
Minicompact	11	3.11	1.23	1.11	23.64	19.85	4.46
Total	36	2.98	1.83	1.35	24.75	50.71	7.12

Table 3-6 displays the same automobile data in terms of driving ease—whether cars come equipped with a manual or automatic transmission. In the Table 3-6 list, cars are separated first by transmission type and then ordered from highest to lowest gasoline mileage. This second arrangement might provide a more meaningful set of comparisons.

Two types of comparisons may be made using summary statistics. These are computed separately for the two data arrangements in Tables 3-7 and 3-8, where the respective computed values for means, variances, and standard deviations are given.

DISCUSSION QUESTIONS

1. What conclusions can you draw from the results displayed in Tables 3-7 and 3-8?
2. What other criteria would you consider before purchasing one of these automobiles?
3. Determine the mode and median values for engine displacement and mileage for each of the categories (i.e., two-seater, minicompact, automatic, manual) and the total.
4. Have the members of your class select the car of their choice (people may select the same automobiles). Compute the mean, median, mode, and standard deviation for your class's list. Compare your results with the answers in Tables 3-7 and 3-8. What conclusions can you draw?

TABLE 3-8 Second Comparison by Transmission Type—Means, Variances and Standard Deviations for Engine Displacement and Highway Mileage

		Engine Displacement (liters)			Highway Mileage (miles per gallon)		
Type	Number	$\bar{X}$	s^2	s	$\bar{X}$	s^2	s
Manual	23	2.90	1.94	1.39	25.48	66.35	8.15
Automatic	13	3.11	1.76	1.33	23.46	23.44	4.84
Total	36	2.98	1.83	1.35	24.75	50.71	7.12

REVIEW EXERCISES

3-48 The following cumulative relative frequency distribution has been obtained for the proportions of weed seed found in boxes of Sod Seeder mixtures.

Proportion of Weed Seed	Cumulative Relative Frequency
.00—under .01	.05
.01—under .02	.12
.02—under .03	.25
.03—under .04	.37
.04—under .05	.50
.05—under .06	.67
.06—under .07	.75
.07—under .08	.84
.08—under .09	.89
.09—under .10	.90
.10—under .11	.95
.11—under .12	.98
.12—under .13	1.00

Determine the following values.

(a) the .90 fractile
(b) the 37th percentile
(c) the first quartile
(d) the third quartile
(e) the interquartile range
(f) the median

3-49 Mr. Chips needs to analyze the grade point data of a random sample of ten students. The possible scores range downward from 4 points for "A" to 0 points for "F." The following data have been obtained from department records.

3	2	4	1	0
3	2	2	2	1

(a) Calculate the (1) range, (2) mean, (3) variance, and (4) standard deviation.
(b) Determine the (1) 25th, (2) 50th, and (3) 75th percentiles.
(c) Calculate the interquartile range.

3-50 The following percentiles have been obtained from a series of aptitude tests taken by all entering freshman at Old Ivy.

Score	Percentile
450	25th
573	50th
615	75th
729	90th
738	95th
752	99th

(a) Determine the (1) first, (2) second, and (3) third quartiles.
(b) Calculate the median score.
(c) Calculate the interquartile range.

3-51 The mean lifetimes for cartons of 100-watt Silk Vane long-life light bulbs have been established to be normally distributed, with mean 1,500 hours

and standard deviation 100 hours. Find the upper and lower bounds for the following limits, and indicate the percentage of all cartons for which the mean lifetimes fall within these limits.
(a) $\mu \pm 1\sigma$ (b) $\mu \pm 2\sigma$ (c) $\mu \pm 3\sigma$

3-52 The following frequency distribution has been obtained for sample data related to the viable shelf life of Pumper's Nickel-a-Slice bread.

Hours to Deterioration	Number of Loaves
90.0–under 110.0	23
110.0–under 130.0	37
130.0–under 150.0	26
150.0–under 170.0	14

Calculate the (a) mean, (b) median, (c) variance, and (d) standard deviation.

3-53 The following cumulative relative frequency distribution has been obtained for sample IQ scores achieved by students at Boston Sanskrit School.

IQ Score	Cumulative Proportion of Students
70–less than 80	.02
80–less than 90	.12
90–less than 100	.24
100–less than 110	.46
110–less than 120	.65
120–less than 130	.79
130–less than 140	.88
140–less than 150	.97
150–less than 160	1.00

(a) Plot the ogive.
(b) Read the following values from your graph. (The figures obtained will be only estimates of the actual values.)
(1) 50th percentile (3) first quartile (5) 90th percentile
(2) .75 fractile (4) median
(c) Use your answers from (b) to calculate the interquartile range.

3-54 The following ungrouped sample examination scores have been obtained for a large lecture course on human sexuality.

84	77	67	94	90
81	56	89	77	88
74	76	28	80	58
66	77	89	81	78
77	72	94	93	79
93				

(a) Calculate the (1) mean and (2) variance.
(b) The following frequency distribution for the sample data given in (a) is provided below.

Class Interval	Frequency
25.0–under 35.0	1
35.0–under 45.0	0
45.0–under 55.0	0
55.0–under 65.0	2
65.0–under 75.0	4
75.0–under 85.0	11
85.0–under 95.0	8
Total	26

Calculate the (1) mean and (2) variance.

(c) Calculating population parameters using grouped data provides only approximations of the population parameters that would be obtained directly from the ungrouped raw data. Find the amount of error in this approximation procedure for the sample mean by subtracting your answer in (b) from the value obtained in (a).

3-55 A plant superintendent fine-tuned a liquid blending operation by experimenting with control settings. The following impurity levels (parts per million) have been obtained for sample runs, with all settings unchanged during a single day.

Day 1	Day 2	Day 3	Day 4	Day 5
50	34	30	39	38
23	45	38	35	37
34	29	35	37	39
26	37	42	37	38
	27	33		
		32		

The superintendent's two objectives for the levels of impurities are (1) to minimize the variability and (2) to minimize the average.

(a) Calculate, for each day, the (1) mean, (2) standard deviation, (3) first quartile, (4) median, and (5) third quartile.

(b) Construct, on the same graph, a box plot for each day's completion times.

(c) Comment on how well the settings that the superintendent found met his goals.

3-56 Refer to the data given in Exercise 3-54.

(a) Construct a stem-and-leaf plot.

(b) Construct an ordered stem-and-leaf plot.

(c) Using the original ungrouped data, calculate the (1) mean, (2) standard deviation, and (3) mode.

(d) Using the original ungrouped data, determine the (1) 10th, (2) 25th, and (3) 75th percentiles.

(e) Calculate the median.

(f) Calculate the (1) range and (2) interquartile range.

(g) Construct the box plot.

STATISTICS IN PRACTICE

3-57 Refer to the master class data from Exercise 1-19.

(a) Use the data for height and find the mean, mode, median, variance, and standard deviation for the ungrouped data.

(b) Group the height data and recalculate the values.

(c) Explain why you grouped the data in the fashion you did. What conclusions can you draw by comparing your answers from parts (a) and (b)?

(d) Do the results demonstrate any skewing or bimodality? Explain why or why not.

(e) Determine the quartiles for your grouped data. What value is nearest the 80th percentile?

(f) Separate the class by sex, compare the height distributions and compare the means and standard deviations with your answers in parts (a) and (b).

(g) Categorize the class data by state, province or country of birth. Create one category for the state or province where your school is located and one for all others. Create a cross tabulation using place of birth versus major or favorite food. Use proportions in place of frequencies.

(h) Use the student age variable in a grouped format and compare the proportions for favorite food or place of birth.

3-58 Refer to your group's class data list developed in Exercise 1-19 and also used in Exercise 2-40. Perform the following operations for describing and displaying statistical data:

(a) For one interval data set find the mean, mode, median, variance, and standard deviation for the ungrouped data.

(b) Using the data from (a), group the data and recalculate the values.

(c) Explain why you grouped the data in the fashion you did. What conclusions can you draw by comparing answers from (a) and (b)?

(d) Do the results demonstrate any skewing or bimodality of the data? Explain the reasons for your results.

(e) Determine the quartiles for your grouped data. Find the 85th percentile.

(f) For one nominal variable, determine the proportion of observations in each category.

(g) Construct a cross tabulation with two nominal variables, determining the proportions for each cell and category.

3-59 *The Last Cold War Olympics—Applied Summary Statistics.* Consider the best way to organize the medal total data in Table 2-15 from the 1988 Games of the Summer Olympics. What summary descriptive measures would be useful in analyzing these data? Demonstrate these measures.

3-60 Table 2-16 shows the twenty most populous countries for the years 1991 and 2100. What summary descriptive measures would be most meaningful in analyzing these data? Demonstrate these measures.

3-61 Table 1-2 provides data on estimates of the location of homeless people.

(a) Determine the mean and median for the total data. Compare the mean to the median value.

(b) Suppose New York City is deleted from the data set. What might

TABLE 3-9 Best-Selling Prerecorded Videos of All Time

Rank/Title	Distributor	Units Sold (millions)
1. E.T.–The Extra Terrestrial	MCA	15.1
2. Batman	Warner	11.5
3. Bambi	Disney	10.5
4. The Little Mermaid	Disney	9.0
5. Teenage Mutant Ninja Turtles	LIVE	8.8
6. Who Framed Roger Rabbit	Touchstone	8.5
7. Cinderella	Disney	7.6
8. Peter Pan	Disney	7.0
9. Pretty Woman	Paramount	6.2
10. Honey, I Shrunk the Kids	Disney	5.8

Source: *The Universal Almanac* 1992: 252.

happen to the summary descriptive measures? Recompute the mean and median. Recompare the mean to the median.

3-62 Using the personal computer sales marketing data in Table 2-12, determine the average per capita installed base for the ten largest markets. What is the standard deviation? According to Chebyshev's theorem, what proportion of the per capita installed base should lie within the mean ± \$400?

3-63 Given the video sales data in Table 3-9, what descriptive summary measures could be used to best summarize the data? Apply the measures you selected to the data.

CASE Ingrid's Hallmark Shop II

As you recall from the Case in Chapter 2, Ingrid's Hallmark Shop is a card and gift shop located in a suburban town. The owner, Ingrid, needs to make operational decisions and plan her financial strategy. Ingrid's concerns include forecasting cash flow, estimating daily sales of staple items such as birthday cards, and assessing the efficiency of her staff in performing various tasks.

Ingrid's son Dan helped to resolve some of the aforementioned business concerns as part of an MBA term project. To begin, Dan obtained the operating data in Table 3-10 for a sample of peak off-season weekdays.

Dan was particularly interested in Ingrid's balloon business. He decided to determine how much time an employee spent completing a balloon order, beginning at that point when the customer's choice has been made and the fresh balloons have been gathered from stock. The employee's task then is to fill the balloons, one at a time, with helium, clamp the ribbon onto the stem (which also secures the contents), and, finally, to tie on a decorative weight. Often the order will be picked up later in the day enabling the employee to handle interruptions between balloons. Over time, Ingrid's employees become more adept at completing balloon orders.

How rapid is the employee's learning process? This is what Dan set out to determine. He prepared a log for Nancy, a new hire, to fill in as she

TABLE 3-10 Sample Operating Data for Ingrid's Hallmark Shop

Number of Transactions	Total Sales
68	$ 563
97	729
133	826
115	633
122	912
85	552
144	1,220
78	464
110	601
112	598
92	653
88	532

completed balloon orders. Table 3-11 is a portion of Nancy's log showing a sample of balloon orders filled during her first month of employment at Ingrid's Hallmark Shop.

Dan also selected a sample of days and asked all the employees to count carefully the number of birthday cards they sold those days. Table 3-12 lists the results Dan obtained.

QUESTIONS

1. One of Ingrid's most important forecasting measures is the individual average transaction (IAT). This is found by dividing the dollar sales by the customer count.

TABLE 3-11 Sample Balloon Order Data from Nancy's Log

Date	Order	Number of Balloons Completed	Elapsed Time (seconds)
8/02	1	5	335
	3	7	454
	6	2	132
	13	9	585
8/04	4	10	528
	5	4	206
	8	1	48
	13	14	732
	15	7	395
8/28	6	5	150
	9	6	185
	14	10	290
	15	12	365
	16	10	310
	17	8	232

(a) Use the operating data given in Table 3-10. Calculate each IAT.
(b) Using your answers to (a), calculate the (1) mean, (2) standard deviation, and (3) median.
(c) Determine the (1) 10th, (2) 25th, (3) 50th, (4) 75th, and (5) 90th percentiles using your answers to (a).
(d) Construct a box plot for the sample IAT data in (a).
(e) What do your results suggest regarding the possibility of having an IAT as small as \$1.50 or as large as \$20.00 on a peak weekday during the off-season?

2. Refer to the daily sales data given in Table 3-12. Repeat Question 1(b)–(d) above.

3. One way to forecast a weekday's dollar sales is to multiply the mean IAT by the customer count estimated for that day. Using your answers to Question 1, forecast the dollar sales when (a) 90, (b) 110, and (c) 120 customers are projected.

4. Ingrid believes that 20% of a day's sales volume, on the average, consists of birthday cards. The average retail value of a birthday card is \$1.50. Thus, on a 100-card day, the expected dollar sales would be

$$(1/.20) \times 1.50 \times 100 = \$750$$

(a) Assuming that your answers to Question 2 are representative, what would Ingrid's average sales be for a typical weekday?
(b) Comment on the appropriateness of the number found in (a) for planning purposes.
(c) Suggest an alternative procedure Ingrid might use to predict daily sales.

5. Refer to the balloon order data given in Table 3-11.
(a) For each sample day, construct a box plot for the average time per balloon Nancy spent while completing an order.
(b) What do you notice about Nancy's balloon-filling skills over time?

TABLE 3-12 Sample Daily Unit Birthday Card Sales for Ingrid's Hallmark Shop

Date	Cards Sold
7/25	113
8/06	155
8/15	78
9/02	63
9/15	206
9/16	125
9/23	132
10/02	95
10/08	118
10/12	188

CHAPTER 4

THE STATISTICAL SAMPLING STUDY

BEFORE READING THIS CHAPTER, MAKE SURE YOU UNDERSTAND:

The distinction between quantitative and qualitative data (Chapter 1).
How data are displayed (Chapter 2).
The various statistical measures and how they give meaning to data (Chapter 3).

AFTER READING THIS CHAPTER, YOU WILL UNDERSTAND:

Why samples should be used.
The stages of a statistical sampling study.
How to avoid bias and control sampling error.
The main types of samples.
The various forms of random sampling.
Some important elements of a statistical experiment.

Now that we have covered the basic elements of descriptive statistics, we are ready to consider **statistical sampling**. To draw conclusions about populations from samples, we must use inferential statistics, which enables us to determine a population's characteristics by directly observing only a portion, or sample, of the population.

We obtain a sample rather than a complete enumeration (a census) of the population for many reasons. Obviously, it is cheaper to observe a part rather than the whole, but we should prepare ourselves to cope with the dangers of using samples. In this chapter, we will investigate various kinds of sampling procedures. Some are better than others, but all may yield samples that are inaccurate and unreliable. We will learn how to minimize these dangers, but some potential error is the price we must pay for the convenience and savings that samples provide.

4-1 THE NEED FOR SAMPLES

There would be no need for statistical theory if a census, rather than a sample, was always used to obtain information about populations. But a census may not be practical and is almost never economical.

Sample information must be relied on for most applications. There are six main reasons for sampling in lieu of the census: economy, timeliness, the large size of many populations, inaccessibility of some of the population, destructiveness of the observation, and accuracy.

THE ECONOMIC ADVANTAGES OF USING A SAMPLE

Obviously, taking a sample—directly observing only a portion of the population—requires fewer resources than a census. For example, consider a consumer survey to determine the reactions of all the owners of a popular automobile to several proposed colors for next year's model. A questionnaire is to be printed and mailed to all owners. Imagine the clerical chore of simply addressing the envelopes, and the cost of the postage alone could easily run into five figures. The bookkeeping problems in tabulating the replies would be overwhelming.

Perhaps the greatest difficulty would be to ensure a 100% response. A high proportion of the questionnaires will simply be ignored along with the plethora of other "junk" mail. Most persons can be reached by telephone, telegram, or personal visit. Invariably, however, an irascible few will slam their doors even in the face of the company president, and some will have to be bribed with a new car to respond. A great many car owners will have moved and will be hard to locate, necessitating the services of a detective agency. Some owners will die without responding before the survey is completed. The company could have more difficulty taking a census of its owner population than the FBI has arresting its ten most wanted men.

As unrealistic as this example is, it does illustrate the very high cost of a census. For the type of information desired, the car manufacturer would be wise to interview a small portion of the car owners. Rarely does a circumstance require a census of the population, and even more rarely is the expense justified.

THE TIME FACTOR

A sample may provide an investigator with needed information quickly. Often speed is of paramount importance, as in a political polling, where the goal is to determine from sample evidence voter preferences toward candidates for public office. The voting public as a whole is extremely fickle; polls have indicated that voters fluctuate in preference right up to the time of the election. If a poll is to be used to gauge public opinion, it must be very current; the opinions must be obtained, tabulated, and published within a very short period of time. Even if it were physically possible to use a census in such an opinion survey, its results would not be valid due to significant shifts in public opinion over the time required to conduct it.

Similarly, managerial decisions based on a population's characteristics must frequently be made very quickly. In a highly competitive environment there may not be enough time to wait for a 100% response before introducing a new product or changing service patterns. Since a census would not be feasible, sample evidence must be relied on.

THE VERY LARGE POPULATION

Many populations about which inferences must be made are quite large. For example, consider the population of high school seniors in the United States—a group numbering about 3,000,000. The plans of these soon-to-be graduates will directly affect the status of universities and colleges, the military, and prospective employers—all of whom must have specific knowledge about the students' plans in order to make compatible decisions to absorb them during the coming year. But the sheer size of the population of postgraduate plans will probably make it physically impossible to conduct a census. Sample evidence may be the only available way to obtain information from high school seniors.

PARTLY INACCESSIBLE POPULATIONS

Some populations contain elementary units so difficult to observe that they are in a sense inaccessible. One example is the population of crashed aircraft: Planes that crash and sink in the deep ocean are inaccessible and cannot be directly studied to determine the physical causes of their failure. Similar conditions hold in determining consumer attitudes. Not all of the users of a product can be queried. Some may be in prisons, nursing homes, or hospitals and have limited contact with the outside world. Others may be insulated from harassment; consider the limited accessibility to the president of the United States or the pope.

Whenever some elementary units are inaccessible, sampling must be used to provide the desired information about the population. These illustrations demonstrate physical inaccessibility, but an elementary unit's accessibility may be limited for economic reasons alone: Those observations deemed too costly to be made are, in a real sense, also inaccessible.

THE DESTRUCTIVE NATURE OF THE OBSERVATION

Sometimes the very act of observing the desired characteristic of the elementary unit destroys it for the use intended. Classical examples of this occur in quality control: To test a fuse to determine whether it is defective, it must be destroyed; to obtain a census of the quality of a shipment of fuses, all of them must be destroyed. This negates any purpose served by quality-control testing. Clearly, a *sample* of fuses must be tested to assess the quality of the shipment.

STATISTICS AROUND US

Indians and Teenage Widows

Two statisticians noticed a very unusual anomaly in the change of two categories between 1940 and 1950.* An abnormally large number of 14-year-old widows were reported in the 1950 figures—20 times as many as in 1940. Indian divorcees, who had also been extremely rare, had increased by a like magnitude. Unable to justify the changes by any sociological trends, the statisticians analyzed the data-gathering and data-processing procedures of the census. They concluded that the figures could have resulted from the erroneous reversal of the entries on a few of the punched cards used to process the data. In this instance, a census seemed to provide far from reliable or credible results.

ACCURACY AND SAMPLING

A sample may be more accurate than a census. A sloppily conducted census can provide less reliable information than a carefully obtained sample. Indeed, the U.S. census of 1950 provides us with an excellent example in the above Statistics Around Us box.

A large utility company had problems of a somewhat different nature with punched cards, described in the box at the bottom of this page.

EXERCISES

4-1 For each of the following situations, indicate whether a sample or a census would be more appropriate. Explain.

(a) AC-DC knows that due to variations in processing, a certain percentage of its spark plugs will be defective. A thorough test of a spark plug

STATISTICS AROUND US

Work Sampling

The procedure for allocating a data center's data entry costs was based on a census compiled from detailed logs maintained by keypunch operators. These records were not very accurate, and record keeping reduced operator productivity. A company statistician found that operators spent 10% of their time maintaining the logs and proposed that management use **work sampling**. At random time intervals, a bell would ring and all operators would stop work and fill out a simplified form. Data entry costs were allocated to the various departments according to the percentage of forms returned, which was accurate since heavier users would accumulate more forms. Operator productivity increased, and everyone was pleased with the greater accuracy.

*Ansley J. Coale and Frederick F. Stephan, "The Case of the Indians and Teen-age Widows," *Journal of the American Statistical Association*, LVII (June 1962): 388–437.

destroys it, but the production output must be tested to determine whether remedial action is necessary.
(b) NASA must determine the quality of the components of a manned space vehicle.
(c) A hospital administrator attempting to improve patient services wishes to determine the attitudes of persons treated.
(d) A medical researcher wants to determine the possible harmful side effects from a chemical that eases the pain of arthritis.

4-2 For each of the following reasons, give an example of a situation for which a census would be less desirable than a sample. Explain.
(a) economy (c) size of population (e) accuracy
(b) timeliness (d) inaccessibility (f) destructive observations

4-2 DESIGNING AND CONDUCTING A SAMPLING STUDY

Much of this book is concerned with how to collect samples so that meaningful conclusions can be drawn about an entire population. Figure 4-1 shows the major stages of a sampling study. The first stage—**planning**—requires careful attention so that the sampling results will achieve the best impact. In the second stage—**data collection**, where the plans are followed—a major goal is to ensure that observations are free from bias. The last phase—**data analysis and conclusions**—is the area to which a major portion of this book will be devoted.

THE IMPORTANCE OF PLANNING

Planning is the most important step in a statistical study. Inadequate planning can lead to needless expense when actual data collection begins. Poor planning may result in the eventual invalidation of the entire study. The outcome of the study may even prove strongly counterproductive. Several extreme cases of poor planning will be given in this chapter.

Planning begins with the identification of a population that will achieve the study's goals. This is followed by the selection of an observation procedure that might require a questionnaire, which would then have to be designed, or an observation-measuring instrument. The latter is a broad category that includes mechanical devices (to record physical data, such as dimensions and weight), various tests (for intelligence, aptitude, personality, or knowledge), sources of data (for example, family income could be obtained from tax records, from employers, or by directly questioning a family member), and survey techniques (written reply, telephone response, or personal interview).

Of equal importance in planning is the choice of the sample type itself. Alternative kinds of samples range from the most "scientific" random sample, like the one used in the major public opinion polls, to the convenience sample taken in campus straw votes, where practically no attention is paid to how representative the sample might be. The random sample is the most important, because statistical theory applies to it alone. As we will see, there are a variety of ways to select a sample.

If proper and valid conclusions are to be drawn from the sample data, planning must include a presampling choice of the statistical procedure to be used later in analyzing the results. Choosing an analytical technique *after* sifting through the

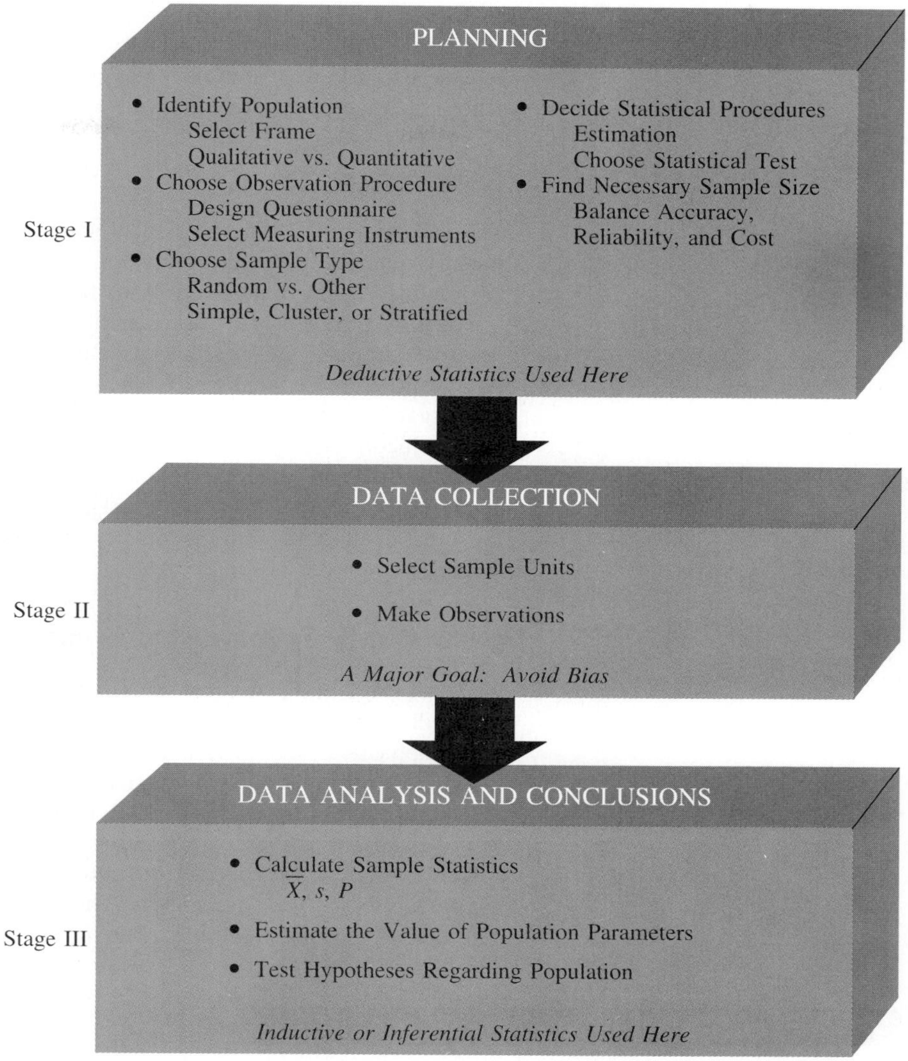

FIGURE 4-1 Major stages in a statistical sampling study.

results may lead to the most insidious kind of bias—the innocent or intentional selection of a tool that strongly supports the desired conclusion.

An important planning consideration in any sampling study is determining how many observations to make. In general, the larger its size, the more closely a random sample is expected to represent its population. But where do we draw the line? Isn't a sample ten times as large ten times as good? The first question will be answered in Chapter 8. To the second, the answer is *no.* As we will see, selection of sample size is largely an economic matter; scarce resources (funds available for gathering data) must be traded off against the accuracy and reliability of the result. A point of diminishing return is soon reached where an extra dollar buys very little in increased sample quality.

Both choosing a statistical procedure and selecting an appropriate sample size involve a great amount of deductive statistics, since both of these planning aspects require us to look at how samples are generated from "textbook" populations whose characteristics are fully known.

DATA COLLECTION

The second phase of the statistical sampling study—obtaining the raw data—usually requires the greatest amount of time and effort. Adequate controls must be provided to prevent observations from becoming biased.

Potential problem areas associated with collecting and managing the data are described in detail in subsequent sections of this chapter. Such problems include observational biases that result when the sample units are measured, queried, or investigated. A poorly asked question and an improperly operated device both lead to incorrect responses. Another source of bias arises because some parts of the population are inaccessible or difficult to observe. Additional problems may appear after the data are collected. The inevitable ambiguities and contradictions must be dealt with and the results processed so that statistical analyses can be made.

DATA ANALYSIS AND CONCLUSIONS

This last stage of a statistical sampling study is extremely important. Here, many of the descriptive tools we discussed earlier are used to communicate the results. Our emphasis, however, is placed on drawing conclusions from the necessarily incomplete information available from any sample. This is the point at which statistical inferences are made. The lion's share of statistical theory is directly related to or in support of making generalizations or **inferences** about populations from samples. Inferences generally fall into the three broad categories of estimation, hypothesis testing, and association. The goals of the study and the resources available dictate the statistical inference and technique that will be used.

4-3 BIAS AND ERROR IN SAMPLING

The manner in which the observed units are chosen significantly affects the adequacy of the sample. Here we will examine some of the pitfalls commonly encountered in sampling and learn how to avoid many of them.

A sample is expected to mirror the population from which it comes. However, there is no guarantee that any sample will be precisely representative of the population; chance may dictate that a disproportionate number of untypical observations will be made. In practice, it is rarely known when a sample is unrepresentative and should be discarded, because some population characteristics are unknown (or else no sample would be needed in the first place). Steps must be taken during the planning of the study to minimize the chance that the sample will be untypical.

SAMPLING ERROR

What can make a sample unrepresentative of its population? One of the most frequent causes is **sampling error**, for which we provide the following.

DEFINITION: **Sampling error** comprises the differences between the sample and the population that are due solely to the particular elementary units that happen to have been selected.

To illustrate sampling error, suppose that a sample of 100 American men are measured and are all found to be taller than seven feet. An obvious conclusion would be that most American males are taller than seven feet. Of course, this is absurd; most people do not know a man who is seven feet tall and might not even be sure one existed if a few basketball players were not that tall. Yet it is possible for a statistician to be unfortunate enough to obtain such a highly unrepresentative sample. However, this is highly unlikely; nature has distributed the rare seven-footers widely among the population.

More dangerous is the less obvious sampling error against which nature offers little protection. It is not difficult to envision a sample in which the average height is overstated by only an inch or two rather than a foot. It is the insidious, unobvious error that is our major concern.

There are two basic causes for sampling error. One is chance: Bad luck may result in untypical choices. Unusual elementary units do exist, and there is always a possibility that an abnormally large number will be chosen. The main protection against this type of error is to use a large enough sample. Another cause of sampling error—sampling bias—is not as easy to remedy.

SAMPLING BIAS

The size of the sample has little to do with the effects of sampling bias. In the present context, we provide the

DEFINITION: **Sampling bias** is a tendency to favor the selection of elementary units that have particular characteristics.

Sampling bias is usually the result of a poor sampling plan. Consider the following classical example from political polling.

STATISTICS AROUND US

The *Literary Digest* Said Roosevelt Would Lose

A poll was conducted by the now defunct *Literary Digest* in 1936, when Franklin D. Roosevelt was running against Republican Alfred M. Landon for the presidency. Based on several million responses obtained from a sample of the voting public, the *Digest* concluded that Landon would win by a record margin. Exactly the opposite happened: Roosevelt won one of the most one-sided victories in American history. The poll's erroneous results were later attributed to sampling bias. The *Digest* had selected its sample from magazine subscription listings and telephone directories. During the Great Depression, both sources contained a disproportionate number of prosperous persons who favored the laissez-faire Republican platform. Because a large proportion of the disgruntled majority, who strongly favored Roosevelt, had no telephones and did not subscribe to magazines, these voters were not adequately represented in the sample.

The avoidance of sampling bias is a major concern of statisticians. A means of selecting the elementary units must be designed to avoid the more obvious forms of bias. In practice, it is difficult (if not impossible) to eliminate all forms of bias. Most notable is the **bias of nonresponse**, when—for whatever reason—some elementary units have no chance of appearing in the sample. The cost considerations involved in making sample observations almost guarantee that this particular form of bias will be present to some degree in any sample.

An excellent example is provided by consumer surveys involving food products. It is relatively cheap to obtain opinions about a company's product from persons who remain at home during the day. But a large proportion of adult residents in many areas are employed and are at home only in the evenings and on weekends. If the sampling survey is conducted during normal working hours, these consumers who make food-buying decisions will not be represented. A company wishing to determine whether to expand its line of prepared frozen foods may obtain survey results indicating that there is not a great demand for such products. But working people have less leisure time and are often enthusiastic users of such items. A sample that neglected their opinions could lead to an erroneous marketing decision.

NONSAMPLING ERROR

The other main cause of unrepresentative samples is nonsampling error. This type of error can occur whether a census or a sample is being used. Like sampling error, nonsampling error may either be produced by participants in the statistical study or be an innocent byproduct of the sampling plans and procedures.

DEFINITION: A **nonsampling error** is an error that results solely from the manner in which the observations are made.

The simplest example of nonsampling error is inaccurate physical measurement due to malfunctioning instruments or poor procedures. Consider the observation of human weights. If persons are asked to state their own weights, no two answers will be of equal reliability. The people will have weighed themselves on different scales in various states of poor calibration. An individual's weight fluctuates diurnally by several pounds, so that the time of weighing will affect the answer. The scale reading will also vary with the person's state of undress. Responses will not be of comparable validity unless all persons are weighed under the same circumstances.

Biased observations due to inaccurate measurement can be innocent but devastating. A French astronomer once proposed a new theory based on spectroscopic measurements of light emitted by a particular star. When his colleagues discovered that the measuring instrument had been contaminated by cigarette smoke, they rejected his findings.

In surveys of personal characteristics, unintended errors may result from (1) the manner in which the response is elicited, (2) the idiosyncrasies of the persons surveyed, (3) the purpose of the study, or (4) the personal biases of the interviewer or survey writer.

The Interviewer's Effect

No two interviewers are alike, and the same person may provide different answers to different interviewers. The manner in which a question is formulated can also result in inaccurate responses. Individuals tend to provide false answers to particular questions. A good example of this is a person's age. Some people will lie about their age. If asked their age in years, most people will give their chronological age at their previous birthday, even if it is more than 11 months past. Both problems can be alleviated by asking the date of birth. It would require quick arithmetic to give a false date, and a date of birth is much more accurate than a person's age on his or her last birthday.

Respondents might also give incorrect answers to impress the interviewer. This is especially prevalent when survey questions are based on a knowledge of current events or on intellectual accomplishments. Many people have said that they "know" about famous people who are fictitious or that they have read books that were never written. This type of error is the most difficult to prevent, because it results from outright deceit on the part of the respondent. It is important to acknowledge that certain psychological factors induce incorrect responses, and great care must be taken to design a study that minimizes their effect.

Knowing Purpose of the Study

Knowing why a study is being conducted may create incorrect responses. A classic example is the answer to the question: What is your income? If a government agency is asking, a different figure may be provided than the respondent would give on an application for a home mortgage. A teacher's union seeking to justify a wage increase may receive a different response from a member than would the brother-in-law of the member. The union would probably not be given (nor would it want to know) the member's full income, incorporating earnings from moonlighting and summer employment, whereas the brother-in-law would probably be informed about the income derived from these sources as well as any successful investments. One way to guard against such bias is to camouflage the study's goals; an independent opinion survey firm might even be employed to keep secret the objective of the investigation. Another remedy is to make the questions very specific, allowing little room for personal interpretation. For example, "Where are you employed?" could be followed by "What is your salary?" and "Do you have any extra jobs?" A sequence of such questions may produce more accurate information.

Induced Bias

Finally, it should be noted that the personal prejudices of either the designer of the study or the data collector may tend to **induce bias**. A person should not design a questionnaire related to a subject he or she feels strongly about. Questions may be slanted in such a way that a particular response will be obtained even though it is inaccurate. An example of this is a preference survey sponsored by the makers of brand A, prefaced by the question "In your opinion, which of the following factors that make brand A a superior-quality product is the most important?" This could be followed by a question asking for a preference ranking of a list of products, including brand A. (Most blatantly, brand A may be the first name on the list.) The preliminary question encourages the respondent to think about the good features of brand A, creating an atmosphere that will make the later comparison unfair. Another instance of induced error may occur in an experiment in which a technical specialist selects the elementary units to be treated with a new product. For example, when doctors favoring a new drug decide which patients are going to receive it, they may select (consciously or not) those they feel have the best chance of benefiting from its administration. An agronomist may apply a new fertilizer to certain key plots, knowing that they will provide more favorable yields than others. To protect against induced bias, an individual trained in statistics should have a measure of control over the design and implementation of the entire statistical study, and someone who is aware of these pitfalls should serve in an auditing capacity.

EXERCISES

4-3 A government official must delegate the responsibility for determining employee attitudes toward a training program conducted by the personnel department. What are the dangers in asking the personnel manager to handle this matter? Suggest a procedure that would overcome these obstacles.

4-4 People who filled out the "long" form for the U.S. Census of 1970 were asked to answer questions about their employment. One question was "How many hours did you work last week?" Successive questions relating to the same work week asked about type of employer, duties, and so on. The public was instructed to provide the data by April 1, 1970. This was the Wednesday right after Easter, and most of the nation's educators had been on a holiday for the entire week in question. Comment on the possible errors that may have resulted from this set of questions. How could the questionnaire have been improved to avoid these errors?

4-5 Greenwall's Drugstore has recently experienced a significant decline in sales due to the presence of some new discount stores in the city. A questionnaire asked customers who visited the store during one week to compare its prices, convenience, and level of service with the discount stores. What do you think about the manner in which the information was obtained? What sampling procedure could you recommend?

4-6 A questionnaire prepared for a study on consumer buying habits contains the question "What is the value of your present automobile(s)?" What errors may result from this question? Suggest a better way to obtain the desired response.

4-7 Many personality profiles require that an individual provide answers to multiple-choice questions. The answers are then compiled, and various trait ratings are found. Comment on the pitfalls of this procedure. Suggest how some may be alleviated.

4-8 Testing a new drug therapy sometimes involves two patient groups. The patients in one group receive the medication under investigation. The other may receive no medication at all or may be given an innocuous substance called a **placebo** (often just a sugar pill) that looks like the drug being tested. Why is the placebo used?

4-9 A well-known television rating agency provides networks and advertisers with estimates of the audience size for all nationally televised programs. These estimates are based on detailed logs, maintained by persons in the households surveyed, that indicate which stations were watched during each period of the day. The agency has a difficult time recruiting households for its sample, because it is bothersome and inconvenient to keep the logs. Independent observers have estimated that an average of 50 families must be approached before one agrees to join the sample. Comment on the pitfalls that may be encountered when the sample results are taken as representative of the nations's television viewing habits. Can you suggest ways to minimize these pitfalls? Do you think that the sample observations obtained are in danger of being untypical? Explain.

4-4 SELECTING THE SAMPLE

In Section 4-3, we examined the most common problems associated with statistical studies. The desirability of a sampling procedure depends on both its vulnerability to error and its cost. However, economy and reliability are competing ends, because to reduce error often requires an increased expenditure of resources.

Of the two types of statistical error, only sampling error can be controlled by exercising care in determining the method for choosing the sample. We have established that sampling error may be due to either bias or chance. The chance component exists no matter how carefully the selection procedures are implemented, and the only way to minimize chance sampling errors is to select a sufficiently large sample. Sampling bias, on the other hand, may be minimized by the judicious choice of a sampling procedure.

There are three primary kinds of samples: the convenience sample, the judgment sample, and the random sample. They differ in the manner in which their elementary units are chosen. Each sample will be described in turn, and its desirable and undesirable features will be discussed.

THE CONVENIENCE SAMPLE

A convenience sample results when the more convenient elementary units are chosen from a population for observation. Convenience samples are the cheapest to obtain. Their major drawback is the extent to which they may be permeated with sampling bias, which tends to make them highly unreliable. An important decision made on the basis of a convenience sample is in great danger of being wrong. The letters received by a member of Congress constitute a convenience sample of constituent attitudes. The legislator does not have to expend any time, money, or effort to receive mail, but the opinions voiced there will rarely be indicative of the attitudes of the entire constituency. Persons who have special interests to protect are far more likely to write than the typical voter.

The bias of nonresponse, when present, usually results in a convenience sample. This type of bias can be expected when the telephone—a very convenient device—is used to obtain responses, because the incidence of nonresponse may be relatively high. Many calls will be unanswered, and some people will have unlisted numbers or no telephones at all.

Despite the obvious disadvantages of convenience samples, they are sometimes suitable, depending on the purpose of the study. If only approximate information about a population is needed, then a convenience sample may be adequate. Or funds for a study may be so limited that only a convenience sample is feasible. But in such cases, the obvious drawbacks must be acknowledged. On the other hand, a convenience sample may result in an insignificant source of bias. For example, when there is no reason to believe that nonrespondents would provide information that would differ on the whole from the data already available, there may be little danger in using a telephone survey; but we can never be sure.

THE JUDGMENT SAMPLE

A judgement sample is obtained according to the discretion of someone who is familiar with the relevant characteristics of the population. The elementary units are selected judgmentally when the population is highly heterogeneous, when the sample is to be quite small, or when special skill is required to ensure a representative collection of observations.

The judgment sample is obviously prone to bias. Its adequacy is limited by the ability of the individual who selects the sample to perceive differences. All of the dangers mentioned in Section 4-3 in connection with induced bias apply to the judgment sample. Clearly, there are instances in which this type of sample is preferred. Indeed, the consumer price index would be unworkable if it were not partly based on judgment samples.

STATISTICS AROUND US

Consumer Price Index

The Consumer Price Index of the U.S. Department of Labor is partly a judgment sample. The items to be included in establishing the index are chosen on the basis of judgment in order to measure a dollar's purchasing power. Thus, only items or commodities that are used by most people are included; for example, television sets are included, but tape recorders are not. Over time, certain items become obsolete and must be replaced by others; for instance, refrigerators have supplanted iceboxes. Judgment must be employed in deciding what will be replaced and what will be substituted. Judgment is also used in establishing weights for each item; toothpaste should only be weighted in proportion to its position in a typical family's total expenditure—and the typical expenditure is itself a matter of judgment. Finally, judgment is employed in selecting the cities to be represented in the surveys; these, too, must be assigned weights.

THE RANDOM SAMPLE

Perhaps the most important type of sample is the random sample. **A random sample allows a known probability that each elementary unit will be chosen.** For this reason, it is sometimes referred to as a **probability sample**.

In its simplest form, a random sample is selected in the manner of a raffle. For example, a random sample of ten symphony conductors from a population of 100 could be obtained by a lottery. The name of each symphony conductor would be written on a slip of paper and placed into a capsule. All 100 capsules would then be placed in a box and thoroughly mixed. An impartial party would select the sample by drawing ten capsules from the box.

In actual practice, a lottery can be physically cumbersome and even its randomness can be questioned, as the following example shows.

STATISTICS AROUND US

The 1970 Draft Lottery Fiasco

The 1970 U.S. draft lottery determined priorities of selection by date of birth. A physical method similar to a raffle was used, but the results appeared to have a pattern. December birth dates were assigned a disproportionate amount of early numbers, and January birth dates were assigned predominantly later numbers. Investigation showed that the undesirable outcome resulted from the fact that the capsules had not been mixed at all. Since the December capsules were the last to be placed in the hopper, many December dates were drawn first. Because persons with these birth dates were almost certain to be drafted, considerable controversy arose and lawsuits were filed to invalidate the entire lottery.

SAMPLE SELECTION USING RANDOM NUMBERS

A more acceptable way to obtain a random sample is to use **random numbers**—digits generated by a lottery process that allows for the equal probability that each possible number will appear next. For example, in a list of five-digit random numbers, each value between 00000 and 99999 has the same chance of appearing at each location. Appendix Table B is a list of five-digit random numbers that was generated by an electromechanical process at the Rand Corporation. These particular numbers have passed many tests and have been certified by the scientific community. If the Selective Service had used such a table of random numbers to select its birth dates, it would have been guiltless in the eyes of everyone except those who were chosen first.

There is no guarantee that a list of random numbers will not exhibit some sort of pattern. For example, 8 may follow 7 more frequently than any other value. But in a long list, any kind of pattern is highly unlikely (8 should follow 7 about 10% of the time).

EXAMPLE: SELECTING SYMPHONY CONDUCTORS AT RANDOM

We select a sample of ten symphony conductors. As a preliminary step, we must assign a number to each member of the population. In this case, we can use two digits; the assigned numbers will therefore range from 00 through 99. It makes no difference how these numbers are assigned, but the person making the assignments should not know which location of the random number table is being used. In Table 4-1, the 100 conductors have been arranged in alphabetical order and assigned the numbers 00 through 99 in sequence. We are now ready to use random numbers to obtain a sample of size $n = 10$.

SOLUTION: We will choose our sample of ten conductors by reading down the first column of the random number table until we obtain ten different values. Note that we only require two-digit numbers but that the table entries contain five digits, so we will use only the first two digits of each entry and ignore the extra digits. If a value is obtained more than once before all ten conductors have been chosen, then that number will be skipped and the next number on the list will be

TABLE 4-1 Alphabetical Listing for a Population of 100 Symphony Conductors

00. Abbado	25. Golschmann	50. Mehta	**74.** Santini
01. André	26. Hannikainen	51. Mitropoulos	76. Sargent
02. Anosov	27. Hollingsworth	52. Monteux	77. Scherchen
03. Ansermet	28. Horenstein	53. Morel	78. Schippers
04. Argenta	29. Horvat	54. Mravinsky	**79.** Schmidt-Isserstedt
05. Barbirolli	30. Jacquillat	**55.** Newman	80. Sejna
06. Beecham	31. Jorda	56. Ormandy	**81.** Serafin
07. Bernstein	32. Karajan	57. Ozawa	**82.** Silvestri
08. Black	33. Kempe	58. Patanè	83. Skrowaczewski
09. Bloomfield	34. Kertesz	59. Pedrotti	84. Slatkin
10. Bonynge	35. Klemperer	60. Perlea	85. Smetácčêk
11. Boult	**36.** Kletzki	61. Prêtre	86. Solti
12. Cantelli	37. Klima	62. Previn	87. Stein
13. Cluytens	38. Kondrashin	63. Previtali	88. Steinberg
14. Dorati	39. Kostelanetz	64. Prohaska	89. Stokowski
15. Dragon	40. Koussevitzky	65. Reiner	**90.** Svetlanov
16. Erede	41. Krips	66. Reinhardt	91. Swarowsky
17. Ferencsik	42. Kubelik	67. Rekai	92. Szell
18. Fiedler	43. Lane	68. Rignold	93. Toscanini
19. Fistoulari	44. Leinsdorf	69. Ristenpart	94. Van Otterloo
20. Fricsay	45. Maag	**70.** Rodzinski	95. Van Remoortel
21. Frühbeck de Burgos	46. Maazel	71. Rosenthal	96. Vogel
22. Furtwängler	47. Mackerras	72. Rowicki	97. Von Matacic
23. Gamba	48. Markevitch	73. Rozhdestvensky	98. Walter
24. Giulini	49. Martin	74. Sanderling	99. Watanabee

used instead. The values obtained by starting at the top of the first column of Appendix Table B and reading down are listed here, with the corresponding conductors who now comprise our sample.

12651	Cantelli	**74**146	Sanderling
81769	Serafin	**90**759	Svetlanov
36737	Kletzki	**55**683	Newman
82861	Silvestri	**79**686	Schmidt-Isserstedt
21325	Frühbeck de Burgos	**70**333	Rodzinski

It does not matter how the random number table is read (from left to right, right to left, top to bottom, bottom to top, or diagonally), but it is important not to read the same number location more than once and not to look ahead before deciding in which direction to proceed. If the numbers are larger than required, the beginning or ending digits can be ignored. If a number on the list has no counterpart in the population (which may happen when the population is smaller than the possible number of random numbers), it should be skipped.

Unlike judgment and convenience samples, random samples are free from sampling bias. No particular elementary units are favored. This still does not guarantee that a random sample will be extremely representative of the population from which it came, because the chance effect may cause it not to be. But it will be possible to assess the reliability of a sample in terms of probability, which can be done only with random samples. When sampling bias is present, an objective basis for measuring its effect does not exist. Therefore, *only the random sample has a theoretical basis for the quantitative evaluation of its quality.* In later chapters, we will see how probability is used for such evaluations.

TYPES OF RANDOM SAMPLES

The way we chose our sample of ten conductors is only one type of a random sampling scheme. At times, it may be desirable to modify the selection procedure without altering the essential features of the random sample. The type of sampling we just discussed is a **simple random sample**, for which we provide the following

DEFINITION: A **simple random sample** is obtained by choosing elementary units in such a way that each unit in the population has an equal chance of being selected.

A simple random sample is free from sampling bias. However, using a random number table to choose the elementary units can be cumbersome. If the sample is to be collected by a person untrained in statistics, then instructions may be misinterpreted and selections may be made improperly. Instead of using a list of random numbers, data collection can be simplified by selecting, say, every 10th or 100th unit after the first unit has been chosen randomly. Such a procedure is called a **systematic random sample**, for which we have the following

DEFINITION: A **systematic random sample** is obtained by selecting one unit on a random basis and choosing additional elementary units at evenly spaced intervals until the desired number of units is obtained.

EXAMPLE: SAMPLING WITH TELEPHONE NUMBERS

A telephone company is conducting a billing study to justify a new rate structure. Data are to be collected by taking a random sample of individual telephone bills from cities and metropolitan areas classified according to population. Billing data are stored by telephone number. A company statistical analyst has designed a procedure for each regional office to employ in collecting the samples.

In one city, 10,000 telephones share the 825 prefix. The telephone numbers range from 825-0000 through 825-9999. A sample size of 200 is required.

SOLUTION: Dividing the number of telephones by 200, the interval width of 50 is obtained. Thus, the bill for every 50th telephone number will be incorporated into the sample. The analyst chooses a number between 0 and 49 at random. Suppose she chooses 37. Her instructions to the regional accounting offices specify that the billing figures for every 50th telephone number, starting with 825-0037, be forwarded to her office. It then becomes a simple manual task for a clerk to pull every 50th telephone bill from the files, and the analyst will receive the figures for 825-0037, 825-0087, 825-0137, 825-0187, and so on.

Sometimes we must ensure that various subgroups of a population are represented in the sample. (In statistics, these subgroups are referred to as **strata**.) To do this, we must collect a sample that contains the sample proportions of each

STATISTICS AROUND US

Problem in Predicting U.S. Presidential Elections

Voter preference polls have been taken prior to each presidential election. Due to the expense involved, the pollsters draw a random sample of voters from the entire United States. Sampling is not conducted independently within each state.

The electoral college determines who will be president. The membership of the college has historically voted as a block by state, and all of a state's votes have gone to the candidate winning in that state. American history shows that the popular vote leader can still lose the election in the electoral college. The winner must only achieve small margins in several large states. Thus, a candidate might win a majority of electoral votes while losing the national plurality. This has happened twice since the Civil War: In 1876, Rutherford B. Hayes beat Samuel J. Tilden, who received a greater number of popular votes; in 1888, Benjamin Harrison beat the larger popular vote getter, Grover Cleveland. The situation is further distorted by the fact that electoral votes are rationed to each state in accordance with its representation in *both* houses of Congress. Thus, Alaska, with about one hundredth the voting population of California, has about one-fourteenth as many electoral votes, making each Alaskan voter about seven times as powerful as a Californian.

A sampling scheme designed to predict the election outcome must treat each state as a separate stratum to adequately cope with the distortion of the electoral college. The sample results must be separately compiled for each state, and the winner of each state must be determined. The results must then be combined in the same proportion as the electoral votes to present a distortion-free prediction.

subgroup as the population itself does. Thus, we obtain a stratified sample, for which we provide the

DEFINITION: A **stratified sample** is obtained by independently selecting a separate simple random sample from each population stratum.

Although it depends on the purpose of the study, stratification is usually required if certain nonhomogeneities are present in the population. There are other reasons why a stratified sample may be desirable. It may be more convenient to collect samples from separate regions. Or there may be some prevailing reason to divide the population, such as to compare strata.

Another form of random sampling is used prevalently in consumer surveying, where it is more economical to interview several persons in the same neighborhood. For example, contrast the time, effort, and expense of collecting 1,000 responses in a city of 100,000 by simple random sampling with the relative ease of completely canvassing a few selected neighborhoods. In the former case, the elementary units are scattered throughout the city; in the latter, the elementary units live next door to each other. Random sampling would therefore require considerable travel between interviews, whereas the door-to-door neighborhood canvass would minimize travel time. Because the interviewer is normally paid by the hour, the simple random sample would be much more expensive.

Neighborhood groupings of people are referred to as **clusters**. Populations may be divided into clusters according to a criterion such as geographical proximity, creating groups that are easy to observe in their entirety. Most often, the clusters that are to be observed are chosen randomly, and so we can state the

DEFINITION: A **cluster sample** is obtained by selecting clusters from the population on the basis of simple random sampling. The sample comprises a census of each random cluster selected.

The only justification for using cluster sampling is that it is economical. Cluster sampling is highly susceptible to sampling bias. In neighborhood surveys, similar responses may be obtained from the entire cluster, as people of similar age, family size, income, and ethnic and educational backgrounds tend to live in the same vicinity. Thus, there is a high risk that persons with certain backgrounds or preferences will not be represented in the sample because the clusters in which they are predominant are not chosen; conversely, other groups may be unduly represented.

At this point, it might be helpful to emphasize the similarities and differences between cluster and stratified samples. Both separate the population into groups, but the basis for distinction is usually the homogeneity within strata versus the accessibility of clusters. In stratified samples, all groups are represented, whereas the cluster sample comprises only a fraction of the groups in a population. In stratified sampling, a sample is taken from within each stratum; in cluster sampling, a census is conducted within each group. The goal of stratified sampling is to eliminate certain forms of bias; the goal of cluster sampling is to do the job cheaply, which enhances the chance of bias.

Systematic, stratified, and cluster sampling are approximations to simple random sampling. To the extent that the statistical theory applicable to simple random sampling is applied to samples obtained via these other procedures, there may be erroneous conclusions. Throughout much of the remainder of this book, techniques will be developed primarily for analyzing simple random samples. The more complex sampling schemes require more complicated methodology.

EXERCISES

4-10 What type of sample does each of the following represent?
(a) Telephone callers on a radio talk show.
(b) The 30 stocks constituting the Dow Jones Industrial Average.
(c) The record of a gambler's individual wins and losses from a day of placing bets of $1 on black in roulette.
(d) The oranges purchased by a shopper from the produce section of a market.

4-11 In the following situations, would you recommend the use of judgment, convenience, or random sampling, or some combination of these? Explain.
(a) A saleswoman for Fly Paper Company is preparing a kit of product samples to carry on her next road trip to printing concerns.
(b) A teacher asks his students for suggestions as to how he can improve curriculum. He plans to use their suggestions as a basis for a questionnaire concerning curriculum preferences.

(c) Gotham City wants to compare the wages of its clerical workers with the wages of persons holding comparable jobs in private industry.

(d) Centralia Bell plans to purchase a fleet of standard-sized cars from one of four different manufacturers. The criterion for selection will be economy of operation.

(e) A *Daily Planet* editor selects letters from the day's mail to print on the editorial page. (Answer from the editor's point of view.)

4-12 Getting Oil Company wishes to obtain a random sample of its customers to estimate the relative proportion of purchases made from other oil companies. An accountant on the operations staff has recommended that a random sample of credit card customers be selected. An independent survey firm would be retained to obtain detailed records of the following month's purchases by brand and quantity for each sample unit. Evaluate this procedure.

4-13 A medical research foundation wishes to obtain a random sample of expectant mothers to investigate postnatal developments in their newborn babies. Various metropolitan areas are to be represented. Suggest a procedure that might be used to select the sample in a particular city.

4-14 A certain U.S. senator is reputed to follow the majority opinion of his constituents on important pending legislation. Over the years, he has accumulated a panel of 20 persons whom his secretary contacts before a major Senate vote. Panel members are replaced only when they die or change their state of residence. The senator's votes usually coincide with the majority of this panel. Comment on this policy.

4-15 A random sample must be obtained in each of the following situations. Indicate whether a cluster, stratified, or combined sampling procedure should be used. Explain.

(a) A WaySafe market wishes to determine its customers' attitudes toward trading stamps. Because the funds for the survey are limited, the sample replies are to be obtained by interviewing customers on the store premises.

(b) A Fast-Gro agronomist wants to take a sample to compare the effectiveness of two fertilizers on a variety of crops under a range of climate and soil conditions.

(c) FlyMe Airlines is taking a sample of its first-class and tourist-class passengers to assess the quality of its in-flight meals. The passengers' ratings must be taken directly after they have eaten their meals.

4-5 SELECTING STATISTICAL PROCEDURES

A complete examination of statistical procedures is made in several later chapters. All of these procedures make generalizations about a population when only sample data are available. We call this process **inductive** or **inferential statistics**. There are several types of inference, and the procedures to be used depend on the goals of the study.

Statistical procedures should be determined during the planning stage. There are many ways to do this. The simplest procedure is to estimate a population's parameter, such as its mean, standard deviation, or proportion. The most complicated procedures test some hypothesis regarding the population's characteristics. Ordinarily, several testing schemes are employed. In all tests, the decision is indicated by the sample results. Many tests actually compare two or more populations and require that a separate sample be obtained from each.

In the fields of education, psychology, and medicine, the two-sample testing procedure is a popular way to decide which of two approaches is better. Often the status quo is compared to a proposed improvement. For example, a new method of teaching reading might be evaluated in terms of comprehension test scores. The population of scores achieved by students in the current reading program could be compared to the test scores achieved by another group of readers exposed to the new program. Because the new program might or might not be adopted, the associated population would not exist yet. Nevertheless, a sample of readers in the new program would represent this potentially large group, making it a target population. The actual comparison would be made between separate samples from both populations.

The readers in the sample from the current program are referred to as the **control group**, because they are not subjected to anything new. The readers in the second sample constitute the **experimental group**, because these students are exposed to a new procedure on a trial basis primarily to evaluate its merit. Control and experimental groups are common in many testing situations, such as in evaluating a new drug or medical procedure, selecting a more effective fertilizer, or checking new safety devices.

The simplest way to conduct a two-sample test is to select the two groups **independently**. Readers in the control and experimental groups would be chosen using separate lists of random numbers. (Ordinarily, both samples would be derived from a common frame of applicable students, because the experimental group represents only a target population.) One drawback to independent sampling is that any differences in the reading comprehension scores of the two groups could be attributed to causes other than the particular reading programs, such as previous level of reading or home environment. The danger that some outside influence might camouflage the actual differences between the two reading programs could be minimized by applying a stratified sampling scheme. Then two separate groups would be selected each from the same categories of student knowledge and background. If large enough, each group should provide a representative cross section of the student body.

A common method for choosing the control and experimental groups is to pair each elementary unit with one that closely matches it in terms of potential extraneous influences. One member of each pair would be assigned to the experimental group; the other member, to the control group. This is called **matched-pairs sampling**. The procedure is epitomized by studies of identical twins, who are genetically the same and who normally share the same environment as well. In our survey, one twin would be assigned to the existing reading program and the other would participate in the new program. Thus, any differences in reading scores between sample groups could be confidently attributed to differences in the reading programs and not to other causes. For practical purposes, twins are rare and are not normally used in such tests, but unrelated individuals might still be paired. For example, a new drug for heart patients could be tested with pairs matched in terms of age, sex, weight, marital status, smoking habits, medical histories, and so on, thereby producing "near twins." Identical twins who were reared apart have been extensively studied in an attempt to isolate the effects of heredity and environment on intelligence.

STATISTICS AROUND US

Evaluating a Beverage Container Law

A new law was about to become effective requiring that all soft drink and beer containers be returnable, in order to eliminate the unsightly refuse problem caused by pop-top cans. Bottles were to be used exclusively. To guarantee that the empty bottles would be returned, a deposit was required by the seller, as it had been throughout the United States 20 years earlier.

To assess the effectiveness of the beverage container law, a study was made to determine how it affected accumulations of roadside litter. A random sample of 30 one-mile stretches of highway was chosen, cleared of all beer and soda cans, and left to the vagaries of normal public neglect and mistreatment for three months before the new law became effective. The 30 miles of highway served as the control group, representing state residents' littering habits when beverage containers were not dictated by law. At the end of three months, the litter was cleared and the cans were counted. For the initial three months under the new law, the same 30 miles—now the experimental group—were again left to accumulate beverage containers (which would only be bottles this time). The accumulations of the two groups were then compared.

This study shows how the same elementary units can sometimes be used in both the control and the experimental groups. In this case, each one-mile segment after the law became effective was matched with itself in a preceding time period. In this way, traffic conditions and local idiosyncrasies were alike and could not be responsible for any differences between the two groups. However, using the same units in both groups is valid only if no bias is induced on the second set of observations by the first set—and this is the point at which the study fell apart. When the beverage litter was measured the second time, very little was found. But all other kinds of litter were practically absent, too, and adjacent stretches of highway were abnormally clean. At first blush, environmental officials were ecstatic at the apparent widespread impact of their new law. But they became embarrassed when it was determined that the pattern prevailed only near the test tracts and not throughout the state.

Who absconded with the litter and why? Perhaps environmentalists—well aware that the new law would be temporary unless it proved effective—tried to help the study along by cleaning up the test stretches. Maybe when the state cleaned the one-mile parcels, local residents were shamed into picking up their own litter.

On the advice of a statistician, officials discarded the second set of test results and matched the original 30 one-mile stretches of highway with 30 similar ones that had not been cleaned. The new areas were checked only once, and only the returnable bottles were counted (the old cans did not have to be).

The Statistics Around Us box on page 134 describes the experiences of one state during the ecology renaissance of the early 1970s. That experience illustrates the pitfalls of inadequate planning when conducting a statistical study.

SUMMARY

1. **Why should samples be used?**
There are several compelling reasons for sampling. The usual reason is that a sample is less expensive than a complete enumeration or **census** of the population. Samples are also more timely and more desirable when the population is large or not totally accessible. The use of samples is mandatory when the observation itself is destructive.

2. **What are the stages of a statistical sampling study?**
There are three stages for a statistical sampling study. First, we have the **planning stage**, where the overall study design is established and the procedures are chosen. *Deductive statistics* is used here. Next, we have the **data collection stage**, which involves the actual work of making the observations. Care must be taken to avoid procedural *errors* and *bias*. Sampling studies are completed during the **data analysis and conclusions stage**. It is here where inductive or inferential statistics comes into play.

3. **How can we avoid bias and control sampling error?**
Although there are no guarantees that a sample will be typical or accurate, good statistical procedures control **sampling error**—the difference between the population and the sample that is due to the particular units selected for observation. You can control sampling error by eliminating **sampling bias**, thereby giving all units the same chance of being selected. You can avoid **nonsampling error** by eliminating inaccuracies in the observation process itself.

4. **What are the main types of samples?**
There are three broad categories of samples: the **convenience sample**, where the easiest observations are made; the **judgment sample**, where particular sample units are chosen to "guarantee" a representative sample; and the **random sample**, where all elementary units have an equal chance of being observed and included in the sample. Only the random sample is free from sampling bias, but it still may involve some unavoidable sampling error.

5. **What are the various forms of random sampling?**
The most common type of random sample is the **simple random sample**, which allows an equal chance that any particular unit will be observed. The sample units are often chosen using a list of **random numbers**. A **systematic random sample** uses a single random number to establish a sequential starting point. A **stratified sample** guarantees inclusion of units from various *strata*. A **cluster sample** involves the complete enumeration of a few randomly selected *clusters*.

6. **What are some of the important elements of a statistical experiment?**
Most statistical methodology assumes that simple random samples will be used. Although one population and sample is the usual case, some statistical investigations involve multiple populations. One common investigation compares a **control group** to an **experimental group**. Often the two samples are selected independently. An efficient alternative is the **controlled experiment**, which uses **matched-pairs sampling**.

REAL-LIFE STATISTICAL CHALLENGE

Selecting the Automobile of Your Dreams

In the last chapter we calculated summary statistics for a set of sports cars. You were asked to select the "car of your dreams" from the list. From a sampling standpoint, you were then using a convenience sample. The sampling process was not random.

Consider selecting your automobile from a larger number of models. Table 4-2 lists 231 makes and models of automobiles. As in Chapter 3, we can compare automobiles in terms of their fuel efficiency. The listed cars are classified by type based primarily on size: two-seater, minicompact, subcompact, compact, midsize, and large.

Table 4-2 shows the model, manufacturer, type of car, transmission type, engine displacement (liters), and miles per gallon (highway). The transmission is either manual (M) or automatic (A or L) and may have different gear configurations (3, 4, 5, or 6 forward). The number in the first column shows a sequence number we will use for our random sampling operations. The first 36 cars are from the same list as in Chapter 3. They are followed by the remaining types of automobiles.

DISCUSSION QUESTIONS

1. Select a random sample of 15 automobiles from the list. What is the median mileage for this list?
2. Use a stratified random sample to select 30 cars from the list. Make sure each size type has equal representation. Compare the median mileage with the sample drawn for Question 1.
3. From the list in this chapter, have members of your class select the car of their choice. (People may select the same automobiles as last time.) Compare the list of cars your classmates derived from the "sporty cars" in Chapter 3 with the list derived from this chapter. Do you think the summary statistics will change? (We will compare the summary statistics for both data sets in a later chapter. It is not required that you calculate the new values at this time.)
4. Several types of vehicles are not included, such as light trucks and vans. Discuss the issues of sampling or nonsampling bias and error.
5. This list includes only 1990 model year cars. What impact would adding data from later years have on your sample?

TABLE 4-2 Mileage Data for 1990 Automobiles Showing Transmission Type, Engine Displacement (Liters) and Highway Mileage per Gallon.

Number	Type	Manufacturer	Model	Transmission Type	Engine Displacement (liters)	Highway Mileage (miles/gallon)
0000	T	Alfa-Romeo	Spider	M5	2.0	30
0001	T	Buick	Reatta	L4	3.8	27
0002	T	Cadillac	Allante	L4	4.5	22
0003	T	Chevrolet	Corvette	L4	5.7	24
0004	T	Chevrolet	Corvette	M6	5.7	25
0005	T	Chrysler	TC/Maserati	M5	2.2	25
0006	T	Chrysler	TC/Maserati	L4	3.0	24
0007	T	Ferrari	Testarossa	M5	4.9	15
0008	T	Honda	Civic CRX	L4	1.5	35
0009	T	Honda	Civic CRX	M5	1.5	35
0010	T	Honda	Civic CRX	M5	1.6	33
0011	T	Honda	Civic CRX-HF	M5	1.5	52
0012	T	Lamborghini	Countach	M5	5.2	10
0013	T	Lotus	Lotus	M5	2.2	27
0014	T	Maserati	Karif	L4	2.8	18
0015	T	Maserati	Karif	M5	2.8	20
0016	T	Maserati	Spyder	L4	2.8	18
0017	T	Maserati	Spyder	M5	2.8	20
0018	T	Mazda	RX-7	L4	1.3	23
0019	T	Mazda	RX-7	M5	1.3	25
0020	T	Mazda	RX-7	M5	1.3	24
0021	T	Mazda	Miata	M5	1.6	30
0022	T	Mercedes-Benz	500 SL	M5	5.0	21
0023	T	Nissan	300ZX	L4	3.0	24
0024	T	Nissan	300ZX	M5	3.0	24
0025	M	Maserati	222E	L4	2.8	18
0026	M	Maserati	222E	M5	2.8	20
0027	M	Nissan	240SX	L4	2.4	25
0028	M	Nissan	240SX	M5	2.4	27
0029	M	Porsche	911-4/2	M5	3.6	24
0030	M	Porsche	911-FWD	M5	3.6	22
0031	M	Porsche	928-S4	A4	5.0	19
0032	M	Porsche	928-S4	M5	5.0	19
0033	M	Porsche	944-S2	M5	3.0	26
0034	M	Volkswagen	Cabriolet	A3	1.8	28
0035	M	Volkswagen	Cabriolet	M5	1.8	32
0036	S	Acura	Integra	L4	1.8	27
0037	S	Acura	Integra	M5	1.8	28
0038	S	Audi	Quattro	M5	2.3	24
0039	S	Audi	80	A3	2.0	27
0040	S	Audi	80	M5	2.0	30
0041	S	Audi	90	A3	2.3	22
0042	S	Audi	90	M5	2.3	26
0043	S	Audi	90 Quat-20V	M5	2.3	24
0044	S	BMW	M3	M5	2.3	29
0045	S	BMW	325i-conv	L4	2.5	23
0046	S	BMW	325i-conv	M5	2.5	25
0047	S	BMW	325i/325s	L4	2.5	22
0048	S	BMW	325i/325s	M5	2.5	23
0049	S	BMW	325ix	L4	2.5	22
0050	S	BMW	325ix	M5	2.5	23
0051	S	Chevrolet	Camaro	L4	3.1	27
0052	S	Chevrolet	Camaro	L4	5.0	24
0053	S	Chevrolet	Camaro	M5	5.0	26
0054	S	Chevrolet	Camaro	L4	5.7	24
0055	S	Chrysler	LeBaron-con	M5	2.2	28
0056	S	Chrysler	LeBaron-con	A3	2.5	23
0057	S	Chrysler	LeBaron-con	L3	2.5	27
0058	S	Chrysler	LeBaron-con	M5	3.0	27
0059	S	Daihatsu	Charade	M5	1.0	42
0060	S	Daihatsu	Charade	A3	1.3	34
0061	S	Daihatsu	Charade	M5	1.3	39
0062	S	Dodge	Colt	L3	1.5	29
0063	S	Dodge	Colt	M4	1.5	36
0064	S	Dodge	Colt	M5	1.5	34
0065	S	Dodge	Colt	L4	1.6	28
0066	S	Dodge	Colt	M5	1.6	28
0067	S	Dodge	Daytona	M5	2.2	28
0068	S	Dodge	Daytona	A3	2.5	23
0069	S	Dodge	Daytona	L3	2.5	27
0070	S	Dodge	Daytona	M5	2.5	32
0071	S	Dodge	Daytona	M5	3.0	27
0072	S	Dodge	Omni	L3	2.2	30
0073	S	Dodge	Omni	M5	2.2	34
0074	S	Eagle	Talon	L4	2.0	27
0075	S	Eagle	Talon	M5	2.0	29
0076	S	Eagle	Talon/4WD	M5	2.0	25
0077	S	Ford	Festiva	A3	1.3	33
0078	S	Ford	Festiva	M5	1.3	41
0079	S	Ford	Mustang	L4	2.3	27
0080	S	Ford	Mustang	M5	2.3	29
0081	S	Ford	Mustang	L4	5.0	25
0082	S	Ford	Mustang	M5	5.0	24
0083	S	Geo	Metro	A3	1.0	40
0084	S	Geo	Metro	M5	1.0	50
0085	S	Geo	Metro LSI	A3	1.0	39
0086	S	Geo	Metro LSI	M5	1.0	50
0087	S	Geo	Metro XFI	M5	1.0	58
0088	S	Geo	Prizm	L3	1.6	29
0089	S	Geo	Prizm	L4	1.6	30
0090	S	Geo	Prizm	M5	1.6	34
0091	S	Geo	Storm	A3	1.6	31
0092	S	Geo	Storm	L4	1.6	32
0093	S	Geo	Storm	M5	1.6	36
0094	S	Honda	Civic	L4	1.5	33
0095	S	Honda	Civic	M4	1.5	37
0096	S	Honda	Civic	M5	1.5	34
0097	S	Honda	Civic	L4	1.6	29
0098	S	Honda	Civic	M5	1.6	32
0099	S	Hyundai	Excel	L4	1.5	32
0100	S	Hyundai	Excel	M4	1.5	33
0101	S	Hyundai	Excel	M5	1.5	36
0102	S	Hyundai	Precis	L4	1.5	32
0103	S	Hyundai	Precis	M4	1.5	33
0104	S	Hyundai	Precis	M5	1.5	36
0105	S	Infiniti	M30	L4	3.0	25
0106	S	Isuzu	Impulse	L4	1.6	32
0107	S	Isuzu	Impulse	M5	1.6	34
0108	S	Maserati	430	L4	2.8	18
0109	S	Maserati	430	M5	2.8	20

(continued on next page)

Source: U.S. Environmental Protection Agency, 1989.
Type: T, Two-Seater; M, Minicompact; S, Subcompact; C, Compact; MS, Mid-Size; L, Large.

TABLE 4-2 (continued)

Number	Type	Manufacturer	Model	Transmission Type	Engine Displacement (liters)	Highway Mileage (miles/gallon)
0110	S	Mitsubishi	Eclipse	L4	1.8	30
0111	S	Mitsubishi	Eclipse	M5	1.8	32
0112	S	Mitsubishi	Eclipse	L4	2.0	27
0113	S	Mitsubishi	Mirage	M5	1.6	28
0114	S	Nissan	Pulsar NX	M5	1.8	30
0115	S	Nissan	Sentra	M5	1.6	36
0116	S	Nissan	Sentra Coupe	M5	1.6	36
0117	S	Nissan	300ZX 22	M5	3.0	24
0118	S	Plymouth	Colt	M5	1.6	28
0119	S	Plymouth	Horizon	M5	2.2	34
0120	S	Plymouth	Laser	M5	2.0	29
0121	S	Pontiac	Firebird	M5	5.0	25
0122	S	Pontiac	Sunbird Con	M5	2.0	33
0123	S	Saab	900 Con	M5	2.0	28
0124	S	Subaru	Justy	M5	1.2	37
0125	S	Subaru	Justy 4WD	M5	1.2	33
0126	S	Subaru	XT	M5	1.8	31
0127	S	Subaru	XT 4WD	M5	1.8	29
0128	S	Suzuki	Swift	M5	1.3	44
0129	S	Suzuki	Swift GT	M5	1.3	36
0130	S	Toyota	Celica	M5	2.2	29
0131	S	Toyota	Corolla	L4	1.6	33
0132	S	Toyota	Supra	L4	3.0	23
0133	S	Toyota	Tercel	L3	1.5	32
0134	S	Volkswagen	Corrado	M5	1.8	28
0135	S	Volkswagen	Fox	M4	1.8	30
0136	C	Acura	Legend	L4	2.7	22
0137	C	BMW	525i	L4	2.5	23
0138	C	BMW	535i	L4	3.4	21
0139	C	Buick	Skylark	L3	3.3	27
0140	C	Chevrolet	Beretta	M5	3.1	28
0141	C	Chevrolet	Cavalier	L3	3.1	27
0142	C	Chrysler	LeBaron	L3	2.5	27
0143	C	Dodge	Shadow	L3	2.5	27
0144	C	Eagle	Summit	M5	1.6	28
0145	C	Ford	Escort	M5	1.9	30
0146	C	Ford	Probe	L4	3.0	26
0147	C	Ford	Tempo	A3	2.3	23
0148	C	Honda	Accord	L4	2.2	28
0149	C	Isuzu	Stylus	M5	1.6	33
0150	C	Jaguar	Jaguar	L4	4.0	22
0151	C	Lexus	ES250	L4	2.5	25
0152	C	Lincoln-Mercury	Topaz	A3	2.3	23
0153	C	Mazda	323/Protege	L4	1.6	33
0154	C	Mitsubishi	Galant	M5	2.0	29
0155	C	Mitsubishi	Sigma	A4	3.0	22
0156	C	Nissan	Stanza	M5	2.4	29
0157	C	Oldsmobile	Calais	L3	3.3	27
0158	C	Peugeot	405	L4	1.9	25
0159	C	Plymouth	Sundance	L3	2.5	27
0160	C	Pontiac	Grand Am	M5	2.5	33
0161	C	Pontiac	LeMans	L3	2.0	30
0162	C	Pontiac	Sunbird	L3	2.0	28
0163	C	Saab	900	A3	2.0	23
0164	C	Subaru	Legacy	M5	2.2	30
0165	C	Subaru	Loyale	L3	1.8	26
0166	C	Toyota	Camry	L4	2.0	31
0167	C	Toyota	Cressida	L4	3.0	24
0168	C	Volkswagen	Golf	M5	1.8	32
0169	C	Volkswagen	GTI	M5	2.0	28
0170	C	Volkswagen	Jetta	M5	1.8	32
0171	C	Volvo	240	M5	2.0	28
0172	C	Volvo	780	A4	2.8	21
0173	MS	ASC	Grand Prix	L4	3.1	25
0174	MS	Audi	V8	L4	3.6	18
0175	MS	Audi	100 Quattro	M5	2.3	24
0176	MS	Audi	200 Quattro	M5	2.2	25
0177	MS	BMW	735i	L4	3.4	21
0178	MS	BMW	750iL	L4	5.0	18
0179	MS	Buick	Century	L4	3.3	29
0180	MS	Buick	Regal	L4	3.1	30
0181	MS	Buick	Riviera	L4	3.8	27
0182	MS	Cadillac	Eldorado	L4	4.5	25
0183	MS	Cadillac	Seville	L4	4.5	25
0184	MS	Chevrolet	Corsica	L3	3.1	27
0185	MS	Chevrolet	Lumina	L4	3.1	30
0186	MS	Chrysler	New Yorker	L4	3.3	26
0187	MS	Dodge	Dynasty	L4	3.3	26
0188	MS	Dodge	Spirit	L3	2.5	27
0189	MS	Ford	Taurus	L4	3.8	28
0190	MS	Ford	Thunderbird	L4	3.8	23
0191	MS	Hyundai	Sonata	L4	2.4	26
0192	MS	Infiniti	Q45	L4	4.5	22
0193	MS	Lexus	LS400	L4	4.0	24
0194	MS	Lincoln-Mercury	Cougar	L4	3.8	23
0195	MS	Lincoln-Mercury	Mark VII	L4	5.0	24
0196	MS	Lincoln-Mercury	Sable	L4	3.8	28
0197	MS	Maserati	228	M5	2.8	19
0198	MS	Mazda	626	L4	2.2	25
0199	MS	Mazda	929	L4	3.0	23
0200	MS	Mercedes-Benz	300 E	L4	3.0	22
0201	MS	Nissan	Maxima	L4	3.0	26
0202	MS	Oldsmobile	Ciera	L4	3.3	29
0203	MS	Oldsmobile	Supreme	L4	3.1	30
0204	MS	Oldsmobile	Trofeo	L4	3.8	27
0205	MS	Plymouth	Acclaim	L3	2.5	27
0206	MS	Pontiac	Grand Prix	L4	3.1	30
0207	MS	Pontiac	6000	L4	3.1	30
0208	MS	Rolls-Royce	Bentley-Cont.	A3	6.8	13
0209	MS	Rolls-Royce	Corniche III	A3	6.8	13
0210	MS	Rolls-Royce	Bentley-8	A3	6.8	13
0211	MS	Rolls-Royce	Silver Spirit	A3	6.8	13
0212	MS	Volkswagen	Passat	L4	2.0	29
0213	MS	Volvo	740	L4	2.3	26
0214	MS	Volvo	740-16	L4	2.3	24
0215	MS	Volvo	760	A4	2.8	21
0216	L	Buick	Electra	L4	3.8	27
0217	L	Buick	LeSabre	L4	3.8	27
0218	L	Cadillac	Brougham	L4	5.7	21
0219	L	Cadillac	Fleetwood	L4	4.5	25
0220	L	Chevrolet	Caprice	L4	5.0	25
0221	L	Chrysler	New Yorker	L4	3.3	25
0222	L	Dodge	Monaco	L4	3.0	26
0223	L	Eagle	Premier	L4	3.0	26
0224	L	Ford	LTD	L4	5.0	24
0225	L	Lincoln	Continental	L4	3.8	25
0226	L	Mercury	Grand Marquis	L4	5.0	24
0227	L	Lincoln	Town Car	L4	5.0	24
0228	L	Oldsmobile	Eighty-Eight	L4	3.8	27
0229	L	Oldsmobile	Ninety-Eight	L4	3.8	27
0230	L	Pontiac	Bonneville	L4	3.8	27
0231	L	Saab	9000	L4	2.0	24

Type: T, Two-Seater; M, Minicompact; S, Subcompact; C, Compact; MS, Mid-Size; L, Large.

REVIEW EXERCISES

4-16 Starting in the fifth column of the random number table (Appendix Table B), select a simple random sample of ten symphony conductors from those listed in Table 4-1. Use only the first two digits of each random number from the table. List the names selected.

4-17 List the names for a systematic random sample of ten symphony conductors chosen from Table 4-1. Assume that the starting random number selects Sir John Barbirolli as the first name.

4-18 Suppose that each successive ten names in Table 4-1 provides a stratum. Redesignate the names in each stratum, starting with 0 and ending with 9, maintaining the original alphabetical sequence. Then select a stratified random sample that contains one conductor from each group. Assume that the following random numbers apply in the respective strata.

6 5 5 2 1 9 8 7 7 0

List the names selected.

4-19 Treat each successive five names in Table 4-1 as a cluster. A random cluster sample of two clusters from the 20 is to be selected. After assigning a number (1 through 20) to each successive cluster, use the random numbers 18 and 4 to select the sample. List the names selected.

STATISTICS IN PRACTICE

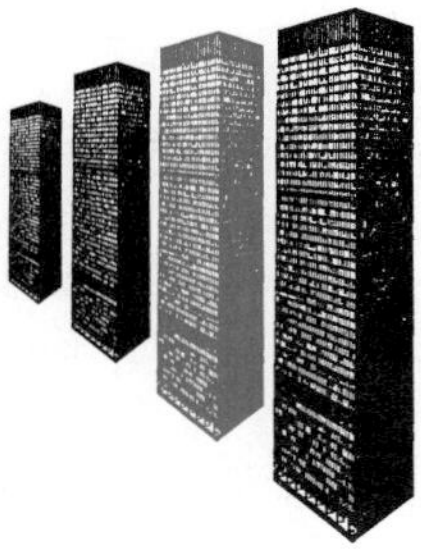

4-20 Using the master class data set that you developed in Exercise 1-19, perform the following statistical sampling study exercises.

(a) Convenience sampling: Look around your classroom and list the names of the five people sitting closest to you in your class. Referring your class data list, do you notice any unusual data patterns (people in your sample sharing a common characteristic)?

(b) Judgment sample: Select a variable from your class list and write the names of those people who share a common characteristic. List the data for these students. Do you notice any patterns in the data for the people you selected?

(c) Random sample: Using the case numbers, collect a sample of 5 people using the table of random numbers. List the data for these students.

(d) Conduct a stratified sample by classifying one variable into three categories. Randomly select 5 names from each stratum. List the data for these students.

(e) Compare the results of your samples from (a)—(d). Comment on any patterns in the data you observe. Are there detectable elements of bias and error in the sampling?

4-21 Using your group's class data from Exercise 1-21, perform the same statistical sampling study exercises listed in (a) through (e) of Exercise 4-20.

4-22 Table 4-3 shows the 20 most populous countries for the year 1991. The data list also includes gross domestic or national product. A global retailer

TABLE 4-3 Population and GNP for World's Most Populous Countries

1991 Rank	Country	Population	GNP or GDP (billions $s)
1	China	1,151,300,000	$350
2	India	859,200,000	333
3	United States	252,800,000	5,233
4	Indonesia	181,400,000	80
5	Brazil	153,300,000	377
6	Russia	147,400,000	1,330
7	Japan	123,800,000	1,914
8	Nigeria	122,500,000	30
9	Pakistan	117,500,000	43
10	Bangladesh	116,600,000	21
11	Mexico	85,700,000	137
12	Germany	79,500,000	1,105
13	Vietnam	67,600,000	14
14	Philippines	62,300,000	41
15	Thailand	58,800,000	65
16	Iran	58,600,000	94
17	Turkey	58,500,000	75
18	Italy	57,700,000	803
19	United Kingdom	57,500,000	818
20	France	56,700,000	820
	Total	3,868,700,000	$13,683

Source: *The 1992 Information Please Almanac* 136, and "Countries of the World Section": 147–286. GDP for Russia estimated by the author.

wishes to survey consumer preferences for the following items: children's toys, sports cars, condoms, and frozen foods. What would be the advantages of using a sample? Which sampling method would you suggest? Which elements of bias and error in the sampling should the market researchers watch for?

4-23 Table 1-2 (page 18) provides data on estimates of the location of homeless people discussed in Chapter 1. Discuss which sampling method would be most appropriate. Which elements of bias and sampling should the researchers watch for?

CASE Boomville

Peggy Jones is a marketing researcher. She has selected the city of Boomville as her marketplace barometer for testing new product concepts. The map of a Boomville test sector is provided in Figure 4-2 and will aid Peggy's evaluation of various research procedures. She has placed homes arbitrarily into "census tracts," each representing a contiguous neighborhood. Household identity, address, and family income data are given in Table 4-4.

To begin Peggy selects sample incomes from the Boomville residents. In later studies, she will observe other types of demographic data. Her present concern is to select a sampling procedure that will be representative of Boomville as a whole. She needs the expertise of a person knowledgeable in statistics.

QUESTIONS

1. To assist Peggy in determining an overall sampling procedure, you select a *simple random sample* of resident incomes from the Boomville sector.

(a) Matching the following random numbers with the corresponding household identity codes, select a simple random sample of ten family incomes.

34 01 17 73 93 05 54 89 42 29

List the results selected.

(b) Calculate the mean.

(c) Comment on the advantages and disadvantages of this procedure.

2. As an alternative procedure, Peggy may use a *systematic random sample.*

(a) Select, from the Boomville sector, a systematic random sample of ten family incomes. To do this, use the identity codes, and pick every tenth household, starting with the randomly selected code 07. List the sample results.

(b) Calculate the mean.

(c) Comment on the advantages and disadvantages of this procedure.

3. A third sampling approach might be for Peggy to take a *cluster sample.*

(a) Treat each census tract as a cluster. Use the first applicable random numbers in the following sequence to select two clusters by matching the appropriate census tract code.

1 6 8 6 3 8 7 4

List the tracts selected.

(b) The sample consists of household incomes for the residences in those tracts. List the sample results.

(c) Calculate the mean.

(d) Comment on the advantages and disadvantages of this procedure.

4. Instead of the cluster sample, Peggy may decide to use a *stratified ran-*

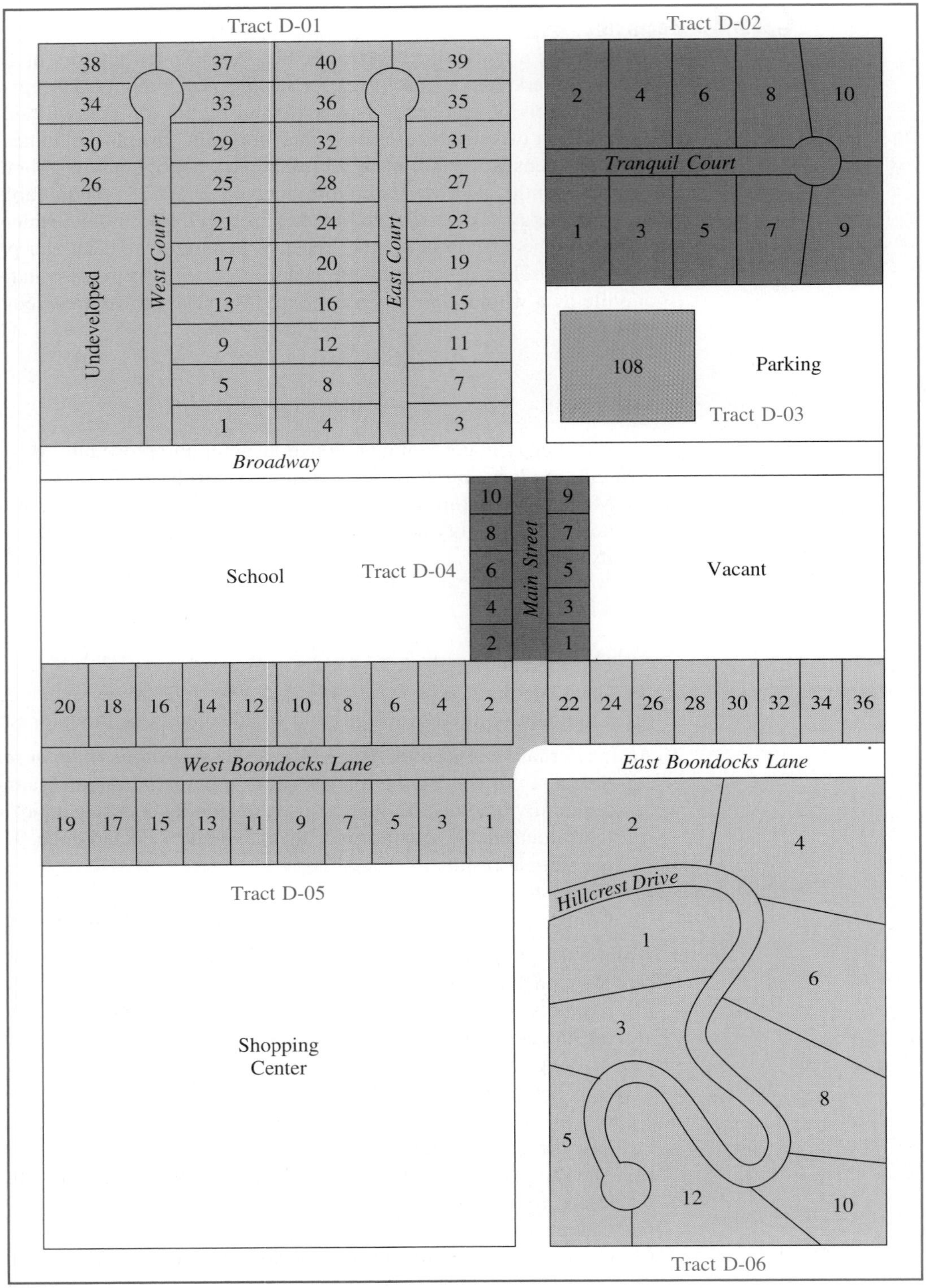

FIGURE 4-2 Map of Boomville test sector and census tracts.

TABLE 4-4 Family Income Data for the Boomville Test Sector

Household	Address	Income
East Boondocks Lane		
01	22	$15,772
02	24	14,667
03	26	21,539
04	28	11,814
05	30	7,644
06	32	12,888
07	34	11,119
08	36	10,024
West Boondocks Lane		
09	1	$ 9,836
10	2	8,448
11	3	10,887
12	4	13,464
13	5	11,118
14	6	12,747
15	7	10,777
16	8	9,007
17	9	12,225
18	10	12,345
19	11	10,554
20	12	13,098
21	13	10,567
22	14	8,553
23	15	11,863
24	16	13,119
25	17	12,225
26	18	10,887
27	19	11,008
28	20	11,080
Main Street		
29	1	$ 4,675
30	2	6,778
31	3	5,558
32	4	8,905
33	5	5,731
34	6	7,088
35	7	6,775
36	8	9,222
37	9	9,776
38	10	5,783
39	108-01	14,453
40	108-02	10,113
41	108-03	8,985
42	108-04	21,119
43	108-05	16,668
44	108-06	10,560
45	108-07	14,554
46	108-08	11,800
Tranquil Court		
47	1	$24,776
48	2	26,123
49	3	30,001
50	4	28,888
51	5	28,998
52	6	23,556
53	7	27,956
54	8	24,665
55	9	29,545
56	10	26,997
East Court		
57	3	$18,998
58	4	13,556
59	7	17,956
60	8	14,665
61	11	19,545
62	12	16,997
63	15	15,305
64	16	15,555
65	19	16,885
66	20	17,554
67	23	21,115
68	24	20,997
69	27	16,666
70	28	17,002
71	31	15,155
72	32	18,444
73	35	15,876
74	36	16,123
75	39	20,001
76	40	18,888
Hillcrest Drive		
77	1	$57,845
78	2	28,553
79	3	42,735
80	4	60,600
81	5	38,887
82	6	71,775
83	8	31,119
84	10	40,000
85	12	56,337
West Court		
86	1	$12,223
87	5	10,678
88	9	14,556
89	13	13,665
90	17	15,997
91	21	14,555
92	25	16,554
93	26	22,115
94	29	19,997
95	30	17,666
96	33	16,002
97	34	16,155
98	37	17,444
99	38	16,876

dom sample. Although strata may be identified in a variety of ways, such as income, education, or occupation, Peggy limits this investigation to locational strata. To do this, treat each census tract as a separate stratum, and take a simple random sample from each.

(a) Obtain Peggy's stratified random sample using two observations per stratum. Begin with tract D-01 and proceed through the tracts with the next highest identity code. Match the following random numbers with the street or apartment number. Be sure to skip the random numbers that do not apply to an address and never go back to an earlier random number. Starting in the upper left-hand corner, proceed horizontally, line by line.

56	04	57	55	85	34	01	17	73	93	05	54	89	42	29	57
69	43	10	77	97	78	17	40	30	23	80	32	94	31	20	91
46	75	29	15	31	82	44	77	32	42	11	09	14	61	19	00
12	05	63	29	23	33	05	49	29	48	21	90	01	58	07	03
24	25	47	16	41	14	61	12	55	86	88	02	39	44	57	56

(b) List the incomes.
(b) Calculate the mean.
(c) Comment on the advantages and disadvantages of this procedure.

5. Peggy may prefer the *convenience sample*, a less sophisticated sampling approach that would enable her to choose sample residences quickly.

(a) Imagine yourself as a canvasser in Boomville, except that you forgot to take along the map. You must return with sample incomes, and you want to work quickly. Take a convenience sample by obtaining only the income data for residents of the apartment house on 108 Main Street. You find nobody home in unit 02. The tenant in unit 05 wants to preserve his privacy and does not open the door. The remaining residents provide the income information you request (listed in Table 4-4). List the sample results.
(b) Calculate the mean.
(c) Comment on the advantages and disadvantages of this procedure.

6. Peggy feels that she may be able to improve the approaches by using her judgment to pick sample incomes. There are many ways for her to take such a *judgment sample*. In order to guarantee an element of locational representation, Peggy decides that there should be one income from each census tract.

(a) Obtain her judgment sample by selecting the household with the lowest identity code in each tract. List the sample incomes.
(b) Calculate the mean.
(c) Comment on the advantages and disadvantages of this procedure.

CHAPTER 5

PROBABILITY

BEFORE READING THIS CHAPTER, MAKE SURE YOU UNDERSTAND:

The distinction between deductive and inductive statistics (Chapter 1).
The advantages of *random* samples (Chapter 4).
How to generate simple random samples (Chapter 4).

AFTER READING THIS CHAPTER, YOU WILL UNDERSTAND:

The basic concepts of probability and how they relate to relative frequency.
Random experiments and the outcomes they generate.
How to use the count-and-divide method to find probabilities for some events.
How to express probabilities for joint events (intersections) and to display the related information.
The advantages of the addition and multiplication laws.
The importance of statistical independence and how that relationship may be verified.
What conditional probabilities are and how they are distinguished from ordinary "unconditional" probabilities.
How to construct and use probability trees.

Probability plays a special role in all our lives, because we use it to measure uncertainty. We are continually faced with decisions leading to uncertain outcomes, and we rely on probability to help us make our choices. Probability is a pivotal factor in most significant business decisions. A department store buyer will order heavily in a new style that is believed likely to sell well. A company will launch a new product when the chance of its success seems high enough to outweigh the possibility of losses due to failure. A new college graduate is hired when the probability for satisfactory performance is judged sufficiently high.

Modern probability theory underlies the methodology of statistics, which is less than a hundred years old. Today's probability theory has roots that were planted over 300 years ago. Since statistics uses the language of probability, some knowledge of this interesting subject is crucial before proceeding.

5-1 BASIC PROBABILITY CONCEPTS

Probability theory treats a probability as a number. Such numbers, too, are common. We are all familiar with the weather forecaster's announcement that "there is a 50 percent chance of rain tomorrow." We may extend our understanding of probability to a family of experiments. The simplest of which is the coin toss, for which there is a 50 percent chance of obtaining either outcome: head or tail.

PROBABILITY AS LONG-RUN FREQUENCY

What does a 50 percent chance of getting a head really mean? It is an expression of the **long-run relative frequency** with which a head will be obtained in a series of coin tosses. In ten tosses, we can expect to get 5 heads (50% of 10). But the exact number is uncertain, and 4 or 6 heads are likely possibilities. Fewer or more heads are possible, although most will agree extreme outcomes would be very untypical. (If everybody in your class tosses a coin ten times, how many people do you think would have 0 or 10 heads or even 1 or 9 heads? And what number do you think would be closest to the overall average number of heads per student?) If a machine were to toss a coin every second, the long-run frequency for head would be the fraction .5, and we say that the probability of getting a head on any particular toss is .5.

How do we know that .5 is the correct value? Without making some assumptions, the only way to find the long-run frequency would be to toss the coin a very long time and then see how often head occurs. But we may *logically deduce* that .5 is the correct figure by examining a coin, seeing that there are two sides—one designated the head and the other the tail. Then, we assume that weight is distributed evenly, so that we would expect any toss to be just as likely to end head-side up as tail-side up. Finally, we rely on a key property common to all situations having equally likely outcomes.

THE RANDOM EXPERIMENT AND ITS ELEMENTARY EVENTS

Probability theory focuses on uncertain events, which are generated through a **random experiment**. A coin toss is one example of a random experiment. The most basic outcomes of interest are called **elementary events**. For a coin toss, the usual elementary events are head and tail. (But we could be interested in other elementary events, such as the number of revolutions, the coin's maximum height, or the angle made by Lincoln's nose with respect to the North Pole.) In a random experiment having N *equally likely* elementary events, the long-run frequency of any one of them must be $1/N$.

Finding the Probability for an Event

We may use the following expression to calculate the

PROBABILITY FOR ONE ELEMENTARY EVENT
(Among Equally Likely Possibilities):

$$\Pr[\text{elementary event}] = \frac{1}{N}$$

For the toss of a perfect coin there are $N = 2$ equally likely sides, and

$$\Pr[\text{head}] = \frac{1}{2} = .5$$

The following gives a detailed example involving an experiment having equally likely events.

EXAMPLE: ROLL OF THE DIE

A die cube has six faces, the first marked with one dot, the second with two dots, and so on, with the sixth face having six dots. Suppose that the die is rolled. One of the following possibilities applies for the up-side face:

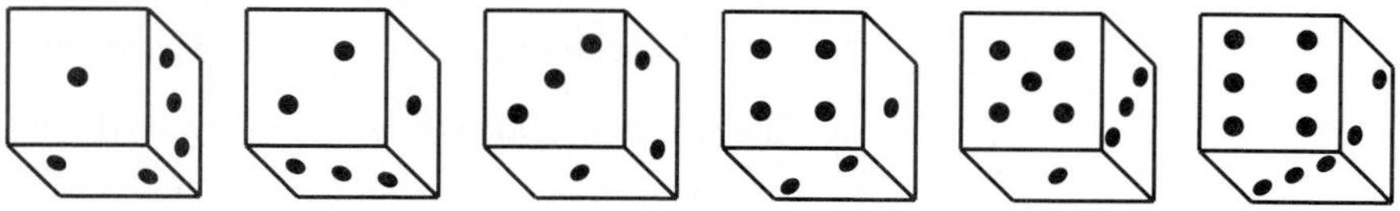

If the cube is perfectly shaped and balanced, then each of the above is an equally likely elementary event. What is the probability that the die stops two-face up?

SOLUTION: There are $N = 6$ equally likely elementary events for this random experiment, so that

$$\Pr[2] = \frac{1}{6} = .1667$$

The above indicates that the long-run frequency for the two-face is 1/6, so that it occurs 16.67% of the time in repeated rolls of the die. Stated equivalently, there is a 16.67% chance of getting a two on any particular roll.

In another example illustrating how to find the probability for an elementary event, suppose that Professor Horatio Dull randomly selects a student to solve one statistics homework problem on the blackboard. If Amy Sax is among the $N = 32$ students in Professor Dull's class, her probability of being chosen is

$$\Pr[\text{AmySax}] = \frac{1}{32} = .03125$$

so that there is a 3.125% chance that she will be chosen. If Prof. Dull always selects a student randomly, then throughout the term Amy Sax would be at the blackboard 3.125% of the time.

COMPLICATING ISSUES

Although many situations involve probabilities that may be computed in the foregoing fashion, complications might arise.

Elementary Events Need Not Be Equally Likely

Some elementary events might be more likely than others. This would be the case if a blob of solder is attached to the head-face or if two opposing die cube faces are shaved. Furthermore, we do not know how much solder might be involved nor where it might be placed; nor do we know how deep into the die the cuts might be made. And, Amy Sax might be chosen more often than other students because she always has the right answers; also, she might get picked only for the hardest problems as the term progresses. Under those circumstances, it is impossible to logically deduce probabilities.

We emphasize that the probabilities for head with a lopsided coin, the 2-face with a shaved die, and picking Amy Sax when she is the teacher's pet are *still long-run frequencies*. But their values must be established through observation of actual outcomes. And, they cannot be known with an exactitude until the random experiment has been repeated a very long time. (Should Amy Sax be chosen with increasing frequency over time, a probability value may never become known.)

Random Experiments May Not Be Repeatable

Consider your grade in statistics. This is strictly a one-shot phenomenon, and only one grade will ever be received. Some uncertainty about the final result undoubtedly exists. But what can we say regarding the probability of getting an "A"? It is obviously not the long-run frequency of "A"; that can happen, if at all, just once. The random experiment of receiving a grade is nonrepeatable.

OBJECTIVE AND SUBJECTIVE PROBABILITIES

Many statisticians would deny the existence of an "A" probability. Others hold that it must be a 0 or a 1, we just do not know which. But most would agree, nevertheless, that an "A" is more likely after hard study than after no studying. We just have difficulty quantifying such an event. Some might attach a value such as .10 or .20. This number is referred to as a **subjective probability**, reflecting that persons might disagree about an appropriate figure. The earlier probability values all arise from repeatable random experiments and are sometimes referred to as **objective probabilities**.

Many important uncertain business events arise from nonrepeatable circumstances. Consider next year's sales of a product, the yearly high of the Dow Jones Average, or your final grade in statistics. Any probabilities given to such events must be based solely on *judgment*. Chapter 20 describes various procedures for determining subjective probabilities.

THE LAW OF LARGE NUMBERS

Suppose a fair coin is tossed 20 times, and a head appears every time. The probability for this happening is less than one-millionth. Does this mean that 20 extra tail outcomes must occur in a long series of future tosses to balance the long-run frequency of occurrence ratio and to coincide with "head" having a probability of 1/2? Also, does this increase the probability for obtaining a tail on the next toss?

The answer to both questions is *no*. First, there are no guarantees that any particular sequence of results will exhibit heads even close to one-half the time. This presents no contradiction, because there is a nonzero probability that any number of heads (say, 10,000) will occur in sequence. All that can be stated is that it is not very likely that there will be many more (or fewer) heads than half the number of tosses. A law of probability, the **law of large numbers**, in essence states that the probability for the result deviating significantly from that indicated by the theoretical long-run frequency of occurrence becomes smaller as the number of repetitions (tosses) increases. Thus, if the coin were tossed several thousand more times, the effect of the 20 "extra" heads on the resulting frequency would be barely noticeable.

If the coin tossing process is fair (that is, if the process is not biased in favor of heads or tails), then we can infer that the probability for obtaining a head should be 1/2. Also, if the process is fair, then a head would be no more likely to follow a head than a tail would. The probability for obtaining a tail should not increase or decrease if it is accepted that fairness is present. After obtaining 20 heads in a row, human reasoning may lead to the inference that the tossing mechanism is unfair. However, this seemingly aberrant result does not constitute proof of unfairness.

EXERCISES

5-1 You buy a raffle ticket for a new convertible. A total of 20,000 tickets have been sold. The winner will be selected at random from these. What is the probability that you win?

5-2 A roulette wheel has 38 slots. Two are green, numbered 0 and 00. Of the remaining pockets, 18 are red and 18 are black. Assuming that all pockets are equally likely, what is the probability that the ball for a spinning wheel lands in the 00 pocket?

5-3 Besides head and tail, a penny toss may have other types of elementary events, such as the angle made by Lincoln's nose relative to true north. Suggest at least another set of outcomes that might serve as the elementary events.

	SUIT			
DENOMINATION	Spades (black)	Hearts (red)	Clubs (black)	Diamonds (red)
King	♠K •	♥K •	♣K •	♦K •
Queen	♠Q •	♥Q •	♣Q •	♦Q •
Jack	♠J •	♥J •	♣J •	♦J •
10	♠10 •	♥10 •	♣10 •	♦10 •
9	♠9 •	♥9 •	♣9 •	♦9 •
8	♠8 •	♥8 •	♣8 •	♦8 •
7	♠7 •	♥7 •	♣7 •	♦7 •
6	♠6 •	♥6 •	♣6 •	♦6 •
5	♠5 •	♥5 •	♣5 •	♦5 •
4	♠4 •	♥4 •	♣4 •	♦4 •
3	♠3 •	♥3 •	♣3 •	♦3 •
Deuce	♠2 •	♥2 •	♣2 •	♦2 •
Ace	♠A •	♥A •	♣A •	♦A •

SAMPLE SPACE

FIGURE 5-1 Sample space for random selection of a playing card.

5-4 A history student writes 20 important names including Napoleon Bonaparte on separate slips of paper. Each name appears on just one slip. She then draws names one at a time from the box; once selected, a name is not returned to the box.
(a) What is the probability that Napoleon is the first name selected?
(b) She has selected 10 names already, not including Napoleon. What is the probability that Napoleon is next?

5-2 PROBABILITIES FOR COMPOSITE EVENTS

To expand our knowledge of probability concepts, let's establish additional important concepts. Consider a deck of playing cards, the contents of which are listed in Figure 5-1. Suppose that the deck is thoroughly shuffled and one card is removed. Each card is an elementary event in this random experiment.

THE SAMPLE SPACE, COMPOSITE EVENTS, AND EVENT SETS

What is the probability that the selected card is a queen? In terms of long-run frequency, the desired probability may be determined by the following calculation.

$$\Pr[\text{queen}] = \frac{4}{52} = .077$$

The above calculation reflects that 4 out of 52 cards are queens, so that in repeated experiments a queen should be obtained about 4/52 of the time. In other words, one of the four queens should be drawn in about 7.7% of all selections. Each queen card constitutes an elementary event for getting a queen. The event "queen" is a **composite event**, since it will occur if any of those elementary events occur.

The following listing of the elementary events may be helpful.

Queen = {♠Q, ♥Q, ♣Q, ♦Q}

Every composite event may be viewed as an **event set** comprising as elements the applicable elementary events. The entire collection of elementary events is an all-inclusive event set sometimes called the **sample space**. Composite events may then be viewed as corresponding to a portion or *subset* of the sample space.

EXAMPLE: TOSSING THREE COINS

Charlie Brown has a penny, a nickel, and a dime, all of which he plans to toss at the same time. Since all three coins will land simultaneously—making one outcome—each outcome, or elementary event, is a different combination of the sides of the coins that will be showing. To impress his friends, Charlie Brown wants to list the sample space.

SOLUTION: His listing is contained in Figure 5-2. In the list, H stands for a head, T for a tail, and the subscripts p, n, and d for the respective coins. Thus, if Charlie Brown tosses his three coins and gets heads with the penny and the nickel and a tail with the dime, he would represent this event as $H_pH_nT_d$.

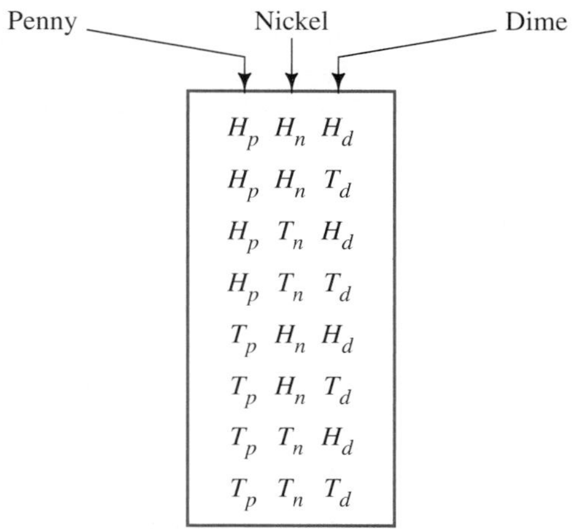

FIGURE 5-2 Sample space for tossing three coins.

THE COUNT-AND-DIVIDE METHOD FOR COMPUTING PROBABILITIES

In the playing card illustration, all cards have the same chance of being selected. The calculation given above for Pr[queen] illustrates the **count-and-divide method** for finding composite event probabilities.

PROBABILITY—COUNT-AND-DIVIDE METHOD (Equally Likely Elementary Events):

$$\text{Pr[event]} = \frac{\text{Number of elementary events in the event set}}{\text{Number of possible elementary events}}$$

Consider a second composite event:

Heart = {♥K, ♥Q, ♥J, ♥10, ♥9, ♥8, ♥7, ♥6, ♥5, ♥4, ♥3, ♥2, ♥A}

Counting the elementary events, we see that there are 13 heart cards, any of which yield the event "heart." The complete deck contains 52 cards, and that is the number of elementary events possible. Thus,

$$\text{Pr[heart]} = \frac{13}{52} = .25$$

Applying the count-and-divide method, you can verify the following:

Pr[face card] = 12/52   Pr[red card] = 26/52   Pr[black jack] = 2/52

To further illustrate the count-and-divide method, we will use the sample space in Figure 5-3, which shows the breakdown of the State University business students who hold scholarships. One student is selected at random from the group of 72. The following probabilities apply.

$$\text{Pr[male]} = \frac{40}{72} = .556 \qquad \text{Pr[female]} = \frac{32}{72} = .444$$

$$\text{Pr[accounting]} = \frac{16}{72} = .222 \qquad \text{Pr[graduate]} = \frac{30}{72} = .417$$

PROBABILITY ESTIMATES

Count-and-divide is one method for determining the long-run frequency at which an event occurs. When we cannot count the possibilities, the count-and-divide approach is unworkable. This is the case for events occurring over time, such as automobile accidents. The true probability for a fatal accident under a given set

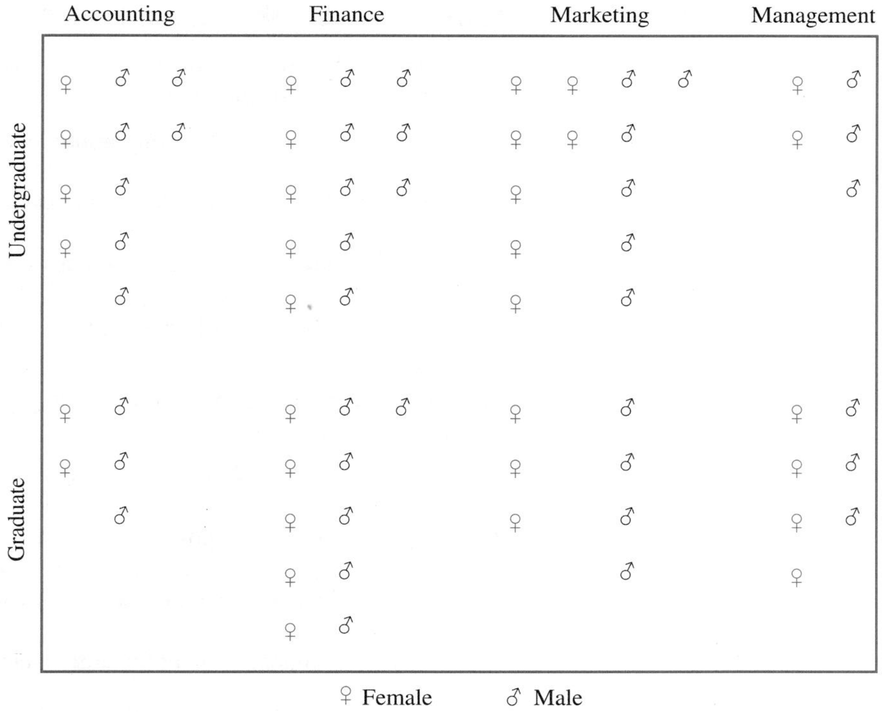

FIGURE 5-3 Sample space for business scholarship students at State University.

of circumstances might be .001—the historical frequency. Such a probability value would ordinarily be an *estimate* of the underlying true probability. The count-and-divide method applies only if the elementary events are *equally likely.* What if, for example, a lopsided coin is tossed? The probability for an event in such a random experiment is still a long-run frequency, but it can only be estimated from the actual results experienced by repeating the experiment (tossing the lopsided coin) many times.

EXAMPLE: DEFECTIVE ITEMS IN A PRODUCTION PROCESS

A quality control inspector removes 100 widgets from production and finds that 14 are defective (D) and 86 are good (G). If you assume that the production process will behave identically in the future, the probability that any particular widget is defective may be *estimated.*

SOLUTION:

$$\Pr[D] = \frac{14}{100} = .14$$

But the above is an estimate, and the true probability remains unknown and could be some other value, such as .175 or .128. The sample space is *not* 100 Ds and Gs for the selected items, but rather the quality for every item that will be produced—possibly millions of elementary events. The total number of Ds and Gs may never be known, thus, the count-and-divide method will not work.

CERTAIN AND IMPOSSIBLE EVENTS

An event's probability is a fraction or decimal between 0 and 1. You can see this by looking at two extreme probabilities. Since an **impossible event** *never* occurs,

$$\text{Pr[impossible event]} = 0$$

Consider the following examples of impossible events.

$$\text{Pr[Dow Jones Average doubles yesterday's close]} = 0$$

$$\text{Pr[student is both undergraduate and graduate]} = \frac{0}{72} = 0$$

Similarly, a **certain event** (for example, "the selected card has a suit") will *always* occur.

$$\text{Pr[certain event]} = 1$$

The following examples apply.

$$\text{Pr[Dow Jones Average closes at some level]} = 1$$

$$\text{Pr[student is either undergraduate or graduate]} = \frac{72}{72} = 1$$

All other probabilities will lie between these two extremes.

ALTERNATIVE EXPRESSIONS OF PROBABILITY

In addition to ratios, probabilities can be expressed as percentages, odds, or chances. These other forms are not inconsistent with our definition, because they can be translated into the basic fraction or ratio form. For example, the probability for obtaining the head side of a coin can be expressed in the following forms:

1. 50% probability for a head. [Divide the percent by 100 to obtain the fraction 1/2.]
2. 50–50 chance for a head. [An even chance; a probability of 50/(50 + 50) = 1/2.]
3. 1 to 1 odds that a head will occur.

To express odds as a fraction, add the two numbers (in this case, 1 + 1 = 2) and place the result in the denominator; then place the first number in the numerator. For 1 to 1 odds, the result is 1/2. As another example, the odds for drawing a queen are 4 to 48 or 1 to 12, so that Pr[queen] = 4/(4 + 8) = 1/(1 + 12) = 1/13.

PROBABILITY AND SAMPLES

Probability is an essential part of statistics. This is primarily due to the uncertainties in making conclusions from samples. Probability concepts are useful in explaining how a sample is generated and what kinds of sample results might be possible when various assumptions are made regarding the parent population.

EXAMPLE: HOW MUCH DO STUDENTS PAY FOR CLOTHES?

The following yearly clothing expenditures apply to Slippery Rock's ten Iota Omega Upsilon pledges.

CT	$786	WR	$915	JB	$125	AB	$321	RT	$980
MJ	$553	TY	$248	BB	$416	HS	$844	NB	$377

Half of the IOU pledges spent more than $500. If one pledge is selected at random, the probability is 5/10 = .5 (5 out of 10) that the chosen person was a high-end spender (that is, over $500).

Viewing the ten IOU expenditures as a population, the figure for the randomly selected person constitutes a *sample* of size $n = 1$, and there is a .5 probability, or 50% chance, that the sample amount exceeds $500.

Suppose that a sample of size $n = 2$ is taken. We can find the probability that the mean sample expenditure lies between $450 and $550.

SOLUTION: To do this we first determine which possibilities might yield such a result:

CT&TY	$517.00	CT&JB	$455.50	WR&JB	$520.00
MJ&BB	$484.50	MJ&NB	$465.00	TY &HS	$546.00
JB &HS	$484.50				

There are altogether 45 possible pledge pairs, 7 of which give a mean that falls in the stipulated range, so that the desired probability is

$$\Pr[\bar{X} \text{ lies between \$450 and \$550}] = \frac{7}{45} = .16$$

Statisticians are often interested in the relation between the interval width and the probability that $\bar{X}$ will lie inside. It is easy to see that the probability is 45/45 = 1 that the sample mean will lie somewhere between $0 and $1,000 (because all 45 sample pairs will have means falling between these values). Likewise, the probability is 0/45 = 0 that the sample mean will fall between $490 and $510 (since there are no pairs with means in that range). Here we see that the looser limits result in a greater probability for getting a result, while tighter limits provide a smaller probability.

EXERCISES

5-5 You are selecting cards at random from a shuffled deck and arguing with your friends over various probabilities. For each of the following composite events, (1) list the corresponding elementary events in the event set, and (2) express the probability as a fraction.

(a) club
(b) five
(c) face card
(d) numbered *and* even
(e) black card
(f) diamond *and* nonface

5-6 In a special study, an accountant found the following information for 850 receivables: (a) 119 were paid early, (b) 340 were settled on time, (c) 221 were paid late, and (d) 170 were uncollectible. Assume that this experience is representative of the future. Estimate the probabilities that a particular receivable will fall into each of the four categories.

5-7 You are asked to toss a pair of six-sided dice, one red and one green. Each side of a die cube has a different number of dots, 1 through 6.
(a) List the possible sums of the number of dots on the two upturned faces.
(b) For each possible sum, list the corresponding elementary events and determine the sum's probability. (Identify your elementary events using a convenient code, such as 2R-5G for 2 dots showing on the red die and 5 on the green.)

5-8 Refer to the sample space in Figure 5-3 for a randomly selected business scholarship student. Determine the probabilities for the following events.
(a) finance major
(b) undergraduate in mangement
(c) graduate in finance
(d) female accounting major
(e) female undergraduate in marketing

5-9 Refer to the sample space in Figure 5-2 for three coins. Determine the following probabilities.
(a) exactly 2 heads
(b) exactly 1 tail
(c) dime and penny agree
(d) dime and penny disagree

5-3 JOINT PROBABILITY AND THE MULTIPLICATION LAW

Important issues are raised by considering two variables. Consider the relationship between SAT scores and college grades or that between college grades and career success. An employer might be interested in how a screening examination score relates to an applicant's future job performance. We now consider how to find the probability for simultaneous occurrence of two events, such as "above 700 on SAT" and "GPA of 4.00," or "pass a screening test" and "satisfactory job performance."

THE JOINT PROBABILITY TABLE

Consider the business scholarship students in Figure 5-3. Considering sex and academic level, the following cross tabulation applies.

	Level		
Sex	**Undergraduate**	**Graduate**	**Total**
Male	24	16	40
Female	18	14	32
Total	42	30	72

Suppose that one student is selected at random. We are interested in the sex (M, F) and level (U, G) for that student, which are now uncertain events. Extending the count-and-divide method to the entire cross tabulation, a complete set of

TABLE 5-1 Joint Probability Table for Randomly Selected Business Scholarship Student

	Level		
Sex	**Undergraduate (U)**	**Graduate (G)**	**Marginal Probability**
Male (M)	24/72	16/72	40/72
Female (F)	18/72	14/72	32/72
Marginal Probability	42/72	30/72	1

probabilities applies. When arranged in an analogous table, the resulting display in Table 5-1 is called a **joint probability table**.

MUTUALLY EXCLUSIVE AND COLLECTIVELY EXHAUSTIVE EVENTS

Joint probability tables convey the essential probabilities used in a two-way classification of events. The rows represent for one category **mutually exclusive events** (only one can occur) and **collectively exhaustive events** (at least one must occur). The columns have the same feature.

JOINT EVENTS AND PROBABILITIES

Each cell in a joint probability table represents an outcome in which the respective row event and column event occur simultaneously. The cell thus signifies a **joint event**. There are four joint events in Table 5-1:

$$M \text{ and } U \qquad M \text{ and } G \qquad F \text{ and } U \qquad F \text{ and } G$$

The numerical values represent the applicable probabilities. Each cell contains the **joint probability** for the respective row and column event. The top left cell of Table 5-1 contains

$$\Pr[M \text{ and } U] = \frac{24}{72}$$

which expresses the probability that the chosen student is both a male (M) and an undergraduate (U).

MARGINAL PROBABILITIES

The margins contain the probability values for the respective row or column event. Because they are located in the *margins* of the table, these are referred to as **marginal probabilities**. The margins of the first row and first column of Table 5-1 contain

$$\Pr[M] = \frac{40}{72} \qquad \Pr[U] = \frac{42}{72}$$

Notice that the joint probabilities within each row sum to the respective marginal probability. (This feature is guaranteed by the nature of the original cross tabulation.) The same fact applies as well to the columns.

THE MULTIPLICATION LAW FOR FINDING *"AND"* PROBABILITIES

As we shall see, the joint probability table is a key element in many probability evaluations. But there may not be a cross tabulation available, and in those cases the count-and-divide method cannot be used in its construction. The needed probabilities must be built using some useful laws provided by probability theory.

The first probability law allows us to compute a joint probability by multiplying together the individual probabilities for the component events. This is the *multiplication law*. Before we state that law, it will be helpful to consider an illustration in which the law may be used.

Consider a quarter that has been flattened on a railroad track:

We want to establish the head and tail probabilities. But there is no reason to believe tosses of this damaged coin will be just as likely to result in a tail as a head. We cannot therefore use 1/2 as the head probability.

A student makes 100 tosses of the bad coin, each time letting it fall free to the floor. She obtained a head on only 35 tosses. The following *estimated* value for the long-run frequency may be used as the approximate head probability:

$$\Pr[\text{head}] = 35/100 = .35$$

The other 65 tosses resulted in a tail, and thus a second approximate probability applies for the tail event:

$$\Pr[\text{tail}] = 65/100 = .65$$

Now consider two later tosses of the bad quarter. Let's denote achieving a head on the first toss as H_1 and use T_1 to represent obtaining a tail. Similarly, for the second toss we use H_2 for a head and T_2 for a tail. We have

$$\Pr[H_1] = \Pr[H_2] = .35 \quad \text{and} \quad \Pr[T_1] = \Pr[T_2] = .65$$

What is the probability that both tosses result in heads?

To answer this question we must use the following

MULTIPLICATION LAW FOR INDEPENDENT EVENTS

$$\Pr[A \text{ and } B] = \Pr[A] \times \Pr[B]$$

The above tells us that when A and B are independent (a relation to be discussed shortly), we may find an unknown joint probability by multiplying together the known probabilities for the individual component events. The joint event's set is the **intersection** of the component events, which are logically joined by "and."

We illustrate this law with the two tosses of the damaged quarter. Multiplying together the H_1 and H_2 probabilities, we have the probability for getting two successive heads:

$$\begin{aligned}\Pr[H_1 \text{ and } H_2] &= \Pr[H_1] \times \Pr[H_2] \\ &= .35(.35) = .1225\end{aligned}$$

The multiplication law applies even when the component events are not elementary events. To see this, let's use it to establish the probability that a randomly selected playing card is both a heart and a queen. Counting and dividing, we first get

$$\Pr[\text{heart}] = \frac{13}{52} \qquad \Pr[\text{queen}] = \frac{4}{52}$$

Then, multiplying the component event probabilities, we get

$$\begin{aligned}\Pr[\text{heart } \textit{and} \text{ queen}] &= \Pr[\text{heart}] \times \Pr[\text{queen}] \\ &= \frac{13}{52} \times \frac{4}{52} \\ &= \frac{1}{52}\end{aligned}$$

SOME ADVICE AND WARNINGS ABOUT THE MULTIPLICATION LAW

With the card example, the multiplication law involves a lot of work. If we had first noted that "heart and queen" is the same as drawing the queen of hearts, we could have more easily just counted-and-divided to establish 1/52 as the probability of getting that card.

You should use the multiplication law when it is advantageous to do so. It is definitely *not mandatory* to use this law when you are finding a joint probability. As we have seen, joint probabilities can sometimes be more easily found by counting and dividing.

The foregoing version of the multiplication law only applies when events are *independent*, a relationship we will define in Section 5-5. When events do not have that relationship, the law will not work. Beginners find it perplexing that the multiplication law can give the *wrong answer*!

JOINT PROBABILITIES INVOLVING MORE THAN TWO EVENTS

The multiplication law for independent events extends to any number of component events.

EXAMPLE: LATE AIRLINE DEPARTURES
Each noon on weekdays, Unified Airways Flight 22 departs from Centralia. This flight experiences late departures 70% of the time, and the takeoff time on any day has no effect on a future day's experience. What is the probability that a particular week will have late departures on every day?

SOLUTION: The probability of a late departure on any particular day is .70. Denoting the respective late-departure events as LMo, LTu, LWe, LTh, and LFr, the multiplication law provides the answer:

$$\begin{aligned}&\Pr[\text{LMo } \textit{and} \text{ LTu } \textit{and} \text{ LWe } \textit{and} \text{ LTh } \textit{and} \text{ LFr}]\\&\quad= \Pr[\text{LMo}] \times \Pr[\text{LTu}] \times \Pr[\text{LWe}] \times \Pr[\text{LTh}] \times \Pr[\text{LFr}]\\&\quad= .7(.7)(.7)(.7)(.7)\\&\quad= (.7)^5 = .168\end{aligned}$$

The above notation tell us that even though 70% of the daily departures are late, only 16.8% of the weeks involve late takeoffs every day.

PROBABILITIES WHEN ELEMENTARY EVENTS ARE NOT EQUALLY LIKELY

The multiplication law may be used to establish probabilities for elementary events that are *not* equally likely.

To illustrate, we return to the damaged coin. The multiplication law allows us to establish probabilities for all two-toss outcomes:

$$\begin{aligned}\Pr[H_1 \textit{ and } H_2] &= \Pr[H_1] \times \Pr[H_2] = .35(.35) = .1225\\\Pr[H_1 \textit{ and } T_2] &= \Pr[H_1] \times \Pr[T_2] = .35(.65) = .2275\\\Pr[T_1 \textit{ and } H_2] &= \Pr[T_1] \times \Pr[H_2] = .65(.35) = .2275\\\Pr[T_1 \textit{ and } T_2] &= \Pr[T_1] \times \Pr[T_2] = .65(.65) = .4225\end{aligned}$$

The outcomes H_1H_2, H_1T_2, and T_1T_2 (abbreviated by removing the *and*) are elementary events for the two-toss random experiment. However, they are *not* equally likely (T_1T_2 has over three times the probability of H_1H_2).

EXERCISES

5-10 The following cross tabulation applies for a consumer testing group.

Occupation	Family Income Low	Medium	High	Total
Homemaker	8	26	6	40
Blue-collar Worker	16	40	14	70
White-collar Worker	6	62	12	80
Professional	0	2	8	10
Total	30	130	40	200

One person is selected at random. Construct a joint probability table for occupation versus income levels.

5-11 The statistics students at Adams College are 60% male. Exactly 20% of the men and 20% of the women are married. Use the multiplication law to determine the probability that a randomly selected student will be classified as the following.
(a) man *and* married
(b) man *and* unmarried
(c) woman *and* married
(d) woman *and* unmarried

5-12 Refer to the sample space in Figure 5-3 for a randomly selected business scholarship student. Construct a joint probability table for sex versus major.

5-13 Refer to the sample space in Figure 5-3 for a randomly selected business scholarship student. Construct a joint probability table for academic level versus major.

5-14 Professor Horatio Dull's statistics class has 3 married men and 5 married women; the rest are unmarried. There are 35 people altogether, 20 of whom are men. One student is selected at random.
(a) Construct the joint probability table for sex versus marital status.
(b) Indicate the probabilities for the following joint events:
(1) man *and* married
(2) woman *and* married
(3) woman *and* unmarried
(4) man *and* unmarried

5-15 List all the possible side-showing elementary events from three tosses of the damaged coin described on page 158. Find for each the joint probability.

5-16 A *fair* coin is tossed 5 times. Two possibilities are

(1) $H_1T_2H_3T_4H_5$
(2) $H_1H_2H_3H_4H_5$

(a) Without computing any probabilities, which outcome do you think is more likely?
(b) Use the multiplication law to determine the probability for each outcome.

5-17 Refer to the sample space for a randomly selected playing card in Figure 5-1.
(a) Use the count-and-divide method to find the following probabilities.

(1) heart (4) black
(2) face (K,Q,J) (5) even-numbered (2,4,6,8,10)
(3) king (6) spade

(b) Use the count-and-divide method to find the following joint probabilities.
(1) heart *and* face (3) black *and* face
(2) king *and* black (4) even-numbered *and* spade

(c) Suit and denomination events are independent. Apply the multiplication law using probabilities found in (a) to compute each joint probability listed in (b).

5-18 Matchless Garments test markets its products with a consumer test panel provided by a consultant. Two panels, each made up of 100 persons, are available. Consider the characteristics of a person selected at random from each group.

(a) Panel A is 50% men and 50% women; 70% of the panel members are married (the rest unmarried), and just as many men as women are married. Thus, any two sex and marital status events are *independent*. Construct a joint probability table by first determining the marginal probabilities and then using the multiplication law to obtain the joint probabilities, which in this case are the products of the two respective marginal probabilities.

(b) Panel B is also 50% men and 50% women, and 70% of the panel members are married. However, only 60% of the men are married, whereas 80% of the women are married. Thus, any two sex and marital status events are *dependent*. This means that the product of the respective marginal probabilities does not equal the corresponding joint probability, so the multiplication law can not be used to find the joint probabilities. Instead, construct the joint probability table using the count-and-divide method.

5-4 FINDING PROBABILITIES USING THE ADDITION LAW

We have seen that the count-and-divide procedure may be used to determine the probabilities for composite events. That method, however, has limited scope. We now consider a more general approach.

To illustrate, let's return to the damaged coin of the previous section. Again, we will toss it twice. We have seen that the sample space comprises these elementary events:

$$H_1H_2 \qquad H_1T_2 \qquad T_1H_2 \qquad T_1T_2$$

What is the probability of exactly one head?

The outcome in question is a composite event having the event set listed below.

$$\text{Exactly one head} = \{H_1T_2, T_1H_2\}$$

The desired probability is *not* equal to 2/4, which is what the count-and-divide method would provide. Counting and dividing works only for equally likely elementary events.

Instead we may get correct values with the following procedure, which uses the probabilities for component events as building blocks.

THE ADDITION LAW FOR FINDING "OR" PROBABILITIES

A second probability law allows us to find the probability of composite events whether or not the elementary events are equally likely. This is the **addition law**, which under special circumstances permits us to add together the component event probabilities. The following states the

ADDITION LAW FOR MUTUALLY EXCLUSIVE EVENTS

$$\Pr[A \textit{ or } B \textit{ or } C] = \Pr[A] + \Pr[B] + \Pr[C]$$

The above expression may be used in finding the unknown probability for a composite event whose event set is the **union** of two or more *mutually exclusive* component events, only one of which can actually occur. Those individual events are logically connected with "or" and have known probabilities.

Continuing with the example of the two damaged coin tosses, we may use the addition law to find the probability of exactly one head:

$$\begin{aligned}\Pr[\text{exactly 1 head}] = \Pr[H_1T_2 \textit{ or } T_1H_2] &= \Pr[H_1T_2] + \Pr[T_1H_2] \\ &= .2275 + .2275 \\ &= .4550\end{aligned}$$

As with the multiplication law, the addition law applies even when the component events are not elementary events. To illustrate, consider again the business scholarship students in Figure 5-3. The following apply to the major of a randomly selected student:

$$\Pr[\text{accounting}] = 16/72 \qquad \Pr[\text{marketing}] = 20/72$$

$$\Pr[\text{finance}] = 24/72 \qquad \Pr[\text{management}] = 12/72$$

Using the above, we may apply the addition law to establish the probability that a nonmanagement major is selected. Note first the equivalency

$$\Pr[\text{nonmanagement}] = \Pr[\text{accounting } \textit{or} \text{ finance } \textit{or} \text{ marketing}]$$

Then, applying the addition law, the correct value is obtained:

$$\begin{aligned}&\Pr[\text{accounting } \textit{or} \text{ finance } \textit{or} \text{ marketing}] \\ &\quad = \Pr[\text{accounting}] + \Pr[\text{finance}] + \Pr[\text{marketing}] \\ &\quad = 16/72 + 24/72 + 20/72 \\ &\quad = 60/72\end{aligned}$$

SOME ADVICE AND WARNING ABOUT THE ADDITION LAW

When the elementary events are equally likely and we can easily count possibilities, a probability for a composite event might be obtained *without* using the addition law. Directly from Figure 5-3, we determine that there are 60 nonmanagement majors (accounting, finance, or marketing) out of 72 business scholarship students, so that a single count-and-divide method more readily provides the same result:

$$\text{Pr[nonmanagement]} = 60/72$$

Like the multiplication law, the addition law does not have to be used every time an *or* joins component events. We should use it only when advantageous to do so. It becomes essential when counting and dividing is impractical or impossible. That is the case in the following example, in which details about the sample space are not provided.

EXAMPLE: REASONS FOR DENIAL OF CREDIT

The credit manager for the Hide-Away Safe Company has several reasons for denying credit to buyers: (1) low income, (2) poor repayment history, (3) high debts, and (4) no collateral. Records of past transactions list one of these as the primary reason for denial of credit. If you assume that past frequencies will apply in the future, you have the following probabilities that the next credit application will be rejected for each primary reason.

$$\text{Pr[low income]} = .15$$

$$\text{Pr[poor repayment]} = .20$$

$$\text{Pr[high debts]} = .25$$

$$\text{Pr[no collateral]} = .40$$

Reasons (3) and (4) apply to what are called "balance sheet deficiencies." We will determine the probability that a balance sheet deficiency will be the reason for the next credit denial.

SOLUTION: We will apply the addition law.

$$\begin{aligned}\text{Pr[balance sheet]} &= \text{Pr[high debts } \textit{or} \text{ no collateral]} \\ &= \text{Pr[high debts]} + \text{Pr[no collateral]} \\ &= .25 + .40 = .65\end{aligned}$$

The addition law can also lead to the *wrong answer*. It requires that the component events be *mutually exclusive*, and it will provide incorrect values if that is not the case.

To illustrate an improper application of the addition law, consider the following calculation for a randomly selected playing card:

$$\text{Pr[heart]} + \text{Pr[queen]} = 13/52 + 4/52 = 17/52$$

The above calculation gives an *incorrect* value for Pr[heart *or* queen]. (Go back to Figure 5-1. How many cards fall into the category of being either a heart or a queen?) Adding the two probabilities is fallacious because heart and queen are *not* mutually exclusive events. Both event sets have the queen of hearts in common, and the above calculation accounts for that possibility twice! (Section 5-7 describes a general version of the addition law that may be used when events are not mutually exclusive.)

MUTUALLY EXCLUSIVE AND COLLECTIVELY EXHAUSTIVE EVENTS

The relevant events from many random experiments are *mutually exclusive*—so that only one of them can occur—and also *collectively exhaustive*—making it certain that one of the events will occur. Consider the outcomes experienced by SoftWhereHaus, which takes a sample of its program diskettes every hour to determine the quality of its final product. If only 10% of the diskettes are defective, then the following probabilities apply for the number of defectives in a sample of 5 diskettes.

Number of Defectives	Probability
0	.5905
1	.3280
2	.0729
3	.0081
4	.0005
5	.0000
	1.0000

The events for "number defective" are mutually exclusive and collectively exhaustive, and their probabilities add up to 1.

APPLICATION TO COMPLEMENTARY EVENTS

When two events are complementary (opposite), their probabilities add up to 1.

$$\Pr[A \text{ or not } A] = \Pr[A] + \Pr[\text{not } A] = \Pr[\text{certain event}] = 1$$

Thus,

$$\Pr[A] = 1 - \Pr[\text{not } A]$$

This is helpful when you want to know an event's probability, but the probability for its complementary event is easier to determine. If you want to determine the probability for "at least 1" defective diskette in the above example, you can use the addition law and add together the probabilities for "exactly 1," "exactly 2," and so on. But you can determine the answer faster if you recognize that "at least 1" is the opposite of "exactly 0." The above example gives the probability for "0 defective" as .5905, so that

$$\begin{aligned}\Pr[\text{at least 1 defective}] &= 1 - \Pr[\text{exactly 0 defective}] \\ &= 1 - .5905 = .4095\end{aligned}$$

EXERCISES

5-19 Refer to the randomly selected playing card sample space in Figure 5-1.

(a) Use the count-and-divide method to find the following probabilities.

(1) club (3) 4 (5) heart (7) ace
(2) king (4) 5 (6) red (8) jack

(b) Use the count-and-divide method to find the following composite event probabilities.

(1) club *or* king (3) club *or* heart (5) ace *or* jack
(2) 4 *or* 5 *or* 6 (4) ace *or* red

(c) Apply the addition law using your probabilities from (a) to attempt to compute each composite event probability listed in (b). Indicate for each whether the obtained result is correct or incorrect because the components are not mutually exclusive events.

5-20 An accountant randomly selects 5 trial balances out of 10. Exactly 4 of the 10 are in error. The following probabilities have been obtained for the number of selected accounts having incorrect balances.

Number of Incorrect Balances	Probability
0	1/42
1	10/42
2	20/42
3	10/42
4	1/42

Determine the probability for the following number of incorrect balances.

(a) at least 2 (c) 1 or more (e) fewer than 4
(b) at most 3 (d) greater than 2 (f) 4 or fewer

5-21 The following joint probability table applies to marital status and job classification of a randomly selected Metropolis worker.

Marital Status	Job Classification: Blue Collar	White Collar	Management	Marginal Probability
Married	.15	.20	.17	.52
Divorced	.12	.02	.04	.18
Widowed	.04	.04	.02	.10
Never Married	.09	.06	.05	.20
Marginal Probability	.40	.32	.28	1.00

(a) What is the probability that the person has a nonmanagement job?
(b) What is the probability that the person is presently unmarried?
(c) What is the probability that the person is a formerly married blue-collar worker?
(d) What is the probability that he or she is a nonmanagement married person?

5-22 The following joint probability table applies to the age group and first college degree held by a randomly selected alumnus of State University.

Age	College Degree: Science	Liberal Arts	Social Science	Professional	Marginal Probability
Under 23	.01	.01	.01	.00	.03
23–29	.02	.02	.04	.06	.14
30–50	.07	.11	.06	.09	.33
Over 50	.10	.05	.18	.17	.50
Marginal Probability	.20	.19	.29	.32	1.00

(a) What is the probability that he is 23 or older?
(b) What is the probability that he is 30 or older?
(c) What is the probability that he is over 50 and has a science or professional degree?
(d) What is the probability that he is under 23 with a science or social science degree?

5-5 STATISTICAL INDEPENDENCE

We have been using the multiplication law to compute various probabilities. That law only works when events are *independent*. We are now ready to formally define this concept.

A DEFINITION OF STATISTICAL INDEPENDENCE

The multiplication law stated earlier applies only for independent events. The following definition applies.

DEFINITION 1: Two events A and B are **statistically independent** whenever

$$\Pr[A \text{ and } B] = \Pr[A] \times \Pr[B]$$

The above indicates that statistical independence is established only by the *probabilities* of two events—not their sequence, cause and effect, timing, or hierarchical ranking.

A BASIC TEST FOR INDEPENDENCE BETWEEN EVENTS

If the probability data are available, we can establish the independence or nonindependence between two events by comparing probabilities.

To illustrate, consider once more the business scholarship students. The following joint probability table for sex versus major applies for a randomly selected undergraduate.

Sex	Major				Marginal Probability
	Accounting	Finance	Marketing	Management	
Male	7/42	8/42	6/42	3/42	24/42
Female	4/42	5/42	7/42	2/42	18/42
Marginal Probability	11/42	13/42	13/42	5/42	1

Consider the events male and marketing. The joint probability for these events is

$$\text{Pr[male } \textit{and} \text{ marketing]} = \frac{6}{42} = .1429$$

Then, multiplying the respective marginal probabilities, we have

$$\text{Pr[male]} \times \text{Pr[marketing]} = \frac{24}{42} \times \frac{13}{42} = .1769$$

Since the above product *differs* from the joint probability, the events male and marketing are *not* statistically independent. Events that are not independent are said to be **dependent events**.

A second comparison with playing card events,

$$\text{Pr[heart } \textit{and} \text{ queen]} = \frac{1}{52} = \frac{13}{52} \times \frac{4}{52} = \text{Pr[heart]} \times \text{Pr[queen]}$$

establishes that heart and queen are statistically independent events.

Statistical independence may apply to any number of events. To have independence, the joint probability of any subset of those events, including the whole, must always equal the product of the individual probabilities. Although the above test is foolproof, the probability values needed to establish independence or dependence may not be readily available.

COMMONLY ENCOUNTERED INSTANCES OF STATISTICAL INDEPENDENCE

In a broad class of random experiments, independence between events may be *assumed*, due to the very nature in which they are generated. This is what we have implicitly been doing all along with coin tosses. To have independence between successive outcomes, a head should be just as likely regardless of whether the preceding toss was a head or a tail. We don't ordinarily need to test for this. (Although a person could sabotage independence by tossing the coin in special ways.)

Drawing a playing card also provides examples where independence may be assumed. Any pair of suit and denomination events involves independent events. This is because the *proportion* of cards with any denomination *is the same value*, regardless of suit. For example, the proportion of face cards (king, queen, jack) among the clubs is 3/13; the same figure applies regardless of suit.

Unequal proportions would occur only in a scrambled card deck constructed from random portions of several decks. Such scrambling is typical with groups of people. With demographic type events—such as those for sex, marital status, occupation, or income—dependence is therefore to be expected. In the case of a randomly selected individual, independence between "married person" and "male" would require that the grouping of people contain exactly the same proportion of married men as married women. Most people will agree that such an arrangement would be very uncommon—except perhaps with groups containing only married couples.

INDEPENDENT EVENTS AND THE MULTIPLICATION LAW

The multiplication law stated earlier requires independence before it can even be used. We use that law only when independence can be safely *assumed.* (And there is obviously no purpose served in comparing the joint probabilities thereby obtained to establish independence, which had to be known at the outset.)

FINDING JOINT PROBABILITIES FOR DEPENDENT EVENTS

When sufficient data are available (as with the business scholarship students), joint probabilities for dependent events may be found by counting and dividing. When no cross tabulation exists, a different procedure must be used. The alternative method works when probabilities are derived from historical frequencies rather than by counting and dividing.

Percentages are common sources of probability data. For instance, a researcher reports that the following apply to Gotham City adults.

5% drive drunk (D).
12% are alcoholics (A).
40% of all drunk drivers are alcholics.

From the above we can readily establish the following probabilities for a randomly selected Gotham City adult.

$$\Pr[D] = .05 \qquad \Pr[A] = .12$$

Multiplying the above, we obtain the product

$$\Pr[D] \times \Pr[A] = .05 \times .12 = .006$$

The above is *not* the joint probability for the two events.

To find the correct value for the joint probability, we use the fact that 40% of the 5% who are drunk drivers are also alcoholics, so that the product of the respective decimal fractions is

$$.40 \times .05 = .02$$

We see that 2% are *both* drunk drivers and alcoholics (D *and* A). This indicates that for a randomly selected adult,

$$\Pr[D \textit{ and } A] = .02$$

Note that D and A are *dependent* events, since

$$\Pr[D \textit{ and } A] = .02 \neq .006 = \Pr[D] \times \Pr[A]$$

CONSTRUCTING A JOINT PROBABILITY TABLE WITHOUT A CROSS TABULATION

We have the essential information for filling in the blanks in the 2-by-2 joint probability table for drunk driving versus alcoholism. We start by inserting the above probabilities:

Driving	Alcoholism: Alcoholic (*A*)	Alcoholism: Nonalcoholic (not *A*)	Marginal Probability
Drunk Driver (*D*)	**.02**		**.05**
Sober (not *D*)			
Marginal Probability	**.12**		

The missing marginal probabilities are filled in next. For the right-hand margin, these must sum to 1.00, because the respective events are *complementary*. Thus, .95 applies for Pr[not *D*]. An analogous condition applies to the bottom margin, and .88 applies for Pr[not *A*]. This gives the following (new values in light face type).

Driving	Alcoholism: Alcoholic (*A*)	Alcoholism: Nonalcoholic (not *A*)	Marginal Probability
Drunk Driver (*D*)	**.02**		**.05**
Sober (not *D*)			.95 ← 1 − .05
Marginal Probability	**.12**	.88 ↑ 1 − .12	1.00

Next, the cell probabilities are obtained. First, the value .03 is found for the empty cell in the *D*-row, establishing Pr[*D and* not *A*]. That value gives cell entries in the *D*-row that sum to the marginal probability of .05 for that row. In the same way, .10 is found for the empty cell in the *A*-column, establishing the value for Pr[not *D and A*]. Then, working with the marginal probability for either the not-*D*-row or the not-*A*-column, the entry for the last empty cell has to be .85, and Pr[not *A and* not *D*] is determined. The completed joint probability table is:

Driving	Alcoholism: Alcoholic (*A*)	Alcoholism: Nonalcoholic (not *A*)	Marginal Probability
Drunk Driver (*D*)	**.02**	.03 ← .05 − .02	**.05**
Sober not (*D*)	.10 ← .12 − .02	.85 ← .88 − .03 or .95 − .10	.95
Marginal Probability	**.12**	.88	1.00

Had the joint probability in the *D and A* cell been different, the other joint probabilities would differ too. In effect, there is only one *degree of freedom* in filling the inside of a 2-by-2 joint probability table. The first cell entry always dictates the joint probability values for the other cells.

EXERCISES

5-23 Consider a randomly selected playing card.
  (a) Show that the following event pairs are independent.
    (1) club, 10 (2) red, king (3) black, queen
  (b) Show that the following event pairs are dependent.
    (1) face, king (2) black, club (3) queen, ten

5-24 A cannery inspector accepts (A) 90% of all peach truckloads inspected and rejects (R) the rest. Historically, she has found that 95% of all truckloads are good (G), the rest bad (B). She rejects 90% of the bad truckloads inspected.
  (a) What percentage of all inspected truckloads are both bad and get rejected?
  (b) Construct the action versus quality joint probability table for the next truckload of peaches inspected.
  (c) What percentage of all inspected loads are (1) good and rejected, (2) good and accepted, and (3) bad and accepted?
  (d) An incorrect action is to accept a bad lot or reject a good load. What is the probability that the inspector takes an incorrect action?

5-25 Refer to the joint probability table in Problem 5-21.
  (a) Show that blue collar and widowed are statistically independent.
  (b) Show that management and never married are statistically dependent.

5-26 Refer to the joint probability table in Problem 5-22.
  (a) Show that over 50 and science are statistically independent.
  (b) Show that under 23 and science are statistically dependent.

5-27 Felina Wild is an oil wildcatter who decides that the probability for striking gas (G) is .40. Felina orders a seismic survey that confirms (C) gas with a probability of .85 in known gas fields and denies (D) gas with a probability of .60 when there is no gas. Construct the joint probability table for geology and survey events.

5-28 A banana inspector accepts only 10% of all bad shipments and rejects only 5% of the good shipments. Overall, 90% of the shipments inspected are good.
  (a) Construct the joint probability table for shipment quality versus inspector action.
  (b) Determine the probability that the inspector will take the wrong action on the next shipment.

5-6 CONDITIONAL PROBABILITY AND THE GENERAL MULTIPLICATION LAW

It is useful to have probability values that apply only when a special condition is met. These are called **conditional probabilities**, and they express the chance that one event will occur given that another occurs. We represent symbolically the conditional probability of A given B by

$$\Pr[A \mid B] \qquad (\Pr[A \textit{ given } B])$$

The probability value for the above pertains to A, computed under the assumption that B will occur.

The weather provides some examples. Consider the events "rain" and "cloudy," for which the following might be true.

$$\Pr[\text{rain} \mid \text{cloudy}] = .70$$

This equation is read, "The probability that there will be rain *given* that it is cloudy is .70." The event "rain" is listed first, and .70 is the probability for this event. The second event, which appears after the vertical bar, is the **given event**, "cloudy." This event establishes the condition under which .70 applies. Given some other event, "rain" could have a different probability. For example,

$$\Pr[\text{rain} \mid \text{low pressure}] = .30$$

In either case, the probability for rain is conditional because it assumes that another event—"cloudy" or "low pressure"—is going to occur. Should no conditions be stipulated for the weather, we might have the value

$$\Pr[\text{rain}] = .20$$

which is an **unconditional probability**.

COMPUTING CONDITIONAL PROBABILITIES

Count-and-Divide Method

The condition, or given event, eliminates extraneous possibilities that would need to be accounted for in establishing unconditional probabilities. For example, consider a randomly selected playing card. You can see that

$$\Pr[\text{jack} \mid \text{face card}] = \frac{4}{12} = \frac{1}{3}$$

since there are only 12 face cards and just 4 cards are jacks. The condition of "face card" effectively reduces the sample space to just 12 cards, and the count-and-divide method can then be applied to the smaller, or restricted, sample space. Without the condition, you would have to consider the entire sample space (all 52 cards), so that

$$\Pr[\text{jack}] = \frac{4}{52} = \frac{1}{13}$$

As another example, consider the student selection experiment in Figure 5-3. You can determine the probability for "finance major given undergraduate" by observing that the condition "undergraduate" eliminates all graduate students.

Therefore, the 42 students in the event set "undergraduate" are the restricted sample space. Of those 42 students, 13 are finance majors, so that

$$\Pr[\text{finance} \mid \text{undergraduate}] = \frac{13}{42}$$

Conditional Probability Identity

If the necessary probability values are known, you may find it helpful to use the

CONDITIONAL PROBABILITY IDENTITY

$$\Pr[A \mid B] = \frac{\Pr[A \textit{ and } B]}{\Pr[B]}$$

This equation states that the conditional probability for an event can be determined by dividing the joint probability for the two events (if known) by the unconditional probability for the given event (if that value is also known). The above calculation provides the long-run relative frequency that A occurs out of all those times that B occurs.

To illustrate, consider the values in the joint probability table found earlier for drunk driving versus alcoholism. The above identity provides the conditional probability that a randomly selected Gotham City adult is an alcoholic given that he or she is a drunk driver:

$$\Pr[A \mid D] = \frac{\Pr[A \textit{ and } D]}{\Pr[D]} = \frac{.02}{.05} = .40$$

The above reflects that 40% of the *drunk drivers only* are alcoholics. Do not confuse *A given D* with the joint event *A and D*, which represents *all adults*, 2% of which are both alcoholics and drunk drivers.

Let's now reverse roles, finding the probability that this person is a drunk driver given that he or she is an alcoholic:

$$\Pr[D \mid A] = \frac{\Pr[D \textit{ and } A]}{\Pr[A]} = \frac{.02}{.12} = .1667$$

The same value as before appears in the numerator, but a different divisor is used because now alcoholic (A) is the given event. The above number tells us that 17% of the alcoholics in Gotham City are drunk drivers. (Be careful when you find conditional probabilities. Reversing the events always gives a different meaning to the result, and the computed value will ordinarily differ as well.)

Although it is always a mathematically correct expression, the conditional probability identity cannot always be used to find conditional probabilities. Consider the following example.

EXAMPLE: FINDING PROBABILITIES FOR SAMPLE DEFECTIVES

The receiving department of Soft Where Haus is sample testing a small shipment of high velocity recording heads. Suppose that out of the 10 heads in the shipment, 2 are defective (D) and the rest are satisfactory (S). (Of course, the inspector doesn't know this fact.) Two heads, represented by the subscripts 1 and 2, are randomly selected one at a time and tested just once. We want to find the various probabilities involving D_1 and D_2.

SOLUTION: You can see that

$$\Pr[D_1] = \frac{2}{10}$$

and given that the first head is defective, only 1 defective is among the 9 remaining heads, so that

$$\Pr[D_2 | D_1] = \frac{1}{9}$$

Should the first head instead be satisfactory, then 2 defectives are left in the remaining 9, and

$$\Pr[D_2 | S_1] = \frac{2}{9}$$

You can not use the conditional probability identity here since you do not know the values for $\Pr[D_1 \textit{ and } D_2]$ or $\Pr[S_1 \textit{ and } D_2]$.

Conditional probability is useful for decision-making purposes.

EXAMPLE: EVALUATING A CLERICAL SKILLS TEST

Probability concepts may be useful in deciding to implement an employment screening test. Consider the experience of Whirl-a-Gigs, a regional children's clothing chain. The company administered on a trial basis a clerical skills test to all employees (who were hired without reference to their test scores). Present hiring policy provides the following historical job performance percentages:

15% unsatisfactory
65% satisfactory
20% excellent

Matching job performance to test scores, the following percentages were obtained:

10% of the unsatisfactory employees received high scores
70% of the satisfactory employees received high scores
85% of the excellent employees received high scores

We want to establish a joint probability table representing job performance and test score events pertaining to a randomly selected Whirl-a-Gigs employee. We will use that table to generate probabilities which may be used to qualify the effectiveness of the test.

SOLUTION: The following table is constructed.

	Test Score		
Performance	**Low (L)**	**High (H)**	**Marginal Probability**
Unsatisfactory (U)	.135	.015	**.150**
Satisfactory (S)	.195	.455	**.650**
Excellent (E)	.030	.170	**.200**
Marginal Probability	.360	.640	1.000

The historical frequencies establish the right-hand marginal probabilities (shown in boldface). The entries in Column H were found using the given percentages to establish the respective proportions of employees. For instance, just 10% of the 15% who were unsatisfactory employees scored high, and

$$\Pr[U \textit{ and } H] = .10 \times .15 = .015$$

The joint probabilities in column L are those values that agree with the requirement that the sum of the cell values in any row equals the respective marginal probability. The bottom marginal probabilities are the sums of the joint probabilities in the respective columns.

The following indicates how good the test would be in screening unsatisfactory employees.

$$\Pr[U|L] = \frac{\Pr[U \textit{ and } L]}{\Pr[L]} = \frac{.135}{.360} = .375$$

The above calculation tells Whirl-a-Gigs that, assuming they would be hired regardless of score, and leaving all other personnel policies the same, 37.5% of the low-scoring applicants would be unsatisfactory employees. This percentage is more than twice as high as the percentage of unsatisfactories currently experienced. This suggests that the test will effectively filter potential unsatisfactories.

The following conditional probabilities tell Whirl-a-Gigs how using the screening test should improve overall employee performance.

$$\Pr[U|H] = \frac{\Pr[U \textit{ and } H]}{\Pr[H]} = \frac{.015}{.640} = .023$$

$$\Pr[S|H] = \frac{\Pr[S \textit{ and } H]}{\Pr[H]} = \frac{.455}{.640} = .711$$

$$\Pr[E|H] = \frac{\Pr[E \textit{ and } H]}{\Pr[H]} = \frac{.170}{.640} = .266$$

Under present hiring policies, if Whirl-a-Gigs were to hire only high-scoring persons, the above equations indicate that only 2.3% of future employees would be unsatisfactory, 71.1% would be satisfactory, and 26.6% would be excellent.

The downside to using the screening test is that a lot of low-scoring people, who may otherwise be satisfactory or excellent employees, would never be hired. Consider the following probability:

$$\begin{aligned}&\text{Pr[may-be-satisfactory-or-excellent-but-not-hired low-scoring applicant]}\\&\quad = \Pr[(S \text{ and } L) \text{ or } (E \text{ and } L)] = \Pr[S \text{ and } L] + \Pr[E \text{ and } L]\\&\quad = .195 + .030 = .225\end{aligned}$$

CONDITIONAL PROBABILITY AND STATISTICAL INDEPENDENCE

Two events are statistically independent if the occurrence of one has no effect on the probability of the other. In terms of conditional probability, an alternative definition of independence applies.

DEFINITION 2: Two events A and B are **statistically independent** whenever

$$\Pr[A \mid B] = \Pr[A] \quad \text{or} \quad \Pr[B \mid A] = \Pr[B]$$

Two events are independent whenever the conditional probability of one event given the second is equal to its *unconditional* probability. In effect, the occurrence, nonoccurrence, or lack of knowledge about the other event has no effect on an event's probability value.

An alternative test for independence would therefore be to compare the unconditional probability for either event to its respective conditional probability. To illustrate, queen and face are dependent, since

$$\Pr[\text{queen}] = 4/52 \neq 4/12 = \Pr[\text{queen} \mid \text{face}]$$

When the above holds, so must the reverse:

$$\Pr[\text{face}] = 12/52 \neq 4/4 = \Pr[\text{face} \mid \text{queen}]$$

And, queen and heart are independent, since

$$\Pr[\text{queen}] = 4/52 = 1/13 = \Pr[\text{queen} \mid \text{heart}]$$

and likewise,

$$\Pr[\text{heart}] = 13/52 = 1/4 = \Pr[\text{heart} \mid \text{queen}]$$

THE GENERAL MULTIPLICATION LAW

The multiplication law used so far pertains just to *independent* events. That requirement does not apply to the following

GENERAL MULTIPLICATION LAW

$$\Pr[A \textit{ and } B] = \Pr[A] \times \Pr[B \mid A]$$

or

$$\Pr[A \textit{ and } B] = \Pr[B] \times \Pr[A \mid B]$$

The above involves the product of one unconditional probability with a conditional probability.

To illustrate, consider the following experience of an accountant. She has established that 60% of all accounts receivable involve incorrect remittances (I), and that 10% of those involve partial payments (P). This history may be expressed in terms of the following probabilities.

$$\Pr[I] = .60$$
$$\Pr[P \mid I] = .10$$

The multiplication law provides the probability that a particular remittance will be both incorrect and a partial payment.

$$\begin{aligned}\Pr[I \textit{ and } P] &= \Pr[I] \times \Pr[P \mid I]\\ &= .60 \times .10\\ &= .06\end{aligned}$$

Thus, 6% of all remittances for accounts receivable will fall into the two categories. (You can verify the result in terms of percentages: 10% of 60% is 6%.)

Illustration: Oil Wildcatting with a Seismic Survey

The owner of the Petroleum Entrepreneurship is a wildcatter who judges that there is a 30% chance of oil (O) beneath his leasehold on Fossil Ridges, with complementary chances that the site is dry (D). That is, the following unconditional probabilities apply.

$$\Pr[O] = .30 \quad \text{and} \quad \Pr[D] = 1 - .30 = .70$$

The wildcatter has the option of drilling now or ordering a seismic survey. Such a test is 90% reliable in predicting favorable (F) when there is actually oil, but only 70% reliable in providing an unfavorable (U) forecast when a site is dry. The given reliability percentages directly express the conditional probabilities

$$\Pr[F \mid O] = .90 \quad \text{and} \quad \Pr[U \mid D] = .70$$

The general multiplication law may be used to establish the joint probability that Fossil Ridges does indeed contain oil and that the seismic survey will be favorable.

$$\begin{aligned} \Pr[O \textit{ and } F] &= \Pr[O] \times \Pr[F \mid O] \\ &= .30 \times .90 = .27 \end{aligned}$$

Similarly, the joint probability for a dry site and an unfavorable seismic survey is

$$\begin{aligned} \Pr[D \textit{ and } U] &= \Pr[D] \times \Pr[U \mid D] \\ &= .70 \times .70 = .49 \end{aligned}$$

CONSTRUCTING A JOINT PROBABILITY TABLE WITH THE ASSISTANCE OF THE GENERAL MULTIPLICATION LAW

As we have seen, even when there are insufficient data to directly apply the count-and-divide method, a joint probability table may be built from percentages, as illustrated with the drunk driving example (Section 5-5) and the foregoing clerical skills test example. The general multiplication law streamlines the procedure.

To demonstrate, we continue with the oil wildcatting illustration, summarized in Table 5-2 by the joint probability table showing geology evens versus seismic results. To fill in the numbers, we applied the general multiplication law (shown earlier) to get two key joint probabilities:

$$\Pr[O \textit{ and } F] = .27 \quad \text{and} \quad \Pr[D \textit{ and } U] = .49$$

They have been placed (in boldface type) in their respective position in Table 5-2. The geology event marginal probabilities

$$\Pr[O] = .30 \quad \textit{and} \quad \Pr[D] = .70$$

have also been positioned in boldface. Using this information, the rest of the table entries were determined. The joint probability for "oil" *and* "unfavorable," .03, is determined by subtracting the joint probability for "oil" *and* "favorable," .27, from the marginal probability for "oil," which is .30. The joint probability for "dry" *and* "favorable," .21, represents the difference between the margin probability for "dry," .70, and the joint probability for "dry" *and* "unfavorable," .49. The marginal probabililities of .48 for a favorable seismic survey and .52 for an unfavorable survey are determined by summing the joint probabilities in each column.

TABLE 5-2 Joint Probability Table for Oil Wildcatting with a Seismic Survey

Geology	Survey Results		Marginal Probability
	Favorable (F)	Unfavorable (U)	
Oil *(O)*	**.27**	.03	**.30**
Dry *(D)*	.21	**.49**	**.70**
Marginal Probability	.48	.52	1.00

EXERCISES

5-29 Refer to the joint probability table in Table 5-1. Determine the conditional probabilities for the following:

(a) male *given* undergraduate (c) female *given* graduate
(b) undergraduate *given* male (d) graduate *given* female

5-30 Refer to the joint probability table in Problem 5-21 for a randomly selected Metropolis worker. Determine the following joint probabilities.

(a) Pr[blue collar|married] (c) Pr[divorced|white collar]
(b) Pr[management|widowed] (d) Pr[widowed|management]

5-31 Refer to the joint probability table in Problem 5-22 for a randomly selected State University alumnus. Determine the following joint probabilities.

(a) Pr[over 50|professional] (c) Pr[social science|30—50]
(b) Pr[professional|over 50] (d) Pr[under 23|science]

5-32 Forty percent of Natti Nitpicker's students have done their probability homework (H). Eighty percent of all students who do homework will pass (P) the probability quiz. Ninety percent of those who do not do the homework will fail (F). Pick a student at random.

(a) Identify the following: (1) Pr[H], (2) Pr[$P|H$]. Then apply the general multiplication law to find (3) Pr[H *and* P].
(b) Find (1) Pr[not H], (2) Pr[$F|$not H], (3) Pr[not H *and* F].

5-33 One Near Miss faculty member is selected from those categorized in Figure 5-4. All instructors have the same chance of being selected. Determine the following conditional probabilities.

(a) Pr[accounting|female]
(b) Pr[finance|male]
(c) Pr[management|male *and* full-time]
(d) Pr[finance|female *and* part-time]
(e) Pr[full-time|female]
(f) Pr[full-time *and* finance|male]
(g) Pr[male|accounting *or* finance]
(h) Pr[part-time *and* accounting|male]

5-34 A card is selected at random from a deck of playing cards. Determine the following probabilities. (Count ace as a "1"—low and odd.)

(a) Pr[heart|red] (d) Pr[jack|face]
(b) Pr[odd-numbered|below 6] (e) Pr[below 6|nonface]
(c) Pr[club|black] (f) Pr[above 3|below 8]

5-35 A State University business scholarship student is randomly selected. Figure 5-2 summarizes the sample space. Let U and G denote level; M and Fe, sex; A, accounting major; and Fi, finance major.

(a) Use the count-and-divide method to determine the following probabilities.

(1)	(2)	(3)	(4)	(5)	(6)
Pr[U]	Pr[Fi]	Pr[Fe]	Pr[G]	Pr[M]	Pr[Fe]
Pr[$Fe|U$]	Pr[$U|Fi$]	Pr[$A|Fe$]	Pr[$M|G$]	Pr[$Fi|M$]	Pr[$U|Fe$]

(b) Apply the multiplication law to each pair of probabilities in (a) to determine the following joint probabilities.

(1) Pr[U *and* Fe] (3) Pr[Fe *and* A] (5) Pr[M *and* Fi]
(2) Pr[Fi *and* U] (4) Pr[G *and* M] (6) Pr[Fe *and* U]

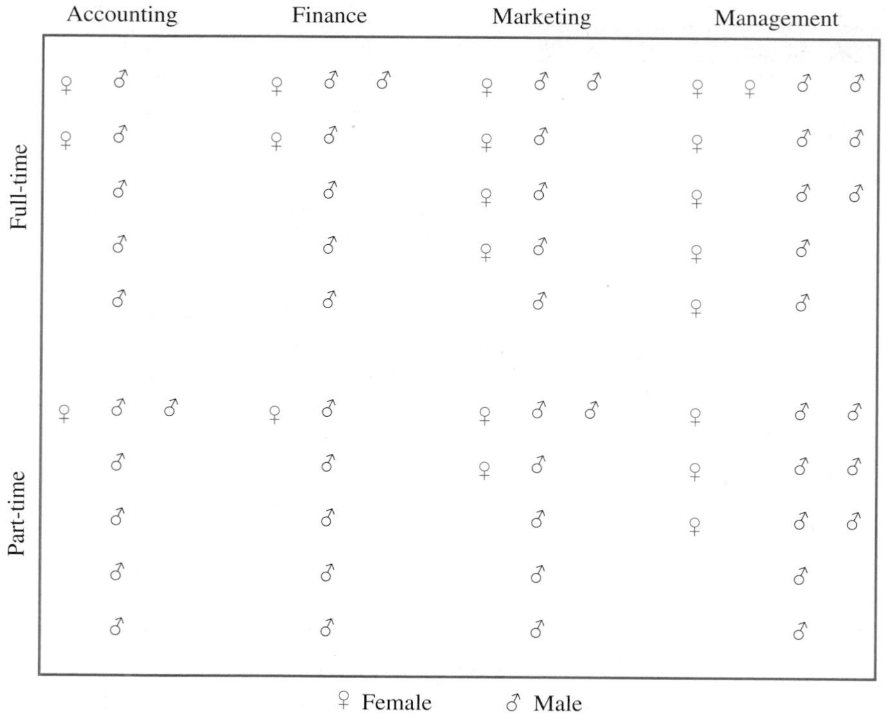

FIGURE 5-4

5-36 Ty Ruth is a switch hitter for baseball's Gotham Flyers. He bats right-handed (R) on 40% of all trips to the plate. In that direction, Ty's batting average is .320. This means that historically he has achieved a hit (H) on 32% of "official" times at bat. He was out (O) on the remainder. Walks, bases on errors, and sacrifices are categorized separately and are not included as "official" at–bats. As a lefty (L), Ruth has hit .360. Consider Ty's next time at bat.

(a) What are the values for the unconditional probabilities (1) $\Pr[L]$ and (2) $\Pr[R]$?

(b) What are the values for the conditional probabilities (1) $\Pr[H|L]$ and (2) $\Pr[H|R]$?

(c) Using your answers to (a) and (b), determine Ty's joint probability table for "official" hitting result (H or O) versus batting direction.

(d) Given that Ty makes a hit, what is the probability that he has batted (1) right-handed? (2) left-handed?

5-37 The general manager of the Gotham City Hellcats is evaluating an employment screening test for the front office clerical staff. During this experiment, all new clerical employees are given the test. Seventy percent pass the test; the rest fail. At a later time, it is determined whether the new clerks are satisfactory or unsatisfactory. Historically, 80% of all clerical hires have been found to be satisfactory, and 75% of the satisfactory clerks in the program have passed the screening test.

(a) From the given information, determine the following values.

(1) Pr[pass] (2) Pr[satisfactory] (3) Pr[pass|satisfactory]

(b) Using your answers to (a), determine Pr[pass *and* satisfactory].

(c) Construct the joint probability table for test results versus employee performance events.

(d) Using your answers in (c), determine the following conditional probabilities.

(1) Pr[fail | unsatisfactory]
(2) Pr[fail | satisfactory]
(3) Pr[pass | unsatisfactory]
(4) Pr[unsatisfactory | fail]
(5) Pr[satisfactory | pass]
(6) Pr[unsatisfactory | pass]
(7) Pr[satisfactory | fail]

(e) Using your answers in (d), determine the following percentages.

(1) failing clerks who prove to be unsatisfactory employees
(2) passing clerks who prove to be satisfactory employees

(f) Government guidelines are that a proper screening test must provide at least 20% for (1) in (e) and at least 60% for (2). Does this test meet those guidelines?

5-38 Two playing card decks are formed from printer's rejects. Deck 1 has no black cards, twice the usual number of hearts or diamonds, equal representations among all denominations, and 52 cards. Deck 2 has 3 sets of kings, 4 sets of queens, and 6 sets of jacks, and no other denominations. Each set has exactly one heart, one diamond, one club, and one spade, so that altogether deck 2 also has 52 cards. One of the decks is selected at random, thoroughly shuffled, and a card drawn and turned over.

(a) Find the joint probabilities for (1) ace of hearts *and* deck 1, (2) ace of hearts *and* deck 2.

(b) Given that an ace of hearts shows, what is the probability that it comes from (1) deck 1? (2) deck 2?

5-7 PROBABILITY TREES AND FURTHER LAWS

We have seen how the joint probability table arranges probability information in a convenient display. We are now ready to discuss a second display that is especially useful for decision making purposes. We then complete our probability introduction by extending the probability laws presented so far and giving some warnings on their misuse.

THE PROBABILITY TREE DIAGRAM

Business decision makers find the joint probability table cumbersome at times. They prefer to organize their probability calculations using a **probability tree**. The probability tree diagram for the preceding oil wildcatting illustration is shown in Figure 5-5. There, each event is represented as a **branch** in one or more **event forks**. This representation is especially convenient when events occur at different times or stages.

In probability trees, time moves from left to right. Since the geology events precede the seismic events, the branches for oil (O) and dry (D) appear in the event fork on the left. Each is followed by a separate event fork representing the seismic events, with a branch for favorable (F) and another for unfavorable (U). Two seismic event forks are required, since the seismic results can occur under two distinct geological conditions. The complete tree exhibits each outcome as a

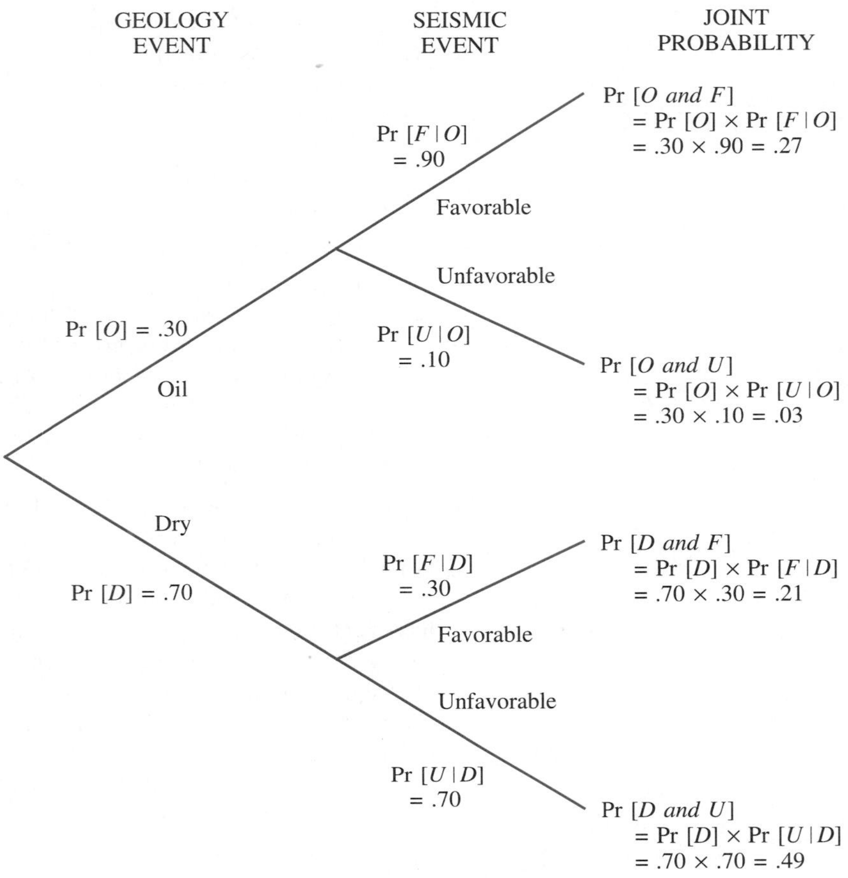

FIGURE 5-5 Probability tree diagram for oil wildcatting with a seismic survey.

single **path** from beginning to end. The probability tree in Figure 5-5 has four paths: oil-favorable, oil-unfavorable, dry-favorable, dry-unfavorable. Each path corresponds to a distinct joint event.

The probabilities for each event are placed alongside its branch. The values listed in the left fork, $\Pr[O] = .30$ and $\Pr[D] = .70$, are unconditional since that event fork has no predecessor. Probabilities for later stage events will all be *conditional* probabilities, with the branch or subpath leading to the branching point signifying the given events. The top seismic event fork lists the probabilities $\Pr[F|O] = .90$ for favorable and $\Pr[U|O] = .10$ for unfavorable. Since that fork is preceded by the oil (O) branch, both conditional probabilities involve O as the given event. A *completely different* set of conditional probabilities, $\Pr[F|D] = .30$ and $\Pr[U|D] = .70$, apply in the bottom event fork; that branching point is preceded by the dry (D) branch, so that D is the given event.

The events emanating from a single branching point are mutually exclusive and collectively exhaustive, so that exactly one must occur. All the probabilities on branches within the same fork must therefore sum to 1.

The probability tree is very convenient for determining joint probabilities. A joint event is represented by a path through the tree, and its probability is determined by multiplying together all the individual branch probabilities for its path. For instance, the topmost path represents the outcome sequence oil-favorable. The corresponding joint probability is

$$\begin{aligned} \Pr[O \textit{ and } F] &= \Pr[O] \times \Pr[F|O] \\ &= .30(.90) \\ &= .27 \end{aligned}$$

All of the joint probabilities for the oil wildcatter are listed in Figure 5-5 at the terminus of the respective event path. Notice that these sum to 1. That is because the joint events themselves are mutually exclusive and collectively exhaustive.

MULTIPLICATION LAW FOR SEVERAL EVENTS

The general multiplication law can be expanded to apply to situations involving more than two component events. For three events,

$$\Pr[A \textit{ and } B \textit{ and } C] = \Pr[A] \times \Pr[B|A] \times \Pr[C|A \textit{ and } B]$$

All terms except the first are conditional probabilities, with the preceding events assumed as given events. There may be any number of component events.

To illustrate, in a particular industry it has been found that 80% of all new firms survive (S) past one year. Of those, 40% close (C) within the second year, half due to bankruptcy (B) and the rest for a number of other reasons. This experience provides the following probabilities for a start-up.

$$\begin{aligned} \Pr[S] &= .80 \\ \Pr[C|S] &= .40 \\ \Pr[B|S \textit{ and } C] &= .50 \end{aligned}$$

The multiplication law provides the joint probability that a particular new firm will survive the first year, close during the second, and then go bankrupt.

$$\begin{aligned} \Pr[S \textit{ and } C \textit{ and } B] &= \Pr[S] \times \Pr[C|S] \times \Pr[B|S \textit{ and } C] \\ &= .80 \times .40 \times .50 \\ &= .16 \end{aligned}$$

EXAMPLE: THE MATCHING BIRTHDAY PROBLEM

Consider the probability that there is at least one matching birthday (day and month) among a group of persons.

SOLUTION: It will be simplest to determine the probability of the complementary event—no matches—by using the general multiplication law. Envision each member of a group of size n being asked in succession to state his or her birthday. We conveniently define our events as follows:

$$A_i = \text{the } i\text{th person queried does not share a birthday with the previous } i - 1 \text{ persons.}$$

TABLE 5-3 Probabilities for at Least One Matching Birthday

Group Size	Pr[no matches]	Pr[at least one match]
3	.992	.008
7	.943	.057
10	.883	.117
15	.748	.252
23	.493	.507
40	.109	.891
50	.030	.970
60	.006	.994

Then Pr[no match] $=$ Pr[A_1 *and* A_2 *and* . . . *and* A_{n-1} *and* A_n], which is the probability of the event that no person shares a birthday with the preceding persons. For simplicity, assume all dates to be equally likely and ignore leap year. Thus,

$$\Pr[A_1] = \frac{365}{365} \qquad \Pr[A_2|A_1] = \frac{364}{365} \qquad \Pr[A_3|A_1 \text{ and } A_2] = \frac{363}{365}$$

so that the nth person cannot have a birthday on the previously cited $n - 1$ dates, $365 - (n - 1) = 365 - n + 1$ days are allowable for his or her birthday. Therefore, we may apply the multiplication law to obtain

$$\Pr[\text{no matches}] = \frac{365}{365} \times \frac{364}{365} \times \frac{363}{365} \times \ldots \times \frac{365 - n + 1}{365}$$

The probability for at least one match may be determined from this:

$$\Pr[\text{at least one match}] = 1 - \Pr[\text{no matches}]$$

One interesting issue is finding the size of the group for which the probability exceeds 1/2 that there is at least one match. Knowing this number, you can amaze your less knowledgeable friends and perhaps win a few bets. The "magical" group size turns out to be 23.

Why such a low group size? If it were physically possible to list all the ways (triples, sextuples, septuples, and so forth) in which 23 birthdays can match (there are several million, and for each a tremendous number of date possibilities), an intuitive appreciation as to why could be attained. Table 5-3 shows the matching probabilities for several group sizes. Note that for groups above 60 there is almost certain to be at least one match.

THE GENERAL ADDITION LAW

The addition law encountered earlier requires that the component events be *mutually exclusive*. That condition is not required by the following

GENERAL ADDITION LAW

$$\Pr[A \textit{ or } B] = \Pr[A] + \Pr[B] - \Pr[A \textit{ and } B]$$

The above acknowledges that when A and B are not mutually exclusive, they have elementary events in common, and the joint probability must be subtracted from the sum of the individual probabilities in order to avoid double accounting of possibilities.

To illustrate, consider a randomly selected playing card. The addition law gives the probability that the card is either heart or queen:

$$\begin{aligned}\Pr[\text{heart } \textit{or} \text{ queen}] &= \Pr[\text{heart}] + \Pr[\text{queen}] - \Pr[\text{heart } \textit{and} \text{ queen}] \\ &= \frac{13}{52} + \frac{4}{52} - \frac{1}{52} \\ &= \frac{16}{52}\end{aligned}$$

The general addition law may always be employed. Should A and B happen to be mutually exclusive, then $\Pr[A \textit{ and } B]$ must be zero. (The original addition law is just the general law applied when $\Pr[A \textit{ and } B] = 0$, so that in those cases the joint probability may be ignored without creating erroneous results.)

COMMON ERRORS IN APPLYING THE LAWS OF PROBABILITY

Some of the most prevalent errors in determining probability values result from the improper use of the laws of probability. Four common mistakes are listed on page 186.

STATISTICS AROUND US

Natural Disasters

Casualty insurance underwriters have determined the probabilities for a city experiencing one of the following natural disasters over the next decade.

Disaster	Probability
Tornado	.5
Flood	.3
Earthquake	.4

We cannot say that the probability for one disaster occurring is .5 + .3 + .4 = 1.2. Two or more of these disasters may occur over a ten-year period, and some may occur more than once.

1. Using the addition law to find the probability for the union of several events when they are *not* mutually exclusive. (See box on page 185.)

2. Using the addition law when the multiplication law should be used, and vice versa. Remember that *or* signifies addition and that *and* signifies multiplication.

   For example, the probability for drawing a red face card is the same as the probability for the event "red *and* face card." Recall that

$$\text{Pr[red]} = \frac{26}{52} \quad \text{and} \quad \text{Pr[face card]} = \frac{12}{52}$$

   If we add these values to determine the joint probability, we obtain a meaningless result.

$$\frac{26}{52} + \frac{12}{52} = \frac{38}{52}$$

   Since "red" and "face card" are independent events,

$$\text{Pr[red } \textit{and} \text{ face card]} = \frac{26}{52} \times \frac{12}{52} = \frac{6}{52}$$

3. Using the multiplication law for independent component events when the events are dependent.

4. Improperly identifying the complement of an event. For example, the complement of "none" is "some," which may be expressed as "one or more"or "at least one."

The incident described in the following Statistics Around Us box on the facing page, which actually happened, dramatically illustrates how ludicrous results may be obtained by applying the probability laws incorrectly.*

EXERCISES

5-39 Refer to Exercise 5-27. Construct a probability tree diagram. Determine the joint probability for each geology and seismic outcome.

5-40 Refer to Exercise 5-28. Construct a probability tree diagram using shipment quality events in the first stage and inspector actions in the second. Determine the joint probabilities for each path outcome.

5-41 For simplicity, suppose that all months of the year are equally likely to be a person's birth month. Several people are comparing their birth months. Determine the probability for at least one matching birth month when this group consists of (a) two people (b) three people, and (c) five people.

5-42 A playing card is randomly selected from a standard deck. Establish for the following (1) the component event and joint probabilities. Then (2) apply the addition law to get the indicated composite event probability.
(a) Pr[diamond *or* face] (c) Pr[face *or* king]
(b) Pr[9 *or* red] (d) Pr[spade *or* odd-numbered]

*For a detailed discussion, see "Trial by Mathematics," *Time* (April 26, 1968), p. 41.

STATISTICS AROUND US

Wrongly Convicted by Probability

An elderly woman was mugged in the suburb of a large city. A couple was convicted of the crime, although the evidence was largely circumstantial. The multiplication law was used to demonstrate the extremely low probability that a couple fitting the description of the muggers could have committed the crime. The events (the characteristics that witnesses ascribed to the couple) are listed below, along with their assumed probabilities.

Characteristic Event	Assumed Probability
Drives yellow car	1/10
Interracial couple	1/1,000
Blond woman	1/4
Woman wears hair in ponytail	1/10
Man bearded	1/10
Man black	1/3

These values were multiplied to obtain the probability that any specific couple, selected at random from the city's population, would have all six characteristics.

$$\frac{1}{10} \times \frac{1}{1{,}000} \times \frac{1}{4} \times \frac{1}{10} \times \frac{1}{10} \times \frac{1}{3} = \frac{1}{12{,}000{,}000}$$

Since the defendants exhibited all six characteristics and the jury was mystified by the overwhelming strength of the probability argument, they were convicted.

The Supreme Court of the state heard the appeal of one of the defendants. The defense attorneys, after obtaining some good advice on probability theory, attacked the prosecution's analysis on two points: (1) the rather dubiously assumed probability values for the events, and (2) the invalid assumption of independence implicit in using the multiplication law in this manner (examples: the proportion of black men having beards may be greater than the proportion of the population as a whole having beards; "interracial couple" and "man black" are not independent events). The judge accepted the arguments of the defense and noted that trial evidence was misleading on another score: A high probability that the defendants were the *only* such couple should have been determined to demonstrate a strong case. Using the prosecution's original figures and its assumptions of independence, it can be demonstrated that the probability was large that at least one other couple in the area had the same characteristics.

5-43 Consider the joint probability table in Exercise 5-22 for a randomly selected State University alumnus. Find the probability for the following.

(a) professional *or* under 23
(b) older than 29 *or* social science
(c) over 22 *or* non-professional
(d) liberal arts *or* under 23

5-44 Consider the joint probability table in Exercise 5-21 for a randomly selected Metropolis worker. Find the probability for the following.

(a) white collar *or* divorced
(b) blue collar *or* never married
(c) management *or* widowed
(d) previously married *or* management

SUMMARY

1. **What are the basic concepts of probability and how do they relate to relative frequency?**
Probability in this book represents the **long-run frequency** with which an uncertain event occurs after repeated random experiments of identical nature. Probability theory is crucial to statistics since it explains how likely various sample results might be.

2. **What are random experiments and the outcomes they generate?**
The term **random experiment** refers to the situation giving rise to the uncertain event, such as a coin toss, a lottery, or a random selection. Random experiments involve **elementary events**, the most detailed outcomes of interest, which may or may not be **equally likely**.

3. **How is the count-and-divide method used to find probabilities for some events?**
When the elementary events are equally likely, the probability for any one of them is one divided by the number of possibilities. And, in that case the **count-and-divide method** provides the probability for any **composite event**; this procedure divides the number of applicable elementary events (size of the **event set**) by the total number possible. But, it works only when the elementary events are equally likely.

4. **How do we express probabilities for joint events (intersections), and how is the related information displayed?**
One special composite event is the **joint event**, which happens when two or more component events occur simultaneously, and they are logically connected by "and" (so that the joint event is the **intersection**). For some random experiments the probability for such a result, called **joint probability**, may sometimes be computed by counting and dividing or established by finding the percentage of the time both occur.
Joint probabilities may be represented in a two-way **joint probability table** as entries in the cells. The row and column totals are then referred to as **marginal probabilities**. Like a cross tabulation, the sum of the entries in any row or column must equal the respective marginal value.

5. **What are the advantages of the multiplication law?**
Should the count-and-divide method not be suitable (either because the elementary events are not equally likely or because counts are not available), joint probabilities might be found using the **multiplication law**, which states that the desired result equals the product of the individual component event probabilities. One stipulation must be met: The component events have to be **statistically independent**.

6. **What is the importance of statistical independence, and how may that relationship be verified?**
Two events are **statistically independent** if the probability of any one of

them is unaffected by the occurrence of the other. One test for this is to check whether the product of the component events does indeed equal the joint probability (found earlier, either by counting and dividing or from an established percentage). Events found not to be independent are **dependent events**.

7. **How do we use the addition law for components joined by "or"?**
A second type of composite event involves components connected by "or" (so that the composite event is their **union**). In some cases, the count-and-divide method can often be used to find the probability for the composite event. When that is not possible, the **addition law** should give the desired value as the sum of the individual probabilities for the components. This law requires that the components be mutually exclusive. It gives rise to the useful **complementary event property**, which allows us to find a probability by taking one minus the probability of the opposite event.

8. **What are conditional probabilities and how are they distinguished from ordinary "unconditional" probabilities?**
Useful values are **conditional probabilities**, which are probabilities that apply for one event under the condition that a given event occur as well. For statistically independent events, the **unconditional** probability of any event will always be equal to its conditional probability given the other event. Conditional probabilities can sometimes be computed by applying the count-and-divide method, counting only those possibilities permissible by the stated condition. When that is not possible, a conditional probability may sometimes be available as given information (perhaps as a historical percentage). Finally, if sufficient probability values are already known, the **conditional probability identity** may be used. That identity works well when the data have been arranged in a joint probability table.

9. **What are the general forms for the multiplication and addition laws?**
General forms exist for the multiplication and addition laws. The **general multiplication law** does not require statistical independence, and the joint probability for two events is found by multiplying the *unconditional* probability for the first event times the *conditional* probability of the second given the first. (The general law still works if the events are independent, since the conditional probability for the second event must then equal its unconditional probability.) The **general addition law** does not require that the component events be mutually exclusive. For two events it corrects for double accounting of possibilities by subtracting their joint probability.

10. **How do we construct and use probability trees?**
Analogous to the joint probability table is the graphical **probability tree diagram**. Trees are especially useful when events occur at different points in time. Each branching point, or fork, in a probability tree represents a collectively exhaustive and mutually exclusive set of events as branches, the probabilities for which sum to 1. The probability values for events preceded by other branches are *conditional* probabilities, given those branches on the path leading to that branch. Each path represents a distinct outcome, or joint event, of the random experiment. The general multiplication law coincides naturally with the probability tree, since any joint event's probability is equal to the product of the branch probabilities for its path.

REAL LIFE STATISTICAL CHALLENGE

Convicted by Your Genes?

The idea of applying probability theory to the successful arrest and conviction of individuals accused of criminal behavior is not new. Unfortunately neither is the misuse of probability theory. (See the box on page 187.) Now questions are being raised concerning one of the most recent scientific applications to crime-stopping—the use of DNA analysis.

Using DNA for Health and the Law

In exploring patterns in human DNA (deoxyribonucleic acid), researchers discovered there are parts of the DNA that can serve to match an individual's sequences of genetic code to samples. This matching procedure has been applied in major areas:

- DNA diagnosis of inheritable diseases passed on from a child's mother or father.
- DNA analysis or "fingerprinting" for comparing samples of unknown origins.

How DNA Is Tested

The procedure for testing either for analysis or diagnosis involves subjecting the DNA to enzymes that break the strands into fragments at "restriction points." The lengths of the fragments will vary from person to person because of mutations that occur to the DNA code as it is transmitted from generation to generation. Through a series of steps the DNA fragments are sorted and tagged with radioactive markers. (The process of sorting is called electrophoresis, where the smallest DNA fragments are drawn furthest across an electrically charged gel.) An X-ray photograph is then taken. The photographic results can then be compared to other X-rays. A sample comparison is displayed in Figure 5-6.

By comparing the pattern for one individual with genetic material gathered from a large sample of people, some scientists argue it is possible to compare how closely individuals may be related. The probability for a close match between a person and a sample is considered to be extremely small. The unlikelihood of a match occurring by chance underlies the idea of genetic "fingerprint" matching. Indeed, genetic markers were first applied to establish probabilities that a particular male was the father of a child. Physical evidence gathered from a crime scene is often used in determining whether an alleged suspect was at the location. Even small pieces of DNA material have been used to aid in the successful conviction of accused individuals. In one multiple murder/rape case, over 3,000 people were sampled in villages and hamlets before the culprit was identified.

The Controversy Concerning DNA "Fingerprinting"

Not everyone is convinced DNA "fingerprinting" will always lead to the conviction of the right man or woman. The heated debate involves a number of respected scholars. Two points are at issue:

- The procedures used to carry out the testing.
- The samples from which the isotopic markers are based.

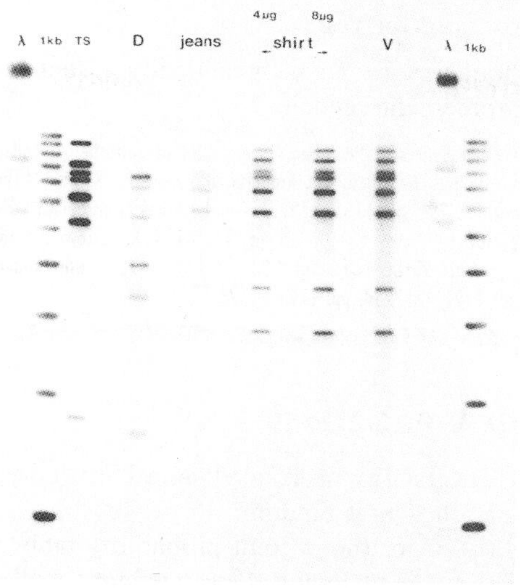

Source: Figure A Cellmark Diagnostics found in Leslie Roberts, "Fight Erupts Over DNA Fingerprinting," *Science* 29 December 1991 Vol. 254, pp. 1721–1723.

FIGURE 5-6 Compelling Evidence. Bands indicate that blood on the defendant's shirt came from the victim (V), not from the defendant (D).

Representing the pro-genetic fingerprinting side is the argument defended by Ranajit Charkraborty (University of Texas at Houston) and Kenneth Kidd (Yale University), "it is the general frequency in the total population that is desired." They further indicate if *proper* procedures are followed in testing samples the results should be accurate enough for use as forensic evidence. (In one case, the odds are as extreme as 738,000,000,000,000 to 1 against a match being based on chance.)

Dissenting views are held by such scholars as Richard C. Lewontin (Harvard University), Daniel L. Hartl (Washington University) and Eric S. Lander (Massachusetts Institute of Technology). They believe that the total population data hide significant *similarities* found within various subgroups, especially among African-Americans and Hispanics. Additional samples of these subgroups are needed. They argue, furthermore, that some of the probability values (such as the above) entered as court testimony are based on faulty statistical methods. Additional issues are raised about the level of regulation needed to ensure proper procedures are followed.

The experts are lined up on both sides. In the realm of DNA "fingerprinting" the courts and the legal system may be faced with a hung jury.

QUESTIONS

1. Put yourself in the position of the defendant's attorney. How would you attack the credibility of the evidence gathered by the prosecution?
2. Reverse your position and develop arguments for the prosecution.

3. Imagine you are on a jury. What type of questions would the discussion in this box raise for you?

4. Should everyone be genetically tested and the results kept on file by law enforcement agencies?

Sources: Tim Beardsley, "Pointing Fingers: DNA Identification Is Called into Question," *Scientific American*, March 1992, Vol. 266, No. 3, pp. 26–27. R. Charkraborty and Kenneth. K. Kidd, "The Utility of DNA Typing in Forensic Work," *Science* 29 December Vol. 254, pp. 1735–1739. Cassandra Franklin-Barbajosa "DNA Profiling The New Science of Identity," *National Geographic*, May 1992, Vol. 181, No. 5, pp. 112–124. R. C. Lewontin and Daniel L. Hartl "Population Genetics in Forensic DNA Typing," *Science* 29 December Vol. 254, pp. 1745–1750. Leslie Roberts, "Fight Erupts Over DNA Fingerprinting," *Science* 29 December 1991, Vol. 254, pp. 1721–1723.

REVIEW PROBLEMS

5-45 The faculty at Transylvania University are represented in Figure 5-7. One is chosen at random.

(a) Construct a joint probability table for sex versus highest degree.

(b) Are male and doctorate statistically independent or dependent events?

(c) Given that the selected professor is female, find the conditional probability that she (1) holds a doctorate, (2) has a master's, as the highest degree.

(d) Given that the selected professor has a doctorate, find the conditional probability that he or she is (1) male, (2) female.

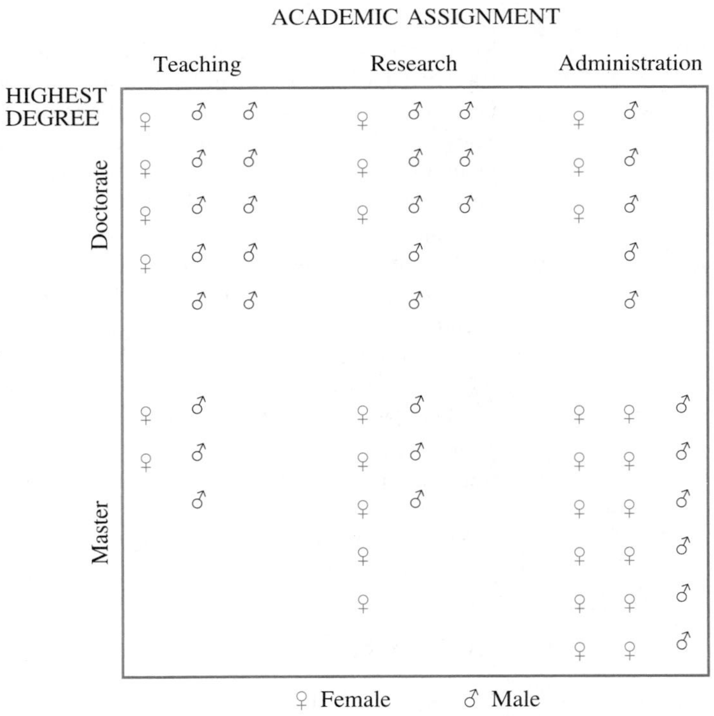

FIGURE 5-7 Sample space for randomly selected Transylvania University faculty member.

5-46 Suppose that the professors in Figure 5-7 are selected at random for various committee assignments. Each person has the same chance of being selected for each successive assignment. Determine the following probabilities.

(a) The next two assignments go to (1) males, (2) females, (3) holders of doctorates.

(b) At least one female professor is selected out of the next (1) 2 assignments, (2) 3 assignments, (3) 4 assignments.

5-47 The faculty at Transylvania University are represented in Figure 5-7. One is chosen at random.

(a) Construct a joint probability table for sex versus academic assignment.

(b) Are female and researcher statistically independent or dependent events?

(c) Given that the selected professor is female, find the conditional probability that she is (1) a researcher, (2) an administrator, (3) teaching.

(d) Given that the selected professor is an administrator, find the conditional probability that he or she is (1) male, (2) female.

5-48 The faculty at Transylvania University are represented in Figure 5-7. One is chosen at random.

(a) Construct a joint probability table for highest degree versus academic assignment.

(b) Are doctorate and researcher statistically independent or dependent events?

(c) Given that the selected professor has a master's degree as the highest degree, find the conditional probability that he or she is (1) a teacher, (2) a researcher, (3) an administrator.

(d) Given that the selected professor is a researcher, find the conditional probability that he or she (1) holds a doctorate, (2) has a master's degree.

5-49 The probability is .95 that a GizMo Corporation traveling sales representative will have no automobile accidents in a year. Assuming that accident frequencies in successive years are independent events, determine the probability that a selected driver (a) goes 5 straight years with no accident; (b) has at least 1 accident in 5 years.

5-50 The Centralia plant of DanDee Assemblers experiences power failures with a probability of .10 during any given month. Assume that power events in successive months are independent. Determine the probability that there will be (a) no power failures during a 3-month span; (b) exactly 1 month involving a power failure during the next 4 months; (c) at least 1 power failure during the next 5 months.

5-51 A new family with two children of different ages has moved into the neighborhood. Suppose that it is equally likely that either child will be a boy or girl. Hence, the following situations are equally likely.

Youngest	Oldest	
boy	boy	(B, B)
boy	girl	(B, G)
girl	boy	(G, B)
girl	girl	(G, G)

(a) Determine Pr[at least one girl].
(b) If you know there is at least one girl, what is the conditional probability that the family has exactly one boy?
(c) Given that at least one child is a girl, what is the conditional probability that there are two girls?

5-52 The Ourman-Friday Employment Agency specializing in clerical and secretarial help classifies candidates in terms of primary skills and years of experience. The skills are bookkeeping, reception, and word processing. (We will assume that no candidate is proficient in more than one.) Experience categories are less than one year, one to three years, and more than three years. There are 100 persons currently on file, and their skills and experience are summarized in the following table.

	Skill			
Experience	**Bookkeeping**	**Reception**	**Word Processing**	**Total**
Less than One Year	15	5	30	50
One to Three Years	5	10	5	20
More than Three Years	5	15	10	30
Total	25	30	45	100

One person's file is selected at random. Determine the probability that the selected person will fall into the following categories.
(a) bookkeeping
(b) less than one year of experience
(c) reception
(d) one to three years of experience
(e) word processing
(f) more than three years of experience

5-53 Refer to Exercise 5-52.
(a) Assume the selected person has less than one year of experience. What is the probability that his or her skill is bookkeeping?
(b) Does the bookkeeping probability in (a) differ from the one you determined in Exercise 5-52? Are bookkeeping and less than one year of experience statistically independent events?
(c) Determine Pr[bookkeeping *and* less than one year of experience]. Can the multiplication law be used to determine this probability?

5-54 Refer to Exercise 5-52.
(a) Use the addition law to determine the probabilities for the following composite events.
(1) bookkeeping *or* reception
(2) word processing *or* reception
(3) less than one year of experience *or* more than three years of experience
(b) Use the count-and-divide procedure to determine the probabilities for the following composite events.
(1) bookkeeping *or* less than one year of experience
(2) reception *or* more than three years of experience
(3) word processing *or* one to three years of experience

5-55 The business faculty at Near Miss University are categorized in Figure 5-4. One instructor is selected at random. Construct a joint probability table for sex versus employment status events.

5-56 Repeat Exercise 5-55 for discipline versus employment status events.

5-57 The following data have been obtained for the employees of the Metropolis branch office of Kryptonite Corporation.

Name	Age	Sex	Salary	Marital Status	Years of Education	Years of Service
Emily Brown	26	female	$150/week	single	12	2
Thomas Duncan	54	male	3/hour	single	8	1
David Eckhart	34	male	400/week	married	18	10
Thelda Hunt	48	female	3/hour	widowed	10	21
James Mohair	33	male	200/week	single	12	7
Irvin Odle	31	male	175/week	married	14	2
Stacy Parker	35	female	190/week	divorced	12	4
Norman Raab	27	male	4/hour	divorced	12	2
Tammy Salazar	28	female	200/week	married	15	1
Ted VanDorn	42	male	500/week	married	16	15

For one person selected at random determine the following probabilities.

(a) Pr[older than 35] (c) Pr[more than 12 years of education]
(b) Pr[paid hourly] (d) Pr[more than 5 years of service]

5-58 An Admiral Motors quality control inspector accepts only 5% of all bad items and rejects only 1% of all good items. Overall production quality of items is such that only 90% are good.

(a) Using the percentages as probabilities for the next item inspected, determine the following probabilities.
(1) Pr[accept | bad] (2) Pr[reject | good] (3) Pr[good]

(b) In the following joint probability table, determine the missing values.

Quality	Inspector Action: Accept	Inspector Action: Reject	Marginal Probability
Good			
Bad			
Marginal Probability			

(c) What is the probability that the inspector will accept or reject the next item incorrectly?

5-59 Applicants to a business school are 70% male. Regardless of their sex, 40% are married. Use the multiplication law to determine the probability for each of the following characteristics for a selected applicant.

(a) man *and* married (c) man *and* unmarried
(b) woman *and* married (d) woman *and* unmarried

5-60 Refer to Exercise 5-57. Consider the characteristics for one employee of Kryptonite Corporation selected at random from those listed.

(a) Construct a joint probability table for sex versus marital status events.

(b) Determine the following probabilities.
(1) Pr[widowed *or* divorced] (3) Pr[male *or* single]
(2) Pr[single *or* divorced] (4) Pr[female *or* married]

5-61 Consider again the random selection of one employee from those listed in Exercise 5-57. In each of the following cases, determine the unconditional probability of event (1). Then determine the conditional probability of event (1) given event (2). Comparing each pair of values, indicate whether the two events are statistically independent or dependent.
(a) (1) age over 35 (2) more than 10 years of service
(b) (1) female (2) hourly worker
(c) (1) married female (2) age under 30
(d) (1) more than 12 years of education (2) single

5-62 Refer to Exercise 5-57. Two employees are selected by pulling names out of a hat. The first name picked is not placed back into the hat.
(a) Construct a probability tree diagram for this experiment, with the sex of the selected employees as the events at each stage. Then, identify the elementary events in the sample space, and determine the joint probability for each.
(b) Determine the probability that the two selections will involve employees of the same sex.

5-63 Suppose that Giant Enterprises increases its computer facilities, so that a busy signal is encountered only 10% of the time. Let B_1 denote that the first message gets a busy signal, D_1 that it goes through directly, and similarly for remaining messages. List all the joint events possible for the first three messages, and determine the probabilities for these events.

5-64 Refer to your answers to Exercise 5-63.
(a) Determine the following probabilities for the number of busy signals encountered in the three messages.
(1) Pr[exactly 0] (3) Pr[exactly 2]
(2) Pr[exactly 1] (4) Pr[exactly 3]
(b) Using your answers to (a), determine the following probabilities for the number of busy signals encountered in the three messages.
(1) Pr[exactly 2 *or* exactly 3] (3) Pr[at least 1]
(2) Pr[at most 2] (4) Pr[at most 1]

5-65 BriDent toothpaste has a 20% market share. Thus, there is a 20% chance that a randomly selected user of toothpaste will be a buyer (B) of BriDent. Suppose that 60% of BriDent buyers remember (R) a funny commercial about the product, while only 10% of nonbuyers do.
(a) Determine the following probabilities.
(1) Pr[B] (2) Pr[not B] (3) Pr[$R|B$] (4) Pr[$R|$not B]
(b) Construct the joint probability table for a person's buying category and memory regarding the commercial.
(c) What percentage of all toothpaste users remember the commercial?

5-66 Consider the first three telecommunications queries by Giant Enterprises. Suppose that the system is busy (B) 20% of the time and that a direct connection (D) is achieved the rest of the time. Assume that the status of the system at each query is independent of that for preceding messages.
(a) Construct a probability tree diagram for the system status encountered by those three queries.

(b) Identify all elementary events.
(c) Determine the joint probability for each event.

5-67 Callers to the Midget Motors switchboard encounter busy signals (B) 20% of the time. The remainder of the time calls are connected directly (D). Because of the slow rate at which calls are placed, the connection status of successive calls is dependent. Records show that half of all calls placed after a preceding call encountered a busy signal will also find the switchboard busy. But 90% of calls placed after the preceding call was directly connected will also be directly connected.

(a) Construct a probability tree diagram for the system status encountered by the first three calls to the Midget Motors switchboard.
(b) Identify all elementary events.
(c) Determine the joint probability for each event.

STATISTICS IN PRACTICE

5-68 Using the master class data from Exercise 1-19, one student will be selected at random. Perform the following probability operations.

(a) Construct a joint probability table using two data sets. Use either your nominal data or create categories for the ordinal or interval data. Possible comparisons include favorite food versus major or sex; place of birth versus age.
(b) Using the joint probability table, create some examples to demonstrate your understanding of the multiplication and addition laws.
(c) Using the joint probability table, create some examples to demonstrate your understanding of mutually exclusive events and conditional probability.

5-69 Using your group's class data list, developed in Exercise 1-21, repeat (a) through (c) of Exercise 5-68.

5-70 The First Post-Cold War Olympics: The following table shows the medal results for the top six countries and the total medals won by participants from other countries in the Albertville, France Winter Olympics of 1992.

Country	Gold	Silver	Bronze	Total
Germany	10	10	6	26
Unified Team	9	6	8	23
Austria	6	7	8	21
Norway	9	6	5	20
Italy	4	6	4	14
United States	5	4	2	11
Others	14	19	23	56
Total	57	58*	56*	171

*Two silver medals were awarded in Woman's Giant Slalom. No bronze medal was awarded.

Source: *San Jose Mercury News* February 24, 1992 p. 6C

One medalist will be chosen at random.

(a) Construct a joint probability table using the data.
(b) What is the probability that the selected medalist came from one of two listed countries bordering on the Swiss Alps?
(c) Assuming an American is chosen what is the probability that he or she won a gold medal.

5-71 Back at the 1988 Summer Olympics. Consider the best way to organize the medal total data presented from the 1988 Summer Olympics (Exercise 2-41). Construct a joint probability table and demonstrate applications of the addition law, multiplication law and conditional probability.

5-72 Use the data in the gas mileage data displayed in Table 3-5 to carry out the following probability operations.
(a) Construct a joint probability table and demonstrate applications of the addition law, multiplication law and conditional probability.
(b) What is the probability of selecting a car at random with a mileage value of less than 20; greater than 26; between 27 and 18 mpg inclusively? Greater than 25 mpg given the vehicle is a two-seater? Create two other examples showing your understanding of conditional probability.

CASE The Three Marketeers

Dar Tan Yun, president of the Three Marketeers, has formed a consumer test panel to help devise a marketing strategy for a line of microwavable gourmet meals. The panel would be responsible for choosing promotions, formulating advertising copy, and selecting advertising media.

Table 5-4 shows a partial breakdown of the 25 panel members. Dar believes that they are a microcosm of the target market. If true, the probability that a potential customer has various characteristics should coincide with the probability that a randomly selected panel member has them also.

QUESTIONS

1. Various two-way joint probability tables might be constructed for the characteristics of a randomly selected panel member.
(a) Including a person's sex as a main feature, how many different joint probability tables may be constructed using the demographic groupings in Table 5-4?
(b) Construct the following joint probability tables.
(1) marital status versus education
(2) education versus home
(3) home versus sibling status
(4) sex versus marital status
(5) marital status versus children at home
(6) sibling status versus education

(c) Using your answers to (b), identify any event pairs that are statistically independent.

(d) What might you conclude regarding the incidence of independence among demographic characteristics in target markets?

2. Determine the following conditional probabilities for a randomly selected panel member.

(a) Pr[bachelor's | married]
(b) Pr[married | bachelor's]
(c) Pr[renter | master's]
(d) Pr[master's | renter]
(e) Pr[firstborn | owner]
(f) Pr[owner | firstborn]
(g) Pr[unmarried | no children at home]
(h) Pr[no children at home | unmarried]

3. A recent survey showed that 20% of the subscribers to the *Rising Loafer* are college graduates. Another 10% of the subscribers have master's degrees, and only 5% never went beyond high school. Determine the probability that a randomly selected panel member who reads this magazine (a) owns his or her home; (b) is married.

4. Half of the subscribers to *Foodaholics NewScooper* have siblings. Of these, 10% are the firstborn, and 30% are the youngest child. Determine the probability that a panel member who subscribes to this newsletter (a) is a homeowner; (b) has a master's degree.

TABLE 5-4 Demographic Breakdown of Three Marketeers Consumer Test Panel

Name	Marital Status	Level of Education	Home	Sibling Status	Children at Home
Ruth Baird	married	high school	renter	firstborn	yes
Ann Schultz	unmarried	some college	renter	youngest	no
Mark Maris	unmarried	bachelor's	renter	firstborn	no
Tom Steel	married	some college	owner	youngest	yes
Bill Adamson	unmarried	master's	renter	only child	yes
Pete Gonzales	unmarried	bachelor's	renter	middle	no
Morris Chin	married	high school	owner	middle	yes
Heidi Gravitz	married	bachelor's	owner	middle	no
Todd Fullmer	unmarried	bachelor's	renter	firstborn	yes
Scott Meadows	unmarried	master's	owner	youngest	no
Harvey Abramovitz	married	bachelor's	owner	firstborn	yes
Andy Pilsner	unmarried	some college	renter	youngest	no
Ann Goldberg	unmarried	some college	renter	only child	yes
Mike O'Hara	married	bachelor's	renter	youngest	yes
Larry Ellington	married	high school	owner	only child	no
Dick Senn	unmarried	bachelor's	renter	firstborn	no
Tom Sellers	married	bachelor's	renter	middle	no
Jack Beringer	unmarried	high school	owner	middle	no
Don McKinsey	unmarried	bachelor's	renter	only child	no
Sally Deerwalker	married	some college	owner	firstborn	yes
Ingrid Folsom	married	bachelor's	owner	only child	yes
Gloria Gravenstein	married	high school	owner	middle	yes
Marsha Markovich	unmarried	some college	renter	middle	yes
Ursula Hernandes	unmarried	bachelor's	renter	only child	no
Tom Fujimoto	unmarried	bachelor's	renter	youngest	no

5. Half of all the people in the target market eat oatmeal. Of these, 30% of the females prefer that dried fruit be added to the premix, whereas only 20% of the men do. Assuming that the same percentages apply to the panel members, determine the probability that a panel member will (a) eat oatmeal; (b) prefer dried fruit in their oatmeal.

6. Crunchy-Munchy is a new snack food. Of the children living with a married parent, only 20% will eat the snack. And of the children living with a single parent, 40% will eat it. Crunchy-Munchy will be marketed if at least 5% of all potential buyers have a child at home who would eat it. Assuming that the panel matches the market, should Crunchy-Munchy be marketed?

PART II

DRAWING CONCLUSIONS FROM SAMPLES: INFERENTIAL STATISTICS

CHAPTER 6

PROBABILITY DISTRIBUTIONS, EXPECTED VALUE, AND SAMPLING

BEFORE READING THIS CHAPTER, MAKE SURE YOU UNDERSTAND:

The distinction between the sample and the population (Chapter 1).

The difference between a sample statistic and a population parameter (Chapter 3).

The advantages of *random* samples (Chapter 4).

The basic concepts of probability (Chapter 5).

How to construct a probability tree (Chapter 5).

The addition and multiplication laws of probability (Chapter 5).

AFTER READING THIS CHAPTER, YOU WILL UNDERSTAND:

About random variables and their probability distributions.

About the two basic types of random variables.

How probability distributions are obtained.

About sampling with and without replacement and the effect on probabilities.

About expected value and variance and their uses.

How to represent sample results as random variables.

About the sampling distributions of the mean and proportion.

About the binomial distribution and how to compute binomial probabilities.

This chapter focuses on **deductive statistics**: determining probabilities for obtaining particular sample results when the population values are known. As an illustration, we will determine the possible sample outcomes for a population of Graduate Management Admissions Test scores. Studying how random samples are generated and learning what to expect when working with *known* populations will lay the essential groundwork for evaluating *unknown* populations.

The average test score, or sample mean, is an important value to use in establishing admissions policies. When its value is uncertain (the case *before* the sample is taken), the sample mean is referred to as a **random variable**. The values of a random variable are treated as uncertain events that occur with a set of probabilities called a **probability distribution**.

We can summarize the information in a probability distribution in terms of central tendency and variability. The "average" figure for a random variable is referred to as its **expected value**. We use expected values to compare probability distributions. In sampling, they enable us to analyze the kinds of results that we might obtain.

6-1 RANDOM VARIABLES AND PROBABILITY DISTRIBUTIONS

We have seen (in Chapter 2) that frequency of occurrence plays an important role in statistics. We also have become familiar with probability (in Chapter 5). We are now ready to combine these concepts, laying the foundation for statistical analysis of samples and for evaluating decisions made under uncertain conditions.

THE RANDOM VARIABLE

A numerical value that may result from a future random experiment is unknown and should be considered a *variable*. The value actually achieved is subject to chance and is therefore determined *randomly*. Such a quantity is given the following

DEFINITION: A **random variable** is a numerical quantity whose value is determined by chance.

All of the following are random variables.

your income next year	your score on the next exam
tomorrow's high temperature	the number of errors in a phone book
how long you wait for a soda	IBM's next quarterly dividend
length of a movie line	the height of the next person you see
amount of money you will lose	your GPA for the present term

A random variable must be a numerical quantity. There can be no random variable for a random experiment involving qualitative outcomes unless points, a cost, or some other number can be associated with the elementary events.

THE PROBABILITY DISTRIBUTION

Random variables are fundamental to statistical theory. The relationship between a random variable's values and their probabilities is summarized by the probability distribution.

DEFINITION: The **probability distribution** provides a probability for each possible value of a random variable.

A probability distribution can be analogous to a relative frequency distribution. To illustrate, a data set was formed by keeping track of the number of customers arriving at the checkout counter at a WaySafe market. The frequency distribution in Table 6-1 applies for each six-minute time interval over a period of five hours on the first day of December.

The relative frequency for each number of customer arrivals is shown in column (3). Recall that the relative frequency indicates the *proportion* of observations falling into a particular category. (Here, the elementary units are six-minute *time spans*, not customers, and the categories are the *number of arrivals*.) Thus, .36, or 36% of the intervals involve exactly 1 arriving customer, while .04, or 4% of the intervals have exactly 4 arrivals.

Now consider a random experiment where one of the 50 time intervals is selected at random and the corresponding number of arrivals determined. The outcome might be the number of customers who arrived during 10:36–10:42, during 12:06–12:12, or within any of the time spans. The number of arrivals during the selected time is the random variable. The probability that the selected segment has exactly 1 arrival is

$$\Pr[\text{exactly 1 arrival}] = \frac{18}{50} = .36$$

Similarly, the probability that it will be one having 4 arrivals is

$$\Pr[\text{exactly 4 arrivals}] = \frac{2}{50} = .04$$

Notice that the probability for any particular number of arrivals matches the relative frequency. The individual probabilities for all possibilities are listed in Table 6-2, which constitutes the probability distribution for the random variable.

The possible values of a random variable are mutually exclusive and collectively exhaustive events. The probabilities in a complete listing must therefore

TABLE 6-1 Frequency Distribution for Customer Arrivals at Checkout Counter

(1) Number of Arrivals	(2) Number of Six-Minute Intervals	(3) Relative Frequency
0	18	.36
1	18	.36
2	8	.16
3	3	.06
4	2	.04
5	1	.02
6	0	.00
7 or more	0	.00
	50	1.00

sum to 1. For mathematical convenience we use symbols. A capital letter represents the random variable itself. Here, X denotes the yet-to-be-determined number of arrivals in the sample time segment. A lower case letter, here x, is the stand-in or **dummy variable** for all possible levels of the random variable. This makes it easier to communicate and permits use of algebraic expressions that summarize statistical procedures. The following example should be helpful.

EXAMPLE: A RAFFLE

A raffle is to be conducted with 10,000 tickets, numbered consecutively from 1 through 10,000. One ticket is to be selected from a barrel after thorough mixing. Because each ticket is equally likely to be selected, the probability that a particular ticket will be selected is 1/10,000. If we define a random variable for the raffle as the number of the selected ticket, to be denoted by X, we can shorten the statement "The number of the selected ticket will be 7,777" to read

$$X = 7{,}777$$

We wish to find the probability distribution for this random variable.

SOLUTION: We express the probability for this event as

$$\Pr[X = 7{,}777] = \frac{1}{10{,}000}$$

Because there are 10,000 possible outcomes, all having the same probability, we can express the probability distribution more concisely by using a statement of the form

$$\Pr[X = x] = \frac{1}{10{,}000} \quad \text{for values of } x = 1, 2, \ldots, 10{,}000$$

which is equivalent to duplicating the previous probability expression 10,000 times, once for each ticket number.

TABLE 6-2 Probability Distribution for Customer Arrivals during Randomly Selected Six-Minute Intervals

Number of Arrivals x	Probability $\Pr[X = x]$
0	.36
1	.36
2	.16
3	.06
4	.04
5	.02
6	.00
7 or more	.00
	1.00

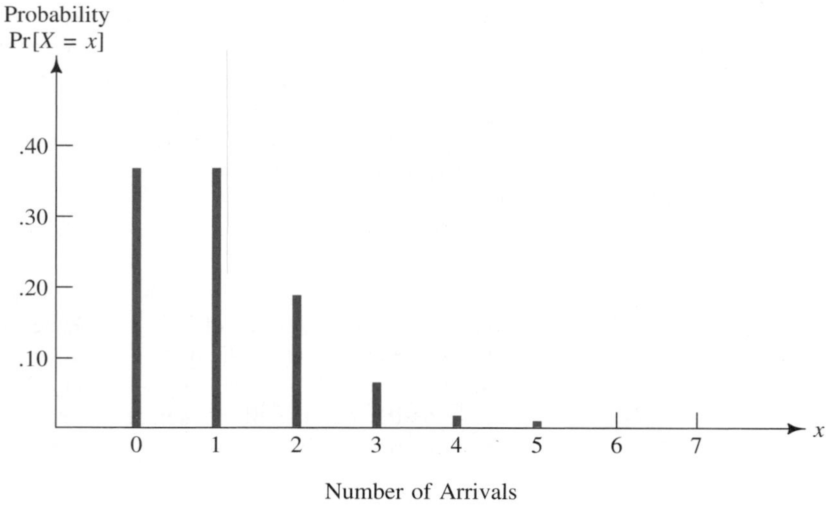

FIGURE 6-1 Graph of the probability distribution for the number of arrivals.

It is important to keep in mind that the capital letter X represents the number of the ticket that *will be* selected and has no determined value until the raffle is completed. The lowercase letter x is a stand-in for *each* ticket number to avoid 10,000 repetitious statements.

Figure 6-1 shows how the WaySafe arrival probability distribution appears on a graph. The values for each possible variable level are on the horizontal axis. The vertical axis provides the probability. For each variable level, a spike is drawn on the graph with a height equal to the appropriate probability.

Many random variables have probability distributions for which individual probabilities can be calculated from a mathematical expression. Later you'll encounter illustrations of those expressions that are applicable to some common probability distributions. Such expressions are called **probability mass functions**.

In a random sampling experiment, the population observations are also the elementary events of the sample space, as in Figure 6-2. Each element of the sample space corresponds to a level $x = 0$, $x = 1$, ... Mathematicians think of X as a function that maps each elementary event onto the x-line.

FINDING THE PROBABILITY DISTRIBUTION

A probability distribution can be established by applying the probability concepts and procedures found in Chapter 5. The following example shows how to create a probability distribution using the multiplication and addition laws.

EXAMPLE: AMOUNT PAID FOR A PERSONAL COMPUTER

Quant Jacques wishes to buy a personal computer made by VBM (Very Big Machines). From past purchases, VBM has established the following breakdown for the percentage of times that a particular component is selected for a system.

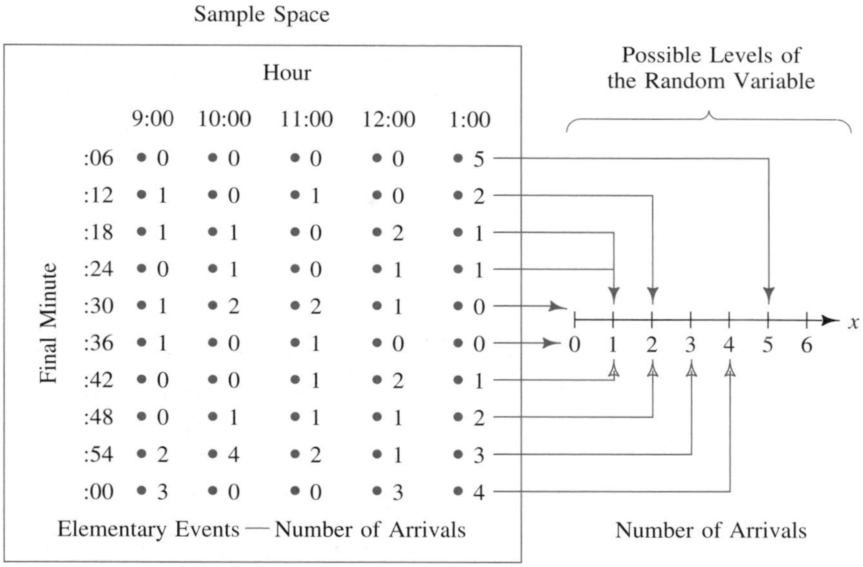

FIGURE 6-2 Illustration of the random variable for a randomly selected time interval.

Computer and Memory	Printer	Monitor
30%–250K ($1500)	50%–Matrix ($500)	60%–Monochrome ($200)
70%–500K ($2000)	50%–Laser ($1000)	40%–Color ($400)

Assuming that Quant selects the three components independently and that the probability for each choice agrees with the percentages given in the table, what is the probability distribution for his total system cost?

SOLUTION: Begin by listing all the possible combinations. You can determine the probability for each by using the multiplication law.

Computer and Memory	Printer	Monitor	Cost	Probability
250K	Matrix	Monochrome	1,500 + 500 + 200 = $2,200	.3(.5)(.6) = .09
250K	Matrix	Color	1,500 + 500 + 400 = 2,400	.3(.5)(.4) = .06
250K	Laser	Monochrome	1,500 + 1,000 + 200 = 2,700	.3(.5)(.6) = .09
250K	Laser	Color	1,500 + 1,000 + 400 = 2,900	.3(.5)(.4) = .06
500K	Matrix	Monochrome	2,000 + 500 + 200 = 2,700	.7(.5)(.6) = .21
500K	Matrix	Color	2,000 + 500 + 400 = 2,900	.7(.5)(.4) = .14
500K	Laser	Monochrome	2,000 + 1,000 + 200 = 3,200	.7(.5)(.6) = .21
500K	Laser	Color	2,000 + 1,000 + 400 = 3,400	.7(.5)(.4) = .14

List the possible costs, applying the addition law as needed, to construct the probability distribution table.

Cost	Probability	
\$2,200		.09
2,400		.06
2,700	.09 + .21 =	.30
2,900	.06 + .14 =	.20
3,200		.21
3,400		.14
		1.00

PROBABILITY TREES AND SAMPLING

Especially important to statistical investigations are probability distributions that summarize the potential results from sampling. Sampling ordinarily involves multiple observations, and, therefore, the probability calculations can be complicated. Probability trees are helpful in organizing those computations.

To illustrate, consider a shipment of 100 printed circuit (PC) boards received by a computer manufacturer. Each board is either defective (D) or good (G). The decision to accept or reject the shipment will be based on a sample of three boards selected at random. The inspector has no way of knowing ahead of time how many defective boards there are. Let's assume that there are exactly 5 defective boards and 95 good boards.

The probability tree in Figure 6-3 summarizes the essential information. The first observation is represented by the two branches in the event fork farthest to the left. We use the abbreviation D_1 to denote the event "the first board is defective" and G_1 to denote the event "the first board is good." The subscripts help

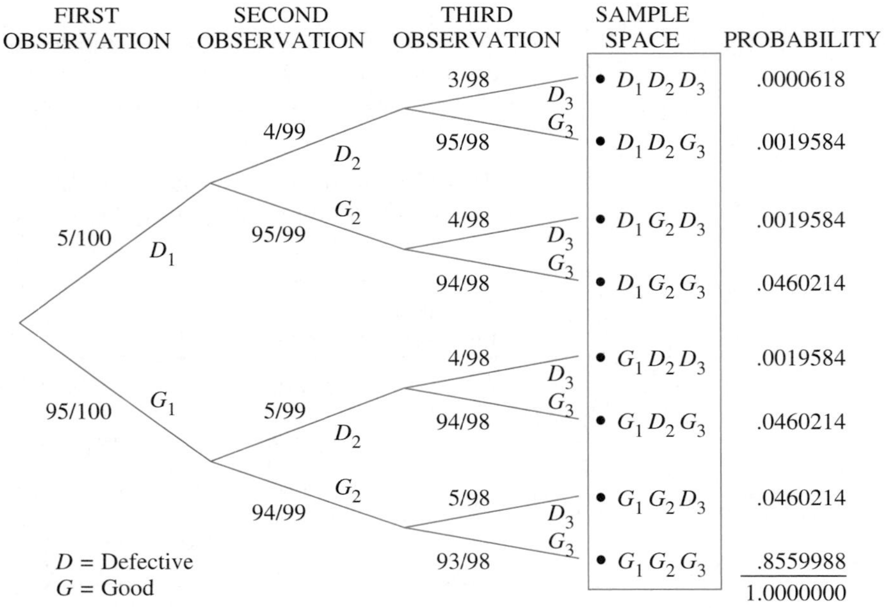

FIGURE 6-3 Probability tree diagram for selecting a sample of three PC Boards without replacement.

to distinguish the results from different observations. Each branch for the first observation leads to a separate event fork for the second. Both forks for the second observation have a D_2 and a G_2 branch. Together, the initial observations create four distinct circumstances under which the third observation might occur, and each of these is represented by a separate fork that has a D_3 and G_3 branch.

The probabilities for each branch are determined using the count-and-divide method, according to the number of defective and good boards remaining up to that point in the tree. The initial fork has probabilities

$$\Pr[D_1] = \frac{5}{100} \quad \text{and} \quad \Pr[G_1] = \frac{95}{100}$$

Because the quality mix of the remaining items varies at the second stage, the probabilities for D_2 and G_2 differ in the two event forks for that observation. The values shown are *conditional probabilities.* The top set applies when D_1 has occurred, when there are only 4 defective boards and 95 good boards remaining. With 99 boards available for testing, the count-and-divide procedure provides

$$\Pr[D_2|D_1] = \frac{4}{99} \quad \text{and} \quad \Pr[G_2|D_1] = \frac{95}{99}$$

Likewise, the lower second stage fork involves

$$\Pr[D_2|G_1] = \frac{5}{99} \quad \text{and} \quad \Pr[G_2|G_1] = \frac{94}{99}$$

since, at that point—with 1 good board removed—the tree indicates that 5 defective and 94 good boards remain.

The forks for the third stage involve probabilities reflecting the respective histories of defective and good for the previously tested items. The fork at the top right is preceded by D_1 and D_2 branches, so that the following conditional probabilities appear.

$$\Pr[D_3|D_1 \text{ and } D_2] = \frac{3}{98} \quad \text{and} \quad \Pr[G_3|D_1 \text{ and } D_2] = \frac{95}{98}$$

It is easy to verify the remaining third stage probabilities.

Each path through the tree in Figure 6-3 corresponds to a distinct outcome, and is summarized in the sample space listed in the box beside the tree. The probability for these elementary events is determined by multiplying together the branch probabilities on its respective path. For instance, to determine the second elementary event probability we have

$$\Pr[D_1D_2G_3] = \frac{5}{100} \times \frac{4}{99} \times \frac{95}{98} = .0019584$$

We are actually applying the multiplication law for several joint events.

$$\Pr[D_1 \text{ and } D_2 \text{ and } G_3] = \Pr[D_1] \times \Pr[D_2|D_1] \times \Pr[G_3|D_1 \text{ and } D_2]$$

TABLE 6-3 Probability Distribution for the Number of Defective PC Boards when Three Sample Items are Inspected without Replacement

Number of Defectives r	Corresponding Elementary Events	Elementary Event Probability	Probability $\Pr[R = r]$
0	$G_1G_2G_3$	.8559988	.8559988
1	$D_1G_2G_3$	.0460214	.1380642
	$G_1D_2G_3$	.0460214	
	$G_1G_2D_3$	.0460214	
		.1380642	
2	$D_1D_2G_3$	.0019584	.0058752
	$D_1G_2D_3$	.0019584	
	$G_1D_2D_3$	.0019584	
		.0058752	
3	$D_1D_2D_3$	.0000618	.0000618
			1.0000000

By itself, the probability tree is too detailed to help the inspector decide how to dispose of a particular shipment. However, she would find useful the probability distribution for the number of defectives R provided in Table 6-3. The table probabilities were determined using the information in the last two columns of Figure 6-3 and then applying the addition law for mutually exclusive events.

Using the values in Table 6-3, the inspector can determine the probability that the shipment would contain more than 1 defective.

$$\begin{aligned}\Pr[R > 1] &= \Pr[R = 2] + \Pr[R = 3] \\ &= .0058752 + .0000618 \\ &= .0059370\end{aligned}$$

If she rejects shipments having more than 1 defective item, less than 1% of similar shipments would be unacceptable.

INDEPENDENT SAMPLE OBSERVATIONS

The preceding illustration involves **sampling without replacement**, since the inspected sample units are set aside. Although it seems inherently wasteful (and even impossible when testing destroys the items), some inspection schemes replace the items in the original population, allowing them the same chance of being selected for each subsequent observation as the other items. Such a procedure is called **sampling with replacement**. As we shall see, sampling with replacement simplifies the probability calculations.

Figure 6-4 shows the probability tree diagram that would apply if the inspector sampled with replacement. Notice that all the D branches have identical probabilities of .05, and, similarly, the probabilities for the G branches are all .95. Since sampled items are replaced, the probabilities for later quality events must be unaffected by what happens earlier. In effect, successive quality events are *statistically independent*. Independence between successive sample observations arises naturally when sampling from a continuing production line, when replacement or

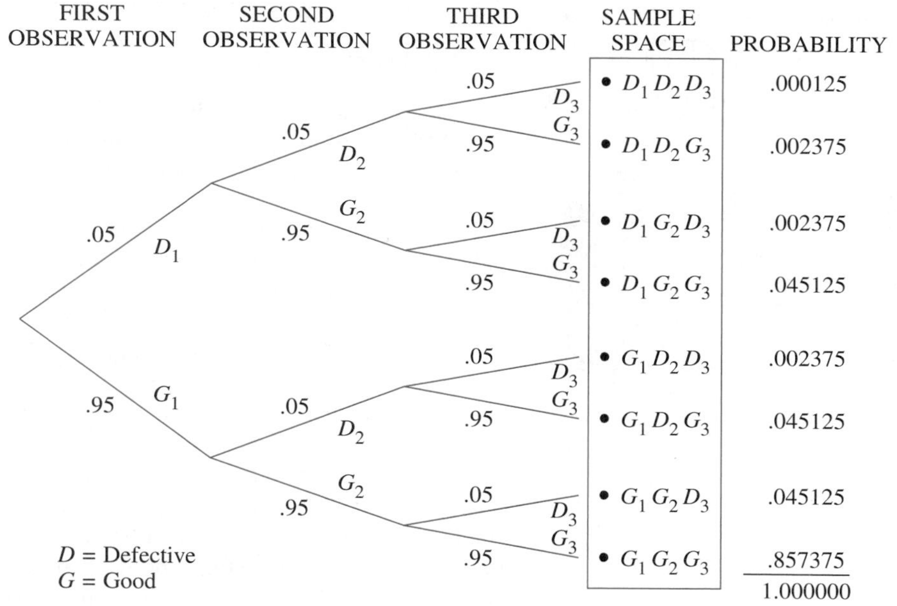

FIGURE 6-4 Probability tree for selecting a sample of three PC Boards with replacement.

nonreplacement would yield identical probabilities due to the theoretically infinite population size.

The probability distribution for the number of defectives found using sampling with replacement is given in Table 6-4. The probabilities are obtained in the same manner as before. To help compare the two procedures, the two sets of probabilities are given side by side.

The two sets of values are very close. As noted earlier, the probabilities computed for sampling without replacement involve cumbersome calculations, and they are often *approximated* using the cleanly computed values that strictly apply for sampling with replacement. The computations for both types of similar distributions can be streamlined. When there is replacement—or, more generally, when successive observations are independent—the *binomial distribution*

TABLE 6-4 Probability Distributions for the Number of Defective PC Boards

Number of Defectives	$Pr[R = r]$ for Sampling	
r	without Replacement	with Replacement
0	.8559988	.857375
1	.1380642	.135375
2	.0058752	.007125
3	.0000618	.000125
	1.0000000	1.000000

STATISTICS AROUND US

No Ball Bearing Is Exact

For use in large motors, precision 1-inch-diameter ball bearings must be machined to within a tolerance of .01 of an inch. Each bearing is assumed to be so nearly perfectly round that no measuring device can perceive otherwise.

Each bearing sold has been inspected at uniform temperature by using a pair of "go-no go" gauges (stands with holes through which a bearing being tested is dropped). The diameter of one hole is 1.01 inches, the other is .99 inch. Each bearing must be small enough to fall through the large gauge but not small enough to fall through the small gauge.

To determine how many of the 1 million bearings produced annually are precisely 1 inch in diameter, a more accurate measuring system must be established. A pair of gauges could determine if bearings were within a hundred-thousandth (.00001) of an inch of being exactly 1 inch in diameter, but only about 1,000 ball bearings would pass this test (assuming nearly equal frequency for all values between .99 and 1.01 inches). Bearings that passed this second stage of testing could be measured again with gauge blocks accurate to within a millionth of an inch. About 100 bearings would pass the test. Optical tests would filter out the majority of these bearings, leaving a handful to be measured even more accurately in a fourth stage. But how many would pass the fourth test? Would greater precision of measurement eliminate all of the bearings?

We cannot be certain whether one or more of the bearings would be precisely 1 inch in diameter, as the standard inch is presently defined and within our capability to measure it. But we can conclude that such ball bearings would be extremely rare. Consider the random selection of one bearing. Taking the diameter of the ball bearing as our random variable, we can conclude that the probability that it will be exactly 1 inch is so small as to be considered zero for all practical purposes.

(described in Section 6-5) applies. Using sampling without replacement in finite populations, the *hypergeometric distribution* (described in Chapter 22) would be applied.

DISCRETE AND CONTINUOUS RANDOM VARIABLES

Any random variable that can assume only integer (whole number) values is classified as **discrete**. An example is the variable for the number of arrivals. But some variables, such as those involving physical measurements or time, might assume any value over a continuous range of possibilities. Those random variables are classified as **continuous**.

Special difficulties arise when random variables do not assume a discrete number of possible values.

The dichotomy of discrete versus continuous random variables is important in probability theory because different mathematical procedures are used to describe the probability distributions of each. However, continuous and discrete random variables share many properties, and the more significant ones attributable to both can be explored using discrete examples.

EXERCISES

6-1 Shirley Smart has assigned the following probabilities for her final grades.

	A	B	C
Statistics	.2	.8	0
Finance	0	.4	.6
Accounting	.5	.5	0
Marketing	0	.2	.8

(a) List all possible elementary events for Shirley's grades.
(b) Assuming independence between courses, apply the multiplication law to determine the probability for each elementary event.
(c) The following grade points have been assigned.

A = 4 B = 3 C = 2

(1) Determine Shirley's total grade points for each elementary event in (a).
(2) Calculate the grade point average (GPA) for each event.
(3) Construct the probability distribution table for GPA X.

6-2 Refer to the personal computer example (pages 206–208). Suppose that the cost of the laser printer is reduced to \$700. Construct the new probability distribution table for total system cost.

6-3 For each of the following, describe a circumstance that would create a random variable.
(a) tomorrow's weather
(b) the sex of an unborn child
(c) the winner of the World Series

6-4 A GizMo Corporation inspector randomly selects three widgets from a production line assumed to yield 90% satisfactory (S) and 10% unsatisfactory (U) output. Assume successive quality events to be independent.
(a) Construct a probability tree diagram, identify all the elementary events in the sample space, and calculate the joint probability for each event.
(b) Determine the probabilities for the following number of unsatisfactory items.
(1) none (3) exactly 2 (5) at least 1
(2) exactly 1 (4) exactly 3 (6) at most 2

6-5 The point spread for tossing two fair dice is the difference between the number of dots showing on the upturned faces. Determine the probability distribution for this random variable. (You may refer to your answer to Exercise 5-7 to obtain the probabilities for the possible dice sums.)

6-6 DanDee Assemblers receives shipments of 50 widgets each from GizMo Corporation. Suppose that a particular shipment contains exactly 90%

satisfactory and 10% unsatisfactory widgets. A sample of three widgets is selected without replacement and the quality of each is determined.

(a) Construct a probability tree diagram, identify all the elementary events in the sample space, and calculate the joint probability for each event.

(b) Determine the probabilities for the following number of unsatisfactory items.

(1) none	(3) exactly 2	(5) at least 1
(2) exactly 1	(4) exactly 3	(6) at most 2

6-7 Refer to the faculty data in Figure 5-4 (page 180). A lottery is held to select the membership of a university grievance panel. Three persons will be selected. Determine the following probabilities.

(a) exactly 2 males will be selected

(b) at least 1 female will be selected

(c) all will be from the finance department

(d) at least 1 part-time instructor will be selected

6-8 "Craps" is a favorite gambling game in which a pair of six-sided dice are tossed. One way to place a bet is to "play the field," where the bettor places a bet with a complicated payoff, depending on which faces of the dice show. If a "field" number (defined by a sum value of 2 through 4 or 9 through 12) occurs, the player wins. If the roll of dice yields any other total, the player loses. A field gamble is further complicated by varying payoffs: 1 to 1 on all field numbers except 2 or 12; 2 to 1 on a 2; and 3 to 1 on a 12. A winning bettor keeps the original bet and is also paid winnings. A losing bettor forfeits the original bet.

(a) For a bet of $1, determine the probability distribution for W, the gambler's net winnings from one field bet in craps. (Refer to your answer to Exercise 5-7 to obtain the probabilities for the possible dice sums.)

(b) Solve (a) for a bet of $2.

6-2 EXPECTED VALUE AND VARIANCE

THE EXPECTED VALUE OF A RANDOM VARIABLE

A probability distribution is similar to the frequency distribution of a quantitative population because both provide a long-run frequency for each possible outcome. In Chapter 3, we saw that the population mean is a desirable summary for comparing populations or for making decisions about a population. It is also useful to find the average of the random variable values to be achieved from repeated circumstances. Because the outcomes are in the future, the average result is called an expected value.

In Chapter 3, we learned that an average can be calculated in several different ways. The computation that we will use to determine the expected value is analogous to the computation used to find the mean of grouped data.

DEFINITION: The **expected value** of a discrete random variable X, denoted by $E(X)$, is the weighted average of that variable's possible values, where the respective probabilities are used as weights.

$$E(X) = \sum x\Pr[X = x]$$

TABLE 6-5 Probability Distribution for the Number of Dots Showing on a Tossed Die

Possible Value x	Probability $Pr[X = x]$
1	1/6
2	1/6
3	1/6
4	1/6
5	1/6
6	1/6
	6/6 = 1

To illustrate how to calculate the expected value of a random variable, let X represent the number of dots on the upturned face after a six-sided die is tossed. The probability distribution for X is provided in Table 6-5. Multiplying each possible result by its corresponding probability produces a weighted value. Summing these results gives the expected value.

$$E(X) = 1\left(\frac{1}{6}\right) + 2\left(\frac{1}{6}\right) + 3\left(\frac{1}{6}\right) + 4\left(\frac{1}{6}\right) + 5\left(\frac{1}{6}\right) + 6\left(\frac{1}{6}\right) = \frac{21}{6} = 3.5$$

On the average, the number of dots obtained for a large number of tosses will be 3.5. Because it is the average value achieved by the random variable X, we sometimes refer to $E(X)$ as the *mean of X.*

The expected value has many uses. In a gambling game, it tells us what our long-run average losses per play will be. Sophisticated gamblers know that slot machines pay poorly in relation to the actual odds and that the average loss per play is less in roulette or dice games. A mathematician, Edward Thorp, caused quite a stir in the early 1960s when he demonstrated that various betting strategies in playing the card game of blackjack result in positive expected winnings.*

THE VARIANCE OF A RANDOM VARIABLE

Just as the expected value of a random variable is analogous to the weighted mean, the variability of random variables may be measured in much the same way as the variability in a population or a sample. The measure we will consider is the variance. Like the mean, the variance of a random variable represents the same thing that it does for the population: the average of the squared deviations from the mean or expected value.

DEFINITION: The **variance** of a discrete random variable X, denoted by $Var(X)$, is the average of the squared deviations from the expected value calculated using probability weights.

$$Var(X) = \sum [x - E(X)]^2 Pr[X = x]$$

**See* Edward Thorp, *Beat the Dealer*, Revised Edition (New York: Random House, 1966). Unlike other gambling games, blackjack allows bets to be placed when the odds are in a player's favor. This is because the card deck may not be reshuffled after each stage of play. By significantly raising bets at these times, a player will make a profit on the average.

As an example, again consider the roll of a six-sided die. Table 6-6 shows how the variance $\text{Var}(X) = 2.924$ is calculated for the number of dots on the upturned face.

The **standard deviation** of a random variable X, which we will abbreviate $\text{SD}(X)$, will have the same meaning as that of the population. It is found by taking the square root of the variance.

$$\text{SD}(X) = \sqrt{2.924} = 1.71$$

EXPECTED VALUE AND VARIANCE IN DECISION MAKING

Expected value often serves as the basis for decision making under uncertainty. A chief executive officer might use rates of return to evaluate various projects, selecting the one providing the greatest expected value. Investors must make evaluations similar to those of CEOs. To illustrate, consider two stocks having the following probability distributions for prices at the year's end.

ChipMont		Gotham Electric	
Price x	**$\Pr[X = x]$**	**Price y**	**$\Pr[Y = y]$**
$10	.10	$28	.20
20	.25	29	.20
30	.30	30	.20
40	.25	31	.20
50	.10	32	.20
	1.00		1.00

Although historical data are important in reaching the probability distributions used to make such evaluations, the greatest role is played by *judgment*. In business decision making, probability distributions typically involve *subjective* probabilities. Chapter 20 describes how these may be found.

If the choice is made solely on the basis of expected value, the two stocks are equally attractive, each having an expected price of $30.00. However, many investors would actually prefer Gotham Electric, concurring that it is less risky.

TABLE 6-6 Variance Calculation for Die Toss

(1) Possible Values of X x	(2) Probability $\Pr[X = x]$	(3) Deviation $x - E(X)$	(4) Squared Deviation $[x - E(X)]^2$	(5) Weighted Value [(2) × (4)] $[x - E(X)]^2 \Pr[X = x]$
1	1/6 = .167	−2.5	6.25	1.044
2	.167	−1.5	2.25	.376
3	.167	−.5	.25	.042
4	.167	.5	.25	.042
5	.167	1.5	2.25	.376
6	.167	2.5	6.25	1.044
				$\text{Var}(X) = 2.924$

TABLE 6-7 Expected Value and Variance Calculations for Future Stock Prices

ChipMont Price			Gotham Electric Price		
x	$x\Pr[X = x]$	$[x - E(X)]^2\Pr[X = x]$	y	$y\Pr[Y = y]$	$[y - E(Y)]^2\Pr[Y = y]$
$10	1.00	40.00	$28	5.60	0.80
20	5.00	25.00	29	5.80	0.20
30	9.00	0.00	30	6.00	0.00
40	10.00	25.00	31	6.20	0.20
50	5.00	40.00	32	6.40	0.80
	30.00 = $E(X)$	130.00 = Var(X)		30.00 = $E(Y)$	2.00 = Var(Y)

Assuming that each stock were bought for the same price, the loss potential for ChipMont is greater, as shown in Table 6-7.

The comparative risks of the two investments may be summarized by the respective *variances* (or standard deviations). We have the following.

ChipMont:	Gotham Electric:
$\text{Var}(X) = 130.00$	$\text{Var}(Y) = 2.00$
$\text{SD}(X) = 11.40$	$\text{SD}(Y) = 1.41$

Notice that the variance for Gotham Electric is $\text{Var}(Y) = 2.00$, while the variance for ChipMont is a much higher $\text{Var}(X) = 130.00$. The same conclusions may be reached by comparing standard deviations.

The variance is a common measure of risk. It is fundamental in some models of portfolio theory, which can be used in prescribing an investment strategy.

EXERCISES

6-9 Using Quant Jacques' probability distribution for personal computer cost (pages 206–208), calculate his expected system cost.

6-10 The following probability distribution table has been obtained for the number of telephone calls arriving at a Centralia Bell switching device during any given millisecond.

x	$\Pr[X = x]$
0	.37
1	.37
2	.18
3	.06
4	.02

Calculate the (a) expected value, (b) variance, and (c) standard deviation of X.

6-11 The following probability distribution table has been obtained for the number of requests Million Bank receives daily for credit verifications.

Number of Requests	Probability
0	.1
1	.2
2	.3
3	.2
4	.1
5	.1

Calculate the expected number of daily verification requests.

6-12 The following probability distribution table has been obtained for the number of customer arrivals during any given minute at a Beta Alpha supermarket.

Number of Arrivals	Probability
0	.1
1	.2
2	.3
3	.3
4	.1

Calculate the (a) expected value, (b) variance, and (c) standard deviation of the number of arrivals.

6-13 Consider the *sum* of the dots on the upturned sides after tossing a pair of fair dice. (Refer to the answer to Exercise 5-7.) Calculate the (a) expected value, (b) variance, and (c) standard deviation of the random variable.

6-14 Willy B. Rich wishes to buy a stock and hold it for one year in anticipation of capital gain. He has narrowed his choice to High-Volatility Engineering or Stability Power. Both stocks currently sell for \$100 per share and yield \$5 dividends. The following probability distributions for next year's price have been judgmentally assessed for each stock, where S_1 = selling price of High-Volatility Engineering and S_2 = selling price of Stability Power.

High-Volatility Engineering		Stability Power	
s	$\Pr[S_1 = s]$	s	$\Pr[S_2 = s]$
\$ 25	.05	\$ 95	.10
50	.07	100	.25
75	.10	105	.50
100	.05	110	.15
125	.10		1.00
150	.15		
175	.12		
200	.10		
225	.12		
250	.14		
	1.00		

(a) Calculate the expected prices for a share of each stock.
(b) Should Willy select the stock with the highest expected value? Discuss.

TABLE 6-8 Population Data and Calculations for Customer Arrivals at Checkout Counter

Number of Arrivals X	Frequency f	Relative Frequency f/n	Weighted Value $X(f/n)$	X^2	fX^2
0	18	.36	.00	0	0
1	18	.36	.36	1	18
2	8	.16	.32	4	32
3	3	.06	.18	9	27
4	2	.04	.16	16	32
5	1	.02	.10	25	25
6	0	.00	.00	36	0
	50	1.00	1.12		134

6-3 POPULATION PARAMETERS AND SAMPLING

Deductive statistics applies probability concepts to the process of sampling. It is appropriate when the sample elementary units are selected *randomly* from the population. In this section, we consider the probability distribution for the level of a quantitative variable pertaining to the selected unit.

POPULATION PARAMETERS

For quantitative populations, the most important parameters are the population mean μ and the population variance σ^2 (and its square root, the population standard deviation σ). The exact values for these parameters are not usually known, since for a variety of reasons discussed in Chapter 4, a census of the population data will not be made. Indeed, a major thrust of inferential statistics is drawing conclusions about the unknown population parameters based largely on the computed values of the sample counterparts.

To lay the foundation for drawing conclusions from the sample, we will now examine the sample results that *might* be obtained when the population is *known.* We illustrate this using an experimental population made by taking the 50 WaySafe market time intervals used earlier.

The first two columns of Table 6-8 provide the frequency distribution for the number of arrivals for this experimental population. With those data, the shortcut expressions are used to obtain the mean number of arrivals, using $n = 50$ as the number of observations.

$$\bar{X} = \sum X(f/n) = 1.12$$

Since all of the population data are represented, the above provides the true value for the population mean, and we have

$$\mu = 1.12$$

Similarly, the variance is computed,

$$s^2 = \frac{\sum fX^2 - n\bar{X}^2}{n-1} = \frac{134 - 50(1.12)^2}{49} = 1.4547$$

TABLE 6-9 Probability Distribution for Customer Arrivals during a Randomly Selected Time Interval

Possible Number of Arrivals x	$\Pr[X = x]$	$x\Pr[X = x]$	$x - E(X)$	$[x - E(X)]^2$	$[x - E(X)]^2\Pr[X = x]$
0	.36	.00	− 1.12	1.2544	.451584
1	.36	.36	− .12	.0144	.005184
2	.16	.32	.88	.7744	.123904
3	.06	.18	1.88	3.5344	.212064
4	.04	.16	2.88	8.2944	.331776
5	.02	.10	3.88	15.0544	.301088
6	.00	.00	4.88	23.8144	.000000
	1.00	$E(X) = 1.12$			$\text{Var}(X) = 1.425600$

Adjusting the above number, we obtain the true value of the population variance.*

$$\sigma^2 = \left(\frac{50 - 1}{50}\right) \times 1.4547 = 1.4256$$

The population standard deviation is

$$\sigma = \sqrt{1.4256} = 1.194$$

PROBABILITY DISTRIBUTION FOR A RANDOMLY SELECTED OBSERVATION

A randomly selected elementary unit should mirror the population from which it comes. Suppose that one of the original five-minute intervals is so chosen. The number of arrivals X for the interval is a random variable. The present example illustrates the following

RELATION: The value of an elementary unit randomly selected from a quantitative population is a random variable. Its expected value equals the population mean and its variance equals the population variance.

The probability distribution for the number of arrivals during a randomly selected time interval is provided in Table 6-9, where calculations are made for finding $E(X)$ and $\text{Var}(X)$. Probabilities are used in the same manner as class frequencies, and the values correspond. We find that $E(X) = 1.12$, $\text{Var}(X) = 1.4256$, and $\text{SD}(X) = 1.194$. These are the same values as the corresponding population parameters, so that

$$E(X) = \mu \qquad \text{Var}(X) = \sigma^2 \qquad \text{SD}(X) = \sigma$$

If the actual values for μ and σ were known, there would be little purpose in collecting a sample, since most of the essential population information would already be known! But whatever μ and σ are—even unknown quantities—it is always true that $E(X) = \mu$ and $\text{SD}(X) = \sigma$.

*Ordinarily, σ^2 is not computed at all, since the complete population is rarely observed 100% (as was the case here). Under the usual circumstances, s^2, computed from sample data only, is used unadjusted as an *estimate* of σ^2.

STATISTICS AROUND US

Auditing Accounts Receivable

Compu-Quik's accounts receivable balances constitute a population. One amount is selected *at random;* you can denote this uncertain quantity as X. Historically, it has been established that the mean balance is μ = \$137.50 and the standard deviation is σ = \$15.20. If these values apply presently, then the expected balance for the selected account is $E(X)$ = \$137.50, and the standard deviation is $SD(X)$ = \$15.20.

Of course, there may be no reason to assume that prior levels for μ and σ still apply.

EXERCISES

6-15 The following frequency distribution applies for a population formed by the number of defective floppy disks found in each of 100 batches.

Number of Defectives	Frequency
0	44
1	21
2	13
3	7
4	6
5	3
6	4
7	2

(a) Find the (1) population mean, (2) variance, and (3) standard deviation. (Multiply s^2 by .99 to get the properly adjusted value for σ^2.)

(b) One of the batches is selected at random. Specify the probability distribution for the number of defectives X in that batch.

(c) Using your probability distribution in (b), determine (1) $E(X)$, (2) $\text{Var}(X)$, (3) $SD(X)$.

6-16 The following frequency distribution applies for the number of absent employees found per day at a branch office of Big-M Corporation during a recent sales campaign.

Number Absent	Frequency
0	2
1	4
2	8
3	5
4	3
5	2
6	1

(a) Find the (1) population mean, (2) variance, and (3) standard deviation. (Multiply s^2 by .96 to get the properly adjusted value for σ^2.)
(b) One of the days is selected at random. Specify the probability distribution for the number of absent employees X during that day.
(c) Using your probability distribution in (b), determine (1) $E(X)$, (2) $\text{Var}(X)$, (3) $\text{SD}(X)$.

6-17 Refer to the probability distribution in Exercise 6-15. Determine the probabilities for the following numbers of defective floppy disks in the randomly selected batch.
(a) at most 7
(b) at least 2
(c) between 2 and 3, inclusively
(d) 4 or more

6-4 THE SAMPLING DISTRIBUTION OF THE MEAN

We are now ready to make the transition from probability theory to statistical planning and analysis. For now, we will assume that many details regarding the population are known, and we will study the kinds of *possible* results that may be obtained for samples taken from the population. Such a deductive viewpoint is not usually encountered in a real sampling situation, because the sample results are known and the population details are unknown. But if we know how sample results are generated and what values are likely, we can easily learn how to generalize about an unknown population from a known sample.

Estimating the population mean μ is an important inference. Usually, we would employ the corresponding sample mean $\bar{X}$ to make this estimate.

In the planning stage of a sampling study, before the data are collected, we can speak of $\bar{X}$ *only in terms of probability.* Its value is not determined and will depend on which particular elementary units happen to be randomly selected. Thus, before the sample results are obtained, $\bar{X}$ is a random variable. We emphasize that at one stage $\bar{X}$ is viewed as a random variable and later as a statistic whose value can be calculated from observed data. The probability distribution of $\bar{X}$ is of key importance. It is called a **sampling distribution**.

The basic concepts underlying the sampling distribution of $\bar{X}$ are illustrated in Figure 6-5. This distribution may be viewed as roughly analogous to the results that would be obtained if many different samples were taken and the sample mean $\bar{X}$ were calculated each time. In practice only one sample will ever be taken. Prob-

TABLE 6-10 Hypothetical Population of GMAT Scores

Name	GMAT Score
Chen	600
Jones	500
O'Hara	700
Sandor	600

$\mu = 600$

$\sigma^2 = 5{,}000$

$\sigma = \sqrt{5{,}000} = 70.71$

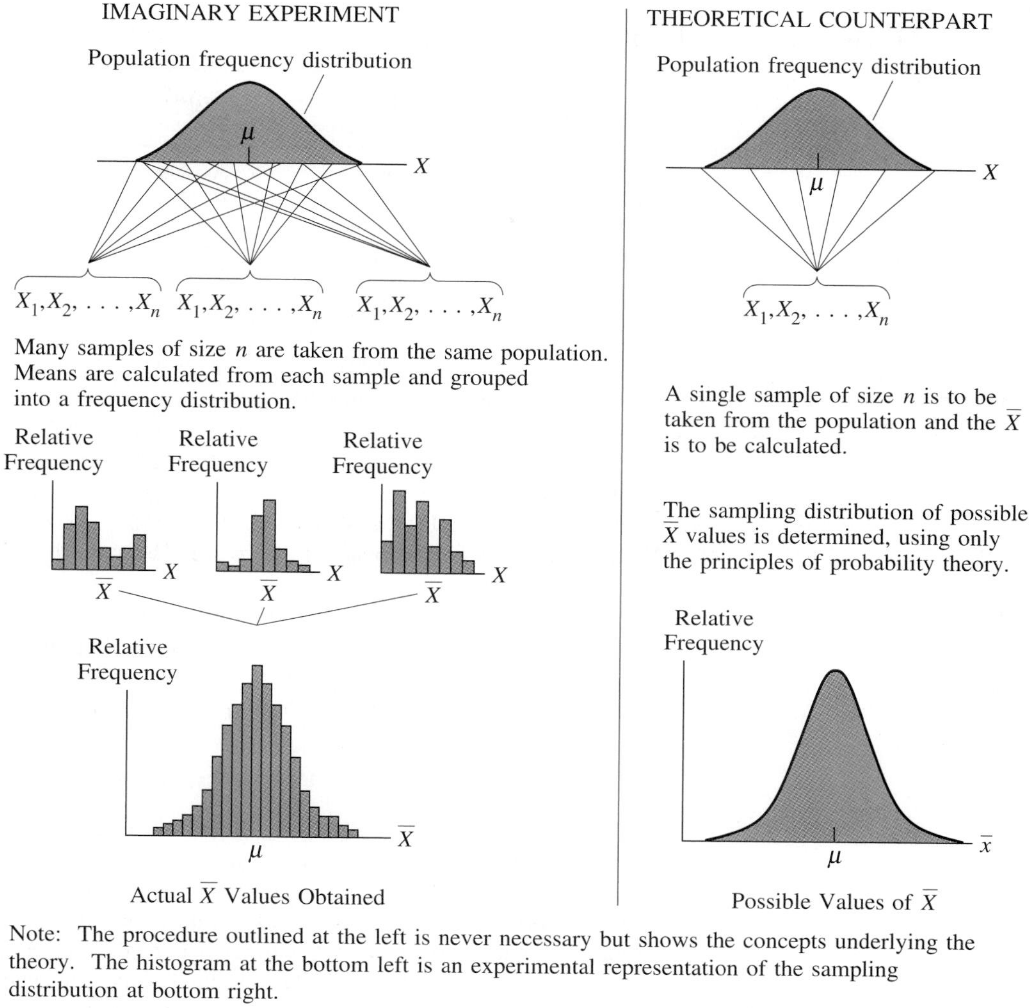
IMAGINARY EXPERIMENT
Population frequency distribution
μ
X
X1,X2, . . . ,Xn X1,X2, . . . ,Xn X1,X2, . . . ,Xn
Many samples of size n are taken from the same population. Means are calculated from each sample and grouped into a frequency distribution.
Relative Frequency
Relative Frequency
Relative Frequency
X
X̄
Relative Frequency
X̄
μ
Actual X̄ Values Obtained
THEORETICAL COUNTERPART
Population frequency distribution
μ
X
X1,X2, . . . ,Xn
A single sample of size n is to be taken from the population and the X̄ is to be calculated.
The sampling distribution of possible X̄ values is determined, using only the principles of probability theory.
Relative Frequency
μ
x̄
Possible Values of X̄
Note: The procedure outlined at the left is never necessary but shows the concepts underlying the theory. The histogram at the bottom left is an experimental representation of the sampling distribution at bottom right.

FIGURE 6-5 Interpretation of a theoretically derived sampling distribution.

ability concepts are used to establish the sampling distribution of $\bar{X}$, represented in the lower right-hand corner of Figure 6-5.

Next, we illustrate how probability concepts can be extended to finding the sampling distribution of the mean. As a matter of convenience, a tiny population is considered.

Table 6-10 shows the population of Graduate Management Admissions Test (GMAT) scores for four hypothetical Slippery Rock University seniors applying to the Harvard Business School. The population mean is $\mu = 600$ and the population variance is $\sigma^2 = 5{,}000$.* Suppose that Harvard will admit exactly two of

*When all the data are available from a population of size N, these are computed from

$$\mu = \frac{\sum X}{N} \qquad \sigma^2 = \frac{\sum (X-\mu)^2}{N}$$

TABLE 6-11 Possible Sample Results for Two GMAT Scores Selected without Replacement

Applicants Selected	GMAT Scores	Sample Mean $\bar{x}$
Chen, Jones	600,500	550
Chen, O'Hara	600,700	650
Chen, Sandor	600,600	600
Jones, O'Hara	500,700	600
Jones, Sandor	500,600	550
O'Hara, Sandor	700,600	650

these applicants by drawing their names from a hat. The scores of the two selected will be a random sample from the population of four.

Table 6-11 shows the six possible sample results and the corresponding values of the sample mean. We can easily determine the probabilities for each possible value. For example, the mean GMAT score for two potential samples is 600, so the probability of this result is 2/6 = 1/3. The sampling distribution of $\bar{X}$ is shown in Table 6-12.

The procedure illustrated serves primarily to establish the conceptual framework for understanding sampling distributions. Populations ordinarily involve too many units for us to catalogue possibilities. Chapter 7 provides a more direct method for establishing the sampling distribution of $\bar{X}$.

SAMPLING WITH AND WITHOUT REPLACEMENT

Our business school admissions illustration is an example of *sampling without replacement*: Once an elementary unit (an applicant) is selected for the sample, it has no chance of being selected again. *As a practical matter, statistics almost always involves sampling without replacement.* However, to help us understand some essential concepts, we will also consider *sampling with replacement,* in which every elementary unit has an equal chance of being selected for each successive observation. In this case, some population units may be represented more than once in the sample. Table 6-13 shows the possible sample results for randomly selecting two of the four GMAT scores when sampling with replacement. There are $4 \times 4 = 16$ equally likely outcomes.

A somewhat different sampling distribution applies depending on whether or not replacement is made. The sampling distribution for mean GMAT scores is given in Table 6-14 for the replacement case.

TABLE 6-12 Sampling Distribution of $\bar{X}$ for GMAT Scores Selected without Replacement

Possible Value $\bar{x}$	Probability $\Pr[\bar{X} = \bar{x}]$
550	1/3
600	1/3
650	1/3
	1

TABLE 6-13 Posssible Sample Results for Two GMAT Scores Selected with Replacement

Applicants Selected	GMAT Scores	Sample Mean $\bar{x}$	Applicants Selected	GMAT Scores	Sample Mean $\bar{x}$
Chen, Chen	600,600	600	O'Hara, Chen	700,600	650
Chen, Jones	600,500	550	O'Hara, Jones	700,500	600
Chen, O'Hara	600,700	650	O'Hara, O'Hara	700,700	700
Chen, Sandor	600,600	600	O'Hara, Sandor	700,600	650
Jones, Chen	500,600	550	Sandor, Chen	600,600	600
Jones, Jones	500,500	500	Sandor, Jones	600,500	550
Jones, O'Hara	500,700	600	Sandor, O'Hara	600,700	650
Jones, Sandor	500,600	550	Sandor, Sandor	600,600	600

Sample outcomes are statistically independent when sampling with replacement and statistically dependent when sampling without replacement. Whether or not sample outcomes are independent influences many statistical procedures that we will encounter later. For example, consider the population of the heights of all adult American males. If the height of the first man randomly selected for the sample is 7′, independence does not permit this height to influence the probability distribution for the height of any other man selected. But if the selection is made without replacement, selecting a man 7′ tall first will influence any probability for the second man's height.

No practical difficulty exists unless the population is small. For instance, if our population contains 1,000 men, exactly one of whom is over 7′ tall, then independence is violated when sampling without replacement. For a very large population, the degree of dependence will be so slight that it can be ignored. For the United States as a whole, the removal of one seven-footer from the population would not appreciably change the remaining proportion of persons who are 7′ tall, but in a small population it could seriously affect the sampling outcome.

AN EMPIRICAL APPROXIMATION OF THE SAMPLING DISTRIBUTION OF THE MEAN

The nature of the sampling distribution of the mean may be illustrated through an approximation involving a series of sampling experiments.

TABLE 6-14 Sampling Distribution of $\bar{X}$ for GMAT Scores Selected with Replacement

$\bar{x}$	$\Pr[\bar{X} = \bar{x}]$
500	1/16
550	4/16
600	6/16
650	4/16
700	1/16
	1

ILLUSTRATION: BASEBALL SUPERSTAR SALARIES

In recent years, salaries of baseball players have increased substantially. For the 1991 season, 127 players listed in Table 6-15 were paid salaries of at least \$2 million. From this population, separate random samples were selected, each having size $n = 10$.

The histograms in Figure 6-6 describe the experimental results. The top histogram portrays the complete population, which is bimodal. Beneath this histogram are those constructed from the data of the first three samples. Included are the respective values of $\bar{X}$ and s. Notice that the value of $\bar{X}$ varies from one sample to the next.

Altogether, 100 random samples were taken without replacement. All players had the same chance of being selected for the successive sample groups.The 100 separate sample means are collectively described by the histogram at the bottom of Figure 6-6. That histogram is the experimental counterpart to the sampling distribution of the mean.

Repeated samples, like those illustrated here, are not really necessary to establish the key features of the sampling distribution of $\bar{X}$. Certain properties of that distribution have already been established theoretically. The bottom histogram in Figure 6-6 illustrates those properties.

Notice that the $\bar{X}$s tend to *cluster tightly* about the value for μ and that their computed mean of 2,634.6 thousand dollars lies very *close* to the population mean of $\mu = 2{,}643.2$. Our intuition should suggest that:

TABLE 6-15 Salaries (thousands of dollars) of Baseball Superstars Earning at Least Two Million Dollars in 1991

1 Larry Anderson 2000	27 Chili Davis 2000	53 Mike Greenwell 2650	79 Fred McGriff 2750	105 Mike Scott 2337
2 Kevin Bass 2000	28 Eric Davis 3600	54 Kevin Gross 2217	80 Mark McGwire 2875	106 Ruben Sierra 2650
3 George Bell 2150	29 Glenn Davis 3275	55 Kelly Gruber 3033	81 Kevin McReynolds 2267	107 Bryn Smith 2133
4 Bert Blyleven 2000	30 Mark Davis 3625	56 Mark Gubicza 2667	82 Kevin Mitchell 3750	108 Lee Smith 2792
5 Mike Boddicker 3167	31 Storm Davis 2367	57 Pedro Guerrero 2283	83 Paul Molitor 3253	109 Lonnie Smith 2042
6 Wade Boggs 2750	32 Andre Dawson 3325	58 Tony Gwynn 2388	84 Jack Morris 3700	110 Ozzie Smith 2225
7 Barry Bonds 2300	33 Jose DeLeon 2367	59 Von Hayes 2200	85 Dale Murphy 2500	111 Zane Smith 2225
8 Bobby Bonilla 2400	34 Jim Deshaies 2100	60 Dave Henderson 2625	86 Eddie Murray 2562	112 Dave Stewart 3500
9 George Brett 3675	35 Bill Doran 2833	61 Rickey Henderson 3250	87 Randy Myers 2000	113 Dave Stieb 3000
10 Hubie Brooks 2317	36 Doug Drabek 3350	62 Tom Henke 2967	88 Pete O'Brien 2038	114 Darryl Strawberry 3800
11 Tom Browning 2650	37 Shawon Dunston 2100	63 Orel Hershiser 3167	89 Lance Parrish 2417	115 Rick Sutcliffe 2275
12 Tom Brunansky 2650	38 Len Dykstra 2217	64 Ted Higuera 2750	90 Tony Pena 2350	116 Greg Swindell 2025
13 Tim Burke 2328	39 Dennis Eckersly 3100	65 Danny Jackson 2625	91 Pascual Perez 2100	117 Danny Tartabull 2250
14 Brett Butler 2833	40 Chuck Finley 2500	66 Howard Johnson 2242	92 Dan Plesac 2267	118 Bobby Thigpen 2417
15 Ivan Calderon 2215	41 Nick Esasky 2100	67 Wally Joyner 2100	93 Kirby Puckett 3192	119 Alan Trammell 2200
16 Tom Candiotti 2500	42 Steve Farr 2400	68 Jimmie Key 2217	94 Tim Raines 3500	120 Andy Van Slyke 2160
17 Jose Canseco 3500	43 Sid Fernandez 2167	69 Mark Langston 3550	95 Jeff Reardon 2608	121 Frank Viola 3167
18 Joe Carter 3792	44 Tony Fernandez 2100	70 Barry Larkin 2100	96 Dave Righetti 2500	122 Bob Welch 3450
19 Jack Clark 3400	45 Carlton Fisk 2455	71 Charlie Leibrandt 2183	97 Jose Rijo 2613	123 Lou Whittaker 2000
20 Will Clark 3775	46 John Franco 2633	72 Craig Lefferts 2042	98 Cal Ripkin Jr. 2433	124 Dave Winfield 3750
21 Roger Clemens 2700	47 Julio Franco 2313	73 Greg Maddux 2425	99 Jeff Russell 2450	125 Mike Witt 2417
22 Vince Coleman 3113	48 Gary Gaetti 2700	74 Dennis Martinez 3348	100 Nolan Ryan 3300	126 Matt Young 2267
23 David Cone 2350	49 Kent Hrbek 2600	75 Don Mattingly 3420	101 Bret Saberhagen 2950	127 Robin Yount 3200
24 Kal Daniels 2025	50 Andres Galarraga 2485	76 Kirk McCaskill 2100	102 Ryne Sandberg 2725	
25 Ron Darling 2067	51 Scott Garrelts 2400	77 Roger McDowell 2200	103 Scott Sanderson 2175	
26 Danny Darwin 3250	52 Dwight Gooden 2467	78 Willie McGee 3563	104 Mike Scioscia 2183	

Source: *New York Times*

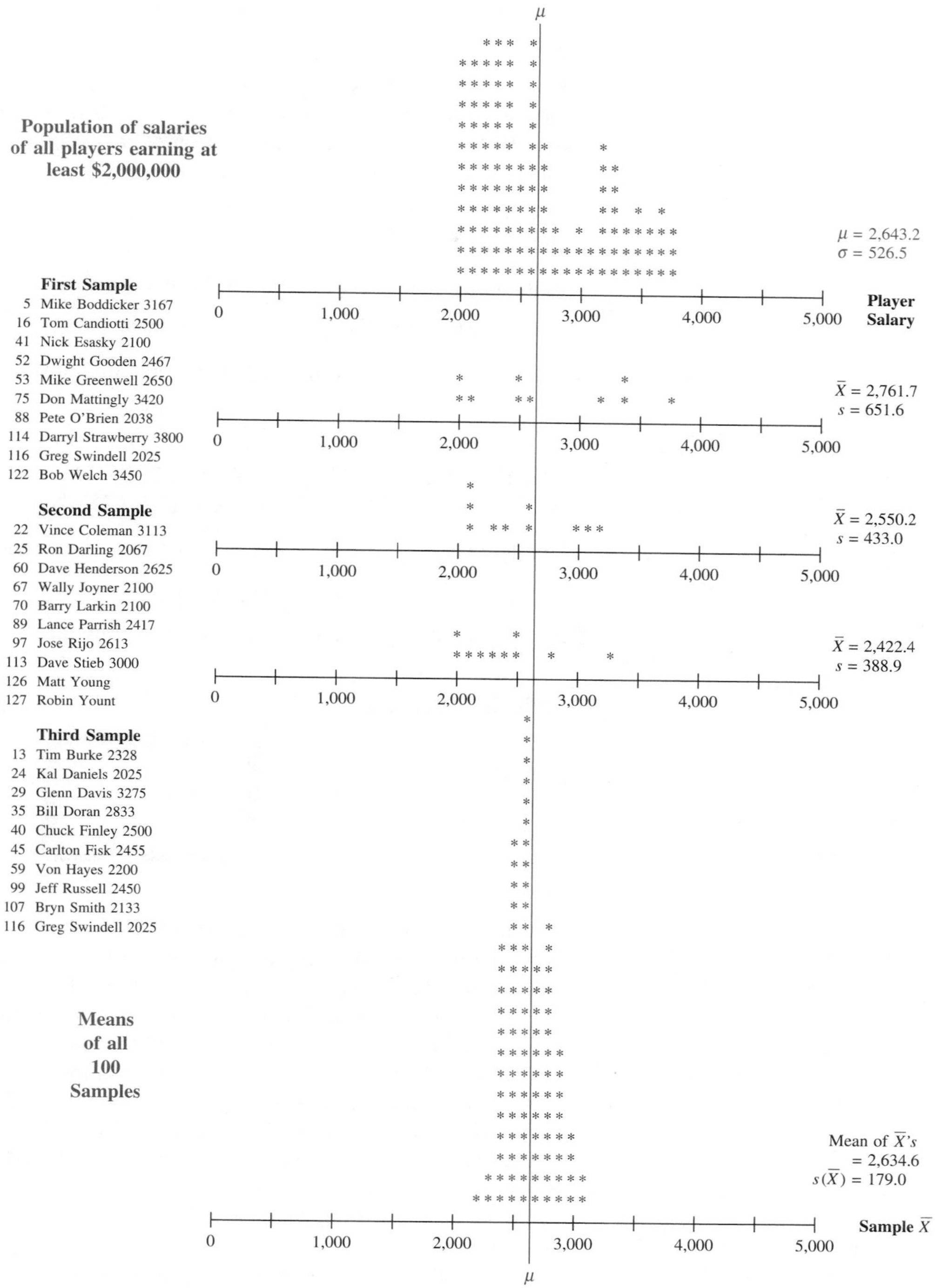
Population of salaries of all players earning at least $2,000,000
μ = 2,643.2
σ = 526.5
Player Salary
First Sample
5 Mike Boddicker 3167
16 Tom Candiotti 2500
41 Nick Esasky 2100
52 Dwight Gooden 2467
53 Mike Greenwell 2650
75 Don Mattingly 3420
88 Pete O'Brien 2038
114 Darryl Strawberry 3800
116 Greg Swindell 2025
122 Bob Welch 3450
X̄ = 2,761.7
s = 651.6
Second Sample
22 Vince Coleman 3113
25 Ron Darling 2067
60 Dave Henderson 2625
67 Wally Joyner 2100
70 Barry Larkin 2100
89 Lance Parrish 2417
97 Jose Rijo 2613
113 Dave Stieb 3000
126 Matt Young
127 Robin Yount
X̄ = 2,550.2
s = 433.0
X̄ = 2,422.4
s = 388.9
Third Sample
13 Tim Burke 2328
24 Kal Daniels 2025
29 Glenn Davis 3275
35 Bill Doran 2833
40 Chuck Finley 2500
45 Carlton Fisk 2455
59 Von Hayes 2200
99 Jeff Russell 2450
107 Bryn Smith 2133
116 Greg Swindell 2025
Means of all 100 Samples
Mean of X̄'s = 2,634.6
s(X̄) = 179.0
Sample X̄
0
1,000
2,000
3,000
4,000
5,000
μ

FIGURE 6-6 Histograms for salaries of high-income baseball players.

On the average, values of $\bar{X}$ should be close to the mean of their parent population.

Notice also that the standard deviation computed from the 100 $\bar{X}$s (each an average of 10 superstar salaries) is $S(\bar{X}) = 179.0$ thousand dollars, a *smaller* value than the population standard deviation of $\sigma = 526.5$ applicable to the individual salaries. This, of course, reflects that:

Sample $\bar{X}$ values tend to be less varied than individual population observations.

A final key point suggested by the $\bar{X}$ histogram is its profile:

The histogram for values of $\bar{X}$ resembles the shape of a bell curve.

The above findings are not accidental and are substantiated by statistical theory.

SOME THEORETICAL PROPERTIES OF THE SAMPLING DISTRIBUTION OF THE MEAN

The tendency of $\bar{X}$ to be close in value to μ is explained by *expected value.*

Expected Value of Sample Mean

For any sampling situation, we have the following relation for the

EXPECTED VALUE OF $\bar{X}$

$$E(\bar{X}) = \mu$$

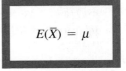

This conclusion is quite plausible. In effect, this expression says that the long-run average value of sample means is the same as the mean of the population from which the sample observations are taken. The rationale for this is simple. If $\bar{X}$ is calculated over and over for different samples taken from the same population, the successive sample means tend to cluster about the population mean. If a sample of 100 men is taken from a population where the mean height is $\mu = 5'10''$, the sample mean $\bar{X}$ is expected to be $5'10''$. This does not imply that $\bar{X}$ cannot be $5'9\frac{1}{2}''$, but *on the average* $\bar{X}$ will equal $5'10''$.

The sampling distribution found earlier for mean GMAT scores (using replacement and $n = 2$) is listed again in Table 6-15, where the expected value is computed to be $E(\bar{X}) = 600$, which equals the population mean of $\mu = 600$ established at the outset.

The variability for any probability distribution is summarized by its variance and standard deviation.

Standard Error of the Sample Mean

When a random variable is the yet-to-be computed value of a sample statistic, its standard deviation is usually referred to as its **standard error**. Because we use

TABLE 6-16 Expected Value and Standard Deviation of $\bar{X}$ for GMAT Scores Selected with Replacement

$\bar{x}$	$\Pr[\bar{X} = \bar{x}]$	$\bar{x}\Pr[\bar{X} = \bar{x}]$	$\bar{x} - E(\bar{X})$	$[\bar{x} - E(\bar{X})]^2$	$[\bar{x} - E(\bar{X})]^2\Pr[\bar{X} = \bar{x}]$
500	1/16	500/16	−100	10,000	10,000/16
550	4/16	2,200/16	−50	2,500	10,000/16
600	6/16	3,600/16	0	0	0
650	4/16	2,600/16	50	2,500	10,000/16
700	1/16	700/16	100	10,000	10,000/16
		$E(\bar{X}) = 600$			$\text{Var}(\bar{X}) = 2{,}500$

$$\sigma_{\bar{X}} = \text{SD}(\bar{X}) = \sqrt{2{,}500} = 50$$

it often, the standard error of $\bar{X}$ is represented by the special symbol $\sigma_{\bar{X}}$. The standard error of $\bar{X}$ is computed in Table 6-16 for the mean GMAT score to be

$$\sigma_{\bar{X}} = \text{SD}(\bar{X}) = 50$$

We have found that $E(\bar{X}) = \mu$. Similarly, $\sigma_{\bar{X}}$ relates to the population standard deviation. *When sampling with replacement or from large population,* we can use the following expression to calculate the

STANDARD ERROR OF $\bar{X}$

$$\sigma_{\bar{X}} = \frac{\sigma}{\sqrt{n}}$$

Both the population standard deviation σ and sample size n influence the level of $\sigma_{\bar{X}}$. In Table 6-9 we found that the population of GMAT scores had a standard deviation of $\sigma = 70.71$. In this illustration, $n = 2$, so that

$$\sigma_{\bar{X}} = \frac{70.71}{\sqrt{2}} = \frac{70.71}{1.414} = 50$$

which is the same value of $\sigma_{\bar{X}}$ calculated in Table 6-16 directly from the sampling distribution.

When samples are taken without replacement from small populations, $\sigma_{\bar{X}}$ does not equal $\sigma/\sqrt{n}$. In such cases, a canceling effect arises from the potential early selection of extremely large or small population values. In Chapter 7, we will learn how to correct for this.

EXERCISES

6-18 The following monthly incomes have been obtained from five residents of Dogpatch.

Identity	Income
Mr. A	\$1,000
Mrs. D	1,200
Mr. J	1,200
Ms. P	1,000
Miss R	900

A sample of two residents is randomly selected *without replacement.* Determine the sampling distribution of the sample mean.

6-19 The number of children in each of the five families who have won the California State Lottery is provided below.

Family	Number of Children
Chavez	2
Luke	5
Markowitz	3
Rogers	4
Williams	1

A sample of two families is randomly selected *without replacement.* Determine the sampling distribution of the sample mean.

6-20 Assume that the sample in Exercise 6-18 is selected *with replacement.*

(a) Determine the sampling distribution of the sample mean.

(b) Calculate the (1) expected value, (2) variance, and (3) standard deviation of the sample mean.

6-21 Refer to the data given in Exercise 6-19, repeat Exercise 6-20.

6-5 BINOMIAL PROBABILITIES: THE SAMPLING DISTRIBUTION OF THE PROPORTION

Until now, we have been considering the sampling distribution of the mean, which involves quantitative data. For qualitative populations, the *sample proportion P* is of primary interest, and at this point we will consider the sampling distribution of *P*. We will begin by describing the **binomial distribution**—one of the most important concepts in statistics. This distribution is concerned with the *number of outcomes* in a particular category.

To illustrate, consider an evenly balanced coin that is tossed fairly five times. The corresponding probability tree diagram appears in Figure 6-7, where the sample space is also listed. Our initial problem is to determine the probability for obtaining exactly two heads. As each of the 32 outcomes is equally likely, the basic definition of probability allows us to find the answer by counting the number of elementary events involving two heads and dividing this result by the total

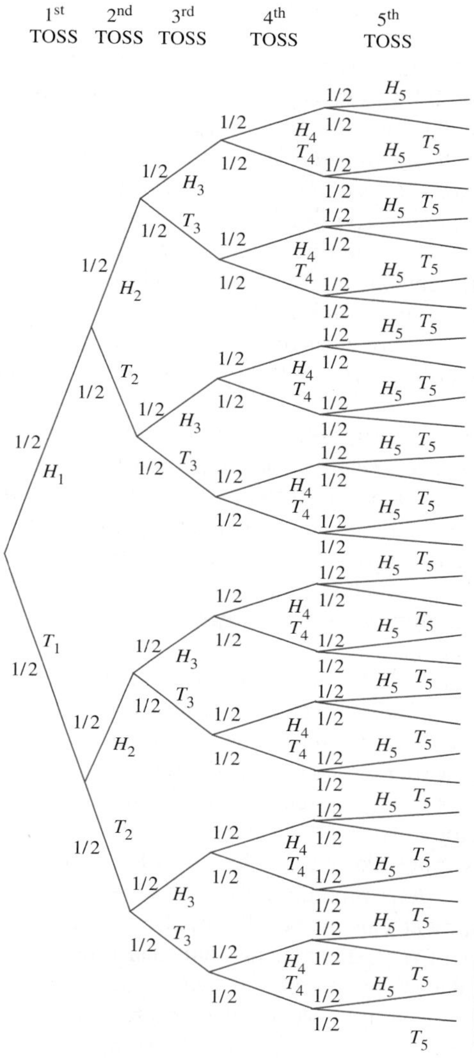

SAMPLE SPACE	PROBABILITY	NO. OF HEADS	TALLY 0	1	2	3	4	5
• $(H_1 H_2 H_3 H_4 H_5)$	1/32	5						*
• $(H_1 H_2 H_3 H_4 T_5)$	1/32	4					*	
• $(H_1 H_2 H_3 T_4 H_5)$	1/32	4					*	
• $(H_1 H_2 H_3 T_4 T_5)$	1/32	3				*		
• $(H_1 H_2 T_3 H_4 H_5)$	1/32	4					*	
• $(H_1 H_2 T_3 H_4 T_5)$	1/32	3				*		
• $(H_1 H_2 T_3 T_4 H_5)$	1/32	3				*		
• $(H_1 H_2 T_3 T_4 T_5)$	1/32	2			*			
• $(H_1 T_2 H_3 H_4 H_5)$	1/32	4					*	
• $(H_1 T_2 H_3 H_4 T_5)$	1/32	3				*		
• $(H_1 T_2 H_3 T_4 H_5)$	1/32	3				*		
• $(H_1 T_2 H_3 T_4 T_5)$	1/32	2			*			
• $(H_1 T_2 T_3 H_4 H_5)$	1/32	3				*		
• $(H_1 T_2 T_3 H_4 T_5)$	1/32	2			*			
• $(H_1 T_2 T_3 T_4 H_5)$	1/32	2			*			
• $(H_1 T_2 T_3 T_4 T_5)$	1/32	1		*				
• $(T_1 H_2 H_3 H_4 H_5)$	1/32	4					*	
• $(T_1 H_2 H_3 H_4 T_5)$	1/32	3				*		
• $(T_1 H_2 H_3 T_4 H_5)$	1/32	3				*		
• $(T_1 H_2 H_3 T_4 T_5)$	1/32	2			*			
• $(T_1 H_2 T_3 H_4 H_5)$	1/32	3				*		
• $(T_1 H_2 T_3 H_4 T_5)$	1/32	2			*			
• $(T_1 H_2 T_3 T_4 H_5)$	1/32	2			*			
• $(T_1 H_2 T_3 T_4 T_5)$	1/32	1		*				
• $(T_1 T_2 H_3 H_4 H_5)$	1/32	3				*		
• $(T_1 T_2 H_3 H_4 T_5)$	1/32	2			*			
• $(T_1 T_2 H_3 T_4 H_5)$	1/32	2			*			
• $(T_1 T_2 H_3 T_4 T_5)$	1/32	1		*				
• $(T_1 T_2 T_3 H_4 H_5)$	1/32	2			*			
• $(T_1 T_2 T_3 H_4 T_5)$	1/32	1		*				
• $(T_1 T_2 T_3 T_4 H_5)$	1/32	1		*				
• $(T_1 T_2 T_3 T_4 T_5)$	1/32	0	*					
Totals	32/32		1	5	10	10	5	1

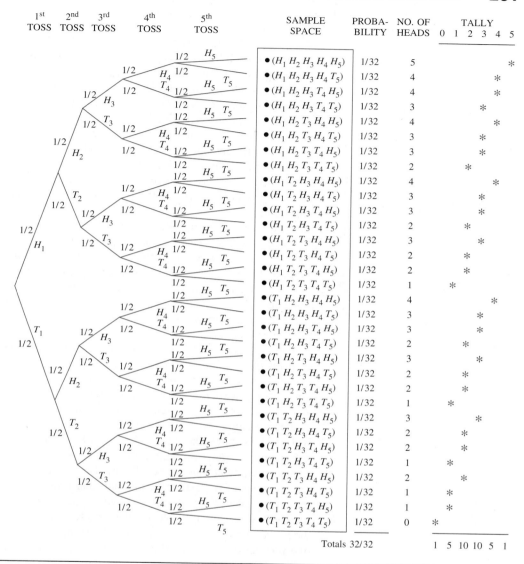

FIGURE 6-7 Probability tree diagram for five coin tosses.

number of equally likely elementary events. The sample space contains 32 elementary events, and Figure 6-7 shows that 10 of these are two-head outcomes. Thus, we can determine that

$$\Pr[\text{exactly two heads}] = \frac{10}{32}$$

It is impractical to list all possible outcomes unless there are only a few. For instance, if 10 tosses were to be considered, the list would contain 1,024 (2^{10}) entries. Before discussing a procedure to simplify finding such probabilities, it will be helpful to relate coin tossing to a similar class of situations.

THE BERNOULLI PROCESS

A sequence of coin tosses is one example of a **Bernoulli process**. A great many circumstances fall into the same category: All involve a series of situations (such as tosses of a coin) that are referred to as **trials**. For each trial, *there are only two possible complementary outcomes*, such as head or tail. Usually one outcome is referred to as a **success**; the other as a **failure**.

Examples include giving birth to a single child in a maternity hospital, where each birth is a trial resulting in a boy or a girl; canning a vegetable, where each trial is a full can that is slightly overweight or underweight (cans of precisely correct weight are so improbable that we can ignore them); and transcribing numerical data, where each completed data block is a trial that will either contain errors or be correct. In all these cases, only two opposite trial outcomes are considered.

What further distinguishes these situations as Bernoulli processes is that *the success probability remains constant* from trial to trial. The probability for obtaining a head is the same, regardless of which toss is considered; this is also true of the probability for delivering a girl for any successive birth in the maternity hospital, picking up an overweight can of vegetables, and receiving a correct data block each time. (The last condition would not hold if the operator tires over time; then the probability would be larger for an earlier block being correct than that for a later block.)

A final characteristic of a Bernoulli process is that *successive trial outcomes must be independent events*. Like a tossed coin, the probability for obtaining a success (head) must be independent of what occurred in previous trials (tosses). The births in a *single family* may violate this requirement if the parents use medical techniques to have a second child of the opposite sex of their first child. Or, a data operator's errors may occur in batches due to fatigue, so that once an error is made it is more likely to be followed by another.

Sampling to determine the impact of advertising, voter preference, or response to drug treatment can all be classified as Bernoulli processes. To preserve the requirements of independence and constant probability for success, we must sample with replacement, thereby allowing each person the same chance of being selected each time and perhaps of being selected more than once.* In each case, the probability for a trial success would be the proportion of persons in the respective population who would provide the desired response.

THE NUMBER OF COMBINATIONS

Now we will derive an algebraic expression for computing binomial probabilities. Looking at Figure 6-7 again, we see that 10 elementary events involve exactly two heads.

$$
\begin{array}{lll}
H_1H_2T_3T_4T_5 & T_1H_2H_3T_4T_5 & T_1T_2H_3H_4T_5 \\
H_1T_2H_3T_4T_5 & T_1H_2T_3H_4T_5 & T_1T_2H_3T_4H_5 \\
H_1T_2T_3H_4T_5 & T_1H_2T_3T_4H_5 & T_1T_2T_3H_4H_5 \\
H_1T_2T_3T_4H_5 & &
\end{array}
$$

*When sampling without replacement, a different probability distribution, the *hypergeometric distribution* (discussed in Chapter 22), should be used. In practice, when the population is large, the conditions of a Bernoulli process are very neatly met and the binomial distribution is acceptable.

Each of these outcomes represents one path of branches in the probability tree. They differ only in terms of which particular two tosses are heads.

If we want to find out the number of two-head outcomes without constructing an entire probability tree we can determine how many different ways there are to pick the two tosses to be heads from the total of five. It will help if each toss is represented by a fork.

Figure 6a
msp 263

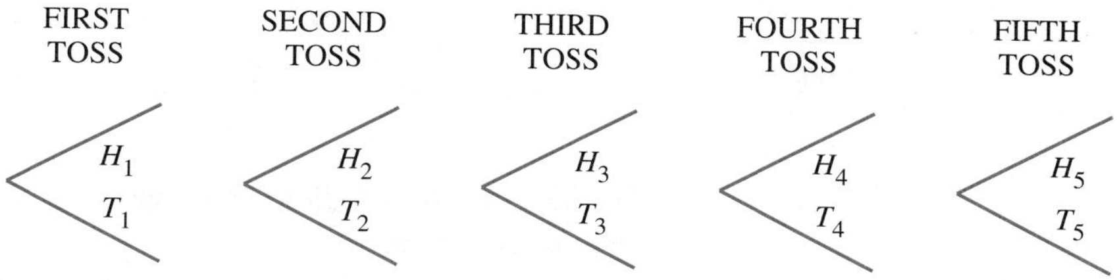

We want to save one branch from each fork. Two of the branches saved will be *H*s; three will be *T*s. Our problem is to determine how many ways there are to pick two *H* branches to save from the five.

If we pick the *H* branches one at a time, we have 5 possibilities for the first choice. No matter which *H* branch is chosen first, 4 *H* branch possibilities remain for the second choice. Multiplying the possibilities gives

$$5 \times 4 = 20$$

This answer is twice as large as it should be because the order of selection is considered. But we don't care whether an H_3H_5 resulted from H_3 being the first or the second choice, so we divide by 2 to avoid accounting for order of selection.

$$\frac{5 \times 4}{2} = 10$$

This calculation can be used to find the **number of combinations** of items for a variety of situations. It will be helpful if we re-express this fraction in the equivalent form

$$\frac{5 \times 4}{2} = \frac{5 \times 4}{2 \times 1} = \frac{5 \times 4 \times 3 \times 2 \times 1}{2 \times 1 \times 3 \times 2 \times 1} = 10$$

Multiplying both the numerator and the denominator of the middle fraction by 3, then by 2, and finally by 1 leaves the result unchanged. The final fraction contains factorial terms. A **factorial** is the product of successive integer values ending with 1. Such a product is denoted by placing an exclamation point after the highest number.

$$2! = 2 \times 1 \quad (= 2)$$

$$3! = 3 \times 2 \times 1 \quad (= 6)$$

$$5! = 5 \times 4 \times 3 \times 2 \times 1 \quad (= 120)$$

We define

$$1! = 1$$

$$0! = 1$$

In factorial notation, the number of two-head sequences in five coin tosses is

$$\frac{5 \times 4 \times 3 \times 2 \times 1}{2 \times 1 \times 3 \times 2 \times 1} = \frac{5!}{2!3!} = 10$$

This result suggests the general procedure for finding the

NUMBER OF COMBINATIONS: The number of combinations of *r* objects taken from *n* objects may be determined from

$$\frac{n!}{r!(n-r)!}$$

In our illustration, there are $n = 5$ tosses and we are considering exactly $r = 2$ heads occurring in those tosses. Thus, the number of two-head sequence combinations is

$$\frac{5!}{2!(5-2)!} = \frac{5!}{2!3!} = 10$$

THE BINOMIAL FORMULA

When the trial outcomes are the results of a Bernoulli process, the number of successes is a random variable having a binomial distribution. The following expression may then be used to determine the probability values. It is referred to as the

BINOMIAL FORMULA

$$\Pr[R = r] = \frac{n!}{r!(n-r)!}\pi^r(1-\pi)^{n-r}$$

where R = number of successes achieved
n = number of trials
π = trial success probability
$r = 0, 1, \ldots, n$

The binomial formula can be used to determine the probability we found earlier for obtaining $r = 2$ heads in $n = 5$ tosses of a fair coin. In this case, $\pi = \Pr[H] = \frac{1}{2}$ and $1 - \pi = \Pr[T] = \frac{1}{2}$, so that

$$\begin{aligned}\Pr[R = 2] &= \frac{5!}{2!(5-2)!}\left(\frac{1}{2}\right)^2\left(1 - \frac{1}{2}\right)^{5-2} \\ &= \frac{5!}{2!3!}\left(\frac{1}{2}\right)^2\left(\frac{1}{2}\right)^3 \\ &= 10\left(\frac{1}{2}\right)^5 = \frac{10}{32}\end{aligned}$$

The product involving 1/2 represents the probability for obtaining any one of the 10 two-head sequences shown in the probability tree in Figure 6-7. Each of these positions is reached by traversing a particular path of 2 head and $5 - 2 = 3$ tail branches. The probability for doing this may be obtained by applying the multiplication law. Since a two-head result can occur in any one of 10 equally likely ways, the addition law of probability tells us to add 10 of the identical product terms together or more simply to multiply by 10. The entire binomial distribution for the number of heads is given in Table 6-17.

Labeling one attribute the "success" is a completely arbitrary designation, but we must be sure to use the appropriate value of π. An interesting feature of the binomial formula is that it can also be used to obtain the probability that some number of failures will occur. For instance, the probability for obtaining exactly three tails in five tosses of the coin has the same value as the probability for obtaining two heads, because whenever there are two heads there must be three tails. In general, *when there are r successes, there must be n − r failures.*

TABLE 6-17 Binomial Distribution for the Number of Heads Obtained in Five Coin Tosses

Possible Number of Heads r	$\Pr[R = r]$
0	$\frac{5!}{0!5!}\left(\frac{1}{2}\right)^0\left(\frac{1}{2}\right)^5 = \frac{1}{32} =$ .03125
1	$\frac{5!}{1!4!}\left(\frac{1}{2}\right)^1\left(\frac{1}{2}\right)^4 = \frac{5}{32} =$ .15625
2	$\frac{5!}{2!3!}\left(\frac{1}{2}\right)^2\left(\frac{1}{2}\right)^3 = \frac{10}{32} =$ .31250
3	$\frac{5!}{3!2!}\left(\frac{1}{2}\right)^3\left(\frac{1}{2}\right)^2 = \frac{10}{32} =$ .31250
4	$\frac{5!}{4!1!}\left(\frac{1}{2}\right)^4\left(\frac{1}{2}\right)^1 = \frac{5}{32} =$ .15625
5	$\frac{5!}{5!0!}\left(\frac{1}{2}\right)^5\left(\frac{1}{2}\right)^0 = \frac{1}{32} =$ .03125
	1.00000

Different Bernoulli processes will have different binomial probability values. Note that the probabilities for all possible values of R depend on the value of π. Different sizes for n will result in a larger or smaller number of possible values for R and will also affect each probability value. *For purposes of calculating probabilities, one Bernoulli process differs from another only by the values of π and the sizes of n.*

IMPORTANT PROPERTIES OF THE BINOMIAL DISTRIBUTION

You should be aware of several important properties of the binomial distribution.

Binomial distributions apply to a family of random variables. Two parameters, n and π, determine which specific binomial distribution applies. It is convenient to view all possible distributions as a *family*, members of which are distinguished by the levels of n and π. An infinite number of members exist. Consider varying one parameter while the other is held fixed.

Role Played by the Trial Success Probability π

Figure 6-8 shows the probability distributions for several levels of π when the number of trials is held fixed at $n = 5$. Notice that there is a skewed spike pattern

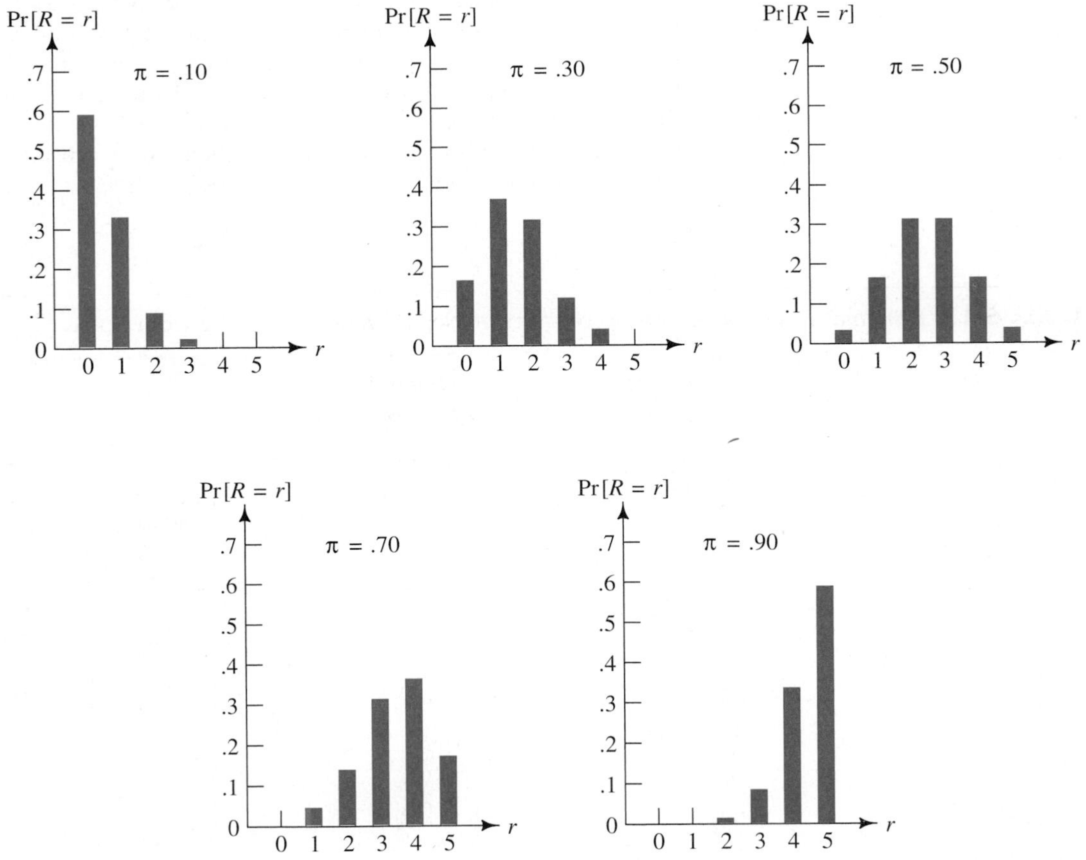

FIGURE 6-8 Binomial probability distributions for several levels of π, when $n = 5$.

except when $\pi = .50$. That symmetrical case applies to the series of coin tosses considered earlier. Notice also that complementary trial success probabilities, $\pi = .10$ and $\pi = .90$ or $\pi = .30$ and $\pi = .70$, have distributions that are mirror images.

EFFECT OF THE NUMBER OF TRIALS n

Figure 6-9 shows the binomial distributions for three levels of n when the trial success probability is fixed at $\pi = .20$. Notice how the spikes grow more numerous and become shorter as n increases. Notice also that the spike clusters take on progressively symmetrical patterns, becoming almost bell-shaped as n gets larger. This is an important feature that you'll learn more about in Chapter 7.

EXAMPLE: AIRCRAFT DELAY PROBABILITY

The Gotham City airport administrator wishes to determine the number of aircraft departure delays that are attributable to inadequate control facilities. A random sample of 10 aircraft takeoffs is to be investigated. If the true proportion of such delays in all departures is .40, what is the probability that 4 of the sample departures will be delayed due to control inadequacies?

SOLUTION: Letting a control-caused delay be a success, the trial success probability is equal to the proportion of such outcomes, so that $\pi = .40$. The probability

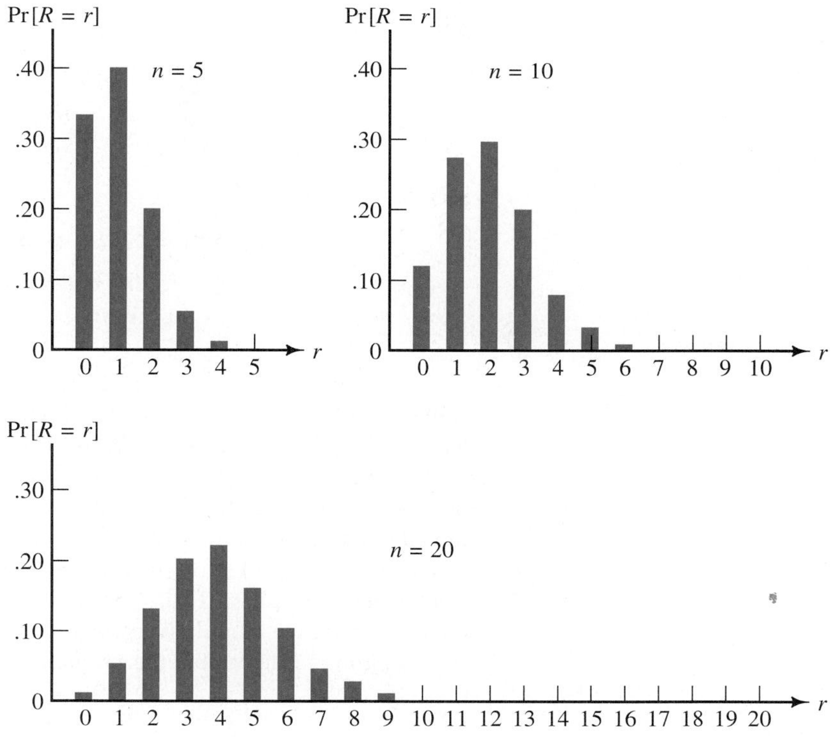

FIGURE 6-9 Binomial probability distributions for three levels of n, when $\pi = .20$.

for $R = 4$ control caused delays (successes), using the binomial formula when $\pi = .40$, $n = 10$, and $r = 4$, is

$$\begin{aligned}\Pr[R = 4] &= \frac{10!}{4!(10 - 4)!}(.40)^4(1 - .40)^{10-4} \\ &= 210(.40)^4(.60)^6 \\ &= 210(.0256)(.046656) \\ &= .2508\end{aligned}$$

The complete probability distribution is given in Table 6-18.

THE CUMULATIVE PROBABILITY DISTRIBUTION

Just as it can be convenient to deal with cumulative frequencies, which are readily determined from the population frequency distribution, we may wish to use **cumulative probabilities** for random variables. These can be simply obtained from the probability distribution for the number R of aircraft delays in the above example by creating column (3) for $\Pr[R \leq r]$, as shown in Table 6-18. The values in this column are obtained by adding all the preceding entries for the values of $\Pr[R = r]$. Thus,

$$\Pr[R \leq 0] = \Pr[R = 0] = .0060$$

and

$$\begin{aligned}\Pr[R \leq 1] &= \Pr[R = 0] + \Pr[R = 1] \\ &= .0060 + .0404 \\ &= .0464\end{aligned}$$

and

$$\begin{aligned}\Pr[R \leq 2] &= \Pr[R = 0] + \Pr[R = 1] + \Pr[R = 2] \\ &= .0060 + .0404 + .1209 \\ &= .1673\end{aligned}$$

The values in columns (1) and (3) constitute the **cumulative probability distribution** of the random variable R. The binomial probability distribution of R and the cumulative probability distribution of R are graphed in Figure 6-10. The cumulative probability value corresponding to any particular proportion value is obtained from the *highest point* directly above on the "stairway." For instance, the cumulative probability of values 5 or less is .8338 (not .6331, which belongs to the lower "step"). Note that the size of each step is the same as the height of the respective spike. Thus, the underlying probability distribution may be obtained from the cumulative probability distribution by finding these step sizes. For example, to determine the probability that $R = 5$, we find the difference

$$\begin{aligned}\Pr[R = 5] &= \Pr[R \leq 5] - \Pr[R \leq 4] \\ &= .8338 - .6331 = .2007\end{aligned}$$

TABLE 6-18 Probability Distribution for the Number of Aircraft Delays (n = 10 and π = .40)

(1) r	(2) $\Pr[R = r]$	(3) $\Pr[R \leq r]$
0	.0060	.0060
1	.0404	.0464
2	.1209	.1673
3	.2150	.3823
4	.2508	.6331
5	.2007	.8338
6	.1114	.9452
7	.0425	.9877
8	.0106	.9983
9	.0016	.9999
10	.0001	1.0000
	1.0000	

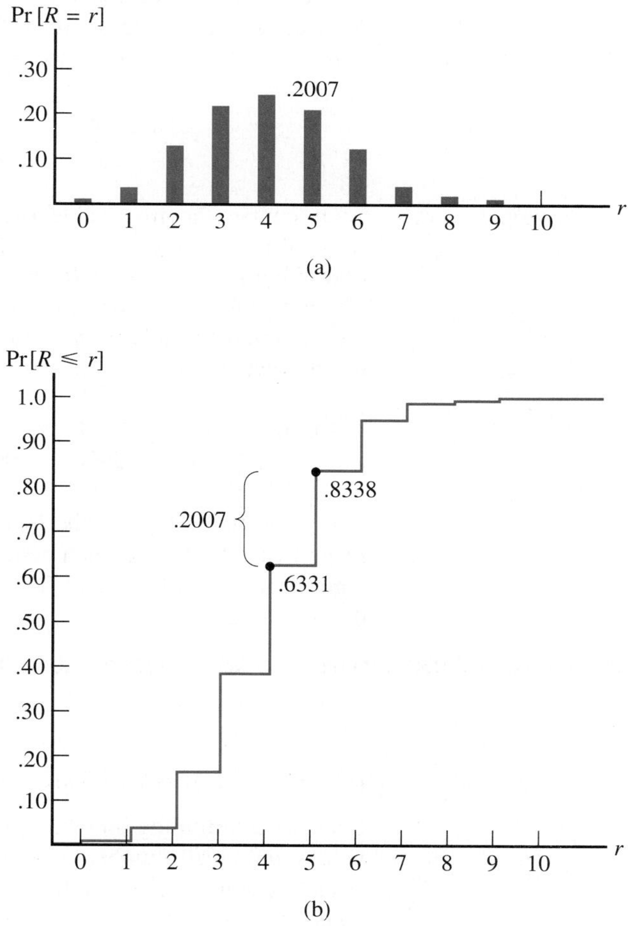

FIGURE 6-10 (a) Binomial probability distribution and (b) cumulative probability distribution (n = 10 and π = .40).

STATISTICS AROUND US

Brand Preference—Skinny Sip vs. Tummy Trim

A TipsiCola Bottling Company marketing researcher wishes to determine whether to recommend introduction of Skinny Sip, a new diet soda that will compete with HokeyCola's Tummy Trim. His final action depends on how high a proportion of the millions of potential customers will prefer Skinny Sip over the other brand.

Some information is provided by the number of sample test subjects R who have been found to prefer Skinny Sip. The researcher is satisfied that the binomial distribution closely approximates the true probabilities for R. The probability that a randomly selected person will prefer the brand equals the true population proportion π. Although that quantity is unknown, the following value might apply.

$$\pi = \Pr[\text{a subject prefers Skinny Sip}] = .40$$

The researcher administered a taste test to $n = 20$ subjects. Although the numbers are large, the binomial formula can be used to establish the probability that 12 of those subjects prefer Skinny Sip.

$$\Pr[R = 12] = \frac{20!}{12!8!}(.40)^{12}(1 - .40)^{8} = .0355$$

Of course the true value of π remains unknown. The actual sample resulted in 8 subjects preferring Skinny Sip. Consider how different levels of π affect the probability for getting that many or fewer positive responses. Using a probability table published by a statistician who originally applied the binomial formula with computer assistance, the researcher determined the following values.

Assumed value:	$\pi = .20$	$\pi = .30$	$\pi = .40$	$\pi = .50$	$\pi = .60$	$\pi = .70$
$\Pr[R \leq 8]$:	.9900	.8867	.5956	.2517	.0565	.0051

For $\pi = .50$ or higher, the probability is small that 8 or fewer positive responses would have been achieved. The researcher's sample evidence is consistent with a low level for π. Therefore, he doesn't recommend introducing Skinny Sip.

USING BINOMIAL PROBABILITY TABLES

Because determining binomial probabilities involves working with large factorial values and small numbers raised to large powers, it is convenient to have them already calculated. Appendix Table C provides cumulative binomial probability values computed for various sizes of n (with separate tabulations for several πs).

We use this table to compute probabilities for the number of successes in the variety of situations described in the following list. Suppose we wish to determine probabilities regarding the number of $n = 100$ patients who will respond favorably (success) to treatment with a new drug. We assume the drug will be successful 30% of the time, so that $\pi = .30$. To simplify our discussion, only a portion of Appendix Table C is reproduced below.

1. **Obtaining a result less than or equal to a particular value.** The probability that 20 or fewer patients will respond favorably is a cumulative probability value that may be read directly from the table when $r = 20$ successes.

$$\Pr[R \leq 20] = .0165$$

2. **Obtaining a result exactly equal to a single value.** Recall that cumulative probabilities represent the sum of individual probability values and are portrayed graphically as a stairway (see Figure 6-10). A single value

		$n = 100$		
	$\pi \cdots$	.20	.30	.40 $\cdots$
r	r/n			
⋮	⋮	⋮	⋮	⋮
19	.19	.4602	.0089	.0000
20	.20	.5595	.0165	.0000
21	.21	.6540	.0288	.0000
22	.22	.7389	.0479	.0001
23	.23	.8109	.0755	.0003
24	.24	.8686	.1136	.0006
25	.25	.9125	.1631	.0012
26	.26	.9442	.2244	.0024 $\cdots$
27	.27	.9658	.2964	.0046
28	.28	.9800	.3768	.0084
29	.29	.9888	.4623	.0148
30	.30	.9939	.5491	.0248
31	.31	.9969	.6331	.0398
32	.32	.9984	.7107	.0615
33	.33	.9993	.7793	.0913
⋮	⋮	⋮	⋮	⋮

probability may be obtained by determining the size of the step between two neighboring cumulative probabilities. For example, the probability that exactly 32 of the patients will respond favorably would be

$$\begin{aligned}\Pr[R = 32] &= \Pr[R \leq 32] - \Pr[R \leq 31] \\ &= .7107 - .6331 \\ &= .0776\end{aligned}$$

3. **Obtaining a result strictly less than some value.** The probability that fewer than 30 successes are achieved is the same as the probability that exactly 29 or fewer successes are obtained, or

$$\Pr[R < 30] = \Pr[R \leq 29] = .4623$$

4. **Obtaining a result greater than or equal to some value.** To determine the probability that at least 20 patients will respond favorably, we look up the cumulative probability that 19 or fewer will respond and subtract this value from 1.

$$\begin{aligned}\Pr[R \geq 20] &= 1 - \Pr[R \leq 19] \\ &= 1 - .0089 = .9911\end{aligned}$$

Note that the situation is similar when the result must be *strictly greater than* some value. Then, we determine the cumulative probability for r itself and subtract this from 1. For example, the probability that more than 20 patients will respond to treatment is 1 minus its complementary probability that 20 or fewer patients will respond, or

$$\begin{aligned}\Pr[R > 20] &= 1 - \Pr[R \leq 20] \\ &= 1 - .0165 = .9835\end{aligned}$$

5. **Obtaining a result that lies between two values.** Suppose we want to determine the probability that the number of successes will lie somewhere between 25 and 35, inclusively. Thus, we want to determine

$$\Pr[25 \leq R \leq 35]$$

In this case, we obtain the difference between two cumulative probabilities.

$$\Pr[R \leq 35] - \Pr[R \leq 24] = .8839 - .1136 = .7703$$

The first term on the left represents all outcomes of 35 or fewer successes. But we do not want to include outcomes of 24 or fewer successes, so we subtract the second cumulative probability from the first, thereby accounting for only outcomes of between 25 and 35 successes.

6. **Finding probabilities when the trial success probability exceeds .50.** For brevity, our binomial table stops at $\pi = .50$. If we wish to determine probabilities for the number of successes when the trial success probability is larger (say, .70), we can still use Appendix Table C by letting R represent the number of failures and π represent the trial failure probability.

   Consider a data operator who receives correct data blocks 99% of the time. Suppose we want to determine the probability that at least 95 of $n = 100$ blocks are correct. Here, a success represents a correct block and $\pi = .99$. At least 95 correct blocks is the same as 5 or fewer incorrect blocks (failures). Using $\pi = 1 - .99 = .01$ as the trial failure probability, from Appendix Table C we determine

$$\Pr[R \leq 5] = .9995$$

This makes use of the fact that for every success event there is a corresponding failure event with the same probability.

EXPECTED VALUE AND VARIANCE OF A BINOMIAL RANDOM VARIABLE

It's not necessary for you to use individual probabilities and take weighted averages to calculate $E(R)$ or $\text{Var}(R)$. It has been mathematically established that the following apply

$$E(R) = n\pi \quad \text{and} \quad \text{Var}(R) = n\pi(1 - \pi)$$

Returning to the coin toss illustration when $n = 5$ and $\pi = 1/2$, you have

$$E(R) = 5\left(\frac{1}{2}\right) = 2.5$$

so that you expect 2.5 heads whenever tossing a fair coin 5 times. That is, if you perform 5 tosses, repeating the experiment many times, you should come close to getting 2.5 heads for every 5 tosses.

Likewise,

$$\text{Var}(R) = 5\left(\frac{1}{2}\right)\left(1 - \frac{1}{2}\right) = 1.25$$

By taking the square root of this answer, you find that the standard deviation for the number of heads is

$$\text{SD}(R) = \sqrt{1.25} = 1.12$$

THE SAMPLING DISTRIBUTION OF THE PROPORTION

Often random samples are taken from qualitative populations. The sample proportion P of observations falling in a particular category may be used to estimate the population proportion π.

You can find the proportion of successes by dividing the number of successes by the number of trials.

$$P = \frac{R}{n}$$

The probability that P assumes any level can be determined by using the probability for the corresponding value for R. Consider the following table, which partially lists the binomial probability distribution for the number of defectives and the proportion of defectives found in a batch of $n = 100$ items arriving from a production line yielding 10% defective, so that $\pi = .10$.

Number of Defectives r	Proportion Defective r/n	Probability $Pr[R = r] = Pr[P = r/n]$
0	0	.0000
1	.01	.0003
2	.02	.0016
3	.03	.0059
4	.04	.0159
5	.05	.0339
6	.06	.0596
7	.07	.0889
8	.08	.1148
9	.09	.1304
10	.10	.1319
⋮	⋮	⋮

When sampling with replacement or when dealing with a large population, *the successive observations are trials in a Bernoulli process.* The probability that a particular observation is a "success" is equal to π. For example, if one-half the population is men, so that the overall proportion of men is $\pi = .50$, there is a .50 chance that any particular person selected at random will be a man. The binomial distribution provides probabilities for various possible levels for the sample proportion P of men observed.

On the average, P will equal π, even though it may differ for a particular sample. The following property applies for the

EXPECTED VALUE OF *P*

$$E(P) = \pi$$

P may turn out to be many possible values. As we did with $\bar{X}$, we may summarize the variability in the sample proportion by its standard deviation or standard error. The following expression, applicable whenever sampling with replacement or from large populations, provides the

STANDARD ERROR OF *P*

$$\sigma_P = \sqrt{\frac{\pi(1 - \pi)}{n}}$$

This expression tells us that the variability in P depends on both the level of the population proportion π and the sample size n.

As an illustration, suppose that a large population of voters is 80% Democrat ($\pi = .80$). A sample of size $n = 100$ is taken. If P represents the sample proportion of Democrats,

$$E(P) = .80$$

$$\sigma_P = \sqrt{\frac{.80(1 - .80)}{100}}$$

$$= \sqrt{\frac{.16}{100}} = .04$$

Knowing how to determine the values of $E(P)$ and σ_P will be quite helpful later when we consider a variety of statistical procedures.

The major obstacle to using the binomial distribution is that in sampling, the assumption of independence between trial outcomes is usually violated. Consider a random sample taken from a population of fixed size N. Unless sampling is done *with replacement* (rarely the case), the proportion of the remaining population having a particular attribute will change as each successive unit is removed and observed. This makes every observation or trial outcome statistically dependent on the earlier findings. The Bernoulli process doesn't strictly apply, and the binomial formula doesn't provide exactly proper probability values.

Another probability distribution, called the *hypergeometric* (which is related to the binomial), can provide exact probabilities when sampling *without replacement.* Unfortunately, that distribution (described in Chapter 22) is very cumbersome to use. However, as long as the population size N is large in relation to the sample size n, the binomial distribution provides a reasonably good approximation of the true probabilities.

EXERCISES

6-22 Calculate the following factorial products.

(a) 4! (b) 6! (c) 7! (d) 8!

6-23 Calculate the following quantities.

(a) $\frac{4!}{2!2!}$ (b) $\frac{6!}{3!3!}$ (c) $\frac{7!}{5!2!}$ (d) $\frac{6!}{2!4!}$

6-24 An evenly balanced coin is tossed fairly seven times.

(a) Determine the probability for obtaining (1) exactly two heads, (2) exactly four heads, (3) no tails, and (4) exactly three tails.

(b) What do you notice about your answers to (2) and (4)? Why is this so?

6-25 Can each of the following situations be classified as a Bernoulli process? If not, state why.

(a) The outcomes of successive rolls of a die, considering only the events "odd" and "even."

(b) A crooked gambler has rigged a roulette wheel, so that whenever the player loses, a mechanism is released that gives the player better odds;

whenever a player wins, the chance of winning on the next spin is somewhat smaller than before. Consider the outcomes of successive spins.

(c) The measuring mechanism that determines how much dye to squirt into paint being mixed occasionally violates the required tolerances. The mechanism is highly reliable when it is new, but, with use it continually wears, becoming less accurate. Consider the outcomes (within or not within tolerance) of successive mixings.

(d) A machine produces items that are sometimes too heavy or too wide to be used. The events of interest express the quality of each successive item in terms of both weight and width.

6-26 The proportion of consumers favoring a new product is $\pi = .70$. A sample of $n = 5$ persons is randomly selected. Use the binomial formula to determine the probabilities for the following number of consumers favoring a new product.

(a) exactly 5 (b) none (c) exactly 3

6-27 The following binomial probabilities have been obtained for the number of successes in $n = 10$ Bernoulli trials when the probability for success is $\pi = .49$.

r	$\Pr[R = r]$
0	.0012
1	.0114
2	.0495
3	.1267
4	.2130
5	.2456
6	.1966
7	.1080
8	.0389
9	.0083
10	.0008
	1.0000

Construct the cumulative probability table.

6-28 From a production process that yields 5% defectives, n parts are randomly selected. What is the expected proportion of defectives?

6-29 A consumer testing agency has contacted a random sample of $n = 50$ persons. The true proportion of all persons favoring a new package is $\pi = .30$. Assuming that the binomial distribution applies, use Appendix Table C to determine the probabilities for the following outcomes relating to the number of favorable responses R.

(a) $R \leq 11$ (c) $R < 18$ (e) $R > 25$
(b) $R = 15$ (d) $R \geq 20$ (f) $17 \leq R \leq 23$

6-30 A fair coin is tossed 20 times. Using Appendix Table C, determine the probabilities for the following number of heads obtained.

(a) less than or equal to 8 (d) greater than or equal to 12
(b) equal to 10 (e) greater than 13
(c) less than 15 (f) between 8 and 14, inclusively

6-31 The following probability distribution table has been obtained for P.

p	$Pr[P = p]$
.0	.59049
.2	.32805
.4	.07290
.6	.00810
.8	.00045
1.0	.00001

Calculate $E(P)$ as a weighted average. (Your answer should equal π, which is .10.)

6-32 The following probability distribution table has been obtained for values when $n = 5$ and $\pi = .70$.

p	$Pr[P = p]$
.0	.00243
.2	.02835
.4	.13230
.6	.30870
.8	.36015
1.0	.16807

Construct the cumulative probability distribution table for P.

6-33 The BugOff Chemical Company chief engineer has established a testing procedure using five sample vials drawn from the final stage of a chemical process at random times over a four-hour period. If one or more vials contain impurities, all the settling tanks are cleaned. Determine the probability that the tanks must be cleaned when the following probabilities of a dirty vial apply.

(a) $\pi = .01$ (b) $\pi = .05$ (c) $\pi = .20$ (d) $\pi = .50$

(*Hint:* Use the fact that Pr[at least one dirty vial] = 1 − Pr[no dirty vials].)

6-34 A process produces defective parts at a rate of .05. If a sample of five items is randomly selected, what is the probability that at least four of the sample will be defective?

6-35 A batch of 100 items in which 5% are defective is sampled *without replacement.* Five items are selected. Does the binomial distribution apply here? Explain.

6-36 A lopsided coin provides a 60% chance of a head on each toss. If the coin is tossed 20 times, determine the probabilities for obtaining the following number of heads.

(a) less than or equal to 8
(b) equal to 9
(c) less than 15
(d) greater than or equal to 12
(e) greater than 13
(f) between 8 and 14, inclusively

6-37 A DanDee Assemblers inspector accepts shipments of parts whenever two or fewer defectives are found in a sample of ten items tested. The following proportion of defectives apply.

(1) $\pi = .01$ (2) $\pi = .05$ (3) $\pi = .10$ (4) $\pi = .20$

(a) Calculate, for each case, the expected number of defectives.
(b) Determine, for each case, the approximate binomial probability for accepting a shipment.

6-38 The proportion π of defective spindles wound on automatic fiber-processing systems is unknown. An inspector requests equipment adjustments whenever one or more spindles are found to be defective in a sample of $n = 100$. Determine the probability for adjustment when the following assumptions apply.

(a) $\pi = .01$ (b) $\pi = .05$ (c) $\pi = .10$ (d) $\pi = .20$

6-6 CONTINUOUS PROBABILITY DISTRIBUTIONS

We will begin our discussion of continuous probability distributions by considering an uncertain situation involving the selection of a sample from a population. The frequency distribution obtained from grouping the years of company service of each of the 22,000 employees of the Wheeling Wire Works is given in Figure 6-11. The height of each bar of this histogram represents the relative frequency for duration of employment in the interval covered by the bar. The random variable of interest, denoted by X, is the length of service of one person randomly selected from the population. The time an employee has worked for the company can be measured on a continuous scale and therefore can be expressed to any desired fraction of the year. This makes X in our example a *continuous random variable*.

The probability that X lies within a particular class interval will be the same as the relative frequency of persons employed for that duration. Recall that the bars of the histogram for a relative frequency distribution have areas proportional to the relative frequency of the variate values in the corresponding interval. Since the relative frequencies must sum to 1, we can consider the total area under the histogram to be equal to 1. There, each class interval is one 5-year unit wide.

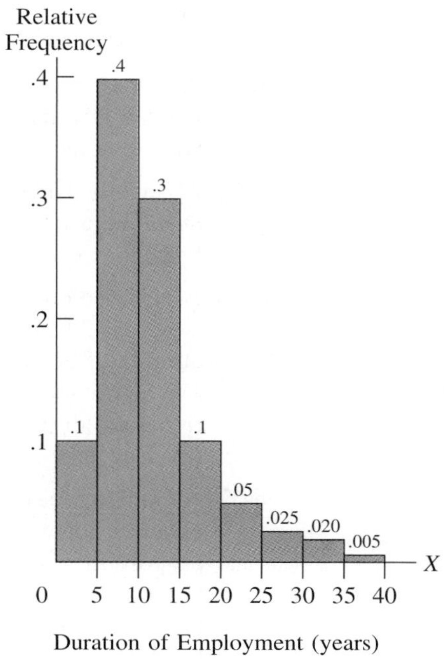

FIGURE 6-11 Frequency distribution for years of employment.

Thus, the probability that X lies inside a particular class interval is equal to the area of the bar covering that interval. Therefore, the probability that our employee served between 10 and 15 years must be .3 (the area under the bar or rectangle of the histogram that covers these values, or width $\times$ height $= 1 \times .3 = .3$).

But what if we want to consider an event that is more specific? For example, we may wish to determine the probability that our selected person was employed between 10.95 and 11.05 years—a range of values lying totally within a single class interval. In this case, the frequency distribution does not provide sufficiently detailed information for us to determine the probability directly.

SMOOTHED CURVE APPROXIMATION

Our problem arises from the fact that the histogram artificially forces us to treat population variates in discrete lumps. Each value is arbitrarily placed into one of very few class intervals. To accurately consider intervals of any width, we may construct a smoothed, continuous approximation to the histogram, like the one in Figure 6-12, where the curve is superimposed on the histogram from Figure 6-11. This approximation may then be used to generate any probability value we desire.

If the smoothed curve is drawn properly, the area under portions of the curve will correspond closely to the area of the histogram bars for that part of the horizontal axis, and the total area under the curve can also be taken as unity. Thus, in Figure 6-12, the shaded area under the portion of the curve covering the points between A and B is nearly the same as the corresponding area under the bar covering the values from A to B. Here, the curve has been drawn so that the wedge-

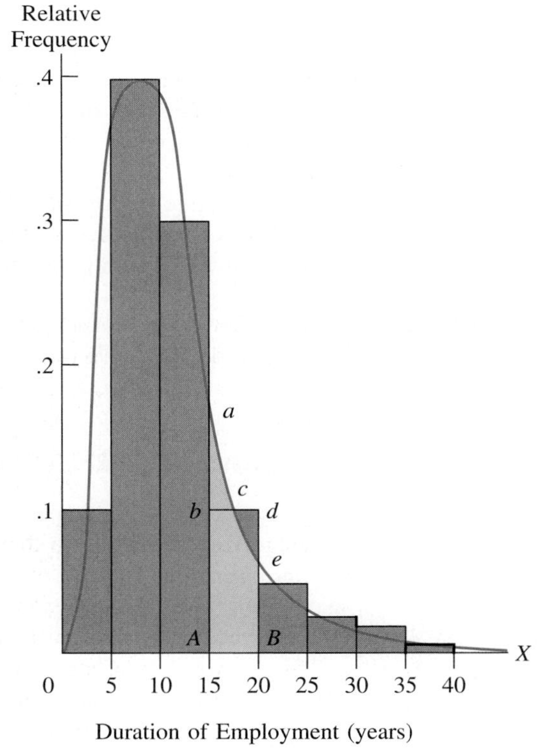

FIGURE 6-12 Frequency distribution from Figure 6-10 approximated by a continuous curve.

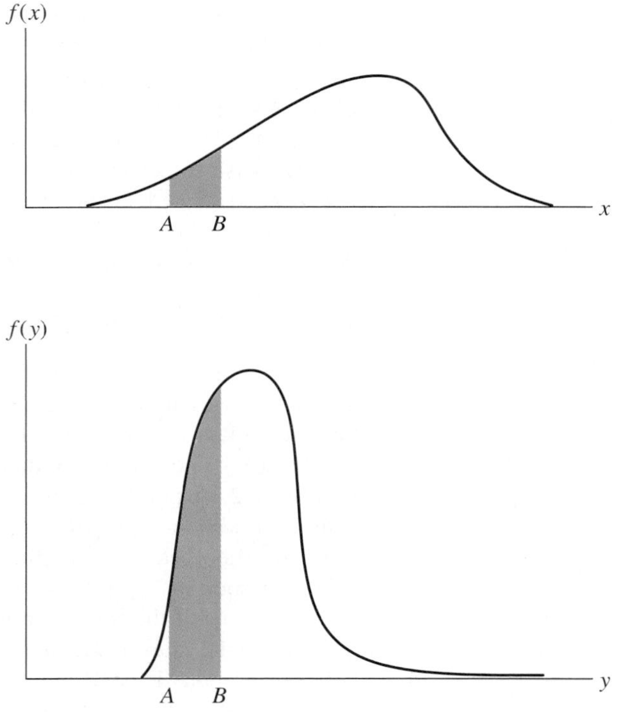

FIGURE 6-13 Two probability density function curves.

shaped area described by the points *a, b, c* is nearly the same as the area described by *c, d, e*. The sum of the areas for portions that are cut off the histogram by the curve should equal the sum of those areas that the curve adds by smoothing the corners.

The relative frequency of the population values lying between *A* and *B* in Figure 6-12 can be approximated by the area under the portion of the curve covering these values. We may therefore conclude the following

PROPERTY: The probability that a continuous random variable assumes some value in an interval is represented by the area under the portion of the continuous curve covering that interval.

PROBABILITY DENSITY FUNCTION

In Chapter 2, we learned that population frequency distribution graphs can be categorized according to their general shapes. We can construct smoothed curve approximations for any of these distributions. Essentially, we select a curve by choosing the appropriate shape.

Curves that have a particular shape can be defined by an equation or function. This allows us to group population frequency distributions according to the mathematical function that defines the curve corresponding most closely to the shape of the population histogram. If we know the function that defines the curve, we can mathematically calculate the area over an interval to obtain the required probability.

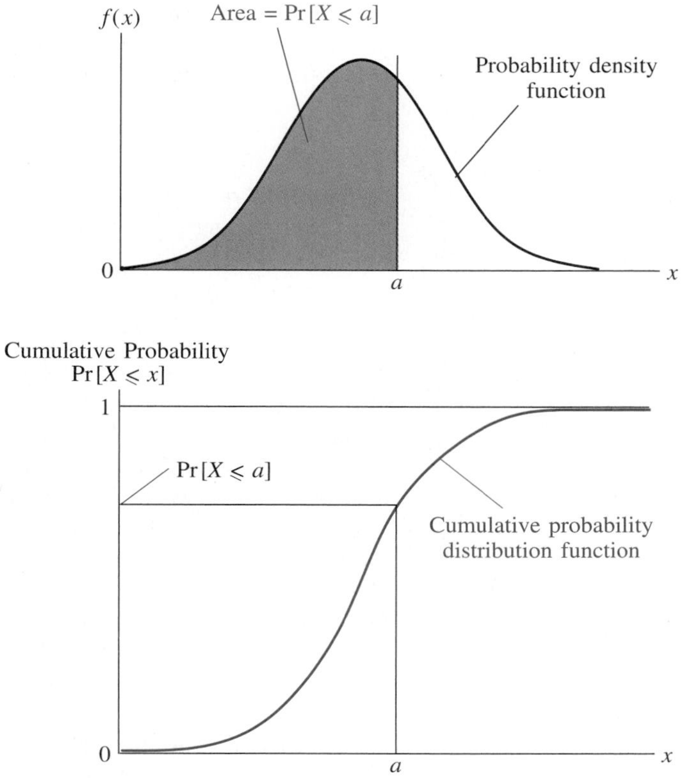

FIGURE 6-14 Graphical expressions of the probability distribution for a continuous random variable.

A unique set of probabilities is obtained from a particular curve. For example, consider the two curves in Figure 6-13 for two random variables, X and Y, whose values range over the same scale. The areas covering the values between points A and B are different for the two curves, because the shapes of the two curves are different. Thus,

$$\Pr[A \leq X \leq B] \neq \Pr[A \leq Y \leq B]$$

so that X and Y have different probability distributions. Note that the thickness or density of the two curves is distributed differently. For this reason, the mathematical expression describing such a curve is sometimes called a **probability density function**. In general, this function is denoted by $f(x)$, where x represents the possible values of the random variable X. The probability density function therefore describes the probability distribution for a continuous random variable, so that a random variable may be categorized by the form of its function.

CUMULATIVE PROBABILITY DISTRIBUTION

The graphic expressions of the probability distribution for a continuous random variable are presented in Figure 6-14. Although the cumulative probability distributions for discrete and continuous random variables are defined identically, the cumulative probability distribution for a continuous random variable resembles a smoothed curve (Figure 6-14) instead of a stairway (Figure 6-10). Both distributions may be expressed algebraically, graphically, or as a table of values.

It follows that for a continuous random variable,

$$\Pr[X \leq x] = \Pr[X < x]$$

because $\Pr[X = x] = 0$. (There is zero area under the portion of the density curve that covers a single *point*, since there is no width.)

THE EXPECTED VALUE AND THE VARIANCE

The expected value of a continuous random variable, like that of a discrete random variable, can be viewed as the long-run average of many repetitions. This is also true of the variance. Both the expected value and the variance can be calculated from the probability density function, but the calculations are beyond the scope of this book. These values have already been determined for the common distributions that we will encounter.

Random variables that have the same basic density function and differ only in terms of the values of the parameters specifying that particular function are said to belong to the same *distribution family*. In Chapter 7, we will discuss one of these families—the normal distribution. Other continuous probability distributions will be introduced in later chapters.

SUMMARY

1. **What is a random variable and its probability distribution?**
   An uncertain quantity whose value is subject to chance is a **random variable**. The set of possible variable values and their probabilities constitutes the **probability distribution** for the random variable. A probability distribution is sometimes graphed.

2. **What are the two basic types of random variables?**
   Discrete random variables are those that assume integer values. A second type is the **continuous** random variable, which may assume any value over a continuous range of possibilities.

3. **How do we obtain a probability distribution?**
   Probability distributions are founded on the basic concepts and laws of probability, and these may be used directly to determine individual probability values. A useful tool for constructing a group of probability distributions is the *probability tree diagram*. Probability trees can help determine the distribution for the number of *sample* units having a particular characteristic.

4. **How do result probabilities for sampling with replacement differ from those applicable to sampling without replacement?**
   An important statistical dichotomy is the way sample units are selected. Different probability values apply when **sampling with replacement** than when **sampling without replacement**. When the sample units are replaced prior to each successive selection, the characteristics of successive items are *statistically independent* events. When sampling without replacement, those events are dependent, unless the population size N is infinite.

5. **What are the expected value and variance of a random variable and how do we find and use them?**

Each random variable has a measure of central tendency, called its **expected value** $E(X)$. This quantity is found by taking a weighted average of the possible variable values, with their associated probabilities serving as weights.

$$E(X) = \sum x\Pr[X = x]$$

Two measures of dispersion, the **variance** Var(X) and the **standard deviation** SD(X), apply to any random variable.

$$\text{Var}(X) = \sum [x - E(X)]^2 \Pr[X = x]$$

$$\text{SD}(X) = \sqrt{\text{Var}(X)}$$

The standard deviation is the more useful of the two, because it does not distort the amount of variability.

6. **When sample results are represented as random variables, how do the expected value and variance relate to the parameters of the parent population?**
Expected value concepts apply to sampling, where each quantitative sample observation may be considered a random variable. The expected value and standard deviation for such an observation are equal to their population parameter counterparts.

7. **What are the characteristics of the sampling distribution of the mean?**
Before sample data are collected, the values of the sample statistics are random variables. The probability distributions for these variables are called **sampling distributions**. The sample mean $\bar{X}$ is a very important statistic. Its sampling distribution may be derived from the known characteristics of the population. Even if the population details are sketchy, the expected value of $\bar{X}$ must always be equal to the population mean μ. The standard deviation of $\bar{X}$ may be derived using the values for n (sample size) and σ (population standard deviation).

$$\sigma_{\bar{X}} = \frac{\sigma}{\sqrt{n}}$$

The quantity σ is usually referred to as the **standard error of $\bar{X}$**. The equation above is theoretically correct when sampling with replacement or when sample observations are statistically independent. Otherwise, it is approximately correct, as long as the population size N is large in relation to the sample size n.

8. **What is the binomial distribution?**
The **binomial distribution** provides probabilities for the number of "successes" (R) in a series of repeated random experiments or trials with only two possible outcomes. Those experiments where the binomial distribution applies are referred to as **Bernoulli processes**, and one example is a series of coin tosses. The requirements of a Bernoulli process are (1) there are just two complementary trial outcomes; (2) the probability of success must remain constant from trial to trial; and (3) successive trial outcomes must be statistically independent events.

9. **How are binomial probabilities computed?**
Binomial probabilities are computed using an algebraic expression called the **binomial formula**. It is easy to see from a probability tree why the formula works. However, it is so computationally cumbersome that in actual practice, tables of binomial probabilities are used instead. These are usually provided for composite groupings of events in terms of **cumulative probabilities** (of the form $R \leq r$).
There are two parameters that determine which particular member of the binomial distribution family applies. These are the **trial success probability** π and the **number of trials** n. Binomial distributions become progressively more skewed as π falls further above or below .5, the only level for that parameter for which the binomial distributions are symmetrical. As n gets larger, the graph of the mass functions has more numerous spikes that tend progressively toward a bell-shaped pattern. The expected value and variance of R, the number of successes, may be computed directly from expressions involving n and π.

$$E(R) = n\pi \quad \text{and} \quad \text{Var}(R) = n\pi(1 - \pi)$$

10. **What are the characteristics of the sampling distribution for the proportion?**
Perhaps the greatest importance of the binomial distribution is that it ordinarily represents the **sampling distribution of the sample proportion** P. That statistic is useful for investigations involving samples from qualitative populations. The binomial distribution usually only serves as an *approximation,* however, since random sampling typically violates the Bernoulli process assumptions of independence and constant trial success probability. That approximation is a good one if the population size N is large in relation to the sample size n.
The proportion of successes is the number of successes divided by the number of trials, $P = R/n$. The probability for any value r/n of P is equal to the probability for the counterpart value of R. The expected value of P is π, and the **standard error** of P is calculated

$$\sigma_P = \sqrt{\frac{\pi(1 - \pi)}{n}}$$

REAL-LIFE STATISTICAL CHALLENGE

Sampling from the Automobile Dream List

In Chapters 3 and 4 we calculated summary statistics and practiced taking random samples from a list of automobile models. Using the concepts of probability distributions we will explore other uses for this data set.

Table 4-2 lists 232 makes and models of automobiles, classified by type based primarily on size. These types include: two-seater, minicompact, subcompact, compact, midsize, and large. The table also gives model, manufacturer, type of

car, transmission type, engine displacement in liters and miles per gallon (highway). The transmissions were either manual (M) or automatic (A or L) and may have had different gear configurations (3, 4, 5 or 6 forward). The numbers in the first column are sequence numbers we use for our random sampling operations.

Using Appendix Table B, three samples of five automobiles each were drawn from the list of 232 autos. The results are listed in Table 6-19. A combined list for the 15 random sampled cars is shown in Table 6-20. The population parameters for engine displacement for all 232 are $\mu = 2.69$ liters and $\sigma = 1.23$ liters. The mileage parameters are $\mu = 27.48$ mpg and $\sigma = 6.23$ mpg.

DISCUSSION QUESTIONS

1. Consider the set of sample data in Table 6-19. Suppose 3 cars are picked at random from this list of 15. Determine the probability that at least two of the automobiles will have a manual transmission.
2. Use the second data list from Table 6-19 and determine the sampling distribution of the sample mean for mileage when sampling *two* automobiles from

TABLE 6-19 Three Random Samples of $n = 5$ for Mileage Data for 1990 Automobiles Showing Transmission Type, Engine Displacement (liters) and Highway Mileage per Gallon

Number	Type	Manufacturer	Model	Transmission Type	Engine Displacement in Liters	Highway Mileage Miles/gallon
0126	Subcompact	Subaru	XT	M5	1.8	31
0140	Compact	Chevrolet	Beretta	M5	3.1	28
0154	Compact	Mitsubishi	Galant	M5	2.0	29
0186	Mid-Size	Chrysler	New Yorker	L4	3.3	26
0213	Mid-size	Volvo	740	L4	2.3	26
					$\bar{X} = 2.50$	$\bar{X} = 28.00$
					$s = 0.67$	$s = 2.12$
0053	Subcompact	Chevrolet	Camaro	M5	5.0	26
0111	Subcompact	Mitsubishi	Eclipse	M5	1.8	32
0149	Compact	Isuzu	Stylus	M5	1.6	33
0151	Compact	Lexus	ES250	L4	2.5	25
0218	Large	Cadillac	Brougham	L4	5.7	21
					$\bar{X} = 3.32$	$\bar{X} = 27.40$
					$s = 1.90$	$s = 5.03$
0026	Minicompact	Maserati	222E	M5	2.8	20
0088	Subcompact	Geo	Prizm	L3	1.6	29
0178	Mid-Size	BMW	750i	L4	5.0	18
0185	Mid-Size	Chevrolet	Lumina	L4	3.1	30
0199	Mid-Size	Mazda	929	L4	3.0	23
					$\bar{X} = 3.10$	$\bar{X} = 24.00$
					$s = 1.22$	$s = 5.34$

Source: United States Environmental Protection Agency, 1989.

REAL-LIFE STATISTICAL CHALLENGE

this list of five cars. First assume you are sampling *without replacement*, then repeat the process by sampling *with replacement*.

3. Develop two examples based on all fifteen cars in Table 6-20 that apply binomial probability concepts. Determine the expected value and variance of R. Determine the expected value and standard error of P.

4. Determine the standard error of the mean, $\sigma_{\bar{X}}$, for the separate and the combined samples (Tables 6-19 and 6-20).

TABLE 6-20 Combined Random Sample of n = 15 for 1990 Automobiles.

Number	Type	Manufacturer	Model	Transmission Type	Engine Displacement in Liters	Highway Mileage Miles/gallon
0026	Minicompact	Maserati	222E	M5	2.8	20
0053	Subcompact	Chevrolet	Camaro	M5	5.0	26
0088	Subcompact	Geo	Prizm	L3	1.6	29
0111	Subcompact	Mitsubishi	Eclipse	M5	1.8	32
0126	Subcompact	Subaru	XT	M5	1.8	31
0140	Compact	Chevrolet	Beretta	M5	3.1	28
0149	Compact	Isuzu	Stylus	M5	1.6	33
0151	Compact	Lexus	ES250	L4	2.5	25
0154	Compact	Mitsubishi	Galant	M5	2.0	29
0178	Mid-size	BMW	750i	L4	5.0	18
0185	Mid-Size	Chevrolet	Lumina	L4	3.1	30
0186	Mid-size	Chrysler	New Yorker	L4	3.3	26
0199	Mid-Size	Mazda	929	L4	3.0	23
0213	Mid-Size	Volvo	740	L4	2.3	26
0218	Large	Cadillac	Brougham	L4	5.7	21
					$\bar{X}$ = 2.97	$\bar{X}$ = 26.47
					s = 1.31	s = 4.47

Source: United States Environmental Protection Agency, 1989.

REVIEW EXERCISES

6-39 The following probability distribution table has been obtained for the number of persons arriving at Shangrila Theater during any specified minute between 8 and 9 P.M.

Persons	Probability
0	.4
1	.3
2	.2
3	.1
	1.0

Calculate the (a) expected value and (b) variance of the number of persons arriving between 8:30 and 8:31 P.M.

6-40 Refer, once more, to the personal computer example (pages 206–208). Suppose that a third choice for a printer is allowed: the hybrid, at a cost of \$1,200. The new probabilities are .3 (matrix), .5 (laser), and .2 (hybrid). Suppose, also, that only the color monitor may be selected. Construct the probability distribution table for the total system cost.

6-41 The following probability distribution table has been obtained for the number of unsatisfactory widgets in a random sample.

x	$\Pr[X = x]$
0	.35
1	.39
2	.19
3	.06
4	.01

Calculate the (a) expected value, (b) variance, and (c) standard deviation of X.

6-42 The proportion of adult U.S. citizens who approve of presidential policy is $\pi = .50$. A sample of $n = 5$ persons is randomly selected. Use the binomial formula to determine the probabilities for the following number of citizens who approve.

(a) exactly 5 (b) none (c) exactly 3

6-43 An inspector for Yellow Giant Corn will remove a random sample of 100 cans. He is interested in the number R of overweight cans. The inspector assumes that 5% are overweight, so that $\pi = .05$ is the probability that any particular can is overweight. Determine the probabilities for the following outcomes.

(a) $\Pr[4 \leq R \leq 10]$ (c) $\Pr[2 \leq R \leq 11]$
(b) $\Pr[7 \leq R \leq 9]$ (d) $\Pr[9 \leq R \leq 11]$

6-44 Twenty percent of the cars leaving a Midget Motors automobile assembly line have defective brakes. A sample of $n = 4$ cars is randomly selected. Determine the probabilities for the following number of defective brake systems.

(a) 1 (b) 2 (c) 0

6-45 A chemical flow control device underfills 10% of all barrels. A sample of five barrels is randomly selected. Determine the probabilities for the following number of underfilled barrels.

(a) exactly 3 (b) exactly 2 (c) zero (d) at least 1

6-46 The ages of the straight-A students in Bill Bernoulli's statistics class are provided below.

Student	Age
Mr. C	24
Miss H	19
Mr. J	21
Mr. M	20
Mrs. T	23

A sample of two students is randomly selected *without replacement.*
(a) Determine the sampling distribution of the mean age $\bar{X}$.
(b) Using your answer to (a), calculate the (1) expected value, (2) variance, and (3) standard deviation of $\bar{X}$.
(c) Calculate the standard deviation of the age *population* of students. Multiply s^2 by .80 to get σ^2.
(d) Using your answers to (c), determine the standard error of $\bar{X}$ if the sample of two students is randomly selected *with replacement.*

6-47 A statistics class provided the following examination grades for five MBA students.

Name	Grade	Grade Points
Ann	B	3
Bob	C	2
Cal	B	3
Don	A	4
Eve	C	2

A sample of two students is randomly selected *without replacement.*
(a) Determine the sampling distribution for the mean number of grade points $\bar{X}$.
(b) Using your answer to (a), calculate, for $\bar{X}$, the (1) expected value, (2) variance, and (3) standard deviation.

6-48 Refer to the student grade point population in Exercise 6-47. A sample of $n = 2$ students is randomly selected without replacement. Construct a table for sampling distributions for the following random variables.
(a) the sample proportion of B's
(b) the sample range (largest value minus smallest value)

6-49 Refer to the student grade point population in Exercise 6-47. Construct a table of probabilities for the sampling distribution of the mean for *three* randomly selected values without replacement.

6-50 Dumpty-Humpty Disposal serves 100 industrial customers. Of these, 15 are delinquent (D) in paying their bills, and the rest are on time (O). An auditor randomly selects 3 accounts, one at a time without replacement. The subscripts 1, 2, and 3 denote the sequence in which the audited bills are selected.
(a) Determine the following probabilities.

(1) $\Pr[D_1]$ (3) $\Pr[D_2|D_1]$ (5) $\Pr[O_2|D_1]$
(2) $\Pr[O_1]$ (4) $\Pr[D_2|O_1]$ (6) $\Pr[O_2|O_1]$

(b) Determine the following probabilities.
(1) $\Pr[D_3|D_1 \textit{ and } D_2]$ (5) $\Pr[O_3|D_1 \textit{ and } D_2]$
(2) $\Pr[D_3|D_1 \textit{ and } O_2]$ (6) $\Pr[O_3|D_1 \textit{ and } O_2]$
(3) $\Pr[D_3|O_1 \textit{ and } D_2]$ (7) $\Pr[O_3|O_1 \textit{ and } D_2]$
(4) $\Pr[D_3|O_1 \textit{ and } O_2]$ (8) $\Pr[O_3|O_1 \textit{ and } O_2]$

STATISTICS IN PRACTICE

6-51 Use the master class data from Exercise 1-19.

(a) For one of your variables, determine the following probabilities for the results of three random selections *without replacement.*

(1) That at least 2 people will be selected that share the same characteristic (such as, liking Italian or Chinese food, gender, or age 21 or older).

(2) That exactly 3 people will be selected who do not have that characteristic.

(b) Using the first five people on your data list, select a quantitative characteristic (such as height or age). Determine the sampling distribution of the sample mean when sampling *two* individuals from this list of five people, assuming (1) sampling *without replacement* and (2) sampling *with replacement.*

(c) Develop two examples based on your data set that apply binomial probability concepts. Determine the expected value and variance of R. Determine the expected value and standard error of P.

6-52 Using your group's class data list developed in Exercise 1-21, repeat (a) through (c) of Exercise 6-51.

6-53 Using Exercise 6-1 as a guide, assign probabilities for *your* final grades in each of *your* classes. (Feel free to be optimistic about your grades. If you are taking only one or two classes add two or three more you expect to take in the next term or two.)

(a) List all possible events for your grades.

(b) Assuming independence between courses, apply the multiplication law to determine the probability for each elementary event.

(c) The following grade points have been assigned:

$$A = 4 \quad B = 3 \quad C = 2 \quad D = 1 \quad F = 0$$

(1) Determine total grade points for each elementary event in (a).

(2) Calculate the grade point average (GPA) for each event.

(3) Construct the probability table for GPA X.

6-54 Refer to the personal computer example on pages 206–208. (Note: The original problem uses simplified data for ease of computation.) Research the costs of two types of computer systems (computer and memory, printer, monitor). Typically these costs can be found in newspaper advertisements.In small groups of 3–5 students, assess the probabilities of purchasing each type (high/low memory, laser/nonlaser printer, color/monochrome monitor).

(a) List all the possible combinations.

(b) Construct the probability distribution table for total system cost.

(c) Determine the expected cost.

(d) Compare your results with those in the example.

6-55 Go to a local store or other retail outlet and determine a frequency distribution for the number of arrivals during each of several one-minute intervals. Be sure to ask permission of the store manager before you engage in this experiment. Assuming that your frequencies are representative, use them to construct a probability distribution for the number of arrivals during any minute. From your distribution, calculate the expected value, variance, and standard deviation. Comment on your results. Be sure to note the *time of day* and the *day of the week.*

CASE AlphaComp

AlphaComp is a specialized microcomputer manufacturer. Mark Wun, the head of procurement and quality assurance, needs to refine company policy regarding the disposal of shipments. To begin, Mark investigates two microcircuit chips: the customized-logic Z-1020 and the A-19, for harddrive controllers. The Z-1020 chips are shipped from a sole supplier in lots of 1,000 chips each. The A-19 chips are sent from a different source in lots of 50.

Mark contemplates two actions for all the microcircuit chip shipments: (1) accept the shipment and install all the chips untested or (2) reject the shipment, test all the chips, and eliminate the defective ones before installation. Accepting a shipment can be very costly, since defective chips will be identified in later system testing and will have to be removed from assembled computers. The late replacement cost is estimated to be \$25 for defective Z-1020s and \$100 for defective A-19s. Individual testing costs for a Z-1020 chip and an A-19 chip are \$2.00 and \$4.00, respectively. But, all of the chips in a rejected lot must be tested, so that the decision to reject a shipment is not necessarily cheaper. The suppliers will replace, for free, all the defective chips, whether or not they have first been installed.

Mark's current acceptance sampling plan for Z-1020 shipments is based on a sample of $n = 5$ chips randomly selected *without replacement.* If the number of sample defectives is 0, the Z-1020 shipment is accepted; otherwise, the shipment is rejected. A similar plan is used for shipments of A-19 chips, but a smaller sample of size $n = 3$ is selected. As for the Z-1020 chips, an A-19 shipment is accepted only when 0 defectives are found.

QUESTIONS

1. Two levels are possible for the proportion of defective chips found in a Z-1020 shipment: (1) $\pi = .05$ and (2) $\pi = .10$.
   (a) For each assumed level of π above, use the binomial distribution to determine the approximate probabilities for the number of defective chips found in a sample of Z-1020s.
   (b) For each level of π, determine the probability that a Z-1020 shipment will be accepted.
   (c) For each level of π, determine the probability that a Z-1020 shipment will be rejected.

2. Two levels are possible for the proportion of defective chips found in an A-19 shipment: (1) $\pi = .10$ and (2) $\pi = .20$.
   (a) For each assumed level of π above, determine the probability distribution for the number of defective chips found in a sample of A-19s. (*Hint:* The binomial distribution cannot be used. To start, construct for each case a probability tree diagram similar to Figure 6-3.)
   (b) For each level of π, determine the probability that an A-19 shipment will be accepted.
   (c) For each level of π, determine the probability that an A-19 shipment will be rejected.

3. Find the breakeven level for the proportion of defectives π found in a shipment of (a) Z-1020s and (b) A-19s. This will be the level for π at which the net cost for accepting a shipment is equal to that for rejecting. (For simplicity, ignore the cost of the sample.)

4. There is a 50% chance that the Z-1020 supplier will send shipments containing either exactly 5% or exactly 10% defectives. Mark has no way of knowing how many defectives a particular shipment contains. Calculate the expected cost for (a) accepting and (b) rejecting every shipment without the benefit of any sample evidence.

5. For a Z-1020 shipment, Mark wants to determine the expected cost of, first, conducting the sampling study and then using the sample results to determine a final action.
   (a) Refer to the probability results from Question 1 and assume that the two levels for π are equally likely. Find the missing values in the following table.

Proportion Defective	**Sample Result**	**Joint Probability**
$Pr[\pi = .05] =$ ____	$Pr[\text{Accept } (R = 0) \mid \pi = .05] =$ ____	$Pr[\pi = .05 \text{ and Accept}] =$ ____
$Pr[\pi = .05] =$ ____	$Pr[\text{Reject } (R > 0) \mid \pi = .05] =$ ____	$Pr[\pi = .05 \text{ and Reject}] =$ ____
$Pr[\pi = .10] =$ ____	$Pr[\text{Accept } (R = 0) \mid \pi = .10] =$ ____	$Pr[\pi = .10 \text{ and Accept}] =$ ____
$Pr[\pi = .10] =$ ____	$Pr[\text{Reject } (R > 0) \mid \pi = .10] =$ ____	$Pr[\pi = .10 \text{ and Reject}] =$ ____

   (b) Determine the expected cost of, first, conducting a sampling study and then using the results to determine whether to accept or reject a Z-1020 shipment. Find the missing values in the following table. Include the cost of the sample.

Proportion Defective	**Sample Result**	**Total Cost**	**Joint Probability**	**Cost × Probability**
$\pi = .05$	Accept $(R = 0)$	____	____	____
$\pi = .05$	Reject $(R > 0)$	____	____	____
$\pi = .10$	Accept $(R = 0)$	____	____	____
$\pi = .10$	Reject $(R > 0)$	____	____	____
			Expected sampling cost =	____

(c) Does sampling provide a lower expected cost than either of the two actions in Question 4?

6. Suppose that Mark raises the acceptance number from 0 to 1 sample defective for shipments of Z-1020 chips. Repeat Questions 5(a) and 5(b). Determine, separately, the joint probabilities and costs for $R = 0$ and $R = 1$ sample defectives. In the cases where sample defectives are found, the total cost must reflect the amount saved as a result of not having to remove the defective chips found before installation.

7. Suppose that Mark increases the sample size of Z-1020s to $n = 10$. Repeat Question 1(a).

8. Suppose that when $n = 10$ Mark would modify further his sampling scheme by raising the acceptance number to 2 sample defectives. Using the analogous ground rules given in Question 6, repeat Questions 5(a) and 5(b).

9. Refer to your answers to Questions 4–8. What might you conclude Mark should do before finalizing his choices of acceptance sampling plans?

CHAPTER 7

THE NORMAL DISTRIBUTION

BEFORE READING THIS CHAPTER, MAKE SURE YOU UNDERSTAND:

The difference between a sample statistic and a population parameter (Chapter 3).

The basic concepts of probability (Chapter 5).

About sampling distributions (Chapter 6).

AFTER READING THIS CHAPTER, YOU WILL UNDERSTAND:

About the properties of the normal distribution and why it is so important.

About the role played by *areas* under the normal curve and how these relate to *probabilities*.

How the *central limit theorem* enables us to use the normal curve to find probabilities for future levels of the sample mean.

How we may use the normal distribution to approximate probabities for future levels of the sample proportion.

The **normal distribution** may be the most important distribution used in statistical applications. The observed frequency distributions for many physical measurements and natural phenomena closely resemble the normal distribution. These include distributions for physical measurement, such as height and weight, as well as other human characteristics, such as IQ. The frequency distributions for these and many more populations closely resemble the **normal curve** in Figure 7-1. But there is a more fundamental reason why the normal distribution is so important in statistics. A theoretical property of the sample mean allows us to use the normal distribution to determine probabilities for various sample results. Thus, the normal curve plays a basic role when inferences are made regarding the population mean and only the sample mean can be calculated directly.

7-1 CHARACTERISTICS OF THE NORMAL DISTRIBUTION

Several features of the normal curve in Figure 7-1 are interesting. Note that the curve is shaped like a bell with a single peak, making it **unimodal**, and that it is **symmetrical** about its center. The mean of a normally distributed population lies at the center of its frequency curve. Due to symmetry, the median and the mode of the distribution also occur at the normal curve's center, so that the mean, median, and mode all have the same value. Although it is impractical to show this on the graph, the tails of a normal curve extend indefinitely in both directions, never quite touching the horizontal axis.

We say that a population with a frequency distribution approximating the shape of the normal curve is *normally distributed.* If the random variable X is the value of an elementary unit selected at random from a normally distributed population, then we say that X is normally distributed. The normal curve also represents the probability density function for X.* The normal curve depends on only two parameters: the mean μ and the standard deviation σ. Whatever the values of μ and σ are, the total area under the normal curve is always 1.

We know that the mean is a measure of central tendency or location. When normal curves for populations having different means are graphed together, they are located at different positions along the horizontal axis. This is illustrated in Figure 7-2 for three different populations with means of 30, 80, and 120, respectively.

Figure 7-2 also illustrates that the shape of a normal curve is determined by the population's standard deviation σ. Distributions with small standard deviations have narrow, peaked "bells," and those with large σs have flatter curves with less pronounced peaks. The three populations in Figure 7-2 have standard deviations of 5, 10, and 2, respectively. A large class of populations belong to the normal family, and each member differs only by its mean and its standard deviation.

The probability that a normally distributed random variable will assume values within a particular interval is equal to the area of the portion of the curve covering that interval. Before we learn to use a table to find the areas under the

*The function denoting the height of the curve is

$$f(x) = \frac{1}{\sqrt{2\pi\sigma^2}} e^{-[(x-\mu)^2/2\sigma^2]}$$

where π is the ratio of the circumference to the diameter of a circle (3.1416), and e is the base of natural logarithms (2.7183).

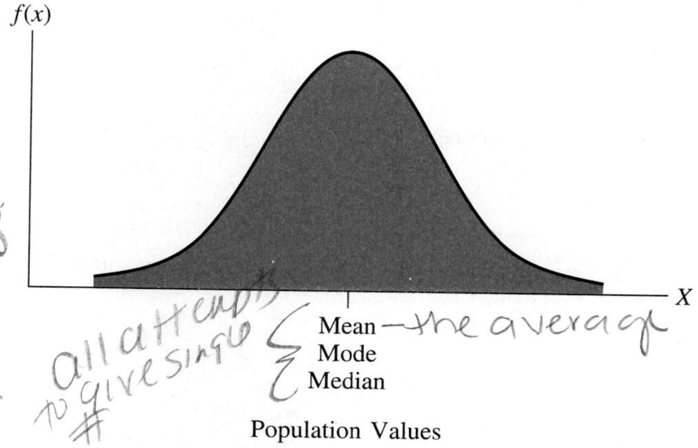

FIGURE 7-1 Frequency curve for the normal distribution.

normal curve, we should note a useful property of any normal distribution (see Figure 7-3).

PROPERTY: The area under the normal curve covering an interval that is symmetrical about the mean is determined solely by the distance that separates the end points from the mean, measured in standard deviations.

For instance, the values of about 68% of the population lie within one standard deviation in either direction from the mean, that is, the area under the curve over the interval $\mu - \sigma$ through $\mu + \sigma$ is .68. This is true no matter what the values of μ and σ are. The values of about 95.5% of the population lie within two standard deviations of the mean, and approximately 99.7% fall within three standard deviations.

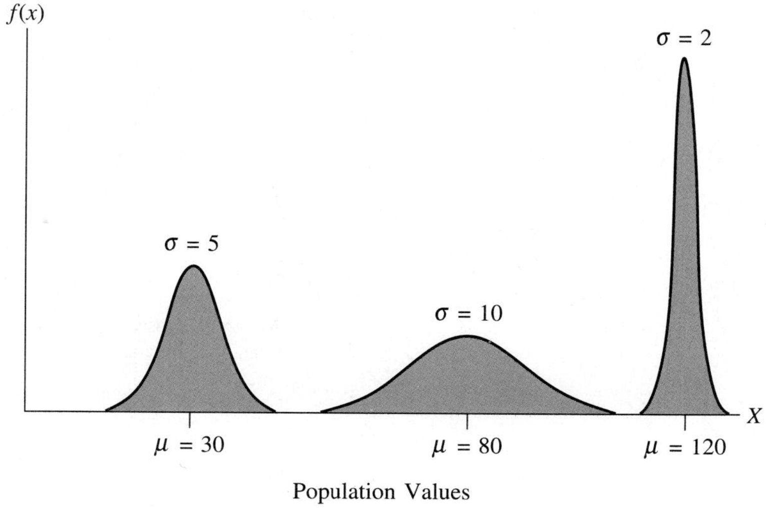

FIGURE 7-2 Three normal distributions graphed on a common axis.

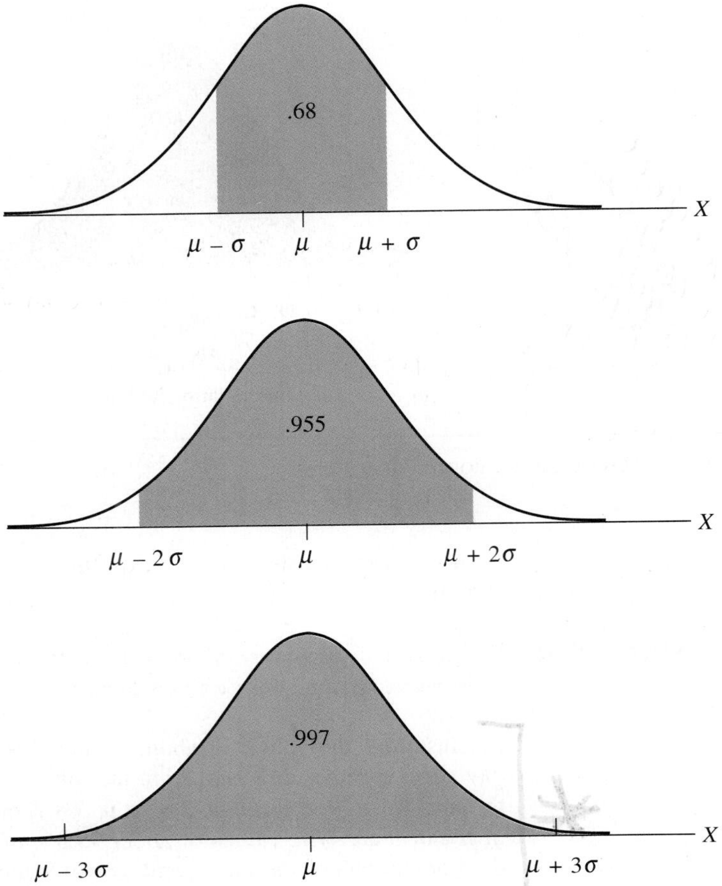

FIGURE 7-3 Relationship between the area under the normal curve and the distance from the mean, expressed in units of standard deviation.

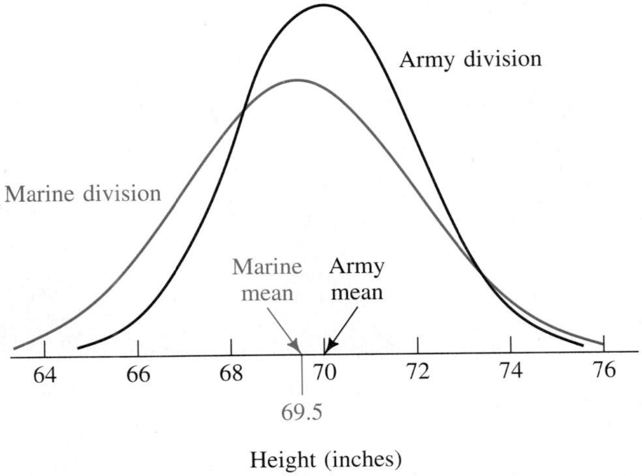

FIGURE 7-4 Normal curves for the heights of the marine and army divisions.

STATISTICS AROUND US

Are Marines Taller than Soldiers?

The commander of an army division has wagered with the commander of a marine division that his army troops are taller. To verify this, the army commander's aide compiles the heights of the army soldiers from their medical records and calculates that the mean height is 70 inches and the standard deviation is 2 inches. The aide also constructs a histogram, which exhibits an almost perfect bell shape, indicating that the heights of the soldiers may be described in terms of the normal distribution.

The marine commander arrives at similar conclusions. The mean height of his men is 69.5 inches, with a standard deviation of 2.5 inches. The two populations are compared in the following table. Figure 7-4 shows the frequency curves for these two populations.

	Army Heights	Marine Heights
Mean (μ)	70 inches	69.5 inches
Standard deviation (σ)	2	2.5
68% from $\mu - \sigma$ to $\mu + \sigma$	68 to 72	67 to 72
95.5% from $\mu - 2\sigma$ to $\mu + 2\sigma$	66 to 74	64.5 to 74.5
99.7% from $\mu - 3\sigma$ to $\mu + 3\sigma$	64 to 76	62 to 77

The army commander claims to have won the bet, because the mean height of the army soldiers is .5 inch greater than the mean marine height. The marine commander objects, noting that his division contains a greater percentage of overly tall men. (Note that the upper tail of the marines' frequency curve lies above the army division's curve.) The army commander agrees but retorts that there is also a higher percentage of shorter marines. (Observe the lower tails of the two frequency curves.)

This example illustrates how difficult it is to compare populations by using a measure of location, such as the mean. The fact that some marines are taller than the tallest army soldiers is due to the difference in population variabilities. The marine division is a more diverse group with a larger standard deviation (2.5 inches compared with 2.0 inches for the army division).

7-2 FINDING AREAS UNDER THE NORMAL CURVE

Before we can obtain probability values for normally distributed random variables, we must find the appropriate area lying under the normal curve by using Appendix Table D. To illustrate, we will determine the desired areas for the time a particular typesetter takes to compose 500 lines of standard type. We will assume that the population of times is normally distributed, with a mean of μ = 150 minutes and a standard deviation of σ = 30 minutes. The time it takes to set any given 500 lines, such as the next 500 to be composed, represents a randomly selected time from this population.

The probability that it takes between 150 and 175 minutes to set 500 lines is represented by the shaded area under the normal curve in Figure 7-5. We know

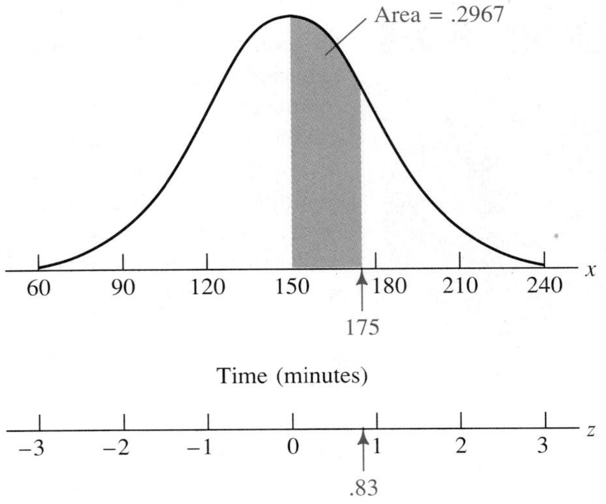

FIGURE 7-5 Determining the area under a normal curve.

that the area beneath the normal curve between the mean and a certain point depends only on the number of standard deviations separating the two points. We see that 175 minutes is equivalent to a distance above the mean of .83 standard deviation. This figure is determined by observing that 175 minutes minus the mean of 150 minutes is equal to 25 minutes. Since the standard deviation is 30 minutes, 25 minutes is only a fraction, 25/30 = .83, of the standard deviation.

Appendix Table D has been constructed for a special curve, called the **standard normal curve**, which provides the area between the mean and a point above it at a specified distance measured in standard deviations. Because this distance will vary, as a convenience it is represented by the letter z. Sometimes the value of z is referred to as a **normal deviate**. The distance z that separates a possible normal random variable value x from its mean, expressed in terms of standard deviations, is given by the following expression for the

NORMAL DEVIATE

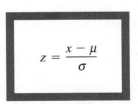

$$z = \frac{x - \mu}{\sigma}$$

A negative value will be obtained for z when x is smaller than μ.

To ease our discussion, a portion of Appendix Table D is reproduced here.

Normal Deviate z	.00	.01	.02	.03	.04	.05	.06	.07	. . .
⋮				⋮					
0.6	.2257	.2291	.2324	.2357	.2389	.2422	.2454	.2486	
0.7	.2580	.2612	.2642	.2673	.2704	.2734	.2764	.2794	
0.8	.2881	.2910	.2939	**.2967**	.2995	.3023	.3051	.3078	
0.9	.3159	.3186	.3212	.3238	.3264	.3289	.3315	.3340	. . .
1.0	.3413	.3438	.3461	.3485	.3508	.3531	.3554	.3577	
1.1	.3643	.3665	.3686	.3708	.3729	.3749	.3770	**.3790**	
1.2	.3849	.3869	.3888	.3907	.3925	.3944	.3962	.3980	
⋮				⋮					

The first column of the table lists values of z to the first decimal place. The second decimal place value is located at the head of one of the remaining ten columns. The area under the curve between the mean and z standard deviations is found at the intersection of the correct row and column. For example, when $z = .83$, we find the area of .2967 by reading the entry in the .8 row and the .03 column. The area under the normal curve for a completion time between 150 and 175 minutes is thus .2967, which represents the probability that it will take this long to set the next 500 lines of print.

USING THE NORMAL CURVE TABLE

Appendix Table D provides areas only between the mean and some point above it, but we can also use this table to find areas encountered in other common probability situations. Each of these areas is described in this section.

(a) Area between the mean and some point below the mean.

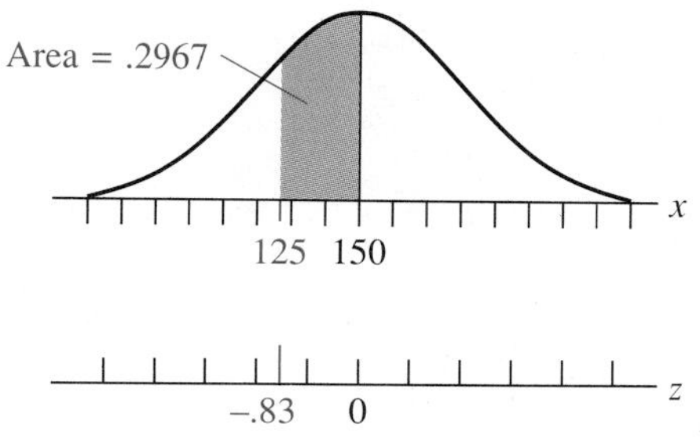

To determine the probability that the completion time lies between 125 and 150 minutes, first we must calculate the normal deviate.

$$z = \frac{x - \mu}{\sigma} = \frac{125 - 150}{30} = -.83$$

Here, z is negative because 125 is a point lying below the mean. Since the normal curve is symmetrical about the mean, this area must be the same as it would be for a positive value of z of the same magnitude (in this case .2967, as before). It is therefore unnecessary to tabulate areas for negative values of z. The area between the mean and a point lying below it will be equal to the area between the mean and a point lying the same distance above it.

(b) Area to the left of a value above the mean.

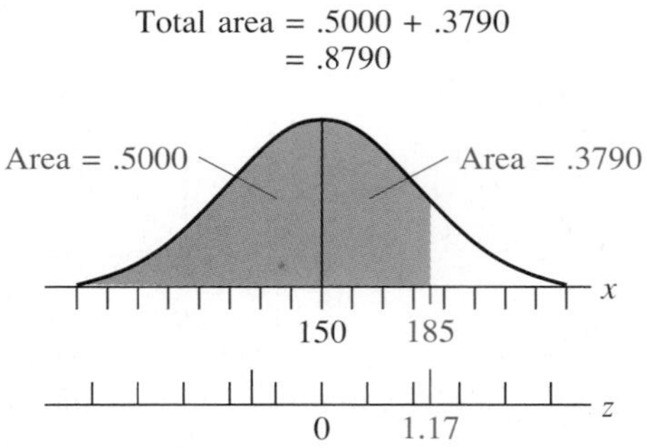

To determine the probability that 500 lines can be set in 185 minutes or less, we must find the entire shaded area below 185. Here, we must consider the lower half of the normal curve separately. Since the entire area of the normal curve is 1, the area under the half to the left of 150 must be .5. The area between 150 and 185 is found from Table D, with $z = (185 - 150)/30 = 1.17$, to be .3790. The entire shaded area below 185 is the sum of the two areas, or $.5000 + .3790 = .8790$.

(c) Area in upper tail.

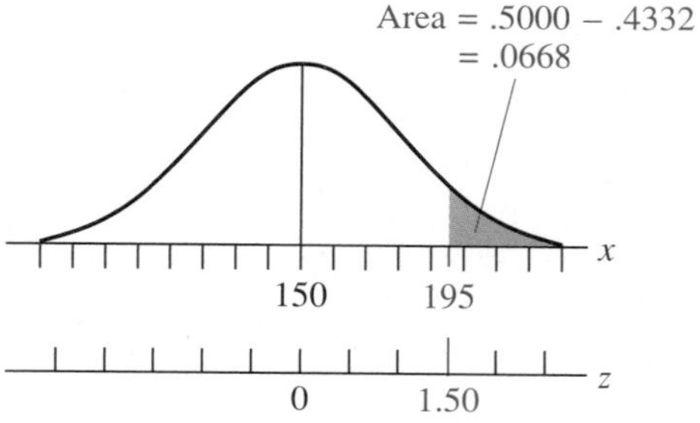

To determine the probability that the number of minutes required exceeds 195, we must first determine the area between the mean and 195. The normal deviate is $z = (195 - 150)/30 = 1.50$; the area from Table D is .4332. Since the area under the upper half of the normal curve is .5, we find the area above 195 by subtracting the unwanted portion: $.5000 - .4332 = .0668$.

Because the total area under the normal curve is 1, we may use the value of the upper tail area to calculate the area to the left of 195. Subtracting the upper tail area of .0668 from 1 gives us $1.0000 - .0668 = .9332$ for the area to the left of 195 (or the probability that the time will be less than 195 minutes). Similarly, when the area to the left of a point is known, the area to its right can be found by subtracting this value from 1. For example, in **(b)** we found that the area to the left of 185 is .8790; thus, the area in the upper tail to the right of 185 must be 1 − .8790 = .1210.

(d) Area in lower tail.

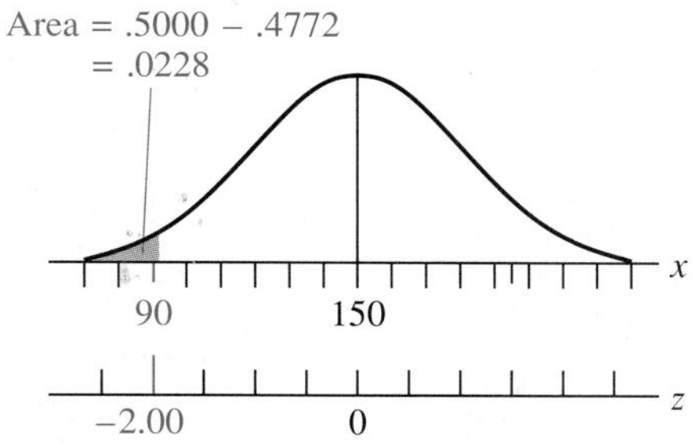

To determine the probability that it will take 90 minutes or less to set the type, we follow two steps similar to those in **(c)**. First, we find the area between 90 and 150. Using $z = (90 - 150)/30 = -2.00$, we obtain .4772 from Table D. Subtracting this value from .5 yields .5000 − .4772 = .0228.

(e) Area to the right of a value below the mean.

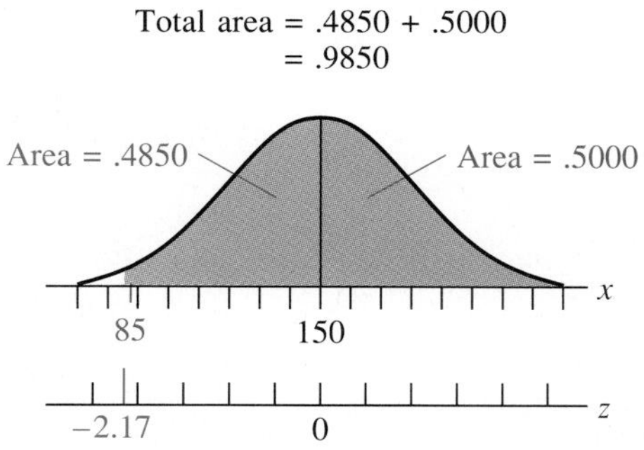

To determine the probability that the completion time will be equal to or greater than 85 minutes, the area between 85 and the mean is added to the area to the right of the mean, which is .5. Here, we calculate $z = (85 - 150)/30 = -2.17$. Adding the area from Table D (.4850) to .5, the combined area is .5000 + .4850 = .9850.

We can find the area in the lower tail below 85 by subtracting .9850 from 1, or 1 − .9850 = .0150. We can also find the area to the right of 90 by subtracting the lower tail area found in **(d)** from 1, or 1 − .0228 = .9772.

To determine the probability that it will take between 140 and 170 minutes to set the 500 lines, we simply add the portion of the shaded area below the mean to the portion above it. The respective normal deviate values are $z = (140 - 150)/30 = -.33$ and $z = (170 - 150)/30 = .67$. From Table D, the lower area is .1293 and the upper area is .2486, so that the combined area is .1293 + .2486 = .3779.

(f) Area under portion overlapping the mean.

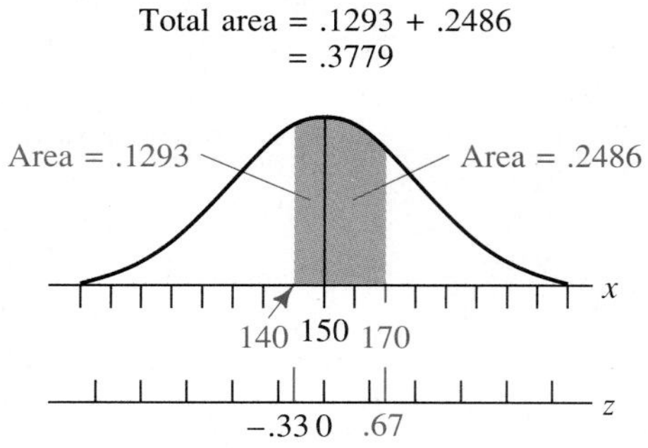

If we wish to determine the probability that it will take between 120 and 180 minutes to set the type, the normal deviates are $z = (120 - 150)/30 = -1$ and $z = (180 - 150)/30 = 1$. From Table D, .3413 is the same area for both sides, so that the combined area is .3413 + .3413 = .6826. Because z expresses the number of standard deviation units from the mean, we see that .6826 is a more precise value for the area between $\mu \pm \sigma$ than the value used in the top graph of Figure 7-3.

(g) Area between two values lying above or below the mean.

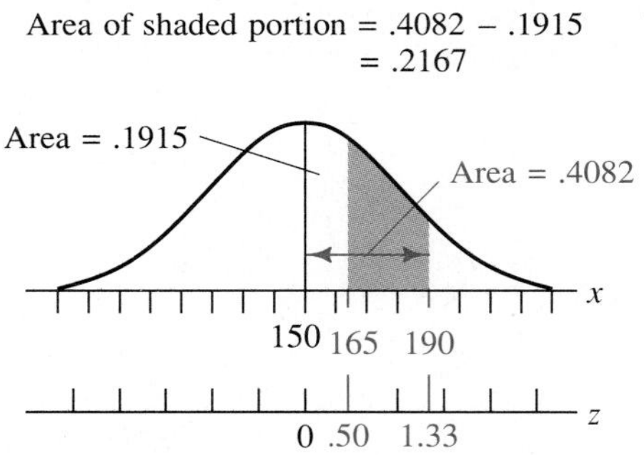

To determine the probability that the composition time is between 165 and 190 minutes, we must first find the areas between the mean and each of these values. The respective normal deviates are $z = (165 - 150)/30 = .50$ and $z = (190 - 150)/30 = 1.33$. From Table D, the area between the mean and 190 is .4082, and the area between the mean and 165 is .1915. Thus, the shaded area is found by subtracting the smaller area from the larger one, or .4082 − .1915 = .2167.

A similar procedure can be applied to an area lying below the mean. It is also possible to find the value for a complementary situation—that the time will be either below 165 minutes or greater than 190 minutes—by subtracting the shaded area from 1, or 1 − .2167 = .7833.

The normal curve represents values that lie on a continuous scale, such as height, weight, and time. There is zero probability that a specific value, such as 129.40 minutes, will occur (there is zero area under the normal curve covering a single point). Thus, in determining probabilities, it does not matter whether we use "strict" inequalities, such as the composition time is "less than" ($<$) 129.40 minutes, or an ordinary inequality, such as the time is "less than or equal to" ($\leq$) 129.40 minutes. Using $z = (129.40 - 150)/30 = -.69$, the area is the same in either case: $.5000 - .2549 = .2451$.

CUMULATIVE PROBABILITIES AND PERCENTILES

Cases **(b)** and **(d)** in our discussion of normal curve areas show us how all the values for a normal cumulative probability distribution can be determined. We have seen that the probability of a time of 185 minutes or less is .8790 and that the probability of 90 minutes or less is .0228. For values above the mean, when z is positive, we obtain the cumulative probabilities from Appendix Table D simply by adding .5 to the tabulated areas. For values below the mean, when z is negative, we subtract the area given in the table from .5 to obtain the cumulative probability.

It is frequently necessary to determine the percentile values of a normally distributed population. Recall from Chapter 3 that a percentile is the population value below which a certain percentage of the population lies and that a percentile or fractile value can be obtained directly from the cumulative relative frequency distribution.

To determine a population percentile, we must read Appendix Table D in *reverse*, since the specified percentage represents an area under the normal curve. For instance, in our example, the 90th percentile is a particular number of minutes, and the area under the normal curve to the left of this value will be .90. Thus, the area between the mean and the number of minutes to be determined will be $.90 - .50 = .40$.

Searching through the body of the table, we select the area that lies closest to this figure—in this case, .3997. Since .3997 is in the $z = 1.2$ row and the .08 column, the corresponding normal deviate is $z = 1.28$. This means that the desired time is 1.28 standard deviations, or $30 \times 1.28 = 38.4$ minutes, above the mean. Adding this to the mean, we determine that the 90th percentile is $150 + 38.4 = 188.4$ minutes.

In general, to determine a percentile, we begin by reading Appendix Table D in reverse to find z. We can then calculate the corresponding population value x from the following expression, which provides the

PERCENTILE FOR A NORMAL POPULATION

$$x = \mu + z\sigma$$

Note that below the 50th percentile, the lower tail area is used to find z, which will be negative in these cases.

EXAMPLE: DESIGNING WITHIN HUMAN LIMITATIONS

Engineers who are designing an aircraft cockpit want to arrange the controls so that 95% of all pilots can reach them while seated. This involves finding the maximum reach radius exceeded by 95% (but not by 5%) of all pilots. Thus, the engineers must find the reach that corresponds to the 5th percentile.

SOLUTION: The maximum reach radii of airline pilots are assumed to be approximately normally distributed, with a mean of $\mu = 48$ inches and a standard deviation of $\sigma = 2$ inches. The engineers seek the point below which the area under the normal curve is equal to .05. This means that Appendix Table D must be searched to find the area closest to $.50 - .05 = .45$. Two areas, .4495 and .4505, are equally close. Therefore, the desired figure lies somewhere between the corresponding normal deviates 1.64 and 1.65. For simplicity, the engineers select 1.64, preferring to err on the side of a larger rather than a smaller tail area. Since the 5th percentile is below the 50th, they are dealing with a lower tail area and their normal deviate is negative, so that $z = -1.64$. (The 5th percentile lies *below* the mean and is smaller, so that a distance of 1.64 standard deviations must be *subtracted* from the mean.) The 5th percentile is therefore

$$x = \mu + z\sigma = 48 - 1.64(2) = 44.72 \text{ inches}$$

THE STANDARD NORMAL RANDOM VARIABLE

The area under any normal curve can be found by using the standard normal curve. This curve provides the probability distribution for the **standard normal random variable**.

In our typesetting illustration, we essentially transformed the original random variable X, the time to complete 500 lines, into the standard normal random variable whenever we used Appendix Table D to find areas under the normal curve.

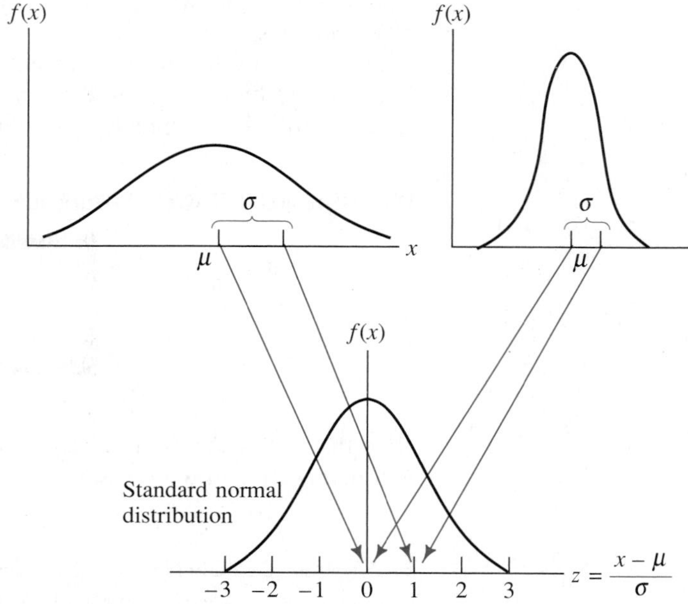

FIGURE 7-6 Illustration of the linear transformation of normal random variables into the standard normal distribution.

This transformation can be accomplished physically by shifting the center of the curve and then stretching or contracting it. To shift the original curve so that its center lies above the point $x = 0$, we subtract μ from each point on the x axis. Then the repositioned curve can be stretched or squeezed until the scale on the horizontal axis matches the scale for the standard normal distribution. If all values of the random variable are divided by its standard deviation, the transformed curve will have the same shape as the standard normal curve in Figure 7-6. The net effect will always be the same, no matter what the values of μ and σ are. The horizontal scale may be either expanded or contracted.

Fortunately, we do not need to physically transform the original random variable X into the standard normal random variable because we can manipulate the possible values of x algebraically.

ILLUSTRATION: TWO IQ TESTS

IQ tests illustrate this concept. These tests are designed so that the scores achieved by a cross section of persons are normally distributed for all practical purposes. One of the most popular, the Stanford-Binet test, has a mean of $\mu = 100$ points and a standard deviation of $\sigma = 16$. Letting X represent the IQ score achieved by a randomly selected person, it is possible to determine various probabilities for the value achieved.

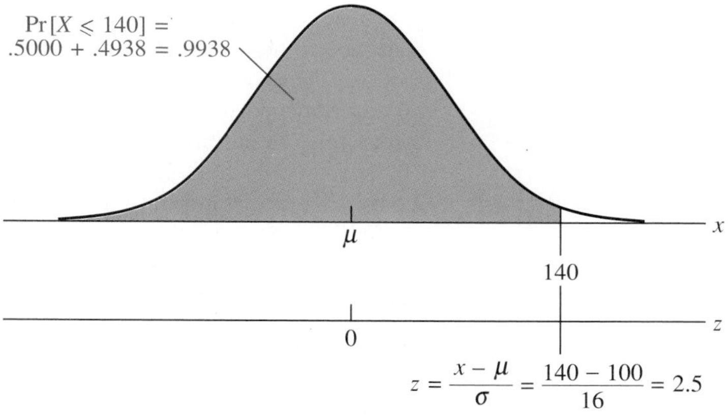

For example, we find the probability that this person's IQ is at most 140. Here, we see that there is better than a 99% chance that this person's IQ falls below 140 on the Stanford-Binet scale.

Other IQ tests have different standard deviations than the Stanford-Binet, although the mean of most IQ tests is 100 points. If we ask the same question using another test with a standard deviation of $\sigma = 10$ points, we have

$$z = \frac{x - \mu}{\sigma} = \frac{140 - 100}{10} = 4.0$$

$$\Pr[X \leq 140] = .50000 + .49997 = .99997$$

Note that IQs above 140 are considerably rarer using this test.

Because various types of IQ tests are scaled differently, it is hard to compare IQ scores. For this reason, intelligence test results are often transformed into **standard scores**, or normal deviate values. In our example, 140 points on the

Stanford-Binet scale provides a standard score of 2.50. Thus, a person scoring 140 points on the second test would exhibit a much higher level of intelligence. (To obtain a standard score equal to 4.0 on the Standford-Binet test, a person would have to be 4 standard deviations above the mean and have an IQ of $100 + 4(16) = 164$ on that scale.)

If σ is smaller than the 10 applicable to the second IQ test, the absolute value of z will be too large to obtain the area from Appendix Table D. Our table has to stop somewhere, but the tails of the normal curve extend indefinitely. In general, whenever z exceeds 4.00, the area between the mean and z is so close to .5 that for practical purposes .5 is used. In such cases, the upper and lower tail areas are so close to 0 that they are *negligible*. For example, the area below $z = 5$ is approximately 1, as is the area above $z = -5$; the areas above $z = 5$ and below $z = -5$ are each approximately 0.

ADDITIONAL REMARKS

The fact that the tails of the normal curve never touch the horizontal axis implies a probability (although tiny) that the random variable can exceed any value. Consider the distribution for heights of men, for instance. The normal curve literally assigns a probability to the event that a man will grow to be more than one mile tall. This seems impossible, but according to the normal curve the probability for this event is not zero, although it is quite remote. The normal curve also assigns a probability to the fact that a man will be negatively tall. Although these implications are absurd, they should not detract from the utility of the normal distribution. They are by-products of the use of a convenient mathematical expression to describe a particular curve that fits some empirical frequency distributions quite accurately. According to Appendix Table D, only about .13% of the area under the normal curve lies beyond a distance of 3σ above the mean. Areas in the tails of the theoretical normal distribution are miniscule for greater distances. (At 4σ, the tail area is only .003%.) Any discrepancy between reality and the theoretical normal curve that occurs beyond 4 standard deviations from the mean can be safely ignored. (A mile-tall man would be more than 40,000 standard deviations from the mean.)

EXERCISES

7-1 Cash balance errors at Do-Nut Dunker Cafés are approximately normally distributed with a mean of \$0 and a standard deviation of \$1.00. Determine the relative frequency for the following balance errors.

(a) less than \$1.25
(b) greater than − \$.75
(c) less than − \$2.50
(d) greater than \$3.50
(e) between \$1.50 and \$1.75
(f) between − \$.50 and − \$.25
(g) less than − \$2.80 or greater than \$.65
(h) less than \$.65 or greater than \$.75

7-2 The lifetime of a disk drive head is normally distributed, with a mean of $\mu = 1{,}000$ hours and a standard deviation of $\sigma = 100$ hours. Determine the probability for each of the following lifetime outcomes for one drive unit. (*Hint:* It will help if you first sketch the normal curve and identify the corresponding area for each outcome.)

(a) between 1,000 and 1,150 hours
(b) between 950 and 1,000 hours
(c) 930 hours or less
(d) longer than 1,250 hours
(e) 870 hours or less
(f) longer than 780 hours
(g) between 700 and 1,200 hours
(h) betweeen 750 and 850 hours

7-3 Determine the following percentiles for the cash balance errors given in Exercise 7-1.
(a) 10th (b) 25th (c) 85th (d) 95th (e) 99th

7-4 The heights of men attending Near Miss University form a normally distributed population with a mean of 69″ and a standard deviation of 2″. One man is selected at random. Determine the probability that his height falls in the following ranges.
(a) between 69″ and 70.5″
(b) between 65″ and 69″
(c) 72″ or taller
(d) taller than 72″
(e) 68″ or shorter
(f) taller than 65″
(g) between 69.5″ and 70″
(h) between 67.6″ and 68.2″

7-5 The wrist circumference of adult males is normally distributed with a mean of $\mu = 6.85''$ and a standard deviation of $\sigma = .40''$. One man is selected at random.
(a) Determine the probabilities for the following possible wrist sizes.
(1) less than 8.00″
(2) between 6.50″ and 7.50″
(3) between 5.75″ and 6.75″
(4) greater than 7.00″
(b) Determine the following percentiles.
(1) 5th (2) 10th (3) 75th (4) 95th

7-6 An architect designing the men's gymnasium at Slippery Rock University wants to make the interior doors high enough, so that 95% of the men will have at least a 1-foot clearance. Assuming that the heights will be normally distributed, with a mean of 70 inches and a standard deviation of 3 inches, how high must the architect make the doors?

7-7 The Precision Die Company quality control manager shuts down an automatic lathe for corrective maintenance whenever a sample of the parts it produces has an average diameter greater than 2.01 inches or smaller than 1.99 inches. The lathe is designed to produce parts with a mean diameter of 2.00 inches, and the sample averages have a standard deviation of .005 inches. Assume that the normal distribution applies.
(a) What is the probability that the quality control manager will stop the process when the lathe is operating as designed, with $\mu = 2.00$ inches? (The manager does not know that the lathe is operating correctly.)
(b) If the lathe begins to produce parts that on the average are too wide, with $\mu = 2.02$ inches, what is the probability that the lathe will continue to operate?
(c) If an adjustment error causes the lathe to produce parts that on the average are too narrow, with $\mu = 1.99$ inches, what is the probability that the lathe will be stopped?

7-3 SAMPLING DISTRIBUTION OF THE SAMPLE MEAN FOR A NORMAL POPULATION

The normal curve describes the frequency distributions for a great many populations, notably measurements of persons and things. Some important questions can be answered by applying the normal curve.

It has been established mathematically that under certain circumstances **when the population frequencies are described by the normal curve, the sampling distribution of $\bar{X}$ itself is also normally distributed.**

SAMPLING DISTRIBUTION OF $\bar{X}$: If $\bar{X}$ is the mean of a random sample taken from a normally distributed population having a mean of μ and a standard deviation of σ, then the sampling distribution for $\bar{X}$ is also normal, its mean is also μ, and its standard deviation is $\sigma_{\bar{X}} = \sigma/\sqrt{n}$. This is true no matter what the size of the sample happens to be.*

The area under the normal curve between μ and a possible level of the sample mean is found by transforming $\bar{X}$ into the corresponding

NORMAL DEVIATE FOR THE SAMPLE MEAN

$$z = \frac{\bar{x} - \mu}{\sigma_{\bar{X}}}$$

Recall that many physical dimensions are closely represented by the normal distribution. In these cases, knowing μ and σ establishes the sampling distribution for the mean of any sample.

Illustration: Normal Distribution for Inseams

To illustrate this concept consider a trousers manufacturer. The president must determine how many pairs of pants to make of various sizes. He is concerned with inseam lengths of its adult male customers. Although μ and σ are not known, suppose that this population is normally distributed and that the following parameters are assumed to apply.

$$\mu = 34.52'' \qquad \sigma = 1.75''$$

The top normal curve in Figure 7-7 represents the frequency distribution of this population.

Suppose the manufacturer hires a statistician as a consultant. The statistician is going to collect a random sample of $n = 100$ men and measure the inseams for each. Many different sample results are possible. Therefore, before any men are selected, $\bar{X}$ is a random variable that is normally distributed with mean $\mu = 34.52''$ (identical to that of the population), and standard deviation

$$\sigma_{\bar{X}} = \frac{\sigma}{\sqrt{n}} = \frac{1.75''}{\sqrt{100}} = .175''$$

The above standard deviation is only one-tenth as large as its population counterpart. This is because possible values for $\bar{X}$ (representing the average of 100 men's inseams) will tend to be more alike than individual population values (inseams of single men). The normal curve for $\bar{X}$ is shown at the bottom of Figure 7-7. Notice that the bottom curve is shaped like a taller, thinner bell. That curve's

*As we will see in Chapter 8, when σ is *also* of unknown value and n is small, it is necessary to use the Student t statistic instead of $\bar{X}$. This statistic has a different sampling distribution.

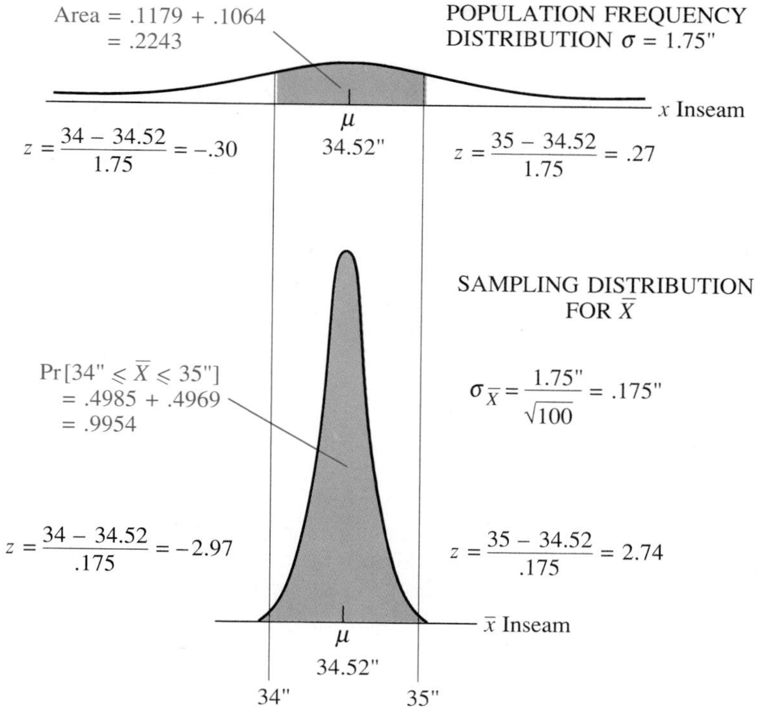

FIGURE 7-7 Population frequency curve and sampling distribution for sample mean inseam of adult males.

mass is concentrated more tightly about the center, reflecting the smaller variability in possible values of $\bar{X}$.

The effect of the smaller variability in $\bar{X}$ is reflected in the shaded areas under each curve. Each area provides the frequency of inseam dimensions falling between 34″ and 35″. The proportion of the inseam population (top curve) falling between these limits is .2243. A much higher probability of .9954 applies for $\bar{X}$ (bottom curve) falling inside the same limits.

To help appreciate the above result, imagine what would happen if the company statistician collected a series of different samples, each involving 100 inseams taken from the same population. For every sample group a different $\bar{X}$ value would be computed. These means would be close to each other in value, and their average should be very near to μ. The several sample means would cluster more tightly about μ than the inseams of individual mean. (This is reflected in a level for $\sigma_{\bar{X}}$ that is smaller than σ.)

THE ROLE OF THE STANDARD ERROR

The standard error of $\bar{X}$ gauges how closely to μ the computed sample mean tends to be. A sampling situation when $\sigma_{\bar{X}}$ is small can be expected to result in a computed $\bar{X}$ falling more closely to the population center than when $\sigma_{\bar{X}}$ is large. The amount of sampling error becomes smaller as $\sigma_{\bar{X}}$ does.

When populations are normally distributed, two factors affect the level for $\sigma_{\bar{X}}$. These are the population standard deviation σ and the sample size n.

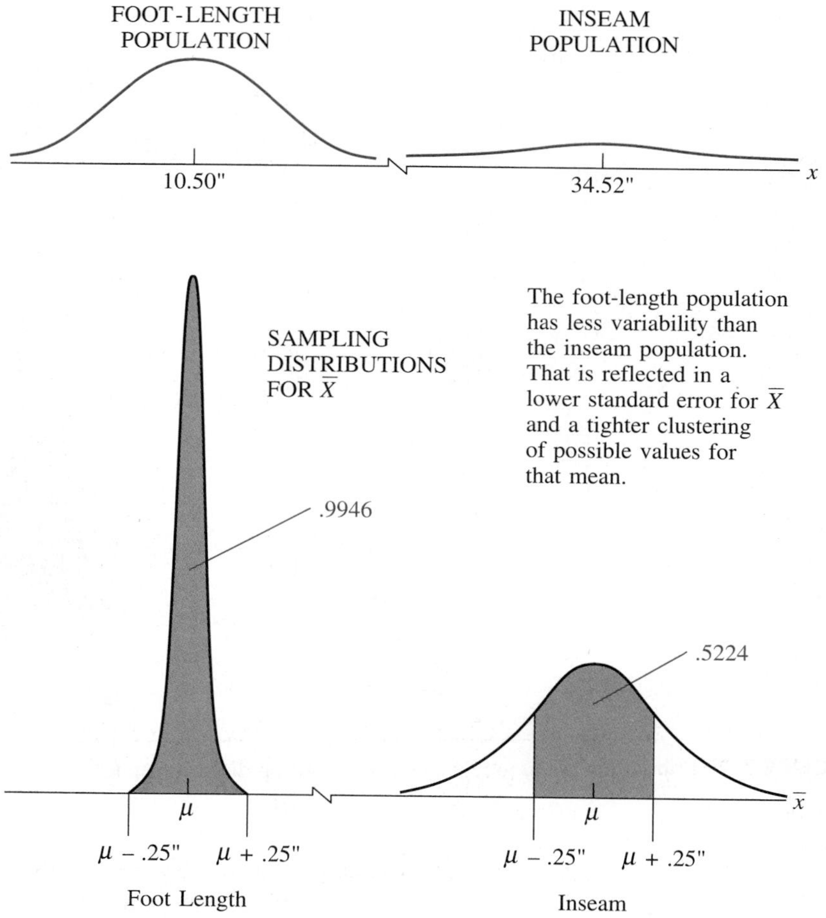
FOOT-LENGTH
POPULATION
INSEAM
POPULATION
10.50"
34.52"
x
SAMPLING
DISTRIBUTIONS
FOR X̄
The foot-length population
has less variability than
the inseam population.
That is reflected in a
lower standard error for X̄
and a tighter clustering
of possible values for
that mean.
.9946
.5224
μ
μ − .25"
μ + .25"
Foot Length
μ
μ − .25"
μ + .25"
Inseam
x̄

FIGURE 7-8 Normal curves for adult male anthropometric data.

Influence of the Standard Deviation

The standard error of $\bar{X}$ is directly proportional to the population standard deviation σ. This means that the amount of error in using the computed $\bar{X}$ to estimate μ is expected to be greater when sampling from a population having a large σ than it would be if a sample of the same size were taken from a population having a smaller σ.

Illustration: Normal Distribution for Foot Length

For example, a men's shoe manufacturer would be interested in the population of foot lengths of adult males. Suppose that the mean is $\mu = 10.50''$ with a standard deviation of $\sigma = .45''$. The standard deviation for this population is smaller than the earlier one for inseam, where $\sigma = 1.75''$. The respective values of $\sigma_{\bar{X}}$ will reflect this difference in σ size. When separate random samples of $n = 25$ measurements are obtained for foot length and for inseam, the respective standard errors are

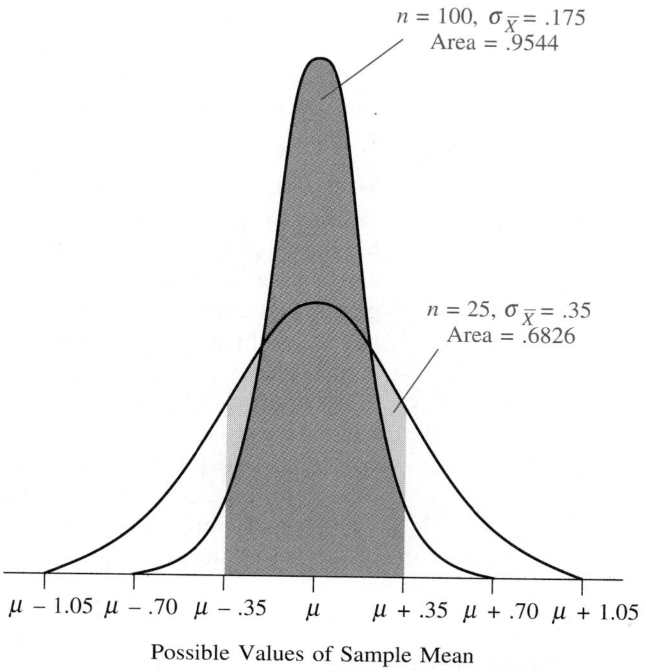

FIGURE 7-9 *The effect of increased sample size on the sampling distribution of $\bar{X}$.*

$$\sigma_{\bar{X}} = \frac{.45''}{\sqrt{25}} = .09'' \qquad \text{(foot length)}$$

$$\sigma_{\bar{X}} = \frac{1.75''}{\sqrt{25}} = .35'' \qquad \text{(inseam)}$$

The respective pairs of normal curves are shown in Figure 7-8. The probability is quite high, .9946, that $\bar{X}$ (foot length) will fall within $\mu \pm .25''$. The analogous chance is only .5224 that $\bar{X}$ (inseam) will fall within .25″ of the mean of the inseam population. The smaller σ for foot length will lead to less sampling error.

Influence of the Sample size

The sample size n is a second influence on $\sigma_{\bar{X}}$. The standard error of $\bar{X}$ is inversely proportional to the square root of n. Greater sample reliability in using $\bar{X}$ can be expected as n becomes larger (making $\sigma_{\bar{X}}$ smaller).

The company statistician for the trousers manufacturer described earlier may want to achieve the lower sampling error that results from increased sample size. Suppose that for a particular market segment the mean inseam μ is unknown, but the same standard deviation as before, $\sigma = 1.75''$, is believed to apply.

Figure 7-9 shows the sampling distibutions for mean inseam $\bar{X}$ when $n = 25$ and $n = 100$. Notice that the normal curve for the larger sample size (and smaller standard error) exhibits less dispersion, with possible levels of $\bar{X}$ clustering more tightly about μ. When $n = 100$, the probability that $\bar{X}$ falls within $\mu \pm .35''$ is

.9544, as compared with only .6826 for the like event when $n = 25$. This indicates that a larger sample size provides a more reliable estimate of μ for the same level of precision. Since a larger sample size is reflected by a smaller value of $\sigma_{\bar{X}}$, we can conclude that the smaller the value of $\sigma_{\bar{X}}$, the more accurate the sample result will be.

DISTINGUISHING $\sigma_{\bar{X}}$ FROM s.
We should be careful not to confuse $\sigma_{\bar{X}}$ with s. They are both standard deviations, but they represent entirely different phenomena—another reason why we usually call $\sigma_{\bar{X}}$ the standard error of $\bar{X}$. Remember that s is the standard deviation of a particular sample result and is actually calculated from the observed sample values at the final stage of sampling; s measures the variability among the observations that are actually made.

In contrast, $\sigma_{\bar{X}}$ measures the variability of the *possible* $\bar{X}$ values that *might be* obtained and is mainly used in the planning stage of sampling. Even though $\bar{X}$ will be assigned only one numerical value, depending on the sample results, we have demonstrated the need to know the pattern of variation among the possible values that $\bar{X}$ might assume. This variation is summarized by the standard error of the sample mean.

EXERCISES

7-8 Random samples of size $n = 100$ are selected from five normally distributed populations with the following standard deviations σ.

(a) .1 (b) 1.0 (c) 5.0 (d) 20 (e) 100

Calculate the value of $\sigma_{\bar{X}}$ for each sample.

7-9 A random sample of 100 Old Ivy men is chosen, and their heights are determined. Assume that the population mean in 69.5″ and the standard deviation is 3″.

(a) Calculate the standard error of $\bar{X}$.
(b) Determine the probability that the mean height for the sample falls in the following ranges.
  (1) between 70″ and 70.3″
  (2) less than 69.5″
  (3) greater than 72″
  (4) less than 68″
  (5) between 69.4″ and 70.3″

7-10 Consider operator reaction time to a warning signal that BugOff Chemical Company is experiencing significant drops in pressure. This variable is normally distributed with a mean of $\mu = 45$ seconds and a standard deviation of $\sigma = 8$ seconds. Calculate (1) the standard error of $\bar{X}$ and (2) the probability that $\bar{X}$ falls within $\mu \pm 1$ second when random samples of the following sizes are selected.

(a) $n = 25$ (b) $n = 100$ (c) $n = 200$ (d) $n = 500$

7-11 The times taken to install bumpers on cars passing along a Midget Motors assembly line are normally distributed with mean time $\mu = 1.50$ minutes and standard deviation $\sigma = .25$ minute. A sample of $n = 25$ cars is selected and the mean bumper installation time $\bar{X}$ is to be calculated.

(a) Calculate $\sigma_{\bar{X}}$.
(b) Determine the probability that $\bar{X}$ will fall in the following ranges.
  (1) between 1.40 and 1.50 minutes
  (2) exceed 1.35 minutes

(3) at or below 1.45 minutes
(4) between 1.52 and 1.58 minutes
(5) exceed 1.65 minutes

7-12 The hand length of adult males is normally distributed with a mean of $\mu = 7.49''$ and a standard deviation of $\sigma = .34''$. One man is selected at random.

(a) Determine the probabilities for the following possible hand sizes.

(1) less than 7.00″
(2) between 6.75″ and 7.25″
(3) between 7.80″ and 8.20″
(4) greater than 8.00″

(b) Determine the following percentiles.

(1) 1st (2) 10th (3) 90th (4) 99th

7-4 SAMPLING DISTRIBUTION OF $\bar{X}$ WHEN THE POPULATION IS NOT NORMAL

The preceding section describes how the normal curve determines the sampling distribution of $\bar{X}$ when samples are taken from a parent population that is normally distributed. In this section we see that, under proper conditions, *the same conclusions may be reached even when the parent population is not normally distributed.* This feature is a theoretical property, the **central limit theorem**.

A MULTIPLE-SAMPLE EXPERIMENT

Before we discuss that theorem in detail, it should be helpful to consider once more the results achieved from a multiple-sample experiment.

ILLUSTRATION: BASEBALL SUPERSTAR SALARIES

In Chapter 6, we investigated properties of samples generated from the population of 1991 salaries of baseball superstars, listed in Table 6-15 on page 226.

The histograms in Figure 7-10 describe the experimental results. The top histogram portrays the complete population, which is positively skewed and bimodal. The population frequency distribution is not even close to the shape of a normal curve.

A series of 100 random samples were taken with replacement from the population for each of three sample sizes. The second histogram in Figure 7-10 summarizes the results with $n = 10$ salaries in each sample. The next two histograms resulted when $n = 25$ and $n = 100$.

Notice that regardless of sample size, the $\bar{X}$ values cluster about the mean of the parent population. This further illustrates the property already established that the expected value of the sample mean is the population mean μ. Notice also that as the sample size increases, the $\bar{X}$ values cluster more tightly about the respective centers. This is consistent with our earlier finding that $\bar{X}$ has a sampling distribution with standard deviation equal to $\sigma/\sqrt{n}$. (Notice how closely the computed standard deviations come to the theoretical counterpart.) Finally, notice that the $\bar{X}$ histograms tend to have the bell shape associated with the normal curve. Although the bell form is only hinted at by the histogram for $n = 10$, the bell shape is very pronounced for the two larger sample sizes.

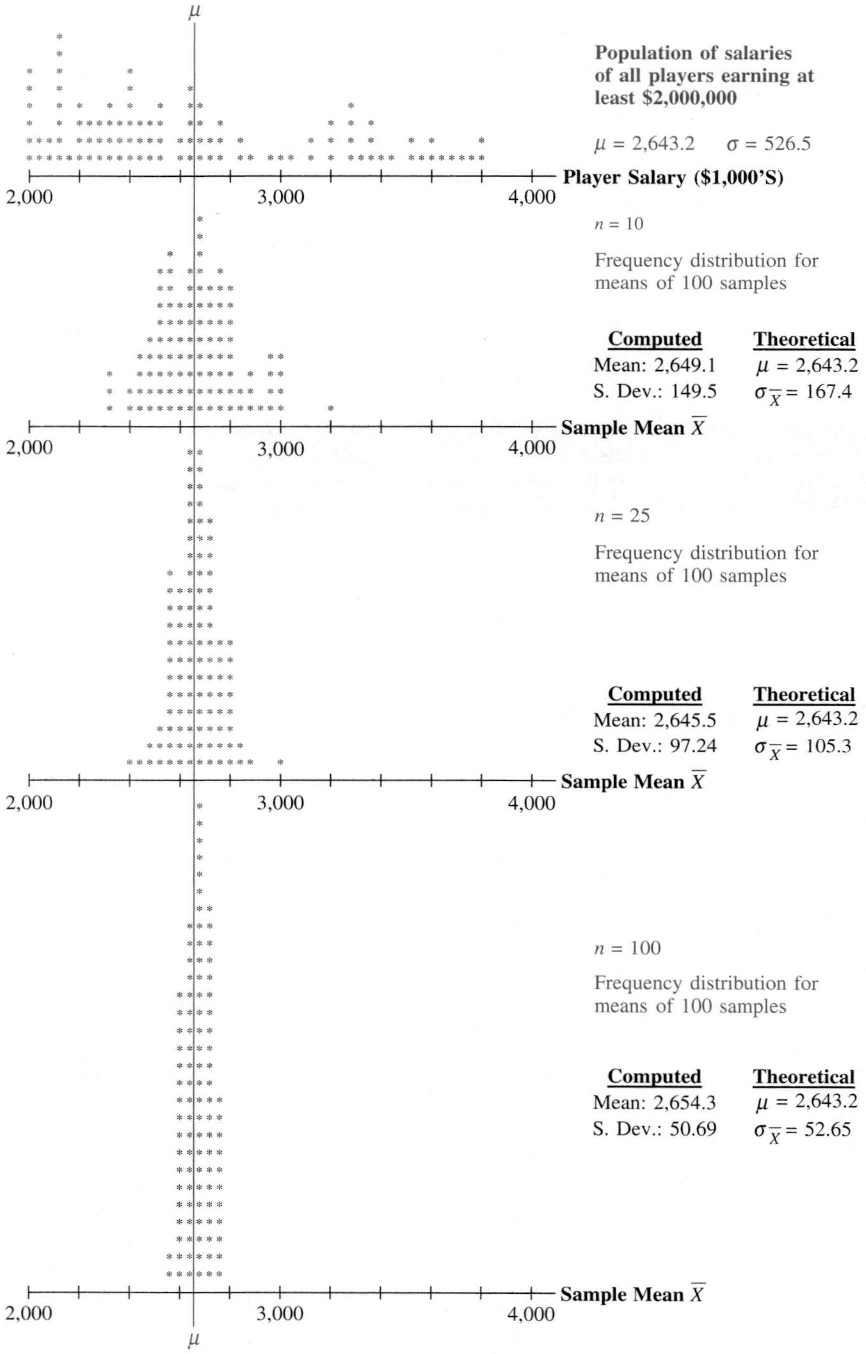

FIGURE 7-10 Frequency distributions for means computed from repeated samples from population of baseball superstar salaries.

The theoretical sampling distribution of $\bar{X}$ for baseball superstar salaries is closely approximated by the normal distribution.

THE CENTRAL LIMIT THEOREM

As the foregoing illustration suggests, it has been established mathematically that the normal distribution may be used as a basis for approximating the sampling distribution of $\bar{X}$. This fact alone makes the normal distribution so fundamentally important in statistics.

We now state the

CENTRAL LIMIT THEOREM: As sample size n becomes large, when each observation is independently selected from a population with a mean of μ and a standard deviation of σ, the sampling distribution of $\bar{X}$ tends to assume a normal distribution with a mean of μ and a standard deviation of $\sigma_{\bar{X}}$.

Note that the central limit theorem can be applied regardless of the shape of the population frequency distribution. It may be used whether the observation random variable is discrete or continuous.* Figure 7-11 shows the sampling distribution of $\bar{X}$ obtained mathematically for samples taken from populations having frequency distributions of various shapes. Note that the sampling distribution of $\bar{X}$ becomes more bell shaped as sample size increases.

The central limit theorem is useful because it permits us to make an inference about a population without knowing anything about its frequency distribution except what we can determine from a sample, although we must still presume a specific value for σ.

EXAMPLE: ESTIMATING MEAN INCOMES FOR SURGEONS AND TEACHERS

Suppose that you are asked to estimate the mean income of persons in various professions. You are to determine this by taking a random sample of persons from each group and calculating the mean income $\bar{X}$.

Consider surgeons and teachers. You are interested in the population mean income μ for each group. These are unknowns, but the following "ballpark" guesses apply for the respective standard deviations.

Teachers	Surgeons
$\sigma = \$2{,}000$	$\sigma = \$25{,}000$

Income data ordinarily provide population frequency curves that are positively skewed, as shown in Figure 7-12. Even though the particular shapes are not known, the central limit theorem allows you to use normal distributions in determining probabilities for $\bar{X}$.

Suppose that you take samples of size $n = 100$ from each population. You want to determine the probability that $\bar{X}$ lies within $\pm$ \$500 of the population mean of each group.

*One restriction is that the population must have a finite variance. This is a theoretical limitation of no practical significance to populations ordinarily encountered in statistical study.

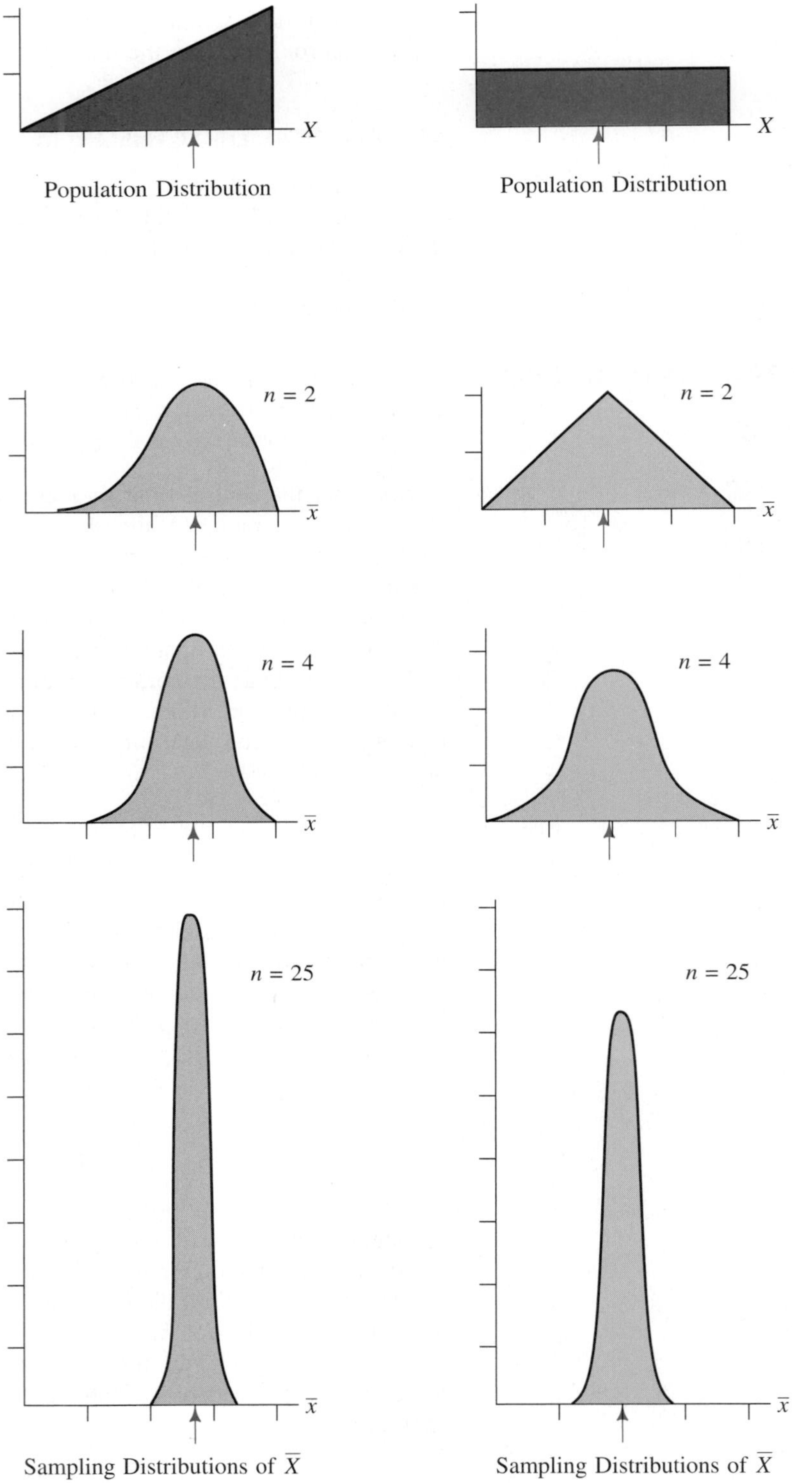

FIGURE 7-11 Illustration of the central limit theorem, showing the tendency toward normality in the sampling distribution of $\bar{X}$ as n increases for various populations.

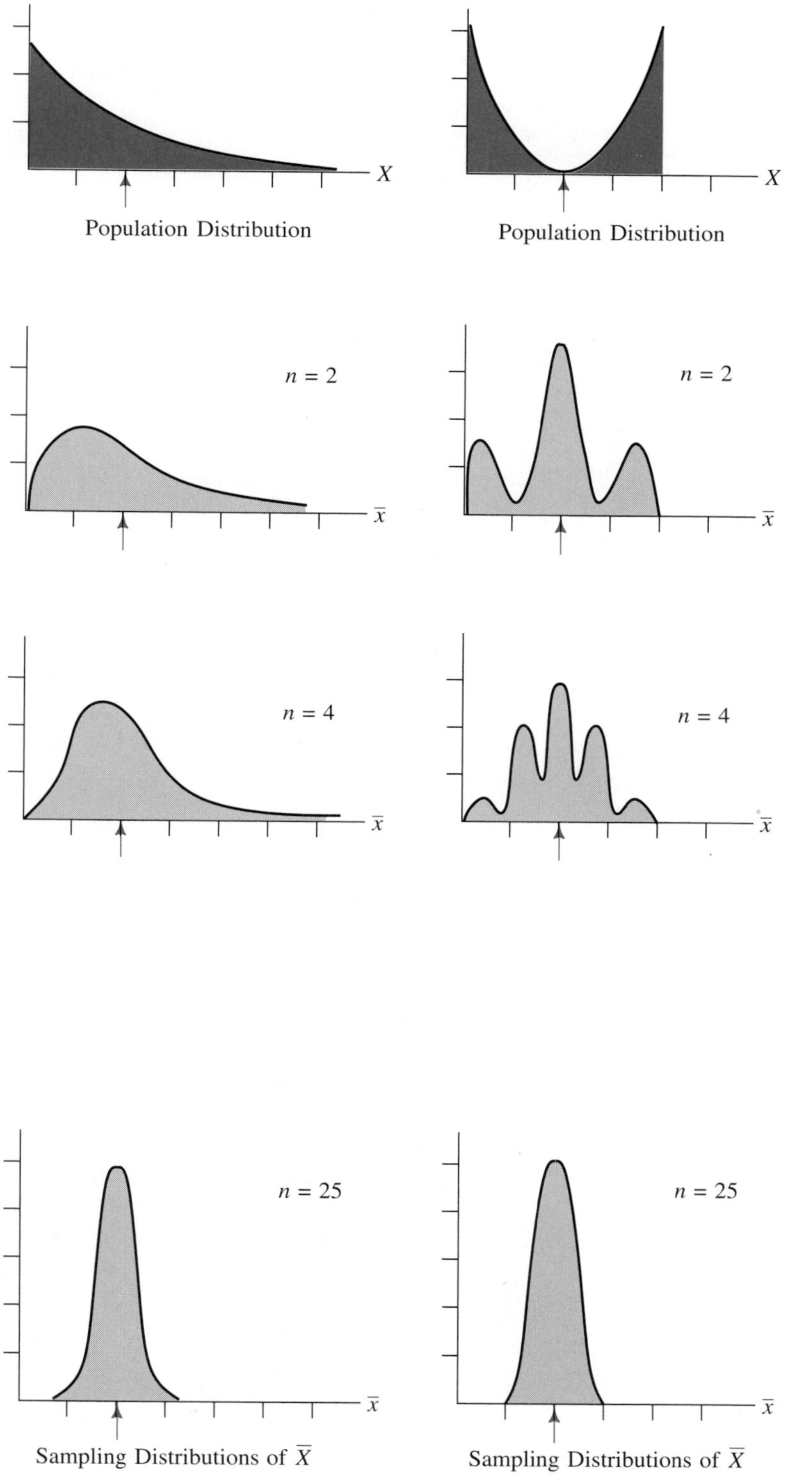

FIGURE 7-11 *(continued)*

SOLUTION: The following standard errors apply for $\bar{X}$.

Teachers	Surgeons
$\sigma_{\bar{X}} = \dfrac{\$2{,}000}{\sqrt{100}}$	$\sigma_{\bar{X}} = \dfrac{\$25{,}000}{\sqrt{100}}$
$= \$200$	$= \$2{,}500$

Find the normal deviates, substituting \$500 for $(\bar{x} - \mu)$ in the equation $z = (\bar{x} - \mu)/\sigma_{\bar{X}}$. Then read the areas from Appendix Table D. Since you wish to obtain a value that is both above and below the means ($\pm$\$500), you must multiply each tabled area by 2.

Teachers	Surgeons
$= \dfrac{\$500}{\$200} = 2.50$	$z = \dfrac{\$500}{\$2{,}500} = .20$
$\Pr[-\$500 \leq \bar{X} - \mu \leq +\$500]$	$\Pr[-\$500 \leq \bar{X} - \mu \leq +\$500]$
$= 2(.4938) = .9876$	$= 2(.0793) = .1586$

As reflected by the shaded areas under the bottom curves in Figure 7-12, there is a higher probability that $\bar{X}$ will be close to its target with teachers than with surgeons. This is because the smaller standard deviation for that more homogeneous income group provides a smaller standard error of $\bar{X}$.

The above example again shows that lower population variability will increase the probability that the computed $\bar{X}$ will be close to μ. And, as the following example shows, greater reliability can be achieved by increasing the sample size.

EXAMPLE: PROBABILITY OF NOT MEETING THE MINIMUM LIFETIME

Idea Lightbulb Company replaces a seam control mechanism whenever a sample of test bulbs has a mean lifetime less than or equal to 450 hours. When the process is exactly on target, the mean lifetime of all bulbs μ is 500 hours. The lifetimes of individual bulbs have a standard deviation σ that is also 500 hours.

Even though individual lifetimes have a frequency distribution that fits the pattern of an exponential curve (reverse J-shaped), the central limit theorem allows Idea's statistician to use the normal curve in determining probabilities for $\bar{X}$.

Present company policy calls for a test sample of $n = 25$ test bulbs, and a manager wants to determine the probability of unnecessarily replacing the control mechanism under this policy.

SOLUTION: The standard error of $\bar{X}$ is $\sigma_{\bar{X}} = 500/\sqrt{25} = 100$. The normal deviate for a possible level of 450 hours is $z = (450 - 500)/100 = -.50$. The tabled normal curve area between the mean and $z = .50$ is .1915. The probability for unnecessary replacement is thus

$$\Pr[\bar{X} \leq 450] = .5000 - .1915 = .3085 \qquad (\text{when } n = 25)$$

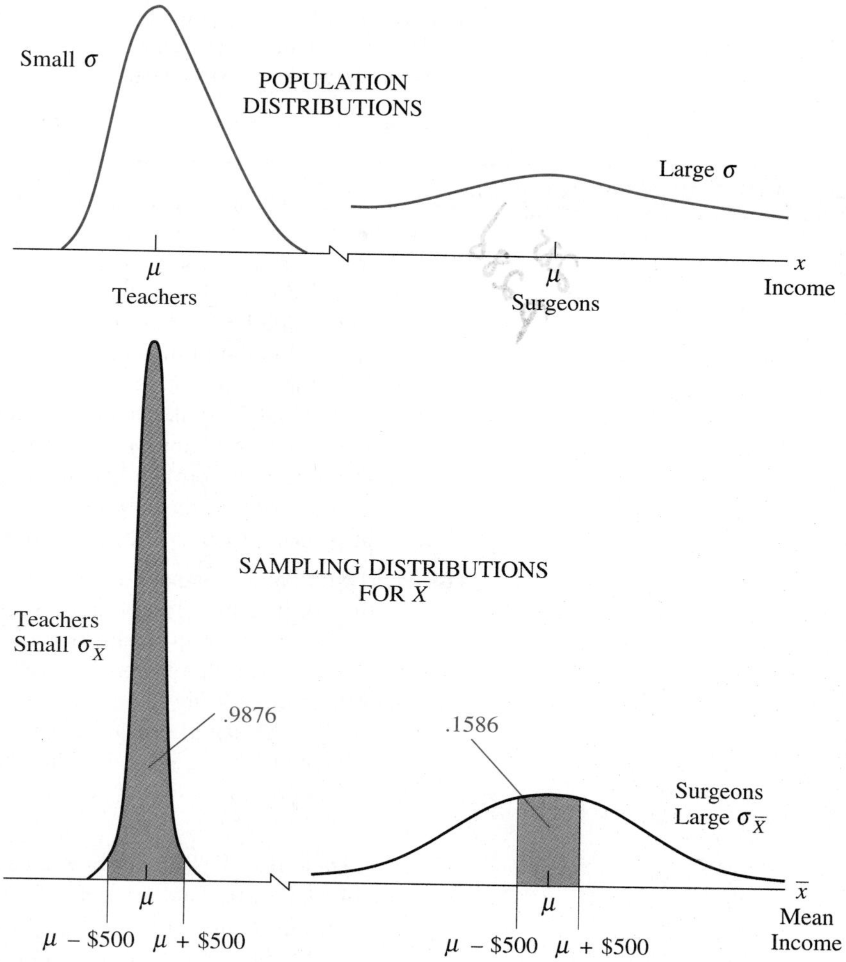

FIGURE 7-12 How the size of σ affects $\sigma_{\overline{X}}$ and thus reliability of $\overline{X}$. (Scales are approximate.)

This probability indicates a substantial chance of unnecessary repairs. The manager wants to see what effect increasing the sample size to $n = 400$ will have. The standard error of $\overline{X}$ now becomes $\sigma_{\overline{X}} = 500/\sqrt{400} = 25$, so that the normal deviate is $z = (450 - 500)/25 = -2.00$, giving a tabled area of .4772. If the company adopts this new policy, the probability for replacing the mechanism when it is functioning correctly will be

$$\Pr[\overline{X} \leq 450] = .5000 - .4772 = .0228 \qquad (\text{when } n = 400)$$

Because the central limit theorem can be applied universally, the normal curve plays a fundamental role in a great portion of statistical theory. In Chapter 8, we will make use of this result in estimating population means. In Chapter 9, the theorem will enable us to develop procedures for making decisions based on the sample mean, which may tend to confirm or deny an assumption regarding the true value of the population mean.

EXERCISES

7-13 An economist serving as a consultant to a large teamsters' local union wishes to estimate the mean annual earnings μ of the membership. He will use the mean $\bar{X}$ of a sample of $n = 100$ drivers as an estimate. Assume that the standard deviation of the membership's annual earnings is $\sigma = \$1{,}500$.

(a) Determine the probability that the estimate will fall within \$200 of the actual population mean.

(b) Increasing n to 400, determine the probability that the estimate will fall within \$200 of the actual population mean. What is the percentage increase in probability over the probability determined in (a)?

(c) Determine the probability that the estimate will fall within \$100 of the true population mean when $n = 100$. What is the percentage reduction in probability over the probability determined in (a)?

7-14 Van Dyke Paint Company is testing a solvent to determine the average drying time of its paint. The population of drying times for individual swatches has an unknown mean μ, and some value must be assumed for the standard deviation. A sample of $n = 25$ swatches will be tested to determine drying times. The underlying population is of unlimited size. Determine the probability that the sample mean drying time deviates from the unknown μ by no more than 1 hour, assuming that the standard deviation has the following values (in hours).

(a) $\sigma = 2$ (b) $\sigma = 4$ (c) $\sigma = 8$ (d) $\sigma = 16$

7-15 Great Dane Buslines wishes to estimate the mean mileage obtained by a new type of radial tire. Due to operating methods, a tire may be used on several buses during its useful life, so that a separate mileage log must be kept for each tire in the sample. Since this procedure is costly, only $n = 100$ tires are to be checked. In a previous study on another type of tire, a standard deviation of $\sigma = 2{,}000$ miles was determined. It is assumed that the same figure will apply to the new tires.

(a) What is the probability that the sample mean will fall within 500 miles of the population mean?

(b) The maintenance superintendent states that the new tires may exhibit greater mileage variability than the tires in current use. Assuming that the standard deviation is increased to $\sigma = 4{,}000$ miles, determine the probability that the sample mean will differ from the population mean by no more than 500 miles.

(c) Compare your answers to (a) and (b). What can you conclude about the effect of increased population variability on the reliability of the sample mean as an estimator?

(d) Suppose that a sample of $n = 200$ tires is used instead. If a standard deviation of $\sigma = 2{,}000$ miles is determined, find the probability that the sample mean will differ from the population mean by no more than 500 miles.

(e) Compare your answers to (a) and (d). What can you conclude about the effect of increased sample size on the reliability of the sample mean as an estimator?

7-16 Hops Brewery has automated filling equipment. To monitor the quantity of ingredients placed in cans, a random production sample is selected each hour, and the average weight $\bar{X}$ is determined. As long as the sample mean falls between 11.9 and 12.1 ounces, the operation continues; otherwise, the equipment is shut down and adjusted. Assuming that the true process mean μ is unknown and that the standard error of $\bar{X}$ is $\sigma_{\bar{X}} = .05$ ounce, determine the following probabilities.

(a) The equipment is operating properly ($\mu = 12$ ounces), but it is adjusted anyway.

(b) The equipment is overfilling ($\mu = 12.05$ ounces), but it is not adjusted.

(c) The equipment is underfilling ($\mu = 11.95$ ounces), and it is adjusted.

7-17 The operations manager of a port authority ordered an extensive study to determine the optimal number of toll booths to open during various times of the week. One unanticipated finding is that the mean time to collect a toll decreases as traffic becomes heavier. For example, on late Friday afternoons, collection times were found to have a mean of $\mu = 10$ seconds, with a standard deviation of $\sigma = 2$ seconds. On less busy Wednesday mornings, the mean was $\mu = 12$ seconds and the standard deviation was $\sigma = 3$ seconds. A consistency check is now being made to determine whether the season of the year affects efficiency. Random samples of $n = 25$ cars are taken on Wednesday mornings and Friday afternoons. Assume that these results are true population parameters.

(a) What is the probability that the Wednesday sample mean will differ by no more than 1 second from the assumed mean?

(b) What is the same probability for Friday?

(c) Why do the probabilities you determined in (a) and (b) differ?

7-5 SAMPLING DISTRIBUTION OF *P* AND THE NORMAL APPROXIMATION

In Chapter 6, we established that the proportion of successes obtained from a Bernoulli process is a random variable having the binomial distribution. A random sample selected from a population of two complementary attributes may be construed to be a Bernoulli process when the population is very large or when sampling with replacement.

ADVANTAGES OF APPROXIMATING THE BINOMIAL DISTRIBUTION

Calculating probabilities from the binomial formula can be a tedious chore that may seem insurmountable in many cases. For example, consider calculating the probability that $R = 324$ convictions are obtained in the next $n = 2{,}032$ criminal cases brought to trial in a state, when the average rate of convictions is $\pi = .537$. This would involve evaluating

$$\frac{2{,}032!}{324!(2{,}032 - 324)!}(.537)^{324}(1 - .537)^{2{,}032 - 324}$$

Such computations would require working with both extremely large and small numbers, making the use of logarithms or other approximations almost mandatory.

Of course, using a high-speed digital computer might make the task manageable. Binomial probabilities can be calculated and tabulated, but then a new problem arises: For what values of π and n should tables be constructed? Obviously, not all π values can be accommodated, because they are infinite in number (all possible values between 0 and 1), and the probability table for a particular π would be quite long for even a moderately large n. Clearly, no table can be constructed that would contain all the binomial probabilities.

THE NORMAL DISTRIBUTION AS AN APPROXIMATION

The difficulties just discussed can be avoided if a satisfactory approximation to the binomial distribution can be used. Remember that a graph of the binomial distribution tends to become bell shaped as n increases (see Figure 6-9). This suggests that for large sample sizes, the binomial distribution approaches the shape of the normal curve.

In fact, the central limit theorem indicates that P tends to have a normal curve as its sampling distribution. To see why this must be so, suppose you assign points to the trial outcomes, with each success getting a 1 and each failure a 0. The outcome of any given trial, then, is a random variable having either of these two values. Let X_1 denote the first trial value, X_2 the second, and so on. Consider the mean of these,

$$\bar{X} = \frac{X_1 + X_2 + \cdots + X_n}{n}$$

This value $\bar{X}$ is the same as the proportion of successes P (because the sum of all the Xs must equal the total number of successes, and P is that value divided by the number of trials n). When n is large, the *central limit theorem* states that $\bar{X}$, and hence P, has a sampling distribution closely approximated by the normal curve.

The commonly accepted guidelines for using the normal approximation are given in Table 7-1. These guidelines have been constructed according to the

TABLE 7-1 Guidelines for Using the Normal Approximation to the Binomial Distribution

Whenever π Equals	Use the Normal Approximation Only if n Is No Smaller than
.5	10
.40 or .60	13
.30 or .70	17
.20 or .80	25
.10 or .90	50
.05 or .95	100
.01 or .99	500
.005 or .995	1,000
.001 or .999	5,000

popular rule that the normal approximation to the binomial distribution is adequate whenever both of the following hold.

$$n\pi \geq 5$$

$$n(1 - \pi) \geq 5$$

Some statisticians insist that even larger sample sizes than those listed in Table 7-1 must be used before the approximation is acceptable. In some cases, a very large sample size should be used, because the skew of the binomial distribution is so pronounced for large or small π that the bell shape is assumed by the binomial distribution only for very large n.

In Chapter 6, we established expressions for the mean and the standard deviation of P. The expected value of P is π and the standard error of P is

$$\sigma_P = \sqrt{\frac{\pi(1 - \pi)}{n}}$$

Using a normal curve centered at π with a standard deviation of σ_P, we can determine for any possible level p of the sample proportion the corresponding

NORMAL DEVIATE FOR THE SAMPLE PROPORTION

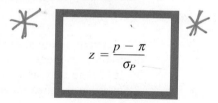

$$z = \frac{p - \pi}{\sigma_P}$$

To illustrate the suitability of the normal approximation, we will consider the two distributions when $n = 10$ and $\pi = .5$. The actual sampling distribution is plotted in Figure 7-13. (The probability values were obtained from Appendix Table C.) To compare this discrete distribution to the continuous normal distribution, the probabilities are presented as bars rather than spikes. The height of each bar represents the probability that P assumes the value at the midpoint of the bar's base. Since the base of each bar may be considered to be of unit width (letting each unit represent a .10 increment on the scale of p), the area of a bar also represents the probability of the P value at the midpoint. The area .3770 of all the bars at or above the point $P = .6$ therefore represents the probability that P will be greater than or equal to .6 (the gray area in Figure 7-13).

We can obtain the normal approximation to the sampling distribution of P. Here, the mean and the standard error are

$$E(P) = \pi = .5$$

$$\sigma_P = \sqrt{\frac{.5(1 - .5)}{10}} = .158$$

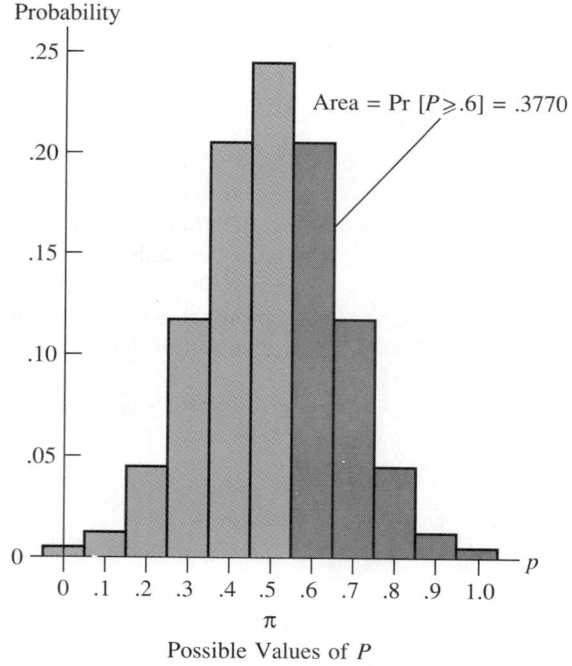

FIGURE 7-13 Binomial sampling distribution of P.

The corresponding normal curve is graphed in Figure 7-14. Treating P as an approximately normal random variable, the probability that P lies at or above .6 is .2643 (the gray area under the approximating normal curve in Figure 7-14).

Note that the area under the normal curve above .6 only approximates the true probability indicated by the gray area under the bars in Figure 7-13. The true probability is .3770, but the normal curve provides a probability of .2643. The discrepancy between the binomial probabilities and the probabilities determined by using the normal curve are negligible for large sample sizes. It is easier to assess the nature of the approximation in Figure 7-15, where the graph for the binomial distribution of P is superimposed on the normal curve. Here, a continuity correction has been applied to obtain a better approximation.*

*In Figure 7-14, we could have obtained a value from the normal curve area above .55 rather than above .60.

$$z = \frac{.55 - .50}{.158} = .32$$

$$\Pr[P \geq .55] = .5000 - .1255 = .3745$$

The value .3745 is much closer to the true binomial probability of .3770. Using .55 instead of .60 applies a continuity correction of $.5/n = .5/10 = .05$. A continuity correction is needed because the *discrete* binomial distribution is being approximated by *continuous* normal distribution. Thus, we may improve our normal curve approximation by subtracting $.5/n$ from the lower limit for P and adding $.5/n$ to the upper limit. The continuity correction will be ignored in this book to make discussion conceptually simpler. For most sample sizes where the normal approximation will be made, n is large enough so that $.5/n$ is relatively small, and the continuity correction only slightly improves the approximation.

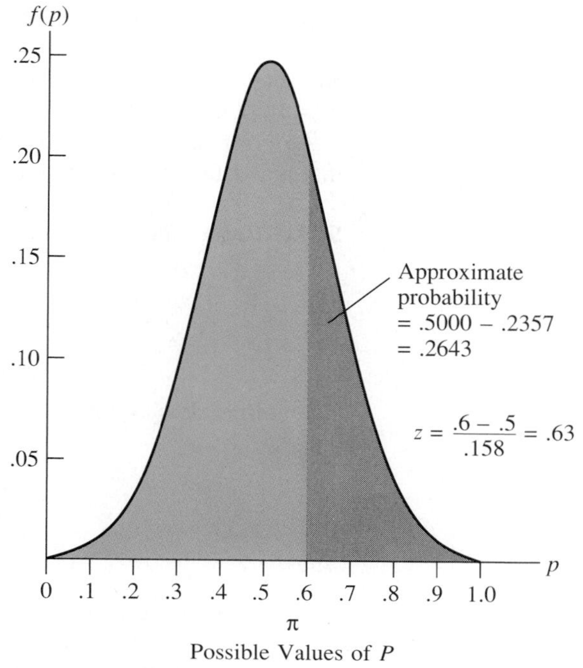

FIGURE 7-14 Normal approximation to the sampling distribution of P when $n = 10$ and $\pi = .5$.

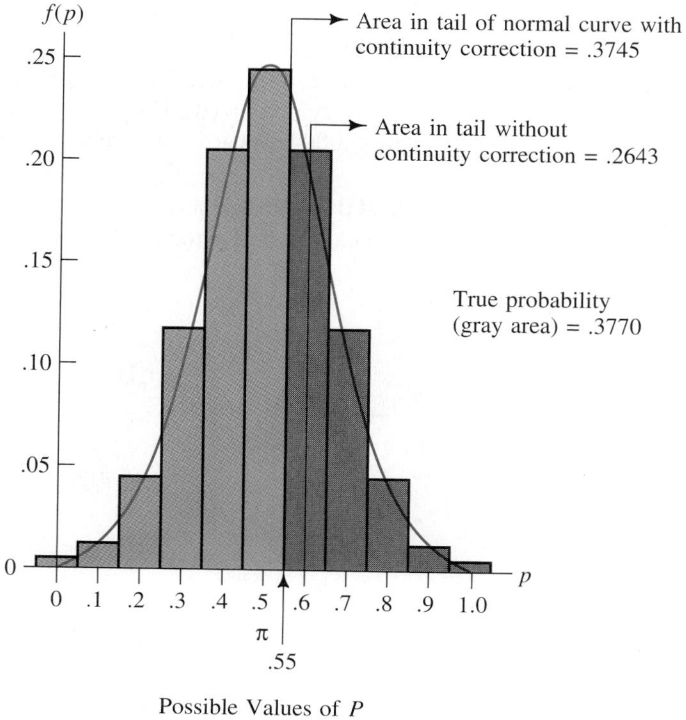

FIGURE 7-15 A comparison of the binomial sampling distribution of P to its normal approximation.

EXAMPLE: WHEN TO REPLACE A RELAY SWITCH

Centralia Bell replaces its relay switches whenever the proportion of erroneous characters in a test transmission is greater than .0003. Each test involves $n = 10{,}000$ characters.

An error rate of $\pi = .0002$ is considered satisfactory. What is the probability that a satisfactory relay is replaced?

SOLUTION: The standard error of P is

$$\sigma_P = \sqrt{\frac{.0002(.9998)}{10{,}000}} = .00014$$

The normal deviate for a sample proportion of level .0003 is

$$z = \frac{.0003 - .0002}{.00014} = .71$$

Thus,

$$\Pr[\text{replacement}] = \Pr[P > .0003] = .5000 - .2612 = .2388$$

About 24% of all tests involving satisfactory relays will involve unnecessary replacement.

EXAMPLE: (continued)

The testing procedure also provides good protection against leaving an unsatisfactory relay switch in place. Suppose that the error rate π is instead a too high $\pi = .0004$. What is the probability that the unsatisfactory switch gets replaced?

SOLUTION: (continued)

The standard error of P is

$$\sigma_P = \sqrt{\frac{.0004(.9996)}{10{,}000}} = .00020$$

The normal deviate is

$$z = \frac{.0003 - .0004}{.00020} = -.50$$

which is negative and so lies below the center of the normal curve. Thus,

$$\Pr[\text{replacement}] = \Pr[P > .0003] = .5000 + .1915 = .6915$$

In about 69% of all tests, such grossly malfunctioning switches will get replaced.

AN APPLICATION OF THE NORMAL APPROXIMATION TO ACCEPTANCE SAMPLING

We can illustrate the usefulness of the normal approximation to the binomial distribution with an example of **acceptance sampling**. A manufacturer who depends on outside suppliers for raw materials or components for production will accept only shipments of some set minimum quality. Due to the expense involved, the decision to accept or reject an incoming shipment is based on a sample of the items received. The procedure for accomplishing this is an acceptance sampling plan—a common approach in quality control.

ILLUSTRATION: INSPECTING CAR HEADLAMPS

Consider an automobile assembly plant that procures headlamps. The supplier has designed its production operation in such a way that, for various reasons, about 5% of its output is defective. The assembly plant quality control manager inspects a sample of $n = 100$ from each shipment. If 7 or fewer (that is, 7% or fewer) items in the sample are defective, the manufacturer will accept the shipment; otherwise, the batch will be rejected and returned to the supplier.

The number 7 is referred to as the **acceptance number**. It forms the basis for a **decision rule**, which specifies the action to be taken regarding a particular batch. We can determine the implications for both the consumer and the producer by using such a rule to calculate various probabilities.

Suppose a large batch of headlamps contains $\pi = .10$ defectives. If the quality control manager knew the value of π, she would reject the shipment. But because only a sample will be taken, she may accept the poor batch. What is the probability that the manager will accept the shipment?

The shipment will be accepted if the sample proportion of defectives P is $\leq .07$. Employing the normal approximation, we first calculate the standard error of P.

$$\sigma_P = \sqrt{\frac{\pi(1-\pi)}{\text{n}}} = \sqrt{\frac{.10(1-.10)}{100}} = .03$$

The probability for accepting the bad batch is then calculated.

$$z = \frac{p - \pi}{\sigma_P} = \frac{.07 - .10}{.03} = -1.00$$

$$\Pr[P \leq .07] = .5000 - .3413 = .1587$$

Thus, there is a .1587 probability that this poor batch of headlamps will be accepted. Because accepting an inferior shipment is an incorrect decision that will hurt some product users, such a probability value is referred to as the **consumer's risk**.

The supplier can be hurt by another kind of erroneous decision. Suppose that an acceptable lot having $\pi = .05$ defectives is shipped. If, by chance, more than 7 defectives are sampled, the good shipment will be rejected. To determine the probability that this will occur, we again use the normal approximation. The standard error of P is

$$\sigma_P = \sqrt{\frac{.05(1-.05)}{100}} = .0218$$

The probability for rejecting the good batch is therefore

$$z = \frac{.07 - .05}{.0218} = .92$$

$$\Pr[P > .07] = .5000 - .3212 = .1788$$

A probability that an acceptable shipment will be erroneously rejected is referred to as the **producer's risk**.

The producer's risk and the consumer's risk are illustrations of the more general Type I and Type II errors of hypothesis testing that we will discuss in Chapter 9. There, we will describe how a decision rule may be constructed to balance both risks and to keep the probabilities for making erroneous decisions at desired levels.

EXERCISES

7-18 A Speak E-Z quality control inspector tests a random sample of 100 video display terminals from each outgoing shipment. In one large shipment, 5% of the units are defective, though the inspector does not know this. If 7% or more of the tested units are defective, she will hold the entire shipment for further testing. Determine the probability that the inspector will hold the shipment.

7-19 A Bernoulli process has a trial success probability of $\pi = .5$. Determine the approximate probability that the proportion P of successes will fall between .4 and .6 when the following number n of trials apply.

(a) 64 (b) 100 (c) 400

(d) What relationship do you notice between the probability values you obtained and the trial size n? How do you explain this relationship?

7-20 A marketing researcher for Big Sky Enterprises believes that the proportion of persons favoring a new package design is $\pi = .6$. Suppose that a sample of $n = 100$ persons is selected at random from the entire market, which numbers in the millions. The sample proportion favoring the new design may be approximated by the normal distribution.

(a) Calculate the standard error of P.

(b) Assuming that the given parameter applies, determine the probability that 70% or more of the persons queried will favor the new package.

(c) Suppose that the parameter value is only $\pi = .57$.

(1) Recalculate the standard error of P.

(2) Determine the probability that 70% or more of the sample persons will favor the new design.

7-21 A robot that shapes metal needs overhauling if it is out of tolerance on 4.5% of the items processed, and it is operating satisfactorily if it is off on only .8% of its output. A test is performed involving 50 sample items. If the sample proportion of out-of-tolerance items is greater than .02, the robot will be overhauled. Otherwise, it will be allowed to continue to operate.

(a) What is the probability that a satisfactory robot will be overhauled unnecessarily?

(b) What is the probability that a robot in need of overhauling will be left in operation?

7-22 The manufacturer of WeeTees is considering reformulating the product. The cereal currently has 30% of the total market. The value .30 is assumed to apply to the proportion of all persons in the market who will favor the reformulated product. The final decision for reformulating will be based on the results of a sample taste test involving 100 randomly selected persons representing the entire market. If more than 25% of the sample likes the new formulation, it will be marketed.

(a) Suppose that the new product tastes so horrible that only 15% of the population likes it. Determine the probability that the new formulation will be adopted.

(b) Suppose that the new WeeTees is so luscious that its market share would immediately jump to 40% if it is reformulated. Determine the probability that it does not get adopted in spite of that.

7-23 A Red Giant cannery accepts a shipment of tomatoes whenever P (the proportion that is ripe in a sample of $n = 100$) is $\geq .90$. Assume that the shipments are sufficiently large that the sampling process can be represented (with only minor error) as a Bernoulli process.

(a) What is the approximate probability for accepting a poor shipment in which the proportion of ripe tomatoes is $\pi = .8$?

(b) What is the approximate probability for rejecting a good shipment in which the proportion of ripe tomatoes is $\pi = .95$?

(c) How do you account for the fact that these probabilities indicate some shipments of poor quality will be accepted and some shipments of good quality will be rejected?

SUMMARY

1. What are the properties of the normal distribution and why is it so important?

The **normal distribution** is used to represent the frequency distributions of many populations that are often encountered—especially those resulting from physical measurements. The frequency curve of such a population is called a **normal curve**. Normal curves have a bell shape, are symmetrical, and have tails extending indefinitely above and below the center. Three measures of central tendency coincide at that point: the mean, the median, and the mode.

2. How are the various normal distributions distinguished?

All normal curves belong to a common family, the members of which are distinguished by their *location* and *scale* parameters, the mean μ and standard deviation σ.

3. What role is played by areas under the normal curve and how do these relate to probabilities?

The *area* under the normal curve between any two points provides the relative frequency for the population values in that range. That area is specified by the **normal deviate**, which is the distance (in units of standard deviations) separating each endpoint from the mean.

When a sample unit from a normally distributed population is observed at random, the possible value achieved is a random variable whose **probability density function** graphs as a normal curve. The probability that such a variable assumes a value in any particular range is equal to the matching area.

4. **How does the *central limit theorem* enable us to use the normal curve to find probabilities for future levels of the sample mean?**
The key role played by the normal distribution in statistics is that it allows us to draw conclusions regarding the *sample mean* $\bar{X}$. According to the **central limit theorem**, $\bar{X}$ is a random variable whose sampling distribution can usually be represented by a normal curve. The mean of that normal distribution is the population mean itself, and its standard deviation is $\sigma_{\bar{X}} = \sigma/\sqrt{n}$ for large populations. The central limit theorem applies even when the population frequency curve isn't normal, although then the normal curve is only an *approximation* that improves as n increases. Before the sample data are available, the normal distribution provides probability values for any possible level of $\bar{X}$.

5. **How may we use the normal distribution to approximate probabilities for future levels of the sample proportion?**
The normal distribution may also approximate the sampling distribution of the *sample proportion P*. This is advantageous primarily from a computational point of view; the normal distribution is easier to work with than the binomial. Care must be taken that n is large enough, and a **continuity correction** can be made to improve the accuracy of the approximation.

REAL-LIFE STATISTICAL CHALLENGE

Applying the Normal Distribution to the Automobile Dream List

We will observe whether the normal distribution would be a good measurement tool for analyzing the automobile data for 232 cars originally listed in Table 4-2. Table 7-2 shows the distributions of both the mileage and engine displacements for the automobiles. The population parameters for engine displacement for all 232 automobiles are $\mu = 2.69$ liters and $\sigma = 1.23$ liters. The mileage parameters are $\mu = 27.48$ mpg and $\sigma = 6.23$ mpg. The percentage of cases that are within one standard deviation of the mean are 79.3% for engine displacement and 79.7% for mileage respectively.

DISCUSSION QUESTIONS

1. Determine how many automobiles would have engine displacements exceeding 4.3 liters assuming that the normal distribution applies. Compare this to the actual number exceeding that displacement.
2. Construct histograms for the two distributions. Are the shapes similar to those of normal curves?
3. Mark the first two standard deviations from the mean for both mileage and displacement. What proportion of the population values should lie between these if the normal distributions apply?
4. Refer to Tables 6-19 and 6-20. Incorporate into your histograms the location of the respective sample means. Comment on your results.

TABLE 7-2 Mileage Data for 1990 Automobiles Showing Engine Displacement (liters) and Highway Mileage per Gallon

Engine Displacement in Liters	Frequency	Highway Mileage Miles/gallon	Frequency
1.0	6	10	1
1.1	0	11	0
1.2	2	12	0
1.3	9	13	4
1.4	0	14	0
1.5	16	15	1
1.6	22	16	0
1.7	0	17	0
1.8	14	18	6
1.9	2	19	3
2.0	19	20	4
2.1	0	21	6
2.2	12	22	10
2.3	12	23	14
2.4	4	24	21
2.5	19	25	20
2.6	0	26	12
2.7	1	27	29
2.8	11	28	18
2.9	0	29	14
3.0	17	30	16
3.1	10	31	3
3.2	0	32	11
3.3	7	33	11
3.4	2	34	7
3.5	0	35	2
3.6	3	36	7
3.7	0	37	2
3.8	13	38	0
3.9	0	39	2
4.0	2	40	1
4.1	0	41	1
4.2	0	42	1
4.3	0	43	0
4.4	0	44	1
4.5	5	45	0
4.6	0	46	0
4.7	0	47	0
4.8	0	48	0
4.9	1	49	0
5.0	14	50	2
5.1	0	51	0
5.2	1	52	1
5.3	0	53	0
5.4	0	54	0
5.5	0	55	0
5.6	0	56	0
5.7	4	57	0
5.8	0	58	1
5.9	0		
6.0	4		
$\mu = 2.69$	$N = 232$	$\mu = 27.48$	$N = 232$
$\sigma = 1.23$		$\sigma = 6.23$	

Source: United States Environmental Protection Agency, 1989.

REVIEW EXERCISES

7-24 The mean μ and standard deviation σ for accountants' salaries is unknown. A sample of $n = 25$ is taken at random from a population of accountants, and the sample mean is calculated. Assume that the population is of large size. Determine the probability that $\bar{X}$ falls within $\mu \pm \$500$ when the following standard deviations apply.

(a) $\sigma = \$1{,}500$ (b) $\sigma = \$2{,}000$ (c) $\sigma = \$2{,}500$

7-25 The height of women is normally distributed with a mean of $\mu = 66$ inches and a standard deviation of $\sigma = 1.5$ inches. Determine the (a) 50th, (b) 15th, (c) 95th, (d) 75th, and (e) 33rd percentiles.

7-26 The annual incomes of consultants constitute a highly positively skewed population. Nevertheless, according to the central limit theorem, it is still possible to find the sampling distribution of the mean for a random sample of these incomes by using the normal distribution. Suppose the population has an unknown mean of μ and a standard deviation of $\sigma = \$10{,}000$. An estimate of μ is to be made using the value of the sample mean $\bar{X}$. This estimate must fall within $\pm\$1{,}000$ of the true mean.

(a) If $n = 100$ incomes, determine the probability that the estimate will meet the desired accuracy.

(b) If a sample $n = 625$ incomes is used instead, determine the probability that the estimate will meet the desired accuracy.

7-27 The time that each payroll waits to be processed at Comp-U-Quik's data service bureau is assumed to have a positively skewed distribution. A sample of 25 waiting times is collected. Both the mean and the standard deviation for individual waiting times are equal to .5 day. A large population size is assumed. Determine the probabilities for the following possible sample mean waiting times.

(a) doesn't exceed .6 day
(b) is greater than .7 day
(c) equals $.5 \pm .1$ day
(d) is between .3 and .7 day

7-28 The weights of "1-ounce" gold ingots cast by Midas Metals are normally distributed, with a mean of $\mu = 28$ grams and a standard deviation of $\sigma = 1$ gram. Consider a shipment of 25 ingots.

(a) What is the probability that the mean ingot weight will be less than 27.5 grams?

(b) Determine the probability that the entire shipment will weigh more than 705 grams.

7-29 The Water Wheelies production process is designed to produce only 10% defective items. Once each day, a sample of 100 items is selected and the proportion of defectives P is determined. If this value lies below .15, production is continued. Otherwise, production is stopped for maintenance.

(a) Assuming that the process is operating as designed, determine the probability that operations will be continued.

(b) Suppose that the process is producing too many defectives, at the rate of 20%, but management does not know this. Determine the probability that the process will be stopped for maintenance.

7-30 A parapsychologist is testing the extrasensory perception of a purported clairvoyant. Using a deck of cards, half of which are red and half of which are black, she selects the top card and asks her subject (who is in another room) to identify its color. The procedure is repeated 100 times. Each successive card is replaced in the deck, and the deck is shuffled before the next card is drawn. A subject with no powers of ESP should identify the correct color 50% of the time, so that $\pi = .5$. Under this assumption, what is the probability that a correct response will be obtained for 65 or more of the 100 cards? Use the normal approximation.

7-31 For each of the following sampling situations, indicate (by *yes* or *no*) whether the sampling distribution of the sample proportion can be approximated by the normal curve.

(a) $\pi = .50; n = 9$
(b) $\pi = .10; n = 36$
(c) $\pi = .83; n = 100$
(d) $\pi = .45; n = 20$
(e) $\pi = .01; n = 1{,}000$

7-32 Assume the population of members of the U.S. Army has a mean height of 70 inches and a standard deviation of 3 inches. A random sample of 100 soldiers is selected. Determine the probabilities for the following mean heights.

(a) between 70 and 70.5 inches
(b) less than 69.5 inches
(c) greater than 72 inches
(d) less than 68 inches
(e) between 69.4 and 70.8 inches

7-33 Procrastinator Pete marks an examination consisting of 36 true-or-false questions by tossing a coin. For each question, he answers "true" for a head or "false" for a tail. Assuming that half the correct answers should be marked "true," what is the probability that the student will pass the examination by marking at least 75% of the answers correctly? Use the normal approximation.

7-34 A clerk at the Fox Box Company measures the quantities in all bulk products purchased. On the average, 1,000-foot rolls of transparent tape should be close to the specified length. In evaluating a shipment, a random sample of 100 rolls of tape is selected, and the mean length is determined. If the mean is greater than or equal to 990 feet, the entire shipment is accepted; otherwise, the shipment is rejected and returned to the manufacturer.

(a) If a shipment has a mean roll length of only 980 feet, with a standard deviation of 50 feet, determine the consumer's risk (probability of accepting these inferior tapes).
(b) If a shipment has a mean roll length of 1,005 feet, with a standard deviation of 60 feet, determine the producer's risk (probability of rejecting these good tapes).

STATISTICS IN PRACTICE

7-35 Using the master class data found for Exercise 1-19, answer the following for one of your quantitative variables (e.g., age or height).

(a) Using all data points, compute the mean and standard deviation. Those values will serve as the μ and σ.
(b) You will select a sample of 5 observations randomly from the list. Find the standard error of the sample mean. After selecting your sample, compute the mean and standard deviation.
(c) Compare the means from (a) and (b). What is the probability of getting

a sample mean as far or farther (in the same direction) from the population mean as the one actually found?

(d) Develop an example based on your data set that demonstrates how the binomial distribution may be approximated by the normal curve in finding probabilities for the sample proportion. Find the probability that the sample proportion falls between .60 and .70.

7-36 Using your group's class data list developed in Exercise 1-21, repeat (a) through (d) of Exercise 7-35. Use $n = 7$ as the sample size and change the limits in (d) to .25 and .75.

7-37 Refer to the data you created in Exercise 6-54 for the personal computer system cost. Assume that the probability distribution found actually represents the relative frequency distribution for the *population* relative frequency distribution.

(a) Compute the mean and standard deviation. Those values will serve as the μ and σ.

(b) Assume a sample size of $n = 100$ is selected. Compute three meaningful probability values for the sample mean system cost.

7-38 In Exercise 6-55 you were asked to go to a local store or other retail outlet and find the number of customer arrivals during each of several one-minute intervals.

(a) For those data, compute the mean and standard deviation for the number of arrivals in any given minute. Assume that these values will serve as the μ and σ.

(b) A sample will be taken of $n = 9$ one-minute intervals. Find the probability that the mean number of arrivals will be (1) less than .5, (2) above 2, (3) between 1 and 3.

CASE MBA Income and Stature

Various statistical populations are associated with an MBA degree. Three Slippery Rock University undergraduates majoring in geography, Georgia Maine, Tex York, and Virginia Washington, are compiling a demographic profile. The subjects of their study are former MBA students who have just completed their first year in the working world.

Georgia sent out questionnaires to a random sample of recent graduates. Tex is particularly interested in MBA salaries (including bonuses and other monetary perquisites). Using the sample data from the completed questionnaires, Tex constructed the sample histogram in Figure 7-16. He then calculated the *sample* mean and variance for the salaries. Although he cannot know the levels of the population counterparts, some judgmental adjustments were made to arrive at $\mu = \$29{,}000$ and $\sigma = \$12{,}000$. Tex wants to use these values to form various probabilistic assessments.

Virginia believes that persons with an MBA are not only motivationally different from other graduate alumni but physically distinct as well. To begin her study, Virginia investigated sample heights. Using the sample data, she constructed the histograms in Figure 7-17. From these results, Virginia used the following values to make probability evaluations.

$$\mu = 70'' \qquad \sigma = 2.6'' \qquad \text{(men)}$$

$$\mu = 67'' \qquad \sigma = 2.3'' \qquad \text{(women)}$$

At this point, the undergraduates need some statistical expertise. You have volunteered to answer their questions concerning statistics.

QUESTIONS

1. Tex asks you to determine probabilities for the salary of a typical MBA selected at random. Comment on the appropriateness of using the normal distribution for this purpose.

2. You assure Tex that the normal distribution may be used to establish probabilities for the mean salary of any sample group randomly selected from the underlying population.

(a) Comment on why you may comfortably make such assurances even though the population frequency curve will most likely resemble the histogram in Figure 7-16.

(b) Suppose that another random sample of size $n = 9$ is selected from the salary population. Determine the following probabilities.

(1) $\Pr[\bar{X} \geq \$40{,}000]$ (3) $\Pr[\bar{X} \leq \$26{,}000]$

(2) $\Pr[\$27{,}000 \leq \bar{X} \leq \$30{,}000]$ (4) $\Pr[\bar{X} > \$31{,}000]$

```
  Class Interval                Frequency
  for Salary                  ----------------------------------------------
                              0    10   20   30   40   50   60   70   80   90
10000. under 15000.     0     :
15000. under 20000.     28    :**************
20000. under 25000.     62    :*******************************
25000. under 30000.     52    :**************************
30000. under 35000.     20    :***********
35000. under 40000.     16    :********
40000. under 45000.     6     :***
45000. under 50000.     4     :**
50000. under 55000.     2     :*
55000. under 60000.     2     :*
60000. under 65000.     0     :
65000. under 70000.     2     :*
70000. under 75000.     2     :*
75000. under 80000.     2     :*
80000. under 85000.     2     :*
85000. under 90000.     0     :
```

Note: Figure generated on an IBM PC using EasyStat.

FIGURE 7-16 Sample histogram for the salaries of former MBA students.

(c) Assume that $n = 100$. Determine the above probabilities.

(d) Compare your answers to (b) and (c). What might you conclude regarding the use of a larger sample size?

3. Virginia asks you to determine various probabilities for the heights of a typical MBA selected at random.

(a) You inform Virginia that there are typical *male* MBA heights and typical *female* MBA heights. But, probabilities should be reported separately. Explain.

(b) Comment on why you may find normal distributions suitable for this purpose in spite of the obstacles you faced with salary.

4. Determine the following probabilities for the height of a randomly selected male MBA.

(a) $\Pr[X \geq 73'']$ (b) $\Pr[X \leq 66'']$

5. Determine the above probabilities for the height of a randomly selected female MBA.

6. Suppose that the sample selected is exactly half men and half women. Consider the mean height of the entire sample, with sexes mixed.

Class Interval for Height (inches)		Frequency (Men) 0 10 20 30		Frequency (Women) 0 10 20 30
60. under 61.	0	:	0	:
61. under 62.	0	:	1	:*
62. under 63.	1	:*	2	:*
63. under 64.	1	:*	5	:***
64. under 65.	2	:*	12	:******
65. under 66.	4	:**	15	:********
66. under 67.	3	:**	21	:***********
67. under 68.	10	:*****	15	:********
68. under 69.	12	:******	13	:*******
69. under 70.	17	:*********	5	:***
70. under 71.	15	:********	4	:**
71. under 72.	16	:********	5	:***
72. under 73.	11	:******	2	:*
73. under 74.	3	:**	0	:
74. under 75.	1	:*	0	:
75. under 76.	4	:**	0	:
76. under 77.	0	:	0	:

Note: Figure generated on an IBM PC using EasyStat.

FIGURE 7-17 Sample histograms for the heights of former MBA students.

(a) Although it may not be very meaningful, the normal distribution may be used to determine probabilities for the sample mean height (with sexes mixed). Why?

(b) When a bimodal population is formed from two component populations, the resulting population mean will be a weighted average of the two separate population means, according to the proportional sizes of the two groups. Suppose that Virginia combines the heights of men and women MBAs. Regardless of the proportional representation of the sexes, her combined population is assumed to have a standard deviation of 3″ (an approximation). Virginia plans to select a random sample of $n = 25$ heights. Assume that the combined population is half men's heights and half women's heights.
  (1) Find the mean height of the combined population.
  (2) Determine $\Pr[\bar{X} \geq 70'']$.
  (3) Determine $\Pr[\bar{X} \leq 68'']$.

(c) Repeat (b) assuming instead that 90% of the combined population observations are men's heights.

(d) Repeat (b) assuming instead that 25% of the combined population observations are men's heights.

7-6 OPTIONAL TOPIC: SAMPLING DISTRIBUTION OF $\bar{X}$ WHEN THE POPULATION IS SMALL

We have established that for independent sample observations, the standard error of $\bar{X}$ may be obtained from the expression $\sigma_{\bar{X}} = \sigma/\sqrt{n}$. Observations are always independent when sampling with replacement, but we usually sample *without replacement*. When populations are large compared to sample size, the probability distributions for successive observations barely change when earlier items are removed. In these cases, we can generally assume independence between observations.

But when the population is small compared to sample size, this fact must be reflected in calculating $\sigma_{\bar{X}}$.

STANDARD ERROR OF $\bar{X}$ (small populations)

$$\sigma_{\bar{X}} = \frac{\sigma}{\sqrt{n}}\sqrt{\frac{N-n}{N-1}}$$

where σ = population standard deviation, N = population size, and n = sample size.

FINITE POPULATION CORRECTION FACTOR

The term $\sqrt{(N - n)/(N - 1)}$ is referred to as the **finite population correction factor**. When n is small in relation to N, the factor is very close to 1. Thus, the standard error obtained from a sample without replacement is close in value to one obtained from a sample with replacement. Note that the numerator in the expression will never be greater than the denominator, so that $\sigma_{\overline{X}}$ will be smaller when a sample is taken without replacement. *In practice, the finite population correction is usually ignored whenever n is less than 10% of N.*

For samples from small populations, the normal distribution approximately describes the sampling distribution of $\overline{X}$, even though the observations are not independent. As an illustration, consider a survey of incomes in two cities. City A has a population of $N = 10{,}000$; city B has a population of $N = 2{,}500$. A standard deviation of $\sigma = \$1{,}500$ is assumed to be common to both populations. A sample of $n = 1{,}000$ is taken from each. The following calculation provides the standard error of $\overline{X}$ for city A.

$$\sigma_{\overline{X}} = \frac{\$1{,}500}{\sqrt{1{,}000}}\sqrt{\frac{10{,}000 - 1{,}000}{10{,}000 - 1}} = \$45.00$$

Analogously, for city B,

$$\sigma_{\overline{X}} = \frac{\$1{,}500}{\sqrt{1{,}000}}\sqrt{\frac{2{,}500 - 1{,}000}{2{,}500 - 1}} = \$36.75$$

Note that the standard error of $\overline{X}$ for city B is smaller than that for city A. This is to be expected, because B is a smaller city. But the standard error of $\overline{X}$ for city A is only about 23% greater, although its population is four times as large.

The probability that $\overline{X}$ *exceeds* the mean by 100 or more can be calculated for each city. For A,

$$z = \frac{\bar{x} - \mu}{\sigma_{\overline{X}}} = \frac{100}{45.00} = 2.22$$

$$\Pr[\overline{X} - \mu \geq 100] = .5000 - .4868 = .0132$$

and for B,

$$z = \frac{100}{36.75} = 2.72$$

$$\Pr[\overline{X} - \mu \geq 100] = .5000 - .4967 = .0033$$

In either case, the probability for obtaining a sample mean that exceeds the respective mean by \$100 or more is relatively small. However, the same sample size provides about the same protection against obtaining extremely large sample values in *both* cities, regardless of the size of either.

When n is small in relation to N, the finite population correction factor approaches 1. Thus, a sample of $n = 1{,}000$ would yield almost the same finite population factor for a population of $N = 100{,}000$ that it would for one of $N = 1{,}000{,}000$ (.9949 versus .9995). Thus, if the standard deviations of the two populations are identical, there would be an imperceptible difference in the respective values of $\sigma_{\bar{X}}$, and the probabilities for possible sample results would be nearly identical. In this case, a sample of $n = 1{,}000$ would be almost as reliable in a large population as in a population one-tenth its size. This is why we concluded in Chapter 4 that a sample of Alaska voters in a presidential election poll would have to be about the same size as a sample of California voters for the sample results to be equally reliable.

OPTIONAL EXERCISES

7-39 A sample of $n = 100$ families is selected at random from the community of Dog Patch. Assume that there are $N = 500$ families in the entire town. The population standard deviation is known to be $\sigma = \$700$.

(a) Calculate the standard error of the sample mean family income.

(b) Then take a random sample of the same size from the residents of Metropolis. Assume $N = 1{,}000{,}000$ and that the same level applies for σ as before. Calculate the value for $\sigma_{\bar{X}}$.

7-40 A random sample of 100 soldiers is selected without replacement from a regiment of 900 men. The mean regiment height is 71 inches, with a standard deviation of 2.5 inches. Determine the probabilities for the following sample mean heights.

(a) between 71 and 71.4 inches.

(b) less than 70.5 inches.

(c) greater than 71.6 inches.

(d) between 70.7 and 71.5 inches.

7-41 The unemployment rates experienced by $N = 210$ medium-sized cities in one year have a mean of $\mu = 7\%$ and a standard deviation of $\sigma = 2\%$. A random sample of 25 of these cities is selected.

(a) Calculate the standard error of the sample mean.

(b) Determine the probability that the sample mean

(1) exceeds 8%.

(2) is smaller than 6.5%.

(3) is between 6.5% and 7.5%.

(4) is between 6.0% and 6.5%.

7-42 A customs official wishes to estimate the mean weight of each of three batches of copper ingots obtained from different smelters. $N = 500$ ingots have arrived from Chile, $N = 1{,}000$ from Bolivia, and $N = 700$ from Arizona. Samples of $n = 100$ ingots from each batch are weighed. Each smelter is assumed to produce batches of ingots with a mean weight of $\mu = 100$ pounds and a standard deviation of $\sigma = 5$ pounds.

(a) Determine the probability that the sample mean of each batch lies between 99 and 101 pounds.

(b) Using the same sample size, determine the analogous probability values when the sample means are obtained from batches ten times as large.

(c) Do your answers differ significantly between smelters? Explain.

7-43 Suppose that the customs official in Exercise 7-42 establishes a rule to enable him to decide when an entire batch of ingots should be individually weighed. Because it is such a time-consuming procedure, he wants to weigh the ingots only when there is strong sample evidence that they are underweight.

Assume that an acceptable batch of $N = 1{,}000$ ingots has a mean weight of $\mu = 100$ pounds, but that the official does not know this value. He takes a sample of $n = 200$ and calculates $\bar{X}$. Suppose that the batch standard deviation is $\sigma = 5$ pounds. The official must consider three decision rules.

(1) Accept batch (do not weigh all 1,000 ingots) if $\bar{X} \geq 100$ pounds.
(2) Accept batch if $\bar{X} \geq 99.5$ pounds.
(3) Accept batch if $\bar{X} \geq 99.0$ pounds.

(a) Determine the probability according to each of these decision rules that the customs official will accept the batch without weighing all the ingots.
(b) If he prefers the rule that maximizes the probability for not weighing all 1,000 ingots, which rule should he choose?

CHAPTER 8

STATISTICAL ESTIMATION

BEFORE READING THIS CHAPTER, MAKE SURE YOU UNDERSTAND:

How to avoid bias in selecting samples and how sampling error arises (Chapter 4).

How to find probabilities for possible results of a random sample (Chapter 6).

The properties of the sampling distribution of the mean (Chapter 6).

About the binomial distribution and its role as the sampling distribution of the proportion (Chapter 6).

About the normal distribution and how to use the normal curve to obtain probabilities for the sample mean (Chapter 7).

How the binomial distribution may be approximated by the normal curve in finding probabilities for the sample proportion (Chapter 7).

AFTER READING THIS CHAPTER, YOU WILL UNDERSTAND:

About estimation and estimators.

What properties are desirable for an estimator.

What two forms are taken by estimates.

About confidence intervals for the mean, and how they are used and constructed.

About the Student *t* distribution and its role in constructing confidence intervals for the mean.

When the Student *t* distribution should be used instead of the normal distribution.

How to use the normal distribution used in constructing confidence intervals for the proportion.

What considerations are important in establishing a sample size.

In this chapter, we will be concerned with the kinds of estimates we make from sample data and the procedures we use to make these estimates. Problems of estimation are crucial to practically every statistical application. This is especially true in business decision making, where often only sample results are available for establishing vital information. For example, samples are used to estimate a product's share of the market—a useful number for many important marketing decisions. Also, statistical estimates provide management with the average times required to complete various production operations, which allows for intelligent planning and better day-to-day control. Similarly, sample data yield median earnings of subscribers to various magazines, a demographic feature useful to merchandisers in choosing where to place advertisements. Estimation problems are perhaps most difficult in economic planning, where the impact of policies can affect the lives of literally every person in an entire nation.

8-1 ESTIMATORS AND ESTIMATES

Using samples to estimate a population parameter is one of the more common forms of statistical inference. A sample statistic that serves this purpose is called an **estimator**. An important segment of statistical theory is concerned with finding statistics that are appropriate estimators. For instance, the sample mean is a particularly good estimator for the population mean. We will learn why this is so.

THE ESTIMATION PROCESS

Parameter estimation requires a great deal of planning. First, we must choose an estimator. Then a major concern is to control the sampling error. The choice of a sampling method—judgment or convenience sampling, or some version of random sampling—will affect this. Our discussion will center on random samples because we know they are free from sampling bias. We also know that small samples tend to be less reliable, so that sampling error can be controlled by using a sufficiently large sample. A practical consideration is to balance the level of reliability, which is influenced by sampling error, against the costs of obtaining the sample.

Due to chance, the value of the sample statistic we obtain may not be close to the population parameter. But unless we take a census of the population, we cannot determine the true parameter value. Therefore, statisticians must be able to assess the reliability of their results even though they can only theoretically determine what values are reasonable.

We are presently concerned only with estimates based on samples taken from already existing populations or from identifiable target populations. This excludes predictions based on other kinds of information—most notably, economic forecasts based on time-series data. For example, although sampling may be involved in forecasting the gross national product, the major role is played by other factors, such as judgment, current trends, contemplated changes in government policies, and the state of international affairs. Some procedures useful in making such predictions will be discussed in Chapter 10. Another category of excluded predictions concerns parameters of some future population. For example, the median annual family income for the United States in the year 2000 cannot be estimated from the usual sample, because the elementary units cannot be presently defined and the variate values themselves lie in the future.

Statistical estimates take two basic forms.

POINT ESTIMATES

You are probably most familiar with the **point estimate**. For example, you may recall the following statements.

> "The mean height of adult males is 5′9″."
> "The proportion of voters approving the president is .40."
> "Our car averages 35 miles per gallon in highway driving."

To be statistically valid, each of the values in these statements must have been obtained in a sampling investigation where the respective findings gave the following computed values: $\bar{X} = 5'9''$, $P = .40$, and $\bar{X} = 35$ mpg.

One drawback to point estimates is that too often they are assumed to be precise and correct. Indeed, lay persons will often believe point estimates to be the levels of the population parameters themselves. You should by now know better! Nevertheless, you will encounter occasions where a point estimate is the preferred form.

INTERVAL ESTIMATES

A sounder way to report findings is to use the **interval estimate**. This type of estimate places the unknown parameter between two limits. Consider the following examples.

> 5′8″–5′10″ for the mean height μ of adult males
> .35–.45 for the proportion π of voters approving the president
> 28.75–39.23 for the mean gasoline mileage μ

An interval estimate acknowledges that the sampling procedure is prone to some error, so that any computed statistic may fall above or below its population parameter target.

It also shows very simply the degree of precision achieved by the results obtained.

Because it represents a range of possible values, an interval estimate implies the presence of uncertainty. It is ordinarily accompanied by a statement indicating the likelihood that the parameter being estimated actually does lie within the stated interval.

There are several ways to symbolically represent the interval estimate. The one adopted in this book is an **inequality**. For example, the population mean height for a group of men would be reported in the form

$$5'8'' \le \mu \le 5'10''$$

Some statisticians favor "strict" inequalities, using $<$ instead of $\le$. Another method is to state the endpoints only—either in parentheses, (5′8″, 5′10″), or with a dash, 5′8″–5′10″.

It is often convenient to adopt the notation for measurement tolerances, really a more compact form of the inequality. This notation applies to most interval estimates, which are usually symmetrical around a point estimator midpoint. For example, the inequality $5'8'' \leq \mu \leq 5'10''$ can be represented equivalently as

$$\mu = 5'9'' \pm 1''$$

Whether a point or an interval estimate is to be made depends on the objective of the statistical study. Interval estimates would be unsuitable to a manufacturer as the basis for placing orders for raw materials, for the supplier cannot accept an order for "something between 2,000 and 3,000 units." Likewise, knowing only that the wattage of a stereo amplifier lies between 50 and 80 makes it difficult to compare that model to other brands. But the superiority of an interval estimate is evident in many kinds of planning or reporting. For example, knowing that next year's sales might lie between 10,000 and 11,000 units, a company president is able to draw up a realistic budget taking into account uncertainties about the sales level. He can visualize the best and worst cases, and thereby obtain a reasonable basis for evaluating the risks involved.

CREDIBILITY AND PRECISION IN ESTIMATION

There are two considerations in establishing the endpoints of an interval estimate. One is the **level of precision** obtained. The other involves the **credibility** of the estimate. You can improve each of these features at the expense of the other, but you can attain improvements in *both* precision and credibility only by increasing the quality of the sample itself.

STATISTICS AROUND US

Credibility vs. Precision—How Tall Are Marlborough Men?

Suppose you are asked to construct an interval estimate of the mean height of adult males in Marlborough County. You would obviously agree that the following estimate is totally believable.

$$4' \leq \mu \leq 8'$$

Indeed, almost any knowledgeable person would accept it as true regardless of what (if any) sample evidence were obtained.

You could take a sample of size 1, measure that person, and from your finding report a very precise result, such as the following

$$5'8.33'' \leq \mu \leq 5'8.34''$$

Although precise to one-hundredth of an inch, this result is not very likely to be true and would be believed by few people.

Although totally credible, the first interval is too wide to be of any practical use. A narrower, more precise interval would be mandatory. The second interval is very precise, but not credible. It is useless as well.

In the next section of this chapter you will see how an interval estimate may be constructed using only the information contained in sample data. In doing this, the statistical investigator has some flexibility in making a trade-off between precision and credibility.

CHOOSING AN ESTIMATOR

Several alternative statistics can be used as estimators. For instance, we can use one of three sample statistics—the mean, median, or mode—to estimate the population mean. We may think that the sample mean is the most suitable estimator, but how can we substantiate our choice?

The most desirable feature of an estimator is that it has a value close to the unknown value of the population parameter. Under certain circumstances, the sample mean, median, and mode will each have a value that lies close to the population mean. The basic questions are therefore: Which statistic will be the most reliable estimator? And which will require the least expenditure of resources in terms of sample size? An important ancillary question is: Is there an easily applied theoretical procedure for determining the probability that the value obtained for the estimator statistic will lie sufficiently close to the parameter?

CRITERIA FOR STATISTICS USED AS ESTIMATORS

Three criteria have been developed to compare statistics in terms of their worth in estimating a parameter. One determines whether there is a tendency, on the average, for the statistic to assume values close to the parameter in question. Another considers the reliability of the estimator. The third indicates whether this reliability improves as sample size increases.

UNBIASED ESTIMATORS

An unbiased estimator is a statistic that has an expected value equal to the population parameter being estimated. A statistic that does not, on the average, tend to yield values equal to the parameter is said to be biased. The sample mean $\bar{X}$ is an unbiased estimator of the population mean μ, because we have established that

$$E(\bar{X}) = \mu$$

Likewise, the sample proportion P is an unbiased estimator of the population proportion π, since $E(P) = \pi$.

Unbiasedness explains why we define the sample variance s^2 as

$$s^2 = \frac{\sum (X - \bar{X})^2}{n - 1}$$

Here, the divisor is $n - 1$ instead of n. It can be proved that s^2 defined using the $n - 1$ divisor is an unbiased estimator of σ^2, since

$$E(s^2) = \sigma^2$$

An intuitive reason why $n - 1$ is used as the divisor is because it provides a somewhat larger value for the sample variance than the n divisor. The estimator that results from using s^2 is larger, reflecting the fact that a sample is ordinarily less diverse than its population (the part is rarely more varied than the whole).

Efficient Estimators

One statistic is a more efficient estimator than another if its standard error is smaller for the same sample size. The sample median is an unbiased estimator of μ when the population is normally distributed. But its standard error is 1.2533 times as great as that of the sample mean. This implies that the sample mean is a more efficient estimator of μ than the sample median. Medians of samples taken from normally distributed populations tend to be more unlike each other than means of the same samples. Thus, the sample mean is always a more reliable estimator of μ.

Maximum Likelihood Estimators

The most efficient estimator among all the unbiased ones is the maximum likelihood estimator. The sample mean is an example of a maximum likelihood estimator.

Consistent Estimators

A statistic is a consistent estimator of a parameter if the probability that it will be close to the parameter's true value approaches unity with increasing sample size. In general, *a statistic whose standard error becomes smaller as n becomes larger will be consistent.* In other words, a consistent estimator is more reliable when larger samples are used.

Both $\bar{X}$ and P are consistent estimators, since

$$\sigma_{\bar{X}} = \frac{\sigma}{\sqrt{n}} \quad \text{and} \quad \sigma_P = \sqrt{\frac{\pi(1-\pi)}{n}}$$

both become smaller as n increases.

Consistency alone does not guarantee reliable sample results; reliability can be achieved only by increasing the sample size. But consistency is a necessary condition if a larger sample is to be more reliable. The net effect is that the use of a consistent estimator allows the statistician to buy greater reliability for the price of a larger sample.

The criteria do not always clearly indicate which statistic will be the most reliable estimator. Usually, the better of any two estimators that are both unbiased and consistent is the more efficient. But if the better statistic is cumbersome or theoretically difficult to apply, the second choice is generally used.

COMMONLY USED ESTIMATORS

We have seen that $\bar{X}$ is the most desirable estimator of μ, because it is unbiased, consistent, and more efficient than other estimators, including the sample median. $\bar{X}$ also has a readily obtainable *normal* sampling distribution when the sample is sufficiently large. As we will see in this chapter, knowing the sampling distribution enables us to select a large enough sample to achieve an estimate with a desired level of reliability. It also allows us to qualify the estimate that we actually obtain after the sample results have been collected and tabulated.

The sample variance s^2 is an unbiased and consistent estimator of the population variance σ^2. We can take the square root of s^2 to estimate the population standard deviation, since σ is the square root of σ^2. In the following example, the sample standard deviation is calculated as $s = 62.65$ words per page. This figure can then be used to estimate σ, the standard deviation of words per page for the entire book.

EXAMPLE: ESTIMATING THE LENGTH OF A BOOK

A publisher wishes to determine the number of words in a 600-page book. An estimate of the mean number of words per page μ is obtained by counting the number of words on each of 30 randomly selected pages. The results are shown in Table 8-1. What are the estimates of μ and the total number of words?

SOLUTION: The sample mean number of words per page is computed in Table 8-1 to be $\overline{X} = 356$. The estimate of μ is 356 words per page. This results in an estimate of

$$356 \times 600 = 213{,}600$$

words in the entire book.

TABLE 8-1 Estimating the Number of Words in a Book

Number of Words X	X^2	Number of Words X	X^2
383	146,689	175	30,625
325	105,625	278	77,284
411	168,921	351	123,201
416	173,056	423	178,929
395	156,025	327	106,929
372	138,384	381	145,161
293	85,849	317	100,489
361	130,321	362	131,044
216	46,656	338	114,244
431	185,761	411	168,921
406	164,836	371	137,641
394	155,236	393	154,449
402	161,604	388	150,544
376	141,376	295	87,025
268	71,824	421	177,241
		Totals 10,680	3,915,890

$\overline{X} = \sum X/n = 10{,}680/30 = 356$ words

$s = \sqrt{(\sum X^2 - n\overline{X}^2)/(n-1)} = \sqrt{(3{,}915{,}890 - 30(356)^2)/29}$

$= \sqrt{3{,}924.48} = 62.65$ words

The population proportion π of elementary units that have a particular attribute can be estimated by the corresponding sample proportion P. We know that $E(P) = \pi$, so that P is an unbiased estimator of π. It is also consistent.

STATISTICS AROUND US

Buying on Impulse

A consumer information service measured the tendency of the average shopper to purchase whatever she or he picks up, whether it is needed or not. Shoppers in a random sample prepared detailed shopping lists. At the store, testers followed each sample shopper and recorded each item touched. The items on the shopper's original list were compared to those purchased. The number of items bought but not on the list was added to the number of items touched but not bought. This sum represented the total number of impulse items not included in the original list.

The proportion P of impulse items bought was then found for every sample shopper. One woman accrued a total of 132 impulse items; of these, she purchased 48. Her value of P was therefore determined to be

$$P = \frac{48}{132} = .364$$

which may be taken as an estimate of the actual proportion of impulse items she would buy under similar circumstances.

The average proportion of impulse purchases was estimated to be .55. The consumer service therefore advised its clients to keep their hands on their carts and rely on their initial grocery buying decisions.

EXERCISES

8-1 For each of the following situations, indicate whether or not a sample may be selected from some population to make a current estimate. Explain.

(a) An estimate is to be made of the mean annual lifetime earnings of recent college graduates.

(b) The taste preferences of the potential buyers of a new product not currently on the market are to be determined.

(c) The responses of heart patients to a new drug, previously untried on humans, are to be measured.

(d) The Federal Power Commission wishes to estimate the kilowatt-hour usage by customers at the end of the coming decade.

8-2 A survey is taken of Trim Cuts hairstyling franchises to determine annual earnings. A random sample of $n = 10$ shops resulted in the following figures (in thousands of dollars, rounded).

15	5	2	7	25	19	11	9	13	42

(a) Find a point estimate of the mean expenditures for all shops as a group.

(b) Find a point estimate of the standard deviation of earnings for the population.

(c) Estimate the proportion of earnings in excess of \$10,000.

(d) Estimate the proportion of earnings under \$5,000.

8-3 For each of the following parameters, indicate whether you would use a point estimate or an interval estimate. Explain.

(a) The mean age of product buyers, to be used in comparing alternative advertising plans.

(b) The proportion of an evening's television viewing population watching a particular program, to be presented to advertisers as evidence of the program's drawing power.

(c) The mean pH value (a measure of acidity) of intermediary ingredients in a chemical process, so that a formula can be developed that indicates the amount of neutralizing agent to apply.

(d) The median income of doctors, to be published in a government report.

8-4 Tossing a die twice in succession can be viewed as taking a random sample of $n = 2$ with replacement from a population of six observable values (corresponding to the number of dots showing on each side of the die).

(a) Calculate the range of this population.

(b) We define the **sample range** to be the difference between the highest and the lowest values obtained from the two tosses. The sampling distribution of the sample range is provided in the table below. Calculate the expected value of the sample range.

(c) Compare your answers in (a) and (b). Do you conclude that the sample range is an unbiased estimator of the population range? Explain.

Possible Sample Range	Elementary Events	Probability
0	(1,1) (2,2) (3,3) (4,4) (5,5) (6,6)	6/36
1	(1,2) (2,1) (2,3) (3,2) (3,4) (4,3) (4,5) (5,4) (5,6) (6,5)	10/36
2	(1,3) (3,1) (2,4) (4,2) (3,5) (5,3) (4,6) (6,4)	8/36
3	(1,4) (4,1) (2,5) (5,2) (3,6) (6,3)	6/36
4	(1,5) (5,1) (2,6) (6,2)	4/36
5	(1,6) (6,1)	2/36
		36/36

8-2 INTERVAL ESTIMATES OF THE MEAN WHEN σ IS KNOWN

Estimates of means are very important. The popular form in most statistical applications is the interval estimate because it acknowledges sampling error. The interval end points make it obvious that the sample results are imprecise. In making estimates of the mean we can put our knowledge of the normal distribution to practical use in quantifying the estimation process in terms of probability.

At the planning stage, statistical investigators can specify their precision and credibility targets before collecting actual data. The actual estimate is found in the later data analysis stage of a sampling study, after the sample results are already known. At that time, $\bar{X}$ has already been calculated and there is no uncertainty about the *sample*. (The *population* uncertainty will persist, however.) That computed mean provides the estimate of the unknown μ, becoming the *center* of the interval estimate. We now see how to establish the end points.

Let's return for now to the planning stage (before the sample results are known). The sample size is n and we assume that the value for the population standard deviation σ is known. We know that $\sigma_{\overline{X}} = \sigma/\sqrt{n}$, and the central limit theorem allows us to use the normal curve to determine probabilities for the level of $\overline{X}$. The probability is .90 that $\overline{X}$ will fall within $\pm$ 1.64 standard deviations of μ.

$$\Pr[\mu - 1.64\sigma_{\overline{X}} \leq \overline{X} \leq \mu + 1.64\sigma_{\overline{X}}] = .90$$

Figure 8-1 shows how the above probability incorporates the middle 90% area of the normal curve for $\overline{X}$, leaving a .05 probability area in each of the two tails. The lower tail begins at a point that is 1.64 standard deviations below μ, the other beginning the same distance above μ. When expressed in standard deviation units, the points where the tails start correspond to the **critical normal deviate** $z_{.05}$. Here, $z_{.05} = 1.64$, and we can restate the above probability expression as

$$\Pr[\mu - z_{.05}\sigma_{\overline{X}} \leq \overline{X} \leq \mu + z_{.05}\sigma_{\overline{X}}] = .90$$

We can transform the above inequality by rearranging the terms inside the brackets, so that we obtain

$$\Pr[\overline{X} - z_{.05}\sigma_{\overline{X}} \leq \mu\mu \leq \overline{X} + z_{.05}\sigma_{\overline{X}}] = .90$$

There is a .90 probability interval inside the brackets, which may be expressed as either

$$\overline{X} - z_{.05}\sigma_{\overline{X}} \leq \mu \leq \overline{X} + z_{.05}\sigma_{\overline{X}}$$

or as

$$\mu = \overline{X} \pm z_{.05}\sigma_{\overline{X}}$$

Similar intervals might correspond to other probability levels than .90. Letting $1 - \alpha$ (one minus lowercase Greek *alpha*) denote the designated probability, each tail will have an area $\alpha/2$. The critical normal deviate may then be expressed as $z_{\alpha/2}$. Figure 8-1 shows the case when $1 - \alpha = .90$ with $\alpha/2 = .05$.

The critical normal deviate for any specified upper tail area may be read from Appendix Table E. For instance, $z_{.025} = 1.96$ and $z_{.01} = 2.33$.

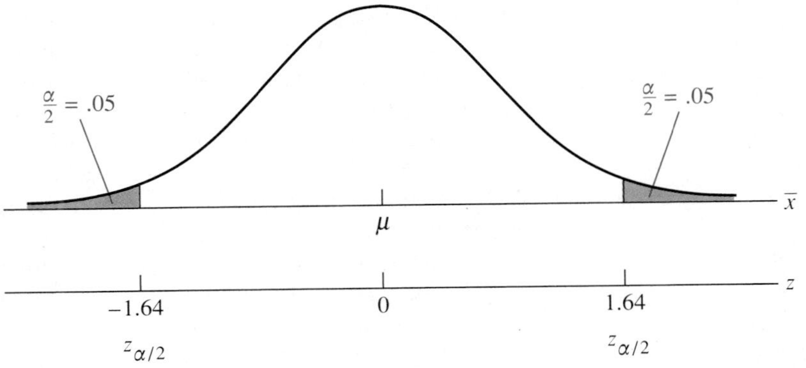

FIGURE 8-1 Illustration of critical normal deviate.

Investigators use an expression similar to the above in calculating the interval estimate.

CONFIDENCE AND MEANING OF THE INTERVAL ESTIMATE

Estimates can be made only *after* the sample data have been collected. At that time it is too late to express a probability that the sample will place μ inside $\bar{X} \pm z_{\alpha/2}\sigma_{\bar{X}}$. The sample mean is then a calculated and known quantity, and it may or may not be close enough to μ. (And, you will ordinarily never know if it is.)

Statisticians use a related concept when expressing their less than perfect certainty regarding the still unknown μ. This is the **confidence level** for which we make the following

DEFINITION: The **confidence level** is the percentage of interval estimates—obtained from many repeated samples, each of size n, from the same population—that will contain the actual value of the parameter being estimated. Although a single sample is ordinarily selected from the population, the confidence level is expressed as a percentage.

For any specified decimal α, the confidence level percentage may be determined from

$$\text{Confidence level} = 100(1 - \alpha)\%$$

And, for the confidence level percentage, the decimal α may be determined from

$$\alpha = 1 - (\text{confidence level }\%)/100\%$$

Figure 8-2 illustrates the concepts underlying the confidence level. A sampling investigation yielding an interval estimate of the mean with 90% confidence can be expected to be correct only 90% of the time. In 100 repetitions of the sampling procedure, about 90 of the constructed intervals, each centered on the computed $\bar{X}$, will contain μ. About 10 will be untrue—the entire interval lying above or below μ. Usually only one sample of n observations is taken, and the *statistician never knows whether the reported interval is true*. This situation can be improved either by raising the confidence level (using a bigger $z_{\alpha/2}$), which reduces the precision, or by increasing the sample size.

The interval estimate is referred to as a **confidence interval**. The level of confidence determines the value of $z_{\alpha/2}$ to be used, with greater confidence resulting in wider confidence intervals.

CONSTRUCTING THE CONFIDENCE INTERVAL

A confidence interval for the mean is centered on the computed value of $\bar{X}$. The following expression is used to calculate the $100(1 - \alpha)\%$

CONFIDENCE INTERVAL ESTIMATE OF THE MEAN WHEN σ IS KNOWN

$$\mu = \bar{X} \pm z_{\alpha/2}\sigma_{\bar{X}} \quad \text{or} \quad \bar{X} - z_{\alpha/2}\sigma_{\bar{X}} \le \mu \le \bar{X} + z_{\alpha/2}\sigma_{\bar{X}}$$

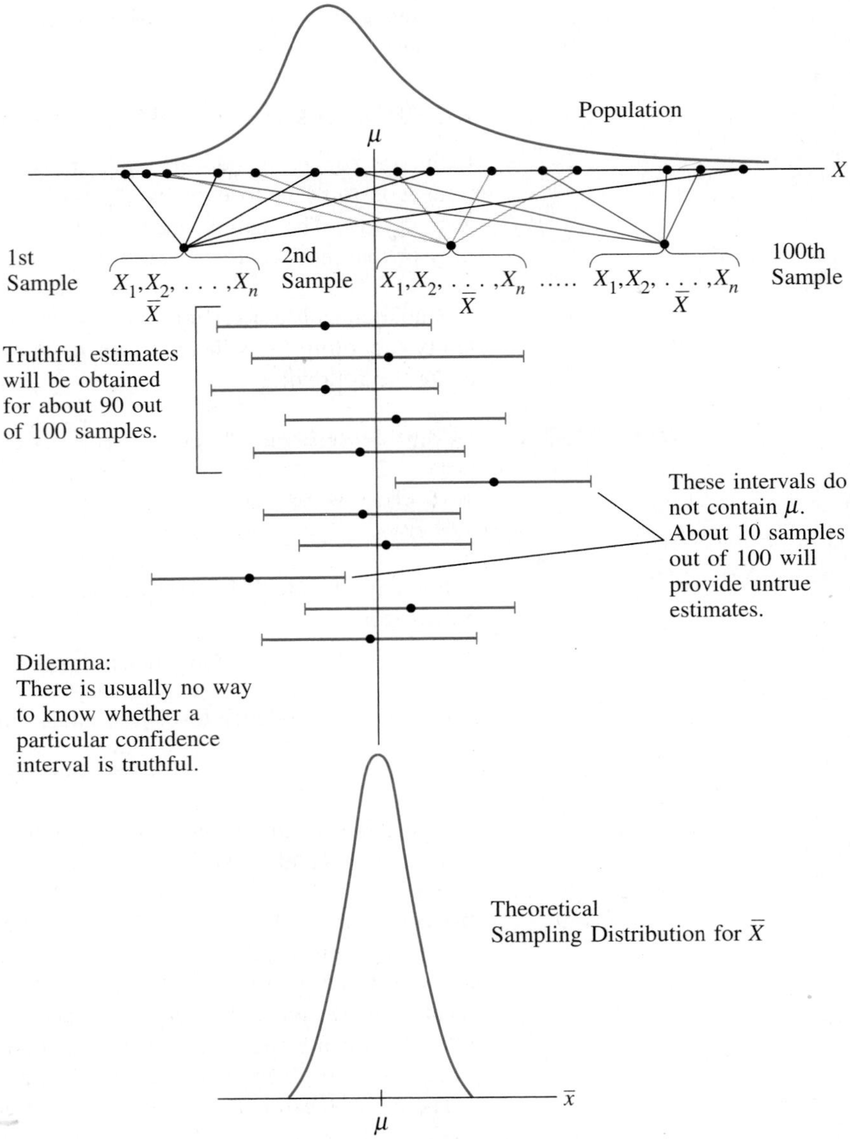

FIGURE 8-2 Illustration of the confidence interval concept.

where the standard error of $\bar{X}$ is

$$\sigma_{\bar{X}} = \frac{\sigma}{\sqrt{n}}$$

and σ must be specified in advance.*

*When the sample size n is large in relation to the population size N, the finite population correction factor should be used to calculate the standard error.

$$\sigma_{\bar{X}} = \frac{\sigma}{\sqrt{n}}\sqrt{\frac{N-n}{N-1}}$$

ILLUSTRATION: FAMILY INCOMES

To illustrate how a confidence interval estimate is obtained, we will assume that a sample of $n = 100$ families is selected from the population of a large city and that the sample mean income is $\bar{X} = \$15{,}549.63$. We have *prior knowledge* that the standard deviation of the population of family incomes is $\sigma = \$5{,}000$. We wish to determine a 99% confidence interval estimate of the true population mean μ.

Using $\alpha = 1 - .99 = .01$, from Appendix Table E the required normal deviate is $z_{\alpha/2} = z_{.005} = 2.57$. The standard error of $\bar{X}$ is

$$\sigma_{\bar{X}} = \frac{\$5{,}000}{\sqrt{100}} = \$500$$

and the 99% confidence interval estimate is

$$\begin{aligned}\mu = \bar{X} \pm z_{\alpha/2}\sigma_{\bar{X}} &= \$15{,}549.63 \pm 2.57(\$500)\\ &= \$15{,}549.63 \pm \$1{,}285.00\end{aligned}$$

and

$$\$14{,}264.63 \leq \mu \leq \$16{,}834.63$$

We *cannot* say there is a .99 probability that the stated interval contains μ. (It either does or does not, but we do not know which case applies.) For the above 99% confidence interval we give the following proper

INTERPRETATION: If we repeated the same procedure often, each time selecting a different sample of 100 families from the same population, then 99 out of every 100 similar intervals we obtained would, on the average, contain μ.

FEATURES DESIRED IN A CONFIDENCE INTERVAL

Although both credibility and precision are desirable features in a confidence interval estimate, they are competing goals. For a fixed sample size, a reduction in the interval width, which causes greater precision, can be achieved only at the expense of reducing z, which lowers the confidence level. Conversely, greater confidence can be obtained only at the expense of precision. Thus, a confidence interval may be very precise but not at all credible, or vice versa. For example, if $z_{\alpha/2}$ is .5 in estimating the mean family income, then the confidence interval would be

$$\mu = \$15{,}549.63 \pm .5(500) = \$15{,}549.63 \pm 250$$

or

$$\$15{,}299.63 \leq \mu \leq \$15{,}799.63$$

which is more precise than before, but the confidence level would be only 38%. Likewise, increasing the confidence level to 99.8%, so that $\alpha = 1 - .998 = .002$ and $z_{.001} = 3.08$, would yield the less precise interval estimate

$$\mu = \$15{,}549.63 \pm 3.08(500) = \$15{,}549.63 \pm \$1{,}540$$

or

$$\$14{,}009.63 \leq \mu \leq \$17{,}089.63$$

The only way to increase both confidence and precision is to collect a larger sample at the start. For example, suppose that $n = 1{,}000$ families are selected and that the *same* sample mean is calculated. The standard error of $\bar{X}$ would then be

$$\sigma_{\bar{X}} = \frac{\$5{,}000}{\sqrt{1{,}000}} = \$158.11$$

and the 99.8% confidence interval would be

$$\mu = \$15{,}549.63 \pm 3.08(\$158.11) = \$15{,}549.63 \pm \$486.98$$

or

$$\$15{,}062.65 \le \mu \le \$16{,}036.61$$

This is a *more precise* interval with a *greater confidence level* than the one originally obtained.

But the larger sample might not be the best to use. The cost of collecting the data must be weighed against the value of the information thereby obtained. More will be said about this later in the chapter.

COMPUTER-GENERATED CONFIDENCE INTERVALS

A confidence interval estimate may be constructed with computer assistance. Although, once the hardest job (calculating the sample mean $\bar{X}$) has been done, there is little advantage to using a computer. Some software packages will supply the confidence interval endpoints immediately on request.

To illustrate, suppose that a random sample of student car owners is selected, and the following annual insurance premiums are reported.

\$520	\$725	\$615	\$435	\$266	\$498

The population standard deviation is assumed to be $\sigma = \$100$. Figure 8-3 shows the computer printout obtained from a computer run using the above data.

The computed value of the sample mean is $\bar{X} = \$508.20$. Although it is not used in constructing the confidence interval, the printout provides the *sample* standard deviation of $s = \$153.90$. This should not be confused with the given value of $\sigma = \$100$ for the *population* standard deviation. (Although s is *expected* to be equal to σ, an actual sample result will ordinarily differ, perhaps considerably so, from the expected level.) Figure 8-3 also reports $\sigma_{\bar{X}} = 40.8$, which is computed by dividing σ (not s) by the square root of the sample size. The end points of the 95% confidence interval are (\$428.0, \$588.3), or

$$\$428.00 \le \mu \le \$588.30$$

(If you are computing by hand, your results may differ slightly from the ones above due to rounding.)

EXERCISES

8-5 The Kryptonite Corporation personnel director wishes to estimate the mean scores for a proposed aptitude test that may be used in screening applicants for clerical positions. The population standard deviation is assumed to be

```
MTB > retrieve 'Shelf'
MTB > AOVOneway c1-c4.

ANALYSIS OF VARIANCE
SOURCE      DF        SS         MS         F          p
FACTOR       3    412.63     137.54     19.07      0.000
ERROR       26    187.53       7.21
TOTAL       29    600.17
                                   INDIVIDUAL 95 PCT CI'S FOR MEAN
                                   BASED ON POOLED STDEV
 LEVEL       N      MEAN      STDEV  ---+---------+---------+---------+---
Two-Foot     5    15.200      3.033                (-----*-----)
Four-Ft.     7     9.143      2.193   (----*----)
Split       10    13.000      2.625             (----*---)
Corner       8    19.375      2.925                              (---*----)
                                     ---+---------+---------+---------+---
POOLED STDEV =     2.686               8.0      12.0      16.0      20.0
```

Note: Figure generated on an IBM PC using Minitab®.

FIGURE 8-3 Computer printout of the confidence interval for sample insurance premiums.

$\sigma = 15$. For a sample of $n = 100$ applicants, the sample mean score is $\bar{X} = 75.6$. Construct a 95% confidence interval estimate of the true mean.

8-6 A random sample of 100 package weights is selected. The population standard deviation is assumed to be .5 ounces. The sample mean is $\bar{X} = 15.9$ ounces. Construct a 95% confidence interval estimate of the mean weight for the items in the entire population.

8-7 The production superintendent for a pharmaceutical manufacturer knows from past history that a particular capsule is produced with varying mean impurity levels, depending on how well the control mechanism performs. The variability in capsule impurities remains nearly constant, so that, regardless of μ, the standard deviation is assumed to be $\sigma = 2.5$ parts per million (ppm). Construct a 95% confidence interval estimate of the true population mean impurity level for the following sample results.

(a) $n = 100$; $\bar{X} = 125.6$ ppm (c) $n = 200$; $\bar{X} = 148.9$ ppm
(b) $n = 25$; $\bar{X} = 153.4$ ppm (d) $n = 500$; $\bar{X} = 206.4$ ppm

8-8 The VBM board of directors is evaluating the performance of the corporation president in order to decide whether to retain him. One director proposes that each director rate the president—on a scale from 1 to 5—as to the quality of his performance in five areas: (1) sales growth, (2) personnel relations, (3) operating efficiencies achieved, (4) attainment of profit potential, and (5) successful new-product development. The ratings will be summarized in terms of frequency distributions, with the mean rating calculated for each category and submitted to the directors at the next meeting, when a vote on retention will take place. The board agrees to the procedure.

The chairman is concerned with the average ratings. He is worried about their precision and wonders what level of confidence should be attached to the results. A trustee who happens to be an expert in statistics diplomatically informs the chairman that these considerations are irrelevant. Explain the basis for the expert's stand.

8-9 A CPA auditing trainee wishes to estimate the errors in accounts payable vouchers. The errors are assumed to have a standard deviation of \$2. In the following cases, suppose that the sample mean error is \$10.

(a) For a sample of size $n = 100$, construct interval estimates of the true mean error level when the confidence level is (1) 90%, (2) 95%, (3) 99%, (4) 99.9%.

(b) Construct 95% confidence interval estimates when the sample size is (1) $n = 10$, (2) $n = 25$, (3) $n = 150$, and (4) $n = 500$.

8-10 *Computer exercise.* The following price/earnings ratios have been obtained for a sample of NYSE stocks selected on a particular day.

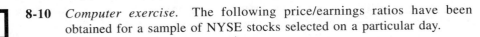

15.3	9.7	12.4	23.0	62.3	9.5	5.3	8.6	29.7	43.4

Assume that $\sigma = 10$. Construct a 90% confidence interval estimate of the mean price/earnings ratio.

8-11 *Computer exercise.* The following annual inventory turnovers have been obtained for a sample of retail gift stores.

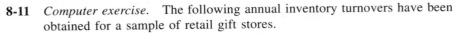

2.7	5.8	6.4	1.9	3.8	3.6	4.3	4.5

Assume that $\sigma = .50$. Construct a 95% confidence interval estimate of the mean annual inventory turnover for the population.

8-3 INTERVAL ESTIMATES OF THE MEAN WHEN σ IS UNKNOWN

In Section 8-2, we constructed confidence interval estimates of the mean when the population standard deviation σ is *known*. But often when μ is unknown, the level of σ may not be known either. In those cases, σ must be estimated with μ. The sample standard deviation s is used for that purpose.

The normal distribution is theoretically *not* correct for making inferences about μ when σ is also unknown. This presents a statistical dilemma and creates the need for a new sampling distribution.

THE STUDENT *t* DISTRIBUTION

W. S. Gosset first studied this dilemma in the early 1900s. Because his employer, a brewery, forbade him to publish, he chose the nom de plume "Student." Gosset derived a probability distribution, now referred to as the Student t distribution, for a random variable t. Whenever the population being sampled is normally distributed,

$$t = \frac{\bar{X} - \mu}{s/\sqrt{n}}$$

In practice, however, the t distribution may be used when samples are taken from any population that is not highly skewed.

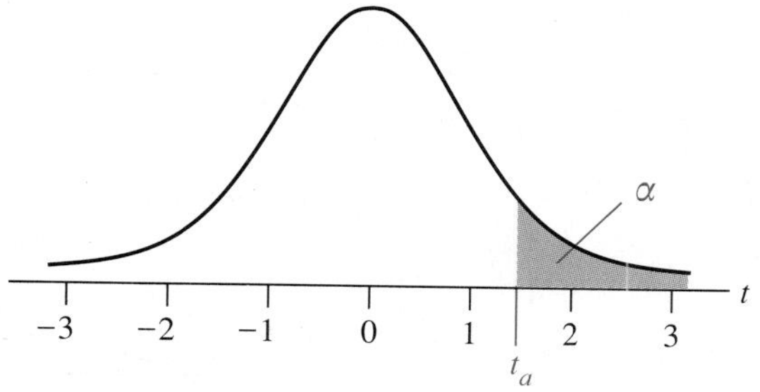

FIGURE 8-4 The Student t distribution.

Like the normal distribution, the Student t distribution has a relative frequency curve that is bell-shaped and symmetrical, as shown in Figure 8-4. The single parameter that determines the shape of its curve is called the *number of degrees of freedom*, which is $n - 1$ (because for a fixed value of $\bar{X}$, there are only $n - 1$ "free choices" for the values of the n observations used to calculate $\bar{X}$ and s).

To determine the probability that t exceeds some value, we must consult the table of areas under the Student t distribution in Appendix Table F. There is a separate distribution—and therefore a separate set of values—for each number of degrees of freedom; these appear in separate rows in the table. It is traditional to use α to represent the upper tail area. The values in the body of the table are the points t_α corresponding to the respective upper tail area α (column) and degrees of freedom (row). To find the point that corresponds to a given upper tail area t_α, so that

$$\Pr[t \geq t_\alpha] = \alpha$$

we read down the column headed by the probability value α, stop at the row corresponding to the number of degrees of freedom, and read the desired t_α value. (Like the normal curve table, there is no need to list separate entries for the left-hand portion of the t curve.) A partial reproduction of Appendix Table F will be helpful.

Degrees of Freedom	Upper Tail Area α									
	.4	.25	.1	.05	.025	.01	.005	.0025	.001	.0005
1	0.325	1.000	3.078	6.314	12.706	31.821	63.657	127.32	318.31	636.62
2	.289	.816	1.886	2.920	4.303	6.965	9.925	14.089	22.327	31.598
3	.277	.765	1.638	2.353	3.182	4.541	5.841	7.453	10.214	12.924
4	.271	.741	1.533	2.132	2.776	3.747	4.604	5.598	7.173	8.610
5	0.267	0.727	1.476	2.015	2.571	3.365	4.032	4.773	5.893	6.869
6	.265	.718	1.440	1.943	2.447	3.143	3.707	4.317	5.208	5.959
7	.263	.711	1.415	1.895	2.365	2.998	3.499	4.029	4.785	5.408
8	.262	.706	1.397	1.860	2.306	2.896	3.355	3.833	4.501	5.041
9	.261	.703	1.383	1.833	2.262	2.821	3.250	3.690	4.297	4.781
10	0.260	0.700	1.372	1.812	2.228	2.764	3.169	3.581	4.144	4.587
11	.260	.697	1.363	1.796	2.201	2.718	3.106	3.497	4.025	4.437
12	.259	.695	1.356	1.782	2.179	2.681	3.055	3.428	3.930	4.318

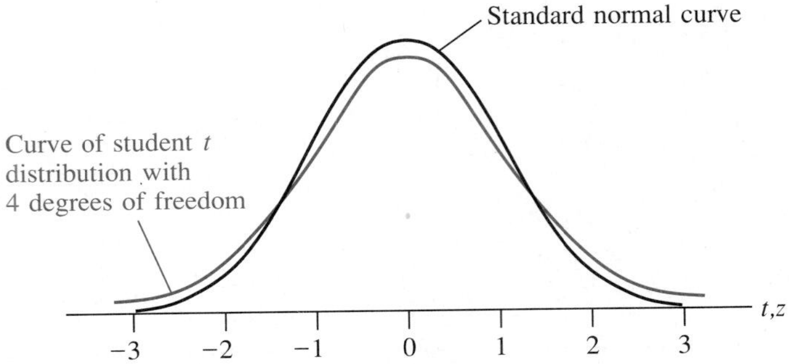

FIGURE 8-5 A comparison of the relative frequency curves for the standard normal distribution and the Student t distribution.

For example, suppose that we wish to find $t_{.01}$ (the value for which the probability is .01 that t is greater than or equal to that value) and that the number of degrees of freedom is 20. From Appendix Table F, $t_{.01} = 2.528$. So

$$\Pr[t \geq 2.528] = .01$$

Figure 8-5 shows the standard normal curve and the t distribution curve when the number of degrees of freedom is 4. Note that the normal curve falls below the t curve for values lying in the tails. This reflects the fact that the t distribution assigns higher probabilities to outcomes of extreme value than the normal distribution does, due to the extra element of uncertainty arising from the unknown value of σ.

A theoretical requirement of the Student t distribution is that the *population* itself be normally distributed. (It is ordinarily acceptable, however, to still employ the Student t as long as the underlying population is unimodal and not highly skewed.) The normal curve comes into play in another more practical way. *For large sample sizes, the Student t distribution tends to coincide with the standard normal distribution.*

CONSTRUCTING THE CONFIDENCE INTERVAL

A confidence interval falls on two sides of the sample mean, which is the center. Thus, two tails are excluded, each of area $\alpha/2$, and the matching critical value $t_{\alpha/2}$ is used in constructing the $100(1 - \alpha)\%$

CONFIDENCE INTERVAL ESTIMATE OF THE MEAN WHEN σ IS UNKNOWN

$$\mu = \bar{X} \pm t_{\alpha/2}\frac{s}{\sqrt{n}} \quad \text{or} \quad \bar{X} - t_{\alpha/2}\frac{s}{\sqrt{n}} \leq \mu \leq \bar{X} + t_{\alpha/2}\frac{s}{\sqrt{n}}$$

To illustrate, we construct a 90% confidence interval estimate of μ, using $\alpha = 1 - .90 = .10$ and $t_{\alpha/2} = t_{.05}$. The results obtained from a survey having

$n = 25$ observations provide $\bar{X} = 10.0$ and $s = 5.0$. The degrees of freedom is $n - 1 = 24$, and, from Appendix Table F, $t_{.05} = 1.711$. The 90% confidence interval estimate of μ is

$$\mu = \bar{X} \pm t_{.05}\frac{s}{\sqrt{n}} = 10 \pm 1.711\frac{5.0}{\sqrt{25}}$$

$$= 10 \pm 1.7$$

so that

$$8.3 \leq \mu \leq 11.7$$

EXAMPLE: ESTIMATING MEAN LOST PRODUCTION TIME

The production manager of Black and Becker is concerned that too little attention has been paid to the cost of labor lost due to stamping machine breakdowns. In the one year in which the plant has been in operation, the stamping machine has failed nine times. Table 8-2 shows the direct labor hours lost for each breakdown. An estimate of the mean number of labor hours lost per breakdown is to be obtained. This estimate may then be multipled by the expected number of breakdowns per year to obtain an estimate of the hours that will be lost annually in the future.

The production manager desires a 95% confidence interval to estimate μ, the mean labor hours lost.

TABLE 8-2 Labor Hours Lost Due to Stamping Machine Breakdowns

	Labor Hours Lost X	X^2
	205	42,025
	1,123	1,261,129
	528	278,784
	359	128,881
	1,421	2,019,241
	723	522,729
	57	3,249
	172	29,584
	25	625
Totals	4,613	4,286,247

$\bar{X} = \sum X/n = 4{,}613/9 = 512.56$ hours

$s = \sqrt{(\sum X^2 - n\bar{X}^2)/(n-1)} = \sqrt{(4{,}286{,}247 - 9(512.56)^2)/8}$

$= 490.1$ hours

SOLUTION: The number of degrees of freedom is $9 - 1 = 8$. Using $\alpha = 1 - .95 = .05$, Appendix Table F provides $t_{\alpha/2} = t_{.025} = 2.306$. The following confidence interval is obtained:

$$512.56 - 2.306(490.1)/\sqrt{9} \leq \mu \leq 512.56 + 2.306(490.1)/\sqrt{9}$$

so that

$$\mu = 512.56 \pm 376.72$$

and

$$135.84 \leq \mu \leq 889.28 \text{ hours}$$

Notice that the confidence interval is quite wide, which is expected with a large sample standard deviation and a small sample size.

COMPUTER-GENERATED CONFIDENCE INTERVALS

As with the estimates in Section 8-2, a computer may be used to construct confidence intervals. Figure 8-6 shows the printout obtained from a computer run using the above data. Except for rounding, exactly the same results have been obtained as before when computing by hand.

CONFIDENCE INTERVALS WHEN *n* IS LARGE

The Student t distribution applies for $(\bar{X} - \mu)/(s/\sqrt{n})$ when σ is unknown—regardless of the sample size—for most populations encountered in business applications. When constructing intervals by hand, there are some special difficulties that arise from tabular limitations. Appendix Table F leaves gaps. It jumps from 30 degrees of freedom to 40, then from 40 degrees of freedom to 60, and finally from 60 degrees of freedom to 120. There is one row for each, with the last row in the table corresponding to an infinite number for the degrees of freedom.

When constructing confidence intervals, the gaps can be filled by using *linear interpolation* to approximate the missing critical values. But, for simplicity, this book uses the nearest tabled entry when Appendix Table F does not list values for a particular number of degrees of freedom. Thus, we use the entry in row 30 when the degrees of freedom are 31, 32, 33, or 34, and the entry in row 40 when the degrees of freedom are 36, 37, 38, or 39. If the number of degrees of freedom is exactly in the middle (e.g., 35), the entries in the neighboring rows are averaged. When the number of degrees of freedom exceeds 120, use the t from the

```
MTB > set c1
      205,1123,528,359,1421,723,57,172,25
MTB > end
MTB > name c1 'Turnover'
MTB > tinterval 95 percent c1

                 N      MEAN    STDEV  SE MEAN    95.0 PERCENT C.I.
 turnover        6   512.556  490.131  163.377  ( 135.705, 889.406)
```

Note: Figure generated on an IBM PC using Minitab®.

FIGURE 8-6 Computer printout of the confidence interval for the sample data in Table 8-2.

∞ row. (You may find slight differences between computer results and hand constructions, since computers obtain more accurate critical values of t.)

If n is large enough to generate degrees of freedom greater than 120, the $t_{\alpha/2}$ values in Appendix Table F are identical to the $z_{\alpha/2}$ critical normal deviates in Appendix Table E. This reflects the property that in the limiting case the Student t and standard normal curves coincide. For this reason, t and z are interchangeable when n is large.

EXAMPLE: ESTIMATING MEAN BILL PAYMENT TIMES

The Million Bank operates a credit card system and wishes to establish policy for mailing customer bills. The time of month must be identified that provides the shortest average time to receipt of cash payment. Three samples of customers are randomly selected, one group to be billed on the 5th of the month, another on the 15th, and the final group on the 25th. In order to avoid any bias due to the transition in billing cycle, figures from the fourth month under the new dates constitute the samples. A total of $n = 500$ customers are selected for each sample group. The following results are obtained.

5th of Month	15th of Month	25th of Month
$\bar{X} = 18.30$ days	$\bar{X} = 17.41$ days	$\bar{X} = 5.42$ days
$s = 6.2$	$s = 5.8$	$s = 2.3$

Interval estimates are to be found using a 99% level of confidence.

SOLUTION: First, find α:

$$\alpha = 1 - (99\%)/(100\%)$$
$$= 1 - .99 = .01$$
$$\alpha/2 = .005$$

Since the number of degrees of freedom exceeds 120, the critical value from the ∞ row of Appendix Table F is used. This value is $t_{.005} = 2.576$.

For the 5th of the month, the confidence interval is

$$18.30 - \frac{2.576(6.2)}{\sqrt{500}} \leq \mu \leq 18.30 + \frac{2.576(6.2)}{\sqrt{500}}$$

or

$$\mu = 18.30 \pm .71$$

so that

$$17.59 \leq \mu \leq 19.01 \text{ days} \qquad \text{(for 5th)}$$

Analogously, the following confidence intervals have been obtained for the other groups.

$$\mu = 17.41 \pm .67 \quad \text{or} \quad 16.74 \leq \mu \leq 18.08 \text{ days} \qquad \text{(for 15th)}$$
$$\mu = 5.42 \pm .26 \quad \text{or} \quad 5.16 \leq \mu \leq 5.68 \text{ days} \qquad \text{(for 25th)}$$

Note that there is so little difference between the results for the 5th and 15th that the confidence intervals overlap. Of the three times of the month, the 25th appears to be the superior billing time. By switching its billing cycle, so that bills are mailed on the 25th instead of at the end of the month, the bank *might* (remember, *we do not know* μ) be able to reduce the average collection time from its present 10 days to some value between 5.17 and 5.68 days, thereby allowing the firm to have longer use of the funds received.

EXERCISES

8-12 Determine the value t_α that corresponds to the following upper tail areas of the Student t distribution.

	(a)	(b)	(c)	(d)	(e)
α	.05	.01	.025	.01	.005
Degrees of freedom	10	13	21	120	30

8-13 Construct 95% confidence interval estimates of the means of populations yielding the following sample results.
(a) $n = 6$; $\bar{X} = \$8.00$; $s = \$2.50$
(b) $n = 15$; $\bar{X} = 15.03$ minutes; $s = .52$ minutes
(c) $n = 25$; $\bar{X} = 27.30$ pounds; $s = 2.56$ pounds

8-14 Construct 99% confidence intervals for (a), (b), and (c) in Exercise 8-13.

8-15 Shirley Smart measures the heights of 35 men in her statistics class. She assumes that the data represent a random sample of all male students in her state. From the data, she calculates $\bar{X} = 70.2''$ and $s = 2.44''$. Construct a 95% confidence interval estimate of the population mean height.

8-16 Rock of Gibraltar Insurance Company is revising its rate schedules. A staff actuary wishes to estimate the average size of claims resulting from fire damage in apartment complexes with between 10 and 20 units. The current year's claim settlements are to be used as a sample. Considering the 19 claim settlements for buildings in this category, the average claim size was \$73,249, with a standard deviation of \$37,246. Construct a 90% confidence interval estimate of the mean claim size.

8-17 The manager of the Nogales Ritz desires to improve the level of room service by increasing personnel. To justify the increase, she must estimate the mean waiting time experienced by guests before being served. From a random sample of $n = 100$ orders, the sample mean waiting time was established at 30.3 minutes, with a standard deviation of 8.2 minutes. Construct a 99% confidence interval that the manager can use to estimate the actual mean waiting time.

(class) **8-18** The Wear-Ever Corporation tested the tread life of a sample of $n = 50$ radial tires. The sample results yielded $\bar{X} = 52{,}346$ miles and $s = 2{,}911$ miles.
(a) Construct a 99% confidence interval estimate of the mean tread life.
(b) What is the interpretation of the interval constructed in (a)?

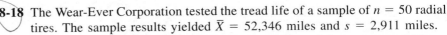

8-19 A hospital administrator intends to improve the level of emergency room service by increasing support personnel. To justify the increase, he must estimate the mean time that patients must wait before being attended to by a physician. For a random sample of $n = 100$ previously recorded emergencies, the sample mean waiting time was 70.3 minutes, with a standard deviation of 28.2 minutes. Construct a 99% confidence interval that the administrator can use to estimate the actual mean waiting time.

8-20 DanDee Assemblers currently trains its chassis assemblers on the job. It has been proposed that new employees be given one week of formal training. To test the quality of the training program, the output rate of ten trainees (Group *A*) was compared to that of ten new employees receiving on-the-job training (Group *B*). Each trainee from Group *A* was matched with one from Group *B*, based on aptitude test scores. After training, each person was given a specific number of chassis to wire, and the completion time was recorded. For each of the $n = 10$ pairs of assemblers, the time of the trainee from Group *A* was subtracted from that of the matching trainee from Group *B*. The sample results yielded $\bar{X} = 3$ minutes and $s = 2$ minutes.

(a) Construct a 95% confidence interval estimate of the mean time difference.

(b) If there is no difference between the two training methods and if the population standard deviation is $\sigma = 2$, use the normal distribution to determine the probability that the sample mean will be 3 or more.

8-21 *Computer exercise.* The following weights (in pounds) have been obtained for a random sample of Dogpatch men.

183	203	148
146	192	159
157	176	165

(a) Compute the sample mean and standard deviation.

(b) Construct a 95% confidence interval estimate of the population mean weight.

8-22 *Computer exercise.* Lily Gilding Company will estimate the mean amount of gold consumed per batch in a plating operation. The following quantities (in ounces) have been obtained for a random sample of 15 batches.

.25	.18	.24	.19	.20
.23	.27	.21	.23	.21
.19	.22	.20	.25	.25

(a) Compute the sample mean and standard deviation.

(b) Construct a 95% confidence interval estimate of the mean gold consumption.

8-23 *Computer exercise.* The Block-Nock tax preparation service provided the following data for the amount of time (in minutes) taken to complete client interviews.

8	12	26	10	23	21
16	22	18	17	36	9

You may assume these data are a representative sample of all client interview times.

(a) Compute the sample mean and standard deviation.

(b) Construct a 99% confidence interval estimate of the population mean interview time.

8-4 INTERVAL ESTIMATES OF THE POPULATION PROPORTION

We can estimate the population proportion π by an interval, using the sample proportion P, in much the same way that we can estimate μ, using $\bar{X}$. To estimate π, we take advantage of the normal approximation to the binomial sampling distribution of P (which we learned in Chapter 7 is allowable only for certain sample sizes).

We will use P to estimate π by an interval in the form

$$P - z_{\alpha/2}\sigma_P \leq \pi \leq P + z_{\alpha/2}\sigma_P$$

Again, we do not know the value of σ_P, because it depends on π—the value we are estimating. So we must determine the value of σ_P from the sample results. We therefore replace π with P in

$$\sigma_P = \sqrt{\frac{\pi(1 - \pi)}{n}}$$

to obtain the point estimate

$$\sqrt{\frac{P(1 - P)}{n}}$$

We can then use this substitution in expressing the $100(1 - \alpha)\%$

CONFIDENCE INTERVAL ESTIMATE OF THE POPULATION PROPORTION

$$\pi = P \pm z_{\alpha/2}\sqrt{\frac{P(1 - P)}{n}}$$

or

$$P - z_{\alpha/2}\sqrt{\frac{P(1 - P)}{n}} \leq \pi \leq P + z_{\alpha/2}\sqrt{\frac{P(1 - P)}{n}}$$

EXAMPLE: PREFERENCE FOR CANNED CORN

To estimate the proportion of buyers who preferred the quality of their canned corn, Yellow Giant researchers randomly selected a panel of $n = 100$ persons. Each panelist was given three cans of brand X and three cans of brand Y, with the labels removed. The testers were asked to rate each can of corn on the basis of four factors: tenderness, sweetness, consistency, and color. The brand receiving the highest aggregate score by a tester was the preferred one. The following test results were obtained.

Number preferring brand X:	59
Number preferring brand Y:	37
Number of ties:	4
Total	100

A 99% confidence interval is desired in estimating π, the proportion of the buying population preferring brand X.

SOLUTION: The critical normal deviate when $\alpha = 1 - .99 = .01$ obtained from Appendix Table E is $z_{\alpha/2} = z_{.005} = 2.57$. The sample proportion of buyers preferring brand X is $P = 59/100 = .59$. The 99% confidence interval is

$$\pi = .59 \pm 2.57\sqrt{\frac{.59(1 - .59)}{100}}$$

$$\pi = .59 \pm 0.13$$

so that

$$.46 \leq \pi \leq .72$$

EXERCISES

8-24 Construct a 95% confidence interval for the proportion of defective items in large shipments yielding the following sample results.
(a) $n = 1{,}000$; $P = .2$ (b) $n = 2{,}000$; $P = .04$ (c) $n = 500$; $P = .01$

8-25 In a poll taken to estimate the president's current popularity, each person in a random sample of $n = 1{,}000$ voters was asked to agree with one of the following statements.

"The president is doing a good job."
"The president is doing a poor job."
"I have no opinion."

A proportion of .59 chose the first statement. Assuming that the actual number of voters is quite large, construct a 95% confidence interval for the population proportion of voters who will choose the first statement.

8-26 The Eureka Lumber Mill cuts redwood logs removed from a very large reforested area into boards of specified dimensions. The individual pieces of board are then sorted by grade. The proportion of boards that are of a high enough quality to be merchandised is to be estimated. A sample of 100 boards from various logs is taken for this purpose.
(a) Suppose that the sample proportion of quality grade boards is .5. Construct a 99% confidence interval estimate of the proportion of all lumber that will be cut and placed in this category.
(b) Suppose that the sample proportion of quality grade boards is .4. Construct a 95% confidence interval estimate of the proportion of all lumber that will be cut and placed in this category.

8-27 The highway patrol director in a certain state has ordered a crackdown on drunk drivers. To see if this safety campaign is working, the director has ordered a sampling study to estimate the proportion of all fatal traffic accidents caused by drinking. In a random sample of $n = 100$ accidents, 42% were attributed to alcohol. Assuming that the accident population is large, construct a 95% confidence interval for the population proportion.

8-28 The Skinny Tinny Company adjusts the settings of a sheet metal roller whenever the proportion π of overthick sheets is .015 or greater. The true level of π is unknown but is periodically estimated from samples of 100 sheets.

(a) In one sample there were 4 overthick sheets. Construct the corresponding 95% confidence interval estimate of π.

(b) Using the normal approximation, determine the probability for getting as many or more thick sheets as in (a) when the true level of π is .01.

8-29 A printer has negotiated a contract with Centralia Bell to print directories. Because disgruntled customers whose names are misspelled or listed with the number of, say, a local mortuary will complain bitterly for a whole year, the telephone company is anxious to minimize directory errors. Its contract therefore states that the printer must forfeit \$100 for every page that contains errors introduced in the printing process.

Counting the errors in a completed directory is an onerous chore. The majority are found by customer complaint, and most of these turn out not to be the printer's fault. Thus, a sample will be taken to determine what penalty fee to charge the printer. It is so difficult to find errors that many persons must search for them independently. A company accountant selects a sample of 50 pages from a 600-page directory and asks 20 people in succession to review each page for errors. An estimate is to be made of the proportion π of pages that contain errors.

(a) Construct a 99.8% confidence interval estimate of π if $P = .37$.

(b) The contract specifies that the estimate of π must be a point estimate. What are the losses to the printer if the estimate is too large by .02?

(c) Determine the probability that the estimator P will be .37 or over if the actual error rate is only $\pi = .35$.

8-5 CHOOSING THE SAMPLE SIZE AND SELECTING THE ESTIMATOR

In this section we consider two important issues in statistical planning. We begin by considering the choice of sample size, which can be viewed as an economic consideration. The n actually used might be dictated by funding or other outside circumstances. But we will see that it can be selected in order to meet reliability and error targets. A related issue is the choice of estimator. As we shall see, sometimes we have a choice whether to estimate a mean quantity using a sample mean or using a sample proportion.

ERROR AND RELIABILITY

Costs are usually incurred when an estimate is erroneous. In many statistical applications, it is quite difficult to place a monetary value on the results of an incorrect estimate. Ideally, a sample size should be chosen that achieves the most desirable balance between the chances of making errors, the costs of those errors, and the costs of sampling. Figure 8-7 illustrates the concepts involved in finding the optimal sample size, which minimizes the total cost of sampling. The costs of collecting the sample data increase with n. But larger samples are more reliable, so that the losses from chance sampling error decline. The total cost of sampling—the sum of collection costs and error costs—will achieve a minimum value for some optimal n. This is the sample size that should be used.

Due to the difficulties associated with finding the costs of sampling error, the procedure illustrated in Figure 8-7 is not usually used. Instead, we focus on a number that separates insignificant errors from decidedly undesirable ones. This

STATISTICS AROUND US

Airlines Sharing Ticket Revenues

Lake Airlines is a small regional carrier feeding the larger airlines. Passengers purchasing a ticket for a cross-country trip are issued a single ticket for the entire journey at the point of embarkation. Lake is entitled to keep only its portion of the revenue and must forfeit shares to the other airlines involved. The reverse occurs for passengers originating with other airlines who use Lake for a single leg. In these cases, Lake must collect its share of the ticket revenue from the other airline. At the end of each month, the airlines balance their accounts based on a detailed enumeration of the inter-airline tickets collected. This has proved to be a very costly and time consuming process.

A consulting statistician has suggested that the airlines balance their accounts by means of random samples of collected tickets, arguing that only a small portion of the tickets must then be analyzed. There would be a certain amount of risk, however, for the samples obtained could provide erroneous figures.

Using a sample has drawbacks. Because of chance sampling error, Lake's claims against other airlines will be understated in some months and overstated in others. Viewing the long-run average or expected revenue losses as the cost of sampling error, the statistician has computed (by a procedure too detailed to discuss here) the costs for various sample sizes.

Sample Size n	Cost of Collecting Sample	Sampling Error Costs	Total Cost of Sampling
100	\$ 100	\$40,222	\$40,322
1,000	1,000	13,059	14,059
5,000	5,000	5,666	10,666
5,200	5,200	5,454	10,654
6,000	6,000	5,202	11,202
10,000	10,000	4,028	14,028

Assuming that each sample ticket processed costs Lake \$1, the costs of sampling have also been calculated. The sample size yielding the minimum cost to Lake is about $n = 5{,}200$.

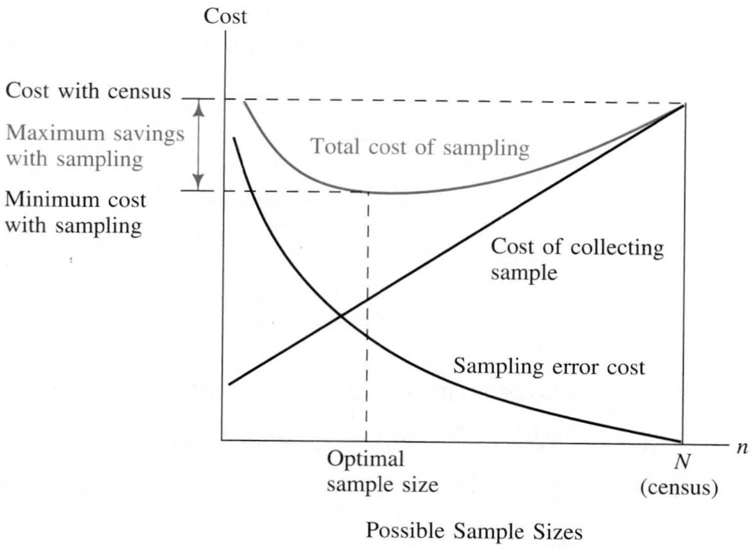

FIGURE 8-7 Relationships among sampling costs.

is called the **tolerable error level**. Accepting some error is the price we pay for using a sample instead of a census.

We denote the tolerable error—the maximum amount the estimate should extend above or below the parameter—by e, which is a number in the same units as the parameter being estimated. As applied in traditional statistics, we define an estimate's reliability in terms of e.

DEFINITION: The **reliability** associated with using $\bar{X}$ to estimate μ is the probability that $\bar{X}$ differs from μ by no more than the tolerable error level e, or

$$\text{Reliability} = \Pr[\mu - e \leq \bar{X} \leq \mu + e]$$

Figure 8-8 illustrates the relationships among reliability, tolerable error, and the sampling distribution of $\bar{X}$ when reliability is .95. The shaded area provides the probability that $\bar{X}$ will lie within $\mu \pm e$.

For a fixed e, only one normal curve has a shape that provides the desired area. If the reliability is lowered to .80, another curve, shown in Figure 8-9, applies. Note that compared with the curve in Figure 8-8, this second curve is flatter and exhibits more variability, so that it must have a larger value of $\sigma_{\bar{X}}$.

Thus, for any specified tolerable error and corresponding reliability, there is a unique level of $\sigma_{\bar{X}}$. Since $\sigma_{\bar{X}} = \sigma/\sqrt{n}$ and σ is *a fixed value*, only the sample size n can be adjusted to achieve the required level of $\sigma_{\bar{X}}$. This means that a given e and reliability require a unique value of n.

STEPS FOR FINDING THE REQUIRED SAMPLE SIZE TO ESTIMATE THE MEAN

To illustrate how to determine the appropriate sample size to use in estimating the mean, consider the problem faced by a government pension analyst who wishes to estimate the mean age at which federal employees retire.

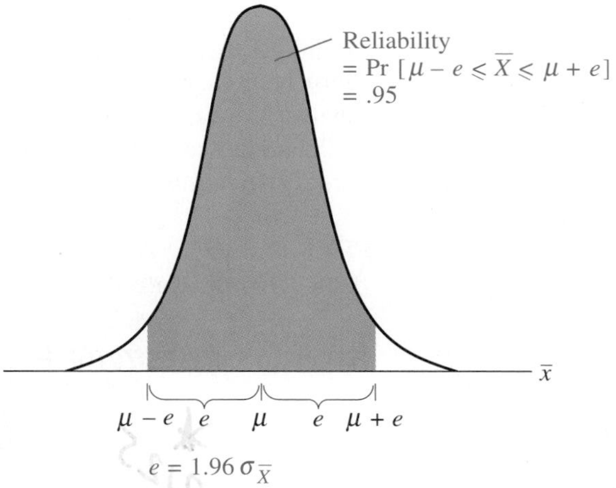

FIGURE 8-8 Relationships among reliability, tolerable error, and the sampling distribution of $\bar{X}$ when reliability (shaded area) = .95.

STEP 1

Set a tolerable error level e. The same units apply to e as to the observed units. The analyst chooses $e = .5$ year as adequate precision for the estimate.

STEP 2

Set a target reliability probability $1 - \alpha$ *and find* $z_{\alpha/2}$. Although the analyst would like to be certain of achieving the desired precision, such perfection cannot be achieved using a sample. She determines that a reliability of .95 will suffice with $\alpha = 1 - .95 = .05$. Appendix Table E provides the critical normal deviate of $z_{\alpha/2} = z_{.025} = 1.96$.

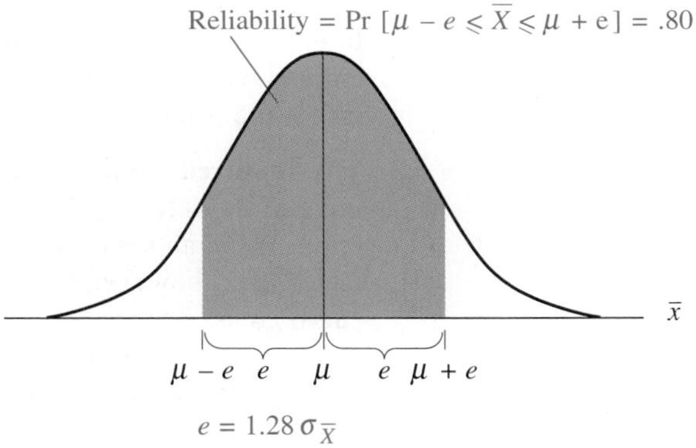

FIGURE 8-9 Relationships among reliability, tolerable error, and the sampling distribution of $\bar{X}$ when reliability (shaded area) = .80.

STEP 3

Establish a value for the population standard deviation σ. Ordinarily, this value must be a *guess*. As an aid, a value from a similar study may be used for σ. The analyst is aware that in a recent study of postal employee retirements, the sample standard deviation for the age of retirement was 3.5 years. Believing that a similar age dispersion applies to federal employees, she uses $\sigma = 3.5$ years.

STEP 4

Calculate the required sample size n:

REQUIRED SAMPLE SIZE FOR ESTIMATING THE MEAN

$$n = \frac{z_{\alpha/2}^2 \sigma^2}{e^2}$$

Using the values

$$e = .5 \qquad z_{.025} = 1.96 \qquad \sigma = 3.5$$

the pension analyst finds the required sample size.

$$n = \frac{(1.96)^2(3.5)^2}{(.5)^2} = 188.2, \text{ or } 189$$

(When n is fractional, the next larger whole number is chosen.)

THREE INFLUENCES ON SAMPLE SIZE

1. **The required sample size is directly proportional to the population variance.** A larger sample size will be required for a population with high dispersion than for a population that exhibits little variability.

2. **The required sample size is inversely proportional to the square of the tolerable error.** Thus, if we reduce e by one-half, we need four times as large a sample if reliability remains constant. Similarly, if we increase e ten times, the sample size will be 1/100th as large.

3. **The required sample size is directly related to the square of the critical normal deviate $z_{\alpha/2}$.** Thus, doubling z will require n to be four times as large. We cannot say that doubling z will ordinarily raise reliability by a factor of 2, however, because z does not have a linear relationship to normal curve areas. For example, decreasing z from 2.57 to 1.28 (a reduction z of about one-half, so that n is about one-fourth as large) lowers the reliability from .99 to .80 (not quite a 20% drop).

The choices of e and z are interrelated, because the targeted reliability usually depends on the selected tolerable error. Because the tolerable error serves merely as a convenient cutoff point between serious and insignificant errors, its choice may be inseparable from the selection of the reliability level.

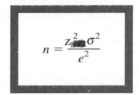

EXAMPLE: ESTIMATING MEAN LEG INSEAM AND FOOT LENGTH

A consultant is helping a clothing conglomerate establish improved standards for sizing products. One division makes pants, and another shoes. A key measure for sizing pants is the leg inseam length, and a counterpart in making shoes is the foot length. The respective population mean values will be estimated from sample mean measurements of two separate groups of randomly selected men. Using related air force anthropometric data, the following planning values have been obtained for the respective standard deviations.

$$\sigma = 1.75'' \text{ (inseam)} \quad \text{and} \quad \sigma = .45'' \text{ (foot length)}$$

To find the desired sample sizes, the tolerable error is $e = .10''$ and the reliability target is .99.

SOLUTION: For $\alpha = 1 - .99 = .01$, Appendix Table E provides a critical normal deviate value of $z_{\alpha/2} = z_{.005} = 2.57$. The desired sample sizes are thus

Inseam	Foot Length
$n = \dfrac{(2.57)^2(1.75'')^2}{(.10'')^2}$	$n = \dfrac{(2.57)^2(.45'')^2}{(.10'')^2}$
$= 2{,}023$	$= 134$

Notice that the n needed for estimating mean leg inseam length is about 16 times as great as the sample size needed to estimate mean foot length. This is because, in absolute terms, leg inseams are considerably more varied than foot lengths, with σ for the former being nearly 4 times as great. Our n formula shows that the required n must be about $(4)^2 = 16$ times as great for leg inseams as feet.

Although the above calculations do not reflect it, the consultant would probably want different es for sizing pants and shoes, accounting for the differences in the relative sizes of legs and feet. He may feel that precision of $\pm .10''$ may be adequate for sizing pant legs, but that a smaller tolerable error of $\pm .01''$ would be better for making shoes. [As an exercise, you might want to find the corresponding n for estimating mean foot length.]

FINDING A PLANNING ESTIMATE OF σ

The choice of sample size takes place in the planning stage of the sampling study before any sample data are collected. Like μ, the population standard deviation σ is ordinarily unknown and to be estimated. A planning level must be assumed for σ in order to calculate the desired n. Should this quantity be too big or too small, the computed level of n will result in undersampling (giving poor reliability or too much error) or in oversampling (being unnecessarily costly).

A statistician can sometimes use a planning σ estimated from another study involving a similar population having observations of about the same magnitude. The air force data in the above example were suitable for this purpose. But what if no such data exist?

A reasonably close "ballpark" level of σ is needed for planning purposes. One satisfactory method is purely judgmental. This is based on a feature of all normal curves.

Recall that normally distributed populations will have over 99.7% of their values falling within $\pm 3\sigma$ of the mean. Only about one out of a thousand population observations will fall below $\mu - 3\sigma$ or above $\mu + 3\sigma$. These quantities are roughly the .1st percentile and the 99.9th percentile. Those quantities span a range approximately equal to six standard deviations. Once these two quantities are specified, a planning value of σ may be computed from

$$\text{Planning } \sigma = \frac{99.9\text{th} - .1\text{st Percentiles}}{6}$$

Of course, if an investigator does not precisely know the above percentiles, she cannot be assured that her σ will be correct. But this indirect approach is easier than directly pulling a σ "from thin air."

EXAMPLE: ESTIMATING MEAN INCOME OF ACCOUNTANTS

You are asked to obtain the sample size necessary to estimate the mean income of accountants. First, you must get a planning σ. After some introspection, you can find a dollar figure at or below which about one accountant out of a thousand will earn in a year. At the high end, you can exercise similar judgment to find a 99.9% point.

SOLUTION: A student, Bob S., chose \$15,000, reasoning that figure to be the lowest offer anyone received in the last recruiting season at his school. Another student, Lisa L., chose \$22,000 because the most junior analyst in her father's CPA firm earns that much.

Bob chose \$150,000 as his 99.9th percentile, simply because it seemed appropriate. He said, "Many lawyers earn over \$100,000, but accountants are not so wealthy. The richest few should make upwards of \$150,000." Lisa reads her father's trade journals, reasons that the high-earners must be partners in big firms, and remembers that one such partner makes \$200,000. She chooses that amount.

The two students calculated the following planning standard deviations.

Bob

$$\sigma = \frac{150{,}000 - 15{,}000}{6} = \$22{,}500$$

Lisa

$$\sigma = \frac{200{,}000 - 22{,}000}{6} = \$29{,}667$$

Using $e = \$5{,}000$ and $z_{.025} = 1.96$, their desired sample sizes are

$$n = \frac{(22{,}500)^2(1.96)^2}{(5{,}000)^2} = 78 \qquad n = \frac{(29{,}667)^2(1.96)^2}{(5{,}000)^2} = 136$$

The underlying populations may not have a normal distribution. (In the above example, the population would be positively skewed.) But Chebyshev's theorem tells us that σ should be close to one computed from the above expression. That is because a substantial percentage of any population will lie within $\mu \pm 3\sigma$, falling inside a 6σ central range. Actual experimentation would be necessary to find a better value of σ.

When the costs of error and sampling are high, under- or oversampling can be serious. A two-stage sampling scheme that involves a small preliminary *pilot sample* might then be appropriate. The resulting sample standard deviation s can then be used as a point estimator of σ and as the planning value in computing the desired n.

STEPS FOR FINDING THE REQUIRED SAMPLE SIZE TO ESTIMATE THE PROPORTION

Using the same type of analysis that we applied to the sample mean, we can find the number of observations required to estimate a population proportion from its sample counterpart. The roles of tolerable error and reliability, as they affect n, are completely analogous. Tolerable error e represents the maximum allowable deviation between π and its estimator P, and e is expressed as a *decimal fraction.* Reliability is the probability that P differs from π by no more than e.

We follow the same procedure for finding the required sample size as we did before. To illustrate, we will consider the problem at a gas company, where there is a continual discrepancy between the cubic feet of gas leaving the storage tanks and the actual consumption reported by company meter readers. Some of the discrepancy may be caused by inaccurate meters and minor leaks, but much of it is believed to be due to the inattention of the meter readers. The proportion of misread meters is to be estimated for each reader. A sample of homes from each meter reader's route is selected to be audited. A company supervisor, whose presence is unknown, will follow each reader on a portion of his or her route and reread the meters. Later, the figures will be compared.

STEP 1

Set a tolerance error level e. This will be a decimal fraction. A tolerable error of $e = .02$ is chosen.

STEP 2

Set a target reliability probability and find α and $z_{\alpha/2}$. A reliability of .90 is considered adequate. The critical normal deviate is $z_{.05} = 1.64$.

STEP 3

Establish a preliminary value for the population proportion π. Initially, it is assumed that 10% of the readings are in error. The preliminary value of the population proportion is therefore $\pi = .10$. (The true value of π remains unknown.)

STEP 4

Calculate the required sample size n:

REQUIRED SAMPLE SIZE FOR ESTIMATING THE PROPORTION

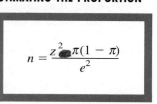

$$n = \frac{z_{\alpha/2}^2 \pi(1 - \pi)}{e^2}$$

Using the values

$$e = .02 \qquad z = 1.64 \qquad \pi = .10$$

the required sample size is

$$n = \frac{(1.64)^2(.10)(1 - .10)}{(.02)^2} = 605.16, \text{ or } 606$$

There may be insufficient knowledge for "ballparking" π. In that case, a preliminary value of $\pi = .50$ might be used. The resulting n is then guaranteed to meet error and reliability targets.

CHOOSING THE ESTIMATOR

The choice of statistical estimator is ordinarily dictated by circumstance. Most of the time we will use $\bar{X}$ as the estimator of μ, s to find σ, and P to get π. But there are situations when P might indirectly serve as the basis for estimating μ. As we shall see, in those cases it could actually be more expensive to use $\bar{X}$ to directly estimate μ.

ILLUSTRATION: WORK SAMPLING

One very important concern of production management is work measurement. Because of the great expense involved in collecting the required data, statistical tools have been developed to make the task more efficient.

A generation ago, procedures for obtaining measurements involved stop-watch methods that required continuous monitoring. Sometimes there was one watcher for each worker, so that the cost of gathering the data was high. The development of a statistical technique called **work sampling** relieved management of the burden of the stopwatch and at the same time removed the worker from its purported tyranny.

The classical procedure for finding the mean time to assemble a bumper on a car required that the worker be watched continuously and the installation times be duly recorded. If a sample of 20 completion times was required, each of about 10 minutes duration, about 200 minutes—or half a day—would be spent by the timer watching just this one worker. If ten workers in the automobile assembly plant install bumpers, and a sample is to be obtained for each, the timer must spend about 5 days measuring this one operation.

Work sampling is an alternative to continuous work measurement that can achieve a manyfold increase in the efficiency of the observer. The advantage of work sampling is that the same information obtainable from continuous observation may be achieved instead by many more shorter observations or "glimpses" taken randomly at scattered moments for an extended duration. Suppose that for a week the observer simply walks by the bumper installation station, making a note of what the worker is doing at that moment. It would be possible to do this many times, placing a check mark on a tally sheet for the particular task being performed at that instant. When the tallies have been accumulated at the end of the week, they would form the basis for estimating the proportion of time a worker spends at each task. The underlying principle of work sampling is that *the amount of time spent in a particular state of activity is proportional to the number of observations made of that state.*

Let us suppose that 100 observations have been made of an automobile bumper assembler; 86 times he was busy installing, and the rest of the time he was idle. Let us take this figure to calculate $P = 86/100 = .86$, which is a point estimate of the actual proportion of time π that the employee was busy installing bumpers. Assuming that all observations were made during the 35 hours in which the installer was officially on station and that he installed 222 bumpers, we may estimate the mean time taken for an installation.

The total time actually spent installing is estimated to be

$$35(.86) = 30.1 \text{ hours}$$

By dividing the time duration by the number of cars completed, the mean installation time μ may be estimated to be

$$\frac{30.1}{222} = .136 \text{ hour per bumper}$$

$$= 8.2 \text{ minutes per bumper}$$

This is the same type of result that would have been obtained through many hours of continuous observation of the single worker. But the 100 work sampling observations represent only minutes of the observer's time. On each pass through the plants he may collect tally marks for dozens of workers, each of whom performs a variety of tasks. Tallies would be obtained at all hours of the day and for every day of the week. No worker need feel uncomfortable about being watched, and the observer need carry no stopwatch.

The above results are only estimates. The same would be true for stopwatch timing. But work sampling is free of the many sources of potential bias of stopwatch studies. Thus, the results may be both more reliable and cheaper.

To find the number of work sampling observations required to estimate the mean time the worker takes to install bumpers, a very "rough" estimate would first have to be made of π. Suppose that we use $\pi = .80$. If a 5% tolerable error is desired with a 95% reliability, then $e = .05$ and $z_{.025} = 1.96$. We obtain

$$n = \frac{(1.96)^2(.8)(1 - .8)}{(.05)^2} = 245.86, \text{ or } 246$$

We may compare this value to the number of stopwatch observations necessary to estimate μ, the mean bumper installation time. Suppose that we know this worker's standard deviation to be $\sigma = 2$ minutes per bumper. With a true value of μ near 8 minutes, a 5% tolerable error would correspond to $8(.05) = .4$ minute. Using $e = .4$ and $z_{.025} = 1.96$, the required sample size would be

$$n = \frac{(1.96)^2(2)^2}{(.4)^2} = 96.04, \text{ or } 97$$

The number of continuous stopwatch observations would be 97 as compared to 246 for work sampling. But recall that the latter would take a few seconds each, whereas the former require several minutes each.

RELIABILITY VERSUS CONFIDENCE AND TOLERABLE ERROR VERSUS PRECISION

It may prove helpful at this point to clarify the key concepts that have been introduced in this chapter. An obvious question is: What is the difference between reliability and confidence? Another might be: How do we distinguish between tolerable error and precision? In both cases, aren't we really dealing with two terms that are synonymous?

In one sense, confidence and reliability mean the same thing. But the distinction between these concepts is that they apply in *different stages* of a sampling study. The notion of reliability is mainly a concern in the *planning stage*, where an appropriate sample size is chosen to satisfy the statistical analyst's goals. Greater reliability may only be achieved either by increasing the sample size, and hence the data collection costs, or by reducing the tolerable error level. In selecting a reliability level, the statistician seeks to find a satisfactory balance between risks of error and cost. The concept of confidence applies in the last phase of a sampling study—the *data analysis and conclusions stage*. At this final point in an investigation, the statistician is concerned with communicating results, so that the overriding concern is with *credibility*. Although often of the same value, the reliability need not be equal to the reported confidence level. Indeed, there are instances when the sample size n is not under the statistician's control, so that reliability considerations do not even enter into the planning.

We have already encountered the notion of precision in constructing confidence intervals. As the limits of the interval estimate become narrower, we can say that the resulting estimate becomes more precise. Like confidence, precision applies in the final stage of a sampling study. At this point in time, all sample data have been collected and precision can be improved only by a compensating reduction in confidence, or vice versa. The tolerable error level, on the other hand, is merely a convenient point of demarcation that separates serious errors from those that may be acceptable. It is used only in the planning stage and, with reliability, serves primarily to guide the statistician in selecting an appropriate sample size. Only when the reliability coincidentally equals the confidence level, and the planning guess as to σ or π is on target, will tolerable error be of equal magnitude to reported precision.

EXERCISES

8-30 The mean time required by Dearborn automobile assemblers to hang a car door is to be estimated. Assuming a standard deviation of 10 seconds, determine the required sample size under the following conditions.

(a) The desired reliability of being in error by no more than 1 second (in either direction) is .99.

(b) The desired reliability is .95 for a tolerable error of 1 second.

(c) A reliability of .99 is desired with a tolerable error of 2 seconds. How does the sample size you obtain compare with your answer to (a)?

(d) Answer (a), assuming that $\sigma = 20$ seconds. By how much does the sample size increase or decrease?

8-31 The Kryptonite Corporation purchasing manager orders supplies from many vendors and has the following policy. The quality of each shipment is to be estimated by means of a sample that will always include 10% of the items, regardless of the size of the shipment. Do you think this is good policy? Explain.

8-32 The following percentiles have been obtained by judgment. Find, in each case, a planning guess for the population standard deviation.

	(a)	(b)	(c)	(d)
.1st	56″	\$20,000	− 20%	.97″
99.9th	80″	\$200,000	220%	1.03″

8-33 An operations research analyst for Centralia Bank wishes to estimate the mean transaction time for a new ATM system. He judges it an almost certainty that 10 seconds will be required and that a transaction will seldom take more than 100 seconds. He wants to achieve 99% reliability and plus or minus one-second precision. How many sample transactions must he monitor?

8-34 The cost of obtaining the sample in Exercise 8-30 is \$1.50 per observation.
(a) For a tolerable error of 1 second, find the reliability that can be achieved by an expenditure of \$300.
(b) For a reliability of .95, find the tolerable error that must correspond to an expenditure of \$300.

8-35 An Ace Widgets quality control manager has a flexible sampling policy. Because there are different quality requirements for different parts, there is a separate policy for each type of part. For example, a pressure seal used on some assemblies must be able to withstand a maximum load of 5,000 pounds per square inch (psi) before bursting. If the mean maximum load of a sample of seals taken from a shipment is less than 5,000 psi, then the entire shipment must be rejected.

The sampling policy for this item requires that a sample be large enough so that the probability that the sample mean differs from the population mean by no more than 10 psi (in either direction) is equal to .95. Historically, it has been established that the standard deviation for bursting pressures of this seal is 100 psi.
(a) Find the required sample size.
(b) If the true mean maximum bursting pressure of the seals in a shipment is actually $\mu = 5{,}010$ psi, use your sample size in (a) to determine the probability that the shipment will be rejected.

8-36 A VBM engineer wishes to determine how many extra batteries to include in the power supply so that a satellite's useful life will be likely to exceed minimum specifications. A random sample of a particular type of battery is selected for testing. The engineer wishes to find the sample size that will provide an estimate of the true proportion π of batteries whose performance will be satisfactory to an accuracy of $e = .05$ with a .95 reliability. We will assume that the population of batteries is quite large.
(a) If π is initially assumed to be .5, find the necessary sample size.
(b) After testing the number of batteries found in (a), only 250 prove satisfactory. What is the point estimate of π? If this were the true value of π, how many more batteries were tested unnecessarily?

8-37 A waiter at Bon Appétit has been observed at 200 random times while on his station. The following tabulation provides the frequency distribution for the tasks he was performing at each observation.

Cleaning tables	10
Taking orders	35
Walking	57
Placing orders	8
Preparing food	20
Picking up orders	15
Delivering orders	10
Calculating bills	10
Preparing or delivering drinks	35

If during the time period over which he was observed he worked a total of 25 hours, exclusive of idle time, and served a total of 1,000 customers, estimate the mean time (in minutes) spent on each of the above tasks per customer.

SUMMARY

1. What are estimation, estimate, and estimator?
Estimation is the simplest form of inferential statistics, which uses known sample evidence to draw conclusions regarding unknown population characteristics. An **estimate** is a numerical value assigned to the unknown population parameter. In statistical investigations, the calculated value of a sample statistic serves as the estimate. That statistic is referred to as the **estimator** of the unknown parameter.

2. What are desirable properties for an estimator?
There are several properties that are desirable for estimators. One is **unbiasedness**, so that the expected value of the estimator is equal to the parameter being estimated. A **consistent** estimator achieves improved reliability and precision as the sample size becomes larger. The more **efficient** of two estimators reaches the investigator's reliability and precision goals with the smaller sample size.

3. What are the two forms of estimates?
Estimates take two forms. The **point estimate** is a single numerical quantity. Statisticians prefer the **interval estimate**, which acknowledges that some sampling error is unavoidable. The statistical art balances precision (interval width) against credibility while at the same time not devoting too many resources to collecting the sample data.

4. What are confidence intervals for the mean, and how are they used and constructed?
Interval estimates are qualified by a **confidence level**, a value stating how often the estimation procedure would provide a truthful solution if it were conducted over and over again with new samples. The estimate itself is called a **confidence interval**. A confidence interval estimate of the population mean is centered on the computed $\bar{X}$.

There are two main ways for finding the endpoints of a confidence interval for μ. When the population standard deviation is known, the following expression is used to construct the $100(1 - \alpha)\%$ confidence interval

$$\mu = \bar{X} \pm z_{\alpha/2}\sigma_{\bar{X}} \qquad (\sigma \text{ known})$$

where $\sigma_{\bar{X}} = \sigma/\sqrt{n}$ is the standard error of $\bar{X}$ and $z_{\alpha/2}$ is the normal deviate that corresponds.

5. **What is the Student t distribution, and what is its role in constructing confidence intervals for the mean?**
When the population standard deviation is unknown, use the critical value $t_{\alpha/2}$ for the **Student t distribution** in place of the normal deviate, and estimate σ using the computed sample standard deviation s. The following expression applies.

$$\mu = \bar{X} \pm t_{\alpha/2}\frac{s}{\sqrt{n}} \qquad (\sigma \text{ unknown})$$

The Student t distribution is characterized by a single parameter, the *number of degrees of freedom.* Its density function provides a bell-shaped curve resembling the normal curve. It applies to the random variable

$$t = \frac{\bar{X} - \mu}{s/\sqrt{n}}$$

which involves two uncertain quantities, $\bar{X}$ and s.

6. **When should the Student t distribution be used instead of the normal distribution?**
The Student t allows us to make inferences about the mean when the population standard deviation σ is unknown. The normal curve for $\bar{X}$, on the other hand, is based on a stipulated value for σ. When the sample size is large, the normal and Student t distributions tend to coincide, and the normal curve is generally applied whenever the sample size is too large to retrieve an accurate $t_{\alpha/2}$ value from the table.

7. **How is the normal distribution used in constructing confidence intervals for the proportion?**
The normal approximation also extends to constructing confidence intervals for the population proportion where

$$\pi = P \pm z_{\alpha/2}\sqrt{\frac{P(1 - P)}{n}}$$

8. **What are the considerations in establishing a sample size, and how can a level for n be established in an objective and systematic manner?**
The *choice of sample size* is an important issue. This may be computed ahead of time. For estimating μ, three quantities determine the appropriate n. These are the **tolerable error** level e, the desired **reliability** level for the estimate, and a good *guess* for σ. The reliability corresponds to the probability $1 - \alpha$ that the estimate will fall within a distance of $\pm\, e$ from its target. Both the tolerable error and reliability are arbitrary choices that reflect sampling costs and the investigator's attitudes toward the risks involved. The reliability gives rise to the **critical normal deviate** $z_{\alpha/2}$. The following expression is used to compute the required sample size.

$$n = \frac{z_{\alpha/2}^2 \sigma^2}{e^2} \qquad \text{(for estimating } \mu\text{)}$$

The required sample size for estimating the proportion is found in a similar fashion. A good *guess* is made for π (the quantity being estimated) and the required sample size is calculated using

$$n = \frac{z_{\alpha/2}^2 \pi(1 - \pi)}{e^2} \qquad \text{(for estimating } \pi\text{)}$$

REAL-LIFE STATISTICAL CHALLENGE

Applying Statistical Estimation to the Automobile Dream List

We will now apply statistical estimation methods to the set of "dream machines," using the 232 autos listed in Table 4-2. Table 8-3 shows the sample means and standard deviations found in Chapter 6 for three samples of size 5 and one of size 15.

Now we can construct a 90 percent confidence interval for mean highway mileage using our first sample of five randomly selected automobiles. The confidence interval is:

$$\mu = 28.00 \pm 2.132(2.12/\sqrt{5})$$

$$\mu = 28.00 \pm 2.02$$

so that

$$25.98 \leq \mu \leq 30.02$$

Now let's consider an example of statistical estimation using the sample proportion. Our population data shows a total of 99, or 43 percent, of the automobiles tested had manual transmissions. We can construct a 95 percent confidence interval for that same proportion of automobiles using the first 15 randomly selected automobiles. (Refer to Table 6-20.) P is equal to 7/15 or .47. The confidence interval is

$$\pi = .47 \pm (1.96)(.13)$$

$$\pi = .47 \pm .25$$

so that

$$.22 \leq \pi \leq .72$$

In Chapter 9 we will apply these results to the topic of hypothesis testing.

DISCUSSION QUESTIONS

1. Construct and compare the 90 percent confidence intervals for mean mileage using the results for samples (2) and (3).

TABLE 8-3 Sample Means and Standard Deviations for Engine Displacement (liters) and Mileage

	Sample 1 $n = 5$		Sample 2 $n = 5$		Sample 3 $n = 5$		Combined $n = 15$	
	Disp.	**MPG**	**Disp.**	**MPG**	**Disp.**	**MPG**	**Disp.**	**MPG**
Mean	2.50	28.00	3.32	27.40	3.10	24.00	2.97	26.47
Standard Deviation	0.67	2.12	1.90	5.03	1.22	5.34	1.31	4.47

2. Construct the 90 percent confidence interval for mean mileage using the combined sample results. Compare this to the intervals found in Question 1.
3. Construct and compare the 95 percent confidence intervals for the proportion of manual transmissions using the results from samples (1)-(3).
4. Develop another example estimating the combined sample proportion. Compare your results to the population data.

REVIEW EXERCISES

8-38 Woody Mills estimates the mean number of square feet of scrap and wasted wood per log in the manufacture of one-half-inch exterior plywood from a random sample of 100 logs of various sizes. Each log's volume was carefully measured, and the theoretical number of square feet of plywood was computed. This value was compared to the actual quantity achieved at the end of production, and the wood loss was calculated. When the study data were assembled, the sample mean and the standard deviation were computed as $\bar{X} = 1{,}246$ square feet and $s = 114.6$ square feet, respectively. Construct a 95% confidence interval estimate of the mean wood loss.

8-39 In estimating the mean time taken by a sheetrocker to nail one 8-foot sheet already in place, a sample of $n = 25$ observations were taken at random times. The worker was found to be nailing during just 5 of these observations.

(a) Make a point estimate of the proportion of all working time spent nailing.

(b) During the 200-minute span of time covering the observations, the sheetrocker hung 20 sheets. Make a point estimate of the mean time per sheet to do the nailing.

8-40 An engineer for BugOff Chemical Company estimates the mean number of gallons of a key ingredient that are wasted in the manufacturing of a ton of pesticide. She selects a random sample of 100 tons and computes the results to be $\bar{X} = 5.4$ gallons and $s = .42$ gallons. Construct a 95% confidence interval of the mean waste.

8-41 *Computer exercise.* The following rates of return were obtained by holding several common stocks for one year. You may assume that these data are a representative sample of a large population of historical rates of return.

5	−4	10	15	11	25	−5	17
−5	0	8	12	14	8	1	5

(a) Compute the sample mean and standard deviation.
(b) Construct a 95% confidence interval estimate of the population mean rate of return.

8-42 *Computer exercise.* The following salaries were obtained for a sample of ten executive secretaries.

\$35,000	\$67,500	\$51,500	\$53,000	\$38,000
\$42,000	\$29,500	\$31,500	\$46,000	\$37,500

(a) Find the value of an efficient, unbiased, and consistent estimator of the mean of the salaries of all executive secretaries.
(b) Find the value of an unbiased and consistent estimator of the variance of the salaries.
(c) Find the value of an unbiased estimator of the proportion of salaries above \$40,000.

8-43 The respective proportions of viewers watching each of the earliest prime time television programs on one network on four successive nights are to be estimated within a tolerance of ±.01, so that there is a 95% chance this precision will be achieved (reliability = .95). The sample proportion P is to be used. Find the required sample sizes for each of the following daily population proportions.
(a) Tuesday: .3 (c) Thursday: .5
(b) Wednesday: .6 (d) Friday: .1

8-44 A psychologist has designed a new aptitude test for life insurance companies to use to screen applicants for beginning actuarial positions. To estimate the mean score achieved by all future applicants who will eventually take the test, the psychologist has administered it to nine persons. The sample mean and the standard deviation have been calculated as $\bar{X} = 83.7$ and $s = 12.9$ points, respectively. Construct the confidence interval estimates of the mean for each of the following levels of confidence.
(a) 99% (b) 95% (c) 90% (d) 99.5%

8-45 The mean time to failure of Try-Hard batteries is estimated from a sample of 100 test items taken from a large population. Sample results provide $\bar{X} = 57.4$ hours and $s = 11.1$ hours. Construct a 99% confidence interval estimate of the population mean time to failure.

8-46 A random sample of $n = 100$ widths for two-by-fours is selected. The sample results yield $\bar{X} = 3.5$ inches and $s = .1$ inches. Construct a 95% confidence interval estimate of the boards in the entire shipment.

8-47 A pharmaceutical house wants to estimate the mean number of milligrams (mg) of drug its machinery inserts into each capsule in four different sizes of pills. In each case, a standard deviation of 1 mg is assumed and a reliability of 95% is desired. However, the amount of error tolerated varies with pill size. Find the following required sample sizes.
(a) tiny pills: .05 mg error (c) medium pills: .2 mg error
(b) small pills: .1 mg error (d) large pills: .5 mg error

8-48 Unified Airways is estimating the mean distance traveled annually by its first-class business travelers. From a random sample of $n = 100$ it was determined that $\bar{X} = 76{,}400$ and $s = 5{,}250$ miles. Construct a 95% confidence interval estimate of the mean distance traveled.

8-49 The work sampling example in Chapter 4 shows how work sampling can be used to allocate the expense of data entry. Suppose that two departments in a company have data entry. Three alternatives are possible for determining the charges assigned to the respective departments. (1) Detailed record keeping (census) at a cost of $200 per day. (2) Stopwatch sampling to estimate the mean daily data entry time per operator for Department *A*; then estimating the total daily time for Department *A* by multiplying this sample mean by the number of operators. (Department *B*'s usage can then be estimated from employee timeclock records.) (3) Work sampling to estimate the proportion of all data entry time for Department *A*, which when applied to total daily data entry time yields an estimate equivalent to that in (2).

(a) Suppose that the daily operator data entry time for Department *A*, determined by stopwatch sampling, has a standard deviation of $\sigma = .5$ hour. A .95 reliability probability is desired, with a tolerable error of $e = .08$ hour. Find the required sample size n.

(b) Suppose that the proportion of time spent on Department *A*, determined by a work sampling study, is presumed to be $\pi = .50$ (a guess). A .95 reliability probability is desired, with a tolerable error of $e = .02$. Determine the required number of observations n.

(c) Suppose that each stopwatch observation costs $1.00, but that each work sampling observation costs only $.05. Determine the daily cost of each method. Which one is least expensive?

STATISTICS IN PRACTICE

8-50 Using the master class data list developed in Exercise 1-19, answer the following (ignoring any finite population corrections).

(a) Select a quantitative variable and *assume* an appropriate value for σ. Then randomly select $n = 4$ observations. Using the normal distribution, construct a 90 percent confidence interval for the mean assuming that σ is known.

(b) Using the same sample observations as in (a), use the Student t distribution to construct a 95 percent confidence interval for the mean.

(c) Comment on differences between the results achieved in (a) and (b).

(d) Select a sample of $n = 5$ observations of a qualitative variable from the data set. Construct a 99 percent confidence interval for the proportion having a particular attribute. If the confidence level were lowered to 90 percent, what would that interval be?

8-51 Repeat Exercise 8-50 using your group's class data list developed in Exercise 1-21.

8-52 In Exercise 6-55 you were asked to go to a local store or other retail outlet and collect data for the number of customer arrivals during each of several one-minute intervals. Treating those data as *sample* observations, construct a 95 percent confidence interval for the mean number of arrivals per minute. Comment on your results.

8-53 Consider genetic diversity in your class and develop a set of questions based on some personal characteristics. Possible factors would be gender, eye color, handedness, ability to roll tongue, and color blindness.

(a) Collect the data. For each variable, these may be assumed to be random samples from the respective general populations.

(b) Construct a 90 percent confidence interval estimate of the proportion of the general population possessing the ability to roll their tongues.

(c) Construct a 95 percent confidence interval estimate of the proportion of persons who are right-handed.

8-54 Who do you want for President? If the election were held today, which candidate would you vote for? Research the most recent pre-election opinion poll from your local newspaper.

(a) Comment on that poll in terms of the investigator's use of statistical estimation methods.

(b) Using the question as it was worded in the newspaper report, conduct your own poll. Then construct a 90 percent confidence interval for the proportion favoring a particular candidate.

(c) Comment on the validity of your results.

CASE Brown and Becker's Budget

Brown and Becker is a consumer products manufacturer. The president has requested budgetary input for the next fiscal year. The head of new product development must generate data for the required funding. This will be done on a product-by-product basis, as if those items are already in existence, already part of the company's regular product mix.

One of the largest cost components for new products is direct manufacturing labor, used almost exclusively in assembling products supplied by Asian vendors. Forecast levels of direct labor will be based partly on the estimated productivity of existing products. For the electronics group, the following specialized data have been obtained for sample production runs.

Units	Direct Labor Cost	Units	Direct Labor Cost
5,240	$ 65,720	12,500	$105,200
8,330	79,249	5,550	49,720
1,125	13,450	3,355	42,060
24,360	261,420	15,610	163,400
8,550	91,050	1,500	17,400

The above data will be helpful in establishing the forecast cost of a new cellular modem.

The ultimate budgetary impact of the cellular modem will depend on the unit sales volume. The demand for the product will remain uncertain until it is on the market, the price has been established, and the marketing plan is in place. Several statistical samples will provide management with information regarding these factors.

QUESTIONS

1. Discuss the advantages of using a point estimate to forecast the labor cost segment of the budget for new product manufacturing. Why might management also require an interval estimate?
2. Convert the sample direct labor cost data to direct labor cost per unit. Calculate the sample mean and standard deviation of the cost per unit.
3. Construct a 95% confidence interval estimate of the mean direct labor cost per unit of all of the electronics group items.
4. Suppose that the unit direct labor cost of assembling cellular modems is estimated to be double that of the sample products. What is the point estimate of this cost component?
5. The product demand will depend, to a great extent, on the proportion of the market targeted to buy the product. Suppose that the modem will cost \$100. A sample of potential users is asked if they would buy one, and the data obtained will be used to estimate the true proportion of would-be buyers.
   (a) Using a guess of .10 for the population proportion, how large must the sample size be for the sample proportion to fall within .02 of the population parameter with probability .95?
   (b) If you are unable to guess where the population proportion will fall, select a sample size that guarantees achieving or exceeding the above specifications.
6. For a sample similar to the one above, the quantity of interest is the most a potential customer would be willing to pay for a cellular modem. Management feels that almost nobody would pay \$500, but that nearly everybody would be willing to pay \$20. The sample size must be chosen to obtain sample responses.
   (a) Suggest an appropriate planning guess for the population standard deviation.
   (b) Using your answer to (a), what sample size is necessary if the population mean maximum price is to be estimated within plus or minus \$10, with reliability .95?
   (c) Suppose that the management can only afford a sample of $n = 100$, and that the standard deviation given in (a) applies.
      (1) What is the resulting reliability if the tolerable error level remains at \$10?
      (2) What is the resulting tolerable error level if the reliability probability .95 remains unchanged?
7. A sample of $n = 100$ is selected to estimate the proportion in Question

5. Four of the sample persons said that they would buy a $100 cellular modem. Construct a 95% confidence interval estimate of the true proportion of the market targeted to buy that priced modem.

8. A sample of $n = 15$ persons is selected for estimating the mean maximum price of the modem. The following results have been obtained.

$100	$50	$200	$700	$10	$300	$150	$250
$75	$150	$50	$350	$400	$250	$90	

(a) Calculate the sample mean and standard deviation.

(b) Construct a 95% confidence interval estimate of the population mean maximum price.

9. Discuss any further sample information that management might find useful in establishing the budget for cellular modems.

CHAPTER 9

HYPOTHESIS TESTING

BEFORE READING THIS CHAPTER, MAKE SURE YOU UNDERSTAND:

How to avoid bias in selecting samples and how sampling error arises (Chapter 4).

The properties of the sampling distribution of the mean and proportion (Chapter 6).

How to use the normal curve to obtain probabilities for the sample mean and proportion (Chapter 7).

About confidence intervals and how they are used and constructed (Chapter 8).

When the Student *t* distribution should be used instead of the normal distribution (Chapter 8).

What considerations are important in establishing a sample size (Chapter 8).

AFTER READING THIS CHAPTER, YOU WILL UNDERSTAND:

About hypothesis testing and how it may be used in decision making.

How the hypothesis testing approach deals with sampling error.

The basic forms of a hypothesis test.

How decisions are reached when testing hypotheses.

About the two basic hypothesis testing procedures and when *z* or *t* should be used.

About the significance level of a test and how it relates to the decision rule and error probabilities.

We have encountered one form of statistical inference, estimation, and we are now ready for another type of inference, **hypothesis testing**. Since it culminates in a decision, the latter is the more dynamic form. Statistical testing is based on two opposite assumptions called **hypotheses** regarding populations that have some unknown features. This chapter considers the most common hypothesis tests involving assumed levels for population parameters. Later chapters consider other forms of hypotheses used to compare two or more populations, pertaining to the manner in which two variables are related, concerned with the structure of the population frequency distribution, or involving tests for randomness of data.

To set the stage, we begin with hypothesis tests for the unknown level of the population mean. Such an evaluation is helpful when there are two complementary actions, the outcomes of which depend on the unknown μ. For example, a supervisor can adjust controls whenever the mean output exceeds some prescribed level. Since the unknown μ cannot be known, the final action must depend on sample data. The sample mean is used as the **test statistic**, with adjustment taking place only if the computed $\bar{X}$ exceeds some critical value.

Unfortunately, the supervisor can never know if a shutdown was really necessary, since samples can give false readings. We can control but never eliminate the underlying sampling error. Unlike estimation, where precision and reliability are the major concerns, hypothesis testing focuses on a **decision rule** that balances the probabilities for taking incorrect actions. A good rule allows the supervisor to keep small the chance of unnecessarily adjusting controls while avoiding leaving bad controls in operation too long. Errors of omission and errors of commission can be managed through hypothesis testing when there has been a judicious choice of decision rule.

9-1 BASIC CONCEPTS OF HYPOTHESIS TESTING: TESTING A NEW DRUG

We will develop the many concepts that link hypotheses together via an extensive illustration based on whether or not the government should approve the manufacturing of a new drug.

A dietary supplement is being tested to determine if it can dissolve cholesterol deposits in arteries. A major cause of coronary ailments is hardening of the arteries caused by the accumulation of cholesterol. The Food and Drug Administration will not allow the product to be marketed unless there is strong evidence that it is effective. A sample of 100 middle-aged men have been selected for the test, and each man is given a standard daily dosage of the supplement. At the end of the experiment, the change in each man's cholesterol level is recorded.

On the basis of the sampling experiment, a government administrator must decide between two courses of action.

1. Release the supplement for public use.
2. Delay the supplement (and request further research).

Some risks are involved due to uncertainty regarding the supplement's true effectiveness (the sample may not be representative of the population as a whole).

THE NULL AND ALTERNATIVE HYPOTHESES

The possible effectiveness states of the supplement are referred to as *hypotheses.* Because the drug administrator is considering only two possibilities—ineffective versus effective—the following hypotheses apply.

1. The supplement is ineffective.
2. The supplement is effective.

The true effectiveness of the supplement is defined by the population of the percentage reduction in cholesterol levels experienced by all middle-aged men who took the supplement. We summarize effectiveness in terms of the population mean.

$$\mu = \text{Population mean percentage reduction in cholesterol levels}$$

The government will classify the drug as effective only if it produces more than a 20% improvement ($\mu > 20\%$). The percentage reduction constitutes a *target population* that does not exist until (and will not exist unless) the supplement is widely available. However, it is still possible to draw a sample from this "imaginary" population.

The first hypothesis is customarily referred to as the null hypothesis. Here, "null" represents no change from the natural variation in cholesterol level. In terms of the population mean μ, we use the following expression for the

NULL HYPOTHESIS

$$H_0\colon \mu \leq 20\% \qquad \text{(Supplement is ineffective.)}$$

The second hypothesis is called the alternative hypothesis. We express the

ALTERNATIVE HYPOTHESIS

$$H_A\colon \mu > 20\% \qquad \text{(Supplement is effective.)}$$

The hypotheses are formulated so that H_0 and H_A are opposites: When one is true, the other is false.

To achieve another special notation in hypothesis testing, we add the subscript 0 to the symbol for the population parameter. In the present example, this gives

$$\mu_0 = 20\%$$

which is the **pivotal value** of the population mean. In general, the null hypothesis holds for all levels of μ that are equal to μ_0 or that fall on one side of this value, and the alternative hypothesis applies otherwise. Unfortunately, we do not know which side actually applies, because the true value of μ remains unknown.

MAKING THE DECISION

The decision as to whether or not to release the dietary supplement coincides with the test results obtained for the sample patients. This decision is based on the value of

$$\bar{X} = \text{Sample mean percentage reduction in cholesterol levels}$$

We refer to $\bar{X}$ as the **test statistic**.

The chosen action must be consistent with the sample evidence. The two choices may be expressed in terms of the following hypotheses.

1. Release the supplement. Conclude that the null hypothesis is false (the supplement is effective). This is expressed as *reject* the null hypothesis.
2. Delay the supplement. Conclude that the null hypothesis is true (the supplement is ineffective). This is expressed as *accept* the null hypothesis.

The government administrator will release the supplement for public use if it provides a large mean reduction $\bar{X}$ in the cholesterol levels of the sample patients, because this result would seem to deny H_0. Similarly, she will delay the supplement's introduction if $\bar{X}$ is small and the supplement has not been very effective during the sample test—evidence that tends to confirm H_0.

In effect, the administrator will decide what action to take when she sets the point of demarcation for $\bar{X}$. For now, we suppose that the value 22 is chosen. This value is commonly referred to as the **critical value** or the **acceptance number**. The test statistic is then used to formulate a decision rule. A decision rule allows us to translate sample evidence into a plan for choosing a course of action.

DECISION RULE

Accept H_0 if $\bar{X} \leq 22$	(Delay the supplement.)
Reject H_0 if $\bar{X} > 22$	(Release the supplement.)

The decision rule identifies **acceptance and rejection regions** for the possible value of $\bar{X}$, which can be illustrated as

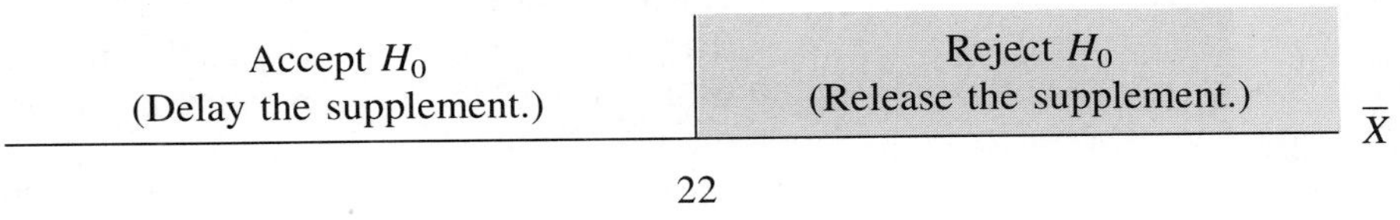

Having established the decision rule, the ultimate action taken by the government agency will be determined by the observed sample results. The computed value of $\bar{X}$ will fall within either the acceptance or the rejection region, and H_0 will be accepted or rejected accordingly. When H_0 is *rejected*, the results are said to be **statistically significant**. Here, we use the word *significant* in a special sense. All hypothesis-testing results are important, but the test is statistically significant only when the null hypothesis is *rejected.*

The structure of the decision is shown in Table 9-1. Two courses of action are considered: *Delay* or *release* the supplement. There are also two population states: The supplement is either *ineffective* or *effective.* For each combination of an action and a supplement quality, the outcome represents a correct decision or an error. Two correct decisions are (1) *accept* a true null hypothesis (delay an ineffective supplement) and (2) *reject* a false null hypothesis (release an effective supplement). The decision rule may also result in two errors.

TYPE I ERROR

Reject H_0 when it is true	(Release an ineffective supplement.)

TYPE II ERROR

Accept H_0 when it is false	(Delay an effective supplement.)

TABLE 9-1 The Decision Structure for the Dietary Supplement

	Course of Action	
Possible Population States	**Accept Null Hypothesis** If $\bar{X} \leq 22$ (Delay the supplement.)	**Reject Null Hypothesis** If $\bar{X} \geq 22$ (Release the supplement.)
Null Hypothesis True $\mu \leq 20$ (μ_0) (Supplement is ineffective.)	**Correct Decision** Probability $= 1 - \alpha$ (Delay the ineffective supplement.)	**Type I Error** Probability $= \alpha$ Significance level $= \alpha$ (Release the ineffective supplement.)
Null Hypothesis False $\mu > 20$ (μ_0) (Supplement is effective.)	**Type II Error** Probability $= \beta$ (Delay the effective supplement.)	**Correct Decision** Probability $= 1 - \beta$ (Release the effective supplement.)

To evaluate the decision rule, we find the probability for committing each error. It is conventional to denote the probabilities for these errors by α and β (the lower case Greek *beta*).

ERROR PROBABILITIES

$$\alpha = \Pr[\text{Type I error}] = \Pr[\textit{Reject } H_0 | H_0 \text{ is true}]$$

$$\beta = \Pr[\text{Type II error}] = \Pr[\textit{Accept } H_0 | H_0 \text{ is false}]$$

The value α is also called the **significance level** of the test.

FINDING THE ERROR PROBABILITIES

How good is the choice of 22 as the critical value? When establishing the decision rule, the decision maker's attitude toward the two types of errors should be reflected in the levels of the α and β probabilities.

To find α, we consider the case when the null hypothesis is true: the population mean μ is ≤ 20. The null hypothesis holds for any value of $\mu = 20$ or less, such as 0, 9.7, or 17.5. We focus on the extreme possibility, when the pivotal value of μ_0 applies, and set the population mean at $\mu = 20$.

The normal curve at the top of the following figure shows the sampling distribution of $\bar{X}$ when the null hypothesis is true and $\mu = \mu_0$ exactly. Although we do not know its actual value, for purposes of illustration we assume that the population standard deviation for reduction in cholesterol levels is $\sigma = 10$. The probability for the Type I error (the shaded area to the right of 22 under the top curve) is

$$\alpha = \Pr[\bar{X} > 22 | H_0 \text{ is true } (\mu = \mu_0 = 20)] = .5 - .4772 = .0228$$

When the null hypothesis is false, a different sampling distribution of $\bar{X}$ applies, as shown in the bottom curve. The dietary supplement is effective for any mean percentage reduction in cholesterol levels greater than 20. In our illustration, $\mu = 23.5$ (and the population standard deviation is assumed to be the same as before). The corresponding probability for the Type II error (the shaded area to the left of 22 under the bottom curve) is

$$\beta = \Pr[\bar{X} \leq 22 | H_0 \text{ is false } (\mu = 23.5)] = .5 - .4332 = .0668$$

A similar β probability can be obtained for any other level of μ greater than 20. For instance, when $\mu = 24.5$ is used, we obtain $\beta = .0062$.

Of course, the number of ways for H_0 to be false is unlimited, and μ might assume any level, with a different β applicable to each. A fundamental dilemma of hypothesis testing is balancing the targeted α with the family of possible β's. This is accomplished by choosing an appropriate decision rule.

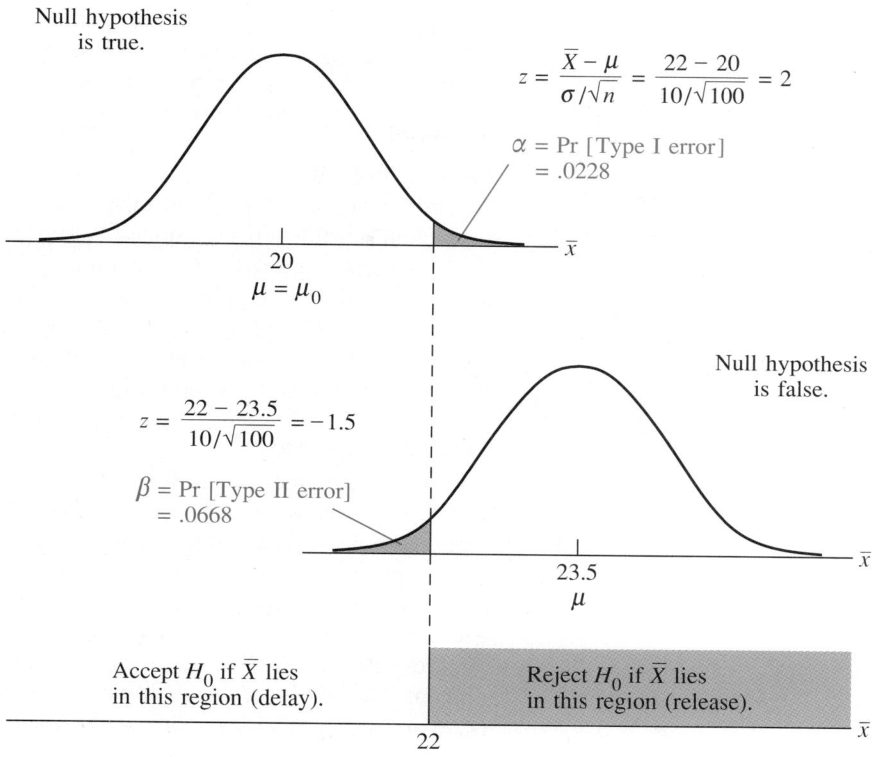

CHOOSING THE DECISION RULE

In hypothesis-testing situations, the decision maker's only real choice is selecting the decision rule. In testing the dietary supplement, the administrator could use a different critical value, such as 23 or 24. Different α and β probabilities would then apply. An ideal decision rule provides a balance between α and β.

In general, the Type I error (rejecting the null hypothesis when it is true) is more serious. In our example, the Type I error is to release an ineffective supplement, because great care is taken in the United States to avoid marketing any drug or food additive that could have serious undesirable side effects. **Decision rules are usually selected to guarantee a target level for α.**

Avoiding the Type I error by keeping α small tends to increase the chances of committing a Type II error (accepting a false null hypothesis). Delaying an effective supplement could result in deaths that could have been prevented by the use of an anticholesterol agent. Both the α and β error probabilities can be kept tolerably small by using a large sample size.

MAKING THE DECISION

Up to this point, our perspective with the dietary supplement decision has been from the planning stage of the sampling investigation. Recall that the planning stage occurs before data have been collected, and it is at that time when the hypotheses are formulated, the sample size is fixed (perhaps by the constraints of a budget), and the decision rule is established in accordance with the prescribed

α. Only after all of this will the sample observations be made.

In the dietary supplement decision, the action taken depends on what sample results are obtained. Consider the following hypothetical scenarios that might apply once the data have been collected.

FIRST SCENARIO

A random sample of $n = 100$ men is selected, administered the supplement, and their cholesterol levels determined before and after the experiment. For each subject the percentage reduction is found. The mean percentage reduction in cholesterol levels is computed to be $\bar{X} = 25.7\%$. This result exceeds the critical value of 22%, providing statistically significant evidence that the supplement is indeed effective. Since $\bar{X}$ falls in the rejection region, the administrator would *reject* her null hypothesis and *release* the supplement for public use.

SECOND SCENARIO

The same experiment is performed, with little change in cholesterol levels. The computed mean percentage reduction is only $\bar{X} = 17.4\%$. This is not strong evidence in support of an effective supplement, and $\bar{X}$ falls in the acceptance region. The administrator must *accept* H_0, concluding that the supplement is ineffective, and *delay* its introduction until further research has been completed. (That same action would be required for any computed level for $\bar{X}$ that is ≤ 22, such as 15.1, 19.2, or even 21.9.) Since H_0 is accepted, the test results are not statistically significant. The administrator should be aware of the β probabilities that this decision is incorrect (since in spite of the sample results μ might nevertheless be bigger than 20).

FORMULATING HYPOTHESES

The null and alternative hypotheses are opposites: When one is true, the other is false. This allows us to consider just two actions and two outcomes for each hypothesis, depending on whether H_0 is true or false. One area of potential confusion is deciding which hypothesis to label H_0. In earlier statistical applications, the null hypothesis corresponded to the assumption that no change occurs, which accounts for the adjective *null*. For example, in testing a drug, the usual hypoth-

STATISTICS AROUND US

Testing Grade Point Averages

A college president wants to show that special admissions students have lower grade point averages (GPAs) than regular students, whose mean GPA is 2.75. Letting μ represent the mean GPA of the special admissions, the following hypotheses apply.

$$H_0: \mu \geq 2.75 \qquad \text{(GPAs are as high.)}$$
$$H_A: \mu < 2.75 \qquad \text{(GPAs are lower.)}$$

The null hypothesis places $\mu \geq 2.75$, since this is what the decision maker wishes to disprove.

esis would be that it yields little or no improvement over nature. The H_0 used in the dietary supplement illustration corresponds to this designation. Another frequently used guideline is to designate the hypothesis that the decision maker wishes to disprove as H_0. *A common practice is to designate as H_0 the hypothesis for which rejection when true is the more serious error.* Thus, the Type I error would be worse than the Type II error. In the dietary supplement illustration, the decision rule was chosen so that this happened to be the case.

The Statistics Around Us box on page 364 and the earlier dietary supplement illustration have hypotheses that place μ to one side of the pivotal level. A statistical investigation involving such hypotheses is referred to as a **one-sided test.** A second form, described below, has hypotheses used in a **two-sided test.**

The Statistics Around Us box on page 366 shows that designation of the null hypothesis can vary with the decision making context.

STATISTICS AROUND US

Testing Cannery Machinery

A cannery inspector must determine whether or not cans are being filled with a mean $\mu = 16$ ounces of tomato paste. Machinery must be adjusted if the cans are being overfilled or underfilled. The inspector uses the following hypotheses.

H_0: $\mu = 16$ ounces	(Machinery is satisfactory.)
H_A: $\mu \neq 16$ ounces	(Machinery must be adjusted.)

The null hypothesis is $\mu = 16$ ounces, so that the machinery is assumed to be satisfactory. The Type I error of rejecting H_0 when it is true (unnecessarily adjusting the machinery when it is satisfactory) is the more serious error. The alternative hypothesis states that $\mu \neq$ (is not equal to) 16 ounces. This can also be stated as $\mu > 16$ ounces (cans are being overfilled) or $\mu < 16$ ounces (cans are being underfilled). This is an example of a *two-sided alternative.*

EXERCISES

9-1 A new slow-dissolving aspirin tablet is being evaluated. The null hypothesis is that the tablet dissolves too fast, with a mean dissolving time of $\mu \leq 10$ seconds. The new aspirin will replace the old one if the sample mean $\bar{X} > 12$ seconds; otherwise, the old tablet will continue to be marketed.

Express the null and alternative hypotheses as inequalities involving μ. Then, construct an appropriate hypothesis-testing decision table similar to Table 9-1. Be sure to identify the Type I and Type II errors. (Do *not* try to find the values of α and β.)

9-2 For each of the following situations, indicate the Type I and Type II errors and the correct decisions.

(a) H_0: New system is not better than the old one.

(1) Adopt new system when new one is better.

STATISTICS AROUND US

Producers, Consumers, and Blenders

A **producer** of lightbulbs must decide whether or not to ship a production batch to its regular customers or to scrap it and sell it as "seconds." The bulbs in any batch may be predominantly good ones with a long mean lifetime μ, or mainly bad ones with a short μ. Ideally, the regular customers would get nothing but good batches, and the bad bulbs would all be scrapped. But since the producer will decide a batch's disposition from sample data, there are two errors.

1. Some good batches will be scrapped.
2. Some bad batches will be shipped.

Producers tend (perhaps shortsightedly) to view the first error as more serious. The null hypothesis would then be that any particular batch is good, so that in terms of mean lifetime μ,

$$H_0\text{: } \mu \geq \mu_0$$

where μ_0 might be the advertised "minimum" lifetime.

The **consumer** of the lightbulbs can refuse or buy any particular shipment. This choice will be based on a sample inspection by the receiving-department. The following two errors apply.

1. Some of the time a bad shipment will be bought.
2. Some of the time a good shipment will be refused.

Consumers are less concerned about inconveniencing suppliers than acquiring defective merchandise, so they judge the first error to be more serious. The null hypothesis is thus that the shipment is bad. In terms of mean lifetime,

$$H_0\text{: } \mu \leq \mu_0$$

where μ_0 might be a barely tolerable mean lifetime.

To achieve color consistency, a **blender** of Scotch whiskey wants to ensure a balance between the levels of dark and light whiskeys. The mixing process is designed so that any batch of barrels yields a mean color index of 100. When the true level for μ is lower, dark ingredients should be added; when it is higher, light additives should be included. Unfortunately, not all barrels can be opened, and μ can't be known. Some batches will be unnecessarily darkened, others improperly lightened. These errors are equally serious, and the following simple null hypothesis applies.

$$H_0\text{: } \mu = \mu_0$$

The value $\mu_0 = 100$ would be appropriate here.

(2) Retain old system when new one is better.
(3) Retain old system when new one is not better.
(4) Adopt new system when new one is not better.

(b) H_0: New product is satisfactory.
(1) Introduce new product when unsatisfactory.
(2) Do not introduce new product when unsatisfactory.
(3) Do not introduce new product when satisfactory.
(4) Introduce new product when satisfactory.

(c) H_0: Batch of transistors is of good quality.
(1) Reject good-quality batch.
(2) Accept good-quality batch.
(3) Reject poor-quality batch.
(4) Accept poor-quality batch.

9-3 Indicate whether the following statements are true or false. If false, explain why.
(a) A Type II error is the same as accepting the alternative hypothesis when it is false.
(b) Either a Type I or a Type II error must occur.
(c) The significance level is the probability of rejecting the null hypothesis when it is true.

9-4 For each of the following hypothesis-testing situations, state the Type I and Type II errors in nonstatistical terms (for example, releasing a poor drug or delaying a good drug).
(a) The null hypothesis is that a new manufacturing process is no improvement over the existing one. If sample evidence indicates that it is better, the new process will be adopted.
(b) A union is negotiating with management for a 4-day workweek with 9-hour working days at a slightly higher wage. The union argues that efficiency and morale will be improved, thereby increasing output. Choosing as its null hypothesis that productivity will not increase, management will sign the contract if there is adequate evidence that the union claims are true. Otherwise, some hard negotiating sessions will follow.
(c) The objective of a statistical study is to determine whether a stronger consumer protection law is favored by more voters than the present one. Taking as its null hypothesis that the new law does not meet greater voter approval, a consumer action group will lobby for the new law if there is significant evidence to the contrary.

9-5 A university introduces a new degree program.
(a) What null and alternative hypotheses are being tested if the Type I error is to incorrectly conclude that the program will succeed?
(b) What hypotheses are being tested if the Type II error is to incorrectly conclude that the program will succeed?

9-6 In testing the hypotheses

$$H_0: \mu \leq \mu_0 \quad \text{and} \quad H_A: \mu > \mu_0$$

use $\mu_0 = 150$.

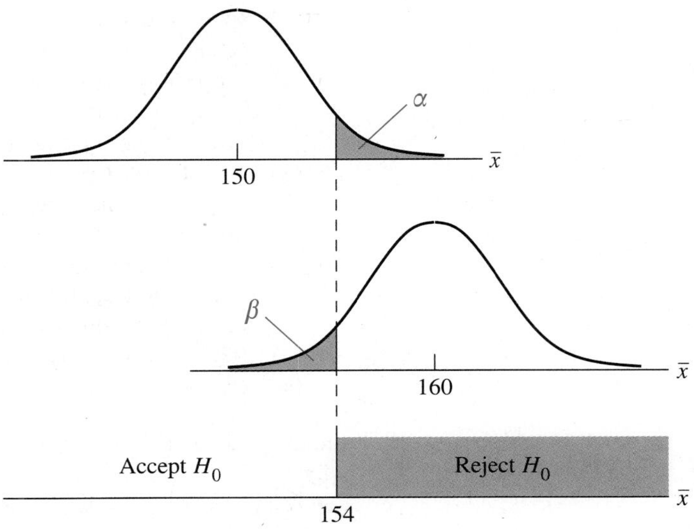

Suppose that the population standard deviation is $\sigma = 30$ and a sample of $n = 100$ is used. Find the Type I error probability α when $\mu = 150$ and the Type II error probability β when $\mu = 160$. Assume that the following decision rule applies.

$$\textit{Accept } H_0 \text{ if } \bar{X} \leq 154$$

$$\textit{Reject } H_0 \text{ if } \bar{X} > 154$$

9-7 Repeat Exercise 9-6 using 156 as the critical value. Is the new α larger or smaller? Is the new β larger or smaller?

9-8 Repeat Exercise 9-6 using a larger sample of $n = 200$. Is the new α larger or smaller? Is the new β larger or smaller?

9-2 TESTING THE MEAN

Now that we have mastered the basic concepts of hypothesis testing, we are ready to apply the procedure. The sampling study begins with the formulation of the hypotheses. After the decision maker establishes a Type I error probability α (significance level) and an appropriate sample size n, everything that follows is largely mechanical. The sample data are collected, and a critical value corresponding to the desired value of α is found. The computed value of the test statistic is then compared to the critical value, and the decision rule indicates the appropriate course of action.

THE HYPOTHESIS-TESTING STEPS

To simplify hypothesis testing with the mean, a five-step procedure will be used.

STEP 1

Formulate the null and alternative hypotheses. The decision parameter is the unknown population mean μ. A pivotal level μ_0 is used to define H_0 and H_A.

ONE-SIDED TESTS

The more serious error establishes which side of μ_0 to include under H_0. One of the following two null hypotheses applies.

$$\mu \leq \mu_0 \quad \text{or} \quad \mu \geq \mu_0$$

There are two types of errors.

1. Taking the wrong action when $\mu \leq \mu_0$.
2. Taking the wrong action when $\mu \geq \mu_0$.

The null hypothesis is H_0: $\mu \leq \mu_0$ if the first error is more serious, and H_0:$\mu \geq \mu_0$ if the second error is more serious.

TWO-SIDED TESTS

In a two-sided test, the following null hypothesis applies.

$$H_0\text{:}\mu = \mu_0$$

Since H_0 is false when $\mu < \mu_0$ and when $\mu > \mu_0$, the testing of the null hypothesis is two-sided.

STEP 2

Select the test statistic and procedure. In testing the mean, $\bar{X}$ is the natural test statistic. When the population standard deviation σ is known, the normal distribution is used as the sampling distribution for $\bar{X}$. Hypothesis testing procedures are developed using probability concepts for the normal distribution. But, when σ is unknown, the testing procedures must instead be based on the

STUDENT t TEST STATISTIC (σ unknown)

$$t = \frac{\bar{X} - \mu_0}{s/\sqrt{n}}$$

There are two types of testing procedures, depending on the nature of the decisions to be made. The **single-decision procedure** tests H_0 just once. The **recurring-decisions procedure** applies when there are a series of decisions to be made, so that H_0 is accepted or rejected over and over again. Both the choice of the test statistic and the form of the decision rule differ under the two procedures.

A recurring-decisions procedure uses one decision rule many times, possibly to be applied by different investigators at various places. The test statistic should be easy to compute and readily understood by all participants. To keep the procedure simple, the population standard deviation value is stipulated for all test applications, so that σ is treated as a *known* quantity.

When σ is known, there are two versions of the decision rule. Both versions utilize the fact that $\bar{X}$ has a normal sampling distribution. The **detailed decision**

rule compares the computed mean $\bar{X}$ to one or two critical values expressed on the same numerical scale. The **abbreviated decision rule** compares instead the computed values of the normal deviate z to one or two values read from the normal curve table. The two versions are used widely and lead to identical results.

A single-decision procedure requires no stipulation on the value of the population standard deviation, and σ may remain *unknown*. In this case, the Student t serves as the test statistic and the decision rule is based on it.

STEP 3

Establish the significance level and identify the acceptance and rejection regions. The probability α of the more serious Type I error, also referred to as the significance level, is prescribed in advance. Figure 9-1 summarizes the three basic test forms. How H_0 is expressed determines which form applies. Each is labeled according to which part of the sampling distribution curve overlaps the rejection region for the computed test statistic values. A test form is either lower-tailed, upper-tailed, or two-sided. The acceptance and rejection regions are defined by the critical value of the test statistic.

In testing the mean when σ is known, these regions are determined by the **critical normal deviate** z_α (or $z_{\alpha/2}$) for which the normal curve upper tail area is α (or $\alpha/2$). When σ is unknown, the critical value of the Student t statistic t_α (or $t_{\alpha/2}$) is used instead.

When a recurring-decisions procedure applies, so that σ is known and $\bar{X}$ serves as the test statistic, the critical normal deviate is used in conjunction with a *detailed decision rule* to compute the

CRITICAL VALUES OF THE SAMPLE MEAN (σ known)

Lower-tailed tests (H_0: $\mu \geq \mu_0$) Upper-tailed tests (H_0: $\mu \leq \mu_0$)

$$\bar{X}^* = \mu_0 - z_\alpha \sigma_{\bar{X}} \qquad \bar{X}^* = \mu_0 + z_\alpha \sigma_{\bar{X}}$$

Two-sided tests (H_0: $\mu = \mu_0$)

$$\bar{X}_1^* = \mu_0 - z_{\alpha/2}\sigma_{\bar{X}} \quad \text{and} \quad \bar{X}_2^* = \mu_0 + z_{\alpha/2}\sigma_{\bar{X}}$$

The computed standard error of $\bar{X}$ is*

$$\sigma_{\bar{X}} = \frac{\sigma}{\sqrt{n}}$$

The *abbreviated decision rule* requires computing the

*When the sample size n is large in relation to the population size N, the finite population correction factor is used to compute $\sigma_{\bar{X}}$.

$$\sigma_{\bar{X}} = \frac{\sigma}{\sqrt{n}}\sqrt{\frac{N-n}{N-1}}$$

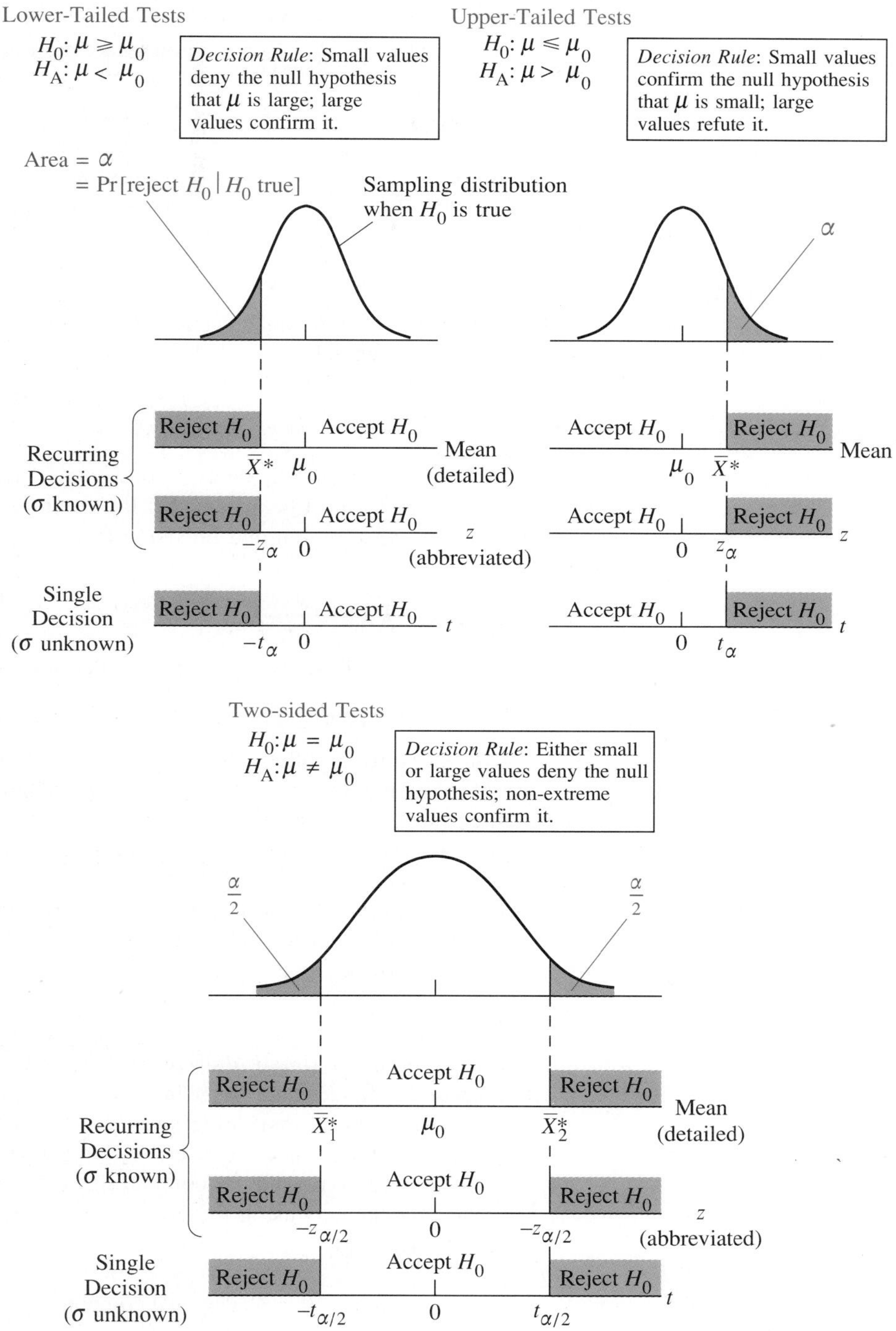

FIGURE 9-1 Three forms of hypothesis testing for the mean.

NORMAL DEVIATE FOR SAMPLE RESULTS (σ known)

$$z = \frac{\bar{X} - \mu_0}{\sigma_{\bar{X}}}$$

STEP 4

Collect the sample and compute the value of the test statistic. This step occurs during the second stage of the statistical sampling study. No revisions to steps 1–3 should be made during or after collecting sample data.

STEP 5

Make the decision. The decision rule established in Step 3 makes the final choice automatic. H_0 must be accepted if the computed value of the test statistic falls in the acceptance region and rejected otherwise.

UPPER-TAILED TESTS

Two detailed illustrations of upper-tailed tests for the mean follow.

SINGLE DECISION: TESTING AUDITING SOFTWARE

Consider how hypothesis testing may be used to evaluate a new software package.

Baskin and Shells is testing a new software package to be used in auditing field sites assisted by a portable personal computer. The test involves a team of two auditors who each examine identical data and complete workups. Judged equally skillful, one member uses the traditional manual procedures, the other the personal computer. A random sample of eight sites have been examined. The teammates switch roles at each new job.

The following steps apply.

STEP 1

Formulate the null and alternative hypotheses. Baskin and Shells will adopt the proposed software and use it in portable personal computers system-wide if the present test shows that doing so is a significant improvement over manual field auditing methods. The most serious error would be to do this when in fact there is not a time savings under computerized auditing. Letting μ represent the actual mean time savings using the computers in field auditing workups, the following hypotheses apply.

H_0: $\mu \leq 0$ (Personal computer software does not save time.)

H_A: $\mu > 0$ (Personal computer software saves time.)

The pivotal level of the population mean is $\mu_0 = 0$.

STEP 2

Select the test statistic and procedure. The firm's decision is made just once. The Student t therefore serves as the test statistic.

STEP 3

Establish the significance level and identify the acceptance and rejection regions. Management wants good protection against the very undesirable Type I error of adopting computerized field auditing when it won't be faster on the average. A small significance level of $\alpha = .01$ is thus chosen. The resulting test is upper-tailed. Using $8 - 1 = 7$ degrees of freedom, Appendix Table F provides the critical value $t_\alpha = t_{.01} = 2.998$. The acceptance and rejection regions are shown below.

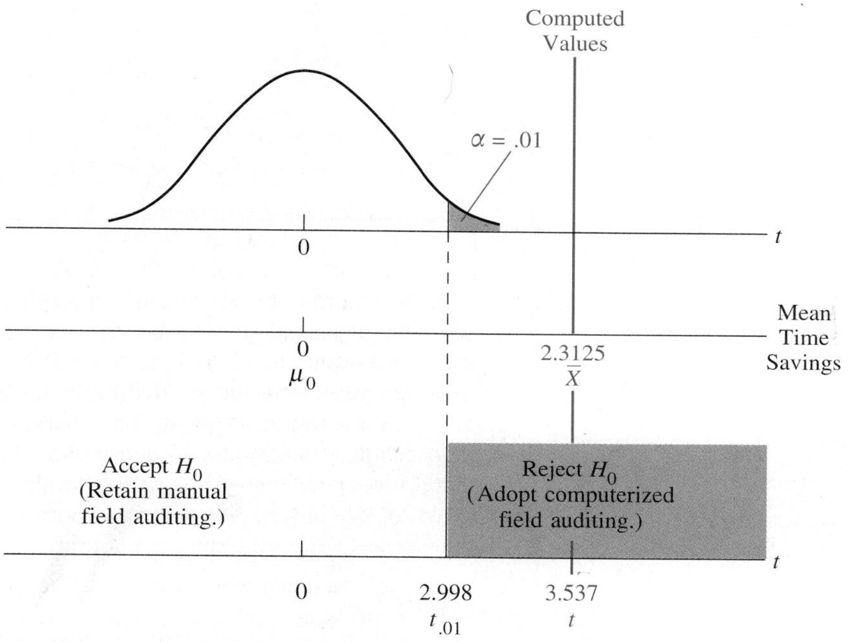

STEP 4

Collect the sample and compute the value of the test statistic. The workup completion times are provided in Table 9-2. To obtain the time savings using the computer, the latter completion times are subtracted from the manual times. The computed value of the test statistic is

$$t = \frac{2.3125 - 0}{1.849/\sqrt{8}} = 3.537$$

STEP 5

Make the decision. Since the computed value of the test statistic falls in the rejection region, the firm must *reject* the null hypothesis that computerized field auditing yields no time savings. Baskin and Shells will adopt a policy of using personal computers with the tested software.

Recurring Decisions: Adjusting Mixing Controls

Consider how hypothesis testing may be used to establish a permanent testing policy for monitoring production.

TABLE 9-2 Test Results of Auditing Software for Personal Computers

Site	Completion Time Manual Procedure	Completion Time Personal Computer	Difference X	X^2
1	4.1 hours	1.7 hours	+2.4 hours	5.76
2	9.5	6.2	+3.3	10.89
3	12.3	13.5	−1.2	1.44
4	18.4	14.8	+3.6	12.96
5	7.5	5.0	+2.5	6.25
6	3.4	3.0	+.4	.16
7	6.5	3.5	+3.0	9.00
8	12.5	8.0	+4.5	20.25
			+18.5	66.71

$$\bar{X} = 18.5/8 = 2.3125$$

$$s = \sqrt{\frac{66.71 - 8(2.3125)^2}{8 - 1}} = 1.849$$

A production superintendent for a pharmaceutical manufacturer must decide when to adjust the mixing controls for the final stage of production of a pain killer. He wants to base these everyday decisions on the mean weight of inert materials per tablet. The desired mean value μ is .5 milligram (mg) for each tablet, although a lower level would be satisfactory. A decision rule needs to be found that technicians may use to determine whether or not to adjust control settings, thereby keeping the mean within the desired limit. A new sample of tablets is taken every eight hours, so that a control-adjustment decision can be made three times a day. The following steps apply.

STEP 1

Formulate the null and alternative hypotheses. The superintendent selects the following hypotheses.

H_0: $\mu \leq .5$mg (Weight is within desired limit.)

H_A: $\mu > .5$mg (Weight is above desired limit.)

The pivotal level of the mean material weight is $\mu_0 = .5$mg per tablet.

The above designation provides a Type I error of unnecessarily adjusting controls when the mean actually falls within the desired limit. The Type II error is failing to adjust controls when the mean level of inert materials is intolerably high. The first error is judged to be more serious.

STEP 2

Select the test statistic and procedure. The sample mean weight $\bar{X}$ serves as the test statistic. From previous testing, the superintendent establishes a value of $\sigma = .2$ mg for the population standard deviation. The standard deviation is assumed to be stable even though the mean fluctuates, and σ is therefore treated as a *known* quantity.

STEP 3

Establish the significance level and identify the acceptance and rejection regions. The superintendent decides that a 5% significance level will adequately protect against the undesirable Type I error. To keep the incidence of the Type II error low, he relies on a fairly substantial sample size of $n = 25$ tablets.

The standard error of $\overline{X}$ is

$$\sigma_{\overline{X}} = \frac{.2}{\sqrt{25}} = .04 \text{ mg}$$

Since a *large* $\overline{X}$ refutes the null hypothesis that the mean level of inert materials falls within the desired limit, the resulting test is *upper-tailed.* Using the significance level of $\alpha = .05$, the critical normal deviate, from Appendix Table E, is $z_{.05} = 1.64$. The critical value of the sample mean is

$$\overline{X}^* = .5 + 1.64(.04) = .566 \text{ mg}$$

The acceptance and rejection regions are shown in the figure that follows.

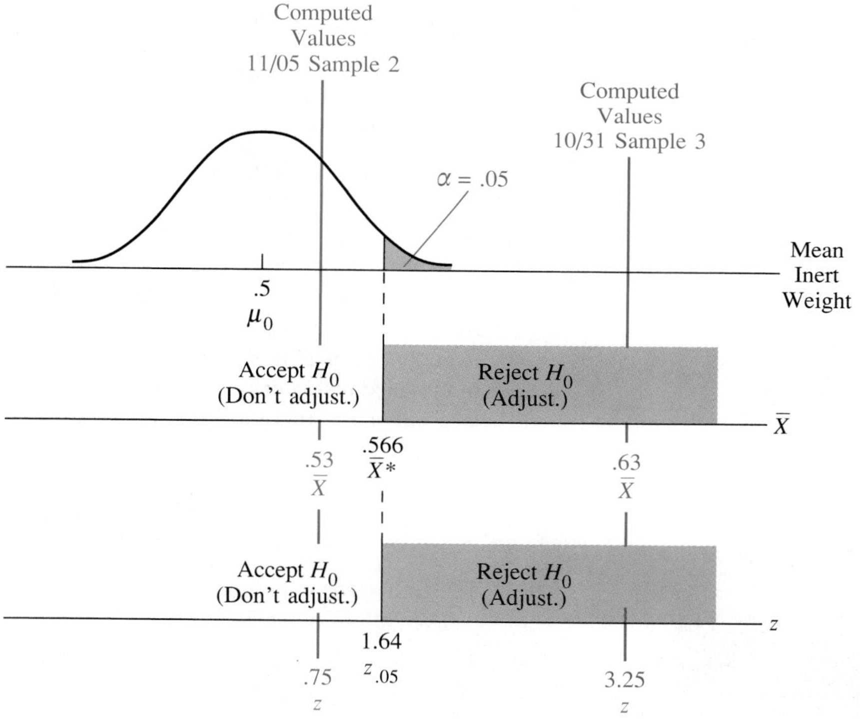

STEP 4

Collect the sample and compute the value of the test statistic. This step is conducted every eight hours. The mean weight of inert materials is computed for each 25-tablet sample.

STEP 5

Make the decision. As in Step 4, a decision is made every eight hours in accordance with the decision rule.

When implemented, the test is run three times daily using a different sample of tablets each time. Two results are illustrated above. On 10/31 during the swing shift, the computed value of the sample mean is $\bar{X} = .63$ mg. Since $\bar{X}$ falls within the rejection region, the null hypothesis must be *rejected* and the controls adjusted. The opposite conclusion is reached on 11/05 during the day shift. The computed value of the sample mean is found to be $\bar{X} = .53$ mg. Since the value falls within the acceptance region, the null hypothesis, for that shift, must be *accepted*, and no control adjustments are made.

The same conclusions may be reached using an abbreviated decision rule. If the computed normal deviate falls above $z_\alpha = z_{.05} = 1.64$, the null hypothesis must be rejected; otherwise it is accepted. We have

10/31 Sample 3	11/05 Sample 2
$z = \dfrac{.63 - .5}{.04} = 3.25$	$z = \dfrac{.53 - .5}{.04} = .75$
Reject H_0	*Accept* H_0

LOWER-TAILED TESTS

Two detailed illustrations of lower-tailed tests for the sample mean follow.

SINGLE DECISION: FINE TUNING AN EMPLOYMENT SCREENING TEST

Consider how hypothesis testing may be used to evaluate an employment screening test.

The Variety Galore Stores have redesigned their employment screening examination for sales clerk positions to eliminate sex bias. Management must decide whether to decrease the new test's difficulty or to adopt it without further modification. The major uncertainty is the mean score μ to be achieved by the clerical applicant pool. If μ is as high or higher than the historical mean score of 70 points, the revised test is easy enough. Should μ be lower, the new test is too hard. Since μ is unknown, there are two types of errors.

1. Decreasing the difficulty when the test is easy enough.
2. Using the new test without modification when it is too hard.

The first error is judged least desirable.

The following steps apply.

STEP 1

Formulate the null and alternative hypotheses. The following hypotheses apply.

H_0: $\mu \geq 70$ (Test is easy enough.)

H_A: $\mu < 70$ (Test needs difficulty decreased.)

The pivotal level of the mean score is $\mu_0 = 70$.

STEP 2

Select the test statistic and procedure. The new test is administered to a random sample of $n = 100$ applicants for the clerical positions. This is a one-time decision. The population standard deviation σ of all the test scores remains unknown, and the Student t serves as the test statistic.

STEP 3

Establish the significance level and identify the acceptance and rejection regions. Although a tiny significance level such as $\alpha = .01$ would be ideal, that would be accompanied by unacceptably high chances of adopting the test with no changes when it is too easy. Management decides that a better balance would be achieved between the Types I and II errors if they set the significance level at the higher level of $\alpha = .05$. Using $100 - 1 = 99$ degrees of freedom, Appendix Table F provides the nearest critical value of $t_{.05} = 1.658$. Since a low value of the sample mean test score $\bar{X}$ refutes the null hypothesis, the test is lower-tailed. Thus, a negative value of t lying below -1.658, will lead to rejection of H_0. The acceptance and rejection regions are shown in the figure that follows.

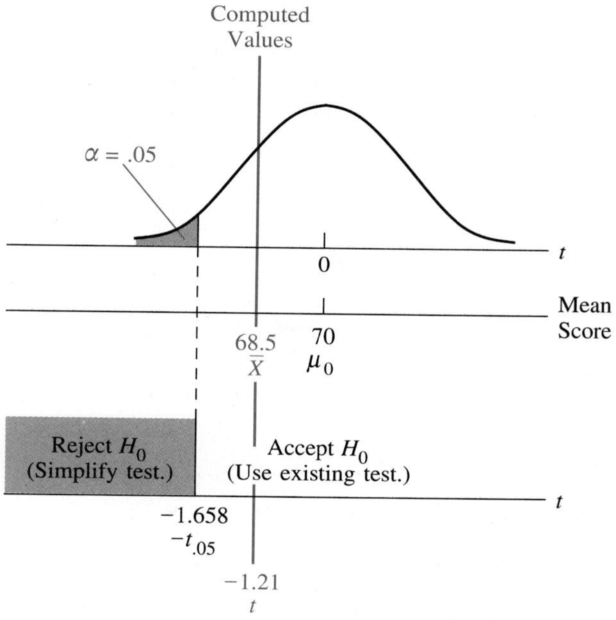

STEP 4

Collect the sample and compute the value of the test statistic. The computed value of the sample mean is $\bar{X} = 68.5$ points, and the value of the sample standard deviation is $s = 12.4$. The computed value of the test statistic t is

$$t = \frac{68.5 - 70}{12.4/\sqrt{100}} = -1.21$$

STEP 5

Make the decision. Since t falls within the acceptance region, the null hypothesis must be *accepted* and the existing test must be used without modification.

RECURRING DECISIONS: TESTING TAPE THICKNESS

Consider how hypothesis testing may be used to evaluate a new laser control.

Scotty Adhesives has installed a new laser control to determine when a roll of cellophane tape has reached the desired thickness. To exceed labeling requirements by an acceptable margin, the mean length μ of individual rolls must be at least 525 inches. Otherwise the control mechanism needs to be replaced.

The following steps apply.

STEP 1

Formulate the null and alternative hypotheses. The following hypotheses apply.

$$H_0: \mu \geq 525'' \quad \text{(Control is working properly.)}$$
$$H_A: \mu < 525'' \quad \text{(Control needs replacement.)}$$

The pivotal level of the mean length is $\mu_0 = 525''$ per roll.

STEP 2

Select the test statistic and procedure. A random sample of $n = 50$ rolls is tested and each is measured to exact length. The sample mean $\bar{X}$ is then computed. Throughout production, the population standard deviation is assumed to be at the historical level of $\sigma = 12''$. The sample mean $\bar{X}$ may therefore serve as the test statistic. The standard error of $\bar{X}$ is

$$\sigma_{\bar{X}} = \frac{12''}{\sqrt{50}} = 1.70''$$

STEP 3

Establish the significance level and identify the acceptance and rejection regions. A significance level of $\alpha = .01$ is chosen. Appendix Table E provides the critical normal deviate of $z_{.01} = 2.33$. Since a low value of $\bar{X}$ refutes the null hypothesis the test is lower tailed. The critical value for the sample mean is

$$\bar{X}^* = 525'' - 2.33(1.70) = 521.04''$$

The acceptance and rejection regions are shown below.

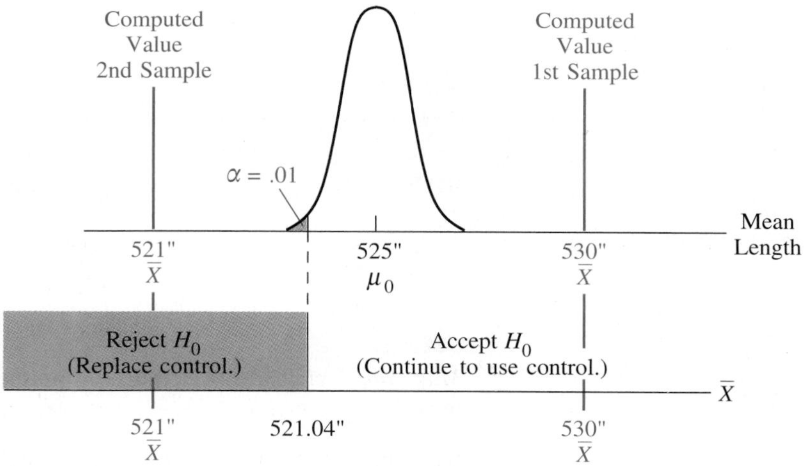

STEP 4

Collect the sample and compute the value of the test statistic. Samples are taken periodically. The computed mean value of the *first* sample is $\bar{X} = 530''$.

STEP 5

Make the decision. Since the first $\bar{X}$ falls within the acceptance region, H_0 must be *accepted* and the control must remain in operation.

A second sample yields a computed mean of value $\bar{X} = 521''$. Since $\bar{X}$ now falls within the rejection region, H_0 must be *rejected* and the control replaced.

TWO-SIDED TESTS

Two detailed illustrations of two-sided tests using a single-decision and a recurring-decisions procedure follow.

SINGLE DECISION: QUALITY CONTROL IN FOOD PROCESSING

Consider how a two-sided hypothesis test may be used to maintain quality control in food production.

A food company advertises that there are 105 chunks of beef in every 15-ounce can of its chili. To verify that its standards are being met in chili production, periodic checks of product quality are made by measuring the quantity of beef in several random samples of 15-ounce cans of chili.

Management cannot be sure that 105 chunks of beef will be added to every can, and can control only the *mean number* of chunks per can.

If current production has a lower mean than 105, remedial action is to be taken. However, because beef is by far the most expensive chili ingredient, a mean higher than 105 will also require remedial action. The management wishes to avoid both high and low extreme values in the mean beef quantity. A sample of $n = 100$ cans is tested.

STEP 1

Formulate the null and alternative hypotheses. The following hypotheses apply.

$$H_0: \mu = 105 \qquad \text{(No correction is required.)}$$
$$H_A: \mu \neq 105 \qquad \text{(Correction is required.)}$$

Here, $\mu_0 = 105$ beef chunks. The two-sided alternative hypothesis states that the quantity of beef differs from μ_0, so that either $\mu > 105$ (too much beef) or $\mu < 105$ (too little beef).

STEP 2

Select the test statistic and procedure. Since the population standard deviation σ is unknown, $\bar{X}$ cannot serve as the test statistic. The Student t is used instead.

STEP 3

Establish the significance level and identify the acceptance and rejection regions. There are two ways the Type I error may occur: to unnecessarily correct for overfilling or for underfilling. Management desires a significance level of $\alpha = .05$. This is split: Half of the value is assigned to the left tail and half to the right tail. Using $100 - 1 = 99$ degrees of freedom, Appendix Table F provides the nearest critical value of $t_{\alpha/2} = t_{.025} = 1.98$. The acceptance and rejection regions are shown in the following figure.

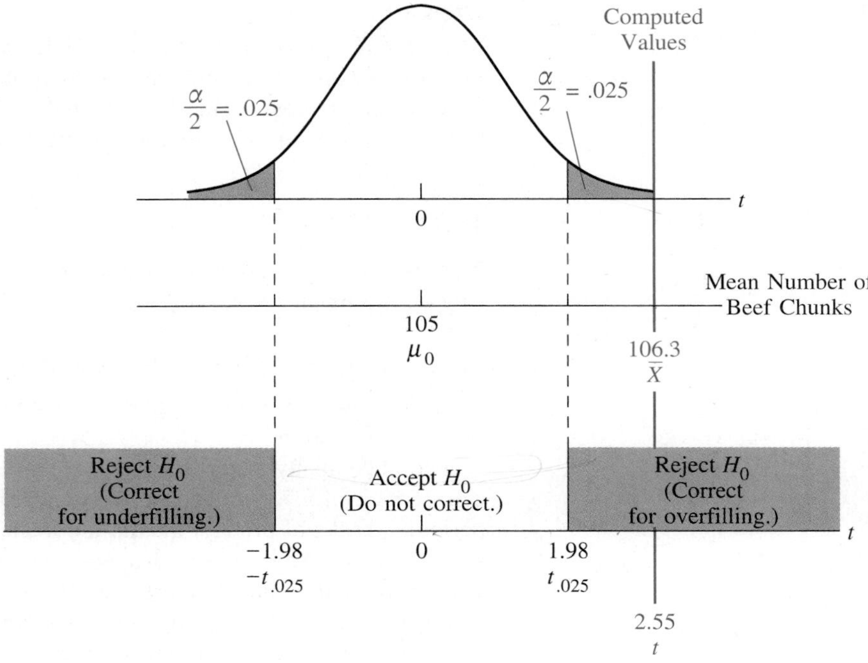

STEP 4

Collect the sample and compute the value of the test statistic. The computed value of the sample mean is $\bar{X} = 106.3$ beef chunks, and the value of the standard deviation is $s = 5.1$ beef chunks. The computed value of the test statistic is

$$t = \frac{\bar{X} - \mu_0}{s/\sqrt{n}} = \frac{106.3 - 105}{5.1/\sqrt{100}} = 2.55$$

STEP 5

Make the decision. Since t falls in the upper rejection region, the null hypothesis must be *rejected.* The test results are significant at the 5% level, and the management must take corrective action to remedy overfilling.

Recurring Decisions: Quality Control in Receiving Shipments

Consider how hypothesis testing may be used to establish a routine maintenance policy.

A brass fixture manufacturer is reformulating its policy for receiving shipments of one-hundred pound ingots. It is too expensive to continue weighing all ingots, since they would have to all be unpackaged. Instead, a sample mean is computed for $n = 100$ ingots, and the shipment will be accepted without further weighing if the computed value is within the limits determined below.

The following steps apply.

STEP 1

Formulate the null and alternative hypotheses. The following hypotheses apply.

$$H_0: \mu = 100 \text{ lbs}$$
$$H_A: \mu \neq 100 \text{ lbs}$$

The pivotal level of the mean ingot weight is $\mu_0 = 100$ lbs. Management uses a two-sided test because the final billing from the smelter is adjusted according to shipment weight when received.

STEP 2

Select the test statistic and procedure. From previous experience, the standard deviation in ingot weights has been firmly established at $\sigma = 2$ lbs. The sample mean $\bar{X}$ may therefore serve as the test statistic. The standard error of $\bar{X}$ is

$$\sigma_{\bar{X}} = \frac{2}{\sqrt{100}} = .2 \text{ lb}$$

STEP 3

Establish the significance level and identify the acceptance and rejection regions. Management has to separately weigh each ingot in a rejected shipment, which is quite costly because of the necessary unpackaging. The significance level has therefore been set at $\alpha = .01$ to keep the incidence of unnecessary weighings low. The critical normal deviate is $z_{\alpha/2} = z_{.005} = 2.57$. The critical values of the sample mean are

$$\bar{X}_1^* = 100 - 2.57(.2) = 99.49 \text{ lbs}$$
$$\bar{X}_2^* = 100 + 2.57(.2) = 100.51 \text{ lbs}$$

The acceptance and rejection regions are shown below.

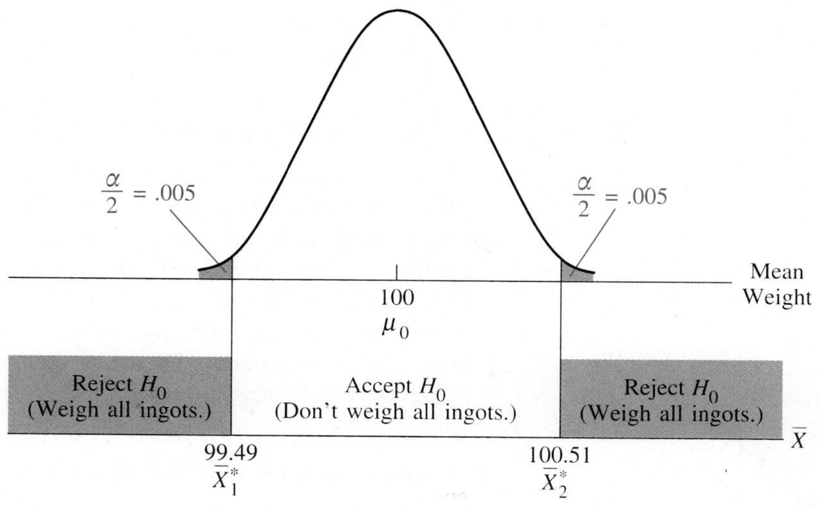

STEP 4

Collect the sample and compute the value of the test statistic. A sample mean is computed for each shipment.

STEP 5

Make the decision. If a computed mean value such as $\bar{X} = 100.2$ lbs falls within the acceptance region, the shipment would be *accepted* without further weighing.

Should a shipment yield a sample mean falling within one of the rejection regions, such as $\bar{X} = 98.7$ lbs or $\bar{X} = 101.1$ lbs, it would be *rejected* and all ingots weighed.

HYPOTHESIS TESTING AND CONFIDENCE INTERVALS

Two-sided hypothesis tests are related to statistical estimation with confidence intervals. We can approach the testing procedure by first constructing a $100(1 - \alpha)\%$ confidence interval from the sample results. If μ_0 falls inside the interval, the null hypothesis must be accepted; otherwise, it is rejected.

Here, α represents the proportion of similarly constructed intervals (found in duplicated sampling experiments) that fail to bracket μ_0 when it is the true mean. This interpretation means that the Type I error of rejecting H_0 when it is true occurs at frequency α.

In the previous quality control illustration, $\bar{X} = 106.3$ beef chunks, $s = 5.1$, and $n = 100$. Using these data to construct a 95% confidence interval gives

$$\mu = \bar{X} \pm t_{\alpha/2}\frac{s}{\sqrt{n}}$$

$$= 106.3 \pm 1.98\frac{5.1}{\sqrt{100}}$$

$$= 106.3 \pm 1.0$$

or

$$105.3 \leq \mu \leq 107.3 \text{ beef chunks}$$

Since the pivotal value $\mu_0 = 105$ does not fall within this interval, H_0 must be *rejected*. This is the same conclusion we reached earlier.

SUMMARY OF TESTING THE MEAN

Figure 9-2 summarizes hypothesis testing with the mean. When σ is known, the normal distribution applies, and the critical normal deviates z_α or $z_{\alpha/2}$ may be found using Appendix Table E. When σ is unknown, the Student t distribution applies, and critical values t_α or $t_{\alpha/2}$ may be found using Appendix Table F. (For degrees of freedom that falls somewhere between the listed tabled values, read the one nearest. You may average the neighboring values if the degrees of freedom falls exactly midway between the two. For large sample sizes, the critical-values should be read from the df = ∞ row.)

VARIATIONS IN HYPOTHESIS-TESTING PROCEDURES

σ is unknown = t-test
σ is known- z-test.

The single-decision and recurring-decisions procedures are useful in sorting situations and choosing an appropriate course of action. A common convention is to simply specify whether or not σ is known. When σ is unknown, the entire hypothesis-testing procedure may be referred to as a ***t*-test**. Likewise, when σ is known, the procedure may be referred to as a ***z*-test**, since it is based on the normal curve.

Not only does the terminology vary, but the procedure may differ also. Two important variations follow.

SIGNIFICANCE OF RESULTS

Instead of concluding that you must either *accept* H_0 or *reject* H_0, and then take the corresponding action, another common approach is to *make no decision at all.* In this case, a conclusion is reached in terms of one of the following statements.

1. The test results are not significant at the α level.
(equivalent to *accept* H_0)

2. The test results are significant at the α level.
(equivalent to *reject* H_0)

This type of reporting is often found in research publications when no specific decision needs to be made. One shortcut is not to mention alpha, which is generally understood to be some conventional level, such as .01.

PROBABILITY FOR GETTING THE SAME RESULT

In published research, when no decision is needed, the reader may be allowed to select a significance level. No level is stipulated for α. Instead, a probability value is determined that establishes the likelihood of getting the reported result were the null hypothesis to actually be true. *Readers draw their own conclusions.*

COMPUTER-ASSISTED HYPOTHESIS TESTING

As with the estimating procedures in Chapter 8, statistical testing may be done with the assistance of a computer. Here, again, computing $\bar{X}$ and s is the hardest part. If the computations have already been done (either by hand, with a calculator, or using a computer), it is very easy to do the rest by hand.

Computer software packages can do various amounts of the work. Many provide just the computed values of $\bar{X}$ and s. The Minitab® software package does a bit more.

t-TEST WHEN σ IS UNKNOWN

Figure 9-3 displays the computer printout of the auditing software data given in Table 9-2. Minitab computes the same values of $\bar{X}$ and s that we found earlier, and reports the *estimated* value of $\sigma_{\bar{X}}$ (s divided by $\sqrt{n}$). The computed value of the test statistic $t = 3.54$, (found previously) is also given. Finally, notice that the **prob. value** of .0047 is provided. This number expresses the likelihood of getting sample results identical to or more extreme than those actually obtained.

z-TEST WHEN σ IS KNOWN

The computer printout of a *z*-test is similar to that of a *t*-test. The level of σ must be provided with the input. Consider, again, the control-adjustment decision for the production of a pain killer. Figure 9-4 displays the computer printout for the sample results for a particular 8-hour shift. The computed value of the test statistic is $z = 1.08$. Since this value falls below the critical normal deviate of $z_{.05} = 1.64$, the null hypothesis must be *accepted*, and the mixing controls are not adjusted. (The same conclusion may be reached by noting that the computer-generated prob. value of .14 exceeds the desired $\alpha = .05$ significance level.)

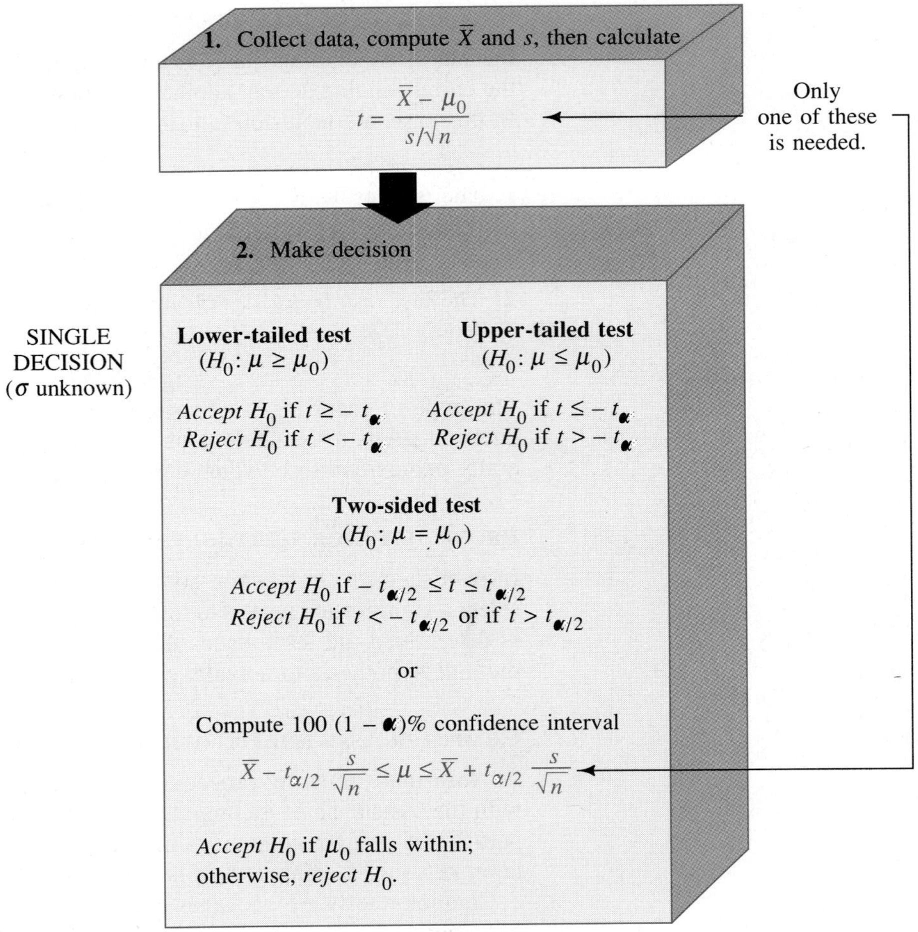

1. Collect data, compute $\overline{X}$ and s, then calculate
$t = \dfrac{\overline{X} - \mu_0}{s/\sqrt{n}}$
Only one of these is needed.
2. Make decision
SINGLE DECISION (σ unknown)
Lower-tailed test
(H_0: $\mu \geq \mu_0$)
Accept H_0 if $t \geq -t_\alpha$
Reject H_0 if $t < -t_\alpha$
Upper-tailed test
(H_0: $\mu \leq \mu_0$)
Accept H_0 if $t \leq -t_\alpha$
Reject H_0 if $t > -t_\alpha$
Two-sided test
(H_0: $\mu = \mu_0$)
Accept H_0 if $-t_{\alpha/2} \leq t \leq t_{\alpha/2}$
Reject H_0 if $t < -t_{\alpha/2}$ or if $t > t_{\alpha/2}$
or
Compute 100 $(1 - \alpha)$% confidence interval
$\overline{X} - t_{\alpha/2}\dfrac{s}{\sqrt{n}} \leq \mu \leq \overline{X} + t_{\alpha/2}\dfrac{s}{\sqrt{n}}$
Accept H_0 if μ_0 falls within; otherwise, *reject* H_0.

FIGURE 9-2 Summary of hypothesis-testing procedures with the mean.

```
MTB > set c1
      2.4, 3.3, -1.2, 3.6, 2.5, 0.4, 3.0, 4.5
MTB > end
MTB > name c1 'Time Sav'
MTB > ttest mu=0 c1;
SUBC> alternative=+1.

TEST OF MU = 0.000 VS MU G.T. 0.000

              N      MEAN     STDEV   SE MEAN        T      P VALUE
Time Sav      8     2.312     1.849     0.654     3.54      0.00475
```

Note: Figure generated on an IBM PC using Minitab®.

FIGURE 9-3 Computer printout for the auditing software hypothesis test.

RECURRING DECISIONS
(σ known)

Identify Procedure

1. Compute $\sigma_{\bar{X}}$, find critical value, and establish decision rule

When $n < .10N$:

$$\sigma_{\bar{X}} = \frac{\sigma}{\sqrt{n}}$$

When $n > .10N$:

$$\sigma_{\bar{X}} = \frac{\sigma}{\sqrt{n}}\sqrt{\frac{N-n}{N-1}}$$

Lower-tailed test (H_0: $\mu > \mu_0$)

$$\bar{X}^* = \mu_0 - z_\alpha \sigma_{\bar{X}}$$

Accept H_0 if $\bar{X} \geq \bar{X}^*$ (if $z \geq -z_\alpha$)
Reject H_0 if $\bar{X} < \bar{X}^*$ (if $z < -z_\alpha$)

Upper-tailed test (H_0: $\mu < \mu_0$)

$$\bar{X}^* = \mu_0 - z_\alpha \sigma_{\bar{X}}$$

Accept H_0 if $\bar{X} \leq \bar{X}^*$ (if $z \leq z_\alpha$)
Reject H_0 if $\bar{X} > \bar{X}^*$ (if $z > z_\alpha$)

Two-sided test (H_0: $\mu = \mu_0$)

$$\bar{X}_1^* = \mu_0 - z_{\alpha/2}\sigma_{\bar{X}}$$
$$\bar{X}_2^* = \mu_0 + z_{\alpha/2}\sigma_{\bar{X}}$$

Accept H_0 if $\bar{X}_1^* \leq \bar{X} \leq \bar{X}_2^*$ (if $-z_{\alpha/2} \leq z \leq z_{\alpha/2}$)
Reject H_0 if $\bar{X} < \bar{X}_1^*$ (if $z < -z_{\alpha/2}$
or if $\bar{X} > \bar{X}_2^*$ or if $z > z_{\alpha/2}$)

2. Collect data, compute $\bar{X}$, and decide using

$$\bar{X} \text{ directly or } z = \frac{\bar{X} - \mu_0}{\sigma_{\bar{X}}}$$

EXERCISES

9-9 In testing the hypotheses

$$H_0: \mu \leq \mu_0 \quad \text{and} \quad H_A: \mu > \mu_0$$

using $\mu_0 = 100$, the desired Type I error probability is $\alpha = .10$. The values $\bar{X} = 102.6$ and $s = 25$ have been computed for a sample of $n = 100$.

(a) Is this a lower- or an upper-tailed test? Sketch this situation; include an appropriate Student t curve.

(b) Find the critical value t_α and indicate the acceptance and rejection regions on your sketch.

(c) Compute the value of the Student t test statistic and indicate in which region it falls. Should the null hypothesis be accepted or rejected?

9-10 In testing the hypotheses

$$H_0: \mu \leq 160 \quad \text{and} \quad H_A: \mu > 160$$

```
MTB > set c1
      .33, .45, .67, .85, .23, .49, 1.01, .76, .41, .30, .25
      .66, .74, .52, .49, .37, .46, .55, .60, .82, .44, .53
      .25, .67, .73
MTB > end
MTB > name c1 'Inert Wt'
MTB > ztest mu=.5, sigma=.2, c1;
SUBC> alternative=+1.

TTEST OF MU = 0.5000 VS MU G.T. 0.5000
THE ASSUMED SIGMA = 0.2000

               N      MEAN     STDEV   SE MEAN        Z    P VALUE
Inert Wt      25    0.5432    0.2055    0.0400     1.08       0.14
```

Note: Figure generated on an IBM PC using Minitab®.

FIGURE 9-4 Computer printout for a sample of tablets.

a significance level of $\alpha = .05$ is desired. The test is upper-tailed, as shown below.

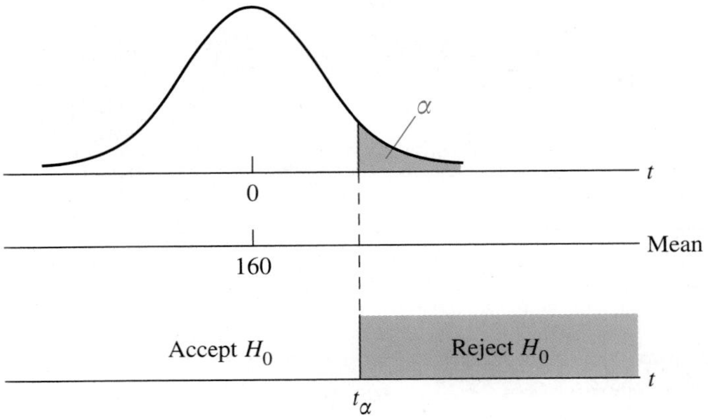

The values $\bar{X} = 170$ and $s = 30$ have been computed for a sample of $n = 25$. Complete the hypothesis-testing steps to determine whether the null hypothesis should be accepted or rejected.

9-11 In testing the hypotheses

$$H_0\colon \mu \geq \mu_0 \quad \text{and} \quad H_A\colon \mu < \mu_0$$

using $\mu_0 = 30$, the desired Type I error probability is $\alpha = .05$. The values $\bar{X} = 25$ and $s = 10$ have been computed for a sample of $n = 100$. Referring to Exercise 9-9, answer (a), (b), and (c).

9-12 A Yellow Giant cannery inspector insists that the mean weight of ingredients in 16-ounce cans be precisely accurate. If the mean weight falls above or below this figure, some remedial action is taken. The inspector assumes that the standard deviation is $\sigma = .3$ ounces. A significance level of $\alpha = .05$ is established for a sampling test, so that the Type I error (taking unnecessary action) is expected 5% of the time. Each hour, a sample of $n = 25$ cans is taken, each can is opened, and the contents are weighed.

(a) Perform the hypothesis-testing Steps 1–3.

(b) Should the inspector take remedial action if (1) $\overline{X} = 15.9$ ounces; (2) $\overline{X} = 16.2$ ounces?

9-13 In testing the hypotheses

$$H_0: \mu = \mu_0 (= 0) \quad \text{and} \quad H_A: \mu \neq \mu_0$$

the values $\overline{X} = 1.2$ and $s = 9.5$ have been computed for a sample of $n = 100$. At the significance level of $\alpha = .05$, should the null hypothesis be accepted or rejected?

9-14 The output of a chemical process for manufacturing Snail Hail is monitored by taking a sample of $n = 25$ vials to determine the level of impurities. The null hypothesis is that the mean level is exactly .05 gram per liter. If the mean level of impurities in the sample is too high, the process will be stopped and the tanks will be purged; if the sample mean is too low, the process will also be stopped and the valves will be readjusted. Otherwise, the process will continue. The test is two-sided, as shown below.

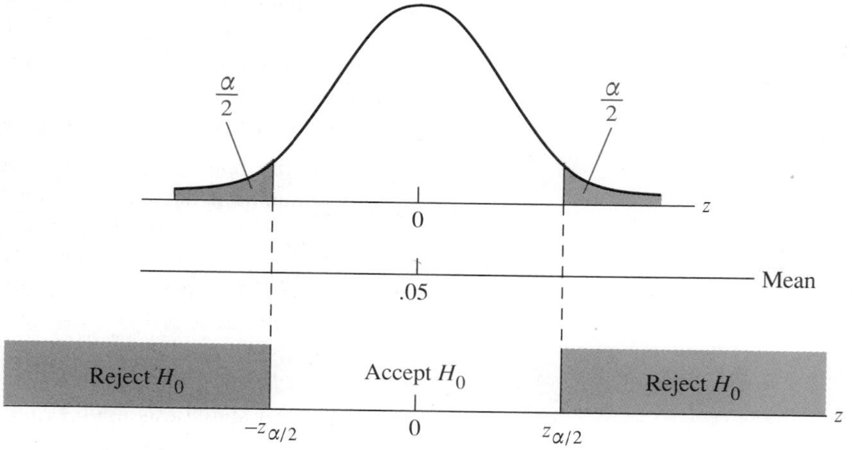

Assume that the population standard deviation is $\sigma = .02$ gram per liter. Sample results provide $\overline{X} = .064$ gram. At a significance level of $\alpha = .01$, should the process be stopped? If so, what type of remedial action is required?

9-15 For each of the following two-sided testing situations, construct a 95% confidence interval for μ. Decide whether H_0 must be accepted or rejected.

(a) $\mu_0 = 10$; $\overline{X} = 10.1$; $s = .3$; $n = 100$

(b) $\mu_0 = .72$; $\overline{X} = .705$; $s = .13$; $n = 169$

(c) $\mu_0 = 0$; $\overline{X} = -.7$; $s = 2.5$; $n = 625$

9-16 In packaging Snow White soap powder, the desired weight is 5 lbs. If the true population mean value μ is above or below this amount, the machinery needs to be adjusted. Management has decided that unnecessary adjustments occur no more than 5% of the time.

Each day a random sample of 100 boxes is selected, and then, based on the sample mean weight, a decision is made whether to leave the equipment alone or to adjust it. Suppose that $\bar{X}$ is 5.1 lbs. and $\sigma = .5$ lbs. What action should be taken?

9-17 Satcom Corporation will use a new power cell in future communications satellites if sample evidence refutes the null hypothesis that it exhibits a mean-time-between-failure no greater than the present cell, which is rated at $\mu = 550$ hours. A sample test of 100 new cells provides a sample mean of $\bar{X} = 565$ hours and a standard deviation of $s = 200$ hours.

Assuming a significance level of 5%, perform all the hypothesis-testing steps. Should the new power cell be used?

9-18 Huey-Packer is evaluating an experimental tuning stand as a possible substitute for the present manual method of calibrating electronic timing devices. The stand will be acquired only if it can calibrate the devices in a mean time μ of less than 15 minutes. A sample of 50 units is to be tested, and nothing is known regarding the population of calibration times.

(a) Assuming a maximum chance of $\alpha = .01$ for acquiring the tuning stand when it takes 15 minutes or longer to complete calibration, express the decision rule.

(b) Test results provide a mean calibration time of 13.5 minutes, and a standard deviation of 3.4 minutes. What action should be taken?

9-19 A special paper has a desired thickness of .05 millimeter. If the mean value differs from this amount, the processing machinery requires adjustment. The value $\bar{X} = .051$ mm has been computed for a sample of $n = 100$ sheets. The assumed standard deviation is $\sigma = .002$ mm. At the $\alpha = .05$ significance level, should the machinery be adjusted or left alone?

9-20 A Wheel-Rite plant produces bearings with a specified 1-inch mean diameter. The standard deviation for all bearings produced is known to be .01 inch. A decision rule is to be established for determining when to correct for oversized or undersized items. This choice is based on a sample of 100 bearings, and the assumption is made that there is only an $\alpha = .01$ chance of taking corrective action when the production process is exactly meeting its mean target.

(a) Formulate the null hypothesis.

(b) What test statistic is appropriate?

(c) Express the decision rule.

(d) What action should be taken if (1) $\bar{X} = .993''$; (2) $\bar{X} = 1.0023''$?

9-21 A structural engineer is testing the strength of a newly designed steel beam required in cantilever construction. As his null hypothesis, he assumes that the mean strength will be at most as great as the 100,000 pounds per square inch (psi) for traditional beams. A test sample of $n = 9$ new beams has provided $\bar{X} = 105{,}000$ psi and $s = 10{,}000$ psi. At the $\alpha = .05$ significance level, should the engineer accept or reject his null hypothesis?

9-22 The product manager for Exonex wants to determine the time in which an experimental drug cures a skin disease. If management concludes that the drug yields a mean cure-time advantage over traditional treatment of more than 2 days, research will continue with the present formulation. Otherwise, a new formulation will be adopted for further testing. The drug will be administered to a sample of $n = 25$ persons and the cure-time advantage determined for each. The Type I error probability has been set at $\alpha = .05$ for switching to a new formulation when the present one achieves the desired advantage.

(a) Formulate the null hypothesis. Indicate which test statistic applies, and determine its critical value. Express the decision rule.

(b) Suppose the sample results for the cure-time advantage are $\bar{X} = 1.6$ days and $s = .4$ day. What action should the manager take?

9-23 P. J. Willy periodically checks the output of a chemical process to determine the level of impurities in the final product. If it contains too many impurities, the product will be reclassified; if it contains too few, an expensive catalyst is being consumed in undesirably large quantities. The process is designed to tolerate impurities of $\mu = .05$ gram per liter. Regardless of the mean impurity level, the historical standard deviation of .025 gram per liter applies.

The level of impurities in a sample of $n = 100$ 1-liter vials is measured at random times during each 4-hour period. The process is stopped if there are too many impurities (the tanks are purged) or too few impurities (the control valves are readjusted). The chief engineer will accept a Type I error probability of $\alpha = .01$ for unnecessarily stopping the process when the true mean level of impurities is at the target level.

(a) Perform hypothesis-testing Steps 1–3.

(b) What action should be taken in the following cases?

(1) At 8 A.M., $\bar{X} = .042$.

(2) At 12:30 P.M., $\bar{X} = .052$.

(3) At 5 P.M., $\bar{X} = .056$.

9-24 Your friend owns a retail store where she plans to give individual arriving customers a short verbal "commercial" message regarding the products for sale. Your friend asks you to determine if this will boost the mean sales transaction level μ, currently at \$5.00. You may assume that the standard deviation per transaction is \$1.00 and that the population is of unlimited size. You will monitor a random sample of $n = 200$ customers given this special treatment and determine the amount purchased by each.

(a) Your friend will adopt a policy of giving messages if sample evidence indicates that sales will improve. She wants most to avoid adopting this policy when the mean sales transaction won't improve. Formulate the null and alternative hypotheses.

(b) Suppose you wish to protect your friend with a probability of $\alpha = .05$ against rejecting the null hypothesis when it is true. Compute the critical value of the sample mean, and express the decision rule.

(c) You collect the sample data. What action should you take if (1) $\bar{X} =$ \$5.37; (2) $\bar{X} =$ \$5.05; (3) $\bar{X} =$ \$4.97; (4) $\bar{X} =$ \$5.20?

9-25 The Sour Grapes Winery is evaluating a modified fermentation process that involves higher temperatures than its present method. Since the new procedure requires specially designed controls, it has been judged economic only if production batches ferment faster than the mean time of 30 hours under the present system. If that isn't supported by testing, the present process will be continued. The test will involve 50 pilot batches to be run under the modified procedure.

(a) The more serious error is to adopt the modified process when it isn't actually the faster one. Express the null hypothesis in terms of the mean fermentation time μ.
(b) The standard deviation in fermentation time is unknown. Assuming a significance level of $\alpha = .01$, express the decision rule.
(c) Suppose the sample results are $\bar{X} = 29.5$ hours and $s = 4.91$ hours. What action should be taken?

9-26 The superintendent of a Deluxe Printing Company plant selects random samples of 100 rolls of paper from every large batch. The average length of the rolls in any shipment is unknown, although the standard deviation in lengths is assumed to always be $\sigma = 50$ feet. His null hypothesis is that $\mu \geq 525$ feet (satisfactory batch) and his alternative hypothesis is that $\mu < 525$ feet (short batch). Any shipment the superintendent believes to be short will be made into 100-foot rolls. Those believed to be satisfactory will be shipped.

Unfortunately, there is no way to be certain about the batch quality. A decision rule needs to be formulated to determine the action for each batch. This should be done, so that satisfactory batches are rendered just 1% of the time.

(a) What type of action is taken when H_0 is (1) accepted; (2) rejected?
(b) What is the significance level? Specify the appropriate test statistic and decision rule.
(c) For each of the following sample results, decide whether the null hypothesis should be accepted or rejected and the appropriate action to take.
(1) $\bar{X} = 514'$ (2) $\bar{X} = 530'$ (3) $\bar{X} = 521'$ (4) $\bar{X} = 508'$

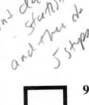

9-27 *Computer exercise.* The accounting firm of Ernest & Whitney achieved the following percentage savings in audit time by using a new computer system for examining transactions.

80	10	37	26
45	29	44	5

(a) Compute the sample mean and standard deviation.
(b) At the $\alpha = .05$ significance level, can the firm conclude that the computer system will yield some level of savings in auditing time?

9-28 *Computer exercise.* You want to test the null hypothesis that the true mean family income in Blahsburg falls at or below \$20,000. Assume that the standard deviation is $\sigma = \$2{,}500$. The following sample results have been obtained.

\$19,874	\$23,496	\$33,520	\$17,442	\$19,002	\$21,003
\$37,720	\$41,352	\$17,246	\$18,010	\$19,240	\$22,207

(a) Find the normal deviate statistic and the prob. value.
(b) Should the null hypothesis be accepted or rejected? Explain.

9-29 *Computer exercise.* A professor obtained the following sample differences in basic mathematics scores.

−7	−13	25	7	8	9	10	12	21	2
0	−2	−10	8	6	12	13	15	1	7

Each value was found by subtracting a student's standardized test score at the beginning of the semester from that achieved at the end. The standard deviation in differences is assumed to be 5 points.

(a) Perform a z-test to evaluate the null hypothesis that mean scores are the same at the beginning and the end of the semester (zero difference). At the 5% significance level, what should you conclude?

(b) Construct a 95% confidence interval for the mean score difference. Is this result consistent with your answer to (a)? Explain.

9-30 *Computer exercise.* The following Wear-Ever tire mileage data (in thousands of miles) have been obtained for a new tread design.

62.3	44.4	49.2	63.3	47.6	60.1
37.4	55.8	57.5	58.3	56.2	54.3

(a) Compute the sample mean and standard deviation.

(b) At the $\alpha = .05$ significance level, should you accept or reject the null hypothesis that, on the average, tires with the new tread will last 50 thousand miles or more?

9-3 TESTING THE PROPORTION

Tests of the proportion are used extensively in statistical applications. The proportion is important in a variety of managerial situations. In quality assurance, testing establishes whether the level of defectives in a shipment or from a production process is too high or too low. In marketing decisions, it is the proportion of product users in various categories that influences whether to change a product or its package, to enter a market, or to modify advertising.

The testing procedures for the proportion are similar to those for the mean. Ordinarily the sample proportion P serves as the test statistic in evaluations of π. The normal approximation closely approximates the sampling distribution for P for many situations, depending on the size for n and π.

USING P AS THE TEST STATISTIC

Tests of the proportion are categorized in the same way as those for the mean. The hypotheses and decision rules take the following forms.

Lower-tailed tests (H_0: $\pi \geq \pi_0$)	Upper-tailed tests (H_0: $\pi \leq \pi_0$)
Accept H_0 if $P \geq P^*$	*Accept* H_0 if $P \leq P^*$
Reject H_0 if $P < P^*$	*Reject* H_0 if $P > P^*$

Two-sided tests (H_0: $\pi = \pi_0$)

Accept H_0 if $P_1^* \leq P \leq P_2^*$

Reject H_0 if $P < P_1^*$ or if $P > P_2^*$

The sampling distribution of P is approximated by a normal curve having mean $E(P) = \pi$ and standard error $\sigma_P = \sqrt{\pi(1 - \pi)/n}$. Critical normal deviates are used in the same manner as in testing the mean. The following expressions are used to find the

CRITICAL VALUES OF THE PROPORTION

Lower-tailed tests

$$P^* = \pi_0 - z_\alpha \sqrt{\frac{\pi_0(1 - \pi_0)}{n}}$$

Upper-tailed tests

$$P^* = \pi_0 + z_\alpha \sqrt{\frac{\pi_0(1 - \pi_0)}{n}}$$

Two-sided tests

$$P_1^* = \pi_0 - z_{\alpha/2} \sqrt{\frac{\pi_0(1 - \pi_0)}{n}} \quad \text{and} \quad P_2^* = \pi_0 + z_{\alpha/2} \sqrt{\frac{\pi_0(1 - \pi_0)}{n}}$$

Some investigators prefer to use instead the normal deviate as the test statistic. That quantity is computed by subtracting π_0 from the computed P and dividing by the standard error.

NORMAL DEVIATE FOR TESTING THE PROPORTION

$$z = \frac{P - \pi_0}{\sqrt{\pi_0(1 - \pi_0)/n}}$$

The hypothesis-testing steps are discussed in the following illustration.

ILLUSTRATION: CONTROLLING ERRORS IN TELEPHONE DIRECTORIES

Liberty Bell Telephone publishes its telephone directory once a year. The state public utilities commission has established very strict quality guidelines. The greatest source of error is in preprocessing, not in typesetting. Historically, Liberty Bell has simply checked the directory against billing records for proper name, address, and telephone number. A new, more expensive procedure involves pasting each listing on the bill itself and asking customers to verify their own entry, placing a check mark by each correct item or making any necessary changes. This procedure will only work if a high proportion of customers respond, since expensive follow-up contacts are required for nonresponders.

A random sample of $n = 1{,}000$ customers has been selected for a test mailing to determine if the proportion π of responses received would be practical. If the sample response rate is sufficiently high, the new procedure will be adopted. Otherwise, the present method will be retained.

The following steps apply.

STEP 1

Formulate the null and alternative hypotheses. The new system is judged to be practical if at least 90% of the customers supply acknowledgement or corrections of their listings. The following hypotheses apply.

$$H_0\colon \pi \geq .90 \qquad \text{(New procedure is practical.)}$$
$$H_A\colon \pi < .90 \qquad \text{(New procedure is impractical.)}$$

The pivotal level for the population proportion of responders is $\pi_0 = .90$. The null hypothesis is designated in such a way that the more serious error corresponds to the Type I error: retaining the old preprocessing check when the new procedure would be practical.

STEP 2

Select the test statistic and procedure. The sample proportion P serves as the test statistic.

STEP 3

Establish the significance level and identify the acceptance and rejection regions. Liberty Bell management will tolerate only a 1% chance of retaining the old method when the new procedure would be practical. Using $\alpha = .01$, the critical normal deviate is $z_\alpha = z_{.01} = 2.33$ for this lower-tailed test. The critical value for P is

$$P^* = .90 - 2.33\sqrt{\frac{.90(1 - .90)}{1{,}000}} = .878$$

The acceptance and rejection regions are shown in the figure that follows.

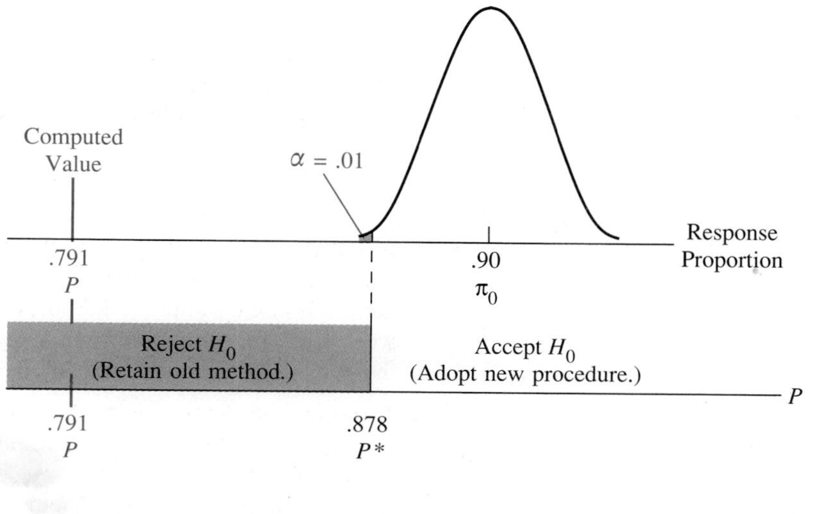

STEP 4

Collect the sample and compute the value of the test statistic. Only 791 listing responses were obtained from the sample mailing. The computed value of the test statistic is

$$P = \frac{791}{1{,}000} = .791$$

STEP 5

Make the decision. Since P falls within the rejection region, the test results are statistically significant. Liberty Bell management must *reject* the null hypothesis that the new procedure would be practical, and retain the old method.

The above test could have been performed using the normal deviate z instead of P as the test statistic. In that case, the computed value of z is

$$z = \frac{.791 - .90}{\sqrt{.90(1 - .90)/1{,}000}} = -11.49$$

Since z falls below $-z_\alpha = -2.33$, in the rejection region, the same conclusion is reached as before.

EXERCISES

9-31 In testing the hypotheses

$$H_0: \pi \leq \pi_0\ (= .5) \quad \text{and} \quad H_A: \pi > \pi_0$$

the desired Type I error probability is $\alpha = .10$. The value $P = .55$ has been computed for a sample of $n = 100$. Complete the hypothesis-testing steps to determine whether the null hypothesis should be accepted or rejected.

9-32 A quality control inspector at ChipMont tests random samples of $n = 100$ from the items in each shipment received from suppliers. If the proportion P of defective items is sufficiently low, the shipment is accepted; otherwise, it is rejected. The null hypothesis is that the true proportion of defectives in a shipment does not exceed the standard: $\pi \leq \pi_0$. In all cases, the significance level is $\alpha = .05$.

(a) Is this a lower- or an upper-tailed test?

(b) For each of the following situations, decide whether the shipment will be accepted or rejected.

(1) $\pi_0 = .05$; $P = .08$

(2) $\pi_0 = .10$; $P = .08$

(3) $\pi_0 = .01$; $P = .04$

9-33 A statistician is testing the null hypothesis that exactly half of all MBAs continue their formal education by taking courses within ten years of graduation. Using a sample of 200 persons, she found that 111 had taken coursework since receiving their MBA. At the $\alpha = .05$ significance level, should the statistician accept or reject her null hypothesis?

9-34 A professional group claims that at least 40% of all engineers employed by aerospace firms switch jobs within three years of being hired. The alternative hypothesis is that the rate of job changing is below 40%. At the $\alpha = .01$ significance level, should the claim be accepted or rejected if the sample results show that 25 out of $n = 100$ engineers changed jobs?

9-35 Liberty Bell Telephone policy is to add an information operator to the pool whenever sample data indicate that all operators are busy an excessive proportion of the time. A Type I error probability of $\alpha = .05$ has been established for unnecessarily adding an operator when the pool is busy 50% of the time or less. A sample of $n = 20$ observations will be made at random times.

(a) The sample proportion of time busy P serves as the test statistic. Express the decision rule.

(b) What action should be taken if all operators are busy during 65% of the sample observation times?

9-36 A sample of $n = 100$ items has been selected at random from a large incoming shipment. The null hypothesis is that the proportion defective is at most .05. The sample proportion defective is .06. At the $\alpha = .05$ significance level, should the null hypothesis be accepted or rejected?

9-4 SELECTING THE TEST

SOME IMPORTANT QUESTIONS

We have covered the basic concepts of hypothesis testing that apply to means and proportions. It is now time to consider some fundamental questions.

1. *What other test statistics can we use?* Many test statistics other than $\bar{X}$ and P can be applied to hypothesis-testing situations. Usually, the nature of the test determines the type of test statistic to be employed. In later chapters, we will learn to use many new statistics to compare the parameters of two or more populations. In lieu of testing with $\bar{X}$, a number of so-called **nonparametric tests** (to be described in Chapter 19) may be used.

2. *How can we determine which test statistic will work best?* Often, we must choose from several alternative procedures. Perhaps the most important factor to consider in making this choice is the relative efficiency of each test.

3. *How can we evaluate a particular decision rule in terms of the protection it provides against both kinds of incorrect decisions, the Type I and Type II errors?* Both types of decision errors should be avoided. But we have seen that when the choice is based on sample data, some probability for each error (α and β) must be tolerated. Ordinarily, only α—the probability for committing the more serious Type I error—is explicitly considered in selecting a decision rule. But the statistician may revise the initial decision rule if it proves to be inadequate in protecting against the Type II error.

4. *What assumptions underlie the proposed testing procedure, and how do they affect its applicability?* The t test assumes that the population itself is normally distributed. Just how critical is such an assumption? At one extreme, an assumption can limit a test so severely that it cannot be applied to many decision-making situations. On the other hand, an assumption may prove to be relatively unimportant. A test that basically accomplishes what it is intended to do even when a requirement is not exactly met is said to be **robust** with respect to a violation of that assumption.

THE POWER CURVE

Usually there are several possible values of β, the Type II error probability. Remember that β is the probability for accepting H_0 when H_0 is false (and H_A is true). Using the alternative hypothesis H_A: $\mu > 20$ in our dietary supplement illustration, we can compute a different β for any particular level of μ greater than 20. On page 362, we computed $\beta = .0668$ when $\mu = 23.5$. Some other values are

$$\beta = .8413 \text{ when } \mu = 21$$

$$\beta = .5000 \text{ when } \mu = 22$$

$$\beta = .0228 \text{ when } \mu = 24$$

These probabilities are represented as points on the graph in Figure 9-5. The curve connecting the points is called a **power curve**. The height of the curve provides the probability $(1 - \beta)$ for rejecting the null hypothesis at the indicated possible level for μ.

The power curve can be useful in evaluating a hypothesis test. The usual hypothesis-testing procedure begins with a prescribed significance level α (the Type I error probability) and set sample size n. These parameters fix the levels of the β probabilities.

The decision maker may study the power curve and conclude that the βs are higher than the desired levels. In our dietary supplement illustration, two remedies are available.

1. Raise the significance level α, so that there is a higher Type I error probability for releasing an ineffective supplement. This shifts the critical value of the test statistic, lowering all the βs and providing a lower Type II error probability for delaying an effective supplement for each μ.

2. Increase the sample size n. This will decrease both the α and β probabilities for all levels of μ.

EFFICIENCY AND POWER

The choice of a test statistic is an important issue in advanced applications of hypothesis-testing theory. In many decision situations, a number of statistical tests can be performed. For instance, rather than find the actual levels of cholesterol reduction in patients treated in the dietary supplement illustration, the statistician could simply determine the proportion P of patients who achieved a major reduction in their cholesterol levels. Instead, the more detailed measure $\bar{X}$—the mean percentage reduction in cholesterol levels—was chosen. Generally, $\bar{X}$ provides more information than P, so that $\bar{X}$ is a more efficient test statistic than P. Thus, for the same sample size and Type I error probability α, the decision rule obtained for $\bar{X}$ should provide smaller Type II error probabilities β (and higher probabilities for rejecting H_0 when it is false). In this case, the $\bar{X}$-test is said to be more **powerful** than the P-test.

9-5 LIMITATIONS OF HYPOTHESIS-TESTING PROCEDURES

In this chapter we presented the *classical* statistical decision analysis. Its applicability to the rather large class of decision problems faced by the modern manager is limited in several ways. Paramount among these is the dependence on

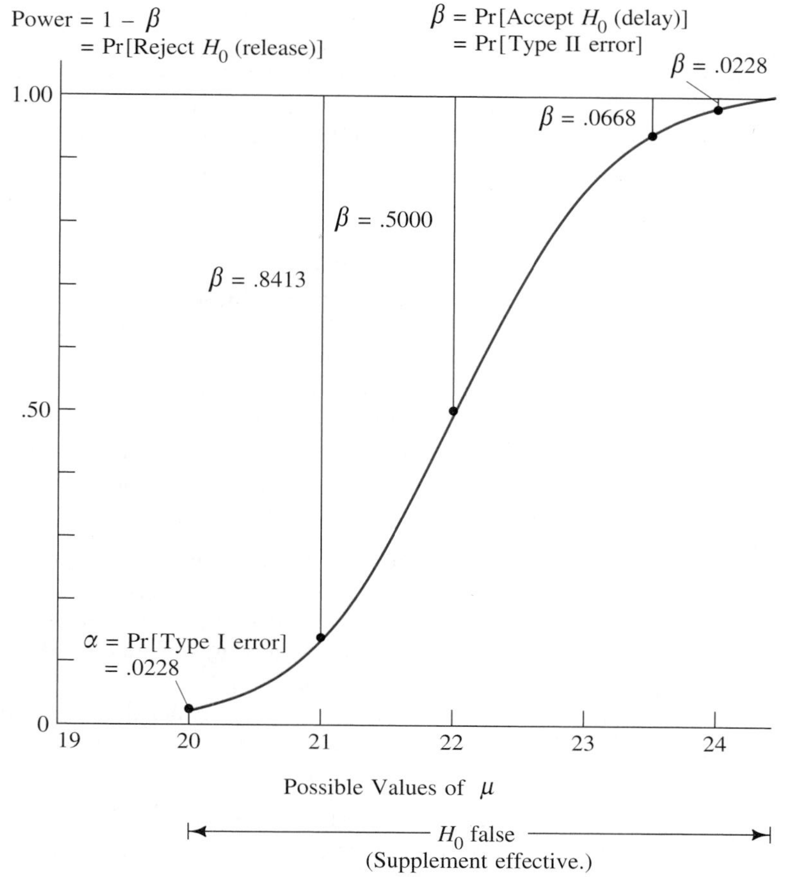

FIGURE 9-5 Power curve for the dietary supplement decision.

samples for obtaining supportive or contradictory evidence. Many significant decisions must be made without first taking a sample, because a sample is too costly or simply unobtainable. For example, in deciding whether to drill for oil, the wildcatter does not collect direct sample evidence by drilling holes at random as the basis for rejecting or accepting the null hypothesis that there is oil. The only way such evidence may be obtained is to sink the shaft, and this can be done only after the decision has already been made to drill. What evidence is obtained must be of an indirect nature, such as results of geological surveys, seismic tests, and nearby drilling experience. Another limitation of hypothesis testing is its restricted applicability to decisions involving two alternatives when so many decisions involve choosing among a multitude of alternatives.

Even when classical hypothesis testing is applicable, there are improvements that can be made. One is to expand the process so that more information can be utilized. For instance, the fact that certain values of the population decision parameter may be more likely than others can be used by the decision maker to reduce the probability for an incorrect decision. Methods for doing this will be described in Chapter 28. A further limitation of the classical approach is that it does not in any way help to resolve the problem faced by a decision maker in assessing the risks associated with the incorrect decisions; this subject is covered further in Chapter 25. The cost of collecting the sample is not explicitly considered in the classical treatment. Chapter 27 shows how we can relate the costs of selecting the sample to the costs of the ensuing risks, so that an optimal course of action can be achieved.

SUMMARY

1. **What is hypothesis testing?**
   Because of its role in decision making, **hypothesis testing** is a more dynamic form of statistical inference than estimation. This chapter considers tests for the mean (μ) and the proportion (π). There are two possible actions, equivalent to accepting or rejecting a **null hypothesis** (H_0). While uncertain, the decision maker must make a choice as to whether or not the null hypothesis is true. The action taken is determined by applying a **decision rule** that specifies what to do for any computed level of the **test statistic**, $\bar{X}$ or P, or z or t.

2. **How does the hypothesis testing approach deal with sampling error?**
   Before sample results are known, the test statistic is a random variable, and there is a chance that the decision will be incorrect—resulting in either a **Type I error** (rejecting the null hypothesis when it is true) or a **Type II error** (accepting the null hypothesis when it is false).
   Statisticians consider the probabilities for these errors when setting a decision rule. These probabilities are

$$\alpha = \Pr[\text{Type I error}] = \Pr[\textit{reject } H_0 | H_0 \text{ true}]$$
$$\beta = \Pr[\text{Type II error}] = \Pr[\textit{accept } H_0 | H_0 \text{ false}]$$

   You ordinarily designate H_0 so that the more undesirable outcome corresponds to the Type I error.

3. **What are the basic forms of a hypothesis test?**
   The pivotal parameter level is denoted by μ_0 in testing the mean and by π_0 in testing the proportion. That value establishes the center of the sampling distribution for the test statistic, and this center is assumed to apply under the extreme case of the null hypothesis. Depending on the form of H_0, the procedure may be a **one-sided test** or a **two-sided test**. One-sided tests may be **lower-tailed** or **upper-tailed**. The following classifications apply.

Lower-tailed test	Upper-tailed test	Two-sided test
H_0: $\mu \geq \mu_0$	H_0: $\mu \leq \mu_0$	H_0: $\mu = \mu_0$
$\pi \geq \pi_0$	$\pi \leq \pi_0$	$\pi = \pi_0$

   For an upper-tailed test, the Type I probability α corresponds to an area in the upper tail of the curve for the sampling distribution of the test statistic, and for a lower-tailed test, it corresponds to an area in the lower tail. For a two-sided test, α is equal to the sum of the matching areas in both tails.

4. How are decisions reached when testing hypotheses?
The decision will be made depending on where the computed level of the test statistic falls. The point(s) of demarcation is (are) the **critical value(s)**. It separates the **acceptance region** from the **rejection region**. The form and placement of these regions is determined by the above test classifications.

5. What are the two basic hypothesis testing procedures for the mean, and when should z or t be used?
In testing the mean, there is a basic dichotomy that depends on knowledge of the population standard deviation.

When σ is unknown, the *Student t statistic* is used to test the hypothesis. It is convenient to designate such a test as a **single-decision procedure**. It is also referred to as a ***t*-test**.

When σ is known, the normal distribution applies for $\bar{X}$. The decision rule then is based on the **critical normal deviate**, z_α or $z_{\alpha/2}$. Ordinarily, more than one decision is made with the same rule when σ is known, and it is convenient to classify this test of the mean as a **recurring-decisions procedure**. There are two versions of the procedure. A **detailed decision rule** involves the critical value(s) of $\bar{X}$ that falls above or below μ_0 at a distance of z_α or $z_{\alpha/2}$ times $\sigma_{\bar{X}}$. An **abbreviated decision rule** compares the computed z to the critical normal deviate. The ***z*-test** is another common designation for a test of the mean when σ is known.

6. What is the significance level of a test, and how does it relate to the decision rule and error probabilities?
Once the null hypothesis is formulated, the decision maker must choose a value for α. This is the **significance level**. The critical value is positioned in accordance with α. A statistical decision rule guarantees that the Type I error probability will equal the significance level. But that rule may provide inadequate protection against the Type II error. Probabilities β for the latter vary, depending on the pivotal level μ_0 or π_0. The adequacy of the decision rule is sometimes assessed by examining the **power curve**.

REAL-LIFE STATISTICAL CHALLENGE

Applying Hypothesis Testing to the Automobile Dream List

In Chapter 8 concepts about statistical estimation were used to analyze populations for 232 autos. We will now apply hypothesis testing methods to the set of "dream machines."

Let us assume that the list of 15 cars in Table 6-20 represents a sample of the cars purchased by a firm for business use. To control costs, the company might be concerned whether the fleet mileage is above certain standards. We will determine for management whether the mileage is significantly above 20 miles per gallon. Our null hypothesis is:

$$H_0\text{: } \mu \leq 20 \qquad \text{(Mileage level is too low)}$$

REAL-LIFE STATISTICAL CHALLENGE

Our alternative hypothesis is:

$$H_A: \mu > 20 \qquad \text{(Mileage level is satisfactory)}$$

The Student t test statistic is used:

$$t = \frac{\bar{X} - \mu_0}{s/\sqrt{n}}$$

For the sample of 15 automobiles $\bar{X} = 26.47$ mpg and $s = 4.47$. The computed t value is:

$$t = \frac{26.47 - 20}{4.47/\sqrt{15}} = 5.60$$

Using significance level $\alpha = .01$ the critical value is $t_{.01} = 2.624$ for $(15 - 1) = 14$ degrees of freedom. Since $t = 5.60$ exceeds the critical value we can *reject* the null hypothesis and conclude that the gasoline mileage level is satisfactory.

The choice of the pivotal value and the level of significance was arbitrary. For example a pivotal value $\mu_0 = 25$ miles per gallon would have yielded $t = 1.27$; and at $\mu_0 = 24$ mpg, $t = 2.13$. In these two cases the null hypothesis would be accepted when $\alpha = .01$. For $\alpha = .05$, the critical value becomes $t_{.05} = 1.761$; we would reject the null hypothesis when $\mu_0 = 24$ (but not when $\mu_0 = 25$).

DISCUSSION QUESTIONS

1. Develop another hypothesis test using the mean gas mileage.
2. Comment on the impact on your test in Question 1 from altering the pivotal value or the sample size.
3. Develop two examples of hypothesis tests using the engine displacement data.
4. Develop a hypothesis for testing the proportion (for example: proportion of cars with manual transmissions, or various combinations of car type, large, midsize, etc.).

REVIEW EXERCISES

9-37 For each of the following situations, find the Type I error probability α that corresponds to the stated decision rule. In all cases, use a sample of $n = 100$.

(a) *Accept* H_0 if $\bar{X} \geq 12$ *Reject* H_0 if $\bar{X} < 12$ $\mu_0 = 14$ and $\sigma = 18$

(b) *Accept* H_0 if $\bar{X} \leq 100$ *Reject* H_0 if $\bar{X} > 100$ $\mu_0 = 97$ and $\sigma = 20$

9-38 For each of the following hypothesis-testing situations, $n = 100$ and $\alpha = .05$. In each case, decide whether H_0 should be accepted or rejected.

(a) H_0: $\mu \geq 25$; H_A: $\mu < 25$; $\bar{X} = 23.0$; $s = 4.7$.

(b) H_0: $\mu \leq 14.7$; H_A: $\mu > 14.7$; $\bar{X} = 15.3$; $s = 1.5$.

(c) H_0: $\mu = 168$; H_A: $\mu \neq 168$; $\bar{X} = 169$; $s = .92$.

9-39 The mean length of a random sample of $n = 20$ rolls of wire is $\bar{X} = 2{,}031$ meters(m), with a standard deviation of $s = 47$ m. The null hypothesis that

$\mu \geq 2{,}000$ m is to be tested. Assuming that $\alpha = .01$, should the null hypothesis be accepted or rejected?

9-40 You are asked to determine whether to accept or reject the null hypothesis that the mean processing time μ for special orders is less than or equal to 10 minutes. There will be a very large number of such orders processed, and you may assume that the standard deviation is 2 minutes per order (the same value that applies to regular orders). A sample of $n = 100$ special orders have been timed.

(a) Formulate the null and alternative hypotheses.

(b) Suppose you wish to protect yourself with a probability of $\alpha = .01$ against rejecting the null hypothesis when it is true. Compute the critical value of the sample mean, and express the decision rule.

(c) Collect the sample data. What action must be taken if (1) $\bar{X} = 10.62$ min; (2) $\bar{X} = 10.47$ min; (3) $\bar{X} = 10.25$ min?

9-41 A presidential candidate plans to campaign in only those primaries that he is preferred by at least 20% of the voters in his party. A random sample of 100 voter preferences is obtained from each state. In each case, the null hypothesis is that the state meets the 20% criterion. The desired Type I error probability is $\alpha = .05$. Decide whether the null hypothesis should be accepted or rejected in each of the following states. Also decide whether or not the candidate will enter the campaign in each of these states.

State	Number Preferring Candidate
(a) New Hampshire	12
(b) Florida	23
(c) Wisconsin	15
(d) Massachusetts	10

9-42 Gizmo Corporation will be manufacturing a bearing with a specified 1/2-inch diameter. The standard deviation in diameter is unknown, and corrective action will be taken based on a sample of 100 items measured.

(a) Formulate the null hypothesis.

(b) What test statistic is appropriate?

(c) Using $\alpha = .01$, express the decision rule.

(d) What action should be taken: (1) if $\bar{X} = .497''$ and $s = .0075''$? (2) if $\bar{X} = .508''$ and $s = .013''$?

9-43 Ace Assemblers is reviewing its employment screening procedures for detail work. Several new persons, none having prior experience, have been hired. They have all been given a manual dexterity test. An investigator wishes to test the null hypothesis that the mean test score μ of newly hired inexperienced persons is just as high as that of the company's experienced workers, for which it has been established that the mean is 81.

Only 15 inexperienced persons take the test. They achieve a mean score of $\bar{X} = 78.3$ with a standard deviation of $s = 5$. At a significance level of $\alpha = .05$, should the null hypothesis be accepted or rejected?

9-44 The Fruty Tooty product manager wishes to determine whether or not to change the package design for the cereal. She feels that it will be worth the bother only if more than 60% of nonusers prefer the new box to the old one. She most wants to avoid changing the box when the preference proportion π is smaller, so that her null hypothesis is $\pi \leq .60$.

The manager selects a random sample of $n = 100$ persons who don't buy Fruty Tooty. She wants to protect herself at the 5% significance level against incorrectly rejecting the null hypothesis when it is true. She finds that 73 sample respondents prefer the new box. What action should she take?

9-45 To assess the time required to cure a disease using an experimental drug, it is administered to a sample of $n = 25$ persons. The pharmaceutical company is basing its decision to continue or terminate its research on whether or not the drug is deemed effective. The desired Type I error probability is $\alpha = .01$ for not continuing the research when the drug actually yields a mean advantage in cure time of at least two days over the present treatment time. If the sample results for the cure-time advantage are $\bar{X} = 1.5$ and $s = .5$ day, should the null hypothesis be accepted or rejected? Should the drug experiment be continued or terminated?

9-46 The plant manager of Very Wide Shoe Company wishes to determine whether or not the sizing department's work is satisfactory. Due to ordinary variability, a shoe does not fall into a precise size category like $8\frac{1}{2}$EEE. Finished shoes must be individually measured and then classified to the nearest appropriate size. To determine whether or not to take corrective action, the manager asks that a sample of 100 randomly selected shoes be meticulously resized. The proportion of shoes that were originally correctly sized is to be determined. As his null hypothesis, the manager assumes that the true proportion of all shoes incorrectly sized is $\leq .05$, the desirable level. He must construct a decision rule that rejects this hypothesis when it is true with a probability of .05.

The sample results show that $P = .062$. Should the null hypothesis be accepted or rejected? Should corrective action be taken?

9-47 A personal director for Kryptonite Corporation wishes to give her standard screening examination to some recent job applicants to decide whether or not today's job seekers achieve higher scores than applicants did ten years ago. If they do, she will use a new examination in the future. The test is to be administered to a random sample of $n = 25$ persons. In analyzing the results, the director wishes to allow only a 1% chance of incorrectly changing procedures when the actual mean screening examination score is ≤ 86, the historical mean figure ten years ago. If the sample group achieves a mean score of 88, with a standard deviation of 10 points, should the present screening examination be retained or changed?

9-48 The VBM personnel manager is testing the physical aptitude of college graduates to determine whether or not they score higher than high school graduates. If they do, the new test will be used in the future to screen college graduates, as well as nongraduates, applying for nonmanagement positions. The test is administered to a random sample of $n = 25$ persons. Management wants only an $\alpha = .05$ chance of incorrectly changing screening procedures when the actual mean aptitude test score is ≤ 86, the historical mean for high school graduates.

(a) Formulate the null hypothesis. Indicate which test statistic applies, and compute its critical value. Express the decision rule.

(b) Suppose the sample results are $\bar{X} = 88$ and $s = 10$. What action should the manager take?

STATISTICS IN PRACTICE

9-49 Consider populations comprising all statistics students. Using as sample data the master class list developed in Exercise 1-19, answer the following. (Note: Be sure to show all your intermediate steps. You may use intermediate answers you developed in earlier chapters to avoid unnecessary effort.)

(a) Test the population for the mean of one of your variables, using either an upper- or lower-tailed test.

(b) Test the population mean of one of your variables, using a two-tailed test.

(c) Test for the population proportion of one of your variables for either an upper- or lower-tailed test.

(d) Perform a hypothesis test for a population proportion using a two-tailed test.

9-50 Repeat Exercise 9-49 using as sample data your group's class data from Exercise 1-21.

9-51 In Exercise 6-55 you were asked to go to a local store or other retail outlet and collect data for the number of arrivals during one minute intervals. Develop a hypothesis test to aid the store manager in decision making.

9-52 Using the data set from Exercise 8-53 based on genetic diversity you may assume that 70 percent of the population possess the ability to roll their tongues and that 90 percent of the people are right-handed. Test whether the data you gathered are significantly different from the population proportion for (a) hand preference and (b) tongue rolling. Comment on your results.

9-53 Who do you want for President? If the election were held today, which candidate would you vote for? Research the most recent pre-election opinion poll from your local newspaper. Comment on the most recent poll in terms of the pollster's use of statistical estimation methods. Conduct your own poll, using the question as it was worded for the nationwide poll. Do your results differ significantly from the national results?

CASE SynerGentex

SynerGentex is a pharmaceutical company specializing in drugs and hormones synthesized through "genetic engineering" using bacterial media. All areas of the company use statistics in a variety of ways and to meet distinct needs. The statistical applications may be conveniently categorized into one of the following four groupings.

1. To determine whether or not a new product or approach is even worth pursuing.

2. To establish the efficacy of a new drug or chemical.

3. To assess the deleterious impact ("side effects") of a new drug or chemical.

4. To settle issues of implementation of promising products, such as effective dosages.

Group 1 applications are strictly in-house investigations and the information thereby gleaned is proprietary. The remaining statistical applications often involve outside entities, such as universities, institutes, other firms and researchers, and government regulators.

Examples of each type of application are given in the following Questions.

QUESTIONS

1. SynerGentex wants to determine if a sizable market exists for a new drug to treat a rare genetic disease. Management will provide the required funding for the development of the substance if a high enough proportion of physicians would potentially prescribe the drug when it is known to give noticeable symptom relief. A sample of 25 potential prescribers were given a brief hypothetical description of the proposed drug, and 19 responded positively. The company will proceed if they can reject the null hypothesis that, at most, half of all treating doctors would prescribe the drug. At the 5% significance level, what action should SynerGentex take?

2. A synthetic steroid for treatment of an induced allergic skin rash is evaluated in terms of the time it takes to clear up the problem. The null hypothesis is that the mean clearing time is at least as long as that of a conventional treatment, known to be 96 hours. If the hypothesis is rejected, the steroid will be passed on to the next phase of testing; otherwise, it will be reformulated. The following sample clearing times have been obtained. At the $\alpha = .01$ significance level, what action should be taken?

22	37	41	55	69	115	138	61	204

3. A new substance is being tested for carcinogenic effects. The research is performed by administering the chemical to laboratory rats at a dosage that would be hundreds of times the anticipated human equivalent. The following results have been obtained for three treatment levels.

(a) 100 × Human	(b) 500 × Human	(c) 1,000 × Human
7 tumorous	18 tumorous	21 tumorous
54 healthy	49 healthy	54 healthy
H_0: $\pi \leq .05$	H_0: $\pi \leq .10$	H_0: $\pi \leq .20$

The results show how many treated rats developed tumors. At a 5% significance level, should the respective null hypotheses be accepted or rejected?

4. A new sleep inducer is being tested to establish a recommended dosage. Again, laboratory rats are used to conduct the research. The null hypothesis is that treated rats will fall to sleep quickly at a mean dosage of $\mu \leq .1$ mg. The following intravenous dosage data have been obtained for a sample of rats.

.15 .07 .09 .22 .08 .08 .11 .07 .06

At a 5% significance level, what conclusion should be made regarding the true level of μ?

CHAPTER 10

REGRESSION AND CORRELATION

BEFORE READING THIS CHAPTER, MAKE SURE YOU UNDERSTAND:

The distinction between the sample and population (Chapter 1).

The role of random samples in statistical evaluations (Chapter 4).

About confidence intervals and how they are used and constructed (Chapter 8).

About the basic concepts of hypothesis testing (Chapter 9).

AFTER READING THIS CHAPTER, YOU WILL UNDERSTAND:

How statistics measures and expresses association between variables.

What the correlation coefficient measures and how to compute it.

The role of the regression line and how it is found.

How to summarize the variability about the regression line and measure its quality.

The theoretical assumptions underlying regression analysis.

How to make statistically confident predictions using the regression line.

About the coefficient of determination and the quality of the regression analysis.

The role of the computer in regression and correlation analysis.

In many important business decisions it is necessary to predict the values of unknown variables. A personnel manager is concerned with predicting the success of a job applicant, which may be expressed in terms of the applicant's productivity. A production manager for a chemical company may wish to predict the levels of impurities in a final product. Many economists make predictions of gross national product (GNP). In each case, knowledge of one factor may be used to better predict another factor. The personnel manager may use screening examination scores as the basis for predicting future on-the-job performance. The production manager may use process temperatures or concentrations of ingredient chemicals to forecast impurities. The economist may use current interest rates, unemployment levels, and government spending to make GNP prognostications.

Regression analysis tells us how one variable is related to another by providing an equation that allows us to use the known value of one or more variables to estimate the unknown value of the remaining variable. For instance, an economist may use regression analysis to show how one variable, such as percentage unemployment, can be used to predict the percentage inflation rate. The resulting mathematical relationship provides a graphical display called the Phillips curve. More than one variable can be used to estimate an unknown variable. When several variables are used to make a prediction, the technique is called **multiple regression**. (We will discuss this topic in Chapter 11.)

Correlation analysis tells us the degree to which two variables are related. It is useful in expressing how efficiently one variable has estimated the value of another variable. Correlation analysis can also identify the factors of a multiple-characteristic population that are highly related, either directly or by a common connection to another variable.

10-1 REGRESSION ANALYSIS

The primary goal of regression analysis is to obtain predictions of one variable using the known values of another. These predictions are made by employing an equation such as $Y = a + bX$, which provides the estimate of an unknown variable Y when the value of another variable X is known. Such an expression is referred to as a **regression equation**. Knowing the regression equation, we can readily predict Y from a given X. Unlike the results from ordinary mathematical equations (such as $A = b \times h$ for the area of a rectangle, or interest $= i \times P \times t$, where i is the rate of interest, P is the principal, and t is the time), we cannot be certain about the value of Y that we obtain from the regression equation. This is due to inherent statistical variability. Predictions made from the regression equation are subject to error and are only *estimates* of the true values.

Regression analysis begins with a set of data involving pairs of observed values, one number for each variable. Table 10-1 shows the observations of distances and transportation times for a sample of ten rail shipments made by an automobile parts supplier. These data will be used to arrive at predictions of transit times for future shipments. From these the regression equation will be determined. Because using a sample gives rise to sampling error, the regression equation obtained may not be truly representative of the actual relationship between the variables. In order to reduce the chances of large sampling error, a sample size considerably greater than ten ought to be used. We have taken such a small number here merely for ease in showing calculations.

TABLE 10-1 Sample Observations of Rail Distances and Transportation Times for Ten Shipments by a Parts Supplier

Customer	Rail Distance to Destination X	Transportation Time (days) Y
1. Muller Auto Supply	210	5
2. Taylor Ford	290	7
3. Auto Supply House	350	6
4. Parts 'n Spares	480	11
5. Jones & Sons	490	8
6. A. Hausman	730	11
7. Des Moines Parts	780	12
8. Pete's Parts	850	8
9. Smith Dodge	920	15
10. Gulf Distributors	1,010	12

THE SCATTER DIAGRAM

A first step in regression analysis is to plot the value pairs as points on a **scatter diagram** as Figure 10-1. The horizontal axis corresponds to values of the variable distance, denoted by the letter X. The vertical scale represents values of the variable time, for which we use the designation Y. A point is found for each shipment. For example, the shipment to Jones & Sons, located at a distance of $X = 490$ miles from the plant, took $Y = 8$ days to arrive. This is represented by the point $(X = 490, Y = 8)$ on the graph.

The parts supplier wishes to use the known rail distance to the customers as the basis for predicting an order's unknown transportation time. It is customary to refer to the variable whose value is known as the **independent variable**, the possible values of which are represented on the X axis of the scatter diagram. The variable whose value is being predicted is called the **dependent variable**, the possible magnitudes of which are represented on the Y axis. Thus, rail distance X is the independent variable, because it is determined by the shipment's destination only, whereas the transportation time Y is the dependent variable, because it is in part predictable from rail distance.

These designations follow from simple algebra, where the X axis represents the independent variable, and the Y axis provides values of the dependent variable by means of a function or an equation. Thus, Y is a function of X. The dependence of Y on X does not necessarily mean that Y is *caused* by X. The type of relationship found by regression analysis is a statistical one. (We can find a *statistical* relationship expressing family household expenditures as a dependent variable that is a function of an independent variable, family disposable income. But having money to spend does not mean that appliances will be purchased. A purchase is a voluntary decision that is merely allowed to occur because money has been made available; a purchase need not be made just because there is sufficient income.)

THE DATA AND THE REGRESSION EQUATION

The second step in regression analysis is to find a suitable function to use for the regression equation, so that it will provide the predicted value of Y for a given

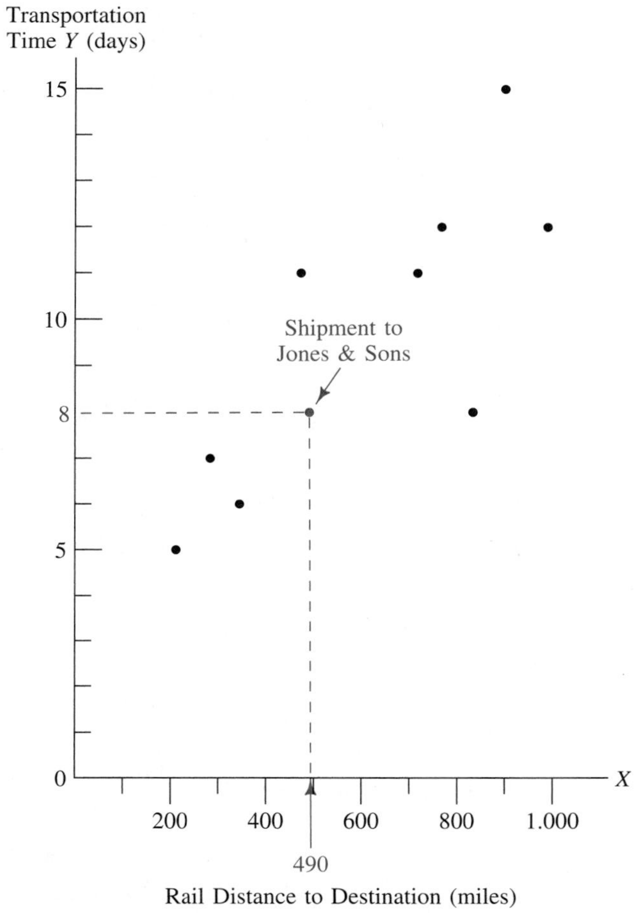

FIGURE 10-1 Scatter diagram for shipments by a parts supplier (Values from Table 10-1).

value of X. The clue to finding an appropriate regression equation can be found in the general pattern presented by the points in the scatter diagram. A quick examination of the parts supplier's data in our example indicates that a straight line, like the one shown in Figure 10-2, might be a meaningful summary of the information provided by the sample. This line seems to "fit" the rough scatter pattern of the data points.

A linear relationship between the variables X and Y is the simplest to visualize. The general equation for a straight line is $Y = a + bX$. The constant a is the value of Y obtained when $X = 0$, so that $Y = a + b(0) = a$. Because this is the value of Y at which the line intersects the Y axis, a is usually referred to as the ***Y* intercept**. The constant b, or the **slope** of the line, represents the change in Y due to a one-unit increase in the value of X. Figure 10-3 shows the line for the equation $Y = 3 + 2X$. Here, the Y intercept is $a = 3$ and the slope is $b = 2$. Y increases by two units for every one-unit change in X.

To review how we determine the value of Y for X, suppose we wish to find the Y that corresponds to $X = 5$. Substituting 5 for X in the expression gives us $Y = 3 + 2(5) = 13$. The same value may be read directly from Figure 10-3 by

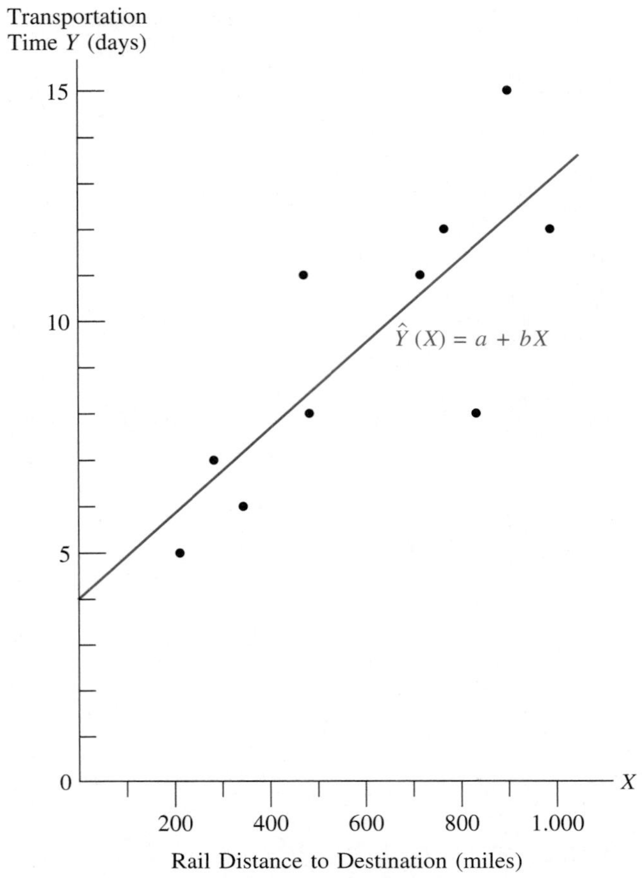

FIGURE 10-2 Fitting a regression line to the parts supplier's data.

following the vertical black line from $X = 5$ to the line relating Y to X. The vertical distance represents the value of Y. Any point on the line, for example ($X = 5$, $Y = 13$), can be described by the horizontal distance (5) and the vertical distance (13) from the origin.

The line used to describe the average relationship between the variables X and Y, or the **estimated regression line**, is generally obtained from sample data. The estimated regression line provides an estimate of the mean level of the dependent variable Y when the value of X is specified. We use the symbol $\hat{Y}(X)$ ("Y-hat of X") to represent the values obtained from the linear

ESTIMATED REGRESSION EQUATION

$$\hat{Y}(X) = a + bX$$

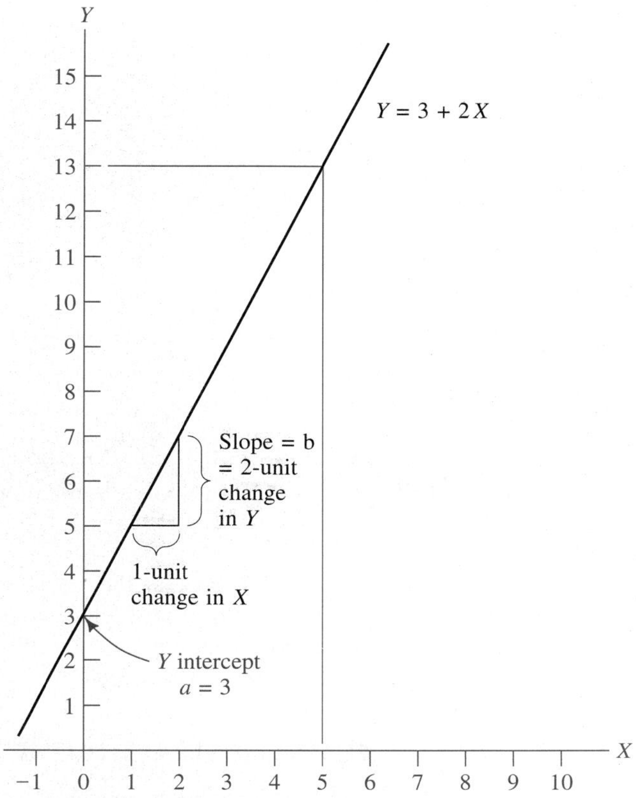

FIGURE 10-3 Slope and Y intercept of a straight line.

The symbol $\hat{Y}(X)$ distinguishes estimates of the dependent variable from the observed data points, which, for simplicity, we denote by the symbol Y. For a specific X, the resulting $\hat{Y}(X)$ is a *predicted* value of the dependent variable. As we will see, the values a and b in this expression are found from sample data and are referred to as **estimated regression coefficients**.

SOME CHARACTERISTICS OF THE REGRESSION LINE

Some important general properties of the regression line and its fit to the data are illustrated in Figure 10-4. First, we will consider the manner in which Y is related to X. There are two basic kinds of regression lines. If the values of the dependent variable Y increase for larger values of the independent variable X, then Y is **directly related** to X, as shown in Figure 10-4(a). Here, the slope of the line is positive, so that $b > 0$; this is because Y will increase as X becomes larger. Figure 10-2 shows that transportation time and rail distance are directly related variables. Other examples of directly related variables are age and salary (during employment years), weight and daily caloric intake, and the number of passengers and the quantity of luggage on commercial aircraft flights. In Figure 10-4(b), the slope of the regression line is negative and $b < 0$. Here, Y becomes smaller for larger

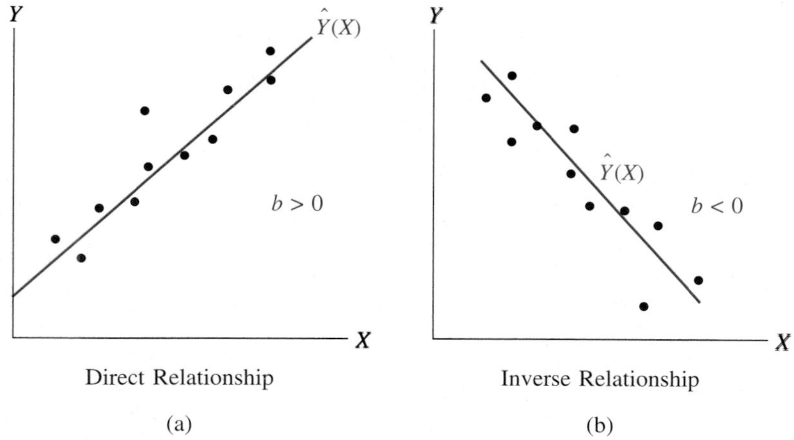

FIGURE 10-4 Properties of the regression line and possible relationships between variables.

values of X, so that the variables X and Y are **inversely related**. Examples of inverse relationships include remaining tire tread and miles driven, crop damage by insects and the quantity of insecticide applied, and the typical economic demand curve where quantity demanded decreases as price increases.

FITTING A STRAIGHT LINE TO THE DATA

How do we determine which particular regression line to use? One simple procedure would be to use our judgment in positioning a straightedge until it appears to summarize the linear pattern of the scatter diagram, and then draw the line. We can find the equation of this regression line by reading its Y intercept and slope directly from the graph. Although this procedure may be adequate for some applications, estimates of Y obtained in this way are often crude. A major drawback to using freehand methods in fitting a line is that two persons will usually draw different lines to represent the same data. Freehand fitting can therefore create unnecessary controversy about the conclusions of the data analysis. Another serious objection is that statistical methodology cannot be used to qualify the estimation errors (by confidence limits, for instance).

These difficulties can be overcome by using a statistical method to fit the line to the data. The most common technique is the **method of least squares**, which we will discuss in Section 10-3. From many different viewpoints, this procedure provides the best possible fit to a set of data and thereby the best possible predictions.

EXERCISES

10-1 On graph paper, plot the following regression lines and indicate whether X and Y are directly or inversely related.
(a) $\hat{Y}(X) = -5 + 2X$ (b) $\hat{Y}(X) = 5 + 3X$ (c) $\hat{Y}(X) = 20 - 2X$

10-2 An economist has established that personal income X may be used to predict personal consumption Y by the relationship $\hat{Y}(X) = -24.0 + .94X$ (billions

of dollars). For each of the following levels of personal income, calculate the predicted value for personal consumption.
(a) \$300 billion (b) \$500 billion (c) \$700 billion.

10-3 The following data represent the years in practice and the annual income (thousands of dollars) for a random sample of certified public accountants.

Years	Income	Years	Income
5	40	3	20
15	40	6	30
24	90	12	30
16	70	27	70
19	60	13	50

Treat income as the dependent variable.
(a) Plot the scatter diagram for the data.
(b) The following estimated regression lines have been recommended. Plot each line on your graph.
(1) $\hat{Y}(X) = 0 + 1X$ (3) $\hat{Y}(X) = 100 - 3X$
(2) $\hat{Y}(X) = 40 + 0X$ (4) $\hat{Y}(X) = 20 + 2X$
(c) Which regression line appears to provide the best fit?

10-4 Consider the two variables, family savings and income. For each of the following studies, indicate which of these two variables would be independent and which would be dependent.
(a) A bank wishes to predict the increase in its time deposits due to a 10% increase in the salaries of state employees, whose incomes are known.
(b) A mutual fund wishes to use its customers' stock purchases (a form of savings) to predict their incomes. This information will be used by salespersons to identify leads for increased business.
(c) An economist wishes to forecast increases in savings due to inflationary wage settlements.

10-2 CORRELATION ANALYSIS

Regression analysis provides an equation for estimating the value of one variable from the value of another variable. Correlation analysis is used to measure the *degree* to which two variables are related—to show how closely two variables can move together.

Correlation analysis is a useful auxiliary tool in regression analysis, because it can indicate how well the regression line explains the relationship between variables. Correlation is used instead of regression when the only question is how strongly two variables are related. One application is isolating statistically related characteristics of a population to explain their differences. For example, a pharmacologist may wish to identify the chemicals that can be formulated into a drug to alleviate various symptoms of a particular disease, such as anemia, pain, and poor appetite. A high positive correlation between dosage X of a specific chemical and appetite Y (measured by the quantity of food consumed) may make the chemical a good candidate for inclusion in the final drug.

Illustration: Baseball Superstar Salaries and Performance

We again use the baseball superstar data first introduced in Chapter 6. Figure 10-5 shows scatter diagrams of selected variables from the data set in Table 10-2, which gives various performance statistics for players paid salaries of at least $2,000,000 in the 1991 baseball season. The positively sloping regression line in

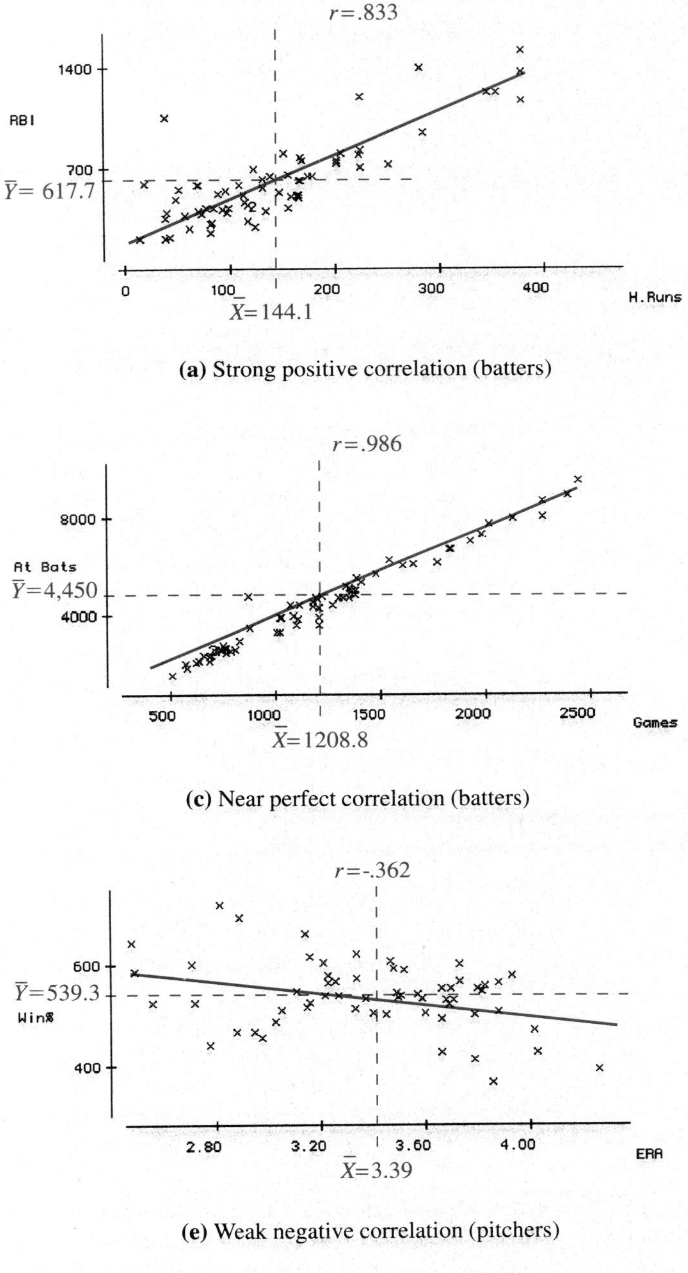

(a) Strong positive correlation (batters)

(c) Near perfect correlation (batters)

(e) Weak negative correlation (pitchers)

FIGURE 10-5 Scatter diagrams and correlations for baseball superstars. (Graphs generated with Minitab®.)

(a) points up, since a player's runs batted in (RBI) ordinarily increase as his number of home runs becomes greater. A different set of variables X and Y applies to the negatively sloping line in (e). That line points down, reflecting the tendency for a pitcher's winning percentage to drop as his earned run average (ERA) rises

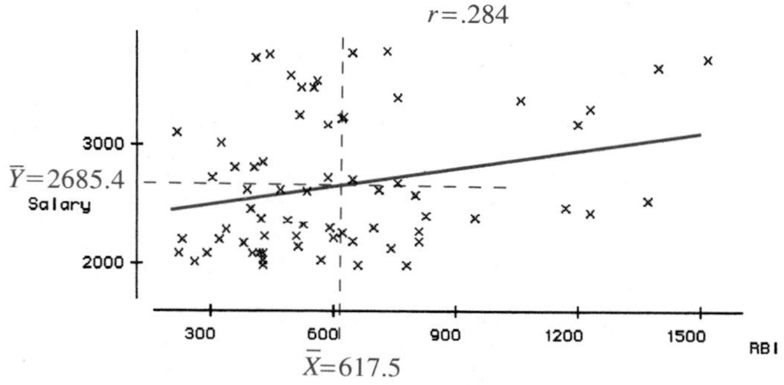

(b) Weak positive correlation (batters)

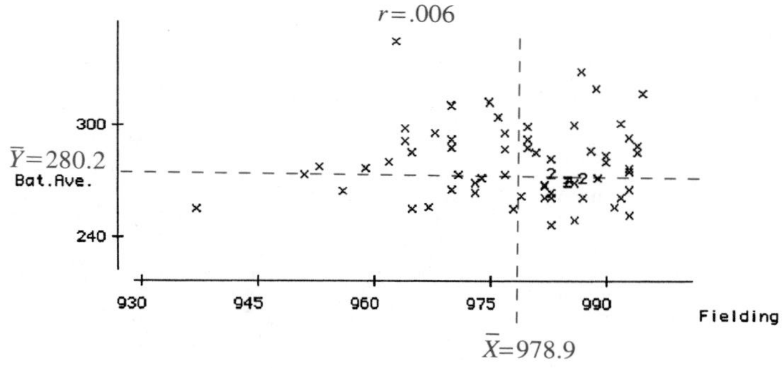

(d) Near zero correlation (batters)

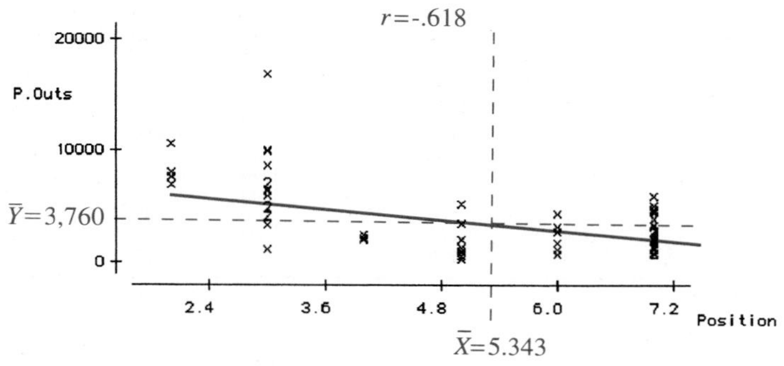

(f) Strong negative correlation (batters)

FIGURE 10-5 (con't)

TABLE 10-2 Baseball Superstar Data for Players Having 1991 Salaries of at Least $2,000,000

1 Player	2 Salary ($1,000)	3 Card Price	4 Position	5 Games	6 At Bats or Innings	7 Bat. Ave. or ERA	8 RBI or Win%	9 Runs or S. Outs	10 Fielding or Walks	11 Home Runs	12 Put Outs
1 Larry Anderson	2,000	6.00	1	534	819.67	3.15	516	589	254	0	0
2 Kevin Bass	2,000	1.25	7	1,008	3,349	274	428	426	983	85	1,694
3 George Bell	2,150	9.00	7	1,181	4,528	286	740	641	965	202	2,018
4 Bert Blyleven	2,000	60.00	1	667	4,837.33	3.27	540	3,631	1,293	0	0
5 Mike Boddicker	3,167	2.00	1	273	1,802.33	3.66	554	1,180	610	0	0
6 Wade Boggs	2,750	35.00	5	1,338	5,153	346	586	912	963	70	1,468
7 Barry Bonds	2,300	4.00	7	717	2,601	265	337	468	983	117	1,605
8 Bobby Bonilla	2,400	3.00	3	761	2,717	279	426	408	953	98	1,219
9 George Brett	3,675	200.00	5	2,279	8,692	311	1,398	1,382	970	281	5,277
10 Hubie Brooks	2,317	2.50	7	1,351	5,082	274	700	561	951	123	1,600
11 Tom Browning	2,650	2.00	1	220	1,439	3.73	604	774	389	0	0
12 Tom Brunansky	2,650	2.50	7	1,376	4,943	248	712	659	983	224	2,818
13 Tim Burke	2,328	.25	1	388	554.33	2.48	645	370	175	0	0
14 Brett Butler	2,833	2.50	7	1,360	5,001	285	362	850	990	39	3,423
15 Ivan Calderon	2,215	1.00	7	660	2,433	273	323	356	974	81	1,283
16 Tom Candiotti	2,500	.25	1	179	1,166.67	3.69	522	711	388	0	0
17 Jose Canseco	3,500	50.00	7	699	2,644	270	525	425	973	165	1,243
18 Joe Carter	3,792	15.00	3	1,024	3,941	262	646	541	982	175	3,467
19 Jack Clark	3,400	20.00	3	1,773	6,109	270	1,060	1,011	986	38	7,016
20 Will Clark	3,775	5.00	3	736	2,700	302	447	452	992	117	6,588
21 Roger Clemens	2,700	13.00	1	206	1,513	2.89	695	1,424	425	0	0
22 Vince Coleman	3,113	1.50	7	878	3,535	265	217	566	973	15	1,660
23 David Cone	2,350	2.75	1	132	784.67	3.14	663	725	276	0	0
24 Kal Daniels	2,025	6.00	7	507	1,665	300	262	316	980	81	817
25 Ron Darling	2,067	5.00	1	240	1,517.67	3.48	595	1,090	586	0	0
26 Danny Darwin	3,250	.70	1	488	1,913.33	3.40	505	1,265	581	0	0
27 Chili Davis	2,000	1.25	7	874	4,720	267	659	652	970	156	2,553
28 Eric Davis	3,600	15.00	7	767	2,572	272	499	515	985	166	1,709
29 Glenn Davis	3,275	2.00	3	830	3,032	262	518	427	992	166	6,951
30 Mark Davis	3,625	1.50	1	469	927	3.86	368	827	392	0	0
31 Storm Davis	2,367	.70	1	265	1,431	3.93	579	831	523	0	0
32 Andre Dawson	3,325	45.00	7	2,018	7,785	283	1,231	1,130	983	346	4,569
33 Jose DeLeon	2,367	.08	1	233	1,417	3.79	415	1,225	636	0	0
34 Jim Deshaies	2,100	.25	1	155	948	3.50	538	638	358	0	0
35 Bill Doran	2,833	.80	4	1,182	4,323	269	409	621	982	70	2,281
36 Doug Drabek	3,350	1.00	1	157	1,003	3.21	605	577	271	0	0
37 Shawon Dunston	2,100	3.00	6	758	2,768	257	290	340	967	61	1,349
38 Len Dykstra	2,217	2.50	7	783	2,628	281	232	432	990	43	1,728
39 Dennis Eckersly	3,100	20.00	1	604	2,815.33	3.49	547	1,938	659	0	0
40 Nick Esasky	2,100	.70	3	810	2,703	250	427	336	986	122	4,180
41 Steve Farr	2,400	.30	1	320	627	3.33	514	512	249	0	0
42 Sid Fernandez	2,167	6.00	1	199	1,212.33	3.26	569	1,153	491	0	0
43 Tony Fernandez	2,100	6.00	6	1,028	3,952	289	404	510	980	40	1,786
44 Chuck Finley	2,500	.90	1	152	767	3.20	539	544	311	0	0
45 Carlton Fisk	2,455	150.00	2	2,278	8,055	272	1,231	1,220	987	354	10,660
46 John Franco	2,633	1.50	1	448	595.67	2.49	588	423	231	0	0
47 Julio Franco	2,313	6.00	4	1,221	4,720	297	593	680	968	69	2,086
48 Gary Gaetti	2,700	5.00	5	1,361	4,989	256	758	646	965	201	1,166
49 Andres Galarraga	2,485	3.50	3	740	2,707	276	400	360	993	97	6,377
50 Scott Garrelts	2,400	.90	1	344	939.67	3.23	567	695	404	0	0
51 Dwight Gooden	2,467	9.00	1	211	1,523.67	2.82	721	1,391	449	0	0
52 Mike Greenwell	2,650	2.75	7	635	2,256	313	388	326	975	73	1,006
53 Kevin Gross	2,217	.35	1	265	1,469.33	4.02	471	996	583	0	0
54 Kelly Gruber	3,033	8.00	5	686	2,219	266	326	321	956	83	498
55 Mark Gubicza	2,667	1.00	1	215	1,407.33	3.57	543	921	540	0	0
56 Pedro Guerrero	2,283	10.00	3	1,378	4,819	305	812	679	976	206	4,795
57 Tony Gwynn	2,388	20.00	7	1,201	4,651	329	488	696	987	49	2,534
58 Von Hayes	2,200	2.00	7	1,324	4,658	272	646	689	987	139	5,144
59 Dave Henderson	2,625	2.00	7	1,205	3,915	262	537	559	983	147	2,676
60 Rickey Henderson	3,250	200.00	7	1,608	6,013	293	622	1,290	980	166	4,016
61 Tom Henke	2,967	1.25	1	381	517	2.72	527	596	165	0	0
62 Orel Hershiser	3,167	5.00	1	235	1,482.33	2.71	604	1,027	438	0	0
63 Ted Higuera	2,750	1.00	1	181	1,255	3.34	622	986	381	0	0
64 Kent Hrbek	2,600	6.00	3	1,299	4,670	290	803	685	994	223	10,127

(because a higher percentage of runs is given up). Notice that in some diagrams the data scatter adheres closely to the regression line, while in others there is a barely discernable pattern or none apparent.

Before we discuss the details for fitting the regression line in Section 10-3, it will be helpful to first introduce the associated statistical measure.

TABLE 10-2 Continued

1 Player	2 Salary ($1,000)	3 Card Price	4 Position	5 Games	6 At Bats or Innings	7 Bat. Ave. or ERA	8 RBI or Win%	9 Runs or S. Outs	10 Fielding or Walks	11 Home Runs	12 Put Outs
65 Danny Jackson	2,625	2.50	1	196	1,206.33	3.66	493	737	473	0	0
66 Howard Johnson	2,242	10.00	5	1,023	3,395	256	512	516	937	159	714
67 Wally Joyner	2,100	.80	3	703	2,657	286	422	759	994	93	6,061
68 Jimmie Key	2,217	1.00	1	251	1,269.67	3.47	608	702	301	0	0
69 Mark Langston	3,550	2.25	1	233	1,597.67	3.88	508	1,448	772	0	0
70 Barry Larkin	2,100	.80	6	572	2,125	293	221	314	970	38	846
71 Craig Lefferts	2,042	.20	1	528	762.33	2.95	470	482	227	0	0
72 Charlie Leibrandt	2,183	.50	1	300	1,735	3.71	532	800	513	0	0
73 Greg Maddux	2,425	2.00	1	140	911	3.68	531	540	319	0	0
74 Dennis Martinez	3,348	2.00	1	460	2,711.33	3.82	549	1,423	804	0	0
75 Don Mattingly	3,420	30.00	3	1,117	4,416	317	759	655	995	169	8,769
76 Kirk McCaskill	2,100	.35	1	162	1,043.33	3.80	553	643	382	0	0
77 Roger McDowell	2,200	.40	1	396	611.33	3.05	512	299	211	0	0
78 Willie McGee	3,563	4.00	7	1,193	4,698	297	560	650	977	52	2,744
79 Fred McGriff	2,750	1.00	3	578	1,944	278	305	348	993	125	4,161
80 Mark McGwire	2,875	3.00	3	623	2,173	253	429	355	993	156	4,913
81 Kevin McReynolds	2,267	7.00	7	1,089	3,997	270	621	550	985	167	2,353
82 Kevin Mitchell	3,750	3.00	5	688	2,378	278	412	369	959	135	953
83 Paul Molitor	3,253	50.00	5	1,540	6,246	299	626	1,053	964	131	2,115
84 Jack Morris	3,700	6.00	1	430	3,043.33	3.73	569	1,980	1,086	0	0
85 Dale Murphy	2,500	60.00	7	1,983	7,312	268	1,171	1,125	982	378	5,997
86 Eddie Murray	2,562	45.00	3	2,135	7,997	294	1,373	1,210	993	379	17,030
87 Randy Myers	2,000	.50	1	251	326.67	2.56	525	362	135	0	0
88 Pete O'Brien	2,038	.70	3	1,209	4,271	267	569	526	993	131	9,972
89 Lance Parrish	2,417	30.00	2	1,656	6,066	257	947	765	991	285	8,166
90 Tony Pena	2,350	2.50	2	1,350	4,676	273	528	500	989	89	7,668
91 Pascual Perez	2,100	2.50	1	193	1,170.33	3.45	504	781	320	0	0
92 Dan Plesac	2,267	.30	1	276	353	2.98	458	333	112	0	0
93 Kirby Puckett	3,192	15.00	7	1,070	4,395	320	586	624	989	108	2,915
94 Tim Raines	3,500	9.00	7	1,405	5,305	301	552	934	986	96	2,782
94 Jeff Reardon	2,608	1.25	1	694	943.33	3.03	488	755	320	0	0
96 Dave Righetti	2,500	2.50	1	522	1,136	3.11	548	940	473	0	0
97 Jose Rijo	2,613	1.00	1	193	872	3.60	505	753	399	0	0
98 Cal Ripkin Jr.	2,433	18.00	6	1,476	5,655	274	828	871	977	225	4,469
99 Jeff Russell	2,450	.20	1	277	778	4.03	430	476	303	0	0
100 Nolan Ryan	3,300	1,400.00	1	740	4,990.33	3.16	526	5,308	2,614	0	0
101 Bret Saberhagen	2,950	5.00	1	224	1,464	3.23	581	957	286	0	0
102 Ryne Sandberg	2,725	45.00	4	1,389	5,508	287	649	872	988	179	2,606
103 Scott Sanderson	2,175	.30	1	343	1,826.33	3.59	535	1,209	478	0	0
104 Mike Scioscia	2,183	7.00	2	1,205	3,680	262	382	340	987	57	7,017
105 Mike Scott	2,337	10.00	1	345	2,061	3.51	539	1,466	623	0	0
106 Ruben Sierra	2,650	3.50	7	748	2,882	274	470	395	971	114	1,378
107 Bryn Smith	2,133	.25	1	310	1,541.67	3.37	533	916	371	0	0
108 Lee Smith	2,792	1.25	1	650	919.33	2.88	470	923	363	0	0
109 Lonnie Smith	2,042	3.00	7	1,269	4,377	292	427	772	964	77	2,085
110 Ozzie Smith	2,225	45.00	6	1,926	7,019	256	600	910	978	19	3,237
111 Zane Smith	2,225	.35	1	223	1,116.33	3.66	429	652	435	0	0
112 Dave Stewart	3,500	12.00	1	393	1,827.67	3.52	591	1,202	677	0	0
113 Dave Stieb	3,000	10.00	1	390	2,667	3.34	574	1,557	937	0	0
114 Darryl Strawberry	3,800	18.00	7	1,109	3,903	263	733	662	979	252	2,054
115 Rick Sutcliffe	2,275	3.25	1	357	2,130.67	3.83	559	1,412	856	0	0
116 Greg Swindell	2,025	1.00	1	120	805	3.88	567	587	195	0	0
117 Danny Tartabull	2,250	6.00	7	691	2,435	281	435	357	962	121	913
118 Bobby Thigpen	2,417	1.00	1	277	382.33	2.78	444	251	141	0	0
119 Alan Trammell	2,200	50.00	6	1,835	6,702	288	810	1,009	977	152	2,880
120 Andy Van Slyke	2,160	3.00	7	1,098	3,632	270	516	530	985	113	2,626
121 Frank Viola	3,167	10.00	1	307	2,107.67	3.7	555	1,469	608	0	0
122 Bob Welch	3,450	15.00	1	396	2,512.33	3.16	618	1,714	801	0	0
123 Lou Whitaker	2,000	20.00	5	1,827	6,693	274	781	1,040	983	167	3,581
124 Dave Winfield	3,750	50.00	7	2,401	8,896	286	1,516	1,384	981	378	4,668
125 Mike Witt	2,417	.80	1	330	2,062	3.79	502	1,343	690	0	0
126 Matt Young	2,267	.15	1	264	956	4.26	395	666	413	0	0
127 Robin Yount	3,200	200.00	7	2,449	9,494	289	1,201	1,433	970	225	4,827

Source: *New York Times, The Sporting News Official Baseball Register—1991*, and *Sports Collectors Digest Baseball Card Pocket Price Guide.*

THE CORRELATION COEFFICIENT

The direction and overall strength of the linear relationship between X and Y is summarized by the **correlation coefficient**, denoted by the letter r. A strong correlation of $r = .833$ applies in diagram (a) of Figure 10-5, where a player's RBI Y is plotted against his number of home runs X. When two variables are highly correlated, the regression line will provide good predictions of Y using only the known level for X, so that the number of home runs could be used in arriving at accurate forecasts of a player's RBI.

Figure 10-5(b) displays data for variables having a much looser linear fit. There, a batter's salary is the Y and his RBI is now the X; a much lower correlation of $r = .284$ applies. The weak correlation suggests that RBI would not be a very accurate predictor of salary. The data in diagram (c), where number of at bats Y is related to the number of games played X, scatter very tightly about the regression line. The correlation coefficient for (c) is $r = .986$, which is very close to the maximum that r might achieve. A **perfect correlation** is achieved when $r = 1$, in which case all data points would fall exactly on the regression line.

The complete lack of correlation is reflected when $r = 0$. A **zero correlation** is almost reached in Figure 10-5(d), where a player's batting average Y has only an $r = .006$ correlation with his fielding percentage X. There is essentially no statistical relationship between the two variables, and the regression line is flat. Therefore, fielding percentage appears to be worthless in predicting batting average.

The correlation coefficient can be negative, as in Figure 10-5(e), in which the regression line has a negative slope. There a pitcher's winning percentage is the Y and his earned run average (ERA) is the X, which provide a correlation coefficient of $r = -.362$. The negative value reflects that winning pitchers tend to give up fewer runs.

The slope of the regression line and correlation coefficient always have the same sign. The computed value for r always falls between -1 and $+1$.

COMPUTING THE CORRELATION COEFFICIENT

The correlation coefficient may be computed by establishing for each data point a collective measure of the distance separating it from the respective sample means, computed in the usual manner:

$$\bar{X} = \frac{\sum X}{n} \quad \text{and} \quad \bar{Y} = \frac{\sum Y}{n}$$

To illustrate, we will use the scatter diagram in Figure 10-6, which relates RBI Y to home runs X. Consider the player Dave Winfield, who is the 66th batter in the superstar data set. The distances of the data point (X_{66}, Y_{66}) from the respective means are the differences $(X_{66} - \bar{X})$ and $(Y_{66} - \bar{Y})$. A collective distance measure is the product of these

$$(X_{66} - \bar{X})(Y_{66} - \bar{Y})$$

The above product is the area of the rectangle having Dave Winfield at one corner and the point $(\bar{X}, \bar{Y})$ diagonal to it. The $(X - \bar{X})$ and $(Y - \bar{Y})$ differences computed for some players will be negative, if their points lie to the left or below $(\bar{X}, \bar{Y})$.

If you imagine the dashed line at $\bar{X}$ as the north-south axis and the dashed line at $\bar{Y}$ as the east-west axis, then the distance products will be negative for data points lying in the northwest and southeast quadrants and positive for points in

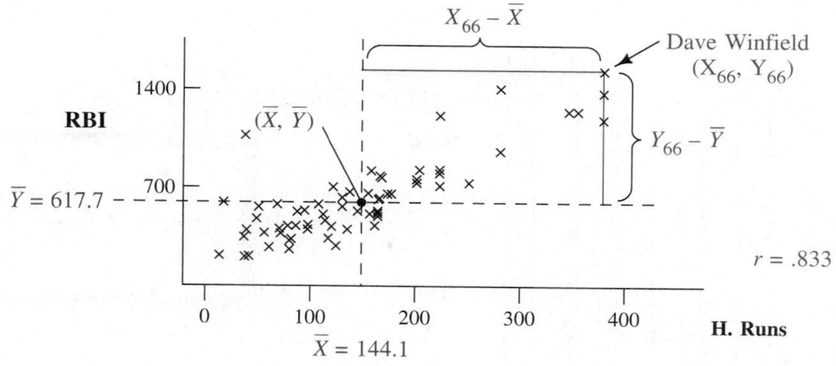

FIGURE 10-6 Scatter diagram for baseball superstar RBI and home runs.

the northeast and southwest quadrants. Positively correlated variables have data points lying predominantly in the northeast and southwest, while negatively correlated ones fall mainly in the northwest and southeast.

The correlation coefficient is based on the average of all distance products. But the distances themselves must be adjusted for scale before determining r. Otherwise, a very big average distance product would be obtained for major league baseball players, and the resulting value could be thousands of times greater than the counterpart measure for younger minor league batters.

All distances are adjusted by dividing by the respective *standard deviations.* These are computed in the usual fashion from the data values separately for each variable:

$$s_X = \sqrt{\frac{\sum (X - \bar{X})^2}{n - 1}} = \sqrt{\frac{\sum X^2 - n\bar{X}^2}{n - 1}}$$

and

$$s_Y = \sqrt{\frac{\sum (Y - \bar{Y})^2}{n - 1}} = \sqrt{\frac{\sum Y^2 - n\bar{Y}^2}{n - 1}}$$

The subscripts X and Y are needed to distinguish between the two variables.

The following transformed distances

$$\frac{(X - \bar{X})}{s_X} \quad \text{and} \quad \frac{(Y - \bar{Y})}{s_Y}$$

are then averaged to compute the correlation coefficient.

$$r = \frac{\sum \left[\frac{(X - \bar{X})}{s_X}\right]\left[\frac{(Y - \bar{Y})}{s_Y}\right]}{n - 1}$$

The following equivalent expression is used to compute the

CORRELATION COEFFICIENT

$$r = \frac{\sum (X - \bar{X})(Y - \bar{Y})}{(n - 1)s_X s_Y}$$

Since the numerator is equal to

$$\sum (X - \bar{X})(Y - \bar{Y}) = \sum XY - n\bar{X}\bar{Y}$$

the following equivalent expression may also be used.

$$r = \frac{\sum XY - n\bar{X}\bar{Y}}{(n - 1)s_X s_Y}$$

When the sample standard deviations are not computed separately, the following expression can also be used.

$$r = \frac{\sum XY - n\bar{X}\bar{Y}}{\sqrt{\left(\sum X^2 - n\bar{X}^2\right)\left(\sum Y^2 - n\bar{Y}^2\right)}}$$

(As we shall see, an alternative procedure is sometimes used to find r using information obtained during regression analysis.)

EXAMPLE: PRICE OF ROOKIE BASEBALL CARD AND PLAYER SALARY

Although a player's *salary* ordinarily expresses his worth to the club's *owner*, an alternative objective measure of worth might apply to the *fans*. We use the player's *rookie baseball card price*. Consider the following superstars having a rookie card valued at least $100 in 1991.

Superstar	Price of Rookie Card	Salary (thousands)
9 George Brett	$ 200	$3,675
45 Carlton Fisk	100	2,455
60 Rickey Henderson	200	3,250
100 Nolan Ryan	1,400	3,300
127 Robin Yount	200	3,200

We will designate price of rookie card as X and the salary as Y, and calculate the correlation coefficient.

SOLUTION: Using $n = 5$, the following calculations apply.

Card Price X	Salary Y	$(X - \bar{X})$	$(\bar{X} - \bar{X})^2$	$(Y - \bar{Y})$	$(Y - \bar{Y})^2$	$(X - \bar{X})(Y - \bar{Y})$
200	3,675	−220	48,400	499	249,001	−109,780
100	2,455	−320	102,400	−721	519,841	230,700
200	3,250	−220	48,400	74	5,476	−16,280
1,400	3,300	980	960,400	124	15,376	121,520
200	3,200	−220	48,400	24	576	−5,280
2,100	15,880	0	1,208,000	0	790,270	220,900

$$\bar{X} = \frac{2{,}100}{5} = 420$$

$$\bar{Y} = \frac{15{,}880}{5} = 3{,}176$$

$$s_X = \sqrt{\frac{\sum (X - \bar{X})^2}{n - 1}} = \sqrt{\frac{1{,}208{,}000}{5 - 1}} = 549.55$$

$$s_Y = \sqrt{\frac{\sum (Y - \bar{Y})^2}{n - 1}} = \sqrt{\frac{790{,}270}{5 - 1}} = 444.49$$

$$r = \frac{\sum (X - {}^{-}X)(Y - \bar{Y})}{(n - 1)s_X s_Y} = \frac{220{,}900}{(5 - 1)(549.55)(444.49)} = .226$$

Although it is not surprising that r is positive, the correlation is a weak one. For these five superstars, owner and fan player valuations are not strongly associated.

Regression or correlation analyses are usually performed using sample data. Inferences may then be made regarding the parent population. The population counterpart to r is the *population* correlation coefficient ρ. That parameter may be estimated using the value for r computed from sample data.

COMPUTING THE CORRELATION COEFFICIENT USING A COMPUTER

The correlation coefficient is ordinarily found using computer assistance. Figure 10-7 shows the correlations for all the baseball superstar batters computed using Minitab.

EXERCISES

10-5 Horatio Dull is a statistics instructor who wants to find the correlation between his students' homework point totals and their average examination scores. The following results have been obtained for a random sample of five students.

Homework Point Total X	Average Examination Score Y
140	90
80	80
90	60
150	80
110	70

```
MTB > Correlation c1-c12.
```

	Player	Salary	Card Pr.	Position	Games	At Bats	Bat.Ave.	RBI
Salary	-0.039							
Card Pr.	0.106	0.308						
Position	-0.013	0.001	0.026					
Games	0.298	0.156	0.654	-0.027				
At Bats	0.276	0.182	0.666	0.012	0.986			
Bat.Ave.	-0.004	0.174	0.216	0.098	0.113	0.166		
RBI	0.203	0.284	0.595	-0.094	0.878	0.881	0.101	
Runs	0.250	0.268	0.735	0.064	0.923	0.942	0.270	0.825
Fielding	0.120	0.067	-0.035	-0.302	0.079	0.057	0.006	0.090
H.Runs	0.181	0.244	0.458	-0.098	0.604	0.603	-0.096	0.833
P.Outs	0.180	0.047	0.245	-0.618	0.455	0.426	0.014	0.534

	Runs	Fielding	H.Runs
Fielding	0.075		
H.Runs	0.573	0.124	
P.Outs	0.375	0.597	0.488

FIGURE 10-7 Minitab output showing correlations between all possible variable pairs for baseball superstar batters.

Calculate the correlation coefficient for the data.

10-6 The following data obtained for sample households in Dogpatch relate the size of the family X to the annual usage Y of a cleaning agent.

Family size X	Bottles Used Y	Family size X	Bottles Used Y
5	2	4	2
8	3	5	3
7	4	5	2
3	2	6	4
2	1	7	5

Calculate the correlation coefficient for the data.

10-7 There are only four baseball superstar catchers listed in Table 10-2. These are indicated by the value 2 as the position in column (4). Compute for the catchers the correlation coefficients for each of the following variable pairs.

(a) Y = salary (2) and X = rookie baseball card price (3)

(b) Y = games played (5) and X = number of putouts (12)

(c) Y = rookie baseball card price (3) and X = number of home runs (11)

10-8 For each of the following situations, indicate whether a correlation analysis, a regression analysis, or both would be appropriate. In each case, give the reasons for your choice.

(a) To choose advertising media, an agency account executive is investigating the relationship between a woman's age and her annual expenditures on a client firm's cosmetics.

(b) A trucker wishes to establish a decision rule that will enable him to determine when to inspect or replace his tires, based on the number of miles driven.

(c) A government agency wishes to identify which field offices of various sizes (based on number of employees) do not conform to the prevailing pattern of working days lost due to illness.

(d) A research firm conducts attitude surveys in two stages. The first stage identifies coincident factors, such as age and income. The second stage is more detailed and involves a separate study to predict the values of one variable using the known values of other variables associated with it in the initial stage.

10-3 FINDING THE REGRESSION EQUATION

An estimated regression line should fit the sample data. To accomplish this, statisticians use a procedure called the method of least squares.

THE METHOD OF LEAST SQUARES

We will begin by applying the method of least squares to our previous parts supplier's data, which are again plotted in Figure 10-8. The least-squares criterion requires that a line be chosen to fit our data so that the *sum of the squares of the vertical deviations separating the points from the line will be a minimum*. The deviations are represented by the lengths of vertical line segments that connect the points to the estimated regression line in the scatter diagram.

To explain how this procedure may be interpreted, we investigate the shipment to Jones & Sons at a distance of $X = 490$ miles from the supplier's plant. Our data (page 408) show that $Y = 8$ days were required for the shipment to arrive. This transportation time is represented on the graph by the vertical distance to the corresponding data point along the dashed line from the X axis at $X = 490$. The predicted or estimated transportation time for the *next* shipment to Jones & Sons equals the vertical distance all the way up to the regression line, a total of $\hat{Y}(X) = \hat{Y}(490) = 8.4$ days. The difference between the observed transportation time, $Y = 8$ days, and the predicted value for Y is the deviation $Y - \hat{Y}(X) = Y - \hat{Y}(490) = 8 - 8.4 = -.4$ days. This is represented by the colored vertical line segment connecting the point to the regression line. Because the observed value of Y lies below the predicted value, a negative deviation is obtained; if the observed Y lay above the line, the deviation would be positive. The vertical deviation represents the amount of *error associated with using the regression line to predict* a future shipment's transportation time. We want to find the values of a and b that will minimize the sum of the squares of these vertical deviations (or prediction errors).

One reason for minimizing the sum of the *squared* vertical deviations is that some of the deviations are negative and others are positive. For any set of data, a great many lines can be drawn for which the sum of the unsquared deviations is zero, but most of these lines would fit the data poorly.

The sum to be minimized is

$$\sum [Y - \hat{Y}(X)]^2 = \sum [Y - a - bX]^2$$

which involves two unknowns, a and b. Mathematically, it may be shown that

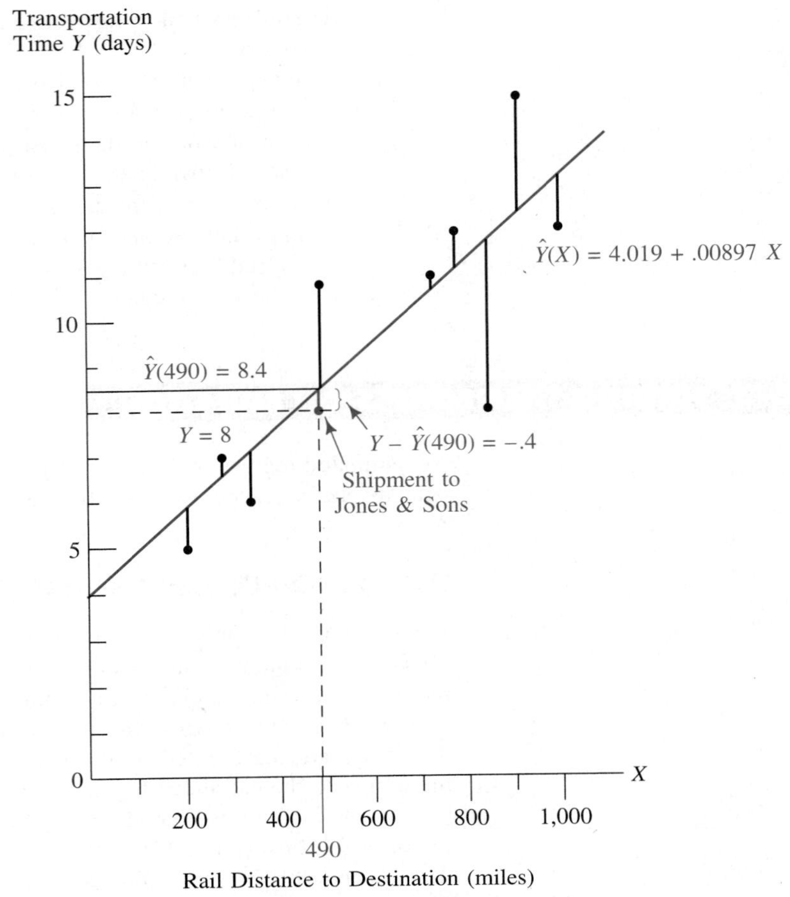

FIGURE 10-8 Fitting the regression line to the parts supplier's data using the method of least squares.

the required values must simultaneously satisfy the following expressions, referred to as the **normal equations**.*

$$\sum Y = na + b\sum X$$
$$\sum XY = a\sum X + b\sum X^2$$

Solving these equations algebraically gives us the following expression for b.

$$b = \frac{n\sum XY - \sum X \sum Y}{n\sum X^2 - (\sum X)^2}$$

We obtain the equation for a by substituting the value of b into the first normal equation. Then

$$a = \frac{1}{n}\left(\sum Y - b\sum X\right)$$

*The word *normal* as used here has nothing to do with the normal curve. Rather, *normal equations* receive their name from a mathematical property of linear algebra.

The expressions for a and b can be simplified further by using the mean values $\bar{X} = \left(\sum X\right)/n$ and $\bar{Y} = \left(\sum Y\right)/n$ to compute the

ESTIMATED REGRESSION COEFFICIENTS

$$b = \frac{\sum XY - n\bar{X}\bar{Y}}{\sum X^2 - n\bar{X}^2}$$

$$a = \bar{Y} - b\bar{X}$$

Note that b must be calculated before a.

The advantage of calculating a and b from these expressions is that every step involves computations with values of moderate size. Although this may increase the danger of rounding errors, such errors are usually negligible.

ILLUSTRATION OF THE METHOD

We are now ready to find the regression equation for the parts supplier's regression line obtained from the $n = 10$ observations. In order to evaluate the expressions for a and b, we must perform a set of intermediate calculations (shown in Table 10-3). To find b, we must calculate $\bar{X}$, $\bar{Y}$, $\sum XY$, and $\sum X^2$. Columns for the values of X, Y, XY, and X^2 are used for this purpose. An extra column for the squares of the dependent variable observations, Y^2, is computed for use in later

TABLE 10-3 Intermediate Calculations for Obtaining the Parts Supplier's Estimated Regression Line

(1) Customer	(2) Rail Distance to Destination X	(3) Transportation Time (days) Y	(4) XY	(5) X^2	(6) Y^2
1. Muller Auto Supply	210	5	1,050	44,100	25
2. Taylor Ford	290	7	2,030	84,100	49
3. Auto Supply House	350	6	2,100	122,500	36
4. Parts 'n Spares	480	11	5,280	230,400	121
5. Jones & Sons	490	8	3,920	240,100	64
6. A. Hausman	730	11	8,030	532,900	121
7. Des Moines Parts	780	12	9,360	608,400	144
8. Pete's Parts	850	8	6,800	722,500	64
9. Smith Dodge	920	15	13,800	846,400	225
10. Gulf Distributors	1,010	12	12,120	1,020,100	144
Totals	6,110 $= \sum X$	95 $= \sum Y$	64,490 $= \sum XY$	4,451,500 $= \sum X^2$	993 $= \sum Y^2$

$$\bar{X} = \frac{\sum X}{n} = \frac{6,110}{10} = 611.0 \qquad \bar{Y} = \frac{\sum Y}{n} = \frac{95}{10} = 9.5$$

discussions of the regression line. Using the intermediate values obtained, we can first find the value of b.

$$b = \frac{\sum XY - n\bar{X}\bar{Y}}{\sum X^2 - n\bar{X}^2} = \frac{64{,}490 - 10(611.0)(9.5)}{4{,}451{,}500 - 10(611.0)^2} = \frac{6{,}445}{718{,}290} = .00897$$

Substituting $b = .00897$, we obtain

$$\begin{aligned} a = \bar{Y} - b\bar{X} &= 9.500 - .00897(611.0) \\ &= 9.500 - 5.481 = 4.019 \end{aligned}$$

Thus, we have determined the following equation for the estimated regression line graphed in Figure 10-8.

$$\hat{Y}(X) = 4.019 + .00897X$$

We may now use the above regression equation to predict the transportation time $\hat{Y}(X)$ for a shipment of known rail distance X from the parts supplier's plant. For instance, when $X = 490$, we have

$$\begin{aligned} \hat{Y}(490) &= 4.019 + .00897(490) \\ &= 8.4 \text{ days} \end{aligned}$$

Thus, the prediction for the transportation time to a customer 490 miles away is $Y(490) = 8.4$ days. This is the same value previously read from the graph of the regression line in Figure 10-8.

The least-squares regression line has two important features. First, it goes through the point $(\bar{X}, \bar{Y})$ that corresponds to the mean of the X and Y observations. Second, the sum of the deviations of the Ys from the regression line is zero, or

$$\sum [Y - \hat{Y}(X)] = 0$$

Thus, the positive and negative deviations from the regression line cancel one another, so that the least-squares line goes through the center of the data scatter. This can be a useful check to determine if any miscalculations have been made in finding a and b.

MEANING AND USE OF THE REGRESSION LINE

Once the regression equation has been obtained, predictions or estimates of the dependent variable may be made. For purposes of planning, the parts supplier now has a basis for determining his order-filling priorities, so that there will be a reasonable chance that shipments will be received by customers at the required times. His estimated regression equation is $\hat{Y}(X) = 4.019 + .00897X$. The value $a = 4.019$ is an estimate of the Y intercept. An interpretation of this value is that about 4 days of "overhead" are built into all rail shipments. This roughly corresponds to the time a shipment spends in delivery to and from the railhead, being loaded and unloaded, and waiting between various stages of the shipping process. The slope $b = .00897$ reflects the impact of distance alone on the total transportation time. For each additional mile, an estimated .00897 day is added to the total time. Stated another way, each additional 100 miles of distance adds roughly .9 day to the transportation time. Note that b is positive, indicating that transportation time varies directly with distance—the greater the distance, the longer, on the average, it will take for a shipment to be delivered.

Knowing that Jones & Sons is 490 miles distant, the $\hat{Y}(490) = 8.4$ days may be used as a point estimate of the transportation time required for the shipment. But the proper interpretation of 8.4 days is that *on the average* all future shipments to Jones & Sons will require about this much time in transit. It is an average because the conditions existing for successive shipments to this customer will vary due to a host of factors, such as freight train schedules, total freight to be handled, loading and unloading conditions, and routing of the box car. The times will vary from shipment to shipment. In general, the dependent variable Y will vary for a given X. Furthermore, the same regression equation will be used for other customers at a 490-mile distance; shipments to these others may travel on roads having different characteristics. This leads us to the next important considerations of regression analysis.

MEASURING VARIABILITY IN RESULTS

The fundamental indication of variability provided by the sample data is the measure of the spread or scatter about the estimated regression line. As we have noted, estimates made from the regression line will be more precise when the data are less scattered. Thus, we can investigate the degree of scatter to determine an expression for the error involved making estimates through regression. We wish to employ a measure that fits naturally into the scheme of least-squares regression. Recall that we obtained the Y intercept a and the slope b of the regression line by minimizing $\sum [Y - \hat{Y}(X)]^2$, the *sum* of the squared deviations about the regression line. As we saw in selecting the fundamental measure of a population's variability, the variance is the average of the squared deviations from the mean. This suggests that we can select as our measure of variability the *mean* of the squared deviations about the regression line. The following expression applies.

$$\frac{\sum [Y - \hat{Y}(X)]^2}{n}$$

The square root of the mean squared deviations is referred to as the **standard error of the estimate** about the regression line. As this suggests, we will use it to estimate the true variability in Y. For convenience, we will modify the preceding expression before taking its square root, using as our standard error of the estimate

$$s_{Y \cdot X} = \sqrt{\frac{\sum [Y - \hat{Y}(X)]^2}{n - 2}}$$

The subscript $Y \cdot X$ indicates that the deviations are about the regression line, which provides values of Y for given levels of X. We divide the sum of the squared deviations by $n - 2$, which will make $s^2_{Y \cdot X}$ an unbiased estimator of the true variance of the Y values about the regression line. We subtract 2 from n to indicate that 2 degrees of freedom are lost, since the values of a and b contained in the expression for $\hat{Y}(X)$ have been calculated from the same data.

The standard error of the estimate resembles the standard deviation calculated for the individual Ys.

$$s_Y = \sqrt{\frac{\sum (Y - \bar{Y})^2}{n - 1}} = \sqrt{\frac{\sum Y^2 - n\bar{Y}^2}{n - 1}}$$

Here, X does not appear in the subscript because s_Y makes no reference to the values of X. The sample standard deviation is the square root of the mean of the squared deviations about the center $\bar{Y}$ of the sample: $(Y - \bar{Y})^2$. Thus, s_Y represents the *total variability* in Y. Ordinarily, the deviations about $\bar{Y}$ are larger than their counterparts about the estimated regression line, so that s_Y will be larger than $s_{Y \cdot X}$. Figure 10-9 illustrates this concept. Note that s_Y and $s_{Y \cdot X}$ summarize the dispersions of separate sample frequency distributions.

To compute the standard error for our parts supplier regression, we first have to compute the estimated shipment time $\hat{Y}(X)$, plugging the distance X for each data point into the estimated regression equation. The resulting values are listed in column (4) of Table 10-4. Subtracting each $\hat{Y}(X)$ from its counterpart Y, the *residuals* $Y - \hat{Y}(X)$ in column (5) are then computed. Those quantities are squared

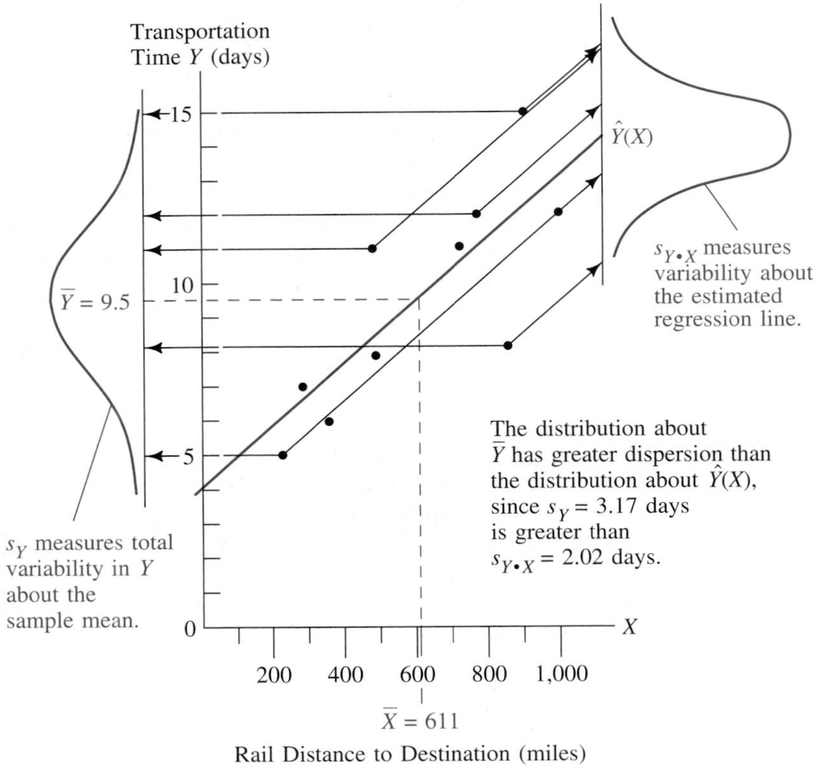

FIGURE 10-9 Illustration of the difference between total variability and variability about the estimated regression line.

TABLE 10-4 Preliminary Computations for Finding Standard Error of the Estimate for the Regression Analysis of the Parts Supplier's Data

(1) Customer	(2) Time Y	(3) Distance X	(4) $\hat{Y}(X) = 4.019 + .00897X$	(5) Residual $Y - \hat{Y}(X)$	(6) $[Y - \hat{Y}(X)]^2$
1	5	210	5.90	−.90	.8100
2	7	290	6.62	.38	.1444
3	6	350	7.16	−1.16	1.3456
4	11	480	8.32	2.68	7.1824
5	8	490	8.41	−.41	.1681
6	11	730	10.57	.43	.1849
7	12	780	11.01	.99	.9801
8	8	850	11.64	−3.64	13.2496
9	15	920	12.27	2.73	7.4529
10	12	1,010	13.08	−1.08	1.1664
				.02	32.6844

in column (6). Substituting the total of column (6) into the above expression, we have

$$s_{Y \cdot X} = \sqrt{\frac{32.6844}{10 - 2}} = 2.02$$

When knowledge of X is ignored, and no regression line is used, the total variability in Y is summarized by the sample standard deviation s_Y, which we calculate

$$s_Y = \sqrt{\frac{993 - 10(9.5)^2}{10 - 1}} = 3.17 \text{ days}$$

This value of s_Y is larger than the value found for $s_{Y \cdot X}$, reflecting the fact that the variability about the regression line is smaller than the total variation in Y. This is illustrated in Figure 10-9, where the underlying frequency curve for deviations about the estimated regression line is more compact than the one that might be constructed for the Ys without a knowledge of X. Thus, a prediction interval calculated using s_Y would be wider. (Section 10-5 discusses how those intervals are constructed.) A general conclusion is that *predictions tend to be more reliable and accurate when X is used as a predictor than when it is not.*

In calculating $s_{Y \cdot X}$, we sometimes use the following mathematically equivalent

SHORTCUT EXPRESSION FOR THE STANDARD ERROR OF THE ESTIMATE

$$s_{Y \cdot X} = \sqrt{\frac{\sum Y^2 - a\sum Y - b\sum XY}{n - 2}}$$

Using the values obtained previously for a and b and the intermediate calculations from Table 10-3, we have

$$s_{Y \cdot X} = \sqrt{\frac{993 - 4.019(95) - .00897(64{,}490)}{10 - 2}} = 2.02 \text{ days}$$

which is identical to the result found earlier.

COMPUTER-ASSISTED REGRESSION ANALYSIS

We have explained the procedures for finding a regression line using an example in which computations were made by hand with a calculator. In actual practice, most regressions involve such a volume of data that it is cumbersome to take this approach. For this reason, computers have been programmed to compute regression lines. Although the details of operation vary with the computer system and software package available, the essential features of a computer regression are provided in the *EasyStat* program for the IBM PC that accompanies this book. The following illustration provides an example of regression using a computer.

ILLUSTRATION: PREDICTING TIME NEEDED TO DUPLICATE REPORTS

A corporate headquarters uses a duplicating center for preparing copies of company reports. Based on the size of the job, the manager gives service requesters an estimated duplication completion time. In order to improve these projections, the manager requests the help of the statistical department.

Based on a sample of 20 jobs, an analyst obtained the following data.

Job i	Number of Copies X	Completion Time (minutes) Y	Job i	Number of Copies X	Completion Time (minutes) Y
1	150	2.9	11	500	4.2
2	310	3.9	12	200	3.4
3	450	3.9	13	50	.9
4	1,150	8.1	14	920	6.2
5	800	7.1	15	500	5.1
6	200	2.6	16	500	5.4
7	300	4.1	17	400	2.7
8	250	3.3	18	750	5.8
9	910	6.1	19	410	3.5
10	100	1.9	20	200	3.5

Figure 10-10 is a printout for the above regression data generated on a computer using *EasyStat*. The data in the two columns X and Y were first entered onto a computer spreadsheet. During data entry, *EasyStat* allows for backing up to fix errors and for final editing. The data can be saved on a file for retrieval at a later time.

EasyStat operates from a series of menus (not pictured). The first menu selection prints the original data as they appear on the spreadsheet. These values are listed in the top portion of the printout. The second menu selection informs *EasyStat* that column Y contains data for the dependent variable and that one independent variable has values listed in the first column. In an instant, *EasyStat* provides the results displayed in the bottom portion of Figure 10-10.

NO. COPIES X	TIME Y
150	2.9
310	3.9
450	3.9
1150	8.1
800	7.1
200	2.6
300	4.1
250	3.3
910	6.1
100	1.9
500	4.2
200	3.4
50	.9
920	6.2
500	5.1
500	5.4
400	2.7
750	5.8
410	3.5
200	3.5

REGRESSION RESULTS

Vari- able	Title	Regression Coefficient	Mean	Standard Deviation	Correl. X vs. Y	Standard Error
X1	NO. COPIES X	0.0054638 *b*	$\bar{X}$ 452.5	s_X 306.81513	0.9331339 *r*	0.0004962 s_b
Y2	TIME Y		$\bar{Y}$ 4.23	s_Y 1.7965171		

Intercept	1.75760926995 *a*
Standard Error of the Estimate	0.66359944416 $s_{Y \cdot X}$
Coefficient of Determination	0.87073878867 r^2

Note: Figure generated on an IBM PC using EasyStat.

FIGURE 10-10 Computer printout for the duplicating center illustration.

For convenience, all of the reported values are annotated in color with their symbol. The following regression equation (rounded) applies.

$$\hat{Y}(X) = 1.758 + .00546X$$

The standard error of the estimate is

$$s_{Y \cdot X} = .664$$

EasyStat generates a variety of other output in conjunction with regression. Popular software packages also provide similar information. Figure 10-11 is the scatter diagram obtained for the above data using *Minitab*. The regression line was inserted by hand. (Many software packages do not graphically display the estimated regression line. This is partly because the printers that are widely available do a poor job of printing diagonal lines.)

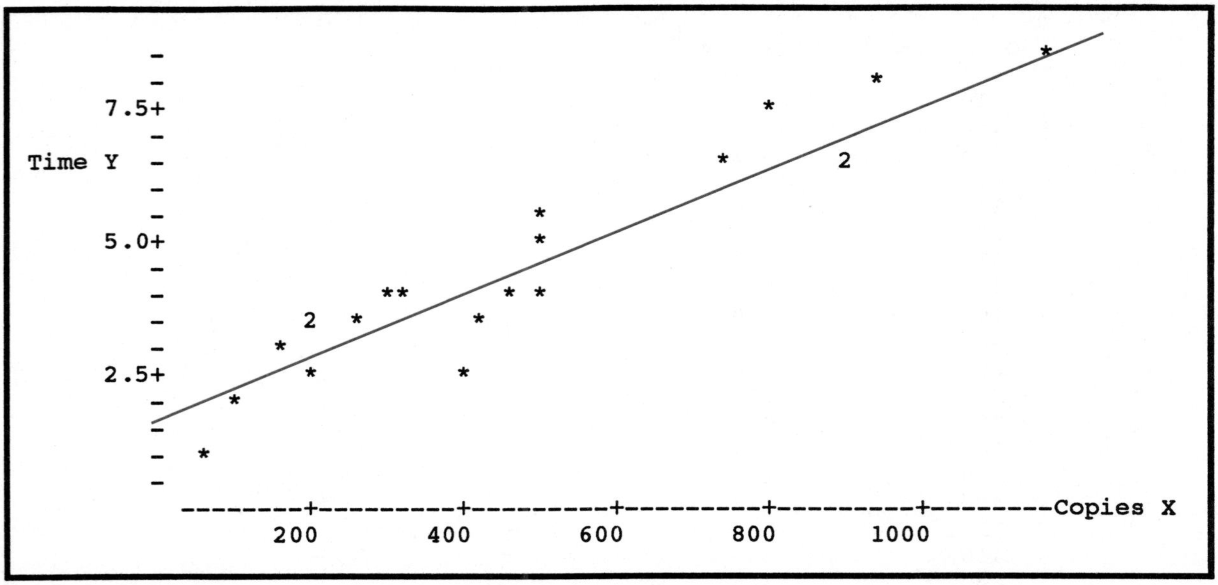

Note: Figure generated on an IBM PC using Minitab®.

FIGURE 10-11 Scatter diagram for the duplicating center illustration.

EXERCISES

10-9 Cost accountant Uriah Heap provided the following sample data for observations obtained during an investigation of the relationship between the volume of an ingredient X and the weight of a production batch Y.

Volume (liters) X	Weight (kilograms) Y	Volume (liters) X	Weight (kilograms) Y
10	61	25	102
24	110	6	38
13	75	10	42
7	47	16	75
9	78	15	91

(a) Determine the estimated regression equation.

(b) Compute, for batch weight, (1) the sample standard deviation and (2) the standard error of the estimate. Does a comparison of these two values indicate that the regression line would be useful in predicting batch weight? Why or why not?

10-10 A statistician for FlyMe Airlines wishes to determine the equation relating destination distance to freight charge for a standard-sized crate. The following data were obtained for a random sample of ten freight invoices.

Distance (hundreds of miles) X	Charge (to nearest dollar) Y
14	68
23	105
9	40
17	79
10	81
22	95
5	31
12	72
6	45
16	93

(a) Plot the scatter diagram for the data.
(b) Using the method of least squares, determine the equation for the estimated regression line.
(c) Check your calculations by computing $\sum [Y - \hat{Y}(X)]$. (Allowing for rounding errors, this should equal zero. If it does not, find your error.) Plot the regression line on your graph.

10-11 A floppy disk drive manufacturer has conducted a regression analysis to estimate the drive lifetime Y (hours) at various force settings X (grams). The regression equation $\hat{Y}(X) = 1{,}300 - 200X$ has been obtained for a sample of $n = 100$ drives that were played at different forces until they were worn out. The standard error of the estimate for drive lifetimes about this line is $s_{Y \cdot X} = 100$ hours.
(a) Plot the regression line on graph paper.
(b) State the meaning of the slope b of the regression line.
(c) Calculate $\hat{Y}(X)$ when $X = 1$, $X = 2$, $X = 3$ grams.

10-12 A food processing manager uses least-squares regression to predict the total cost of Crunchola production runs. The following data apply.

Production Quantity (tons) X	Total Cost (thousands of dollars) Y
400	200
150	85
220	115
500	200
300	140
100	65
150	70
150	65
240	125
350	190

(a) Using the method of least squares, determine the equation for the estimated regression line.
(b) State the meaning of the slope b and intercept a of the regression line.

(c) Using your answer to (a), calculate the predicted value of total cost per production run for the following quantities.
(1) 200 (2) 350 (3) 400

10-13 Consider the baseball superstar first-basemen in Table 10-2. These are identified in column (4) by position number 3. Determine, for the first-basemen only, the estimated regression equation for each of the following variable pairs.
(a) Y = salary (2) and X = number of runs (9)
(b) Y = price of rookie baseball card (3) and X = no. of games played (5)

10-14 Consider the baseball superstar shortstops in Table 10-2. These are identified in column (4) by position number 6. Determine, for the shortstops only, the estimated regression equation for each of the following variable pairs.
(a) Y = salary (2) and X = runs batted in (8)
(b) Y = price of rookie baseball card (3) and X = no. of home runs (11)

10-15 *Computer exercise.* A WaySafe market provided the following data for the number of arriving customers X per hour and the total hourly waiting time Y at the checkout counter.

Number of Customers X	Waiting Time (minutes) Y	Number of Customers X	Waiting Time (minutes) Y
105	44	435	208
511	214	275	138
401	193	55	34
622	299	128	73
330	143	97	52
211	112	187	103
332	155	266	110
322	131		

(a) Determine the estimated regression equation.
(b) Compute for total waiting time, (1) the sample standard deviation, and (2) the standard error of the estimate.

10-16 *Computer exercise.* Ace Widgets provided the following data for the time required to inspect outgoing batches of their deluxe model for various percentages of defective items.

Percentage Defective X	Inspection Time (minutes) Y	Percentage Defective X	Inspection Time (minutes) Y
17	48	10	49
9	50	14	55
12	43	18	63
7	36	19	55
8	45	6	36

(a) Plot the scatter diagram for the data.

(b) Determine the estimated regression equation, and plot the estimated regression line on your graph.
(c) Compute, for inspection time, (1) the sample standard deviation, and (2) the standard error of the estimate.

10-4 ASSUMPTIONS AND PROPERTIES OF LINEAR REGRESSION ANALYSIS

In Section 10-3, we were introduced to the mechanical process of fitting a regression line to the data. In this section, we will examine the assumptions and properties of the theoretical model for regression analysis.

ASSUMPTIONS OF LINEAR REGRESSION ANALYSIS

Suppose that in our parts supplier illustration we consider each possible transportation time Y for *all* shipments, past and future, to customers at a specified distance X from the plant. For this fixed X, the values of Y represent a population, and they will fluctuate and cluster about a central value. Similarly, for any other rail distance X, there will be a corresponding population of Y values. Since the means of these populations depend on the respective values for X, we may represent them symbolically by $\mu_{Y \cdot X}$, where, as before, the subscript $Y \cdot X$ signifies that the values of Y are for a given value of X.

Figure 10-12 illustrates how several populations for Y fit into the context of linear regression. This graph is three dimensional, having an extra axis perpendicular to the XY plane. This vertical axis represents the relative frequency of Y at a specified level X. The curves are drawn with their centers at a distance $\mu_{Y \cdot X}$ from the X axis. Thus, we may refer to $\mu_{Y \cdot X}$ as the **conditional mean** of Y

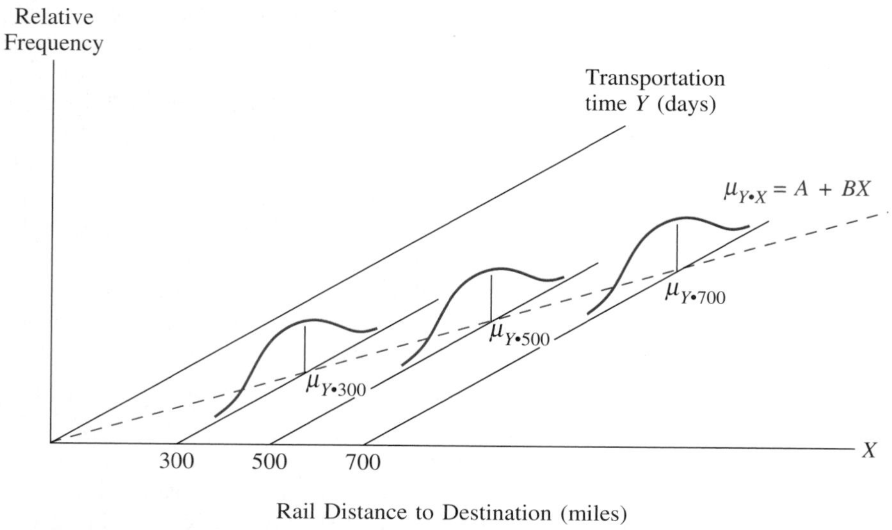

FIGURE 10-12 Populations for Y at various given values of X.

given X. There will be a different frequency curve for each X. Here, we show these curves for all shipments to destinations of $X = 300$, $X = 500$, and $X = 700$ miles. The respective conditional means are denoted by $\mu_{Y \cdot 300}$, $\mu_{Y \cdot 500}$, and $\mu_{Y \cdot 700}$.

In linear regression analysis, the following four theoretical assumptions about the populations for Y apply.

1. All populations have the same standard deviation, denoted by $\sigma_{Y \cdot X}$, no matter what the value of X is.
2. The means $\mu_{Y \cdot X}$ all lie on the same straight line, given by the equation

$$\mu_{Y \cdot X} = A + BX$$

   which is the expression of the **true regression line**.
3. Successive sample observations are independent.
4. The value of X is known in advance.

It is convenient to express each observation in terms of the expression

$$Y = A + BX + \varepsilon$$

where ε is the **error term**. Ordinarily, the εs are assumed to be independent and have a normal distribution with mean 0 and standard deviation $\sigma_{Y \cdot X}$. For any specific level of X, the Ys would then be normally distributed with mean $\mu_{Y \cdot X}$ and standard deviation $\sigma_{Y \cdot X}$.

SAMPLING AND REGRESSION ANALYSIS

The true regression line is not usually known. Ordinarily, a regression analysis is performed using *sample* data. A single sample of size n is usually all we ever see. But it will be helpful in understanding the process if we consider a special experiment in which the population is *known* and repeated samples are selected, with regressions performed on each.

For this experiment, the baseball superstar data in Table 10-2 were used. The dependent variable is the price Y of a batter's rookie baseball card; the independent variable is his number of runs X. To avoid wild oscillations from sample to sample, six players having unusually high-priced cards (Brett, Canseco, Fisk, Henderson, Murphy, and Yount) were removed from the population. (The data for these players may be categorized as *outliers*. This concept will be discussed in Section 10-6.) A regression analysis for the population provides the true regression equation.

$$\mu_{Y \cdot X} = -16.2 + .0454X$$

The above is plotted in color as the regression line in Figure 10-13.

In this experiment, 100 separate samples were selected, each with $n = 20$ players, and the respective regression line determined. The following representative results were obtained.

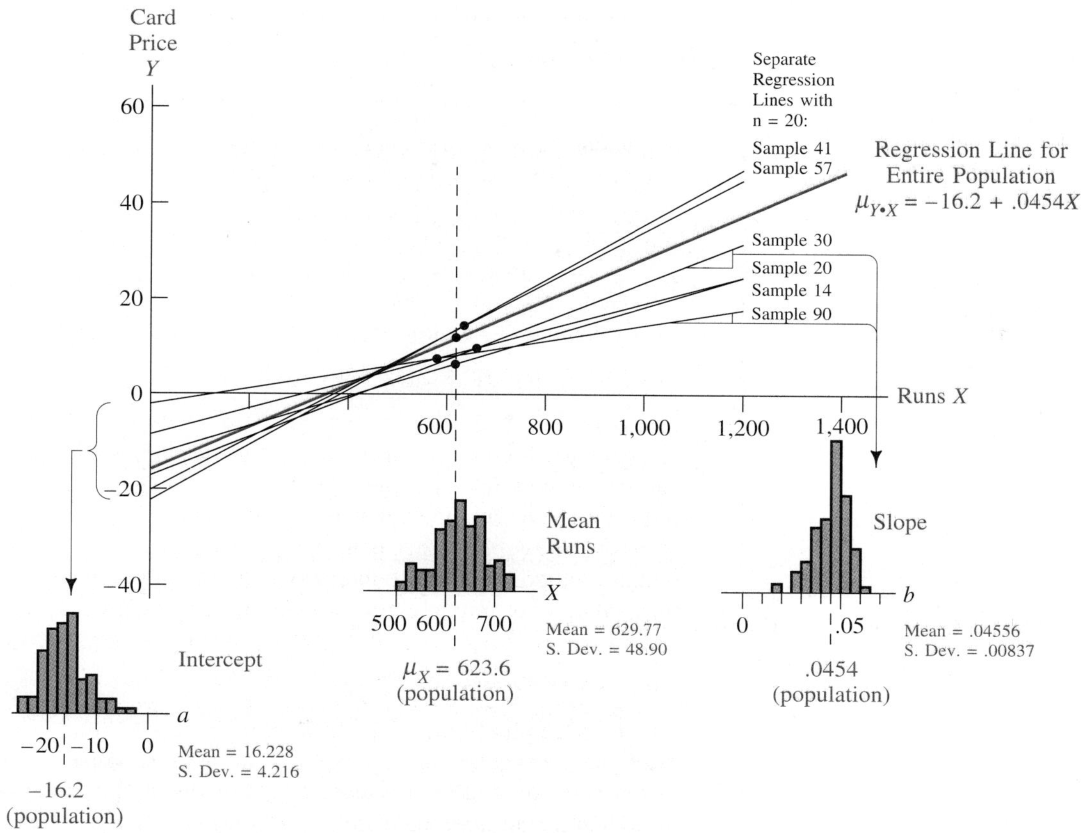

FIGURE 10-13 Results from 100 separate regressions, each using $n = 20$ random observations from truncated population of baseball batter superstars.

Sample 14:	$\hat{Y}(X) = -\ \ 8.56 + .0275X$	$\bar{X} = 554.60$
Sample 20:	$\hat{Y}(X) = -12.74 + .0321X$	$\bar{X} = 623.55$
Sample 30:	$\hat{Y}(X) = -17.40 + .0408X$	$\bar{X} = 661.05$
Sample 41:	$\hat{Y}(X) = -22.24 + .0577X$	$\bar{X} = 631.10$
Sample 57:	$\hat{Y}(X) = -20.97 + .0557X$	$\bar{X} = 634.05$
Sample 90:	$\hat{Y}(X) = -\ \ 2.30 + .0167X$	$\bar{X} = 548.60$

Each of the above lines is plotted in Figure 10-13. Notice that the intercepts and slopes vary, as well as the mean level for $\bar{X}$. The regression line for any particular sample can differ substantially from the true regression line.

Histograms are plotted in Figure 10-13 for the intercepts a, slopes b, and sample means $\bar{X}$ for the independent variable. The computed means for each of these lie close in value to their population counterparts. That fact is not a coincidence, and it exhibits an essential feature to the theory underlying regression analysis.

```
MTB > Regress c2 1 c1.

The regression equation is
Time Y = 4.02 + 0.00897 Dist. X

Predictor        Coef         Stdev     t-ratio       p
Constant       4.018a.        1.591        2.53   0.036
Dist. X     0.008973b.     0.002384        3.76   0.006

s = 2.021       R-sq = 63.9%      R-sq(adj) = 59.4%

Analysis of Variance

SOURCE        DF        SS          MS        F        p
Regression     1    57.829      57.829    14.16    0.006
Error          8    32.671       4.084
Total          9    90.500
```

FIGURE 10-14 Minitab printout for regression analysis with parts supplier data.

ESTIMATING THE TRUE REGRESSION EQUATION

We have learned how to use the method of least squares to derive the estimated regression equation $\hat{Y}(X) = a + bX$. Now we will investigate how this equation is related to the true regression equation $\mu_{Y \cdot X} = A + BX$. The values of A and B, which we call the **true regression coefficients**, are generally unknown. We will use $\hat{Y}(X)$ to estimate $\mu_{Y \cdot X}$ in the same way that we used $\overline{X}$ to estimate μ in Chapter 8. The estimated regression equation differs from the true regression equation only in the values of the Y intercept and slope. We can consider a and b, calculated from the sample data, to be point estimates of A and B, respectively.

The calculated values of a and b depend on the sample observations obtained. The equation $\hat{Y}(X) = 4.019 + .00897X$ was determined from the particular transportation times for the sample of ten shipments selected. A regression equation for some other sample of ten shipments would probably have differed—perhaps considerably—from the one we found.

When a and b are calculated by the method of least squares, they are *unbiased estimators* of the true coefficients A and B. This means that if the experiment of collecting samples is repeated a large number of times and the regression line is found by the least-squares method each time, the average value of the Y intercepts a will tend to be close to the true Y intercept A. Likewise, on the average, the values of b will tend to be close to B. As we mentioned in Chapter 8, unbiasedness is a desirable property of an estimator. In addition, the least-squares criterion provides the estimators of smallest variance, making the method of least squares the *most efficient* of all unbiased estimators of linear regression coefficients. Therefore, a and b minimize chance sampling error, so that estimates made from the regression line $\hat{Y}(X) = a + bX$ are the most reliable ones that can be attained for a fixed sample size. The values of a and b obtained by the least-squares method are also *consistent* and *maximum likelihood* estimators of A and B. Recall from Chapter 8 that a consistent estimator becomes progressively closer to the target parameter with increasing sample size. This can be attributed to the sampling distributions of a and b, whose variances decrease with n.

INFERENCES REGARDING REGRESSION COEFFICIENTS

The normality assumption of the error terms permits us to employ statistical theory in establishing sampling distributions for the regression coefficients a and b. For both of these quantities, the Student t statistic may be used to qualify the results obtained. A detailed discussion of how that is done is provided in optional Section 10-9.

Computer programs generally provide computed values for the respective ts under the assumption that the regression line is flat (the case of zero correlation). This is illustrated in Figure 10-14, which provides the *Minitab* computer printout for a regression analysis using the same parts supplier data seen earlier. The constant row provides the values for the intercept a, and the distance row gives the values for the slope b. That t-ratio column provides 3.76 for the slope. The adjacent entry in the p column indicates a prob. value of .006. (That means that under the assumption of a flat regression line there would be only a .6% chance of getting, from a sample of n = 10 random shipments, a slope as big or greater than the one actually computed.)

EXERCISES

10-17 Suppose that the theoretical regression line for predicting assembly time Y (minutes) from the number of components X is

$$\mu_{Y \cdot X} = 35.0 + 5.1X$$

Individual Y values may be computed from the above by plugging in a level for X and adding the error term ε. Those error terms are normally distributed with mean zero and standard deviation $\sigma_{Y \cdot X} = 10$. We represent a random normal deviate as z, so that error terms may be generated from

$$\varepsilon = 0 + z\sigma_{Y \cdot X}$$

(a) Complete the following table for 10 levels of X and random normal deviates.

Number of Components X	Theoretical Time $\mu_{Y \cdot X}$	Random Normal Deviate z	Error Term ε	Simulated Actual Time Y
5	______	−1.13	______	______
7	______	1.09	______	______
10	______	−.30	______	______
12	______	−.95	______	______
13	______	2.14	______	______
15	______	.25	______	______
16	______	.47	______	______
20	______	−.08	______	______
22	______	.53	______	______
25	______	1.22	______	______

(b) Plot a scatter diagram using the above levels for Y and their matching value for X.

10-18 *Continuation.*
(a) Plot the *true* regression line on a graph.
(b) Using the above values for Y and X, determine the estimated regression equation.
(c) Plot on the same graph the *estimated* regression line.

10-19 *Continuation.*
(a) Compute $s_{Y \cdot X}$ using the regression results from Exercise 10-18(a).
(b) Why does $s_{Y \cdot X}$ differ from $\sigma_{Y \cdot X}$?

10-20 *Continuation.*
(a) Complete the following table.

(1) Number of Components X	(2) Simulated Actual Time Y	(3) Theoretical Time $\mu_{Y \cdot X}$	(4) Estimated Time $\hat{Y}(X)$	(5) Error Term $\varepsilon = Y - \mu_{Y \cdot X}$	(6) Residual $Y - \hat{Y}(X)$
5	______	______	______	______	
7	______	______	______	______	______
10	______	______	______	______	______
12	______	______	______	______	______
13	______	______	______	______	______
15	______	______	______	______	______
16	______	______	______	______	______
20	______	______	______	______	______
22	______	______	______	______	______
25	______	______	______	______	______

(b) Compare the values in columns (3) and (4). Should these be identical or not?
(c) Compare the values in columns (5) and (6). Should these be identical or not?

10-5 PREDICTIONS AND STATISTICAL INFERENCES USING THE REGRESSION LINE

We use the estimated regression line to make a variety of inferences, which can be grouped into two broad categories: (1) predictions of the dependent variable and (2) inferences regarding the regression coefficients A and B. Because predictions are made more often, we will discuss them first.

PREDICTIONS USING THE REGRESSION EQUATION

The major goal of regression analysis is to predict Y from the regression line at given levels of X. This may be done either by (1) predicting the value of the conditional mean $\mu_{Y \cdot X}$ or (2) predicting an individual Y value, rather than a mean.

As an example of the first kind of prediction, the parts supplier might want to predict the mean transportation time that will be achieved by all shipments over a distance of 500 miles. In this case, $X = 500$, and the best point estimate of $\mu_{Y \cdot X}$ will be the fitted Y value from the regression line.

$$\begin{aligned}\hat{Y}(500) &= a + b(500) \\ &= 4.019 + .00897(500) \\ &= 8.50 \text{ days}\end{aligned}$$

The computed value 8.50 may also be used to estimate the transportation time for a particular shipment over the same distance. To distinguish an individual value from a mean value, both of which can only be estimated from the sample, we use the special symbol Y_I.

Either kind of estimate will involve sampling error, which can be acknowledged and expressed in terms of confidence intervals. Because of the special nature of regression analysis, the numbers obtained are usually referred to as **prediction intervals**.

PREDICTION INTERVALS FOR THE CONDITIONAL MEAN

We determine prediction intervals in a manner similar to the way we derived confidence intervals in Chapter 8. There, we used

$$\mu = \bar{X} \pm t_{\alpha/2}\frac{s}{\sqrt{n}} \qquad \text{(when } \sigma \text{ is unknown)}$$

where $s/\sqrt{n}$ is the estimator of $\sigma_{\bar{X}}$.

In regression analysis, Y (not X) is the variable being estimated. Intervals of analogous form are required to estimate a conditional mean of Y.

$$\mu_{Y \cdot X} = \hat{Y}(X) \pm t_{\alpha/2} \text{ estimated } \sigma_{\hat{Y}}$$

The standard error of $\hat{Y}(X)$, denoted by $\sigma_{\hat{Y}}$, represents the amount of variability in possible $\hat{Y}(X)$values at the particular level for X that a prediction is desired. In the context of transportation time, a somewhat different line $\hat{Y}(X) = a + bX$ [such as $\hat{Y}(X) = 3.5 + .011X$ or $\hat{Y}(X) = 4.2 + .009X$] might have fitted the least-squares method if some other random sample of ten shipments had been selected. Thus, for some other sample $\hat{Y}(500)$ might have computed to a value different from 8.50 days. But nevertheless, for each particular value of X, a potential set of $\hat{Y}(X)$ values would have a distribution with a standard deviation of $\sigma_{\hat{Y}}$.

There are two components of the variability in $\hat{Y}(X)$.

$$\sigma^2_{\hat{Y}} = \begin{array}{c}\text{Variability in the} \\ \text{mean of } Y\text{s}\end{array} + \begin{array}{c}\text{Variability caused by the} \\ \text{distance of } X \text{ from } \bar{X}\end{array}$$

The first source is analogous to the variability in the sample mean, which, as we saw in Chapter 8, depends on the population standard deviation and the sample size. The second source of variation is associated with the distance that X lies from $\bar{X}$. Figure 10-15 shows why this is so. Here, several estimated regression lines have been plotted, each representing different samples of shipments taken from the same population. (Although each sample involves the same Xs and thus

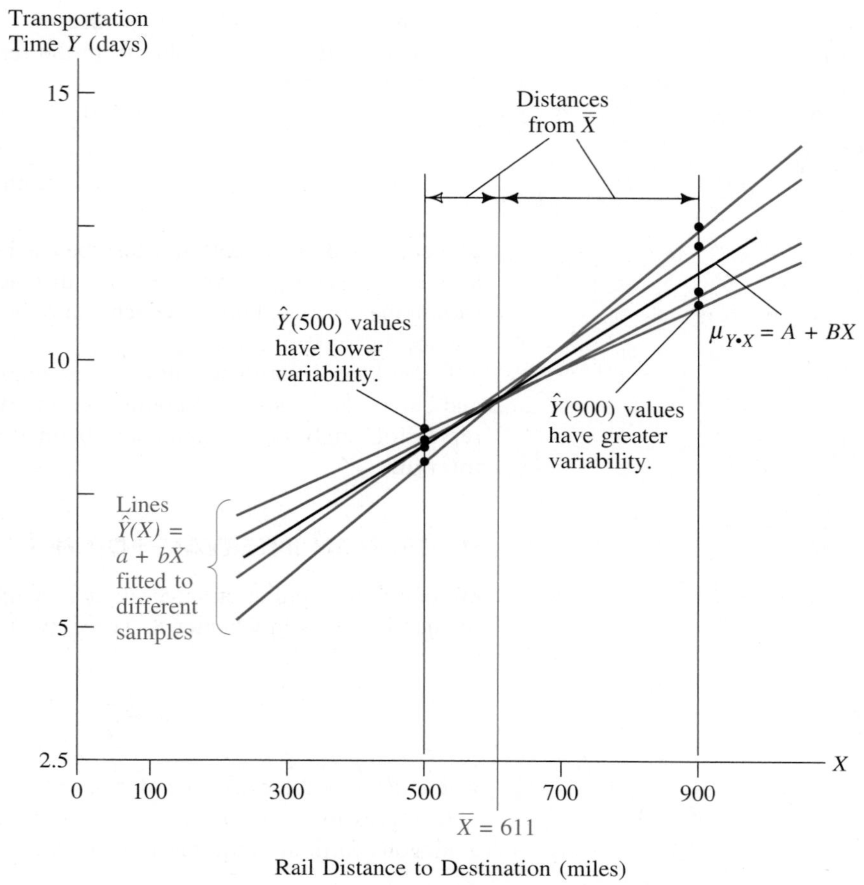

FIGURE 10-15 Illustration of how variability in $\hat{Y}(X)$ increases for larger distances separating X from $\bar{X}$.

the same level for $\bar{X}$, each involves slightly different values for a, b, and $\bar{Y}$.) Note that these lines tend to diverge and that their separations become greater as the distance between X and $\bar{X}$ increases. Therefore, the values of $\hat{Y}(X)$ become more varied the farther X is from $\bar{X}$.

The following expression is used to construct the $100(1 - \alpha)\%$

PREDICTION INTERVAL FOR THE CONDITIONAL MEAN

$$\mu_{Y\cdot X} = \hat{Y}(X) \pm t_{\alpha/2}s_{Y\cdot X}\sqrt{\frac{1}{n} + \frac{(X - \bar{X})^2}{\sum X^2 - n\bar{X}^2}}$$

where $t_{\alpha/2}$ is found from Appendix Table F for $n - 2$ degrees of freedom. (When using Appendix Table F, if the required critical value of t is not listed, use the

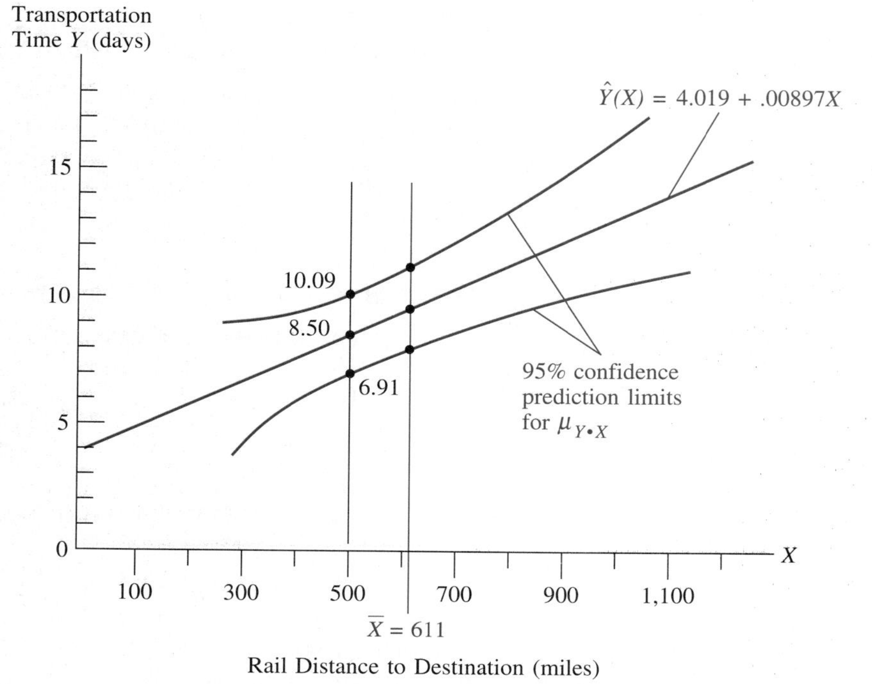

FIGURE 10-16 Confidence limits for predictions of mean transportation time.

nearest tabled entry. If the value is exactly in the middle, average the entries in the two neighboring rows. And, when the number of degrees of freedom exceeds 120, use the value of t from the df $= \infty$ row.)

Representing $\mu_{Y \cdot X}$ when $X = 500$ as $\mu_{Y \cdot 500}$, we may construct the 95% prediction interval for the conditional mean transportation time using $10 - 2 = 8$ degrees of freedom. Since $\alpha/2 = .025$, we find that $t_{\alpha/2} = t_{.025} = 2.306$, and therefore

$$\mu_{Y \cdot 500} = \hat{Y}(500) \pm t_{.025} s_{Y \cdot X} \sqrt{\frac{1}{n} + \frac{(500 - \bar{X})^2}{\sum X^2 - n\bar{X}^2}}$$

$$= 8.50 \pm 2.306(2.02) \sqrt{\frac{1}{10} + \frac{(500 - 611)^2}{4{,}451{,}500 - 10(611)^2}}$$

$$= 8.50 \pm 1.59$$

or

$$6.91 \le \mu_{Y \cdot 500} \le 10.09 \text{ days}$$

We therefore conclude that the transportation time for destinations 500 miles from the plant is *on the average* somewhere between 6.91 and 10.09 days. Our confidence that this statement is correct rests on the procedure used, which provides similar intervals containing the true mean about 95% of the time.

We may calculate 95% prediction intervals for the other values of X, thus obtaining prediction limits for $\mu_{Y \cdot X}$ over the entire range of X. In Figure 10-16, this has been done for the parts supplier's data. Note that the width of the confidence band depends on the distances that the X values lie from the mean.

PREDICTION INTERVALS FOR AN INDIVIDUAL VALUE OF *Y* GIVEN *X*

Predicting an individual value of Y given X is similar to predicting the mean. If our parts supplier wished to predict the transportation time for the next shipment over a distance of $X = 500$ miles, then the same point estimate, $\hat{Y}(500) = 8.50$ days, would be made from the regression equation. The following expression provides the $100(1 - \alpha)\%$

PREDICTION INTERVAL FOR AN INDIVIDUAL *Y*

$$Y_I = \hat{Y}(X) \pm t_{\alpha/2} s_{Y \cdot X} \sqrt{\frac{1}{n} - \frac{(X - \bar{X})^2}{\sum X^2 - n\bar{X}^2} + 1}$$

This expression is the same as the one for $\mu_{Y \cdot X}$, except for the addition of " + 1." This reflects the fact that when $\hat{Y}(X)$ is used to estimate Y_I, a third source of variability is present—the dispersion of individual Y values about the regression line. (Even if the true regression line were known, the Ys at a particular level of X would have a variance of $\sigma^2_{Y \cdot X}$.)

We may now construct a 95% prediction interval for Y_I, using the parts supplier's data when $X = 500$.

$$\begin{aligned} Y_I &= \hat{Y}(500) \pm t_{.025} s_{Y \cdot X} \sqrt{\frac{1}{n} + \frac{(500 - \bar{X})^2}{\sum X^2 - n\bar{X}^2} + 1} \\ &= 8.50 \pm 2.306(2.02) \sqrt{\frac{1}{10} + \frac{(500 - 611)^2}{4{,}451{,}500 - 10(611)^2} + 1} \\ &= 8.50 \pm 4.92 \end{aligned}$$

or

$$3.58 \leq Y_I \leq 13.42 \text{ days}$$

Note that this interval is considerably wider than the interval obtained previously for $\mu_{Y \cdot 500}$. This is to be expected, because Y_I is the estimate of the transportation time for *a particular shipment*, not a mean, and the greater width is attributable to the added variability that would be present even if the true regression line were available in making the prediction.

COMPUTER-GENERATED INTERVAL ESTIMATES

The procedures for finding confidence intervals in regression analysis involve computations that are cumbersome to do by hand. Certain computer software packages will generate these estimates concurrently with the regression. Figure 10-17 displays a computer printout for the above estimates. Notice that, in the figure, the quantity $\hat{Y}(500) = 8.504$ days is referred to as the "Fit." The *Minitab* software package provides 95% prediction intervals. The first, narrower interval applies to $\mu_{Y \cdot X}$; the second interval applies to Y_I.

```
MTB > Regress 'Time Y' on 1 'Dist.X';
SUBC> predict 500.
```

```
The regression equation is
Time Y = 4.02 + 0.00897 Dist. X


     Fit   Stdev.Fit          95% C.I.             95% P.I.
   8.504       0.692    (  6.909, 10.100)   (  3.577, 13.431)
```

Note: Figure generated on an IBM PC using Minitab®.

FIGURE 10-17 Portion of a computer printout for the parts supplier illustration.

INFERENCES REGARDING THE SLOPE OF THE REGRESSION LINE

Second in importance to prediction intervals are inferences regarding the slope B of the true regression line. This is especially true in statistical applications where the underlying relationship between X and Y is more important than predicting Y at a particular level for X. For example, much economic theory relies on regression analysis to substantiate hypothetical models requiring supply and demand curves. The *coefficients* of these demand and supply equations—not the predicted quantities for a given price—are our main interest. Similarly, a metallurgist might use regression analysis to develop a mathematical relationship between alloy concentrations and strength properties. He might be more concerned with predicting how much extra shearing force is needed to break a metal for each unit increase in alloy material than with predicting a particular force (that is, he might wish to estimate B rather than $\mu_{Y \cdot X}$).

A prediction interval can be constructed for B, and hypotheses regarding the true level of B can be tested. An optional discussion of these procedures appears in Section 10-9.

EXERCISES

10-21 The estimated regression line $\hat{Y}(X) = 150 + .1X$ provides the yield (bushels) per acre of corn when X pounds of nitrate fertilizer are applied. This result was obtained for a sample of $n = 100$ acres for which $s_{Y \cdot X} = 5$ bushels. Construct the 95% prediction intervals for $\mu_{Y \cdot X}$ and Y_I when $X = 50$ pounds. Assume that $\bar{X} = 50$ pounds.

10-22 The relationship between the total weight Y (pounds) of luggage stored in an aircraft's baggage compartment and the number of passengers X on the flight manifest is $\hat{Y}(X) = 250 + 27X$. Airport superintendents will use this equation to determine how much additional freight can be stored safely on a flight, after considering the fuel load and the weight of the passengers themselves. The data have been obtained for a sample of $n = 25$ flights. The sample results yield $s_{Y \cdot X} = 100$ pounds, $s_Y = 300$ pounds, $\sum X^2 = 64{,}000$, and $\bar{X} = 50$. Construct the 95% prediction intervals for $\mu_{Y \cdot X}$ and Y_I when (a) $X = 50$; (b) $X = 75$; (c) $X = 100$.

10-23 Refer to the Crunchola data given in Exercise 10-12 and to your answers. Construct the 95% prediction intervals for (a) the mean total cost of production runs of 200 tons and (b) the cost of an individual run of 400 tons.

10-24 Refer to the FlyMe Airlines' data given in Exercise 10-10 and to your answers. Construct the 99% prediction intervals for (a) the mean freight charge for shipments over a distance of six hundred miles and (b) the freight charge for an individual shipment over a distance of nine hundred miles.

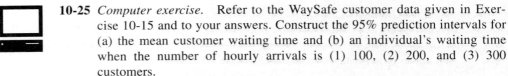

10-25 *Computer exercise.* Refer to the WaySafe customer data given in Exercise 10-15 and to your answers. Construct the 95% prediction intervals for (a) the mean customer waiting time and (b) an individual's waiting time when the number of hourly arrivals is (1) 100, (2) 200, and (3) 300 customers.

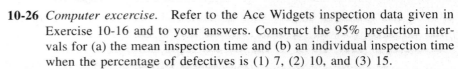

10-26 *Computer excercise.* Refer to the Ace Widgets inspection data given in Exercise 10-16 and to your answers. Construct the 95% prediction intervals for (a) the mean inspection time and (b) an individual inspection time when the percentage of defectives is (1) 7, (2) 10, and (3) 15.

10-27 The credit manager of a department store has determined that the regression equation for a customer credit rating index X and the proportion of customers Y who eventually incur bad debts is $\hat{Y}(X) = .09 - .002X$. The index values range from 0 to 40. A sample of $n = 25$ is selected. The sample results yield $\sum X^2 = 23{,}000$, $s_{Y \cdot X} = .02$, and $\bar{X} = 30$.

(a) Construct the 90% prediction interval for the mean proportion of customers with ratings of $X = 20$ who will incur bad debts.

(b) The proper interpretation of Y_I in this case is the *probability* that a particular individual will incur a bad debt. Construct the 90% prediction interval for Y_I when $X = 20$.

10-6 ASSESSING THE QUALITY OF REGRESSION ANALYSIS

One way of assessing the overall quality of regression analysis is to measure the strength of the relationship between the dependent and independent variables. Another means of assessment explores whether the data are consistent with the theoretical assumptions of the regression model. An *analysis of residuals* may pinpoint potential trouble spots that tend to weaken or even invalidate the conclusions drawn from regression analysis.

THE COEFFICIENT OF DETERMINATION

In Section 10-2, we saw the degree to which the correlation coefficient indicates the direction and strength of association between X and Y. A related index, the **coefficient of determination**, expresses the amount of variation in the levels of Y that is explained by the regression analysis. As a foundation for understanding this coefficient, we first take the difference between the observed Y and its mean and break it into three *deviations*. To help illustrate, consider, again, the parts supplier's data.

Figure 10-18 shows the regression line found earlier for the parts supplier's original transportation times. Suppose the parts supplier predicts how long the next order will take to ship without using that line. That sample mean would then give a suitable estimate, providing the following

$$\bar{Y} = 9.5 \text{ days} \qquad \text{(prediction without regression)}$$

The estimate ignores how far the shipment will go. Suppose that this shipment goes to Smith Dodge, for which the distance is known to be $X = 920$ miles. This information allows the supplier to make a better forecast,

$$\hat{Y}(920) = 12.3 \text{ days} \qquad \text{(prediction using regression line)}$$

Although the actual time of the next shipment to Smith Dodge is uncertain, it can be represented by the time originally observed in the sample,

$$Y = 15.0 \text{ days} \qquad \text{(observed time)}$$

The first prediction falls wide of the mark, providing a **total deviation** of $Y - \bar{Y} = 15.0 - 9.5 = 5.5$ days, none of which can be explained. The second prediction is better since it yields a smaller prediction error of $Y - \hat{Y}(X) = 15.0 - 12.3 = 2.7$ days. By using the regression line, the total error is reduced by the amount $\hat{Y}(X) - \bar{Y} = 12.3 - 9.5 = 2.8$ days. Thus, part of the total error may be attributed to using the regression line, so that $\hat{Y}(X) - \bar{Y} = 2.8$ days is the **explained deviation**. The remaining portion of the error is due to unidentifiable

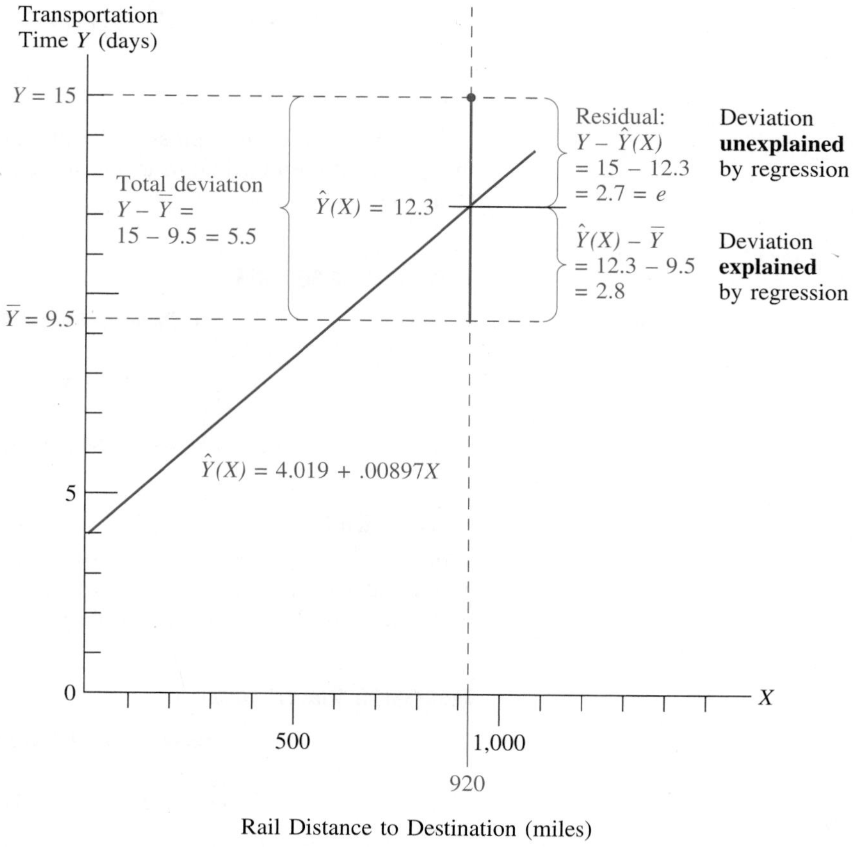

FIGURE 10-18 Illustration of total, explained, and unexplained variation in Y.

causes, so that $Y - \hat{Y}(X) = 2.7$ days is an **unexplained deviation**. The total deviation of the observed Y may then be expressed as

$$[Y - \bar{Y}] = [\hat{Y}(X) - \bar{Y}] + [Y - \hat{Y}(X)]$$

Stated in words, we have

Total deviation = Explained deviation + Unexplained deviation

The unexplained deviations are often referred to as the **residuals** and are defined by the differences

$$e_i = Y_i - \hat{Y}(X_i)$$

The es may be considered as the *observed* errors. Although similar, they differ from the *actual* errors ε of the theoretical model, the values of which remain unknown.

By squaring the above deviations and then summing, we extend the relationship to the entire collection of observations.

$$\begin{array}{ccccc} \text{Total variation} & = & \text{Explained variation} & + & \text{Unexplained variation} \\ \sum [Y - \bar{Y}]^2 & = & \sum [\hat{Y}(X) - \bar{Y}]^2 & + & \sum [Y - \hat{Y}(X)]^2 \\ SSTO & = & SSR & + & SSE \end{array}$$

The total variation expresses the amount that the individual Ys deviate from their mean $\bar{Y}$ without regard to the regression relationship. The result is referred to as the

TOTAL SUM OF SQUARES

$$SSTO = \sum [Y - \bar{Y}]^2$$

As shown in Figure 10-18, the distance between Y and the regression line at X explains a portion of the deviation in the observed Y from its mean $\bar{Y}$. The explained variation summarizes the collective squared distances between the regression line $\hat{Y}(X)$ and the sample mean $\bar{Y}$. This is expressed by the

REGRESSION SUM OF SQUARES

$$SSR = \sum [\hat{Y}(X) - \bar{Y}]^2$$

The final component of total variation involves the residuals and measures the overall observed error in the sample. This is the

ERROR SUM OF SQUARES

$$SSE = \sum [Y - \hat{Y}(X)]^2$$

The method of least squares selects the regression coefficients a and b, so that the above quantity is minimized. The above term expresses the collective dispersion in Y about the regression line. The regression line leaves those deviations *unexplained.*

Rearranging the terms, the identity

$$\begin{matrix} \text{Explained variation} & = & \text{Total variation} & - & \text{Unexplained variation} \\ SSR & = & SSTO & - & SSE \end{matrix}$$

is used to construct a useful index. Dividing the explained variation by the total variation provides the **coefficient of determination**. The following expression applies.

$$r^2 = \frac{\text{Explained variation}}{\text{Total variation}} = \frac{SSTO - SSE}{SSTO} = \frac{\sum [Y - \bar{Y}]^2 - \sum [Y - \hat{Y}(X)]^2}{\sum [Y - \bar{Y}]^2}$$

An equivalent expression is

$$r^2 = \frac{\text{Explained variation}}{\text{Total variation}} = 1 - \frac{\sum [Y - \hat{Y}(X)]^2}{\sum [Y - \bar{Y}]^2}$$

which may be expressed equivalently as

$$r^2 = 1 - \frac{SSE}{SSTO}$$

The coefficient of determination expresses the proportion of the total variation in Y explained by the regression line. The above summations are the numerators of $s^2_{Y \cdot X}$ and s^2_Y. The following expression is most commonly used in computing the

COEFFICIENT OF DETERMINATION

$$r^2 = 1 - \frac{s^2_{Y \cdot X}}{s^2_Y}\left(\frac{n - 2}{n - 1}\right)$$

For the parts supplier's data, the above expression provides

$$r^2 = 1 - \frac{(2.02)^2}{(3.17)^2}\left(\frac{10-2}{10-1}\right) = .639$$

The computed value $r^2 = .639$ signifies that 63.9% of the total variation or scatter of transportation time Y about their mean can be explained by the relationship between this variable and the corresponding rail distance X, as estimated by the regression line for X and Y.

The coefficient of determination is computed automatically using the popular software packages. When working by hand, it may be convenient to express the sample coefficient of determination by means of the mathematically equivalent equation

$$r^2 = \frac{a\sum Y + b\sum XY - n\bar{Y}^2}{\sum Y^2 - n\bar{Y}^2}$$

In the parts supplier illustration, we may calculate r^2 using $a = 4.019$, $b = .00897$, and the intermediate calculations from Table 10-3.

$$r^2 = \frac{4.019(95) + .00897(64{,}490) - 10(9.5)^2}{993 - 10(9.5)^2}$$

$$= \frac{57.78}{90.50} = .64$$

The *population* coefficient of determination is denoted by ρ^2. This parameter ordinarily remains unknown, so that r^2 serves as the point estimate of its population counterpart ρ^2.

Relation to the Correlation Coefficient

Choosing r^2 to denote the sample coefficient of determination is no coincidence. The following relationship applies.

$$\text{Coefficient of determination} = (\text{Correlation coefficient})^2$$

Thus, the absolute value of the correlation coefficient is the square root of the coefficient of determination.

$$|r| = \sqrt{r^2} \quad \text{and} \quad |\rho| = \sqrt{\rho^2}$$

The sign for r or ρ and the slope of the corresponding regression line must agree. Thus, for the parts supplier illustration, the sample correlation coefficient is

$$r = \sqrt{.639} = +.80$$

The above relationship provides another perspective on how the coefficient of determination measures the strength of association between X and Y. In the special case when all the data points fall directly on the regression line, so that there is a perfect correlation and $r = +1$ or $r = -1$, all of the variation in Y is explained and r must be equal to one. At the other extreme, a horizontal regression line is obtained when X and Y exhibit zero correlation, so that all of the variation in Y is unexplained and r^2 must then be equal to zero.

APPROPRIATENESS OF THE MODEL: RESIDUAL ANALYSIS

The residual values computed for the parts supplier's data are listed in Table 10-4. The first step in residual analysis is to construct the scatter plot. Figure 10-19 illustrates the residual scatter diagram for the data given in Table 10-5.

All inferences made from the regression relationship are based on theoretical properties discussed in Section 10-4. Should the underlying population and sampling process deviate from the model described, the regression analysis will be based on false assumptions. Residual analysis can be helpful in uncovering the violations of the model.

The parts supplier's residual data reflect the aforementioned linear relationship, with the individual es falling within a narrow horizontal band. Such a plot has

```
MTB > Regress 'Time Y' on 1 'Dist.X';
SUBC> residuals c3.
    .
    .
    .
MTB > name c3 'Y-Y(X)'
MTB > plot c3 c1
```

```
        -
        -
    2.5+                     *                            *
        -
Y-Y(X)  -
        -                                         *
        -        *                             *
    0.0+
        -                      *
        -   *        *                                           *
        -
        -
   -2.5+
        -
        -                                              *
        -
        -
          --------+---------+---------+---------+---------+--------Dist. X
                300       450       600       750       900
```

Note: Figure generated on an IBM PC using Minitab®.

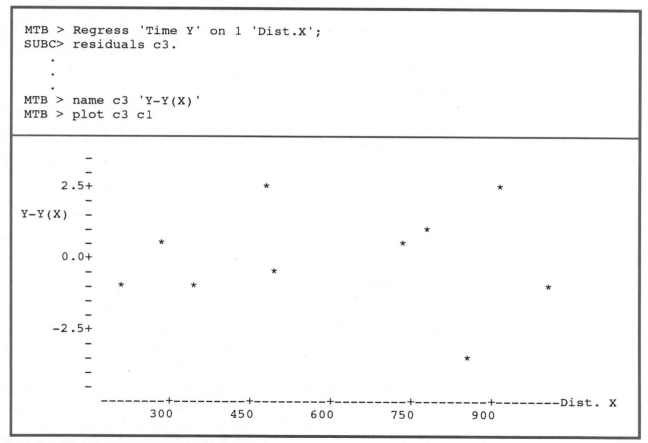

FIGURE 10-19 Residual scatter plot for the parts supplier illustration.

TABLE 10-5 Residual Calculations for Parts Supplier's Data

Customer	Rail Distance to Destination X	Transportation Time (days) Y	Predicted Time from Regression Line $\hat{Y}(X) = 4.019 + .00897X$	Residual $e = Y - \hat{Y}(X)$
1	210	5	5.9027	−.9027
2	290	7	6.6203	.3797
3	350	6	7.1585	−1.1585
4	480	11	8.3246	2.6754
5	490	8	8.4143	−.4143
6	730	11	10.5671	.4329
7	780	12	11.0156	.9844
8	850	8	11.6435	−3.6435
9	920	15	12.2714	2.7286
10	1,010	12	13.0787	−1.0787

an appearance ideal for a regression analysis. The three scatter diagrams in Figure 10-20 illustrate other situations where critical assumptions of regression analysis are violated.

NONLINEARITY

Diagram (a) in Figure 10-20 shows a *nonlinear* relationship, with the *e*s exhibiting a pronounced curve. Section 10-8 considers nonlinear regression analysis.

NONCONSTANT VARIANCE

Figure 10-20(b) is a plot representing the regression analysis for a hypothetical experiment where the computer processing time Y for scheduling shipments in a distribution system is related to the number of destinations X. Notice that the band of *e*s gets wider as X increases. This indicates a *nonconstant variance* in the *e*s as the level of X becomes greater. This violates the theoretical assumption that errors have constant variance $\sigma^2_{Y \cdot X}$. We may remedy the problem by substituting a nonlinear regression for the original.

TIME DEPENDENCY

Figure 10-20(c) illustrates the residual plot for a regression model where adjustment time Y for temperature settings in a chemical process is related to the final output volume X of the production batch. The horizontal axis is the *time sequence* of the observation (rather than X). Notice that the *e*s increase over time, which indicates a *lack of independence*. This could be due to a variety of explained causes, such as operator fatigue. (We may avoid this difficulty by collecting all the data for production batches run on different days, at about the same time of day.)

OUTLIERS: BASEBALL BATTING SUPERSTARS

Residual analysis extends to two other types of regression model violations where a conventional scatter diagram is less useful. One violation involves **outliers**, isolated observations that are so extreme that they do not appear to belong with the rest. If an identifiable cause exists (such as a power outage or an absent operator), the data point may be safely discarded.

Figure 10-21 shows the *Minitab* results for a regression analysis with the baseball superstar data from Table 10-2 (batters only). The rookie baseball card price

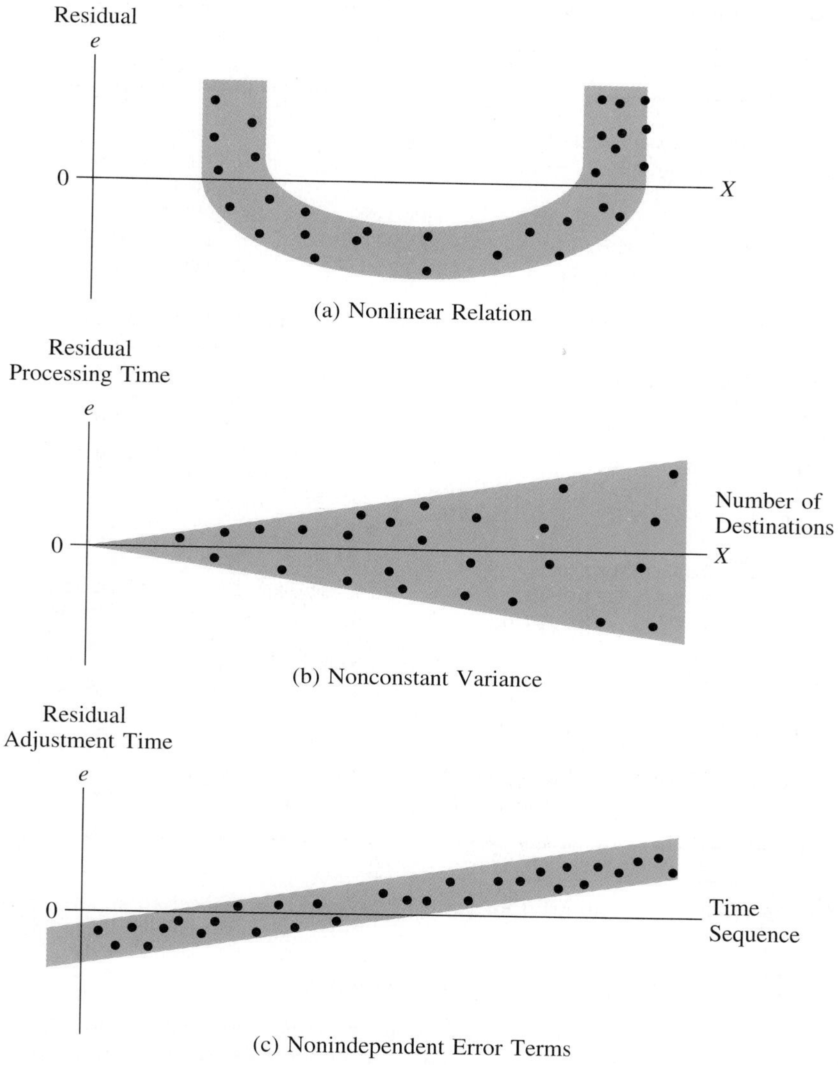

FIGURE 10-20 Residual scatter diagrams reflecting regression model violations.

Y is the dependent variable and the number of runs *X* is the independent variable. The program output lists the players whose data involve outliers. The outlying players are:

George Brett   Carlton Fisk   Rickey Henderson   Robin Yount

(The data do not show that these players are held in abnormally high esteem by fans because of their longevity, records, all-star performance, and World Series participation. Those extras have given added boost to their card prices.) A fifth listed player, Dave Winfield, is not classified as an outlier because his data point lies closer to the estimated regression line. But because of his high run production, he does have a greater influence on the positioning of that line.

```
MTB > Regress c3 1 c9.

The regression equation is
Card Pr. = - 49.8 + 0.110 Runs
Ŷ(X)                    X
Predictor        Coef        Stdev      t-ratio        p
Constant      -49.841        9.218        -5.41    0.000
Runs          0.10997      0.01257         8.75    0.000

s = 30.61       R-sq = 54.1%      R-sq(adj) = 53.4%

Analysis of Variance

SOURCE        DF         SS          MS          F        p
Regression     1      71717       71717      76.56    0.000
Error         65      60885         937
Total         66     132602

Unusual Observations
Obs.   Runs  Card Pr.       Fit  Stdev.Fit   Residual    St.Resid
  6    1382    200.00    102.14       9.69      97.86      3.37RX
 26    1220    150.00     84.32       7.85      65.68      2.22R
 36    1290    200.00     92.02       8.64     107.98      3.68R
 66    1384     50.00    102.36       9.72     -52.36     -1.80 X
 67    1433    200.00    107.75      10.29      92.25      3.20RX
          X         Y      Ŷ(X)                 Y-Ŷ(X)
R denotes an obs. with a large st. resid.
X denotes an obs. whose X value gives it large influence.
```

FIGURE 10-21 Minitab printout from regression using baseball superstar data.

NON-NORMALITY

Another violation, not easy to identify on a residual diagram, is non-normality in the *e*s. Chapter 23 describes *goodness-of-fit tests* that may establish whether or not the *e*s are normally distributed.

EXERCISES

10-28 The following data represent disposable personal income and personal consumption expenditures (billions of dollars) for the United States during the five-year period from 1964 through 1968. (Source: *Economic Report of the President*, February 1970.)

Year	Disposable Income X	Consumption Expenditures Y
1964	438	401
1965	473	433
1966	512	466
1967	547	492
1968	590	537

(a) Using the method of least squares, determine the estimated linear regression equation that provides consumption expenditure predictions for specified levels of disposable income.
(b) Is the Y intercept negative or positive? Why do you think this is so?
(c) State the meaning of the slope b of the regression line.
(d) Using your intermediate calculations in (a) and the values found for the estimated regression coefficients, calculate the coefficient of determination.

10-29 To help evaluate the effectiveness of a retraining program, the MakeWave Corporation personnel manager is studying the following results obtained for a sample of $n = 10$ employees. The data in the table that follows provide productivity indexes before and after retraining.
(a) Using the method of least squares, determine the equation for the estimated regression line.
(b) Calculate the sample coefficient of determination.

Student	Prior Score X	Current Score Y
Grace Brown	90	83
Patrick Gray	75	72
Lisa White	80	84
Homer Black	65	76
John Green	85	77
Linda Jones	90	82
Carl Smith	95	95
Freddy Tyler	75	68
Lisa Adams	70	78
Karen Johnson	60	55

(c) What percentage of the total variation in Y is explained by the estimated regression line?

10-30 Refer to the data given in Exercise 10-28.
(a) What percentage of the total variation in Y is explained by the regression line?
(b) Calculate the correlation coefficient.

10-31 Refer to the FlyMe Airlines' data in Exercise 10-10 for the distance X and the freight charge Y of a shipment.
(a) Calculate the sample correlation coefficient directly from the data.
(b) Using your earlier regression results, calculate the sample coefficient of determination.
(c) What percentage of the total variation in freight charge Y is explained by the estimated regression line?

10-32 Refer to the FlyMe Airlines' data given in Exercise 10-10 and to your answers.
(a) Compute, for each observation, the residual values.
(b) Plot the residual scatter diagram for the data.
(c) What do you conclude regarding consistency with the theoretical assumptions of the regression model?

10-33 Repeat Exercise 10-32(a)–(c) for the Crunchola data given in Exercise 10-12.

10-34 *Computer exercise.* Refer to the Ace Widgets data given in Exercise 10-16 and to your answers.
(a) Calculate (1) the sample coefficient of determination and (2) the sample correlation coefficient.
(b) Plot the residual scatter diagram for the data.

10-35 *Computer exercise.* Repeat Exercise 10-34(a) and (b) for the WaySafe customer data given in Exercise 10-15.

10-7 COMMON PITFALLS AND LIMITATIONS OF REGRESSION AND CORRELATION ANALYSIS

There are several pitfalls and limitations associated with linear regression and correlation analysis that should be given special mention. These may be categorized as being due to (1) violations of the theoretical assumptions, (2) improper use of the regression equation and correlation coefficient, and (3) misinterpretation of these coefficients. Regression and correlation are powerful tools, but ludicrous conclusions may be drawn if they are not used properly.

DANGERS OF EXTRAPOLATION IN REGRESSION ANALYSIS

The set of observations used to establish a regression equation covers a limited range of values of the independent variable X. Caution must be exercised in making predictions of the dependent variable Y whenever X falls outside this range. Such predictions are called **extrapolations**.

In the parts supplier illustration, the regression line was determined for ten shipments whose distances ranged from 210 to 1,010 miles. Suppose we wished to use our results to predict the transportation time for a shipment to a customer separated from the plant by 2,000 miles, a distance considerably greater than the largest used in determining the regression line. How reliable would such an extrapolation be?

This depends on whether our assumption of a linear relationship between time and distance is valid for shipments over great distances. There is simply no way to know this without including some longer shipments in the sample. As noted earlier in this chapter, the selection of a straight line was motivated by the general appearance of the data's scatter. Perhaps with a few additional points for distances between 1,000 and 2,000 miles, a curvilinear relationship might provide a better fit.

There may be a good logical basis for assuming that a line will prevail—but then we might expect its slope to be flatter or steeper because of the influence of additional data points. On the other hand, there are reasonably sound arguments that longer distances ought to involve less time-consuming recomposition of trains (adding and removing box cars), so that the additional time per extra mile (that is, the slope of the regression curve) decreases for longer trips.

Regression analysis is limited only to the range of actual observations. These observations—and not qualitative reasoning—are used to quantify the relationship between X and Y. Qualitative reasoning is useful initially in selecting the form of the regression equation (linear versus curvilinear) and later in interpreting the results, but it cannot be used in place of actual observation. We are not ruling out extrapolation here but are merely indicating its potential pitfalls. If there are no data available beyond the range of required predictions, then extrapolation may be the only suitable alternative. Keep in mind that *extrapolation assigns values using a relationship that has been measured for circumstances differing from those for the prediction.*

Circumstances may differ for reasons other than extrapolation. Should the underlying populations change over time—as would be the case for changes in railroad operations or technology—then the regression line would not represent the shipments in subsequent years. Often, a regression analysis is short lived in its applicability because underlying relationships can change over time.

RELEVANCY OF PAST DATA

Care must be taken in using past data to determine a future relationship. Regression analysis is often used in forecasting with time series, which we will discuss in Chapter 12. There the independent variable is time, with the dependent variable Y being forecast. The source of data is history, so that often a time span of many years is encompassed by the observed Y values. A very serious danger is that the underlying Y populations may change character over time. The regression equation assumes that variance in Y is constant. Thus, if there is reason to believe that the values of Y are becoming more or less volatile over time, a critical assumption of regression analysis is violated. In addition to difficulties with the variance, the observations over the years are usually statistically *dependent* violating another assumption of regression theory. The net effect of such violations is that probabilistic interpretations of inferences are invalid and cannot be used.

Because relationships are apt to change over time, special care should be taken when past data are used to predict a future value of the dependent variable. The hazards are most pronounced in forecasting with time series, but similar difficulties may arise whenever the data are collected over a long time period. This would be the case in attempting to express the cost of a production run by means of a regression line relating it to quantity produced.

A very useful result of such an analysis is identification of fixed and variable cost components, so that the Y intercept is the estimated fixed cost per production run, while the slope of the regression line provides an estimate of variable costs per unit. Since production runs may be infrequent, obtaining sufficient data points for predictions precise enough to be useful may require historical experience from several years. But during this period, a great many changes—in labor and material costs, in efficiency (due to technological improvements), or in facilities—can cause unknown changes in the relationship between cost and production volume.

The regression assumptions presume that the same conditions prevail at all levels of production, which is probably not the case. For example, low production volumes may predominate in early time periods, with higher volumes in later years. The slope of the regression line obtained may be unduly steep, exaggerating the true cost–volume relationship if prices have been increasing over the duration. If there is inflation, labor rates and per-unit material prices will rise with time, so that all basic historical accounting data ought to be recalculated at present wage and price levels prior to regression analysis, if that is at all possible.

CORRELATION AND CAUSALITY

The correlation coefficient measures only the strength of *association* between two variables. This is a statistical relationship, and a large positive or negative value of r does not indicate that a high value of one variable necessarily *causes* the other variable to be large. Examples of nonsense or *spurious* correlations abound.

Regression and correlation analysis only provides a *statistical* relationship between two variables. It cannot tell us whether the values of X cause the values of Y. There may be a cause-and-effect relationship, but not necessarily. Possibly there is not even a logical reason for a relationship. (Although for any practical problem there is ordinarily some reasonable connection.) Often the relationship between two variables may be explained by their interactions with a common factor. Thus, we might find that a straight line provides a very close fit to the scatter diagram that relates the number of major oil slicks polluting our coasts to the number of electrical power failures. Clearly, one set of events is not caused by the other, but both may be explained by a common linkage: the demand for energy.

STATISTICS AROUND US

Sperm Whales and Stock Prices

Consider the correlation between the number of sperm whales Y caught between 1964 and 1968 and *Standard and Poor's Price Index* for 500 stocks X during the same time period. In the following table, $r = -.89$ is calculated, indicating a high negative correlation between X and Y. How do we interpret this result? Clearly, there is no apparent logical connection between whaling and the New York Stock Exchange prices of common stocks. The values of X and Y have simply moved in opposite directions by approximately the same relative amounts for the five years considered. Statistically, large values of X have occurred with small values of Y, and vice versa. Obviously, r does not measure **causality** here, because we cannot say that increasing stock prices have caused a decline in the number of sperm whales caught, or the reverse.

Year	Number of Whales Caught (thousands) X	Standard and Poor's Price Index Y	X^2	Y^2	XY
1964	29	81	841	6,561	2,349
1965	25	88	625	7,744	2,200
1966	27	85	729	7,225	2,295
1967	26	92	676	8,464	2,392
1968	24	99	576	9,801	2,376
Totals	131	445	3,447	39,795	11,612
	$= \sum X$	$= \sum Y$	$= \sum X^2$	$= \sum Y^2$	$= \sum XY$

$$\bar{X} = 26.2 \qquad \bar{Y} = 89$$

$$r = \frac{\sum XY - n\bar{X}\bar{Y}}{\sqrt{(\sum X^2 - n\bar{X}^2)(\sum Y^2 - n\bar{Y}^2)}} = \frac{11{,}612 - 5(26.2)(89)}{\sqrt{[3{,}447 - 5(26.2)^2][39{,}795 - 5(89)^2]}} = -.89$$

Sources: *Yearbook of Fishery Statistics*, Food and Agricultural Organization, United Nations; *Economic Report of the President*, February 1970.

10-8 NONLINEAR REGRESSION ANALYSIS

It must be emphasized that a straight line is not always an appropriate function relating Y to X. The scatter diagrams in Figure 10-22 illustrate cases for which various types of nonlinear functions fit the data more closely. Notice that all the functions are curves. Such relationships between X and Y are called **curvilinear** relationships.

Figure 10-22(a) shows the relationship between crop yield Y and quantity X of fertilizer applied. The curve fits data obtained for test plots to which various amounts of fertilizer have been applied. As the amount of fertilizer increases to a certain point, it proves beneficial in increasing the harvest. But beyond this point, the benefits become negative, because additional fertilizer burns plant roots and causes the crop yield to decline. The greatest increases in Y occur for small values of X, with Y increasing at a decreasing rate. The peak value of Y may be referred to as the "point of negative returns," after which Y decreases at an increasing rate. This curve expressing Y as a function of X has the shape of an inverted U. A regression equation in the form $Y = a + bX - X^2$ could be used here.

This is contrasted to the U-shaped curve in Figure 10-22(b), where the incremental or marginal cost Y of production is plotted against volume X. This regression equation assumes the form $Y = a + bX + cX^2$. Here, data points have been obtained for the various levels of production activity in a plant. At low levels of plant activity, all factors of production are employed less efficiently. But as volume increases, the cost of additional units declines as factors are employed more efficiently. Increases in efficiency become less pronounced, until a point is reached after which extra production can be handled—but less efficiently than before—and marginal costs begin to rise.

In Figure 10-22(c), the size Y of a population of *Drosophila* (fruit flies) is shown as a function of the number of generations X since the colony was established. The data points represent observations made after successive hatchings. There are no natural checks on the population growth, because the flies are reared in an artificial environment. The curve obtained is an exponential or geometric growth curve, so that Y is related to X by an expression like $Y = a^X$ or $Y = X^c$. Plots for the world's human population growth during the past several centuries assume the same basic shape. With exponential growth, Y increases at an increasing rate for larger values of X.

This is contrasted to the negative exponential curve in Figure 10-22(d), where the percentage appreciation Y in the value of each share of a mutual fund is plotted against the total money invested X by the fund. The points represent several successful mutual funds at various stages of growth. The appropriate regression equation would be in the form $Y = ae^{-bX}$. Negative exponential curves correspond to values of Y that decrease at a decreasing rate as X becomes larger. A rationale for such a result is that a small mutual fund can be highly selective in choosing its portfolio, giving it the opportunity to buy small company stocks that may appreciate greatly. But as the fund grows larger, it cannot buy as heavily into the rather limited number of small, growing companies and must invest more money in the stocks of larger, less promising firms.

Figure 10-22(e) shows a logarithmic curve relating the percentage Y of the original components of a particular type that have failed to the age X of the system.

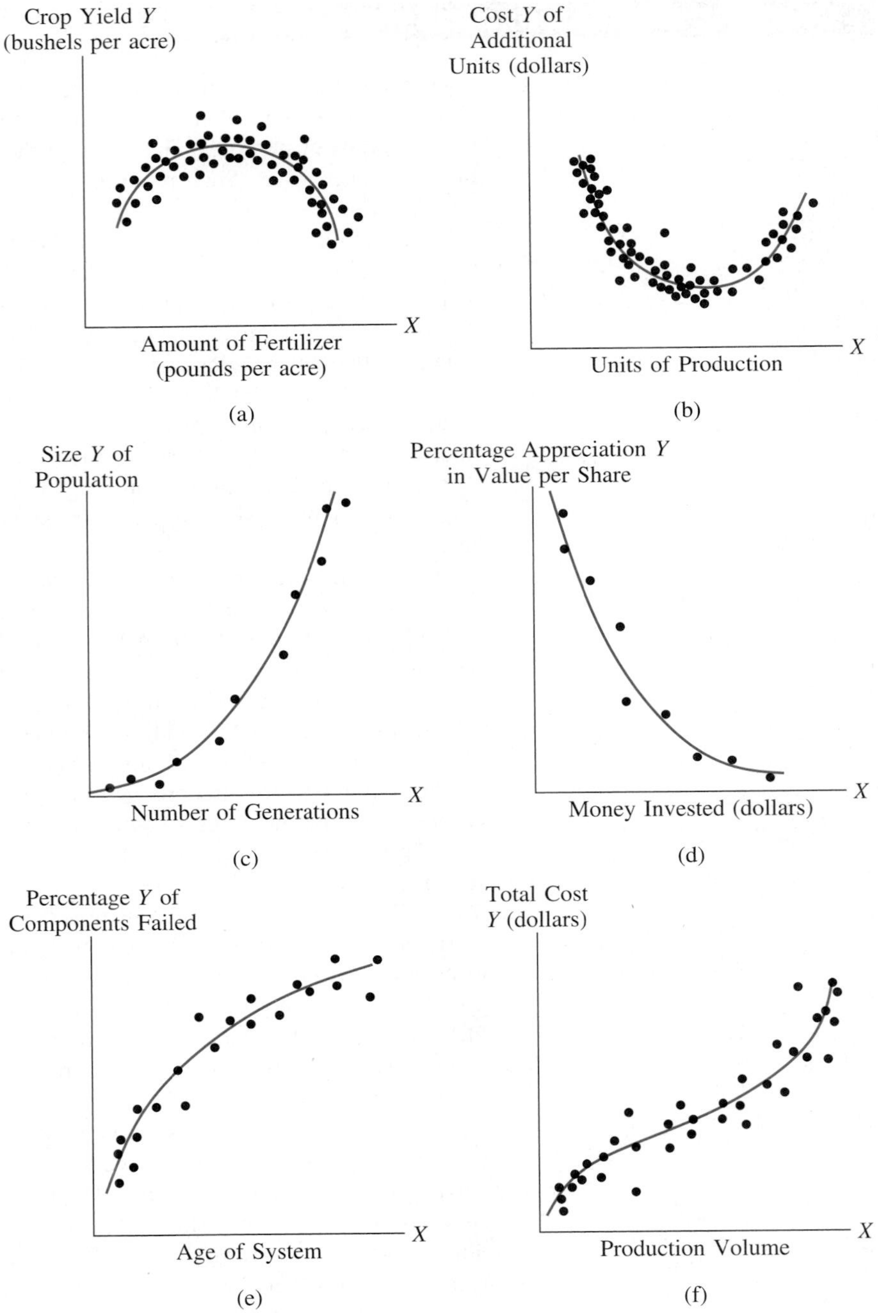

FIGURE 10-22 Scatter diagrams for examples of curvilinear relationships.

The points were obtained from the histories of several systems. Some components survive almost indefinitely, but most original components fail early. Here, values of Y increase at a decreasing rate as X becomes larger. We can express Y in terms of X by using the equation $Y = a + b \log(1 + X)$.

In Figure 10-22(f), the total cost Y of production for a plant over a particular time period is plotted against the associated levels of production activity X. These points are fitted by a curve that shows total cost increasing at a decreasing rate as greater volumes of production are achieved. Beyond a point of diminishing returns for X, the larger volume reduces incremental efficiency, and the curve shows the values of Y increasing at an increasing rate.

Throughout this chapter, we have considered only linear relationships. The procedure we use to determine the particular line that best fits the data is called *linear regression analysis*. One reason for our emphasis on linear equations is that they are easier to explain. The methods of analysis are also simpler and may be directly extended to curvilinear relationships. Straight lines are useful for describing a great many phenomena, so they are among the most common regression relationships.

SOLVING BY TRANSFORMATION OF VARIABLES

Linear regression analysis may be used to solve some nonlinear problems by first making a transformation of the variables. The dependent variable may be transformed using logarithms, so that $\log(Y)$ becomes the independent variable. The predicted values can then be converted back to original units by taking the antilogarithm. In Chapter 12 we will see in more detail how this may be done in conjunction with time-series analysis.

With the use of a computer, either X or Y may be transformed easily and followed by a linear regression analysis performed on the new variables. In doing this, the least-squares method minimizes the sum of the vertical deviations in the *transformed* units. But then the assumptions of the underlying model may not apply, so that care must be taken when making inferences.

FITTING A POLYNOMIAL

In Chapter 11, we will investigate in detail *multiple regression*. The procedures involved may be adapted to a simple nonlinear regression analysis involving just one predictor X. The estimated regression equation

$$\hat{Y}(X) = a + b_1X + b_2X^2 + b_3X^3 + \cdots$$

may be found by treating X^2, X^3, . . . as separate independent variables. The resulting regression equation is a **polynomial**.

EXERCISES

10-36 Plot the scatter diagram for each of the following sets of data. Sketch the shape of the regression curve that seems to be the best fit for each relationship.

(a)

Number of Workers X	Output per Labor Hour Y
5	10
8	4
1	3
1	2
1	7
8	8
7	10
10	2
3	5
3	8

(b)

Number of Units X	Total Cost Y
600	$11,000
50	3,100
470	10,200
910	15,700
160	6,300
950	19,500
690	13,900
90	1,800
310	8,800
1,000	25,700

(c)

Minutes between Rest X	Pounds Lifted per Minute Y
5.5	350
9.6	230
2.4	540
4.4	390
.5	910
7.9	220
2.0	680
3.3	590
13.1	90
4.2	520

SUMMARY

1. **How does statistics measure and express *association* between two or more variables?**
   Regression and correlation analyses are concerned with the *association* between two or more variables, each representing a separate quantitative population. The relationship between two variables may be suggested graphically by the **scatter diagram**.

2. **How is the correlation coefficient computed and what does it measure?**
   The **correlation coefficient**

$$r = \frac{\sum (X - \bar{X})(Y - \bar{Y})}{(n-1)s_X s_Y}$$

   measures the strength and direction of the relationship between X and Y. This value can help determine when there exists a potentially useful linear relationship between two variables. **Perfect correlation** is approached as r becomes near to 1 or -1. X and Y are **uncorrelated** whenever $r = 0$.

3. **What is the role of the regression line and how is its equation found?**
   Regression analysis predicts the level of the **dependent variable** Y when only the value of the **independent variable** X is known. You compute the predicted Y by plugging a specific X into the **estimated regression equation**

$$\hat{Y}(X) = a + bX$$

   This is also called the **estimated regression line**, which you establish by the **method of least squares** from the sample data. The Y intercept a and the slope b are the **regression coefficients**, found by the following equations.

$$b = \frac{n\sum XY - (\sum X)(\sum Y)}{n\sum X^2 - (\sum X)^2} = \frac{\sum XY - n\bar{X}\bar{Y}}{\sum X^2 - n\bar{X}^2}$$

$$a = \bar{Y} - b\bar{X}$$

   These values describe the regression line that best fits the data.

4. **How do we summarize the amount of variability in Y about the regression line and thereby achieve an important measure of the overall quality of the regression analysis?**

The overall quality of the regression line is reflected by the **standard error of the estimate**

$$s_{Y \cdot X} = \sqrt{\frac{\sum [Y - \hat{Y}(X)]^2}{n - 2}}$$

This quantity reflects the capacity of the regression line to "explain" some of the variability in values of Y. A satisfactory regression line will yield a value of $s_{Y \cdot X}$ that is considerably smaller than the sample standard deviation of Y, s_Y.

5. **What are the theoretical assumptions underlying regression analysis?**
The theory underlying regression and correlation assumes that X and Y may be related by a **true regression line**

$$\mu_{Y \cdot X} = A + BX$$

that can only be estimated by the sample results. The height of this line $\mu_{Y \cdot X}$ at any given level of X is called the **conditional mean** of the underlying population of Y values assumed to exist for that X.

Any inferences made rest upon further theoretical assumptions, among which are the normality and independence of **error terms** ε and constant variance $\sigma^2_{Y \cdot X}$ in Y populations, regardless of X. An analysis of **residuals** $e = Y - \hat{Y}(X)$ can help to assess how well those assumptions are met.

6. **How can we use the regression equation to make predictions with statistical confidence?**
Several statistical inferences may be made in conjunction with regression analysis. Especially important to business applications are **prediction intervals.** These are confidence intervals for estimating either the **conditional mean** $\mu_{Y \cdot X}$ or an individual value Y_I, both of which have a common point estimate—the height $\hat{Y}(X)$ of the estimated regression line at the given level of X. The interval for $\mu_{Y \cdot X}$ is narrower, and the width of both depends on the distance separating X from its mean $\bar{X}$.

7. **What other inferences may be made in regression analysis?**
Estimates or tests may also be made regarding the **true regression coefficients** A and B (using the sample counterparts a and b) and the **population correlation coefficient** ρ.

8. **What is the coefficient of determination and how does it relate to the quality of the regression analysis?**
The overall quality of the regression analysis may be summarized by the **coefficient of determination**, r^2.

$$r^2 = 1 - \frac{s^2_{Y \cdot X}}{s^2_Y}\left(\frac{n - 2}{n - 1}\right)$$

The coefficient of determination expresses the proportion of the variability in Y that is explained by the regression line.

9. **What is the role of the computer in regression analysis?**
Computer assistance is especially valuable in regression analysis because of the large volume of calculations needed. Popular software packages will not only find the estimated regression equation and plot scatter diagrams, but they may compute r, r^2, $s_{Y \cdot X}$, and most information needed for making inferences.

REAL-LIFE STATISTICAL CHALLENGE

Regression and Correlation Applied to the Automobile Dream List

In Chapter 9 hypothesis testing concepts were used to help analyze various populations for 232 autos. We will now apply regression and correlation testing methods to the set of "dream machines."

What factors could determine mileage? Weight of the vehicle? Transmission type? Driving skill? Engine size? To keep things simple we will investigate how gasoline mileage varies with engine size.

Using gasoline mileage Y as the dependent variable and engine size X as the independent variable, the regression equation for the population is:

$$\mu_{Y \cdot X} = 36.40 - 3.32X$$

The results are not really surprising—cars with bigger engines generally have lower mileage ratings.

In Chapter 6 three samples of $n = 5$ and one sample of $n = 15$ were described in Tables 6-19 and 6-20. The regression data for those samples are shown in Table 10-6. Observe how the slopes for the subgroups are similar to the overall population.

DISCUSSION QUESTIONS

1. Graph the regression lines for the population and the combined sample (15 cars). Comment on what you observe.
2. Graph the regression lines for all four samples. What do you observe?
3. Using the data for the combined sample, calculate the 95 percent prediction interval for the conditional mean of Y when $X = \bar{X}$.
4. Using the data for the combined sample, calculate the 95 percent prediction interval for an individual value of Y given X when $X = \bar{X}$.

TABLE 10-6 Regression Results for the 1990 Automobiles Mileage Data by Engine Displacement (X) and Highway Mileage (Y) per Gallon

	Regression Results			
	First Sample	Second Sample	Third Sample	Combined
Constant	33.34	34.82	33.15	33.56
Stand. Error of Est.	1.82	3.12	4.55	3.32
R Squared	0.45	0.71	0.46	0.49
No. of Observations	5	5	5	15
Degrees of Freedom	3	3	3	13
Slope	−2.13	−2.23	−2.95	−2.39
Stand. Error of Coeff.	1.36	0.82	1.86	0.68

REVIEW EXERCISES

10-37 The Dean at Old Ivy provided the following data for the number of outside activities X and the GPA Y for a sample of ten students.

Number of Activities X	GPA Y	Number of Activities X	GPA Y
10	3.9	3	2.8
0	3.1	4	3.3
5	3.4	5	2.6
2	2.8	4	2.5
0	1.9	3	3.2

(a) Determine the estimated regression line for predicting a student's GPA from the number of his or her activities.
(b) Compute, for GPA, (1) the sample standard deviation and (2) the standard error of the estimate.
(c) Compute (1) the sample coefficeint of determination and (2) the sample correlation coefficient.
(d) What is the predicted GPA of a student who has the following number of activities?
(1) 5 (2) 2 (3) 4 (4)10

10-38 A security analyst wants to be convinced that the efficiency of capital utilization, expressed by the annual turnover of inventory, actually does have an effect on a manufacturer's earnings. The following data have been obtained for a sample of five firms selected at random.

Company	Inventory Turnover X	Earnings as a Percentage of Sales Y
A	3	10
B	4	8
C	5	12
D	6	15
E	7	13

Calculate the correlation coefficient.

10-39 A California rancher has kept records over the past $n = 10$ years of the amount of rainfall X (inches) in his county and of the number of alfalfa bales Y he has had to buy to supplement grazing grass for his herd until he has been able to sell his excess cattle. The following estimated regression line has been obtained: $\hat{Y}(X) = 20{,}000 - 500X$. The rancher has calculated $s_Y = 1{,}000$ bales, $s_{Y \cdot X} = 500$ bales, and $\sum X^2 = 2{,}500$. The mean rainfall for the time period considered has been $\bar{X} = 15$ inches. To arrange bank financing, the rancher wishes to predict how much alfalfa he must buy for the remainder of the current year. Since the dry season has arrived, he knows how much rain has fallen. Construct the 95% prediction intervals for the required number of bales if this year's rainfall is (a) 15, (b) 20, and (c) 10 inches.

10-40 An economist has established that personal income X may be used to predict personal savings Y by the relationship $\hat{Y}(X) = 24.0 + .06X$ (billions of dollars). For each of the following levels of personal income, calculate the predicted value of personal savings.
(a) \$300 billion (b) \$500 billion (c) \$700 billion

10-41 BugOff Chemical Company determined the estimated regression line for total ingredient cost of chemical batches of size X (thousands of liters) to be $\hat{Y}(X) = \$30{,}000 + \$5{,}000X$. This result was obtained for a sample of $n = 100$ production runs, for which $s_{Y \cdot X} = \$400$ and $\bar{X} = 10$ thousand liters.

(a) Construct the 95% prediction interval for the conditional mean batch cost $\mu_{Y \cdot X}$ when $X = 10$ thousand liters.
(b) Construct the 99% prediction interval for the total cost of the next 10-thousand-liter batch.

10-42 A Fast-Gro agronomist believes that over a limited range of fertilizer levels X (gallons per acre) she can obtain a prediction of crop yield Y (bushels per acre) using the method of least squares. For a sample of $n = 25$ plots, she has established that $\hat{Y}(X) = 50 + .05X$, with $s_Y = 8$ and $s_{Y \cdot X} = 2$ bushels per acre; $\bar{X} = 210$ gallons, and $\sum X^2 = 1{,}105{,}000$. Construct the 95% prediction intervals for (a) the mean bushels per acre when the level of fertilizer applied is 200 gallons and (b) the yield of an individual 1-acre plot with the same amount of fertilizer as in (a).

STATISTICS IN PRACTICE

10-43 Consider the populations comprising all statistics students. Using as sample data the master class data list developed in Exercise 1-19, answer the following. (Note: Be sure to show all your intermediate steps. You may use intermediate answers you developed in earlier chapters to avoid unnecessary effort. If needed gather additional data such as weight, age, commute time to work or distance to work.)

(a) Select one variable as the independent variable X and one as the dependent variable Y.
(b) Determine the estimated regression equation.
(c) For the dependent variable determine the sample standard deviation and the standard error of the estimate.
(d) Calculate the sample coefficient of determination and the sample correlation coefficient.
(e) Predict the value of the dependent variable for four different independent variable values (see Exercise 10-37 as an example).
(f) Demonstrate how to calculate the 95 percent prediction interval for the conditional mean when $X = \bar{X}$.
(g) Demonstrate how to calculate the 95 percent prediction interval for an individual value of Y given X when $X = \bar{X}$.

10-44 Repeat Exercise 10-43 using your group's class data from Exercise 1-21.

10-45 Carry out a hypothesis test for the results you found in either Exercise 10-43 or 10-44. (See Section 10-9 for additional details.)

10-46 Exercise 10-37 asked you to examine the relationship between the number of outside activities and a student's GPA. Select several of your classmates (groups of at least five would work best) and list the number of outside activities and your GPAs.

(a) Add your data to the "Old Ivy" data and recalculate the estimated regression equation for predicting a student's GPA from the number of his or her activities.

(b) Compute for the GPA the sample standard deviation and the standard error of the estimate.

(c) Compute the sample coefficient of determination and the sample correlation coefficient.

(d) What is the predicted GPA for each of your group members?

(e) If you previously answered Exercise 10-37, compare the answers and comment on any similarities or differences.

10-47 *Comparing Commute Time and Distance to Work.* The following data is from a sample of graduate students who work in the Silicon Valley (San Jose, Calif.) and attend school at night.

Commute Time (Min.)	Distance (Kilometers)	Data (Rounded) (Miles)
20	8	5
20	13	8
35	21	13
45	26	16
25	24	15
30	28	17
20	20	12
45	54	33
30	28	17
15	4	3
10	8	5
20	8	5
35	31	19
35	37	23
25	18	11
5	3	2

(a) Calculate the estimated regression line for predicting a student's commute time given the distance traveled to work.

(b) Compute for the commute time the sample standard deviation and the standard error of the estimate.

(c) Compute the sample coefficient of determination and the sample correlation coefficient.

(d) What is the predicted commute time for someone living 12 miles from the office?

CASE La Boutique Fantasque

Anna Respighi runs a gift shop located in the Gentrytown Mall. The shop, La Boutique Fantasque, specializes in merchandise with a ballet theme, including objets d'art, music boxes, and figurines. Anna has hired a study group of statistics students from the local college campus to help her answer important questions about her store.

The store's 19X1 operating statements provide the following data.

Month	Wages	Utilities	Sales Volume
January	$1,500	$200	$26,000
February	2,200	250	31,500
March	1,850	225	27,450
April	1,920	185	26,450
May	2,350	195	42,440
June	1,750	210	21,010
July	1,660	195	18,075
August	1,550	180	16,350
September	1,620	200	19,330
October	2,050	210	25,370
November	2,250	235	32,340
December	3,150	305	58,730

Anna buys her merchandise from various suppliers and marks it up, so that after paying for all the freight, damage, shrinkage, and obsolescence costs, she achieves an average gross margin of 50%. Thus, for a $20 sale her cost of goods will be $10. Anna's lease requires that she pay a monthly minimum of $2,000 plus 10% of any sales over $40,000. All of her other costs, except rent, wages, and utilities, take 10% from each sales dollar.

QUESTIONS

1. Using the above data, determine the estimated regression equations for predicting (a) wages and (b) utilities from sales volume.
2. Calculate the coefficients of determination for the above equations. Comment on the quality of each regression.
3. Using the estimated regression equation found in Question 1(a), comment on the suitability of a prediction interval for mean wages.
4. Anna needs to forecast her operating profit for 19X2. She projects that month-by-month sales will be 20% higher than their 19X1 levels.
   (a) Determine her projected sales for each month of 19X2.
   (b) Using the estimated regression equations found in Question 1, predict (1) wages and (2) utilities for each month of 19X2.
   (c) Using the forcasted sales data, compute the predicted levels of rent and other costs for each month. Then, compute Anna's predicted monthly operating profit.
   (d) What will Anna's projected operating profit be for the year of 19X2?

10-9 OPTIONAL TOPIC: INFERENCES REGARDING REGRESSION COEFFICIENTS

In some applications of regression analysis, the major concern is not predictions but instead the nature of the regression equation itself. The slope and intercept of the true regression equation

$$\mu_{Y \cdot X} = A + BX$$

can be estimated or tested, so that inferences regarding A or B could be made. Such investigations are usually limited to the slope B.

CONFIDENCE INTERVAL ESTIMATE OF B

An unbiased estimate of slope B of the true regression line may be obtained from its sample counterpart b. We construct the $100(1 - \alpha)\%$

CONFIDENCE INTERVAL ESTIMATE OF SLOPE

$$B = b \pm t_{\alpha/2} \frac{s_{Y \cdot X}}{\sqrt{\sum X^2 - n\bar{X}^2}}$$

where $t_{\alpha/2}$ is found from Appendix Table F for $n - 2$ degrees of freedom.*

We may use our parts supplier illustration to apply this procedure. Suppose that a 95% confidence interval is desired for the true regression coefficient B. Using $\alpha = .05$ and $10 - 2 = 8$ degrees of freedom, we have, from Appendix Table F, $t_{\alpha/2} = t_{.025} = 2.306$. Using the intermediate calculations from Table 10-3 and the values previously determined for b and $s_{Y \cdot X}$, we construct the following 95% confidence interval.

$$B = .00897 \pm 2.306 \frac{2.02}{\sqrt{4{,}451{,}500 - 10(611)^2}} = .00897 \pm .00550$$

or

$$.00347 \leq B \leq .01447$$

*Here we use the principle that

$$B = b \pm t_{\alpha/2} \text{ (estimated } \sigma_b)$$

It can be established that

$$\sigma_b = \frac{\sigma_{Y \cdot X}}{\sqrt{\sum X^2 - n\bar{X}^2}}$$

Using $s_{Y \cdot X}$ in place of $\sigma_{Y \cdot X}$, we obtain an estimate of the standard error s_b for b.

This means that we are 95% confident that the true value of B, the mean number of days required for transporting a shipment each additional mile, falls between .00347 and .01447. (Repeating this procedure for 100 different samples, then, about 95% of the time we will construct an interval containing the true value of B.)

This interval estimate of B is not very precise and would probably be of little use to the parts supplier. As with the confidence interval for the population mean discussed in Chapter 8, precision can be increased by using a large sample—considerably larger than the one used in this illustration.

TESTING HYPOTHESES ABOUT *B*

We may extend hypothesis testing to inferences about B. Ordinarily, the fact of greatest importance in testing for the value of B is whether it equals zero. Figure 10-23 illustrates a regression line having zero slope. Note that no matter what the value of X, $\mu_{Y \cdot X}$ remains at A, parallel to the X axis. Thus, if $B = 0$, then since the population distributions of Y have the same mean and variance, we may usually conclude that the Y distributions are identical for all values of X. This means that there is no statistical relationship between X and Y. Thus, if $B = 0$, regression analysis will be of no value in making predictions of Y.

The following hypotheses apply for a two-sided testing situation.

$$H_0\colon B = 0 \quad \text{and} \quad H_A\colon B \neq 0$$

If we choose $\alpha = .05$ (to match the previous confidence level) as our significance level, then we only need to determine if our confidence interval contains the point $B = 0$. If it does not, we must reject the null hypothesis. Since the lower limit of the 95% confidence interval calculated previously is .00347, a number greater than $B = 0$, the null hypothesis must be *rejected* at a .05 significance level. We conclude that rail distance does affect transportation time.

It may be appropriate instead to employ an upper-tailed test with $H_0\colon B \leq 0$ and $H_A\colon B > 0$. This would be better if Y varies directly with X, as seems natural in the case of transportation time and distance. The first step is to calculate the

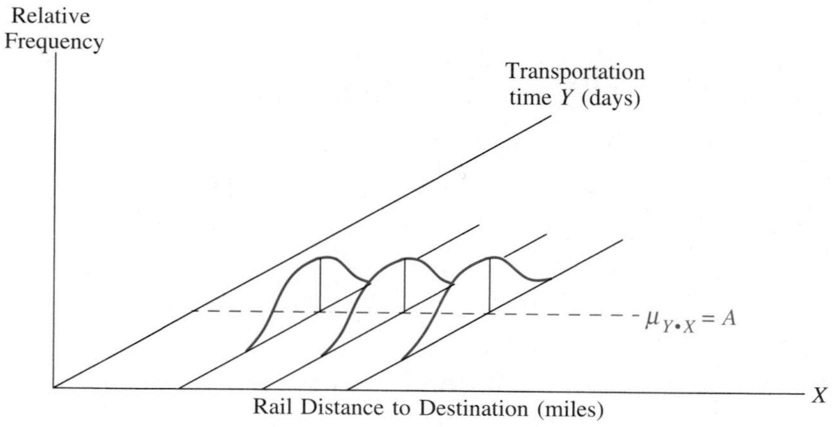

FIGURE 10-23 Illustration of a true regression line having zero slope, so that X and Y are uncorrelated.

STUDENT *t* STATISTIC FOR THE SLOPE

$$t = \frac{b - 0}{s_b} = \frac{b}{\dfrac{s_{Y \cdot X}}{\sqrt{\sum X^2 - n\bar{X}^2}}}$$

The computed value is then compared to the critical value t_α that corresponds to the prescribed significance level α. If t is smaller than t_α the null hypothesis is accepted. The opposite is true for a lower-tailed test, where the alternative is that $B < 0$ (the case when Y bears an inverse relationship to X).

We may illustrate the one-sided test using the parts supplier's results. For example, using $\alpha = .005$ and $10 - 2 = 8$ degrees of freedom, from Appendix Table F we obtain the critical value $t_{.005} = 3.355$. The computed value of the test statistic is

$$t = \frac{.00897}{\dfrac{2.02}{\sqrt{4{,}451{,}500 - 10(611)^2}}} = 3.769$$

Since $t = 3.769$ exceeds 3.355, the null hypothesis must be *rejected* at the significance level of $\alpha = .005$. This indicates that the slope of the true regression line is greater than zero.

USING *B* TO MAKE STATISTICAL INFERENCES ABOUT ρ

The population correlation coefficient ρ is the square root of the population coefficient of determination. The latter is defined as 1 minus the ratio of the variance of Y about the true regression line to the variance of Y about its mean. In order to make probability statements regarding ρ, *both* X and Y must be treated as random variables. Correlation theory requires this before we can qualify inferences about ρ. When using r as the estimator, one additional restrictive—and often unrealistic—assumption is ordinarily made to avoid mathematical difficulties in finding the sampling distribution of r. This is that X and Y have a particular joint probability distribution called the **bivariate normal distribution**. Since discussion of this distribution is beyond the scope of this book, we cannot describe the sampling distribution of r or discuss construction of the confidence interval estimates of ρ.

The far more common inference desired is a test to decide whether $\rho = 0$—that is, whether there is any statistical relationship at all between X and Y. For this purpose, we may substitute the test regarding the slope of the regression line. Recall that a slope of zero for the regression line indicates a zero correlation. Thus, a test of whether $B = 0$ may be used to reject or to accept the null hypothesis $\rho = 0$. *A test rejecting the null hypothesis that $B = 0$ will also reject the assumption that $\rho = 0$.*

```
MTB > Regress 'Time Y' 1 'Copies X'

The regression equation is
Time Y = 1.76 + 0.00546 Copies X

Predictor        Coef        Stdev    t-ratio        p
Constant       1.7576       0.2691       6.53    0.000
Copies X    0.0054638    0.0004962      11.01    0.000

s = 0.6636      R-sq = 87.1%     R-sq(adj) = 86.4%

Analysis of Variance

SOURCE         DF          SS          MS         F        p
Regression      1      53.395      53.395    121.25    0.000
Error          18       7.927       0.440
Total          19      61.322
```

Note: Figure generated on an IBM PC using Minitab®.

FIGURE 10-24 Computer printout for the duplicating center illustration.

COMPUTER-ASSISTED INFERENCES ABOUT REGRESSION COEFFICIENTS

As with prediction intervals, the computations needed to make inferences about B are burdensome. Fortunately, the popular software packages often provide the necessary information as part of regression analysis. Consider the printout in Figure 10-24 for the regression analysis of the duplicating center illustration.

The applicable values regarding inferences about the slope are found in the "Copies X" row. Listed first is the value $b = .00546$ (rounded). Next, we find the value of the standard error to be .0004962. The computed value $t = 11.01$ follows for the null hypothesis that $B = 0$. The achieved result has a prob. value of zero, to three places of accuracy.

The printout also provides analogous information for making inferences about the intercept A. The corresponding values appear in the "Constant" row.

The bottom portion of the printout contains other information, the meaning and use of which will be described in Chapter 11.

OPTIONAL EXERCISES

10-48 Refer to the information given in Exercise 10-22.

(a) Construct a 99% confidence interval estimate of the slope B of the true regression line.

(b) In testing H_0 that $B = 0$ against the two-sided alternative that $B \neq 0$, should the null hypothesis be accepted or rejected at the .01 significance level?

(c) In testing H_0 that $B \leq 0$ against the one-sided alternative that $B > 0$, should the null hypothesis be accepted or rejected at the .01 significance level?

10-49 Refer to the information given in Exercise 10-27.

(a) Construct a 95% confidence interval estimate of the slope B of the true regression line.

(b) In testing H_0 that $B = 0$ against the two-sided alternative that $B \neq 0$, should the null hypothesis be accepted or rejected at the .05 significance level?

(c) In testing H_0 that $B \geq 0$ against the one-sided alternative that $B < 0$, should the null hypothesis be accepted or rejected at the .05 significance level?

CHAPTER 11

MULTIPLE REGRESSION AND CORRELATION

BEFORE READING THIS CHAPTER, MAKE SURE YOU UNDERSTAND:

The distinction between the sample and population (Chapter 1).
The role of random samples in statistical evaluations (Chapter 4).
About confidence intervals and how they are used and constructed (Chapter 8).
About the basic concepts of hypothesis testing (Chapter 9).
The basic concepts of regression and correlation analysis (Chapter 10).

AFTER READING THIS CHAPTER, YOU WILL UNDERSTAND:

What the difference is between multiple regression and simple regression.
How to establish the multiple regression equation.
What assumptions underlie multiple regression analysis and what potential pitfalls may be encountered.
What inferences may be made with multiple regression analysis.
How to assess the overall quality of a regression analysis.
How to find a predictive regression model.
How dummy variables can be used in conjunction with multiple regression.

In Chapter 10, we learned to construct a regression equation to make predictions of a dependent variable when the value of a single independent variable is known. The techniques we used there are referred to as **simple regression and correlation analysis**. We have already noted that such predictions may be too imprecise for practical application, because a substantial amount of the variation in Y cannot be explained by X. In this chapter, these techniques will be expanded to include **multiple regression and correlation analysis**, which involves *several* independent predictor variables. The total variation in Y can then be explained by two or more variables, which permits us to make a more precise prediction in many situations than is possible in simple regression analysis.

The essential advantage in using two or more independent variables is that it allows greater use of available information. For example, a regression line expressing a new store's sales in terms of the population of the city it serves should yield a poorer sales forecast than an equation that also considers median income, number of nearby competitors, and the local unemployment rate. A plant manager ought to predict more precisely the cost of processing a new order if he considers, in addition to the size of that order, the total volume of orders, his current manpower level, or the production capacity of available equipment. A marketing manager ought to gauge more finely the sales response to a magazine advertisement by considering, in addition to its circulation, the demographical features of its readers, such as median age, median income, or proportion of urban readers.

11-1 LINEAR MULTIPLE REGRESSION INVOLVING THREE VARIABLES

In linear multiple regression analysis, we extend simple linear regression analysis to consider two or more independent variables. In the case of two independent variables, denoted by X_1 and X_2, we use the

ESTIMATED MULTIPLE REGRESSION EQUATION

$$\hat{Y} = a + b_1X_1 + b_2X_2$$

As before, $\hat{Y}$ denotes values of Y calculated from the estimated regression equation. Here, we must consider two independent variables and one dependent variable, or a total of three variables. The sample data will consist of three values for each sample unit observed, so that a scatter diagram for these observations will be three–dimensional.

REGRESSION IN THREE DIMENSIONS

To explain how sample data can be portrayed in three dimensions, we will use the analogy of the walls and the floor of a room. Letting a corner of the room represent the situation when all three variables have a value of zero, the data

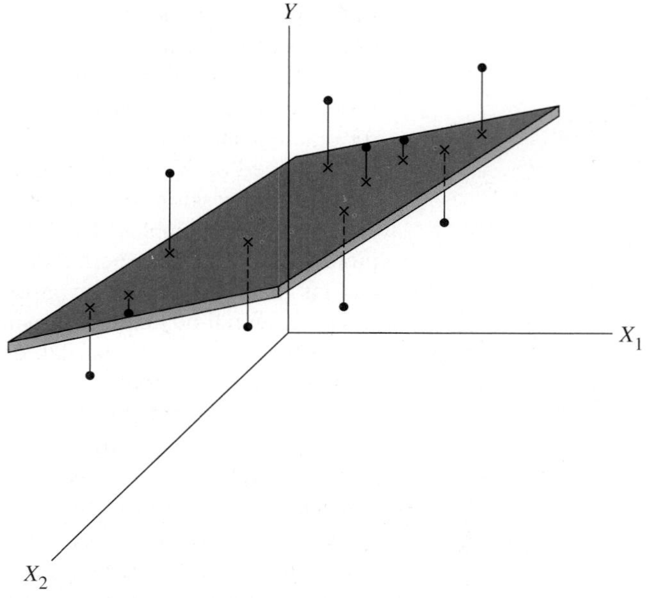

FIGURE 11-1 Scatter diagram and regression plane for multiple regression using three variables.

points may be represented by marbles suspended in space at various distances from the floor and the two walls. A marble's height above the floor can be the value of Y for that observation. Its distance along the right wall can represent the observed value of X_1, and its distance along the left wall can express the value of X_2. Figure 11-1 is a pictorial representation of one three-dimensional scatter for a hypothetical set of data.

The estimated multiple regression equation corresponds to a **plane**,* which must be slanted in the way that provides the best fit to the sample data. This results in a three-dimensional surface called the **regression plane**. Choosing this plane is analogous to determining how to position a pane of glass through the suspended marbles so that its incline approximates that of the pattern of scatter. Of course, everyone should obtain the same regression plane, so we will adapt the method of least squares to three dimensions.

The constants a, b_1, and b_2 in the equation of the regression plane $\hat{Y} = a + b_1X_1 + b_2X_2$ are called the **estimated regression coefficients**. As with $\hat{Y}(X) = a + bX$, a is the value of Y where the regression plane intersects the Y axis, so that we still refer to a as the Y intercept. However, the interpretations of b_1 and b_2 are somewhat different in multiple regression. The constant b_1 expresses the net change in Y for a one-unit increase in X_1, holding X_2 at a constant value. We can view b_1 as the slope of the edges obtained by slicing the

*Although Y is related to X_1 and X_2 by a plane instead of a line, we still say that the relationship is linear. The three-dimensional extension of a two-dimensional line is a plane. Although a line can also exist in three dimensions, it is defined as the intersection of two planes. Thus, a three-dimensional line is like a point in two dimensions, which can be defined by the intersection of two lines.

regression plane with cuts made parallel to the X_1 axis at a distance X_2 from the origin. Likewise, b_2 is the net change in X_2, holding X_1 constant. Because b_1 or b_2 by itself only indicates part of the total movement in Y in response to increases in its respective independent variable, b_1 and b_2 are referred to as **estimated partial regression coefficients**.

ILLUSTRATION: PREDICTING COLLEGE GPA

For example, suppose that college grade point average (GPA) Y (on a scale of 4) is related to high school GPA, denoted by X_1, and Scholastic Aptitude Test (SAT) score X_2 (hundreds of points) by the equation $\hat{Y} = -1.8 + .8X_1 + .3X_2$. Here $a = -1.8$, so that the regression plane cuts the Y axis at $Y = -1.8$. The regression coefficient $b_1 = .8$ signifies that a student's college GPA can be predicted to be .8 point higher for each additional point in her high school GPA, regardless of how well she has done on the SAT. The constant $b_2 = .3$ indicates that each additional 100 points on the SAT is estimated to add .3 point to a student's college GPA, no matter what her high school GPA. Thus, a "straight A" high school student (GPA = 4.0) scoring 750 on the SAT would have a predicted college GPA of

$$\hat{Y} = -1.8 + .8(4.0) + .3(7.5) = 3.65$$

which is an "A minus" average. Because the sample of students used to obtain the above regression equation will exhibit individual differences in background, motivation, study load, high school grading levels, and so forth, we cannot assume that this particular student will necessarily achieve a 3.65 GPA. As noted in Chapter 10, we must account for variability in Y, both inherent and due to sampling error.

11-2 MULTIPLE REGRESSION USING THE METHOD OF LEAST SQUARES

Mathematically, we use the method of least squares to position the regression plane so that the sum of the squared vertical deviations from its surface to the data points is minimized. The dots in Figure 11-1 represent the observed data points, and the vertical deviations of these points from the plane are shown as line segments. The crosses indicate the corresponding points on the regression plane that have identical values of X_1 and X_2. The height of a cross above the X_1X_2 plane (or the floor in our analog) represents the value of $\hat{Y}$ computed from $\hat{Y} = a + b_1X_1 + b_2X_2$. The deviation between the observed and the computed heights, $Y - \hat{Y}$, will be positive for dots lying above the regression plane and negative for dots lying below, so that the method of least squares minimizes

$$\sum (Y - \hat{Y})^2$$

As in simple regression, we determine the coefficients of the estimated regression plane by solving a set of three equations in three unknowns. As before, these are referred to as the

NORMAL EQUATIONS

$$\sum Y = na + b_1 \sum X_1 + b_2 \sum X_2$$
$$\sum X_1Y = a \sum X_1 + b_1 \sum X_1^2 + b_2 \sum X_1X_2$$
$$\sum X_2Y = a \sum X_2 + b_1 \sum X_1X_2 + b_2 \sum X_2^2$$

These equations may be obtained from the equation for a plane $Y = a + b_1X_1 + b_2X_2$. The first normal equation is found by summing each term of the plane equation, using the fact that $\sum a = na$. The second normal equation is obtained by multiplying every term in the plane equation by X_1 and summing the results. The third equation is found by multiplying every term by X_2 and summing.*

We will not introduce separate expressions for the regression coefficients here, because the resulting equations would be too complicated and cumbersome. Instead, we find a, b_1, and b_2 by calculating the required sums from the data for the various combinations of Y, X_1, and X_2 and substituting these sums into the normal equations, which are solved simultaneously.

ILLUSTRATION: PREDICTING SUPERMARKET PROFITS

In order to illustrate how to find the estimated multiple regression equation, we consider the problem of predicting profit Y for supermarkets in a large metropolitan area. As independent variables, we use the total sales X_1 of foods and X_2 of nonfoods. For simplicity of calculation, we use only the ten hypothetical observations shown in Table 11-1.

TABLE 11-1 Profit and Sales of Food and Nonfood Items

Supermarket Number	Profit (thousands of dollars) Y	Food Sales (tens of thousands of dollars) X_1	Nonfood Sales (tens of thousands of dollars) X_2
1	20	305	35
2	15	130	98
3	17	189	83
4	9	175	76
5	16	101	93
6	27	269	77
7	35	421	44
8	7	195	57
9	22	282	31
10	23	203	92

*This procedure is a mnemonic aid. Calculus was used to actually derive these equations.

One reason for splitting total sales into food and nonfood categories is that stores will differ significantly from each other in the nonfood items offered. Virtually all stores handle tobacco and cleaning agents. But some have liquor departments, offer lines of convenience hardware and small appliances, or handle clothing articles. The nonfood items typically have higher markups and move more slowly off the shelf. Thus, treating food and nonfood sales separately ought to provide a better prediction of a store's profit than total sales.

The intermediate calculations necessary to find the regression equation are shown in Table 11-2. The first eight columns contain the individual variable values and the squared and product terms. Column (9) contains the values for Y^2, which are not needed to obtain the regression coefficients but will be used later. Substituting the appropriate column totals, we obtain the following normal equations

$$191 = 10a + 2{,}270b_1 + 686b_2$$

$$48{,}690 = 2{,}270a + 594{,}832b_1 + 139{,}565b_2$$

$$12{,}569 = 686a + 139{,}565b_1 + 52{,}682b_2$$

Solving these equations simultaneously for the unknowns a, b_1, and b_2, the following solutions are obtained.

$$a = -23.074 \qquad b_1 = .1148 \qquad b_2 = .2349$$

The simultaneous solution of three normal equations by hand can be quite a chore. This task, as we will see later in this chapter, can be simplified by using a computer.

The above values for a, b_1, and b_2 provide the following estimated multiple regression equation.

$$\hat{Y} = -23.074 + .1148X_1 + .2349X_2$$

This equation may then be used to forecast the profit of a particular store. Suppose

TABLE 11-2 Intermediate Calculations for Obtaining Regression Coefficients

(1) Y	(2) X_1	(3) X_2	(4) X_1Y	(5) X_2Y	(6) X_1X_2	(7) X_1^2	(8) X_2^2	(9) Y^2
20	305	35	6,100	700	10,675	93,025	1,225	400
15	130	98	1,950	1,470	12,740	16,900	9,604	225
17	189	83	3,213	1,411	15,687	35,721	6,889	289
9	175	76	1,575	684	13,300	30,625	5,776	81
16	101	93	1,616	1,488	9,393	10,201	8,649	256
27	269	77	7,263	2,079	20,713	72,361	5,929	729
35	421	44	14,735	1,540	18,524	177,241	1,936	1,225
7	195	57	1,365	399	11,115	38,025	3,249	49
22	282	31	6,204	682	8,742	79,524	961	484
23	203	92	4,669	2,116	18,676	41,209	8,464	529
191 $= \sum Y$	2,270 $= \sum X_1$	686 $= \sum X_2$	48,690 $= \sum X_1Y$	12,569 $= \sum X_2Y$	139,565 $= \sum X_1X_2$	594,832 $= \sum X_1^2$	52,682 $= \sum X_2^2$	4,267 $= \sum Y^2$

that a new store is built that will have estimated sales of $2,500,000 for foods and $750,000 for nonfoods. To match the sample data, the food and nonfood sales are both expressed in increments of $10,000, so that $X_1 = 250$ and $X_2 = 75$. The estimated store profit for these sales levels would be

$$\begin{aligned}\hat{Y} &= -23.074 + .1148(250) + .2349(75)\\ &= 23.244 \text{ (thousand dollars) or } \$23{,}244\end{aligned}$$

We may interpret the value $b_1 = .1148$ as follows. For each $10,000 increase in food sales there will be an estimated increase of .1148 thousand dollars, or $114.80, in profits, holding the sales of nonfood items at any fixed level. Likewise, each additional $10,000 in nonfood sales results in an estimated profit increase of $b_2 = .2349$ thousand dollars, or $234.90, for any fixed amount of food sales. Thus the marginal contribution of nonfoods to profits is, dollar for dollar, slightly more than twice that of the foods. The result $a = -23.074$ signifies that $23,074 of "fixed" costs, on the average, must be absorbed before a store can show a profit. These correspond to those expenses, such as rent, that continue whether or not the store is open. The $23,074 figure may vary considerably from the actual fixed costs of any particular store, because of sampling error and due to different store characteristics. It also depends on (1) the linear model being appropriate and (2) the validity of extrapolation down to zero sales for both types of items.

ADVANTAGES OF MULTIPLE REGRESSION

Two interesting questions may be posed regarding the use of multiple rather than simple regression analysis. First, is the simultaneous analysis of two independent variables through multiple regression any improvement over that obtained through two separate simple regressions? Second, how can we show that the accuracy of predictions is improved by the use of multiple regression analysis? We will begin to answer these questions by continuing with our supermarket illustration.

Three two-dimensional diagrams for the supermarket data are shown in Figure 11-2. In Figure 11-2(a), profit is plotted against food sales. Food sales X_1 by itself might be a fairly reliable predictor of profit Y, since there is a high value of .76 for the sample correlation coefficient. Denoting this particular sample correlation coefficient by the double-subscripted symbol r_{Y1}, where $Y1$ indicates that the strength of association between the variables Y and X_1 is being measured, we have $r_{Y1} = .76$. A similar figure may be obtained for any pair of the three variables. Thus, analysis relating profit Y to nonfood sales X_2 provides another sample correlation coefficient, $r_{Y2} = -.29$. A cursory examination of this second relationship, shown in Figure 11-2(b), seems to indicate that nonfood sales have little effect on profits. Does this indicate that nonfood sales would be a poor predictor of a store's income? Two-variable analysis seems to contradict our previous finding that profit will increase by an estimated $234.90 for each additional $10,000 in nonfood sales. How might we explain this?

A comparison of food sales X_1 to nonfood sales X_2, as represented by the scatter diagram in Figure 11-2(c), shows a pronounced negative correlation between these two variables. We distinguish the sample correlation coefficient in this case from the others by using the subscript 12; here, $r_{12} = -.77$. Supermarkets having higher than average food sales tend to have lower than average nonfood sales,

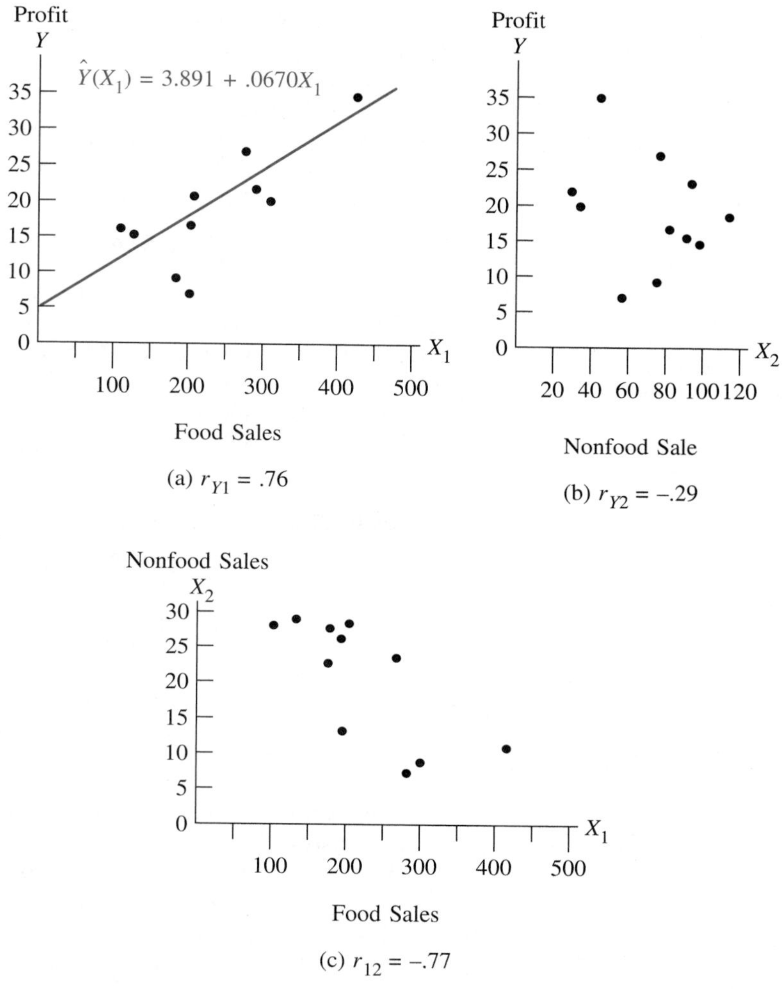

FIGURE 11-2 Scatter diagrams for variable pairs using supermarket data.

whereas the reverse is true for stores with below average food sales. By specializing heavily in nonfood items, the operators having a low volume of food sales manage to survive and achieve profits in the face of competition from stores more successful at selling food. The two stores having annual food sales below \$1.5 million have extraordinarily large profits, which are not very well explained by food sales alone. Their data points lie considerably above the regression line in Figure 11-2(a). The impact of nonfood sales is camouflaged by the interaction of food and nonfood sales.

This illustrates a general inadequacy in using simple regression to separately determine how a dependent variable relates to several independent variables. The same is true of correlation. Separate simple correlations of Y versus X_1 and Y versus X_2 seem to indicate that food sales would be a far better predictor of profit than nonfood sales. A two-variable analysis indicates that X_2 has a negligible correlation with Y of $r_{Y2} = -.29$. But it would be a blunder to discard X_2 because it shows such a small correlation with Y. This is because X_2 is highly negatively correlated with X_1, $r_{12} = -.77$, so that its influence on Y can be explained only by considering how Y relates to both X_1 and X_2 through multiple regression. The interactions between the predictor variables themselves must first be determined before a variable can be discarded. We will later present techniques of multiple regression and correlation analysis used to provide this information.

RESIDUALS AND THE STANDARD ERROR OF THE ESTIMATE

We have seen that the errors in making predictions from the regression line are smaller when the scatter of the data is less pronounced. The degree of such variation in Y can be expressed by the standard error of the estimate for values of Y. The same is true in multiple regression. The standard error of the estimate for values of Y about the regression *plane* is computed in the same way. This is determined from the following expression for the

STANDARD ERROR OF THE ESTIMATE

$$S_{Y \cdot 12} = \sqrt{\frac{\sum (Y - \hat{Y})^2}{n - 3}}$$

We use a different subscript notation, $Y \cdot 12$, to show that two independent variables X_1 and X_2 are being used to predict Y. As in simple regression, we find the standard error of the estimate by taking the square root of the mean squared deviations of observed Y values from the estimated regression plane. The divisor $n - 3$ is chosen because 3 degrees of freedom are lost in estimating the regression coefficients. This makes $S^2_{Y \cdot 12}$ an unbiased estimator of the variance of Y about the true regression plane.

As in simple regression, the vertical deviations $Y - \hat{Y}$ are referred to as **residuals**. This terminology reflects that the sum of the squared residuals represents the variation in Y left unexplained by the regression analysis. It is the unexplained variation in the evaluation that remains, and thus provides the residual. By including one more independent predictor variable in an expanded regression analysis, there may be a resulting reduction in the unexplained variation. The expanded regression would then provide a sum of the squared residuals that is smaller.

The predicted and residual values for the supermarket illustration are computed in Table 11-3. Notice that the residual values (vertical deviations) sum to zero (except for rounding errors). The least-squares procedure guarantees this outcome. The standard error of the estimate is

$$S_{Y \cdot 12} = \sqrt{\frac{132.2522}{10 - 3}} = 4.347 \text{ (thousand dollars)}$$

When performing the regression calculations by hand with a calculator, it may be simpler to use the following

SHORTCUT EXPRESSION FOR THE STANDARD ERROR

$$s_{Y \cdot 12} = \sqrt{\frac{\sum Y^2 - a\sum Y - b_1 \sum X_1 Y - b_2 \sum X_2 Y}{n - 3}}$$

because it does not require $\hat{Y}$ to be calculated for every data point.

Using the data in Table 11-2 and the regression constants found previously, we calculate the standard error of the estimate

$$s_{Y \cdot 12} = \sqrt{\frac{4{,}267 - (-23.074)(191) - .1148(48{,}690) - .2349(12{,}569)}{10 - 3}}$$

$$= 4.343 \text{ (thousand dollars)}$$

(Due to rounding this value differs slightly from the earlier result.)

This value may be compared to the corresponding standard error found in a simple regression for profit Y and food sales X_1. Using X_1 as the only independent variable, and then applying the procedures of Chapter 10 to the supermarket data, we find the regression line

$$\hat{Y}(X_1) = 3.891 + .0670X_1$$

The scatter of data about this regression *line* is summarized by the standard error of the estimate

$$s_{Y \cdot X_1} = 5.719 \text{ (thousand dollars)}$$

TABLE 11-3 Actual, Predicted, and Residual Values for Three-Variable Regression Analysis Using the Supermarket Data

Actual Profit Y	Predicted Value $\hat{Y}$	Residual Value $Y - \hat{Y}$	Squared Deviation $(Y - \hat{Y})^2$
20	20.1615	−0.1615	0.0261
15	14.8702	0.1298	0.0168
17	18.1199	−1.1199	1.2542
9	14.8684	−5.8684	34.4381
16	10.3665	5.6335	31.7363
27	25.8945	1.1055	1.2221
35	35.5924	−0.5924	0.3509
7	12.7013	−5.7013	32.5048
22	16.5815	5.4185	29.3601
23	21.8412	1.1588	1.3428
191	189.9974	0.0026	132.2522

Comparing this with the standard error of the estimate about the regression *plane*, $S_{Y\cdot 12} = 4.343$, we see that multiple regression provides a better interpretation of the data. As we noted earlier, the standard error expresses the amount of variation in Y that is left unexplained by regression analysis. Since $S_{Y\cdot 12}$ is smaller than $s_{Y\cdot X_1}$, our regression plane (incorporating both food and nonfood sales as *two* independent variables) explains more of the variation in Y than the regression line does (where food sales serves as the *single* independent variable and there is more unexplained variation). This indicates that all inclusion of nonfood sales data in the analysis will indeed provide better predictions of store profit.

ASSUMPTIONS OF MULTIPLE REGRESSION

The assumptions of linear multiple regression are similar to those of simple regression. The least-squares method provides a plane that is an estimate of

$$\mu_{Y\cdot 12} = A + B_1X_1 + B_2X_2$$

where $\mu_{Y\cdot 12}$ denotes the **conditional mean** of Y, given X_1 and X_2. The values of the true regression coefficients A, B_1, and B_2 remain unknown and are estimated by a, b_1, and b_2, respectively. For each combination of X_1 and X_2 there is a corresponding point on the true regression plane. The height of this point is $\mu_{Y\cdot 12}$, the mean of the corresponding population of Y.

The theoretical model expresses each observation in terms of the expression

$$Y = A + B_1X_1 + B_2X_2 + \varepsilon$$

where ε is the error term. Ordinarily, the ε's are assumed to be independent and normally distributed with mean 0 and standard deviation $\sigma_{Y\cdot 12}$. For any specified levels of X_1 and X_2, the Ys would then be normally distributed with mean $\mu_{Y\cdot 12}$ and standard deviation $\sigma_{Y\cdot 12}$.

CHALLENGES AND PITFALLS OF MULTIPLE REGRESSION ANALYSIS

There are several challenges associated with regression analysis involving several variables. It is a process fraught with pitfalls. A few issues and difficulties should be addressed.

VIOLATIONS OF THE UNDERLYING MODEL

Multiple regression analysis is subject to all of the potential complications discussed in Section 10-6 for simple regression. These include nonlinear relationships between variables, nonconstant variance in the error terms, outliers, and nonnormality in error terms. As in Chapter 10, *residual analysis* may be helpful in identifying some of the problem areas, and many of the same remedies apply in multiple regression. We will see that greater challenges are created by the existence of several variables and their interrelationships.

MULTICOLLINEARITY

A potential problem in multiple regression applications can arise when two independent variables are highly correlated. Business applications are especially prone to such high correlations. For example, consider retail sales and foot traffic or magazine advertising revenue and number of pages. In a three-variable situation, such a relationship would provide sample data that are scattered closely about a single line lying inside the least-squares regression plane. Although the estimated regression equation can be found with no special difficulty when X_1 and X_2 are highly correlated, a second set of sample observations may result in drastically different regression coefficients, even when the second line of scatter is nearly identical to the first one. Because many different regression planes can contain the same line, the regression exhibits **multicollinearity**.

The inherent instability of multicollinearity is reflected in imprecise regression coefficients that would vary widely from sample to sample. If the investigator is only interested in making predictions or estimating the conditional mean, multicollinearity presents no problem. But if the primary concern is in separate assessments of the effects of the independent variables, it may be better to evaluate X_1 and X_2 each in a separate study. In some cases, including a third independent variable will eliminate the problem created by the multicollinearity.

Time-Series Data

Some of the more interesting applications of regression involve data generated over time. This is epitomized by the problem economists face when they must use regression analysis to establish the mathematical forms of various relationships, such as those involving supply and demand curves. When data for evaluations are collected at regular intervals from monthly, quarterly, or annual reports, they are referred to as **time-series data**.

Time-series data may present special difficulties arising from a **serial correlation** between observations made in successive time periods. A serial correlation or **autocorrelation** exists whenever there is a tendency for similar values to follow the earlier number. For example, the following successive monthly seasonally adjusted unemployment rates show a serial correlation.

7.3 7.4 7.6 7.5 7.3 7.1 7.0 6.9 6.9 7.1 7.2 7.3

Notice that each successive monthly rate lies close to the preceding level, reflecting the inertia in the economy.

Serial correlations are common in time-series data. Difficulties arise when the error terms, or deviations $Y - \hat{Y}$, are serially correlated. Key assumptions of the underlying regression model are thereby violated, making the least-squares method inefficient and invalidating the inferences made. The problem might be alleviated by including another independent variable which is itself serially correlated. For example, a regression where the dependent variable is company profit and the independent variable is number of orders would involve a high serial correlation in error terms due to inflation (which raises unit prices, and thus, revenue and profits); inclusion of the consumer price index as a second independent variable might eliminate the difficulties.

Procedures exist for testing for serial correlation. A detailed discussion may be found in many of the references listed in the back of this book.

Computational Demands

Multiple regression analysis involves a substantially greater amount of computation than we encountered for simple regression in Chapter 10. It takes a great deal of patience and devotion to detail to successfully wade through those calculations by hand. The following example comprehensively illustrates all the steps involved in determining an estimated regression equation.

After working through one multiple regression problem by hand (or just carefully following all the steps in the example), the need for computer assistance becomes obvious. When four or more variables are involved a computer is almost mandatory. Section 11-3 describes in detail computer-assisted multiple regression analysis.

EXAMPLE: WEETEES PRODUCTION COSTS

Consider the problem of estimating the total cost Y of a production batch of WeeTees using quantity produced X_1 and grain price index X_2 as the independent variables. The following sample data apply.

Sample i	Total Cost (thousands of dollars) Y	Production Quantity (tons) X_1	Grain Price Index X_2
1	200	400	120
2	85	150	134
3	115	220	115
4	200	500	90
5	140	300	85
6	65	100	140
7	70	150	95
8	65	150	80
9	125	240	96
10	190	350	125

SOLUTION: The multiple regression procedure begins with the calculation of sums and sums of squares and products.

Y	X_1	X_2	$X_1 Y$	$X_1 X_2$	$X_2 Y$	X_1^2	X_2^2	Y^2
200	400	120	80,000	24,000	48,000	160,000	14,400	40,000
85	150	134	12,750	11,390	20,100	22,500	17,956	7,225
115	220	115	25,300	13,225	25,300	48,400	13,225	13,225
200	500	90	100,000	18,000	45,000	250,000	8,100	40,000
140	300	85	42,000	11,900	25,500	90,000	7,225	19,600
65	100	140	6,500	9,100	14,000	10,000	19,600	4,225
70	150	95	10,500	6,650	14,250	22,500	9,025	4,900
65	150	80	9,750	5,200	12,000	22,500	6,400	4,225
125	240	96	30,000	12,000	23,040	57,600	9,216	15,625
190	350	125	66,500	23,750	43,750	122,500	15,625	36,100
1,255 $=\sum Y$	2,560 $=\sum X_1$	1,080 $=\sum X_2$	383,300 $=\sum X_1 Y$	135,215 $=\sum X_2 Y$	270,940 $=\sum X_1 X_2$	806,000 $=\sum X_1^2$	120,772 $=\sum X_2^2$	185,125 $=\sum Y^2$

The appropriate values are placed in the normal equations.

$$1{,}255 = 10a + 2{,}560b_1 + 1{,}080b_2$$
$$383{,}300 = 2{,}560a + 806{,}000b_1 + 270{,}940b_2$$
$$135{,}215 = 1{,}080a + 270{,}940b_1 + 120{,}772b_2$$

To solve these normal equations, we eliminate all but one of the unknowns. We start by combining the first two equations to eliminate a.

$$\left.\begin{array}{r} -256(1{,}255 = 10a + 2{,}560b_1 + 1{,}080b_2) \\ 383{,}300 = 2{,}560a + 806{,}000b_1 + 270{,}940b_2 \end{array}\right\} \rightarrow \begin{array}{rl} -321{,}280 = & -2{,}560a - 655{,}360b_1 - 276{,}480b_2 \\ 383{,}300 = & 2{,}560a + 806{,}000b_1 + 270{,}940b_2 \\ \hline 62{,}020 = & 0a + 150{,}640b_1 - 5{,}540b_2 \end{array}$$

We next combine the first and the third equations, again eliminating a.

$$\left.\begin{array}{r} -108(1{,}255 = 10a + 2{,}560b_1 + 1{,}080b_2) \\ 135{,}215 = 1{,}080a + 270{,}940b_1 + 120{,}772b_2 \end{array}\right\} \rightarrow \begin{array}{rl} -135{,}540 = & -1{,}080a - 276{,}480b_1 - 116{,}640b_2 \\ 135{,}215 = & 1{,}080a + 270{,}940b_1 + 120{,}772b_2 \\ \hline -325 = & 0a - 5{,}540b_1 + 4{,}132b_2 \end{array}$$

By combining the two resulting equations and eliminating b_2, we find the value of b_1.

$$\left.\begin{array}{r} 4{,}132(62{,}020 = 150{,}640b_1 - 5{,}540b_2) \\ 5{,}540(\ -325 = -5{,}540b_1 + 4{,}132b_2) \end{array}\right\} \rightarrow \begin{array}{rl} 256{,}266{,}640 = & 622{,}444{,}480b_1 - 22{,}891{,}280b_2 \\ -1{,}800{,}500 = & -30{,}691{,}600b_1 + 22{,}891{,}280b_2 \\ \hline 254{,}466{,}140 = & 591{,}752{,}880b_1 + 0b_2 \end{array}$$

$$b_1 = .430$$

We substitute b_1 into either of the equations having two variables to find the value of b_2.

$$62{,}020 = 150{,}640(.430) - 5{,}540b_2$$
$$62{,}020 = 64{,}775.2 - 5{,}540b_2$$
$$5{,}540b_2 = 2{,}755.2$$
$$b_2 = .497$$

We substitute b_1 and b_2 into one of the original equations with three variables to find the value of a.

$$1{,}255 = 10a + 2{,}560(.430) + 1{,}080(.497)$$
$$1{,}255 = 10a + 1{,}100.80 + 536.76$$
$$1{,}255 = 10a + 1{,}637.56$$
$$-10a = 382.56$$
$$a = -38.3$$

Substituting the values found for a, b_1, and b_2 into the estimated multiple regression equation, we get

$$\hat{Y} = -38.3 + .430X_1 + .497X_2$$

The predicted cost of WeeTees production runs can be made from the estimated regression equation. Consider the following.

Production Quantity (tons) X_1	Grain Price Index X_2	Predicted Cost (thousands of dollars) $\hat{Y}$
100	90	$\hat{Y}=-38.3+.430(100)+.497(90)\ =49.4$
150	110	$\hat{Y}=-38.3+.430(150)+.497(110)=80.9$
200	70	$\hat{Y}=-38.3+.430(200)+.497(70)\ =82.5$

EXERCISES

11-1 Determine the predicted level of Y for each of the following situations.

(a) $\hat{Y} = 10 + 2X_1 + 3X_2$ given $X_1 = 5$ and $X_2 = 10$.

(b) $\hat{Y} = -20 + 4X_1 + 5X_2$ given $X_1 = 1$ and $X_2 = .5$.

(c) $\hat{Y} = 14.67 + .23X_1 - .58X_2$ given $X_1 = 55$ and $X_2 = 27$.

11-2 Solve the following system of simultaneous equations.

a = -8.167
b₁ = 4.25
b₂ = -3.417

$$5 = 2a + 1b_1 - 5b_2$$
$$2 = 1a + 4b_1 + 2b_2$$
$$-1 = 2a + 2b_1 - 2b_2$$

11-3 An economist wishes to predict the incomes of restaurants that are more than two years old using total floor space X_1 and number of employees X_2 as independent variables. The following data have been obtained for a sample of $n=5$ restaurants.

Income (thousands of dollars) Y	Floor Space (thousands of square feet) X_1	Number of Employees X_2
20	10	15
15	5	8
10	10	12
5	3	7
10	2	10

(a) Determine the estimated regression equation.

(b) State the meaning of the partial regression coefficients b_1 and b_2.

11-4 A college admissions director wishes to predict college GPA Y from the regression equation

$$\hat{Y} = .5 + .8X_1 + .003X_2$$

Using high school GPA X_1 and IQ score X_2 as independent variables, calculate the predicted college GPA for the following students.

	High School GPA X_1	IQ Score X_2
(a)	2.9	123
(b)	3.0	118
(c)	2.7	105
(d)	3.5	136

11-5 A Crunchola food processing manager wishes to predict the total cost Y of production runs from a least-squares regression. As independent variables she uses production quantity X_1 and wheat price index X_2. The following data apply.

Total Cost (thousands of dollars) Y	Production Quantity (tons) X_1	Wheat Price Index X_2
1,950	3,750	118
910	1,450	128
1,130	2,300	119
2,100	5,100	85
1,370	3,100	90
700	950	137
690	1,450	100
710	1,450	82
1,300	2,500	94
2,010	3,750	126

(a) Determine the estimated regression equation.

(b) By how much do these results indicate that total cost will increase if one additional ton is produced? If the wheat price index goes up one point?

11-6 The editor of a statistics journal wishes to predict the total typing hours Y for article drafts. As independent variables, she uses the number of words in the draft X_1 (tens of thousands) and an index X_2 for level of difficulty on a scale from 1 (least difficult) to 5 (most difficult). The following intermediate calculations have been obtained.

$$n=25 \qquad \sum Y=200 \qquad \sum X_1=100 \qquad \sum X_2=75$$

$$\sum X_1Y = 1{,}000 \qquad \sum X_2Y = 800 \qquad \sum X_1^2 = 600$$

$$\sum X_2^2 = 325 \qquad \sum Y^2 = 3{,}800 \qquad \sum X_1X_2 = 200$$

(a) Determine the equation for the regression plane $\hat{Y} = a + b_1X_1 + b_2X_2$.

(b) State the meaning of the values you obtain for b_1 and b_2.

11-7 A real estate appraiser wishes to predict the selling price of a home Y using building size X_1 and lot size X_2 as independent variables. The following data apply.

Price (thousands of dollars) Y	Building Size (hundreds of square feet) X_1	Lot Size (thousands of square feet) X_2
45	21	21
37	16	23
26	17	7
32	14	9
34	19	11
49	18	45
53	23	12
65	22	10
71	24	10
88	26	22

(a) Calculate the sums and the sums of squares and product terms.
(b) Express the normal equations, and solve them simultaneously to obtain the estimated multiple regression coefficients. Then, determine the estimated multiple regression equation.
(c) Compute the standard error of the estimate.

11-8 Refer to the intermediate calculations given in Exercise 11-6.
(a) Determine the equation for the estimated regression line $\hat{Y}(X_1) = a + bX_1$ using a *single* independent variable X_1.
(b) Compute $s_{Y \cdot X_1}$ using X_1 instead of X in the expression for $s_{Y \cdot X}$ on page 429. Then, compute $S_{Y \cdot 12}$ using the expression on page 483. Do you think more accurate predictions result if the variable X_2 is included than if X_1 is the sole predictor? Why?

11-3 MULTIPLE REGRESSION: COMPUTER APPLICATIONS

Multiple regression may involve more than two independent variables. For example, in predicting college GPA, we could also include the number of extracurricular high school activities, since this information is usually considered in making college admissions decisions. Including this third independent variable, denoted by X_3, would provide the regression equation

$$\hat{Y} = a + b_1X_1 + b_2X_2 + b_3X_3$$

To determine the regression coefficients, additional product sums involving X_3 must be computed and four normal equations must be solved simultaneously.

In multiple regression using X_1, X_2, and X_3, we compute the standard error of the estimate about the regression **hyperplane**. (Including Y, there are now four variables, and the regression surface can no longer be graphed in only three dimensions. Mathematicians call a four-dimensional plane a "hyperplane.") The standard error, denoted by $S_{Y \cdot 123}$, is calculated in the same way that we calculate $S_{Y \cdot 12}$, but with the extra term $-b_3 \sum X_3Y$ in the numerator. The denominator will be $n - 4$. The number of degrees of freedom will also be $n - 4$, and we calculate the prediction intervals as we did before, except using this reduced value.

When more predictor variables are added, we can expand the regression analysis by including X_4, X_5, and so on. When there are m total variables (one dependent and $m - 1$ independent), the number of degrees of freedom will be $n - m$, which is used as the denominator in computing the standard error and in finding $t_{\alpha/2}$ when constructing prediction intervals.

A computer application will now be discussed to illustrate multiple regression using three independent variables.

COMPUTER-ASSISTED MULTIPLE REGRESSION ANALYSIS

A computer generally provides greater levels of accuracy due to its superior capability of handling a large number of significant figures. It is not necessary for users to prepare their own computer programs to perform regression and correlation analysis. The widely available software packages vary considerably in format and type of output data, but they usually include determinations of the regression coefficients (a, b_1, b_2, and so on), standard errors, and correlation coefficients. These packages can be elaborate enough to include lower-dimensional regression equations for several variable combinations, values of the t statistics (used in making inferences regarding regression coefficients), and coefficients of partial determination (to be discussed in Section 11-5). The most complex programs provide inference-making computations that are too sophisticated to discuss here.

To explain the use of the computer, we will expand our supermarket illustration to include a third independent variable—the size of the store in thousands of square feet. Our previous sample data are augmented by including the ten observations for X_3 provided in Table 11-4.

A multiple regression run using the augmented supermarket data was performed and the computer printout in Figure 11-3 was generated. The top portion of the printout shows the data entered and the necessary commands for the program. Next, is the regression run, broken down into three parts. First, we find the information regarding the estimated regression equation; second, the analysis of variance (to be discussed in Section 11-4); and third, the printout provides the

TABLE 11-4 Sample Data for Supermarket Profits, Augmented

Supermarket Number	Food Sales (tens of thousands of dollars) X_1	Nonfood Sales (tens of thousands of dollars) X_2	Store Size (thousands of square feet) X_3	Profit (thousands of dollars) Y
1	305	35	35	20
2	130	98	22	15
3	189	83	27	17
4	175	76	16	9
5	101	93	28	16
6	269	77	46	27
7	421	44	56	35
8	195	57	12	7
9	282	31	40	22
10	203	92	32	23

```
MTB > Print c1-c4
```

```
ROW   Food  Nonfood   Size  Profit
      X1    X2        X3    Y
  1    305      35      35      20
  2    130      98      22      15
  3    189      83      27      17
  4    175      76      16       9
  5    101      93      28      16
  6    269      77      46      27
  7    421      44      56      35
  8    195      57      12       7
  9    282      31      40      22
 10    203      92      32      23
```

```
MTB > Name c5 = 'SRES1' c6 = 'FITS1' c7 = 'RESI1'
MTB > Regress c4 3 c1-c3 'SRES1' 'FITS1';
SUBC>   Residuals 'RESI1'.
```

```
The regression equation is
Profit = - 10.2 + 0.0270 Food + 0.0971 Nonfood + 0.525 Size

Predictor        Coef          Stdev       t-ratio        p
Constant      -10.170 a        3.473 s_a     -2.93     0.026
Food          0.02704 b1     0.01204 s_b1     2.25     0.066
Nonfood       0.09705 b2     0.03015 s_b2     3.22     0.018
Size          0.52468 b3     0.05916 s_b3     8.87     0.000

s = 1.250          R-sq = 98.5%         R-sq(adj) = 97.7%
    S_Y·123              R^2
Analysis of Variance

SOURCE         DF          SS               MS             F         p
Regression      3      609.53 SSR      203.18 MSR    130.06     0.000
Error           6        9.37 SSE        1.56 MSE
Total           9      618.90 SSTO

SOURCE         DF      SEQ SS
Food            1      357.56
Nonfood         1      129.09
Size            1      122.88
```

```
MTB > Print c1 c4 c6 c7 c5.
```

```
ROW   Food   Profit     FITS1      RESI1      SRES1

  1    305       20   19.8368    0.16315    0.15738
  2    130       15   14.3987    0.60131    0.55938
  3    189       17   17.1615   -0.16154   -0.13975
  4    175        9   10.3322   -1.33221   -1.27938
  5    101       16   16.2774   -0.27738   -0.34409
  6    269       27   28.7111   -1.71110   -1.64730
  7    421       35   34.8649    0.13509    0.18844
  8    195        7    6.9303    0.06973    0.08087
  9    282       22   21.4501    0.54987    0.72267
 10    203       23   21.0369    1.96309    1.82476
       X1        Y      Ŷ         ε=Y-Ŷ
```

Note: Figure generated on an IBM PC using Minitab®.

FIGURE 11-3 Computer printout for the augmented supermarket data.

actual Y and predicted or fitted $\hat{Y}$ values—with residuals—computed for all of the observations.

Although the presentation may vary, most computer programs provide the same information as shown in Figure 11-3. The more important values are identified with annotated symbols added to the printout. The results indicate that store profit may be predicted from the estimated regression equation

$$\hat{Y} = -10.170 + .027X_1 + .097X_2 + .525X_3$$

We may interpret the values for the partial regression coefficients. The value $b_1 = .027$ indicates that a store's profit will increase by an estimated .027 thousand dollars or $27, for each additional $10,000 in food sales, holding other variables fixed. This is smaller than the value for b_1 found in the previous three-variable regression, but b_1 has a different meaning here. Instead of a single additional variable, two variables, both nonfood sales and store size, are accounted for and are being held constant. Likewise, $b_2 = .097$ indicates that holding store size and food sales constant, store profits will increase by an estimated $97 for each $10,000 in nonfood sales. The independent variable X_3, store size, has a partial regression coefficient of value $b_3 = .525$, indicating that a supermarket can increase its profits by an estimated $525 for each thousand square feet of additional floor space.

The substantial changes in the values a, b_1, and b_2 from the earlier multiple regression indicate that including store size X_3 as one of the independent variables should lead to better profit predictions. This improvement can be seen by comparing the standard error of the estimate of $S_{Y \cdot 123} = 1.250$ (shown in the computer printout) to the earlier one of 4.343. Including the additional variable X_3 for store size reduces the standard error of the estimate of Y considerably. This indicates that profit can be predicted with greater precision when store size is included as well as food and nonfood sales.

EXERCISES

11-9 An economist wishes to predict total spending for a sample of 10 families using income, family size, and additional savings as the three independent variables. The following data apply.

Family	Total Spending Y	Income X_1	Family Size X_2	Additional Savings X_3
A	$ 8,000	$10,000	3	$1,000
B	7,000	10,000	2	1,500
C	7,000	9,000	2	700
D	12,000	16,000	4	1,800
E	6,000	7,000	6	200
F	7,000	9,000	4	500
G	8,000	8,000	6	0
H	7,000	8,000	5	100
I	10,000	12,000	6	200
J	8,000	11,000	2	1,000

(a) Determine the coefficients for the estimated regression line $\hat{Y}(X_1) = a + bX_1$, and calculate $s_{Y \cdot X_1}$.
(b) Determine the coefficients for the estimated regression plane $\hat{Y} = a + b_1X_1 + b_2X_2$, and calculate $S_{Y \cdot 12}$.
(c) Does a comparison of the values of $S_{Y \cdot 12}$ and $s_{Y \cdot X_1}$ suggest that including family size X_2 as an independent variable improves total spending predictions? Explain.

11-10 *Computer exercise.* Refer to the data given in Exercise 11-9.
(a) Determine the coefficients for $\hat{Y} = a + b_1X_1 + b_2X_2 + b_3X_3$.
(b) Calculate the value of $S_{Y \cdot 123}$.
(c) Does a comparison of the values of $S_{Y \cdot 123}$ and $S_{Y \cdot 12}$ suggest that including additional savings as the third variable improves total spending predictions?

11-11 The Environmental Protection Agency wishes to predict the fuel consumption of one popular car model using speed, altitude, and passenger weight as the independent variables. The following data apply.

Trip	Fuel Consumption (mpg) Y	Average Speed (mph) X_1	Altitude (thousands of feet) X_2	Passenger Weight (hundreds of pounds) X_3
1	28	50	2	2
2	26	55	0	3
3	28	44	1	2
4	18	46	5	4
5	31	57	0	2
6	25	53	2	3
7	24	54	4	3
8	21	60	4	2
9	23	59	1	5
10	26	52	1	4

(a) Determine the coefficients for the estimated regression line $\hat{Y}(X_1) = a + bX_1$, and calculate $s_{Y \cdot X_1}$.
(b) Determine the coefficients for the estimated regression plane $\hat{Y} = a + b_1X_1 + b_2X_2$, and calculate $S_{Y \cdot 12}$.
(c) Does a comparison of the values of $S_{Y \cdot 12}$ and $s_{Y \cdot X_1}$ suggest that including altitude as a variable improves fuel consumption predictions? Explain.

11-12 *Computer exercise.* Refer to the data given in Exercise 11-11.
(a) Determine the coefficients for $\hat{Y} = a + b_1X_1 + b_2X_2 + b_3X_3$.
(b) Determine the value of $S_{Y \cdot 123}$.
(c) Does a comparison of the values of $S_{Y \cdot 123}$ and $S_{Y \cdot 12}$ suggest that including weight as the third variable improves fuel consumption predictions? Explain.

11-13 A VBM (Very Big Machines) systems programmer wishes to predict run times of payroll programs run on a particular software—hardware configuration. The following data have been obtained for 20 runs.

Run Time (minutes) Y	Required Memory (thousands of bytes) X_1	Amount of Output (thousands of lines) X_2	Amount of Input (thousands of lines) X_3
11.3	24	10	5
8.7	8	6	5
5.5	14	8	2
7.4	35	6	2
9.1	11	9	4
6.1	23	4	3
15.2	24	11	11
18.2	110	9	3
5.0	20	5	2
22.7	75	21	9
15.9	28	13	9
4.0	20	4	1
10.2	19	4	7
11.9	74	13	2
6.8	7	4	5
14.0	26	8	5
10.2	37	9	4
6.4	16	3	2
5.9	21	3	3
25.5	96	22	7

(a) Using required memory and amount of output as the independent variables and run time as the dependent variable, determine the equation for the estimated multiple regression equation.

(b) Using your regression plane from (a), compute the standard error of the estimate for run time.

11-14 *Computer exercise.* A Druid's Drayage truck dispatcher wishes to predict how many driver hours it will take to deliver less-than-truckload shipments over any one of a number of routes. Using four independent variables, he has collected the following 20 sample observations.

Driver Time (hours) Y	Distance (miles) X_1	Initial Load (tons) X_2	Deliveries X_3	Speed (mph) X_4
3.0	90	1.5	1	50
7.2	150	3.7	3	35
4.5	65	4.9	3	42
4.3	74	2.6	5	37
6.4	60	3.1	8	40
3.1	70	1.9	2	45
7.0	120	4.7	5	48
5.2	48	3.4	4	29
5.4	125	4.1	3	43
9.2	156	3.4	7	40
5.9	121	2.9	4	46
6.1	98	3.0	6	42
5.5	91	4.5	6	53
5.0	65	4.0	7	42
7.3	74	4.0	8	37

(continued on next page)

Driver Time (hours) Y	Distance (miles) X_1	Initial Load (tons) X_2	Deliveries X_3	Speed (mph) X_4
4.7	83	3.6	5	39
4.5	44	2.7	3	48
1.9	33	1.9	1	29
4.2	106	2.0	2	46
4.4	73	3.0	3	37

Determine the estimated multiple regression equation.

11-15 *Computer exercise.* Refer to the data given in Exercise 11-13. Include the amount of input X_3 as the third independent variable. Determine the estimated multiple regression equation.

11-4 INFERENCES IN REGRESSION ANALYSIS

Since the estimated multiple regression equation is derived from sample information, any conclusions based on it are subject to sampling error. As in simple regression, several types of inferences may be drawn. Most important of these are prediction intervals, testing for nonzero regression coefficients, and estimates of the coefficients.

PREDICTION INTERVALS IN MULTIPLE REGRESSION

The procedures used to construct prediction intervals to qualify estimates made from the regression plane are similar to those used in simple regression. In Chapter 10 we saw that the level of the single independent variable affects both the center and width of those intervals. In multiple regression analysis the levels of *all* the independent variables collectively establish the prediction intervals. Mathematically, the values of X_1, X_2, . . . are elements of a *vector* and must be combined algebraically with a complex *matrix* to find the specific end points of the prediction interval for both a conditional mean $\mu_{Y \cdot 12 \ldots}$ and for an individual value Y_I. (A detailed discussion of the matrix algebra is beyond the scope of this book.)

Finding prediction intervals by hand using a calculator is a demanding task and is not ordinarily done—except to make approximations. Computer programs are available and should be used to properly handle this task.

To illustrate, we will use the supermarket data, augmented to include store size X_3 as the third independent predictor. Consider stores having food sales of \$2,000,000, nonfood sales of \$500,000, and size of 30,000 square feet. Thus (in \$10,000 units), $X_1 = 200$, $X_2 = 50$, and $X_3 = 30$. The corresponding height of the regression plane is

$$\hat{Y} = -10.170 + .027(200) + .097(50) + .525(30) = 15.830 \text{ (thousand dollars)}$$

The computer printout in Figure 11-4 shows the results of a run using the augmented supermarket data. The top portion of the printout provides the 95% prediction intervals for $\mu_{Y \cdot 123}$ and Y_I given the above levels for the X's. Both of the intervals are centered at $\hat{Y} = 15.830$.

```
MTB > retrieve 'supermkt'
MTB > regress c4 3 c1-c3;
SUBC> predict 200 50 30.
```

```
The regression equation is
Profit = - 10.2 + 0.0270 Food + 0.0971 Nonfood + 0.525 Size
     .
     .
     .
     Fit  Stdev.Fit        95% C.I.            95% P.I.
  15.830      0.884   ( 13.666, 17.994)  ( 12.083, 19.577)
```

```
MTB > regress c4 3 c1-c3;
SUBC> predict c1-c3.
```

```
     .
     .
     .
     Fit  Stdev.Fit        95% C.I.            95% P.I.
  19.837      0.698   ( 18.128, 21.546)  ( 16.333, 23.341)
  14.399      0.638   ( 12.838, 15.959)  ( 10.964, 17.833)
  17.162      0.475   ( 15.998, 18.325)  ( 13.888, 20.435)
  10.332      0.691   (  8.640, 12.024)  (  6.836, 13.828)
  16.277      0.955   ( 13.940, 18.615)  ( 12.427, 20.128)
  28.711      0.695   ( 27.010, 30.413)  ( 25.211, 32.212)
  34.865      1.024   ( 32.359, 37.371)  ( 30.910, 38.819)
   6.930      0.905   (  4.716,  9.145)  (  3.154, 10.707)
  21.450      0.992   ( 19.023, 23.877)  ( 17.545, 25.355)
  21.037      0.636   ( 19.480, 22.594)  ( 17.604, 24.470)
```

Note: Figure generated on an IBM PC using Minitab®.

FIGURE 11-4 Portion of a computer printout for the augmented supermarket data.

The first prediction interval provides

$$13.666 \leq \mu_{Y \cdot 123} \leq 17.994 \text{ (thousand dollars)}$$

We are 95% confident that the mean profit of *all* stores having the given levels for the independent variables will lie between \$13,666 and \$17,994. The second prediction interval provides

$$12.083 \leq Y_I \leq 19.577 \text{ (thousand dollars)}$$

This interval is wider than the first and expresses 95% confidence that an individual store will have a profit that lies between \$12,083 and \$19,577.

The remaining information shown in Figure 11-4 is a portion of the output from a third run using the supermarket data. This optional segment provides the prediction interval sets for all observed levels of the X's. Notice that both the center and the width of these intervals vary, depending on the levels of the independent variables.

INFERENCES REGARDING REGRESSION COEFFICIENTS

The computed values of the intercept a and partial regression coefficients b_1, b_2, . . . are statistical estimators of the true regression coefficients A, B_1, B_2, ... Ordinarily, confidence intervals for the B's are not constructed until the null hypothesis

$$H_0\text{: } B_1 = B_2 = \cdots = B_{m-1} = 0$$

has been tested. The regression results are statistically significant when the hypothesis is rejected. The procedure for making this determination is based on the *analysis of variance* approach (discussed in more detail in Chapters 17 and 18), which focuses on sums of squares.

Analogous to simple regression, the least-squares method minimizes the sum of the vertical deviations about the regression plane. Each deviation consists of an explained and unexplained component. Summing the squares of the individual components, the following relationship applies to the entire collection of observations.

$$\begin{array}{ccccc} \text{Total variation} & = & \text{Explained variation} & + & \text{Unexplained variation} \\ \sum [Y - \bar{Y}]^2 & = & \sum [\hat{Y} - \bar{Y}]^2 & + & \sum [Y - \hat{Y}]^2 \\ SSTO & = & SSR & + & SSE \end{array}$$

The **total sum of squares** $\boldsymbol{SSTO}$ expresses the variation in observed Y's about their mean $\bar{Y}$ without regard to the regression relationship. Although not ordinarily computed by hand, the following expression applies.

$$SSTO = \sum [Y - \bar{Y}]^2$$

The **regression sum of squares** $\boldsymbol{SSR}$ summarizes the explained variation in estimated Y's about the sample mean. The following expression applies.

$$SSR = \sum [\hat{Y} - \bar{Y}]^2$$

The **error sum of squares** $\boldsymbol{SSE}$ expresses the unexplained variation in observed Y's about the estimated regression plane. The following expression applies.

$$SSE = \sum [Y - \hat{Y}]^2 = (n - m)\, S^2_{Y \cdot 12 \ldots}$$

The sums of squares in a multiple regression analysis are considered standard output for the popular computer software packages.

The Analysis of Variance Approach

To test the null hypothesis that all partial regression coefficients are equal to zero, we must compare the explained and unexplained variations in Y. This is accomplished by employing a composite test statistic based on the *means* of the squared deviations for the explained and unexplained variations. The first of these, the **regression mean square *MSR***, is

$$MSR = \frac{SSR}{m - 1}$$

where m is the total number of variables in the regression analysis. The denominator $m-1$ is the number of degrees of freedom for the explained variation. The second mean, the **error mean square *MSE***, is

$$MSE = \frac{SSE}{n - m} = s^2_{Y \cdot 12 \ldots}$$

where $n - m$ is the number of degrees of freedom for the unexplained variation.

Recall that the sample variance is found by averaging the squared deviations about the central value. Both MSR and MSE are computed this way, and, thus, both of the mean squares are actually sample variances. Since these form the basis of the test, the procedure is called analysis of *variance* (even though the null hypothesis itself says nothing about variance).

The following expression provides the regression test statistic.

$$F = \frac{\text{Variance explained by regression}}{\text{Unexplained variance}} = \frac{MSR}{MSE}$$

The above quantity has the F distribution, discussed in detail in Chapter 17. That distribution allows us to find probabilities for getting the results achieved when the null hypothesis is true.

The value $F = 130.06$, from the printout in Figure 11-3, was computed for the augmented supermarket data during the multiple regression run. The corresponding prob. value is 0.000, indicating that those results are inconsistent with the null hypothesis, which must be *rejected.* The regression relationship found earlier is statistically very significant.

Estimating Regression Coefficients

After the null hypothesis that all B's are equal to zero has been rejected, investigators will generally estimate the coefficients using a set of intervals applicable at a *collective* level of confidence. The following expression provides the $100(1 - \alpha)\%$

BONFERRONI COLLECTIVE CONFIDENCE INTERVAL FOR A REGRESSION COEFFICIENT

$$B_k = b_k \pm t_{\alpha/2(m-1)} s_{b_k}$$

where the $n-m$ degrees of freedom apply.

Using the supermarket data given in Figure 11-3, the following intervals apply jointly at the 85% confidence level. The critical value $t_{.025} = 2.447$ is read from Appendix Table F using $10 - 4 = 6$ degrees of freedom.

$$B_1 = .027 \pm 2.447(.012)$$

or

$$-.002 \leq B_1 \leq .056 \qquad \text{(food sales)}$$

also

$$.024 \leq B_2 \leq .170 \qquad \text{(nonfood sales)}$$

$$.381 \leq B_3 \leq .669 \qquad \text{(store size)}$$

The first interval indicates that B_1, the profit obtained for \$10,000 of food sales, does not differ significantly from zero. Both nonfood sales and store size have partial regression coefficients (B_2 and B_3) and are significantly nonzero.

EXERCISES

11-16 *Computer exercise.* Refer to Exercise 11-10 and to your answers.
(a) Construct the 95% prediction intervals for (1) the mean and (2) individual family spending when the income is \$10,000, the family size is 4, and additional savings is \$1,000.
(b) Using a collective confidence level of 97%, construct the interval estimates of the partial regression coefficients for (1) income, (2) size, and (3) additional savings.

11-17 *Computer exercise.* Refer to Exercise 11-12 and to your answers.
(a) Construct the 95% prediction intervals for (1) the mean and (2) individual fuel consumption when the average speed is 50 mph, the altitude is 4 thousand feet, and the passenger weight is 2 hundred pounds.
(b) Using a collective confidence level of 97%, construct the interval estimates of the partial regression coefficients for (1) average speed, (2) altitude, and (3) passenger weight.

11-18 *Computer exercise.* Refer to Exercise 11-14 and to your answers.
(a) Construct the 95% prediction intervals for (1) the mean and (2) individual driver time when the distance is 100 miles, the initial load is 4.0 tons, the number of deliveries is 5, and the speed is 50 mph.
(b) Using a collective confidence level of 96%, construct the interval estimates of the partial regression coefficients for (1) distance, (2) initial load, (3) number of deliveries, and (4) speed.

11-19 *Computer exercise.* Refer to Exercise 11-15 and to your answers.
(a) Construct the 95% prediction intervals for (1) the mean and (2) run time when the required memory is 100 thousand bytes, there are 15 thousand lines of output and there are 10 thousand lines of input.
(b) Using a collective confidence level of 85%, construct the interval estimates of the partial regression coefficients for (1) required memory, (2) amount of output, and (3) amount of input.

11-5 MULTIPLE CORRELATION

COEFFICIENT OF MULTIPLE DETERMINATION

The concept of correlation can be extended to multiple variables. As we did in our earlier discussion of simple linear relationships, we will begin by describing the **coefficient of multiple determination** as an index of association. When a multiple regression involves only two independent variables, X_1 and X_2, this is denoted symbolically by $R^2_{Y\cdot 12}$, which represents the ratio of the variation in Y that is explained by the regression plane to the total variation, or

$$R^2_{Y\cdot 12} = \frac{\text{Explained variation}}{\text{Total variation}} = 1 - \frac{\sum (Y - \hat{Y})^2}{\sum (Y - \bar{Y})^2}$$

The **multiple correlation coefficient** is defined as the square root of the coefficient of multiple determination, or $R_{Y\cdot 12} = \sqrt{R^2_{Y\cdot 12}}$. The sign of $R_{Y\cdot 12}$ is always considered positive.

A shorter, equivalent expression is used to calculate the

COEFFICIENT OF MULTIPLE DETERMINATION

$$R^2_{Y\cdot 12} = 1 - \frac{S^2_{Y\cdot 12}}{s^2_Y}\left(\frac{n - m}{n - 1}\right)$$

As before, m represents the number of variables used.

To illustrate this computation, we will again use our earlier results from the multiple regression for store profit Y when food sales X_1 and nonfood sales X_2 are the only independent variables. The standard deviation in profit is

$$s_Y = \sqrt{\frac{\sum Y^2 - n\bar{Y}^2}{n - 1}} = \sqrt{\frac{4{,}267 - 10(19.1)^2}{9}} = 8.293$$

From before, we have $S_{Y\cdot 12} = 4.343$. Here, $m = 3$. Using these values we calculate

$$R^2_{Y\cdot 12} = 1 - \frac{(4.343)^2}{(8.293)_2}\left(\frac{10 - 3}{10 - 1}\right) = .787$$

The interpretation of $R^2_{Y\cdot 12} = .787$ is that an estimated 78.7% of the total variation in Y may be explained by knowledge of the regression plane and the values of X_1 and X_2. Only $100 - 78.7 = 21.3\%$ of the variation in Y is estimated due to other causes, such as chance, plus factors not explicitly considered—for example, store size, location, and advertising.

When the supermarket data were expanded to include an additional independent variable for store size, X_3, the estimated regression equation was recalculated to be $\hat{Y} = -10.170 + .027X_1 + .097X_2 + .525X_3$. As noted earlier, the standard error of the estimate for Y about this higher-dimensional regression hyperplane was significantly smaller than when store size was ignored. This indicates that, in this case, more of the total variation in Y may be explained by raising the number of regression variables. To see how far the total variation in Y that is explained by regression has risen, we obtain the coefficient of multiple determination when X_3 is included in the analysis. The computer printout in Figure 11-3 provides the value $R^2_{Y \cdot 123}=.985$. Thus, the total variation in Y that is explained by regression increases from 78.7% to 98.5% when store size X_3 is included as an additional independent variable. This further illustrates that expanding regression analysis to include more variables may increase the reliability of predictions.

We now consider a set of indexes helpful in determining whether or not it is worthwhile to include additional variables in the regression analysis.

PARTIAL CORRELATION

Let's begin by comparing the results of a simple regression analysis relating store profit Y to food sales X_1 alone. As we have seen, the equation for the estimated regression line is

$$\hat{Y}(X_1) = 3.891 + .0670X_1$$

and the simple coefficient of determination is $r^2_{Y1} = (.760)^2 = .578$. Suppose we now incorporate nonfood sales X_2 as a second independent variable. We have seen that better predictions for Y will result from doing this. To quantify the improvement achieved with a higher-dimensional regression analysis, we can calculate the proportional reduction in previously explained variation. This provides a further index of association, $r^2_{Y2 \cdot 1}$, called the **coefficient of partial determination,** that measures the correlation between Y and X_2 when the other independent variable X_1 is still considered but held constant. The subscript $Y2 \cdot 1$ indicates this.

COEFFICIENT OF PARTIAL DETERMINATION

$$r^2_{Y2 \cdot 1} = \frac{\text{Reduction in unexplained variation}}{\text{Previously unexplained variation}} = \frac{R^2_{Y \cdot 12} - r^2_{Y1}}{1 - r^2_{Y1}}$$

Substituting our earlier values, we obtain

$$r^2_{Y2 \cdot 1} = \frac{.787 - .578}{1 - .578} = .495$$

The difference, $R^2_{Y \cdot 12} - r^2_{Y1}$, represents the reduction in unexplained variation (which is also the increase in explained variation). The value $r^2_{Y2 \cdot 1} = .495$ tells us that 49.5% of the variation in store profit Y that was left unexplained by a simple regression with food sales X_1 alone can be explained by the regression obtained from including nonfood sales X_2.

In multiple regression analysis, the coefficient of partial determination or its square root, the **partial correlation coefficient**, provides an index of the correlation between two variables *after* the effects of all the other variables have been considered. Thus, the value .495 expresses the net association between store profit Y and nonfood sales X_2 when food sales X_1 are held constant but still accounted for.

The value $r^2_{Y2 \cdot 1} = .495$ may be compared to the *simple* coefficient of determination between Y and X_2, $r^2_{Y2} = (-.286)^2 = .082$. The former provides a truer impact of including X_2 in the multiple regression analysis than would be indicated by a simple correlation analysis using only X_2. When evaluating the potential merits of a predictor variable, the coefficients of partial determination (or the partial correlation coefficients) are sometimes employed in determining which independent variables to include (a superior method to using the simple counterpart coefficient). We can illustrate how the coefficient of partial determination may be used to do this.

In discussing a third independent variable X_3 (size of store), a multiple regression was run on the computer. The coefficient of partial determination may be found from

$$r^2_{Y3 \cdot 12} = \frac{\text{Reduction in unexplained variation}}{\text{Previously unexplained variation}} = \frac{R^2_{Y \cdot 123} - R^2_{Y \cdot 12}}{1 - R^2_{Y \cdot 12}}$$

Substituting the coefficients of multiple determination obtained from the previous two multiple regressions for the supermarket data, we have

$$r^2_{Y3 \cdot 12} = \frac{.985 - .787}{1 - .787} = .930$$

Thus, $r^2_{Y3 \cdot 12} = .930$ tells us that there is a 93.0% reduction in previously unexplained variation by including X_3. This additional variable has been quite effective in increasing the sharpness of the multiple regression analysis.

Table 11-5 shows how the amount of variation in Y that is explained by regression has increased through successive inclusions of additional variables. Note how the variation in Y is reduced from $s_Y = 8.293$, which was obtained when no regression was performed. Variation is expressed by the successive standard errors of the estimates of Y about the respective regression surfaces (line, plane, and hyperplane) shown in column (3). Paralleling the declining standard errors are increases in the proportion of variation explained by regression, shown in column (4). Column (5) shows the proportional reduction in previously unexplained variation in Y resulting from the additional variable.

The total explained variations in Y will not always be reduced by including additional variables. It is not always obvious that an additional factor will sharpen rather than cloud the predictive powers of regression analysis. Good common sense must be exercised in selecting variables for which there is a meaningful nonstatistical explanation of their influence on the dependent variable. Sales is one factor used to calculate profit, so it has a logical connection. Likewise, a larger store requires a greater investment in facilities and may be operated more efficiently than a smaller one, so store size can also be reasoned to have a direct relation to profits.

The supermarket coefficients of partial determination listed in Table 11-5 are what would apply if the successive Xs were added to the regression sequence in 1-2-3 order, according to their subscripts. But other sequences are possible. The tree in Figure 11-5 shows the various possible sequences for adding new variables

TABLE 11-5 How Explained Variation in Y Increases as Additional Variables Are Included

(1) Independent Variables Included	(2) Additional Variable	(3) Standard Error of Estimate (thousands of dollars)	(4) Proportion of Variation Explained	(5) Proportional Reduction in Previously Unexplained Variation
none	—	$s_Y = 8.293$	0.000	—
X_1	X_1	$s_{Y \cdot X_1} = 5.719$	$r^2_{Y1} = .578$*	$\frac{.578 - 0}{1 - 0} = .578 = r^2_{Y1}$
X_1, X_2	X_2	$S_{Y \cdot 12} = 4.343$	$R^2_{Y \cdot 123} = .787$	$\frac{.787 - .578}{1 - .578} = .495 = r^2_{Y2 \cdot 1}$
X_1, X_2, X_3	X_3	$S_{Y \cdot 123} = 1.250$	$R^2_{Y \cdot 123} = .985$	$\frac{.985 - .787}{1 - .787} = .930 = r^2_{Y3 \cdot 12}$

*This value is the simple coefficient of determination calculated for the regression line $\hat{Y}(X_1) = 3.891 + .0670X_1$.

in obtaining the next higher-dimensional regression analysis. Altogether, the supermarket illustration involves three steps, each involving the choice of which remaining candidate should be added to the set of independent variables.

In Section 11-6 we will investigate how the coefficients of partial determination may be used in stepwise regression to select which variables to include in a regression analysis.

EXERCISES

11-20 An economist wishes to predict annual family spending Y using income X_1, size X_2, and annual savings X_3. The following intermediate calculations have been obtained for a sample of $n = 100$ families. All monetary figures are in thousands of dollars.

$$\bar{Y} = 10 \qquad \bar{X}_1 = 12 \qquad \bar{X}_2 = 5 \qquad \bar{X}_3 = 1$$

$$\sum Y^2 = 11{,}400 \quad \sum X_1Y = 13{,}000 \quad \sum X_2Y = 6{,}000 \quad \sum X_3Y = 500$$

$$\text{Plane } A\text{:} \quad \hat{Y} = 1.7 + .4X_1 + .7X_2 \qquad \text{(excluding } X_3\text{)}$$

$$\text{Hyperplane } B\text{:} \quad \hat{Y} = 4.3 + .3X_1 + .6X_2 - .9X_3 \qquad \text{(including } X_3\text{)}$$

(a) Calculate $S_{Y \cdot 12}$ and $R^2_{Y \cdot 12}$. What percentage of the variation in Y is explained by regression plane A?

(b) If $S_{Y \cdot 123} = .722$ and $R^2_{Y \cdot 123} = .964$, what percentage of the variation in Y is explained by regression hyperplane B?

(c) Has the inclusion of X_3 in the regression analysis reduced the standard error of the estimate of Y?

(d) Use the regression equations for planes A and B to determine the proportions of unexplained variation in Y. What proportional change in previously unexplained variation is achieved by adding X_3 to the analysis? Does this increase or decrease the unexplained variation?

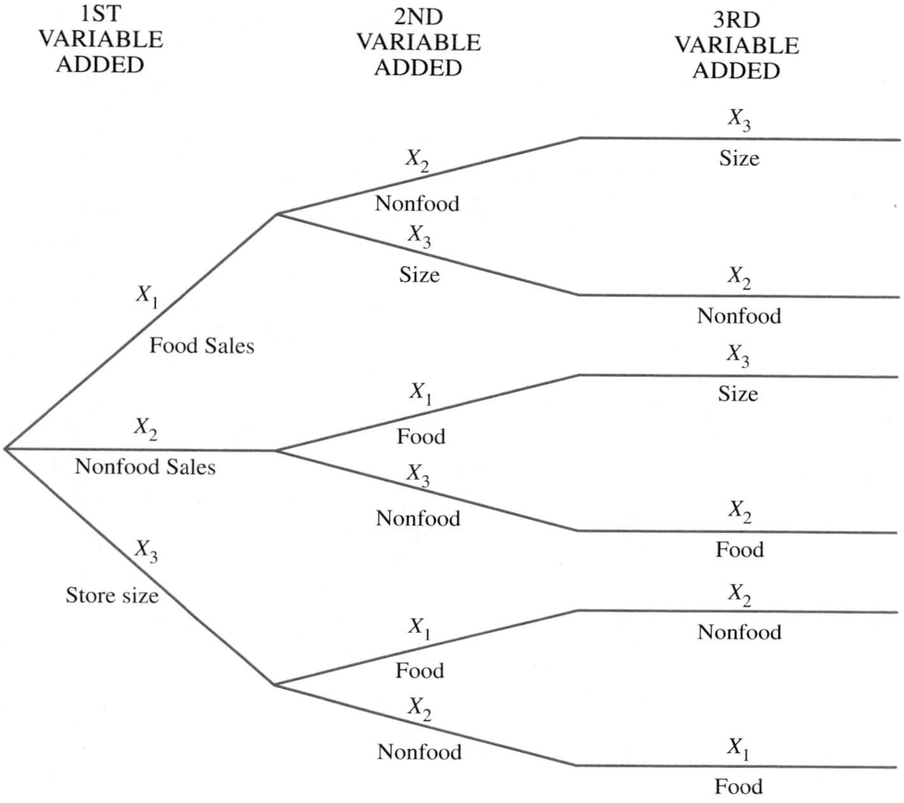

FIGURE 11-5 Tree diagram all of the regression sequences possible for adding predictor of supermarket sales.

11-21 Refer to the data given in Exercise 11-5. The following results have been obtained for predicting Crunchola production cost Y from quantity X_1 and wheat price index X_2.

$$r_{Y1}^2 = .9270 \qquad r_{Y2}^2 = .0052 \qquad R_{Y\cdot 12}^2 = .9715$$

(a) Compute the coefficient of partial determination $r_{Y2\cdot 1}^2$ for production cost and wheat price index, holding production quantity constant.

(b) Compute the coefficient of partial determination $r_{Y1\cdot 2}^2$ for production cost and quantity, holding wheat price index constant.

11-22 Refer to the data given in Exercise 11-11. The following regression results have been obtained for predicting fuel consumption Y from average speed X_1, altitude X_2, and passenger weight X_3.

$$s_Y = 3.742$$

$$s_{Y\cdot X_1} = 3.968 \qquad r_{Y1}^2 = .0003$$

$$s_{Y\cdot X_1} = 2.427 \qquad r_{Y2}^2 = .6261$$

$$S_{Y\cdot 12} = 2.522 \qquad R_{Y\cdot 12}^2 = .6465$$

$$S_{Y\cdot 123} = 1.794 \qquad R_{Y\cdot 123}^2 = .8467$$

Compute the following coefficient of partial determination.
(a) $r^2_{Y2 \cdot 1}$ (b) $r^2_{Y1 \cdot 2}$ (c) $r^2_{Y3 \cdot 12}$
(d) What is the percentage reduction in unexplained variation achieved by adding X_3 as the third independent variable? Does this suggest that including passenger weight should improve fuel consumption predictions? Explain.

11-23 Suppose that the economist in Exercise 11-20 has determined, *for another sample*, that the simple coefficient of determination is .50 between Y and X_1 and that it is .60 between Y and X_2. She has also found that the coefficient of multiple determination is .75, considering only X_1 and X_2.
(a) Compute the coefficients of partial determination $r^2_{Y1 \cdot 2}$ and $r^2_{Y2 \cdot 1}$.
(b) State the meaning of the values that you obtained in (a).
(c) Compare the values in (a) to their respective simple coefficients of determination. Why may the corresponding values differ?

11-24 Speed-E-Print, a wholesale distributor of business forms, has developed three predictors of sales Y (thousands of dollars) achieved by its representatives in the field. For each salesperson, X_1 represents the score on a sales aptitude test, X_2 the score on a motivation test, and X_3 the total years of sales experience. The following intermediate calculations have been obtained for sample data representing $n=30$ salespersons.

$$\bar{Y} = 50 \qquad \bar{X}_1 = 10 \qquad \bar{X}_2 = 5 \qquad \bar{X}_3 = 5$$

$$\sum Y^2 = 80{,}600 \quad \sum X_1Y = 16{,}000 \quad \sum X_2Y = 8{,}500 \quad \sum X_3Y = 8{,}100$$

$$\text{Plane } A\text{:} \quad \hat{Y} = 10 + 3X_1 + 2X_2 \qquad \text{(excluding } X_3\text{)}$$

$$\text{Hyperplane } B\text{:} \quad \hat{Y} = 5 + 2X_1 + 1X_2 + 4X_3 \qquad \text{(including } X_3\text{)}$$

(a) Calculate $S_{Y \cdot 12}$ and $R^2_{Y \cdot 12}$. What percentage of the variation in Y is explained by the regression plane A?
(b) $R^2_{Y \cdot 123}=.964$. What percentage of the variation in Y is explained by the regression hyperplane B?
(c) Compute the coefficient of partial determination for adding X_3 to the analysis. What is the percentage reduction in previously unexplained variation achieved by adding X_3 as the third independent variable?
(d) Should years of sales experience be included in predictions of sales performance? Why?

11-6 FINDING A PREDICTIVE REGRESSION MODEL

In any data set comprising several variables, one will be the dependent variable Y whose value will be forecast from the known levels of one or more of the remaining variables. We now consider the problem of finding which variables in a data set might be used as independent predictor variables, serving as the Xs.

GOALS FOR A PREDICTIVE MODEL

There are two primary goals in establishing a predictive model.

1. Achieve a regression surface (line, plane, hyperplane) that explains a high

proportion of variability in Y. One measure useful for this purpose is the coefficient of multiple determination.

2. Keep the regression equation simple. In a multiple regression, this is achieved by minimizing the number of predictors. Limiting the number of predictors gives stability to predictions made from different data sets.

Unfortunately, the two goals are contradictory, since the amount of variation left unexplained can only increase as each further independent predictor variable is brought into the next higher-dimensional analysis. Some trade-off must be made between achieving a high R^2 and finding a stable set of predictors.

SEARCHING FOR THE BEST PREDICTORS: ALL REGRESSIONS

To find the best predictors, all regressions might be performed. For the supermarket illustration, the possibilities are listed in Table 11-6. A similar list of possibilities for a data set having four predictors would contain 15 separate predictor sets, each with a distinct regression equation. In general, for a data set having p possible predictors the number of possible different regressions would be

$$2^p - 1$$

With an 11-variable data set, excluding the Y there are $p = 10$ candidate predictors. The number of possible regressions would be

$$2^{10} - 1 = 1{,}023$$

When the number of candidate predictor variables is large, a prodigious amount of work would be necessary to complete all possible regressions. A streamlined procedure breaks the process of selecting predictors into steps.

STEPWISE REGRESSION

To minimize computational effort, statisticians add independent predictor variables to the predictor set one at a time. The process is called **stepwise regression**. The first step involves simple regression analyses; each analysis is performed

TABLE 11-6 All Possible Regressions for Supermarket Illustration

Predictor Set	Regression Equation	Coefficient of Determination
X_1	$\hat{Y} = 3.88 + .067X_1$	$r^2_{Y1} = .578$
X_2	$\hat{Y} = 25.6 - .095X_2$	$r^2_{Y2} = .082$
X_3	$\hat{Y} = .21 + .602X_3$	$r^2_{Y3} = .958$
X_1, X_2	$\hat{Y} = -23.1 + .115X_1 + .235X_2$	$R^2_{Y\cdot 12} = .786$
X_1, X_3	$\hat{Y} = .42 - .0038X_1 + .623X_3$	$R^2_{Y\cdot 13} = .959$
X_2, X_3	$\hat{Y} = -3.76 + .0431X_2 + .634X_3$	$R^2_{Y\cdot 23} = .972$
X_1, X_2, X_3	$\hat{Y} = -10.17 + .0270X_1 + .0971X_2 + .525X_3$	$R^2_{Y\cdot 123} = .985$

separately with a different possible candidate as the single independent variable. This procedure is summarized in Figure 11-6. The decision tree in (a) shows the four choices, including the possibility of adding no predictor. Various criteria are employed for selecting the best predictor, which will be kept for future steps. For the supermarket illustration, the coefficient of partial determination is used to make this choice.

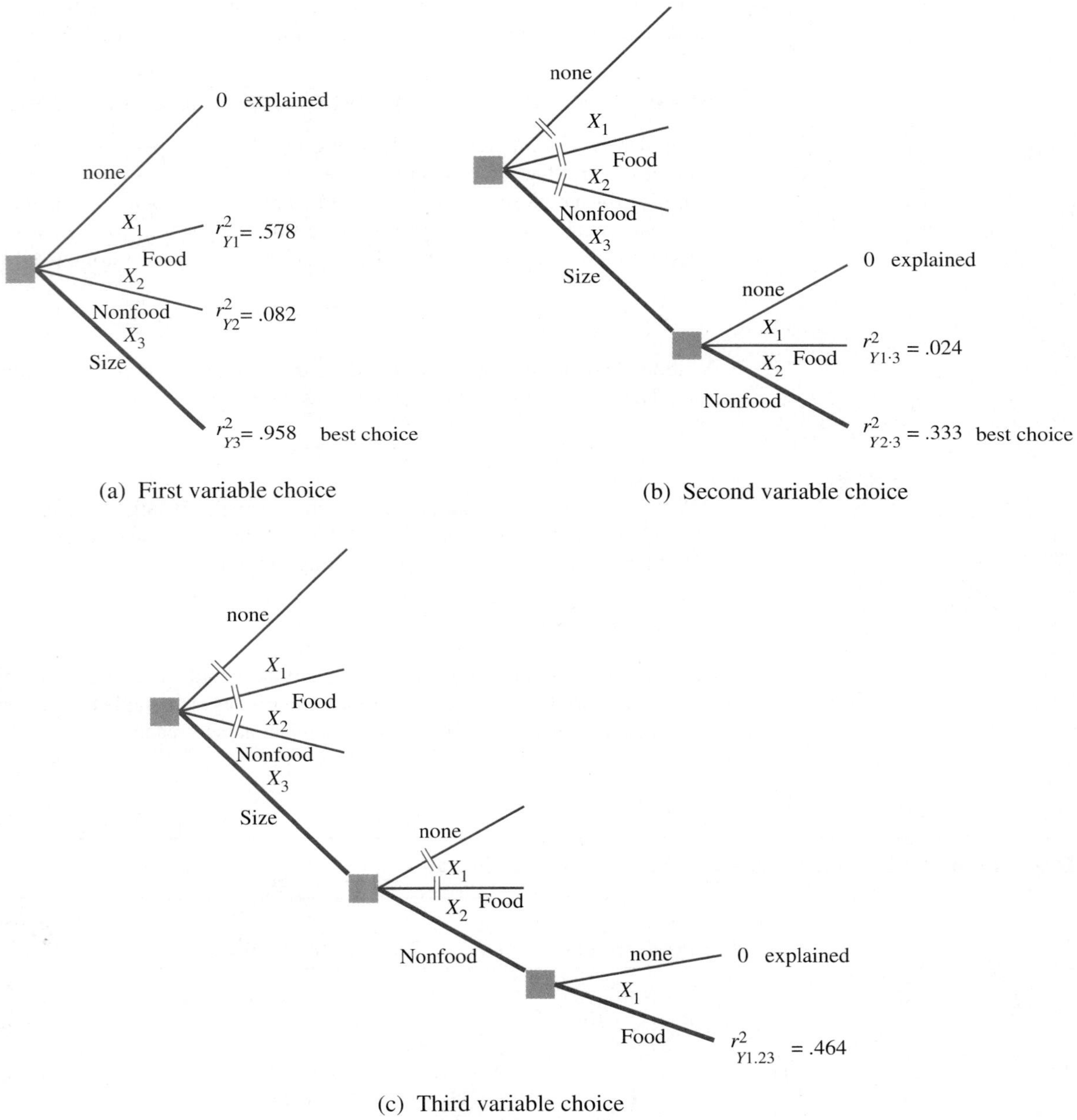

FIGURE 11-6 Decision tree showing stepwise regression choices for selecting predictors of supermarket sales.

Of the three possible first Xs in Figure 11-6(a), the most promising is X_3 (store size) which has the greatest coefficient of $r_{Y3}^2 = .958$. (Since there are no independent variables to begin with, a coefficient of *partial* determination does not exist, and the respective *ordinary* coefficients of determination serve for making the first choice.) The first predictor variable added to the set is therefore X_3 (store size). The second step is shown in Figure 11-6(b), where either X_1 or X_2 can be chosen for the second predictor. (Again, it is possible to pick none, in which case the selection process would end.) The greatest coefficient of partial determination is $r_{Y2 \cdot 3}^2 = .333$, achieved by adding X_2 (nonfood sales). That variable gets picked as the second predictor.

The remaining choices are shown in Figure 11-6(c): to select *no more* predictors or to include X_1 (food sales) in the predictor set. The coefficient of partial determination is $r_{Y1 \cdot 23}^2 = .464$, indicating that including food sales as a predictor would bring about a major reduction in that variation in Y which is presently left unexplained by regression with the latest predictor set. The best choice is therefore to include X_1 (food sales) in the predictor set.

ILLUSTRATION: PERFORMANCE PREDICTORS FOR BASEBALL BATTER SUPERSTAR SALARY

Using batter superstar data from Table 10-2, a stepwise regression was performed in order to determine which of the following predictors to use for a regression model for forecasting salary Y.

X_4 = position code	X_9 = number of runs
X_5 = games played	X_{10} = fielding percentage
X_6 = number of at bats	X_{11} = number of home runs
X_7 = batting average	X_{12} = number of putouts
X_8 = runs batted in (RBI)	

This is summarized by the decision tree in Figure 11-7. Step 1 involves nine simple regression analyses, each using just one of the above Xs as the *single* independent variable. The largest coefficient of determination achieved is .081 from using X_8 (RBI). Step 2 then includes eight multiple regressions using X_8 plus one of each of the above as the *two* independent variables. Computing the coefficients of partial determination for each, the greatest value of .041 occurs with X_5 (games played), and that variable is added to the predictor set.

Step 3 repeats the process, this time including X_5 and X_8 along with just one of the remaining predictors in seven separate multiple regressions, each involving *three* independent variables. The maximum coefficient of partial determination is .101, found for the regression in which X_9 (number of runs) is the third independent variable. That variable joins X_5 and X_8 as the permanent predictors for Step 4. In that step, six separate multiple regressions were made with *four* independent variables (X_5, X_8, X_9, and one other). The coefficients of partial determination were all below .01, so that bringing a fourth predictor into the model would only reduce the remaining unexplained salary variation by less than 1%. Since little would be gained in predictive power by adding a fourth predictor, it was decided to terminate the steps at this point, adding no new variables to the predictor set.

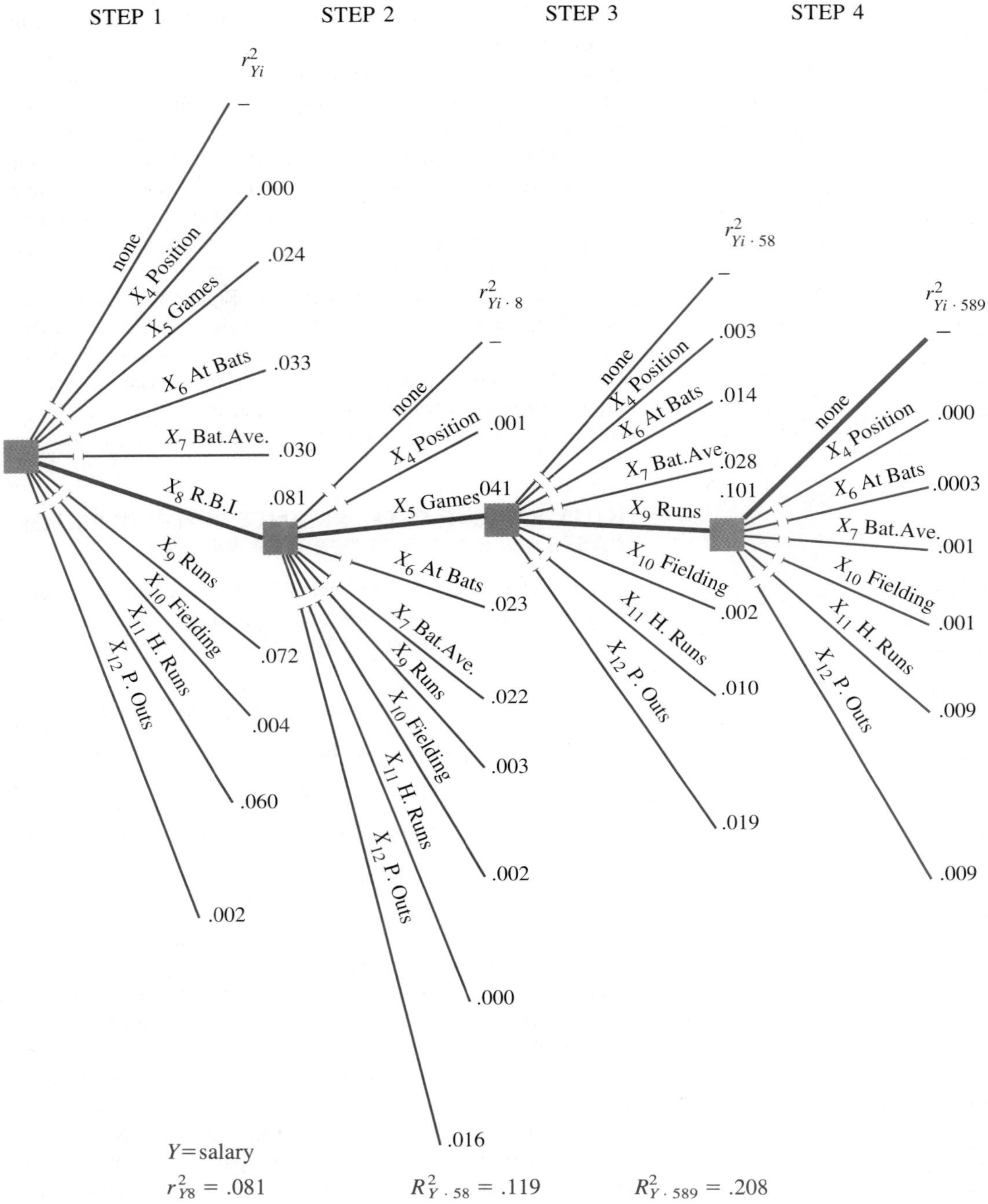

FIGURE 11-7 Decision tree showing stepwise regression choices for finding predictors of baseball batting superstar salaries.

Using the above predictors, the computer printout in Figure 11-8 is obtained. The regression equation (in thousands of dollars) is

$$\hat{Y} = 2{,}513 - 1.25X_5 + 1.13X_8 + 1.47X_9$$

The above regression equation might be used in making predictions about future player salaries. (Although the overall coefficient of determination is itself only $R^2_{Y \cdot 589} = .208$, which indicates that this model would be a very weak one.)

FINE-TUNING THE MODEL I: ELIMINATING OUTLIERS

Recall from Chapter 10 that outliers are data points that have unusually large residual values $Y - \hat{Y}$. In Figure 11-8 we see that there are four outliers—Joe

```
MTB > Regress c2 3 c5 c8 c9.

The regression equation is
Salary = 2513 - 1.25 Games + 1.13 RBI + 1.47 Runs

Predictor        Coef        Stdev     t-ratio        p
Constant       2513.3        170.0       14.78    0.000
Games         -1.2503       0.3995       -3.13    0.003
RBI            1.1338       0.4510        2.51    0.015
Runs           1.4667       0.5527        2.65    0.010

s = 517.0       R-sq = 20.8%      R-sq(adj) = 17.0%

Analysis of Variance

SOURCE       DF          SS          MS          F        p
Regression    3     4410688     1470230       5.50    0.002
Error        63    16838788      267282
Total        66    21249476

SOURCE       DF      SEQ SS
Games         1      516936
RBI           1     2011799
Runs          1     1881954

Unusual Observations
Obs.   Games     Salary       Fit Stdev.Fit   Residual    St.Resid
 12     1024     3792.0    2758.9      90.2     1033.1       2.03R   Joe Carter
 17      874     2000.0    3124.0     151.8    -1124.0      -2.27R   Chili Davis
 36     1608     3250.0    3100.0     257.3      150.0       0.33 X  Rickey Henderson
 39      703     2100.0    3226.0     226.3    -1126.0      -2.42RX  Wally Joyner
 46      688     3750.0    2661.4      98.2     1088.6       2.14R   Kevin Mitchell
 60     1926     2225.0    2120.1     225.0      104.9       0.23 X  Ozzie Smith

R denotes an obs. with a large st. resid.
X denotes an obs. whose X value gives it large influence.
```

FIGURE 11-8 Minitab printout for final baseball batter regression model selected through stepwise regression.

Carter, Chili Davis, Wally Joyner, and Kevin Mitchell. The regression analysis indicates that each of these players, when compared with their peers, is either overpaid or underpaid by over a million dollars. Eliminating explainable outliers can sometimes result in an improved regression model.

After removing the data points for the above four players, a second regression analysis provides the regression equation

$$\hat{Y} = 2{,}574 - 1.85X_5 + 1.22X_8 + 2.39X_9$$

The new equation has a much lower partial regression coefficient for number of games X_5 and a greater one for number of runs X_9. The negative multiplier for X_5 reflects a pattern by owners to reward "new blood" and discount the value of veterans. The coefficient of 1.22 for X_8 indicates that an additional run batted in (RBI) should boost a superstar's salary by 1.22 thousand dollars. But the 2.39 coefficient for X_9 indicates that a player's own run justifies about twice the salary increase.

The coefficient of multiple determination for the new regression equation nearly doubles, to $R^2_{Y \cdot 589} = .367$, so that about 37% of the variation in a batting superstar's salary can be explained by the new regression equation. This is a big improvement.

The elimination of outliers may also be cause to change the predictors. A new stepwise regression with the reduced data set indicates that four further variables—home runs, fielding, batting average, and at bats, in that order—could be worthwhile predictors if added to the regression model. The expanded model is

$$\hat{Y} = 2{,}931 - 3.34X_5 + .285X_6 - 5.65X_7 + 2.36X_8 \\ +2.63X_9 + 7.36X_{10} - 2.97X_{11}$$

The amount of salary variation explained by the above is a higher 44%, but this increase is a small one and does not seem to justify the further model complexity.

KINDS OF STEPWISE REGRESSION

Stepwise regression can be elaborate when done with a computer. One variation involves a backward procedure, in which all predictors are included as independent variables in a multiple regression of maximum dimension as the first step. Predictors are then *deleted* from the set in successive steps in a reverse process to the forward procedure described above. The forward procedure is elaborated in some programs, so that weaker members of the current predictive set might be deleted whenever a new variable is added.

A stepwise procedure can automatically screen predictors that do not improve the predictive worth of the evolving model. That might be done by excluding any candidate X for which the new regression would result in a low coefficient of partial determination. Another screening trigger would be to avoid variables too highly correlated with any of the current predictors.

STEPWISE REGRESSION WITH A COMPUTER

Stepwise regression is ordinarily done with computer assistance. Figure 11-9 shows the output from a Minitab stepwise regression run with the baseball super-

```
MTB > Stepwise c2 c4-c12;
SUBC>   FEnter 1;
SUBC>   FRemove 1.

 STEPWISE REGRESSION OF  Salary  ON  9 PREDICTORS, WITH N =   67

    STEP          1          2          3
CONSTANT       2348       2496       2513

RBI            0.55       1.23       1.13
T-RATIO        2.39       2.62       2.51

Games                    -0.47      -1.25
T-RATIO                  -1.66      -3.13

Runs                                 1.47
T-RATIO                              2.65

S               548        541        517
R-SQ           8.09      11.90      20.76
```

FIGURE 11-9 Minitab printout of stepwise regression with baseball batting superstar data.

star batter data. The details of individual regressions are not provided, but those can be established in later regular regression runs.

The resulting set of predictors is listed in each step column. These are identical to the results achieved earlier. An equivalent criterion is used by the Minitab program for selecting predictors based on the F statistic. The steps continue until no new regression yields an F value greater than the screening level. The cutoff point was $F = 1.0$ in the current illustration. The t-ratio values shown in Figure 11-9 are the square roots of the computed F values.

Many assumptions concerning the *linearity* of the data are automatically made by such computer programs. As with any other application, in multiple regression analysis the computer does not eliminate the need for good judgment. Computer printouts must be thoroughly evaluated to determine if there is a meaningful explanation of why some variables are excluded and others are included. A variable may be rejected because it does not reduce the unexplained variation, but this may actually be due to a strong curvilinear relation between the variable and Y.

SELECTING SCREENING PARAMETERS

The decision when to terminate the stepwise regression is an arbitrary one. Termination always eliminates some further reduction in unexplained Y variation for the current data set. But too many predictors, yielding a model overly fine-tuned to one data set, can contribute to unstable predictions over time. Generally, the looser the cutoff specifications for screening parameters (r^2 or F), the greater will be the number of steps and predictors.

Illustration: Predicting Baseball Card Price for Pitching Superstars

A second data set involving just *pitchers* was formed from the baseball superstar data in Table 10-2. A stepwise regression analysis was performed for predicting rookie baseball card price Y. As we shall see, this dependent variable for pitchers exhibits a much tighter relationship with players' performance statistics than did batter salaries. The following predictor candidates are used.

X_2 = salary

X_5 = games played

X_6 = innings pitched

X_7 = earned run average (ERA)

X_8 = winning percentage

X_9 = strikeouts

X_{10} = walks

Figure 11-10 shows the results obtained.

```
MTB > Stepwise c3 c2 c5-c10;
SUBC>   FEnter 1;
SUBC>   FRemove 1;
SUBC>   Steps 5.
```

```
 STEPWISE REGRESSION OF Card Pr. ON  7 PREDICTORS, WITH N =   60
                            Y
    STEP         1        2        3        4        5
CONSTANT   -165.11  -105.60   -82.91    49.75   124.90

Walks        0.389    0.797    0.474    0.534    0.558 X10
T-RATIO       9.59    10.55     5.43     5.62     5.78

Innings             -0.181   -0.274   -0.254   -0.249 X6
T-RATIO              -5.97    -8.96    -7.75    -7.55

S. Outs                       0.261    0.215    0.204 X9
T-RATIO                        5.28     3.73     3.52

ERA                                      -42      -46 X7
T-RATIO                                -1.50    -1.64

Salary                                         -0.027 X2
T-RATIO                                         -1.26

S              113     89.6     73.8     73.0     72.6
R-SQ         61.32    76.20    84.11    84.74    85.17
```

These steps give little improvment in predictive power.

FIGURE 11-10 Minitab printout of stepwise regression with baseball pitching superstar data.

Notice that five predictors are chosen, and that the coefficients of multiple determination R^2 for each successive regression (shown in the bottom row of the printout as percentages) are substantial. However, in steps 4 and 5 there is very little improvement. A tighter screening level for the F statistic should bring about an earlier stop to the search. A second computer run using a limit of 4.0 for the computed F terminated the predictor search after step 3.

The regression results using the three predictors are provided in Figure 11-11. The following regression equation is obtained.

$$\hat{Y} = -82.90 - .274X_6 + .261X_9 + .474X_{10}$$

The coefficient of multiple determination is quite substantial, $R^2_{Y \cdot 6910} = .841$,

```
MTB > Regress c3 3 c6 c9 c10.

The regression equation is
Card Pr. = - 82.9 - 0.274 Innings + 0.261 S. Outs + 0.474 Walks

Predictor        Coef        Stdev     t-ratio        p
Constant       -82.91        18.66       -4.44    0.000
Innings      -0.27358      0.03053       -8.96    0.000
S. Outs       0.26084      0.04938        5.28    0.000
Walks         0.47417      0.08726        5.43    0.000

s = 73.81       R-sq = 84.1%     R-sq(adj) = 83.3%

Analysis of Variance

SOURCE        DF         SS          MS        F        p
Regression     3    1615346      538448    98.83    0.000
Error         56     305092        5448
Total         59    1920437

SOURCE        DF     SEQ SS
Innings        1     570704
S. Outs        1     883768
Walks          1     160873

Unusual Observations
Obs. Innings  Card Pr.      Fit  Stdev.Fit  Residual   St.Resid
  2     4837     60.00   153.87      50.45    -93.87    -1.74 X   Bert Blyleven
 13     1417      0.08   150.51      13.41   -150.43    -2.07R    Jose DeLeon
 30     1598      2.25   223.74      16.81   -221.49    -3.08R    Jimmy Key
 45     4990   1400.00  1175.80      67.44    224.20     7.47RX   Nolan Ryan

R denotes an obs. with a large st. resid.
X denotes an obs. whose X value gives it large influence.
```

FIGURE 11-11 Minitab printout applying selected regression model with baseball pitching superstar data.

signifying that the regression explains 84% of the variation in rookie baseball card price.

An interpretation of the above leads to some surprising conclusions.

FINE-TUNING THE MODEL II: FINDING A REGRESSION EQUATION THAT MAKES SENSE

The negative regression coefficient $-.274$ for the number of innings pitched X_6 indicates that veteran superstar pitchers' cards lose value as their careers get longer, about 25 cents per inning pitched. That does seem odd, since card prices generally rise as a player ages. The coefficient .261 for number of strikeouts X_9 gives added card value of \$.26 for each strikeout. Most interesting is the coefficient .474 for the number of walks X_{10}, which adds \$.474 to the value of a card for each walk. Walks are generally *bad* for pitching performance, and we should expect a predictive model to reflect that by assigning a *negative* regression coefficient for X_{10}. The model does not make a lot of sense.

Some of the explanation of the odd regression equation might be attributed to the *outliers*—especially Nolan Ryan, having a card value of \$1,400. Ryan has pitched much longer than the other superstar pitchers, and his long-term popularity is reflected in the price of his rookie baseball card. When Nolan Ryan is removed, a new stepwise regression with F limit of 4.0 leaves innings pitched X_6 out of the final predictor set.

The following regression equation applies.

$$\hat{Y} = -6.45 + .0227X_9 - .0247X_{10} \qquad \text{(without Nolan Ryan)}$$

This indicates that card prices will go up by about 2 cents for each strikeout and down by about the same for each walk. That is what we should intuitively expect. The coefficient of multiple determination, $R^2_{Y \cdot 910} = .775$, is somewhat smaller than before, so that less variation in Y gets explained by the regression equation. But removing Ryan gives the new model much better predictive accuracy, the standard error of the estimate dropping from \$73.81 to a much smaller $S_{Y \cdot 910} =$ \$4.15. Even better, the new model has simplicity and seems to make sense.

EXERCISES

11-25 Refer to the economist's family data in Exercise 11-9. Construct a tree showing all possible regression sequences that might be taken when adding successive predictor variables, one at a time, to obtain regression equations of successively higher dimensions for predicting total spending. Do not actually perform the regressions, and do not compute the coefficients of partial determination.

11-26 Refer to the economist's family data in Exercise 11-9 used to forecast total spending.

(a) Determine the following estimated regression equations and compute the respective coefficients of determination.

(1) $\hat{Y}(X_1) = a + bX_1$ (2) $\hat{Y}(X_2) = a + bX_2$ (3) $\hat{Y}(X_3) = a + bX_3$

(b) As the first step in a stepwise regression, the best variable to include in the predictor set is X_1 (income). Why is this so?

(c) Perform the next stage of stepwise regression. To do this, first determine the following estimated regression equations.

(1) $\hat{Y} = a + b_1X_1 + b_2X_2$ (2) $\hat{Y} = a + b_1X_1 + b_3X_3$

Then compute the respective coefficients of multiple determination. Finally, calculate the respective coefficient of partial determination, assuming that X_1 was the predictor added in stage 1. The best stage-2 variable to add to the predictor set is X_2 (family size). Why is this so?

11-27 Consider the data given in Table 11-7 for first-basemen superstars. The following data apply for regressions for predicting salary from one or more *X*s.

$r^2_{Y5} = .598$	$R^2_{Y \cdot 56} = .841$	$R^2_{Y \cdot 567} = .842$	$R^2_{Y \cdot 5689} = .905$
$r^2_{Y6} = .680$	$R^2_{Y \cdot 57} = .637$	$R^2_{Y \cdot 589} = .841$	$R^2_{Y \cdot 5678} = .900$
$r^2_{Y7} = .170$	$R^2_{Y \cdot 58} = .838$	$R^2_{Y \cdot 578} = .848$	$R^2_{Y \cdot 5789} = .845$
$r^2_{Y8} = .735$	$R^2_{Y \cdot 68} = .752$	$R^2_{Y \cdot 568} = .898$	$R^2_{Y \cdot 58\ 10\ 11} = .841$
$r^2_{Y9} = .581$	$R^2_{Y \cdot 78} = .751$	$R^2_{Y \cdot 58\ 10} = .839$	$R^2_{Y \cdot 689\ 10} = .761$
$r^2_{Y10} = .020$	$R^2_{Y \cdot 8\ 10} = .741$	$R^2_{Y \cdot 689} = .755$	$R^2_{Y \cdot 678\ 11} = .783$
	$R^2_{Y \cdot 79} = .595$		

(a) Ignoring any regression combinations not represented in the above, find the predictor variables selected in each stage of a stepwise regression that uses maximum coefficient of partial determination (regular determination in the first step) as the criterion for selection. Do this for (1) step 1 (single predictor), (2) step 2 (two predictors), (3) step 3 (three predictors), and (4) step 4 (four predictors).

(b) Do you think it is worthwhile to include four predictors? Explain.

11-28 *Computer exercise.* Consider the data given in Table 11-7 for first-basemen superstars.

(a) Perform a multiple regression analysis for predicting price of a player's rookie baseball card using games played, at bats, and runs batted in (RBI) as the only predictors. What is the regression equation and standard error?

(b) Determine for each player the predicted card value and calculate the residuals.

(c) An outlier may be identified as any data point having a residual that is in absolute value greater than twice the standard error of the estimate. The ninth player on the list, Kent Hrbek, is the only such player. Delete him from the data set and rerun the same regression. What is the new regression equation and standard error? Do you think that improved predictions might be made from the newest regression equation?

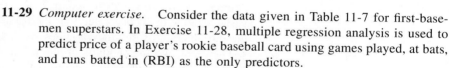

11-29 *Computer exercise.* Consider the data given in Table 11-7 for first-basemen superstars. In Exercise 11-28, multiple regression analysis is used to predict price of a player's rookie baseball card using games played, at bats, and runs batted in (RBI) as the only predictors.

(a) Determine the following correlation coefficients.

(1) games played vs. RBI

TABLE 11-7 Data Set for First-Basemen Superstars

Player i	Salary	Card Price Y	Games Played X_5	At Bats X_6	Batting Average X_7	RBI X_8	Number of Runs X_9	Fielding Percent X_{10}	Home Runs X_{11}	Put-Outs X_{12}
8	2,400	3.00	761	2,717	279	426	408	953	98	1,219
18	3,792	15.00	1,024	3,941	262	646	541	982	175	3,467
19	3,400	20.00	1,773	6,109	270	1,060	1,011	986	38	7,016
20	3,775	5.00	736	2,700	302	447	452	992	117	6,588
29	3,275	12.00	830	3,032	262	518	427	992	166	6,951
40	2,100	.70	810	2,703	250	427	336	986	122	4,180
49	2,485	3.50	740	2,707	276	400	360	993	97	6,377
56	2,283	10.00	1,378	4,819	305	812	679	976	206	4,795
64	2,600	6.00	1,299	4,670	290	803	685	994	223	10,127
67	2,100	.80	703	2,657	286	422	759	994	93	6,061
75	3,420	30.00	1,117	4,416	317	759	655	995	169	8,769
79	2,750	1.00	578	1,944	278	305	348	993	125	4,161
80	2,875	3.00	623	2,173	253	429	355	993	156	4,913
86	2,562	45.00	2,135	7,997	294	1,373	1,210	993	379	17,030
88	2,038	.70	1,209	4,271	267	569	526	993	131	9,972

(2) games played vs. at bats
(3) at bats vs. RBI

(b) At bats is highly correlated with both games played and RBI. This indicates that at bats is not a strong predictor and could cause potential difficulties. Using all originally listed players, perform a multiple regression using just games played and RBI as the predictors. Provide the estimated regression equation and standard error of the estimate.

(c) Which model, the above or the one found in Exercise 11-28(a), would you prefer for making predictions of baseball card prices for future first-basemen superstars? Explain.

11-7 DUMMY VARIABLE TECHNIQUES

It is sometimes necessary to determine how a dependent variable is related to quantitative independent random variables when there are nonhomogeneous factors influencing their interaction. Often such factors are qualitative in nature. For example, in printing a book, the cost of typesetting can be expressed by an equation involving the size of the book and the number of figures and tables. But this cost is also affected by the kind of book. A technical book using many special symbols and characters (like this one) requires a considerable amount of handwork and is, page for page, more expensive to set than a literary anthology. "Kind of book" can be viewed as a qualitative variable that influences composition cost. Although regression analysis requires all variables to be quantitative, qualititative variables may be incorporated into the framework of multiple regression through the introduction of dummy variables.

There are two major kinds of statistical studies where dummy variables may be used. Those made with sample data collected at a single point in time are sometimes referred to as **cross-sectional studies**. Studies made using observations collected over an extended time period use time-series data. In business and

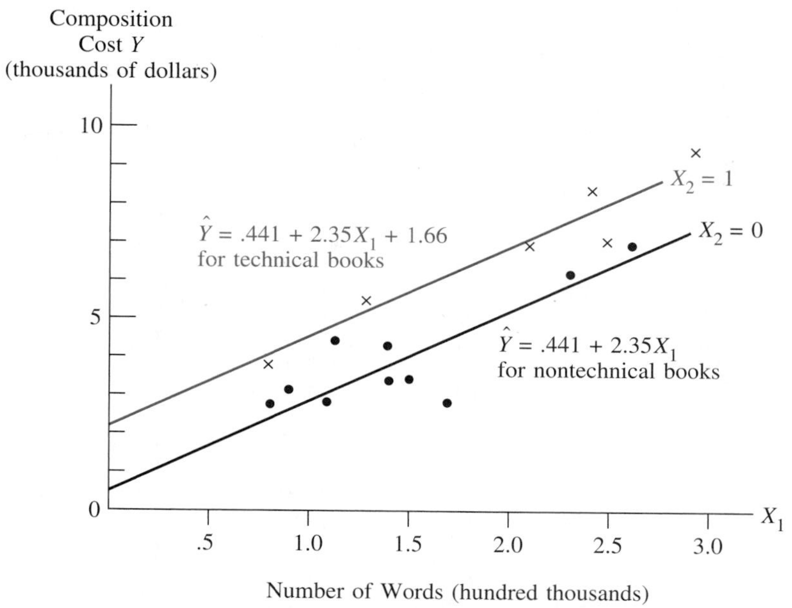

FIGURE 11-12 Multiple regression results using a dummy variable for typesetting cost illustration.

economics, time-series data are very important because observations of a dependent variable, such as consumption of electricity or gross national product, can only be obtained periodically. Often, time itself becomes the independent variable. Unavoidable historical heterogeneous influences, such as war or recession, may be treated as qualitative variables, and their effects must be identified somehow. Another important use for qualitative variables in time series is to identify seasonal influences and to relate them to the dependent variable.

USING A DUMMY VARIABLE

We illustrate the dummy variable technique in Figure 11-12 for data relating composition costs to total number of words for a hypothetical sample of textbooks. The books have been printed during one year by a firm under contract to various publishers. The data points for technical books are shown as crosses; the dots represent nontechnical texts. As we have noted, the technical books tend to be more costly, so that the crosses cluster higher than the dots. Two parallel lines have been constructed for the scatter diagram. The top one, fitting the data for the technical books, represents an upward shift in composition costs due to extensive hand typesetting.

These lines have been obtained by means of a linear least-squares *multiple* regression with two independent variables, word length X_1 and type of book X_2 . X_2 is a **dummy variable** that takes on only two values, 1 or 0, depending on whether or not a book is technical. We may envision X_2 as a "switching" variable that is "on" when an observation is made for a technical book and "off" for an ordinary text. The estimated multiple regression equation is of the form

$$\hat{Y} = a + b_1X_1 + b_2X_2$$

TABLE 11-8 Intermediate Calculations for Multiple Regression Using a Dummy Variable

Cost* Y	Length* X_1	X_2	X_1Y	X_2Y	X_1X_2	X_1^2	X_2^2	Y^2
4.2	1.4	0	5.88	0	0	1.96	0	17.64
2.8	1.1	0	3.08	0	0	1.21	0	7.84
3.3	1.4	0	4.62	0	0	1.96	0	10.89
3.9	.8	1(T)	3.12	3.9	.8	.64	1	15.21
6.7	2.6	0	17.42	0	0	6.76	0	44.89
7.0	2.5	1(T)	17.50	7.0	2.5	6.25	1	49.00
9.3	2.9	1(T)	26.97	9.3	2.9	8.41	1	86.49
2.7	.8	0	2.16	0	0	.64	0	7.29
6.9	2.1	1(T)	14.49	6.9	2.1	4.41	1	47.61
2.8	1.2	0	3.36	0	0	1.44	0	7.84
5.4	1.3	1(T)	7.02	5.4	1.3	1.69	1	29.16
6.1	2.3	0	14.03	0	0	5.29	0	37.21
8.3	2.4	1(T)	19.92	8.3	2.4	5.76	1	68.89
3.3	1.5	0	4.95	0	0	2.25	0	10.89
3.1	.9	0	2.79	0	0	.81	0	9.61
75.8	25.2	6	147.31	40.8	12.0	49.48	6	450.46
$=\sum Y$	$=\sum X_1$	$=\sum X_2$	$=\sum X_1Y$	$=\sum X_2Y$	$=\sum X_1X_2$	$=\sum X_1^2$	$=\sum X_2^2$	$=\sum Y^2$
			$\bar{Y} = 5.053$	$\bar{X}_1 = 1.680$	$\bar{X}_2 = .4$			

*Cost Y (thousands of dollars); length X_1 (hundreds of thousands of words).

where $X_2 = 0$ for nontechnical books and $X_2 = 1$ for technical books. This is the equation for a plane in three-dimensional space. However, we have restricted X_2 in such a way that only two parallel slices through the plane at $X_2 = 0$ and $X_2 = 1$ are possible. These are projected onto the X_1Y plane as the two estimated regression lines in Figure 11-12, the equations for which are

$$\hat{Y} = a + b_1X_1 + b_2 \qquad \text{(technical books)}$$

$$\hat{Y} = a + b_1X_1 \qquad \text{(nontechnical books)}$$

The value of a is the Y intercept for nontechnical books. The value of b_1 is the incremental or variable cost per additional word for either type of book. The amount b_2 represents the additional estimated cost—here assumed to be fixed in nature—associated with setting the type for a technical book. Thus, the Y intercept for technical books is a total fixed cost estimated to be $a + b_2$.*

Table 11-8 shows the data for this example. Solving the corresponding normal equations, the following regression constants are obtained.

$$a = .441 \qquad b_1 = 2.35 \qquad b_2 = 1.66$$

The estimated regression equation is

$$\hat{Y} = .441 + 2.35X_1 + 1.66X_2$$

*A more general model would allow for different variable costs for technical books, which might be more realistic and would allow lines of different slope for the two types of tests.

For the two values of X_2, the multiple regression equation provides

$$\hat{Y} = .441 + 2.35X_1 \qquad \text{(nontechnical books)}$$

and

$$\hat{Y} = .441 + 2.35X_1 + 1.66$$

or

$$\hat{Y} = 2.101 + 2.35X_1 \qquad \text{(technical books)}$$

We may interpret these lines as follows. The value $a = .441$ represents an estimated setup or fixed cost of \$441 applicable, on the average, to every book set in type. The partial regression coefficient value $b_1 = 2.35$, which is also the slope of each of the lines for the two kinds of books, is the estimated average variable cost of \$2,350 for each additional 100,000 words in length, or 2.35 cents per additional word. This applies to both technical and nontechnical books. The other partial regression coefficient, $b_2 = 1.66$, applies only to technical texts and indicates the estimated additional average fixed cost of handsetting special characters, \$1,660 per book, so that these books involve an average fixed cost estimated to be \$441 + \$1,660 = \$2,101 each.

The importance of treating kind of book as a separate variable is that this allows us to properly identify the relationship between composition cost and book length. Using the dummy variable X_2, we can treat the two kinds of books separately and yet still glean the common information that both types yield in relating book length to cost. We certainly should not ignore the kind of book in determining the relationship between these primary variables. Doing so can lead to very erroneous conclusions, as is shown in Figure 11-13, where a simple linear regression line relates Y to X_1. This line does not fit the data nearly as well as the two lines obtained for multiple regression, and the amount of scatter about this single line

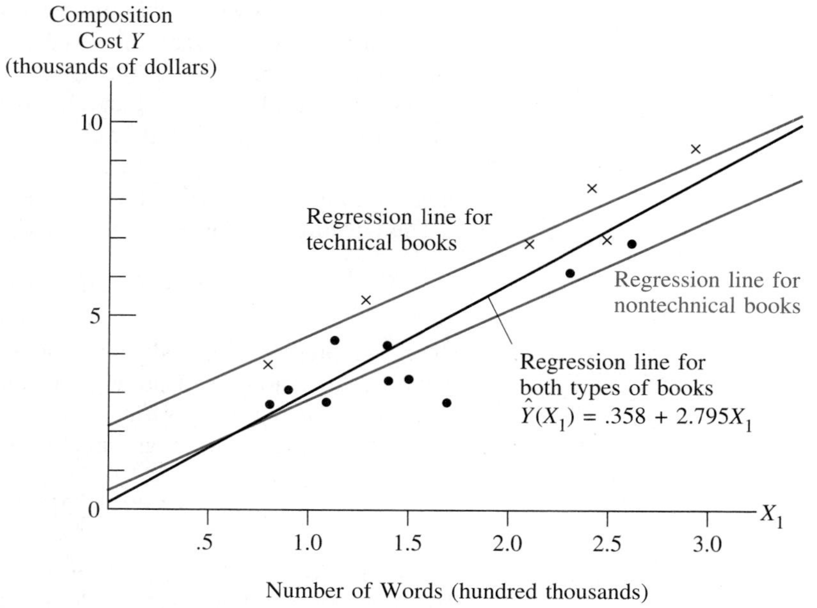

FIGURE 11-13 Linear least-squares regression and multiple regression using a dummy variable.

is substantially greater than that achieved for the parallel lines obtained for multiple regression analysis using a dummy variable.

But why can't we do just as well by making two separate linear regression analyses, splitting the observations into separate samples for technical and nontechnical books? If the sample sizes are large, this would be more desirable than the above approach. Later in this section we will see how the dummy variable technique can be generalized through an interactive mode. Such a variation provides projected lines which may have different *slopes*. (That technique would permit technical and nontechnical books to have different variable costs if the raw data suggest it.)

USING A DUMMY VARIABLE WITH TIME SERIES

We have noted situations where regression analysis using dummy variables with time-series data may be advantageous. One of these involves isolation of the effect of nonhomogeneous influences—such as war and peace or recession and economic expansion—on the relationship between two or more variables. Such variables are characterized by the uncontrollability of the sampling experiment, so that observations can be collected only as they occur over time. The statistician or economist cannot make a large number of "peacetime-only" observations in order to determine a relationship between personal consumption expenditures and disposable personal income, for the data are available only with peacetime and war years intermingled. Separate analyses would be less reliable, because of the scarcity of observations, than a multiple regression analysis treating war as a dummy variable. The procedure for the latter is completely analogous to the one illustrated for textbook composition. A regression plane is fitted to the three-dimensional data array, with values for personal consumption expenditure and disposable personal income variables, and with the dummy variable taking the value 0 for peacetime and 1 for wartime.

Figure 11-14 shows the two projected regression lines obtained for the regression plane using disposable personal income and war to predict personal consumption expenditures for the United States, using data from 1935–1949. Because of World War II's dramatic disruptions of personal lives and the economy, there was a significantly different pattern of consumer spending during the 1942–1945 period. This was due to a host of factors, such as rationing and the appropriation of production facilities for military material.

The equation for the regression plane is

$$C = 1.49 + .915Y_D - 22.66W$$

where C represents personal consumption expenditures, Y_D is the traditional economist's designation for disposable income (taken here to be an independent variable), and W is a dummy variable ($W = 0$ for peacetime and $W = 1$ for wartime). When $W = 0$, the regression plane becomes the line

$$C = 1.49 + .915Y_D \qquad \text{(in peacetime)}$$

which may be interpreted as an estimate of the *aggregate consumption function*. The slope of this line, .915, is the personal consumption expenditure for each dollar increase in disposable income. For the economy as a whole, 91.5 cents from each extra dollar of personal income is estimated to be spent on consumption. In

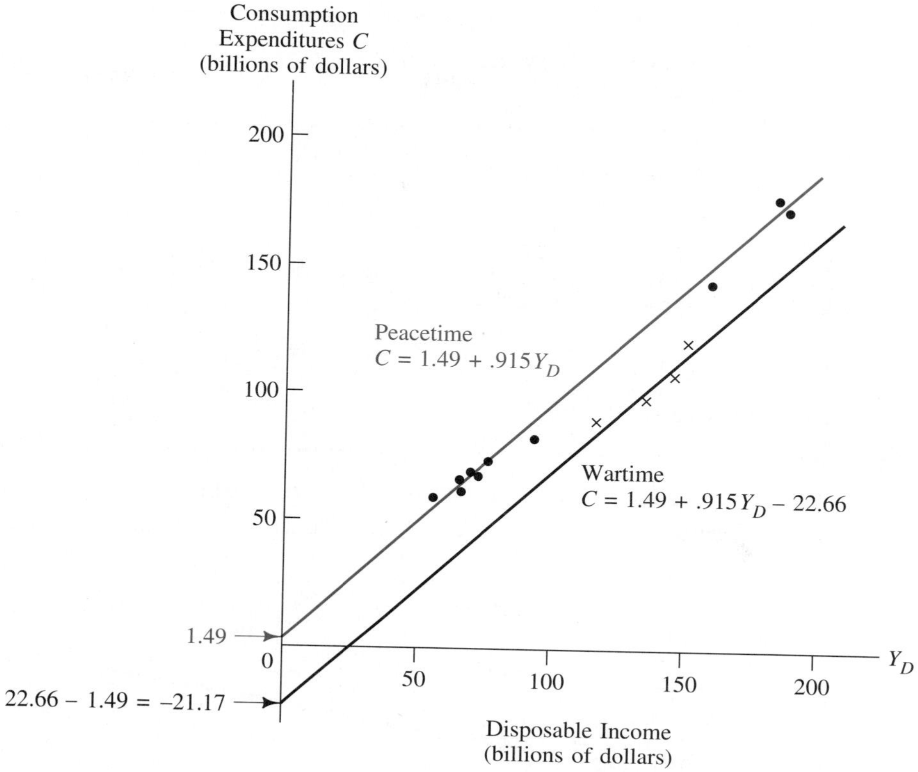

FIGURE 11-14 Multiple regression using a dummy variable for consumption function during wartime and peacetime.

the terminology of economics, .915 is the *marginal propensity to consume.* When $W = 1$, then with $b_2 = -22.66$ the regression line (the consumption function) shifts downward by an amount of $22.66 billion, reflecting a general drop in personal expenditures due to the shortage of many goods formerly purchased by individuals. Notice that this shifted regression line has the same slope, reflecting the fact that the marginal propensity to consume is the same as before.*

If the time-series data were expanded to include the 1950s and 1960s, the effects of two other wars, in Korea and Vietnam, would be much less pronounced. These wars were not as disruptive to consumer spending habits, since there were no major shortages or rationing. For this reason, a better fit to the time series could be obtained by treating these later war years like peacetime (so that perhaps the dummy variable, wartime *rationing*, would then be a better designation).

USING A DUMMY VARIABLE IN INTERACTIVE MULTIPLE REGRESSION

The preceding illustrations involve identical slopes for the individual regression lines projected onto the regression plane. The procedure may be generalized

*As we have noted, this may not be realistic but it is a necessary consequence of the linear multiple regression model.

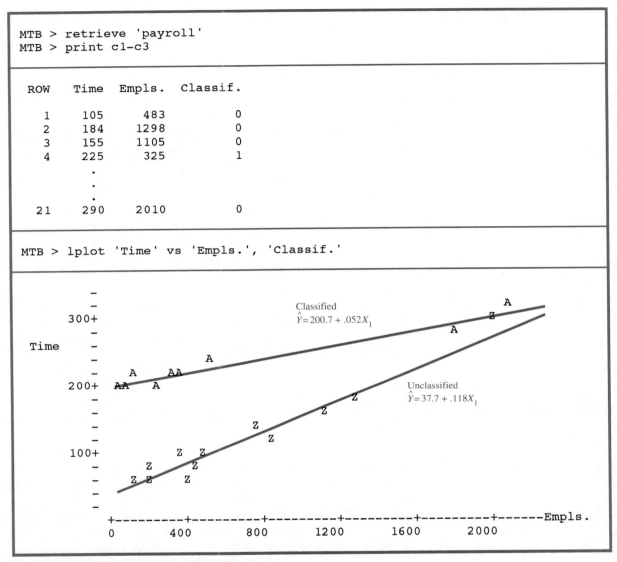

```
MTB > retrieve 'payroll'
MTB > print c1-c3
```

```
ROW   Time   Empls.   Classif.

  1    105     483        0
  2    184    1298        0
  3    155    1105        0
  4    225     325        1
        .
        .
        .
 21    290    2010        0
```

```
MTB > lplot 'Time' vs 'Empls.', 'Classif.'
```

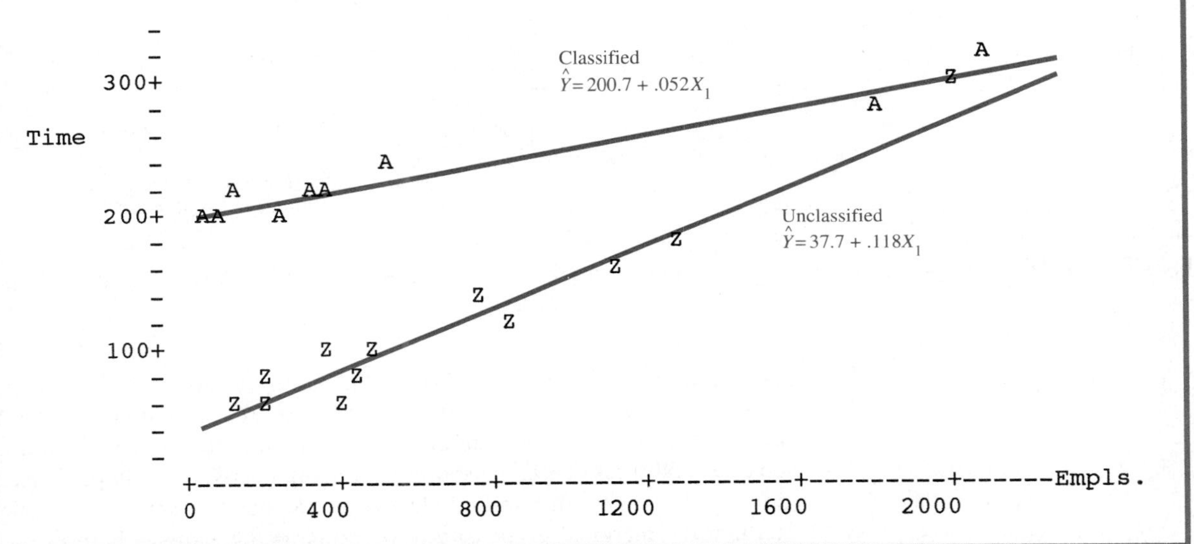

Note: Figure generated on an IBM PC using Minitab®.

FIGURE 11-15 Scatter diagram for the accounting service's payroll data.

slightly to allow for a different slope under the settings of the dummy variable. To accomplish this, find the coefficients of the multiple regression equation

$$\hat{Y} = a + b_1X_1 + b_2X_2 + b_3X_1X_2$$

where $X_2 = 0$ or 1 (dummy variable) and a third independent variable is expressed as

$$X_3 = X_1X_2$$

Two lines result from the two-dimensional projections obtained for the above regression plane.

$$\hat{Y} = a + b_1X_1 \qquad \text{(when } X_2 = 0\text{)}$$
$$\hat{Y} = (a + b_2) + (b_1 + b_3)X_1 \qquad \text{(when } X_2 = 1\text{)}$$

To illustrate the procedure, Figure 11-15 shows a computer-generated scatter diagram for data obtained from an accounting service. Each data point represent a sample payroll processed by the services. The dependent variable Y is payroll processing time (seconds) and the independent variable X_1 is number of employees. The dummy variable is X_2. The payrolls include a mixture of small and large firms, so that the data for firms with predominantly classified (hourly) employees ($X_2 = 1$) are plotted as A's and the firms with mostly unclassified (salaried) employees ($X_2 = 0$) are plotted as Z's. (The projection lines were added by hand after the estimated multiple regression equation was found.)

Figure 11-16 is the printout for a multiple regression run using the payroll data. The estimated regression equation is

$$\hat{Y} = 37.7 + .118X_1 + 163X_2 - .066X_1X_2$$

Using the above equation when X_2=0, the projected regression line is

$$\hat{Y} = 37.7 + .118X_1 \qquad \text{(unclassified employee payrolls)}$$

and, when $X_2 = 1$, the equation provides

$$\begin{aligned}\hat{Y} &= (37.7 + 163) + (.118 - .066)X_1 \\ &= 200.7 + .052X_1 \qquad \text{(classified employee payrolls)}\end{aligned}$$

These lines indicate that payrolls for classified employees have a fixed processing-time component that is about six times as long as that of the payrolls for unclassified employees. That may be attributable to the higher computational setup requirements for determining pay from hours worked for classified (largely hourly) employees. Computing basic pay for unclassified employees should be simpler, since they receive mainly a fixed salary. But the slope is less than half of the counterpart for classified payrolls. This may be due to the richer mix of benefits and salary perquisite items that are included for unclassified (largely white-collar) employees.

EXERCISES

11-30 Six women and four men have taken a test that measures their manual dexterity and patience in handling tiny objects. Each has then gone through a week of intensive training as electronics assemblers, followed by a month at actual assembly, during which their productivity was measured by a relative index having values ranging from 0 to 10 (with 10 being the value for the most productive worker). The data in the following table have been obtained.

Subject	Productivity Index Y	Test Score X_1	Sex
A	5.2	5.8	F
B	6.0	8.5	M
C	6.5	8.2	F
D	2.0	3.5	F
E	2.7	6.5	M
F	10.0	9.5	F
G	6.4	9.8	M
H	6.6	9.2	M
I	3.5	4.0	F
J	4.0	5.5	F

(a) Plot a scatter diagram using different symbols for women and men.

(b) Using a dummy variable having value $X_2 = 1$ for women and $X_2 = 0$ for men, determine the coefficients of the equation $\hat{Y} = a + b_1X_1 + b_2X_2$ for the estimated regression plane. Plot the lines corresponding to $X_2 = 0$ and $X_2 = 1$ on your scatter diagram.

(c) State the meaning of the partial regression coefficients.

(d) Determine the estimated regression line obtained when the sex of the subjects is ignored. Plot the line on your scatter diagram.

11-31 The data in the following table have been obtained for personal savings and personal income (billions of dollars) for the time period 1935–1949.

(a) Plot the scatter diagram using dots for peacetime and crosses for wartime.

(b) Using a dummy variable having value $X_2 = 0$ for peacetime and $X_2 = 1$ for wartime, determine the estimated regression equation $\hat{Y} = a + b_1X_1 + b_2X_2$.

(c) Plot the two lines corresponding to wartime and peacetime on your scatter diagram.

Year	Personal Savings Y	Personal Income X_1	War Year
1935	2	60	
1936	4	69	
1937	4	74	
1938	1	68	
1939	3	73	
1940	4	78	
1941	11	96	
1942	28	123	yes
1943	33	151	yes
1944	37	165	yes
1945	30	171	yes
1946	15	179	
1947	7	191	
1948	13	210	
1949	9	207	

Source: *Economic Report of the President,* February 1970.

```
MTB > let c4=c2*c3
MTB > name c4 'EmpxClas'
MTB > print c1-c4
```

```
 ROW   Time  Empls.  Classif.  EmpxClas

   1    105     483         0         0
   2    184    1298         0         0
   3    155    1105         0         0
   4    225     325         1       325
   5    203      52         1        52
   6    210     125         1       125
   7     56     210         0         0
   8     99     355         0         0
   9    220     378         1       378
  10    208     224         1       224
  11     64     106         0         0
  12     81     425         0         0
  13    231     515         1       515
  14    315    2067         1      2067
  15    285    1810         1      1810
  16    125     844         0         0
  17    135     771         0         0
  18    199      94         1        94
  19     75     186         0         0
  20     50     409         0         0
  21    290    2010         0         0
```

```
MTB > Regress c1 3 c2-c4.
```

```
The regression equation is
Time = 37.7 + 0.118 Empls. + 163 Classif. - 0.0659 EmpxClas

Predictor        Coef       Stdev    t-ratio        p
Constant       37.683       6.430       5.86    0.000
Empls.       0.117874    0.007404      15.92    0.000
Classif.      162.943       8.827      18.46    0.000
EmpxClas    -0.065930    0.009760      -6.75    0.000

s = 13.74        R-sq = 97.6%      R-sq(adj) = 97.1%
```

Note: Figure generated on an IBM PC using Minitab®.

FIGURE 11-16 Computer printout for the payroll data.

11-32 Refer to Exercise 11-30, and to your answers.

(a) Compute the average test scores separately for the men and the women. Then, compute the average productivity index for men and for women.

(b) Based on these averages, what conclusion can you draw with respect to the average test score results for the sample men as compared to those for the women? Can the same conclusion be drawn for the productivity index?

(c) How do you reconcile your conclusion in (b) with the interpretation of the partial regression coefficient b_2?

11-33 A statistician used the following data to illustrate the cows–acres paradox.

Farm	Number of Cows Y	Number of Acres X_1	Primary Product
1	280	650	beef
2	250	400	beef
3	350	200	milk
4	370	350	milk
5	200	480	beef
6	420	340	milk
7	300	600	beef
8	320	130	milk
9	320	280	milk
10	250	450	beef

(a) Plot a scatter diagram using different symbols for farms whose main product is beef and for farms producing primarily milk.

(b) Determine the estimated regression equation expressing number of cows Y in terms of the single independent variable, number of acres X_1. Plot this line on your scatter diagram. Your line should indicate that Y (number of cows) decreases as X_1 (number of acres) increases. Explain.

(c) Using a dummy variable having value $X_2 = 0$ for beef and $X_2 = 1$ for milk, determine the estimated regression equation $\hat{Y} = a + b_1X_1 + b_2X_2$. Plot the lines corresponding to $X_2 = 0$ and $X_2 = 1$ on your graph. (In each case, a positive slope indicates that the predicted number of cows should be greater for larger acreages.)

11-34 Repeat Exercise 11-33 (a) and (b) using the interactive dummy-variable model.

11-35 Repeat Exercise 11-30 (a) and (b) using the interactive dummy-variable model.

SUMMARY

1. What is *multiple* regression and how does it differ from *simple* regression? **Multiple regression** incorporates two or more independent predictor variables. The method of least squares provides an *estimated regression plane* (or hyperplane) described by an **estimated multiple regression equation** of the form

$$\hat{Y} = a + b_1X_1 + b_2X_2 + \cdots + b_kX_k$$

The quality of predictions reached using the higher-dimensional regression plane is often greater than that obtained from a **simple regression** involving a single independent variable.

2. **How do we establish the multiple regression equation?**
The Y intercept a and **estimated partial regression coefficients** (b_1, b_2, . . .) may be computed simultaneously solving a system of *normal equations*. In an $m = 3$ variable evaluation, so that there is a dependent variable Y and two independent variables X_1 and X_2, the normal equations are

$$\sum Y = na + b_1 \sum X_1 + b_2 \sum X_2$$
$$\sum X_1 Y = a \sum X_1 + b_1 \sum X_1^2 + b_2 \sum X_1 X_2$$
$$\sum X_2 Y = a \sum X_2 + b_1 \sum X_1 X_2 + b_2 \sum X_2^2$$

The normal equations become more elaborate as m increases.
A computer is ordinarily used to perform a multiple regression analysis.

3. **What are the assumptions of regression analysis and the potential pitfalls?**
The underlying theoretical assumptions are analogous to those for simple regression. One notable difficulty is **multicollinearity** which can cause instability in predictions. Another challenge arises from **serial correlation**, which might be alleviated by including an additional predictor variable.

4. **What inferences may be made with multiple regression analysis?**
Multiple regression has analogous theoretical assumptions to those of simple regression and involves the same types of inferences, including prediction intervals for the conditional mean $\mu_{Y \cdot 12 \ldots}$ and an individual value Y_I and hypothesis tests and estimates of the partial regression coefficients. The necessary computations for these are often standard computer output. A **collective confidence level** is required for estimating the b's using simultaneous **Bonferroni intervals**.

5. **How do we assess the overall quality of a regression analysis?**
The overall quality of the multiple regression analysis in explaining deviations in Y can be measured by the **coefficient of multiple determination. Partial correlation** is a useful concept, with the net contribution of one variable measured by the **coefficient of partial determination**. These statistics may be used in a **stepwise multiple regression** to determine which X predictors to include in the final evaluation.

6. **How can we find a predictive regression model?**
Multiple regression analysis can be extended to include a search for best predictors that meet the dual goals of *explaining* a high proportion of variability in Y and achieving *simplicity*. The primary technique is **stepwise regression**, in which a series of regressions is performed in stages. The best predictor found at each step is added to the growing set of predictor variables. In a forward procedure, the new variable gives the greatest possible reduction in unexplained Y variation, and the respective *coefficients of partial determination* can be used for this purpose. Stepwise regression should be done with computer assistance, with criterion of choice varying among software packages. Ideally, the process should stop when a point of diminishing returns in improvement is reached. Some programs will drop variables from the

predictive set as well. Regardless of how predictors are chosen, the final model should make sense, so that variables having coefficients of opposite sign to what is logical can be dropped. Predictive stability can be enhanced by not including a predictor that is highly correlated with other independent variables and through judicious elimination of outliers.

7. **How might dummy variables be used in conjunction with multiple regression?**
Multiple regression can be helpful in certain situations involving a *single* main predictor. When the sample data are placed into homogeneous groupings according to some category, a second predictor or **dummy variable** may be used. Dummy variable techniques can be especially helpful when sample sizes are too small to obtain statistically reliable results through separate simple regressions.

REAL-LIFE STATISTICAL CHALLENGE

Multiple Regression and Correlation Applied to the Automobile Dream List

In Chapter 10 concepts of regression and correlation were used to analyze the list of 232 autos. We will now apply multiple regression and correlation testing methods to the list of "dream machines."

Again we consider what factors could determine mileage—weight of the vehicle, transmission type, driving skill, and engine size. With multiple regression we can assess the impact of several factors on gas mileage. The data we will work with are shown in Table 11-9. To simplify things we will compare gas mileage with engine size plus two dummy variables for size of the vehicle and transmission type. Size is categorized into either large and midsized or all others (two-seater, etc.). Transmission is either automatic (A or L) or manual (M). Large and midsized cars are assigned a value of 0 and small ones a value of 1. Automobiles with automatic transmissions are assigned a value of 0; those with manuals, a value of 1. The dependent variable is gas mileage and the three independent variables are engine size, model type and transmission type.

The multiple regression results for the samples are shown in Table 11-10. Observe how the results for each pair of independent variables compare to the result for the regression result when all three independent variables are used. The results are not really surprising—larger cars with bigger engines and automatic transmissions generally have lower mileage ratings.

Discussion Questions

1. Observations in two dimensions:
   (a) Plot a single scatter diagram comparing the data in Table 11-9 for larger (mid-size, large) versus smaller (compact, subcompact, minicompact) cars in terms of their respective engine displacements X and mileage ratings Y.
   (b) Determine the estimated regression equations for each group separately and plot these on your graph. Comment on what you observe.

TABLE 11-9 Data for a Sample of 1990 Automobiles Showing Mileage, Transmission Type, Engine Displacement (liters) and Highway Mileage per Gallon

Number	Type	Manu-facturer	Model	Trans-mission Type	Highway Mileage Miles/gallon	Engine Displacement in Liters	Dummy Variable Model	Dummy Variable Trans-mission
10026	Minicompact	Maserati	222E	M5	20	2.8	1	1
10053	Subcompact	Chevrolet	Camaro	M5	26	5.0	1	1
10088	Subcompact	Geo	Prizm	L3	29	1.6	1	0
10111	Subcompact	Mitsubishi	Eclipse	M5	32	1.8	1	1
10126	Subcompact	Subaru	XT	M5	31	1.8	1	1
10140	Compact	Chevrolet	Beretta	M5	28	3.1	1	1
10149	Compact	Isuzu	Stylus	M5	33	1.6	1	1
10151	Compact	Lexus	ES250	L4	25	2.5	1	0
10154	Compact	Mitsubishi	Galant	M5	29	2.0	1	1
10178	Mid-Size	BMW	750i	L4	18	5.0	0	0
10185	Mid-Size	Chevrolet	Lumina	L4	30	3.1	0	0
10186	Mid-Size	Chrysler	New Yorker	L4	26	3.3	0	0
10199	Mid-Size	Mazda	929	L4	23	3.0	0	0
10213	Mid-Size	Volvo	740	L4	26	2.3	0	0
10218	Large	Cadillac	Brougham	L4	21	5.7	0	0
			Sample	Average	26.47	2.97		
			Sample	St. Dev.	4.47	1.31		

Source: United States Environmental Protection Agency, 1989.

2. With car size as a dummy variable, determine the estimated multiple regression using the data in Table 11-9. What do you think about making predictions from this equation rather than those found in (b)?

TABLE 11-10 Multiple Regression Results for 1990 Automobile Sample Data

	1st Regression	2nd Regression	3rd Regression	4th Regression
Y	mpg	mpg	mpg	mpg
Constant	32.34	31.86	31.89	24.00
Standard Error	3.40	3.26	3.39	4.24
R^2	.55	.54	.51	.23
n	15	15	15	15
m	4	3	3	3
X_1: **Displacement**	included	included	included	out
b_1	−2.23	−2.15	−2.11	—
X_2: **Transmission**	included	included	out	included
b_2	2.63	2.12	—	3.00
X_3: **Model**	included	out	included	included
b_3	−.76	—	1.43	3.46

3. Using the data in Table 11-10 for the first regression, answer the following.
(a) Calculate the 95 percent prediction interval for the conditional mean of Y when $X_1 = \bar{X}_1$, $X_2 = \bar{X}_2$, and $X_3 = \bar{X}_3$.
(b) Calculate the 95 percent prediction interval for an individual value of Y given X when $X_1 = \bar{X}_1$, $X_2 = \bar{X}_2$, and $X_3 = \bar{X}_3$.

4. Refer again to Table 11-10. Which regression results do you prefer in making predictions of gasoline mileage? Discuss and substantiate.

REVIEW EXERCISES

11-36 A college admissions director wishes to predict college GPA Y of applicants using high school GPA X_1 and verbal SAT score X_2 as independent variables. The following data apply.

Student	College GPA Y	High School GPA X_1	Verbal SAT Score X_2
1	3.8	4.0	750
2	2.7	3.7	380
3	2.3	2.2	580
4	3.2	3.8	510
5	3.5	3.8	620
6	2.4	2.8	440
7	2.6	3.0	540
8	3.0	3.4	650
9	2.7	3.3	480
10	2.8	3.0	550

(a) Determine the estimated regression equation.
(b) Using your answer to (a), calculate the predicted college GPA for the following applicants.

	High School GPA X_1	SAT Score X_2
(1)	3.4	550
(2)	2.8	400
(3)	3.2	650
(4)	3.7	450

11-37 Refer to the data given in Exercise 11-36. The estimated regression equation for predicting college GPA Y using only high school GPA X_1 is

$$\hat{Y}(X_1) = .4957 + .7286X_1$$

The values of the standard error of the estimate and coefficient of determination are

$$s_{Y \cdot X_1} = .268 \qquad r_{Y1}^2 = .721$$

with the standard deviation in Y having value $S_Y = .478$. The standard error of the estimate when verbal SAT score X_2 is included as an independent variable is

$$S_{Y \cdot 12} = .110$$

(a) Compute the coefficient of multiple determination when both X_1 and X_2 are used to predict Y.

(b) Compute the coefficient of partial determination ($r_{Y2 \cdot 1}^2$) for adding SAT score X_2 to the regression analysis. What is the percentage reduction in unexplained variation in Y achieved by adding SAT score X_2 as the second independent variable? Does this suggest that including SAT score should improve college GPA predictions? Explain.

11-38 *Computer exercise.* A third independent variable, number of extracurricular activities X_3, is added to the college GPA prediction problem in Exercise 11-36. The following data apply.

Student	Number of Activities X_3
1	7
2	6
3	5
4	6
5	3
6	2
7	8
8	2
9	7
10	4

Determine the coefficients for $\hat{Y} = a + b_1X_1 + b_2X_2 + b_3X_3$.

11-39 (*Continuation of Exercise 11-38*):

(a) Calculate the value of $S_{Y \cdot 123}$.

(b) Compared to the value $S_{Y \cdot 12} = .110$, does a comparison of the values $S_{Y \cdot 123}$ and $S_{Y \cdot 12}$ suggest that including the number of high school activities improves college GPA predictions? Explain.

(c) Compute the coefficient of partial determination ($r_{Y3 \cdot 12}^2$) for including X_3 in the regression analysis. What is the percentage reduction in previously unexplained variation achieved by adding number of activities as the third independent variable?

11-40 *Computer exercise.* Suppose that the real estate appraiser in Exercise 11-7 also gathered data for the median neighborhood selling price to include as her third independent variable X_3. The following data (in thousands of dollars) apply.

Price Y	Median X_3
45	35
37	40
26	23
32	32
34	39
49	45
53	49
65	70
71	66
88	91

(a) You have been asked to run a higher-dimensional multiple regression for the appraiser. Determine the estimated multiple regression equation.

(b) The standard error of the estimate for selling price using the regression hyperplane is $S_{Y \cdot 123}=3.912$. Does it appear that including the additional independent variable improves the regression analysis?

11-41 *Computer exercise.* The data set in Table 11-11 applies to baseball superstar third-basemen and shortstops.

(a) Determine the regression equation for predicting rookie baseball card price using runs batted in and number of home runs as independent variables.

(b) What is the proportion of variation in card price explained by the regression equation from (a)?

(c) Determine the regression equation for predicting salary using runs batted in and number of home runs as independent variables.

(d) What is the proportion of variation in salary explained by the regression equation from (c)?

TABLE 11-11 Data Set for Third-Basemen and Shortstop Superstars (X_4 = 0 for third basemen, X_4 = 1 for shortstop).

Player i	Salary	Card Price	Pos. X_4	Games X_5	At Bats X_6	Bat. Ave. X_7	RBI X_8	Runs X_9	Fielding X_{10}	Home Runs X_{11}	Put-Outs X_{12}
6	2,750	35.00	0	1,338	5,153	346	586	912	963	70	1,468
9	3,675	200.00	0	2,279	8,692	311	1,398	1,382	970	281	5,277
48	2,700	5.00	0	1,361	4,989	256	758	646	965	201	1,166
54	3,033	8.00	0	686	2,219	266	326	321	956	83	498
66	2,242	10.00	0	1,023	3,395	256	512	516	937	159	714
82	3,750	3.00	0	688	2,378	278	412	369	959	135	953
83	3,253	50.00	0	1,540	6,246	299	626	1,053	964	131	2,115
123	2,000	20.00	0	1,827	6,693	274	781	1,040	983	167	3,581
37	2,100	3.00	1	758	2,768	257	290	340	967	61	1,349
43	2,100	6.00	1	1,028	3,952	289	404	510	980	40	1,786
70	2,100	.80	1	572	2,125	293	221	314	970	38	846
98	2,433	18.00	1	1,476	5,655	274	828	871	977	225	4,469
110	2,225	45.00	1	1,926	7,019	256	600	910	978	19	3,237
119	2,200	50.00	1	1,835	6,702	288	810	1,009	977	152	2,880

```
MTB > Stepwise c3 c2 c4-c12;
SUBC>   FEnter 1;
SUBC>   FRemove 1.

 STEPWISE REGRESSION OF Card Pr. ON 10 PREDICTORS, WITH N =   14

    STEP          1        2        3        4        5        6
CONSTANT     -54.34   -55.07   -23.42   -74.76   601.82  1235.50

RBI           0.142    0.201    0.425    0.360    0.383    0.347
T-RATIO        5.21     4.55     4.20     3.44     3.61     3.31

H.Runs                 -0.28    -0.67    -0.62    -0.69    -0.71
T-RATIO                -1.63    -3.08    -2.98    -3.18    -3.43

Games                          -0.091   -0.064   -0.063   -0.069
T-RATIO                         -2.38    -1.60    -1.58    -1.81

Salary                                   0.019    0.014    0.015
T-RATIO                                   1.52     1.08     1.21

Fielding                                          -0.69    -1.35
T-RATIO                                           -1.06    -1.70

P.Outs                                                     0.014
T-RATIO                                                     1.34

S              29.7     27.8     23.3     21.9     21.8     20.7
R-SQ          69.32    75.32    84.25    87.48    89.02    91.27
```

FIGURE 11-17 Minitab stepwise regression results for baseball superstar data set in Table 11-11.

(e) Which regression model, (a) or (c), would provide better predictions? Explain.

11-42 Figure 11-17 provides the results of a computer stepwise regression using the data in Table 11-11 to predict the price of a player's rookie baseball card.

(a) Do you think it would be worthwhile to use more than three predictors? Explain.

(b) If you were going to do a detailed regression analysis, which three predictors would you use?

11-43 *Computer exercise.* The data set in Table 11-11 applies to baseball superstar third basemen and shortstops.

(a) Determine the regression equation for predicting rookie baseball card price using number of games played, runs batted in, and number of home runs as independent variables.

(b) What is the proportion of variation in card price explained by the regression equation from (a)?

(c) Determine a 95% prediction interval for a player who has played 1,000 games, having 1,000 RBIs and producing 300 home runs.

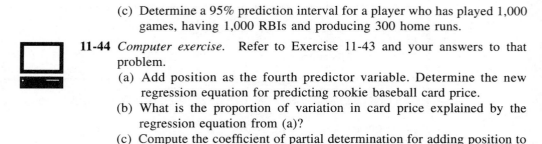

11-44 *Computer exercise.* Refer to Exercise 11-43 and your answers to that problem.

(a) Add position as the fourth predictor variable. Determine the new regression equation for predicting rookie baseball card price.

(b) What is the proportion of variation in card price explained by the regression equation from (a)?

(c) Compute the coefficient of partial determination for adding position to the predictor set. What percentage reduction in previously unexplained variation is achieved by including position as the fourth predictor?

11-45 *Computer exercise.* The data set in Table 11-12 applies to baseball superstar catchers and shortstops.

(a) Determine the regression equation for predicting rookie baseball card price using runs batted in and number of home runs as independent variables.

(b) What is the proportion of variation in card price explained by the regression equation from (a)?

(c) Determine the regression equation for predicting salary using runs batted in and number of home runs as independent variables.

(d) What is the proportion of variation in salary explained by the regression equation from (c)?

(e) Which regression model, (a) or (c), would provide better predictions? Explain.

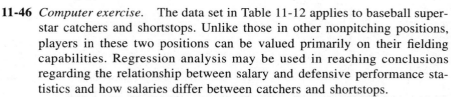

11-46 *Computer exercise.* The data set in Table 11-12 applies to baseball superstar catchers and shortstops. Unlike those in other nonpitching positions, players in these two positions can be valued primarily on their fielding capabilities. Regression analysis may be used in reaching conclusions regarding the relationship between salary and defensive performance statistics and how salaries differ between catchers and shortstops.

(a) Determine the regression equation for predicting salary using position, fielding percentage, and number of putouts as independent variables.

TABLE 11-12 Data Set for Catcher and Shortstop Superstars ($X = 0$ for catcher, $X = 1$ for shortstop).

Player i	Salary Y	Card Price	Pos. X_4	Games X_5	At Bats X_6	Bat. Ave. X_7	RBI X_8	Runs X_9	Fielding X_{10}	Home Runs X_{11}	Put-Outs X_{12}
45	2,455	150.00	0	2,278	8,055	272	1,231	1,220	987	354	10,660
89	2,417	30.00	0	1,656	6,066	257	947	765	991	285	8,166
90	2,350	2.50	0	1,350	4,676	273	528	500	989	89	7,668
104	2,183	7.00	0	1,205	3,680	262	382	340	987	57	7,017
37	2,100	3.00	1	758	2,768	257	290	340	967	61	1,349
43	2,100	6.00	1	1,028	3,952	289	404	510	980	40	1,786
70	2,100	.80	1	572	2,125	293	221	314	970	38	846
98	2,433	18.00	1	1,476	5,655	274	828	871	977	225	4,469
110	2,225	45.00	1	1,926	7,019	256	600	910	978	19	3,237
119	2,200	50.00	1	1,835	6,702	288	810	1,009	977	152	2,880

(b) What is the proportion of variation in salary explained by the regression equation?

(c) Should fielding percentage be kept as a predictor? Using information contained in your computer printout, make a case for keeping or dropping this variable.

11-47 *Computer exercise.* Continuation of Exercise 11-46.

(a) Determine the regression equation for predicting salary using position and number of putouts as independent variables.

(b) What is the proportion of variation in salary explained by the regression equation?

(c) What is the interpretation of the regression coefficient for position? In using the regression equation from (a) to predict salary, who would we expect to make more, catchers or shortstops?

STATISTICS IN PRACTICE

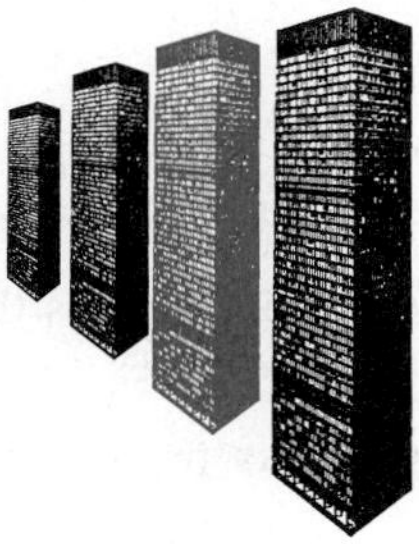

11-48 Consider populations comprising all statistics students. Using as sample data the master class data list developed in Exercise 1-19, perform the following regression and correlation operations. (Note: Be sure to show all your intermediate steps. You may use intermediate answers you developed in earlier chapters to avoid unnecessary effort. If needed, gather additional data.)

(a) Select two variables as the independent variables X_1 and X_2 and one as the dependent variable Y.

(b) Find the estimated regression equation.

(c) Determine the sample standard deviation and the standard error of the estimate for the dependent variable.

(d) Calculate the sample coefficient of multiple determination and the sample partial correlation coefficients.

(e) Predict the value of the dependent variable for four different sets of independent variable values.

(f) Demonstrate how to calculate the 95 percent prediction interval for the conditional mean of Y when $X_1 = \bar{X}_1$ and $X_2 = \bar{X}_2$.

(g) Demonstrate how to calculate the 95 percent prediction interval for an individual value of Y given $X_1 = \bar{X}_1$ and $X_2 = \bar{X}_2$.

11-49 Repeat Exercise 11-48 using your group's class data developed in Exercise 1-21.

11-50 *Comparing Commute Time and Distance to Work.* The following data is from a sample of graduate students who work in the Silicon Valley (San Jose, Calif.) and attend school at night.

(a) Use gender as a dummy variable and calculate the estimated regression plane for predicting a student's commute time given the distance traveled to work.

(b) Compute the sample standard deviation and the standard error of the estimate for commute time.

(c) Compute the sample coefficient of multiple determination and the sample partial correlation coefficients.

(d) What is the predicted commute time for a female living 12 miles from the office?

Gender	Commute Time (Min.)	Distance (Kilometers)	Distance (Miles)
Male	20	8	5
Male	20	13	8
Male	35	21	13
Male	45	26	16
Male	25	24	15
Female	30	28	17
Male	20	20	12
Female	45	54	33
Female	30	28	17
Male	15	4	3
Female	10	8	5
Male	20	8	5
Female	35	31	19
Female	35	37	23
Female	25	18	11
Male	5	3	2

11-51 Given your results in Exercises 11-48, 11-49, or 11-50, discuss the challenges and pitfalls you faced in carrying out these exercises.

CASE Adventures in Regression Land

Cal Crunch, an economist for Million Bank, wonders about the quality of econometric investigations that are based largely on regression analysis. He wishes to explore various facets of multiple regression using his personal computer. Cal plans to submit his findings to his professor as an extra credit report for his MBA core statistics course.

Using his EasyStat software package, Cal generates the following data for a random sample of 25 heads of households using the U.S. census data for 1,000 Sacramento, California, homeowners. Although 14 variables are represented in the data base, Cal has decided to limit his investigations to the six variables listed in the table.

Income Y	Level of Education X_1	Home Value X_2	Age X_3	Mortgage Payment X_4	Sex* X_5
$ 5,705	16	$ 55,300	28	$285	1
20,005	16	88,900	39	398	0
24,005	14	61,400	34	202	0
16,425	15	55,000	38	344	0
33,005	14	86,000	37	317	0

(continued)

Income Y	Level of Education X_1	Home Value X_2	Age X_3	Mortgage Payment X_4	Sex* X_5
19,810	04	30,300	56	087	0
40,005	20	90,000	53	152	0
28,005	13	69,600	51	115	0
50,585	19	111,400	58	263	0
9,885	18	41,800	30	098	1
22,005	14	61,600	49	419	0
9,745	16	45,300	30	312	1
20,005	16	53,000	29	258	0
14,520	15	57,400	22	415	1
22,010	22	112,400	40	900	0
7,370	10	30,700	63	139	1
25,510	20	86,500	31	326	0
20,505	14	49,500	44	307	0
14,005	17	25,600	55	187	1
27,370	20	80,000	40	120	0
9,095	14	31,300	69	090	1
13,005	18	30,800	32	117	0
13,005	14	60,900	57	190	0
23,125	16	54,500	39	149	0
16,005	16	63,500	50	271	0

*Male = 0 and female = 1 for this variable.

Cal then decides to determine the estimated multiple regression equation for predicting income using various Xs as independent predictor variables. To do this, he adapts the regression model to the above sample data. To conclude, Cal wishes to see how well that model will perform with different samples from the same population.

You decide to accept Cal's invitation to join his study group and volunteer to answer the following questions.

QUESTIONS

Computer assistance should be available to answer the following questions.

1. Run a multiple regression to predict income from known levels of education and home value only.
   (a) Determine the estimated multiple regression equation.
   (b) What percentage of the variation in Y is explained by the multiple regression equation?
   (c) Determine the predicted levels of the conditional mean income using the following values for the independent predictor variables.

	Level of Education	Home Value
(1)	16	\$100,000
(2)	10	50,000
(3)	12	75,000

2. Attempt to increase the percentage of explained variation in Y by including a third predictor variable. This will be done based on your results from three separate multiple regressions including successively (a) age, (b) mortgage payment, and (c) sex as the new third independent variable. Determine the following for each multiple regression.
   (1) The respective estimated multiple regression equation.
   (2) The respective percentage of variation in Y that is explained by the multiple regression.
   (3) The partial coefficient of determination for adding the respective third independent variable to the regression analysis.

3. Which of the above, if any, do you recommend for inclusion in further multiple regressions? Explain.

4. Run a multiple regression simultaneously using all five predictor variables for estimating income.
   (a) Determine the estimated multiple regression equation.
   (b) What percentage of the variation in Y is explained by the multiple regression equation?

5. To gain a different perspective on what variables to include in a multiple regression, consider dropping variables. To do this, use separate multiple regressions and, in each, drop just (a) education, (b) home value, (c) age, (d) mortgage payment, and (e) sex. Determine the following for each multiple regression.
   (1) The respective estimated multiple regression equation.
   (2) The respective percentage of variation in Y that is explained by the multiple regression.

6. If it is dropped, which potential independent variable appears to be (a) least damaging and (b) most damaging in the resulting regression's ability to explain variation in income?

7. Cal feels that three independent variables will provide more stable results in future multiple regressions. After perusing your answers and doing further experimentation, Cal decides to use home value, mortgage payment, and sex as the only independent predictor variables for income.
   (a) Determine his final estimated regression equation.
   (b) Calculate the coefficient of multiple determination.
   (c) Determine the predicted mean income when the home value is \$100,000, the mortgage payment is \$400, and the homeowner is male.

8. Cal wishes to assess the overall quality of the regression procedure.
   (a) Using your answers to Question 7, determine the Bonferroni interval estimates of the three partial regression coefficients (b's) using a collective confidence level of 94%.
   (b) Using EasyStat, Cal generated 10 new separate random samples of $n = 25$ from the population data base. The following results were obtained. The predicted mean is based on $X_2 = 100{,}000$, $X_4 = 400$, and $X_5 = 0$.

Sample	Estimated Regression Line $\hat{Y} = a + b_2X_2 + b_4X_4 + b_5X_5$	Predicted Mean
1	$\hat{Y} = 18{,}339 - .010X_2 + 6.78X_4 - 10{,}389X_5$	\$20,051
2	$\hat{Y} = 15{,}638 + .043X_2 + 3.66X_4 - 8{,}742X_5$	21,042
3	$\hat{Y} = 25{,}244 + .001X_2 - 13.49X_4 - 6{,}923X_5$	19,948
4	$\hat{Y} = 8{,}392 + .223X_2 + 5.97X_4 - 7{,}632X_5$	33,080
5	$\hat{Y} = 24{,}922 - .030X_2 - 4.18X_4 + 1{,}744X_5$	20,250
6	$\hat{Y} = 16{,}011 + .041X_2 + 9.90X_4 - 3{,}245X_5$	24,071
7	$\hat{Y} = 14{,}867 + .205X_2 - 21.57X_4 - 2{,}728X_5$	26,739
8	$\hat{Y} = 451 + .380X_2 + .41X_4 - 5{,}711X_5$	38,615
9	$\hat{Y} = 5{,}521 + .247X_2 + 3.21X_4 - 3{,}398X_5$	31,505
10	$\hat{Y} = 18{,}730 + .206X_2 - 13.78X_4 - 8{,}376X_5$	33,818

Using Cal's results and your answers to (a) and Question 7, what do you conclude regarding the following.

(1) Pitfalls in selecting independent predictor variables when the regression equation is adapted to one particular sample.

(2) Variability in predictions and in partial regression coefficients.

11-8 OPTIONAL TOPIC: POLYNOMIAL REGRESSION

In Chapter 10, we learned that nonlinear relationships between X and Y are common functions. The methods of multiple regression may be adapted to find which curves best fit the data. Mathematically, the resulting regression equations are called **polynomials**. The functions express the dependent variable as a combination of the independent variable X raised to various powers. Here, we may extend the least-squares method to establish polynomial regression equations in the following forms.

$$\hat{Y} = a + b_1X + b_2X^2 \qquad \text{(parabola)}$$

$$\hat{Y} = a + b_1X + b_2X^2 + b_3X^3 \qquad \text{(third-degree polynomial)}$$

(Although higher-degree polynomials can be accommodated in a regression analysis, in business applications, we do not ordinarily encounter data for which those polynomials are appropriate.)

The type of curve selected to best fit the data depends on the form of the scatter diagram, but there may be a previously established basis for selecting a particular shape.

Consider the curve shown in Figure 11-18 for an assembly line experiment, where the data points represent productivity index Y obtained for various assembly line speeds X. The data suggest the parabolic curve plotted on the graph. This type of curve best fits the data given in Table 11-13 for a multiple regression using

$X_1 = X$ and $X_2 = X^2$ as the dependent variables. The estimated regression equation assumes the form

$$\hat{Y} = 13.4 + 265.5X - 267.3X^2$$

At slow or fast levels of line speed, we see that productivity is very low. Maximum productivity occurs at a level of around .50 mph. A **parabola** is the proper form to use when the underlying curve is everywhere convex or everywhere concave in shape, achieving a readily identifiable maximum or minimum level.

The second type of curve form is the **third-degree polynomial**. It is the proper form to use when an *inflection point* is present in the underlying shape. The plotted data points are best fitted by a curve that shows a progression from concave to convex, or vice versa. Such a curve will have a slope that steadily increases before it decreases, or that steadily decreases before it increases.

In Figure 11-19 the total cost Y of production for a plant is plotted against the volume X. As suggested by the data in the figure, this economic production function assumes the form of a common shape. Here, data points have been obtained for the various levels of production activity in the plant. The curve best fits the

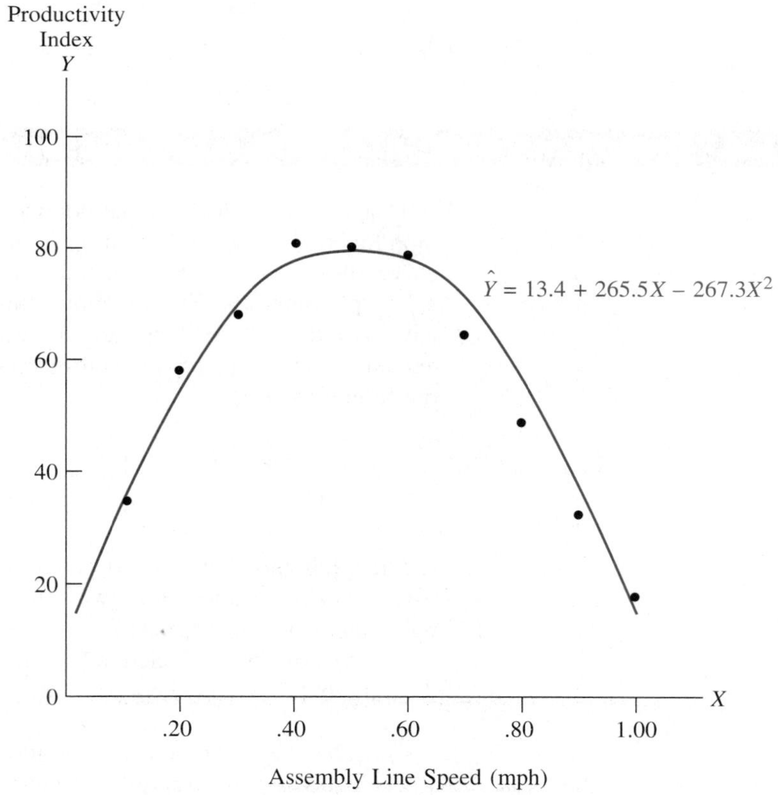

FIGURE 11-18 Regression parabola for the assembly line experiment.

TABLE 11-13 Sample Data for the Assembly Line Experiment

Productivity Index Y	Line Speed (mph) $X_1 = X$	$X_2 = X_2$
77	.60	.3600
81	.40	.1600
35	.10	.0100
80	.50	.2500
64	.75	.5625
48	.80	.6400
32	.90	.8100
68	.30	.0900
57	.20	.0400
17	1.00	1.0000

data given in Table 11-14 for a multiple regression using $X_1 = X$, $X_2 = X^2$, and $X_3 = X^3$ as the independent variables. The estimated regression equation is

$$\hat{Y} = -\ \$18{,}361 + 304.8X - .9546X^2 + .00099X^3$$

At low levels of production activity, this function reflects *decreasing marginal cost* (slope) as greater volumes of production are achieved. But a point is reached

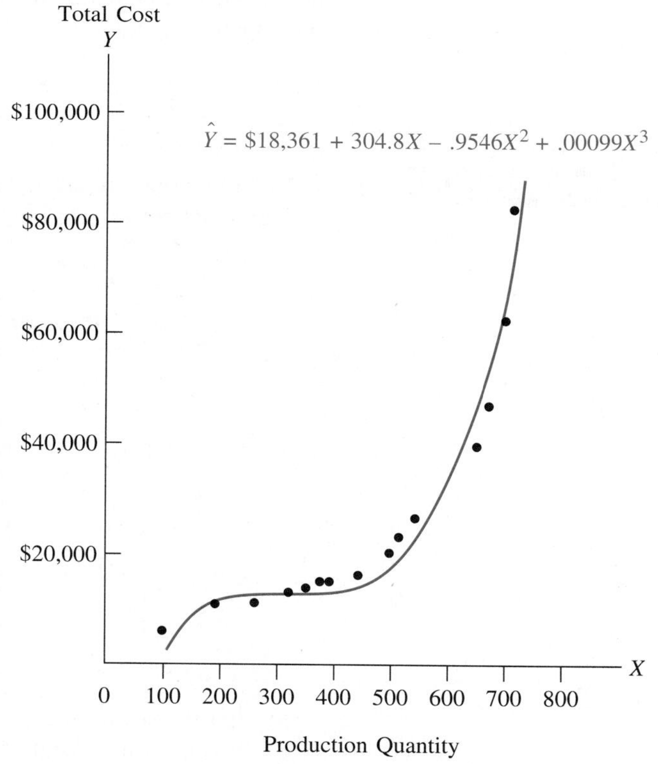

FIGURE 11-19 Third-degree polynomial regression for the production function of a plant.

TABLE 11-14 Sample Data for the Production Function

Total Cost Y	Production Quantity $X_1 = X$	$X_2 = X^2$	$X_3 = X^3$
$ 5,680	100	10,000	1,000,000
9,200	185	34,225	6,331,625
14,100	350	122,500	42,875,000
14,800	390	152,100	59,319,000
22,900	520	270,400	140,608,000
19,800	490	240,100	117,649,000
26,100	550	302,500	166,375,000
39,600	640	409,600	262,144,000
11,300	250	62,500	15,625,000
14,500	370	136,900	50,653,000
46,200	670	448,900	300,763,000
62,100	690	476,100	328,509,000
81,300	720	518,400	373,248,000
16,000	440	193,600	85,184,000
12,800	320	102,400	32,768,000

at around 400 units where all factors are operating most efficiently and greater volume can only be achieved at a disproportionately higher cost. There the plant reaches its maximum level of economic productivity, after which the increase in volume reduces incremental efficiency and the curve shows increasing marginal cost at an increasing rate.

OPTIONAL EXERCISES

11-52 The following sample data have been obtained by an Agragroup staff agronomist who is working to develop new grain hybrids.

Yield (bushels per acre) Y	Rainfall (inches) X
25	37
48	11
123	14
62	44
107	15
119	21
63	33
91	12
152	22
98	29
126	23

(a) Plot the scatter diagram for the data.

(b) Which form, a parabola or third-degree polynomial, appears to best fit the data? Select whichever curve shape seems to provide an appropriate explanation of the underlying relationship.

(c) Using the method of least squares, determine the estimated regression equation for the curve form selected in (b).
(d) Sketch the shape of the regression curve on your scatter diagram.
(e) At around what level of rainfall does maximum crop yield occur?
(f) Using your answer to (c), calculate the predicted crop yield when the level of rainfall is 30 inches.

11-53 A chemical engineer for GetGo provided the following fuel consumption data for sample test car runs.

Fuel Consumption (mpg) Y	Speed (mph) X
28.9	56
30.2	34
29.3	32
23.8	59
29.5	25
29.5	40
27.3	22
29.8	47
26.3	57
28.6	21
29.9	28
28.8	52

(a)–(d) Repeat Exercise 11-52 using the above data.
(e) At what speed does optimal fuel consumption occur?
(f) Using your answer to (c), calculate the predicted miles per gallon when the speed is 35 miles per hour.

11-54 A product manager for ZysTech obtained the following data results from the logbooks of sample communications systems.

Number of Component Failures Y	System Lifetime (years) X
7	5.1
2	10.5
22	2.0
19	1.5
3	7.3
14	3.8
22	1.2
20	3.6
2	6.2

(a)–(d) Repeat Exercise 11-52 using the above data.
(e) Present a verbal summary of the relationship between the number of failed components and the lifetime of the system.
(f) Using your answer to (c), calculate the predicted number of failures when the systems are not replaced until they have been in operation for 3 years.

11-55 An economist for McBurger obtained the following data relating sales to longevity for a random sample of similar franchises.

Sales Y	Longevity (years) X
$210,000	.5
950,000	4.8
405,000	2.8
193,000	1.2
375,000	2.3
930,000	4.2
690,000	3.1
906,000	5.2
310,000	1.8

(a)–(d) Repeat Exercise 11-52 using the above data.

(e) The regression form obtained is an example of a *growth curve*. Present a verbal charaterization of the curve.

(f) Using your answer to (c), calculate the predicted level of sales for a similar McBurger franchise in its second year of operation.

PART III

IMPORTANT BUSINESS APPLICATIONS OF STATISTICS

CHAPTER 12

FORECASTING WITH TIME SERIES

BEFORE READING THIS CHAPTER, MAKE SURE YOU UNDERSTAND:

The types of statistical data (Chapter 1).
How to describe and display data (Chapter 2).
How to summarize data (Chapter 3).
The basic concepts of regression analysis (Chapter 10).

AFTER READING THIS CHAPTER, YOU WILL UNDERSTAND:

About time series analysis and the classical time series model.
How to isolate the trend and seasonal time series components.
About exponential smoothing and how to employ it in time series analysis.
About two-parameter and three-parameter (seasonal) exponential smoothing and their advantages.
How to measure the quality of forecasts.

Every successful business and organization must plan for the future. Quite a dazzling array of statistical tools are available to facilitate this task. In this chapter, we focus on statistical methodology that can transform past experience into forecasts of future events. Thus, a government economist may forecast annual personal income five years into the future by projecting from the trend indicated by the levels of personal income in previous years, and use this information to predict future tax revenue. An electric company may decide that the demand for power will grow at a rate similar to that which has prevailed during the previous decade in order to project its generating capacity requirements five, ten, or twenty years into the future. A department store buyer may use past experience to decide when to make purchases and in what quantities. In each case, values of the variable being predicted are available for several past periods of time. Such data are called **time series**. Statistical procedures that use such values are called **time-series analysis**.

12-1 THE TIME SERIES AND ITS COMPONENTS

Time series are best described in terms of a graph like the one shown in Figure 12-1, in which the gross national product (GNP) of the United States is plotted against time for the period 1929–1988. The graph shows that the GNP has grown over the years, but that this growth has been erratic, being faster in some years than in others. Wide swings are evident, the GNP declining during the Great Depression of the 1930s and then rising rapidly in the 1970s. One goal of time-series analysis is to identify the swings and fluctuations of a time series and sort them into various categories. This is done through arithmetic manipulation of the numerical values obtained.

Several models may be used to characterize time series. The classical model used by economists provides the clearest explanation of the following four time-series components of variation and their relation to each other.

1. Secular trend (T_t)
2. Cyclical movement (C_t)
3. Seasonal fluctuation (S_t)
4. Irregular variations (I_t)

These components may be related to the forecast variable by mathematical equations. The forecast variable is denoted by the symbol Yt, where the subscript t refers to a period of time. Examples of Y are annual sales, passenger miles flown by domestic airlines, and acre-feet of water supplied to a city.

Secular trend is defined as the long-range general movement in Y over an extended period of time. In this chapter, we will develop methods for isolating trend from other variational components in a time series. **Cyclical movement** in time-series data is characterized by wide swings—usually a year or more in duration—upward or downward from the secular trend. Cyclical movements are temporary in nature and are typified by alternating periods of economic expansion and contraction or recession. **Seasonal fluctuation** is a generally recurring upward and downward pattern of movement in Y, usually on an annual basis. A classic example of seasonal fluctuation is the household consumption of fossil fuels, such as oil, coal, or natural gas. **Irregular variations** are characterized by

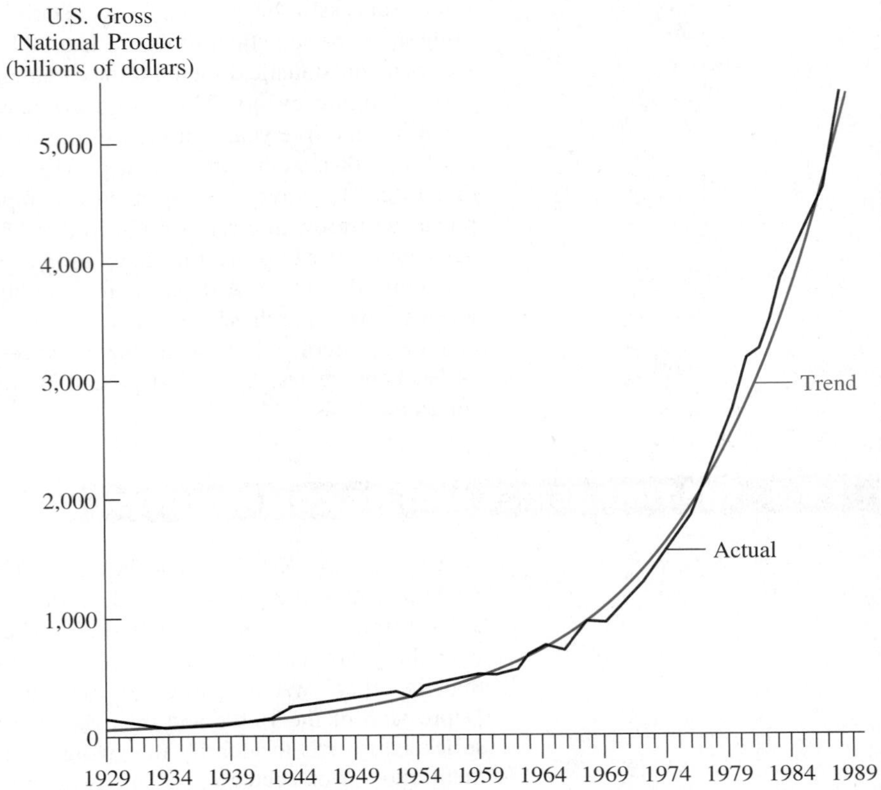

Source: *Economic Report of the President*, 1989.

FIGURE 12-1 U.S. gross national product.

events that are completely unpredictable. These variations, sometimes referred to as random factors, may be the most perplexing.

12-2 THE CLASSICAL TIME-SERIES MODEL

The classical time-series model originally used by economists combines the four components of time-series variation in the equation

$$Y_t = T_t \times C_t \times S_t \times I_t$$

This equation states that factors associated with each of these components may be multiplied together to provide the value of the dependent variable.

ILLUSTRATION: A TIME SERIES FOR STEREO SPEAKER SALES

This model may be explained by means of a hypothetical time series—the sales Y_t of stereo speakers by the Speak E-Z Company. To construct this time series, we will begin with the trend component T_t, shown in Figure 12-2 as a straight

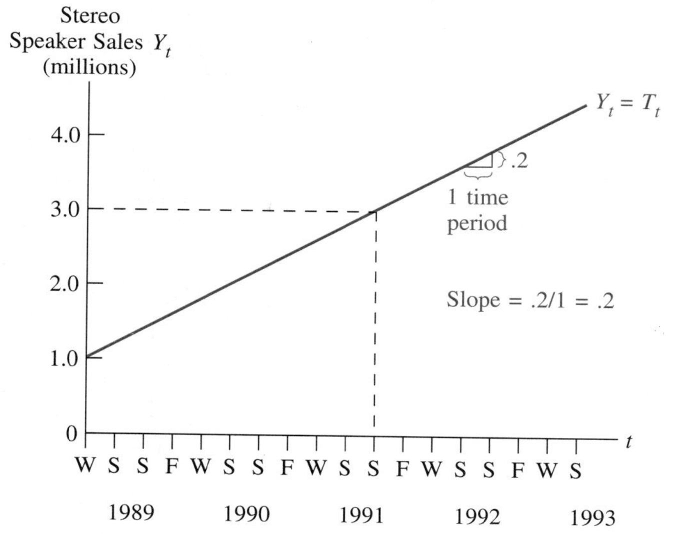

FIGURE 12-2 Trend line T_t for Speak *E-Z* sales.

line relating sales to time period. Each successive quarter raises the level of sales by .2 million. Thus, initial sales of 1 million units have grown by the summer of 1991 (10 periods later) to 1 + .2(10) = 3 million units.

Now let's consider the influence on the series of cyclical movement that produces sales temporarily above the trend in good years or below it in lean years. For convenience, we express the cyclical effect as a percentage of trend, as shown in Figure 12-3(a). The average value of C_t throughout an entire cycle is considered to be 100%. In the summer of 1991, the value of C_t is 150%, indicating that sales are 50% above the trend during that quarter. The time series for speaker sales with this added component is graphed in Figure 12-3(b), where the curve for C_t has been superimposed on the trend line.

We follow the same procedure in dealing with seasonal fluctuations in stereo speaker sales, which may be viewed as short-term swings about the longer-term sales level indicated by the combined trend and cyclical components. Sales will lie above this level during the busy season and below it during slack times. Thus, we consider S_t to be a proportion of the long-term sales level established by T_t and C_t, also expressed as a percentage.

The values of S_t, referred to as **seasonal indexes**, are shown in Figure 12-4. For the summer of 1991, the seasonal index is S_t = 60%, indicating that sales were only 60% of "normal" during this period. The time series obtained by superimposing the seasonal fluctuations on longer-term sales is shown in Figure 12-5.

We must still consider the irregular component of variation in speaker sales. As in the case of C_t and S_t, this variation is represented by a percentage I_t. Viewing all irregular movement as short term in nature, we consider I_t to be the last factor—the one that raises or lowers sales from the level established by the regular pattern of systematic factors that we have already considered. The values

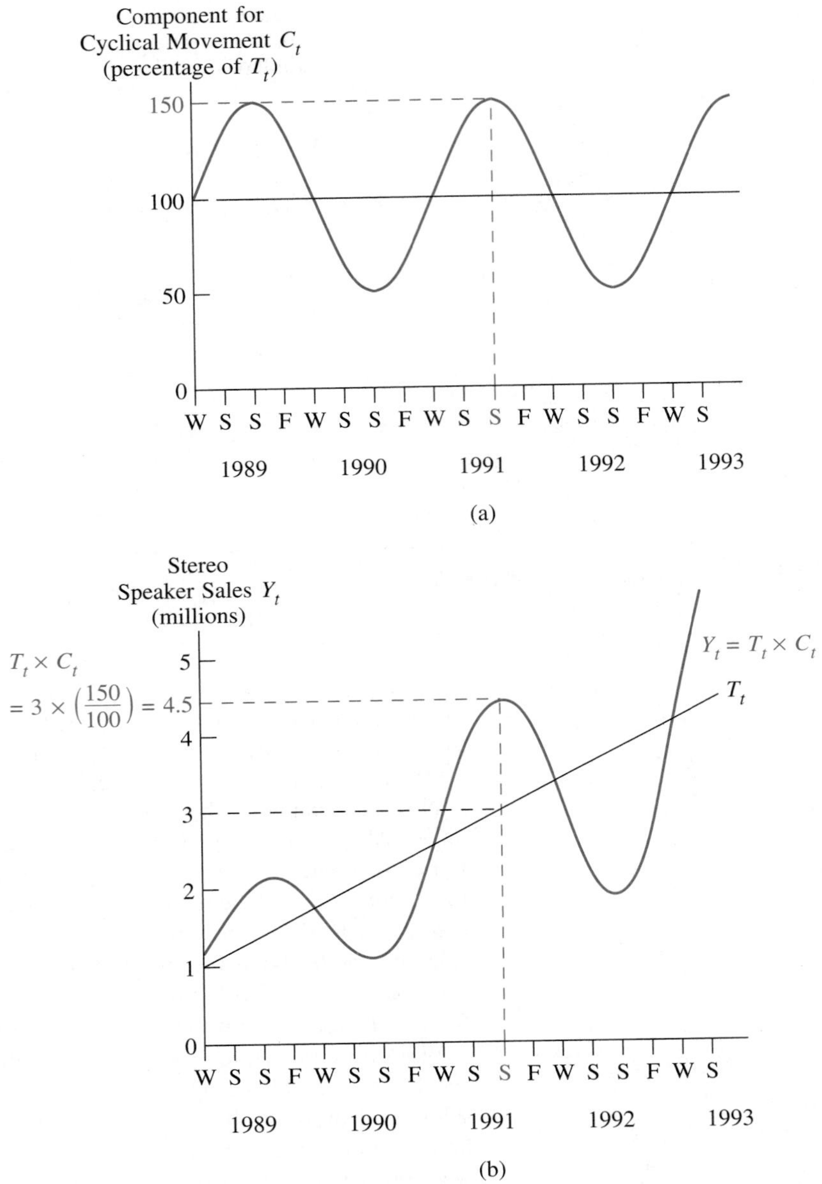

FIGURE 12-3 (a) Cyclical component for Speak *E-Z* sales and (b) trend and cyclical components combined.

used to construct the graph for I_t in Figure 12-6 have been obtained randomly, so that the long-run average value of I_t is 100%.

For the summer of 1991, I_t is 97% of "normal." These irregular variations may be superimposed on the curve that we obtained previously for T_t, C_t, and S_t to provide a complete hypothetical time series for Speak E-Z's sales. The variational influence of each component is summarized in Figure 12-7, where the final time series is obtained.

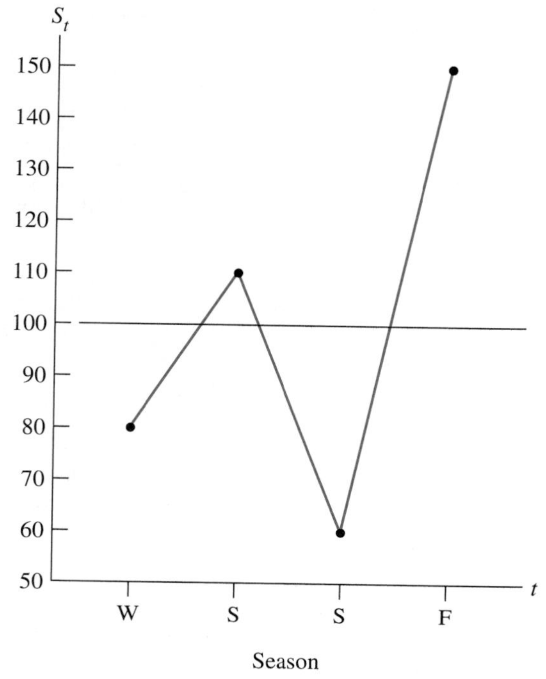

FIGURE 12-4 Seasonal fluctuations of Speak *E-Z* sales.

This illustration has shown us how a hypothetical time series may be synthesized from the assumed characteristics of the four components. In actual applications, however, we may not know anything about T_t, C_t, S_t, or I_t. Usually, we begin with the raw time-series data and reverse the procedure, shifting the data to sort out and identify the components. We will discuss some examples of this technique in this chapter.

The classical time-series model has limitations. The multiplicative relationship between trend, cyclical, seasonal, and irregular components has been criticized as being oversimplified and unrealistic. A large number of possible relationships other than multiplicative may exist between T_t, C_t, S_t, and I_t, and some of these may be more appropriate. Other models use more factors; for example, Y_t is sometimes assumed to also depend on Y_{t-1}, the value from the preceding time period. As we will see, several different techniques are available for isolating the components themselves, so that for a specific time series the classical model yields no unique solution. In spite of these difficulties, the model is easy to understand and to explain and provides a basis for useful time-series analysis.

More sophisticated time-series models have been developed. The field of **econometrics**, which employs specialized statistical tools to explain and predict economic activity, embodies regression techniques for analyzing time-series data. An especially powerful tool uses variables from several different time series to predict values of other variables of interest. To do this, variables called **leading indicators**, which have historically moved upward and downward ahead of the time series being analyzed, are identified and combined mathematically. The general

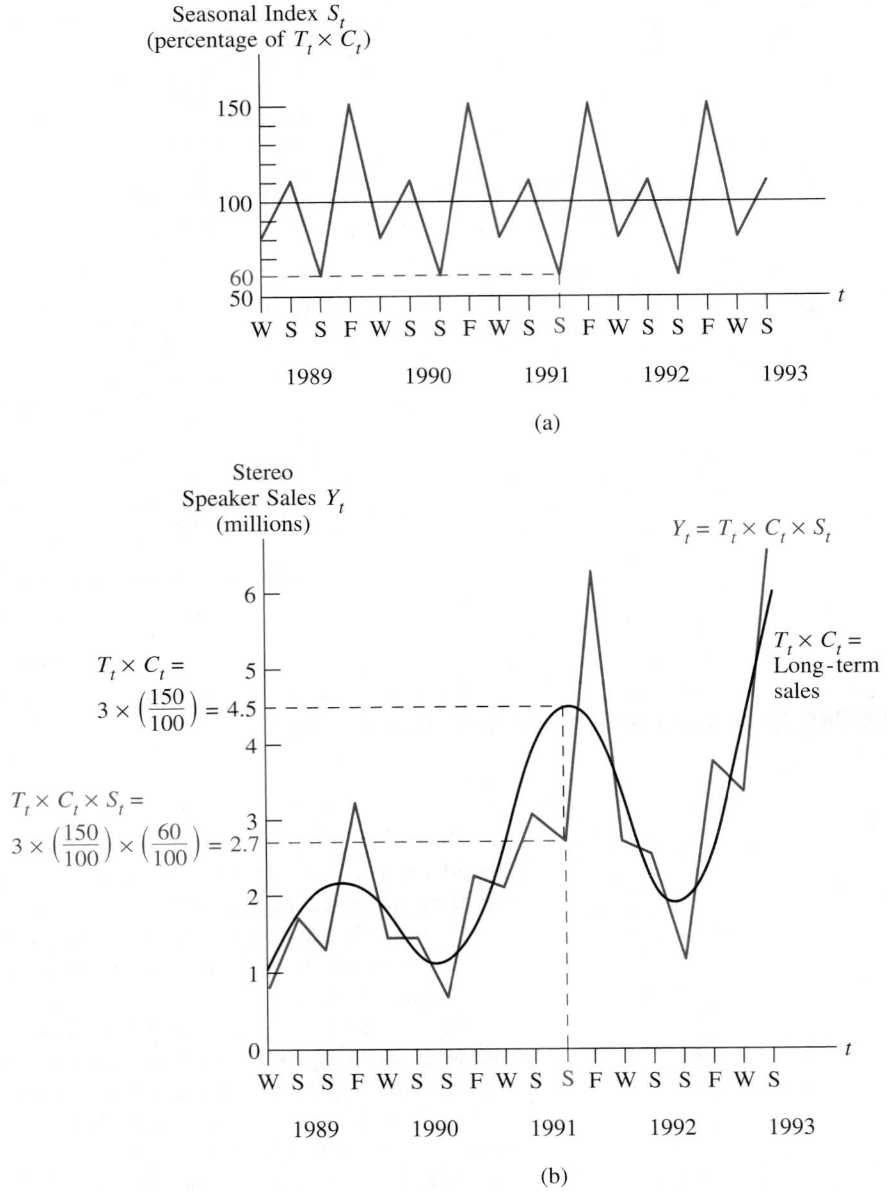

FIGURE 12-5 (a) Seasonal index component for Speak *E-Z* sales and (b) trend, cyclical, and seasonal components combined.

level of economic activity in a future time period may be predicted by a relationship between such leading indicators as business inventories, housing starts, and new durable goods orders.

Other models explain time-series movement in terms of its past behavior only, without isolating seasonal and cyclical components. Later in the chapter, we

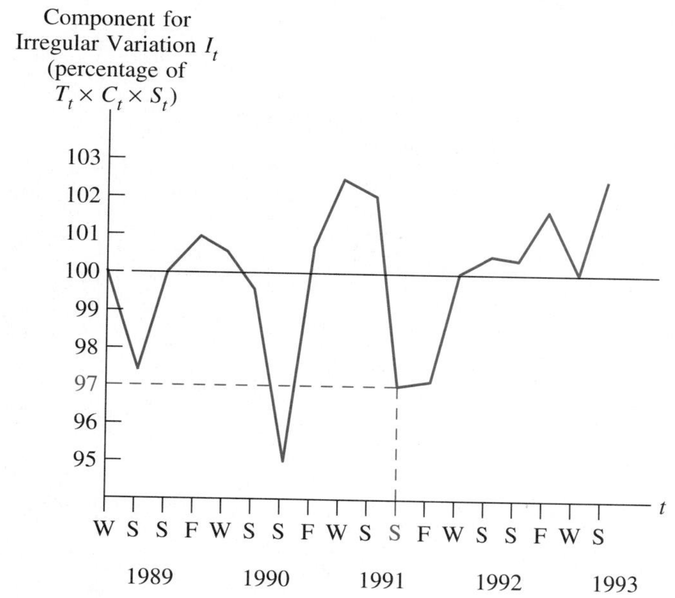

FIGURE 12-6 Component for irregular fluctuation of Speak *E-Z* sales.

describe one technique for doing this, **exponential smoothing**, which involves the averaging of past data, giving greater weight to current values.

EXERCISES

12-1 Blitz Beer Company has projected that sales for 19X2 will grow by \$100,000 per quarter. Assuming that sales during the fall quarter of 19X1 are \$1,000,000, determine the trend sales levels for the winter, spring, summer, and fall quarters of 19X2.

12-2 Pear Peripherals had sales of \$1,000,000 in the fall of 19X1. The trend indicates that sales are growing at a compound rate of 9% per quarter. Determine the trend levels for the winter, spring, summer, and fall quarters of 19X2.

12-3 Use the multiplicative time-series model to determine the actual values for each of the following quarters.

t	T_t	C_t	S_t	I_t
Winter	2,000	80	120	105
Spring	2,200	90	100	100
Summer	2,400	100	70	98
Fall	2,600	110	110	95

12-4 Find the missing values to complete the following quarterly sales data for BugOff Chemical Company.

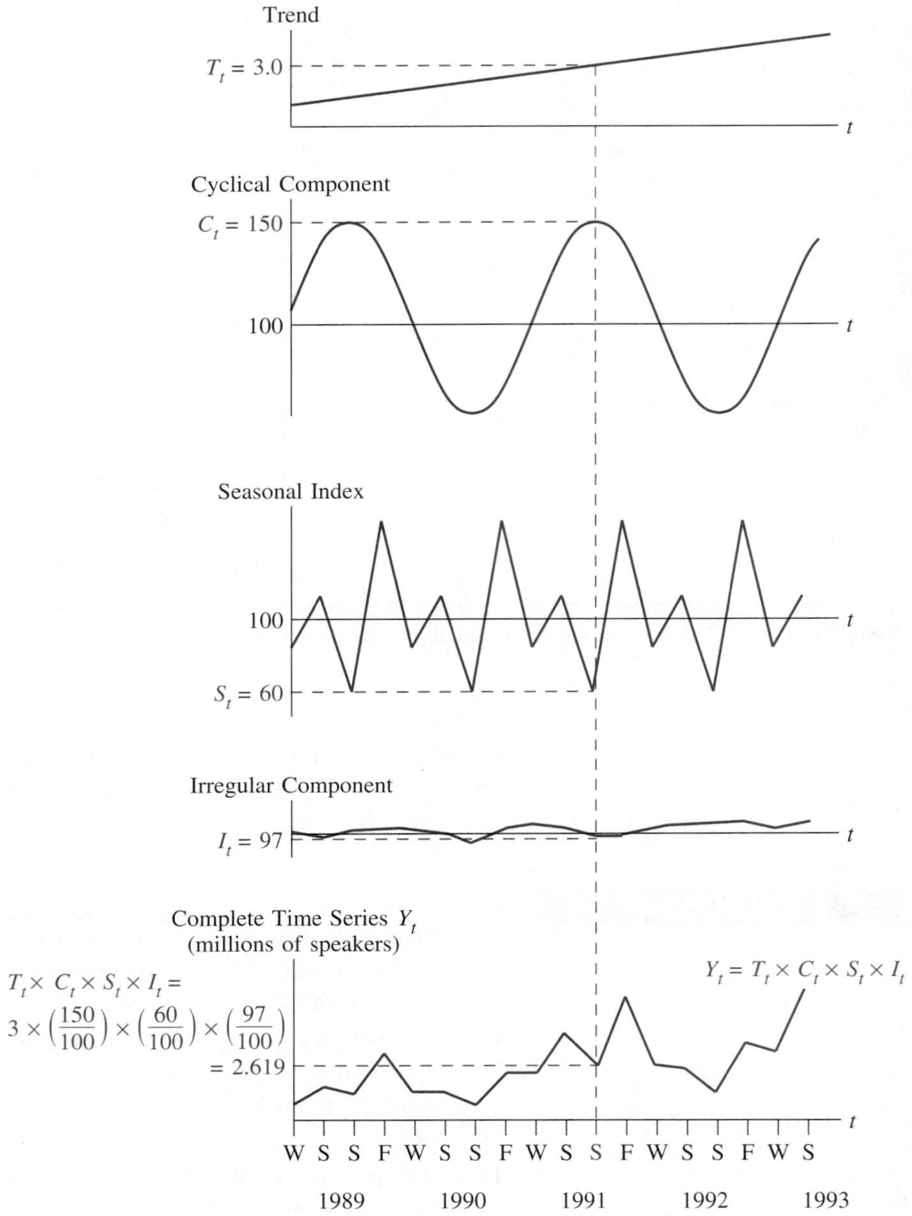

FIGURE 12-7 Complete time series for Speak *E-Z*'s sales, constructed from individual components.

Quarter	Trend	Cyclical (%)	Seasonal (%)	Irregular (%)	Sales
Winter	$100,000	110	50	100	
Spring	110,000	100	70		$ 76,460
Summer	120,000	90		96	124,416
Fall	130,000		160	100	197,600

12-3 ANALYSIS OF SECULAR TREND

The trend component of a time series is perhaps the most valuable in making forecasts using time-series data. Trend analysis focuses on finding an appropriate trend line that summarizes the movement of the series over an extended period of time. As we have seen, a trend line often takes the form of a curve. In this section, several approaches for determining trend are investigated. All of these involve treating the historical data points like a scatter diagram, which we first encountered in conjunction with regression analysis in Chapter 10. The objective of trend analysis is similar to that of regression: To find a trend curve that summarizes the historical scatter of the dependent variable Y_t over time.

The regression techniques discussed in Chapter 10 are severely limited when applied to time-series data. Most of the assumptions, such as independence, normality, and constant variance, are usually not relevant to time-series data. Thus, it is impossible to attach a measure of statistical confidence to a prediction made from a trend line. This should be evident because a forecast must deal with the future, using the past only as a guide. There are no assurances that future influences on the time series will operate like those in the past. Furthermore, a prediction using a trend curve is a projection beyond the range of observations (there are no future data points), so that forecasting with the time series is subject to the major difficulty of extrapolation usually avoided in regression analysis.

DESCRIBING TREND

In the hypothetical time series for stereo speaker demand that was discussed in Section 12-2, secular trend was represented by a straight line. A straight-line trend assumes that Y_t changes at a constant rate. An increasing series will thus have a positively sloping trend line, whereas a declining one will be represented by a line with a negative slope.

Most time series do not involve long-term behavior that changes constantly over time. In business or economic situations, a variable will usually increase or decline at a rate that itself changes from period to period. Some basic shapes of nonlinear trend curves frequently encountered are provided in Figure 12-8. For example, consider the movement in GNP levels over a prolonged period. The GNP for the United States has increased by more in the recent past than it did following World War II, so that the trend is represented best by a curve with increasing and positive slope as in Figure 12-8(a). In absolute terms, the U.S. GNP has been increasing in recent times at an increasing rate.*

Diagram (b) in Figure 12-8 shows the trend for a time series that decreases at a decreasing rate. The level of activity for a declining industry may sometimes be represented by such a curve. The decline is initially dramatic but becomes more gradual with time. An example of such a trend is the number of railroad passengers carried in the United States each year during the past four decades.

The long-range growth of a firm or an industry may sometimes be explained in terms of a trend having the shape shown in Figure 12-8(c). Here, output

*The *percentage* rate of *growth* in real GNP has been more or less constant at about 3%, even though the absolute rate of increase in GNP has been rising. Percentage growth rate is expressed relative to the current position and works like compound interest paid by a bank. The original savings account balance will increase at an increasing rate, so that the shape in diagram (a) applies over time, even though the percentage rate of interest or growth remains constant.

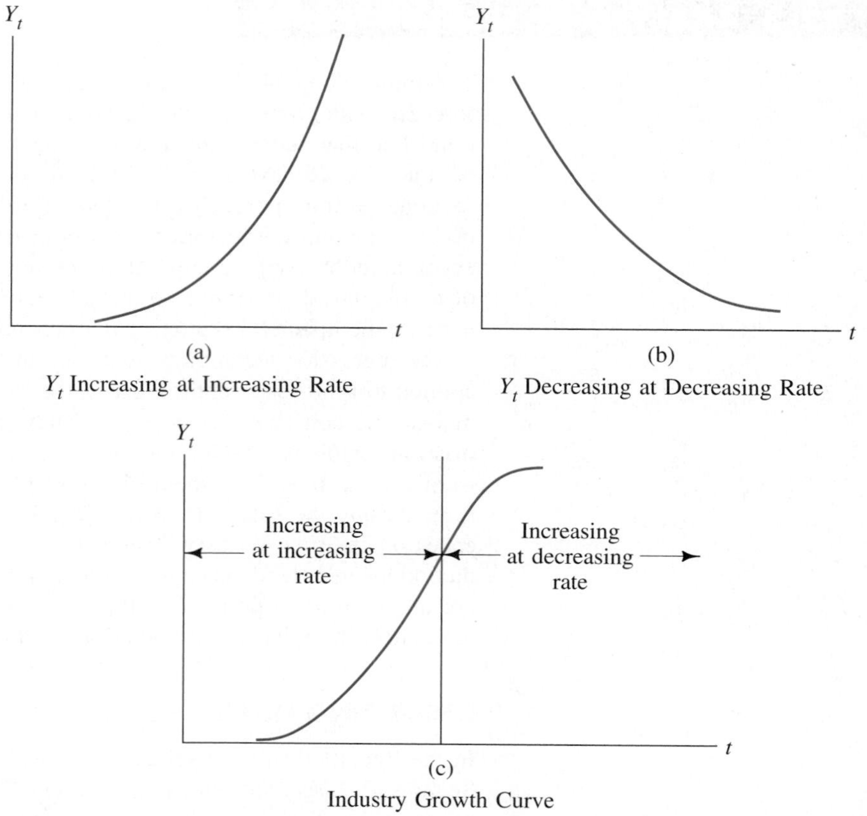

FIGURE 12-8 Basic shapes of common trend curves.

increases at an increasing rate when innovative products are brought onto the market to satisfy emerging needs. As the industry matures, rapid growth is replaced by a period of gradual increases; product sales still increase, but at a decreasing rate. Ultimately, sales peak and a period of stagnation begins. Such S-shaped curves are therefore called **growth curves**. Two growth curves frequently encountered in statistics are the logistic and the Gompertz.

The particular shape to portray the trend of a specific time series is selected partly by studying the scatter of the data on a graph. The choice should be a basic shape that not only seems to fit the historical data closely but also coincides with good judgment about how it should be related to future data. There are no rules to tell us which shape must be used. Judgment and experience play the dominant role, so that fitting a trend curve to make forecasts is as much an art as a science.

DETERMINING LINEAR TREND USING LEAST SQUARES

Time series covering a small number of years usually may be fitted by a straight line. The procedure is to adapt the method of least squares, finding the

REGRESSION EQUATION

$$\hat{Y}(X) = a + bX$$

Chapter 10 describes in detail the procedure for finding values for the regression coefficients a and b. $\hat{Y}(X)$ represents the computed value for the dependent variable of the time series, in keeping with our previous regression notation. The letter X represents the time period, which serves as the independent variable. We use X instead of t because the task of computing the regression coefficients may be considerably simplified by expressing time relative to some base period. For example, suppose that the time series comprises observations for the years 1989, 1990, 1991, and 1992. Rather than using the four-digit year numbers for X, we instead let $X = 0$ represent 1989, $X = 1$ stand for 1990, which is one time period later than 1989, and so forth. Thus, the successive values used for X in these four years would be 0, 1, 2, and 3. The values of $\hat{Y}(X)$ are used to obtain the corresponding trend values T_t.

ILLUSTRATION: TREND IN CIVILIAN EMPLOYMENT

We will illustrate this procedure using the total level of civilian employment in the United States from 1978 through 1987. The time-series data are provided in the first two columns of Table 12-1. The results are $b = 1.68$ and $a = 95.35$, so that the trend equation is $\hat{Y}(X) = 95.35 + 1.68X$ with $X = 0$ at 1978.

This equation indicates that the trend value for 1978 is an employment level of 95.35 million and that Y_t increases by 1.68 million per year. Because we have transformed the calendar years, it is important to indicate the base year: $X = 0$ at 1978. The trend line and time series obtained are plotted in Figure 12-9.

The trend line may be used to project the level of employment for 1998. We must use $X = 20$, because this year is $X = 1998 - 1978 = 20$ periods beyond the base year. From the trend equation, we project employment for 1998 as

$$\begin{aligned}\hat{Y}(20) &= 95.35 + 1.68(20)\\ &= 128.95 \text{ million}\end{aligned}$$

The projected trend line is shown in Figure 12-9 as the portion of the colored line extending beyond the time periods actually observed. It is emphasized that the estimate of 128.95 million is an *extrapolation*; its validity depends on the assumption that the ensuing ten years has exhibited growth similar to that existing in the past. The assumption of linearity is perhaps a poor one to use here, for the labor force grows in the same manner as the population, which for the United States has been nonlinear. Had more past years been used, a curve with slope increasing over time would have provided a closer fit to the actual time-series data. Even then, good judgment would be an essential element. Ordinarily many more than ten years are required to determine a basic pattern for trend.

TABLE 12-1 Computations for Fitting Least-Squares Line to Employment Data

Year	Year in Transformed Units X	Total Civilian Employment (millions) Y	XY	X^2
1978	0	96.1	0	0
1979	1	98.8	98.8	1
1980	2	99.3	198.6	4
1981	3	100.4	301.2	9
1982	4	99.5	398.0	16
1983	5	100.8	504.0	25
1984	6	105.0	630.0	36
1985	7	107.2	750.4	49
1986	8	109.6	876.8	64
1987	9	112.4	1,011.6	81
	45 $= \sum X$	1,029.1 $= \sum Y$	4,769.4 $= \sum XY$	285 $= \sum X^2$

$$n = 10 \qquad \bar{X} = 4.5 \qquad \bar{Y} = 102.91$$

$$b = \frac{\sum XY - n\bar{X}\bar{Y}}{\sum X^2 - n\bar{X}^2} = \frac{4{,}769.4 - 10(4.5)(102.91)}{285 - 10(4.5)^2} = 1.68$$

$$a = \bar{Y} - b\bar{X} = 102.91 - 1.68(4.5) = 95.35$$

$$\hat{Y}(X) = 95.35 + 1.68X \quad (X = 0 \text{ at } 1978)$$

Source: *Economic Report of the President*, 1989.

MODIFYING TREND FOR PERIODS SHORTER THAN ONE YEAR

Trend values are usually obtained from annual data to avoid distortions brought about by seasonal and irregular fluctuations. When time-series analysis is extended to consider the seasonal and cyclical components, it may be necessary to modify a trend equation to obtain monthly or quarterly values. Consider, for example, the following trend line for civilian employment.

$$\hat{Y}(X) = 95.35 + 1.68X$$

with X in years and $X = 0$ at the *middle* of 1978. Suppose we wish to obtain monthly trend values. The new values of X will represent the number of months from the base and will be centered at the middle of each month. Thus, we want to have $X = 0$ at January 15, 1978, which is 5.5 months prior to the middle of 1978 (July 1, 1978). Each successive month will increase $\hat{Y}(X)$ by one-twelfth the annual increment: $b/12 = 1.68/12 = .14$. The slope of the new line will be .14. The intercept a will be reduced by an amount $5.5(.14) = .77$, so that the new Y intercept is $95.35 - .77 = 94.58$. The equation of the modified trend line is

$$\hat{Y}(X) = 94.58 + .14X$$

with X in months and $X = 0$ at January 15, 1978.

The same general approach would apply to finding quarterly trend equations. The slope would be one-fourth as large, and the point $X = 0$ would be shifted to

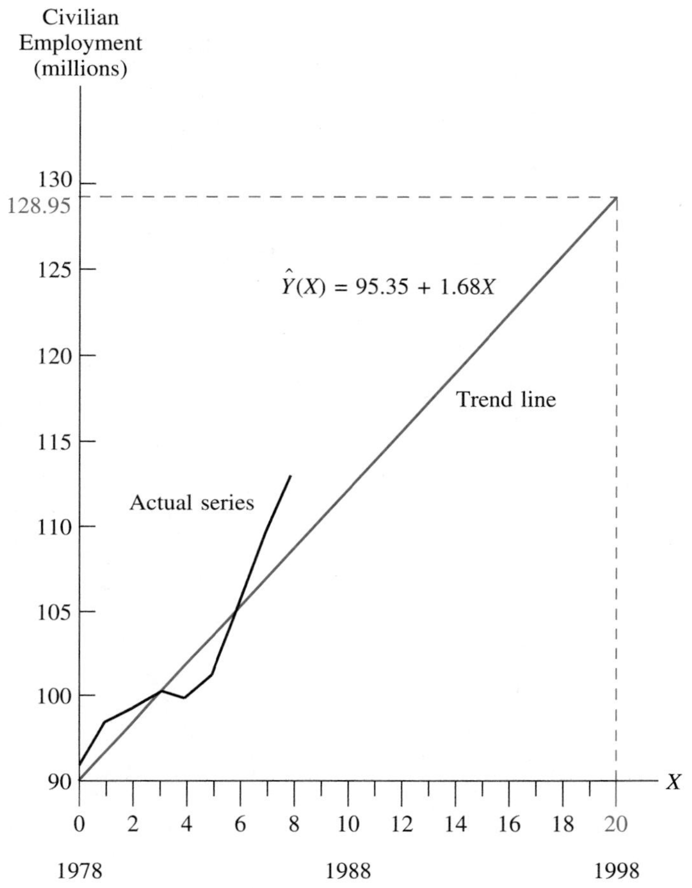

FIGURE 12-9 Actual data and trend line for U.S. civilian employment.

the middle of the winter quarter, February 15, which is 1.5 quarters from the middle of the year. When trend is itself fitted directly to deseasonalized quarterly or monthly data, the trend equation need not be modified.

FORECASTING SALES USING A TREND LINE

In business decision making, sales must often be forecast for planning purposes. Figure 12-10 shows the trend line for BriDent toothpaste using the data in Table 12-2.

The regression coefficients are calculated as

$$b = \frac{3{,}701.2 - 10(4.5)(79.56)}{285 - 10(4.5)^2} = 1.47$$

$$\bar{X} = 45/10 = 4.5 \quad \text{and} \quad \bar{Y} = 795.6/10 = 79.56$$

$$a = 79.56 - 1.47(4.5) = 72.95$$

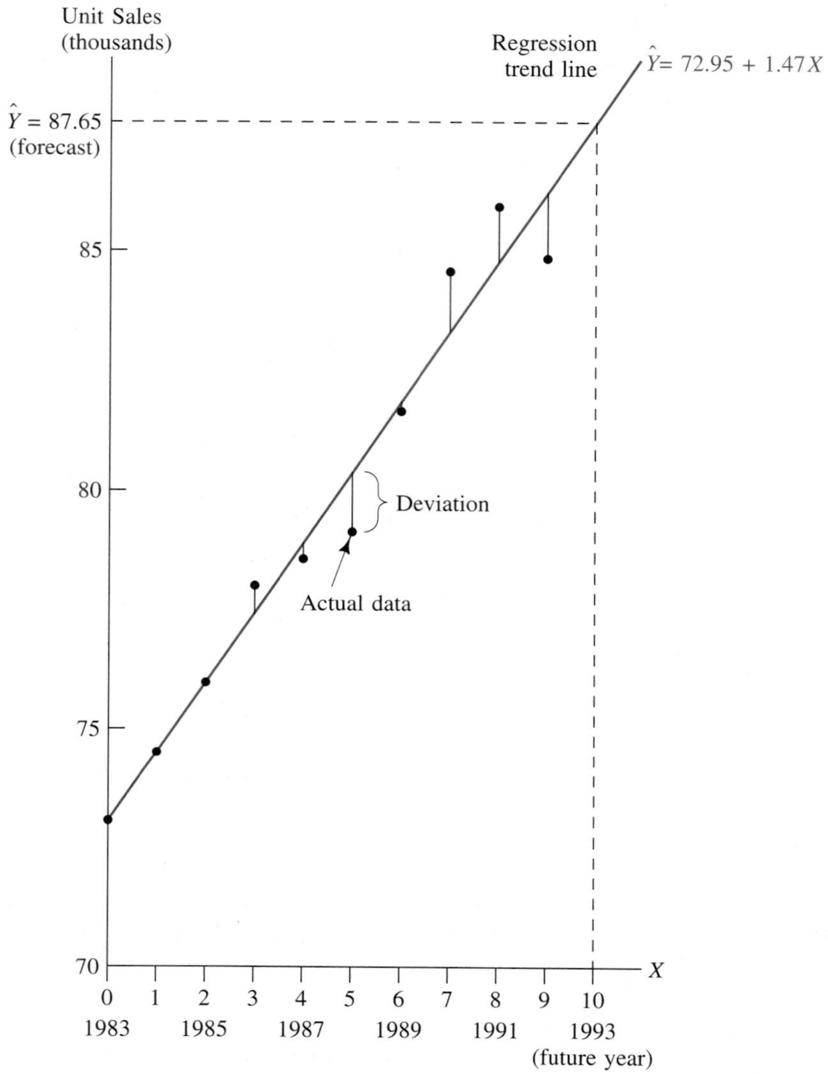

FIGURE 12-10 Regression line for trend in unit sales of BriDent toothpaste.

The regression equation for the trend line in BriDent toothpaste sales (in thousands) is therefore

$$\hat{Y}(X) = 72.95 + 1.47X \qquad (X = 0 \text{ for } 1983)$$

This equation indicates that for 1983 the trend value is sales of 72.95 thousand units and that Y_t increases by 1.47 thousand per year. Because the calendar years have been transformed, it is important to indicate the base year: $X = 0$ for 1983.

We can forecast BriDent sales for 1993 on the basis of the trend line. To do this, we must use $X = 10$, because this year is $X = 1993 - 1983 = 10$ periods beyond the base year. From the trend equation, we can project that 1993 BriDent sales will be

$$\hat{Y}(10) = 72.95 + 1.47(10) = 87.65 \text{ thousand}$$

TABLE 12-2 Computations for Fitting Trend Line to BriDent Toothpaste Sales

Year	Year in Transformed Units X	Unit Sales (thousands) Y	XY	X^2
1983	0	72.9	0	0
1984	1	74.4	74.4	1
1985	2	75.9	151.8	4
1986	3	77.9	233.7	9
1987	4	78.6	314.4	16
1988	5	79.1	395.5	25
1989	6	81.7	490.2	36
1990	7	84.4	590.8	49
1991	8	85.9	687.2	64
1992	9	84.8	763.2	81
	$45 = \sum X$	$795.6 = \sum Y$	$3{,}701.2 = \sum XY$	$285 = \sum X^2$

NONLINEAR TREND: EXPONENTIAL TREND CURVE

For many time series, a straight line provides a poor fit to the data. A straight line assumes that Y_t increases (or decreases) by a constant amount each year. This assumption is not valid for most time series, where Y_t may change at either an increasing or decreasing rate.

ILLUSTRATION: AIRLINES TAKE AWAY RAILROAD PASSENGERS

Figure 12-11 shows the time series for domestic airline fare-paying passengers from 1946 to 1969. Here, the number of passengers has increased at an increasing rate over time. This is contrasted with the number of railroad passengers carried, also shown, for which the trend is decreasing but at a seemingly decreasing rate.

Part of the railroad passenger drop may be explained by a preference for airplane travel and partly by wider use of the automobile. Few passenger trains run over long distances in the United States, and these have been declining so very fast that the government now runs railroad passenger service. The leveling-off at around 300 million passengers may be attributed to the growing significance of commuters, who now comprise a high proportion of rail passengers.

Either of these time series may be fitted by a J-shaped or exponential curve. For the airline passenger data, the equation would be of the form

$$\hat{Y}(X) = ab^X$$

where b is a constant (always positive) raised to the power of the number of time periods beyond the base year, and a is a constant multiple. The railroad passenger series has a negative exponential shape, so that the appropriate equation is

$$\hat{Y}(X) = ab^{-X}$$

where the minus sign before the X is used because $\hat{Y}(X)$ decreases for increasing X.

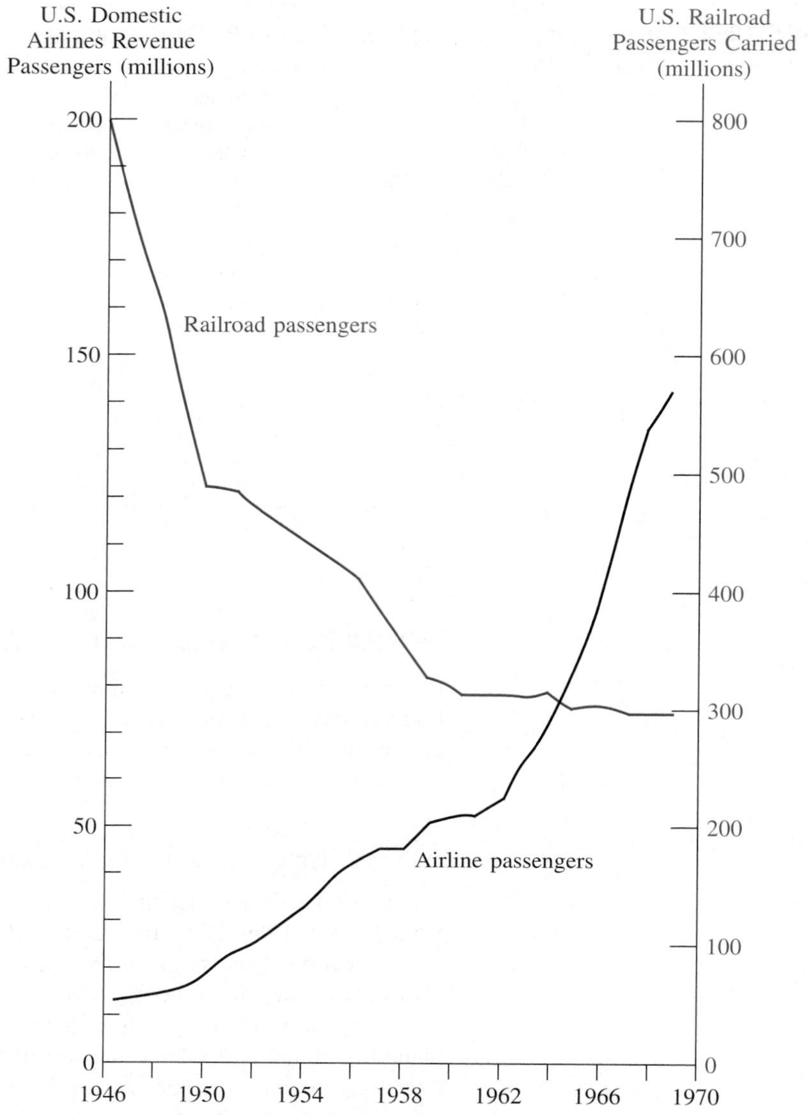

Source: *Moody's Transportation Manual*, 1988.

FIGURE 12-11 Airline and railroad passenger data.

The advantage of using an exponential curve for fitting a trend is evident when taking the logarithm of both sides of $\hat{Y}(X) = ab^X$. When an exponential trend curve is converted in this manner, we have the equation for the

LOGARITHMIC TREND LINE

$$\log \hat{Y}(X) = \log a + X \log b$$

This equation has the form of a straight line using log $\hat{Y}(X)$ for the values on the vertical scale, with intercept of log a and slope of log b.

Figure 12-12(a) shows the graph of the exponential trend curve $\hat{Y}(X) = 5(7)^X$, so that $a = 5$ and $b = 7$. We have

$$\log \hat{Y}(X) = \log 5 + X \log 7$$
$$= .6990 + .8451\,X$$

The logarithm values are obtained from Appendix Table A. The logarithmic trend line in Figure 12-12(b) is drawn with log $\hat{Y}(X)$ expressing height, so that the vertical axis is expressed in log Y units. Both the exponential trend curve and the corresponding logarithmic trend line provide the same information, and values of $\hat{Y}(X)$ may be obtained from the value for log $\hat{Y}(X)$, and vice versa.

This suggests the possibility of fitting historical time-series data to an exponential trend curve, using the method of least squares to first find the logarithmic

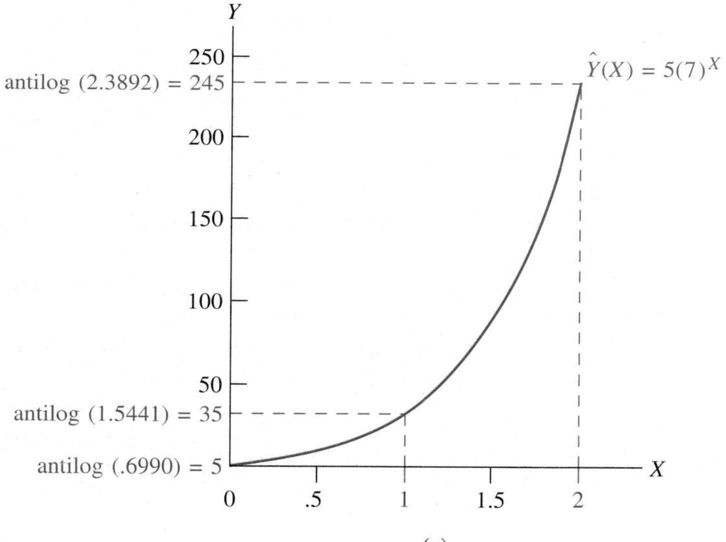

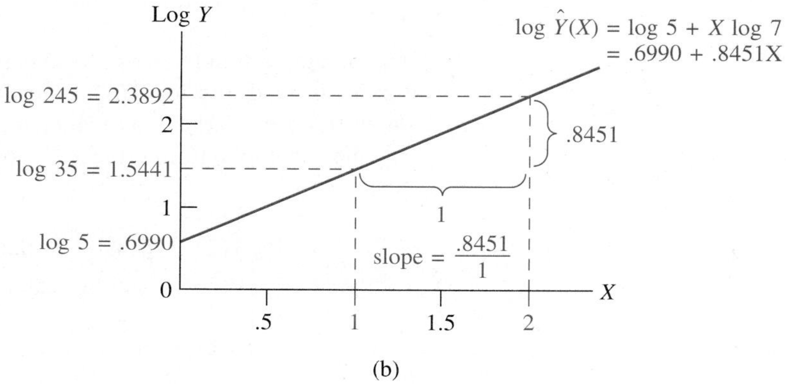

FIGURE 12-12 Graphs of the exponential curve and corresponding logarithmic trend line.

trend line. This may be accomplished by taking the logarithm of the observed time-series values Y, determining the regression coefficients log a and log b. For this purpose we modify the earlier equations for a and b, obtaining the

LOGARITHMIC REGRESSION COEFFICIENTS

$$\log b = \frac{\sum X \log Y - \bar{X} \sum \log Y}{\sum X^2 - n\bar{X}^2}$$

$$\log a = \frac{\sum \log Y}{n} - \bar{X} \log b$$

These expressions replace a, b, and Y values by log a, log b, and log Y.

The procedure is illustrated by the calculations in Table 12-3 using more current airline passenger data. The logarithmic regression coefficients are

$$\log b = \frac{637.161 - 11.5(52.73077)}{4{,}324 - 24(11.5)^2} = .0267$$

$$\log a = (52.73077)/24 - 11.5(.0267) = 1.8901$$

The logarithmic trend line has the equation

$$\log \hat{Y}(X) = 1.8901 + .0267X$$

The values for a and b may be found by taking the antilogs of the coefficients in the previous equation.

$$a = \text{antilog}(1.8901) = 77.64$$

$$b = \text{antilog}(.0267) = 1.063$$

The equation for the exponential trend curve is then

$$\hat{Y}(X) = 77.64(1.063)^X \qquad (X = 0 \text{ at } 1964)$$

In computing trend values, the equation form $\hat{Y}(X) = ab^X$ would not ordinarily be used. Instead, the log $\hat{Y}(X)$ values would be calculated from the fitted logarithmic trend line. The $\hat{Y}(X)$ values may be easily obtained from the antilogs of these. For example, to find the $\hat{Y}(X)$ for 1987, we have $X = 1987 - 1964 = 23$. Thus,

$$\log \hat{Y}(23) = 1.8901 + .0267(23) = 2.5042$$

$$\hat{Y}(23) = \text{antilog}(2.5042) = 319.3 \text{ million passengers}$$

The value is fairly close to the actual figure of 349.2 million passengers carried in 1987.

The trend curve and the original time series are shown in Figure 12-13. This graph has an *arithmetic* vertical scale. The time-series behavior in the early years

TABLE 12-3 Computations for Fitting Exponential Trend Curve to Airline Passenger Data

Year	Years Beyond Base Period X	Revenue Passenger Origin (millions) Y	log Y	X log Y	X^2
1964	0	60.5	1.781755	0	0
1965	1	69.9	1.844477	1.844477	1
1966	2	79.4	1.899820	3.799641	4
1967	3	97.2	1.987666	5.962999	9
1968	4	118.8	2.074817	8.299266	16
1969	5	126.3	2.101404	10.50702	25
1970	6	122.9	2.089552	12.53731	36
1971	7	124.3	2.094471	14.66130	49
1972	8	136.6	2.135451	17.08360	64
1973	9	144.8	2.160769	19.44692	81
1974	10	148.0	2.170262	21.70262	100
1975	11	147.4	2.168497	23.85347	121
1976	12	160.5	2.205475	26.46570	144
1977	13	172.2	2.236033	29.06843	169
1978	14	196.1	2.292477	32.09469	196
1979	15	211.6	2.325516	34.88274	225
1980	16	222.0	2.346353	37.54165	256
1981	17	205.4	2.312600	39.31421	289
1982	18	208.4	2.318898	41.74016	324
1983	19	223.7	2.349666	44.64365	361
1984	20	242.4	2.384533	47.69065	400
1985	21	268.4	2.428783	51.00443	441
1986	22	300.9	2.478422	54.52529	484
1987	23	349.2	2.543074	58.49070	529
	276	4,136.9	52.73077	637.16100	4,324
	$= \sum X$		$= \sum \log Y$	$= \sum X \log Y$	$= \sum X^2$
		$n = 24$	$\bar{X} = 11.5$		

Source: *Moody's Transportation Manual,* 1988.

is hardly noticeable, whereas the points in later years rise by progressively larger amounts. So as not to exaggerate the importance of the later data, exponential trend curves are sometimes graphed with a compressed vertical scale called the **semilogarithmic**. The ruling on such a scale is made so that equal vertical distances correspond to values of Y that have increased by the same percentage. This is accomplished by spacing the scale marks at distances that correspond to the logarithm of their heights.

Figure 12-14 shows the airline passenger time series and trend plotted with a semilogarithmic vertical scale. The exponential trend curve plots as a straight line, indicating that the number of passengers grew at a constant percentage rate during the period shown. The value $b = 1.063$ indicates that this rate was .063, or 6.3%, per year.*

*Recall that the expression for determining the amount A to which a principal amount P will grow at an interest rate i per year is $A = P(1 + i)^n$, where n is the number of time periods. The trend starts in 1964 at 77.64, and $\hat{Y}(X) = 77.64(1.063)^X = 77.64(1 + .063)^X$. The .063 represents the percentage rate of growth in passengers and is analogous to i, whereas 77.64 is similar to P, and X, like n, is the number of years beyond 1964.

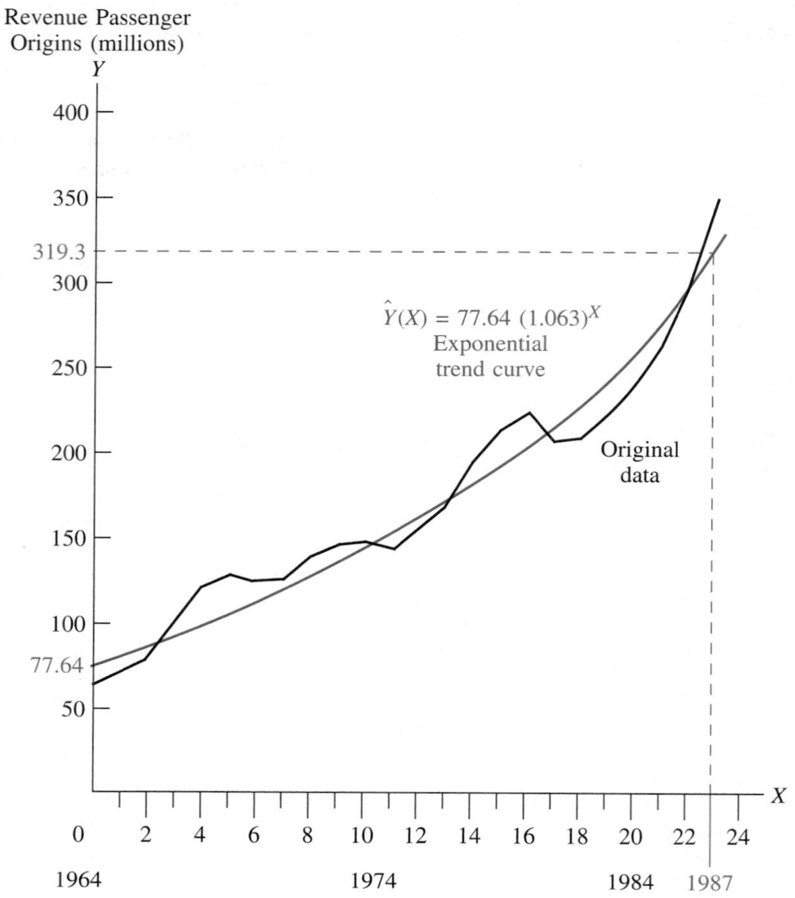

FIGURE 12-13 Exponential trend curve and original data for airline passengers.

EXERCISES

12-5 McFadden's has experienced the following annual sales.

Year	Sales	Year	Sales
1982	$18 million	1988	$ 82 million
1983	28	1989	89
1984	26	1990	108
1985	43	1991	121
1986	55	1992	155
1987	54		

(a) Plot the time-series data on ordinary graph paper.
(b) Would a straight line provide a suitable summary of the trend in sales? Explain.

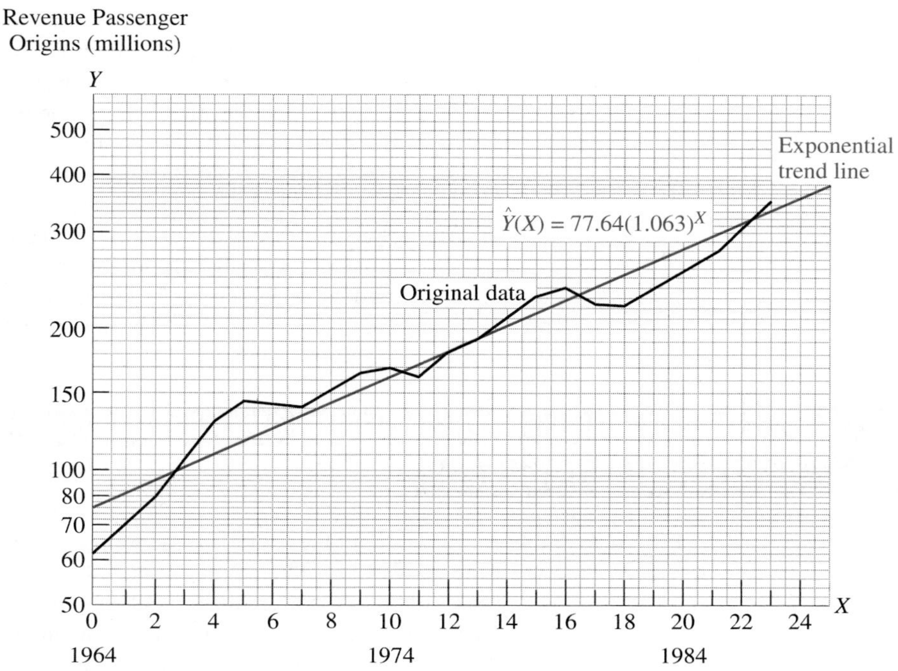

FIGURE 12-14 Airline passenger data plotted on semilogarithmic graph paper.

12-6 The electricity usage (millions of kilowatt-hours) in a region served by Centralia Power from 1983 through 1992 is provided below.

Year	Consumption	Year	Consumption
1983	205	1988	241
1984	206	1989	267
1985	223	1990	268
1986	234	1991	277
1987	231	1992	290

(a) Plot the time-series data on a graph.

(b) Using the method of least squares, determine the equation for the estimated regression line $\hat{Y}(X) = a + bX$ with X in years and $X = 0$ at 1983. Plot this line on your graph.

(c) Using your answer to (b), estimate the electricity consumption for 2001.

12-7 Refer to the data provided in Exercise 12-5.

(a) Representing sales by Y, use least-squares regression of log Y on X, where X is in years and $X = 0$ at 1982, to find the logarithmic trend line, $\log \hat{Y}(X) = \log a + X \log b$.

(b) Determine the exponential trend equation $\hat{Y}(X) = ab^X$.

(c) What is the annual percentage growth in sales indicated by the trend equation found in (b)?

(d) Using the trend equation from (a), what is the projected sales level for 1997?

12-8 For each of the following trend equations, make the required modifications.

(a) $\hat{Y}(X) = 1{,}000{,}000 + 120{,}000X$, with X in years and $X = 0$ at July 1, 1990. This expresses the number of employees in a utility industry. Find (1) $\hat{Y}(X)$ for monthly employment, with X in months and base January 15, 1990, and (2) $\hat{Y}(X)$ for quarterly employment, with X in quarters and base Winter 1990 (February 15, 1990).

(b) $\hat{Y}(X) = 10{,}000 + 600X$, with X in years and $X = 0$ at July 1, 1991. This expresses the number of welfare recipients in a particular county. Find (1) $\hat{Y}(X)$ for the number of welfare recipients, with X in months and base January 15, 1989, and (2) $\hat{Y}(X)$ for the number of welfare recipients, with X in quarters and base February 15, 1989.

12-4 FORECASTING WITH MOVING AVERAGES AND SEASONAL INDEXES

In this section, we will examine a procedure for isolating seasonal fluctuations in time-series data. Identifying seasonal patterns is a necessary first step in short-range planning. The management of a firm whose business drops in May is not alarmed if it is only the beginning of an annual seasonal trough. Likewise, government economists recognize that the consumer price index will rise or fall in certain months due to the influence of seasonal factors, such as changing varieties of produce on the market. To monitor the performance of a business or an economy, it is useful to "deseasonalize" time-series data to determine whether a current drop or rise is greater than normal.

RATIO-TO-MOVING-AVERAGE METHOD

The **ratio-to-moving-average method** is widely used to isolate seasonal fluctuations. Beginning with the actual time series, the trend and cyclical elements are isolated together in what is referred to as a "smoothed" time series. The isolation of the long-term elements is accomplished by means of **four-quarter moving averages**.

In the context of the classical time-series model, the ratio-to-moving-average method is summarized by the expression

$$\frac{Y_t}{\text{Moving average}} = \frac{T_t \times C_t \times S_t \times I_t}{T_t \times C_t} = S_t \times I_t$$

The moving average provides both trend and cycle, so that $T_t \times C_t$ is obtained for each time period. Dividing Y_t by the moving average is therefore equivalent to canceling the $T_t \times C_t$ terms from the multiplicative model, so that only the seasonal and irregular components, expressed by $S_t \times I_t$, remain.

The procedure is carried out in a number of steps. First, the first four successive values in the original time series are summed. That total is divided by 4 to get the first four-quarter moving average, which represents one complete year. These computations are repeated, except the initial quarter is dropped and the fifth is added, so that the second four-quarter average also represents a full year. The process is continued until you have run out of new quarters. The final step is to center the data by computing for each period the **centered moving average**. This is accomplished by averaging each successive pair of four-quarter averages.

ILLUSTRATION: FORECASTING ICE CREAM SALES

To illustrate the procedure, Table 12-4 provides data for Haskin-Dobbins ice cream sales (thousands of gallons). The first four-quarter average is found by adding the actual sales for the quarters of 1988 and dividing by 4.

$$\frac{5{,}100 + 9{,}800 + 15{,}200 + 11{,}300}{4} = 10{,}350$$

This value corresponds to that point in time when the Spring 1988 quarter ends and the Summer 1988 quarter begins—midnight, June 30, 1988.

TABLE 12-4 Time-Series for Haskin-Dobbins Data

(1) Quarter	(2) Sales	(3) Four-Quarter Moving Average	(4) Centered Moving Average	(5) Original as a Percentage of Moving Average	(6) Seasonal Index	(7) Deseasonalized Data
1988						
Winter	5,100				53.58	9,518
Spring	9,800				101.04	9,699
		10,350				
Summer	15,200		10,475	145.11	144.97	10,485
		10,600				
Fall	11,300		10,913	103.55	100.40	11,255
		11,225				
1989						
Winter	6,100		11,625	52.47	53.58	11,385
		12,025				
Spring	12,300		12,263	100.30	101.04	12,173
		12,500				
Summer	18,400		12,638	145.59	144.97	12,692
		12,775				
Fall	13,200		13,000	101.54	100.40	13,147
		13,225				
1990						
Winter	7,200		13,513	53.28	53.58	13,438
		13,800				
Spring	14,100		14,000	100.71	101.04	13,955
		14,200				
Summer	20,700		14,375	144.00	144.97	14,279
		14,550				
Fall	14,800		14,850	99.66	100.40	14,741
		15,150				
1991						
Winter	8,600		15,575	55.22	53.58	16,051
		16,000				
Spring	16,500		16,213	101.77	101.04	16,330
		16,425				
Summer	24,100		16,575	145.40	144.97	16,624
		16,725				
Fall	16,500		17,088	96.56	100.40	16,434
		17,450				
1992						
Winter	9,800		18,113	54.10	53.58	18,290
		18,775				
Spring	19,400		18,988	102.17	101.04	19,200
		19,200				
Summer	29,400				144.97	20,280
Fall	18,200				100.40	18,127

The second four-quarter average is found by dropping sales for Winter 1988 and including the figure for Winter 1989.

$$\frac{9{,}800 + 15{,}200 + 11{,}300 + 6{,}100}{4} = 10{,}600$$

As before, this value applies to the point in time separating Summer 1988 from Fall 1988—midnight, September 30. Since the values apply between quarters, the column of four-quarter averages is positioned one-half line off the rest of the table.

Column (4) contains the centered moving averages. The first of these is found by averaging the first two four-quarter averages.

$$\frac{10{,}350 + 10{,}600}{2} = 10{,}475$$

This value applies to the midpoint of Summer 1988, coinciding in time with the original data.

Next we divide the original sales data by the centered moving average to obtain the **percentage of moving average**. This ratio provides $S_t \times I_t$ values.

The first percentage of moving average is computed for Summer 1988 by dividing the original sales level of 15,200 by that quarter's centered moving average of 10,475. This is then multiplied by 100.

$$\frac{15{,}200}{10{,}475} \times 100 = 145.11$$

Sales for Summer 1988 were thus 145.11% of the trend and cyclical components. The remaining values are provided in column (5) of Table 12-4.

FINDING THE SEASONAL INDEXES

Table 12-5 shows all the percentages of moving averages, grouped by quarters.

The irregular component must be removed before a final set of seasonal indexes may be obtained. This is accomplished by first finding for each season the *median* percentage of moving average for the applicable quarters. (Although the mean may be used, the median is preferred because it is less affected by unusually large or small values.) Then the median percentages are adjusted so that the final indexes average to 100% for the entire year.

There are four percentages for each quarter, with the median obtained by averaging the middle-sized two. The sum of the medians is 400.79. To obtain indexes that sum to 400% (and that average to 100% throughout the year), each median is multiplied by 400/400.79. These seasonal indexes provide the S_t values for ice cream sales.

MONTHLY TIME-SERIES DATA

When the original time series is given by months, the general procedures illustrated for quarterly data may also be applied. A year's worth of successive monthly figures is averaged to provide twelve-month moving averages. Each successive pair of these is then averaged to obtain the **twelve-month centered moving average**. The resulting monthly seasonal indexes must sum to 1,200%.

TABLE 12-5 Calculation of Seasonal Indexes for Haskin-Dobbins Sales

	Quarter			
Year	**Winter**	**Spring**	**Summer**	**Fall**
1988			145.11	103.55
1989	52.47	100.30	145.59	101.54
1990	53.28	100.71	144.00	99.66
1991	55.22	101.77	145.40	96.56
1992	54.10	102.17		
Median	53.69	101.24	145.26	100.60
Sum of medians = 400.79				
Seasonal index = Median × $\frac{400}{400.79}$				
	53.58	101.04	144.97	100.40

DESEASONALIZED DATA

The ratio-to-moving-average method isolates the seasonal indexes. The seasonal indexes may be used to deseasonalize the original time-series data, which is often an asset in analyzing long-term movement in a time series. A deseasonalized series is sometimes used in place of smoothed data to identify cyclical activity and may be used to determine whether a turning point has been reached. For example, inflation may be expressed in terms of the consumer price index (CPI), which is computed by the U.S. Bureau of Labor Statistics. The CPI measures the percentage change in current prices beyond a base period. Government economists base current monetary and fiscal policies on the level of the CPI after the seasonal influence has been removed. Thus, a slower increase in the deseasonalized CPI may indicate that the peak of an inflationary period has been reached. Monthly deseasonalized CPI values may also be converted on an annual basis. Thus, an increase of .5% over the previous month's value would be multiplied by 12 to provide an annual rate of inflation of 6%.

Seasonal fluctuations are removed by dividing the original time-series data points by the corresponding seasonal indexes. In terms of the classical model, this is expressed symbolically as

$$\text{Deseasonalized value} = \frac{Y_t}{\text{Seasonal index}} = \frac{T_t \times C_t \times S_t \times I_t}{S_t}$$
$$= T_t \times C_t \times I_t$$

Dividing Y_t by the seasonal index removes the S_t component from the series, leaving only the trend, cyclical, and irregular components, $T_t \times C_t \times I_t$. The seasonal indexes—the values corresponding to the respective quarter in each year—are

TABLE 12-6 Calculations of the Monthly Forecasts for Department Store 1993 Sales

(1) Month	(2) X	(3) Seasonal Index	(4) Monthly Sales Trend Level $\hat{Y}(X)$	(5) Monthly Sales Forecast [(3) × (4)] ÷ 100
January	0	56.7	$1,025,000	581,175
February	1	64.5	1,075,000	693,375
March	2	62.1	1,125,000	698,625
April	3	99.9	1,175,000	1,173,825
May	4	83.6	1,225,000	1,024,100
June	5	67.4	1,275,000	859,350
July	6	58.2	1,325,000	771,150
August	7	100.1	1,375,000	1,376,375
September	8	110.6	1,425,000	1,576,050
October	9	137.7	1,475,000	2,031,075
November	10	167.3	1,525,000	2,551,325
December	11	191.9	1,575,000	3,022,425
		1,200.0		

entered in column (6) of Table 12-4. The original data values in column (2) are then divided by the seasonal index in column (6) and multiplied by 100. The resulting values, shown in column (7), are deseasonalized. For instance, the actual sales for Winter 1988 were 5,100 thousand gallons and the seasonal index is 53.58. Thus, for this time period

$$\text{Deseasonalized value} = \frac{5{,}100}{53.58} \times 100 = 9{,}518$$

MAKING THE FORECAST

Seasonal indexes are useful in making short-term forecasts. First, a trend over the annual period is determined, and then seasonal adjustments are made for each period within the year. For example, suppose that the managers of a department store who wish to forecast monthly sales for 1993 determine the following trend equation.

$$\hat{Y}(X) = 1{,}025{,}000 + 50{,}000X$$

where X is in months and $X = 0$ at January 15, 1993. Calculations of the monthly forecasts for department store sales are provided in Table 12-6. The 12 monthly seasonal indexes appear in column (3), and the monthly sales trend levels are calculated in column (4) from the managers' trend equation. For January, the trend value of $1,025,000 is multiplied by 56.7% to obtain the forecast sales of $581,175. The sales forecasts for all 12 months are listed in column (5).

EXERCISES

12-9 Extend the department store sales forecasts from Table 12-6 one more year, through 1994. Keep $X = 0$ at January 15, 1993, and use $X = 12$ for January 1994.

12-10 BugOff Chemical made forecasts of sales volume for Caterpillar Chiller over 1992–93. The trend for the number of gallons sold in any quarter is $\hat{Y}(X) = 10{,}000 + 800X$ ($X = 0$ in Winter 1992) and the seasonal indexes are

Winter	50
Spring	200
Summer	125
Fall	25

Determine BugOff's quarterly forecasts for 1992 and 1993.

12-11 The following percentages of moving average values have been obtained for the sales of High Tower Books. Determine the seasonal index for each quarter.

	Quarter			
Year	**Winter**	**Spring**	**Summer**	**Fall**
1986			156	111
1987	49	92	137	109
1988	53	93	148	108
1989	52	91	162	104
1990	51	89	153	110
1991	51	90	151	112
1992	48	88		

12-12 Beauty Boutiques has experienced the following number of transactions (thousands).

1988 Winter	125	
Spring	57	
Summer	108	
Fall	127	
1989 Winter	141	
Spring	55	
Summer	119	
Fall	149	
1990 Winter	146	
Spring	59	
Summer	122	
Fall	161	
1991 Winter	150	
Spring	62	
Summer	125	
Fall	158	
1992 Winter	157	
Spring	67	
Summer	133	
Fall	180	

(a) Determine the four-quarter moving averages, centered moving averages, and percentages of moving averages.
(b) Determine the seasonal index for each quarter.

12-13 Garment Suspenders has experienced the following quarterly sales data (millions of dollars) for the years 1988–92.

	1988	**1989**	**1990**	**1991**	**1992**
Winter	3.9	7.8	12.9	13.9	13.5
Spring	6.1	10.6	15.2	14.4	18.2
Summer	4.3	6.9	10.3	10.2	14.2
Fall	10.8	13.5	18.7	17.3	20.7

(a) Plot the time-series data on a graph.
(b) Determine the four-quarter moving averages.
(c) Calculate the percentage of moving average values and determine the seasonal indexes.
(d) Deseasonalize the original sales data and plot the results on your graph.

12-14 In arranging for short-term credit with its bank, the Make-Wave Corporation must project its cash needs on a monthly basis. To help in doing this, seasonal indexes must be developed from the following historical data on cash requirements (hundreds of thousands of dollars).
(a) Using 12-month moving averages, determine the seasonal index number for each month by means of the ratio-to-moving-average method.
(b) Make-Wave's cash needs for the coming year are forecast to be on the average equal to $1,000,000 per month. Using the seasonal indexes calculated in (a), estimate the cash requirements for each month.

	1988	1989	1990	1991	1992
January	2.7	2.9	3.5	2.5	4.2
February	5.4	6.4	7.3	8.1	9.6
March	9.3	10.1	11.3	7.9	12.4
April	2.4	4.1	3.8	5.2	6.2
May	6.1	7.8	8.1	9.2	8.7
June	7.3	7.4	6.9	8.1	8.3
July	6.5	5.5	6.5	7.6	6.6
August	9.7	9.6	8.9	9.3	9.8
September	13.4	13.5	14.3	15.8	16.3
October	10.6	10.7	11.5	12.6	13.4
November	5.1	4.8	6.5	7.2	6.9
December	3.4	2.8	3.9	4.1	6.1

12-15 Make-Wave Corporation obtained the following seasonal indexes.

Month	Index	Month	Index
January	40	July	90
February	100	August	120
March	140	September	180
April	60	October	140
May	110	November	80
June	90	December	50
		Total	1,200

(a) Use these indexes to deseasonalize the data provided in Exercise 12-14.
(b) Plot the original data for 1991 and 1992 on a graph. Then plot the deseasonalized data for both years on the same graph.
(c) Is the rise in 1992 cash requirements from August to September abnormally large? Explain.

12-5 IDENTIFYING CYCLES AND IRREGULAR FLUCTUATION

Cyclical movement is the most troublesome systematic component of time-series data to analyze. Unlike seasonal fluctuation, which is repetitious and fairly regular from year to year, longer-term oscillations, or cycles, tend to be erratic. It is virtually certain, for example, that a department store will achieve greater sales in the fall quarter than in any other period within a particular year. With cyclical variation, however, the peak may occur at any point within a calendar year, and the cycle's duration may vary one to several years. Cyclical activity usually varies in both intensity and distance from peak to successive peak, making the task of forecasting a cycle formidable—if not impossible.

Identifying past cycles in time-series data is difficult in itself. One problem is that it is normally impossible to achieve a true separation of trend and cyclical movement using the statistical tools available. Determining a trend curve is largely a matter of judgment. For instance, other methods in addition to the least-squares method may be used to fit the data to a regression line. The number of time periods to be included and the particular procedure to be used are matters of individual choice. Different trend forecasts will result from the various techniques used. Procedures for identifying cycles are described in the selected references at the back of the book.

Because irregular fluctuations reflect no systematic influence, they are not ordinarily computed and are of little use in traditional forecasting methods.

12-6 EXPONENTIAL SMOOTHING

Exponential smoothing is a popular forecasting procedure that offers two basic advantages: It simplifies forecasting calculations, and its data-storage requirements are small. Exponential smoothing produces self-correcting forecasts with built-in adjustments that regulate forecast values by increasing or decreasing them in the opposite direction of earlier errors, much like a thermostat.

The basic exponential-smoothing procedure provides the next period's forecast directly from the current period's actual and forecast values. The following expression is used to compute the

FORECAST VALUE (single-parameter smoothing)

$$F_{t+1} = \alpha Y_t + (1 - \alpha)F_t$$

where t is the current time period F_{t+1} and F_t are the forecast values for the next period and the current period, respectively, and Y_t is the current actual value. α (the lowercase Greek *alpha*) is the **smoothing constant**—a chosen value lying between 0 and 1. Since only one smoothing constant is used, we refer to this procedure as **single-parameter exponential smoothing**.

ILLUSTRATION: FORECASTING BEER SALES

To illustrate, we will suppose that actual sales of Blitz Beer in period 10 (October 1992) were $Y_{10} = 5{,}240$ barrels and that $F_{10} = 5{,}061.6$ had been forecast earlier for this period. Using a smoothing constant of $\alpha = .20$, the forecast for period 11 (November 1992) sales can be calculated as

$$\begin{aligned} F_{11} &= .20Y_{10} + (1 - .20)F_{10} \\ &= .20(5{,}240) + .80(5{,}061.6) = 5{,}097.3 \text{ barrels} \end{aligned}$$

Elementary exponential smoothing is extremely simple, because only one number—last period's forecast—must be saved. But, in essence, the entire time series is embodied in that forecast. If we express F_t in terms of the preceding actual Y_{t-1} and forecast F_{t-1} values, then the equivalent expression for next period's forecast is

$$F_{t+1} = \alpha Y_t + \alpha(1 - \alpha)Y_{t-1} + (1 - \alpha)^2 F_{t-1}$$

Continuing this for several earlier periods shows us that all preceding Y's are reflected in the current forecast. The name for this procedure is derived from the successive weights α, $\alpha(1 - \alpha)$, $\alpha(1 - \alpha)^2$, $\alpha(1 - \alpha)^3$, . . . , which *decrease exponentially*. Thus, the more current the actual value of the time series is, the greater its weight is. Progressively less forecasting weight is assigned to older Y's, and the oldest Y's are eventually wiped out. The forecasting procedure can be modified at any time by changing the value of α.

Table 12-7 provides the actual and forecast Blitz Beer sales for 20 periods when $\alpha = .20$. There, the actual sales figure for period 1 has been used for the initial forecast for period 2. (Eventually, the same F's will be achieved in later time periods, regardless of the initial value.)

The actual and forecast values may be compared in the plot provided in Figure 12-15. Notice that the forecast values deviate considerably from the actual values. This reflects a poorness of fit in using this particular model and level for α. The overall forecasting quality may be assessed in terms of the forecasting errors.

FORECASTING ERRORS

The errors in a forecasting procedure are determined by subtracting the forecasts from their respective actual values,

$$\varepsilon_t = Y_t - F_t$$

α should be set at a level that minimizes these errors. Often several separate sets of forecasts are required to "tune" the smoothing constant to past data. Large α levels assign more weight to current values, whereas small α levels emphasize past data. By trial and error, an optimal level can be found for α that minimizes *variability* in forecasting errors.

For any set of actual and forecast values, the **mean squared error**, denoted as *MSE*, is used to summarize this variability. The following expression is used to compute the mean squared error.

$$MSE = \frac{\sum (Y_t - F_t)^2}{n - m}$$

TABLE 12-7 Forecast of Blitz Beer Sales by Single-Parameter Exponential Smoothing ($\alpha = .20$)

Month	Period t	Actual Sales Y_t	Forecast Sales F_t	Error $Y_t - F_t$	Error² $(Y_t - F_t)^2$
January 1992	1	4,890	—	—	—
February	2	4,910	4,890.0	20.0	400.00
March	3	4,970	4,894.0	76.0	5,776.00
April	4	5,010	4,909.2	101.8	10,160.64
May	5	5,060	4,929.4	130.6	17,056.36
June	6	5,100	4,955.5	144.5	20,880.25
July	7	5,050	4,984.4	65.6	4,303.36
August	8	5,170	4,997.5	172.5	29,756.25
September	9	5,180	5,032.0	148.0	21,904.00
October	10	5,240	5,061.6	178.4	31,826.56
November	11	5,220	5,097.3	122.7	15,055.29
December	12	5,280	5,121.8	158.2	25,027.24
January 1993	13	5,330	5,153.5	176.5	31,152.25
February	14	5,380	5,188.8	191.2	36,557.44
March	15	5,440	5,227.0	213.0	45,369.00
April	16	5,460	5,269.6	190.4	36,252.16
May	17	5,520	5,307.7	212.3	45,071.29
June	18	5,490	5,350.2	139.8	19,544.04
July	19	5,550	5,378.1	171.9	29,549.61
August	20	5,600	5,412.5	187.5	35,156.25
September	21	—	5,450.0	—	—
					460,797.99

$MSE = 460{,}797.99/19 = 24{,}252.53$

where n denotes the number of time periods and m is the number of smoothing parameters. A value of $MSE = 24{,}252.53$ applies to the Blitz Beer data in Table 12-7.

TWO-PARAMETER EXPONENTIAL SMOOTHING

The forecast sales found earlier for Blitz Beer are smaller than (lag behind) the actual sales. Whenever there is a pronounced upward trend in actual data (here, increasing sales), forecasts resulting from the single-parameter exponential smoothing will be consistently low.

Two-parameter exponential smoothing eliminates such a lag by explicitly accounting for trend by using a second smoothing constant for the slope of the line. A total of three equations is employed in computing the

FORECAST VALUES (two-parameter smoothing):

$$T_t = \alpha Y_t + (1 - \alpha)(T_{t-1} + b_{t-1}) \qquad \text{(smooth the data to get trend)}$$

$$b_t = \gamma(T_t - T_{t-1}) + (1 - \gamma)b_{t-1} \qquad \text{(smooth the slope in trend)}$$

$$F_{t+1} = T_t + b_t \qquad \text{(forecast)}$$

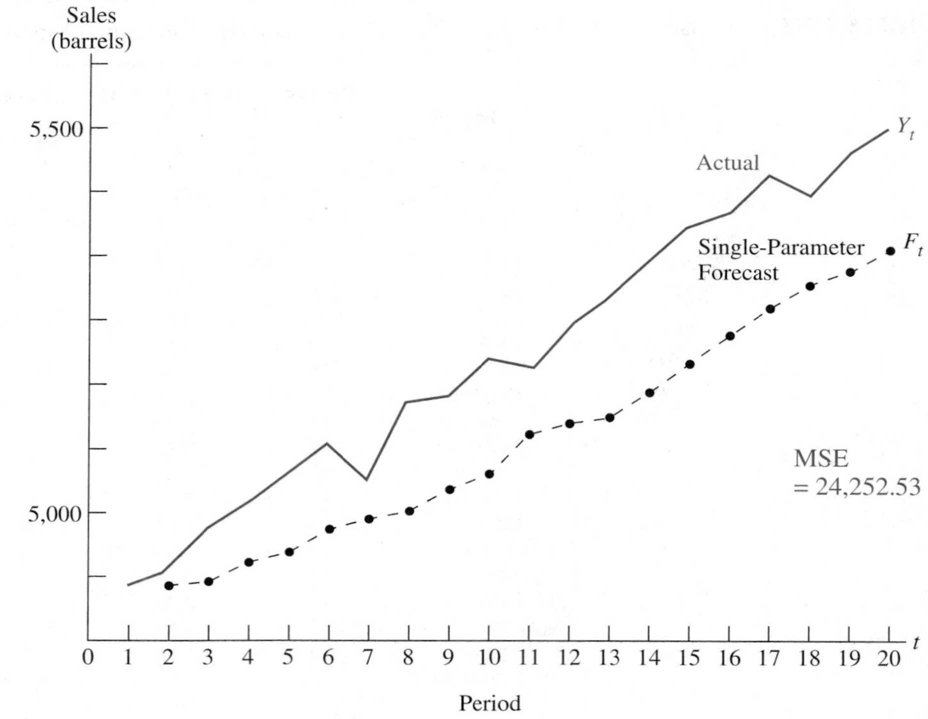

FIGURE 12-15 Single-parameter exponential smoothing results for Blitz Beer sales ($\alpha = .20$).

Here T_t represents the smoothed value for period t. This quantity conveys the underlying *trend* in the data. The difference between the current and the prior trend values provides the current slope in trend: $T_t - T_{t-1}$. The second equation contains the **slope-smoothing constant** γ (the lowercase Greek letter *gamma*), which is used to obtain smoothed-trend line slopes, represented by b_t. The third equation provides the forecast.

Table 12-8 lists the forecasts of Blitz Beer sales when $\alpha = .20$ and $\gamma = .30$. (The initial trend value of $T_2 = 4{,}890$ is the actual sales for period 1. The first slope value of $b_2 = 20$ is the difference in actual sales for periods 1 and 2.) The actual and forecast values are plotted in Figure 12-16.

As an illustration, to forecast period 8 sales, first we obtain the smoothed-data value or trend for period 7.

$$
\begin{aligned}
T_7 &= .20Y_7 + (1 - .20)(T_6 + b_6) \\
&= .20(5{,}050) + .80(5{,}045 + 35.7) \\
&= 5{,}075 \text{ barrels}
\end{aligned}
$$

Then we compute the smoothed slope in trend for period 7,

$$
\begin{aligned}
b_7 &= .30(T_7 - T_6) + (1 - .30)b_6 \\
&= .30(5{,}075 - 5{,}045) + .70(35.7) \\
&= 34.0
\end{aligned}
$$

TABLE 12-8 Forecast of Blitz Beer Sales by Two-Parameter Exponential Smoothing ($\alpha = .20$ and $\gamma = .30$)

Month	Period t	Actual Sales Y_t	Trend T_t	Trend Slope b_t	Forecast Sales F_t	Error $Y_t - F_t$	Error² $(Y_t - F_t)^2$
January 1992	1	4,890	—	—	—	—	—
February	2	4,910	4,890	20.0	—	—	—
March	3	4,970	4,922	23.6	4,910.0	60.0	3,600.00
April	4	5,010	4,958	27.3	4,945.6	64.4	4,147.36
May	5	5,060	5,000	31.7	4,985.3	74.7	5,580.09
June	6	5,100	5,045	35.7	5,031.7	68.3	4,664.89
July	7	5,050	5,075	34.0	5,080.7	−30.7	942.49
August	8	5,170	5,121	37.6	5,109.0	61.0	3,721.00
September	9	5,180	5,163	38.9	5,158.6	21.4	457.96
October	10	5,240	5,210	41.3	5,201.9	38.1	1,451.61
November	11	5,220	5,245	39.4	5,251.3	−31.3	979.69
December	12	5,280	5,283	39.0	5,284.4	−4.4	19.36
January 1993	13	5,330	5,324	39.6	5,322.0	8.0	64.00
February	14	5,380	5,367	40.6	5,363.6	16.4	268.96
March	15	5,440	5,414	42.5	5,407.6	32.4	1,049.76
April	16	5,460	5,457	42.7	5,456.5	3.5	12.25
May	17	5,520	5,504	44.0	5,499.7	20.3	412.09
June	18	5,490	5,536	40.4	5,548.0	−58.0	3,364.00
July	19	5,550	5,571	38.8	5,576.4	−26.4	696.96
August	20	5,600	5,608	38.3	5,609.8	−9.8	96.04
September	21	—	—	—	5,646.3	—	—
							31,528.51

$MSE = 31{,}528.51/18 = 1{,}751.58$

which indicates that sales were increasing at a rate of 34.0 barrels per period at that time. The forecast for period 8 is the sum of the preceding period's trend and slope values.

$$F_8 = T_7 + b_7 = 5{,}075 + 34.0 = 5{,}109.0 \text{ barrels}$$

The forecasts that result from this procedure are close to the actual sales values. The current trend itself is readjusted for each period to coincide with the latest growth in the raw data.

Notice, in Figure 12-16, how closely the forecasts from two-parameter smoothing lie to the actual sales figures. When the underlying time series exhibits a pronounced trend, two-parameter exponential smoothing will ordinarily provide better forecasts than those made with a single parameter. The *MSE* will then be smaller, as is the case with the two sets of Blitz Beer forecasts.

$$MSE = 24{,}252.53 \quad \text{(single parameter)}$$

$$MSE = 1{,}751.58 \quad \text{(two parameters)}$$

MSE can also be used to gauge how well different levels for α and γ provide forecasts that fit past time-series data.

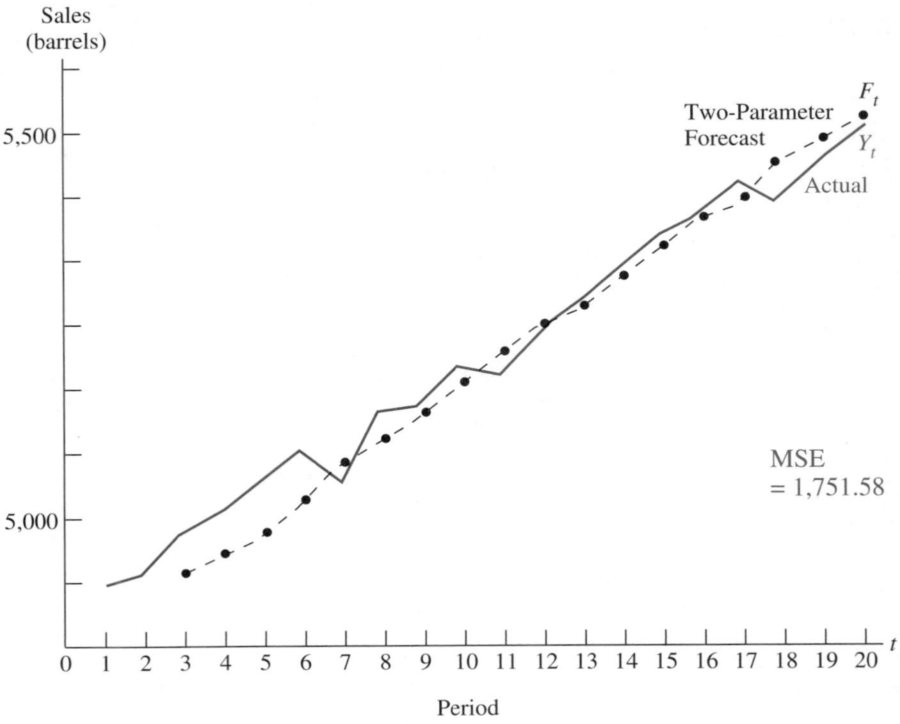

FIGURE 12-16 Two-parameter exponential smoothing results for Blitz Beer sales ($\alpha = .20$, $\gamma = .30$).

COMPUTER APPLICATIONS

Computer assistance is an obvious advantage when performing exponential smoothing. It is helpful for tuning the model (by adjusting the smoothing constants) to the historical data and obtaining a best fit. Figure 12-17 shows a portion of the output from a *QuickQuant* computer run using the Blitz Beer sales data given in Table 12-8.

One of the *QuickQuant* menu choices automatically begins a search for the best α and γ. It does this by creating a set of F_t's with each possible combination of levels for those parameters, starting with $\alpha = .10$ and $\gamma = .10$, in progressive increments of .10. The program computes the *MSE* for each forecast set; the results are shown in Figure 12-17. There, the lowest *MSE* is found to be 1,422.656, when $\alpha = .50$ and $\gamma = .20$. Those parameter settings give a preliminary best fit.

During the optional second *QuickQuant* pass, a finer search is performed in the vicinity of these parameter levels, using increments of .01; the results are shown in the top portion of Figure 12-18. The second search yields the final best fit. The *MSE* is found to be 1,418.864, when $\alpha = .45$ and $\gamma = .23$. The bottom portion of Figure 12-18 shows the detailed forecast information using these parameters.

QuickQuant allows the user to specify the α and γ levels, skipping the search for best fit. Notice the entry in the last row. There, we find a forecast value of $F_{21} = 5{,}631.82$ for the upcoming time period.

SEARCH FOR BEST PARAMETERS

	Gamma=0.10	Gamma=0.20	Gamma=0.30	Gamma=0.40	Gamma=0.50
Alpha=0.10	8141.006	4891.918	3427.73	2766.359	2434.959
Alpha=0.20	3075.86	2055.992	1734.646	1599.476	1542.317
Alpha=0.30	1971.451	1560.416	1463.605	1458.579	1499.119
Alpha=0.40	1623.858	1436.934	1427.561	1470.517	1534.031
Alpha=0.50	1503.587	1422.663	1454.753	1517.952	1591.364
Alpha=0.60	1479.107	1458.945	1517.591	1598.097	1687.513
Alpha=0.70	1509.43	1531.624	1613.768	1714.242	1824.316
Alpha=0.80	1582.042	1640.485	1748.522	1874.433	2011.893
Alpha=0.90	1697.219	1793.918	1936.154	2099.759	2281.257
Alpha=1.00	1863.989	2009.157	2203.039	2429.158	2689.537

	Gamma=0.60	Gamma=0.70	Gamma=0.80	Gamma=0.90	Gamma=1.00
Alpha=0.10	2228.561	2072	1945.865	1849.443	1784.779
Alpha=0.20	1538.043	1572.49	1633.84	1713.055	1802.729
Alpha=0.30	1564.229	1638.92	1711.791	1775.041	1825.443
Alpha=0.40	1602.391	1667.689	1728.08	1785.915	1845.341
Alpha=0.50	1667.626	1745.934	1828.357	1917.52	2015.101
Alpha=0.60	1782.741	1884.007	1991.673	2105.212	2222.808
Alpha=0.70	1941.791	2065.814	2195.354	2329.095	2466.143
Alpha=0.80	2159.339	2316.54	2484.026	2663.55	2858.417
Alpha=0.90	2481.764	2704.735	2955.844	3243.674	3580.03
Alpha=1.00	2991.957	3349.014	3779.02	4307.898	4972.222

Best Fit: Alpha =0.50 Gamma =0.20 MSE = 1422.663

FIGURE 12-17 Portion of QuickQuant report showing the first phase of a search for best-fitting parameters using the Blitz Beer sales data.

QuickQuant will also perform all the calculations for single-parameter exponential smoothing and for the three-parameter procedure, to be discussed next.

SEASONAL EXPONENTIAL SMOOTHING WITH THREE PARAMETERS

The two exponential-smoothing procedures described thus far ignore any seasonal aspects. Consider the quarterly sales data for Stationer's Supply, plotted in Figure 12-19. A retail outlet, Stationer's Supply has historically experienced two busy periods, Spring and Fall, interspersed with the more quiet Summer and Winter quarters. The results show a very pronounced seasonal pattern that gives a saw-toothed effect to the time series.

Seasonal exponential smoothing makes forecasts by isolating the trend and seasonal time-series components as separate smoothed series. The underlying model extends the two-parameter procedure, incorporating the **seasonal smoothing**

SEARCH FOR BEST PARAMETERS

	Gamma=0.15	Gamma=0.16	Gamma=0.17	Gamma=0.18	Gamma=0.19
Alpha=0.45	1451.592	1442.042	1434.555	1428.812	1424.558
Alpha=0.46	1447.074	1438.395	1431.701	1426.66	1423.048
Alpha=0.47	1443.37	1435.514	1429.552	1425.181	1422.19
Alpha=0.48	1440.427	1433.354	1428.083	1424.349	1421.911
Alpha=0.49	1438.193	1431.85	1427.232	1424.083	1422.194
Alpha=0.50	1436.607	1430.958	1426.962	1424.378	1423.001
Alpha=0.51	1435.664	1430.662	1427.252	1425.216	1424.318
Alpha=0.52	1435.299	1430.911	1428.073	1426.524	1426.105
Alpha=0.53	1435.486	1431.698	1429.384	1428.331	1428.35
Alpha=0.54	1436.212	1432.991	1431.186	1430.594	1431.029

	Gamma=0.20	Gamma=0.21	Gamma=0.22	Gamma=0.23	Gamma=0.24
Alpha=0.45	1421.594	1419.748	1418.879	1418.859	1419.606
Alpha=0.46	1420.68	1419.362	1418.989	1419.433	1420.609
Alpha=0.47	1420.36	1419.561	1419.648	1420.53	1422.1
Alpha=0.48	1420.606	1420.29	1420.824	1422.111	1424.051
Alpha=0.49	1421.386	1421.525	1422.471	1424.145	1426.46
Alpha=0.50	1422.663	1423.223	1424.573	1426.62	1429.272
Alpha=0.51	1424.422	1425.399	1427.133	1429.53	1432.499
Alpha=0.52	1426.631	1428.015	1430.092	1432.819	1436.117
Alpha=0.53	1429.288	1431.03	1433.464	1436.525	1440.119
Alpha=0.54	1432.358	1434.457	1437.242	1440.603	1444.489

Best Fit: Alpha =0.45 Gamma =0.23 MSE = 1418.859

SMOOTHED DATA WITH BEST PARAMETERS

Alpha =0.45 Gamma =0.23 MSE = 1418.859

Period t	Actual Yt	Smoothed Vt	Trend Bt	Forecast Ft	Error Yt-Ft
1	4890.00	--	--	--	--
2	4910.00	4890.00	20.00	--	--
3	4970.00	4937.00	26.21	4910.00	60.00
4	5010.00	4984.27	31.05	4963.21	46.79
5	5060.00	5035.42	35.68	5015.32	44.68
6	5100.00	5084.11	38.67	5071.10	28.90
7	5050.00	5090.03	31.14	5122.77	-72.77
8	5170.00	5143.14	36.19	5121.16	48.84
9	5180.00	5179.63	36.26	5179.33	0.67
10	5240.00	5226.74	38.76	5215.89	24.11
11	5220.00	5245.02	34.05	5265.50	-45.50
12	5280.00	5279.49	34.14	5279.07	0.93
13	5330.00	5321.00	35.84	5313.63	16.37
14	5380.00	5367.26	38.23	5356.83	23.17
15	5440.00	5421.02	41.81	5405.49	34.51
16	5460.00	5461.56	41.51	5462.83	-2.83
17	5520.00	5510.69	43.27	5503.07	16.93
18	5490.00	5525.17	36.65	5553.95	-63.95
19	5550.00	5556.50	35.42	5561.82	-11.82
20	5600.00	5595.56	36.26	5591.92	8.08
21	--	--	--	5631.82	--

FIGURE 12-18 Portion of QuickQuant report showing the final phase of a search for best-fitting parameters using the Blitz Beer sales data.

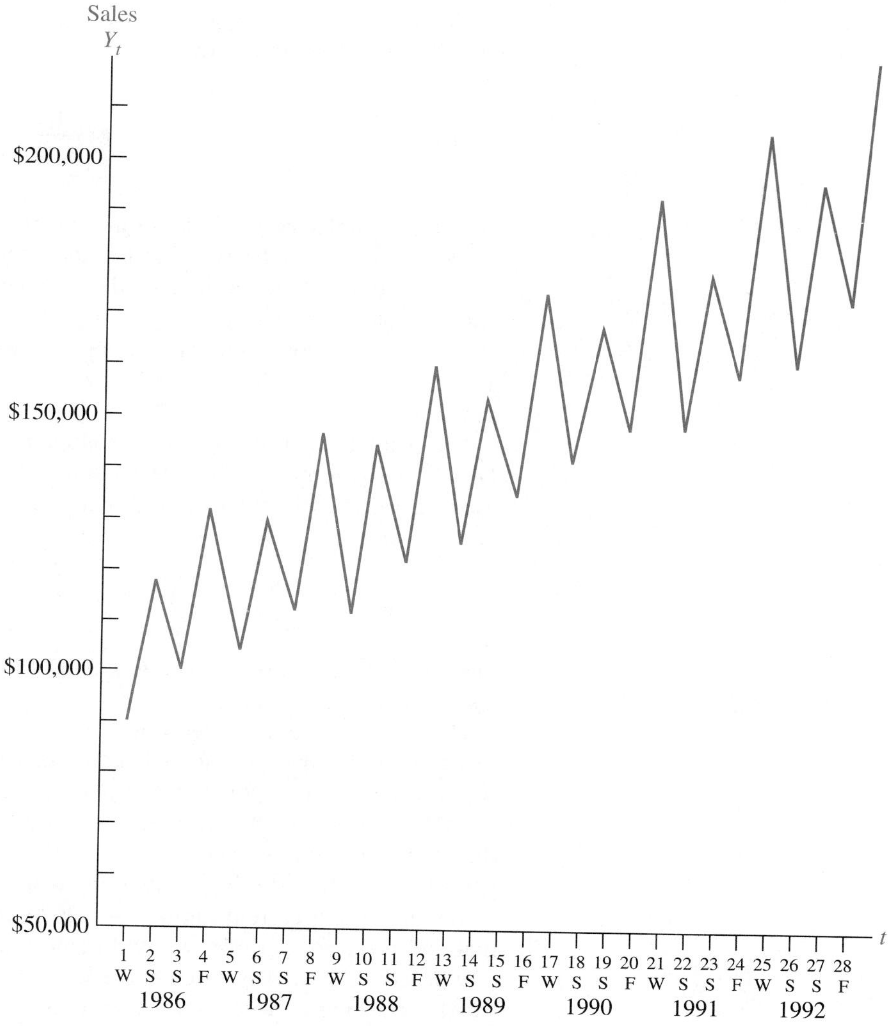

FIGURE 12-19 Actual quarterly sales data for Stationer's Supply.

constant β (Greek lowercase letter *beta*) as the third parameter. The following four equations are used to determine the

FORECAST VALUES (seasonal smoothing with three parameters):

$$T_t = \alpha\left(\frac{Y_t}{S_{t-p}}\right) + (1-\alpha)(T_{t-1} + b_{t-1}) \quad \text{(smooth data to get trend)}$$

$$b_t = \gamma(T_t - T_{t-1}) + (1 - \gamma)b_{t-1} \quad \text{(smooth slope in trend)}$$

$$S_t = \beta\left(\frac{Y_t}{T_t}\right) + (1 - \beta)S_{t-p} \quad \text{(smooth seasonal factor)}$$

$$F_{t+1} = (T_t + b_t)S_{t-p+1} \quad \text{(forecast)}$$

The first equation smooths the past data to obtain the trend. In doing this, the current value Y_t is first *deseasonalized.*

$$\frac{Y_t}{S_{t-p}}$$

This is accomplished by dividing the actual by the latest applicable seasonal factor, S_{t-p}. The $t-p$ subscript signifies that the seasonal factor is taken from p periods earlier. The letter p denotes the number of periods during a major period. There would be $p = 4$ *quarters* in a year, $p = 12$ *months* in a year, and $p = 7$ *days* in a week. For Stationer's Supply, the data are quarterly, and $p = 4$, so that the current Spring sales is divided by the S applicable for the preceding Spring, and so on.

The second equation smooths the slope in trend, just as in the previous model. The third equation smooths the seasonal factor. The current portion of the seasonal factor is defined by the following ratio.

$$\frac{Y_t}{T_t}$$

The above ratio receives a weight β and is added to $1 - \beta$ times the prior matching seasonal factor value.

The final equation creates a new deseasonalized projection, adding the prior period's trend and the latest slope in trend. The quantity is multiplied by the latest applicable known seasonal factor S_{t-p} (*not* S_t) to give the forecast value.

Table 12-9 shows the detailed summary obtained from applying the above to the Stationer's Supply sales data, with $\alpha = .4$, $\gamma = .5$, and $\beta = .7$. We will use period 20 to illustrate the calculations with the seasonal model.

Taking, as the current period, $t = 20$ (Fall 1990) and all available data from that and the prior periods, we will determine the forecast for period 21 (Winter 1991). The first step is to compute the smoothed values for trend and slope in trend, averaging current values with those of period 19.

$$\begin{aligned} T_{20} &= .40\left(\frac{Y_{20}}{S_{16}}\right) + (1 - .40)(T_{19} + b_{19}) \\ &= .40\left(\frac{\$190{,}400}{1.09}\right) + .60(\$169{,}823.34 + \$3{,}376.46) \\ &= \$173{,}810.45 \end{aligned}$$

$$\begin{aligned} b_{20} &= .50(T_{20} - T_{19}) + (1 - .50)b_{19} \\ &= .50(\$173{,}810.45 - \$169{,}823.34) + .50(\$3{,}376.46) \\ &= \$3{,}681.79 \end{aligned}$$

Notice that $S_{16} = 1.09$ (Fall 1989) is used as the divisor to find T_{20}, not S_{20} (which cannot be available until T_{20} has been computed). The seasonal factor for period 20 is computed with the above, however, since it will be needed to make future-period calculations.

TABLE 12-9 Seasonal Exponential Smoothing Results for Stationer's Supply ($\alpha = .4$, $\gamma = .5$, $\beta = .7$)

Quarter	t	Actual Y_t	Trend T_t	Slope b_t	Seasonal S_t	Forecast F_t	Error $Y_t - F_t$
1986 W	1	90,640	—	—	—	—	—
S	2	115,540	90,640.00	24,900.00	1.27	—	—
S	3	99,190	109,000.00	21,630.00	.91	—	—
F	4	128,800	129,898.00	21,264.00	.99	—	—
1987 W	5	102,350	131,637.20	11,501.60	.78	—	—
S	6	127,440	125,873.46	2,868.93	1.09	182,460.92	− 55,020.92
S	7	112,530	126,709.17	1,852.32	.89	117,155.58	− 4,625.58
F	8	145,080	135,663.61	5,403.38	1.05	127,474.79	17,605.21
1988 W	9	110,490	141,482.77	5,611.27	.78	109,681.81	808.20
S	10	143,000	140,679.34	2,403.92	1.04	160,498.08	− 17,498.08
S	11	119,700	139,367.03	545.81	.87	128,011.98	− 8,311.98
F	12	157,760	144,273.64	2,726.21	1.08	146,355.97	11,404.03
1989 W	13	123,710	151,647.84	5,050.21	.81	114,647.37	9,062.63
S	14	153,360	153,066.75	3,234.56	1.01	162,791.25	− 9,431.25
S	15	131,950	154,474.06	2,320.93	.86	135,922.52	− 3,972.52
F	16	173,160	158,254.92	3,050.90	1.09	169,220.94	3,939.06
1990 W	17	135,900	164,310.22	4,553.10	.82	129,853.54	6,046.46
S	18	164,780	166,383.72	3,313.30	1.00	171,059.64	− 6,279.64
S	19	146,010	169,823.34	3,376.46	.86	145,738.78	271.22
F	20	190,400	173,810.45	3,681.79	1.09	188,736.47	1,663.53
1991 W	21	145,070	177,220.66	3,545.99	.82	145,627.08	− 557.08
S	22	175,960	179,044.81	2,685.08	.99	180,252.36	− 4,292.36
S	23	155,480	181,397.27	2,518.76	.86	156,194.73	− 714.73
F	24	202,960	184,576.81	2,849.16	1.10	201,153.27	1,806.73
1992 W	25	157,500	189,364.59	3,818.47	.83	153,529.97	3,970.03
S	26	192,240	193,811.88	4,132.88	.99	190,688.30	1,551.70
S	27	168,330	197,257.61	3,789.30	.85	169,803.64	− 1,473.64
F	28	218,960	200,407.03	3,469.36	1.09	220,716.22	− 1,756.22
1993 W	29	—	—	—	—	168,800.52	—
S	30	—	—	—	—	205,365.31	—
S	31	—	—	—	—	180,182.80	—
F	32	—	—	—	—	234,460.20	—

$$S_{20} = .70\left(\frac{Y_{20}}{T_{20}}\right) + (1 - .70)S_{16}$$

$$= .70\left(\frac{\$190,400}{\$173,810.45}\right) + .30(1.09)$$

$$= 1.09$$

Finally, the forecast is made for period 21.

$$F_{21} = (T_{20} + b_{20})S_{17}$$

$$= (\$173,810.45 + \$3,681.79)(1.09)$$

$$= \$145,627.08$$

The complete set of forecast values is plotted alongside the actual sales figures in Figure 12-20. Notice that the F_t's become close to the Y_t values only after the

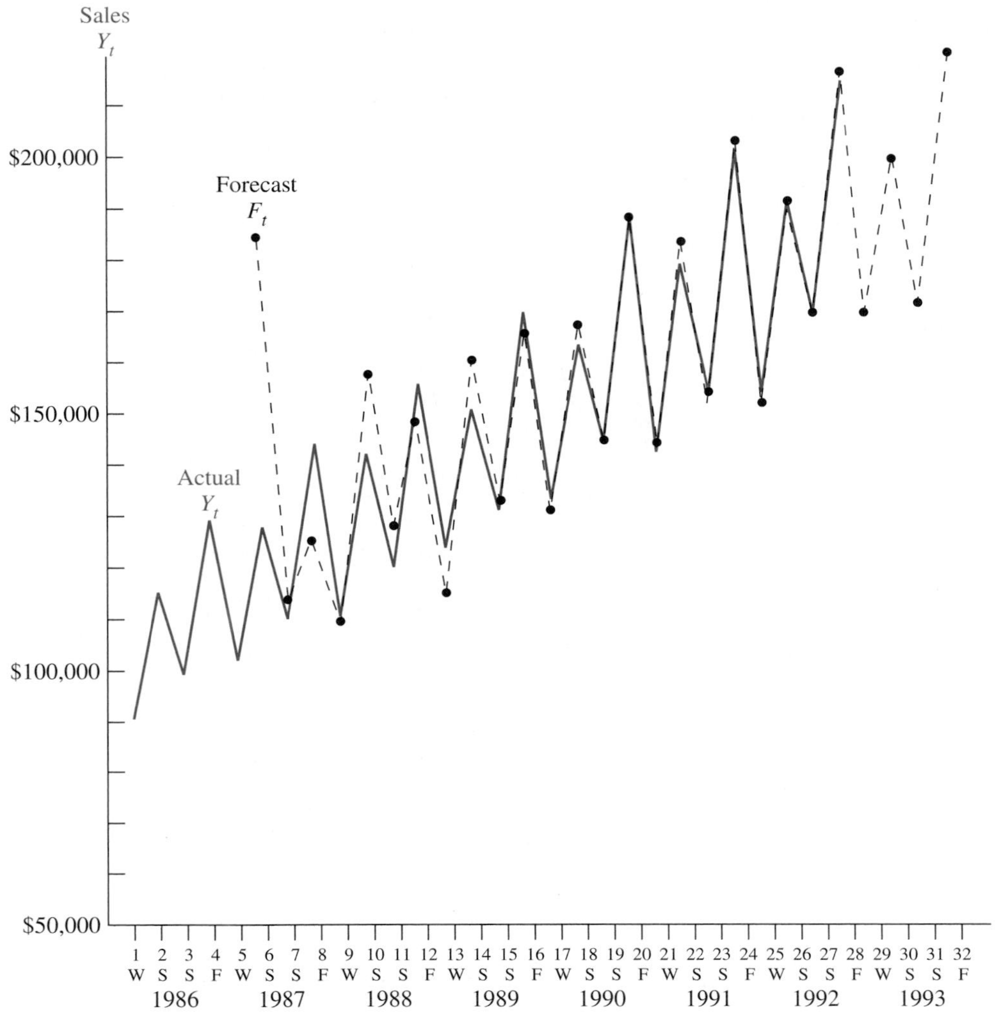

FIGURE 12-20 Actual and quarterly sales data for Stationer's Supply ($\alpha = .4$, $\gamma = .5$, $\beta = .7$).

process has settled down, after three full years of data have been incorporated. This slowness in attaining forecasting accuracy is mainly due to poor starting values. Rather than rely on guesswork, the illustrated procedure uses the actual Y_1 as the first T_2 (which appears to be quite low in relation to the later T's). That in turn distorts the initial seasonal values. (Although *QuickQuant* does not employ them, a quicker start might be achieved by making good guesses for the starting S's.) As with any exponential-smoothing process, earlier inaccuracies eventually wash out.

When applying the seasonal model, forecasts may be found for the entire seasonal cycle using the following expression.

$$F_{t+m} = (T_t + b_t m)S_{t-p+m}$$

The above was used to obtain the last set of four Stationer's Supply forecast values, shown in Figure 12-20 and at the bottom of Table 12-9.

FINE-TUNING EXPONENTIAL-SMOOTHING PARAMETERS

With computer assistance, it is practicable to fine-tune the parameters to the historical data, thereby achieving a best fit (minimum *MSE*). Generally, the following applies to any parameter.

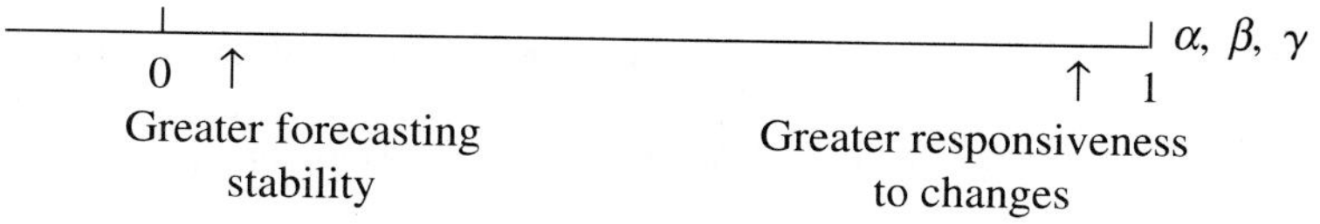

The fine-tuning of parameters to past data does indeed provide a best historical fit. But, there are no guarantees that the parameters thereby obtained will continue to fit the actual data well. And, should the historical fit result in a parameter that is very close to 0 or to 1, it may be wise to choose a less extreme number that sacrifices past *MSE* for greater future stability or responsiveness.

Figure 12-21 shows the results of using different β levels with the Stationer's Supply data (all with the same α and γ as before). Each *MSE* value was obtained with a separate *QuickQuant* run. Notice that *MSE* declines steadily as β is increased, but the curve flattens out around $\beta = .7$. That number appears to be a good compromise for future forecasts of Stationer's Supply sales, allowing for

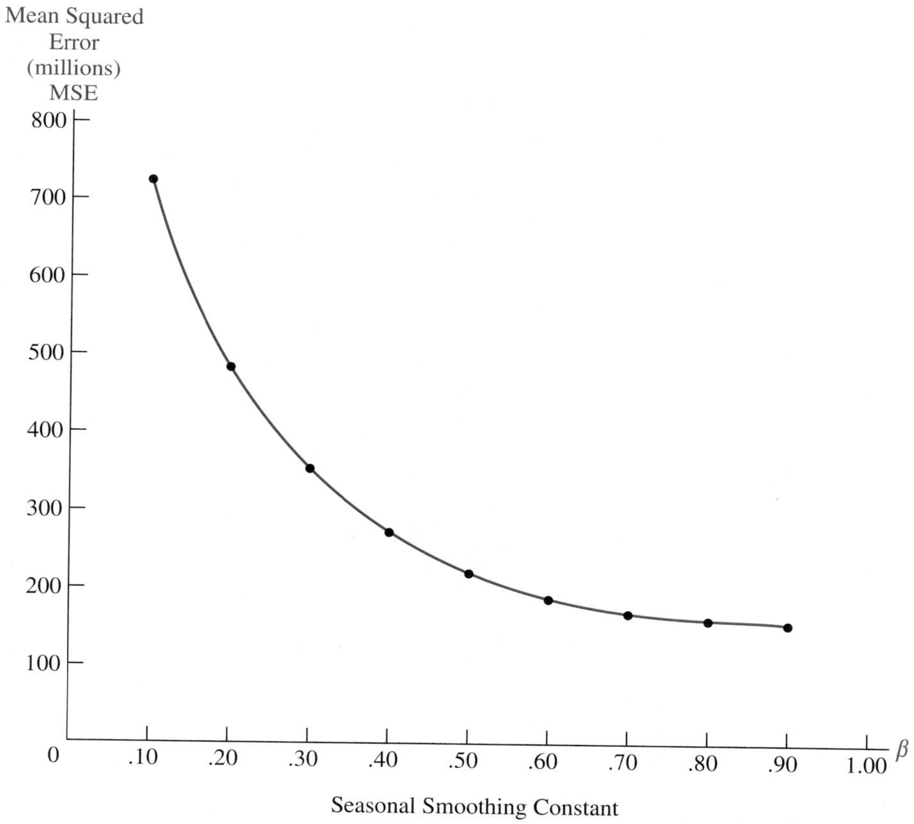

FIGURE 12-21 Relationship between MSE and level for β using Stationer's Supply data ($\alpha = .40$, $\gamma = .50$).

both stability and responsiveness to a seasonal pattern that will likely prevail with little change. Using that β, the other parameters were fine-tuned. Figure 12-22 shows a portion of the *QuickQuant* report obtained.

FURTHER EXPONENTIAL-SMOOTHING PROCEDURES

A wide variety of exponential-smoothing procedures is available. One popular group employs *adaptive response*, involving changes to one or more smoothing constants as conditions change from one period to the next. More elaborate procedures explicitly allow for nonlinear trend. The references in the back of this

Alpha =0.42 Gamma =0.67 Beta =0.70 MSE = 1.683232E+08

Period t	Actual Yt	Trend Tt	Slope bt	Seasonal St	Forecast Ft	Error Yt-Ft
1	90640.00	--	--	--	--	--
2	115540.00	90640.00	24900.00	1.27	--	--
3	99190.00	108673.00	20299.11	0.91	--	--
4	128800.00	128899.82	20250.68	1.00	--	--
5	102350.00	129494.30	7081.02	0.79	--	--
6	127440.00	121203.40	-3218.19	1.12	174094.34	-46654.34
7	112530.00	120212.51	-1725.87	0.93	107689.60	4840.42
8	145080.00	129703.10	5789.14	1.08	118394.90	26685.12
9	110490.00	137298.60	6999.41	0.80	107090.70	3399.34
10	143000.00	137393.00	2373.04	1.06	161387.70	-18387.66
11	119700.00	135175.53	-702.58	0.90	129854.62	-10154.62
12	157760.00	139189.30	2457.35	1.12	145601.40	12158.59
13	123710.00	147067.54	6089.37	0.83	113378.81	10331.19
14	153360.00	149362.32	3547.00	1.04	162973.82	-9613.83
15	131950.00	150360.93	1839.58	0.88	137402.24	-5452.25
16	173160.00	153314.60	2586.01	1.13	170193.90	2966.14
17	135900.00	159277.71	4848.68	0.85	129234.60	6665.44
18	164780.00	161869.60	3336.60	1.02	170357.40	-5577.38
19	146010.00	165201.50	3333.46	0.88	146019.84	-9.84
20	190400.00	168765.00	3487.61	1.13	189783.12	616.88
21	145070.00	171931.80	3272.63	0.84	145716.24	-646.25
22	175960.00	173791.40	2325.92	1.02	179405.00	-3444.97
23	155480.00	176032.00	2268.75	0.88	155659.53	-179.53
24	202960.00	179014.12	2746.73	1.13	201044.73	1915.27
25	157500.00	183759.20	4085.61	0.85	153482.31	4017.69
26	192240.00	188425.00	4474.32	1.02	190836.70	1403.31
27	168330.00	191909.31	3811.04	0.88	170412.30	-2082.27
28	218960.00	194764.31	3170.50	1.13	221536.60	-2576.59
29	--	--	--	--	168896.92	--
30	--	--	--	--	204916.50	--
31	--	--	--	--	179562.71	--
32	--	--	--	--	233695.00	--

FIGURE 12-22 Portion of QuickQuant report for Stationer's Supply data, using parameters $\alpha = .42$, $\gamma = .67$, and $\beta = .7$.

book list sources for more information on these and other exponential-smoothing procedures.

EXERCISES

12-16 Refer to the data in Table 12-7.
(a) Use single-parameter exponential smoothing with $\alpha = .40$ to forecast sales levels.
(b) Compute the mean squared error.

12-17 Tuti-Fruti Yogurt's seasonally adjusted quarterly sales data (thousands of gallons) are given below.

Period	Sales	Period	Sales
1	2	9	12
2	3	10	14
3	5	11	15
4	7	12	17
5	6	13	18
6	8	14	22
7	9	15	24
8	10	16	27

(a) Use single-parameter exponential smoothing with $\alpha = .20$ to forecast sales levels.
(b) Compute the mean squared error.

12-18 Repeat Exercise 12-16. Use $\alpha = .50$.

12-19 Refer to the Tuti-Fruti data in Exercise 12-17.
(a) Use two-parameter exponential smoothing with $\alpha = .40$ and $\gamma = .10$ to forecast sales levels.
(b) Compute the mean squared error.

12-20 Refer to the data given in Table 12-8.
(a) Use two-parameter exponential smoothing with $\alpha = .30$ and $\gamma = .20$ to forecast sales levels.
(b) Compute the mean squared error.

12-21 Big Mountain Power serves a region in which the following amounts of annual electricity usage (millions of kilowatt-hours) have been recorded.

Year	Consumption	Year	Consumption
1983	205	1988	241
1984	206	1989	267
1985	223	1990	268
1986	231	1991	277
1987	234	1992	290

(a) Plot the time-series data on graph paper.
(b) Use single-parameter exponential smoothing with $\alpha = .20$ to forecast values for each past year. Then, compute the *MSE* and find the forecast usage for 1993.
(c) Repeat (b), using two-parameter exponential smoothing with $\alpha = .30$ and $\gamma = .20$.
(d) Which forecast appears better? Explain.

12-22 Garment Suspenders recorded the following quarterly sales data (millions of dollars).

	1988	1989	1990	1991	1992
Winter	3.9	7.8	12.9	13.9	13.5
Spring	6.1	10.6	15.2	14.4	18.2
Summer	4.3	6.9	10.3	10.2	14.2
Fall	10.8	13.5	18.7	17.3	20.7

(a) Plot the time-series data on graph paper.
(b) Use three-parameter seasonal exponential smoothing with $\alpha = .3$, $\gamma = .2$, and $\beta = .4$ to forecast sales levels for the past quarters.
(c) Determine quarterly sales forecasts for 1993.

12-23 In arranging for short-term credit with its bank, the Make-Wave Corporation must project its cash needs on a monthly basis. Management wishes to use the following historical data to project monthly cash requirements (hundreds of thousands of dollars).

	1988	1989	1990	1991	1992
January	2.7	2.9	3.5	2.5	4.2
February	5.4	6.4	7.3	8.1	9.6
March	9.3	10.1	11.3	7.9	12.4
April	2.4	4.1	3.8	5.2	6.2
May	6.1	7.8	8.1	9.2	8.7
June	7.3	7.4	6.9	8.1	8.3
July	6.5	5.5	6.5	7.6	6.6
August	9.7	9.6	8.9	9.3	9.8
September	13.4	13.5	14.3	15.8	16.3
October	10.6	10.7	11.5	12.6	13.4
November	5.1	4.8	6.5	7.2	6.9
December	3.4	2.8	3.9	4.1	6.1

(a) Use three-parameter seasonal exponential smoothing with $\alpha = .2$, $\gamma = .1$, and $\beta = .3$ to forecast cash requirements for past months.
(b) Determine forecast monthly requirements for 1993.

12-24 *Computer exercise.* Telesat Corporation obtained the following message volumes (thousands) relayed on successive days by a new communications satellite.

Day	Vol.	Day	Vol.	Day	Vol.	Day	Vol.	Day	Vol.
1	990	11	1038	21	1064	31	1088	41	1112
2	998	12	1041	22	1069	32	1093	42	1107
3	876	13	1039	23	1071	33	1099	43	1115
4	1014	14	1042	24	1069	34	1101	44	1118
5	1009	15	1045	25	1073	35	1098	45	1119
6	1017	16	1040	26	1074	36	1104	46	1123
7	1023	17	1052	27	1076	37	1103	47	1121
8	1015	18	1057	28	1078	38	1106	48	1123
9	1028	19	1063	29	1079	39	1108	49	1124
10	1035	20	1061	30	1080	40	1110	50	1125

Use two-parameter exponential smoothing to forecast message volumes. Compute the mean squared error for each of the following cases.

(a) $\alpha = .10;\ \gamma = .10$ (c) $\alpha = .10;\ \gamma = .30$
(b) $\alpha = .10;\ \gamma = .20$ (d) $\alpha = .20;\ \gamma = .10$
(e) Which of the above parameter levels provides the best fit to the actual data?

SUMMARY

1. What is time series analysis and the classical time series model?
Time-series data are values arising from fixed periods, such as days, months, or quarters. These may be represented symbolically by Y_t, with t denoting the time period. **Time-series analysis** attempts to uncover patterns in these data. The **classical model** expresses the data as the *product* of four components.

$$Y_t = T_t \times C_t \times S_t \times I_t$$

These components, expressed as percentages, are **trend** T_t, **cyclical movement** C_t, **seasonal index** S_t, and **irregular fluctuation** I_t. Both the trend T_t and seasonal index S_t are considered regular components, and the classical analysis focuses on establishing these.

2. How do we isolate the trend and seasonal time series components?
The trend may be isolated by conducting a least-squares regression, using the original or smoothed data as the dependent variable and time period as the independent variable. The smoothed data may also be used directly to express trend. The classical model smoothes the data using **moving averages**. The **ratio-to-moving-average method** is used to isolate the seasonal fluctuations. Very useful results are **deseasonalized data**, which are often used to establish the **trend line**

$$\hat{Y}(X) = a + bX$$

Curvilinear relationships may be summarized in terms of a logarithmic trend line.

3. What is exponential smoothing, and how is it employed in time series analysis?
Modern forecasting methods are often based on **exponential smoothing**. This procedure applies weights to past data points, giving greater weight to more current values. A single parameter α may serve for this purpose, so that the forecast for period $t+1$ is based on the latest forecast and the current actual value.

$$F_{t+1} = \alpha Y_t + (1 - \alpha)F_t$$

The parameter α is the **smoothing constant**.

4. What are two-parameter and three-parameter (seasonal) exponential smoothing and what are their advantages?
Better estimates may be obtained using a second **slope-smoothing constant** γ for *trend*. The following expressions are used.

$$T_t = \alpha Y_t + (1 - \alpha)(T_{t-1} + b_{t-1}) \quad \text{(smooth the data to get trend)}$$
$$b_t = \gamma(T_t - T_{t-1}) + (1 - \gamma)b_{t-1} \quad \text{(smooth the slope in trend)}$$
$$F_{t+1} = T_t + b_t \quad \text{(forecast)}$$

Three-parameter exponential smoothing incorporates a **seasonal smoothing constant** β. The following expressions are used.

$$T_t = \alpha\left(\frac{Y_t}{S_{t-p}}\right) + (1-\alpha)(T_{t-1} + b_{t-1}) \quad \text{(smooth the data to get trend)}$$

$$b_t = \gamma(T_t - T_{t-1}) + (1-\gamma)b_{t-1} \quad \text{(smooth the slope in trend)}$$

$$S_t = \beta\left(\frac{Y_t}{T_t}\right) + (1-\beta)S_{t-p} \quad \text{(smooth the seasonal factor)}$$

$$F_{t+1} = (T_t + b_t)S_{t-p+1} \quad \text{(forecast)}$$

5. **How may we measure the quality of forecasts?**
The overall quality of forecasts made with exponential smoothing may be summarized by the **mean squared error** *MSE*. It is even possible to fine tune smoothing constants to past data, finding the levels for α, γ, and β that minimize past *MSE*.

REAL-LIFE STATISTICAL CHALLENGE

Feeling in Debt?

Over the past few decades the federal debt has risen considerably. Debt level can be measured in a number of ways: total, per capita, interest paid, or annual percentage changes. Table 12-10 shows the total *accumulated* public debt for the U.S. government for the years 1940 to 1991. (This public debt does not include debt incurred by individuals, corporations or state and local government.) The dollar amount added each year is not shown but it can be derived from the percentage change data. The per capita debt is calculated using the total population (children, adults, working, nonworking or retired) divided by the total debt. The total interest paid is the amount paid for the listed year either through taxes or through issuing new debt. The percentage of federal outlay is the proportion of each year's federal budget devoted to just paying interest on the outstanding debt.

Until recently a straight line regression equation seemed to explain trends in the national debt. It appears that a different regression function may be required for predicting short-term (5- to 10-year) debt trends.

DISCUSSION QUESTIONS

1. What would be the best way to construct a time-series analysis for the national debt data?
2. Comment on the debt patterns in terms of fluctuations caused by World War II and the Korean and Vietnam Conflicts.
3. Use only the data in Table 12-10 to forecast per capita debt for next year.
4. Use only the data in Table 12-10 to forecast federal interest payments during the year after next.

REAL-LIFE STATISTICAL CHALLENGE

TABLE 12-10 Federal Public Debt and Interest Paid, 1940–90

Year	Public Debt			Interest Paid	
	Total (billions)	Average Annual Percent Change	Per Capita	Total (billions)	Percent of Federal Outlay
1940	$ 43.0	8.4%	$ 325	$ 1.0	10.5%
1945	258.7	43.0	1,849	3.8	4.1
1950	256.1	− 0.1	1,688	5.7	13.4
1955	272.8	1.3	1,651	6.4	9.4
1960	284.1	0.9	1,572	9.2	10.0
1965	313.8	2.0	1,613	11.3	9.6
1970	370.1	3.3	1,814	19.3	9.9
1971	397.3	7.4	1,921	21.0	10.0
1972	426.4	7.3	2,037	21.8	9.4
1973	457.3	7.2	2,164	24.2	9.8
1974	474.2	3.7	2,223	29.3	10.9
1975	533.2	12.4	2,475	32.7	9.8
1976	620.4	16.4	2,852	37.1	10.0
1977	698.8	10.1	3,170	41.9	10.2
1978	771.5	10.4	3,463	48.7	10.6
1979	826.5	7.1	3,669	59.8	11.9
1980	907.7	9.8	3,985	74.9	12.7
1981	997.9	9.9	4,338	95.6	14.1
1982	1,142.0	14.4	4,913	117.4	15.7
1983	1,377.2	20.6	5,870	128.8	15.9
1984	1,572.3	14.2	6,640	153.8	18.1
1985	1,823.1	16.0	7,616	178.9	18.9
1986	2,125.3	16.6	8,793	187.1	18.9
1987	2,350.3	10.6	9,630	195.4	19.5
1988	2,602.3	10.9	10,556	214.1	20.1
1989	2,857.4	9.8	11,540	241.0	21.1
1990	3,233.3	13.2	13,000	264.9	21.2

Source: U.S. Department of Treasury and Bureau of the Census, 1991.

REVIEW EXERCISES

12-25 The following trend equation represents the demand for electricity by a particular city.

$$\hat{Y}(X) = 10{,}000 + 20X \text{ kilowatt-hours} \qquad (X = 0 \text{ at } 1979)$$

For each of the following years determine the demand trend level.
(a) 1991 (b) 1981 (c) 1986 (d) 1996

12-26 Find the missing values to complete the following quarterly sales data for ChipMont Corporation.

Quarter	Trend	Cyclical (%)	Seasonal (%)	Irregular (%)	Sales
Winter	$100,000	100		90	$ 99,000
Spring	200,000		80	100	168,000
Summer	300,000	110		110	
Fall	400,000	120	120		604,800

12-27 The following percentages of moving average values have been obtained for Speak E-Z sales of portable stereos.

	Quarter			
Year	Winter	Spring	Summer	Fall
1987			25	149
1988	125	98	36	145
1989	115	95	31	157
1990	108	106	29	148
1991	123	107	30	152
1992	120	101		

Determine the seasonal index for each quarter.

12-28 A CPA firm achieved the following number of new accounts.

Year	Number of New Accounts	Year	Number of New Accounts
1983	300	1988	417
1984	321	1989	464
1985	342	1990	488
1986	383	1991	495
1987	406	1992	531

(a) Determine the equation for the regression line using $X = 0$ at 1983.

(b) Forecast the number of new clients established in the following years.

(1) 1994 (2) 1999 (3) 2004

12-29 Refer to the new account data in Exercise 12-28. Apply two-parameter exponential smoothing to obtain the forecast number of new accounts for 1993. Use $\alpha = .2$ and $\gamma = .3$.

12-30 Albers, Crumbly, and Itch has experienced the following quarterly sales data (thousands) for bottles of Malabug, a mosquito repellent.

	1988	1989	1990	1991	1992
Winter	21	35	39	78	54
Spring	42	54	82	146	114
Summer	60	91	117	136	160
Fall	12	14	38	30	29
Total	135	194	276	390	357

(a) Determine the trend line regression equation using annual sales.
(b) Determine the trend level of sales for 1992.

12-31 Refer to the Malabug sales data in Exercise 12-30.
(a) Determine the seasonal index for each quarter.
(b) Plot the original time-series data and the four-quarter moving averages on a graph.

12-32 The trend for number of bottles of Malabug sold in any quarter is $\hat{Y}(X) = 35 + 3X$ ($X = 0$ at February 15, 1988) and the seasonal indexes are

Winter	60
Spring	120
Summer	180
Fall	40

Determine the quarterly forecasts and deseasonalize the data given in Exercise 12-30.

12-33 Determine the equation for the semilogarithmic trend line for the Malabug quarterly sales data given in Exercise 12-30. What sales level is forecast for Winter 1992?

12-34 WearEver Brake Linings has experienced the following quarterly sales data (millions of dollars).

1988	Winter	8.5	1989	Winter	9.5	1990	Winter	10.4
	Spring	10.4		Spring	12.2		Spring	13.5
	Summer	7.5		Summer	8.8		Summer	9.7
	Fall	11.8		Fall	13.6		Fall	13.1
1991	Winter	9.5	1992	Winter	10.9			
	Spring	11.7		Spring	13.7			
	Summer	8.4		Summer	10.1			
	Fall	12.9		Fall	15.0			

(a) Determine the four-quarter moving averages, centered moving averages, and percentages of moving averages.
(b) Determine the seasonal index for each quarter.
(c) Find the deseasonalized time-series data.
(d) Using your deseasonalized data in (c), determine the equation for the trend line for WearEver sales using least squares regression.
(e) Find the quarterly forecast sales levels for 1993.

12-35 Refer to the data in Exercise 12-34. Apply three-parameter exponential smoothing to determine forecast sales levels for 1993. Apply two-parameter exponential smoothing to obtain the forecast quarterly sales for 1993. Use $\alpha = .2$, $\beta = .5$, and $\gamma = .3$.

STATISTICS IN PRACTICE

12-36 *Investing in ketchup?* Heinz Corporation is well known for its food products line. Its yearly sales, net income and net income per common share for the years 1979 to 1991 are shown below.

(a) Plot the regression lines for $X = 0$ at 1979.
(b) Compare the slopes of the regression lines. Comment on any differences or similarities.
(c) Forecast the yearly sales, net income and net income per common share for the following years:

(1) 1993 (2) 1999 (3) 2005

Year	Sales (in thousands)	Net Income (in thousands)	Net Income per Common Share
1979	$2,470,883	$108,404	$0.79
1980	2,924,774	131,497	0.96
1981	3,568,889	160,827	0.58
1982	3,688,500	192,802	0.68
1983	3,738,445	214,250	0.75
1984	3,953,761	237,530	0.85
1985	4,047,945	265,978	0.96
1986	4,366,177	301,734	1.10
1987	4,639,486	338,506	1.24
1988	5,244,230	386,014	1.45
1989	5,800,877	440,230	1.67
1990	6,085,687	504,451	1.90
1991	6,647,118	567,999	2.13

Source: Heinz Corporation.

12-37 *Investing in industrial products?* Ingersoll-Rand Company manufactures a variety of industrial products. It is well known for its construction and mining equipment product lines. Its yearly sales, net income and net income per common share for the years 1981 to 1991 are shown below.

Year	Sales (in thousands)	Net Income (in thousands)	Net Income per Common Share
1981	$3,377,564	$193,338	$3.88
1982	2,774,725	52,271	0.94
1983	2,274,075	(112,166)	(2.38)
1984	2,478,120	58,895	1.08
1985	2,637,421	79,581	1.51
1986	2,799,481	93,874	1.79
1987	2,647,900	117,691	2.17
1988	3,021,352	161,588	3.00
1989	3,447,407	210,751	3.95
1990	3,737,847	185,343	3.55
1991	3,586,220	150,589	2.91

Source: Ingersoll-Rand Company.

(a) Plot the regression lines for $X = 0$ at 1981.
(b) Compare the slopes of the regression lines. Comment on any differences or similarities.
(c) Forecast the yearly sales, net income and net income per common share for the following years.

(1) 1993 (2) 1999 (3) 2005

12-38 *Investing in a local company?* Look up some recent annual reports for one of the larger publicly owned companies in your local community. Or, select a firm where you or a relative or friend works. List the yearly sales, net income and net income per common share for the past 10 to 15 years. (These reports are usually found at the reference desk of your library.)
(a) Plot regression lines using $X = 0$ for the first year in your data set.
(b) Compare the slopes of the regression lines. Comment on any differences or similarities.
(c) Forecast the yearly sales, net income and net income per common share in the following years.
(1) two years from the most recent report.
(2) five years.
(3) ten years.

12-39 *Seasonal patterns at Ingersoll-Rand.* The following table shows the quarterly sales data for Ingersoll-Rand Company for the years 1988 to 1991.

		Net Amounts (thousands)			Common Stock		
Year	Quarter	Sales	Earnings	Earnings per Share	High	Low	Dividend
1988	First	$711,035	$33,622	$0.62	$41.250	$31.000	$0.26
	Second	779,850	40,045	0.75	44.625	36.875	0.26
	Third	715,383	29,608	0.54	42.625	35.000	0.26
	Fourth	815,084	58,313	1.09	37.500	31.250	0.26
1989	First	801,779	49,207	0.93	39.875	33.625	0.26
	Second	907,402	52,356	0.98	44.750	37.125	0.30
	Third	845,256	44,348	0.82	49.875	41.000	0.30
	Fourth	892,970	64,840	1.22	50.250	40.875	0.30
1990	First	902,260	45,558	0.86	56.875	46.125	0.30
	Second	931,997	53,943	1.03	60.500	51.000	0.30
	Third	936,586	40,156	0.78	60.000	39.625	0.33
	Fourth	967,004	45,686	0.88	41.125	28.500	0.33
1991	First	864,193	28,438	0.55	53.750	35.000	0.33
	Second	922,578	32,769	0.63	53.750	44.000	0.33
	Third	865,547	34,681	0.67	53.125	44.750	0.33
	Fourth	933,902	54,701	1.06	55.000	42.125	0.33

Source: Ingersoll-Rand Company.

(a) Determine the four-quarter moving averages, centered moving averages, and percentages of moving averages.

(b) Determine the seasonal index for each quarter.
(c) Find the deseasonalized time series data.
(d) Using your deseasonalized data from (c), determine the equation for the trend line for Ingersoll-Rand using least squares regression.

12-40 Look up some recent annual or quarterly reports for one of the larger publicly owned companies in your local community. Or, select a firm where you or a relative or friend works. (These reports are usually found at library reference desks.) Use at least four years of quarterly data.
(a) Determine the four quarter moving averages, centered moving averages, and percentages of moving averages.
(b) Determine the seasonal index for each quarter.
(c) Find the deseasonalized time series data.
(d) Using your deseasonalized data in (c), determine the equation for the trend line for your local company using least squares regression.

12-41 Compare the results of the companies analyzed in Exercises 12-37 through 12-40. What similarities or differences did you observe?

12-42 *Trends in discount rates.* The following table shows the discount rate paid by the Federal Reserve Bank of New York from 1976 to 1991.

Effective Date	Rate per Year	Effective Date	Rate per Year	Effective Date	Rate per Year
Jan. 19, 1976	5.50%	Feb. 15, 1980	13.00%	Nov. 22, 1982	9.00%
Nov. 22, 1976	5.25	May 30, 1980	12.00	Dec. 15, 1982	8.50
Aug. 31, 1977	5.75	June 13, 1980	11.00	Apr. 9, 1984	9.00
Oct. 26, 1977	6.00	July 28, 1980	10.00	Nov. 21, 1984	8.50
Jan. 9, 1978	6.50	Sept. 26, 1980	11.00	Dec. 24, 1984	8.00
May 11, 1978	7.00	Nov. 17, 1980	12.00	May 20, 1985	7.50
July 3, 1978	7.25	Dec. 5, 1980	13.00	Mar. 7, 1986	7.00
Aug. 21, 1978	7.75	May 5, 1981	14.00	Apr. 21, 1986	6.50
Sept. 22, 1978	8.00	Nov. 2, 1981	13.00	July 11, 1986	6.00
Oct. 16, 1978	8.50	Dec. 4, 1981	12.00	Aug. 21, 1986	5.50
Nov. 1, 1978	9.50	July 20, 1982	11.50	Sept. 4, 1987	6.00
July 20, 1979	10.00	Aug. 2, 1982	11.00	Aug. 9, 1988	6.50
Aug. 17, 1979	10.50	Aug. 16, 1982	10.50	Feb. 24, 1989	7.00
Sept. 19, 1979	11.00	Aug. 27, 1982	10.00	Dec. 19, 1990	6.50
Oct. 8, 1979	12.00	Oct. 12, 1982	9.50	Feb. 1, 1991	6.00

Source: Board of Governors of the Federal Reserve System, Federal Reserve Bulletin, and Annual Statistical Digest. From The Universal Almanac, 1992

(a) What would be the best way to analyze this data?
(b) Carry out a time series analysis of the data.
Note: You can update the data by referring to such sources as *The Wall Street Journal* or *Business Week.*

CASE BugOff Chemical Company

BugOff Chemical Company is a manufacturer of environmentally safe pesticides that break down rapidly to harmless compounds. The leading product is BugaCider. BugOff also supplies other firms with a technical base used in formulating a variety of specialty chemical pesticides.

The following annual data (thousands of gallons) apply to the number of bottles of BugaCider sold.

	Quarter				
Year	Winter	Spring	Summer	Fall	Total
1987	18	80	30	22	150
1988	24	105	54	27	210
1989	33	141	48	38	260
1990	40	150	75	45	310
1991	35	180	55	50	320
1992	48	205	70	57	380

For planning purposes, management wants to make detailed forecasts of 1993 quarterly sales. Management also wants to make short-range and long-range annual forecasts.

The total national production of the interchangeable technical base products has been determined by an industry trade association. The following data (thousands of gallons) have been provided.

Year	Production Quantity	Year	Production Quantity
1983	587	1988	1,639
1984	648	1989	2,059
1985	815	1990	2,655
1986	1,050	1991	3,050
1987	1,359	1992	3,546

QUESTIONS

1. Determine the seasonal indexes for the BugaCider sales data.
2. Deseasonalized sales values for any given quarter may be found by dividing actual sales by the seasonal index. Determine, for each quarter, the deseasonalized BugaCider sales values.
3. Determine the regression trend line for annual BugaCider sales. Use your regression line to predict sales for (a) 1993, (b) 1997, and (c) 2002.
4. Using your above forecast for 1993 sales, apply the seasonal indexes from Question 1 to make BugaCider sales forecasts for each quarter in 1993.

5. An alternative procedure is to use seasonal exponential smoothing. Determine BugOff's forecast BugaCider quarterly sales for 1993 using $\alpha = .5$, $\gamma = .5$, and $\beta = .5$. Compute the *MSE*.

6. Compare your answers to Questions 4 and 5. Which procedure do you prefer? Explain.

7. Exponential smoothing may be used to forecast future production levels of the technical base. For the following smoothing parameters, use the actual data to determine the forecast values. Compute the *MSE*. Which set appears to best fit the actual data?
(a) $\alpha = .20$; $\gamma = .40$ (b) $\alpha = .30$; $\gamma = .30$

8. BugOff management assumes that its 40% share of the technical market will be maintained. Using the better set of parameters from Question 7, forecast the 1993 industry production quantity. From that quantity, determine BugOff's forecast technical chemical sales for 1993.

CHAPTER 13

STATISTICAL QUALITY CONTROL

BEFORE READING THIS CHAPTER, MAKE SURE YOU UNDERSTAND:

The types of statistical data (Chapter 1).
How to describe and display data (Chapter 2).
How to summarize data (Chapter 3).
The basic concepts of statistical estimation (Chapter 9).
The basic concepts of hypothesis testing (Chapter 10).

AFTER READING THIS CHAPTER, YOU WILL UNDERSTAND:

About statistical quality control.
The basic types of control charts.
How to use a control chart to trigger remedial action.
About acceptance sampling and how to use it.
How acceptance sampling relates to hypothesis testing.
About sequential sampling and how to use it.

In recent years, **statistical quality control** has been growing in importance. This is largely due to the role quality control plays in manufacturing, becoming increasingly significant with mushrooming international trade. These same statistical procedures have always been important in nonproduction applications—in services, retail, and transportation—as well as in the public sector. This chapter focuses on the two groupings of statistical methods for quality control.

Acceptance sampling involves items or services supplied externally. The goal of acceptance sampling is to determine whether individual batches and shipments should be accepted or rejected. The procedures consider the existing *items* themselves. Any difficulties with their creation are not directly addressed.

The second area of statistical quality control focuses on the *creation* of end products, either goods or services. These applications involve the *process* by which the goods are created or services are rendered. Managers monitor such processes by means of **statistical controls**, which are applied continuously during various stages of production or service.

The foundation has been laid in earlier chapters for understanding statistical quality control. The methods are based on familiar descriptive statistics, including the *sample mean*, *range*, *proportion*, and *standard deviation*. Parallel procedures apply to quantitative and qualitative data.

13-1 THE CONTROL CHART FOR QUALITATIVE DATA

Production applications are historically the main source of statistical quality control procedures. The methods help managers fine tune production processes through early detection of problems, followed by quick remedies. Successfully employed, modern statistical controls prevent the creation of defective goods, perhaps avoiding the manufacture of thousands of items that would eventually be scrapped. At least as significant, statistical controls provide a framework that fosters the systematic search for improvements of both the end products and the process whereby they are created.

Statistical control is achieved by establishing limits within which observed units should fall; corrective actions are generated automatically whenever too many items fall outside these bounds. A *sample* becomes the device that triggers those remedial actions. The limits must be wide enough to compensate for any *chance variation* that would be expected to arise naturally even under perfect circumstances. At the same time, the limits must be narrow enough so that samples do not become "hairpin" triggers which generate false signals of nonexisting problems.

When a sample falls outside the prescribed limits, the control procedure flags the results to signal that the violators may arise from some *assignable cause*. Good follow-up action then involves a thorough search for the problem source. Common assignable causes include equipment malfunctions, operator errors, poor materials, and external disturbances. Appropriate remedies include adjusting equipment controls, improving the working atmosphere, changing suppliers, and stabilizing the plant environment.

The instrument used to accomplish this monitorship is the **control chart**. Control charts may be based either on quantitative data or on qualitative data. The following illustration will demonstrate the latter.

ESTABLISHING CONTROL LIMITS FOR THE PROPORTION

ILLUSTRATION: DEFECTIVE DISKETTES

The quality assurance manager for a diskette manufacturer requested that a sample of $n = 1{,}000$ units be taken from each day's production run. There are many reasons why a diskette may prove unacceptable, such as poor casing, thin spots, or unevenness in ferrite layering. Rather than keeping track of each cause, the inspectors were asked to determine whether each sample diskette was defective or satisfactory. During the month of October, the data in Table 13-1 were obtained.

The data are plotted in Figure 13-1, with one dot representing each daily sample. Note that the dots oscillate around a central value. This is the **combined proportion defective $\bar{P}$.** The quantity is calculated by combining all 31 samples into one group, so that, for the composite sample, the proportion defective is

$$\bar{P} = \frac{\text{Combined number of defectives}}{\text{Combined sample size}} = \frac{2{,}126}{31{,}000} = .0686$$

In a general sense, sample proportions P generated under this procedure are random variables, each having a binominal distribution with parameters n and π. The true value of the population proportion π remains unknown. That parameter may be estimated from the sample results.

The procedure described here assumes that π remains *constant* for each successive sample observation as long as the process is *in control.*

As the scatter of the data in Figure 13-1 suggests, the observed P's vary from

TABLE 13-1 Sample Data for Disk Production

Day	Number of Defectives	Proportion Defective P	Day	Number of Defectives	Proportion Defective P
10/01	52	.052	10/17	82	.082
2	81	.081	18	72	.072
3	76	.076	19	47	.047
4	48	.048	20	65	.065
5	66	.066	21	62	.062
6	115	.115	22	48	.048
7	122	.122	23	47	.047
8	61	.061	24	51	.051
9	144	.144	25	63	.063
10	65	.065	26	67	.067
11	73	.073	27	66	.066
12	51	.051	28	49	.049
13	68	.068	29	74	.074
14	47	.047	30	76	.076
15	52	.052	31	55	.055
16	81	.081		2,126	

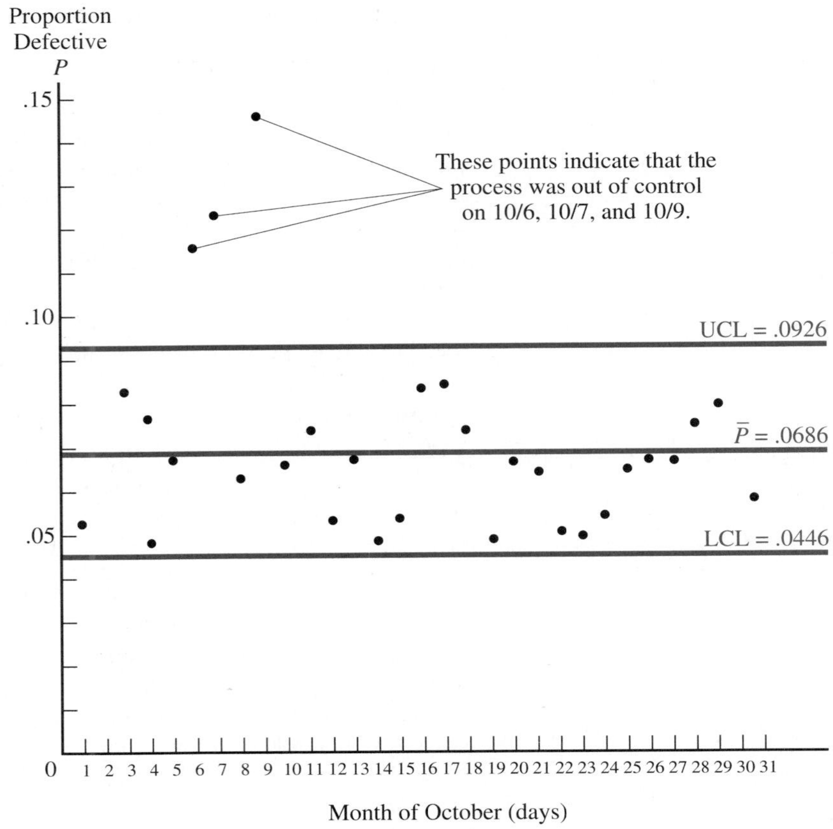

FIGURE 13-1 Preliminary control chart for proportion of defective diskettes.

one observation to the next. We summarize this variability in terms of the standard error of P, the theoretical value of which is

$$\sigma_P = \sqrt{\frac{\pi(1 - \pi)}{n}}$$

Using $\bar{P}$ as the estimator of π, the above quantity may be estimated from the expression

$$\sqrt{\frac{\bar{P}(1 - \bar{P})}{n}}$$

The above expression is used to establish the **control limits** that determine whether or not the process is in statistical control. For this purpose 3-*sigma limits* are popular. That choice follows from a key property of the normal curve stating that about 99.7% of the possible values will lie within $\mu \pm 3\sigma$. For large n's, since the normal distribution approximates the binomial, a similar percentage of possible values for P should fall within $\pi \pm 3\sigma_P$. It would be extremely rare for a sample P to fall outside those limits when π is the true level of the population proportion.

But the true value of π, and hence σ_P, remains unknown. Also, π may shift to abnormally high levels, at which time the process needs remedial action. The control chart is designed to detect those critical periods. Substituting $\bar{P}$ for π and using the estimated σ_P given above, we will use the following expressions to compute the 3-sigma

CONTROL LIMITS FOR THE PROPORTION DEFECTIVE

$$\text{LCL} = \bar{P} - 3\sqrt{\frac{\bar{P}(1-\bar{P})}{n}}$$

$$\text{UCL} = \bar{P} + 3\sqrt{\frac{\bar{P}(1-\bar{P})}{n}}$$

The abbreviation LCL denotes the **lower control limit**, and UCL denotes the **upper control limit**. We define the process as "out of control" whenever the computed value of P lies above the UCL or below the LCL. If the computed value of the LCL is negative, that limit is set to zero.

Using the data from our diskette sampling illustration, we compute the following control limits.

$$\begin{aligned}\text{LCL} &= .0686 - 3\sqrt{\frac{.0686(1-.0686)}{1{,}000}}\\ &= .0686 - 3(.0080)\\ &= .0446\end{aligned}$$

and

$$\begin{aligned}\text{UCL} &= .0686 + 3(.0080)\\ &= .0926\end{aligned}$$

In Figure 13-1, these limits are represented by the colored horizontal lines on the control chart.

APPLYING THE CONTROL CHART

Note the three points in Figure 13-1 that lie above the UCL. These points are .115 (October 6), .122 (October 7), and .144 (October 9). We assume that the production process was out of control on those dates. Those problems went undetected until the above control limits were established. (Subsequent investigations show that key personnel were absent on those dates.)

Out-of-control data points ideally should be eliminated from the underlying data base before the control chart is used in actual production decisions. Figure 13-2 shows the revised control chart used to monitor diskette production during the following month of November. The recomputed value of the combined proportion defective is $\bar{P} = 1{,}745/28{,}000 = .0623$. The corresponding new control limits are LCL = .0394 and UCL = .0852.

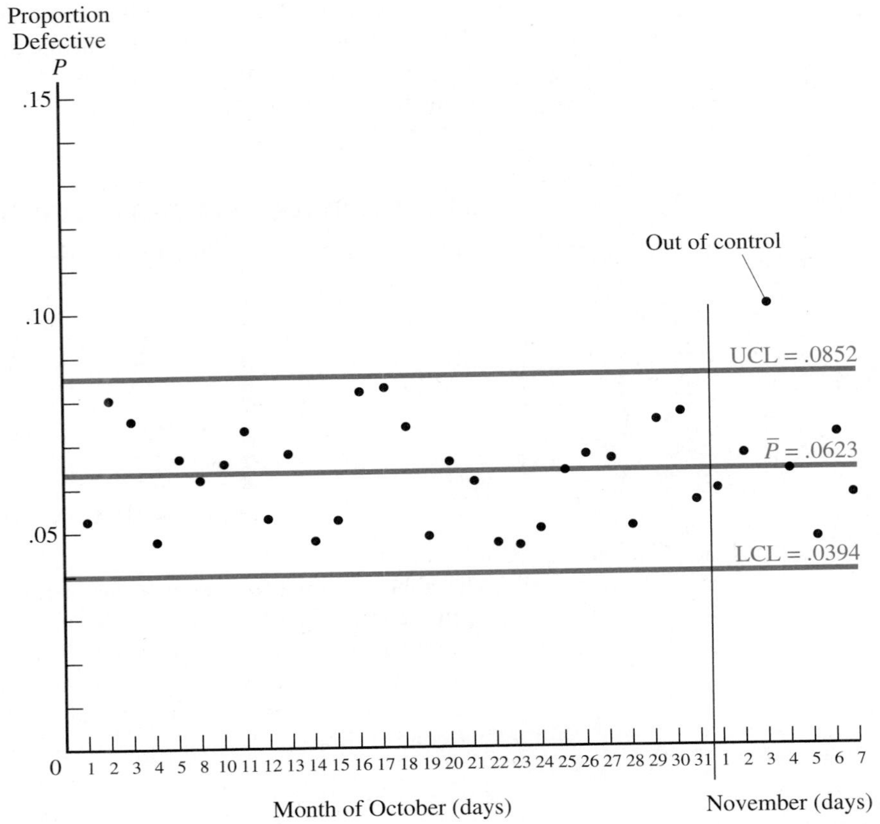

FIGURE 13-2 Final control chart for proportion of defective diskettes.

During the first week in November, the following observations were made.

Day	Proportion Defective P	Signaled Status
11/01	.058	in control
2	.071	in control
3	.098	out of control
4	.063	in control
5	.047	in control
6	.071	in control
7	.058	in control

The sample result for November 3 signaled that an abnormally high proportion of defective diskettes had been produced. A thorough investigation showed that the ferrite compound was contaminated by impurities. To avoid repetitions, improved storage was implemented for all critical materials.

FURTHER REMARKS

It may seem curious that an LCL even exists for the proportion defective. After all, are not low levels of P desirable? Usually, that is the case and zero is often set as the LCL, so that the statistical procedure becomes one-sided. But abnormally low levels of P may also arise from problems in need of fixing. Low P's may result from much more expensive care than originally intended. Or, they may signify a breakdown in the inspection process itself, with too many defects going undetected. And, some undiscovered *improvement* to the process may be uncovered when investigating the cause for a low P.

The traditional 3-sigma limits are intended to provide an optimal balance between triggering excessive false alarms and letting a poor-quality operation continue undetected. A better balance may be achieved with narrower limits (say, 2-sigma) or with wider ones. The issue is analogous to the tradeoff between the Type I error (unnecessarily searching for nonexistent assignable causes when the violation is just due to chance) and the Type II error (letting an out-of-control process continue uncorrected).

EXERCISES

13-1 Determine the LCL and UCL for each of the following situations.

(a) $\bar{P} = .10$; $n = 500$ (c) $\bar{P} = .05$; $n = 1{,}000$
(b) $\bar{P} = .20$; $n = 100$ (d) $\bar{P} = .075$; $n = 200$

13-2 Ace Widgets obtained the following numbers of defectives in successive samples of 1,000 deluxe models removed at random from that day's production.

Day	Number of Defectives	Day	Number of Defectives
6/11	86	6/21	115
12	47	22	82
13	67	23	73
14	54	24	66
15	60	25	75
16	49	26	55
17	66	27	71
18	49	28	128
19	79	29	49
20	70	30	62

(a) Determine the 3-sigma control limits for the sample proportion defective. Plot your results and the above data on a chart.
(b) Identify any days on which the production process was out of control.
(c) Remove the violators from the data base and recompute the control limits. For each of the following numbers of defectives selected from a sample of $n = 1{,}000$, indicate whether the process is in control or out of control.
(1) 86 (2) 112 (3) 48 (4) 125 (5) 98

13-3 DanDee Assemblers obtained the following numbers of defectives in successive samples of 100 final assemblies removed at random from that day's production.

Day	Number of Defectives	Day	Number of Defectives
8/11	6	8/21	11
12	8	22	8
13	7	23	13
14	10	24	14
15	11	25	15
16	5	26	12
17	13	27	7
18	9	28	34
19	9	29	28
20	10	30	8

(a)–(b) Repeat Exercise 13-2.

(c) Remove the violators from the data base and recompute the control limits. For each of the following numbers of defectives selected from a sample of $n = 100$, indicate whether the process was found to be in control or out of control.

(1) 5 (2) 29 (3) 7 (4) 10 (5) 17

13-4 Refer to the data in Table 13-1. Determine the 2-sigma control limits for the sample proportion. Indicate on which days the process was out of control.

13-5 Repeat Exercise 13-3 using 2-sigma control limits instead.

13-6 Refer to the diskette production illustration. Determine the probability that on any given day the process will be in control with the first set of limits when each of the following true population proportion defective applies. Use the normal approximation.

(a) $\pi = .10$ (b) $\pi = .05$ (c) $\pi = .08$ (d) $\pi = .06$

13-2 THE CONTROL CHART FOR QUANTITATIVE DATA

Process quality may be assessed in terms of some *quantity*, such as service time, volume, weight, strength, or yield. Analogous to the *P*-chart described in Section 13-1, a control chart may be constructed for quantitative data. Since central tendency and variability are both important considerations in such evaluations, separate control charts monitor each.

The most common control charts are based on the *sample mean*. Control charts for monitoring variability may be based either on the *sample range* or the *sample standard deviation*. Anyone who has taken a statistics course should be familiar with the standard deviation, but for those with little statistical background, the underlying concepts may be hard to handle. Thus, it is more common to see control charts based on the sample range; the type we will present in this chapter.

Statistical control procedures are more elaborate when using quantitative data. Since quantitative data provide a higher degree of information, the procedures are more sensitive than the *P*-charts. This allows for inspection schemes with smaller *n*s, which, in turn, permit quicker identification of assignable causes for process abnormalities. We will use the following example to illustrate the procedure.

ILLUSTRATION: MONITORING FILLING CONTROLS

As with others in the food processing business, Boxwell House must adhere to truth in labeling laws. Most critical are weights and measures of ingredients. Although it is unlikely that any particular one-pound jar of instant coffee will contain precisely 16 ounces, Boxwell House's objective is to come very close to that target.

To launch a quality control scheme for monitoring the contents weights, the Boxwell House superintendent requested that a sample of $n = 5$ jars be removed from production and the contents carefully weighed. Each half hour over a portion of a day's production operation the data in Table 13-2 were obtained. From the results given, the superintendent implemented a statistical control system designed to meet two objectives: (1) *mean* weight per jar should be close to the labeled 16 ounces and (2) *variability* in contents weights should not be excessive.

The procedure, described here, uses two triggers for corrective action. These are the computed values for the sample mean $\bar{X}$ and the sample range R. The data in Table 13-2 is used to establish control limits for these. During this initial phase, the filling process is assumed to be in control.

The Boxwell House data are plotted in Figure 13-3. The chart in Figure 13-3(a) was constructed using the sample means $\bar{X}$ and serves to gauge shifts in the filling process mean μ. Chart (b) in Figure 13-3 was constructed using the sample ranges R and serves to detect shifts in the process variability.

The procedure for constructing the control charts in Figure 13-3 is similar to that used for the P-chart.

TABLE 13-2 Sample Contents Weights Data for One-Pound Jars of Instant Coffee

Sample	Contents Weight (ounces)					Mean $\bar{X}$	Range R
1	15.75	16.12	16.22	15.87	16.22	16.036	0.47
2	16.23	16.35	16.11	16.48	15.90	16.214	0.58
3	15.88	15.95	16.07	16.33	16.05	16.056	0.45
4	16.67	15.60	16.22	15.65	15.71	15.970	1.07
5	15.56	15.82	15.95	15.76	15.82	15.782	0.39
6	16.20	16.35	16.05	15.90	16.11	16.122	0.45
7	15.88	16.22	16.35	15.71	15.88	16.008	0.64
8	16.10	16.25	16.05	16.11	15.90	16.082	0.35
9	15.70	15.55	16.08	16.21	15.72	15.852	0.66
10	16.15	16.16	16.34	15.88	15.80	16.066	0.54
11	16.22	16.08	16.07	15.55	15.72	15.928	0.67
12	15.66	15.78	16.22	15.85	15.91	15.884	0.56
13	16.44	15.71	15.93	16.12	16.10	16.060	0.73
14	16.21	16.34	16.05	15.87	15.61	16.016	0.73
15	15.55	15.78	15.82	15.60	16.24	15.798	0.69
16	16.05	16.22	16.28	15.90	15.85	16.060	0.43
17	16.10	16.08	15.70	15.82	16.12	15.964	0.42
18	15.67	15.91	15.88	16.10	15.84	15.880	0.43
19	15.95	15.81	16.12	16.07	15.64	15.918	0.48
20	16.04	16.29	16.18	15.76	15.99	16.052	0.53
						319.748	11.27

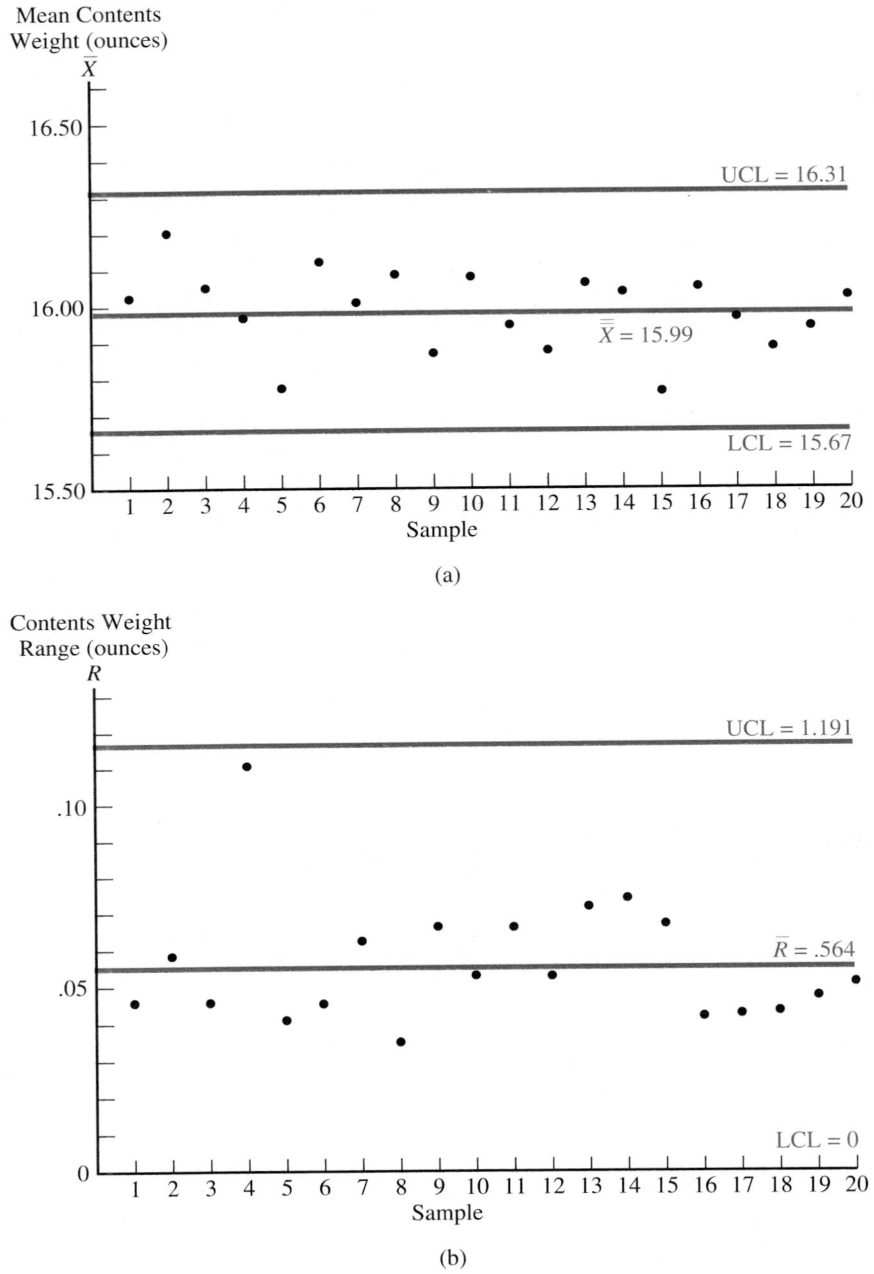

FIGURE 13-3 Control charts for contents weights of jars of instant coffee.

THE CONTROL CHART FOR THE SAMPLE MEAN

As with the *P*-chart, the sample results are pooled, so that an overall average, the **grand mean** $\bar{\bar{X}}$ is obtained. This value serves as the estimator of the underlying population mean. The computed value of $\bar{\bar{X}}$ establishes the center line of the

$\bar{X}$-chart, with individual sample means oscillating about this central value. For our instant coffee sample data we calculate

$$\bar{\bar{X}} = \frac{319.748}{20} = 15.99 \text{ ounces}$$

The process mean μ is estimated to be 15.99 ounces per jar of instant coffee, so that the center line of the $\bar{X}$-chart in Figure 13-3(a) is placed at a height of 15.99.

As with the P-chart, 3-sigma limits must be found to obtain the LCL and UCL for $\bar{X}$. Although earlier in this book we consistently used the sample standard deviation s to estimate the population standard deviation σ, the traditional quality control procedures are based instead on the sample range R. Using R's to estimate σ proves to be easier from an operational point of view and provides nearly identical results.

Using the **overall mean range** $\bar{R}$, the following expression computes the

ESTIMATED POPULATION STANDARD DEVIATION

$$\hat{\sigma} = \frac{\bar{R}}{d_R}$$

where the **range conversion constant** d_R is read from Appendix Table M.

For the Boxwell House data, the computed mean of the sample ranges is

$$\bar{R} = \frac{11.27}{20} = .5635$$

Using $n = 5$ as the individual sample size, Appendix Table M provides the range conversion constant $d_R = 2.326$. We then compute the estimated standard deviation to be

$$\hat{\sigma} = \frac{.5635}{2.326} = .242$$

To establish the 3-sigma control limits, the standard error of $\bar{X}$ is estimated by $\hat{\sigma}/\sqrt{n}$. The following expressions provide the

CONTROL LIMITS FOR THE SAMPLE MEAN

$$\text{LCL} = \bar{\bar{X}} - 3\frac{\hat{\sigma}}{\sqrt{n}} \qquad \text{UCL} = \bar{\bar{X}} + 3\frac{\hat{\sigma}}{\sqrt{n}}$$

For our instant coffee sample results, the above expressions provide

$$\text{LCL} = 15.99 - 3\left(\frac{.242}{\sqrt{5}}\right) = 15.99 - .32 = 15.67 \text{ ounces}$$

$$\text{UCL} = 15.99 + .32 = 16.31 \text{ ounces}$$

The above are plotted as colored horizontal lines in Figure 13-3(a).

THE CONTROL CHART FOR THE SAMPLE RANGE

An analogous procedure is used to find the control limits for successive R's. The following expression computes the

ESTIMATED STANDARD ERROR OF THE SAMPLE RANGE

$$\hat{\sigma}_R = \bar{R}\,\frac{\sigma_w}{d_R}$$

where the **standard deviation conversion constant** σ_w expresses the ratio of the true level for σ_R to the actual population standard deviation σ. Like d_R, this quantity varies with n and is read from Appendix Table M.

Applying the above expression to the Boxwell House instant coffee data when $n = 5$, Appendix Table M provides a value for σ_w of .8641. Using this value and the quantity $d_R = 2.326$ found earlier, we compute the estimated standard error of R to be

$$\hat{\sigma}_R = .5635\left(\frac{.8641}{2.326}\right) = .209$$

The following expressions are used to compute the 3-sigma

CONTROL LIMITS FOR THE SAMPLE RANGE

$$\text{LCL} = \bar{R} - 3\hat{\sigma}_R \qquad \text{UCL} = \bar{R} + 3\hat{\sigma}_R$$

As with P, the LCL is set to zero whenever the computed lower limit is negative.

Returning to the Boxwell House instant coffee data, the following control limits (rounded to three figures) were obtained.

$$\text{LCL} = .564 - 3(.209) = .564 - .627 = -.063 \quad \text{or} \quad 0 \text{ ounces}$$

$$\text{UCL} = .564 + .627 = 1.191 \text{ ounces}$$

These are plotted as colored horizontal lines in Figure 13-3(b), with the center line located at a height equal to the computed mean of the sample ranges, $\bar{R} = .5635$.

IMPLEMENTING STATISTICAL CONTROL

The Boxwell House superintendent implemented the statistical control procedure over several days. From the first 300 half-hourly samples of one-pound jars, $\bar{X}$ exceeded the UCL three times and fell below twice. Assignable causes included defective control mechanisms, blocked laser beams, and lumps in the coffee granules. The latter problem was traced to excessive moisture in the holding vats; a problem remedied by repairing a broken dehumidifier. In three samples, the level of R exceeded the UCL. Assignable causes included oversized coffee crystals, a damaged timer, and operator error. The problem of oversized crystals was remedied by incorporating sifting into the final processing.

Most of the problems identified by the statistical controls were fixed immediately. The more permanent solutions led to further refinements in the filling process and to some improvements in the final product itself. Without the quality management capability provided by the control charts, the problems would have been discovered and corrected much later, and tens of thousands of undersized or oversized jars would have gone to market. The superintendent was so pleased with the success of the statistical controls that he implemented them in the roasting and separating processes for making the product itself.

EXERCISES

13-7 For each of the following situations, determine the LCL and UCL for the (1) sample mean $\bar{X}$ and (2) sample range R.

(a) $\bar{\bar{X}} = .20$; $\bar{R} = .050$; $n = 10$
(b) $\bar{\bar{X}} = 5.80$; $\bar{R} = .55$; $n = 5$
(c) $\bar{\bar{X}} = .002$; $\bar{R} = .005$; $n = 4$
(d) $\bar{\bar{X}} = 1.25$; $\bar{R} = .17$; $n = 7$

13-8 The Boxwell House superintendent obtained the following sample results during the initial phase of the control system for the coffee filling process.

Sample	Contents Weight (ounces)				
1	15.85	16.21	15.91	16.08	16.12
2	15.51	16.10	16.76	15.85	15.92
3	16.21	16.55	16.62	16.68	16.50
4	15.62	15.94	15.72	15.55	15.64
5	15.74	16.21	16.05	16.01	16.17

(a) Calculate the mean and range for each sample.
(b) Using the control limits in Figure 13-3, indicate, for each sample, whether the process is in control or out of control.

13-9 The Boxwell House superintendent introduced statistical controls for five-pound cans of ground coffee. The following sample data were obtained.

Sample	Contents Weight (pounds)			
1	4.85	5.27	5.35	5.09
2	4.62	4.35	4.55	4.62
3	4.95	5.11	5.12	4.88
4	4.69	4.80	5.20	5.15
5	5.64	5.75	5.41	5.64
6	4.78	5.21	5.09	4.85
7	4.22	5.05	5.55	4.84
8	5.12	5.07	5.05	4.95
9	5.11	5.08	4.91	4.89
10	4.79	5.10	5.17	4.95

(a) Calculate the mean and range for each sample. Then calculate the grand mean and overall mean range.

(b) Determine the control limits for $\bar{X}$ and construct the control chart, plotting the data point for each sample. Indicate which, if any, of the samples were generated when the process was out of control.

(c) Determine the control limits for R and construct the control chart, plotting the data point for each sample. Indicate which, if any, of the samples were generated when the process was out of control.

(d) Eliminate the samples where the process was found to be out of control in either (a) or (b). Determine revised control limits for (1) $\bar{X}$ and (2) R.

13-10 The following sample data were obtained for the thickness (millimeters) of aluminum sheets.

Sample	Thickness				
1	4.9	5.1	4.9	5.0	4.9
2	4.9	4.7	5.1	5.2	5.1
3	4.8	5.0	4.9	5.0	5.0
4	5.1	4.8	4.8	4.9	4.6
5	4.8	5.0	5.2	4.5	4.9
6	5.3	4.8	4.9	5.1	4.6
7	4.7	5.3	4.9	5.1	5.2
8	5.3	4.9	4.9	4.8	5.0
9	5.3	5.2	5.2	4.9	4.9
10	5.0	5.0	5.1	5.0	5.1
11	4.9	4.8	4.6	4.9	5.1
12	5.3	5.4	5.4	5.4	5.3
13	5.5	5.2	5.3	5.4	5.2
14	4.7	5.2	5.1	5.0	5.1
15	5.0	4.7	4.9	5.2	4.9
16	5.1	4.9	5.2	5.0	4.9
17	5.0	5.0	4.8	4.8	4.9
18	4.9	4.4	5.4	5.0	5.1
19	4.8	4.8	5.2	5.1	5.0
20	4.8	5.1	4.9	5.2	5.0
21	5.2	4.8	5.2	5.2	5.2
22	4.8	4.8	4.9	5.2	5.2
23	5.0	4.9	5.1	4.7	4.6
24	5.0	5.0	4.9	5.0	5.1
25	4.8	5.0	4.8	4.7	4.9

Repeat Exercise 13-9(a)–(d).

13-11 Assume that the control limits for the sample mean (page 614) apply to one-pound jars of Boxwell House instant coffee. Determine the probability that a particular sample mean $\bar{X}$ will flag the process as out of control when the true mean jar contents is represented by a population with the following values.

(a) $\mu = 16.1$; $\sigma = .3$
(b) $\mu = 15.8$; $\sigma = .2$
(c) $\mu = 16.0$; $\sigma = .25$
(d) $\mu = 15.6$; $\sigma = .4$

13-3 ACCEPTANCE SAMPLING

The second major area of statistical quality control is acceptance sampling. The primary focus of these applications is to determine how to dispose of items that have already been provided by a supplier. The main consideration is the **lot**, which is the underlying statistical population with unknown parameters. A lot is either a production batch (such as subassemblies to be inserted into the main units), a shipment (such as logic chips for computer mother boards), or a grouping of rendered services (such as tax returns prepared by a CPA).

One of two actions may be taken in acceptance sampling: to *accept* the lot or to *reject* it. These actions are predicated on the assumption that the lot is *good* or *bad*. A rejected lot may be returned to the supplier (a typical action with raw materials), be scrapped or reworked (often the case with assembled units), or serve as the basis for extracting contractual penalties (the case with batches of already-rendered services).

Ordinarily, acceptance sampling is conducted when it is uneconomic or impractical to use census data. The underlying concepts of the procedure were encountered earlier, in Chapter 9, with the introduction of hypothesis testing. We will review some of those concepts here, in the context of quality control.

BASIC CONCEPTS OF ACCEPTANCE SAMPLING

Inspected items from a lot are classified as either *satisfactory* or *defective*. These designations apply even when the observations themselves are quantitative, so that a defective item may be so classified because it is too heavy, it could not meet a minimal strength, or it failed to survive an endurance test. A working definition of a good lot is one that has a low proportion of defectives n. Although the level of π remains unknown, various values are assumed when selecting statistical *decision rules*. As discussed earlier, although such rules are based on the sample proportion P, traditional acceptance sampling procedures are based on the number of sample defectives D. Decision rules are then distinguished by the pivotal level for the number of sample defectives. This is the **acceptance number**, denoted by C. The decision rule is of the form

Accept the lot if $D \leq C$
Reject the lot if $D > C$

The decision structure may be explained in terms of the more general hypothesis-testing procedures. The *null hypothesis* is that the lot is good, so that the true proportion of defectives is low and $\pi \leq \pi_0$, while the *alternative hypothesis* is that the proportion is high and $\pi > \pi_0$. The quantity π_0 is the **acceptable quality level** and serves as a benchmark for selecting an appropriate decision rule.

Accepting or rejecting the lot is analogous to accepting or rejecting the null hypothesis. Correct actions will be to accept good lots and reject bad ones. Of course, good lots may be rejected and bad lots may be accepted. These are analogous to the Type I and Type II errors.

PRODUCER'S AND CONSUMER'S RISK

The Type I error of a customer rejecting a good lot is the most undesirable from the supplier's point of view. The probability for this error is referred to as the **producer's risk**. The Type II error of accepting a bad lot is least desired by the customer and is referred to as the **consumer's risk**. Of course the supplier wants to avoid both types of errors. There is no long-term advantage in having customers accept bad shipments, since they would then be stuck with excessive defectives and may switch suppliers.

SELECTING THE DECISION RULE

The decision rule, or choice of C, is determined in such a way that the Type I error probability meets the prescribed *significance level* α. The following expression applies.

$$\Pr[\textit{Reject } H_0 | H_0 \text{ true}] = \Pr[D > C | \pi = \pi_0] \leq \alpha$$

The binomial distribution is used to establish the level of C that achieves this specification. (Keep in mind that for lots of fixed size N and when sampling without replacement, the *hypergeometric distribution* provides the correct probabilities for D. But since that distribution is computationally so cumbersome, the binomial distribution is used to *approximate* those probabilities, usually with accuracy.)

ILLUSTRATION: ACCEPTANCE SAMPLING IN A CANNERY

Yellow Giant uses acceptance sampling to determine whether incoming truckloads should be accepted and emptied directly into washing bins or rejected and sent to a sorting area. Since the grower must pay for the labor involved, the penalty for rejecting a truckload is substantial.

Inspectors classify individual asparagus spears as satisfactory or defective, depending on ripeness, damage, infestation, and rot. Yellow Giant's acceptable quality level for the proportion π of defective asparagus is $\pi_0 = .01$. This level was negotiated with the growers and represents a reasonable quality standard. The contractual sampling scheme is based on a random sample of $n = 100$ spears from each truckload. The agreed acceptance number C guarantees the growers that no more than 5% of good loads (having a true π equal to π_0) will be incorrectly rejected, so that $\alpha = .05$. This level for α is also a negotiated target which reflects grower reluctance to have good shipments rejected unnecessarily. From Appendix Table C, the closest probability not exceeding .05 is

$$\Pr[D > 3] = 1 - .9816 = .0184$$

so that $C = 3$ is the asparagus acceptance number.

A different decision rule applies to sugar beets, for which the acceptable quality level is $\pi_0 = .05$. Using the same sample size and significance level, the closest binomial probability not exceeding .05 is

$$\Pr[D > 9] = 1 - .9718 = .0282$$

so that $C = 9$ is the sugar beet acceptance number.

Decisions made with the above values of C allow for some chance of the Type II error, arising whenever a poor shipment is accepted. Type II error probabilities may be determined for levels of π greater than the acceptable quality level. In the case of asparagus, Appendix Table C provides the following values.

$$\Pr[accept|\text{poor}] = \Pr[D \le 3|\pi = .05] = .2578$$

$$\Pr[accept|\text{poor}] = \Pr[D \le 3|\pi = .10] = .0078$$

The decision rules give Yellow Giant fair protection from accepting somewhat bad shipments. As the true level of π increases, the probability for accepting the poorer-quality loads decreases dramatically.

SEQUENTIAL SAMPLING

The acceptance sampling process can be based on more than one sample, so that the procedure involves **sequential sampling**. A succession of samples is taken and a decision is made each time to either (1) accept the lot, (2) reject the lot, or (3) continue sampling. The decision rule involves an **acceptance number** A_n and a **rejection number** R_n, where the subscript n represents the *cumulative* sample size. The chart in Figure 13-4 shows Yellow Giant's sequential sampling plan for truckloads of cherries. The results obtained from a particular load have also been plotted on the chart.

Sequential sampling schemes tend to be more efficient than single-sample plans. For specified Type I and Type II error probability targets, sequential sam-

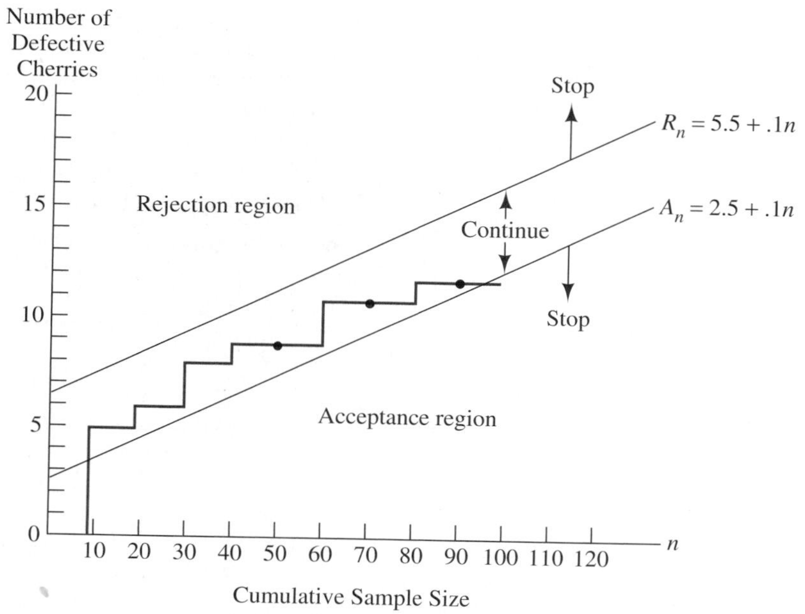

FIGURE 13-4 Sequential sampling scheme and sample results for Yellow Giant cherries.

pling tends to use fewer sample observations. That advantage comes at a steep price—a far more elaborate procedure must be used. A detailed discussion of sequential sampling is beyond the scope of this book. The selected references section of the book lists additional sources of information.

EXERCISES

13-12 A sample of $n = 50$ items is taken from a lot containing 10,000. Assuming an acceptable quality level of .10, use the binomial approximation to determine the acceptance number when the following values apply.
(a) $\alpha = .01$ (b) $\alpha = .05$ (c) $\alpha = .10$

13-13 Repeat Exercise 13-12, assuming a sample size of $n = 100$.

13-14 Repeat Exercise 13-12, assuming an acceptable quality level of .05.

13-15 Refer to the Yellow Giant acceptance sampling procedure for sugar beets. Determine the probability that a poor quality shipment will be accepted given that the true proportion defective is
(a) $\pi = .10$ (b) $\pi = .20$ (c) $\pi = .30$

13-16 A Midget Motors quality assurance inspector sets .10 as the acceptable quality level for outside-supplied spring locks. Each incoming shipment will be assessed using a random sample of $n = 20$.
(a) Assuming a significance level of .10, determine the acceptance number.
(b) Indicate for each of the following results whether the incoming shipment should be accepted or rejected.
(1) $D = 1$ (2) $D = 3$ (3) $D = 5$

13-17 A Computronics purchasing manager has established .01 as the acceptable quality level for printed circuit boards. Incoming shipments are sampled by a thorough testing with $n = 100$ randomly selected boards.
(a) Assuming a significance level of .025, determine the acceptance number.
(b) Indicate for each of the following results whether the incoming shipment should be accepted or rejected.
(1) $D = 4$ (2) $D = 2$ (3) $D = 7$ (4) $D = 3$

13-18 Consider the following numbers of defectives in successive samples of 10 items.

Sample	Number of Defectives
1	2
2	0
3	2
4	1
5	1
6	1
7	1
8	0
9	1
10	2

Determine for each of the following sequential sampling plans which of the above is the final set of observations. Indicate whether the lot should be accepted or rejected.

(a) $A_n = .05n$; $R_n = 1 + .05n$ (b) $A_n = .2n$; $R_n = 1 + .2n$ (c) $A_n = 1 + .1n$; $R_n = 3 + .1n$ (d) $A_n = 2 + .05n$; $R_n = 4 + .05n$

SUMMARY

1. **What is statistical quality control?**
There are two major areas of **statistical quality control**. When the major concern is the *process* of creating products or services, quality controls may be achieved using the **control chart**. The control chart graphically documents a procedure whereby sample data trigger remedial actions. The second type of statistical quality control is **acceptance sampling**, described below.

2. **What are the basic types of control charts?**
For qualitative observations, the ***P*-chart** is used. Two charts are used for quantitative observations: the **$\bar{X}$-chart** for monitoring central tendency and the ***R*-chart** for assessing process variability.

3. **How is a control chart used to trigger remedial action?**
Control charts display a **lower control limit** LCL and an **upper control limit** UCL for the applicable statistic. Observations falling outside these limits correspond to times when the process is *out of control*. An essential feature of a successful quality control plan is the search for **assignable causes** for the unusually large or small observations that result. Since they are ordinarily based on 3-*sigma* deviations, the LCL and UCL should be far enough apart that random causes alone will rarely trigger a search for nonexistent assignable causes.

4. **What is acceptance sampling and how is it used?**
Acceptance sampling places the focus on *items* already produced or *services* already rendered. There are two possible actions that may be taken when sampling the population or **lot**. It may be *accepted* or *rejected*. The *proportion defective*, the value of which remains unknown, is the primary issue. A pivotal level, the **acceptable quality level** π_0, is the focus in establishing a *decision rule*. The rule compares the number of sample defectives D to an **acceptance number** C. The lot must be *accepted* when $D \leq C$ and *rejected* otherwise.

5. **How does acceptance sampling relate to hypothesis testing?**
Acceptance sampling is a direct application of *hypothesis testing*. The procedure uses a specified **significance level** α, which establishes the level for C once the sample size is specified. The value of C represents an upper limit of the probability for the *Type I error* of rejecting a good shipment ($\pi = \pi_0$). That probability is referred to as the **producer's risk**. The *Type II error* of accepting a bad shipment ($\pi > \pi_0$) is also to be avoided. The corresponding probability is referred to as the **consumer's risk**.

6. **What is sequential sampling and how is it used?**
Ordinarily, acceptance sampling schemes are based on single samples. More elaborate procedures may involve **sequential sampling** where a succession of smaller-sized samples are taken, each resulting in either acceptance, rejection, or the choice to continue sampling.

REAL-LIFE STATISTICAL CHALLENGE

Designing Products to Last

For businesses to survive into the next century terms such as quality control and total quality management need to mean more than faddish buzz words. Genichi Taguchi, an engineer with Toyota Motor Cars of Japan, argues that "Quality is a virtue of design." From this premise a body of manufacturing quality assurance techniques has collectively become known as the Taguchi method.

Some Features of the Taguchi Method

The Taguchi Method incorporates a number of statistical, financial analysis, and heuristic measures. (A heuristic measure uses rules of thumb to find solutions to questions.) We will examine four of these measures.

- Designing robustness into products.
- The "Quality Loss Function."
- Striving for consistent products, beginning with design through manufacturing and continuing beyond the plant into the field.
- Robust products have a high internal and external signal-to-noise ratio.

Product Robustness

Mr. Taguchi, in his article with Don Clausing published in the *Harvard Business Review*, puts forth the concept that the " 'robustness' of products is more a function of good design than of on-line control."* Over their useful lives products are subjected to greater variation in the field—due to dust, electrical conditions, and other factors. Therefore, measures to reduce product failure in the field should also reduce failures during manufacturing.

The "Quality Loss Function"

Taguchi makes use of a heuristic quality loss function (defined as the cost to fix a problem in the field after customers complain) shown as the formula:

$$L = D^2 \times C$$

where D is the deviation from the target and C is the cost of the countermeasure to get back on target. For example, if it would cost a manufacturer \$50 per unit as a countermeasure to get a product part on target, the quality loss function provides values of \$50, \$200, \$450, and \$800 at deviations of 1, 2, 3, and 4 from the target.

Striving for Consistency

In general, scattered deviations within specifications are more difficult to correct than consistent deviations outside of specifications. With scattered deviations, a number of factors may be interacting to create a product that eventually will fail or lead to customer dissatisfaction. Consistent error outside the target may be corrected by changing one or a few isolated factors rather than fixing many possible factors.

REAL-LIFE STATISTICAL CHALLENGE

High Signal-to-Noise Ratios

Robust products have a high internal and external signal-to-noise ratio. The signal-to-noise ratio is a metaphor applied by Taguchi to all product behavior—not just electrical parts where the term has a precise physical definition.

The signal is what the product or service is trying to deliver. Noise is any interference internal or external to the product. Designers need to consider three factors in maximizing the ratio:

1. Determine the specific objective for developing the best signal-to-noise ratio.
2. Define feasible design options—physical characteristics such as dimensions and other physical characteristics.
3. Select the option that provides the greatest robustness.

The selection can be achieved through the process of multiple factor analysis (a set of techniques related to the multiple correlation concepts discussed in Chapter 11).

Further Considerations

There are other elements to the Taguchi Method that focus on cost/benefit trade-off issues and other financial measures.

The Taguchi method is one of many quality assurance techniques that have been used in a wide range of industries.** Nonmanufacturing and government and non-profit organizations may find adapting some of these "Total Quality Methods" may lead to greater customer satisfaction and repeat business.

DISCUSSION QUESTIONS

1. If the cost of a countermeasure is $120 per unit, what will be the losses from not correcting at 2 and 3 deviations.

2. For the company where you work, how could robustness be enhanced for a product? For a service?

3. Traditional quality control, as described in the chapter, focuses on piecemeal improvements and corrections. Do you think that Taguchi's approach contradicts those methods?

REFERENCES

*Genichi Taguchi and Don Clausing, "Robust Quality," in *Harvard Business Review*, January–February 1990, pp. 65–75.

**James B. Dilworth, "Total Quality Management," in *Operations Management: Design Planning and Control for Manufacturing and Services*. New York: McGraw-Hill, 1992, pp. 606–629.

REVIEW EXERCISES

13-19 Yellow Giant wishes to establish a control chart for the weights of canned foods. The data in the following table have been obtained over several days.

(a) Calculate the mean and range for each sample. Then calculate the grand mean and overall mean range.

(b) Determine Yellow Giant's control limits for $\bar{X}$ and R.

Day	Contents Weight (ounces)				
1	15.67	16.23	16.08	15.92	16.17
2	16.14	16.33	16.08	16.39	15.82
3	15.76	15.97	16.25	16.19	16.22
4	16.74	15.65	15.66	16.22	15.75
5	15.82	15.95	15.82	15.76	15.56
6	16.38	16.20	16.00	15.80	16.01
7	15.70	16.20	15.71	16.30	15.77
8	16.14	16.05	16.25	15.92	16.10
9	15.65	15.75	16.18	16.03	15.79
10	16.34	16.16	16.15	15.80	15.88

(c) For each of the following sample results, indicate whether the process is in control or out of control.

(1) 15.40 15.60 15.55 15.70 15.80
(2) 15.66 16.05 16.39 16.10 16.07
(3) 15.20 16.80 16.00 15.80 15.90
(4) 15.60 16.25 16.22 15.90 16.05

13-20 A Midget Motors inspector has established the following control limits for the amount of paint needed to cover a car.

$\bar{X}$: LCL = 1.8 gallons UCL = 2.2 gallons

R: LCL = 0.5 gallons UCL = 0.8 gallons

For each of the following sample results, indicate whether the painting process is (1) in control; (2) out of control because of the mean; (3) out of control because of the variability; or (4) out of control due to both the mean and variability.

(a) 1.6 2.2 2.1 1.8 (c) 2.0 1.3 2.7 1.9
(b) 2.4 2.2 1.7 1.6 (d) 0.9 2.0 2.1 1.3

13-21 Shirley Smart is responsible for quality control at SoftWhereHaus. She wishes to determine an acceptance sampling plan for floppy disk drives.

(a) The following plans are being considered. Determine, for each, the acceptance number.

(1) $\pi_0 = .01$; $n = 20$; $\alpha = .10$
(2) $\pi_0 = .05$; $n = 50$; $\alpha = .05$
(3) $\pi_0 = .10$; $n = 100$; $\alpha = .025$

(b) Using your answer to (a), determine the probability that a shipment will be accepted when the true proportion defective disk drives is .30.

13-22 Refer to Exercise 13-21. Suppose that Shirley Smart establishes an acceptable quality level of $\pi_0 = .05$ and a sample size $n = 100$.

(a) At a significance level of $\alpha = .02$, determine the acceptance number.

(b) Using your answer to (a), indicate for each of the following sample results whether she should accept or reject the shipment.
(1) $D = 5$ (2) $D = 1$ (3) $D = 2$ (4) $D = 9$

CASE Billings, Kidd, and Hickock

Billings, Kidd, and Hickock is a large, multiple-city, public accounting firm. The partners have several quality control concerns about the services it provides and that the firm procures from contractors.

Their first concern is with the accuracy of tax-return workups. A random sample of 100 files from each branch office has been selected, along with the computer input sheets. A detailed analysis yields the following numbers of returns that have major preparation errors.

Branch Office	Number of Errors	Branch Office	Number of Errors	Branch Office	Number of Errors
1	25	6	12	11	9
2	14	7	10	12	9
3	2	8	12	13	15
4	16	9	28	14	24
5	17	10	15	15	14

The firm prepares the payrolls for hundreds of medium-sized business clients. Each month, a sample of payrolls processed by the branch offices will be selected and each client employee's workup time will be determined. The following first month's data have been obtained.

Office	Workup Time per Employee (minutes)			
1	7.5	9.4	13.5	5.2
2	15.4	11.5	17.8	20.3
3	5.6	7.1	8.3	4.9
4	19.4	4.7	8.6	7.5
5	6.5	9.5	11.2	8.2
6	10.3	9.8	13.4	11.2
7	8.7	20.5	7.9	6.5
8	11.3	8.7	11.5	12.2
9	9.0	8.8	10.2	11.5
10	15.4	13.6	17.5	17.5
11	4.4	5.1	3.6	3.5
12	10.2	14.6	11.4	13.1
13	7.9	8.5	9.1	9.9
14	12.5	6.9	11.4	7.0
15	9.5	8.2	9.4	5.8

Billings, Kidd, and Hickock contracts out data transcription to a firm that flies records to Jamaica, where the actual work is done. The firm needs to establish an acceptance sampling scheme and to negotiate terms with the contractor. The plan is to return for reprocessing any rejected batches of transcribed data, which the contractor will redo for free.

The firm has retained a statistical consultant to help evaluate the above issues.

QUESTIONS

1. A control chart will help to identify which branches are out of line with the firm's present standards for preparing tax returns. Using the sample error data, construct a *P*-chart. Indicate which, if any, branch offices appear to need remedial attention from the managing partner.
2. A control chart will also help to identify which employees are out of line with the standard workup time for processing payrolls. Construct an $\bar{X}$-chart and an *R*-chart for the given data. Identify which offices appear to violate the firm's suggested norms and state the form of those violations.
3. Discuss why the firm may be concerned with payroll $\bar{X}$'s that are too small as well as too large.
4. Discuss why the firm may expect a great deal of payroll processing variability and also what type of problem may be signaled by too little variability.
5. Discuss how the firm may reach an acceptable quality level for the error rate in transcribing data.
6. Discuss the key issues in setting the significance level and determining the sample size.
7. Suppose that $n = 100$ transactions are selected at random from each data-processed lot and that the acceptable quality level is an error rate of .01. At a significance level of .015, determine the acceptance number that the firm will propose to the contractor.

CHAPTER 14

INDEX NUMBERS

BEFORE READING THIS CHAPTER, MAKE SURE YOU UNDERSTAND:

The types of statistical data (Chapter 1).
How to describe and display data (Chapter 2).
How to summarize data (Chapter 3).

AFTER READING THIS CHAPTER, YOU WILL UNDERSTAND:

What index numbers are.
About the simplest price indexes and how they are computed.
About the three most common weighted price indexes.
About the consumer price index and how it is computed and used.

Inflation is a decrease in the purchasing power of money, evident to consumers as a pervasive increase in the prices of goods and services over a period of time. Many factors may contribute to inflation, but whatever the causes at any particular time, the first step in prescribing possible remedies is to measure the amount of inflation. This is most commonly accomplished by measuring changes in price levels.

How do we measure changes in price? We only have to shop for groceries to notice that it is natural for prices to fluctuate. Some items, such as watermelon, are seasonal and sell at "outrageous" prices before they reach their peak supply and then sell for a small fraction of their previous cost. Other items have no seasonal explanation for their price fluctuations. To obtain a meaningful measure of inflation, the prices of all goods and services must somehow be represented.

14-1 PRICE INDEXES

A numerical value that summarizes price levels is called a **price index**. For such an index, the seasonal rise in the price of a commodity such as strawberries should not have any significant influence. But increases in strawberry prices from one May to the next should. Likewise, only goods that are important to a great many people ought to be considered. Van Gogh paintings have increased steadily in price over the past 80 years, but such a price rise affects a minuscule percentage of persons and may be ignored.

Measuring price changes in the United States is an official task of the Department of Labor. Its Bureau of Labor Statistics periodically publishes the well-known consumer price index (CPI).

It was the question of price changes that led to the development of the first price index more than 200 years ago by G. R. Carli, an Italian who compared the change in the prices of grain, wine, and oil from the years 1500 to 1750.* Carli's original index was crude compared to today's CPI, which is quite elaborate and complicated.

Price indexes have other uses besides being barometers of inflation. Economic models deal with *real* wages and *real* income, so that wages and income are adjusted to account for changing price levels by means of index numbers. Actual economic growth is ordinarily expressed in terms of change in real national product, which is found by using a price index to adjust annual gross national product (GNP) values computed at current price levels to values comparable to those of a prior period.

The simplest price index measures the change over time in the price of a single item. Such an index is illustrated by Table 14-1, which gives the retail prices per pound of frying chicken sold at a particular store from 1982 through 1992. The **base period**, the point in time to which all later prices are compared, is 1982. This is expressed by the equation 1982 = 100, which means that the index expresses all prices relative to that of 1982. Index numbers are ordinarily expressed in percentages. In 1982, the price of chicken was \$0.94 per pound. The **price relative** for 1983, when chicken cost \$0.90 per pound, is the ratio of the

*Bruce D. Mudgett, *Index Numbers* (New York: John Wiley & Sons, 1951), p. 6.

TABLE 14-1 Percentage Price Relatives Index for Frying Chicken

Year	Price per Pound	Price Relative to 1982	Index
1982	$0.94	1.00	100
1983	0.90	.96	96
1984	0.82	.87	87
1985	0.78	.83	83
1986	0.74	.79	79
1987	0.76	.81	81
1988	0.80	.85	85
1989	0.84	.89	89
1990	1.02	1.09	109
1991	1.14	1.21	121
1992	1.26	1.34	134

two prices, .90/.94 = .96, which indicates that in 1983 the price of chicken was 96% as high as in 1982. The price index for 1983 is thus 96. In a similar manner, the 1984 price of $0.82 is divided by the 1982 price, .82/.94 = .87, so that for 1984 the index is 87, or 87% of the price that prevailed in 1982; this is a 100 − 87 = 13% price reduction. Index values so obtained are called **percentage price relatives**.

Expressed symbolically in terms of the base period price p_0 and the price p_n in a given period, we have the

PERCENTAGE PRICE RELATIVES INDEX

$$I = \frac{p_n}{p_0} \times 100$$

It is sometimes convenient to use the calendar years as subscripts, so that, for 1990, the price index would be expressed as

$$I = \frac{p_{90}}{p_{82}} \times 100 = \frac{1.02}{.94} \times 100 = 109$$

Price relatives for a single item are limited in usefulness. Price changes in a single commodity such as chicken do not indicate the general movement in prices. Of greater importance in economic planning and in comparing conditions from year to year is a composite price index that covers many different items. The rise in the price of chicken will not significantly affect the lifestyles of most persons. But a rise in food prices may, especially for those whose incomes are fixed. Thus, an index that considers several food items helps us measure the change in the standard of living of a large number of people.

14-2 AGGREGATE PRICE INDEXES

In Table 14-2, the prices for selected meats, poultry, and fish sold at the same retail outlet are provided for the years 1990, 1991 and 1992. A price index for several items may be determined in a manner similar to that used previously for frying chicken. An **aggregate** of the prices for each year is calculated by summing together the prices for the four items. Such an aggregate may be either unweighted or weighted. Extending the previous notation, we determine the

UNWEIGHTED AGGREGATE PRICE INDEX

$$I = \frac{\sum p_n}{\sum p_0} \times 100$$

Using 1990 = 100, we obtain the following price aggregate.

$$\sum p_{90} = \$2.40 + \$1.80 + \$2.24 + \$1.02 = \$7.46$$

For 1991, the price aggregate is

$$\sum p_{91} = \$2.70 + \$1.84 + \$1.98 + \$1.14 = \$7.66$$

so that the unweighted aggregate price index is

$$I = \frac{\sum p_{91}}{\sum p_{90}} \times 100 = \frac{\$7.66}{\$7.46} \times 100 = 103 \text{ (rounded)}$$

Thus, the aggregate price of these foods has increased by 3% from 1990 to 1991.

Simple unweighted price aggregates are subject to certain difficulties. One problem is that the price index obtained is affected by a factor other than price, the *units* on which the prices are based. In computing the above index numbers, each food item was expressed in the same units of 1 pound. Except for canned tuna, the foods listed are sold by the pound. If instead we had used $6\frac{1}{2}$ ounces, the weight of a standard can of tuna, as the unit of measurement, we would have obtained (rounded to the nearest cent) \$0.91 for 1990, \$0.80 for 1991, and \$0.88 for 1992. Thus, the price index for 1991 would have been 106 instead of 103.

TABLE 14-2 Prices per Pound for Selected Meats

Year	Rib Roast	Pork Chops	Canned Tuna	Frying Chicken
1990	\$2.40	\$1.80	\$2.24	\$1.02
1991	2.70	1.84	1.98	1.14
1992	2.94	2.16	2.16	1.26

One way to eliminate potential distortion caused by choice of units is to weight items in such a way that any units may be used. As a bonus, a weight may be given to each item in relation to its importance, thereby yielding a more meaningful measure of price change. For most households, the prices of rib roast and other beef products are much more significant than the price of canned tuna, since beef is more of a staple item and should weigh more heavily in the index.

The weights traditionally used in price indexes are quantities, denoted by q. The product $p \times q$ represents total value and is unaffected by the units chosen, because p is price per unit and q is the number of units. A meaningful price index is one that uses quantities in proportion to the importance or usage of the item. Thus, in establishing an index intended to measure a family's purchasing power, the quantities of each item purchased by a typical family would be used. When the $p \times q$ terms are summed for several items, the resulting value is referred to as **weighted price aggregate**, which is denoted by $\sum pq$.

Various indexes may be computed from weighted price aggregates. The differences between those presented in this book are due to the choice of quantities used. We first consider the

LASPEYRES INDEX

$$I = \frac{\sum p_n q_0}{\sum p_0 q_0} \times 100$$

The numerator $\sum p_n q_0$ represents the value of all the items purchased in time period n. The Laspeyres index uses quantity weights q_0 from the base period, so that only the prices are allowed to change. The denominator $\sum p_0 q_0$ provides the value of the same quantities of these commodities when they are purchased in the base period.

Table 14-3 shows the weekly quantities (pounds) of selected food items assumed to be purchased by a typical family in 1990, the base period. The Laspeyres index for 1991 is calculated using the quantities for 1990 and prices

TABLE 14-3 Price and Quantity Data for Calculating Laspeyres Index (1990 = 100)

	Price per Pound 1990	Price per Pound 1991	Quantity (pounds) 1990	Value of Items 1990	Value of Items 1991
Item	p_{90}	p_{91}	q_{90}	$p_{90}q_{90}$	$p_{91}q_{90}$
Rib roast	\$2.40	\$2.70	5	\$12.00	\$13.50
Pork chops	1.80	1.84	2	3.60	3.68
Canned tuna	2.24	1.98	1	2.24	1.98
Frying chicken	1.02	1.14	4	4.08	4.56
				\$21.92	\$23.72

for 1990 and 1991.

$$I = \frac{\sum p_{91}q_{90}}{\sum p_{90}q_{90}} \times 100 = \frac{\$23.72}{\$21.92} \times 100 = 108$$

Thus the prices for the selected items in 1991 are 8% higher than in the 1990 base period, which has index value 100.

Another commonly used weighted aggregate price index is the

PAASCHE INDEX

$$I = \frac{\sum p_n q_n}{\sum p_0 q_n} \times 100$$

The Paasche index is similar to the Laspeyres, but the quantities q_n from the *current* period are used to calculate the price aggregate. If the quantities of the various items consumed by a typical family change over time, the two indexes will provide different percentage changes.

For example, in 1991 the market for canned tuna was seriously disturbed by concern over the porpoises killed in tuna nets. This possibly caused a drop in the level of consumption of tuna from the previous year. For the sake of illustration, suppose that the typical family in 1991 consumed only $\frac{1}{2}$ pound of tuna per week, raising its consumption of chicken to $4\frac{1}{2}$ pounds, while the quantities of rib roast and pork chops remained constant at 5 and 2 pounds. The weighted price aggregates are, for 1990,

$$\sum p_{90}q_{91} = \$2.40(5) + \$1.80(2) + \$2.24(\tfrac{1}{2}) + \$1.02(4\tfrac{1}{2}) = \$21.31$$

and for 1991,

$$\sum p_{91}q_{91} = \$2.70(5) + \$1.84(2) + \$1.98(\tfrac{1}{2}) + \$1.14(4\tfrac{1}{2}) = \$23.30$$

The Paasche index is

$$I = \frac{\sum p_{91}q_{91}}{\sum p_{90}q_{91}} \times 100 = \frac{\$23.30}{\$21.31} \times 100 = 109$$

According to this index, the prices in 1991 were 9%, not 8%, higher than in 1990.

Ordinarily the discrepancies between the Laspeyres and Paasche indexes may be expected to grow as the time differential between the base period and current period becomes greater. There are two basic causes for widening disagreement. The primary one is the changing tastes of consumers. Newer items used in the Paasche index will, over the time, tend to supplant the older ones in importance. We need only list some of the meat products heavily purchased 50 years ago to illustrate this point. Kidneys, tripe, heart, brains, and tongue are today hard to find in the ordinary supermarket, and are now largely used in processed meats, such as frankfurters. The Laspeyres index would use the earliest quantities for all items, giving high weight to some items hardly consumed at all and little weight to newer but more popular ones.

A second explanation for the discrepancy between the Paasche and Laspeyres indexes is that in a period of inflation there may be a downward shift in quantities consumed of higher-priced items. Persons of fixed income will buy less beef and eat more chicken as prices rise. If wages rise as fast as or faster than prices, the reverse may be true.

The Paasche index may be more realistic than the Laspeyres, because changes in taste and earnings—as reflected in revised quantity weights—are considered as well as price. However, for reasons indicated below, the Paasche index is more difficult to work with than the Laspeyres, so that a generalized version of the latter is usually preferred. To overcome the difficulties of shifting consumer emphasis on various items, the base period may be revised from time to time to bring an index up to date. The consumer price index, for example, is revised to a new base period about every ten years.

Generally, the use of base period quantities to weight prices, as with the Laspeyres index, is preferred to the use of current quantities, as with the Paasche index. One reason for this is that it is expensive to collect data to find quantity weights, so that to do so every year would require a greater expenditure of resources than to use a single set of quantities for all years. Another difficulty in using current weights is that the base period's weighted aggregate must be recomputed for each new period considered.

It is convenient to consider a price index similar to the Laspeyres that uses arbitrarily chosen quantity weights q_a. This is the

FIXED-WEIGHT AGGREGATE PRICE INDEX

$$I = \frac{\sum p_n q_a}{\sum p_0 q_a} \times 100$$

This equation provides the Laspeyres price index when $q_a = q_0$. The major advantages of this more general index are that, like the Laspeyres, it is free from period-to-period changes in the quantity weights and that, unlike the Laspeyres, its weights are not tied to a single base period.

EXERCISES

14-1 A random sample of 100 households has been selected in order to establish a price index for housing utilities. The following average annual figures have been obtained.

	Price (dollars per unit)				Quantity			
	1989	1990	1991	1992	1989	1990	1991	1992
Electricity	1.97	2.05	2.09	2.10	62	64	68	70
Gas	7.90	8.25	8.60	8.80	8.7	9.0	9.5	10.1
Water	.29	.30	.31	.32	296	297	298	300
Telephone	2.40	2.45	2.50	2.50	55	56	58	60

The units are as follows: thousands of kilowatt-hours for electricity, hundreds of therms for gas, hundreds of cubic feet for water, and hundreds of message-unit equivalents for telephone.

Calculate the unweighted aggregate price indexes for 1990–1992, using 1989 = 100.

14-2 Refer to the data in Exercise 14-1, with 1989 = 100. Calculate the Laspeyres price indexes for 1990–1992, using the 1989 quantities as weights. What is the percentage increase in 1992 prices over those of 1989?

14-3 Refer to the data in Exercise 14-1, with 1989 = 100. Calculate the Paasche indexes for 1990–1992, using the quantities for the current year as weights. What is the percentage increase in 1992 prices over those of 1989?

14-4 Refer to the data in Exercise 14-1. Assume the quantity weights are 65, 10, 300, and 50 for electricity, gas, water, and telephone, respectively.

(a) For a 1991 base, calculate the fixed-weight aggregate price index for 1992. What is the percentage increase in 1992 prices over those of 1991?

(b) For a 1992 base, calculate the fixed-weight aggregate price index for 1991. What is the percentage increase in 1992 prices using these index numbers? Is your answer the same as in (a)? Explain.

14-5 A consumer finance rate index will be established using the following hypothetical interest rate data. As quantities, total loans made that year are used.

	Rate				Quantity (billions)			
	1989	1990	1991	1992	1989	1990	1991	1992
Home mortgage	9%	10%	13%	15%	100	150	100	70
Car loan	12	12	15	15	50	55	60	60
Credit card	15	16	17	18	30	35	40	45
Signature loan	18	19	20	22	5	6	8	10

Calculate the unweighted consumer finance rate (price) indexes for 1990–1992, using 1989 = 100.

14-6 Refer to the data in Exercise 14-5, with 1989 = 100. Calculate the Laspeyres price indexes for 1990–1992, using the 1989 quantities as weights. What is the percentage increase in 1992 rates over those of 1989?

14-7 Refer to the data in Exercise 14-5, with 1989 = 100. Calculate the Paasche indexes for 1990–1992, using the quantities for the current year as weights. What is the percentage increase in 1992 rates over those of 1989?

14-8 Refer to the data in Exercise 14-5. Assume the quantity weights are 100, 60, 40, and 7 for home mortgages, car loans, credit cards, and signature loans, respectively.

(a) For a 1991 base, calculate the fixed-weight aggregate price index for 1992. What is the percentage increase in 1992 rates over those of 1991?

(b) For a 1992 base, calculate the fixed-weight aggregate price index for 1991. What is the percentage increase in 1992 rates using these index numbers? Is your answer the same as in (a)? Explain.

14-3 THE CONSUMER PRICE INDEX

The consumer price index measures changes in prices that affect the cost of living for a large fraction of the U.S. population.* This is achieved by means of a "market basket" of goods and services that consists of about 400 items. These comprise most major expenses incurred by a typical city wage earner, including food, clothing, medical treatment, entertainment, rent, and transportation. Table 14-4 shows the major goods and services categories comprising the CPI and the number of items in each. Also shown is the relative importance, as a percentage of the total market basket, given to the items in each major grouping.

The CPI has been published continuously since 1913, although major modifications have been made in the method of computation, data collection, contents of the market basket, and base period. Since World War II there have been four base periods: 1947–1949, 1957–1959, the single year 1967 and 1982–1984. The CPI closely resembles the Laspeyres index, which, as we have noted, uses fixed quantities for weights. Because of the shifting importance of items, it is advantageous to revise the weights periodically. The weight revisions for the CPI do not necessarily occur at the same time as the shift of base, which is one reason why the CPI is not a Laspeyres index.

The CPI is based on sample data, so sampling error is present. Furthermore, only a few key items are included, because it would be prohibitively expensive to collect data on all products and services provided in the United States. Even for the limited number of items, it would be impossible to monitor every transaction in order to obtain exact prices. Instead, average prices are used as estimates. These are obtained for all of the larger metropolitan areas and for a select group of smaller ones. Separate price indexes are computed for each city and then averaged by means of population weights, so that price levels in the larger cities have greater importance.

The data collecting procedures are far too elaborate for detailed discussion in this book.** A few key features are important. The price data are obtained from a few randomly selected stores in each area. The store types are chosen to be representative of the merchandise classes from a recent census of retail trade. The selection is made by **quota sampling**, where a specified number or quota of stores from each category is sought.

A very significant problem encountered in obtaining pricing data is that of product quality changes. When a product's quality declines while its price is fixed, it amounts to the same thing as a price increase. The nickel candy bar, now gone, is a good example. For over 50 years, the price of many brands of candy bars had been held at 5 cents, even though inflation had been recurrent. The amount of candy bar was gradually reduced in order to cover the rising costs of manufacture. The Bureau of Labor Statistics has published detailed quality specifications on the items included in the price index in order to measure the real changes in price.

*A nontechnical discussion of the CPI is contained in U.S. Department of Labor, *The Consumer Price Index: 1987 Revision*, Report 736, January 1987.

**For a comprehensive discussion, see Doris P. Rothwell, *The Consumer Price Index Pricing and Calculation Procedures* (Preliminary), (Washington, D.C.: U.S. Bureau of Labor Statistics, March 17, 1964).

TABLE 14-4 Relative Importance of Goods and Services Priced for the 1982–1984 Consumer Price Index

Major Group	Relative Importance	Major Group	Relative Importance
All items	100.000	Transportation	18.696
		Private transportation	17.303
Food and beverages	17.840	New vehicles	5.497
Food	16.283	Used cars	1.271
Food at home	10.136	Motor fuel	4.800
Cereals and bakery products	1.351	Automobile maintenance and repair	1.538
Meats, poultry, fish, and eggs	3.177	Other private transportation	4.197
Dairy products	1.350	Public transportation	1.393
Fruits and vegetables	1.677		
Other food at home	2.584	Medical care	4.796
Food away from home	6.145	Medical care commodities	.946
Alcoholic beverages	1.558	Medical care services	3.850
		Professional services	2.546
Housing	42.637	Hospital and related services	1.178
Shelter	26.283	Health insurance	.125
Rent, residential	7.485	Entertainment	4.380
Homeowners' costs	18.569	Entertainment commodities	2.200
Maintenance and repairs	.230	Entertainment services	2.180
Fuel and other utilities	8.519		
Fuels	5.187	Other goods and services	5.128
Fuel and other fuel commodities	.571	Tobacco products	1.120
Gas (piped) and electricity	4.617	Personal care	1.236
Other utilities and public services	3.331	Toilet goods and personal care appliances	.672
Household furnishings and operation	7.835	Personal care services	.564
Housefurnishings	4.974	Personal and educational expenses	2.772
Housekeeping supplies	1.253	School books and supplies	.182
Housekeeping services	1.608	Personal and educational services	2.590
Apparel and upkeep	6.524		
Apparel commodities	5.981		
Men's and boys' apparel	1.614		
Women's and girls' apparel	2.642		
Infants' and toddlers' apparel	.233		
Footwear	.918		
Other apparel commodities	.573		
Apparel services	.544		

Source: *U.S. Bureau of Labor Statistics, Report 736,* January 1987.

The CPI is a hybrid of two indexes discussed previously. In the early periods following a switch of base periods, it is the same as the Laspeyres index. But because the (quantity) weights used in recent times have been switched several periods after the base period was revised, the computations for a fixed-weight index must be used. The reason for this complicated scheme is that CPI base periods have been changed whenever the current index level was judged too high for further meaningful comparisons. The value data necessary for revising weights are obtained from special studies.

Table 14-5 shows the consumer price index values for the years 1946–1990, with 1982–1984 = 100.

TABLE 14-5 Consumer Price Index Values (1992–1984 = 100)

Year	CPI	Year	CPI	Year	CPI
1946	19.5	1961	29.9	1976	56.9
1947	22.3	1962	30.2	1977	60.6
1948	24.1	1963	30.6	1978	65.2
1949	23.8	1964	31.0	1979	72.6
1950	24.1	1965	31.5	1980	82.4
1951	26.0	1966	32.4	1981	90.9
1952	26.5	1967	33.4	1982	96.5
1953	26.7	1968	34.8	1983	99.6
1954	26.9	1969	36.7	1984	103.9
1955	26.8	1970	38.8	1985	107.6
1956	27.2	1971	40.5	1986	109.6
1957	28.1	1972	41.8	1987	113.6
1958	28.9	1973	44.4	1988	118.3
1959	29.1	1974	49.3	1989	124.0
1960	29.6	1975	53.8	1990	130.7

Source: *Economic Report of the President*, 1991.

EXERCISES

14-9 The 1990 *Economic Report of the President* does not list the CPI levels before the year 1946. The following values have been obtained for those earlier years.

Year	CPI (1967 = 100)
1940	42.0
1941	44.1
1942	48.8
1943	51.8
1944	52.7
1945	53.9
1946	58.5

Splice the CPI values for 1940—1945 to those in Table 14-5. To do this, use the common year 1946. First, determine the prices for each year 1940–1945 as a proportion of the 1946 prices (base 1967 = 100). Then, multiply those proportions by the 1946 index from the time series with a base 1982–1984 = 100.

14-10 Consider the CPI time-series data in Table 14-5. *Shift* the base period to 1946. To do this, divide all index numbers by the index for 1946 and then multiply by 100.

14-4 DEFLATING TIME SERIES USING INDEX NUMBERS

A major use of a price index such as the CPI is to measure the "real" values of economic time-series data expressed in monetary amounts. For example, the U.S. gross national product is calculated in current dollars, so that price changes over

TABLE 14-6 Actual U.S. Gross National Product, Consumer Price Index, and Real GNP

Year	(1) Consumer Price Index (1982–1984 = 100)	(2) Actual GNP in Current Dollars (billions)	(3) Real GNP (billions) [(2) ÷ (1)] × 100
1960	29.6	$ 515.3	$1,740.9
1961	29.9	533.8	1,785.3
1962	30.2	574.6	1,902.6
1963	30.6	606.9	1,983.3
1964	31.0	649.8	2,096.1
1965	31.5	705.1	2,238.4
1966	32.4	777.0	2,398.1
1967	33.4	816.4	2,444.3
1968	34.8	892.7	2,565.2
1969	36.7	963.9	2,626.4
1970	38.8	1,015.5	2,617.3
1971	40.5	1,102.7	2,791.6
1972	41.8	1,212.8	2,901.4
1973	44.4	1,359.3	3,061.5
1974	49.3	1,472.8	2,987.4
1975	53.8	1,598.4	2,971.0
1976	56.9	1,782.8	3,133.2
1977	60.6	1,990.5	3,284.7
1978	65.2	2,249.7	3,450.5
1979	72.6	2,508.2	3,454.8
1980	82.4	2,732.2	3,315.8
1981	90.9	3,052.6	3,358.2
1982	96.5	3,166.0	3,280.8
1983	99.6	3,405.7	3,419.4
1984	103.9	3,772.2	3,630.6
1985	107.6	4,014.9	3,731.3
1986	109.6	4,240.3	3,868.9
1987	113.6	4,526.7	3,984.8

Source: *Economic Report of the President,* 1989, 1991.

time are reflected in the original data. GNP is the basic measure of economic growth, so that to determine how much the physical goods and services have grown over time, increases in value due to price should not be included. It is possible for the quantity of goods and services to actually fall during a recession, whereas inflation causes the GNP to rise due solely to price increases. Real economic growth may be determined by using a price index to *deflate* GNP values.

Table 14-6 provides the values for GNP and CPI for the years 1960–1987. Note that the index values have been continually increasing. The GNP has also been rising during this period of inflation. To isolate the changes in real GNP, the effect of rising prices may be found by transforming the actual values obtained for current dollars into their equivalent in 1982–1984 base dollars. This is achieved by dividing the original GNP data by the respective CPI value. In 1963 the GNP was 606.9 billion dollars, and the CPI was 30.6. Since prices were lower in 1963 than for the average base period, *real* GNP should have been higher and is found by dividing 606.9 by 30.6%.

$$\text{Real 1963 GNP} = \frac{606.9}{30.6} \times 100 = 1{,}983.3 \text{ billion dollars}$$

The original data show that in 1974, a recession year, the GNP grew from 1,359.3 to 1,472.8 billion dollars. But prices grew faster. The high levels of unemployment in 1974 actually caused a drop in real GNP, from 3,061.5 billion 1982–1984 dollars to 2,987.4 billion 1982–1984 dollars, the latter being found by dividing the 1974 current-dollars GNP by the CPI value of 49.3.

Economic models are often expressed in terms of real or price-adjusted values. We may use price indexes to find real wages, real income, or real production. To determine whether a typical worker's salary has risen enough to provide an increased standard of living, a price index may be used to compare take-home wages to prices. If wages grow by 5% when prices grow by 6%, there has been a change in real wages (and hence, in living standard) of $105/106 - 1 = -.01$, or a 1% decline. If a union has enough clout, its workers' standard of living may rise even during a period of inflation. Thus, a 10% wage increase when there is a 6% CPI rise results in $110/106 - 1 = .038$, or a 3.8% increase in real wages.

EXERCISES

14-11 The average gross weekly earnings by persons employed in manufacturing, as reported in the 1976 *Economic Report of the President*, are provided below.

Year	Earnings	Year	Earnings
1963	$ 99.63	1970	$133.73
1964	102.97	1971	142.44
1965	107.53	1972	154.69
1966	112.34	1973	166.06
1967	114.90	1974	176.40
1968	122.51	1975	189.51
1969	129.51		

Using the CPI values in Table 14-5, deflate the above time series to obtain current "real" gross earnings with a base 1982–1984 = 100.

14-12 The following data pertain to a large manufacturer's equipment.

Year	Book Value	Replacement Price Index (1984 = 100)
1988	$ 954,000	120
1989	1,236,000	135
1990	1,544,000	148
1991	2,020,000	165
1992	2,400,000	187

Deflate the book value data to determine the "real" equipment worth with a base 1984 = 100.

SUMMARY

1. What are index numbers?

Index numbers are used to facilitate comparisons of time-series data from different periods. **Price indexes** are especially useful in expressing price changes over time, thereby gauging inflation, a condition of rising prices that permeates the modern world.

Price indexes relate the current period's prices to those of a **base period**. These are expressed in percentages, so that an index value of 120 signifies that current prices are 20% higher than they were in the base period.

2. **What are the simplest price indexes and how are they computed?**
The simplest price index is the **percentage price relatives index** which applies to a single item.

$$I = \frac{p_n}{p_0} \times 100$$

Prices of several items may be measured by the **unweighted aggregate price index**, computed by dividing the sum of current prices by the sum of base period prices for the same items and converting that ratio to a percentage.

$$I = \frac{\sum p_n}{\sum p_0} \times 100$$

That index is less common than *weighted* indexes.

3. **What are the most common weighted price indexes?**
The **Laspeyres index** uses base period *quantities* as weights.

$$I = \frac{\sum p_n q_0}{\sum p_0 q_0} \times 100$$

Such quantities may include the production volume of items, the typical amount consumed, or some other useful numbers. A similar index is the **Paasche index**, for which the current quantities serve as the weights.

$$I = \frac{\sum p_n q_n}{\sum p_0 q_n} \times 100$$

The Laspeyres index is easier to compute, since the divisor remains the same for all periods, while the Paasche index has the advantage of reflecting the latest changes in item usage (or production). The **fixed-weight aggregate price index** uses quantities not tied to a specific period.

$$I = \frac{\sum p_n q_a}{\sum p_0 q_a} \times 100$$

4. **What is the consumer price index, and how is it computed and used?**
The **consumer price index** or CPI is the most familiar U.S. price index. It is a hybrid index representing the prices of a market basket of urban workers' goods and services. The CPI is especially important because of the "indexing" of wages, pensions, and government benefits, which are often changed when the CPI moves up. Price indexes such as the CPI are often used to transform time series for income data into "real" values by **deflating** the original data to their equivalents in the base period.

REAL-LIFE STATISTICAL CHALLENGE

An Index for Virtually Every Season

Economists are often called upon to predict the business cycle. To help them in their efforts they turn to sets of data called economic indicators. Three major indicators used are:

- Index of Leading Economic Indicators—reflecting likely changes months in advance for future business cycles.
- Index of Current Economic Indicators—a snapshot of current economic activity.
- Index of Trailing Economic Indicators—used to measure when changes in a business occur.

Each index is made up of a number of submeasures. For the Index of Leading Economic Indicators the factors include measures for consumer expectations, change in unfilled durable goods orders and changes in the average work week and unemployment claims. The Index of Current Economic Indicators includes number of people employed, sales data, and personal income. The Index of Lagging Economic Indicators encompass measures of commercial and consumer credit outstanding, and elements of the Consumer Price Index. Table 14-7 shows a composite list for all three indicators.

TABLE 14-7 Composite Index of Leading, Coincident, and Lagging Indicators

Year	Leading Indicators	Coincident Indicators	Lagging Indicators
1969	83.1	82.0	87.6
1970	79.0	83.5	93.2
1971	79.8	81.5	89.3
1972	88.1	85.4	85.4
1973	97.3	94.4	87.6
1974	95.5	96.3	97.7
1975	78.0	87.2	102.5
1976	93.0	89.8	88.0
1977	98.5	95.3	86.9
1978	101.9	101.1	92.5
1979	105.3	110.5	98.8
1980	101.2	111.0	108.3
1981	102.8	108.5	101.2
1982	97.2	102.1	104.9
1983	106.8	97.9	91.9
1984	123.5	109.1	94.1
1985	121.5	114.7	105.5
1986	127.9	117.8	111.0

(continued on next page)

REAL-LIFE STATISTICAL CHALLENGE

TABLE 14-7 (continued)

Year	Leading Indicators	Coincident Indicators	Lagging Indicators
1987	136.2	119.4	112.2
1988	138.7	125.6	114.0
1989	145.9	132.4	117.6
1990	145.4	131.9	119.2
1991	138.8	127.4	119.9

Note: Figures are for January of the year shown.
Source: U.S. Dept of Commerce unpublished data 1991. From The Universal Almanac 1992.

DISCUSSION QUESTIONS

1. Graph the index data and note at which dates the lines intersect.
2. Update the table from either *The Wall Street Journal* or another business magazine or newspaper with the current indexes. Compare the current data with the data shown in Table 14-7.
3. Which index do you think is more relevant for your decision making about buying a new car? Shopping for next week's groceries? Choosing your major?

REVIEW EXERCISES

14-13 Ace Widgets' dollar sales for the years 1981–1990 are provided below.

Year	Sales	Year	Sales
1981	$1,500,000	1986	$4,250,000
1982	1,650,000	1987	4,790,000
1983	1,880,000	1988	5,635,000
1984	2,945,000	1989	6,880,000
1985	2,675,000	1990	8,025,000

The above sales data were obtained from a period of rising prices and therefore do not reflect the actual level of business activity.

(a) Using the CPI values in Table 14-5, deflate the above time series to obtain "real" gross sales with a base 1982–1984.

(b) In constant dollars, determine the percentage change in sales for the following time periods.

(1) 1983 to 1984 (3) 1987 to 1988
(2) 1984 to 1985 (4) 1989 to 1990

14-14 Refer to the data in Table 14-5. Determine the percentage change in prices for the following time periods.

(a) 1970 to 1971 (c) 1950 to 1960
(b) 1986 to 1987 (d) 1977 to 1987

14-15 The indexes in the following table apply to the prices of the raw materials used in the manufacture of containers.

(a) Shift the base for Index A, so that 1980 = 100. Compute the new index values for each year.

Year	Index A (1970 = 100)
1970	100
1971	106
1972	107
1973	111
1974	121
1975	128
1976	140
1977	151
1978	156
1979	168
1980	181

Year	Index B (1980 = 100)
1980	100
1981	115
1982	120
1983	123
1984	130
1985	135
1986	132
1987	136
1988	140
1989	144

(b) Combine your answers to (a) with the values for Index B to provide a single spliced series (1980 = 100). Use that series to determine the percentage change in prices for the following time periods.
(1) 1975 to 1985 (2) 1979 to 1981

14-16 Refer to Exercise 14-15 and to your answers. Shift the base of the spliced series, so that 1970 = 100. Compute the new index values for each year.

STATISTICS IN PRACTICE

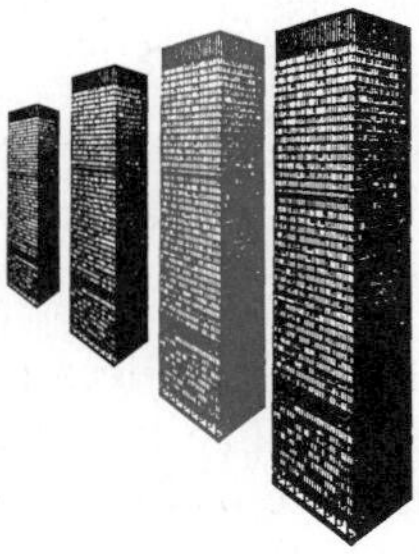

14-17 *Student Price Index Comparison.* The Consumer Price Index developed by the U.S. Bureau of Labor statistics is a good measure for the cost of living for families with children residing in urban areas. But what about other groups of people—retirees, families living in rural areas, or students attending college? Are their costs different? Are their expense patterns different? Working in groups of four to five students, determine the average expenses for a college student in your class. Use the categories in Table 14-8 as a guide (expenses may be estimated, as exact prices may be hard to verify).

14-18 Refer to Table 14-5 "Consumer Price Index Values" and Table 14-6 "Actual Gross National Product and Real GNP." The actual GNP in current dollars for the years 1988–1990 in billions of dollars are

1988 = \$4,864.3 1989 = \$5,200.8 1990 = \$5,465.1.

(a) Calculate the real GNP in billions for the years 1988–1990.
(b) If the wages at a company increase by 5% compounded for each of the three years what would happen to the real wages for the workers at that company?
(c) If the wages stay constant at 1987 values what would the real wages for the worker in 1990 be?

REAL-LIFE STATISTICAL CHALLENGE

TABLE 14-8 Dollar Value and Relative Importance of Goods and Services Priced for a Student Price Index

Group	$ Amount	Relative Importance
Total:	________	________
Food and beverages:	________	________
Food:	________	________
Food at home:	________	________
Food away from home:	________	________
Alcoholic beverages:	________	________
Housing:	________	________
Shelter:	________	________
Fuel and utilities:	________	________
Household furnishings and operation:	________	________
Apparel and upkeep:	________	________
Apparel commodities:	________	________
Apparel services:	________	________
Transportation:	________	________
Private transportation:	________	________
Public transportation:	________	________
Medical care:	________	________
Entertainment:	________	________
Other goods and services:	________	________
Tobacco products:	________	________
Personal care:	________	________
Personal and educational expenses and services:	________	________
School books and supplies:	________	________

(d) How much would wages for a worker need to rise to keep pace with inflation over the period 1988–1990?

14-19 Refer to Exercise 14-11. What would real wages be in 1990 for a worker who earned $189.51 per week in 1975 in order to keep pace with inflation.

14-20 The Producer Price Index measures average changes in prices received by all producers of all commodities. This index, unlike the Consumer Price Index, is often thought of as a "wholesale price index." Using the data below, suppose a manufacturer purchased the following categories of items in millions of dollars in 1975:

Commodity	Millions of $
Farm Products	7.5
Industrial	6.0
Energy	3.0
Metals	2.0

Use the index data in Table 14-9 to find the total cost in 1982 dollars.

TABLE 14-9 Producer Price Indexes—Major Commodity Groups 1950–1990 (1982 = 100)

Year	All Commodities	Farm Products	Industrial Commodities	Energy	Metals and Metal Products
1950	27.3	37.7	25.0	12.6	22.0
1955	29.3	36.6	27.8	13.2	27.2
1960	31.7	37.7	30.5	13.9	30.6
1965	32.3	39.0	30.9	13.8	32.0
1970	38.1	44.9	35.2	15.3	38.7
1975	58.4	74.0	54.9	35.4	61.5
1980	89.8	98.3	88.0	82.8	95.0
1985	103.2	100.7	103.7	91.4	104.4
1990	116.3	118.6	115.8	82.2	123.0

Farm products includes processed foods and feeds.
Energy incudes fuels, related products and power.

Source: U.S. Bureau of Labor Statistics, Product Price Indexes (monthly and yearly). From The Universal Almanac, 1992.

CASE The Variety Galore Stores

The Variety Galore Stores is a small chain of shops specializing in gifts, crafts, and party supplies. Working on her MBA at night, the owner, Anita Miller, is using her store records to explore index numbers. She wants to construct and maintain a measure for gauging overall supplier price changes. She plans to use the following historical data obtained from the "flagship" store. The quantities represent the number of units ordered.

Item	Price				Quantity			
	1989	1990	1991	1992	1989	1990	1991	1992
Candles (12″ taper)	.35	.37	.40	.42	144	192	168	192
Picture frames (7″ × 10″)	5.00	6.50	7.15	7.65	144	144	168	192
Gift wrap (yard roll)	1.85	2.15	2.25	2.45	1,000	950	900	850
Mugs	2.75	2.50	2.75	2.90	576	624	672	720
Ball point pens	.13	.12	.14	.15	2,304	2,352	2,496	2,640

You have volunteered to help Anita with her project.

QUESTIONS

1. Calculate the unweighted aggregate price indexes, with 1989 = 100.
2. Calculate the Laspeyres price indexes, with 1989 = 100.
3. Calculate the Paasche indexes, with 1989 = 100.
4. Which index do you recommend Anita use as the most realistic one for measuring changes in prices? Explain.
5. If you had to maintain the index time series indefinitely, which index would involve the least amount of work? Explain.

PART IV

FURTHER TOPICS IN INFERENTIAL STATISTICS

CHAPTER 15

CONTROLLED EXPERIMENTS: TWO-SAMPLE INFERENCES

BEFORE READING THIS CHAPTER, MAKE SURE YOU UNDERSTAND:

The statistical sampling study (Chapter 4).

Statistical estimation (Chapter 8).

Hypothesis testing (Chapter 9).

AFTER READING THIS CHAPTER, YOU WILL UNDERSTAND:

How two-sample experiments are generally structured.

About the two basic sampling schemes for comparing two populations.

The basic procedures for drawing inferences using independent samples.

The procedure for drawing inferences with matched-pairs samples.

How to test hypotheses regarding two population proportions.

A very important area of statistical decision making involves comparing two populations in order to establish what alternative course of action provides better results. Many business applications involve such choices, such as deciding whether to change to a new procedure, package, or product design. Statistical methodology originally developed for biological and medical research can be employed in a wide variety of such business applications.

15-1 THE NATURE OF TWO-SAMPLE INFERENCES

The procedures described in this chapter involve two samples. One sample is selected at random from population *A*, the other from population *B*. Both populations have unknown characteristics. Inferences are made regarding these populations. The letters *A* and *B* are used symbolically as subscripts to separate the two sample groups, so that the sizes of the samples are denoted by n_A and n_B respectively.

CONTROLLED EXPERIMENTS

We will be focusing on **controlled experiments** which use separate samples drawn from the two populations. The sample results culminate in an inference, either an estimate or a hypothesis test. One population is usually traditional, representing observations that would be generated by the status quo, and the second population consists of observations that would arise if a major change is made. For example, a bank might substitute automatic teller machines (ATMs) for human workers. A statistical sampling study may involve two sets of customer waiting times. One set may be for customers attempting machine transactions and another set for customers dealing with human tellers.

The observed waiting times obtained for the ATM sampling study are designated as the **experimental group**. The observed times obtained for the human tellers constitute the **control group**. The sampling study is a controlled experiment, since the investigator attempts to ensure that any differences between groups may be explained by differences in the populations rather than by the testing procedure itself.

INDEPENDENT AND MATCHED-PAIRS SAMPLES

Two basic methods are used to conduct a controlled experiment with two samples. One involves sample observations selected independently for the two groups. The second approach matches elementary units for the two groups. It is simpler to use **independent samples** which allow for different group sample sizes. More careful control is required for **matched-pairs samples**, where smaller group sizes may be used advantageously to achieve the desired reliability, precision, and error protection.

THE SAMPLE SIZE DICHOTOMY

Two parallel methodologies apply when making inferences regarding two means. The choice of method depends on the sample sizes used.

In Chapter 7, we learned that when a *single* sample is selected at random from a population with parameters μ and σ, the central limit theorem states that $\bar{X}$ is approximately normally distributed with mean μ and standard deviation $\sigma/\sqrt{n}$. But the value of σ must be *known* for the normal curve to be used in making probability statements regarding levels of $\bar{X}$. When σ is unknown, the Student t distribution provides the basis for making inferences about μ. Recall also that the Student t distribution approaches the normal distribution as the sample size becomes large.

Using two independent samples, with mean values $\bar{X}_A$ and $\bar{X}_B$, the same issues apply. For large sample sizes, the normal curve is used as the sampling distribution for the difference $\bar{X}_A - \bar{X}_B$ even though the population standard deviations σ_A and σ_B remain unknown. That is strictly an *approximation* which improves with larger n's. One important advantage to using the normal distribution in this fashion is that σ_A and σ_B are allowed to have *different*, if even unknown, levels.

When the n's are small, the normal approximation is poor. In these cases, the Student t distribution is used to make inferences regarding the population means. But in doing so, populations A and B must have *identical standard deviations* of some unknown level.

15-2 CONFIDENCE INTERVALS FOR THE DIFFERENCE BETWEEN MEANS

The simplest two-sample inference involves estimating the difference between two population parameters. We begin by constructing a confidence interval estimate of the difference between the two population means.

For convenience, we will designate the populations as A and B.

POPULATION MEANS

μ_A = Mean of population A

μ_B = Mean of population B

The population that is presumed to have the larger mean is usually denoted by A, although this designation is completely arbitrary. The difference between population means $\mu_A - \mu_B$ may be estimated from the sample results. To do this, the observations may be made either independently or by matching pairs.

INDEPENDENT SAMPLES

It is a simpler procedure to select the sample observations independently. Sample means from the respective populations are denoted by $\bar{X}_A$ and $\bar{X}_B$. As an unbiased estimator of $\mu_A - \mu_B$, we use the

DIFFERENCE BETWEEN THE SAMPLE MEANS

$$d = \bar{X}_A - \bar{X}_B$$

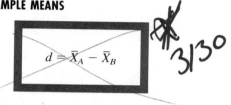

The samples may vary in size.

The sampling distributions of $\bar{X}_A$ and $\bar{X}_B$ may be approximated by the normal curve for sufficiently large samples. Because the samples are selected independently, d will also be approximately normally distributed, with mean $\mu_A - \mu_B$ and standard deviation

$$\sigma_d = \sqrt{\frac{\sigma_A^2}{n_A} + \frac{\sigma_B^2}{n_B}}$$

where σ_A^2 and σ_B^2 are the population variances.*

Ordinarily, the values of σ_A and σ_B are unknown. Two parallel procedures apply for estimating $\mu_A - \mu_B$, depending on the sample sizes.

Large Sample Sizes

When n_A and n_B are both greater than or equal to 30, the following expression is used as an estimator of σ_d.

$$s_d = \sqrt{\frac{s_A^2}{n_A} + \frac{s_B^2}{n_B}}$$

We are now ready to construct the confidence interval estimate of the difference between population means. We select a normal deviate z corresponding to the desired confidence level, so that we estimate the difference between population means by the interval

$$\mu_A - \mu_B = d \pm z s_d$$

However, it is more convenient to use the following expression to compute the $100(1 - \alpha)\%$

CONFIDENCE INTERVAL FOR THE DIFFERENCE BETWEEN MEANS USING INDEPENDENT SAMPLES (large n's)

$$\mu_A - \mu_B = \bar{X}_A - \bar{X}_B \pm z_{\alpha/2}\sqrt{\frac{s_A^2}{n_A} + \frac{s_B^2}{n_B}}$$

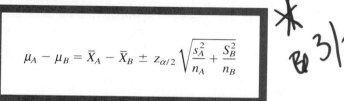

*Here, we make use of the fact that $\bar{X}_A$ and $\bar{X}_B$ are independent random variables, so that the variance of their sum or difference equals the sum of the individual variances.

$$\sigma_d^2 = \sigma^2(\bar{X}_A - \bar{X}_B) = \sigma^2(\bar{X}_A) + \sigma^2(\bar{X}_B) = \frac{\sigma_A^2}{n_A} + \frac{\sigma_B^2}{n_B}$$

Illustration: Comparing Two Textbooks

A statistics professor wishes to compare a new textbook with the textbook she currently uses. She teaches two sections of the same course. The professor continues to use the old book in section B and begins to use the new book in section A. Both sections contain 30 students, and the classes are conducted almost identically. Because the quality of the new book is being evaluated, we will refer to section A as the experimental group and to section B as the control group. The students have been randomly assigned to section A or B, and each may be viewed as a sample of all students taking statistics in the professor's classes.

The effectiveness of each textbook may be measured in terms of the combined examination scores achieved by the students on common tests given throughout the term. Population A represents the potential scores of all students at the university who might use the new textbook in a course taught by this particular professor; population B represents the potential scores these same students would receive using the old textbook.

The sample results are provided in Table 15-1. We will use these data to estimate the difference between mean population scores, $\mu_A - \mu_B$. For this study, $n_A = n_B = 30$. It is not necessary for both samples to be the same size. The following data apply.

$$\bar{X}_A = \frac{2{,}295}{30} = 76.5 \qquad \bar{X}_B = \frac{2{,}223}{30} = 74.1$$

$$s_A^2 = \frac{179{,}607 - 30(76.5)^2}{30 - 1} = 139.29 \qquad s_B^2 = \frac{169{,}043 - 30(74.1)^2}{30 - 1} = 148.92$$

The professor constructs the following 95% confidence interval for $\mu_A - \mu_B$ using normal deviate $z_{.025} = 1.96$.

$$\mu_A - \mu_B = \bar{X}_A - \bar{X}_B \pm z_{.025}\sqrt{\frac{s_A^2}{n_A} + \frac{s_B^2}{n_B}} = 76.5 - 74.1 \pm 1.96\sqrt{\frac{139.29}{30} + \frac{148.92}{30}}$$

$$= 2.4 \pm 6.08$$

or

$$-3.68 \le \mu_A - \mu_B \le 8.48$$

Thus, the mean difference between scores is estimated to lie between -3.68 and 8.48. The limit -3.68 indicates the *disadvantage* in mean scores using book A might be 3.68 points (so that book B might be better), and 8.48 tells us that the *advantage* in mean scores using book A might be as great as 8.48 points.

The interval indicates that if this experiment were repeated several times, the resulting interval estimates would contain the true $\mu_A - \mu_B$ difference about 95% of the time. Note that this estimate is not very precise and does not clearly indicate much difference in effectiveness between the two books.

The following example illustrates the procedure when samples of different size are used.

EXAMPLE: MEASURING THE ADVANTAGE OF SHELF POSITION

A large greeting card chain conducted an experiment to estimate the mean sales advantage due to favorable location of promotional cards. In group A stores, the cards were interspersed within the regular line. In group B stores, the same pro-

TABLE 15-1 Sample Results for Students in Two Classes Using New and Old Books

Students Using New Book (*A*)			Students Using Old Book (*B*)		
Student's Initials	Combined Exam Score X_A	X_A^2	Student's Initials	Combined Exam Score X_B	X_B^2
C.A.	95	9,025	C.A.	85	7,225
L.A.	87	7,569	J.A.	74	5,476
A.B.	84	7,056	O.A.	59	3,481
I.B.	79	6,241	P.A.	71	5,041
P.B.	78	6,084	W.A.	48	2,304
B.C.	93	8,649	D.B.	78	6,084
M.C.	72	5,184	D.C.	94	8,836
D.D.	92	8,464	M.C.	75	5,625
E.E.	89	7,921	B.E.	92	8,464
S.F.	68	4,624	F.E.	85	7,225
T.G.	73	5,329	J.F.	76	5,776
V.G.	53	2,809	S.G.	69	4,761
G.I.	81	6,561	G.H.	82	6,724
F.L.	90	8,100	F.J.	76	5,776
M.L.	77	5,929	J.K.	85	7,225
N.L.	86	7,396	S.L.	70	4,900
G.M.	83	6,889	K.M.	69	4,761
H.M.	91	8,281	M.M.	71	5,041
T.M.	68	4,624	D.N.	80	6,400
N.N.	81	6,561	A.O.	91	8,281
Q.P.	75	5,625	L.P.	77	5,929
P.R.	76	5,776	A.S.	90	8,100
P.S.	64	4,096	B.S.	88	7,744
S.S.	63	3,969	T.S.	60	3,600
W.S.	61	3,721	W.S.	47	2,209
M.T.	83	6,889	L.T.	74	5,476
S.T.	72	5,184	N.T.	63	3,969
W.T.	69	4,761	T.T.	63	3,969
T.W.	59	3,481	L.V.	71	5,041
W.W.	53	2,809	P.W.	60	3,600
	2,295	179,607		2,223	169,043

motional cards were located in a separate special location. Sales of those cards were recorded for two independent random samples. The following data apply.

$$n_A = 50 \qquad n_B = 100$$
$$\bar{X}_A = \$1{,}257 \qquad \bar{X}_B = \$928$$
$$s_A = \$152 \qquad s_B = \$129$$

Find the 95% confidence interval estimate for $\mu_A - \mu_B$.

SOLUTION: Using $z_{.025} = 1.96$, the following 95% confidence interval estimate applies to the difference in mean sales for all stores where promotional cards were displayed.

$$\mu_A - \mu_B = \$1{,}257 - \$928 \pm 1.96\sqrt{\frac{(152)^2}{50} + \frac{(129)^2}{100}}$$

$$= \$329 \pm 49$$

or

$$\$280 \leq \mu_A - \mu_B \leq \$378$$

With 95% confidence, promotional card sales are on the average between \$280 and \$378 higher when interspersed with regular cards.

SMALL SAMPLE SIZES

When $n_A < 30$ or $n_B < 30$, the Student t distribution is used to estimate the difference between population means. The key theoretical assumption is that *both populations must have the same variance.* We must assume that $\sigma_A^2 = \sigma_B^2 = \sigma^2$. We express the standard error of d in a slightly different form than before.

$$\sigma_d = \sqrt{\frac{\sigma^2}{n_A} + \frac{\sigma^2}{n_B}} = \sigma\sqrt{\frac{1}{n_A} + \frac{1}{n_B}}$$

To fulfill this requirement, s_A^2 and s_B^2 must serve as unbiased estimators of σ^2. We obtain an even better estimate of σ^2 by pooling the sample results. Thus, σ_d may be estimated by taking the square root of a weighted average of the sample variances, providing the following expression for the

STANDARD ERROR OF THE DIFFERENCE IN SAMPLE MEANS (small *n*'s)

$$s_{d\text{-small}} = \sqrt{\frac{(n_A - 1)s_A^2 + (n_B - 1)s_B^2}{n_A + n_B - 2}}\sqrt{\frac{1}{n_A} + \frac{1}{n_B}}$$

(Note that the denominator of the first term has been reduced by 2 to yield an unbiased estimator.)

The following expression is used to compute the $100(1 - \alpha)\%$

CONFIDENCE INTERVAL FOR THE DIFFERENCE BETWEEN MEANS USING INDEPENDENT SAMPLES (small *n*'s)

$$\mu_A - \mu_B = \bar{X}_A - \bar{X}_B \pm t_{\alpha/2}s_{d\text{-small}}$$

We find $t_{\alpha/2}$ from Appendix Table F using the α that corresponds to the confidence level. The number of degrees of freedom is $n_A + n_B - 2$. In effect, the combined sample size $n_A + n_B$ must be reduced by 2, because one degree of freedom is lost in calculating each of the two sample variances.

EXAMPLE: COST SAVINGS FOR AUTOMATED TELLERS

A large bank estimated the cost per transaction for customer cash withdrawals from checking accounts. The mean cost of human teller processing is μ_A, while that for automated teller processing is μ_B. Using the weekly costs per transaction for $n_A = 10$ branches and for $n_B = 15$ automated teller sites, the bank obtained the following data.

$n_A = 10$ $\quad$ $n_B = 15$

$$\bar{X}_A = \$.13 \qquad \bar{X}_B = \$.09$$

$$s_A = \$.021 \qquad s_B = \$.018$$

Find the 90% confidence interval estimate of the difference in mean costs.

SOLUTION: Using $t_{.05} = 1.714$, from Appendix Table F for $10 + 15 - 2 = 23$ degrees of freedom, we find the following

$$\mu_A - \mu_B = \$.13 - \$.09 \pm 1.714 \sqrt{\frac{(10 - 1)(.021)^2 + (15 - 1)(.018)^2}{10 + 15 - 2}} \sqrt{\frac{1}{10} + \frac{1}{15}}$$

$$= \$.04 \pm .013$$

or

$$\$.027 \leq \mu_A - \mu_B \leq \$.053$$

With 90% confidence, the mean cost savings for automated tellers lie between \$.027 and \$.053 per transaction.

MATCHED-PAIRS SAMPLES

To obtain a **matched-pairs sample**, each observation from population *A* is made in such a way that the selected elementary unit is matched with a "twin" from population *B*. For example, in evaluating a new drug, each patient in the control group would have an experiment partner of the same sex, as well as age, weight, height, build, and other physiological characteristics. In educational testing, partners would be matched by aptitude and intelligence, family background, socio-economic level, and achievement. In every case, matching would be based on factors that might influence the characteristic being measured.

The individual differences between each pair can be used to estimate population differences. Thus, matched-pairs sampling attempts to explain the differences between individual pairs in terms of differences caused by the factor under examination, while minimizing variability in extraneous influences. The net effect is to reduce the impact of sampling error and thereby obtain greater sampling efficiency.

To illustrate how we obtain matched pairs, we will expand the textbook-comparison sampling study. Suppose that the statistics professor decides to match the students in the two classes. Each matched pair should be closely alike in statistical aptitude and achievement in related areas. Because the students *should be matched before the actual sample observations are made*—a safeguard that minimizes bias in selecting pairs—the professor cannot base her matching criteria on the two classes' performance on statistics tests given during the year.

However, the professor can use the quantitative SAT scores currently on file as a matching criterion for statistical aptitude. As a measure of achievement, she might use the students' grades in the prerequisite mathematics course. Suppose the professor uses these indicators to match her students. Table 15-2 shows one matching assignment, using mathematics grades as the main ranking device and quantitative SAT scores to distinguish between students who have identical mathematics grades. In terms of these criteria, two "A" students having respective SAT scores of 706 and 713 constitute the first pair; similarly, two "C" students scoring 455 and 454 are the nineteenth pair. The sample observations are denoted by X_{A_i} and X_{B_i} for the respective population partner in the ith matched pair.

For each sample we find the

MATCHED-PAIRS DIFFERENCE

$$d_i = X_{A_i} - X_{B_i}$$

Note that d_i should not be confused with the unsubscripted d that we used earlier to express the difference between the means of two independent samples rather than individual pairs.

In the usual manner, we find the

MEAN OF THE MATCHED-PAIRS DIFFERENCES

$$\bar{d} = \frac{\sum d_i}{n}$$

where n is the *number of pairs* observed in the sampling study. Analogously, we determine the

STANDARD DEVIATION OF THE MATCHED-PAIRS DIFFERENCES

$$s_{d\text{-paired}} = \sqrt{\frac{\sum d_i^2 - n\bar{d}^2}{n - 1}}$$

Here, $\bar{d}$ represents the mean of n separate matched-pairs differences and has an expected value of $\mu_A - \mu_B$.

TABLE 15-2 Matching Students in Two Classes Using Mathematics Grades and Quantitative SAT Scores

	Students Using New Book (*A*)			Students Using Old Book (*B*)		
Pair	Student's Initials	Mathematics Grade	Quantitative SAT Score	Student's Initials	Mathematics Grade	Quantitative SAT Score
1	A.B.	A	706	A.O.	A	713
2	B.C.	A	702	A.S.	A	698
3	C.A.	A	674	B.E.	A	685
4	D.D.	A	660	B.S.	A	659
5	E.E.	A	622	C.A.	A	610
6	F.L.	B	685	D.C.	A	507
7	G.M.	B	683	D.N.	B	671
8	G.I.	B	623	D.B.	B	654
9	H.M.	B	583	F.J.	B	612
10	I.B.	B	582	F.E.	B	596
11	L.A.	B	581	G.H.	B	575
12	N.L.	B	525	J.K.	B	533
13	M.T.	B	489	J.F.	B	477
14	M.L.	B	425	J.A.	B	454
15	M.C.	C	523	K.M.	B	426
16	N.N.	C	512	L.P.	C	544
17	Q.P.	C	510	L.T.	C	523
18	P.R.	C	468	L.V.	C	481
19	P.B.	C	455	M.C.	C	454
20	P.S.	C	421	M.M.	C	409
21	S.F.	C	411	N.T.	C	408
22	S.S.	C	394	O.A.	C	402
23	S.T.	C	359	P.A.	C	383
24	T.M.	C	342	P.W.	C	336
25	T.G.	C	326	S.L.	C	326
26	T.W.	C	308	S.G.	C	315
27	W.S.	C	295	T.S.	D	435
28	W.T.	D	421	T.T.	D	386
29	V.G.	D	351	W.A.	D	321
30	W.W.	D	288	W.S.	D	317

Although two populations, *A* and *B*, generate the respective samples, it is helpful to consider the hypothetical single *population of paired differences*. Theoretically, inferences regarding that population may be made in exactly the same way as for any single population, like those presented in Chapters 8 and 9. Usually the standard deviation of the paired-difference population is unknown, so that the Student *t* distribution is used.

The following expression is used to compute the $100(1 - \alpha)\%$

CONFIDENCE INTERVAL FOR THE DIFFERENCE BETWEEN MEANS USING MATCHED PAIRS

$$\mu_A - \mu_B = \bar{d} \pm t_{\alpha/2} \frac{s_{d\text{-paired}}}{\sqrt{n}}$$

* 3/30/94

We find the critical value $t_{\alpha/2}$ from Appendix Table F for $n - 1$ degrees of freedom.

Returning to the statistic professor's problem of estimating the difference between population mean scores using the new and old books, the values of the matched-pairs differences are given in Table 15-3. For $n = 30$ pairs, the professor obtained the following results.

$$\bar{d} = 2.4 \qquad s_{d\text{-paired}} = 5.01$$

Note that 2.4 is the same point estimate for $\mu_A - \mu_B$ that we found earlier using the same data as independent samples. We may now construct a 95% confidence

TABLE 15-3 Calculation of Matched-Pairs Differences for Student Scores Using New and Old Books

	Student Pair		Combined Exam Scores			
i	Group A Student	Group B Student	Group A X_{A_i}	Group B X_{B_i}	Difference d_i	d_i^2
1	A.B.	A.O.	84	91	− 7	49
2	B.C.	A.S.	93	90	3	9
3	C.A.	B.E.	95	92	3	9
4	D.D.	B.S.	92	88	4	16
5	E.E.	C.A.	89	85	4	16
6	F.L.	D.C.	90	94	− 4	16
7	G.M.	D.N.	83	80	3	9
8	G.I.	D.B.	81	78	3	9
9	H.M.	F.J.	91	76	15	225
10	I.B.	F.E.	79	85	− 6	36
11	L.A.	G.H.	87	82	5	25
12	N.L.	J.K.	86	85	1	1
13	M.T.	J.F.	83	76	7	49
14	M.L.	J.A.	77	74	3	9
15	M.C.	K.M.	72	69	3	9
16	N.N.	L.P.	81	77	4	16
17	Q.P.	L.T.	75	74	1	1
18	P.R.	L.V.	76	71	5	25
19	P.B.	M.C.	78	75	3	9
20	P.S.	M.M.	64	71	− 7	49
21	S.F.	N.T.	68	63	5	25
22	S.S.	O.A.	63	59	4	16
23	S.T.	P.A.	72	71	1	1
24	T.M.	P.W.	68	60	8	64
25	T.G.	S.L.	73	70	3	9
26	T.W.	S.G.	59	69	− 10	100
27	W.S.	T.S.	61	60	1	1
28	W.T.	T.T.	69	63	6	36
29	V.G.	W.A.	53	48	5	25
30	W.W.	W.S.	53	47	6	36
			2,295	2,223	72	900

$$\bar{d} = \frac{\sum d_i}{n} = \frac{72}{30} = 2.4$$

$$s_{d\text{-paired}} = \sqrt{\frac{\sum d_i^2 - n\bar{d}^2}{n - 1}} = \sqrt{\frac{900 - 30(2.4)^2}{29}}$$

$$= \sqrt{25.0759} = 5.01$$

interval estimate of $\mu_A - \mu_B$. Using $\alpha/2 = .025$ and $30 - 1 = 29$ degrees of freedom, Appendix Table F provides the critical value $t_{.025} = 2.045$. Thus,

$$\mu_A - \mu_B = \bar{d} \pm t_{.025}\frac{s_{d\text{-paired}}}{\sqrt{n}} = 2.4 \pm 2.045\left(\frac{5.01}{\sqrt{30}}\right)$$

$$= 2.4 \pm 1.87$$

so that

$$.53 \leq \mu_A - \mu_B \leq 4.27$$

This confidence interval is more precise than the one found previously using the student test data as independent samples.

EXAMPLE: EVALUATING A NEW COMPUTER MEMORY

A systems analyst for the Marlborough County Data Center has proposed adopting the virtual memory used in neighboring Kent County. The counties have identical computers and otherwise identical software. A special test is to be administered to estimate the savings in mean "throughput" time required to process regular job batches under the proposed system. Designating Marlborough's present system A and the new system B, a random sample of $n = 25$ batches has been run twice, once in each county. Thus, the two processing times for one batch constitute the observations of a matched pair. For the ith batch, d_i represents the throughput time on the Marlborough computer run minus the throughput time on the Kent run. The following results apply.

$$\bar{d} = 25 \text{ minutes} \qquad s_{d\text{-paired}} = 20 \text{ minutes}$$

A 95% confidence interval estimate of the savings in mean batch throughput time using virtual memory may then be constructed.

SOLUTION: Using $t_{.025} = 2.064$ for $25 - 1 = 24$ degrees of freedom, the estimated mean time advantage is

$$\mu_A - \mu_B = 25 \pm 2.064\frac{20}{\sqrt{25}}$$

$$= 25 \pm 8.3$$

so that

$$16.7 \leq \mu_A - \mu_B \leq 33.3 \text{ minutes per batch}$$

This confidence interval indicates that Marlborough's present computer software may be improved by using virtual memory. Mean batch processing time will be reduced by a value that lies between 16.7 and 33.3 minutes.

MATCHED-PAIRS COMPARED TO INDEPENDENT SAMPLES

Is independent sampling or matched pairs the better procedure? We begin to answer this question by comparing the sample sizes required to provide identical levels of estimation reliability for the same tolerable error.

In general, the comparative advantage of matched-pairs sampling depends on how closely the matching scheme correlates population A values with population

B values. A good matching criterion should eliminate most extraneous sources of variation, so that this correlation would ordinarily be quite high.

It is easier to compare samples if an equal number of observations are taken from A and B, so that $n_A = n_B$. We may also presume that population variabilities are similar, so that σ_A and σ_B are approximately equal. Under these conditions, it is possible to prove mathematically that *matched-pairs sampling requires a smaller sample size than independent sampling and that this reduction in required sample size is proportional to the population correlation coefficient.* Thus, if A and B have a correlation coefficient of .9, a 90% savings in sample size can be achieved by using matched pairs; that is, 10 times as many observations are required for independent samples to yield as precise and reliable results as matched pairs. If the correlation coefficient is .99, independent sampling would require 100 times as many observations as matched-pairs sampling.

Returning to our original question, we may ask why independent samples are used at all. In part, independent sampling is prevalent because it is often difficult to match pairs and because it is time consuming to make each observation. Sometimes it is possible to match elementary units advantageously. Successful matching generally requires that a large amount of data be collected for every unit. Not only must these data be studied to establish relevant matching criteria—perhaps using multiple regression and correlation techniques—but they must also be carefully applied when the sample units are paired. Once this has been accomplished, further sampling costs are comparable, observation by observation, to independent sampling costs. For a study involving continued monitorship over a long period of time, matched-pairs samples have a distinct cost advantage. Thus, they are preferable in medical studies, where the fixed cost of establishing the sample pairs is small in comparison to total expenses.

EXERCISES

15-1 The dean of the business school at State University wishes to compare the GMAT scores of his graduate students to those of nonbusiness students. Scores have been obtained for two independent random samples. The following data apply.

Business Students	Nonbusiness Students
$n_A = 100$	$n_B = 150$
$\bar{X}_A = 620.1$	$\bar{X}_B = 576.4$
$s_A^2 = 1{,}874$	$s_B^2 = 2{,}057$

Construct a 95% confidence interval for the difference between population means.

15-2 Independent random samples have been obtained for the fuel consumption (miles per gallon) of two car models. The following results apply.

Car A	Car B
$n_A = 10$	$n_B = 10$
$\bar{X}_A = 24$	$\bar{X}_B = 22.5$
$s_A^2 = 2$	$s_B^2 = 2.5$

Construct a 95% confidence interval estimate of the difference between mean fuel consumptions.

15-3 Suppose that the drivers of the two cars in Exercise 15-2 have been matched according to their driving skills. By subtracting car *B*'s mpg from car *A*'s mpg, the following results were obtained for the mean and the standard deviation.

$$\bar{d} = 1.5 \text{ mpg} \qquad s_{d\text{-paired}} = 1.2 \text{ mpg}$$

Construct a 95% confidence interval for the difference between mean fuel consumptions.

15-4 CompTel Corporation has collected independent random samples for the transaction times (seconds) of two computer teleprocessing monitors. The following data apply.

Monitor A			
12.7	13.4	14.5	11.7
10.6	11.4	12.2	13.7
14.1	13.3	12.6	12.2
11.3	12.5	12.3	13.7
15.1	13.7	12.5	14.4
12.5	13.3	13.3	14.5
12.5	13.3	13.5	12.5
10.7	10.5	12.4	11.9
12.0	13.5	14.1	

Monitor B			
9.8	10.4	12.6	13.7
12.3	11.7	12.1	10.8
12.6	11.9	10.1	9.9
12.3	12.1	11.6	10.8
13.1	11.5	10.9	11.4
10.2	10.4	12.7	12.6
11.2	11.7	12.4	13.1
11.0	12.0	13.1	12.0

Construct a 99% confidence interval estimate of the difference between mean processing times.

15-5 In a sample test evaluation of assembly operations, MakeWave Corporation considered two different sequences. A sample of $n = 100$ workers were timed for batches of parts assembled under sequence *A*. The same workers were timed for another group of the same parts assembled under sequence *B*. The average time per part was found for each sequence and worker. Subtracting each worker's sequence *B* average time from that of sequence *A*, the mean difference was found to be .25 minute with a standard deviation of .75 minute. Construct a 95% confidence interval estimate of the difference between population mean assembly times.

15-6 The following student GPA data have been obtained for matched pairs randomly selected from two populations at Old Ivy University. Group *A* consists of students who work less than 20 hours a week. Group *B* consists of students who hold full-time jobs.

A	B	A	B	A	B	A	B
3.65	3.71	2.84	2.75	3.22	3.15	3.61	3.40
3.25	2.96	2.86	2.91	3.11	2.95	3.55	3.35
3.33	3.17	3.55	3.51	4.00	3.86	3.74	3.55
2.54	2.27	2.85	2.62	3.45	3.28	3.61	3.48
3.44	3.42	3.65	3.51	3.12	2.88	3.05	3.12
3.14	3.02	3.67	3.50	3.24	3.18	3.15	2.91
3.29	3.17	3.64	3.52	3.78	3.42	3.20	2.95
2.65	2.90	2.85	2.69	3.53	3.37	3.15	3.11
3.22	2.84	3.55	3.65	3.52	3.44		

Construct a 95% confidence interval for the difference between mean GPA for all students in the respective populations.

15-7 Mirror Images collected the following annual operating cost sample for two high-volume copiers.

Copier A			Copier B		
$12,366	$12,575	$13,589	$ 7,024	$11,115	$10,443
11,950	13,820	12,276	18,203	6,450	4,255
11,786	12,479	13,125	12,357	19,204	4,158
12,659			23,425	3,718	8,295
			6,225	4,870	9,146

(a) Compute the mean and standard deviation for each sample.

(b) Construct a 95% confidence interval estimate of the difference between mean costs for the two copiers.

15-8 Gotham City's manager wished to determine the amount of savings in fuel consumption that would result if the tires were converted on all city cars. New tires were ordered for 200 cars; half of these cars were equipped with steel radial tires and the rest with the standard cord variety. Cars in the two groups were matched by make, model, age, use (police, building inspection, and so on), and general condition. A month-long test revealed that the mean decrease in fuel consumption when radial tires were used was 2 miles per gallon. The standard deviation in savings for the paired cars was also 2 miles per gallon. Construct a 95% confidence interval estimate of the savings advantage in mean fuel consumption that would result if radial tires were used on all city cars.

15-9 Elegante Printers wishes to determine the advantage of splitting its large custom order catalog into two segments that are easier to handle. The company conducted a sampling investigation using group *A* retail stores, where the split catalog was displayed, and group *B* stores, where the large catalog was used. Stores from each group were paired according to historical sales, size, geographical location, and many other factors. The following sales data apply.

Store	Sales		Store	Sales		Store	Sales	
i	X_{A_i}	X_{B_i}	i	X_{A_i}	X_{B_i}	i	X_{A_i}	X_{B_i}
1	$1,052	$ 987	11	$8,950	$9,235	21	$2,050	$1,975
2	4,226	3,929	12	5,025	4,810	22	550	375
3	2,550	2,743	13	2,714	2,705	23	840	525
4	980	540	14	922	741	24	2,250	2,170
5	1,105	1,024	15	4,455	3,693	25	1,777	1,523
6	4,885	3,901	16	2,500	3,100	26	1,627	1,552
7	833	904	17	1,125	1,084	27	902	822
8	1,770	1,550	18	666	522	28	1,220	1,110
9	2,565	1,945	19	2,005	1,814	29	4,250	4,527
10	3,220	3,175	20	1,615	1,922	30	943	602

Construct a 95% confidence interval estimate of the difference between mean sales for the two catalog versions.

15-3 HYPOTHESIS TESTS FOR COMPARING TWO MEANS

In addition to estimating the difference between two population means, hypothesis-testing procedures can be used to determine whether or not population A values are significantly larger or smaller than population B values. These methods permit choices to be made. Thus, an experimental compensation program may be adopted because the statistical test concludes that workers paid under it attain a higher mean productivity than those paid under the existing program. A new drug may be rejected by a hospital staff because its mean relief level does not significantly exceed that of a drug currently in use. The owner of a taxicab fleet may find that sample results indicate a new tire supplier should be awarded a contract because his tires wear longer than the present brand. In each case, sample data are required for both the control and the experimental groups.

In two-sample tests, the null hypothesis may be stated in any one of the following forms.

H_0: $\mu_A \geq \mu_B$	or	H_0: $\mu_A - \mu_B \geq 0$	(lower-tailed test)
H_0: $\mu_A \leq \mu_B$	or	H_0: $\mu_A - \mu_B \leq 0$	(upper-tailed test)
H_0: $\mu_A = \mu_B$	or	H_0: $\mu_A - \mu_B = 0$	(two-sided test)

The equivalent expressions on the right are found by subtracting μ_B on both sides of the original inequalities. As in estimating the difference between two means, two-sample hypothesis tests can be applied to independent samples as well as to matched pairs.

INDEPENDENT SAMPLES

When samples are selected independently, an appropriate test statistic is $d = \bar{X}_A - \bar{X}_B$. As in estimating $\mu_A - \mu_B$, there are two methods for testing H_0, depending on whether the sample sizes are large or small.

Large Sample Sizes

When $n_A \geq 30$ and $n_B \geq 30$, the normal deviate serves as the test statistic. The following expression is used to compute the

NORMAL DEVIATE FOR INDEPENDENT SAMPLES (large *n*'s)

$$z = \frac{d}{s_d} = \frac{\bar{X}_A - \bar{X}_B}{\sqrt{\dfrac{s_A^2}{n_A} + \dfrac{s_B^2}{n_B}}}$$

*411

We will illustrate this procedure by conducting a comparison of automobile exhaust emissions.

Illustration: Testing Exhaust Emissions

In evaluating how effectively a new automobile engine controls exhaust emissions, the U.S. Environment Protection Agency might conduct a sampling study like the one we will describe here. The experimental group (A) consists of a sample of $n_A = 50$ prototype turbocharged engines proposed to replace conventional engines. The control group (B) contains a sample of $n_B = 100$ fuel injection engines equipped with catalytic converters. (Note that different sample sizes were used for the two groups.)

STEP 1

Formulate the null hypothesis. The EPA wishes to use the null hypothesis that the mean sulfur-dioxide emissions level in parts per million (ppm) for all turbocharged engines is at least as great as that for the current fuel injection engines. The following null hypothesis applies.

$$H_0\colon \mu_A \geq \mu_B$$

STEP 2

Select the test statistic and procedure. The normal deviate z serves as the test statistic.

STEP 3

Establish the significance level and identify the acceptance and rejection regions. Because rejecting the null hypothesis will permit a manufacturer to install the turbocharged engine in all its cars, the EPA has established an $\alpha = .01$ significance level for the test; that is, there is a 1% chance of making the incorrect decision and concluding that turbocharged engines are cleaner than fuel injection engines when the opposite is true. From Appendix Table E, we find $z_{.01} = 2.33$. Because a large negative difference between sample means will refute the null hypothesis, the test is lower-tailed. The acceptance and rejection regions are shown below.

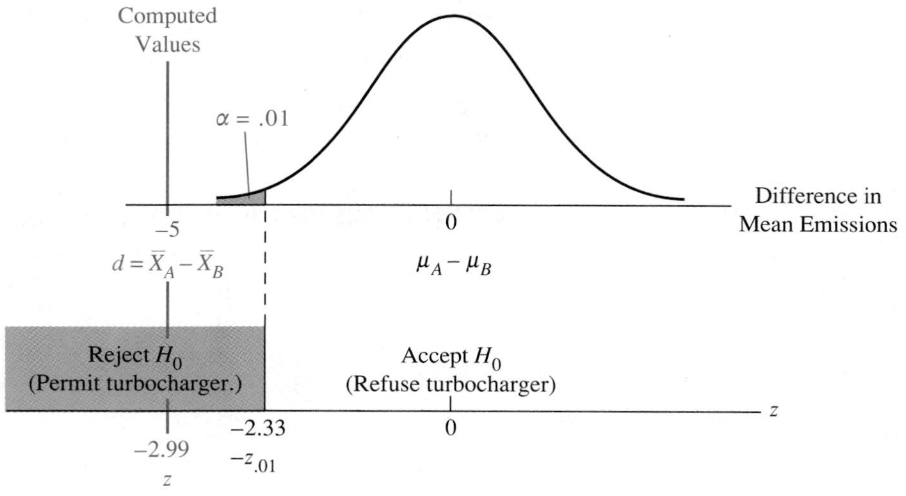

STEP 4

Collect the sample and compute the value of the test statistic. The following sample results have been obtained for sulfur-dioxide emissions.

Turbocharged Engine	Fuel Injection Engine
$\overline{X}_A = 25$ ppm	$\overline{X}_B = 30$ ppm
$s_A^2 = 90$	$s_B^2 = 100$

The computed value of the normal deviate z is

$$z = \frac{\overline{X}_A - \overline{X}_B}{\sqrt{\dfrac{s_A^2}{n_A} + \dfrac{s_B^2}{n_B}}} = \frac{25 - 30}{\sqrt{\dfrac{90}{50} + \dfrac{100}{100}}} = -2.99$$

STEP 5

Make the decision. Since $z = -2.99$ falls in the rejection region, the null hypothesis must be *rejected.* The EPA must permit the turbocharged engine to be installed.

The above example involves a lower-tailed test. An upper-tailed test with H_0: $\mu_A \le \mu_B$ has a rejection region with large positive values of z. A two-sided test (when H_0: $\mu_A = \mu_B$) has a double rejection region.

The two-sided test is often conducted in conjunction with a confidence interval estimate of $\mu_A - \mu_B$. In the beginning of this chapter, we found that the 95% confidence interval for the difference between population mean statistics scores for students using a new book A and students using an old book B is

$$-3.68 \le \mu_A - \mu_B \le 8.48$$

Since this interval contains the value 0, the null hypothesis for those data—H_0: $\mu_A = \mu_B$ or $\mu_A - \mu_B = 0$—must be *accepted* at an $\alpha = 1 - .95 = .05$ significance level.

Small Sample Sizes

When $n_A < 30$ or $n_B < 30$, the testing procedure is based on the Student t distribution. The following expression is used to compute the

STUDENT t STATISTIC FOR INDEPENDENT SAMPLES (small n's)

$$t = \frac{\overline{X}_A - \overline{X}_B}{\sqrt{\dfrac{(n_A - 1)s_A^2 + (n_B - 1)s_B^2}{n_A + n_B - 2}}\sqrt{\dfrac{1}{n_A} + \dfrac{1}{n_B}}}$$

We find the critical value corresponding to the desired significance level α from Appendix Table F for $n_A + n_B - 2$ degrees of freedom. The following example illustrates this procedure.

ILLUSTRATION: FORMULATING A SOAP

Laboratory researchers for a home products company are formulating a new soap. They plan to recommend version A if it is found to be significantly more effective than version B. The effectiveness of a soap is measured from wash tests by finding the mean percentage reduction in stain area μ.

STEP 1

Formulate the null hypothesis. The researchers assume that version A is not more effective. The following null hypothesis applies.

$$H_0: \mu_A \leq \mu_B$$

STEP 2

Select the test statistic and procedure. The Student t serves as the test statistic because both $n_A = 10$ and $n_B = 15$ are less than 30.

STEP 3

Establish the significance level and identify the acceptance and rejection regions. The researcher chooses an $\alpha = .05$ significance level. For $10 + 15 - 2 = 23$ degrees of freedom, Appendix Table F provides $t_{.05} = 1.714$. Since a large positive value of $d = \bar{X}_A - \bar{X}_B$ will refute the null hypothesis, the test is upper-tailed. The acceptance and rejection regions are shown in the following figure.

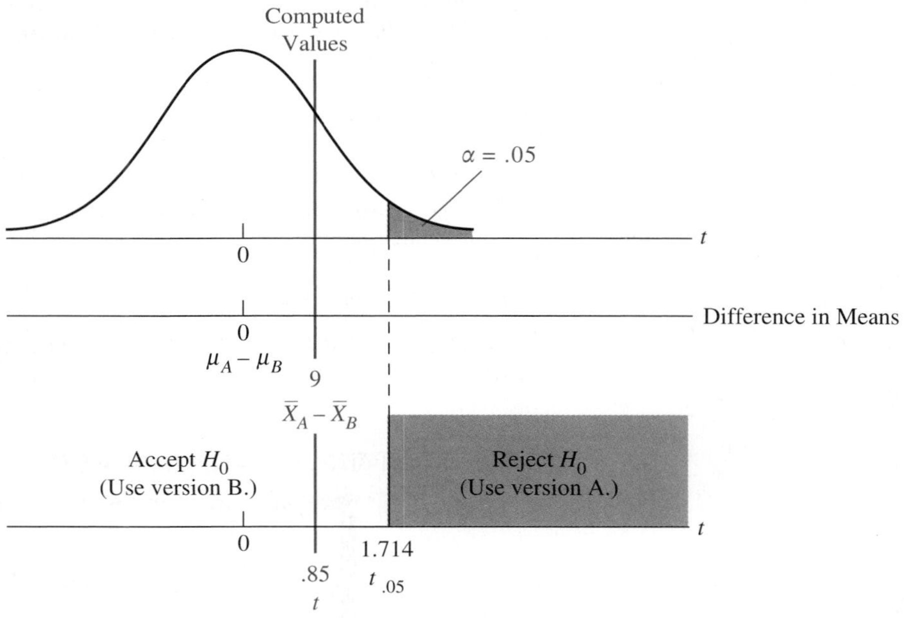

STEP 4

Collect the sample and compute the value of the test statistic. The following sample results have been obtained for each sample.

Version A	**Version B**
$\bar{X}_A = 45\%$	$\bar{X}_B = 36\%$
$s_A^2 = 706$	$s_B^2 = 654$

The computed value of the test statistic t is

$$t = \frac{45 - 36}{\sqrt{\frac{9(706) + 14(654)}{23}}\sqrt{\frac{1}{10} + \frac{1}{15}}} = .85$$

STEP 5

Make the decision. The computed value $t = .85$ falls within the acceptance region. The null hypothesis that version A is not more effective must be *accepted.*

MATCHED-PAIRS SAMPLES

When matched pairs are used, we find the pair differences $d_i = X_{A_i} - X_{B_i}$ and calculate their mean $\bar{d}$ and standard deviation $s_{d\text{-paired}}$. Since the standard deviation of the matched-pairs differences is ordinarily unknown, the Student t distribution applies regardless of the number of sample pairs.

STUDENT *t* STATISTIC FOR MATCHED PAIRS

$$t = \frac{\bar{d}}{s_{d\text{-paired}}/\sqrt{n}}$$

We find the critical value t_α of the desired significance level α from Appendix Table F, using $n - 1$ degrees of freedom. For a two-sided test, we use $t_{\alpha/2}$ as the critical value.

To illustrate this procedure, we will conduct a one-tailed test using the computer system evaluation data for the example on page 659.

STEP 1

Formulate the null hypothesis. The systems analyst wishes to test whether Kent County's new virtual memory system (B) is as slow as or slower (not faster) than Marlborough's present system (A). The following null hypothesis applies.

$$H_0\text{: } \mu_A \leq \mu_B$$

STEP 2

Select the test statistic and procedure. The Student t serves as the test statistic.

STEP 3

Establish the significance level and identify the acceptance and rejection regions. A significance level of $\alpha = .05$ is desired. For $n - 1 = 24$ degrees of freedom, the critical value of the test statistic is $t_{.05} = 1.711$. Since a large positive value of $\bar{d}$ (and therefore t) will refute the null hypothesis, the test is upper-tailed. The acceptance and rejection regions are shown below.

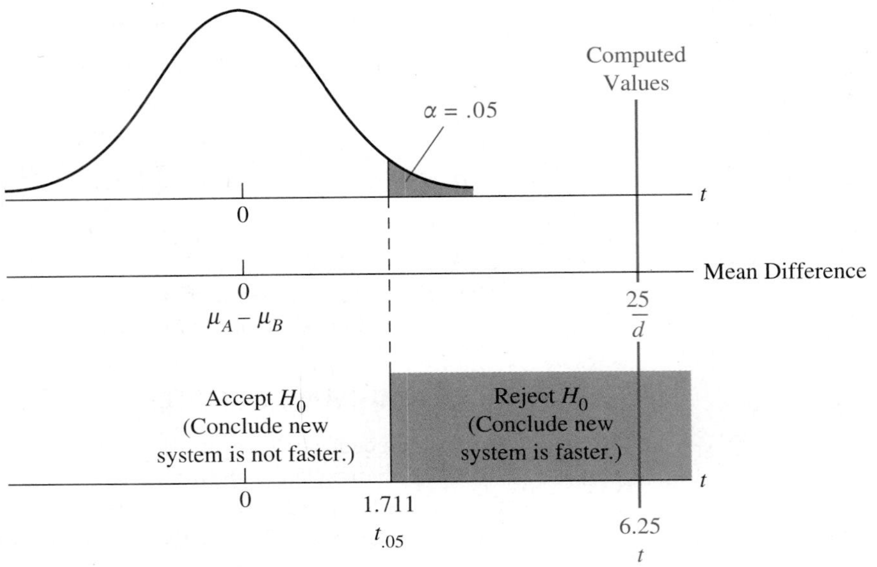

STEP 4

Collect the sample and compute the value of the test statistic. The computed value of the test statistic is

$$t = \frac{25}{20/\sqrt{25}} = 6.25$$

STEP 5

Make the decision. Since $t = 6.25$ falls in the rejection region, the null hypothesis must be *rejected.* The analyst must conclude that Kent County's new virtual memory system is faster than Marlborough's present system.

EXAMPLE: DOES METALLIC PAINT LAST LONGER THAN ACRYLIC PAINT?

You wish to test the null hypothesis that acrylic paint lasts at least as long as metallic paint. You paint 15 metal plates on one side with acrylic paint (A) and on the other with metallic paint (B). In terms of the mean paint lifetimes, the following null hypothesis applies.

$$H_0\text{: } \mu_A \geq \mu_B$$

You deliver the plates to an environmental testing laboratory where they are subjected to abuse until both paints are so worn that they must be replaced. The lab technicians note the time until each paint is worn out. Suppose you compute $\bar{d} = -1.4$ months with $s_{d\text{-paired}} = 2$ months. Does metallic paint last longer?

SOLUTION: You select an $\alpha = .05$ significance level, using the critical value for $15 - 1 = 14$ degrees of freedom, so that $t_{.05} = 1.761$. After subtracting the survival time of the metallic paint from that of the acrylic, you average the pair differences, compute their standard deviation, and find t. The following decision rule applies.

Accept H_0 if $t \geq -1.761$ (Conclude acrylic paint lasts at least as long as metallic.)

Reject H_0 if $t < -1.761$ (Conclude metallic paint outlasts acrylic.)

You compute the value of the test statistic to be

$$t = \frac{-1.4}{2/\sqrt{15}} = -2.711$$

Since this value lies in the rejection region, you *reject* H_0 and conclude that metallic paint outlasts acrylic paint.

EXAMPLE: TIRE TREAD LIFETIME

A tire manufacturer will cancel the scheduled revision of its tire tread template only if the new design exhibits significantly worse mileage than the present one. Letting A represent the present design and B the new one, the respective mean tire tread lifetimes are μ_A and μ_B. The following null hypothesis applies.

H_0: $\mu_A \leq \mu_B$ (New design is longer-lived.)

A sample of 100 cars was driven with tires of the present design on one side and those of the new design on the other. After 30,000 miles of driving, an estimate was made for each car of the remaining lifetime for the two types of tires. Then the value for the revised tire was subtracted from that for the present tire. The following sample results have been obtained.

$\bar{d} = 76$ miles $s_{d\text{-paired}} = 421$ miles

What should the tiremaker do?

SOLUTION: Since a large positive value of $\bar{d}$ will refute the null hypothesis, the test is upper-tailed. A significance level of $\alpha = .01$ is desired. Using $n - 1 = 100 - 1 = 99$ degrees of freedom, Appendix Table F provides the nearest tabled value of $t_{.01} = 2.358$ from the df $= 120$ row. The following decision rule applies.

Accept H_0 if $t \leq 2.358$ (Revise the template.)

Reject H_0 if $t > 2.358$ (Cancel the revision.)

The computed value of the test statistic is

$$t = \frac{76}{421/\sqrt{100}} = 1.81$$

Since this value does not exceed the critical value, H_0 is *accepted*, and the tire tread template must be revised.

THE EFFICIENCY OF MATCHED-PAIRS TESTING

The earlier arguments for and against matched-pairs sampling apply to hypothesis testing as well. A matched-pairs test is much more efficient or powerful than a test of independent samples. In matched-pairs sampling, a much smaller sample size can generally be used to provide similar protection against committing the Type I and Type II errors. However, matched-pairs sampling is more costly and should be used only when suitable matching criteria and supporting data are available.

EXERCISES

15-10 Sly Fox is a real estate property manager who wishes to compare net monthly incomes for two different leasing agreements. Plan *A* has tenants sign for a lower rent but requires them to pay for all small repairs themselves. Plan *B* has tenants pay more rent but they are not responsible for repairs. As the null hypothesis, the manager assumes that plan *B* yields at least as great a mean income as plan *A*. The following data have been obtained for independent random samples of 15 leases each.

Plan A	Plan B
$\bar{X}_A = \$132.45$	$\bar{X}_B = \$128.06$
$s_A^2 = 123$	$s_B^2 = 95$

At a 5% significance level, should the manager reject the null hypothesis?

15-11 To evaluate two alternative assembly procedures, a Hoopla Hoops production manager has gathered independent sample data from pilot runs of both. She wishes to protect herself from erroneously concluding that the procedures are equally fast, in terms of mean assembly times, at an $\alpha = .05$ significance level. She has collected the following data.

$$n_A = 100 \qquad n_B = 100$$
$$\bar{X}_A = 10.8 \text{ minutes} \qquad \bar{X}_B = 10.6 \text{ minutes}$$
$$s_A = .21 \text{ minutes} \qquad s_B = .19 \text{ minutes}$$

What conclusion should the manager reach?

15-12 Refer to the data for teleprocessing transaction times given in Exercise 15-4. Test the null hypothesis that monitor *A* involves times that are on the average less than or equal to those of monitor *B*. At a 1% significance level, should you accept or reject H_0?

15-13 To combat aphid infestation, Rich Sod must decide whether he should spray his fruit trees with pesticide or inundate them with ladybugs. He sprays 250 trees and uses ladybugs on another 250 trees. The farmer's null hypothesis is that spraying (A) produces a mean yield at least as great as the yield obtained using natural predators (B). His sample results for spraying provide a mean of 10 bushels of good fruit per tree, with a standard deviation of 3 bushels. Using ladybugs, the mean is 10.5 bushels of good fruit per tree, with a standard deviation of 1 bushel. Should the farmer accept or reject the null hypothesis at a .05 significance level?

15-14 Refer to the student GPA data given in Exercise 15-6. Test the null hypothesis that full-time job holders achieve GPA's at least as great as those of nonworking students. At a 1% significance level, should you accept or reject H_0?

15-15 Slalomander is a ski equipment manufacturer comparing two types of ski bindings. A total of 100 matched pairs of skiers participated in the study. Group A consisted of skiers with loosely adjusted bindings, group B skiers had tightly adjusted bindings. The number of accidents per hour of skiing was determined for each skier. The following results were obtained.

$$\bar{d} = .05 \qquad s_{d\text{-paired}} = .01$$

(a) Construct a 95% confidence interval estimate of the difference in mean accident rates.

(b) At a 5% significance level, should the manufacturer accept or reject the null hypothesis that tightness of bindings makes no difference in the mean ski accident rate?

15-16 Refer to the confidence interval you found in Exercise 15-8 for the savings in mean fuel consumption using radial tires. Should the city manager accept or reject the null hypothesis that mean fuel consumption is the same for radial and standard tires at an $\alpha = .05$ significance level?

15-17 A consumer testing service asks you to compare gas and electric ovens by baking one type of bread in each type of oven. The following baking times have been obtained.

Gas	Electric
$n_A = 10$	$n_B = 12$
$\bar{X}_A = 2.1$ hours	$\bar{X}_B = 2.3$ hours
$s_A = .3$ hours	$s_B = .4$ hours

(a) Construct a 95% confidence interval estimate of the difference in mean baking times for the two ovens.

(b) At an $\alpha = .05$ significance level, should you accept or reject the null hypothesis of identical means?

15-18 TipsiCola wants to determine whether or not noncaloric drinks help people with weight problems. Although these drinks do reduce caloric intake, they do not reduce overall appetite levels as sugared drinks do. The company dietician matched 36 pairs of obese persons in terms of weight, sex, diet, lifestyle, eating habits, and prior weight problems. The experimental group (A) was asked to use only diet soft drinks and artificial sweeteners. Both groups were to continue with their regular diets, but the control group (B) was asked to avoid noncaloric beverages of any kind. At the end of six months, the weight change was determined for each person. As her null hypothesis, the dietician assumes that the mean weight reduction will be the same for both groups. The mean of the matched-pairs differences was a 1-pound reduction in favor of noncaloric drinks, and the standard deviation was 2 pounds. If an $\alpha = .01$ significance level is desired for this two-sided test, what conclusion should the dietician reach?

15-19 Inter-Rupter's telephone salespeople are all currently salaried. To improve incentives, management will convert the compensation to either a commission-only basis or to a salary-plus-commission plan. The null hypothesis is that the mean sales per solicitor will be the same under either plan. To test the schemes, random samples of 25 salespeople from each of two different offices were matched into pairs according to past sales records. After a trial six months, the sales of the salary-plus-commission partner were subtracted from the corresponding figure for the commission-only person. A mean difference of \$100 was obtained with a standard deviation of \$25. At a 5% significance level, which compensation plan, if any, is the better one?

15-4 HYPOTHESIS TESTS FOR COMPARING PROPORTIONS

Qualitative populations can be compared in terms of their respective proportions. We can extend the hypothesis-testing concepts that we applied in Section 15-3, using sample proportions as the basis for comparison. This type of testing may be useful, for example, to a politician who must determine whether or not the popularity of new legislation differs between two groups of constituents. Similarly, a network television director, debating whether or not to reschedule programs, might wish to compare the proportions of potential audiences that prefer two of the network's comedies over a third, all shown on different nights.

As before, the two population proportions are represented by π_A and π_B. The respective sample proportions are designated as P_A and P_B. The difference between population proportions, $\pi_A - \pi_B$, may be estimated by the

DIFFERENCE IN SAMPLE PROPORTIONS

$$d = P_A - P_B$$

The null hypotheses may be stated in one of the following forms.

H_0: $\pi_A \geq \pi_B$	or	H_0: $\pi_A - \pi_B \geq 0$	(lower-tailed test)
H_0: $\pi_A \leq \pi_B$	or	H_0: $\pi_A - \pi_B \leq 0$	(upper-tailed test)
H_0: $\pi_A = \pi_B$	or	H_0: $\pi_A - \pi_B = 0$	(two-sided test)

Ordinarily, the sampling distributions of P_A and P_B can be approximated by the normal curve when sample sizes are large enough. Because the samples are selected independently, it follows that d can be assumed to be normally distributed, with a mean of $\pi_A - \pi_B$ and a standard deviation of*

$$\sigma_d = \sqrt{\frac{\pi_A(1 - \pi_A)}{n_A} + \frac{\pi_B(1 - \pi_B)}{n_B}}$$

Under any of the preceding null hypotheses, we can assume that $\pi_A = \pi_B$, so that $\pi_A - \pi_B = 0$, and we can treat the sample results as if they applied to the same population. As an estimator of either π_A or π_B, the sample results may be used to compute the

COMBINED SAMPLE PROPORTION

$$P_C = \frac{n_A P_A + n_B P_B}{n_A + n_B}$$

The standard deviation of d is then estimated by

$$s_d = \sqrt{P_C(1 - P_C)\left(\frac{1}{n_A} + \frac{1}{n_B}\right)}$$

The following expression is used to compute the

NORMAL DEVIATE FOR COMPARING TWO PROPORTIONS

$$z = \frac{P_A - P_B}{\sqrt{P_C(1 - P_C)\left(\dfrac{1}{n_A} + \dfrac{1}{n_B}\right)}}$$

TO Find P_C

ILLUSTRATION: REDUCING WORD-PROCESSING ERRORS

In the rush to convert to word processing and direct composition, proofreading—once done at a less frenetic pace with hard copy (on paper)—is now done at the video display terminal. One newspaper publisher believes that restoring hard copy to the proofreading step might reduce the incidence of typographical errors.

*As in estimating the difference between independent sample means, it follows that the variance of $d = P_A - P_B$ is the sum of the respective variances of the individual sample proportions.

STEP 1

Formulate the null hypothesis. Not wanting to slow down procedures unnecessarily, the publisher tests the null hypothesis that the proportion of errors is at least as high with hard copy (A) as it is without it (B). That is,

$$H_0\colon \pi_A \geq \pi_B$$

STEP 2

Select the test statistic and procedure. One sample of 100 text segments processed with hard copy was to be carefully inspected for typographical errors and the proportion P_A of lines having mistakes noted. A second sample of the same size processed without hard copy was to be collected and P_B found. From these, the normal deviate z serves as the test statistic.

STEP 3

Establish the significance level and identify the acceptance and rejection regions. Negative differences in sample proportions tend to refute the null hypothesis for this lower-tailed test. The publisher chooses an $\alpha = .01$ significance level. The acceptance and rejection regions are shown below.

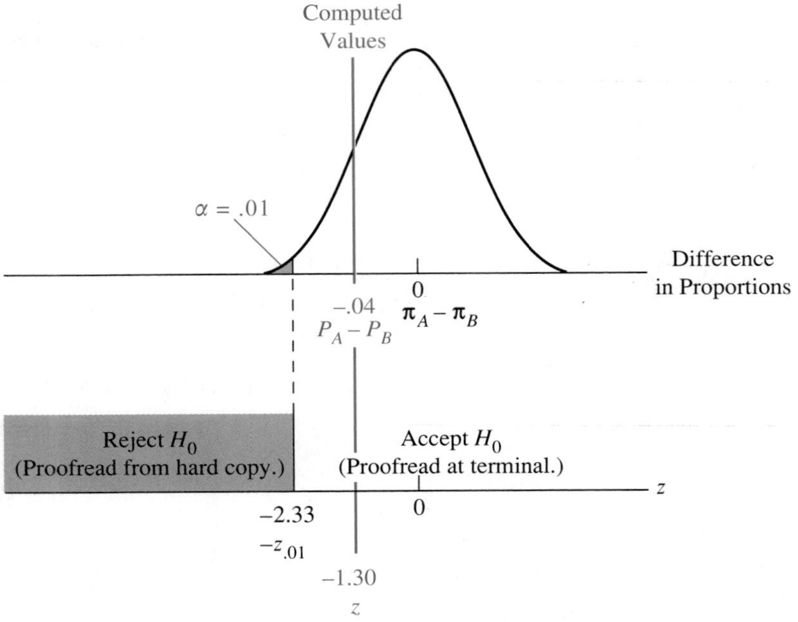

STEP 4

Collect the sample and compute the value of the test statistic. For $n_A = n_B = 100$, the respective sample proportions are

$$P_A = .03 \quad \text{and} \quad P_B = .07$$

These results provide the difference between proportions

$$d = P_A - P_B = .03 - .07 = -.04$$

The combined sample proportion of errors is

$$P_C = \frac{100(.03) + 100(.07)}{100 + 100} = .05$$

The computed value of the test statistic is

$$z = \frac{.03 - .07}{\sqrt{.05(1 - .05)(\frac{1}{100} + \frac{1}{100})}} = -1.30$$

STEP 5

Make the decision. Since the computed value of z falls in the acceptance region, the publisher must *accept* the null hypothesis and continue to have proofreading done at the video display terminals.

EXERCISES

15-20 You have selected samples of size $n_A = 100$ and $n_B = 25$, and have computed the sample proportions $P_A = .19$ and $P_B = .24$. At an $\alpha = .01$ significance level, test the following null hypothesis.

$$H_0\colon \pi_A \geq \pi_B$$

15-21 In determining how to allocate advertising expenditures, an Admiral Mills manager wishes to test the null hypothesis that the proportion of persons in the North (A) that prefer WeeTees is at least as great as it is in the South (B). For samples of 100 obtained for each region, 38 northern and 42 southern subjects are found to prefer WeeTees. At an $\alpha = .05$ significance level, should the director accept or reject the null hypothesis?

15-22 You are asked to compare two chemical processes in terms of proportion of unsatisfactory batches yielded. You find that 100 sample batches from process A yield 5% unsatisfactory, while the same number of runs made under process B yield 7% unsatisfactory. At an $\alpha = .05$ significance level, should you accept or reject the null hypothesis of identical proportions unsatisfactory?

15-23 A Traktronics statistician is evaluating a prototype aircraft radar system to see if it can detect a plane passing through the edges of the radar horizon better than the existing system. Two independent samples of 100 test flights have been made using both systems, and the respective proportions of planes detected have been computed. The statistician desires 5% protection against incorrectly concluding that the new system (A) has a detection probability (a population proportion of flights detected at the horizon) higher than the old system (B). The test results yield $P_A = .80$ and $P_B = .70$. Based on the sample results, can the statistician conclude that the new system is better?

SUMMARY

1. **How are two-sample experiments generally structured?**
   Statistical investigations involving **controlled experiments** typically compare

the parameters of *two* populations, commonly the means (μ_A and μ_B) or the proportions (π_A and π_B). Separate samples are selected from each population. One sample may be referred to as the **control group** and the other sample the **experimental group**.

2. **What are the two basic sampling schemes for comparing two populations?** In making inferences regarding the means, the actual observations may constitute **independent samples**. When practicable, greater efficiency may be achieved using **matched-pairs samples**. In either case, the focus is placed on the difference $\mu_A - \mu_B$.

   For *independent samples*, the estimating and testing procedures involve the sample statistics $\bar{X}_A$, $\bar{X}_B$, s_A, and s_B computed separately for the two samples. There are two basic approaches, depending on *sample sizes* used.

3. **What are the basic procedures for drawing inferences using *independent samples*?**
   For **large independent samples**, the *normal approximation* is used to establish the confidence interval

$$\mu_A - \mu_B = \bar{X}_A - \bar{X}_B \pm z_{\alpha/2}\sqrt{\frac{s_A^2}{n_A} + \frac{s_B^2}{n_B}}$$

   In a hypothesis test the normal deviate serves as the test statistic computed from

$$z = \frac{\bar{X}_A - \bar{X}_B}{\sqrt{\dfrac{s_A^2}{n_A} + \dfrac{s_B^2}{n_B}}}$$

   As in Chapter 9, hypothesis tests are classified as lower-tailed, upper-tailed, or two-sided, depending on the direction of the difference $\mu_A - \mu_B$.

   For **small independent samples,** the Student t distribution is employed. The confidence intervals are computed using

$$\mu_A - \mu_B = \bar{X}_A - \bar{X}_B \pm t_{\alpha/2}\sqrt{\frac{(n_A - 1)s_A^2 + (n_B - 1)s_B^2}{n_A + n_B - 2}}\sqrt{\frac{1}{n_A} + \frac{1}{n_B}}$$

   and the following expression is used to compute the test statistic.

$$t = \frac{\bar{X}_A - \bar{X}_B}{\sqrt{\dfrac{(n_A - 1)s_A^2 + (n_B - 1)s_B^2}{n_A + n_B - 2}}\sqrt{\dfrac{1}{n_A} + \dfrac{1}{n_B}}}$$

   Key assumptions of the applications involving the Student t is that the *population standard deviations must be identical* and that the parent populations should be normally distributed.

4. **What is the procedure for drawing inferences with matched-pairs samples?**
   In *matched-pairs samples,* the pairwise differences $d_i = X_{A_i} - X_{B_i}$ are treated as *single* observations from one population of potential pairwise differences. This allows greater flexibility in using the Student t distribution, which applies

regardless of the sample sizes used. The inferences are based on the following computed sample results.

$$\bar{d} = \frac{\sum d_i}{n} \qquad s_{d\text{-paired}} = \sqrt{\frac{\sum d_i^2 - n\bar{d}^2}{n-1}}$$

The confidence intervals are constructed using

$$\mu_A - \mu_B = \bar{d} \pm t_{\alpha/2} \frac{s_{d\text{-paired}}}{\sqrt{n}}$$

The computed value of the test statistic is

$$t = \frac{\bar{d}}{s_{d\text{-paired}}/\sqrt{n}}$$

5. **How do we test hypotheses regarding two population proportions?** In testing for the difference in proportions, the samples are pooled to compute the **combined sample proportion**.

$$P_C = \frac{n_A P_A + n_B P_B}{n_A + n_B}$$

The testing procedure employs the normal approximation, and P_C is used to compute the test statistic z.

$$z = \frac{P_A - P_B}{\sqrt{P_C(1 - P_C)\left(\frac{1}{n_A} + \frac{1}{n_B}\right)}}$$

REAL-LIFE STATISTICAL CHALLENGE

Applying Two-Sample Hypothesis Testing to the Automobile Dream List

In Chapter 9 concepts about single sample hypothesis testing were used to analyze the list of 232 autos. We will now apply two-sample hypothesis testing methods to the set of "dream machines."

Let's compare mileage for cars with engines that are less than two liters in displacement with those that are greater than or equal to two. We have drawn two samples. The sample data for seven cars with small engines and eight with large engines are listed below in Table 15-4.

Our null hypothesis is that the mean mileage for cars with smaller engines does not exceed the mileage for cars with larger engines.

$$H_0: \mu_S \leq \mu_L$$

The significance level will be set at $\alpha = .025$. The critical value of t is 2.160 at $(15 - 2) = 13$ degrees of freedom. The computed value for the test statistic is:

$$t = \frac{34.43 - 24.50}{\sqrt{\dfrac{(7-1)(7.93^2) + (8-1)(3.85^2)}{7+8-2}}\sqrt{\dfrac{1}{7} + \dfrac{1}{8}}}$$

$$= \frac{9.93}{(6.083)(.5175)} = 3.154$$

Since the above exceeds the critical value, we must *reject* the null hypothesis. As we discussed in Chapter 9, the choice of the significance level was arbitrary. (For example, a significance level of $\alpha = .001$ yields a critical t value of 3.852, which would compel us to *accept* the null hypothesis.)

TABLE 15-4 Sample Data for Small (Less than 2.0 Liters) and Large (2.0 Liters or Greater) Engines.

Number	Type	Manufacturer	Model	Transmission Type	Highway Mileage Miles/gallon	Engine Displacement in Liters
0011	Two-seater	Honda	Civic CRX-HF	M5	52	1.5
0088	Subcompact	Geo	Prizm	L3	29	1.6
0107	Subcompact	Isuzu	Impulse	M5	34	1.6
0149	Compact	Isuzu	Stylus	M5	33	1.6
0110	Subcompact	Mitsubishi	Eclipse	L4	30	1.8
0111	Subcompact	Mitsubishi	Eclipse	M5	32	1.8
0126	Subcompact	Subaru	XT	M5	31	1.8
0199	Mid-Size	Mazda	929	L4	23	3.0
0140	Compact	Chevrolet	Beretta	M5	28	3.1
0185	Mid-Size	Chevrolet	Lumina	L4	30	3.1
0186	Mid-Size	Chrysler	New Yorker	L4	26	3.3
0053	Subcompact	Chevrolet	Camaro	M5	26	5.0
0178	Mid-Size	BMW	750i	L4	18	5.0
0054	Subcompact	Chevrolet	Camaro	L4	24	5.7
0218	Large	Cadillac	Brougham	L4	21	5.7
				All Engines: $\bar{X}$	29.13	3.04
				s	7.79	1.58
				n	.15	5
				Small Engines: $\bar{X}$	34.43	1.67
				s	7.93	0.13
				n	7	7
				Large Engines: $\bar{X}$	24.50	4.24
				s	3.85	1.22
				n	8	8

Source: United States Environmental Protection Agency, 1989.

DISCUSSION QUESTIONS

1. Develop another difference of means hypothesis test using the mean gas mileage.
2. Develop two examples of difference of means hypotheses tests using the engine displacement data.
3. Conduct a hypothesis test for the differences between proportions (for example: proportion of cars with manual transmissions, or various combinations of car type, size, etc.).
4. Comment on the impact on your test results for altering the critical value of the test statistic or the sample size. How would the Type I error probability be affected?

REVIEW EXERCISES

15-24 Consider the following sample data for the weights and ages of athletic and nonathletic men, all approximately 6 feet tall and of medium build.

(a) Calculate the sample means and variances of the weights of the two groups.

(b) Treating the weights as independent random samples, should the null hypothesis that the population mean weight of athletic men is at least as large as that of nonathletic men be accepted or rejected at an $\alpha =$ .10 significance level?

Athletic (*A*)		Nonathletic (*B*)	
Weight	Age	Weight	Age
151	22	152	21
148	24	153	26
156	31	149	33
155	37	162	35
157	41	165	39
161	42	168	44
158	49	157	47
168	51	178	49
149	55	161	57
174	61	186	59

15-25 Hand Crafter's production planners measured the drop-off in manual dexterity from midmorning to midafternoon by giving a sample of $n = 20$ workers a test in the morning and again in the afternoon. By pairing each person's morning score (A) with his or her afternoon score (B), the planners obtained the following results.

$$\bar{d} = 15.7 \qquad s_d = 2.3$$

Construct a 90% confidence interval estimate of the difference in mean manual dexterity scores.

15-26 Refer to Exercise 15-24. Assume that the data represent observation pairs matched by age.

(a) Compute the weight differences between each pair, subtracting the nonathlete's weight from the athlete's. Then calculate the mean and the standard deviation of these matched-pairs differences.

(b) Treating the weights as matched-pairs samples, should the null hypothesis that the population mean weight of athletic men is at least as great as that of nonathletic men be accepted or rejected at an $\alpha = .10$ significance level?

15-27 Before organizing his strategy in the final weeks of the campaign, a congressional candidate has retained a political polling firm to determine whether he is stronger in the suburbs (A) or in the cities (B). Independent random samples of 100 voters in each category have been polled, and the data indicate that the candidate is preferred by 48% in the suburbs and 53% in the cities. As his null hypothesis, the candidate assumes that he is equally strong in both areas. At an $\alpha = .05$ significance level, should he accept or reject the null hypothesis?

15-28 Getting Oil Company currently processes its bills from regional data centers. A sampling study will establish whether a new centralized teleprocessing system will speed the total time taken for bills to reach customers. One drawback of the new system is that the completed bills will travel greater distances through the mail.

The mean time needed for bills to be processed and received by customers under the new procedure (A) and under the present procedure (B) are denoted by μ_A and μ_B. The null hypothesis is that the new system is no faster. The following sample data were obtained.

$$n_A = 500 \qquad n_B = 1{,}000$$

$$\bar{X}_A = 4.3 \text{ days} \qquad \bar{X}_B = 4.5 \text{ days}$$

$$s_A = 1.1 \text{ days} \qquad s_B = 1.3 \text{ days}$$

At an $\alpha = .05$ significance level, what action should be taken?

15-29 WeeTees tested two cereals to determine the taste preferences of potential buyers. Two different panels of persons were selected. The individuals on one panel tasted brand A; the others tasted brand B. Then, each person was asked if he or she would buy the product. The results follow.

	Cereal *A*	**Cereal *B***
Number who would buy	75	80
Number who would not buy or who were undecided	50	60
	125	140

Consider the null hypothesis that there is no difference in the proportion of potential buyers who would prefer to buy either product. At a 5% significance level, should H_0 be accepted or rejected?

15-30 The Blahsburg city manager wants to estimate the mean lifetime of a new type of tire compared to an existing tire. In a test, 10 taxis from the same company were equipped with two of each type of tire. Each car's total mileage was recorded until both tires of the same type had to be replaced. For each car, the replacement mileage for the present tire (B) was subtracted from the corresponding figure for the new tire (A). The mean mileage difference was 2,000, with a standard deviation of 2,000 miles.

(a) Construct a 95% confidence interval estimate of the difference between mean tire lifetimes.

(b) Should the null hypothesis that the mean tire lifetimes are identical be accepted or rejected at a 5% significance level?

15-31 Suppose that a test similar to the one in Exercise 15-30 was performed on another group of cars. Here, 15 cars were fully equipped with the new tire (A), and 10 cars were fully equipped with the old tire (B). No attempt was made to match the cars. All four tires were replaced when driving each car became hazardous. The following mileage results were obtained.

$$\bar{X}_A = 35{,}000 \text{ miles} \qquad \bar{X}_B = 33{,}000 \text{ miles}$$

$$s_A^2 = 6{,}500{,}000 \qquad s_B^2 = 7{,}000{,}000$$

(a) Construct a 95% confidence interval estimate of the difference between mean tire lifetimes.

(b) Should the null hypothesis that the mean tire lifetimes are identical be accepted or rejected at a 5% significance level?

15-32 Rent-a-Lemon wishes to determine which of two types of fuel provides more miles per gallon. Two independent random samples of 15 cars were selected, and each car was driven 2,000 miles by employees on normal business. A different type of fuel was used in each sample. The following results were obtained.

Type A	Type B
$\bar{X}_A = 25.0$ mpg	$\bar{X}_B = 24.8$ mpg
$s_A^2 = 1.44$	$s_B^2 = .81$

(a) Construct a 95% confidence interval estimate of the difference between mean fuel consumptions.

(b) Should the null hypothesis that there is no difference between the fuel be accepted or rejected at an $\alpha = .05$ significance level?

15-33 A Fast-Gro agronomist wishes to compare the corn yield per acre on which a nitrate-based fertilizer was used with the yield from a sulfate-based fertilizer. A sample of 100 acres fertilized with nitrates (A) yields an average of 56.2 bushels per acre, with a variance of 156.25. A sample of 150 acres fertilized with sulfates (B) yields an average of 52.6 bushels per acre, with a variance of 190.44. For each of the following null hypotheses, indicate whether H_0 must be accepted or rejected at a significance level of $\alpha = .05$.

(a) There is no difference in crop yields between the two fertilizers.

(b) The nitrates provide at least the yield of the sulfates.

(c) The sulfates provide at least the yield of the nitrates.

15-34 Suppose that Rent-a-Lemon in Exercise 15-32 matches the cars using fuel A with those using fuel B, that the cars in each pair are nearly identical in many respects (make, age, engine size, accessories, and so on), and that both groups of cars are driven over the same route by the same professional driver. The results indicate that the mean difference between the fuel consumption of the cars using fuel A and the cars using fuel B is .2 mile per gallon, with a standard deviation of .1.

(a) Construct a 95% confidence interval estimate of the difference between mean fuel consumptions.

(b) Should the null hypothesis that there is no difference between fuel consumptions be accepted or rejected at an $\alpha = .05$ significance level?

15-35 Suppose that the plots used to test the nitrate- and sulfate-based fertilizers in Exercise 15-33 were selected so that the two types of fertilizers were placed on neighboring 1-acre plots and that the yield of each sulfate-fertilized acre (B) was subtracted from the yield of its nitrate-fertilized neighbor (A). From a total of 100 pairs, the mean matched-pairs difference is 1.3 bushels, with a standard deviation of 3.2 bushels. Should the null hypothesis that there is no difference in yields due to choice of fertilizer be accepted or rejected at an $\alpha = .05$ significance level?

STATISTICS IN PRACTICE

15-36 Using the master class data list from Exercise 1-19, perform the following statistical estimates and hypotheses tests. (Note: Be sure to show all your intermediate steps. You may use intermediate answers you developed in earlier chapters to avoid unnecessary effort.)

(a) Construct a 95 percent confidence interval estimate of the difference between two means. Comment on the results.

(b) Construct a 95 percent confidence interval estimate for the difference between two proportions.

(c) Perform a hypothesis test for the difference between means for one of your data sets for either an upper- or lower-tailed test.

(d) Perform a hypothesis test for the difference of means of one of your data sets for a two-sided test.

(e) Perform a hypothesis test for the difference between two proportions for one of your data sets for either an upper- or lower-tailed test.

(f) Perform a hypothesis test for the difference between two proportions of one of your data sets for a two-sided test.

15-37 Repeat Exercise 15-36, using instead your group's class data from Exercise 1-21.

15-38 Refer to the hypothesis test you developed in Exercise 9-52. Describe how you can use a two-sample hypothesis test with those data. Would additional data be required? (You do not need to carry out the test—simply describe the method you would use.)

15-39 In Exercise 6-55 you were asked to go to a local store or other retail outlet and construct a probability distribution for the mean arrival times for one-minute intervals. In Exercise 9-51 you were asked to carry out a hypothesis test for a single sample. Describe a two-sample hypothesis test for different patterns in store traffic, such as peak versus nonpeak times. (You do not need to carry out the test—simply describe the method you would use.)

15-40 In Exercise 9-52 you carried out a hypothesis test using the data set from Exercise 8-53 based on genetic diversity. Design a matched-pair, two-sample hypothesis test for different genetic patterns. (You do not need to carry out the test—simply describe the method you would use.)

CASE The MBA Mystique

In recent years, the MBA has achieved a certain mystique, with degree holders from top schools rivaling attorneys and physicians in prestige. As a research project, MBA student Wilhelmena "Willie" Loman conducted a statistical analysis of recent graduates. She wishes to assess certain issues involving prestige, prior background, and gender.

Through a vigorous mail campaign, Willie obtained a data base for about two hundred business school graduates. She believes that the sample group represents a microcosm of the over one hundred thousand people who have recently received degrees.

Using various media lists, Willie categorized her MBAs as having attended either "Top-20" schools or second-tier schools. She is interested in comparing the ages and first-year salaries of the two groups.

The following sample ages were selected at random for the data base.

Top-20 School				
30	27	28	31	25
28	29	29	30	26
27	28	28	29	30
33	35	28	29	30
28	29	27	28	29
31	30	29	29	30
32	30	26	27	27
28	28	29	30	29

Second-Tier School				
23	29	25	41	43
24	35	37	29	24
26	27	33	37	45
24	25	25	24	38
25	25	47	52	39
55	39	38	35	25
36	35	27	28	39
30	31	32	28	25

Using GMAT scores, MBA concentration, GPA, undergraduate major, and pre-MBA experience as matching criteria, Willie obtained the following matched pairs for first-year earned incomes (thousands of dollars).

Top-20	Second-Tier
38.5	39.6
63.2	44.8
55.6	52.0
73.5	38.6
37.3	29.1

Top-20	Second-Tier
42.4	45.0
54.0	43.5
48.1	53.4
42.0	35.4
31.0	27.5

A final set of sample data have been obtained for the earnings of men and women MBAs, which Willie wants to compare. For a variety of reasons, Willie chose to first separate MBAs into two groups, those making a fresh career start (under 30 years old) and those making a career change (over 40 years old). The following independent sample data earnings (thousands of dollars per year) were obtained.

Under 30 Years Old		Over 40 Years Old	
Men	Women	Men	Women
33.5	34.6	48.2	41.3
34.7	41.5	39.2	42.5
28.5	35.0	35.8	40.1
42.0	28.8	35.7	34.5
35.0	37.2	44.3	37.2
44.0	42.5	65.3	42.0
29.9		45.5	
31.0		40.2	
33.3		51.5	
28.2			

QUESTIONS

1. Consider the sample age data for MBAs from top-20 and second-tier schools.
   (a) Do the two groups differ significantly in mean age?
   (b) Construct separate histograms for the two samples. What conclusions may be drawn from your graphs regarding the age distributions of the two business school groupings?
   (c) Using your answer to (b), what might you conclude regarding the quality of the analysis performed in (a)?
2. Referring to Willie's sample data, use the statistical tools presented in this chapter to draw meaningful conclusions regarding differences between mean earnings for top-20 MBAs and second-tier MBAs.
3. Sample data for MBA earnings may be used to assess the graduate school's overall quality. Comment on the validity of doing so and suggest some pitfalls involved.
4. Comment on the possible reasons why Willie decided to compare men's and women's earnings only after first separating the MBAs into two career-cycle groupings.
5. Referring to Willie's sample earnings and data, keeping the two career-cycle groupings separate, use the statistical tools presented in this chapter to draw meaningful conclusions regarding differences between mean earnings for men and women.

CHAPTER 16

CHI-SQUARE APPLICATIONS

BEFORE READING THIS CHAPTER, MAKE SURE YOU UNDERSTAND:

The statistical sampling study (Chapter 4).
Statistical estimation (Chapter 8).
Hypothesis testing (Chapter 9).

AFTER READING THIS CHAPTER, YOU WILL UNDERSTAND:

About the chi-square distribution.
About independence between qualitative variable.
What contingency tables are and how they relate to actual and expected frequencies.
How to conduct the chi-square test for independence.
How to test for the equality of several proportions.

Until now, we have described procedures using the normal and Student t distributions, but many important statistical applications cannot be represented by these distributions. In this chapter, we will expand our basic repertoire considerably by investigating the **chi-square distribution**.

We will begin by applying the chi-square distribution to sample data *to test whether or not two variables are independent.* We have seen in applications of probability that statistical independence between sample observations permits us to steamline procedures markedly. It may be important to know if variables are independent when alternative methods and treatments are being evaluated.

When population variables are qualitative characteristics (such as marital status, political affiliation, sex, state of health, type of treatment, or kind of response), the presence or absence of independence between variables can be used to draw important conclusions. A doctor who knows that preventive measures (vaccinated, unvaccinated) and resistance (diseased, not diseased) are dependent can conclude whether a vaccine is effective. A marketing researcher who learns that highest education level (elementary, high school, college) and brand preference (candidates A, B, C) are dependent might use this information to help choose advertising media. If severity of automobile accidents (property damage, injury, fatalities) is found to be dependent on where the accidents occur (city streets, rural roads, highways), a public safety director may decide to revise traffic law enforcement.

In this chapter, we will also examine a second area of statistical inference—*comparing several population proportions.* This application is closely related to testing for independence. We have already learned to compare two populations in Chapter 15, but when three or more populations are tested, we follow a different procedure that uses the chi-square distribution.

Although these two applications of the chi-square distribution are the most common in business decision making, others exist. Inferences regarding the population variance are discussed as an optional topic later in this chapter. Chapter 23 considers a chi-square procedure called the goodness-of-fit test.

16-1 TESTING FOR INDEPENDENCE AND THE CHI-SQUARE DISTRIBUTION

The first new application of statistical inference that we will investigate is the testing procedure used to determine if two qualitative population variables are independent. In doing this, we will describe a special test statistic with the chi-square sampling distribution.

INDEPENDENCE BETWEEN QUALITATIVE VARIABLES

To describe what we mean by independence between two qualitative variables or population characteristics, we will briefly consider a basic concept of probability. Remember that two events A and B are statistically independent if the occurrence of either event does not affect the probability for the other. For example, drawing an *ace* from a fully shuffled deck of 52 ordinary playing cards is statistically independent of drawing a *club.*

$$\Pr[\text{ace}\,|\,\text{club}] = \frac{1}{13} = \frac{4}{52} = \Pr[\text{ace}]$$

This is true because the proportion of aces in the club suit (1/13) is the same as the proportion of aces in the entire deck (4/52).

We may extend this concept of statistical independence to populations and samples. Consider a population whose elementary units may be classified in terms of two qualitative variables A and B. If variable A represents, say, a person's sex, it will have two possible attributes—male and female; if variable B represents political party, its attributes will be Democrat, Republican, and so on. If we assume that men occur in the same proportion throughout the entire population as they do among Democrats, then for the attributes of a randomly selected person,

$$\Pr[\text{male} \mid \text{Democrat}] = \Pr[\text{male}]$$

so that the *events* "male" and "Democrat" are statistically independent. If this is true, the multiplication law of probability for independent events tells us that

$$\Pr[\text{male } \textit{and} \text{ Democrat}] = \Pr[\text{male}] \times \Pr[\text{Democrat}]$$

If a similar fact holds for all attribute combinations, the population variables will exhibit a very important property.

DEFINITION: Two qualitative population variables A and B are **independent** if the proportion of the total population having any particular attribute of A is the same as it is in the part of the population having a particular attribute of B, no matter which attributes are considered. This implies that the frequency of units having any particular attribute pair may be found by multiplying the respective frequencies for the individual attributes and dividing by the total number of observations.

(The box on page 688 illustrates independence, and the one on page 689 shows dependence.)

When the population frequencies are unknown, the presence or absence of independence between two variables is also unknown. A sample can be used to test for independence, but to do this we must extend the principles of hypothesis testing that we used earlier. It will be helpful to develop an example as an illustration.

Illustration: Testing Customer Preference for Service Station Type

Superior Oil Company markets its products through two distinctly different kinds of service station outlets. One is a company-owned chain, selling gasoline and other products under the Superior label. The other is a chain of franchised dealerships—independently owned and managed—advertised with Superior but also identified as Sentinel stations. The reason for the double identity is twofold.

1. By creating two types of stations, the company believes that it appeals to two segments of the market: (1) those who prefer to buy from a big operator, and (2) those who like to buy from a local dealer (thereby receiving more individual attention and service).
2. The company-owned stations are major operations, located in high-volume traffic areas where the capital investment must be huge. A company-owned station in these locations is believed to be most effective and profitable. Franchise locations are mainly in neighborhoods and small towns.

Another advantage is that when traveling on major highways, a customer who trades at a Sentinel station will stop at conveniently located company-owned stations. Likewise, an urban customer of Superior's company-owned stations will be

STATISTICS AROUND US

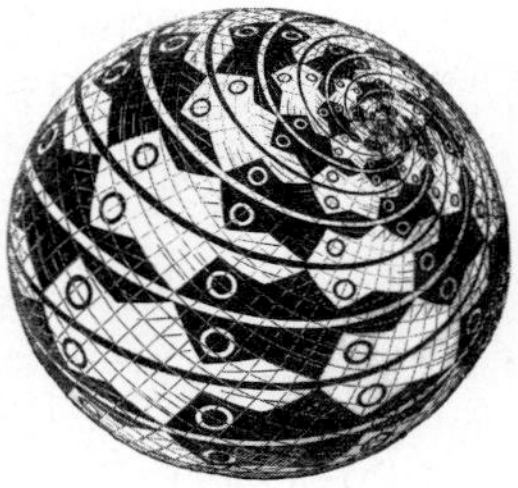

Symphony Orchestra

There are 100 members in a symphony orchestra: 70 men and 30 women. Each member is categorized by the type of instrument he or she plays: woodwind, brass, string, or percussion. The following table shows the frequencies of the members in terms of two characteristics: sex and instrument. Here, the two characteristics are independent. The ratio of male woodwind players to the total number of woodwind players is 21/30 = .7. The same ratio is obtained for male brass, string, or percussion players: 14/20, 21/30, and 14/20, respectively. All equal .7, which is the proportion of men in the orchestra. Similarly, the ratio of female woodwind players to total woodwind players is .3, which is the same ratio obtained for any other instrument played by females and is also the proportion of females in the orchestra.

Sex	Instrument Category				Total
	(1) Woodwind	(2) Brass	(3) String	(4) Percussion	
(1) Male	21	14	21	14	70
(2) Female	9	6	9	6	30
Total	30	20	30	20	100

Because sex and instrument are independent, the frequency of male string players is equal to the product of the frequencies of the respective attributes divided by the total number of players in the orchestra, or

$$\frac{70 \times 30}{100} = 21$$

The frequency of female string players is determined by multiplying the number of females by the number of string players and dividing by 100.

$$\frac{30 \times 30}{100} = 9$$

more likely to trade at a Sentinel station when traveling on side roads or in rural areas.

Superior's new chairman is concerned about the value of operating in this fashion. He wonders whether the extra promotional costs are really justified and, more importantly, whether there are actually two separate market segments. He has requested that his chief statistician conduct a survey to determine whether there is any significant difference between the Sentinel customers and those trading at company-owned stations.

The statistician mailed a questionnaire to a random sample of 200 credit card customers. The replies received have been partially tabulated in Table 16-1. Each subject has been categorized as preferring Sentinel or company stations. The primary reason given for each person's preference is placed in one of six categories:

STATISTICS AROUND US

Driver Preference and Traits

A researcher tested the following variables pertaining to the characteristics of drivers and the car style they prefer.

Preferred Body Style	Driving Traits
Sporty	Adventuresome
Conventional	Conservative
Utilitarian	Abusive

She found that drivers who like sporty cars are predominantly adventuresome but also heavily abusive and hardly conservative at all. Those preferring conventional or utilitarian cars are mainly conservative. She concluded that the two variables are *dependent*.

location, quality of service, cleanliness, personal attention, mechanical service, and staff appearance.

CONTINGENCY TABLES AND EXPECTED FREQUENCIES

In Table 16-1, the customer preference variable is represented by a column for each station type and the second variable by a row for each primary reason given for preferring a particular type of station. The value within each cell is the tally for those subjects classified as having the corresponding attributes. These cell numbers are referred to as **actual frequencies**. Such an arrangement of data is called a **contingency table**, because it accounts for all combinations of the factors being investigated—in other words, for all contingencies.

TABLE 16-1 Contingency Table for Superior Oil's Actual Sample Results

	Customer Preference		
Reason	(1) Sentinel Station	(2) Company Station	Total
(1) Location	32	8	40
(2) Quality of Service	12	2	14
(3) Cleanliness	13	3	16
(4) Personal Attention	56	35	91
(5) Mechanical Service	11	13	24
(6) Staff Appearance	6	9	15
Total	130	70	200

TABLE 16-2 Contingency Table for Superior Oil's Expected Sample Results

	Customer Preference		
Reason	**(1) Sentinel Station**	**(2) Company Station**	**Total**
(1) Location	40 × 130/200 = **26.00**	40 × 70/200 = **14.00**	40
(2) Quality of Service	14 × 130/200 = **9.10**	14 × 70/200 = **4.90**	14
(3) Cleanliness	16 × 130/200 = **10.40**	16 × 70/200 = **5.60**	16
(4) Personal Attention	91 × 130/200 = **59.15**	91 × 70/200 = **31.85**	91
(5) Mechanical Service	24 × 130/200 = **15.60**	24 × 70/200 = **8.40**	24
(6) Staff Appearance	15 × 130/200 = **9.75**	15 × 70/200 = **5.25**	15
Total	130	70	200

Using the statistician's data, we wish to determine whether or not the customer's primary stated reason for choosing where to trade actually matters in the final selection of the particular type of station. The null hypothesis is that the type of station preferred is not related to the stated reason. Stated another way, *the null hypothesis is that the two variables are independent.*

The first step in accepting or rejecting H_0 is to determine the kind of results that might be expected if the variables were truly independent. As a basis for comparison, we use the sample results that would be obtained on the average if the null hypothesis of independence was true. These hypothetical data are referred to as the **expected sample results.**

Table 16-2 is the contingency table for the expected results of this study. The total numbers of observations for each reason and type of station are the same. Because they are calculated in a manner consistent with the null hypothesis of independence, the cell entries are referred to as **expected frequencies**. These frequencies are denoted by the symbol f_e and appear in color in the table. The following expression summarizes the calculation of the

EXPECTED FREQUENCIES

$$f_e = \frac{\text{Row total} \times \text{Column total}}{n}$$

For example, the entry in row (1) and column (1) is

$$f_e = \frac{40 \times 130}{200} = 26.00$$

TABLE 16-3 Combined Contingency Table for Actual and Expected Frequencies

Reason	Customer Preference (1) Sentinel Station f_a	(1) Sentinel Station f_e	(2) Company Station f_a	(2) Company Station f_e	Total
(1) Location	32	26.00	8	14.00	40
(2) Quality of Service	12	9.10	2	4.90	14
(3) Cleanliness	13	10.40	3	5.60	16
(4) Personal Attention	56	59.15	35	31.85	91
(5) Mechanical Service	11	15.60	13	8.40	24
(6) Staff Appearance	6	9.75	9	5.25	15
Total	130		70		200

It is not necessary for the expected frequencies to be whole numbers. (Usually extending the frequency to two decimal places provides adequate accuracy.)

Now that the actual and the expected frequencies have been obtained, they must be compared before the null hypothesis of independence can be accepted or rejected. For this, a new statistic, the chi square, should be used.

THE CHI-SQUARE STATISTIC

A decision rule for determining independence must be established that provides a desirable balance between the probabilities for committing both the Type I error of rejecting independence when it actually exists and the Type II error of accepting independence when it does not exist. In practice, when the sample size is fixed in advance—as it is in our Superior Oil illustration—we can control only the Type I error probability α.

The test statistic we use must (1) measure the amount of deviation between the actual and the expected results and (2) have a sampling distribution that enables us to determine the Type I error probability α. Such a statistic is based on the individual differences between the actual and the expected frequencies in each cell. It is convenient to place both types of frequencies in a single combined contingency table, as shown in Table 16-3.

The following expression is used to calculate the test statistic, which we call the

CHI-SQUARE STATISTIC

$$\chi^2 = \sum \frac{(f_a - f_e)^2}{f_e}$$

where the symbol χ is the lowercase Greek *chi* (pronounced "kie") and χ^2 is read "chi-square." The summation is taken over all cells in the contingency table. Table 16-4 shows the χ^2 calculations for the Superior Oil study results. There, we find that $\chi^2 = 16.929$.

The possible values of χ^2 range upwards from zero. If the deviation between f_a and f_e is large for a particular cell, the squared deviation $(f_a - f_e)^2$ is also large. In calculating χ^2, the squared deviations are divided by f_e before they are summed to ensure that any differences are not exaggerated simply because a large number of observations have been obtained. Large $(f_a - f_e)^2/f_e$ ratios occur when the actual and the expected results differ considerably, making the size of χ^2 large. Therefore, the more the sample results deviate from what would be expected if independence were true, the larger the value of χ^2 will be, and vice versa.

Before we can draw any conclusions regarding customer preference and reason variables, we must determine whether or not the value of χ^2 that we obtained from the sample is inconsistent with the null hypothesis that these variables are independent. As in earlier hypothesis-testing procedures, the sampling distribution of χ^2 will be used to obtain the critical value of this test statistic.

TABLE 16-4 Chi-Square Calculation for Superior Oil's Results

(Row, Column)	Actual Frequency f_a	Expected Frequency f_e	$f_a - f_e$	$(f_a - f_e)^2$	$\frac{(f_a - f_e)^2}{f_e}$
(1,1)	32	26.00	6.00	36.0000	1.385
(1,2)	8	14.00	−6.00	36.0000	2.571
(2,1)	12	9.10	2.90	8.4100	.924
(2,2)	2	4.90	−2.90	8.4100	1.716
(3,1)	13	10.40	2.60	6.7600	.650
(3,2)	3	5.60	−2.60	6.7600	1.207
(4,1)	56	59.15	−3.15	9.9225	.168
(4,2)	35	31.85	3.15	9.9225	.312
(5,1)	11	15.60	−4.60	21.1600	1.356
(5,2)	13	8.40	4.60	21.1600	2.519
(6,1)	6	9.75	−3.75	14.0625	1.442
(6,2)	9	5.25	3.75	14.0625	2.679
	200	200.00	0.00		$\chi^2 = 16.929$

THE CHI-SQUARE DISTRIBUTION

The chi-square distribution is a theoretical probability distribution that, under the proper conditions, may be used as the sampling distribution of χ^2. It is described by a single parameter—the number of degrees of freedom—that has much the same meaning as it did in our discussion of the Student t distribution. (The procedure used to determine the number of degrees of freedom will be given later in this section.)

Figure 16-1 shows curves for the chi-square distributions when the degrees of freedom are 2, 4, 10, and 20. Note that these curves are positively skewed, but that the degree of skew declines as the number of degrees of freedom increases, until eventually the chi-square distribution approaches the normal distribution.

Appendix Table H provides upper tail areas for the chi-square distribution. We use the symbol χ^2_α to represent the chi-square value for which the upper tail area is α.

$$\alpha = \Pr[\chi^2 \geq \chi^2_\alpha]$$

Like the Student t distribution, there is a separate chi-square distribution for each number of degrees of freedom, and a row corresponding to each of these numbers appears in the table of upper tail areas. The tail areas are given at the head of each column, and the entries in the body of the table are the corresponding values of χ^2_α. A portion of this table is reproduced here.

Degrees of Freedom	Upper Tail Area					
	...	.90	...	.10	.05	...
1		.0158		2.706	3.841	
2		.211		4.605	5.991	
3		.584		6.251	7.815	
4		1.064		7.779	9.488	
5		**1.610**		**9.236**	**11.070**	
6		2.204		10.645	12.592	
⋮		⋮		⋮	⋮	

The curve for the chi-square distribution with 5 degrees of freedom is shown in Figure 16-2. To find the upper 5% value of χ^2, denoted by $\chi^2_{.05}$, we read the entry in the row for 5 degrees of freedom and the column for area .05, obtaining $\chi^2_{.05} = 11.070$. Thus, we have

$$.05 = \Pr[\chi^2 \geq 11.070]$$

We also use Appendix Table H to find areas above points lying in the lower portion. For example, for an upper tail area of .90, we obtain the value $\chi^2_{.90} = 1.610$ at 5 degrees of freedom (see Figure 16-2).

Remember that we used row and column totals to estimate the expected frequencies in Table 16-2 for the Superior Oil study. We found the cell entries in that contingency table by multiplying the respective marginal totals for each row and column and then dividing by the sample size. Because the six row totals must sum to n, the values of any five rows automatically fix the value of the sixth row.

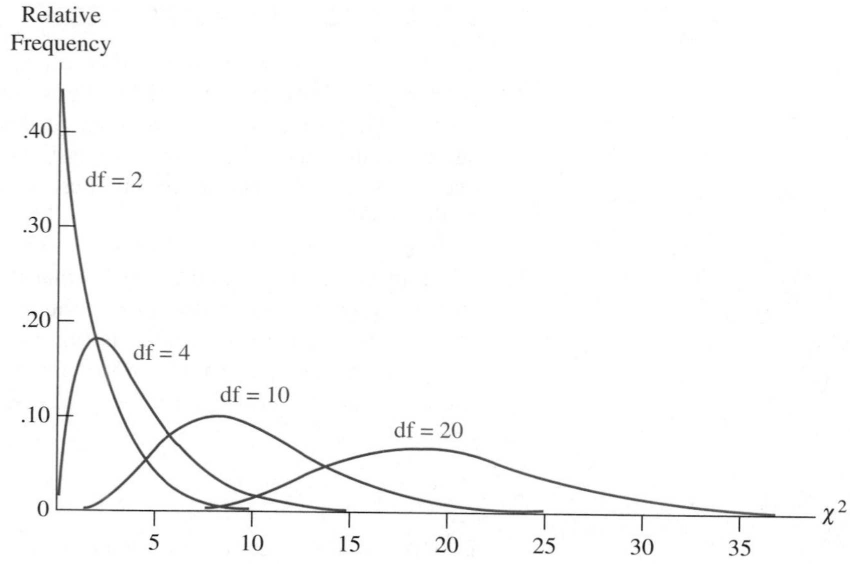

FIGURE 16-1 Various curves for the chi-square distribution.

We can say that five of the row totals are "free" and the sixth is "fixed." Likewise, one of two column totals is free and the second is fixed. Although there are $6 \times 2 = 12$ cells, we are free to specify only $5 \times 1 = 5$ of these cells. Our number of degrees of freedom is therefore 5. In general, we establish the

RULE FOR THE NUMBER OF DEGREES OF FREEDOM

$$(\text{Number of rows} - 1) \times (\text{Number of columns} - 1)$$

THE HYPOTHESIS-TESTING STEPS

STEP 1

Formulate the null hypothesis. The researcher tests the null hypothesis that a customer's preferred station type and the reason given for choosing it are independent.

$$H_0\text{: The two variables are independent.}$$

STEP 2

Select the test statistic and procedure. The chi-square serves as the test statistic.

STEP 3

Establish the significance level and identify the acceptance and rejection regions. Suppose that our researcher wants to protect himself at an $\alpha = .05$ significance

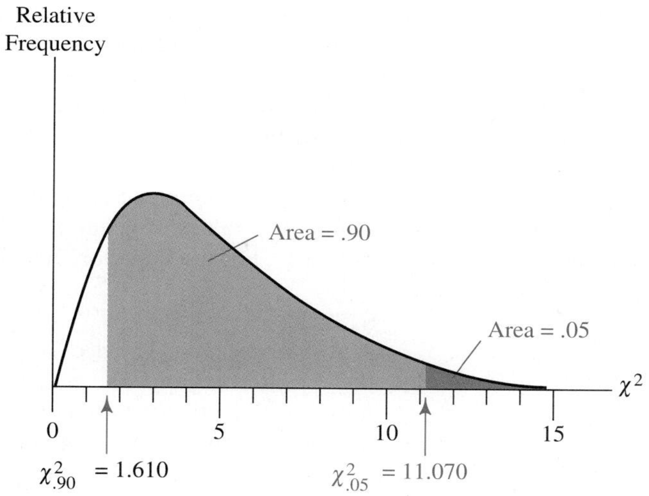

FIGURE 16-2 Chi-square curve for 5 degrees of freedom.

level against making the Type I error of concluding that the selected station type and the stated reason for that choice are dependent when these variables are actually independent. From Appendix Table H, we have already found that $\chi^2_{.05} = 11.070$ for 5 degrees of freedom. The acceptance and rejection regions are shown below.

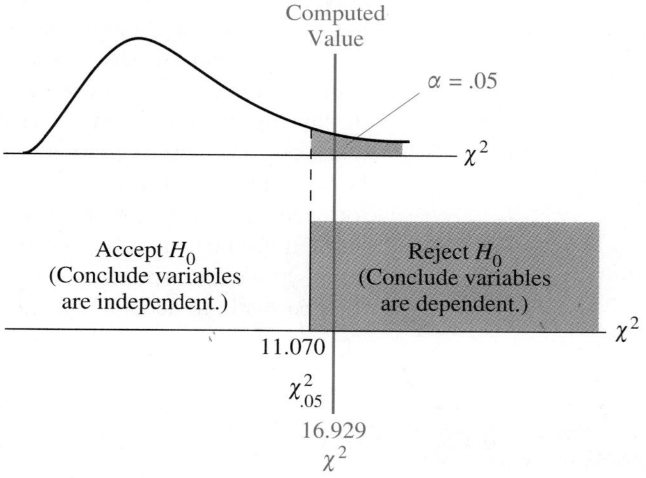

The interpretation of $\chi^2_{.05} = 11.070$ is that due to chance sampling error, this number will be exceeded on the average by only 5% of all χ^2 values calculated from repeated samples, each taken from a population where the null hypothesis is true. Thus, if the two variables are independent, about 5% of the sample results will disagree so much that independence will be rejected. Each of these samples will have a value, such as 13.5 or 14.2, that exceeds 11.070.

The preceding decision rule illustrates a convenient feature of this procedure. *Whenever a chi-square test is used to compare frequencies, it is upper tailed.* Stated another way, large χ^2 values tend to refute H_0, whereas small χ^2 values confirm the null hypothesis.

STEP 4

Collect the sample and compute the value of the test statistic. This step includes finding the values of f_a and f_e for the combined contingency table and then computing χ^2. For the Superior Oil study results, we have already found $\chi^2 = 16.929$.

STEP 5

Make the decision. The decision maker's computed value of $\chi^2 = 16.929$ falls in the rejection region. The null hypothesis must be *rejected,* and the statistician must conclude that the type of station preferred depends on the customer's stated primary reason for choosing where he or she trades.

SPECIAL CONSIDERATIONS

If a smaller significance level of, say $\alpha = .001$, were desired, the researcher would have obtained $\chi^2_{.001} = 20.517$ from Appendix Table H for 5 degrees of freedom, and because this value is larger than the 16.929 computed from sample data, the null hypothesis of independent variables would have been accepted. In such cases, there may be a considerable chance of committing the Type II error of accepting H_0 when the variables are not independent. (In our illustration, this would mean concluding that a *reason* for choosing a service station does not influence the consumer's *type* preference when it does influence choice.) These errors may occur in many ways, and finding β probabilities is too difficult a task to undertake here. The chance of committing a Type II error can be kept within reasonable boundaries only by making the sample size large.

The true sampling distribution of χ^2 that is calculated for testing independence is only approximated by the chi-square distribution. This approximation is similar to substituting the normal distribution for the binomial distribution in certain instances. The approximation is usually adequate if the sample size is sufficiently large. In practice, the sample will be large enough when the expected frequencies for each cell are 5 or more. If some expected cell frequencies are smaller than 5, this requirement may be met by combining two rows or columns before calculating χ^2. A corresponding reduction in the number of degrees of freedom must then be made to account for the lower number of cells.

EXERCISES

16-1 Determine the value of the chi-square statistic that corresponds to each upper tail area α and each number of degrees of freedom (df) provided below.

	(a)	(b)	(c)	(d)	(e)
α	.05	.01	.99	.10	.80
Degrees of freedom	10	20	18	6	29

16-2 A marketing researcher wishes to determine whether a person's sex is independent of a preference for fruits. For each of the following situations, where the sample results have been summarized, (1) determine the number of degrees of freedom and the critical value; and (2) indicate whether the null hypothesis of independence should be accepted or rejected.

(a) Bananas, apples, and pears are considered. $\chi^2 = 7.85$ and $\alpha = .05$.

(b) Pineapples, guavas, papayas, and passionfruit are considered. $\chi^2 = 15.23$ and $\alpha = .01$.

(c) Boysenberries, blueberries, huckleberries, blackberries and strawberries are considered. $\chi^2 = 7.801$ and $\alpha = .10$.

(d) Plums, apricots, peaches, cherries, persimmons, and nectarines are considered. $\chi^2 = 10.99$ and $\alpha = .05$.

16-3 Various random samples have been selected and the chi-square statistics have been computed for the following independence-testing situations. (1) Determine the number of degrees of freedom. (2) Calculate the corresponding critical value for the stated significance level. (3) Indicate whether the null hypothesis should be accepted or rejected.

(a) Sex (male, female) versus attitude toward a product (preferred, not preferred). $\chi^2 = 3.54$ and $\alpha = .05$.

(b) College major (liberal arts, science, social science, professional) versus political affiliation (Democrat, Republican, other). $\chi^2 = 15.231$ and $\alpha = .010$.

(c) Number of bedrooms (1, 2, 3, 4 or more) versus family size (1, 2, 3, 4 or more). $\chi^2 = 15.018$ and $\alpha = .10$.

(d) Type of car (import, large domestic, small domestic) versus sexual attitude (repressive, permissive). $\chi^2 = 7.955$ and $\alpha = .01$.

16-4 The following contingency table containing actual sample frequencies has been provided.

	Marital Status		
Preference	**(1) Single**	**(2) Married**	**Total**
(1) Brand A	20	10	30
(2) Brand B	20	50	70
Total	40	60	100

(a) Perform hypothesis-testing Step 3.
  (1) Determine the number of degrees of freedom.
  (2) Calculate the critical value of the test statistic and identify the acceptance and rejection regions. Assume a significance level of $\alpha = .01$.

(b) Perform hypothesis-testing Step 4.
  (1) Determine the expected frequencies for the null hypothesis of independence between marital status and brand preference. Arrange the data in a combined contingency table.
  (2) Calculate the chi-square statistic.

(c) Should the null hypothesis that marital status and brand preference are independent be accepted or rejected?

16-5 The brand manager for Jiffy Spiffy wishes to determine whether there are any significant differences in regular series program preferences between male and female television viewers. A random sample of persons has been interviewed, and each person has been asked to indicate which one of five program types he or she prefers. The following results were obtained.

Preferred Program Type	Viewer's Sex (1) Male	(2) Female	Total
(1) Western	32	18	50
(2) Situation Comedy	17	13	30
(3) Drama	27	33	60
(4) Comedy	13	7	20
(5) Variety	24	16	40
Total	113	87	200

The null hypothesis is that a viewer's sex and program preference are independent.

(a) Determine the expected results.
(b) Calculate the chi-square statistic.
(c) How many degrees of freedom are associated with this test statistic?
(d) If the advertiser wishes to protect herself against committing the Type I error of incorrectly concluding sex is dependent on program preference at a significance level of $\alpha = .01$, determine the critical value for the test statistic. Should the null hypothesis of independence be accepted?
(e) Would your conclusion in (d) change if an $\alpha = .05$ significance level were chosen instead? Explain.

16-6 A Hoopla Hoops marketing manager wishes to determine whether there are any significant differences between regions in terms of a new product's degree of acceptance. The following results have been obtained for a random sample of customers.

Degree of Acceptance	Region (1) East	(2) Middle	(3) South	(4) West	Total
(1) Poor	22	35	0	5	62
(2) Moderate	84	55	8	24	171
(3) Strong	25	17	22	12	76
Total	131	107	30	41	309

The null hypothesis is that the region and the degree of product acceptance by any given customer are independent.

(a) Determine the expected sample results.
(b) Calculate the chi-square statistic.
(c) How many degrees of freedom are associated with this test statistic?
(d) Assuming that the manager will tolerate a 1% chance of incorrectly

concluding that degree of acceptance differs from region to region when this is not true, determine the critical value for the test statistic. Should the null hypothesis of independence be accepted or rejected?

16-7 Carmena Wheeler wishes to test the null hypothesis that a person's amount of driving and preferred car style are independent variables. She mailed a questionnaire to a random sample of drivers and, from the replies she received, provided the following table.

Amount of Driving	Preferred Car Style (1) Sporty	(2) Conventional	(3) Utility	Total
(1) Light	12	8	13	33
(2) Moderate	7	15	22	44
(3) Heavy	3	22	15	40
Total	22	45	50	117

At a 1% significance level, should Carmena accept or reject the null hypothesis of independence?

16-2 TESTING FOR EQUALITY OF SEVERAL PROPORTIONS

An important statistical question involves a comparison of several population parameters. In Chapter 15, we described the inferences regarding two populations and the tests used to compare *two* population means or proportions. There, we determined which of two proofreading procedures creates fewer errors by using the proportions of two independent samples taken from different populations. If we wish to compare more than two procedures, we may still make pair comparisons as we did in Chapter 15. But sometimes it is better to test the population proportions simultaneously to see if they really differ. In comparing three or more population proportions, we take a different approach and apply the procedures that we used earlier in testing for independence.

ILLUSTRATION: TESTING ADVERTISEMENTS FOR MEMORY RECALL

We will illustrate the procedure for testing several proportions with a situation commonly encountered in the advertising field. An advertising agency wishes to determine whether there are any differences in terms of reader recall among three kinds of magazine advertisements. One ad is humorous, the second is quite technical, and the third is a pictorial comparison with competing brands. A national magazine with three regional editions is chosen for the test, and a different quarter-page advertisement is placed in each of its editions. A random sample of persons is chosen from a list of subscribers in each region, and one month after the ads have appeared, the people in each sample are visited. All participants are shown five ads of similar format, four of which are fakes, and are asked if they remember any of the five ads. Those selecting the correct ad are included in the tally of rememberers, and those unable to select the correct ad are classified as nonrememberers. A brief quiz is administered after the identification test to determine whether or not the magazine was read (to avoid prestige bias by persons who falsely claim to have read the ad), and nonreaders are eliminated from the sample.

STEP 1

Formulate the null hypothesis. The null hypothesis is that there are no differences in the mnemonic properties of the three kinds of advertisements. This may be expressed in terms of the proportions of the readers of the three magazine editions who remembered the advertisements. Thus, letting π_1 represent the proportion remembering the first ad, π_2 the second, and π_3 the third, we express the null hypothesis as

$$H_0: \pi_1 = \pi_2 = \pi_3$$

The results are provided in Table 16-5. Recall that in testing for independence, the expected cell frequencies are determined by assuming equal ratios or proportions. In testing for independence, we are really testing for equality of proportions.

STEP 2

Select the test statistic and procedure. The chi-square serves as the test statistic.

STEP 3

Establish the significance level and identify the acceptance and rejection regions. Each of the three types of advertisements are represented by a column in the contingency table. The rememberers and nonrememberers are represented by rows. The number of degrees of freedom is

$$(\text{Number of rows} - 1) \times (\text{Number of columns} - 1) = (2 - 1) \times (3 - 1) = 2$$

The desired level of significance is $\alpha = .01$. From Appendix Table H, the critical value of $\chi^2_{.01} = 9.210$ is provided. The acceptance and rejection regions are shown below.

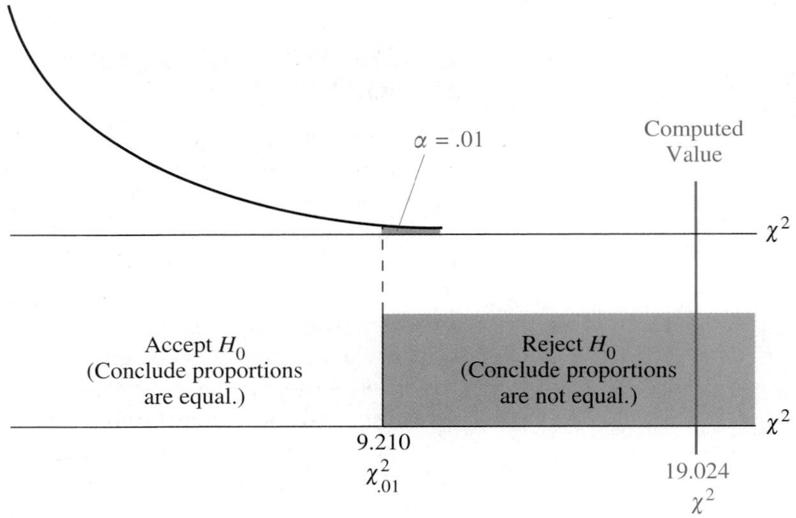

TABLE 16-5 Results of Mnemonic Advertising Samples

	Type of Advertisement		
	(1) Humorous	(2) Technical	(3) Comparative
Number of rememberers	25	10	7
Number of nonrememberers	73	93	108
Number of readers	98	103	115
Proportion of rememberers	$P_1 = .255$	$P_2 = .097$	$P_3 = .061$

STEP 4

Collect the sample and compute the value of the test statistic. Table 16-6 is the combined contingency table for the actual and the expected results. The chi-square statistic is calculated in the same manner as it is in testing for independence. These calculations are provided in Table 16-7.

STEP 5

Make the decision. Since the computed value of $\chi^2 = 19.024$ falls in the rejection region, the null hypothesis of equal proportions must be *rejected* at the .01 significance level. The agency must conclude that the three ads are not equally easy to remember. (The results are also significant at the .001 level, because $\chi^2_{.001} = 13.815$.)

EXERCISES

16-8 The quality control manager of one of Pear Peripheral's electronics assembly plants wishes to determine whether the day of the week influences the number of erroneous cable harness assemblies. He suspects that on Mondays and Fridays the error rate is significantly higher. If he finds that the day of the week does make a difference, he will conduct a more detailed study to determine on which days the error rate is higher and will recommend that

TABLE 16-6 Combined Contingency Table for Mnemonic Advertisement Study

	Type of Advertisement			
	(1) Humorous	(2) Technical	(3) Comparative	Total
(1) Rememberers	25 / **13.025**	10 / **13.690**	7 / **15.285**	42
(2) Nonrememberers	73 / **84.975**	93 / **89.310**	108 / **99.715**	274
Total	98	103	115	316

TABLE 16-7 Chi-Square Calculations for Mnemonic Advertisement Study

(Row, Column)	Actual Frequency f_a	Expected Frequency f_e	$f_a - f_e$	$(f_a - f_e)^2$	$\frac{(f_a - f_e)^2}{f_e}$
(1,1)	25	13.025	11.975	143.4006	11.010
(1,2)	10	13.690	−3.690	13.6161	.995
(1,3)	7	15.285	−8.285	68.6412	4.491
(2,1)	73	84.975	−11.975	143.4006	1.688
(2,2)	93	89.310	3.690	13.6161	.152
(2,3)	108	99.715	8.285	68.6412	.688
	316	316.000	0.000		χ^2 = 19.024

cables be assembled only on special days. The manager has collected a random sample of assemblies produced on different days of the week and obtained the following results.

	Day of the Week				
	(1) Monday	(2) Tuesday	(3) Wednesday	(4) Thursday	(5) Friday
Number of erroneous assemblies	32	12	15	18	27
Number of correct assemblies	95	87	91	79	73

At an $\alpha = .05$ significance level, should the manager accept or reject the null hypothesis that the proportions of erroneous assemblies are identical?

16-9 An auditor selects random samples of 100 transactions from each of three branch offices. The proportions of errors found are .07 (branch 1), .13 (branch 2), and .09 (branch 3). At a 5% significance level, should the auditor conclude that the error rate differs among the branches?

16-10 A printer wishes to determine whether the proportion of lines typeset with errors is affected by the complexity of the text. The following sample data have been obtained.

Need to total

	Complexity		
	(1) Low	(2) Medium	(3) High
Number of lines with errors	42	28	29
Number of lines correct	118	43	29

At a 1% significance level, should the printer conclude that the error rate is the same or different for all complexities?

16-11 The quality control manager at Admiral Electric wishes to determine whether the proportion of defective toasters is affected by the speed of the assembly line. She has selected three samples of 100 toasters from the line when it was running at three different speeds. The proportions of defectives obtained are .05 for 100 parts per hour, .07 for 150 parts per hour, and .10 for 200 parts per hour.

Will the manager conclude that the proportions differ if she wishes to protect herself at the $\alpha = .01$ level of significance against making the wrong decision? What is the lowest significance level at which the results will lead her to conclude that the proportion of defectives varies with line speed?

16-12 Cafeteria dietician Buddy Brave wishes to determine whether the time of day influences the tendency to consume coffee. The following data represent the beverage purchases for a random sample of cafeteria customers.

	Time of Day			
	(1) Early A.M.	(2) Late A.M.	(3) Early P.M.	(4) Late P.M.
Number for coffee	3	5	8	11
Number for other	52	48	51	47

At an $\alpha = .05$ significance level, should the dietician accept or reject the null hypothesis that the proportions of coffee purchases throughout the day are identical?

16-3 OTHER CHI-SQUARE APPLICATIONS

As mentioned earlier, testing for independence and comparing several population proportions are the most common uses of the chi-square distribution in business decision making. But this versatile distribution has wider applications.

Optional Section 16-4 tells us how the chi-square distribution may be used to make inferences about the population variance. Until now, we have not estimated the population variance σ^2 by means of *confidence intervals* or tested *hypotheses about* σ^2. Although important, inferences concerning σ^2 are less common than inferences regarding μ and π, where $\bar{X}$ and P are used as estimators and test statistics. We have waited until this point to examine this area of inference because the chi-square distribution plays a role in the sampling distribution of s^2—the test statistic used in making inferences about σ^2.

Chapter 23 considers a fourth chi-square application—the **goodness-of-fit test**. This procedure is useful in determining whether a variety of technical assumptions hold with respect to the characteristics of the population sampled. The goodness-of-fit test also allows us to decide whether a particular probability distribution actually applies.

SUMMARY

1. What is the chi-square distribution?

A large class of statistical procedures and applications makes use of the **chi-square distribution**. Like the Student t, there is a different distribution for each value of χ^2, depending on the **number of degrees of freedom** that applies for the particular test.

2. **What is *independence* between qualitative variables?**
One important chi-square application involves testing two qualitative variables for independence. Two qualitative population variables A and B are *independent* if the proportion of the total population having any particular attribute of A remains the same for the part of the population having a particular attribute of B, no matter which attributes are considered.

3. **What are contingency tables and how do they relate to actual and expected frequencies?**
The actual sample data are arranged in a **contingency table** involving one row for each attribute of the first variable and one column for each attribute of the second. The cell entries in this matrix are the **actual frequencies** for the respective attribute pairs. The corresponding **expected frequencies**, f_e, are computed from the following expression.

$$f_e = \frac{\text{Row total} \times \text{Column total}}{n}$$

The sample size is n. Once all f_e values have been determined, they may be arranged in a second contingency table.

4. **How do we obtain the chi-square statistic for testing independence?**
Matching the actual and expected frequencies from the respective cells, the following expression establishes the **chi-square test statistic**.

$$\chi^2 = \sum \frac{(f_a - f_e)^2}{f_e}$$

5. **How is the chi-square test for independence conducted?**
All tests of independence are upper-tailed, and at a significance level α there corresponds a critical value χ^2_α found in Appendix Table H. The number of degrees of freedom is computed from the expression

$$\text{df} = (\text{Number of rows} - 1) \times (\text{Number of columns} - 1)$$

If the computed value χ^2 exceeds χ^2_α, the null hypothesis of independence must be *rejected*; otherwise it must be *accepted.*

6. **How may the independence-testing procedure be adapted to test for the equality of several proportions?**
An analogous procedure involves testing for the equality of several proportions. The test statistic is computed in exactly the same way, and the number of degrees of freedom and the critical value are also determined by an identical procedure.

REVIEW EXERCISES

16-13 Slim Sales wishes to test the null hypothesis that people's sexual attitudes are independent of the kinds of cars they own. A random sample of 100 persons has been interviewed and placed into a dominant sexual-attitude category. The following results were obtained.

Dominant Sexual Attitude	Previously Purchased Car			
	(1) Foreign	(2) Small	(3) Large	Total
(1) Repressed	3	6	11	20
(2) Ho-Hum	13	25	12	50
(3) Swinger	14	9	7	30
Total	30	40	30	100

At an $\alpha = .05$ significance level, should Slim accept or reject the null hypothesis?

16-14 A sales manager wants to formulate a marketing strategy. To do this, he must determine whether his product's appeal is generally broad or whether it varies from region to region. A sampling study provided the following regional data.

	Region			
	(1) East	(2) Central	(3) South	(4) West
Number preferring	21	29	23	16
Number not preferring	39	41	27	24

At an $\alpha = .01$ significance level, should the manager conclude that his product is equally preferred in all regions?

16-15 Wright Aviation wants to establish important categories for plane owners. The following data have been obtained.

Amount of Usage	Aircraft Size			
	(1) Small	(2) Medium	(3) Large	Total
(1) Low	34	19	12	65
(2) Moderate	24	28	5	57
(3) High	7	12	22	41
Total	65	59	39	163

At a 5% significance level, should the manufacturer accept or reject the null hypothesis that amount of usage and aircraft size are independent?

16-16 Suppose that the sales manager in Exercise 16-14 wishes to test the null hypothesis that his product is equally strong in the East and the West. At an $\alpha = .05$ significance level, what should he conclude?

16-17 A market researcher for Gimble and Proctor wishes to determine whether the amount of time that people spend watching daytime television influences their choice of laundry bleach. A random sample of 260 persons was selected and their viewing habits and the type of bleach they use most often was determined. The following results apply.

Television Viewing Time	Type of Bleach (1) Liquid Chlorine	(2) Dry Chlorine	(3) Oxygen	Total
(1) Light	53	5	38	96
(2) Moderate	29	10	35	74
(3) Heavy	45	8	37	90
Total	127	23	110	260

At an $\alpha = .05$ significance level, should the researcher accept or reject the null hypothesis that television viewing time and type of bleach used are independent?

16-18 Lou Pole is investigating the effectiveness of computer programs for preparing tax returns. He has collected the following data pertaining to the number of returns that require reprocessing.

Program Type	Type of Return (1) Short Form	(2) Long Form	(3) Multiple Exhibits	(4) Corporate	Total
(1) Interactive	35	15	0	10	60
(2) Batched	40	10	10	15	75
Total	75	25	10	25	135

At a 5% significance level, should he accept or reject the null hypothesis that type of program and type of return are independent?

STATISTICS IN PRACTICE

16-19 Using the master class data list developed in Exercise 1-19, test for independence between two qualitative variables (such as gender and favorite food).

16-20 Using your group's class data from Exercise 1-21, test for independence between two qualitative variables.

16-21 Changes in legislative voting: Comparing 1964 to 1990. We can use chi-square methods to compare voting patterns in our legislatures. Here are examples of two votes separated by nearly thirty years of American history. The votes were cast in the U.S. Senate. States were categorized into four demographic groups based on the estimated percentage of African-Americans residing in the state:

Category	Percentage of African-Americans
Southern (S):	≥ 16%
Border/Southern (B):	<16%
Northern/Western-Homogeneous (N-Hom):	<4%
Northern/Western-Heterogeneous (N-Het):	≥ 4%

The 1964 Civil Rights Act

Category	Yes	No
S	2	20
B	10	2
N-Hom	35	5
N-Het	22	0

(Passed)

The 1990 Civil Rights Act

Category	Yes	No
S	16	6
B	7	5
N-Hom	21	15
N-Het	19	7

(Presidential Veto-Override Failed)

Source: Richard P. Young, Jerome S. Burstein, and Robert Higgs, "The Dynamics of Federalism and the Demise of Prescriptive Racism in the United States," presented at the Annual Meeting of the Public Choice Society, New Orleans, March 16, 1991.

(a) Carry out two tests for independence using the data separately for each vote.
(b) Carry out a test for independence across the two votes for Border/Southern states.

16-22 *Ethics and high technology companies.* Ethical standards (or lack of them) make the news quite often these days. This is especially so in the area of high technology. Do high-technology firms exhibit less ethical behavior? Table 16-8 shows the percentages for two groups—members

TABLE 16-8 Survey Results for Association for Systems Management (ASM) Members and non-ASM Subsamples Indicating Acceptable Behavior at Their Company

Behavior	ASM Members	Non-ASM	Behavior Type
Taking mood altering drugs during company time:	0	3	Safety
Giving certain clients better deals than others:	11	20	Cheating Third Party
Using the copy machine for making personal copies:	25	16	Cheating Company

Note: These three questions are drawn from full set of 19 questions covering acceptable behavior.
Source: Nancie Fimbel and Jerome Burstein, "Defining the Ethical Standards of the High-Technology Industry." *Journal of Business Ethics,* December 1990, v. 9, n. 12, p. 929 (20).

of a high-tech oriented professional association and general members of the population surveyed at random from three metropolitan areas (Boston, Charlotte, and San Jose). Three general types of ethical behavior were selected: safety, cheating the company or cheating a third party. Are behavior type and ASM membership independent?

CASE Gumball's Attitude Survey

The marketing manager for Gumball's Department Store has designed a questionnaire to obtain information regarding the quality of service. The key portion of the questionnaire is reproduced below.

5. What is the most attractive feature of Gumball's?
(a) Prices (c) Choices (e) Ambiance
(b) Access (d) Service

6. What was most annoying about your last Gumball's transaction?
(a) Rudeness (c) Waiting (e) Nothing
(b) Crowds (d) Pushiness

7. What is the most important aspect of good service?
(a) Helpfulness (c) Communication
(b) Quickness (d) Friendliness

8. On a scale of 1 (terrible) to 5 (outstanding), how would you rate the service you received during your last visit to Gumball's?
(a) 1 (b) 2 (c) 3 (d) 4 (e) 5

The manager uses the questionnaire in a small "pilot" investigation to help him plan a more detailed survey.

Several customers were selected at random and their responses are summarized in Table 16-9. These data have been sorted using answers to item 5, with a minor sort using responses to item 6.

You have been asked to do a preliminary analysis of Gumball's questionnaire.

QUESTIONS

1. Refer to the responses given to items 5 (attractive features) and 6 (most annoying).
(a) Construct contingency tables for the actual and expected frequencies of responses to the two service queries. (Group together responses "a" with "b" and "d" with "e" for item 5. For item 6, group "a" with "b" and "c" with "e.")
(b) Calculate the chi-square statistic.
(c) At a 5% significance level, are most attractive and most annoying features independent?

TABLE 16-9 Summary of Partial Results for the Gumball's Survey

Item				Item				Item				Item			
5	6	7	8	5	6	7	8	5	6	7	8	5	6	7	8
a	a	a	1	c	a	a	1	c	d	a	5	d	d	a	1
a	a	b	3	c	a	b	3	c	d	b	1	d	d	b	2
a	b	b	3	c	b	b	3	c	d	c	2	d	e	c	5
a	b	a	4	c	b	c	4	c	d	d	4	d	e	c	5
a	b	c	4	c	b	d	4	c	d	d	3	d	e	d	4
a	c	d	5	c	b	d	2	c	d	a	5	d	e	a	4
a	d	a	2	c	b	c	3	c	d	b	5	d	e	b	5
b	a	c	1	c	b	c	4	c	e	b	4	d	e	b	5
b	a	c	3	c	b	a	3	c	e	c	3	d	e	a	2
b	b	a	3	c	c	b	5	d	a	c	1	d	e	a	3
b	b	a	4	c	c	b	5	d	a	c	2	d	e	c	4
b	b	b	4	c	c	a	5	d	b	a	1	e	a	d	1
b	c	b	5	c	c	b	2	d	b	d	1	e	a	b	1
b	c	b	4	c	d	c	2	d	b	d	2	e	a	a	5
b	d	b	1	c	d	d	2	d	b	b	3	e	b	a	1
b	d	c	2	c	d	c	1	d	b	d	5	e	c	b	3
b	d	d	4	c	d	d	3	d	c	c	4	e	d	d	2
b	e	d	5	c	d	a	1	d	c	a	5	e	d	c	5
c	a	a	2	c	d	b	2	d	c	a	5	e	d	c	4
c	a	a	1	c	d	c	4	d	c	b	1	e	e	d	4

(d) Suggest how Gumball's should use this information in the follow-on survey.

2. Repeat Question 1, using instead the responses given to items 5 (attractive features) and 7 (good service). (Group together responses "a," "b," and "e" for item 5. For item 7, combine response "c" with "d.")

3. Repeat Question 1, using instead the responses given to items 6 (most annoying) and 8 (service rating). (Group together responses "a," "b," and "c" for item 6. Also for item 6, group into second category responses "d" and "e.")

4. Based on your answers to the above questions, do you have any immediate advice regarding what Gumball's should do to rapidly achieve improvements in perceived service?

16-4 OPTIONAL TOPIC: INFERENCES REGARDING THE POPULATION VARIANCE

We have seen that knowledge of population variability is an important element of statistical analysis. For instance, an educator may choose a particular teaching method because it provides low dispersion in student achievement levels, thereby making the teacher's job less demanding than a high-variability procedure would. A bank policy might favor a single waiting line that feeds into several teller windows rather than separate lines, because it has been estimated that a single line will minimize variability in patron waiting times—even though the mean time spent in line is the same in either case. In a car pool, tires with a low variability in wear may be preferred to more durable tires with greater variability in useful lifetime, simply because it is cheaper to replace an entire set of tires periodically for each car.

Like the population mean, σ^2 is ordinarily unknown and its value must be estimated using sample data. Until now, we have been using the sample variance

$$s^2 = \frac{\sum X^2 - n\bar{X}^2}{n - 1}$$

to make point estimates of σ^2. These estimates have been made as an adjunct to inferences regarding μ, where confidence intervals and hypothesis-testing decision rules have been constructed using s^2 in place of σ^2.

Inferences about σ^2 are made in a similar way to inferences about μ, in that s^2 may be used as an unbiased and consistent estimator of the population variance, playing the analogous role with σ^2 that $\bar{X}$ does with μ. Thus, s^2 serves as the basis either for constructing confidence interval estimates or for testing hypotheses regarding σ^2.

PROBABILITIES FOR THE s^2 VARIABLE

In the *planning stage* of a sampling study, s^2 must be treated as a random variable, because its value is not yet determined and is subject to chance variation. In discussing how to apply probability analysis to s^2, it will be helpful to briefly review our earlier treatment of $\bar{X}$.

Recall that when σ^2 is unknown, the Student t distribution is used to make inferences about the population mean. The chi-square distribution assigns a role to s^2 that is similar to the role the Student t distribution assigns to $\bar{X}$. *Before the sample data are collected, s^2 must be viewed as a random variable* (just like $\bar{X}$). Multiplying s^2 by $n - 1$ and dividing by σ^2 converts it into the

CHI-SQUARE RANDOM VARIABLE

$$\chi^2 = \frac{(n - 1)s^2}{\sigma^2}$$

which exhibits the chi-square distribution.* The number of degrees of freedom is $n - 1$.

*As is true of the Student t distribution, to apply the chi-square distribution, the *population* must be normally distributed.

To illustrate this, suppose that a sample of $n = 25$ heights has been randomly selected from a population of men with a standard deviation of $\sigma = 3$ inches. To find the probability that s^2 falls within a range of numbers, two limits must be chosen for the chi-square variable. This may be done so that χ^2 is just as likely to fall below its *lower limit*, denoted by $\chi^2_{1-\alpha/2}$, as it is to fall above its *upper limit* $\chi^2_{\alpha/2}$. For example, if these limits are to be chosen for a 0.90 probability, then using $\alpha = .10$

$$.90 = \Pr\left[\chi^2_{.95} \leq \frac{(n-1)s^2}{\sigma^2} \leq \chi^2_{.05}\right]$$

In this case, χ^2 values are found from Appendix Table H for $n - 1 = 25 - 1 = 24$ degrees of freedom. The upper tail areas are .95 for the lower limit and .05 for the upper limit, and the area under the portion of the chi-square curve between these limits is .90.

$$\chi^2_{1-\alpha/2} = \chi^2_{.95} = 13.848$$
$$\chi^2_{\alpha/2} = \chi^2_{.05} = 36.415$$

Two separate table values are required to find the chi-square limits, because the chi-square distribution is *positively skewed.* This is in contrast to our earlier applications involving the normal and the Student t curves, both of which are symmetrical.

Using $\sigma = 3$ inches ($\sigma^2 = 9$),

$$.90 = \Pr\left[13.848 \leq \frac{24s^2}{9} \leq 36.415\right]$$

so that

$$.90 = \Pr\left[\frac{9(13.848)}{24} \leq s^2 \leq \frac{9(36.415)}{24}\right] = \Pr[5.19 \leq s^2 \leq 13.66]$$

Thus, there is a 90% chance that a sample of $n = 25$ observations from a population having $\sigma = 3$ inches will provide a sample variance of between 5.19 and 13.66. (In other words, there is a 90% probability that s will lie between $\sqrt{5.19} = 2.3$ and $\sqrt{13.66} = 3.7$ inches.)

CONFIDENCE INTERVAL ESTIMATE OF σ^2

The foregoing probability analysis presumes that the value of the population variance is known. However, this is not usually the case in a sampling situation. *After the sample data are collected,* s^2 may be calculated and may serve as the basis for making inferences about σ^2. Treating σ^2 as the unknown and s^2 as the known quantities, we may transform the probability interval for s^2 into the form for determining an interval estimate of σ^2. The following expression is used to construct the $100(1 - \alpha)\%$

CONFIDENCE INTERVAL ESTIMATE OF σ^2

$$\frac{(n-1)s^2}{\chi^2_{\alpha/2}} \leq \sigma^2 \leq \frac{(n-1)s^2}{\chi^2_{1-\alpha/2}}$$

Here, $\chi^2_{1-\alpha/2}$ and $\chi^2_{\alpha/2}$ must be chosen from Appendix Table H using $n - 1$ degrees of freedom, to correspond to the confidence level desired.

EXAMPLE: VARIABILITY IN PORTFOLIO RATES OF RETURN

A financial analyst for Toro, Oso, and Toro estimated the variability in rates of return that her firm's clients experience on their stock investments. She obtained the following sample results for $n = 25$ client portfolios.

$$\bar{X} = 14.5\% \qquad s = 11.2\%$$

She constructed a 98% confidence interval estimate of the variance σ^2 in rates of return.

SOLUTION: Using $\alpha/2 = .01$ and $1 - \alpha/2 = .99$, with df $= 25 - 1 = 24$, she found the following critical values from Appendix Table H.

$$\chi^2_{.01} = 42.980 \qquad \chi^2_{.99} = 10.856$$

The desired interval is thus

$$\frac{(25-1)(11.2)^2}{42.980} \leq \sigma^2 \leq \frac{(25-1)(11.2)^2}{10.856}$$

or

$$70.0 \leq \sigma^2 \leq 277.3$$

The units of this interval are in *square* units. By taking the square root of these limits, she obtained the 98% confidence interval estimate of the population standard deviation σ.

$$8.4\% \leq \sigma \leq 16.7\%$$

TESTING HYPOTHESES REGARDING σ^2

Hypothesis tests concerning σ^2 may be conducted in a manner similar to the tests described in earlier chapters. The null hypothesis regarding σ^2 may be either one- or two-sided, and decision rules may be constructed in terms of the chi-square variable, which serves as the test statistic. For a hypothesized value of the population variance, denoted by σ_0^2, we use the appropriate

TEST STATISTIC FOR THE VARIANCE

$$\chi^2 = \frac{(n-1)s^2}{\sigma_0^2}$$

The significance level α establishes the critical values of this statistic.

For one-sided tests, the decision rule is based on χ^2_α, which must correspond to the upper tail of the chi-square curve, or on $\chi^2_{1-\alpha}$, which must correspond to the lower tail of that curve. This is true because the critical value of χ^2 for a lower-tailed test must be the point *below* which the area is α. The cases may be summarized using the following expressions.

Lower-Tailed Test	Upper-Tailed Test
H_0: $\sigma^2 \geq \sigma_0^2$	H_0: $\sigma^2 \leq \sigma_0^2$
Critical value = $\chi^2_{1-\alpha}$	Critical value = χ^2_α

Illustration: Variability in Waiting Time

That predictability and variability are related may be illustrated by the attitudes of people who wait in lines. A lengthy waiting time is more acceptable if the variability is smaller, even though the average wait may be the same. When the variability is smaller, the inconvenience of waiting becomes more predictable. This accounts for the fact that many businesses and government offices dealing with the public have instituted a "single-line" policy to replace the chaotic procedure of maintaining independent lines at various service areas (like supermarket checkout counters or windows at a post office). Although the mean waiting time is not greatly affected by the single-line policy, the variability in waiting time is.

A particular postmaster has determined that the current procedure of separate lines yields a standard deviation in waiting times on December mornings of $\sigma_0 = 10$ minutes per customer. He wishes to implement the single-line policy on a trial basis to see if a reduction in variability is achieved. A sample of 30 customers were monitored, and their waiting times determined.

STEP 1

Formulate the null hypothesis. As his null hypothesis, the postmaster assumes that the variability in waiting times will be at least as great under the experimental procedure, or

$$H_0: \sigma^2 \geq \sigma_0^2 \qquad (10^2 = 100)$$

STEP 2

Select the test statistic and procedure. The chi-square serves as the test statistic.

STEP 3

Establish the significance level and identify the acceptance and rejection regions. This test is lower-tailed, since the null hypothesis is refuted by a small value of

s^2 (and therefore χ^2). A significance level of $\alpha = .01$ is desired. For $30 - 1 = 29$ degrees of freedom, the critical value of the chi-square statistic is

$$\chi^2_{1-\alpha} = \chi^2_{.99} = 14.256$$

The postmaster's acceptance and rejection regions are shown below.

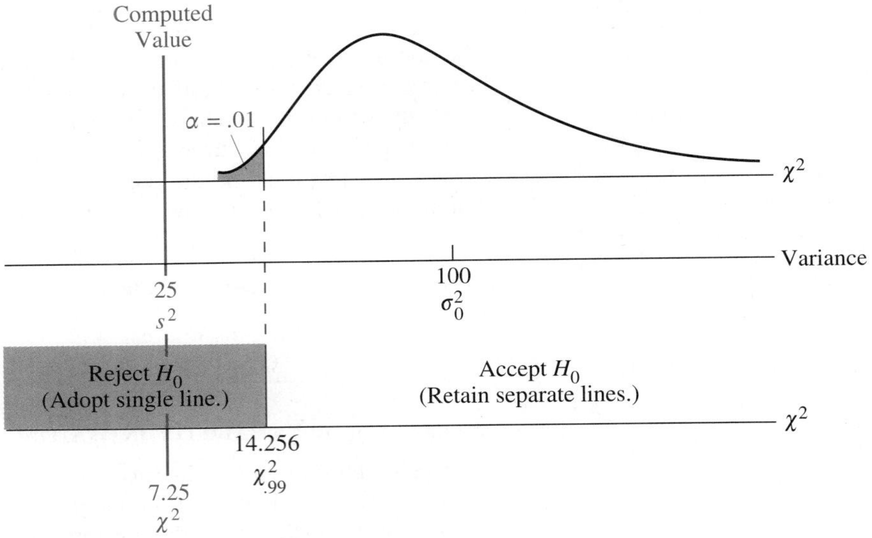

STEP 4

Collect the sample and compute the value of the test statistic. A sample standard deviation of $s = 5$ minutes has been obtained. The computed value of the test statistic is

$$\chi^2 = \frac{(30 - 1)(5)^2}{(10)^2} = 7.25$$

STEP 5

Make the decision. Since the computed value of $\chi^2 = 7.25$ falls in the rejection region, the null hypothesis must be *rejected.* The postmaster should adopt the new single-line policy.

When the null hypothesis takes the form H_0: $\sigma^2 = \sigma_0^2$, a two-sided test applies. Large or small values of the sample variance tend to refute H_0. Thus, either a large or a small calculation for χ^2 will result in a rejection of H_0. As with the two-sided tests that we discussed in earlier chapters, a convenient procedure for making a decision is to construct a confidence interval that corresponds to the significance level. If σ_0^2 falls outside this interval, H_0 must be *rejected*; if the interval contains σ_0^2, H_0 must be *accepted.*

To illustrate this procedure, we will again consider the variability in rates of return for the example on page 712. There, we obtained the 98% confidence interval

$$70.0 \le \sigma^2 \le 277.3$$

Now, suppose the analyst wishes to test the null hypothesis that the return variability in client portfolios is the same as the return variability of portfolios in the community, assumed to have a standard deviation of $\sigma_0 = 10\%$. Thus, her null hypothesis is

$$H_0\text{: } \sigma^2 = \sigma_0^2 \qquad (10^2 = 100)$$

Since $\sigma_0^2 = 100$ lies inside the 98% confidence interval found earlier, H_0 must be *accepted* at an $\alpha = .02$ significance level.

NORMAL APPROXIMATION FOR LARGE SAMPLE SIZES

Appendix Table H does not list chi-square distributions above 30 degrees of freedom. *For values of n larger than 30, we can use the normal curve to approximate the chi-square distribution.* It may be shown that χ^2 has a mean equal to the degrees of freedom and a variance equal to twice that amount. Thus, we may use the following expression to compute the applicable normal deviate.

$$z = \frac{\chi^2 - (n-1)}{\sqrt{2(n-1)}}$$

This expression is useful for testing hypotheses about σ^2. To construct a confidence interval, however, it is more convenient to express the critical values of χ^2 in terms of the tabled value of z by using the equivalent expressions.

$$\chi^2_{1-\alpha/2} = n - 1 - z_{\alpha/2}\sqrt{2(n-1)}$$

and

$$\chi^2_{\alpha/2} = n - 1 + z_{\alpha/2}\sqrt{2(n-1)}$$

EXAMPLE: EFFECTIVENESS OF A TRANQUILIZER

A medical researcher for a drug manufacturer who wishes to determine how effectively a particular tranquilizer induces sleep administered the drug to a sample of $n = 100$ patients. The sample standard deviation in times required to onset of sleep was $s = 7.3$ minutes. The researcher constructed a 95% confidence interval for the variability in time to sleep and used it to test a hypothesis regarding σ^2.

SOLUTION: For a 9.5% confidence level, $\alpha = .05$. Using $z_{.025} = 1.96$, the following limits for the chi-square variable were obtained.

$$\begin{aligned} \chi^2_{.975} &= 99 - 1.96\sqrt{2(99)} \\ &= 99 - 27.58 = 71.42 \\ \chi^2_{.025} &= 99 + 27.58 = 126.58 \end{aligned}$$

Using these values, with $s = 7.3$ and $n = 100$, the researcher constructed the following

$$\frac{(n-1)s^2}{\chi^2_{\alpha/2}} \leq \sigma^2 \leq \frac{(n-1)s^2}{\chi^2_{1-\alpha/2}}$$

$$\frac{99(7.3)^2}{126.58} \leq \sigma^2 \leq \frac{99(7.3)^2}{71.42}$$

$$41.68 \leq \sigma^2 \leq 73.87$$

Taking the square root of each term reveals a 95% confidence that the population standard deviation will fall between 6.46 and 8.59 minutes.

Our researcher wishes to test the null hypothesis that the variability in the new sleeping drug is the same as the variability in the old drug, for which previous records show the standard deviation is 8 minutes. Then, the null hypothesis is

$$H_0\colon \sigma^2 = \sigma_0^2 \qquad (8^2 = 64)$$

Since $\sigma_0^2 = 64$ falls inside the 95% confidence interval for σ^2, the researcher must *accept* H_0 at an $\alpha = .05$ significance level and conclude that the two drugs are identical in variability of time necessary to induce sleep.

OPTIONAL EXERCISES

16-23 For each of the following situations, construct a 90% confidence interval estimate of the population variance.

(a) $s^2 = 20.3$; $n = 25$ (c) $s^2 = .53$; $n = 15$
(b) $s^2 = 101.6$; $n = 12$ (d) $s^2 = 7.78$; $n = 20$

16-24 For each of the following hypothesis-testing situations, (1) indicate whether the test is lower- or upper-tailed; (2) calculate the critical value of the chi-square statistic at the indicated significance level; and (3) calculate χ^2 and determine whether H_0 must be accepted or rejected.

(a) $H_0\colon \sigma^2 \geq 16$; $n = 25$; $\alpha = .05$; $s^2 = 19$
(b) $H_0\colon \sigma^2 \leq 100$; $n = 10$; $\alpha = .01$; $s^2 = 105$
(c) $H_0\colon \sigma^2 \geq .64$; $n = 19$; $\alpha = .10$; $s^2 = .59$
(d) $H_0\colon \sigma^2 \leq 6.1$; $n = 17$; $\alpha = .05$; $s^2 = 10.1$

16-25 The following sample data have been obtained for check cashing transaction times (seconds) at Million Bank.

25	18	24	19	20
23	27	21	23	21
19	22	20	25	25

Construct a 90% confidence interval estimate of the standard deviation in transaction times.

16-26 Suppose that the researcher in the example on page 715 administers another drug to a sample of $n = 200$ patients and that the standard deviation for time to sleep is $s = 8.2$ minutes.

(a) Construct a 95% confidence interval for the population variance of the time to sleep.

(b) Suppose that the researcher wishes to test the null hypothesis that this drug will exhibit the same variability as the current drug, for which the standard deviation is 8 minutes. At an $\alpha = .05$ significance level, should he accept or reject the null hypothesis?

16-27 Druid's Drayage provided the following sample data for the transportation costs (dollars) of moving a pallet of raw materials 500 miles.

105	110	108	97	99
104	112	103	98	105

Construct 90% confidence interval estimates of (a) the variance and (b) the standard deviation in cost per pallet.

16-28 A consumer agency has tested a random sample of $n = 100$ sets of Treadmore radial tires. The sample standard deviation for tire-set lifetimes is $s = 2{,}000$ miles.

(a) Construct a 99% confidence interval estimate of the population variance of radial tire lifetimes.

(b) At an $\alpha = .01$ significance level, should the agency accept or reject the null hypothesis that radial tires have a different lifetime variability than nonradial tires, which have a population standard deviation of 2,500 miles?

CHAPTER 17

ANALYSIS OF VARIANCE

BEFORE READING THIS CHAPTER, MAKE SURE YOU UNDERSTAND:

The statistical sampling study (Chapter 4).

Statistical estimation (Chapter 8).

Hypothesis testing (Chapter 9).

AFTER READING THIS CHAPTER, YOU WILL UNDERSTAND:

The role of analysis of variance.

About the theoretical model for analysis of variance.

How to test whether the population means are identical.

How to compute the *F* statistic for testing.

How to find the critical value for the *F* statistic.

About the ANOVA table.

About other inferences that may be made from the sample data.

In this chapter, we will examine procedures for analyzing several quantitative populations. Our central focus will be a statistical application called **analysis of variance**, which is actually a method for comparing the means of more than two populations.

This kind of analysis is useful in many areas of decision making and research. A manufacturer can use it in determining the most effective packaging for a product. It can indicate to a production manager whether various ingredient combinations really make a difference in the quality of the final product. In drug research, it can help to determine whether a patient's recovery is influenced by different treatments. In agriculture, it may help to determine if crop yields differ according to the type of fertilizer or pesticide used.

The basic questions that we will consider in this chapter have already been posed in Chapter 15, where we compared two population means using samples from control and experimental groups. When more than two samples are involved, however, a radically different approach is required.

Analysis of variance may appear to be misnamed, because it deals with means, but we will see that *this procedure achieves its goal by comparing sample variances*. To do this, a new probability distribution—the ***F* distribution**—is employed.

17-1 ANALYSIS OF VARIANCE AND THE *F* DISTRIBUTION

Analysis of variance uses sample data to compare several **treatments** to determine if they achieve different results. Here, we use the word *treatment* in a broad sense that includes not only medical therapy, but other factors that a researcher might investigate. Thus, an agronomist may consider several concentrations of fertilizer to be treatments for crops. Similarly, each company training program may be a different treatment for employee development. Sample data may be obtained by applying the respective treatments to different samples. These sample data may then be analyzed to determine if the treatments differ.

TESTING FOR EQUALITY OF MEANS: EVALUATING THREE FERTILIZERS

Consider the data in Table 17-1 obtained for three different fertilizer treatments being evaluated by a sod farmer. Here, the total dosages are the same, but the quantities applied and the fertilizing frequencies are varied. The sample observations represent the number of square yards of marketable sod obtained from random plots of 100 square yards, all seeded with the same variety of grass mix. In each case, a random sample of 5 plots was subjected to one of the three treatments.

The analysis of variance procedure used to determine whether fertilization affects sod yield involves two variables. We note some similarities between this situation and regression analysis. The method of fertilizing is a qualitative variable, referred to as the **treatment variable**. The treatment variable is analogous to the independent variable in regression analysis. The sod yield is the **response variable**, which must be quantitative. Because the response achieved may depend on the particular treatment used, this variable plays a role similar to the dependent variable in regression analysis. Although analysis of variance primarily involves *qualitative treatments*, it may be used with quantitative ones as well; in such

TABLE 17-1 Experimental Layout for Sample Sod Yields (square yards) from Three Fertilizer Treatments

	Fertilizer Treatment		
Observation	(1) Quarter Dosage, Once Weekly	(2) Half Dosage, Every Two Weeks	(3) Full Dosage, Every Four Weeks
1	77	83	80
2	79	91	82
3	87	94	86
4	85	88	85
5	78	85	80
Totals	406	441	413
Means	$\bar{X}_1 = 81.2$	$\bar{X}_2 = 88.2$	$\bar{X}_3 = 82.6$

$$\bar{\bar{X}} = \frac{406 + 441 + 413}{5(3)} = 84$$

cases, the treatments are fixed at a few key levels and constitute *quantitative categories* rather than continuous variates.

The sod farmer must compare the alternative fertilizer techniques to see if they provide different mean yields of marketable sod. In effect, he wishes to test the null hypothesis that the population mean yield per 100 square yards of seeded surface is the same for each treatment. Using subscripts 1, 2, and 3 to denote the respective treatments, we may express the

NULL HYPOTHESIS

$$H_0: \mu_1 = \mu_2 = \mu_3$$

The corresponding alternative hypothesis is that the means are not equal, or that at least one pair of the μ's differs.

The procedures described in this chapter actually test a somewhat stronger null hypothesis—that the treatment populations are identical, or that they have the same frequency distribution form. In particular, this assumption means that each treatment population has the same common value for its variance.

The concepts underlying this procedure are illustrated in Figure 17-1. When the sample data are combined, they appear to be observations from a single population with high dispersion, as shown in Figure 17-1(a). But when each treatment is viewed separately, these same sod yields appear to belong to three separate populations with smaller variances, as indicated in Figure 17-1(b). Under the null hypothesis, however, the treatment populations have identical means and the same variance, so that an identical frequency curve like the one in Figure 17-1(c) applies for each fertilization method.

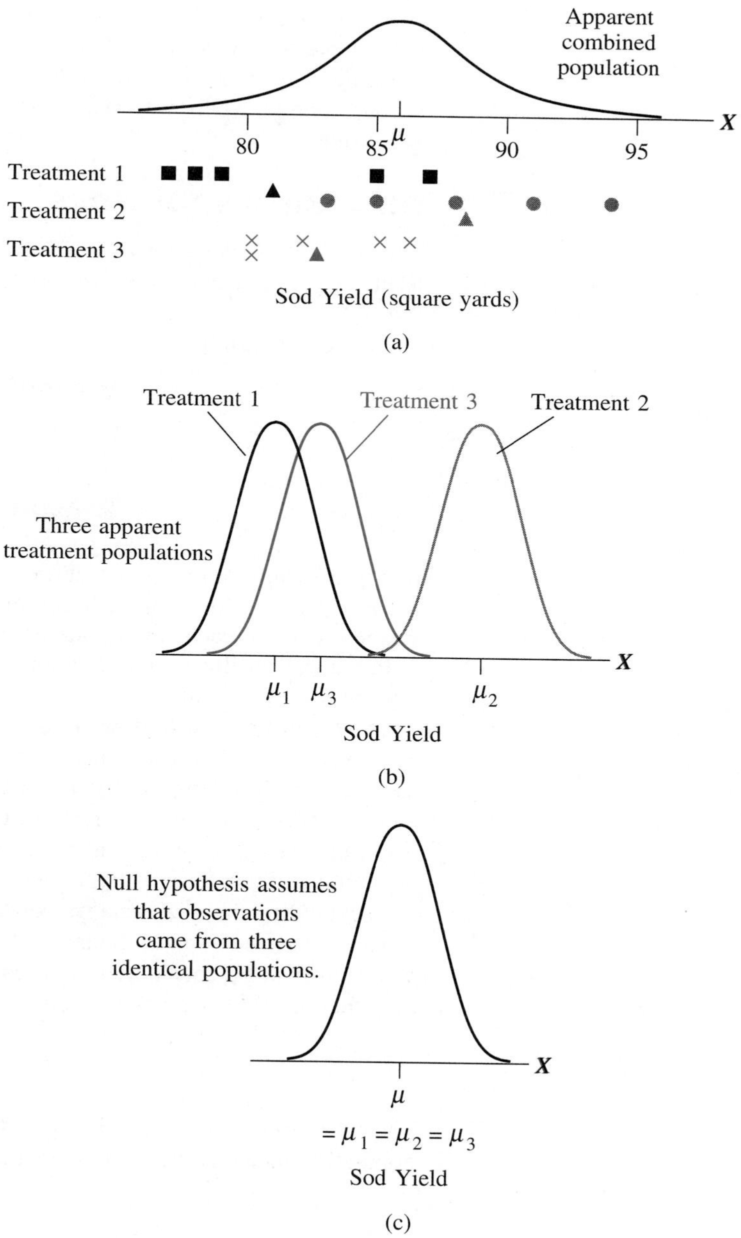

FIGURE 17-1 Concepts underlying analysis of variance.

As in earlier hypothesis-testing procedures, we must convert the sample data into a test statistic and determine if the value achieved refutes H_0. Before we do this, it is necessary to establish some notation and concepts.

Each sample plot yield in Table 17-1 may be represented by a symbol X_{ij}, where i refers to the row or observation number and j refers to the column. This matrix format provides the **experimental layout**. In each column, the values are the sample observations made from the corresponding treatment populations. For example, $X_{32} = 94$ square yards—the sod yield for the third test plot in the second sample, where treatment (2) of half the fertilizer dosage every two weeks was used.

THE SINGLE-FACTOR MODEL

The concepts underlying analysis of variance treat each sample observation in terms of components. Here, we use the

SINGLE-FACTOR MODEL

$$X_{ij} = \mu_j + \varepsilon_{ij}$$

to express each sample observation in terms of two components. Altogether there are c treatments (one for each column) and $j = 1, 2, \ldots, c$. There are r observations (one for each row) made using each treatment.

In the sod-fertilization illustration there are $c = 3$ treatments with $r = 5$ sample observations per treatment.

The **treatment population mean** μ_j is ordinarily a constant of unknown value. The **error term** for each observation is denoted by ε_{ij}. The error terms are assumed to be independent normally distributed random variables with mean 0 and standard deviation σ. It follows that each sample observation is expected to equal the respective treatment population mean and to have a common standard deviation σ, regardless of treatment.

In extending the analytical framework to multiple factors, it may be convenient to view each treatment as the level of a **factor**. The jth treatment population mean μ_j would then be considered the **mean for factor-level** $\boldsymbol{j}$. Each population mean may then be expressed as the sum of two components.

$$\mu_j = \bar{\mu} + B_j$$

The first term is the **overall population mean** $\bar{\mu}$. The model treats the overall population mean as the average of the individual treatment population means.

$$\bar{\mu} = \frac{\sum_j \mu_j}{c}$$

The term B_j is defined as the

EFFECT FOR FACTOR-LEVEL j

$$B_j = \mu_j - \bar{\mu}$$

The null hypothesis of equal factor-level (treatment population) means may be expressed equivalently as

$$H_0: B_1 = B_2 = \cdots = B_c$$

SAMPLE MEANS

Two types of sample means are used to test the above null hypothesis. One set of means corresponds to the treatments, and the other set to the collective sample.

The following expression is used to compute the

SAMPLE MEAN FOR THE jth TREATMENT COLUMN

$$\bar{X}_j = \frac{\sum_i X_{ij}}{r}$$

where all the observations in the jth column are summed and divided by r, the number of observations per treatment or the number of rows. In our illustration, $j = 1, 2,$ or 3, depending on which treatment is being considered. The sample mean of the first treatment is found by summing the values in column (1) and dividing by $r = 5$.

$$\bar{X}_1 = \frac{77 + 79 + 87 + 85 + 78}{5} = 81.2 \text{ square yards}$$

The other sample means are calculated similarly as $\bar{X}_2 = 88.2$ and $\bar{X}_3 = 82.6$ square yards.

To facilitate testing the null hypothesis, the data for the three samples are pooled in calculating the

GRAND MEAN

$$\bar{\bar{X}} = \frac{\sum_j \sum_i X_{ij}}{rc}$$

Here, the grand mean is denoted by $\bar{\bar{X}}$ ("X double bar"). The double summation indicates that we obtain the column totals first and then sum these figures for all treatments. The resultant total is divided by the combined sample size. We denote the number of treatments or columns by the letter c. There are $c = 3$ treatments in this illustration, so the combined sample size is $rc = 5(3) = 15$. The grand mean in our example is computed in Table 17-1 as $\bar{\bar{X}} = 84$ square yards.

USING VARIABILITY TO IDENTIFY DIFFERENCES

In any testing problem, the test statistic should (1) highlight the differences between the observed sample results and the expected results of the null hypothesis and (2) have a convenient sampling distribution to measure the effect of chance sampling error. We have seen that it is easy to estimate the amount of sampling error from the variability in the sample results. We may also use the variability in the results to express differences. For instance, if several values are unalike, their dispersion—expressed by a range, variance, or standard deviation—will be greater than it will be if the values are close to one another. When many values are involved, their collective differences may be summarized by one of these measures of variability.

Further conceptual framework must be erected before we are ready to perform the basic test.

DEVIATIONS ABOUT SAMPLE MEANS

The analytical process may be explained in terms of three types of deviations, as shown in Figure 17-2 for the sod-fertilization experiment. The **total deviations** for each individual observation are shown as bars connecting the data points to the grand mean in Figure 17-2(a). To illustrate, subtract the grand mean from the first observation for treatment (1) to obtain the

$$\text{Total deviation: } X_{11} - \bar{\bar{X}} = 77 - 84 = -7$$

which is negative, since X_{11} lies below $\bar{\bar{X}}$.

The bars plotted in Figure 17-2(b) represent the **treatments deviations**, obtained for each factor level by subtracting the grand mean from the corresponding treatment (column) sample mean. For treatment (1), the following difference provides the

$$\text{Treatment deviation: } \bar{X}_1 - \bar{\bar{X}} = 81.2 - 84 = -2.8$$

Figure 17-2(c) shows the bars for the **error deviations** obtained by subtracting the respective computed value of the treatment sample mean from each individual observation. Again, using the first observation for treatment (1), we obtain the following

$$\text{Error deviation: } X_{11} - \bar{X}_1 = 77 - 81.2 = -4.2$$

Each total deviation may be partitioned as

$$\begin{array}{ccccc} \text{Total} & & \text{Treatments} & & \text{Error} \\ \text{deviation} & = & \text{deviation} & + & \text{deviation} \\ (X_{11} - \bar{\bar{X}}) & = & (\bar{X}_1 - \bar{\bar{X}}) & + & (X_{11} - \bar{X}_1) \end{array}$$

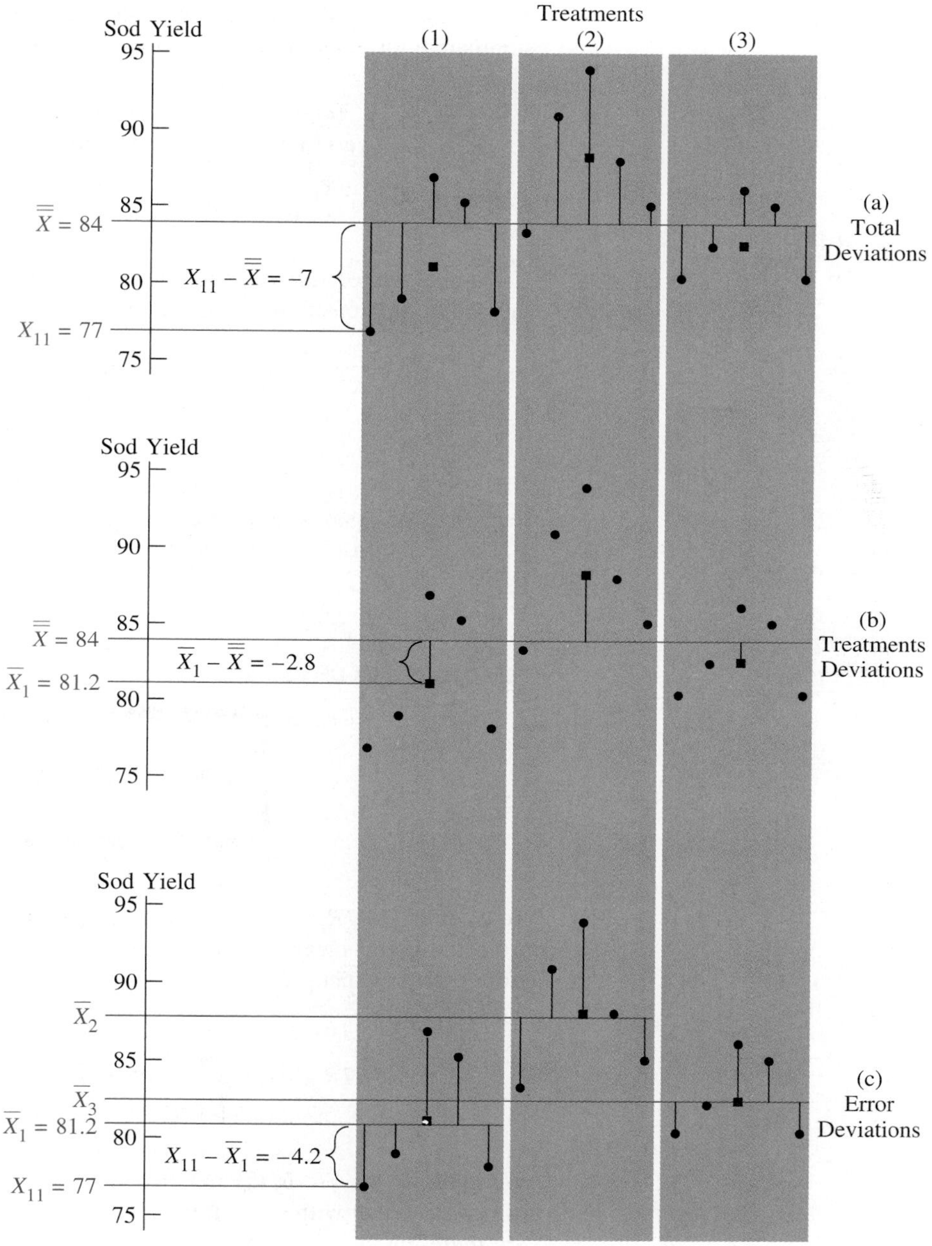

FIGURE 17-2 Three types of deviations for the sod-fertilization experiment.

The above expression gives some justification to the following procedure for summarizing variation in sample data.

SUMMARIZING VARIATION IN SAMPLE DATA

The analysis of variance procedure considers the collective sums of individual *squared* deviations. These express the amount of *variation* about the respective means that is exhibited by the sample values. The following expressions summarize the relationships thereby obtained.

$$\begin{array}{ccccc} \text{Total variation} & = & \text{Treatments variation} & + & \text{Error variation} \\ \sum_i \sum_j (X_{ij} - \bar{\bar{X}})^2 & = & r\sum_j (\bar{X}_j - \bar{\bar{X}})^2 & + & \sum_i \sum_j (X_{ij} - \bar{X}_j)^2 \end{array}$$

Using the *sum of squares* notation discussed previously for regression analysis, the above relationship may be expressed as

$$\begin{array}{ccccc} \text{Total variation} & = & \text{Treatments variation} & + & \text{Error variation} \\ SSTO & = & SSTR & + & SSE \end{array}$$

Each sum of squares may be computed using the expressions that follow.

The variability *between* sample groups or treatment columns is summarized by the

TREATMENTS SUM OF SQUARES

$$SSTR = r\sum (\bar{X}_j - \bar{\bar{X}})^2$$

To calculate $SSTR$, we sum the squared deviations of the sample treatment means from the grand mean and then multiply by the number of observations r made from each treatment. Using the earlier results for our sod-fertilization experiment, we find

$$\begin{aligned} SSTR &= 5[(81.2 - 84)^2 + (88.2 - 84)^2 + (82.6 - 84)^2] \\ &= 5(7.84 + 17.64 + 1.96) = 137.20 \end{aligned}$$

We multiply by $r = 5$, the number of observations per treatment (or the number of rows), so that with $c = 3$ treatments or columns, all of the $rc = 15$ observations are represented.

By expressing the variation between columns (samples), the treatments sum of squares is often called the **explained variation**, because $SSTR$ is obtained from differences in the sample means. Thus, $SSTR$ summarizes the differences in sample results that may be due to inherent differences in the treatment populations rather than to chance alone.

The variability *within* sample groups or treatment columns is determined by summing the squared deviations of the individual observations about their respec-

TABLE 17-2 Calculation of the Error Sum of Squares for the Sod-Fertilization Experiment

j	$(X_{i1} - \bar{X}_1)^2$	$(X_{i2} - \bar{X}_2)^2$	$(X_{i3} - \bar{X}_3)^2$
1	$(77 - 81.2)^2 = 17.64$	$(83 - 88.2)^2 = 27.04$	$(80 - 82.6)^2 = 6.76$
2	$(79 - 81.2)^2 = 4.84$	$(91 - 88.2)^2 = 7.84$	$(82 - 82.6)^2 = .36$
3	$(87 - 81.2)^2 = 33.64$	$(94 - 88.2)^2 = 33.64$	$(86 - 82.6)^2 = 11.56$
4	$(85 - 81.2)^2 = 14.44$	$(88 - 88.2)^2 = .04$	$(85 - 82.6)^2 = 5.76$
5	$(78 - 81.2)^2 = 10.24$	$(85 - 88.2)^2 = 10.24$	$(80 - 82.6)^2 = 6.76$
	80.80	78.80	31.20

$$SSE = \sum \sum (X_{ij} - \bar{X}_j)^2 = 80.80 + 78.80 + 31.20 = 190.80$$

tive sample means. This variability is summarized by the following expression for the

ERROR SUM OF SQUARES

$$SSE = \sum \sum (X_{ij} - \bar{X}_j)^2 = SSTO - SSTR$$

Table 17-2 shows the calculation of the error sum of squares for the results of the sod-fertilization experiment. There, we obtain $SSE = 190.80$. In performing this calculation, it is convenient to maintain the same column arrangement we used initially: We total the squared deviations for each treatment first, then sum these figures to obtain SSE. Like $SSTR$, SSE accounts for each individual sample observation made.

The error sum of squares SSE expresses **unexplained variation**, because it measures differences between sample values that are due to chance (or residual) variation, for which no identifiable cause may be found. This is in contrast to $SSTR$, which explains the variation between samples in terms of differences in treatment populations.

If we initially ignore the groupings of the sample observations, we may determine the sum of squares for a single combined sample. The result is the

TOTAL SUM OF SQUARES

$$SSTO = \sum \sum (X_{ij} - \bar{\bar{X}})^2 = SSTR + SSE$$

We may calculate the total sum of squares for our 15 observations.

$$SSTO = (77 - 84)^2 + (79 - 84)^2 + \cdots + (80 - 84)^2 = 328$$

Note that by adding the treatments and error sums of squares, the same value is obtained.

$$SSTO = SSTR + SSE = 137.20 + 190.80 = 328.00$$

When sample sizes are large, sum of squares calculations may become quite burdensome and may be simplified considerably by using shortcut expressions for *SSTR* and *SSE*. Because the more straightforward procedures presented here work equally well for small samples, shortcut expressions are not included in this book. Instead, *it is recommended that large problems be run on a computer.*

THE BASIS FOR COMPARISON

We have just seen that the two components of total variation are explained (*SSTR*) and unexplained (*SSE*) variations. We must determine whether the explained variation is significant enough to warrant rejecting the null hypothesis that the treatment populations have identical means.

As our test statistic, we must use a summary measure to express how much the sample results deviate from what is expected when the null hypothesis is true. This may be achieved by comparing the explained and the unexplained variations. Whether or not H_0 is true, it is natural in any random-sampling experiment to expect some error or unexplained variation within each sample. But according to the H_0 that the population means are identical for each fertilizer treatment, the amount of unexplained variation between sample treatments should be small; that is, the respective sample means should be about the same. If, in fact, the population means are equal, then the components of the explained and the unexplained variations should be of comparable size.

We may use the ratio between the variation explained by treatments and the error or unexplained variation as a basis of comparison. To find this ratio, we cannot immediately divide the sums of squares. Recall that *SSE* is the sum of $r \times c$ squared differences (for the 15 observations in our example), but that only c squares (representing the 3 samples in our example) are used to calculate *SSTR*. Each sum of squares must be converted to an average before *SSE* and *SSTR* are comparable. This gives us sample variances, which we will call *mean squares* to avoid confusion with population variances. Mean squares may be viewed as estimators of population variances, which, under the assumption that the samples are taken from identical populations, are equal to a common value of σ^2. These estimators are unbiased when the proper divisors are chosen. We express the

TREATMENTS MEAN SQUARE

$$MSTR = \frac{SSTR}{c - 1}$$

Similarly, we define the

ERROR MEAN SQUARE

$$MSE = \frac{SSE}{(r-1)c}$$

Returning to our sod-fertilization illustration, we have

$$MSTR = \frac{137.20}{3-1} = 68.60 \quad \text{and} \quad MSE = \frac{190.80}{(5-1)3} = 15.90$$

Note that the treatments mean square is more than four times as large as the error mean square. Under the null hypothesis of identical population means, these mean squares should be nearly the same. Such a large difference seems unlikely, but it may be "explained" by differences between the populations. We have yet to determine exactly how unlikely this large a discrepancy would be if the populations were in fact identical.

THE ANOVA TABLE

It is helpful to summarize the computations for analysis of variance in the format shown in Table 17-3. For simplicity, this is referred to as an **ANOVA table.** (ANOVA is a contraction of "ANalysis Of VAriance".) This table is important in organizing the ANOVA computations, because it provides the degrees of freedom, the sum of squares, and the mean square for each source of variation. The degrees of freedom are the divisors that we use to calculate the mean squares. The test statistic, which will be discussed next, is the value in column *F*.

THE *F* STATISTIC

We now have two sample variances, *MSTR* and *MSE*. To conform to our earlier discussions, we will refer to the treatments mean square as the variance explained

TABLE 17-3 ANOVA Table for the Sod-Fertilization Experiment

Variation	Degrees of Freedom	Sum of Squares	Mean Square	F
Explained by treatments (between columns)	$c - 1 = 2$	$SSTR = 137.20$	$MSTR = 137.20/2 = 68.60$	$MSTR/MSE = 68.60/15.90 = 4.31$
Error or unexplained (within columns)	$(r-1)c = 12$	$SSE = 190.80$	$MSE = 190.8./12 = 15.90$	
Total	$rc - 1 = 14$	$SSTO = 328.00$		

by treatments and to the error mean square as the unexplained variance. By calculating the ratio of these variances, we obtain the

TEST STATISTIC FOR ANALYSIS OF VARIANCE

$$F = \frac{\text{Variance explained by treatments}}{\text{Unexplained variance}} = \frac{MSTR}{MSE}$$

For our example, we calculate

$$F = \frac{68.60}{15.90} = 4.31$$

Under the null hypothesis, we expect values of F to be close to 1, because $MSTR$ and MSE are both unbiased estimators of the common population variance σ^2. Because they have the same expected value when H_0 is true, similar values of $MSTR$ and MSE should in that case be obtained from the sample, and the ratio of these values should be near 1.

To formulate a decision rule, we must establish the sampling distribution for this test statistic. From this, we may then determine a critical value that will tell us whether the calculated value of F is large enough to reject the null hypothesis. The probability distribution we use to do this is called the F distribution. Before describing this distribution, we must clarify what we mean by degrees of freedom.

We may view the divisor $c - 1$ in the calculation for $MSTR$ as the number of degrees of freedom associated with using $MSTR$ to estimate σ^2. Here, finding the sum of squares involves calculating $\bar{\bar{X}}$, which may be expressed in terms of the $\bar{X}_j$'s. For a fixed $\bar{\bar{X}}$, all except one of the c $\bar{X}_j$'s are free to vary.

Analogously, the $(r - 1)c$ divisor in the calculation of MSE is the number of degrees of freedom associated with using MSE to estimate σ^2. This is true because in finding the sum of squares, each term involves an $\bar{X}_j$ calculated from the X_{ij} values. For a given value of $\bar{X}_j$, only $r - 1$ of the X_{ij}'s are free to assume any value. For c treatments, the number of free variables is therefore only $(r - 1)c$.

Thus, a pair of degrees of freedom is associated with the F statistic. This pair sums to the total number of observations minus 1. In our sod-fertilization experiment, $r = 5$ and $c = 3$, so that the following degrees of freedom apply.

$$c - 1 = 3 - 1 = 2 \qquad \text{(numerator)}$$

$$(r - 1)c = (5 - 1)3 = 12 \qquad \text{(denominator)}$$

The total number of degrees of freedom is $2 + 12 = 14$, a value of one less than the total number of observations. That total may also be found from

$$rc - 1 = 5(3) - 1 = 14$$

THE *F* DISTRIBUTION

Under the proper conditions, we may employ the F distribution to obtain probabilities for possible values of F. Like the t distribution, the F distribution is characterized by degrees of freedom. Because the F statistic is defined as a ratio, however, the F distribution has two kinds of degrees of freedom—one associated with the numerator and one associated with the denominator.

Figure 17-3 illustrates curves for the F distribution when the degrees of freedom for the numerator and denominator are 6 and 6, 20 and 6, and 30 and 30, respectively. Note that the F distribution curve is positively skewed, with possible values ranging from zero to infinity. There is a different distribution and curve for each pair of degrees of freedom.

The F distribution is continuous, so that probabilities for the values of F are provided by the areas under the curves. The critical values of upper tail areas for the F distribution are given in Appendix Table G. The table is constructed in the same manner as the tables for the t and chi-square distributions. Due to space limitations, only two upper tail areas are considered.

In Appendix Table G, the rows correspond to the number of degrees of freedom for the denominator and the columns correspond to the number of degrees of freedom for the numerator. The entries in the body of the table are critical values, designated as F_α, where $\alpha = .01$ or $.05$. A portion of this table is reproduced here.

Degrees of Freedom for Denominator	Degrees of Freedom for Numerator						
	1	2	3	4	5	6	. . .
1	161 **4,052**	200 **4,999**	216 **5,403**	225 **5,625**	230 **5,764**	234 **5,859**	
2	18.51 **98.49**	19.00 **99.00**	19.16 **99.17**	19.25 **99.25**	19.30 **99.30**	19.33 **99.33**	
3	10.13 **34.12**	9.55 **30.82**	9.28 **29.46**	9.12 **28.71**	9.01 **28.24**	8.94 **27.91**	
4	7.71 **21.20**	6.94 **18.00**	6.59 **16.69**	6.39 **15.98**	6.26 **15.52**	6.16 **15.21**	. . .
5	6.61 **16.26**	5.79 **13.27**	5.41 **12.06**	5.19 **11.39**	5.05 **10.97**	4.95 **10.67**	
6	5.99 **13.74**	5.14 **10.92**	4.76 **9.78**	4.53 **9.15**	4.39 **8.75**	4.28 **8.47**	
⋮				⋮			

To find $F_{.01}$ and $F_{.05}$ when the numerator and the denominator degrees of freedom are 6 and 6, we read the entries from column 6 and row 6. Shown in color in the above table, $F_{.01}$ is the boldface value and $F_{.05}$ is the lightface value, so that $F_{.01} = 8.47$ and $F_{.05} = 4.28$. Thus

$$\Pr[F \geq 8.47] = .01$$

$$\Pr[F \geq 4.28] = .05$$

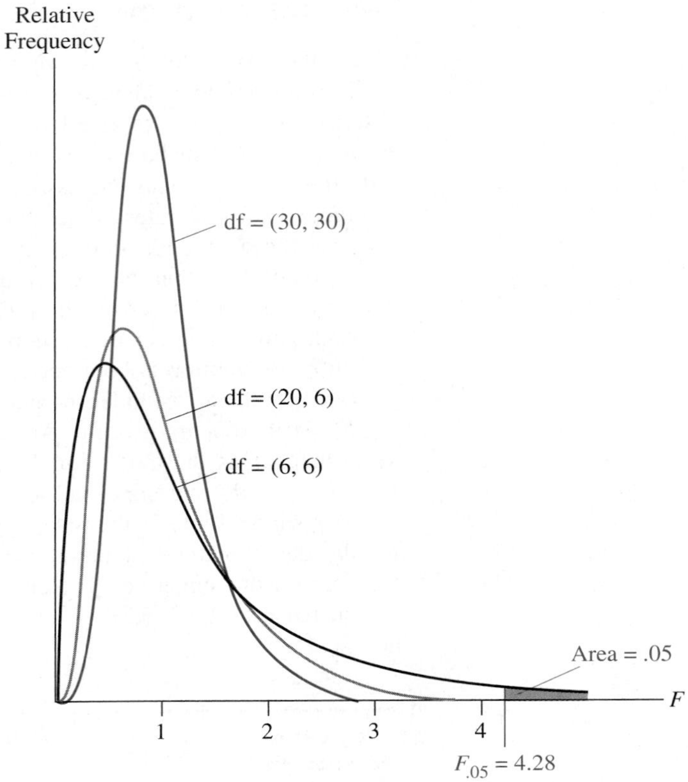

FIGURE 17-3 Various curves for the F distribution.

The second probability is represented by the shaded area under the curve for this distribution, beginning at $F_{.05} = 4.28$. Since the tails of the F curve are long and narrow, the graph in Figure 17-3 does not show the area above $F_{.01}$. These values signify that in repeated experiments, the value of F will exceed 4.28 an average of 5% of the time and will exceed 8.47 about 1% of the time.

TESTING THE NULL HYPOTHESIS

To illustrate the procedure, we will conduct a test using the data from the sod-fertilization experiment.

STEP 1

Formulate the null hypothesis. The sod farmer wishes to determine whether the mean yields of all fertilizer treatments are identical. The following null hypothesis applies

$$H_0: \mu_1 = \mu_2 = \mu_3$$

STEP 2

Select the test statistic and procedure. A value of F serves as the test statistic.

STEP 3

Obtain the significance level and identify the acceptance and rejection regions. A Type I error probability of $\alpha = .05$ is desired for incorrectly concluding that the population means of the various fertilizer treatments are not identical. Earlier, we found the degrees of freedom to be 2 for the numerator and 12 for the denominator. Appendix Table G provides the critical value of $F_{.05} = 3.89$. The acceptance and rejection regions are shown below. Note that large values of F tend to refute the H_0 of equal means.

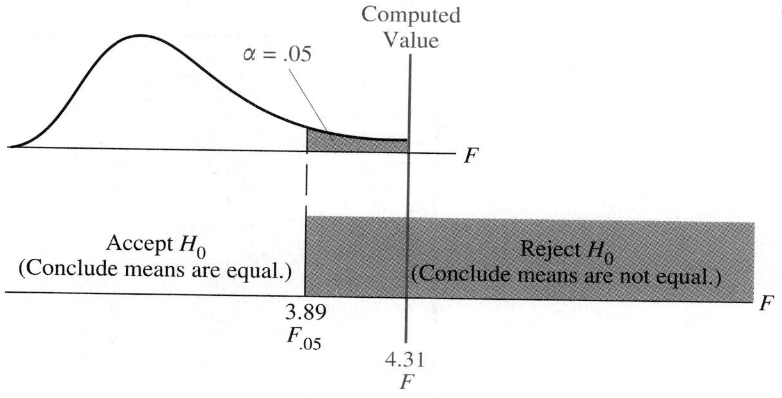

STEP 4

Collect the sample and compute the value of the test statistic. This step includes all the preliminary calculations for the construction of the ANOVA table. Earlier, we found the computed value of the test statistic to be $F = 4.31$.

STEP 5

Make the decision. Since the computed value of $F = 4.31$ falls in the rejection region, the null hypothesis must be *rejected.* The sod farmer must conclude that the fertilization methods have different mean yields.

If the farmer required greater protection against committing the Type I error and used a smaller significance level of $\alpha = .01$, he would reach the opposite conclusion. The critical value would be $F_{.01} = 6.93$, which is larger than the computed value of F, and 4.31 would fall in the acceptance region.

COMPUTER-ASSISTED ANALYSIS

The analysis of variance procedure involves cumbersome computations. To avoid errors and to save time, investigators ordinarily use a computer to perform the calculations. Figure 17-4 displays the computer printout for the sod-fertilization illustration. The top portion of the printout provides the necessary program commands and the input data. The lower portion provides the ANOVA table, nearly identical in format to Table 17-3.

FURTHER CONSIDERATIONS

There are several important issues to consider for an analysis of variance. A few of these are discussed below.

```
MTB > name c1='Trtmnt 1' c2='Trtmnt 2' c3='Trtmnt 3'
MTB > read c1-c3
Data> 77 83 80
Data> 79 91 82
Data> 87 94 86
Data> 85 88 85
Data> 78 85 80
Data> end
MTB > aovoneway c1-c3
```

```
ANALYSIS OF VARIANCE
SOURCE      DF        SS         MS        F        p
FACTOR       2     137.2       68.6     4.31    0.039
ERROR       12     190.8       15.9
TOTAL       14     328.0

 LEVEL       N       MEAN
Trtmnt 1      5    81.200
Trtmnt 2     5    88.200
Trtmnt 3     5    82.600

POOLED STDEV =    3.987
```

Note: Figure generated on an IBM PC using Minitab®.

FIGURE 17-4 Computer printout for the sod-fertilization data.

Deciding a Course of Action: Comparing Treatment Means

What should the sod farmer do after rejecting the null hypothesis of identical population means? Obviously, he should pick the fertilizer treatment that will maximize mean sod yield. But his results are only sample data, which are subject to sampling error. He could arrive at a decision by comparing individual treatments. (This procedure will be described in Sections 17-2 and 17-3.)

More Discriminating Testing Procedures

The analysis of variance procedure that we have described thus far has considered only one type of treatment—sod fertilization. This one factor explained enough of the variation in sod yield to justify our conclusion that the fertilizer treatments produce different effects. But there may be other explanations for the differences in sample yields—for example, varying soil conditions or watering schedules. We discussed procedures for analyzing two or more factors in Chapter 15. As more factors are included, the testing procedures become more discriminating and efficient.

THE TYPE II ERROR

Because we have already established the sample sizes, we are free only to set the value of the Type I error probability α for falsely rejecting the null hypothesis of identical fertilizer treatment means. We saw in Chapter 9 that no matter what the sample size, a critical value may always be obtained to guard against erroneously rejecting the null hypothesis. But when H_0 is accepted after comparing F to the critical value, there may be a very large chance of committing the Type II error and accepting a false hypothesis. To protect against erroneous acceptance, much larger samples should generally be used than those in our sod-fertilization experiment.

VIOLATIONS OF THE UNDERLYING MODEL

The F test is predicated on the theoretical assumptions regarding the error terms. As for regression analysis, serious violations of the model may cause invalid conclusions to be drawn. Two violations may present problems.

First, the error terms, and therefore the X_{ij}'s and $\bar{X}_j$'s, are assumed to be normally distributed. As for procedures based on the Student t distribution, this condition is ordinarily of little consequence as long as the treatment populations are unimodal and not highly skewed.

The second violation arises when the variance in error terms is nonconstant. As a practical matter, the nonconstant variance is serious only in the more complex procedures involving random effects (which are beyond the scope of this book). When factor effects are fixed (as they are in this book), the standard procedures still perform well and are therefore *robust* against this violation.

An alternative procedure may be used to entirely avoid these problems. This procedure, discussed in Chapter 19, is the nonparametric Kruskal-Wallis test.

EXAMPLE: EVALUATING TRAINING ALTERNATIVES

A recently hired MBA for Ace Widgets thinks she can improve the training of production workers. Training, until now, has been only on the job. She has developed three alternative programs involving classroom sessions. These three alternatives are compared, along with the existing procedure, as four methods or treatments.

1. On-the-job training only.
2. Classroom training only.
3. Heavy on-the-job training with light classroom work.
4. Light on-the-job training with heavy classroom work.

Each method is conducted using a different sample group of 8 trainees. A placement examination is given to each trainee on completion of the program and the investigator uses the scores as the response variable.

The following sample results apply.

$$\bar{X}_1 = 50.2 \qquad \bar{X}_2 = 44.9 \qquad \bar{X}_3 = 78.5 \qquad \bar{X}_4 = 82.3 \qquad \bar{\bar{X}} = 64.0$$

TABLE 17-4 ANOVA Table for the Training Program Evaluation

Variation	Degrees of Freedom	Sum of Squares	Mean Square	F
Explained by treatments: type of training (between columns)	$c - 1 = 3$	$SSTR = 8{,}803.12$	$MSTR = SSTR/3 = 2{,}934.37$	$MSTR/MSE = 9.74$
Error or unexplained (within columns)	$(r - 1)c = 28$	$SSE = 8{,}431.31$	$MSE = SSE/28 = 301.12$	
Total	$rc - 1 = 31$	$SSTO = 17{,}234.43$		

SOLUTION: The ANOVA table is provided in Table 17-4. Using a significance level of $\alpha = .01$, with 3 degrees of freedom for the numerator and 28 for the denominator, the investigator finds the critical value $F_{.01} = 4.57$. Since the computed value of $F = 9.74$ for the test statistic exceeds that value, she rejects the null hypothesis that all training methods result in identical mean examination scores. (Further analysis will be performed in Section 17-2 to help her select the best treatment to adopt.)

EXERCISES

17-1 Determine the critical value T_α for the F statistic that corresponds to each tail area α and each pair of degrees of freedom (df) provided below.

	(a)	(b)	(c)	(d)
α	.01	.05	.05	.01
Numerator df	10	12	5	10
Denominator df	10	8	26	5

17-2 A Fast-Gro agronomist is investigating the effect of water dispersal on crop growth. Five different plots have each been watered at three settings, and the results recorded. The null hypothesis of equal growth rate for each water treatment is tested at an $\alpha = .05$ significance level.

(a) Determine the critical value of the test statistic. For each of the following crops considered, indicate whether the agronomist should accept or reject H_0.

(b) Alfalfa is considered. $F = 6.42$.

(c) Sugar beets are considered. $F = 5.07$.

(d) Tomatoes are considered. $F = 3.22$.

17-3 A SynTron experimenter investigated the impact of temperature settings on the yield of a chemical process. He used four different settings for samples of five production runs each. He computed the following values.

$$SSTR = 390 \qquad SSE = 120$$

(a) Construct the ANOVA table.

(b) Using an $\alpha = .01$ significance level, should the experimenter accept or reject the null hypothesis of identical mean yields?

4/15

17-4 Quicker Oats is contemplating changing the shape of its box from the quaint cylinder presently in use. Different random samples were selected from five stores of similar size in the same region, and one of the three candidate boxes was substituted for the cylinder for several days. The following results were obtained for the total number of boxes sold.

	Box Shape		
Store	**(1) Pyramid**	**(2) Rectangle**	**(3) Cube**
1	110	57	92
2	85	65	81
3	69	73	66
4	97	49	71
5	78	77	70

(a) Perform hypothesis-testing Step 3.
   (1) Determine the degrees of freedom for the numerator and the denominator.
   (2) Determine the critical value of the test statistic and identify the acceptance and rejection regions using an $\alpha = .05$ significance level.

(b) Perform hypothesis-testing Step 4.
   (1) Calculate the individual sample means and the grand mean.
   (2) Determine the treatments and the error sums of squares. Using these values, find the total sum of squares.
   (3) Construct the ANOVA table and compute the value of *F*.

(c) Should the null hypothesis that the mean sales are identical regardless of box shape be accepted or rejected?

17-5 A security analyst for Oso, Toro, and Oso evaluated the effect of a sample of five different stock-trading rules on five series of simulated trades. The following rates of return were obtained.

	Trading Rule				
Series	**(1) Buy and Hold**	**(2) Sell on Good News**	**(3) Buy on Bad News**	**(4) Sell on Bad News**	**(5) Buy on Good News**
1	32%	17%	−5%	15%	2%
2	−11	23	8	−5	−10
3	14	15	2	−10	−5
4	9	7	12	8	2
5	16	13	10	−2	4

don't change to decimals!

The null hypothesis of identical mean rates of return is tested at an $\alpha = .05$ significance level.

(a) Determine the critical value of the test statistic.

(b) Compute (1) the sample means, (2) the sums of squares, (3) the mean squares, and (4) the F statistic.
(c) Construct the ANOVA table.
(d) Should the analyst accept or reject the null hypothesis?

17-6 A Relax-a-Seltzer statistican assessed the impact of the level of impurities in a particular ingredient on the solubility of aspirin tablets. Three different samples were selected from five test batches. The following dissolving times (seconds) were obtained.

	Level of Impurities		
Observation	**(1) 1%**	**(2) 5%**	**(3) 10%**
1	2.01	1.95	2.30
2	1.82	2.21	2.29
3	1.74	2.14	2.17
4	1.90	1.93	2.06
5	2.03	2.07	2.58

Using an $\alpha = .05$ significance level, should the statistician accept or reject the null hypothesis that the mean dissolving time is the same regardless of the level of impurity?

17-7 Gimbel-Prompter advertises that its detergent will remove all stains, except oil-base paint, in any kind of water. A consumer information service reporting on detergent quality is testing this claim. Batches of washings were run in five randomly chosen homes having a particular type of water—hard, moderate, or soft. Each batch contained an assortment of rags and cloth scraps stained with food products, grease, and dirt over a 100-square-inch area. After washing, the number of square inches that were still stained was determined and the following results were obtained.

	Type of Water		
Observation	**(1) Hard**	**(2) Moderate**	**(3) Soft**
1	5	4	4
2	3	7	0
3	2	8	1
4	10	3	3
5	6	2	2

(a) Using an $\alpha = .01$ significance level, should the consumer service conclude that the type of water affects the effectiveness of the detergent?
(b) What factors other than water type might explain the sources of variation?

17-8 Refer to the sod-fertilization experiment in Section 17-1. Assume that $\mu_1 = 80$, $\mu_2 = 87$, and $\mu_3 = 85$.
(a) Compute the value of $\bar{\mu}$.
(b) Compute, for each treatment, the value of B_j.
(c) Construct a table providing the associated error term for each observation.

```
MTB > name c1='Config 1' c2='Config 2' c3='Config 3' c4-'Config 4'
MTB > read c1-c4
Data> 10.4      15.5      11.3      17.8
Data>  9.3      14.7      12.5       9.5
Data> 11.2      13.7      13.0      17.4
Data> 10.5      16.1      10.2      16.9
Data> 13.7      15.3      11.5      18.5
Data> 12.1      11.1      11.6      17.0
Data>  9.8      15.2       9.3      20.2
Data> end
MTB > aovoneway c1-c4
```

```
ANALYSIS OF VARIANCE
SOURCE      DF        SS         MS         F         p
FACTOR       3    157.53      52.51     11.54     0.000
ERROR       24    109.20       4.55
TOTAL       27    266.73

 LEVEL       N      MEAN      STDEV
Config 1     7    11.000      1.499
Config 2     7    14.514      1.680
Config 3     7    11.343      1.269
Config 4     7    16.757      3.395

POOLED STDEV =     2.133
```

Note: Figure generated on an IBM PC using Minitab®.

FIGURE 17-5 Computer printout for the supermarket queueing study.

17-9 Figure 17-5 shows the results of an analysis of variance computer run. The sampling study considers the mean waiting times (minutes) of four operational configurations for supermarket checkout areas.

What should you conclude regarding mean waiting times of the respective configurations?

17-2 ESTIMATING TREATMENT MEANS AND DIFFERENCES

Once the null hypothesis of equal treatment population means has been rejected, what do we do next? Continuing with the sod farmer's experiment, we have concluded that the sod yields differ according to the fertilizer treatment used. But what should the farmer do? In this section and the next, we will examine additional procedures that extend the analysis of variance results and enable us to formulate a course of action.

To set the stage, we will individually estimate the mean of a treatment population and compare treatments by estimating the differences between a pair of population means. In both cases, the confidence interval estimation techniques used earlier in this book may be applied.

A second category of inferences encompasses an entire family of estimates or tests. These allow for **multiple comparisons** to be made.

CONFIDENCE INTERVAL FOR A TREATMENT POPULATION MEAN

Remember that a confidence interval for a single sample can be constructed for the population mean by using the expression

$$\mu = \bar{X} \pm t_{\alpha/2} \frac{s}{\sqrt{n}}$$

When several samples have been taken from different populations, only slight modifications are necessary to obtain a similar expression for each of the respective population means $\mu_1, \mu_2, \ldots$.

Remember that the treatment populations were presumed to have identical variance σ^2. Thus, we can obtain a better estimator for σ^2 by pooling the sample results, using the unexplained variance MSE in place of a single sample variance s^2. We can use the sample treatment mean $\bar{X}_j$ to estimate μ_j, the population mean for the jth treatment. We replace n with the number of observations r made using that treatment. Finally, the number of degrees of freedom used to find $t_{\alpha/2}$ is $(r - 1)c$ (the same figure we used to compute MSE). Thus, we obtain the following expression for computing the $100(1 - \alpha)\%$

CONFIDENCE INTERVAL ESTIMATE OF INDIVIDUAL μ_j

$$\mu_j = \bar{X}_j \pm t_{\alpha/2} \sqrt{\frac{MSE}{r}}$$

Consider the Ace Widgets example in the preceding section. The investigator estimated the mean test score of all employees trained using method 3, heavy on-the-job training with light classroom work. She constructed a 99% confidence interval estimate. Using $(r - 1)c = (8 - 1)4 = 28$ degrees of freedom, Appendix Table F provides $t_{.005} = 2.763$. Thus,

$$\mu_3 = \bar{X}_3 \pm t_{.005} \sqrt{\frac{MSE}{8}}$$

$$= 78.5 + 2.763 \sqrt{\frac{301.12}{8}}$$

$$= 78.5 \pm 17.0$$

or

$$61.5 \le \mu_3 \le 95.5$$

PAIRWISE COMPARISONS OF TREATMENT MEANS

In Chapter 15, we examined various procedures for using two sample means to estimate the difference between population means. In the case of independent samples, we used a confidence interval of the form

$$\mu_A - \mu_B = \bar{X}_A - \bar{X}_B \pm t_{\alpha/2} s_{d\text{-small}}$$

where $s_{d\text{-small}}$ estimates the standard error of the difference $d = \bar{X}_A - \bar{X}_B$ that is found by pooling the sample standard deviations. Although we are using number subscripts here, this procedure may be extended to any treatment pair. We replace $s_{d\text{-small}}$ with $\sqrt{2MSE/r}$, again reflecting the fact that the common population variance is estimated by MSE. The 2 indicates that the variability is additive for two samples. Thus we have the following $100(1 - \alpha)\%$

CONFIDENCE INTERVAL FOR THE PAIRWISE DIFFERENCE $\mu_2 - \mu_1$

$$\mu_2 - \mu_1 = \bar{X}_2 - \bar{X}_1 \pm t_{\alpha/2}\sqrt{\frac{2MSE}{r}}$$

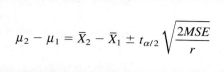

The degrees of freedom are $(r - 1)c$, as before. Applying this expression to the result of the sod-fertilization experiment, the 95% confidence interval for the difference between the mean sod yields of treatments (2) and (1) is constructed. Using $(5 - 1)3 = 12$ degrees of freedom, Appendix Table F provides $t_{.025} = 2.179$. Thus,

$$\mu_2 - \mu_1 = \bar{X}_2 - \bar{X}_1 \pm t_{.025}\sqrt{\frac{2MSE}{5}}$$

$$= 88.2 - 81.2 \pm 2.179\sqrt{\frac{2(15.9)}{5}}$$

$$= 7 \pm 5.5$$

or

$$1.5 \le \mu_2 - \mu_1 \le 12.5 \text{ square yards}$$

Thus, we estimate that the advantage of using treatment (2) over treatment (1) is somewhere between 1.5 and 12.5 square yards.

We may use this confidence interval to test the null hypothesis that the treatment means are equal. The fact that the interval does not overlap zero indicates that H_0: $\mu_1 = \mu_2$ may be *rejected*, and we conclude that μ_1 and μ_2 differ at the $1 - .95 = .05$ significance level. The sod farmer may therefore choose treatment (2) over treatment (1) with only a .05 probability that this action will be incorrect.

COMPUTER-GENERATED CONFIDENCE INTERVALS

Although confidence intervals may be constructed by hand using the data from the ANOVA table, popular software packages also provide this information as optional or standard output for an analysis of variance computer run. Figure 17-6

```
                          INDIVIDUAL 95 PCT CI'S FOR MEAN
                          BASED ON POOLED STDEV
 LEVEL          N         -------+---------+---------+---------
Trtmnt 1        5         (---------*---------)
Trtmnt 2        5                            (---------*---------)
Trtmnt 3        5               (---------*---------)
                          -------+---------+---------+---------
                               80.0      84.0      88.0
```

Note: Figure generated on an IBM PC using Minitab®.

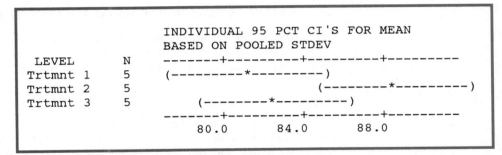

FIGURE 17-6 Portion of the computer printout for the sod-fertilization experiment.

shows a very convenient result provided by a computer for the sod-fertilization experiment. In the printout, the 95% confidence intervals are represented graphically together for each of the individual treatment means.

Users of this version of the Minitab program must compute precise intervals by hand. Using $(r-1)c = (5-1)3 = 12$ degrees of freedom, Appendix Table F provides $t_{.025} = 2.179$. The interval estimate of the treatment (1) population mean is

$$\mu_1 = \bar{X}_1 \pm t_{.025}\sqrt{\frac{MSE}{r}}$$

$$= 81.2 \pm 2.179\sqrt{\frac{15.9}{5}}$$

$$= 81.2 \pm 3.9$$

or

$$77.3 \leq \mu_1 \leq 85.1 \text{ square yards}$$

The remaining individual 95% confidence intervals are the same width.

$$84.3 \leq \mu_2 \leq 92.1 \text{ square yards}$$

$$78.7 \leq \mu_3 \leq 86.5 \text{ square yards}$$

We must be very careful interpreting the above intervals. Although each applies to a *single* estimate at a 95% level, the *collective* level of confidence is less than the reported 95%. We will discuss this further in the next section.

EXERCISES

17-10 A Conformity Systems analyst conducted a study to determine whether a person's attitude toward his or her present job influences the number of years he or she has remained in that position. The treatments were three different job attitudes: (1) dislike, (2) indifference, and (3) enjoyment. A sample of four persons was used for each treatment. The following ANOVA table and mean calculations were obtained.

Variation	Degrees of Freedom	Sum of Squares	Mean Square	F
Treatments	2	104	52	8.7
Error	9	54	6	
Total	11	158		

$\bar{X}_1 = 2$ years $\quad \bar{X}_2 = 4$ years $\quad \bar{X}_3 = 9$ years $\quad \bar{\bar{X}} = 5$ years

(a) Construct a 95% confidence interval for the population mean of treatment (3).
(b) Construct a 95% confidence interval for the difference $\mu_3 - \mu_1$.
(c) Referring to your answer to (b), are the population means of attitudes (3) and (1) signifcantly different at a 5% level?

17-11 Refer to Exercise 17-4.
(a) Construct a 95% confidence interval estimate of the mean sales of the pyramid-shaped box.
(b) Construct a 95% confidence interval for the difference in mean sales between the rectangular box and the pyramid box. Do the two box shapes have different mean sales at an $\alpha = .05$ significance level?

17-12 Refer to Exercise 17-6. Determine whether 1% and 10% impurity levels provide significantly different mean dissolving times at an $\alpha = .05$ significance level.

17-3 MULTIPLE COMPARISONS

There are two potential pitfalls when making estimates or testing further hypotheses using results from the analysis of variance. First, the foregoing procedures apply to only a single estimate with $100(1 - \alpha)\%$ confidence or to just one test at significance level α. If several intervals are to be constructed using expressions from the preceding section, the resulting series of estimates must have as a *family* a lower level of confidence than indicated. And, the hypothesis test for individual μ's and for pairwise μ differences must each involve greater significance levels than α.

This problem might be alleviated by using wider confidence intervals than otherwise, which could be achieved by increasing the level of confidence for the individual intervals (reducing α). But the trickiest issue is: What inferences will be made? To amend the foregoing procedures, the investigator must know, prior to getting the sample results, exactly which μ's will be estimated and which pairwise comparisons will be made. *It is not permissable to look at the data before making those choices.* Doing so will further reduce statistical confidence or significance, in an unsystematic way.

In a one-factor analysis, there is little difficulty deciding which inferences will be made. The most important issue is determining which factor levels (treatments) provide the better mean response and which are not significantly different. Usually this is determined by making every pairwise comparison of the population means.

TABLE 17-5 Sample Results for Solvent Composition Cost

	Chemical Composition (treatment)			
Observation	**(1) High-Acid**	**(2) Low-Acid**	**(3) Non-Acid**	**(4) Staged**
1	\$1,360	\$1,340	\$1,650	\$1,720
2	1,420	1,380	1,590	1,780
3	1,210	1,290	1,690	1,660
4	1,260	1,410	1,730	1,620
5	1,320	1,230	1,540	1,800
	$\bar{X}_1 = 1{,}314$	$\bar{X}_2 = 1{,}330$	$\bar{X}_3 = 1{,}640$	$\bar{X}_4 = 1{,}716$
		$\bar{\bar{X}} = 1{,}500$		

We will use the following illustration to help describe the multiple comparison procedures.

ILLUSTRATION: CHEMICAL COMPOSITION COST

Consider the direct cost data in Table 17-5 obtained for five batches of a solvent manufactured using four slightly different chemical compositions. Each of the $c = 4$ compositions is viewed as a separate treatment, and 5 batches were processed for each treatment. The batch direct cost is the response variable.

The ANOVA table in Table 17-6 provides a computed value of $F = 36.64$ for the test statistic. This result establishes that the population means for at least one pair of the treatments are significantly different.

Figure 17-7 shows a plot for the sample data. The data clusters appear to give both compositions (1) and (2) substantially lower direct costs than either composition (3) or (4). We find, in Table 17-5, that the first pair of treatments provides very close sample mean values, as does the latter pair of treatments. The procedures described next will be used to determine whether or not the differences in mean cost between the two groups are significant. We begin with the construction of confidence intervals for the pairwise differences.

TABLE 17-6 ANOVA Table for Solvent Composition Evaluation

Variation	Degrees of Freedom	Sum of Squares	Mean Square	F
Explained by treatments	$c - 1 = 3$	$SSTR = 648{,}760$	$MSTR = 216{,}253$	36.64
Error or unexplained	$(r - 1)c = 16$	$SSE = 94{,}440$	$MSE = 5{,}903$	
Total	$rc - 1 = 19$	$SSTO = 743{,}200$		

```
MTB > name c1='1 HiAcid' c2='2 LoAcid' c3='3 NoAcid' c4='4 Staged'
Data> 1360      1340      1650      1720
Data> 1420      1380      1590      1780
Data> 1210      1290      1690      1660
Data> 1260      1410      1730      1620
Data> 1320      1230      1540      1800
Data> end
MTB > dotplot c1-c4;
SUBC> same.
```

```
    .   .    .  .    .
---+---------+---------+---------+---------+---------+---1 HiAcid

      .    .   .  .  .
---+---------+---------+---------+---------+---------+---2 LoAcid

                               .    .    .  .  .
---+---------+---------+---------+---------+---------+---3 NoAcid

                                      .  .    .    . .
---+---------+---------+---------+---------+---------+---4 Staged
1200      1320      1440      1560      1680      1800
```

Note: Figure generated on an IBM PC using Minitab®.

FIGURE 17-7 Dot plot for solvent batch cost using different chemical compositions.

MULTIPLE COMPARISONS OF THE TREATMENT POPULATION MEANS

There are two methods for estimating the differences between a pair of population means. The first is the Tukey method, which generally provides the narrowest confidence intervals. It presumes that every pair of μ_j's will be compared and requires equal sample sizes for all treatments. When fewer pairwise differences are of interest, the more general Bonferroni method provides more precise estimates.

TUKEY METHOD

This procedure is based on the **studentized range distribution**, using critical values q listed in Appendix Table K. Like the F distribution, the q distribution is characterized by two parameters that specify which particular distribution applies. Each treatment must have the same sample size r (number of rows in the experimental layout). The following expression is used to compute the $100(1 - \alpha)\%$.

TUKEY COLLECTIVE CONFIDENCE INTERVAL ESTIMATES OF THE DIFFERENCES BETWEEN FACTOR-LEVEL MEANS

$$\mu_j - \mu_k = \bar{X}_j - \bar{X}_k \pm q_{1-\alpha}\sqrt{\frac{MSE}{r}}$$

where the parameters for the numerator and the denominator are c and $(r - 1)c$ respectively.

To illustrate how the Tukey intervals are constructed, let's consider our solvent composition cost evaluation. Altogether there are six pairs among the μ_j's. Using a 90% collective level of confidence, interval estimates may be constructed for each. All use the critical value $q_{.90}$, which has parameters $c = 4$ for the numerator and $(r - 1)c = 16$ for the denominator. Appendix Table K provides the critical value $q_{.90} = 3.52$.

Using $MSE = 5{,}903$, the following interval is constructed for the difference in mean direct cost between the non-acid (3) and the high-acid (1) chemical compositions.

$$\mu_3 - \mu_1 = \bar{X}_3 - \bar{X}_1 \pm q_{.90}\sqrt{\frac{MSE}{r}}$$

$$= \$1{,}640 - \$1{,}314 \pm 3.52\sqrt{\frac{5{,}903}{5}}$$

$$= \$326 \pm 120.95$$

or

Non-acid − High-acid: $\$205.05 \leq \mu_3 - \mu_1 \leq \$446.95$ (significant)

Since the above confidence interval lies entirely to one side of zero, the mean direct costs of compositions (3) and (1) are significantly different at an $\alpha = .10$ collective level of confidence.

The remaining five pairwise differences have the same width. The following confidence intervals apply.

Low-acid − High-acid:	$-\$104.95 \leq \mu_2 - \mu_1 \leq \$136.95$	
Staged − High-acid:	$\$281.05 \leq \mu_4 - \mu_1 \leq \$552.95$	(significant)
Non-acid − Low-acid:	$\$189.05 \leq \mu_3 - \mu_2 \leq \$430.95$	(significant)
Staged − Low-acid:	$\$265.05 \leq \mu_4 - \mu_2 \leq \$506.95$	(significant)
Staged − Non-acid:	$-\$44.95 \leq \mu_4 - \mu_3 \leq \$196.95$	

Again, since the respective intervals do not contain zero, significant cost differences exist between the staged composition alloy and either the high-acid or low-acid compositions and also between the latter two. Neither the high-acid versus low-acid nor the staged versus non-acid pairings result in significant mean cost differences.

Bonferroni Method

This procedure is based on the *Student t distribution.* Unlike the Tukey method, not every pairwise comparison need be included, but the total number of required estimates must be specified in advance. The following expression is used to compute the 100(1 − α)%

BONFERRONI COLLECTIVE CONFIDENCE INTERVAL ESTIMATES OF THE DIFFERENCES BETWEEN FACTOR-LEVEL MEANS

$$\mu_j - \mu_k = \bar{X}_j - \bar{X}_k \pm t_{\alpha/2s}\sqrt{\frac{2MSE}{r}}$$

where the number of intervals constructed is denoted by s and the number of degrees of freedom by $(r - 1)c$.

To illustrate, refer again to the direct cost data given in Tables 17-5 and 17-6. Altogether there are $s = 6$ pairwise differences for which interval estimates may be constructed, using the same 90% overall level of confidence. The critical value of t corresponds to $(r - 1)c = 16$ degrees of freedom, for which the upper tail area is $\alpha/2s = .10/2(6) = .00833$. From Appendix Table F, we find that the critical value lies between $t_{.01} = 2.583$ and $t_{.005} = 2.921$. Using linear interpolation, we compute the following value for the distance that $t_{.00833}$ lies between the tabled quantities.

$$t_{.00833} = 2.921 + \left(\frac{.00833 - .005}{.01 - .005}\right)(2.583 - 2.921) = 2.696$$

The confidence interval estimate of the difference in mean batch direct cost between treatments (3) and (1) is

$$\begin{aligned}\mu_3 - \mu_1 &= \bar{X}_3 - \bar{X}_1 \pm t_{.00833}\sqrt{\frac{2MSE}{r}} \\ &= \$1{,}640 - \$1{,}314 \pm 2.696\sqrt{\frac{2(5{,}903)}{5}} \\ &= \$326 \pm 131.00\end{aligned}$$

or

$$\text{Non-acid} - \text{High-acid:}\quad \$195.00 \le \mu_3 - \mu_1 \le \$457.00 \qquad \text{(significant)}$$

Like our earlier analysis, this interval lies entirely above zero, so that the two chemical compositions are again shown to yield significantly different mean batch costs. Applying the Bonferroni method, all of the pairwise differences in population means will have interval estimates of identical widths, and similar conclusions will be reached as before.

Comparing the Tukey and Bonferroni Methods

The Bonferroni confidence intervals are wider than those constructed for the Tukey method (as the above evaluation shows). When all pairwise comparisons are to be made, the Tukey intervals are preferred. But the Bonferroni method provides more precise estimates when less than all pairs of means are included. (Although, the investigator must then identify *ahead of time* which particular paired differences will be estimated.)

Also, as with any statistical evaluation, the choice of which procedure to use must be made in advance. Thus, either the Tukey or Bonferroni intervals would be constructed for the pairwise differences, but *not both* sets. (Here, we used both methods with the same data just to facilitate comparison of the two.)

COMPUTER-ASSISTED EVALUATIONS

As noted in Section 17-1, computer-assisted evaluation may be very helpful in conducting an analysis of variance. Some software packages generate collective confidence interval estimates of all pairwise differences in treatment population means.

Using a different computer program with the sod-fertilization data, the Tukey interval estimates of all pairwise differences have been constructed at a 95% collective level of confidence. Figure 17-8 shows the computer printout for the results obtained.

Since all intervals overlap zero, none of the pairwise differences are found to be significant. (This contradicts our previous conclusion found on page 741, where only a single inference was made. Here, three pairs are weighed simultaneously and slightly wider intervals apply.)

ESTIMATING INDIVIDUAL TREATMENT POPULATION MEANS

Bonferroni intervals may be constructed for individual treatment population means. The following expression is used to compute the $100(1 - \alpha)\%$

BONFERRONI COLLECTIVE CONFIDENCE INTERVAL ESTIMATES OF INDIVIDUAL TREATMENT POPULATION MEANS

$$\mu_j = \bar{X}_j \pm t_{\alpha/2s}\sqrt{\frac{MSE}{r}}$$

```
                 ANALYSIS OF VARIANCE PROCEDURE

TUKEY'S STUDENTIZED RANGE (HSD) TEST FOR VARIABLE: TEST SCORE
NOTE: THIS TEST CONTROLS THE TYPE I EXPERIMENTWISE ERROR RATE

    ALPHA=.05  CONFIDENCE=0.95  DF=12  MSE=15.9
    CRITICAL VALUE OF STUDENTIZED RANGE=4.20

COMPARISONS SIGNIFICANT AT THE 0.05 LEVEL ARE INDICATED BY '***'

                        SIMULTANEOUS                 SIMULTANEOUS
                           LOWER       DIFFERENCE       UPPER
   EST. PROD. COST      CONFIDENCE      BETWEEN      CONFIDENCE
     COMPARISON            LIMIT          MEANS          LIMIT

  TRTMT1   -   TRTMT2     -14.490        -7.000          0.490
  TRTMT1   -   TRTMT3      -8.890        -1.400          6.090
  TRTMT2   -   TRTMT3      -1.890         5.600         13.090
```

Note: Figure generated on an IBM PC using Minitab®.

FIGURE 17-8 Computer printout for the sod-fertilization experiment.

where the number of intervals constructed is denoted by s and the number of degrees of freedom by $(r-1)c$.

To illustrate, consider again the results given in Table 17-1 for the sod-fertilization experiment. Altogether there are $s = 3$ treatment population means to be estimated using a 95% collective level of confidence. The critical value of t corresponds to $(r-1)c = 12$ degrees of freedom, for which the upper tail area is $\alpha/2s = .05/2(3) = .00833$. From Appendix Table F, we find that the critical value lies between $t_{.01} = 2.681$ and $t_{.005} = 3.055$. Using linear interpolation, we compute the following value for the distance that $t_{.00833}$ lies between the tabled quantities.

$$t_{.00833} = 3.055 + \left(\frac{.00833 - .005}{.01 - .005}\right)(2.681 - 3.055) = 2.806$$

The confidence interval estimate of μ_1 is

$$\begin{aligned}\mu_1 &= \bar{X}_1 \pm t_{.00833}\sqrt{\frac{MSE}{r}}\\ &= 81.2 \pm 2.806\sqrt{\frac{15.9}{5}}\\ &= 81.2 \pm 5.0\end{aligned}$$

or

$$76.2 \le \mu_1 \le 86.2 \text{ square yards}$$

Notice that this confidence interval is wider than the single interval constructed on page 742. Again, the above interval reflects that *three* estimates are being made, so that all intervals apply jointly. The remaining population means are computed in a similar fashion. The following confidence interval estimates apply.

$$83.2 \leq \mu_2 \leq 93.2 \text{ square yards}$$

$$77.6 \leq \mu_3 \leq 87.6 \text{ square yards}$$

COMBINING TWO FAMILIES OF COLLECTIVE ESTIMATES

Two separate groupings or families of inferences may be combined. Doing so only affects the overall collective confidence (significance) level. Consider the following two families of estimates, each constructed using its own confidence level.

Family	Confidence level
1	$100(1 - \alpha_1)\%$
2	$100(1 - \alpha_2)\%$

The overall confidence level for the two families combined is at least

$$100(1 - \alpha_1 - \alpha_2)\%$$

This property may be illustrated using the data for the sod-fertilization experiment. Combine (1) the Bonferroni interval estimates constructed above for the *individual* treatment population means with (2) the Tukey intervals for the *pairwise differences* in means listed in Figure 17-8.

Both sets of estimates have separate 95% collective levels of confidence, so that $\alpha_1 = \alpha_2 = .05$. The combined grouping of six confidence intervals will have a collective level of confidence of at least

$$100(1 - .05 - .05) = 90\%$$

EXERCISES

17-13 An investigator rejects the null hypothesis of an analysis of variance involving six observations using each of four treatments. The following results apply.

$$\bar{X}_1 = 72 \quad \bar{X}_2 = 69 \quad \bar{X}_3 = 47 \quad \bar{X}_4 = 46 \quad X = 58.5 \quad SSE = 7.51$$

Construct Bonferroni interval estimates of the following differences, using a 94% collective level of confidence.

(a) $\mu_2 - \mu_1$ (c) $\mu_4 - \mu_1$ (e) $\mu_4 - \mu_2$
(b) $\mu_3 - \mu_1$ (d) $\mu_3 - \mu_2$ (f) $\mu_4 - \mu_3$

17-14 Refer to Exercise 17-4 and to your answers.

(a) Using a 94% collective level of confidence, construct Bonferroni interval estimates of the difference in mean sales between (1) the pyramid and rectangle, (2) the pyramid and cube, and (3) the cube and rectangle.

(b) Which shape, if any, yields significantly higher sales for each pair?

17-15 Repeat Exercise 17-13, using a 95% collective level of confidence to construct Tukey intervals instead.

17-16 Repeat Exercise 17-14, using a 95% collective level of confidence to construct Tukey intervals instead.

17-17 Consider the Ace Widgets example in Section 17-1.
(a) Construct 96% Bonferroni confidence interval estimates of individual mean test scores.
(b) Construct 94% Bonferroni confidence interval estimates of the pairwise differences in mean test scores.
(c) At a 6% collective level of confidence, which pairs of means, if any, are significantly different?
(d) Which training method(s) appear to yield the significantly highest test scores?

17-18 Refer to Exercise 17-9 and to your answers.
(a) Construct 98% Bonferroni confidence interval estimates of the mean waiting times for the individual operational configurations.
(b) Construct 95% Tukey confidence interval estimates of the pairwise differences in mean waiting times.
(c) At a 5% collective level of confidence, which pairs of means, if any, are significantly different?
(d) Combining the estimates you found in (a) and (b), what is the overall collective level of confidence?
(e) If management wants to eliminate the configurations that yield significantly higher waiting times than the rest, which one(s) should be eliminated?

17-19 Refer to Exercise 17-6 and to your answers.
(a) Using an 88% collective level of confidence, construct Bonferroni interval estimates of the difference in mean dissolving time between the (1) 10% and 1%, (2) 10% and 5%, and (3) 1% and 5% levels of impurity.
(b) Which level of impurities, if any, yields significantly longer dissolving time for each pair?
(c) Suppose that any level of inert substance may be included in the final chemical composition. In order to minimize dissolving time, which of the three levels does the data suggest would be best to use?

17-4 DESIGNING THE EXPERIMENT

The analysis of variance procedure extends to a wide variety of experimental situations. These may be categorized into several major groupings, referred to as **experimental designs**. The selection of an appropriate experimental design is crucial during the planning of investigations involving multiple populations.

So far in this chapter, we have described a one-factor experimental design. More elaborate designs consider two or more factors. Each factor may involve several levels, and there is one treatment for each combination. (See the box at the top of page 752.)

Another type of two-factor design involves treatments from just one factor. The second factor serves as a **blocking variable**. Such a factor is often beyond the decision maker's control, but its presence must be acknowledged in order to iso-

STATISTICS AROUND US

Ingrid's Hallmark Shops

Ingrid's Hallmark Shops are concerned with pricing a five-dollar mug and with identifying effective mug merchandising displays. One of the employees suggests a statistical sampling study. As the response variable, he recommends unit mug sales. Four different prices ($4.95, $4.99, $5.00, and $5.05) are to be evaluated, each at three merchandise display arrangements (one four-foot shelf, two two-foot shelves, one one-by-four-foot kiosk). Altogether there are 12 different treatments, one for each combination of price and display as provided below.

Price	Display	Price	Display
$4.95	4 foot	$5.00	4 foot
4.95	two 2-foot	5.00	two 2-foot
4.95	kiosk	5.00	kiosk
4.99	4 foot	5.05	4 foot
4.99	two 2-foot	5.05	two 2-foot
4.99	kiosk	5.05	kiosk

late that portion of the response which is due to the treatment, the level of which may be chosen. (See the box below.)

In Chapter 18, the sod-fertilization experiment will again be evaluated using *parcel* as the blocking variable. Such an experiment is called a **randomized block design**. The sample units within each parcel are randomly assigned to treatments, thereby nullifying slight differences between plots within parcels. Thus, no plot systematically influences the results—as might be true, say, if the plot receiving the best irrigation was always heavily fertilized. Often an important element in sampling studies, the assignment of sample units to treatments is referred to as **randomization**. For example, in evaluating the effectiveness of training programs, it is important to account for the differences between instructors. This may be accomplished by randomly assigning a particular training program to each instructor.

Also in our illustrations until now, we have set levels in advance for the factors under investigation. For instance, the three fertilizer treatments were established before the data were collected. That study involved a **fixed-effects experiment**, in contrast to a **random-effects experiment** in which the factor levels are not

STATISTICS AROUND US

Television Commercials and WeeTees Sales

The manufacturer of WeeTees breakfast cereal compared four versions of a television spot (each being a treatment) in terms of sales increase (the response). Each commercial ran for one month during a four-month test period. Television stations in three test cities ran the experimental commercials for the study. Because each city may respond differently to each commercial, *city* served as the blocking variable.

established in advance but are subject to chance, as when the levels constitute a sample from a larger population. For example, suppose a medical society is studying doctors' incomes, based on the factors "specialty" and "region where educated." Data might be compiled from one medical school in each region, so that the school selected is just a sample; the levels of the education factor would also be samples. A detailed discussion of random-effects experiments is beyond the scope of this book.

Statisticians use the word **replication** to indicate that an experiment is repeated. The number of repetitions is the number of replications. When a single sample is used, this number is the sample size. In hypothesis-testing situations, the chance of committing the Type II error of accepting a false null hypothesis becomes smaller as the level of n is raised. When two or more samples are used, we compare population parameters or estimate their differences. The advantages of using large sample sizes are accrued in either case, but large sample sizes are naturally more expensive.

The sod-fertilization experiment involved replication, with each treatment administered to five plots. Two-factor evaluations may be made with or without replication. The primary advantage of having more than one observation per treatment combination is that conclusions may then be made regarding **interactions** between levels of the two factors. The combined effect might have greater influence than either factor does individually.

When an observation is made of each combination of factor levels, the experiment has a **complete factorial design**. But sometimes only a fraction of the combinations may be studied, because a complete study would be prohibitively expensive or infeasible (in our example, the soil in some parcels may not absorb heavy applications of fertilizer). Such experiments are said to have a **fractional factorial design**. At times, it may be useful to omit certain combinations of factors but still to incorporate all factorial levels in the experiment. This is called an **incomplete factorial design**. A useful experiment in this category is conducted using a **Latin square design**. This procedure analyzes three factors and will be described in Chapter 18.

EXERCISES

17-20 In designing a sampling experiment for each of the following situations, suggest (1) appropriate factor(s) and possible levels that define the treatments, (2) a meaningful response variable, and (3) a possible blocking variable.

(a) A utility company evaluates day-of-week for the placement of newspaper ads.

(b) A retail drug chain compares how various locations and levels of floorspace within stores influence pet food sales.

(c) A taxi company evaluates tires in terms of rotation cycle and pressure settings.

(d) A statistics instructor compares how various strategies for assigning and grading homework influence student performance.

17-21 Give an example of a two-factor experiment where interactions may be an important consideration.

SUMMARY

1. What is analysis of variance?

Analysis of variance compares several populations, each representing a level of the **treatment variable**. The null hypothesis that every **treatment** results in an identical mean for the **response variable** is tested. Sample data are arranged in an **experimental layout**, forming a matrix. The layout involves r rows (one for each observation) and c columns (one for each treatment).

2. What is the theoretical model for analysis of variance?

This chapter describes a **single-factor analysis of variance**, sometimes referred to as a **one-way analysis**. Each treatment may be thought of as a **factor level**. The analytical procedure is based on a theoretical model, which assumes that each observation X_{ij} ($i = 1, 2, \ldots, r$ and $j = 1, 2, \ldots, c$) may be represented by the sum

$$X_{ij} = \mu_j + \varepsilon_{ij}$$

where the **error terms** ε_{ij} are *independent, normally distributed*, and have a *common standard deviation*. (In practice, the procedure is usually workable unless these assumptions are flagrantly violated.)

Each **treatment population mean** μ_j (mean for factor-level j) may be expressed as the sum of two components.

$$\mu_j = \bar{\mu} + B_j$$

where μ is the **overall population mean** and B_j is the **effect** for treatment (factor-level) j. The null hypothesis that all μ_j's are identical is tested.

3. How do we test whether the population means are identical?

The procedure will reject H_0 if the variation in response that is explained by or attributed to different treatments is significantly greater than the variation that is left unexplained. This is accomplished by an elaborate procedure leading to a computed value of F, which serves as the test statistic.

4. How do we compute the F statistic for testing?

In analysis of variance, the **sample treatment mean** is computed using the expression

$$\bar{X}_j = \frac{\sum_i X_{ij}}{r}$$

The **grand mean** uses the pooled sample data and may be expressed

$$\bar{\bar{X}} = \frac{\sum_j \sum_i X_{ij}}{rc}$$

Applying these two means and the original data values, the **treatments sum of squares** is computed using

$$SSTR = r \sum (\bar{X}_j - \bar{\bar{X}})^2$$

and the **error sum of squares** using

$$SSE = \sum \sum (X_{ij} - \bar{X}_j)^2 = SSTO - SSTR$$

The following expression summarizes the **total sum of squares**.

$$SSTO = \sum \sum (X_{ij} - \bar{\bar{X}})^2 = SSTR + SSE$$

To compute the test statistic, the **treatments mean square** and the **error mean square** must first be found using

$$MSTR = \frac{SSTR}{c - 1} \quad \text{and} \quad MSE = \frac{SSE}{(r - 1)c}$$

We may then determine that

$$F = \frac{\text{Variance explained by treatments}}{\text{Unexplained variance}} = \frac{MSTR}{MSE}$$

5. **How do we find the critical value for the F statistic?**
The critical F values may be read from Appendix Table G. But first, the **numbers of degrees of freedom**, a pair of values determined for the analysis, must be established by the following rule.

$$\text{Numerator:} \quad c - 1$$

$$\text{Denominator:} \quad (r - 1)c$$

The tests are *upper-tailed*, so the null hypotheses for computed levels of F exceeding the critical value must be rejected.

6. **What is the ANOVA table?**
The ANOVA table summarizes the sums of squares and mean squares used in computing the test statistic.

Variation	Degrees of Freedom	Sum of Squares	Mean Square	F
Explained by treatments (between columns)	$c - 1$	$SSTR$	$MSTR$	$MSTR/MSE$
Error or unexplained (within columns)	$(r - 1)c$	SSE	MSE	
Total	$rc - 1$	$SSTO$		

7. Besides the basic test for equality of means, what other inferences may be made from the same data?

If the null hypothesis of identical treatment population means is rejected, further analysis ordinarily is required prior to deciding on a final course of action. This analysis is based on **multiple comparisons**, the key feature of which is a set of confidence intervals for *pairwise differences* in treatment population means. The intervals are constructed using a **collective level of confidence**.

Two different methods may be used, resulting in either **Tukey intervals** or **Bonferroni intervals**. Underlying each procedure, is a different sampling distribution. But both utilize *MSE*, which is treated as a *pooled* sample variance. Either set of intervals will be wider than their counterparts found for *single* inferences. Care should be taken when drawing conclusions from intervals computed separately without using a collective level of confidence.

Whenever any pairwise difference has a confidence interval that does not overlap zero, the respective μ_j's are then *significantly different.*

Collective Bonferroni confidence intervals may be constructed as well for *individual* treatment population means. These may even be combined with the foregoing intervals, but doing so reduces the overall collective confidence.

REVIEW EXERCISES

17-22 The following results were obtained from an experiment using six treatment levels, with five observations per treatment.

$$SSTR = 78 \qquad SSTO = 183$$

(a) Construct the ANOVA table.

(b) At an $\alpha = .01$ significance level, what conclusion should be reached regarding the null hypothesis of equal population means for the treatment levels of the respective factors?

17-23 A financial analyst for Breez Inns wishes to compare mean amounts of time taken to acquire building permits regionally. The regions are (1) East, (2) South, (3) Midwest, and (4) West. A sample of eight projects was collected from each. The following ANOVA table and sample means were obtained.

Variation	Degrees of Freedom	Sum of Squares	Mean Square	F
Treatments	3	4.25	1.42	3.23
Error	28	12.42	.44	
Total	31	16.67		

$\bar{X}_1 = 1.3$ years $\quad \bar{X}_2 = .8$ years $\quad \bar{X}_3 = .9$ years $\quad \bar{X}_4 = .6$ years
$\bar{\bar{X}} = .9$ years

(a) Using a 94% collective level of confidence, construct Bonferroni interval estimates of the following differences.

(1) $\mu_2 - \mu_1$ (3) $\mu_4 - \mu_1$ (5) $\mu_4 - \mu_2$
(2) $\mu_3 - \mu_1$ (4) $\mu_3 - \mu_2$ (6) $\mu_4 - \mu_3$

(b) Referring to your answers to (a), for which regional pairs are the permit acquisition times significantly different?

17-24 A WeeTees product manager is evaluating several different cereal preservatives for useful shelf life. The following data (in months) were obtained.

	Preserving Agent			
Sample	**(1)**	**(2)**	**(3)**	**(4)**
1	5	6	5	7
2	6	8	7	6
3	5	9	7	5
4	5	9	7	5
5	6	8	7	6
6	5	9	8	7
7	7	8	6	6
8	5	9	7	7

(a) Construct the ANOVA table.

(b) Using $\alpha = .01$, should the manager conclude that the mean shelf lives are different for the agents?

17-25 A business school curriculum committee is evaluating formats for laboratory sections in beginning accounting. They requested an experiment where laboratory sections are to be taught using three different methods. The following mean scores on a standard examination were achieved by each sample class.

	Laboratory Method		
Class	**(1) Lecture**	**(2) Computer**	**(3) Mixed**
1	78	77	83
2	85	86	91
3	64	71	75
4	77	75	78
5	81	80	82
6	75	77	80

Using $\alpha = .05$, what should the committee conclude regarding the mean scores of all accounting classes taught using the respective methods?

17-26 Refer to Exercise 17-24 and to your answers.

(a) Using a 95% collective level of confidence, construct Tukey interval estimates of difference in mean scores between all six pairs of preserving agents. [Use the designations in Exercise 17-23(a).]

(b) Which preserving agent, if any, yields a significantly longer mean shelf life for each pair?

(c) Which agent yields a significantly longer shelf life than all others?

17-27 A Shale-Bituminous Processors chemical engineer is evaluating four methods for processing oil shale to obtain synthetic fuel. Nine random samples were selected from batches of raw material processed using each method. The following yields of usable liquid (milliliters per ton) were obtained.

	Processing Method			
Sample	**(A)**	**(B)**	**(C)**	**(D)**
1	−5	11	15	8
2	11	14	10	10
3	13	22	25	18
4	−5	0	2	1
5	25	35	40	28
6	21	24	28	27
7	11	15	19	17
8	33	30	28	32
9	105	224	328	276

(a) Using $\alpha = .01$, should the engineer conclude that some methods for processing shale might be better than others?
(b) What factors other than processing method might explain variation in yield?

17-28 The manager of a CompTel telecommunications network is evaluating various strategies for routing calls. The following data represent the percentage of calls successfully completed during sample intervals of time.

	Call-routing Algorithm				
Observation	**(1) East-West**	**(2) North-South**	**(3) Central**	**(4) Random**	**(5) Shortest**
1	90%	99%	95%	98%	87%
2	92	97	96	98	93
3	94	98	97	99	90
4	93	98	97	99	91
5	92	99	96	98	89

(a) Construct the ANOVA table.
(b) Determine the critical value of the test statistic, and identify the acceptance and rejection regions, using $\alpha = .01$.
(c) Should the manager accept or reject the null hypothesis of identical mean percentages of calls completed?

17-29 Refer to Exercise 17-28 and to your answers.
(a) Using a 99% collective level of confidence, construct Bonferroni interval estimates of the difference in mean scores between every possible treatment pair.
(b) If the manager wants to maximize the mean percentage of successfully completed calls, which algorithms do the data suggest he not use? Which algorithms might be best to use?

CASE GOODY SELLERS

Goodwin "Goody" Sellers is a marketing major at State University. As a marketing research project, Goody performed a series of experiments in a local retail variety store chain. Goody's objective is to assess the effectiveness of various merchandising schemes for advertised specials. His experiments consider in-store location, display density, and product adjacency.

Since the stores vary tremendously in clientele, floor space, and foot traffic, and since the test products themselves vary in customer appeal, Goody concluded that unit sales per se would be inadequate as the response variable. Instead, he chose the test product's percentage of dollar-sales per square foot relative to the store as a whole. For example, if on March 1 the test items use 6 square feet of floor space and bring \$12 in sales, while the store itself uses 1,000 square feet and generates \$500 in sales, then the following relative percentage applies.

$$\frac{\$12/6}{\$500/1{,}000} \times 100 = \frac{\$2.00}{\$.50} \times 100 = 400\%$$

In March, Goody investigated fifteen stores; five each used one of three in-store locations for advertised specials. The following sample results for percentage of sales were obtained.

In-Store Location		
(1) At Rear	(2) Near Front	(3) In Department
75%	150%	110%
72	206	98
99	132	121
66	142	105
70	155	112

During the month of April, Goody arranged the displays for advertised specials in sixteen stores, using four different levels. The following results for percentage of sales were obtained.

Display Density			
(1) Scattered	(2) Low	(3) Medium	(4) High
86%	120%	98%	102%
95	107	112	89
101	133	82	114
85	117	102	99

During the month of May, Goody tested five different primary adjacent departments for the advertised specials. Using three sample stores for each treatment, the following results were obtained.

Primary Adjacent Department				
(1) Candy	(2) Stationery	(3) Cards	(4) Notions	(5) Candles
133%	82%	148%	110%	94%
114	67	133	105	112
156	104	162	120	78

QUESTIONS

1. The primary role of advertised specials is to bring customers into the store. Comment on the appropriateness of Goody's response variable in assessing the overall impact of a particular merchandising scheme.
2. Refer to the sample results for the month of March, using each in-store location as a separate treatment.
   (a) Compute the individual sample treatment means. Then, construct the ANOVA table.
   (b) Using a 95% collective level of confidence, construct Tukey interval estimates of all pairwise differences.
   (c) Give an overall summary statement of the results.
3. Refer to the sample results for the month of April, using the four display densities as treatments. Repeat Question 2(a)–(c).
4. Refer to the sample results for the month of May, using the five primary adjacent departments as separate treatments. Repeat Question 2(a)—(c).
5. Goody expects to use his experimental results to recommend a policy regarding location, display density, and departmental adjacency of advertised specials. Assuming that management wishes to maximize the chosen response variable, what would you suggest to Goody as a possible store policy?
6. Goody will be conducting an identical investigation for another retail chain. Suggest ways to improve the experiment.

17-5 OPTIONAL TOPIC: UNEQUAL SAMPLE SIZES

The procedures discussed in sections 17-1 and 17-3 may be generalized to include the possibility of unequal sample sizes. This results in slightly more complex mathematical expressions, but exactly the same concepts are involved. Computer software programs are available that will automatically accept data for unequal sample sizes.

TABLE 17-7 Sample Results for a Retail Chain's Adjusted Percentage of Gift Sales

	Shelf Arrangement			
Observation	(1) Two-Foot	(2) Four-Foot	(3) Split Level	(4) Corner Unit
1	15%	8%	12%	19%
2	14	11	14	22
3	17	10	17	18
4	11	7	10	17
5	19	10	12	17
6	—	6	14	16
7	—	12	9	24
8	—	—	17	22
9	—	—	12	—
10	—	—	13	—

ILLUSTRATION: SHELF ARRANGEMENTS IN STORES

To illustrate this procedure, consider the sample data given in Table 17-7. These results have been obtained from an investigation where $c = 4$ different shelf arrangements of a specialty gift line were tested in sample stores selected from a large retail chain. During the experimental run, sales were carefully monitored and the percentages of specialty gift sales per total gift sales were determined for each store. Adjusted for size differences, the sample percentage results serve as the response variable.

It was not practical to obtain the same number of sample stores for each shelf arrangement. Accordingly, the number of X_{ij}'s in each column of the experimental layout may vary. The number of sample observations made using treatment j is denoted by n_j. In our illustration, $n_1 = 5$, $n_2 = 7$, $n_3 = 10$, and $n_4 = 8$. The **combined sample size** is

$$n_T = \sum_j n_j$$

For the shelf-arrangement investigation,

$$n_T = 5 + 7 + 10 + 8 = 30$$

(The procedure presented previously in this chapter is a special case, where $n_1 = n_2 = \cdots n_c = r$.)

The respective sample means are computed by averaging the observed values in each treatment column. The grand mean is computed by averaging all observations, and may be expressed

$$\bar{\bar{X}} = \frac{\sum_{j=1}^{c} \sum_{i=1}^{n_j} X_{ij}}{n_T}$$

when the values are added together column by column. The sums of squares are computed using the following expressions.

$$SSTR = \sum_{j=1}^{c} n_j(\bar{X} - \bar{\bar{X}})^2$$

```
MTB > retrieve 'Shelf'
MTB > AOVOneway c1-c4.

ANALYSIS OF VARIANCE
SOURCE      DF        SS         MS          F         p
FACTOR       3    412.63     137.54      19.07     0.000
ERROR       26    187.53       7.21
TOTAL       29    600.17
                                   INDIVIDUAL 95 PCT CI'S FOR MEAN
                                   BASED ON POOLED STDEV
 LEVEL       N      MEAN      STDEV  ---+---------+---------+---------+---
Two-Foot     5    15.200      3.033               (-----*-----)
Four-Ft.     7     9.143      2.193   (----*----)
Split       10    13.000      2.625            (----*---)
Corner       8    19.375      2.925                         (---*----)
                                     ---+---------+---------+---------+---
POOLED STDEV =     2.686                8.0      12.0      16.0      20.0
```

Note: Figure generated on an IBM PC using Minitab®.

FIGURE 17-9 Computer printout for shelf-arrangement investigation.

$$SSE = \sum_{j=1}^{c}\sum_{i=1}^{n_j}(X_{ij} - \bar{X}_j)^2 \qquad SSTO = \sum_{j=1}^{c}\sum_{i=1}^{n_j}(X_{ij} - \bar{\bar{X}})^2$$

The mean squares are computed from

$$MSTR = \frac{SSTR}{c-1} \qquad MSE = \frac{SSE}{n_T - c}$$

As before, the F statistic is the ratio of the above, and the number of degrees of freedom is $c - 1$ for the numerator and $n_T - c$ for the denominator.

Although the results for the shelf-arrangement investigation may be computed with ease by hand, most investigators prefer to use a computer. See Figure 17-9.

The choice of multiple comparison procedures is limited when unequal sample sizes are used. The Tukey method may not be used, so that *pairwise differences* in treatment population means must be estimated using Bonferroni intervals:

$$\mu_j - \mu_k = \bar{X}_j - \bar{X}_k \pm t_{\alpha/2s}\sqrt{MSE\left(\frac{1}{n_j} + \frac{1}{n_k}\right)}$$

where s is the number of intervals and $n_T - c$ is the number of degrees of freedom. *Individual* population means may be estimated using Bonferroni intervals:

$$\mu_j = \bar{X}_j + t_{\alpha/2s}\sqrt{\frac{MSE}{n_j}}$$

where s is the number of intervals constructed using $n_j - 1$ degrees of freedom.

CHAPTER 18

MULTIPLE-FACTOR ANALYSIS OF VARIANCE

BEFORE READING THIS CHAPTER, MAKE SURE YOU UNDERSTAND:

The statistical sampling study (Chapter 4).
Statistical estimation (Chapter 8).
Hypothesis testing (Chapter 9).
Analysis of variance for single factors (Chapter 17).

AFTER READING THIS CHAPTER, YOU WILL UNDERSTAND:

The role of multiple-factor analysis of variance.
About the theoretical model for multiple-factor analysis of variance.
Which sample means serve as the basic building blocks for evaluation.
How to compute the sums of squares used to compute the various test statistics.
Which hypotheses may be tested in a multiple-factor evaluation.
How the respective *F* statistics are computed.
Which follow-on procedures may be applied in multiple-factor evaluations.
Which special experimental designs may be used in multiple-factor analysis of variance.

Chapter 17 laid the conceptual framework for analysis of variance. A detailed discussion was given there of experiments involving one treatment for each of several levels of one factor. Those applications are referred to as single-factor experiments. This chapter extends those concepts to multiple factors. The simplest procedure involves a randomized block design, wherein a second factor may reduce the amount of unexplained variation, thereby increasing test discrimination. For example, in evaluating alternative training procedures in terms of productivity, a personnel analyst might want to separate test subjects by their level of experience. This would remove experience as one source of variation in measured productivity.

A second factor may play a more direct role, joining with the first in creating a separate treatment from each combination of levels for both factors. For example, a newspaper advertiser might be concerned with how audience recall is affected both by the *placement* of its copy and by *day* of week. It would be inefficient to conduct separate experiments on Mondays, Fridays, and Sundays, each of which would test response to placements of ads within news, business, and sports sections. Less time and resources would be consumed in a single experiment that simultaneously incorporates both placement and day.

Multiple-factor studies provide further information not available when a single factor is considered. Of particular interest are interactions between various levels of the factors. For example, the above advertiser might find that the sports section results in higher recall on Sunday ads than on any other day, while the business section is weakest on Mondays.

A third factor may sometimes be useful. This chapter concludes with a procedure employing two blocking variables and one treatments factor. This method is based on the Latin-square design and proves to be very efficient when limited resources restrict the number of observations.

18-1 THE TWO-FACTOR ANALYSIS OF VARIANCE

The analysis of variance procedure involves two factors, denoted by A and B. Each factor involves several levels, so that the experimental layout takes the form of the matrix in Table 18-1. There are r levels (rows) for factor A and c levels (columns) for factor B. A separate treatment (cell) applies for each combination of factor levels.

TABLE 18-1 Experimental Layout for Two-Factor Analysis of Variance

Factor *A* Level	Treatment Population Mean					Factor *A* Level Population Mean
	Factor *B* Level					
	(1)	(2)	(3)	(4)	(5)	
(1)	μ_{11}	μ_{12}	μ_{13}	μ_{14}	μ_{15}	$\mu_{1.}$
(2)	μ_{21}	μ_{22}	μ_{23}	μ_{24}	μ_{25}	$\mu_{2.}$
(3)	μ_{31}	μ_{32}	μ_{33}	μ_{34}	μ_{35}	$\mu_{3.}$
(4)	μ_{41}	μ_{42}	μ_{43}	μ_{44}	μ_{45}	$\mu_{4.}$
Factor *B* Level Population Mean	$\mu_{.1}$	$\mu_{.2}$	$\mu_{.3}$	$\mu_{.4}$	$\mu_{.5}$	$\mu_{..}$

THE POPULATIONS AND MEANS

For this experimental layout, there are $r \times c$ treatment populations, each having a

TREATMENT (CELL) POPULATION MEAN

μ_{ij} = Population mean with factor A at level i and factor B at level j

There is a separate population for each factor level as well. The centers of these are represented by the marginal data in Table 18-1, where each value listed in the right margin is a

FACTOR *A* LEVEL (ROW) POPULATION MEAN

$\mu_{i.}$ = Factor A population mean at level i

In the above subscript, the dot serves as a reminder that a second dimension, or factor, exists and is to be considered. The dot preserves the double-subscript format, which will be maintained throughout the chapter. The dot may also signify that an averaging process will be used to arrive at the quantity represented. The placement of the dot in the second position, following the variable i, indicates that the presence of factor B is acknowledged.

There is a different factor A level mean for each row of the experimental layout. Each $\mu_{i.}$ is the mean of the cells μ_{ij}, or treatment population means, in its row. Thus,

$$\mu_{i.} = \frac{\sum_{j=1}^{c} \mu_{ij}}{c}$$

The subscript dot for $\mu_{i.}$ appears in the second or "j" position since the μ_{ij}'s are averaged over all the levels of j.

Each value in the bottom margin of the experimental layout is a

FACTOR *B* LEVEL (COLUMN) POPULATION MEAN

$\mu_{.j}$ = Factor B population mean at level j

There is a different factor B level mean for each column of the experimental layout. Each $\mu_{.j}$ is the mean of the cells μ_{ij}, or treatment population means, in its column. Thus,

$$\mu_{.j} = \frac{\sum_{i=1}^{r} \mu_{ij}}{r}$$

The subscript dot for $\mu_{.j}$ appears in the first or "i" position since the μ_{ij}'s are averaged over all the levels of i.

The two-factor analysis is based on the collective population of all responses regardless of factor levels. The **overall population mean** $\mu_{..}$ is equal to the average of the factor-level (marginal) means of both the rows and the columns.

$$\mu_{..} = \frac{\sum_{i=1}^{r} \mu_{i.}}{r} \quad \text{and} \quad \mu_{..} = \frac{\sum_{j=1}^{c} \mu_{.j}}{c}$$

The overall population mean is also equal to the average of all treatment (cell) means.

$$\mu_{..} = \frac{\sum_{i=1}^{r}\sum_{j=1}^{c} \mu_{ij}}{rc}$$

THE UNDERLYING MODEL

The additive model for two-factor analysis of variance expresses the cell means as the sum of four components.

$$\mu_{ij} = \mu_{..} + A_i + B_j + (AB)_{ij}$$

The first component is the overall mean. This component is followed by the effects parameters. There are three types of

TWO-FACTOR EFFECT PARAMETERS

A_i = Main effect for factor A at level i

B_j = Main effect for factor B at level j

$(AB)_{ij}$ = Interaction effect with factor A at level i and factor B at level j

The effects parameters A_i, B_j, and $(AB)_{ij}$ may be expressed in terms of the population means as

$$A_i = \mu_{i\cdot} - \mu_{\cdot\cdot}$$
$$B_j = \mu_{\cdot j} - \mu_{\cdot\cdot}$$
$$(AB)_{ij} = \mu_{ij} - \mu_{i\cdot} - \mu_{\cdot j} + \mu_{\cdot\cdot}$$

The parameters are in the same units as the response variable. The following relationships apply.

$$\sum_i A_i = \sum_j B_j = \sum_i \sum_j (AB)_{ij} = 0$$

The effects parameters are helpful in explaining how the factor levels influence the response variable and any interactions between factors. The following examples will illustrate the various cases.

An airline wishes to experiment with their reservation system. Figure 18-1 shows the hypothetical means that may exist. Transaction time is the response variable. Factor A is service type, with three levels, and factor B is ticketing complexity, also with three levels. The plot for the means shows that factor B has *nonzero* effects, since the mean transaction times differ for each level of ticketing complexity. The horizontal lines indicate that factor A has *zero* effects, since the

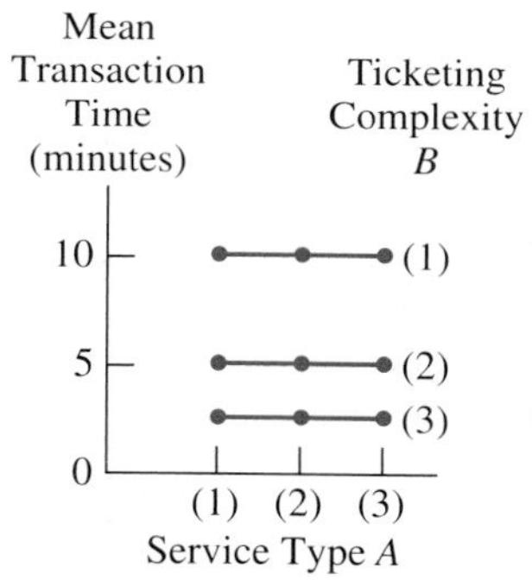

Service Type A	Ticketing Complexity B (1) Low	(2) Medium	(3) High	
(1) *Solo*	$\mu_{11} = 10$	$\mu_{12} = 5$	$\mu_{13} = 3$	$\mu_{1\cdot} = 6$
(2) *Assisted*	$\mu_{21} = 10$	$\mu_{22} = 5$	$\mu_{23} = 3$	$\mu_{2\cdot} = 6$
(3) *Automated*	$\mu_{31} = 10$	$\mu_{32} = 5$	$\mu_{33} = 3$	$\mu_{3\cdot} = 6$
	$\mu_{\cdot 1} = 10$	$\mu_{\cdot 2} = 5$	$\mu_{\cdot 3} = 3$	$\mu_{\cdot\cdot} = 6$

Zero Factor A Effects:

$$A_1 = \mu_{1\cdot} - \mu_{\cdot\cdot} = 6 - 6 = 0$$
$$A_2 = \mu_{2\cdot} - \mu_{\cdot\cdot} = 6 - 6 = 0$$
$$A_3 = \mu_{3\cdot} - \mu_{\cdot\cdot} = 6 - 6 = \underline{0}$$
$$0$$

Nonzero Factor B Effects:

$$B_1 = \mu_{\cdot 1} - \mu_{\cdot\cdot} = 10 - 6 = 4$$
$$B_2 = \mu_{\cdot 2} - \mu_{\cdot\cdot} = 5 - 6 = -1$$
$$B_3 = \mu_{\cdot 3} - \mu_{\cdot\cdot} = 3 - 6 = \underline{-3}$$
$$0$$

No Interactions:

$$(AB)_{11} = \mu_{11} - \mu_{1\cdot} - \mu_{\cdot 1} + \mu_{\cdot\cdot} = 10 - 6 - 10 + 6 = 0$$

all $(AB)_{ij}$'s $= 0$

FIGURE 18-1 Reservation transaction experiment.

mean transaction times for each level of ticketing complexity do not differ with the type of service.

Figure 18-2 provides a similar example. A data processing department is evaluating the extent to which the percentage of data entry error is affected by discipline A (two levels) and job size B (three levels). The plots show decreasing error rates for factor A from lax discipline (1) to strict discipline (2) and also for factor B from small jobs (1) to medium jobs (2) and then to large jobs (3). Thus, both factors have nonzero effects. The parallel plot lines indicate that the effects for one factor are equal at any level of the other factor. This indicates that there are *no interactions* among the factors.

The presence of interactions is shown in Figure 18-3. A hypothetical experiment is conducted to assess the impact of network size A (four levels) and memory need B on the performance (processing time) of a network processing algorithm. Factor B has two levels: low (1) and high (2). Note that both factors tend to provide higher mean responses for successive levels. Moreover, the performance gap between levels of factor B, low-memory need (1) and high-memory need (2), becomes wider as the level of factor A increases. Thus, there are underlying *interactions* between the factors. The presence of the interactions is reflected in Figure 18-3 by the nonparallel plots.

Of course, the levels for the population means and the effects parameters ordinarily will be unknown. Inferences are to be made regarding these unknown quantities from the sample data. Next, we consider testing hypotheses for the factor

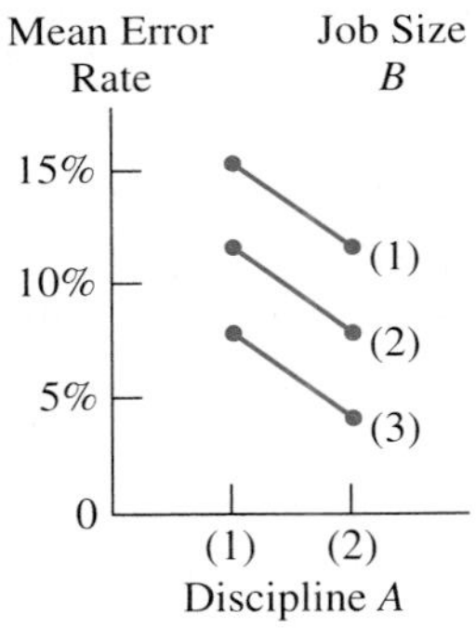

Discipline A	*Job Size B* (1) *Small*	(2) *Medium*	(3) *Large*	
(1) *Lax*	$\mu_{11} = 8$	$\mu_{12} = 12$	$\mu_{13} = 16$	$\mu_{1\cdot} = 12$
(2) *Strict*	$\mu_{21} = 4$	$\mu_{22} = 8$	$\mu_{23} = 12$	$\mu_{2\cdot} = 8$
	$\mu_{\cdot 1} = 6$	$\mu_{\cdot 2} = 10$	$\mu_{\cdot 3} = 14$	$\mu_{\cdot\cdot} = 10$

Zero Factor A Effects:

$$A_1 = 12 - 10 = 2$$
$$A_2 = 8 - 10 = \underline{-2}$$
$$0$$

Nonzero Factor B Effects:

$$B_1 = 6 - 10 = -4$$
$$B_2 = 10 - 10 = 0$$
$$B_3 = 14 - 10 = \underline{4}$$
$$0$$

No Interactions:

$$(AB)_{11} = 8 - 12 - 6 + 10 = 0$$

all $(AB)_{ij}$'s $= 0$

FIGURE 18-2 Data entry evaluation.

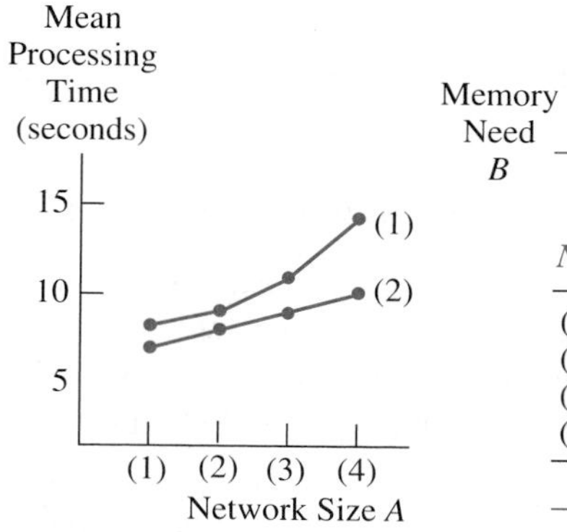

Network Size A	Memory Need B (1) Low	Memory Need B (2) High	
(1) *Tiny*	$\mu_{11} = 8$	$\mu_{12} = 7$	$\mu_{1\cdot} = 7.5$
(2) *Medium*	$\mu_{21} = 9$	$\mu_{22} = 8$	$\mu_{2\cdot} = 8.5$
(3) *Large*	$\mu_{31} = 11$	$\mu_{32} = 9$	$\mu_{3\cdot} = 10.0$
(4) *Huge*	$\mu_{41} = 14$	$\mu_{42} = 10$	$\mu_{4\cdot} = 12.0$
	$\mu_{\cdot 1} = 10.5$	$\mu_{\cdot 2} = 8.5$	$\mu_{\cdot\cdot} = 9.5$

Nonzero Factor A Effects:

$A_1 = 7.5 - 9.5 = -2.0$
$A_2 = 8.5 - 9.5 = -1.0$
$A_3 = 10.0 - 9.5 = 0.5$
$A_4 = 12.0 - 9.5 = \underline{2.5}$
0

Nonzero Factor B Effects:

$B_1 = 10.5 - 9.5 = 1.0$
$B_2 = 8.5 - 9.5 = \underline{-1.0}$
0

Nonzero Interactions:

$(AB)_{11} = 8 - 7.5 - 10.5 + 9.5 = -0.5$
$(AB)_{12} = 7 - 7.5 - 8.5 + 9.5 = 0.5$
$(AB)_{21} = 9 - 8.5 - 10.5 + 9.5 = -0.5$
$(AB)_{22} = 8 - 8.5 - 8.5 + 9.5 = 0.5$
$(AB)_{31} = 11 - 10.0 - 10.5 + 9.5 = 0.0$
$(AB)_{32} = 9 - 10.0 - 8.5 + 9.5 = 0.0$
$(AB)_{41} = 14 - 12.0 - 10.5 + 9.5 = 1.0$
$(AB)_{42} = 10 - 12.0 - 8.5 + 9.5 = \underline{-1.0}$
0

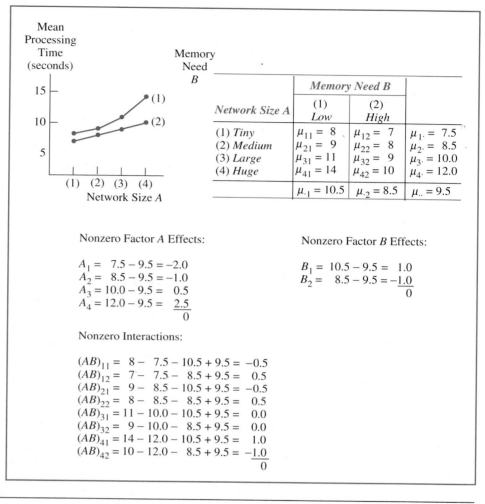

FIGURE 18-3 Algorithm performance experiment.

levels. In Section 18-2, we will construct a variety of confidence intervals for differences and contrasts in means.

TESTING THE NULL HYPOTHESES

Recall from Chapter 17 that the analysis of variance procedure actually tests for equality of the respective population means. In a two-factor evaluation, there are *three* null hypotheses that may be tested. The first two involve the factor A and factor B level population means and test the hypothesis that there is no main effect. For factor A, we have

$$H_0: \mu_{1\cdot} = \mu_{2\cdot} = \cdots = \mu_{r\cdot} \qquad \text{(all } A_i\text{'s} = 0)$$

and for factor B

$$H_0: \mu_{\cdot 1} = \mu_{\cdot 2} = \cdots = \mu_{\cdot c} \qquad \text{(all } B_j\text{'s} = 0)$$

And, the third tests the hypothesis that there are no interaction effects using

$$H_0\colon \mu_{ij} = \mu_{..} + A_i + B_j \text{ for all cells} \qquad (\text{all } (AB)_{ij}\text{'s} = 0)$$

SAMPLE DATA FOR TWO-FACTOR EXPERIMENTS

The procedure requires that exactly n observations be made for each treatment cell and that the same sample sizes apply to each combination of factor levels. The kth sample observation, when factor A is at level i and B is at level j, is denoted by X_{ijk}. The additive model provides

$$X_{ijk} = \mu_{ij} + \varepsilon_{ijk}$$

or

$$X_{ijk} = \mu_{..} + A_i + B_j + (AB)_{ij} + \varepsilon_{ijk}$$

The quantity ε_{ijk} expresses the residual value or **error term**. As with the model in Chapter 17, the analytical framework presented here assumes that the ε's are independent and normally distributed with mean zero and common standard deviation σ.

The interaction effects may not be assessed unless $n > 1$. In that case, sampling is performed with **replication**.

APPLYING THE PROCEDURE: PLACEMENT AND DAY FOR ADVERTISING

A mail order merchandiser builds its catalog subscription base from coupons clipped from local newspapers. An experiment is conducted using an identical quarter-page ad placed in $r = 3$ sections (news, sports, and business) on $c = 4$ different days (Sunday, Monday, Friday, and Saturday). One newspaper is chosen for a 12-week-long test during which sectional placement is rotated on successive test days until $n = 4$ observations are obtained for each factor level combination. The response variable is the number of returned coupons from the ad (which are distinguished by a code printed in the coupon). The 48 observations in Table 18-2 represent random samples from the corresponding target populations of coupons returned.

The sample results provided in Table 18-2 are arranged in matrix form similar to the experimental layout introduced earlier for the population means. The counterpart *sample* mean values are computed using the following expressions.

CELL SAMPLE MEAN FOR TREATMENT COMBINATION (i, j)

$$\bar{X}_{ij.} = \frac{\sum_k X_{ijk}}{n}$$

TABLE 18-2 Sample Results for Newspaper Advertisement Study

Sectional Position A	Day of Week B				Factor A Sample Mean
	(1) Sunday	(2) Monday	(3) Friday	(4) Saturday	
(1) News	X_{111} (966)	X_{121} (979)	X_{131} (1,240)	X_{141} (990)	
	X_{112} (1,004)	X_{122} (975)	X_{132} (1,247)	X_{142} (1,018)	
	X_{113} (993)	X_{123} (985)	X_{133} (1,253)	X_{143} (1,003)	
	X_{114} (979)	X_{124} (998)	X_{134} (1,237)	X_{144} (1,000)	
Cell Mean	$\bar{X}_{11} =$ 985.50	$\bar{X}_{112} =$ 984.25	$\bar{X}_{113} =$ 1,244.25	$\bar{X}_{14} =$ 1,002.75	$\bar{X}_{1} =$ 1,054.19
(2) Sports	X_{211} (1,217)	X_{221} (989)	X_{231} (1,022)	X_{241} (1,018)	
	X_{212} (1,171)	X_{222} (988)	X_{232} (1,011)	X_{242} (1,045)	
	X_{213} (1,178)	X_{223} (1,002)	X_{233} (1,030)	X_{243} (1,037)	
	X_{214} (1,230)	X_{224} (992)	X_{234} (996)	X_{244} (1,058)	
Cell Mean	$\bar{X}_{21.} =$ 1,199.00	$\bar{X}_{22} =$ 992.75	$\bar{X}_{23} =$ 1,014.75	$\bar{X}_{24} =$ 1,039.50	$\bar{X}_{2} =$ 1,061.50
(3) Business	X_{311} (1,021)	X_{321} (871)	X_{331} (889)	X_{341} (851)	
	X_{312} (1,015)	X_{322} (864)	X_{332} (948)	X_{342} (867)	
	X_{313} (1,041)	X_{323} (835)	X_{333} (872)	X_{343} (838)	
	X_{314} (995)	X_{324} (874)	X_{334} (919)	X_{344} (872)	
Cell Mean	$\bar{X}_{31.} =$ 1,018.00	$\bar{X}_{32} =$ 861.00	$\bar{X}_{33} =$ 907.00	$\bar{X}_{34} =$ 857.00	$\bar{X}_{3} =$ 910.75
Factor B Sample Mean	$\bar{X}_{.1} =$ 1,067.50	$\bar{X}_{.2} =$ 946.00	$\bar{X}_{.3} =$ 1,055.33	$\bar{X}_{.4} =$ 966.42	$\bar{\bar{X}}_{...} =$ 1,008.81

ROW SAMPLE MEAN FOR FACTOR *A* AT LEVEL *i*

$$\bar{X}_{i..} = \frac{\sum_{j} \bar{X}_{ij.}}{c}$$

COLUMN SAMPLE MEAN FOR FACTOR *B* AT LEVEL *j*

$$\bar{X}_{.j.} = \frac{\sum_{i} \bar{X}_{ij.}}{r}$$

GRAND OVERALL SAMPLE MEAN

$$\bar{\bar{X}}_{...} = \frac{\sum_{i}\sum_{j} \bar{X}_{ij.}}{rc} = \frac{\sum_{i} \bar{X}_{i..}}{r} = \frac{\sum_{j} \bar{X}_{.j.}}{c}$$

In accordance with the underlying model, the above sample means ($\bar{X}$'s) are unbiased least-squares estimators of the respective unknown treatment population means (μ's).

ANALYTICAL FRAMEWORK

As with the single-factor procedures, the analytical framework for two-factor experiments may be explained in terms of the following three types of deviations.

$$\begin{array}{ccccc} \text{Total deviation} & = & \text{Treatments deviation} & + & \text{Error deviation} \\ (X_{ijk} - \bar{\bar{X}}_{...}) & = & (\bar{X}_{ij.} - \bar{\bar{X}}_{...}) & + & (X_{ijk} - \bar{X}_{ij.}) \end{array}$$

The above expression *partitions* the total deviation about the grand mean into the treatments and error deviation components. The two-factor analysis may further partition the treatments deviation as

$$\begin{array}{ccccccc} \text{Treatments deviation} & = & A\text{ main effect deviation} & + & B\text{ main effect deviation} & + & AB\text{ interaction effect deviation} \\ (\bar{X}_{ij.} - \bar{\bar{X}}_{...}) & = & (\bar{X}_{i..} - \bar{\bar{X}}_{...}) & + & (\bar{X}_{.j.} - \bar{\bar{X}}_{...}) & + & (\bar{X}_{ij.} - \bar{X}_{i..} - \bar{X}_{.j.} + \bar{\bar{X}}_{...}) \end{array}$$

As with the single-factor experiments, the collective sums of individual squared deviations are used to express the amount of variability for various groups. The first expression below is generalized in terms of sums of squares as

$$\begin{array}{ccccc} \text{Total variation} & = & \text{Treatments variation} & + & \text{Error variation} \\ SSTO & = & SSTR & + & SSE \end{array}$$

And, the treatments sum of squares is partitioned as

$$\begin{array}{ccccccc} \text{Treatments variation} & = & A\text{ main effect variation} & + & B\text{ main effect variation} & + & AB\text{ interaction effect variation} \\ SSTR & = & SSA & + & SSB & + & SSAB \end{array}$$

The respective computed sums of squares form the basis for evaluation and are most helpful when arranged in an ANOVA table.

THE TWO-FACTOR ANOVA TABLE

The general organization of the two-factor ANOVA table is shown in Table 18-3. There, the expressions for computing the sums of squares are provided. Recall that the mean squares are obtained by dividing the sums of squares by the respective degrees of freedom. The degrees of freedom are obtained from the dimensions—reduced by 1—of the experimental layout matrix.

Note that there are three test statistics, or values for F—one for testing each of the respective hypotheses.

TABLE 18-3 Expressions for Elements in Two-Factor Analysis and Format of the ANOVA Table

Variation	Degrees of Freedom	Sum of Squares	Mean Square	F
Explained by factor *A* (between rows)	$r-1$	$SSA = nc\sum_i (\bar{X}_{i..} - \bar{\bar{X}}_{...})^2$	$MSA = \dfrac{SSA}{r-1}$	$\dfrac{MSA}{MSE}$
Explained by factor *B* (between columns)	$c-1$	$SSB = nr\sum_j (\bar{X}_{.j.} - \bar{\bar{X}}_{...})^2$	$MSB = \dfrac{SSB}{c-1}$	$\dfrac{MSB}{MSE}$
Explained by interactions (between cells)	$(r-1)(c-1)$	$SSAB = n\sum_i\sum_j (\bar{X}_{ij.} - \bar{X}_{i..} + \bar{X}_{.j.} + \bar{\bar{X}}_{...})^2$	$MSAB = \dfrac{SSAB}{(r-1)(c-1)}$	$\dfrac{MSAB}{MSE}$
Error or unexplained (residual)	$rc(n-1)$	$SSE = \sum_i\sum_j\sum_k (X_{ijk} - \bar{X}_{ij.})^2$	$MSE = \dfrac{SSE}{rc(n-1)}$	
Total	$nrc-1$	$SSTO = \sum_i\sum_j\sum_k (X_{ijk} - \bar{\bar{X}}_{...})^2$		

Calculating Sums of Squares

Ordinarily, a set of streamlined expressions, equivalent to those in Table 18-3, would be used when making computations by hand with a calculator. Since their use does not significantly ease the computational burden, those expressions are not presented here. Rather, it is recommended that a *computer* be used when performing an analysis of variance. The sums of squares are then computed automatically and appear in the ANOVA table which is standard output for all of the popular statistical computer software packages.

Continuing with our advertising illustration, the following sums of squares are computed using the sample data.

$$\begin{aligned} SSA &= 4(4)[(1{,}054.19 - 1{,}008.81)^2 + (1{,}061.50 - 1{,}008.81)^2 \\ &\quad + (910.75 - 1{,}008.81)^2] \\ &= 231{,}221.5 \end{aligned}$$

$$\begin{aligned} SSB &= 4(3)[(1{,}067.50 - 1{,}008.81)^2 + (946.00 - 1{,}008.81)^2 \\ &\quad + (1{,}055.33 - 1{,}008.81)^2 + (966.42 - 1{,}008.81)^2] \\ &= 136{,}207.6 \end{aligned}$$

$$\begin{aligned} SSAB &= 4[(985.50 - 1{,}054.19 - 1{,}067.50 + 1{,}008.81)^2 \\ &\quad + (984.25 - 1{,}054.19 - 946.00 + 1{,}008.81)^2 \\ &\quad + \cdots + (857.00 - 910.95 - 966.42 + 1{,}008.81)^2] \\ &= 230{,}033.0 \end{aligned}$$

TABLE 18-4 ANOVA Table for Newspaper Advertisement Experiment

Variation	Degrees of Freedom	Sum of Squares	Mean Square	F
Explained by factor A: Position (between rows)	$r - 1 = 2$	$SSA = 231{,}221.5$	$MSA = SSA/2 = 115{,}610.75$	$MSA/MSE = 348.72$
Explained by factor B: Day of Week (between columns)	$c - 1 = 3$	$SSB = 136{,}207.6$	$MSB = SSB/3 = 45{,}402.53$	$MSB/MSE = 136.95$
Explained by interactions (between cells)	$(r - 1)(c - 1) = 6$	$SSAB = 230{,}033.0$	$MSAB = SSAB/6 = 38{,}338.83$	$MSAB/MSE = 115.64$
Error or unexplained (residual)	$rc(n - 1) = 36$	$SSE = 11{,}935.2$	$MSE = SSE/36 = 331.53$	
Total	$nrc - 1 = 47$	$SSTO = 609{,}397.3$		

$$SSE = (966 - 985.50)^2 + (1{,}004 - 985.50)^2 + \cdots + (872 - 857.00)^2$$
$$= 11{,}935.2$$
$$SSTO = (966 - 1{,}008.81)^2 + (1{,}004 - 1{,}008.81)^2 + \cdots + (872 - 1{,}008.81)^2$$
$$= 609{,}397.3$$

The ANOVA table is provided in Table 18-4.

Testing first the null hypothesis that there are *no interactions*, the computed value of the test statistic is

$$F = \frac{MSAB}{MSE} = 115.64$$

From Appendix Table G, using 6 degrees of freedom for the numerator and 36 for the denominator, the critical value when $\alpha = .01$ is $F_{.01} = 3.35$. Since the computed value exceeds the critical value, the null hypothesis of no interactions must be *rejected.*

Analogously, the computed value of $F = 348.72$ permits rejection at the $\alpha = .01$ level of the null hypothesis of identical mean returns at all levels of factor A—advertisement sectional position—since the critical value is only $F_{.01} = 5.25$ with 2 degrees of freedom for the numerator and 36 for the denominator. The computed value of $F = 136.95$ in testing equality of mean returns for factor B—day of week—also permits rejection at an $\alpha = .01$ significance level (when $F_{.01} = 4.38$ for 3 and 36 degrees of freedom).

DECIDING A COURSE OF ACTION

The preceding data indicate that the mean number of coupons returned differs both by newspaper section and by day of week. Furthermore, the presence of interactions proves that, for some sections, ads on a particular day may provide a higher mean response than in other sections.

Multiple Comparison Procedures

Depending on which of the null hypotheses is rejected, the next phase of the analysis involves comparing (1) specific factor-level means, (2) individual treatment (cell) means, or (3) various groupings of treatment means. Section 18-2 describes the procedures for doing this. Depending on whether or not the sample data indicate the presence of interactions, one of the following approaches will be taken.

1. *Significant interactions found.* Search the sample data for significant differences in treatment population (cell) means. The sample results may suggest further interesting comparisons.

2. *No interactions are significant.* Compare all factor-level means in each set for which the F test results in rejection of the null hypothesis of identical means. Isolate those pairs of means that differ significantly.

The mail order merchandiser in the present illustration should take the first approach.

COMPUTER-ASSISTED ANALYSIS

A high volume of calculations must be performed for a two-factor analysis, and the use of a computer is highly desirable. Figure 18-4 shows a computer printout of an analysis of variance run using the data for the advertising experiment.

SPECIAL CASE—ONE OBSERVATION PER CELL

A two-factor experiment may be conducted with a single observation per cell. In such cases, the investigation provides no replication and there is only $n = 1$ sample value for each treatment combination. The experiment is less discriminating than one that provides replication. Perhaps the greatest drawback is that the preceding procedure does not allow us to make inferences regarding interactions when only one observation is made from each cell. (However, an alternative procedure does exist but is beyond the scope of this text.)

The earlier notation is somewhat simplified, since when $n = 1$, $\bar{X}_{ij\cdot}$ is equal to the single observation in the cell. It is replaced here by X_{ij} (with no overbar). Also, the third dot is dropped from all subscripts in symbols representing the various sample means. The sums of squares SSA and SSB are computed as before. There is no $SSAB$ term. There are also some necessary modifications in computing $SSTO$ and SSE, and the number of degrees of freedom changes for the respective sources of variation. Table 18-5 shows the modified elements for constructing the ANOVA table.

EXAMPLE: TESTING SWIMMING POOL CHEMICALS AND ALKALINITY

A manufacturer of swimming pool chemicals is publishing a manual for everyday pool maintenance. An experiment is conducted to establish ground rules for homeowners when adding chlorine and acid. The data in Table 18-6 have been

COUPONS	OBS.	SUNDAY	MONDAY	FRIDAY	SATURDAY
NEWS	1	996	979	1240	990
	2	1004	975	1247	1018
	3	993	985	1253	1003
	4	979	998	1237	1000
SPORTS	1	1217	989	1022	1018
	2	1171	988	1011	1045
	3	1178	1002	1030	1037
	4	1230	992	996	1058
BUSINESS	1	1021	871	889	851
	2	1015	864	948	867
	3	1041	835	872	838
	4	995	874	919	872

Sample Means

COUPONS	SUNDAY	MONDAY	FRIDAY	SATURDAY	Sample Mean A
NEWS	985.5	984.25	1244.25	1002.75	1054.1875
SPORTS	1199.	992.75	1014.75	1039.5	1061.5
BUSINESS	1018.	861.	907.	857.	910.75
Sample Mean B	1067.5	946.	1055.333	966.4166	

Grand Mean = 1008.8125

ANOVA TABLE

Variation	Degrees of Freedom	Sum of Squares	Mean Square	F
Explained by Factor A	2	231217.875	115608.9375	348.810673204
Explained by Factor B	3	136214.729167	45404.9097222	136.99388187
Explained by Interactions	6	230032.958333	38338.8263889	115.674377187
Error or Unexplained	36	11931.75	331.4375	
Total	47	609397.3125		

Note: Figure generated on an IBM PC using EasyStat.

FIGURE 18-4 Computer printout for the newspaper advertisement study.

TABLE 18-5 Special Case—$n = 1$: Expressions for Modified Elements and Format of the ANOVA Table

Variation	Degrees of Freedom	Sum of Squares	Mean Square	F
Explained by factor *A* (between rows)	$r - 1$	$SSA = c \sum_{i=1}^{r} (\bar{X}_{i.} - \bar{\bar{X}}_{..})^2$	$MSA = \frac{SSA}{r - 1}$	$\frac{MSA}{MSE}$
Explained by factor *B* (between columns)	$c - 1$	$SSB = r \sum_{j=1}^{c} (\bar{X}_{.j} - \bar{\bar{X}}_{..})^2$	$MSB = \frac{SSB}{c - 1}$	$\frac{MSB}{MSE}$
Error or unexplained (residual)	$(r - 1)(c - 1)$	$SSE = \sum_{i=1}^{r} \sum_{j=1}^{c} (\bar{X}_{ij} - \bar{X}_{i.} - \bar{X}_{.j} + \bar{\bar{X}}_{..})^2$	$MSE = \frac{SSE}{(r - 1)(c - 1)}$	
Total	$rc - 1$	$SSTO = \sum_{i=1}^{r} \sum_{j=1}^{c} (X_{ij} - \bar{\bar{X}}_{..})^2$		

obtained from a random sample of swimming pools. In the table, factor *A* (chlorine concentration) and factor *B* (acidity level) are used to explain the monthly drop in alkalinity in parts per million (ppm). Pool acidity and chlorine are set at various levels to satisfy sanitation requirements, and for each combination of these factor levels, the drop in alkalinity must be offset periodically by adding soda ash. The null hypotheses of identical factor level means are tested.

SOLUTION: The ANOVA table is provided in Table 18-7. At $\alpha = .05$ levels of significance, the critical values are $F_{.05} = 5.14$ for chlorine *A* (with 2 and 6 degrees of freedom) and $F_{.05} = 4.76$ for acidity *B* (with 3 and 6 degrees of freedom). For both factors the null hypothesis of identical means at all levels must be *rejected.*

TABLE 18-6 Sample Results for Swimming Pool Chemical Experiment

Chlorine Concentration *A*	Acidity Level *B* (1) pH 7.2	(2) pH 7.4	(3) pH 7.6	(4) pH 7.8	Sample Mean
(1) Low	23	18	9	7	$\bar{X}_{1.} = 14.25$
(2) Medium	10	12	8	4	$\bar{X}_{2.} = 8.50$
(3) High	9	9	7	4	$\bar{X}_{3.} = 7.25$
Sample Mean	$\bar{X}_{.1} = 14$	$\bar{X}_{.2} = 13$	$\bar{X}_{.3} = 8$	$\bar{X}_{.4} = 5$	$\bar{X}_{..} = 10$

Note: Response = Monthly drop in swimming pool alkalinity (ppm).

TABLE 18-7 ANOVA Table for Swimming Pool Chemical Experiment

Variation	Degrees of Freedom	Sum of Squares	Mean Squares	F
Explained by factor A: Chlorine concentration (between rows)	$r - 1 = 2$	$SSA = 111.5$	$MSA = 111.5/2 = 55.75$	$MSA/MSE = 55.75/10.08 = 5.53$
Explained by factor B: Acidity level (between columns)	$c - 1 = 3$	$SSB = 162$	$MSB = 162/3 = 54$	$MSB/MSE = 54/10.08 = 5.36$
Error or unexplained (residual)	$(r - 1)(c - 1) = 6$	$SSE = 60.5$	$MSE = 60.5/6 = 10.08$	
Total	$rc - 1 = 11$	$SSTO = 334$		

EXERCISES

18-1 An investigator performs an analysis of variance involving 5 observations under each combination of levels for factor A and factor B. Factor A has 4 levels and factor B has 3 levels. The following results apply.

$$SSA = 532 \qquad SSB = 294 \qquad SSAB = 112 \qquad SSE = 24 \qquad SSTO = 962$$

(a) Construct the ANOVA table.

(b) At an $\alpha = .05$ significance level, indicate whether the investigator should accept or reject each of the following hypotheses.
   (1) H_0: no interactions between factor levels
   (2) H_0: identical means for all levels of factor A
   (3) H_0: identical means for all levels of factor B

18-2 The firm of Albers, Crumbly, and Itch wishes to conduct an experiment to assess what impact product display density and lighting brightness have on sales. The following sample unit sales are obtained.

Density A	Lighting Brightness B (1) Dim	(2) Low	(3) Medium	(4) High
(1) Loose	244	201	241	220
	244	204	235	222
	250	196	243	220
	242	199	241	218
(2) Tight	210	225	242	260
	212	226	245	260
	211	223	245	262
	207	226	249	266

(a) Compute the sample means and construct the ANOVA table.

(b) At the $\alpha = .05$ levels of significance, indicate whether the retailer should accept or reject each of the following hypotheses.
(1) H_0: no interactions between density and brightness
(2) H_0: identical means for all product densities
(3) H_0: identical means for all levels of brightness

(c) Using your answers to (b), indicate which of the following comparisons of mean unit sales, if any, should be made in a follow-on analysis.
(1) factor-level means for density
(2) factor-level means for brightness
(3) cell treatment means for density and brightness combinations

18-3 Spillsberry Bakeries wishes to conduct an experiment to assess what impact time of day and positioning of television spots have on telemarketing response. The following sample data provide the number of calls placed to the 800 number following a sample broadcast of the test spot.

Time of day A	Spot Position B			
	(1) On the Hour	(2) On the Half Hour	(3) Early in Program	(4) Late in Program
(1) Morning	55 51 53 51	65 66 59 65	72 69 66 73	44 38 40 38
(2) Afternoon	65 62 66 67	85 81 79 85	85 80 82 83	50 52 54 54
(3) Evening	85 78 83 84	95 88 91 86	85 88 83 84	40 42 39 39

(a) Compute the sample means and construct the ANOVA table.

(b) At the $\alpha = .01$ levels of significance, indicate whether the advertiser should accept or reject each of the following hypotheses.
(1) H_0: no interactions between timing and positioning
(2) H_0: identical means for all spot times
(3) H_0: identical means for all spot positions

(c) Using your answers to (b), which of the following comparisons of mean number of calls placed, if any, should be made in a follow-on analysis?
(1) factor-level means for time of day
(2) factor-level means for spot position
(3) cell treatment means for various combinations of time of day and spot position

18-4 A graduate student wishes to investigate what impact personal computer availability and undergraduate major have on building quantitative reasoning. She administers a quantitative skills test to four randomly selected students in each combination of factor levels listed below. The following sample scores achieved by the students were obtained.

Primary Computer A	Major B (1) IRM	(2) Management Science	(3) Accounting	(4) Finance
(1) PC at Home	97	85	88	75
	84	98	89	77
	93	67	97	73
	95	90	86	75
(2) Campus Lab	91	78	71	68
	85	80	89	68
	72	66	60	85
	77	88	64	51

(a) Compute the sample means and construct the ANOVA table.

(b) At the $\alpha = .05$ levels of significance, indicate whether the student should accept or reject each of the following hypotheses.
  (1) H_0: no interactions between primary computer and major
  (2) H_0: identical means for computer availabilities
  (3) H_0: identical means for all majors

(c) Using your answers to (b), indicate which of the following comparisons of mean quantitative skills test scores, if any, should be made in the follow-on analysis.
  (1) factor-level means for computer availability
  (2) factor-level means for major
  (3) cell treatment means for various combinations of computer availability and major

18-5 A production manager wishes to assess what impact assembly line speed and worker mobility have on production efficiency. He orders five pilot assembly runs under each combination of three different line speeds with two worker-stationing modes. The following number of defective assemblies per 1,000 units was determined for each and are provided below.

Line Speed A	Stationing Mode B (1) Fixed	(2) Mobile
(1) .5 mph	48	40
	53	38
	43	57
	59	34
	37	36
(2) .7 mph	58	50
	50	58
	53	43
	64	44
	65	55
(3) .9 mph	63	55
	69	45
	60	60
	68	60
	55	55

(a) Compute the sample means and construct the ANOVA table.
(b) At the $\alpha = .05$ levels of significance, indicate whether the manager should accept or reject each of the following hypotheses.
  (1) H_0: no interactions between line speed and stationing mode
  (2) H_0: identical means at various line speeds
  (3) H_0: identical means for all stationing modes
(c) Using your answers to (b), indicate which of the following comparisons of mean number of defective assemblies, if any, should be made in the follow-on analysis.
  (1) factor-level means for line speed
  (2) factor-level means for stationing mode
  (3) cell treatment means for various combinations of line speed and stationing mode

18-6 As an MBA research project, Shirley Smart conducted a sampling experiment using graduate applicants to the business school at her university. She uses GMAT scores as her response variable, with experience and major as the factors. The following data are obtained.

Primary Work Experience A	Undergraduate Major B (1) Business	(2) Technical	(3) Nontechnical
(1) Sales	605	595	555
	600	590	560
	595	590	545
	605	590	565
	605	605	555
(2) Staff	650	710	545
	625	695	555
	630	690	570
	645	685	565
	650	700	550
(3) Management	590	600	585
	575	615	570
	560	580	570
	550	570	600
	595	605	595
(4) Nonbusiness	575	650	580
	590	630	605
	595	635	560
	600	635	575
	600	650	595

(a) Compute the sample means and construct the ANOVA table.
(b) At the $\alpha = .01$ levels of significance, indicate whether the student should accept or reject each of the following hypotheses.
  (1) H_0: no interactions between experience and major
  (2) H_0: identical means for all types of experience
  (3) H_0: identical means for all majors
(c) Using your answers to (b), indicate which of the following comparisons of mean GMAT score, if any, should be made in the follow-on analysis.
  (1) factor-level means for primary experience
  (2) factor-level means for major
  (3) cell treatment means for various combinations of experience and major

18-7 The Old Ivy MBA Association wishes to assess the effects of alumni specialty A (six levels) and type of employment B (four levels) on the salary of persons who received their degrees between ten and fifteen years ago. The following data represent observations of one randomly chosen person from each category combination.

$$SSA = 640{,}000 \qquad SSB = 710{,}000 \qquad SSTO = 1{,}500{,}000$$

(a) Construct a one-factor ANOVA table using specialty as the only treatment. At an $\alpha = .01$ significance level, do you conclude that the treatment means differ?
(b) Construct a one-factor ANOVA table using type of employment as the only treatment. At an $\alpha = .01$ significance level, do you conclude that the treatment means differ?
(c) Construct a two-factor ANOVA table using both specialty and type of employment as factors. At an $\alpha = .01$ significance level, what conclusion is drawn regarding the respective null hypotheses of identical mean salaries for specialties and for types of employment?

18-8 An economist wishes to assess the effects of factor A (education) with five levels and factor B (occupation) with four levels on a person's annual earnings. The following data have been obtained in each category for 20 randomly chosen persons.

$$SSA = 800{,}000 \qquad SSB = 900{,}000 \qquad SSTO = 2{,}000{,}000$$

(a) Construct a one-factor ANOVA table using education as the only treatment. At an $\alpha = .05$ significance level, do you conclude that the treatment means differ?
(b) Construct a one-factor ANOVA table using occupation as the only treatment. At an $\alpha = .05$ significance level, do you conclude that the treatment means differ?
(c) Construct a two-factor ANOVA table using both education and occupation as treatments. At an $\alpha = .01$ significance level, what conclusion

is drawn regarding the respective null hypotheses for identical mean incomes for education levels and for occupations?

(d) Is there any discrepancy between the one-factor and the two-factor results? Explain.

18-2 ANALYSIS OF FACTOR EFFECTS

We find that constructing the ANOVA table and testing the null hypotheses are the easiest parts of a two-factor evaluation. The next phase is concerned with the analysis of factor effects, accomplished largely by comparing various means.

In the absence of any significant interactions, pairwise comparisons may be made of the factor-level means, either for the rows ($\mu_{i.}$'s), for the columns ($\mu_{.j}$'s), or for both, in accordance with which of these groups is found to have significantly different means by the respective F test. By constructing a set of collective confidence intervals, we are able to identify those pairs of means that significantly differ.

When the F test indicates the presence of interactions between factors, the analysis instead involves pairwise comparisons of the treatment (cell) population means (μ_{ij}'s). Again, this is done by constructing collective confidence intervals and then identifying μ's that significantly differ.

Recall, from Chapter 17, that multiple comparisons must be made under the umbrella of a collective confidence level. Here, two methods, the Tukey and Scheffé, will be described for doing this. The Tukey method applies when no significant interactions were found in the analysis of variance phase. The Scheffé method applies when interactions were found previously. Both methods maximize the comparisons that may be made (at some small price in reduced precision over alternative procedures). One important advantage of the Tukey and Scheffé methods is that *they free the investigator of any concern over identifying, in advance, which comparisons to make.*

NO INTERACTIONS CASE: MULTIPLE PAIRWISE COMPARISONS OF FACTOR-LEVEL MEANS

Two procedures, the Tukey and the Bonferroni, were discussed in Chapter 17 for comparing factor-level means. Although both methods may be extended to multiple-factor analyses, the Tukey method tends to provide the more precise set of interval estimates when *all* mean pairs are to be examined.

TUKEY METHOD

This procedure is based on the studentized range distribution (with critical values listed in Appendix Table K). A separate set of intervals must be constructed independently for each factor—but only for those factors for which the respective H_0 of equal means (no main effects) has already been rejected. When the H_0's for both have been rejected, the overall level of confidence must be split for the two interval groups. Consider the following examples.

Family	Group Collective Confidence Level: Factor A $100(1 - \alpha_1)\%$	Group Collective Confidence Level: Factor B $100(1 - \alpha_2)\%$	Family Collective Confidence Level $100(1 - \alpha_1 - \alpha_2)\%$
1	$100(1 - .05) = 95\%$	$100(1 - .05) = 95\%$	$100(1 - .05 - .05) = 90\%$
2	$100(1 - .01) = 99\%$	$100(1 - .01) = 99\%$	$100(1 - .01 - .01) = 98\%$
3	$100(1 - .05) = 95\%$	$100(1 - .01) = 99\%$	$100(1 - .05 - .01) = 94\%$
4	$100(1 - .05) = 95\%$	$100(1 - .10) = 90\%$	$100(1 - .05 - .10) = 85\%$

The following expressions for factors A and B are used to compute the $100(1 - \alpha_1 - \alpha_2)\%$

TUKEY COLLECTIVE CONFIDENCE INTERVAL ESTIMATES OF THE DIFFERENCES BETWEEN FACTOR-LEVEL MEANS

$$\mu_{i\cdot} - \mu_{m\cdot} = \bar{X}_{i\cdot\cdot} - \bar{X}_{m\cdot\cdot} \pm q_{1-\alpha_1}\sqrt{\frac{MSE}{cn}} \qquad \text{(factor } A\text{)}$$

where the parameters for the numerator and the denominator are r and $rc(n - 1)$, respectively. And, we have

$$\mu_{\cdot j} - \mu_{\cdot k} = \bar{X}_{\cdot j\cdot} - \bar{X}_{\cdot k\cdot} \pm q_{1-\alpha_2}\sqrt{\frac{MSE}{rn}} \qquad \text{(factor } B\text{)}$$

where the parameters for the numerator and the denominator are c and $rc(n - 1)$, respectively.

Any pairwise differences having confidence intervals lying totally above or totally below zero correspond to factor-level means that are significantly different at the family collective level $\alpha_1 + \alpha_2$.

ILLUSTRATION: EVALUATING A BANK'S CHECK PROCESSING PROCEDURES

To illustrate the procedure, consider the results in Table 18-8. The data were obtained from a bank's evaluation of its check processing procedures. This sampling experiment involves $n = 5$ observations per treatment, one for each combination of $r = 4$ factor A levels (sorting scheme) and $c = 3$ factor B levels (encoding method). The response variable is the error rate (errors per thousand checks).

F tests establish that the factor-level means differ both for sorting scheme A and encoding method B, although no significant interactions are present.

TABLE 18-8 Summary Sample Results (Error Rates) for Check Processing Evaluation

Sorting Scheme A	Encoding Method B (1) On-Line	(2) Batched	(3) Off-Line	Factor B Mean
(1) Full Re-sorting	$\bar{X}_{11.} = 11.0$	$\bar{X}_{12.} = 14.2$	$\bar{X}_{13.} = 25.6$	$\bar{X}_{1..} = 16.93$
(2) No Re-sorting	$\bar{X}_{21.} = 23.4$	$\bar{X}_{22.} = 26.4$	$\bar{X}_{23.} = 34.2$	$\bar{X}_{2..} = 28.00$
(3) Partial Re-sorting	$\bar{X}_{31.} = 12.0$	$\bar{X}_{32.} = 16.0$	$\bar{X}_{33.} = 29.2$	$\bar{X}_{3..} = 19.07$
(4) Terminal Sort	$\bar{X}_{41.} = 11.0$	$\bar{X}_{42.} = 15.2$	$\bar{X}_{43.} = 26.8$	$\bar{X}_{4..} = 17.67$
Factor A Mean	$\bar{X}_{.1.} = 14.35$	$\bar{X}_{.2.} = 17.95$	$\bar{X}_{.3.} = 28.95$	$\bar{\bar{X}}_{...} = 20.42$

The ANOVA table is provided in Table 18-9. We use 90% as the collective family confidence level, to be split evenly between both factors, so that $\alpha_1 = \alpha_2 = .05$. Then, using parameters $[4, 4(3)(5-1)] = (4, 48)$ for factor A and (3,48) for factor B, the critical values of q are read from Appendix Table K. With linear interpolation, these values are $q_{.95} = 3.77$ for factor A and $q_{.95} = 3.42$ for factor B.

Let's first consider factor A, sorting scheme. The following interval is constructed for the difference in mean error rates between the no re-sorting (2) and full re-sorting (1) schemes.

$$\mu_{2.} - \mu_{1.} = \bar{X}_{2..} - \bar{X}_{1..} \pm q_{.95}\sqrt{\frac{MSE}{3(5)}}$$

$$= 28.00 - 16.93 \pm 3.77\sqrt{\frac{11.37}{15}}$$

$$= 11.07 \pm 3.28$$

or

No − Full re-sorting: $7.79 \le \mu_{2.} - \mu_{1.} \le 14.35$ (significant)

TABLE 18-9 ANOVA Table for Check Processing Evaluation

Variation	Degrees of Freedom	Sum of Squares	Mean Square	F
Explained by factor *A* Sorting scheme	$r - 1 = 3$	$SSA = 1{,}185.38$	$MSA = 395.13$	34.76
Explained by factor *B*: Encoding Method	$c - 1 = 2$	$SSB = 2{,}314.13$	$MSB = 1{,}157.07$	101.79
Explained by interactions	$(r-1)(c-1) = 6$	$SSAB = 65.47$	$MSAB = 10.91$	0.96
Error or unexplained	$rc(n-1) = 48$	$SSE = 545.60$	$MSE = 11.37$	
Total	$nrc - 1 = 59$	$SSTO = 4{,}110.58$		

All remaining factor A pairwise differences have the same width. The following confidence intervals apply.

$$\begin{aligned}
\text{Partial} - \text{Full re-sorting:}\quad & -1.14 \leq \mu_{3.} - \mu_{1.} \leq 5.42 \\
\text{Terminal sort} - \text{Full re-sorting:}\quad & -2.54 \leq \mu_{4.} - \mu_{1.} \leq 4.02 \\
\text{Partial} - \text{No re-sorting:}\quad & -12.21 \leq \mu_{3.} - \mu_{2.} \leq -5.65 \text{ (significant)} \\
\text{Terminal sort} - \text{No re-sorting:}\quad & -13.61 \leq \mu_{4.} - \mu_{2.} \leq -7.05 \text{ (significant)} \\
\text{Terminal sort} - \text{Partial re-sorting:}\quad & -4.68 \leq \mu_{4.} - \mu_{3.} \leq 1.88
\end{aligned}$$

The above intervals show a significant difference between $\mu_{2.}$ (no re-sorting) and each of the other sorting scheme means. But since the remaining intervals all overlap zero, no significant differences exist between the mean error rates for partial (3) and either full re-sorting (1) or terminal sort (4), nor between the latter two schemes. It appears that level (2) of factor A, no re-sorting, provides significantly higher error rates than any other sorting scheme, while the other schemes do not have significantly different mean error rates.

Because factor B, encoding method, has a different number of levels, confidence intervals for its pairwise differences will have a different width. The following interval is constructed for the difference in mean error rates between batched (2) and on-line encoding (1).

$$\begin{aligned}
\mu_{.2} - \mu_{.1} &= \bar{X}_{.2.} - \bar{X}_{.1.} \pm q_{.95}\sqrt{\frac{MSE}{4(5)}} \\
&= 17.95 - 14.35 \pm 3.42\sqrt{\frac{11.37}{20}} \\
&= 3.60 \pm 2.58
\end{aligned}$$

or

$$\text{Batched} - \text{On-line:}\quad 1.02 \leq \mu_{.2} - \mu_{.1} \leq 6.18 \quad \text{(significant)}$$

All remaining factor B pairwise differences have the same width (which is narrower than the one used for the preceding set of intervals). The following confidence intervals apply.

$$\begin{aligned}
\text{Off-line} - \text{On-line:}\quad & 12.02 \leq \mu_{.3} - \mu_{.1} \leq 17.18 \quad \text{(significant)} \\
\text{Off-line} - \text{Batched:}\quad & 8.42 \leq \mu_{.3} - \mu_{.2} \leq 13.58 \quad \text{(significant)}
\end{aligned}$$

The mean error rates differ significantly for all pairs of factor B levels for the encoding method.

Thus, we may conclude at the $\alpha_1 + \alpha_2 = .05 + .05 = .10$ family collective significance level that no re-sorting (2-A) provides higher mean error rates than any other sorting scheme, and the other sorting schemes do not differ. We may also conclude that all encoding methods provide different mean error rates, with the on-line method (1-B) yielding the lowest mean error rate and the off-line method (3-B) the highest.

Special Case—One Observation per Cell

When there is only $n = 1$ cell observation for each factor-level combination, the above procedure still applies but the q-parameter must be modified by replacing the term $rc(n - 1)$ with $(r - 1)(c - 1)$.

SIGNIFICANT INTERACTIONS CASE: MULTIPLE CONTRASTS AMONG TREATMENT MEANS

When there are interactions, the individual treatment (cell) population means may be meaningfully compared. Thus, collective confidence intervals involving the μ_{ij}'s may be constructed and will pinpoint specific significant differences. Various groupings of cell means—not just pairs—may be compared. Such comparisons may be made in terms of **contrasts**. The following expression provides the

CONTRAST IN TREATMENT (CELL) POPULATION MEANS

$$L = \sum_{i=1}^{r} \sum_{j=1}^{c} w_{ij}\mu_{ij} \qquad \text{where} \qquad \sum_{i=1}^{r} \sum_{j=1}^{c} w_{ij} = 0$$

All contrasts involve weighted sums of the cell population means, with the requirement that the weights be real numbers and sum to zero. (*Pairwise differences* in the μ_{ij}'s are contrasts where one weight equals $+1$, a second weight is -1, and the remaining weights are zero.)

SCHEFFÉ METHOD

The Scheffé method allows collective confidence intervals to be constructed for *any number* of contrasts, without requiring that they be specified in advance. This allows the investigator to "snoop," sifting and sorting the data to find meaningful comparisons.

Being able to look at the data first is a very important advantage of the Scheffé method—especially in multiple-factor investigations where the number of pairwise differences may be huge. (For example, in an 8 by 4 experimental layout there are $rc = 8(4) = 32$ cells, so that there are 496 possible pairings of μ_{ij}'s.) And, for any investigation there is an unlimited number of contrast possibilities.

The following expression is used in constructing the $100(1 - \alpha)\%$

SCHEFFÉ COLLECTIVE CONFIDENCE INTERVAL ESTIMATES OF MULTIPLE CONTRASTS

$$L = \sum_{i=1}^{r} \sum_{j=1}^{c} w_{ij}\bar{X}_{ij\cdot} \pm \sqrt{(rc - 1)F_{\alpha}\left(\frac{MSE}{n}\right) \sum_{i=1}^{r} \sum_{j=1}^{c} w_{ij}^2}$$

where the number of degrees of freedom is denoted by $rc - 1$ for the numerator and $rc(n - 1)$ for the denominator.

To illustrate the Scheffé method, we will continue with the newspaper advertisement study illustrated in Section 18-1. But before we express any particular contrasts and construct the corresponding confidence intervals, it is helpful to examine in detail the sample data to see which comparisons are meaningful.

Finding Meaningful Comparisons: Plotting the Data

When the number of treatments (cells) is large, it is helpful to plot the sample results. In Figure 18-5, each data point shown has been obtained from Table 18-2. The mean responses are plotted for the levels of factor A (sectional position), with a separate set of connected points provided for the levels of factor B (day of week).

The presence of significant interactions between sectional position A and day of week B are reflected by lines that oscillate and even cross. (The lines for factor B would tend to be parallel if no interaction existed.)

Much of the fluctuation in plot lines is to be expected and may be attributed to chance sampling error. The Scheffé method helps us to sort things out by isolating pairwise differences and other contrasts that differ significantly from zero. In identifying the significant pairwise differences it is not necessary to construct confidence intervals for each. This is because *all such intervals will have identical widths*, so that the essential information is given by the first confidence interval constructed. The cell pairs having significantly different means are those with $\bar{X}_{ij.}$'s separated by more than half the width of the first interval found. For our present illustration, a collective confidence level of 95% ($\alpha = .05$) will be used.

Constructing the Intervals

Although any cell pair may serve as the first interval, we use the μ_{ij}'s with the biggest gap. Thus, we consider the difference between the mean coupons returned from ads in the news section (1) on Friday (3) [cell (1,3)] and the business section (3) on Saturday (4) [cell (3,4)]. This difference provides the contrast

$$L_1 = \mu_{13} - \mu_{34} \qquad \text{(where } w_{13} = 1, w_{34} = -1 \text{ and all other } w_{ij}\text{'s} = 0)$$

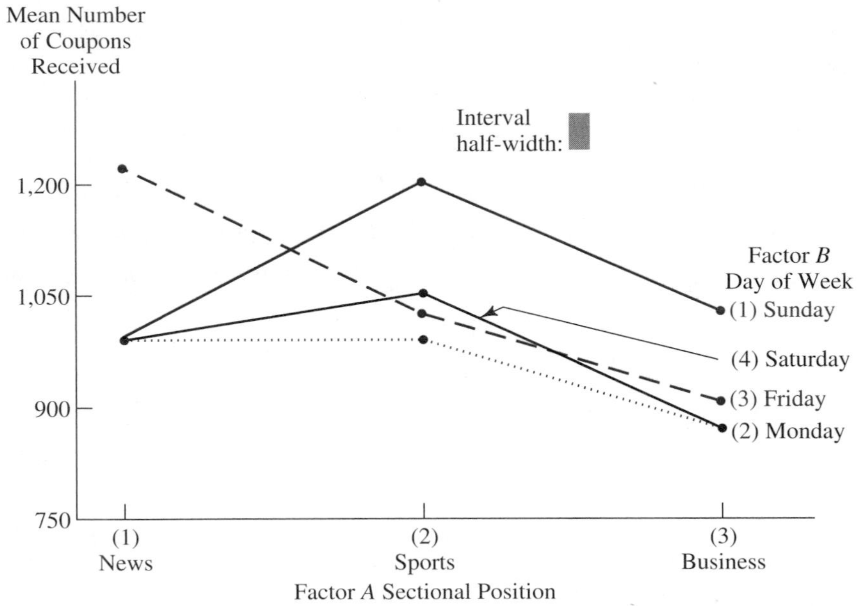

FIGURE 18-5 Sample treatment (cell) means for newspaper advertisement study.

When degrees of freedom are $rc - 1 = 11$ for the numerator and $rc(n - 1) = 36$ for the denominator, Appendix Table G provides the critical value $F_{.05} = 2.06$. Using $MSE = 331.53$ and the sample means from Table 18-2, the following confidence interval applies.

$$L_1 = \mu_{13} - \mu_{34} = (1)\bar{X}_{13\cdot} + (-1)\bar{X}_{34\cdot}$$

$$\pm \sqrt{[3(4) - 1](2.06)\left(\frac{331.53}{4}\right)[(1)^2 + (-1)^2]}$$

$$= 1{,}244.25 - 857.00 \pm 61.29$$

$$= 387.25 \pm 61.29$$

or

$$\begin{matrix}\text{News} \\ \text{on Friday}\end{matrix} - \begin{matrix}\text{Business} \\ \text{on Saturday:}\end{matrix}\ 325.96 \leq \mu_{13} - \mu_{34} \leq 448.54 \qquad \text{(significant)}$$

Since the above interval lies wholly above zero, the difference $\mu_{13} - \mu_{34}$ is significantly nonzero at an $\alpha = .05$ collective confidence level.

All other pairwise cell mean comparisons having a difference exceeding 61.29 in absolute value share this property. Slightly more than half of the 66 possible pairs of cell means provide significant differences. Of course, the mail order merchandiser would only be interested in a few of these.

The greatest mean coupon returns occur when ads are placed in the news section on Fridays and in the sports section on Sundays. Although the corresponding means μ_{13} and μ_{21} do not differ significantly, each is greater than any of the other μ_{ij}'s. Also, the lowest returns occur when ads are placed in the business section on Mondays and Saturdays. Both of the corresponding population means, μ_{32} and μ_{34}, are significantly smaller than all but μ_{33} (business section on Friday).

Quick perusal of Figure 18-5 shows that, on a section-by-section basis, the following means are significantly different.

(1) News	**(2) Sports**	**(3) Business**
(Fri.) $\mu_{13} > \mu_{14}$ (Sat.)	(Sun.) $\mu_{21} > \mu_{23}$ (Fri.)	(Sun.) $\mu_{31} > \mu_{33}$ (Fri.)
(Fri.) $\mu_{13} > \mu_{11}$ (Sun.)	(Sun.) $\mu_{21} > \mu_{22}$ (Mon.)	(Sun.) $\mu_{31} > \mu_{32}$ (Mon.)
(Fri.) $\mu_{13} > \mu_{12}$ (Mon.)	(Sun.) $\mu_{21} > \mu_{24}$ (Sat.)	(Sun.) $\mu_{31} > \mu_{34}$ (Sat.)

We see that the Friday news section provides the strongest mean response. The sports section is best on Sunday and strong on Saturday, while business ads perform best on Sunday.

On a daily basis, it is easy to verify that sports provides the greatest mean coupon return on all days but Friday, when news is the highest-return section. On no day does the business section provide the strongest mean response.

In addition to pairwise differences, some *group comparisons* are suggested by the data plot. It appears that the weekends provide the strongest responses, but just for the sports section. The following comparison is suggested.

Sports on weekends versus Sports on weekdays

The difference in the average of the respective cell means provides the following contrast.

$$L_2 = \frac{\mu_{21} + \mu_{24}}{2} - \frac{\mu_{22} + \mu_{23}}{2}$$

The respective weights are +.50 for the two cells represented by the first term and −.50 for the two cells in the last term. In this contrast, all remaining cells have weights of zero. The point estimate of the above is

$$\begin{aligned} &.50(\bar{X}_{21\cdot}) + (-.50)(\bar{X}_{22\cdot}) + (-.50)(\bar{X}_{23\cdot}) + .50(\bar{X}_{24\cdot}) \\ &\quad = .50(1{,}199.00) - .50(992.75) - .50(1{,}014.75) + .50(1{,}039.50) \\ &\quad = 115.50 \end{aligned}$$

and the sum of squared weights is

$$(.50)^2 + (-.50)^2 + (-.50)^2 + (.50)^2 = 1.00$$

Thus,

$$\begin{aligned} L_2 &= 115.50 \pm \sqrt{[3(4) - 1](2.06)\left(\frac{331.53}{4}\right)(1.00)} \\ &= 115.50 \pm 43.34 \end{aligned}$$

or

$$\begin{matrix}\text{Sports} \\ \text{on weekends}\end{matrix} - \begin{matrix}\text{Sports} \\ \text{on weekdays:}\end{matrix} \quad 72.16 \le L_2 \le 158.84 \qquad \text{(significant)}$$

The data plot in Figure 18-5 suggests the following third contrast for Sunday versus Monday placement of ads.

$$L_3 = \frac{\mu_{11} + \mu_{21} + \mu_{31}}{3} - \frac{\mu_{12} + \mu_{22} + \mu_{32}}{3}$$

Each of the first three cells listed above has weight +1/3 and the last three each have weight −1/3, with zero weight applying to the unlisted cells. The point estimate of the above is

$$\begin{aligned} &(1/3)(\bar{X}_{11\cdot} + \bar{X}_{21\cdot} + \bar{X}_{31\cdot}) + (-1/3)(\bar{X}_{12\cdot} + \bar{X}_{22\cdot} + \bar{X}_{32\cdot}) \\ &\quad = (1/3)(985.50 + 1{,}199.00 + 1{,}018.00) + (-1/3)(984.25 + 992.75 + 861.00) \\ &\quad = 121.50 \end{aligned}$$

and the sum of squared weights is

$$3(1/3)^2 + 3(-1/3)^2 = .667$$

Thus,

$$\begin{aligned} L_3 &= 121.50 \pm \sqrt{[3(4) - 1](2.06)\left(\frac{331.53}{4}\right)(.667)} \\ &= 121.50 \pm 35.39 \end{aligned}$$

or

$$\text{Sunday} - \text{Monday:} \quad 86.11 \leq L_3 \leq 156.89 \qquad \text{(significant)}$$

A final contrast suggested by the data is one that may be used to compare nonbusiness to business placements of ads, regardless of day.

$$L_4 = \frac{\mu_{11} + \mu_{12} + \mu_{13} + \mu_{14} + \mu_{21} + \mu_{22} + \mu_{23} + \mu_{24}}{8} - \frac{\mu_{31} + \mu_{32} + \mu_{33} + \mu_{34}}{4}$$

The corresponding sample means provide

$$\begin{aligned}&(1/8)(\bar{X}_{11\cdot} + \bar{X}_{12\cdot} + \bar{X}_{13\cdot} + \bar{X}_{14\cdot} + \bar{X}_{21\cdot} + \bar{X}_{22\cdot} + \bar{X}_{23\cdot} + \bar{X}_{24\cdot})\\ &\quad - (1/4)(\bar{X}_{31\cdot} + \bar{X}_{32\cdot} + \bar{X}_{33\cdot} + \bar{X}_{34\cdot})\\ &\quad = 147.09\end{aligned}$$

The eight cells have weight + 1/8, outnumbering the last four cells that have negative weight of − 1/4. The sum of squared weights is

$$8(1/8)^2 + 4(-1/4)^2 = .375$$

Thus,

$$\begin{aligned}L_4 &= 147.09 \pm \sqrt{[3(4) - 1](2.06)\left(\frac{331.53}{4}\right)(.375)}\\ &= 147.09 \pm 26.54\end{aligned}$$

or

$$\text{Nonbusiness} - \text{Business:} \quad 120.55 \leq L_4 \leq 173.63 \qquad \text{(significant)}$$

Confidence Summary Statement

At the overall collective level of confidence, the separate statements may be combined into an omnibus statement. The following 95% confidence summary statement applies to the present illustration.

The greatest mean coupon returns occur when ads are placed in the news section on Fridays and in the sports section on Sundays. Also, the lowest returns occur when ads are placed in the business section on Mondays and Saturdays. A sectional breakdown shows that on Friday, news placement is best. On Sunday, sports does best, and also on Sunday, business achieves its highest mean response. A daily breakdown shows that placement of ads in the sports section gives the highest mean response on all days but Friday, when the news section is best. Regardless of day, business is never the strongest section. Further comparisons show that, on the average, the sports section does best on weekends while Sundays have a higher mean coupon return than Mondays. Furthermore, the average performance of the two nonbusiness sections exceeds that of the business section.

EXERCISES

18-9 Refer to Exercise 18-5 and to your answers. Assume that no significant interactions are found. Using a 90% collective level of confidence, construct Tukey interval estimates of each pairwise difference in factor-level means. Use $\alpha_1 = \alpha_2$. What should you conclude?

18-10 Refer to Exercise 18-4 and to your answers. Assume that no significant interactions are found. Using a 94% collective level of confidence, construct Tukey interval estimates of each pairwise difference in factor-level means. Use $\alpha_1 = .01$ and $\alpha_2 = .05$. What should you conclude?

18-11 Refer to Exercise 18-3 and to your answers. All conclusions are to be made at an overall 95% collective confidence level.

(a) Using time of day as the horizontal axis and mean number of calls placed as the vertical axis, plot on a common graph the sample cell means for each spot position.
(b) Construct a confidence interval estimate of the difference $\mu_{21} - \mu_{11}$.
(c) For which cell pairs do the means significantly differ?
(d) Express the contrast for each of the following comparisons in terms of differences in average cell means for applicable groupings. Then, construct interval estimates of each.
   (1) Daytime versus evening
   (2) On the hour versus other times
(e) Incorporating any further contrasts you deem important, give an overall summary statement at a 95% collective confidence level.

18-12 Refer to the swimming pool chemical example in Section 18-1. Using an 80% collective level of confidence, construct Tukey interval estimates of each pairwise difference in factor-level means. Use $\alpha_1 = \alpha_2$. What should you conclude?

18-13 Refer to Exercise 18-6 and to your answers. All conclusions are to be made at an overall 95% collective confidence level.

(a) Plot the cell mean response against levels of factor A, with one set of data points for each level of factor B.
(b) Construct a confidence interval estimate of the difference $\mu_{21} - \mu_{11}$.
(c) For which cell pairs do the means significantly differ?
(d) Express the contrast for each of the following comparisons in terms of differences in average cell means for applicable groupings. Then, construct interval estimates of each.
   (1) Technical versus nontechnical
   (2) Sales versus nonsales
(e) Incorporating any further contrasts you deem important, give an overall summary statement at a 95% collective confidence level.

18-14 Refer to Exercise 18-2 and to your answers. All conclusions are to be made at an overall 99% collective confidence level.

(a)–(c) Repeat Exercise 18-13.
(d) Express the contrast for each of the following comparisons in terms of differences in average cell means for applicable groupings. Then, construct interval estimates of each.
   (1) Weak light (dim or low) versus good light
   (2) Loose versus tight
(e) Incorporating any further contrasts you deem important, give an overall summary statement at a 99% collective confidence level.

18-3 THE RANDOMIZED BLOCK DESIGN

An important class of two-factor studies involves a randomized block design. Here, the second factor is used primarily to reduce the amount of unexplained

TABLE 18-10 Randomized Block Design for Sod Yield (square yards)

	Fertilizer Treatment			
Blocks	**(1) Quarter Dosage, Once Weekly**	**(2) Half Dosage, Every Two Weeks**	**(3) Full Dosage, Every Four Weeks**	**Mean Yield**
(1) Parcel *A*	77	83	80	$\bar{X}_{1\cdot} = 80$
(2) Parcel *B*	79	91	82	$\bar{X}_{2\cdot} = 84$
(3) Parcel *C*	87	94	86	$\bar{X}_{3\cdot} = 89$
(4) Parcel *D*	85	88	85	$\bar{X}_{4\cdot} = 86$
(5) Parcel *E*	78	85	80	$\bar{X}_{5\cdot} = 81$
Mean Yield	$\bar{X}_{\cdot 1} = 81.2$	$\bar{X}_{\cdot 2} = 88.2$	$\bar{X}_{\cdot 3} = 82.6$	$\bar{\bar{X}}_{\cdot\cdot} = 84$

variation in response, thereby increasing the efficacy of the analysis of variance over what is achieved with a single factor (treatment variable).

ILLUSTRATION: EVALUATING THREE DIFFERENT FERTILIZER TREATMENTS

In our analysis of the sod-yield data in Chapter 17, the test results were barely significant to warrant rejecting the H_0 of identical treatment means at a 5% level. At $\alpha = .01$, however, H_0 must be accepted, because there would be too much unexplained variation in sod yields to justify rejecting H_0 at this lower level. Is it possible to lower the level of unexplained variation by explaining a portion of it in terms of another factor? Perhaps some differences in yield may be explained by varying soil qualities, slopes of plots, or watering methods—all of which may be influential factors if the plots were in homogeneous parcels of land.

Suppose that every sample observation consisted of three neighboring plots in each of five separate parcels owned by the farmer and that each treatment was randomly assigned to one plot in every parcel. We may then treat the parcel as a second factor in the analysis. Although the farmer wishes to determine how sod yields are affected by fertilizer treatments (not by the parcels themselves, which are permanent features of the farm), considering the parcels as a second factor may explain some of the differences in yields. In this section, we will describe a procedure employed for this purpose.

Each parcel of land is referred to as a **block**. In Table 18-10, the original sod-yield data are arranged by block and treatment.* This arrangement is called a **randomized block design**, because treatments have been randomly assigned to units within each block. Although the blocks in our illustration are represented as contiguous, presumably rectangular areas (like "city blocks"), the term actually refers to a second factor in the analysis that is used primarily to reduce the unexplained variation by ensuring that the sample units in each block are homogeneous.

*Of course, both the single-factor and randomized-blocking procedures should not be used for the same sample data. The same data set is used here just for purposes of illustration.

The sod farmer is still faced with his earlier question: Are mean sod yields affected by fertilizer treatments? His null hypothesis is the same as before.

$$H_0\colon \mu_1 = \mu_2 = \mu_3$$

Extending the procedure outlined in Chapter 17, which we now refer to as **one-factor analysis of variance**, provides us with another source of variation. In addition to treatments and error variation, **blocks variation**—attributable to differences between blocks—is a third component of total variation.

ANALYTICAL FRAMEWORK AND THEORETICAL MODEL

The underlying model for a two-factor randomized block design treats each observation as the following sum.

$$X_{ij} = \mu_{..} + B_i + T_j + \varepsilon_{ij}$$

where $\mu_{..}$ denotes the overall population mean, B_i is the blocking effect for block i, T_j is the treatment effect, and ε_{ij} denotes the error term. The ε's are assumed to be independent normally distributed random variables with mean zero and standard deviation σ. There are r blocks (levels of the blocking variable), one for each row. There is a separate column for each treatment (level of the treatments variable), and there are c of these. There must be exactly one observation under each treatment and for each block, and every treatment is represented exactly once by each block. Thus, $n = 1$ observation per cell.

The two-factor notation is simplified, with X_{ij} (with no overbar) used in place of $\bar{X}_{ij..}$. Also, a third dot is not needed in the subscripts of symbols representing the various sample means. The analytical framework may be explained in terms of the following partitioning of the deviations.

$$\begin{array}{ccccccc} \text{Total deviation} & = & \text{Treatments deviation} & + & \text{Blocks deviation} & + & \text{Error deviation} \\ (X_{ij} - \bar{\bar{X}}_{..}) & = & (\bar{X}_{.j} - \bar{\bar{X}}_{..}) & + & (\bar{X}_{i.} - \bar{\bar{X}}_{..}) & + & (X_{ij} - \bar{X}_{i.} - \bar{X}_{.j} + \bar{\bar{X}}_{..}) \end{array}$$

As with the earlier procedures, the collective sums of individual squared deviations are used to express the amount of variability for the several groups.

$$\begin{array}{ccccccc} \text{Total variation} & = & \text{Treatments variation} & + & \text{Blocks variation} & + & \text{Error variation} \\ SSTO & = & SSTR & + & SSBL & + & SSE \end{array}$$

The respective computed sums of squares form the basis for evaluation and are most helpful when arranged in an ANOVA table. Table 18-11 shows the general form of the ANOVA table. There, the expressions are given for the sums of squares, mean squares, and number of degrees of freedom.

The following null hypothesis of equal treatment population means is to be tested.

$$H_0\colon \mu_{.1} = \mu_{.2} = \cdots = \mu_{.c}$$

TABLE 18-11 Randomized Block Design: Expressions for Elements and Format of the ANOVA Table

Variation	Degrees of Freedom	Sum of Squares	Mean Square	F
Explained by treatments (between columns)	$c - 1$	$SSTR = r\sum_{j=1}^{c} (\bar{X}_{.j} - \bar{\bar{X}}_{..})^2$	$MSTR = \frac{SSTR}{c - 1}$	$\frac{MSTR}{MSE}$
Explained by blocks (between rows)	$r - 1$	$SSBL = c\sum_{i=1}^{r} (\bar{X}_{i.} - \bar{\bar{X}}_{..})^2$	$MSBL = \frac{SSBL}{r - 1}$	*
Error or unexplained (residual)	$(r - 1)(c - 1)$	$SSE = \sum_{i=1}^{r} \sum_{j=1}^{c} (X_{ij} - \bar{X}_{i.} - \bar{X}_{.j} + \bar{\bar{X}}_{..})^2$	$MSE = \frac{SSE}{(r - 1)(c - 1)}$	
Total	$rc - 1$	$SSTO = \sum_{i=1}^{r} \sum_{j=1}^{c} (X_{ij} - \bar{\bar{X}}_{..})^2$		

*In the randomized block design, F is not ordinarily computed for blocks.

This is accomplished in the usual manner by computing the F statistic using

$$F = \frac{\text{Variation explained by treatments}}{\text{Unexplained variation}} = \frac{MSTR}{MSE}$$

TESTING THE NULL HYPOTHESIS FOR ONE FACTOR

The ANOVA table for our sod-fertilization experiment under the randomized block design appears in Table 18-12. Some of the values ($SSTR$ and $SSTO$) are unchanged from the single-factor evaluation in Chapter 17. There is a new row for the blocks variation, and SSE is now smaller. The degrees of freedom are also different.

The following hypothesis-testing steps apply.

STEP 1

Formulate the null hypothesis. We wish to test whether the mean yields of all fertilizer treatments are equal. The following null hypothesis applies.

$$H_0: \mu_{.1} = \mu_{.2} = \mu_{.3}$$

STEP 2

Select the test statistic and procedure. The test statistic is calculated from

$$F = \frac{\text{Variance explained by treatments}}{\text{Unexplained variance}} = \frac{MSTR}{MSE}$$

TABLE 18-12 ANOVA Table for Sod-Fertilization Experiment under Randomized Block Design

Variation	Degrees of Freedom	Sum of Squares	Mean Square	F
Explained by treatments (between columns)	$c - 1 = 2$	$SSTR = 137.2$	$MSTR = 137.2/2 = 68.6$	$MSTR/MSE = 68.6/3.6 = 19.06$
Explained by blocks (between rows)	$r - 1 = 4$	$SSBL = 162$	$MSBL = 162/4 = 40.5$	
Error or unexplained (residual)	$(r - 1)(c - 1) = 8$	$SSE = 28.8$	$MSE = 28.8/8 = 3.6$	
Total	$rc - 1 = 14$	$SSTO = 328$		

STEP 3
Establish the significance level and identify the acceptance and rejection regions. A 1% ($\alpha = .01$) significance level is assumed. The degrees of freedom are $c - 1 = 3 - 1 = 2$ for the numerator and $(r - 1)(c - 1) = 4(2) = 8$ for the denominator. Appendix Table G provides the critical value of $F_{.01} = 8.65$. The acceptance and rejection regions are shown below.

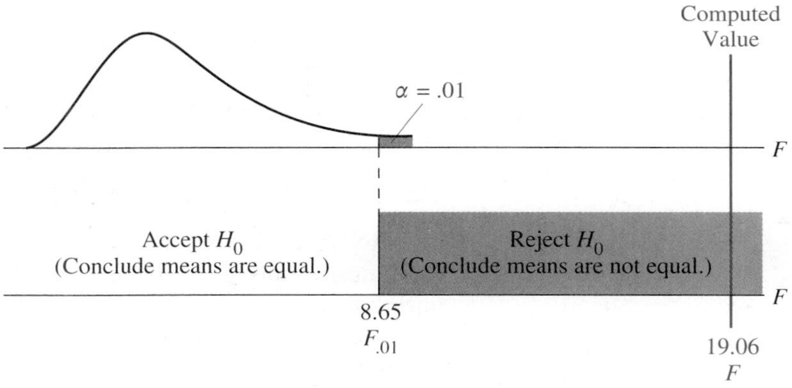

STEP 4
Collect the sample and compute the value of the test statistic. We obtained the ANOVA table values earlier. The computed value of the test statistic is

$$F = \frac{MSTR}{MSE} = \frac{68.6}{3.6} = 19.06$$

Although it is possible to use *MSBL* to calculate a value of *F* for blocks, this variable is of secondary interest and is used primarily to permit a finer discrimination to be made between treatments.

STEP 5

Make the decision. The computed value of $F = 19.06$ falls in the rejection region, indicating that the sod farmer must *reject* the null hypothesis and conclude that the fertilizer treatment means are unequal.

Our example illustrates how the randomized block design may be more efficient than one-factor analysis. We obtained a much larger value of F for treatments than before, allowing us to reject H_0 (equal fertilizer population means) at a smaller significance level than we could in the one-factor analysis. This is because including parcels as a blocking variable considerably reduced the previously unexplained variation in sod yield.

COMPUTER-ASSISTED ANALYSIS

It is advantageous to use a computer to perform the calculations for studies having randomized block designs. Figure 18-6 shows the printout for our sod-fertilization data. Many computer software packages provide ANOVA results for randomized block designs as well as the general two-factor evaluations as standard output.

MULTIPLE COMPARISONS OF FACTOR-LEVEL MEANS

The Tukey procedure for constructing several interval estimates at a collective level of confidence applies here. It is modified somewhat from the two-factor counterpart, since pairwise differences are estimated using *column* means ($\mu_{.j}$'s) only. (There is only one alpha, and the Scheffé method for estimating contrasts in the μ_{ij}'s does not apply.) Adapting the subscript notation, and changing the denominator parameter for q, the following expression provides the $100(1-\alpha)\%$

TUKEY COLLECTIVE CONFIDENCE INTERVAL ESTIMATES OF DIFFERENCES BETWEEN TREATMENT MEANS UNDER RANDOMIZED BLOCK DESIGN

$$\mu_{.j} - \mu_{.k} = \bar{X}_{.j} - \bar{X}_{.k} \pm q_{1-\alpha}\sqrt{\frac{MSE}{rc}}$$

where the parameters for the numerator and for the denominator are c and $(r-1)(c-1)$, respectively.

The following example illustrates this procedure.

EXAMPLE: EVALUATING SHELF HEIGHT FOR SPILLSBERRY DOUGHBOY

Whitey "Doughboy" Cook is the marketing manager for Spillsberry Bakeries. He wishes to determine whether the shelf height of his products affects supermarket sales. As a test he selects a sample of ten stores. During each of four successive weeks, company drivers shelve donuts at a different height. The unit sales (dozens) are provided in Table 18-13.

Treatment Column	Name	Mean
1	TREATMENT 1	81.2
2	TREATMENT 2	88.2
3	TREATMENT 3	82.6

Block Row	Name	Mean
1	BL1	80.
2	BL2	84.
3	BL3	89.
4	BL4	86.
5	BL5	81.

Grand Mean = 84.

ANOVA TABLE

Variation	Degrees of Freedom	Sum of Squares	Mean Square	F
Explained by Treatments	2	137.2	68.6	19.0555555556
Explained by Block	4	162.	40.5	
Error or Unexplained	8	20.8	3.6	
Total	14	328.		

Note: Figure generated on an IBM PC using EasyStat.

FIGURE 18-6 Computer printout for the sod-fertilization experiment under randomized block design.

SOLUTION: As his blocking variable, Doughboy uses the "store." The ANOVA table is provided in Table 18-14. The computed value of $F = 23.60$ establishes that mean sales for shelf heights differ at the $\alpha = .01$ level (for which the critical value is $F_{.01} = 4.60$).

Using the sample data in Tables 18-13 and 18-14, Doughboy makes all pairwise comparisons of mean sales. He uses a collective confidence level of 95%, so that with q-parameters of 4 for the numerator and $(10 - 1)(4 - 1) = 27$ for the denominator, Appendix Table K provides the critical value $q_{.95} = 3.88$ (found with linear interpolation). The following interval is constructed for the difference in mean sales between lower-level (2) and floor level (1) shelves.

TABLE 18-13 Sample Results for Spillsberry Doughboy Shelf Height Experiment

Block i	Shelf Height j (1) Floor	(2) Lower	(3) Upper	(4) Top	Mean Unit Sales
1	28	31	31	29	$\bar{X}_{1.} = 29.75$
2	26	30	29	27	$\bar{X}_{2.} = 28.00$
3	29	31	33	30	$\bar{X}_{3.} = 30.75$
4	30	31	33	31	$\bar{X}_{4.} = 31.25$
5	28	29	29	27	$\bar{X}_{5.} = 28.25$
6	31	32	33	31	$\bar{X}_{6.} = 31.75$
7	26	29	28	26	$\bar{X}_{7.} = 27.25$
8	32	32	32	31	$\bar{X}_{8.} = 31.75$
9	25	28	27	26	$\bar{X}_{9.} = 26.50$
10	29	30	32	29	$\bar{X}_{10.} = 30.00$
Mean Unit Sales	$\bar{X}_{.1} = 28.4$	$\bar{X}_{.2} = 30.3$	$\bar{X}_{.3} = 30.7$	$\bar{X}_{.4} = 28.7$	$\bar{\bar{X}}_{..} = 29.525$

$$\mu_{.2} - \mu_{.1} = \bar{X}_{.2} - \bar{X}_{.1} \pm 3.88\sqrt{\frac{.555}{10(4)}}$$

$$= 30.3 - 28.4 \pm .5$$

$$= 1.9 \pm .5$$

or

$$1.4 \leq \mu_{.2} - \mu_{.1} \leq 2.4 \text{ dozen} \qquad \text{(significant)}$$

The five remaining pairwise differences have the same width. The following confidence intervals apply.

$$1.8 \leq \mu_{.3} - \mu_{.1} \leq 2.8 \text{ dozen} \qquad \text{(significant)}$$

$$-.2 \leq \mu_{.4} - \mu_{.1} \leq .8$$

$$-.1 \leq \mu_{.3} - \mu_{.2} \leq .9$$

$$-2.1 \leq \mu_{.4} - \mu_{.2} \leq -1.1 \qquad \text{(significant)}$$

$$-2.5 \leq \mu_{.4} - \mu_{.3} \leq -1.5 \qquad \text{(significant)}$$

From the above, Doughboy concludes that both floor level (1) and top level (4) locations provide significantly lower mean sales than either lower (2) or upper (3) shelves. Furthermore, the middle heights (2) and (3) do not differ significantly

TABLE 18-14 ANOVA Table for Spillsberry Doughboy Experiment

Variation	Degrees of Freedom	Sum of Squares	Mean Square	F
Explained by treatments (between columns)	$c - 1 = 3$	$SSTR = 39.275$	$MSTR = 39.275/3 = 13.092$	$13.092/.555 = 23.60$
Explained by blocks (between rows)	$r - 1 = 9$	$SSBL = 131.725$	$MSBL = 131.725/9 = 14.636$	
Error or unexplained (within columns)	$(r - 1)(c - 1) = 27$	$SSE = 14.975$	$MSE = 14.975/27 = .555$	
Total	$rc - 1 = 39$	$SSTO = 185.975$		

among themselves and similarly for the outside heights (1) and (4). Doughboy urges his sales people to strive for the middle shelf positions in supermarkets.

EXERCISES

18-15 A randomized block design is being employed to test the null hypothesis that mean responses are identical under five treatments. Using four levels for the blocking factor, the following data are obtained.

$$SSTR = 84 \qquad SSBL = 132 \qquad SSTO = 288$$

(a) Construct the ANOVA table.
(b) At an $\alpha = .01$ level of significance, should the null hypothesis of identical population means be accepted or rejected?

18-16 Suppose the sample data in Exercise 17-4 represent three observations from stores in each of five regions. Treat "region" as the blocking variable, and refer to your answers to that exercise.
(a) Calculate the sample means of each row, and then compute the blocks sum of squares.
(b) Construct the ANOVA table.
(c) Compare the value of *SSE* to the one you obtained in Exercise 17-4. What do you conclude about the effect on unexplained variation of adding the blocking variable?
(d) At an $\alpha = .01$ significance level, should the null hypothesis of identical mean sales for each box shape be accepted or rejected?

18-17 A financial analyst for Money Tree Savings and Loan is evaluating three rules for triggering changes in variable rate mortgages. Using randomly generated market interest rate scenarios as the blocking variable, she obtained the following sample data for loan portfolio yields from computer simulations.

	Rule		
Scenario	**(1) *A***	**(2) *B***	**(3) *C***
1	11.3	12.4	10.9
2	14.2	14.3	13.7
3	14.9	15.2	14.7
4	12.2	11.3	12.5

At a 5% significance level, what should the manager conclude regarding the mean yields?

18-18 Refer to the results of the sod-fertilization experiment on pages 795–797.

(a) Using a 95% collective level of confidence, construct interval estimates of the difference in mean yields between (1) half and quarter dosages, (2) half and full dosages, and (3) full and quarter dosages.

(b) Which dosages, if any, yield significantly higher sales for each pair?

(c) Which dosage does the data suggest the sod farmer use in order to maximize yield?

18-19 Refer to the information in Exercise 17-25. Suppose that each row represents a different instructor, with the three class averages representing a separate class taught by that instructor using a different method. Treat "instructor" as the blocking variable.

(a) Compute the sample means.

(b) Calculate (1) the sums of squares, (2) the mean squares, and (3) the F statistic.

(c) Construct the ANOVA table.

(d) Compare the value of SSE found for this problem to the one obtained in Exercise 17-25. Does the blocking variable appear to reduce unexplained variation in average class score?

(e) At an $\alpha = .01$ significance level, should the committee accept or reject the null hypothesis of identical mean examination scores under each teaching method?

18-20 Refer to Exercise 18-19 and to your answers.

(a) Using a 95% collective level of confidence, construct interval estimates of the difference in mean scores between (1) the computer and lecture methods, (2) the mixed and lecture methods, and (3) the mixed and computer methods.

(b) Which method, if any, yields significantly higher mean scores for each pair?

18-21 Refer to the information in Exercise 17-27. Suppose that each row represents a different type of shale material, with the four yields representing a different portion of the same type of raw material. Treat "type of shale" as the blocking variable.

(a) Construct the ANOVA table.

(b) Compare the value of SSE found for this problem to the one obtained in Exercise 17-27. Does the blocking variable appear to reduce unexplained variation in yield?

(c) At an $\alpha = .01$ significance level, should the engineer accept or reject the null hypothesis of identical mean yield under each processing method?

18-4 THREE-FACTOR EXPERIMENTS: THE LATIN-SQUARE DESIGN

Until this point, we have discussed only one- and two-factor designs. We will now consider a **three-factor analysis** involving one treatment factor of interest and two blocking variables.

ILLUSTRATION: COMPARING TRAINING METHODS

A psychologist conducting an experiment to evaluate the effects of three different training methods on achievement test performance may wish to use a design that incorporates other factors to explain performance variability, such as a trainee's aptitude and age. To do this, the psychologist blocks the sample subjects in terms of three levels of aptitude and three levels of age. A total of 9 blocks are necessary—one for each aptitude- and age-level combination. In a complete design, three treatments must be considered for each case, so that a minimum of 27 subjects are required. In the case of four treatments and two blocking variables, each also having four levels, a minimum of $4^3 = 64$ subjects are necessary for a complete design. Because a large number of sample units may be required for a moderate number of levels, such experiments may be very expensive.

One way to reduce the number of sample units is to use an incomplete design that does not represent all combinations of treatments and blocks. An efficient procedure for this is the **Latin-square design**, which limits the number of treatments to the number of levels used for the blocks. In the training-method evaluation, only 9 instead of 27 subjects are required for a Latin-square design. The data obtained in this experiment for a sample of 9 persons appear in Table 18-15. The letters in the cells identify the particular program applied. These same letters form the

LATIN SQUARE

A	*B*	*C*
B	*C*	*A*
C	*A*	*B*

This arrangement of Latin letters is designed so that each letter appears exactly once in each column and in each row. Other Latin squares for four and five letters are

A	*B*	*C*	*D*
B	*A*	*D*	*C*
C	*D*	*A*	*B*
D	*C*	*B*	*A*

A	*B*	*C*	*D*	*E*
B	*A*	*E*	*C*	*D*
C	*D*	*A*	*E*	*B*
D	*E*	*B*	*A*	*C*
E	*C*	*D*	*B*	*A*

Because a letter represents a particular treatment, and because a different level of the blocking variables corresponds to each column and row, *the Latin-square*

TABLE 18-15 Latin-Square Design for Evaluating Training Programs Using Achievement Test Scores

Row Blocking Variable (Aptitude)	Column Blocking Variable (Age)			Sample Mean for Row
	(1) Young	(2) Middle	(3) Old	
(1) Low	A 82	B 87	C 80	$\bar{X}_{1.} = 83$
(2) Medium	B 92	C 82	A 81	$\bar{X}_{2.} = 85$
(3) High	C 90	A 83	B 88	$\bar{X}_{3.} = 87$
Sample Mean for Column	$\bar{X}_{.1} = 88$	$\bar{X}_{.2} = 84$	$\bar{X}_{.3} = 83$	$\bar{\bar{X}}_{..} = 85$
Treatment: Training Program Sample Mean	*A* $\bar{X}_A = 82$	*B* $\bar{X}_B = 89$	*C* $\bar{X}_C = 84$	

design permits each treatment to be applied exactly once under each level of both blocking variables.

The sample means of the rows and columns in Table 18-15 have been calculated in the usual manner. The treatment sample means are found by summing the cell responses with the same letter and then dividing by the number of cells having that letter. The values of the respective means, denoted by $\bar{X}_A$, $\bar{X}_B$, and $\bar{X}_C$, are given in Table 18-15. For training program *A*, the sample mean is calculated as

$$\bar{X}_A = \frac{82 + 81 + 83}{3} = 82$$

In Latin-square designs the numbers of rows and columns are the same, so that $c = r$ ($= 3$ in the present illustration). The ANOVA table has the generalized form in Table 18-16, where the expressions are given for the sums of squares, mean squares, and the numbers of degrees of freedom.

The ANOVA table appears in Table 18-17. The degrees of freedom are $r - 1 = 2$ for all factors and $(r - 1)(r - 2) = 2$ for the error. The mean squares are calculated in the usual manner. The test statistic is

$$F = \frac{MSTR}{MSE} = 13.0$$

From Appendix Table G, with the numerator and the denominator each having 2 degrees of freedom, $F_{.01} = 99.00$ and $F_{.05} = 19.00$. Because both critical values are larger than the calculated value of *F*, the null hypothesis of identical treatment population means must be *accepted*, and we must conclude that the training programs do not differ.

The primary advantage of the Latin-square design is that it reduces the number of sample units required to conduct a three-factor analysis of variance. But our illustration also points out an important disadvantage of this design: The Latin-

TABLE 18-16 Expressions for Elements in Three-Factor Analysis and Format of the ANOVA Table

Variation	Degrees of Freedom	Sum of Squares	Mean Square	F
Explained by treatments (between letters)	$r - 1$	$SSTR = r \sum_{k=A,B,\cdots} (\bar{X}_k - \bar{\bar{X}}_{..})^2$	$MSTR = \dfrac{SSTR}{c - 1}$	$\dfrac{MSTR}{MSE}$
Explained by row blocks (between rows)	$r - 1$	$SSROW = c \sum_{i=1}^{r} (\bar{X}_{i.} - \bar{\bar{X}}_{..})^2$	$MSROW = \dfrac{SSROW}{r - 1}$	
Explained by column blocks (between columns)	$r - 1$	$SSCOL = r \sum_{j=1}^{c} (\bar{X}_{.j} - \bar{\bar{X}}_{..})^2$	$MSCOL = \dfrac{SSCOL}{r - 1}$	
Error or unexplained (residual)	$(r - 1)(c - 2)$	$SSE = SSTO - SSROW - SSCOL$	$MSE = \dfrac{SSE}{(r - 1)(c - 2)}$	
Total	$rc - 1$	$SSTO = \sum_{i=1}^{r} \sum_{j=1}^{c} (X_{ij} - \bar{\bar{X}}_{..})^2$		

square design has a small number of degrees of freedom, making it difficult to reject the null hypothesis of identical population means unless *SSTR* is quite large in relation to *SSE*. However, this type of test becomes more discriminating if several observations are made for each cell or if the number of treatments is increased. Another drawback to the Latin-square design is that it is limited to testing situations where exactly the same number of levels are used for both the blocking variables and the treatments.

TABLE 18-17 ANOVA Table for Training Experiment under Latin-Square Design

Variation	Degrees of Freedom	Sum of Squares	Mean Square	F
Explained by treatments (between programs)	$r - 1 = 2$	$SSTR = 78$	$MSTR = 78/2 = 39$	$MSTR/MSE = 39/3.0 = 13.0$
Explained by column blocks (between ages)	$r - 1 = 2$	$SSCOL = 42$	$MSCOL = 42/2 = 21.0$	*
Explained by row blocks (between aptitudes)	$r - 1 = 2$	$SSROW = 24$	$MSROW = 24/2 = 12$	*
Error or unexplained (residual)	$(r - 1)(r - 2) = 2$	$SSE = 6$	$MSE = 6/2 = 3.0$	
Total	$r^2 - 1 = 8$	$SSTO = 150$		

*F is not usually calculated for blocking variables.

EXERCISES

18-22 The following sums of squares were obtained using a 4-by-4 Latin-square design.

$$SSTR = 97 \qquad SSCOL = 53$$

$$SSROW = 48 \qquad SSTO = 236$$

Construct the ANOVA table. At an $\alpha = .05$ level of significance, what do you conclude about the treatment means?

18-23 Indicate whether or not each of the following arrangements forms a Latin square.

(a)

A	*B*
B	*A*

(b)

A	*B*	*C*	*D*
B	*C*	*D*	*A*
C	*D*	*A*	*B*

(c)

A	*B*	*C*
B	*C*	*A*
C	*A*	*C*

(d)

E	*A*	*D*	*C*	*B*
A	*C*	*B*	*D*	*E*
D	*E*	*C*	*B*	*A*
B	*D*	*A*	*E*	*C*
C	*B*	*E*	*A*	*D*

(e)

D	*C*	*B*	*A*
C	*D*	*A*	*B*
B	*A*	*C*	*D*
A	*B*	*D*	*C*

18-24 Bill Bird is a production manager evaluating various materials for use in constructing printed circuit boards for avionics systems. Using five each of test boards made from different materials, he conducted an experiment using vibration and stress levels as blocking variables. The following data were obtained for the number of fractures.

Row Blocking Variable (Stress)	Column Blocking Variable (Vibrations)				
	(1) None	(2) Low Medium	(3) Medium	(4) Moderately High	(5) High
(1) Low	*A* 41	*B* 44	*C* 45	*D* 45	*E* 44
(2) Low Medium	*B* 45	*A* 46	*E* 52	*C* 45	*D* 46
(3) Medium	*C* 41	*D* 44	*A* 45	*E* 45	*B* 41
(4) High	*D* 41	*E* 44	*B* 45	*A* 41	*C* 38
(5) Very High	*E* 41	*C* 39	*D* 45	*B* 41	*A* 38

Construct the ANOVA table. At an $\alpha = .01$ level, what do you conclude regarding the mean number of fractures for the different board materials?

18-25 An efficiency expert for Conformity Systems wishes to determine how workers' performance ratings are affected by their skill levels. Three levels are considered.

A = Unskilled B = Semiskilled C = Skilled

The following data were obtained from a sample of three workers from each level, with "productivity" and "attitude" serving as blocking variables.

	Attitude		
Productivity	**(1) Poor**	**(2) Fair**	**(3) Good**
(1) Low	A 50	B 79	C 105
(2) Medium	B 74	C 106	A 63
(3) High	C 98	A 61	B 93

(a) Calculate the sample means and the sums of squares.
(b) Construct the ANOVA table for the Latin-square design.
(c) At an $\alpha = .01$ significance level, what do you conclude about the effect of skill level on the mean performance ratings?

SUMMARY

1. What is multiple-factor analysis of variance?
Multiple-factor analysis of variance may involve treatments defined by the levels of two or more factors. In the general two-factor analysis, the experimental layout involves a *matrix*, with the levels of factor A represented by *rows* and the levels of factor B by *columns*. The basic null hypothesis tested is that the **factor-level means**, denoted as $\mu_{i\cdot}$ (row means for factor A) or $\mu_{\cdot j}$ (column means for factor B), of the same factor are identical. Each cell in the matrix represents a separate treatment, so that there is a **treatment population** with mean μ_{ij} for each cell (combination of levels for the two factors). When more than one sample observation is made per cell, it is possible to test a third hypothesis, that there are no **interactions** between factors.

2. What is the theoretical model for multiple-factor analysis of variance?
The general model for a two-factor analysis stipulates that the kth sample observation X_{ijk} under treatment combination (i, j) is the sum of several components.

$$X_{ijk} = \mu_{\cdot\cdot} + A_i + B_j + (AB)_{ij} + \varepsilon_{ijk}$$

where $\mu_{\cdot\cdot}$ is the **overall population mean**, A_i is the **main effect** for level i of factor A, B_j is the main effect for level j of factor B, and $(AB)_{ij}$ is the **interaction effect** when the two factors have levels i and j. The **error terms** ε_{ijk} are assumed to be independent and normally distributed with mean 0 and standard deviation σ.

Over all cells, the interaction effects sum to zero. And, for all rows the main A effects sum to zero, while for all columns the main B effects sum to zero. Ordinarily, inferences are made regarding the *population means* rather than the effects, whose role is primarily conceptual.

3. **Which sample means serve as the basic building blocks for evaluation?** In the general two-factor analysis there are r rows, c columns, and $r \times c$ cells. The **cell sample mean** for treatment combination (i, j), $\bar{X}_{ij\cdot}$, is the average of the n observations made with those factor levels. All cells have the same n. The **row sample mean** for factor A at level i, $\bar{X}_{i\cdot\cdot}$, is the average of the $\bar{X}_{ij\cdot}$'s in row i. Likewise, the **column sample mean** for factor B at level j, $\bar{X}_{\cdot j\cdot}$, is the average of the $\bar{X}_{ij\cdot}$'s in column j. The **grand overall sample mean** $\bar{\bar{X}}$ is the average of the computed cell means; it also equals the average of both the row means and the column means.

4. **What are the sums of squares used to compute the various test statistics?** The total variation in sample results, $SSTO$, is summarized in terms of the sum of squared deviations in individual observations about the grand mean.

$$SSTO = \sum_i \sum_j \sum_k (X_{ijk} - \bar{\bar{X}}_{\cdot\cdot\cdot})^2$$

The above may be partitioned into component sums of squares.

$$\begin{matrix} \text{Total variation} & = & \text{Treatments variation} & + & \text{Error variation} \\ SSTO & = & SSTR & + & SSE \end{matrix}$$

The treatments sum of squares may be further partitioned as

$$SSTR = SSA + SSB + SSAB$$

The above terms are identified and computed using the following expressions.

A main effect variation: $$SSA = nc \sum_i (\bar{X}_{i\cdot\cdot} - \bar{\bar{X}}_{\cdot\cdot\cdot})^2$$

B main effect variation: $$SSB = nr \sum_j (\bar{X}_{\cdot j\cdot} - \bar{\bar{X}}_{\cdot\cdot\cdot})^2$$

AB interaction variation: $$SSAB = n \sum_i \sum_j (\bar{X}_{ij\cdot} - \bar{X}_{i\cdot\cdot} - \bar{X}_{\cdot j\cdot} + \bar{\bar{X}}_{\cdot\cdot\cdot})^2$$

The error sum of squares may be computed from

$$SSE = \sum_i \sum_j \sum_k (X_{ijk} - \bar{X}_{ij\cdot})^2$$

From the above, the respective mean squares may be computed using

$$MSA = \frac{SSA}{r-1} \qquad MSB = \frac{SSB}{c-1} \qquad MSAB = \frac{SSAB}{(r-1)(c-1)} \qquad MSE = \frac{SSE}{rc(n-1)}$$

5. Which hypotheses may be tested in a multiple-factor evaluation?
The F test may be applied in testing the respective null hypotheses.

$$H_0\colon \mu_{1\cdot} = \mu_{2\cdot} = \cdots = \mu_{r\cdot} \qquad \text{(factor } A\text{)}$$

$$H_0\colon \mu_{\cdot 1} = \mu_{\cdot 2} = \cdots = \mu_{\cdot c} \qquad \text{(factor } B\text{)}$$

$$H_0\colon \mu_{ij} = \mu_{\cdot\cdot} + A_i + B_j \text{ for all } (i, j) \qquad \text{(interactions)}$$

6. How are the respective F statistics computed?
The respective test statistic is computed by dividing the corresponding mean square by MSE. The critical values for F are selected in accordance with the respective numbers of degrees of freedom (matching the divisors in the above mean squares). Each null hypothesis is rejected if the respective computed F exceeds the applicable critical value.

7. Which follow-on procedures may be applied when a multiple-factor null hypothesis is rejected?
The follow-on actions for the second analytical stage will depend on what H_0's are rejected. If the H_0 for no interactions is accepted, but one of the others is rejected, then pairwise comparisons are to be made of the respective *factor-level means* for either the $\mu_{i\cdot}$'s (for rows), the $\mu_{\cdot j}$'s (for columns), or both sets. **Tukey** collective confidence intervals are used for this purpose to isolate those factor levels having significantly greater or smaller means than some of the others.

Should the H_0 for no interactions be rejected, the next step would instead involve pairwise comparisons of *treatment population means*, the μ_{ij}'s (for cells). Such comparisons are made using **Scheffé** collective confidence intervals. These are not limited to pairwise comparisons and may be constructed for any **contrast** in the μ_{ij}'s. Such a contrast is a weighted sum involving weights that sum to zero. Any number of contrasts may be so evaluated, and these *need not* be identified in advance. All conclusions may be combined into a single collective summary statement applicable at the collective confidence level.

8. What are some of the special experimental designs used in multiple-factor analysis of variance?
A multiple-factor analysis may also involve treatments that correspond to levels of a single factor, with the remaining factors serving as **blocking variables**. The common case is the **randomized block design**, which may serve as an alternative to the single-factor analysis of Chapter 17. One advantage of the randomized block design is the reduction in error variation SSE, which may result in a more discriminating test procedure. When there are two blocking variables, the procedure may result in a **Latin-square design**.

Parallel procedures apply in the randomized block design. Since there is then only one observation per cell, the notation is simplified. An evaluation using a Latin-square design extends the randomized block scheme into three dimensions.

REVIEW EXERCISES

18-26 A VBM purchasing manager conducted a sampling study to determine if the mean delivery delay for custom electronic jobs differs between size of vendor and also by type of product. The following sample data (days late) were obtained.

Product Type	Vendor (1) Tiny	(2) Small	(3) Medium	(4) Large
(1) Raw Material	8 11 11	− 3 − 6 − 6	10 8 6	12 15 18
(2) Unassembled	22 27 11	− 8 − 3 − 4	35 28 27	36 40 41
(3) Assembled	2 1 − 3	0 − 5 − 1	3 0 0	7 10 10

(a) Construct the two-factor ANOVA table.
(b) At an $\alpha = .05$ significance level, can the manager conclude that there are no interactions between product type and vendor?
(c) At an $\alpha = .05$ significance level, can the manager conclude that the product types differ in terms of mean delivery delays?
(d) At an $\alpha = .05$ significance level, can the manager conclude that the vendor types differ in terms of mean delivery delays?

18-27 Cal Quick is a computer-programming instructor wishing to determine the effects on student achievement of the computer languages taught and the types of computers used. Over a period of four terms, Cal taught 16 classes and gave each class a standard achievement test. The following mean scores of the respective classes were obtained.

Type of Computer	Language (1) BASIC with No Pascal	(2) BASIC with Some Pascal	(3) Pascal with No BASIC	(4) Pascal with Some BASIC
(1) Home Computer	64	74	68	69
(2) Shared Computer	86	83	85	84
(3) Network	88	90	84	87
(4) Main Frame	84	92	69	89

(a) Compute the row, column, and grand means.
(b) Construct the two-factor ANOVA table.
(c) At an $\alpha = .01$ significance level, can the instructor conclude that "language" makes a difference in achievement?
(d) At an $\alpha = .01$ significance level, can Cal conclude that "computer type" makes a difference in achievement?

18-28 Refer to Exercise 18-26 and to your answers. All conclusions will be made at an overall 95% collective confidence level.
(a) Using product type as the horizontal axis and mean number of days late as the vetical axis, plot on a common graph the sample cell means for each vendor size.

RESPONSE	TREATMENT 1	TREATMENT 2	TREATMENT 3	TREATMENT 4
POSITION 1	247	253	235	260
POSITION 2	252	263	253	278
POSITION 3	264	275	267	291
POSITION 4	305	316	310	328

Treatment Column	Name	Mean
1	TREATMENT 1	267.
2	TREATMENT 2	276.75
3	TREATMENT 3	266.25
4	TREATMENT 4	289.25

Block Row	Name	Mean
1	POSITION 1	248.75
2	POSITION 2	261.5
3	POSITION 3	274.25
4	POSITION 4	314.75

Grand Mean = 274.8125

ANOVA TABLE

Variation	Degrees of Freedom	Sum of Squares	Mean Square	F
Explained by Treatments	3	1386.1875	462.0625	34.3505420754
Explained by Block	3	9807.1875	3269.0625	
Error or Unexplained	9	121.0625	13.4513888889	
Total	15	11314.4375		

Note: Figure generated on an IBM PC using EasyStat.

FIGURE 18-7

(b) Construct a confidence interval estimate for the difference $\mu_{21} - \mu_{11}$.

(c) For which cell pairs do the means significantly differ?

(d) At the collective level of confidence construct an interval estimate of the contrast little vendor (tiny or small) versus big vendor (medium or large).

(e) Give an overall summary statement at a 95% collective confidence level.

18-29 Refer to Exercise 18-27 and your answers. Using a 90% overall collective level of confidence, construct Tukey interval estimates of each pairwise difference in factor-level means. Use $\alpha_1 = \alpha_2$. What should you conclude?

18-30 A Centralia Bell systems analyst is evaluating four versions of a computer program (*A*, *B*, *C*, and *D*) in terms of the run time (milliseconds). Several test runs were made using job type and complexity as the blocking variables. The following data were obtained.

Row Blocking Variable (Complexity)	Column Blocking Variable (Job Type)			
	(1) Payroll	(2) Financial	(3) Technical	(4) Non-Technical
(1) Low	*A* 31	*B* 43	*C* 28	*D* 29
(2) Medium	*B* 29	*A* 44	*D* 29	*C* 28
(3) High	*C* 27	*D* 38	*A* 26	*B* 27
(4) Very High	*D* 22	*C* 37	*B* 27	*A* 25

Construct the ANOVA table. At an $\alpha = .01$ significance level, what do you conclude regarding the mean run time under the respective versions?

18-31 A researcher obtains the results in Figure 18-7 from an investigation evaluating four treatments for a particular disease.

(a) At the 1% significance level, should the researcher conclude that the treatments have different means?

(b) Suppose that the effect of the blocking variable is ignored. Construct the one-factor ANOVA table.

(c) At the 1% significance level and ignoring the blocking factor, what must the researcher conclude regarding the treatment population means?

CASE Making a Commercial Success

The advertising firm of B. O. & O. B. is making a humorous commercial for a new deodorant. The team in charge uses a series of statistical analyses to help determine the final form of their television spot.

As a first step, the type of script is evaluated. The statistical analysis is based on the responses achieved with a series of four studio audiences. Each viewer uses an electronic device to rate scripts in terms of overall quality, and from these an aggregate rating is found. Altogether, nine scripts were evaluated, one for each of three types of humor and one for each of three focuses. The following data were obtained.

Type of Humor	Focus (1) Comparative	(2) Product Strengths	(3) Perceptions
(1) Satire	78.3	82.4	67.5
	71.0	88.3	72.5
	82.0	79.5	62.0
	83.4	78.6	68.3
(2) Puns	81.5	77.2	73.5
	84.0	72.4	79.8
	76.2	66.9	62.5
	82.5	85.3	77.4
(3) Slapstick	85.0	75.0	75.5
	85.3	77.9	68.4
	72.9	68.0	85.5
	91.5	82.5	71.4

After evaluating the above results, the final script was chosen. The story line involves a couple. Two factors were considered in establishing the final form: the age of the characters and the setting. Using essentially the same dialog, a second experiment was conducted with eight different versions, one for each combination of two ages and four settings. Three audience readings were obtained for each, with the following results.

Ages of Couple	Setting (1) Home	(2) Work	(3) Vacation	(4) Vehicle
(1) Under 30	72.4	85.6	81.5	68.5
	68.0	88.3	77.5	75.0
	77.0	92.0	86.0	61.0
(2) Over 40	83.5	68.2	87.0	79.0
	81.0	69.0	91.0	84.3
	85.7	62.3	91.8	75.1

QUESTIONS

1. To be technical, in order to not violate the assumptions of the underlying model, how many separate studio audiences would be required just to test the scripting?
2. What do you think B. O. & O. B. should do in future commercial testing to minimize sampling expenses?

3. Consider the results of the scripting experiment.

(a) Compute the sample means. Then construct the ANOVA table.

(b) Referring to your answers to (a), do whichever one of the following is appropriate.

(1) Estimate the factor level pairwise differences using the Tukey method. Use 95% confidence for each factor.

(2) Construct the Scheffé 95% collective level of confidence interval estimate for $\mu_{21} - \mu_{11}$. Then rank all cell means.

(c) What combination of factor levels do you think correspond to the final choice? Explain.

4. Consider the results of the age-setting experiment.
Repeat (a)–(c) as in Question 3.

CHAPTER 19

NONPARAMETRIC STATISTICS

BEFORE READING THIS CHAPTER, MAKE SURE YOU UNDERSTAND:

The statistical sampling study (Chapter 4).
Statistical estimation (Chapter 8).
Hypothesis testing (Chapter 9).
Controlled experiments using two samples (Chapter 15).
Correlation analysis (Chapter 10).
Analysis of variance (Chapter 17).

AFTER READING THIS CHAPTER, YOU WILL UNDERSTAND:

About nonparametric statistics and its advantages.
About the Wilcoxon rank-sum test for independent samples.
About the sign test for matched pairs.
About the Wilcoxon signed-rank test for matched pairs.
About the number-of-runs test for randomness.
About the Spearman rank correlation coefficient.
About the Kruskal-Wallis test.

Most of the hypothesis-testing procedures discussed earlier in this book involved inferences concerning population parameters, such as the mean. These tests are referred to as **parametric tests**, and their test statistics are sometimes called **parametric statistics**. The sampling distributions of the statistics used in parametric tests are usually based on assumptions about the *populations* from which the samples were obtained. The assumptions of the Student t statistic (used to test means when sample sizes are small) and the F statistic (used in analysis of variance) are particularly stringent. An assumption of both the t and the F sampling distributions is that the sampled populations are normal.

Short of complete enumeration, there is no way we can be sure that the populations are actually normal. Even if the population distribution is known, the normal distribution serves only as a mathematically convenient representation, because we know that no real population is truly normal. Slight deviations from normality may be tolerated when the t and the F tests are used, but sometimes a population that does not meet the assumption of normality may invalidate the results of the statistical test.

19-1 THE NEED FOR NONPARAMETRIC STATISTICS

In this chapter, we will examine statistical tests that make no assumptions about the shape of the population distribution. For this reason, such tests are often said to be "distribution-free." Because many of the test statistics require no assumptions about the population parameters, they are commonly referred to as **nonparametric statistics**. We have already used the nonparametric statistic χ^2 to test for independence. In doing this, we made no assumptions about the distribution for the populations, and our hypotheses did not involve suppositions about parameters.

ADVANTAGES OF NONPARAMETRIC STATISTICS

One of the many convenient properties of nonparametric statistics is that they are easy to calculate. In addition, their sampling distributions may often be explained by the simplest laws of probability. But their major advantage is that they are burdened by very few restrictive assumptions, which is particularly important when, for various reasons, samples may not be large. For instance, nonparametric statistics are vital in business applications because large samples are rarely employed in long-term experiments involving human subjects.

In addition to explicit assumptions regarding the shape of a population, certain parametric tests are based on assumptions about the population parameters that are *not being tested.* For example, equal variances are assumed when the Student t statistic is used to test for differences in population means with independent samples (see Section 15-3). Another assumption often implicit in parametric tests involving means is that the population values are continuous. Many populations involve variates whose values are not continuous, and a large class of these values cannot be combined arithmetically.

Many practical research problems involve subjective ratings on a numerical scale. For example, a subject who rates the taste of brand A beets as 5, brand C beets as 4, and brand B as 3 is really expressing an order of preference: A is better than C, which is better than B. The numbers have no real meaning in themselves: Ratings of 999, 2, and -30, respectively, would express the same thing, and the mean of such numbers is not very meaningful.

Numbers that primarily express such things as preference, ranking, and hierarchy are convenient symbols that convey order. In Chapter 2 we saw that such values belong to an ordinal scale. Because the distance between values has no inherent meaning, standard arithmetic operations cannot be consistently applied to ordinal numbers. Any statistical test requiring the calculations of means or variances would be largely invalid when applied to samples from populations with ordinal variates. *Usually, only nonparametric tests are valid for such populations.*

Another deficiency of parametric tests is a preoccupation with the mean and the variance, which is largely due to the convenient mathematical properties of the measures. Except in symmetrical distributions, the median is a more meaningful measure of central tendency than the mean. Various interfractile ranges depict dispersion more vividly than the standard deviation. For example, knowing that the incomes of 90% of all doctors in a particular region lie between $20,000 and $150,000 is more meaningful to most people than knowing that σ = $25,000. Some nonparametric tests are best suited to testing hypotheses regarding medians, but the popular parametric tests are limited to the less meaningful mean. Furthermore, medians are equally valid measures whether the variates are continuous or ordinal.

DISADVANTAGES OF NONPARAMETRIC STATISTICS

The primary drawback of nonparametric statistics is a tendency to ignore much sample information that may be derived from parametric statistics. But although nonparametric statistics are less efficient, researchers often have more confidence in their methodology than in the unsubstantiable assumptions inherent in parametric tests like the Student t test. Another handicap of nonparametric tests is that they are so numerous that researchers must pay more attention to efficiency than when a parametric test is used.

19-2 COMPARING TWO POPULATIONS USING INDEPENDENT SAMPLES: THE WILCOXON RANK-SUM TEST

Two methods—independent sampling and matched-pairs sampling—for choosing the population with the greater mean were examined in Chapter 15, but these tests are adequate only when the populations are normally or nearly normally distributed. Another procedure—the **Wilcoxon rank-sum test**—that is free of the possibly invalid assumptions of normality may also be used to test independent samples. This test is named after the statistician Frank Wilcoxon, who first proposed it in 1945.

DESCRIPTION OF THE TEST

The Wilcoxon test compares two samples—a control and an experimental group—taken from two populations. All null hypotheses tested under this procedure share a common assumption that the samples were selected from identical populations, which is more stringent than assuming that they have identical means. The Wilcoxon test is therefore based on the principle that the two samples may be treated as if they came from a common population. The data for the two samples may be combined under the various null hypotheses. The observed values in the pooled sample are then ranked from smallest to largest; the smallest value

TABLE 19-1 Sample Results for the Fertilizer Test

	Yield (bushels)	
Sample	**Fertilizer *A***	**Fertilizer *B***
1	42.3	61.4
2	38.7	45.3
3	42.8	46.4
4	35.6	53.1
5	47.2	50.1

is assigned a rank of 1, the next smallest value is ranked 2, and so forth. The samples are then separated and the sums of the ranks are calculated for each sample. The rank sums obtained are used as test statistics.

ILLUSTRATION: COMPARING TWO FERTILIZERS

As an illustration, we will compare the effectiveness of fertilizers *A* and *B* in increasing corn yield. In this experiment, ten farmers set aside one-acre plots for testing. Five acres chosen at random will be treated with fertilizer *A*, and five will be treated with fertilizer *B*. It is assumed that the two fertilizers are equally effective, so that the hypotheses are

H_0: Fertilizers *A* and *B* are equally effective.

H_A: Fertilizers *A* and *B* differ in effectiveness.

H_0 will be accepted or rejected on the basis of the yields of the sample plots. In effect, the *null hypothesis states that the population of yields for plots fertilized with A is identical to the corresponding population using B*. The alternative hypothesis is that the two populations differ somehow. Because the alternative may be true if *A* is better than *B* or if *B* is better than *A*, this experiment involves a *two-sided test.*

The yields obtained from the sample plots are provided in Table 19-1, and the pooled sample results are ranked in Table 19-2. If the fertilizers are equally effective, *A* should be ranked low and high about as many times as *B*. A convenient comparison may be made in terms of the sums of the ranks obtained for the respective samples. *For this purpose, the sum of the ranks for A determines the test statistic*. Using the ranks in Table 19-2 and letting W represent this rank sum, we have

$$W = 1 + 2 + 3 + 4 + 7 = 17$$

Under the hypothesis of identical effectiveness, any five of the ten ranks for the pooled samples may belong to population *A*; that is, the first rank is no more likely to apply to *A* than to *B*. This holds for any rank. In other words, if the fertilizers are equally effective, then the smallest yield is just as likely to be

TABLE 19-2 Ranks of the Fertilizer Experiment Yields

Fertilizer	*A*	*A*	*A*	*A*	*B*	*B*	*A*	*B*	*B*	*B*
Yield	35.6	38.7	42.3	42.8	45.3	46.4	47.2	50.1	53.1	61.4
Rank	1	2	3	4	5	6	7	8	9	10

obtained from a plot where fertilizer A has been applied as from a plot where fertilizer B has been used; this is also true of the highest yield or of any yield in between. Thus, assuming that the null hypothesis is true, we may view the sample results as only one possible outcome from an uncertain situation with as many equally likely outcomes as there are ways to select five ranks for sample A out of a total of ten ranks.

The sampling distribution of W may also be found by listing all of the rank combinations. Treating these elementary events as equally likely, we may determine exact probabilities for rank sums such as 16, 17, 18, 19, and so on. In most testing situations, however, this would be a tedious procedure.

Instead, we approximate the distribution of W by using the normal curve, which applies to most sample sizes. For this purpose, the following expression is used to calculate the

NORMAL DEVIATE FOR THE WILCOXON RANK-SUM TEST

$$z = \frac{W - \dfrac{n_A(n_A + n_B + 1)}{2}}{\sqrt{\dfrac{n_A n_B(n_A + n_B + 1)}{12}}}$$

where n_A and n_B represent the number of sample observations made from populations A and B, respectively.

The usual decision rules apply to the rank-sum test. For one-sided tests, the critical normal deviate z_α that corresponds to the desired significance level is obtained from Appendix Table E. For two-sided tests, $z_{\alpha/2}$ is used. If a significance level of $\alpha = .05$ is desired in the fertilizer experiment, $z_{.025} = 1.96$. The decision rule is illustrated below.

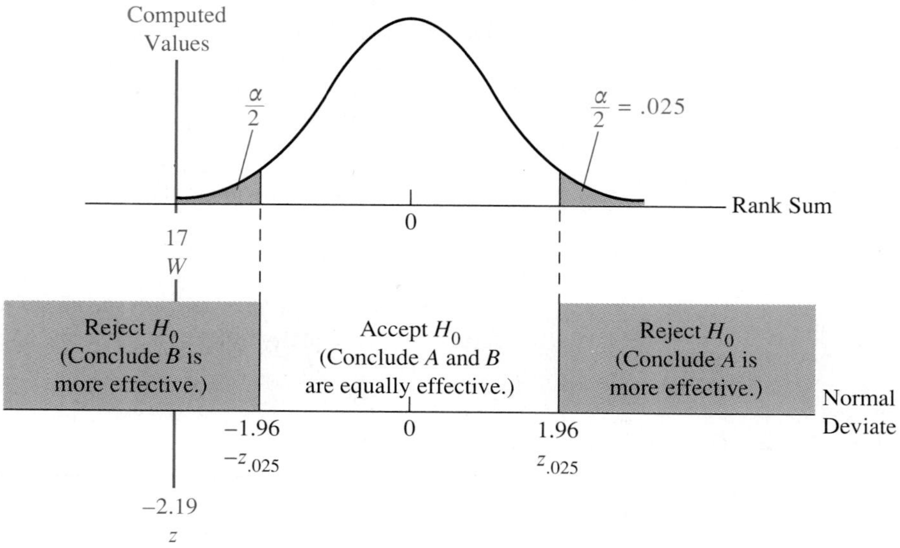

Small values of W, and therefore negative zs, indicate that smaller ranks have been assigned to sample A, which is consistent with a situation in which the values of population A are smaller than the values of B. For large Ws and positive zs, the reverse holds.

Substituting $n_A = n_B = 5$ and $W = 17$ into the expression for z, we may calculate the normal deviate for the sample results.

$$z = \frac{17 - \dfrac{5(5 + 5 + 1)}{2}}{\sqrt{\dfrac{5(5)(5 + 5 + 1)}{12}}} = \frac{17 - 27.5}{\sqrt{22.9167}} = -2.19$$

Since the computed value of the normal deviate $z = -2.19$ falls in the lower rejection region, H_0 must be *rejected.* The sample results indicate that fertilizer B is more effective at the $\alpha = .05$ significance level.

ONE-SIDED TEST APPLICATIONS: EVALUATING COMPENSATION PLANS

To show how this procedure may be applied to a one-sided test, we will consider the case of a statistician for a toy manufacturer who wishes to compare two compensation plans. One plan uses an incentive wage; the other plan calls for a straight hourly wage. A sample of 10 employees has been selected for the incentive plan (A). This group is to be compared to a sample of 15 employees selected for hourly compensation (B). The sample results are provided in Table 19-3.

STEP 1

Formulate the null hypothesis. The statistician assumes that the productivity of the employees under the incentive plan is not greater than that of the hourly employees. The following null hypothesis applies.

$$H_0\text{: Population } A \text{ values} \leq \text{Population } B \text{ values}$$

STEP 2

Select the test statistic and procedure. The test statistic is based on the productivity rank sum for the incentive-compensation sample A. The normal deviate z serves as the test statistic.

STEP 3

Establish the significance level and identify the acceptance and rejection regions. The statistician selects a significance level of $\alpha = .05$. Thus, $z_{.05} = 1.64$. Since a larger number of high ranks for sample A will refute H_0, the test is upper-tailed. The acceptance and rejection regions are shown below.

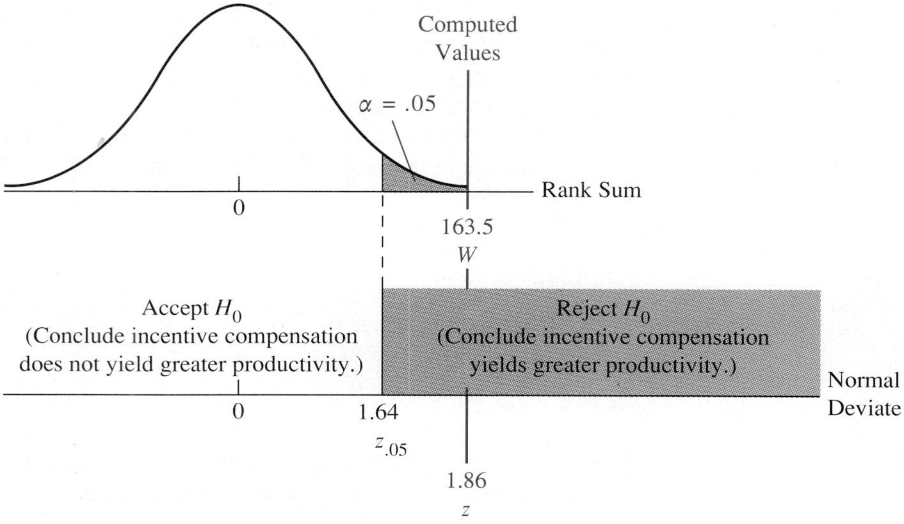

STEP 4

Collect the sample and compute the value of the test statistic. The combined sample data are ranked in Table 19-3. (The special handling of tie scores is explained below.) The rank sum for the sample A productivity is

$$W = 5 + 7.5 + 11 + 12 + 17 + 19 + 20 + 23 + 24 + 25 = 163.5$$

Using sample sizes $n_A = 10$ and $n_B = 15$, the computed value of the test statistic is

$$z = \frac{W - \dfrac{n_A(n_A + n_B + 1)}{2}}{\sqrt{\dfrac{n_A n_B(n_A + n_B + 1)}{12}}} = \frac{163.5 - \dfrac{10(10 + 15 + 1)}{2}}{\sqrt{\dfrac{10(15)(10 + 15 + 1)}{12}}} = \frac{33.5}{\sqrt{325}} = 1.86$$

STEP 5

Make the decision. The computed value of $z = 1.86$ falls in the rejection region. The statistician must *reject* the null hypothesis that the productivity of population A is not larger than that of population B and conclude that incentive compensation yields greater productivity than does hourly compensation.

THE PROBLEM OF TIES

Several ties were encountered in ranking the data in Table 19-3. For instance, two sample A employees shared the productivity level of 148, and two sample B employees achieved the level of 147. *As long as ties occur within the same sample group, successive ranks may be assigned arbitrarily to the tying sample observations.* Thus, we ranked the two 147 levels as 9 and 10 and the two 148 levels as 11 and 12.

TABLE 19-3 Sample Results for Comparing Two Compensation Plans

Productivity (units)			
Incentive Compensation X_A	**Hourly Compensation X_B**	X_A^2	X_B^2
148	143	21,904	20,449
146	137	21,316	18,769
152	149	23,104	22,201
157	151	24,649	22,801
144	146	20,736	21,316
148	155	21,904	24,025
160	147	25,600	21,609
154	150	23,716	22,500
154	147	23,716	21,609
156	138	24,336	19,044
1,519	145	230,981	21,025
	153		23,409
	155		24,025
	149		22,201
	138		19,044
	2,203		324,027

Sample	*B*	*B*	*B*	*B*	*A*	*B*	*A*	*B*	*B*	*B*	*A*	*A*	*B*	*B*
Productivity	137	138	138	143	144	145	146	146	147	147	148	148	149	149
Rank	1	2	3	4	5	6	7.5	7.5	9	10	11	12	13	14

Sample	*B*	*B*	*A*	*B*	*A*	*A*	*B*	*B*	*A*	*A*	*A*
Productivity	150	151	152	153	154	154	155	155	156	157	160
Rank	15	16	17	18	19	20	21	22	23	24	25

$n_A = 10 \qquad n_B = 15$

$$X_A = \frac{1{,}519}{10} = 151.90 \qquad X_B = \frac{2{,}203}{15} = 146.87$$

$$s_A^2 = \frac{230{,}981 - 10(151.90)^2}{9} = 27.21 \qquad s_B^2 = \frac{324{,}027 - 15(146.87)^2}{14} = 33.22$$

A difficulty arises, however, when ties occur between sample groups, because the choice of ranks affects *W*. *When ties occur between sample groups, each observation is assigned the average of the ranks for that value.* The ranks of 7 and 8 would have applied to the two levels of 146 had they been in the same sample. However, since one employee in *each* sample achieved the same productivity level, the values receive equal ranks of $(7 + 8)/2 = 7.5$.

COMPARING THE WILCOXON TEST AND STUDENT *t* TEST

The data from the compensation illustration may be used to compare the Wilcoxon rank-sum test to the Student *t* test for independent samples. Substituting the intermediate calculations from Table 19-3, we obtain

$$t = \frac{\bar{X}_A - \bar{X}_B}{\sqrt{\dfrac{(n_A - 1)s_A^2 + (n_B - 1)s_B^2}{n_A + n_B - 2}}\sqrt{\dfrac{1}{n_A} + \dfrac{1}{n_B}}}$$

$$t = \frac{151.90 - 146.87}{\sqrt{\dfrac{9(27.21) + 14(33.22)}{10 + 15 - 2}}\sqrt{\dfrac{1}{10} + \dfrac{1}{15}}}$$

$$= \frac{5.03}{\sqrt{30.8682}\sqrt{.1667}} = 2.218$$

Using $\alpha = .05$ with $n_A + n_B - 2 = 23$ degrees of freedom, Appendix Table F provides $t_{.05} = 1.714$. Since the computed value of t is larger than 1.714, the t test also indicates that H_0 must be *rejected.*

Similar results were obtained using both tests. (Once again, it should be emphasized that a particular test should be chosen in advance of sampling and that only one test would ordinarily be used for any given data. Both tests were applied here only to compare the two techniques.) Generally, the t test is more efficient or powerful than the Wilcoxon test, so, using the same data, the t test should provide a lower probability α of incorrectly rejecting H_0. However, the Student t test requires that the *populations* be normally distributed, which is often not the case.* Also, the Wilcoxon test may be used for experiments where the observations are measured on an ordinal scale, whereas the t test may not. *The Wilcoxon rank-sum test may therefore be more widely used.*

EXERCISES

19-1 Yellow Jacket Taxi Company intends to replace its brand A batteries with brand B batteries if testing shows that brand B is more effective. The null hypothesis is that brand A is at least as effective as B. Ten new brand A batteries were used in a random sample of taxicabs; 15 new brand B batteries were used in another random sample. The following results were obtained for the number of days until each battery required replacement.

Brand A		Brand B		
323	603	421	504	504
178	496	327	183	312
246	328	609	455	513
195	213	433	365	497
402	187	519	615	723

(a) Rank the sample results and calculate W.

(b) If management wishes to protect itself against incorrectly changing battery brands at a significance level of .05, should the battery brands be changed?

19-2 Refer to Exercise 19-1. Suppose that the company installed 100 brand A batteries and 150 brand B batteries, and that $W = 11{,}500$. Should manage-

*Both procedures require equal population variances.

ment reject the null hypothesis that brand A is at least as effective as B at a .05 significance level?

19-3 A shipper applies the Wilcoxon rank-sum test to a sample of 8 boxes sent using carrier A and a sample of 10 boxes sent using carrier B. She obtains the following results for the number of hours required for receipt.

Carrier A		Carrier B	
5	14	7	4
9	9	8	13
12	10	10	11
22	15	7	5
		7	6

(a) Rank the sample data and calculate W.

(b) The null hypothesis is that the transportation times are identical. In the future, she will use the faster carrier. Otherwise she will test further. What action should the shipper take at an $\alpha = .05$ significance level?

19-4 Solar Flare is evaluating two energy conservation methods to determine which provides the hotter water. The following data represent the temperatures, in degrees Fahrenheit, of independent samples of the water generated by the two methods.

Method A		Method B	
185	233	197	248
206	250	235	234
217	206	245	224
251	215	211	231
190	224	225	216
		245	258

Apply the Wilcoxon rank-sum test to evaluate the null hypothesis that the water generated by method A is at least as hot as that generated by method B. Use an $\alpha = .05$ significance level.

19-5 Two Oso, Toro, and Oso security analysts for a mutual fund wish to compare their trading strategies. Each selected a random sample of 10 stocks and traded them for a year. Analyst A's procedure was somewhat unorthodox, so the null hypothesis was that analyst B's method would provide percentage rates of return at least as great as A's. The following results (for percentage rates of return) were obtained.

Strategy A		Strategy B	
10	57	11	−4
−5	−51	27	−8
15	203	9	53
23	33	9	112
113	44	18	6

(a) Rank the sample results and calculate W.

(b) Should H_0 be accepted or rejected at an $\alpha = .10$ significance level?

19-3 THE MANN-WHITNEY *U* TEST

The *Mann-Whitney U test* is often used to compare two populations using independent samples. This procedure is equivalent to the Wilcoxon rank-sum test, and both tests lead to the same conclusions.

In the Mann-Whitney U test—as in the Wilcoxon test—the combined sample data are ranked, and then the sum W of the sample A ranks is calculated. The test statistic is

$$U = n_A n_B + \frac{n_A(n_A + 1)}{2} - W$$

The normal curve also serves as the approximate sampling distribution of U. The normal deviate for the sample results is provided by

$$z = \frac{U - \dfrac{n_A n_B}{2}}{\sqrt{\dfrac{n_A n_B(n_A + n_B + 1)}{12}}}$$

Because the Wilcoxon procedure is equivalent to the U test and involves a shorter computation, the use of the Wilcoxon rank-sum test is recommended.

19-4 COMPARING TWO POPULATIONS USING MATCHED PAIRS: THE SIGN TEST

In this section, we will discuss a nonparametric test for the differences between two populations that involves samples of *matched pairs*. This is the **sign test**, so named because it considers only the direction of difference in each sample pair, which may be expressed by either a plus or a minus sign. Like the Wilcoxon rank-sum test for independent samples, the sign test may be applied to a wider variety of situations than the parametric t test that we described in Chapter 15. However, the sign test makes no assumptions whatsoever about the shape or the parameters of the population frequency distributions.

DESCRIPTION OF THE TEST: COMPARING TWO RAZOR BLADES

The Blue-Beard Razor Blade Company wishes to compare its prototype "Rapier" blade with a competitor's "Scimitar" brand to determine whether the Rapier is of superior quality. The Rapier blade will be marketed only if testing indicates that Rapier is superior to Scimitar; otherwise, more effort will be devoted to improving Rapier.

A random sample of a representative cross section of 20 men is chosen for the test. Each man is to shave one side of his face with the Rapier blade and the other side with Scimitar for five consecutive days. At the end of the test, each man will rate the two blades in each of five categories: closeness of shave, shaving comfort, durability, shaving ease, and residual facial discomfort during the day. The highest rating is 10 points, and the lowest is 0. The points in each category are added together, so that a blade that rates highest in all five categories will be given a score of 50 and a blade that rates lowest in all categories will be given a score of 0. Fractional scoring is allowed.

Blades are randomly assigned by tossing a coin to determine which side of each man's face will be shaved with the Rapier blade. The brands of the blades are not known to the men participating in the experiment. The same blade is to be used on the same side of a subject's face throughout the experiment.

The null and alternative hypotheses are expressed as

$$H_0\text{: Rapier ratings} \leq \text{Scimitar ratings}$$

$$H_A\text{: Rapier ratings} > \text{Scimitar ratings}$$

The data obtained from the experiment are provided in Table 19-4. A test statistic must now be determined that will enable the company to accept or reject the null hypothesis.

The null hypothesis includes the special case of the blades being of equal quality. If the blades are identical, any differences in the scores for Rapier and Scimitar will result from which side of the face each man finds easier to shave. For instance, the first subject in Table 19-4 has assigned a higher score to Rapier. This may be due to the blade, but it may also be due to the fact that he is right-handed and shaved the left side of his face with Scimitar, which would be more cumbersome. In the latter case, the coin flip—not the blade quality—would be responsible for difference in ratings. Under the presumption of equal quality, the

TABLE 19-4 Sample Results for Razor Blade Test

	Score			
Subject	**Rapier**	**Scimitar**	**Difference**	**Sign**
1	48.0	37.0	+ 11.0	+
2	33.0	41.0	− 8.0	−
3	37.5	23.4	+ 14.1	+
4	48.0	17.0	+ 31.0	+
5	42.5	31.5	+ 11.0	+
6	40.0	40.0	0.0	tie
7	42.0	31.0	+ 11.0	+
8	36.0	36.0	0.0	tie
9	11.3	5.7	+ 5.6	+
10	22.0	11.5	+ 10.5	+
11	36.0	21.0	+ 15.0	+
12	27.3	6.1	+ 21.2	+
13	14.2	26.5	− 12.3	−
14	32.1	21.3	+ 10.8	+
15	52.0	44.5	+ 7.5	+
16	38.0	28.0	+ 10.0	+
17	17.3	22.6	− 5.3	−
18	20.0	20.0	0.0	tie
19	21.0	11.0	+ 10.0	+
20	46.1	22.3	+ 23.8	+

opposite scores would be assigned if the coin toss resulted in a tail instead of a head: The score for Rapier would be 37.0, and the score for Scimitar would be 48.0.

The differences between the sample values of the matched pairs are then determined. In our illustration, the differences in Table 19-4 are obtained by subtracting the Scimitar score from the Rapier score.

The company may now determine whether the data support or refute the null hypothesis. For this purpose, only the signs of the difference for each pair are used. The rating scheme in the experiment resulted in three ties. In these cases, it is assumed that the subject liked the blades equally well. The tied outcomes are therefore eliminated from the analysis, leaving $20 - 3 = 17$ pairs with sign differences.

Because the larger number of positive signs in Table 19-4 indicates that Rapier is preferred over Scimitar, the decision may be based on the number of positive signs represented by R. In our illustration, $R = 14$. Although this value is larger than the number of negative signs because a majority of the subjects rated Rapier blades higher than Scimitar blades, the company must still determine whether R is large enough to warrant rejecting H_0. The first step will be to find the sampling distribution of R.

Presuming blade quality is identical, each sign in Table 19-4 could have been reversed; that is, the probability of a positive sign difference for each matched pair is .5, just as if the results had been determined by the toss of a coin. Thus, the probability of how untypical our results are under the null hypothesis can be determined by using the binomial distribution. The probability of obtaining a positive sign difference for any particular pair is $\pi = .5$, and $n = 17$ pairs.

Although the test may be performed directly using binomial probabilities, it is more convenient to use the normal approximation (which is satisfactory for most sample sizes encountered). The following expression is used to calculate the

NORMAL DEVIATE FOR THE SIGN TEST

$$z = \frac{2R - n}{\sqrt{n}}$$

where R is the number of pairs having positive differences and n is the number of non-tying pairs. The following normal deviate is computed for the Blue Beard results.

$$z = \frac{2(14) - 17}{\sqrt{17}} = 2.67$$

A significance level of $\alpha = .05$ is desired, which corresponds to a critical normal deviate of $z_{.05} = 1.64$. The test is upper-tailed, since a large value of R (of z) tends to refute the null hypothesis. The decision rule is shown in the figure that follows.

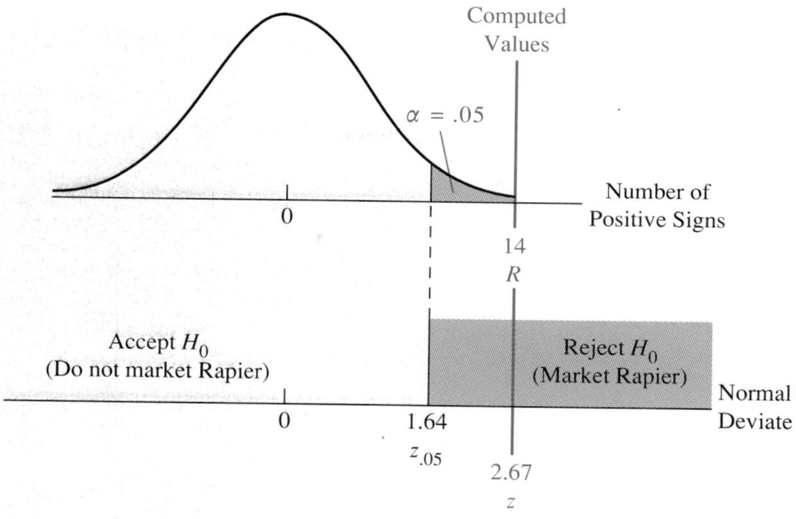

Since the computed value of $z = 2.67$ falls in the rejection region, the null hypothesis that Rapier is not superior to Scimitar must be *rejected* at an $\alpha = .05$ significance level. The Blue-Beard Razor Blade Company should market its new Rapier blade. There is less than a .05 chance that this action will prove incorrect.

ILLUSTRATION: EVALUATING A NEW TRAINING PROCEDURE FOR TELEPHONE OPERATORS

A consultant conducted an experiment for a large telephone company to determine if the existing on-the-job training procedure would be improved when augmented by classroom sessions. Recently hired trainees were divided into two groups. Those in the control group *A* received straight on-the-job training. The trainees in the experimental group *B* alternated regular shift work with classroom sessions for conversational technique and overall system orientation.

Every trainee in group *B* was matched with a partner in group *A* who had similar skills and aptitudes. At the end of training, both groups were given an operator skills test.

STEP 1

Formulate the null hypothesis. The consultant assumes that the new procedure does not improve job performance, as measured by scores on the skills test. The following null hypothesis applies.

$$H_0\text{: Control group } A \text{ scores} \geq \text{Experimental group } B \text{ scores}$$

STEP 2

Select the test statistic and procedure. The test statistic is based on the number of positive signs R. The normal deviate z serves as the test statistic.

STEP 3

Establish the significance level and identify the acceptance and rejection regions. At the chosen significance level of $\alpha = .05$, the critical normal deviate is

$z_{.05} = 1.64$. Since a small value of R (of z) will refute the null hypothesis, the test is lower-tailed. The acceptance and rejection regions are shown below.

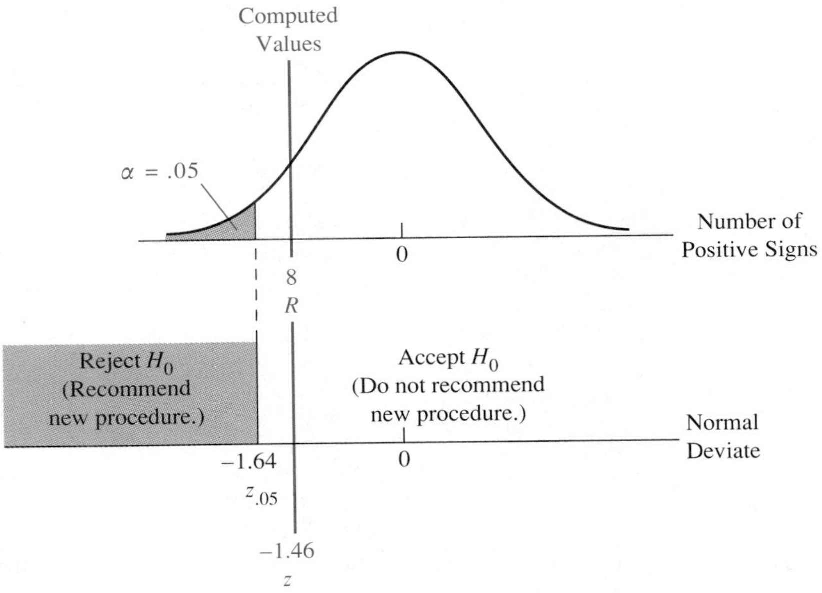

STEP 4

Collect the sample and compute the value of the test statistic. The sample data are provided in Table 19-5. The two tied outcomes are eliminated, which leaves $n = 23$ pairs to consider. The number of positive signs is $R = 8$. Thus, the computed value of the test statistic is

$$z = \frac{2(8) - 23}{\sqrt{23}} = -1.46$$

STEP 5

Make the decision. Since the computed value of $z = -1.46$ falls in the acceptance region, the consultant must *accept* H_0. The new procedure is no improvement and should not be adopted.

COMPARING THE SIGN TEST AND THE STUDENT t TEST

The sign test may be compared to the analogous parametric procedure described in Chapter 15 for matched-pairs testing. There, we used the Student t test with small samples. In our current illustration, given $n = 25$ and substituting into the expression the mean of the matched-pairs differences and their estimated standard error calculated in Table 19-5, we find

$$t = \frac{\bar{d}}{s_{d\text{-paired}}/\sqrt{n}} = -\frac{3.24}{6.35/\sqrt{25}} = -2.551$$

For $25 - 1 = 24$ degrees of freedom at an $\alpha = .05$ significance level, Appendix Table F provides $t_{.05} = 1.711$. The acceptance and rejection regions are shown in the figure on the opposite page.

TABLE 19-5 Sample Results for Comparing Two Training Procedures

	Combined Test Score				
Pair i	Control Group A X_{A_i}	Experimental Group B X_{B_i}	Difference $d_i = X_{A_i} - X_{B_i}$	Sign	d_i^2
1	65	67	− 2	−	4
2	72	66	+ 6	+	36
3	74	77	− 3	−	9
4	81	90	− 9	−	81
5	76	72	+ 4	+	16
6	95	95	0	tie	0
7	63	68	− 5	−	25
8	85	95	− 10	−	100
9	90	98	− 8	−	64
10	64	60	+ 4	+	16
11	78	72	+ 6	+	36
12	86	94	− 8	−	64
13	89	96	− 7	−	49
14	75	73	+ 2	+	4
15	93	96	− 3	−	9
16	78	90	− 12	−	144
17	92	92	0	tie	0
18	67	63	+ 4	+	16
19	88	95	− 7	−	49
20	79	88	− 9	−	81
21	60	75	− 15	−	225
22	90	95	− 5	−	25
23	82	78	+ 4	+	16
24	73	85	− 12	−	144
25	86	82	+ 4	+	16
			− 81		1,229

$\bar{d} = -\dfrac{81}{25} = -3.24$ $\qquad s_{d\text{-paired}} = \sqrt{\dfrac{1,229 - 25(-3.24)^2}{25 - 1}} = 6.35$

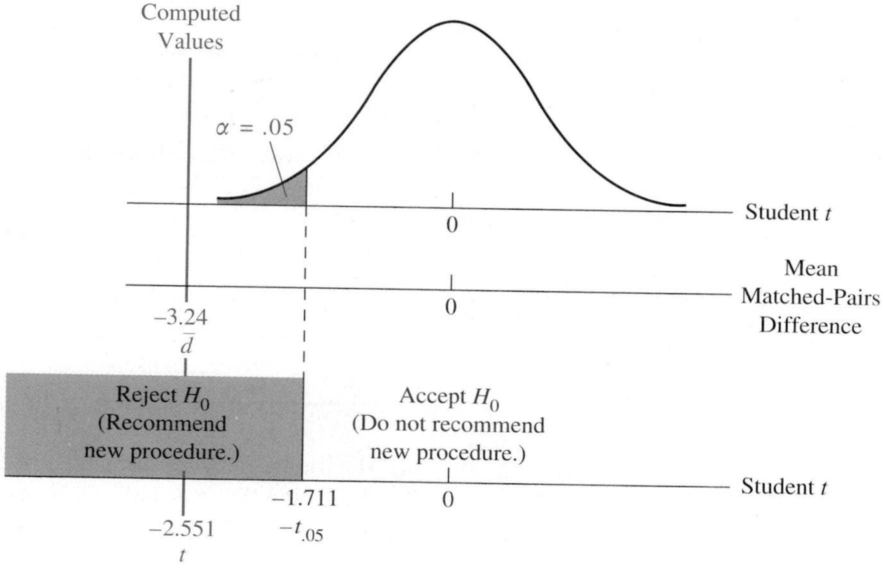

Since the computed value of $t = -2.551$ falls in the rejection region, the Student t test indicates that H_0 should be *rejected.* This conclusion is the reverse of the decision we reached using the sign test for the same data, reflecting the fact that *when applicable* the t test is more powerful and therefore more efficient than the sign test, as well as the Wilcoxon test. The t test is more discriminating because the relative sizes of the matched-pairs differences—as well as their signs—are used in calculating t. However, to use the t test, the *populations* of all potential matched-pairs differences must be normally distributed (or nearly so). *When this requirement is not met,* the sign test is the valid test to use.

EXERCISES

19-6 Use the sign test to determine the appropriate action to take for each of the following situations. Find the acceptance and rejection regions, and indicate whether H_0 should be accepted or rejected at the stated significance level for each result provided.

(a)	(b)	(c)	(d)
H_0: A's $\geq$ B's	H_0: A's $\leq$ B's	H_0: A's $\geq$ B's	H_0: A's $\leq$ B's
$n = 18$	$n = 100$	$n = 50$	$n = 19$
$\alpha = .05$	$\alpha = .01$	$\alpha = .01$	$\alpha = .05$
$R = 4$	$R = 58$	$R = 13$	$R = 13$

19-7 Rent-a-Jalopy wishes to determine whether their cars should burn gasohol (A) or unleaded gasoline (B). A random sample of 15 pairs of cars are selected. One car from each pair uses gasohol; the other uses unleaded. The cars in each pair are nearly identical and are driven over the same routes by drivers with similar driving styles. The null hypothesis is that unleaded gasoline provides at least the same fuel consumption (mpg) as gasohol. The following sample results are obtained.

	Fuel Consumption (mpg)			Fuel Consumption (mpg)	
Pair	**Gasohol (A)**	**Unleaded (B)**	**Pair**	**Gasohol (A)**	**Unleaded (B)**
1	15.3	14.7	9	15.0	13.8
2	18.1	17.9	10	16.2	16.1
3	14.9	15.0	11	15.9	14.2
4	17.3	17.3	12	21.3	20.6
5	13.7	12.3	13	18.4	17.7
6	11.8	9.2	14	19.3	17.4
7	20.3	19.7	15	9.8	7.6
8	15.2	14.7			

(a) Determine the sign difference ($A - B$) for each pair.
(b) Assuming that gasohol will be used if it provides better miles per gallon, will A be used at a significance level of $\alpha = .001$?

19-8 Refer to Exercise 19-7. Smertz conducted a study, testing the same null hypothesis at an $\alpha = .05$ significance level for $n = 100$ automobile pairs. Assuming $R = 60$, which type of fuel will be used?

19-9 A researcher found the signs of differences in mean age for contracting angina pectoris by subtracting the onset age of the nonsmoker (B) from that of the smoker (A) and obtained $R = 30$ positive signs. As the null hypothesis, the researcher assumed that smoking does not affect the speed of the disease. At an $\alpha = .01$ significance level, what should the researcher conclude about the effect of smoking on the age when angina occurs?

19-10 A researcher for Pill Hill wishes to determine whether a new appetite suppressant reduces weight more effectively than the one it now markets. The new suppressant will replace the current one if it proves more effective. A random sample of 40 persons are paired so that all factors believed to influence weight gain are nearly the same for each pair: Women are paired with women; smokers are paired with smokers; physically inactive people are paired; and so on. One pair member is given the new suppressant; the other is given the old one. The null hypothesis is that the new suppressant is at most as effective as the old one. A suppressant is said to be more effective if it results in a greater percentage of weight reduction after three months of use. The following sample results were obtained.

	Reduction (percent)			Reduction (percent)	
Pair	New Supplement	Old Supplement	Pair	New Supplement	Old Supplement
1	10	− 2	11	15	8
2	5	3	12	13	12
3	7	1	13	14	10
4	8	10	14	13	5
5	4	2	15	7	8
6	15	11	16	11	3
7	12	13	17	− 2	− 3
8	18	5	18	0	− 2
9	3	− 2	19	16	9
10	8	12	20	9	8

(a) Determine the sign difference (new − old) for each pair.
(b) At an $\alpha = .05$ significance level, what course of action is indicated by the sample results?

19-11 Puff-n-Stuff wishes to determine whether its new preservative will provide a longer shelf life for bread. A random sample of 10 bakeries have used the new preservative in some of their dough and have provided the supplier with two fresh loaves of standard bread—one baked with their regular preservative and one baked with the new preservative. The following sample results have been obtained.

	Shelf Life (days)	
Bakery	**Old Preservative**	**New Preservative**
1	5.7	6.3
2	4.2	3.9
3	6.5	6.7
4	3.4	3.6
5	6.1	6.3
6	5.3	5.7
7	4.9	5.2
8	3.7	3.7
9	2.8	3.7
10	4.3	4.5

(a) At an $\alpha = .05$ significance level, use the sign test to determine whether to accept or reject the null hypothesis that the new preservative yields shelf lives that are at most as long as those provided by the old preservative.

(b) Repeat this test using the Student t test statistic.

19-5 THE WILCOXON SIGNED-RANK TEST FOR MATCHED PAIRS

Thus far, we have described three nonparametric procedures. The first is based on rank sums and applies to independent samples; the second, the Mann-Whitney U test, is equivalent to the first; and the third, the sign test, is applicable when the sample data are matched into pairs. The first test deals only with the ranking of sample data and does not account for the relative magnitudes of the differences between sample groups. The third test considers the direction but not the size of the differences between sample pairs.

A test that considers both the direction and the magnitude of the differences between matched sample pairs is the **Wilcoxon signed-rank test**, proposed by Frank Wilcoxon. We will now describe this procedure, which is based on both rank sums and the signs of paired differences.

DESCRIPTION OF THE TEST

The Wilcoxon signed-rank test is based on matched-pairs differences. Ignoring signs, the *absolute values* of the differences are ranked from low to high, and the ranks corresponding to the original positive matched-pairs differences are summed. This procedure may be summarized in three steps.

1. Calculate the differences $d_i = X_{A_i} - X_{B_i}$ between all sample pairs.
2. Ignoring signs, rank the absolute values of the d_is. Do *not* rank 0 differences.
3. Calculate V, the sum of ranks for positive d_is.

The V statistic may be used to test the same hypotheses that are associated with the sign test. In every application, H_0 includes the special case of the *A and B values being generated by identical populations*. If this is true, then each matched-pair difference has a 50–50 chance of having a positive or a negative sign, and positive or negative differences of the same absolute size should be equally likely. This indicates that under H_0, about half of the ranks should correspond to positive differences, and that the sum of these ranks V should be close to half of the total rank-sum value. To determine whether the value of V significantly refutes H_0, we must examine its sampling distribution.

As in the earlier Wilcoxon test, a detailed probability accounting will provide the exact sampling distribution of V. However, for most sample sizes, we may apply the normal distribution instead. The following expression is used to calculate the

NORMAL DEVIATE FOR THE WILCOXON SIGNED-RANK TEST

$$z = \frac{V - \dfrac{n(n+1)}{4}}{\sqrt{\dfrac{n(n+1)(2n+1)}{24}}}$$

The value of n is the number of nonzero differences found in the sample. As in the sign test, we ignore tied sample pairs, because they provide matched-pairs differences of zero.

ILLUSTRATION: EVALUATING A NEW TRAINING PROGRAM FOR TELEPHONE OPERATORS

To illustrate, we will reconsider the comparison of two methods for training telephone operators. The data obtained by the consultant are provided in Table 19-6. The hypothesis to be tested is that group A scores are at least as great as Group B scores (the new procedure is no improvement over the old).

Since small values of V and the resulting negative z values indicate that the group B scores are predominately larger than the group A scores—the opposite of what the null hypothesis implies—this test is *lower-tailed.* At an $\alpha = .05$ significance level, $z_{.05} = 1.64$. The decision rule is shown below.

Ignoring the signs, the ranks for the nonzero matched-pairs differences in Table 19-6 were assigned to the absolute amounts, with 1 representing the lowest value. We assign absolute values to pairs of opposite signs in exactly the same way as we did in the Wilcoxon rank-sum test. Thus, the pairs with differences -2 and $+2$, which are tied for the smallest absolute value, both receive the average of the two lowest ranks $(1 + 2)/2 = 1.5$. As before, ties between positive or negative differences only are ignored.

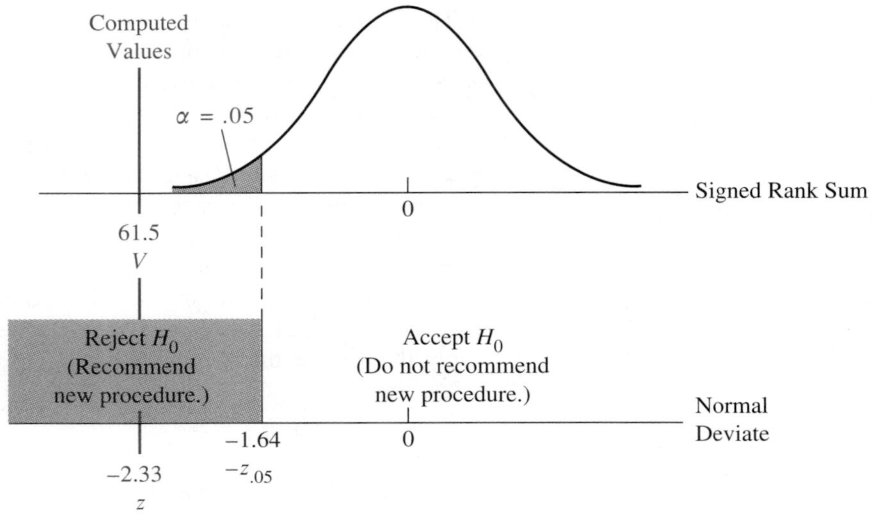

TABLE 19-6 Sample Results for Comparing Two Training Procedures

	Combined Test Score				
Pair i	Control Group A X_{A_i}	Experimental Group B X_{B_i}	Difference $d_i = X_{A_i} - X_{B_i}$	Sign	Rank of Absolute Values of Matched-Pairs Differences
1	65	67	− 2	−	1.5
2	72	66	+ 6	+	12
3	74	77	− 3	−	3
4	81	90	− 9	−	18
5	76	72	+ 4	+	5
6	95	95	0	tie	—
7	63	68	− 5	−	10
8	85	95	− 10	−	20
9	90	98	− 8	−	16
10	64	60	+ 4	+	6
11	78	72	+ 6	+	13
12	86	94	− 8	−	17
13	89	96	− 7	−	14
14	75	73	+ 2	+	1.5
15	93	96	− 3	−	4
16	78	90	− 12	−	21
17	92	92	0	tie	—
18	67	63	+ 4	+	7
19	88	95	− 7	−	15
20	79	88	− 9	−	19
21	60	75	− 15	−	23
22	90	95	− 5	−	11
23	82	78	+ 4	+	8
24	73	85	− 12	−	22
25	86	82	+ 4	+	9

The sum of the ranks for the eight positive differences is

$$V = 12 + 5 + 6 + 13 + 1.5 + 7 + 8 + 9 = 61.5$$

For $n = 23$ nonzero pair differences, the computed value of the corresponding normal deviate test statistic is

$$z = \frac{61.5 - \dfrac{23(24)}{4}}{\sqrt{\dfrac{23(24)(46 + 1)}{24}}} = -\frac{76.5}{\sqrt{1{,}081}} = -2.33$$

Since the computed value of $z = -2.33$ falls in the rejection region, the Wilcoxon signed-rank test indicates that the null hypothesis must be *rejected*. The consultant should conclude that the experimental training program is an improvement over the existing procedure.

COMPARING THE WILCOXON SIGNED-RANK TEST AND THE SIGN TEST

Using the same sample data, the sign test indicates that H_0 should be *accepted*, whereas the Wilcoxon signed-rank test indicates that H_0 should be *rejected* at the identical significance level. For the sign test, $z = -1.46$, which corresponds to a lower tail area of $.5 - .4279 = .0721$ (the lowest significance level at which H_0 may be rejected using the sign test). For the Wilcoxon signed-rank test, $z = -2.33$, which corresponds to a lower tail area of $.5 - .4901 = .0099$. Thus, the probability of incorrectly rejecting H_0 is much lower if the Wilcoxon test is used than if the sign test is used. This reflects the fact that the Wilcoxon signed-rank test is more powerful—for the same sample size, it is more discriminating or efficient than the sign test.

The Wilcoxon procedure derives more information from the sample data, because it accounts for the sizes of the differences as well as for their signs. Then why is the less efficient sign test used at all? One reason for its popularity is that the sign test is simpler to use. Another is that when there are a great many ties between differences of opposite signs, the Wilcoxon signed-rank test must be adjusted to be applicable. A *further advantage of the sign test is that its assumptions are less restrictive than the Wilcoxon signed-rank test.* The sign test does not assume that A and B values have identical population frequency distributions (and hence equal variances), as the Wilcoxon test does.

EXERCISES

19-12 Use the Wilcoxon signed-rank test to determine the appropriate action to take for each of the following situations. Find the acceptance and rejection regions, and indicate whether H_0 should be accepted or rejected at the stated significance level for each result provided.

(a)	(b)	(c)	(d)
H_0: A's $\leq$ B's	H_0: A's $\geq$ B's	H_0: A's $\leq$ B's	H_0: A's $\geq$ B's
$n = 18$	$n = 100$	$n = 50$	$n = 19$
$\alpha = .05$	$\alpha = .01$	$\alpha = .01$	$\alpha = .05$
$V = 40$	$V = 2{,}065$	$V = 890$	$V = 44$

19-13 A financial analyst for Million Bank wishes to determine whether to recommend processing checks in house (A), replacing the present outside (B) processor. That action will be taken if the analyst can show that the operating costs are significantly lower with in-house processing. The null hypothesis is that in-house processing would be at least as expensive as the present procedure. The following sample costs of check processing have been obtained from a test where the same batches of checks were processed in both ways.

	Processing Cost	
Pair	**In house (A)**	**Outside (B)**
1	\$.18	\$.20
2	.17	.18
3	.23	.23
4	.19	.18
5	.21	.24
6	.23	.27
7	.19	.21
8	.22	.22
9	.19	.24
10	.20	.26

Using a significance level of .05, what action should the analyst recommend?

19-14 You wish to test two methods of training. Forty test subjects have been paired in terms of aptitude and experience. You train one member of each pair under method A, the partner under method B. The following scores are obtained by rating subsequent on-the-job performance.

	Score			Score	
Pair	**Method A**	**Method B**	**Pair**	**Method A**	**Method B**
1	87	85	11	62	77
2	55	73	12	67	43
3	62	62	13	77	75
4	51	68	14	71	67
5	48	53	15	58	42
6	66	39	16	58	81
7	53	56	17	61	66
8	24	38	18	51	33
9	91	83	19	80	75
10	63	60	20	44	55

Your null hypothesis is that method A scores are at least as high as those achieved by subjects who trained under method B. What conclusion will you reach at the 1% significance level?

19-15 You wish to evaluate a new food preservative compound. Ten sample batches have been prepared with the old preservative (A) and ten batches with the new formulation (B). Each A batch is matched with a B batch, and each pair is then sorted under a variety of environmental conditions. Following are the observed times until serious decomposition.

	Shelf Life (days)	
Pair	**Old Preservative (A)**	**New Preservative (B)**
1	15.3	16.4
2	17.4	18.0
3	11.5	13.0
4	12.0	11.7
5	14.8	15.1
6	9.2	11.5
7	6.3	7.3
8	10.0	12.6
9	12.2	12.3
10	11.5	11.5

At an $\alpha = .05$ significance level, test the null hypothesis that the old preservative lasts at least as long as the new one.

19-16 Refer to the data provided in Table 15-3 (page 658) for the examination scores achieved by two groups of students, one using a new statistics book (A) and the other using an old statistics book (B). There, the professor chose the null hypothesis of identical scores for the two groups.

(a) Find the professor's acceptance and rejection regions at an $\alpha = .05$ significance level.

(b) Calculate the test statistic V. What conclusion should the professor reach, based on this value?

19-17 Refer to the data provided in Exercise 19-11. Calculate the test statistic V. Should the null hypothesis that the new preservative yields shelf lives that are at most as long as those provided by the old preservative be accepted or rejected at an $\alpha = .05$ significance level?

19-18 Refer to the sample data provided in Exercise 19-7. Apply the Wilcoxon signed-rank test. If gasohol will be used only if it provides significantly better miles per gallon than unleaded gasoline, which fuel will be used at an $\alpha = .001$ level?

19-6 TESTING FOR RANDOMNESS: THE NUMBER-OF-RUNS TEST

THE NEED TO TEST FOR RANDOMNESS

We have seen that observations must be randomly obtained if probabilities are to be used to qualify inferences about populations based on sample results. Determining whether or not a sample is random is especially critical when observations about rare occurrences are collected over time. For example, data about production delays due to equipment malfunctions, the causes or costs of aircraft accidents, or the IQs of identical twins reared apart may be collected only historically—not by short-term random sampling. In such cases, the samples obtained are not random in the usual sense. But if the data appear to be random, they can be analyzed as if they were.

Sample data collected over time are not random if they exhibit some sort of serial dependency, so that the order in which particular attributes or variates of similar size occur is affected by previous events. To apply statistical methodology in such circumstances, we must verify that the order in which the observations are obtained is similar to the order that we would expect to find in a random sample.

THE NUMBER-OF-RUNS TEST

A useful procedure for determining randomness is to separate the sample results into two opposite categories: defective, nondefective; above 80, 80 or below; fatal, nonfatal. Then the data may be represented chronologically as a string of categorical designations. For example, suppose a university department wishes to assess future admissions on the basis of test scores recorded for 20 graduate students admitted over the last two years. Denoting a score below the median by *a* and a score above the median by *b*, the results may be represented by a string of *a*'s and *b*'s, as in

$$\text{Sequence 1:}\quad \underbrace{a}\ \underbrace{b\ b}\ \underbrace{a\ a\ a}\ \underbrace{b\ b}\ \underbrace{a}\ \underbrace{b\ b\ b\ b}\ \underbrace{a\ a\ a}\ \underbrace{b\ b}\ \underbrace{a\ a}$$

The braces indicate **runs** of a particular category—in this sequence, 5 of *a* and 4 of *b*. A *run is a succession of one or more observations in the same category.* The number of runs is employed in hypothesis-testing procedures to determine randomness.

The rationale for using runs for randomness is that too few or too many runs are unlikely if the sample is truly random over time. For instance, consider the two-run result in

$$\text{Sequence 2:}\quad \underbrace{a\ a\ a\ a\ a\ a\ a\ a\ a\ a}\ \underbrace{b\ b\ b\ b\ b\ b\ b\ b\ b\ b}$$

The first 10 students admitted all scored poorly, and the last 10 all scored above the median. Such an outcome is rarely the result of a random process. It might be explained by a change in screening procedure—the institution of a tougher admissions policy, for example. On the other hand, a random run of 20 results is also highly unlikely, as in

$$\text{Sequence 3:}\quad b\ a\ b\ a\ b\ a\ b\ a\ b\ a\ b\ a\ b\ a\ b\ a\ b\ a\ b\ a$$

Such an outcome could result if the department attempted to maintain a balance in student abilities or a fixed ratio of disadvantaged students.

The number-of-runs test is based on the following null hypothesis.

> H_0: The sampling is random. Therefore, each sequence position has the same prior chance of being assigned an a as any other.

The alternative is that the sample is not random.

The test statistic is based on the number of runs for category a, denoted by R_a. (We could just as easily use the number of runs for category b or the total number of runs; either of these would provide nearly the same results.) For the screening test results of sequence 1, the number of a runs is $R_a = 5$; likewise, $R_a = 1$ for sequence 2, and $R_a = 10$ for sequence 3.

It will be easier to formulate an appropriate decision rule if we describe the sampling distribution of R_a first. Basic concepts of probability may be applied to show that R_a exhibits the hypergeometric distribution. The probabilities for this distribution—like those for the binomial distribution—are usually presented in tables, because they are tedious to compute. It is more convenient to approximate these probabilities from the normal distribution. The following expression is used to calculate the

NORMAL DEVIATE FOR THE NUMBER-OF-RUNS TEST

$$z = \frac{R_a - \dfrac{n_a(n_b + 1)}{n_a + n_b}}{\sqrt{\dfrac{n_a(n_b + 1)(n_a - 1)}{(n_a + n_b)^2}\left(\dfrac{n_b}{n_a + n_b - 1}\right)}}$$

where n_a and n_b represent the number of a's and b's in the sample. For the three test score sequences, $n_a = n_b = 10$, and the following normal deviates are calculated for the sample results

$$\text{Sequence 1:}\quad z = \frac{5 - \dfrac{10(10 + 1)}{10 + 10}}{\sqrt{\dfrac{10(10 + 1)(10 - 1)}{(10 + 10)^2}\left(\dfrac{10}{10 + 10 - 1}\right)}}$$

$$= \frac{5 - 5.5}{\sqrt{1.3026}} = \frac{5 - 5.5}{1.14} = -.44$$

$$\text{Sequence 2:}\quad z = \frac{1 - 5.5}{1.14} = -3.95$$

$$\text{Sequence 3:}\quad z = \frac{10 - 5.5}{1.14} = 3.95$$

To continue with our screening test illustration, suppose we desire an $\alpha = .05$ significance level for the probability of incorrectly concluding that the test scores were randomly generated. The critical normal deviate is $z_{.025} = 1.96$. *The testing procedure is two-sided,* since either too few or too many *a* runs will refute the null hypothesis. The appropriate decision rule is illustrated as follows.

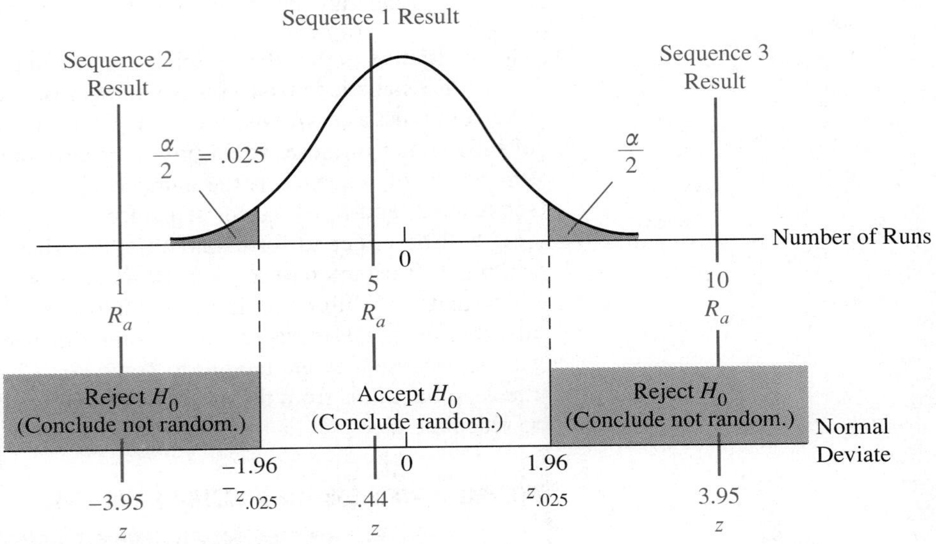

For sequence 1, since the normal deviate $z = -.44$ falls within the acceptance region, H_0 must be *accepted.* At a 5% significance level, we must conclude that the test scores in sequence 1 were randomly generated. Since the normal deviates for sequences 2 and 3 fall outside the acceptance region, we must *reject* H_0 for either sequence and conclude that in both cases the test scores were not randomly generated.

ILLUSTRATION: TESTING THE 1970 DRAFT LOTTERY FOR RANDOMNESS

We will now analyze further the 1970 draft lottery, which we mentioned in an earlier chapter as an example of a poor statistical procedure.

In December 1969, the U.S. Selective Service initiated a new procedure for determining the priorities for inducting young men into compulsory military service. Beginning with the 19-years-olds born in 1950, a revised policy was implemented to draft these younger men before the older ones. A 19-year-old man who was not drafted in 1970 would have a lower priority of being drafted in 1971 than a 19-year-old man born in 1951. Because the manpower requirements for draftees in 1970 were considerably less than the number of available men, a method was devised to determine the induction priorities for 1970 by lottery.

Capsules were to be drawn from a barrel. Those men whose birthdays were drawn first would almost certainly be drafted in 1970. Men who were born on dates chosen near the end of the lottery would almost certainly never have to enter military service.

Newspapers devoted wide coverage to the lottery. Some drew an imaginary line at 183 (half the number of days in a leap year), concluding that those with numbers 183 or below were "vulnerable" and those with numbers greater than 183 were "safe."

The calendar dates and the corresponding draft priority numbers obtained from the lottery in December 1969 are provided in Table 19-7. Note that a greater number of birthdays early in the year tend to be safe and that a greater number of birthdays late in the year tend to be vulnerable. This leads us to question whether the lottery was truly random. To help identify the runs in priority numbers, safe values are labeled *S* and vulnerable values are labeled *V*.

We may use the number-of-runs test here to determine randomness, because the draft lottery fits all the necessary assumptions, with one slight interpretation. The capsules contained *dates*, so the sequence in which a date was drawn determined the draft priority number for that date. It will be simpler if we envision that capsules containing the numbers 1 through 366 are drawn one at a time—the first capsule corresponding to January 1, the second to January 2, and so forth throughout the year. The number inside each capsule represents the draft priority for that date. All possible sequences of priority numbers are equally likely, so that our underlying assumption regarding the sampling distribution of R_a is met.

TABLE 19-7 Runs for High-Priority (*V*) and Low-Priority (*S*) Numbers for the 1970 Draft Lottery

Birthday	Draft Priority Numbers											
	Jan.	Feb.	March	April	May	June	July	Aug.	Sep.	Oct.	Nov.	Dec.
1	S305	86V	108V	32V	S330	S249	93V	111V	S225	S359	19V	129V
2	159V	144V	29V	S271	S298	S228	S350	45V	161V	125V	34V	S328
3	S251	S297	S267	83V	40V	S301	115V	S261	49V	S244	S348	157V
4	S215	S210	S275	81V	S276	20V	S279	145V	S322	S202	S266	165V
5	101V	S214	S293	S269	S364	28V	S188	54V	82V	24V	S310	56V
6	S224	S347	139V	S253	155V	110V	S327	114V	6V	87V	76V	10V
7	S306	91V	122V	147V	35V	85V	50V	168V	8V	S234	51V	12V
8	S199	181V	S213	S312	S321	S366	13V	48V	S184	S283	97V	105V
9	S194	S338	S317	S219	S197	S335	S277	106V	S263	S342	80V	43V
10	S325	S216	S323	S218	65V	S206	S284	21V	71V	S220	S282	41V
11	S329	150V	136V	14V	37V	134V	S248	S324	158V	S237	46V	39V
12	S221	68V	S300	S346	133V	S272	15V	142V	S242	72V	66V	S314
13	S318	152V	S259	124V	S295	69V	42V	S307	175V	138V	126V	163V
14	S238	4V	S354	S231	178V	S356	S331	S198	1V	S294	127V	26V
15	17V	89V	169V	S273	130V	180V	S322	102V	113V	171V	131V	S320
16	121V	S212	166V	148V	55V	S274	120V	44V	S207	S254	107V	96V
17	S235	S189	33V	S260	112V	73V	98V	154V	S255	S288	143V	S304
18	140V	S292	S332	90V	S278	S341	S190	141V	S246	5V	146V	128V
19	58V	25V	S200	S336	75V	104V	S227	S311	177V	S241	S203	S240
20	S280	S302	S239	S345	183V	S360	S187	S344	63V	S192	S185	135V
21	S186	S363	S334	62V	S250	60V	27V	S291	S204	S243	156V	70V
22	S337	S290	S265	S316	S326	S247	153V	S339	160V	117V	9V	53V
23	118V	57V	S256	S252	S319	109V	172V	116V	119V	S201	182V	162V
24	59V	S236	S258	2V	31V	S358	23V	36V	S195	S196	S230	95V
25	52V	179V	S343	S351	S361	137V	67V	S286	149V	176V	132V	84V
26	92V	S365	170V	S340	S357	22V	S303	S245	18V	7V	S309	173V
27	S355	S205	S268	74V	S296	64V	S289	S352	S233	S264	47V	78V
28	77V	S299	S223	S262	S308	S222	88V	167V	S257	94V	S281	123V
29	S349	S285	S362	S191	S226	S353	S270	61V	151V	S229	99V	16V
30	164V		S217	S208	103V	S209	S287	S333	S315	38V	174V	3V
31	S211		30V		S313		S193	11V		79V		100V

STEP 1

Formulate the null hypothesis. We will test the null hypothesis that the lottery is random.

STEP 2

Select the test statistic and procedure. Based on the number of runs of vulnerable (high-priority) dates R_a, the normal deviate z serves as the test statistic.

STEP 3

Establish the significance level and identify the acceptance and rejection regions. At a significance level of $\alpha = .01$, Appendix Table E provides a critical normal deviate of $z_{.005} = 2.57$. The acceptance and rejection regions are shown below.

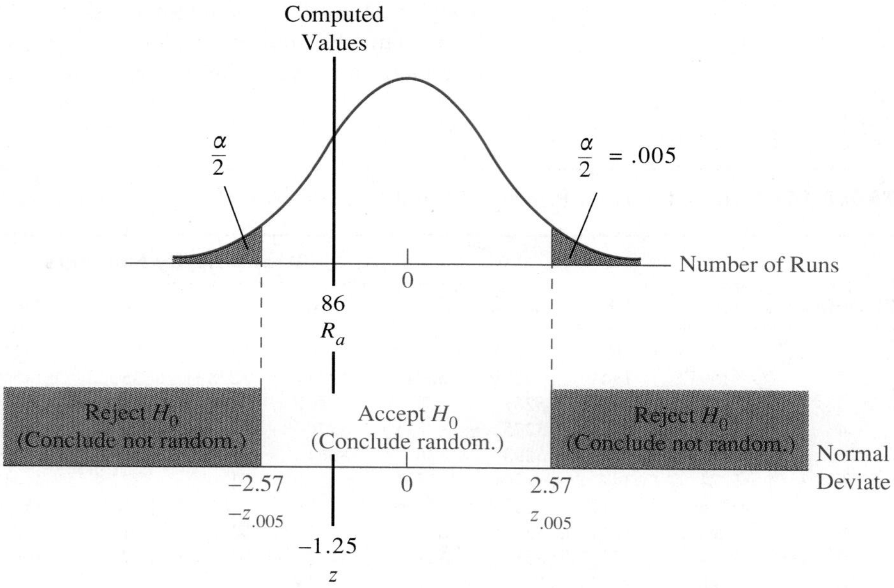

STEP 4

Collect the sample and compute the value of the test statistic. From Table 19-7, we observe that there are 86 runs of vulnerable (high-priority) a's and 86 runs of safe (low-priority) b's. Thus, $R_a = 86$. For $n_a = n_b = 183$, the computed value of the test statistic is

$$z = \frac{R_a - \dfrac{n_a(n_b + 1)}{n_a + n_b}}{\sqrt{\dfrac{n_a(n_b + 1)(n_a - 1)}{(n_a + n_b)^2}\left(\dfrac{n_b}{n_a + n_b - 1}\right)}}$$

$$= \frac{86 - \dfrac{183(183 + 1)}{183 + 183}}{\sqrt{\dfrac{183(183 + 1)(183 - 1)}{(183 + 183)^2}\left(\dfrac{183}{183 + 183 - 1}\right)}} = -1.25$$

STEP 5

Make the decision. Since the computed value of $z = -1.25$ falls in the acceptance region, the null hypothesis must be *accepted.* At an $\alpha = .01$ significance level, we must conclude that the draft lottery numbers were randomly selected. Refer to Appendix Table D. The value of $z = 1.25$ corresponds to a lower tail area of about .105. The null hypothesis must be *rejected* at twice as great a level of significance, or approximately $\alpha = .21$.

THE MEANING OF THE DRAFT LOTTERY RESULTS

The draft lottery example has been included in this book partly because the U.S. Selective Service was vehemently criticized for the way in which the capsules had been selected, due to the disparity in the draft priority numbers shown in Table 19-7. An investigation of the procedure revealed that the capsules were placed in the barrel on a monthly basis, beginning with January and ending with December. The capsules were superficially mixed, so that more December dates than January dates, for example, were on top. It has been convincingly argued that the 1970 draft lottery was unfair to young men whose birthdays were late in the year. Several lawsuits were initiated to invalidate the lottery for this reason.

But our number-of-runs test does not provide sufficient evidence to refute the hypothesis of random selection. The lowest possible significance level that leads to rejection is very high—greater than .20. In many scientific applications, for example, a significance level as low as .01 or .001 may be required before the results are worthy of inclusion in the body of the theory. In general, a level of .20 is considered highly insignificant in establishing that the null hypothesis is untrue. At or above the .20 level, either judgment would be reserved or the null hypothesis would be accepted.

This example points out a major inadequacy of using hypothesis testing as a basis for drawing conclusions about how well data fit a particular assumption. This adequacy is fundamental to the entire statistical approach of explaining outcomes in terms of probabilities. Our number-of-runs model is not refined enough to incorporate all information (for example, the manner in which the capsules were supposedly mixed and then selected). It focuses only on the results of the selection process; all other relevant information is ignored. The same statistician who would conclude that the *results* are not significant enough to warrant the rejection of H_0 would, on hearing a *description of the procedure* for capsule selection, be almost certain to dismiss the same null hypothesis with full conviction, *regardless of what results were obtained.*

One important question remains. Why was such a typical run statistic value calculated for the 1970 draft lottery, when it was so convincingly argued that the lottery was far from random? Although circumstances were far from ideal, there was *some mixing* of the capsules. Capsules were often drawn by plunging the fingers deeply into the barrel, so that all of the top capsules were not withdrawn early and all of the bottom capsules were not immune from an early grasp. These factors contributed some randomness to the lottery. As the numbers in Table 19-7 indicate, the number of vulnerable dates for February, May, June, July, September, and October did not deviate very much from half the number of days in these months respectively.

Undoubtedly embarrassed and goaded by public pressure, the selective service revised its procedures for the 1971 draft lottery. Two sets of capsules were used: One contained dates; the other, priority numbers. Mixing machines were employed, and the drawings consisted of simultaneously selecting a capsule from each barrel and matching the respective date and priority number. The randomness of this procedure was beyond reproach.

OTHER TESTS FOR RANDOMNESS

We have only considered one type of test for randomness, based on the *number* of runs. A similar test that will not be described here is based on the *lengths* of runs. Number-of-runs tests consider only the *sequence* of numbers. In some situations, it is desirable to test for other features, such as the *frequency* of various values or their *serial correlation* (which measures the tendency of certain numbers to be followed by other numbers).

To illustrate the need to consider all these features, we will examine the problem of testing the suitability of using computer-generated random numbers (which only appear to be random and are properly called *pseudorandom numbers*) to select sample units. A number-of-runs test would accept as random the sequence of digits

1 9 9 9 1 1 1 9 9 1 1 1 9 9 9 1 1 1 9 9

Clearly, such a sequence would prove inadequate in selecting a random sample. The number-of-runs test does not detect the frequency with which each digit (in this case, 0 through 9) occurs. In a list of true random numbers, each digit is expected to occur 10% of the time, so that the uniform distribution represents the underlying population of values. A testing procedure (the *goodness-of-fit test*) may be used to determine whether or not the above sequence came from a uniformly distributed population. Such a test would reject this particular sequence of computer-generated numbers as nonrandom.

A test for serial correlation may be applied to the sequence.

2 7 6 9 5 3 2 1 0 7 6 9 5 4 3 8 7 6 4 0

to detect nonrandom patterns (that each occurrence of 7 is followed by a 6, for example). Such quirks are ignored by both number-of-runs and goodness-of-fit tests. Either of these tests would permit us to accept this sequence as consistent with its respective null hypothesis.

A detailed discussion of the various tests of randomness and how they may be combined in a series is beyond the scope of this book.*

EXERCISES

19-19 The following sequences represent the order in which 10 men and 10 women were admitted to four different graduate programs.

(1) *M W M W W W M M W M M W M W M W W M M W*
(2) *M W M M W M W W M W M M W M W W M W M W*
(3) *M M M M W W W W W M M M M M M W W W W W*
(4) *M W W M W M M W M W M W M W M W M W W M*

*For a comprehensive discussion about testing the randomness of number lists, see J. W. Schmidt and R. E. Taylor, *Simulation and Analysis of Industrial Systems* (Homewood, Ill.: Richard D. Irwin, 1970), Chapter 6.

(a) At an $\alpha = .05$ significance level, identify the appropriate acceptance and rejection regions for testing the null hypothesis that the sexes of the graduates were randomly determined for each successive admission. Let R_a represent the number of runs of women.

(b) Applying your decision rule found in (a), indicate whether an H_0 of randomness should be accepted or rejected for each sequence.

19-20 A fair coin tossed 16 times produced a total of 8 heads and 8 tails. Let R_a represent the number of runs of heads. Apply the normal approximation to determine whether the H_0 that the tosses were random events should be accepted or rejected for each of the following sequences at an $\alpha = .05$ significance level.

(a) *H T T T H T T H T T H H T H H H*
(b) *H H H T T T T H H H H H T T T T*
(c) *H T H T H T T H H T H T H T H T*
(d) *H H T T H H T T T H H H T H T T*

19-21 Refer to the results of the 1971 draft lottery provided in Table 19-8.

TABLE 19-8 1971 Draft Lottery Results

	Draft Priority Numbers											
Birthday	**Jan.**	**Feb.**	**March**	**April**	**May**	**June**	**July**	**Aug.**	**Sep.**	**Oct.**	**Nov.**	**Dec.**
1	133	335	14	224	179	65	104	326	283	306	243	347
2	195	354	77	216	96	304	322	102	161	191	205	321
3	336	186	207	297	171	135	30	279	183	134	294	110
4	99	94	117	37	240	42	59	300	231	266	39	305
5	33	97	299	124	301	233	287	64	295	166	286	27
6	285	16	296	312	268	153	164	251	21	78	245	198
7	159	25	141	142	29	169	365	263	265	131	72	162
8	116	127	79	267	105	7	106	49	108	45	119	323
9	53	187	278	223	357	352	1	125	313	302	176	114
10	101	46	150	165	146	76	158	359	130	160	63	204
11	144	227	317	178	293	355	174	230	288	84	123	73
12	152	262	24	89	210	51	257	320	314	70	255	19
13	330	13	241	143	353	342	349	58	238	92	272	151
14	71	260	12	202	40	363	156	103	247	115	11	348
15	75	201	157	182	344	276	273	270	291	310	362	87
16	136	334	258	31	175	229	284	329	139	34	197	41
17	54	345	220	264	212	289	341	343	200	290	6	315
18	185	337	319	138	180	214	90	109	333	340	280	208
19	188	331	189	62	155	163	316	83	228	74	252	249
20	211	20	170	118	242	43	120	69	261	196	98	218
21	129	213	246	8	225	113	356	50	68	5	35	181
22	132	271	269	256	199	307	282	250	88	36	253	194
23	48	351	281	292	222	44	172	10	206	339	193	219
24	177	226	203	244	22	236	360	274	237	149	81	2
25	57	325	298	328	26	327	3	364	107	17	23	361
26	140	86	121	137	148	308	47	91	93	184	52	80
27	173	66	254	235	122	55	85	232	338	318	168	239
28	346	234	95	82	9	215	190	248	309	28	324	128
29	277		147	111	61	154	4	32	303	259	100	145
30	112		56	358	209	217	15	167	18	332	67	192
31	60		38		350		221	275		311		126

(a) Determine the number of runs of vulnerable dates (those having a draft priority of 183 or less).
(b) Remembering that there are only 365 dates, calculate the normal deviate corresponding to your result.
(c) What is the lowest significance level at which the null hypothesis of random selection must be rejected? (Recall that the number-of-runs test is two-sided.)

19-22 Toss a coin 30 times, recording whether a head or a tail occurs for each toss. Test your results for randomness, using the number-of-runs test and applying the normal approximation. At a significance level of .10, should you reject the null hypothesis that you are a fair coin tosser?

19-23 The successive terms in the expansions of certain constants, such as $\pi = 3.1416\ldots$, have been proposed as substitutes for random numbers. A statistician testing for one property of these numbers obtained 45 four-digit numbers at or above 5,000 (a), and 55 numbers below 5,000 (b). Test the null hypothesis of randomness (or, more correctly, the *appearance* of randomness) at the $\alpha = .05$ significance level, using $R_a = 26$. What should the statistician conclude about the "randomness" of successive terms in the π expansion?

19-24 Before random number tables were constructed, a group of British statisticians used the London telephone directory to select random samples. Determine whether your local directory may be used for this purpose.
(a) Select a page from the telephone directory, and determine the number of runs of even last digits for the telephone numbers. Using the normal approximation, should you accept or reject the null hypothesis that the sequence of odd and even last digits is not random at a significance level of .01?
(b) Regardless of your answers to (a), do you think that telephone numbers would be suitable random numbers? Discuss.

19-7 THE RANK CORRELATION COEFFICIENT

In Chapter 10, the sample correlation coefficient r was introduced as an index used to measure the degree of association between two variables X and Y. Nonparametric statistics may be employed to provide alternative measures of correlation. One such statistic is the

SPEARMAN RANK CORRELATION COEFFICIENT

$$r_s = 1 - \frac{6 \sum (X - Y)^2}{n\,(n^2 - 1)}$$

where X and Y are the *ranks* of the two variables being measured.

The rank correlation coefficient is derived directly from the conventional correlation coefficient, except that X and Y represent ranks instead of observation values themselves. The fact that the rank means and the sums of the rank squares are automatically known for each sample size n (for example, when $n = 5$, $\sum X = 1 + 2 + 3 + 4 + 5 = 15$ and $\bar{X} = 15/5 = 3$,) always permits us to use the equivalent and simpler calculation for the rank correlation coefficient.

To illustrate the rank correlation coefficient, consider the data in Table 19-9. Here, observations have been made for the average number of weekly hours that a sample of $n = 10$ university students spent studying and their grade point averages (GPA's) for the term.

Beginning with 1 for the lowest value, the observations for each variable in Table 19-9 have been ranked. *The tied observations received a value for the average of the successive ranks that would have been assigned if the values had been different.* Thus, both observations of 17 study hours received equal ranks of $(2 + 3)/2 = 2.5$, and the two GPA's of 3.6 each received a rank of $(7 + 8)/2 = 7.5$.

The differences in ranks have been determined and their squares calculated. The sum of the squared rank differences is $\sum(X - Y)^2 = 9.00$. The rank correlation coefficient between average weekly study hours and GPA is

$$r_s = 1 - \frac{6(9.00)}{10(10^2 - 1)} = 1 - \frac{54}{990} = .946$$

indicating a high correlation between study time and GPA.

USEFULNESS OF RANK CORRELATION

The rank correlation coefficient may be used in many situations for which the conventional correlation coefficient is unsuitable. In Chapter 10, we learned that the conventional r is based on the assumption that the underlying relationship is linear. The study time and GPA data in Table 19-9 are plotted in Figure 19-1. The graph shows a pronounced, curvilinear relationship between these variables, which is summarized by the colored curve. Here, GPA increases with study

TABLE 19-9 Rank Correlation Calculations for Study Hours and GPA

Variable		Rank			
Study Hours	GPA	Study Hours X	GPA Y	Rank Difference $X - Y$	$(X - Y)^2$
24	3.6	6	7.5	− 1.5	2.25
17	2.0	2.5	1	1.5	2.25
20	2.7	4	4	.0	.00
41	3.6	8	7.5	.5	.25
52	3.7	10	9	1.0	1.00
23	3.1	5	5	0	.00
46	3.8	9	10	− 1.0	1.00
17	2.5	2.5	3	− .5	.25
15	2.1	1	2	− 1.0	1.00
29	3.3	7	6	1.0	1.00
				0.0	9.00

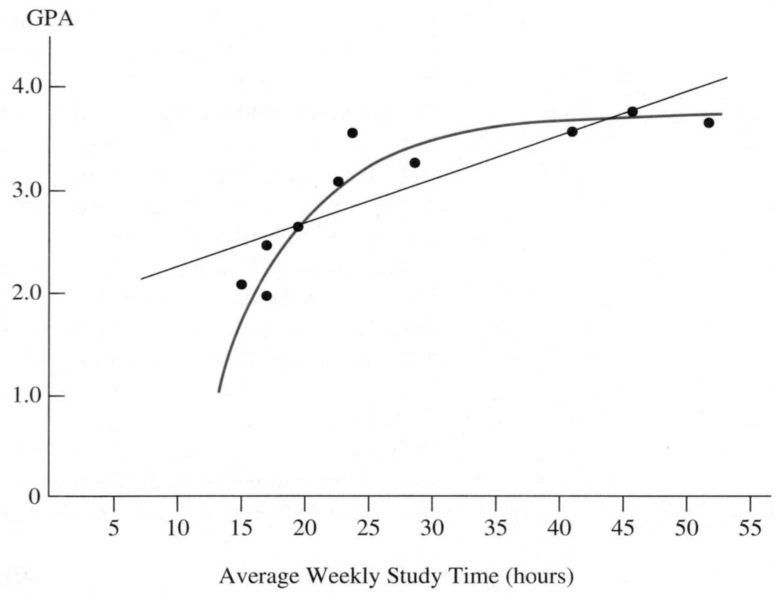

FIGURE 19-1 Graphical relationships between GPA and study time.

time, but each additional hour of study time produces a progressively smaller improvement in GPA. A least-squares regression would fit the black line to the sample data, and the conventional correlation coefficient (through the coefficient of determination r^2) would express the proportion of variation in GPA explained by this line. Obviously, the regression line poorly fits the data here, which is confirmed by the much lower conventional correlation value of $r = .58$ that we obtain.

EXERCISES

19-25 The following data have been obtained on a daily basis for a sample of $n = 10$ smokers who drink coffee.

Packs Smoked	Cups Drunk
.5	3
1.0	4
.5	5
1.5	6
2.0	4
2.5	6
1.0	3
.5	2
1.5	7
2.0	5

Calculate the rank correlation coefficient.

19-26 Refer to Exercise 10-29 on page 455. Determine the rank correlation coefficient for prior and current productivity scores.

19-27 Refer to Exercise 10-6 on page 422. Determine the rank correlation coefficient for family size and bottles used.

19-28 Refer to Exercise 10-37 on page 465. Determine the rank correlation coefficient for number of student activities and GPA.

19-8 ONE-FACTOR ANALYSIS OF VARIANCE: THE KRUSKAL-WALLIS TEST

ALTERNATIVE TO THE *F* TEST

In Chapter 17, we examined a testing procedure for determining whether differences exist between several means—using the *F* test to perform analysis of variance. A very serious drawback to the *F* test is that it requires the populations to be normal, and, as we have already noted, this assumption may invalidate the testing procedure.

An alternative to the *F* test is the Kruskal-Wallis one-factor analysis of variance, introduced by W. H. Kruskal and W. A. Wallis in 1952. This procedure is an extension of the Wilcoxon rank-sum test comparing more than two samples.

DESCRIPTION OF THE TEST: COMPARING PROGRAMMING APTITUDES BY MAJOR

The primary difference between the *F* test and the Kruskal-Wallis test is that the latter is based on a test statistic computed from ranks determined for pooled sample observations. Its null hypothesis is that the rank assigned to a particular observation has an equal chance of being any number between 1 and n, regardless of the sample group to which it belongs. We will describe this procedure with the following illustration.

A college computer-science instructor wishes to determine whether there really is any difference in programming aptitudes between students in different majors. The student body at the college where he teaches may be classified into four major groups: science, liberal arts, business, and engineering. The instructor decided to administer a computer-programming aptitude test to a random sample of students from each category. Their scores and score ranks appear in Table 19-10. (Note that there was no need to average ranks, since no ties between sample groups occurred.)

At a significance level of $\alpha = .05$, the instructor tests the null hypothesis that there are no programming aptitude differences between major groups. The alternative hypothesis is that college major makes a difference in aptitude.

As with the Wilcoxon tests, the null hypothesis implies that the four sample groups are obtained from the same population. Under the null hypothesis, therefore, each score in Table 19-10 has the same prior probability for receiving any rank of 1 through 20.

For his test statistic, the instructor chooses to compare variabilities in the ranks within each column. The sum of ranks for each category T_j is computed. A sum of the squares of these sums—each term weighted by the reciprocal of the sample size n_j of the jth group—is then obtained. The following expression is used to calculate the

KRUSKAL-WALLIS TEST STATISTIC

$$K = \frac{12}{n(n+1)}\left(\sum \frac{T_j^2}{n_j}\right) - 3(n+1)$$

where $n = \sum n_j$.

The sampling distribution of K is approximately a chi-square distribution, with $m - 1$ degrees of freedom, where m is the number of categories. To find the critical value, we use Appendix Table H, which provides critical values for specified tail areas.

In our example, $m = 4$, so that there are $m - 1 = 4 - 1 = 3$ degrees of freedom. Letting $\alpha = .05$, Appendix Table H provides the critical value of $\chi^2_{.05} = 7.815$. The decision rule is shown below.

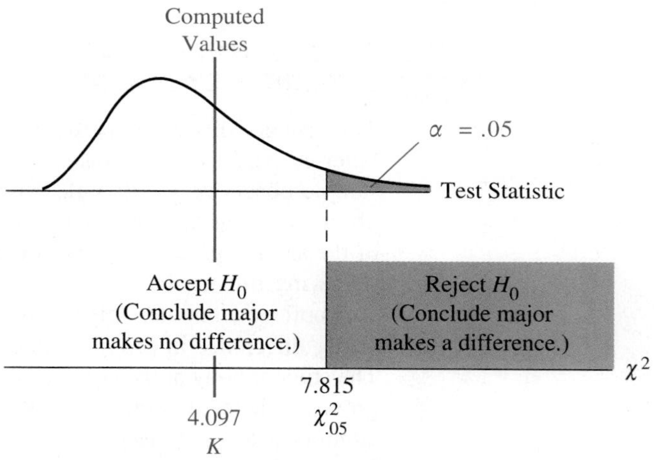

For a sample size of $n = 20$ observations and substituting the values from Table 19-10 into the expression, we find the computed value of the test statistic is

$$K = \frac{12}{20(20+1)}(952.2 + 336.2 + 384.0 + 676.0) - 3(20+1)$$
$$= 4.097$$

Since the computed value of $K = 4.097$ falls in the acceptance region, the instructor must *accept* the null hypothesis that there are no aptitude differences between majors.

TABLE 19-10 Sample Results for Comparing Computer Programming Aptitude by Major

(1) Science		(2) Liberal Arts		(3) Business		(4) Engineering	
Score	Rank	Score	Rank	Score	Rank	Score	Rank
85	12	95	19	67	3	90	15
73	7	54	1	74	8	65	2
96	20	72	6	84	11	92	17
91	16	81	10	68	4	94	18
18	14	69	5	87	13		
				77	9		
$T_1 = 69$		$T_2 = 41$		$T_3 = 48$		$T_4 = 52$	
$T_1^2 = 4{,}761$		$T_2^2 = 1{,}681$		$T_3^2 = 2{,}304$		$T_4^2 = 2{,}704$	
$n_1 = 5$		$n_2 = 5$		$n_3 = 6$		$n_4 = 4$	
$\frac{T_1^2}{n_1} = 952.2$		$\frac{T_2^2}{n_2} = 336.2$		$\frac{T_3^2}{n_3} = 384.0$		$\frac{T_4^2}{n_4} = 676.0$	

Score	54	65	67	68	69	72	73	74	77	81	84	85	87	88	90	91	92	94	95	96
Rank	1	2	3	4	5	6	7	8	9	10	11	12	13	14	15	16	17	18	19	20

EXERCISES

19-29 A chemical engineer wishes to determine whether the mean time required to complete a chemical reaction is affected by the proportion of impurities present. The following reaction times (minutes) have been obtained from sample reactions conducted at several different impurity levels.

Reaction Time (minutes)			
.001	.01	.05	.10
103	104	153	207
111	113	127	183
107	117	143	173
105	120	119	
	113	138	
		143	

(a) Rank the sample results and calculate the test statistic K. How many degrees of freedom are associated with this test statistic?
(b) At an $\alpha = .05$ significance level, should the engineer reject the null hypothesis that impurity level does not affect reaction time?

19-30 Refer to the sod-yield data in Table 17-1 (page 720). Apply the Kruskal-Wallis test to the null hypothesis that mean yields are identical for all fertilizer treatments at an $\alpha = .05$ significance level. What conclusion should be made?

19-31 An insurance company wishes to determine whether the type of profession makes any difference in the mean amount of whole life insurance held by its professional policyholders. The following results are obtained for a random sample of policyholders.

Insurance Coverage		
Physicians	**Lawyers**	**Dentists**
\$200,000	\$ 50,000	\$ 80,000
150,000	100,000	45,000
40,000	95,000	155,000
35,000	10,000	325,000
110,000	300,000	
	75,000	

Determine whether the null hypothesis that there are no coverage differences between professions must be accepted or rejected at a .05 significance level.

SUMMARY

1. What is nonparametric statistics and what are its advantages?

Nonparametric statistics are used primarily in statistical decision making as a substitute for traditional methods. These measures may be necessary if the assumptions of procedures, such as the Student t test, or such as the normality of the underlying populations and equal variances, do not apply. The nonparametric tests make no assumptions regarding population parameters or distributions, and are sometimes referred to as "distribution-free."

2. What is the Wilcoxon rank-sum test for independent samples?

The **Wilcoxon rank-sum test** (equivalent to the Mann-Whitney U test) is used to compare two populations, with the null hypothesis taking two forms. In a *two-sided test*, H_0 is that populations A and B are *identical*. In a *one-sided test*, H_0 stipulates that the values from population A are either $\leq$ or $\geq$ those of population B. The n_A sample observations from population A are assumed to be *independent* of the n_B observations from the other group.

The pooled results are ranked from lowest to highest; the lowest value receives a rank of 1. The next smallest value is ranked 2, and so on. The test is based on the **rank sum W** computed by summing all the ranks corresponding to the sample A observations. Although it is simple to determine probabilities for W under H_0, the *normal approximation* is usually employed in establishing a decision rule. The normal deviate is computed using the expression

$$z = \frac{W - \dfrac{n_A(n_A + n_B + 1)}{2}}{\sqrt{\dfrac{n_A n_B(n_A + n_B + 1)}{12}}}$$

3. What is the sign test for matched pairs?

Two nonparametric procedures are popular for testing with matched pairs. The first procedure is the **sign test**. The test statistic is calculated by subtracting each group B observation from its group A partner, with the sign (+ or −) noted for each pair. The **number of positive differences R** out of the n pairs, after eliminating the tied outcomes, establishes whether H_0 should be accepted or rejected. As with the Wilcoxon test, a normal approximation may be used to establish a decision rule. The normal deviate is computed using

$$z = \frac{2R - n}{\sqrt{n}}$$

4. **What is the Wilcoxon signed-rank test for matched pairs?**
The second matched-pairs test considers more sample information, using both the sign and *magnitude* of the pairwise differences. The procedure we are describing is the **Wilcoxon signed-rank test**. After computing each difference, the *absolute values* are ranked from lowest to highest. The test statistic is the **sum of ranks V for the positive differences**. As with the sign test, the normal approximation is used and the normal deviate is computed from the expression

$$z = \frac{V - \dfrac{n(n+1)}{4}}{\sqrt{\dfrac{n(n+1)(2n+1)}{24}}}$$

5. **What is the number-of-runs test for randomness?**
A popular nonparametric test for *randomness* is the **number-of-runs test**. This procedure isolates the number of a runs, with the total of these denoted by R_a. Abnormally large or small values for R_a refute the null hypothesis of randomness. As with the above tests, the normal deviate may be computed to establish the acceptance and rejection regions (see page 839).

6. **What is the Spearman rank correlation coefficient?**
The nonparametric counterpart to the correlation coefficient described in Chapter 10 is the **Spearman rank correlation coefficient**. Based on the *ranks* of the observed X and Y values, this measure is advantageous in gauging the strength of a relationship that is nonlinear (see page 846).

7. **What is the Kruskal-Wallis test?**
The analysis of variance procedures in Chapters 17 and 18 are actually concerned with comparisons of *means* for three or more populations. The nonparametric counterpart to those tests is the **Kruskal-Wallis test**. The Kruskal-Wallis test is an extension of the first Wilcoxon test for independent samples and utilizes a test statistic constructed from rank sums for each sample group. (See pages 849–851 for a detailed discussion.)

REVIEW EXERCISES

19-32 The following product-rating data apply to two brands of toothpaste. Each observation pair represents an evaluation by a test subject who used both brands. (The higher the rating, the more favorable the evaluation.)

Subject	Rating: Brident (*A*)	Rating: Flossaway (*B*)	Subject	Rating: Brident (*A*)	Rating: Flossaway (*B*)
1	45	39	11	39	29
2	88	71	12	36	36
3	40	42	13	52	50
4	32	27	14	43	34
5	29	28	15	73	51
6	34	30	16	48	42
7	59	50	17	61	61
8	55	60	18	48	45
9	62	51	19	44	32
10	50	48	20	51	43

(a) Construct a 99% confidence interval estimate for the difference in mean ratings between the two brands.

(b) Should the null hypothesis of identical means be accepted or rejected at a 1% significance level?

19-33 In testing the null hypothesis that formulation *A* yields relief from sinus headaches for at least as long as formulation *B*, a Pill Hill statistician selects two independent samples of 30 sinus sufferers and asks a physician to administer drug *A* to one group and drug *B* to the other. The number of pills taken over a fixed time period is used to compute each sufferer's mean relief duration score. In ranking the scores of the two groups, the statistician found that $W = 826$. Should H_0 be accepted or rejected at an $\alpha = .05$ significance level?

19-34 Suppose that the statistician in Exercise 19-33 grouped the patients into 30 pairs, matched on the basis of medical history, age, sex, and lifestyle. Also assume that the same individuals received the respective drugs. The difference in relief duration of each pair was found by subtracting the mean time of each drug *B* patient from the mean time of each corresponding drug *A* patient. A total of $R = 5$ positive differences resulted, and there were 5 ties. Should H_0 be accepted or rejected at an $\alpha = .05$ significance level? (*Note*: We would never use both the Wilcoxon rank-sum test and the sign test for matched pairs on the same data. This is done here only to illustrate how results may vary between the two tests.)

19-35 Refer to the data in Exercise 19-32. Apply the Wilcoxon signed-rank test to evaluate the null hypothesis that Brident yields ratings that are no greater than those of Flossaway. At a 5% significance level should H_0 be accepted or rejected?

19-36 A statistics professor asked her students to construct their own random number lists from scratch to demonstrate how faulty this procedure may be. One student obtained the following list. Proceeding down one column at a time, find the number of runs of small values (0 through 4), and determine whether the null hypothesis of randomness should be accepted or rejected at an $\alpha = .05$ significance level.

4	6	9	9	0
8	1	2	3	6
3	9	8	8	2
7	2	3	2	3
9	4	7	7	4
0	8	1	5	8
2	7	7	1	5
1	6	3	7	3
8	0	4	0	8
5	3	6	5	0

19-37 Refer to Exercise 19-34. Apply the Wilcoxon signed-rank test assuming that the sample data provide $V = 30$.

19-38 You wish to compare the grades achieved by nonworking students (A) to those of working students (B). The following results were obtained from samples selected independently.

Nonworking Students (*A*)				Working Students (*B*)			
GPA	SAT	GPA	SAT	GPA	SAT	GPA	SAT
3.3	655	3.2	712	3.1	588	2.7	578
3.9	722	3.5	690	3.8	716	3.7	695
2.9	623	2.8	575	3.1	627	3.2	634
3.3	710	3.8	690	3.5	713	3.9	730

(a) Construct a 95% confidence interval estimate for the difference in population mean GPA's for nonworking and working students.

(b) Apply the Student t test for the null hypothesis that nonworking students earn grades that are at least as high as those of working students. At a 5% significance level, should the null hypothesis be accepted or rejected?

(c) Test the same null hypothesis using the Wilcoxon rank-sum test. What conclusion should be reached at a 5% significance level?

19-39 Refer to the GPA data in Exercise 19-38. Using SAT scores as the basis for assignment, match each nonworking student with a partner in the working group. Assume that these were the matched pairs from the outset of the investigation.

(a) Construct a 95% confidence interval estimate for the difference in population mean GPA's for nonworking and working students.

(b) Apply the Student t test for the null hypothesis that nonworking students earn grades that are at least as high as those of working students. At the 5% significance level, should you accept or reject the hypothesis?

(c) Test the same null hypothesis using the Wilcoxon signed-rank test. What conclusion should you reach at the 5% significance level?

19-40 Refer to the data in Exercise 10-6 (page 422). Calculate the rank correlation coefficient.

CASE Brimbow, Hatter, and Baldwin

The boutique hat-making firm of Brimbow, Hatter, and Baldwin developed a questionnaire for use in screening members for a consumer testing panel. A portion of their questionnaire is reproduced below.

I. Evaluate the advertising copy in each of the following categories.

	A	B	C	D	E
1 MESSAGE	Lacking	Skewed	Boring	Okay	Succinct
2 HUMOR	Funeral	Dull	Knock-knock	Giggly	Outrageous
3 REMEMBERABLE	Emmies	Birthdays	Illness	Storm	Earthquake
4 IMPRESSION	Litter	Junk Mail	Ho-Hum	Tax Bill	Free Trip
5 APPEAL	Tax Bill	Flat Tire	Bore	Sunset	Hot Tubbing

II. Rate the product in each of the following categories.

	A	B	C	D	E
1 DESIGN	Horrible	Yucky	Tacky	Appealing	Gorgeous
2 COLORS	Revolting	Scary	Laughable	Nice	Outstanding
3 FUNCTIONAL	Halloween	Poor	So-So	Okay	Very Good
4 FASHIONABLE	Garrish	Wiggish	Nebbish	Kiddish	Trendish
5 APPEAL	Spider	Mud Hen	Bland	Cute	Sexy

The following sample results were obtained from part I in response to a possible ad.

Male Subject	Response 1	2	3	4	5
Tom C.	A	B	C	C	C
Bill W.	B	A	D	C	C
Dick S.	C	B	C	C	E
Al B.	D	B	C	B	C
Joe S.	C	C	B	D	C
Tom P.	C	E	D	C	C
Bob S.	E	D	C	D	C
Tom G.	D	C	D	D	C

Female Subject	Response 1	2	3	4	5
Ann J.	D	D	B	C	E
Sue B.	C	D	E	C	B
Marge A.	D	E	C	D	C
Jill K.	D	D	E	D	C
Jan W.	D	D	E	D	C
Lisa L.	E	C	B	D	E

To fine tune the panel selection process and explore ways to refine their questionnaire, the partners of the firm retained a statistics consultant to conduct some exploratory evaluations. As part of a class project, you have offered to help the consultant answer the following questions.

QUESTIONS

1. On a numerical scale, each questionnaire response E, D, C, B, and A has been rated as 5, 4, 3, 2, and 1, respectively. For each sample subject, determine the aggregate score using the responses to part I.
2. Compare male (A) and female (B) aggregate scores obtained for Question 1. Use the Wilcoxon rank-sum test to test the null hypothesis that the ad appeals more to men than to women. At a 10% significance level, what conclusion do you reach?
3. In comparing questionnaire responses to part II regarding a particular men's hat, panelists were classified geographically as Western and Eastern. Subjects in one group were matched with partners in the other group, using age, sex, income, and other demographic characteristics. The following data were obtained.

	Aggregate Score	
Pair	Western (A)	Eastern (B)
1	21	23
2	17	15
3	18	18
4	16	17
5	23	18
6	23	15
7	19	16
8	23	20
9	24	15
10	17	17
11	11	8
12	17	15
13	16	10
14	15	11
15	18	16

Apply the sign test to evaluate the null hypothesis that the hat does not have greater appeal in the West. Use $\alpha = .05$. What is the lowest significance level at which the null hypothesis may be rejected?

4. Repeat Question 3, using instead the Wilcoxon signed-rank test.
5. For four different age groups, the following aggregate scores were obtained from part II in evaluating a line of Tam O'Shanters. (Respondents' ages appear in parentheses.)

(1) Teen-Aged	(2) Younger	(3) Middle-Aged	(4) Seniors
7 (15)	11 (22)	15 (39)	16 (63)
6 (19)	13 (34)	17 (51)	21 (58)
9 (19)	10 (31)	20 (44)	19 (75)
12 (18)	13 (28)	15 (51)	18 (60)
	14 (26)		20 (70)
			22 (65)

Apply the Kruskal-Wallis test to evaluate the null hypothesis that the product line has identical appeal, regardless of age grouping. At a 5% significance level, what do you conclude?

6. Refer to the data in Question 5. Calculate the rank correlation coefficient for aggregate score and respondent age. What should you conclude regarding the appeal of Tam O'Shanters to various ages?

PART V

PROBABILITY APPLICATIONS FOR BUSINESS ANALYSIS

CHAPTER 20

SUBJECTIVE PROBABILITY IN BUSINESS DECISIONS

BEFORE READING THIS CHAPTER, MAKE SURE YOU UNDERSTAND:

Basic concepts of probability (Chapter 5).

Probability distributions and expected value (Chapter 6).

Normal distribution (Chapter 7).

AFTER READING THIS CHAPTER, YOU WILL UNDERSTAND:

About subjective probabilities and the role of judgment in establishing their values.

How to overcome the philosophical objections to using subjective probabilities.

How 50–50 gambles can establish a subjective normal probability distribution.

About the interview method for establishing a subjective probability distribution.

About the actual/forecast ratio method for establishing a subjective probability distribution.

How the graph for subjective cumulative probabilities can be used to find a tabular representation.

Although probability concepts have been extensively used in earlier chapters, little discussion has been devoted to **subjective probabilities**. Subjective probabilities are applicable to nonrepeatable circumstances, such as introducing a new product or drilling a wildcat oil well, and must be arrived at through *judgment*. This is in contrast to the long-run frequencies used to establish **objective probabilities**, which are valid only when elements of repeatability are present. Because so many business decisions involve one-shot situations that never recur exactly, there is a strong need for subjective probabilities when analyzing decision making under uncertainty. In this chapter, we will examine the procedures for translating judgment into the subjective probability values so useful for evaluating real-world decision problems.

20-1 PROBABILITIES OBTAINED FROM HISTORY

Historical experience can be a convenient starting point for assigning probabilities. To calculate the historical frequency of an event, we need to know only two things: the number of times the event has occurred in the past and the number of opportunities when it could have occurred. This is how fire insurance underwriters obtain probabilities for determining the expected claim sizes that are used to establish policy charges. With tens of thousands of buildings involved, the *event frequencies themselves define the probabilities*, because in the traditional sense, probability fundamentally expresses long-run frequency of occurrence.

There are inherent difficulties in using historical frequencies as probabilities. One is the limited extent of history—the available data may only provide a crude frequency estimate. Unless the number of similar past circumstances is large, statistical estimates of event frequencies may be unreliable. Past history may be suitable for setting fire insurance rates. But past frequencies cannot be wholly adequate—indeed, are unavailable—to determine the probability distributions for a great many variables encountered in business, such as the demand for a new product. As the following Statistics Around Us box shows, another serious difficulty is that conditions change over time.

20-2 SUBJECTIVE PROBABILITIES

To apply basic decision-making models based on expected payoffs, we must employ probabilities. Past history may sometimes provide probability values that fit into the mold of long-run frequencies. But the applicability of such data is limited to events with a rich history, such as insurance claims. And even when they are available, these data may be misleading, owing to the forces of change.

In many business decisions, the only recourse is to use subjective probabilities, which are not tied to a long-run frequency of occurrence, because so many decisions involve one-shot situations that may be characterized by essentially nonrepeatable uncertainties. Good *judgment* may be the only method available to transform such uncertainties into a set of probabilities for the various events involved.

We have seen that decision making under uncertainty is analogous to gambling. Unlike card games, lotteries, dice, or roulette, however, most real life gambles may be analyzed only with the help of subjective probabilities, which reflect the decision-maker's judgment and experience. How do we obtain a subjective probability?

STATISTICS AROUND US

Car Insurance Industry Was Poorly Served by Past Frequencies

The recent experience of automobile-casualty insurance firms serves as an example of how changing conditions can make historical frequencies unsuitable for obtaining probabilities. Car insurers, who have consistently complained about losing money on collision and comprehensive coverage, have found that past experience has proved to be a poor predictor of future levels of damage claims. This is due not to sampling error, which is virtually nonexistent because the data obtained constitute a census, but rather to changing circumstances. Cars are becoming less and less sturdy, so that minor impacts that would hardly have dented an older car may seriously damage a new one. Repair costs have also been rising in a pronounced inflationary spiral. More cars are sharing roads that are not increasing at the same rate, and driving habits are changing accordingly, affecting the accident rate. Automobile thefts have also been increasing as the result of new social pressures.

Using historical frequencies to estimate the probabilities for future automobile insurance claims may be compared to tossing a die, some side of which is shaved before each toss. We do not know which side has been shaved or by how much. Under these circumstances, we may never obtain a reasonable probability distribution for the respective sides from historical frequencies alone.

BETTING ODDS

Subjective probabilities may be considered betting odds; that is, they may be treated just like the probabilities that the decision maker would desire in a lottery situation of his or her own design in which the payoffs are identical in every respect to the possible payoffs from the actual decision being evaluated. For example, suppose that a contractor assigns a subjective probability of .5 to the event of winning a contract that will increase profits by \$50,000 and that losing the contract will cost \$10,000. This contractor ought to be indifferent between preparing a bid for the contract and gambling on a coin toss where a head provides a \$50,000 win and a tail results in a \$10,000 loss. The subjective probability for winning the contract may therefore be transformed directly into an "objective" .5 probability for obtaining a head from a coin toss. Assuming indifference between the real gamble and a hypothetical coin toss, we then substitute the latter into the decision analysis.

One practical benefit of substituting a hypothetical gamble for an actual uncertainty is that subjective probabilities may be used in conjunction with the traditional long-run frequencies of occurrence. In effect, apples and oranges may be mixed, permitting wider acceptance of decision-theory analysis. More significantly, a hypothetical gamble or lottery provides a convenient means of obtaining the subjective probability value itself. Consider the following illustration.

SUBSTITUTING A HYPOTHETICAL LOTTERY FOR THE REAL GAMBLE: PROBABILITIES FOR DESIGNING A SONAR

A project engineer must choose between two technologies in designing a prototype sonar system. She may use Doppler shift or acoustic ranging. If the Doppler

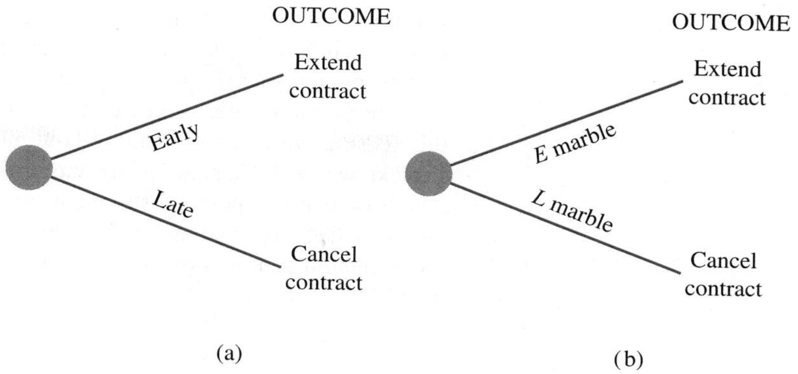

FIGURE 20-1 A project engineer's actual gamble (a) and a hypothetical lottery (b) yielding identical outcomes.

shift is used, time becomes a crucial factor. To analyze this decision, the engineer must determine the probability for completing the project on time. If she is late, the project will be canceled and she will be out of a job. But if she is early or on time, her contract will be extended for two more years. The event fork of concern appears in Figure 20-1(a).

Suppose that the engineer considers the hypothetical lottery shown in Figure 20-1(b), in which one marble is to be randomly selected from a box of 100. Some marbles are labeled *E* (for early); the rest are marked *L* (for late). In this hypothetical gamble, selecting an *E* marble will result in an extended contract, but drawing an *L* marble will result in a canceled contract. Our engineer determines the mix of *L* and *E* marbles. She is asked what mixture will make her *indifferent* between letting her future be decided by trying the Doppler shift design or by selecting a marble from the box.

Suppose that the engineer determines that 70 *E* marbles and 30 *L* marbles would make her indifferent. This means that the probability for selecting an *E* marble is .70. This value may be considered the engineer's **judgmental assessment** that the project will be early or on time if the Doppler shift is used. Thus, our decision maker lets .70 represent the probability for being early or on time in analyzing her decision and place .70 on the early event branch of the fork in Figure 20-1(a).

Arriving at subjective probabilities by substituting the actual gamble for an equally preferred lottery is a useful procedure when the number of possible events is small. But this method may be quite cumbersome when the situation involves more than a handful of events. In business applications, we are often faced with variables, such as product demand, which can be measured on many possible levels. It is best to use an entire *probability distribution* to represent such uncertain quantities.

SUBJECTIVE PROBABILITY DISTRIBUTIONS

We have seen that probability distributions can be divided into two categories. *Discrete probability distributions* apply to variables, such as the demand for cars, that must be a whole number. *Continuous probability distributions* represent variables, such as time, that may be expressed on a continuous scale and measured to any degree of precision desired. When the number of possibilities is great, discrete variables are often treated as if they are approximately continuous. For this reason, we focus on finding continuous probability distributions.

Next we will consider using judgment to determine the normal distribution, which constitutes perhaps the most common distribution family encountered in business decision making with continuous variables. We will then discuss the more general problem of establishing a probability distribution for *any* uncertain quantity.

EXERCISES

20-1 Discuss whether historical frequencies are meaningful in estimating the probabilities for each of the following cases.
(a) the first-year salary levels of business school graduates
(b) the faces obtained by tossing an asymmetrical die
(c) the deaths during the next year of people in various age, health, sex, and occupational categories

20-2 Use your judgment to assess the probability that you will receive an A on your next examination. Imagine that your instructor will let you obtain your grade by lottery, so that 100 slips of paper (some labeled A; the rest, not A) will be put into a hat and mixed. You will draw one of these slips at random, and the letter obtained will be the grade that you receive. How many A slips must there be to make you indifferent between letting your grade be determined by lottery or by earning it?

20-3 DETERMINING A NORMAL CURVE JUDGMENTALLY

The normal distribution plays an important role in decision making. This is largely due to the fact that the probabilities for sample means can usually be characterized by a normal curve. But the normal curve may be applied in many situations other than sampling. The frequency patterns of physical measurements often approximate the normal curve. This feature makes it especially important in production applications, where natural fluctuations in size, density, concentration, and other factors cause individual units to vary according to the normal distribution. Test scores used to determine personal aptitude or achievement are also often characterized by the normal curve. Questions of facility design as it relates to waiting lines in manufacturing, retailing, or data-processing situations must take into account the time needed to produce units, service customers, or complete jobs; these service times are often normally distributed.

Since the normal distribution is prevalent in such a broad spectrum of decision-making situations, we will give it special emphasis in this chapter. We have seen that any normal distribution is uniquely defined in terms of two parameters—the mean μ and the standard deviation σ. Except in the rare circumstances when these parameters are known precisely, it is impossible to measure their values directly without expensive sampling procedures. It may be more convenient to exercise judgment in determining μ and σ. With these two quantities, we can specify the entire normal distribution. (In fact, it may be optimal not to take samples at all—

a question that we will consider in Chapter 27. Often sampling itself is impossible because no population currently exists from which observations may be taken.)

FINDING THE MEAN

The mean of the subjective normal curve for any quantity X believed to have a normal distribution may be established by selecting the *midpoint* of all possible values. *The subjective mean* μ is that point judged to have a 50–50 chance for any value X to lie at or above it versus below it. The value is actually the *median* level, since it is just as likely that X will fall below or above the identified point. Because the normal curve is symmetrical, this central value must also equal the mean.

ILLUSTRATION: TELEPROCESSOR'S PRINTING RATE

Suppose that an engineer is evaluating a new teleprocessing terminal design to determine if a prototype should be fabricated. Based on the physical characteristics of the unit compared with existing equipment of similar scope, the engineer concludes that messages could be printed at a rate of between 30 and 70 lines per second, depending on the type of message. Because the unit has never been built, the true rate X for a typical message is uncertain. The engineer assumes that this quantity is normally distributed, because similar data in related applications have been found to fit well to the normal curve.

To determine the mean printing rate, the engineer is asked to establish a level such that it is equally likely for X to fall above or below it. This decision may be phrased in terms of a coin toss: "Suppose that you had to find a middle value such that it would be difficult for you to choose whether the actual printing rate X lies above or below it. If your professional reputation depended on being correct and you had to make a prediction for X, you would be willing to select one side or the other of that value by tossing a coin. Where would your midpoint lie?" After some thought the engineer might reply, "I think it is a coin-tossing proposition that the printing rate experienced in actual testing may fall above or below 50 lines per second." This establishes the desired midpoint and therefore the mean of the subjective probability distribution, so that $\mu = 50$ lines per second.

Relating the judgmental evaluation to coin tossing makes the problem easy for a person who is not used to dealing with probability. The 50–50 gamble is the easiest to envision. We may extend this concept to finding the standard deviation as well. *The subjective standard deviation* σ *can be found by establishing a middle range of values centered at* μ *such that X is judged to have an equal chance of lying inside or outside that interval.* To see how this works, let's review some properties of the normal curve.

FINDING THE STANDARD DEVIATION

In Chapter 7, we saw that the area under the normal curve between any two points is established by the distances separating each point from the mean, which are expressed in units of standard deviation. This standardized distance may be represented by a value of the normal deviate z, where for any particular point x, the corresponding normal deviate may be computed from

$$z = \frac{x - \mu}{\sigma}$$

We seek two possible values of X that are equally distant from μ such that the area between them is .50. This means that the area between μ and the upper limit must be one-half this value, or .25. From the normal curve areas in Appendix Table D, the normal deviate value of $z = .67$ provides the closest area, .2486. We use $z = .67$ to find σ.

Figure 20-2 illustrates the underlying principles involved. The area between μ and $\mu + .67\sigma$ is about .25, so that the area in the interval $\mu \pm .67\sigma$ is about .50. If we know the distance separating the upper limit $\mu + .67\sigma$ and the mean μ, or the *half-width* of the interval, we determine the corresponding value of σ by setting $.67\sigma$ equal to that distance.

$$.67\sigma = \text{Upper limit} - \mu$$

Dividing both sides by .67, we obtain the expression for the

JUDGMENTAL STANDARD DEVIATION

$$\sigma = \frac{\text{Upper limit} - \mu}{.67} = \frac{\text{Half-width}}{.67}$$

Thus, to find σ, we need to establish only the width of the middle range (covered by the shaded area in Figure 20-2). This quantity is sometimes called the **interquartile range**. This evalutaion is tantamount to establishing the half-width such that there is a 50–50 chance that any particular value of X will fall within μ plus or minus this quantity.

The engineer in our example is now asked to establish the half-width of the central interval. This problem may be formulated: "Select the range of values centered at $\mu = 50$ lines per second so that the actual printing rate will be just

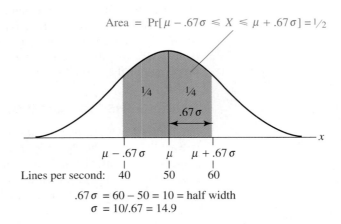

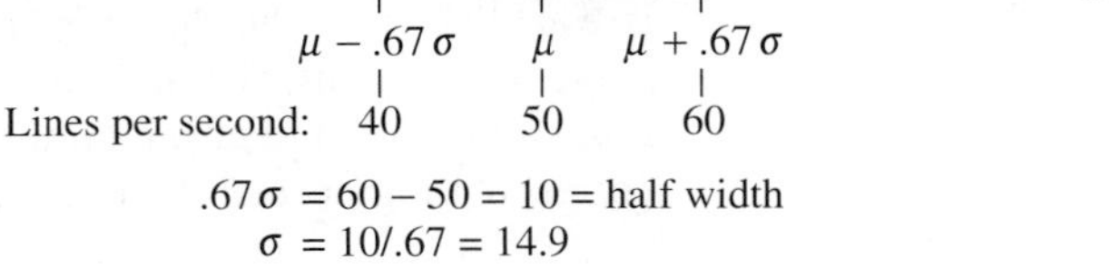

FIGURE 20-2 Finding the standard deviation of a subjective normal distribution.

as likely to fall inside or outside of it. To find the interval, determine an amount such that μ plus or minus that quantity establishes the range." The engineer might respond: "I would guess that ± 10 lines per second is suitable for this purpose. This means that it is a coin-tossing proposition that the actual printing rate will fall somewhere between $50 - 10 = 40$ and $50 + 10 = 60$ lines per second." This establishes the half-width of 10 lines per second for the middle range, and we calculate the standard deviation to be

$$\sigma = \frac{10}{.67} = 14.9 \text{ lines per second}$$

The subjective probability distribution for the actual printing time of the proposed terminal is now specified. Combining this with economic data, the decision maker may then apply decision-theory concepts to evaluate various alternatives regarding the manufacturing or marketing of the proposed unit.

EXERCISES

20-3 An automobile production manager believes that the time it takes to install a new car bumper is normally distributed. He has established that it is a 50–50 proposition that this task will take more than 60 seconds and that it is "even money" that the required time for any particular car will be between 45 and 75 seconds.

(a) Calculate the mean and the standard deviation of the subjective probability distribution.

(b) Determine the probabilities that the installation for a particular car will take

(1) between 50 and 70 seconds

(2) less than 25 seconds

(3) more than 1 minute

(4) between 20 and 90 seconds

20-4 Establish your own subjective probability distribution for the heights of adult males residing within 50 miles of your campus. Use the normal curve that you obtain to establish the probabilities that a randomly chosen man is (a) less than 6′2″; (b) taller than 5′6″; (c) taller than your father.

20-4 THE JUDGMENTAL PROBABILITY DISTRIBUTION: THE INTERVIEW METHOD

The procedure we have just examined is a limited one. Although the normal distribution is very common, it is the exception. We will now consider how judgment may be exercised to determine probability distributions. Our procedure applies to any variable with a large number of possible values, such as product demand.

A natural and fairly simple procedure for obtaining a probability distribution judgmentally is to use cumulative probabilities. By posing a series of 50–50 gambles, it is quite simple to make a judgmental determination of the cumulative probability distribution for a random variable. Each response provides a point that may be plotted on a graph; a smoothed curve can then be drawn through the points. This curve completely specifies the underlying probability distribution. The following illustration shows how this procedure may be carried out.

ILLUSTRATION: JUDGMENTAL PROBABILITY DISTRIBUTION FOR DEMAND

The president of a food manufacturing concern wishes to obtain the probability distribution for the demand for a new snack product. This will be used to help the president decide whether or not to market the product. A statistical analyst asks the president a series of questions to obtain answers that will be used to formulate later questions. The interview follows.*

Q. What do you think the largest and smallest possible levels of demand are?
A. Certainly demand will exceed 500,000 units. But I would set an upper limit of 3,000,000 units. I don't think that under the most favorable circumstances we could sell more than this amount.

Q. Okay, we have determined the range of possible demand. Now I want you to tell me what level of demand divides the possibilities into two equally likely ranges. For example, do you think demand will be just as likely to fall above 2,000,000 as below?
A. No, I'd rather pick 1,500,000 units as the 50–50 point.

Q. Very good. Now let's consider the demand levels below 1,500,000. If demand were to fall somewhere between 500,000 and 1,500,000 units, would you bet that it lies above or below 1,000,000?
A. Above. I would say that a demand of 1,250,000 units would be a realistic dividing point.

Q. We will use that amount as our 50–50 point. Let's do the same thing for the upper range of demand.
A. If I were to pick a number, I would choose 2,000,000 units. I feel that demand is just as likely to fall into the 1.5 to 2 million range as into the 2 to 3 million range.

Q. Excellent. We're making good progress. To get a finer fix on the points obtained so far, I now want you to tell me whether you think demand is just as likely to fall between 1.25 and 2 million units as it is to fall outside that range.
A. No. I think it is more likely to fall inside. I suppose this means I am being inconsistent.

Q. Yes, it does. Let's remedy this. Do you think that we ought to raise the 1,250,000 dividing point or lower the 2 million unit figure?
A. Lower the 2 million figure to 1.9 million.

Q. Let's check to see if this disturbs our other answers. Do you think that 1,500,000 splits demand over the range from 1,250,000 to 1,900,000 into two equally likely regions?
A. Yes, I am satisfied that it does.

*This procedure was inspired by Howard Raiffa, *Decision Analysis: Introductory Lectures on Choices Under Uncertainty* (Reading, Mass.: Addison-Wesley, 1968).

Q. Just a few more questions. Suppose demand is above 1,900,000. What level splits this demand range into two equally likely regions?
A. I'd say 2,200,000.

Q. Good. Now if demand is between 2,200,000 and 3,000,000, where would you split?
A. I would guess that 2,450,000 units would be the 50–50 point.

Q. How about when demand is below 1,250,000?
A. Try 1,100,000 units.

Q. And when demand is between 500,000 and 1,100,000 units?
A. I think demand is far more likely to be close to the higher figure. I would bet on 950,000 units.

Table 20-1 shows the information obtained from this interview. The initial decision to divide demand at 1,500,000 units makes this level the 50% point or median. Since .5 has been judged the probability that demand will be below 1,500,000, we will refer to this as the **.5 fractile**. This means that the probability is .5 that the actual demand will be 1,500,000 units *or less*. Our decision maker has chosen to divide the range from 500,000 to 1,500,000 units at a demand level of 1,250,000. Believing that the chance of demand falling into this range is .5, the president has judged the chance that demand will be at or below 1,250,000 units to be .5(.5) = .25; thus, we refer to 1,250,000 units as the .25 fractile. This establishes a .25 probability that demand will be less than or equal to 1,250,000. The median of the range from 1,500,000 to 3,000,000 units is 1,900,000, which becomes the .75 fractile, since the probability is .5 + .5(.5) = .75 that demand will fall somewhere below 1,900,000 units. The analyst has proceeded to find the medians of the regions by working outward from previously determined 50% points. Thus, the .125 fractile of 1,100,000 units is the median demand for possible levels below the .25 fractile (1,250,000 units), which had to be determined first. The median of demands above 1,900,000 units is the .875 fractile of 2,200,000 units. Similarly, the median of the demands below 1,100,000 is the .0625 fractile of 950,000 units, whereas the median demand level above 2,200,000 is the .9375 fractile of 2,450,000.

The fractiles and the corresponding demands are plotted as points in Figure 20-3. The vertical axis represents the cumulative probability for demand. A curve has been smoothed through these points, which serves as an approximation of the

TABLE 20-1 Judgmental Assessment of Fractiles for Snack Food Demand

Fractile	Quantity
0	500,000
.0625	950,000
.125	1,100,000
.25	1,250,000
.50	1,500,000
.75	1,900,000
.875	2,200,000
.9375	2,450,000
1.000	3,000,000

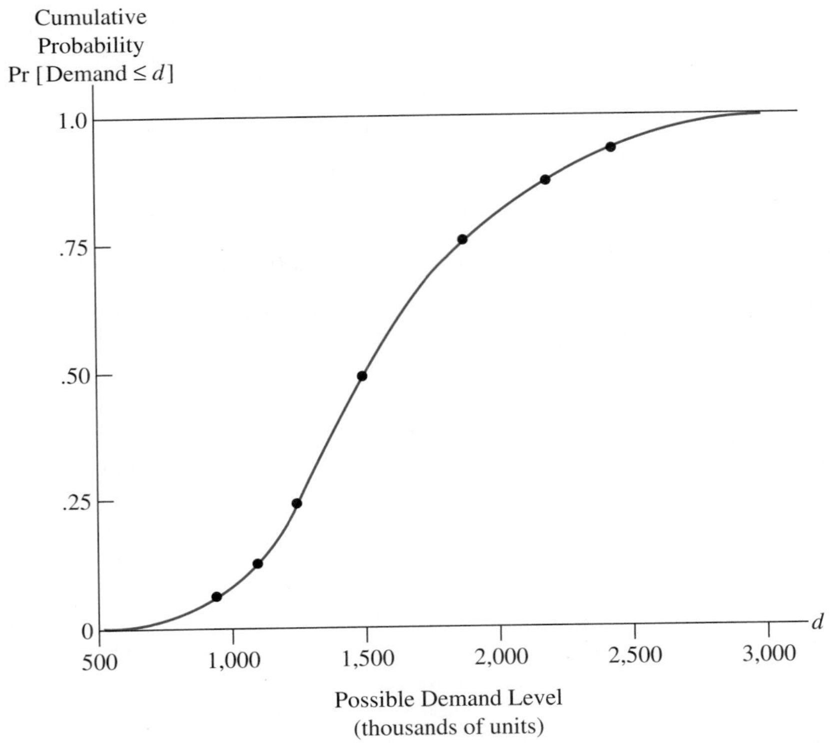

FIGURE 20-3 Cumulative probability distribution for a new snack product.

cumulative probability distribution for the first-year demand for the snack product. The curve has an S shape; its slope increases initially and then decreases over higher levels of demand. The slope changes most rapidly for large and small demands, so that more points in these regions provide greater accuracy. This is why we work outward from the median in assessing the demand fractiles.

This example illustrates how we obtain a very detailed measurement of judgment by posing a few 50–50 gambles. As a rule of thumb, the seven fractile values ranging from .0625 to .9375 in Table 20-1 are adequate for this purpose. Little may be gained from obtaining more fractiles, since further gambles might result in a lumpy curve and would probably not alter the basic shape anyway. Besides, there is no reason to "gild the lily" or to try the decision maker's patience. A curve obtained by following this procedure provides about as accurate a judgmental assessment as is humanly possible.

COMMON SHAPES OF SUBJECTIVE PROBABILITY CURVES

Ordinarily, subjective probability distributions obtained by judgmental assessment provide S-shaped graphs that are elongated at either the top or the bottom. Such graphs represent underlying probability distributions that are skewed to the left or to the right, as the corresponding frequency curves in Figure 20-4(a) and (b) show. Although skewed distributions are most common for business and economic variables, a symmetrical distribution, shown in Figure 20-4(c), is also possible.

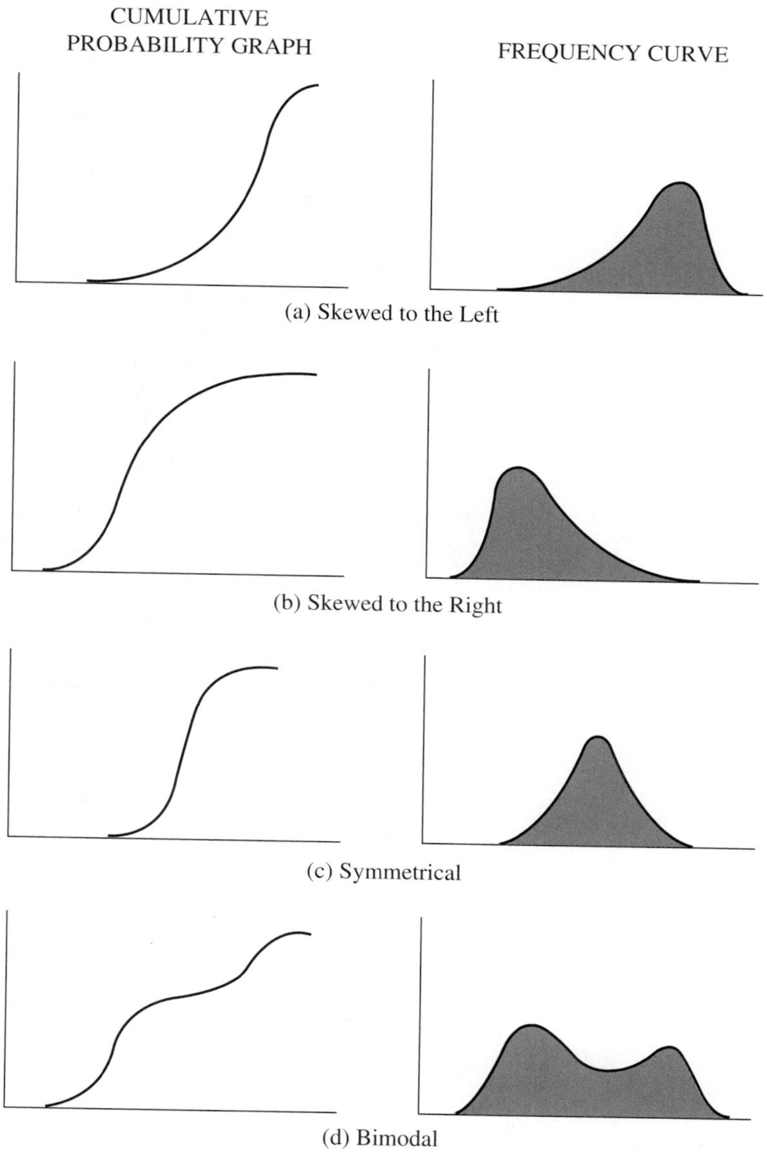

FIGURE 20-4 Possible shapes of subjective probability distributions.

Lumpy cumulative probability graphs with two stacked S-shaped curves, like the one in Figure 20-4(d), are to be avoided. The corresponding frequency curve has the two-humped shape that typifies a *bimodal distribution*. Such distributions reflect some underlying nonhomogeneous influence that operates differently for the lower-valued possibilities than it does for the higher-valued possibilities. The bimodal distribution is epitomized by combining the heights of men and women. In statistics, it is more meaningful to portray male and female heights in terms of two separate curves.

Similarly, if such a result occurs in assessing subjective probability distributions, some identifiable factor in the decision maker's mind might explain the bimodality. A good example would be determining the demand for automobiles in the next model year. If there is a possibility of an oil embargo, as in 1973–1974, or an energy crisis, as in 1978–1980, the assessment should be broken down into greater detail: (1) Find a subjective probability for a gasoline shortage; (2) determine the subjective probability distribution for automobile demand assuming a shortage occurs; and (3) establish a second separate distribution for demand given that no shortage occurs.

If there is no identifiable explanation, lumpiness in the cumulative probability graph may be due to inconsistencies in expressing judgment, which may be resolved by moving one or more points to the left or right and posing again the succeeding 50–50 gambles. One easy consistency check is to see if there is actually a 50–50 chance of the factor under consideration falling inside or outside the interquartile range, from the .25 fractile (1,250,000 units in our example) to the .75 fractile (1,900,000 units). If the decision maker judges the inside to be more likely, then the middle range should be narrowed, either by raising the .25 fractile (perhaps to 1,300,000 units) or by reducing the .75 fractile (perhaps to 1,800,000 units). Conversely, if the outside is more unlikely, then one of the fractiles should be changed in the opposite direction.

APPROXIMATING THE SUBJECTIVE PROBABILITY DISTRIBUTION

It is difficult to employ the cumulative S curve directly in decision analysis, where expected values must be determined. Expected values are ordinarily calculated

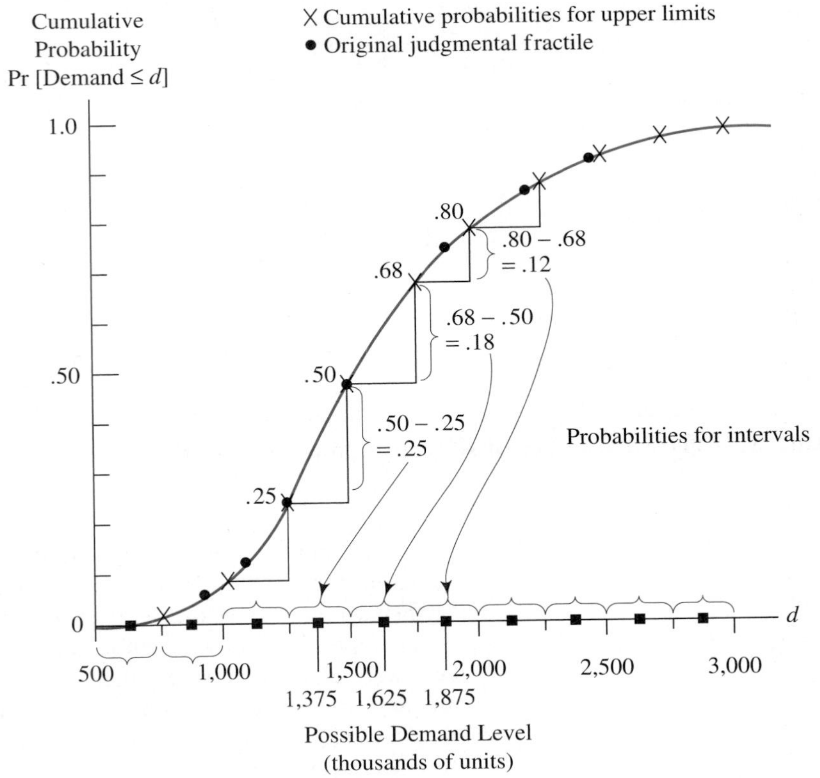

FIGURE 20-5 Approximating the cumulative probability distribution using 10 intervals.

TABLE 20-2 Subjective Demand Probabilities and Approximating the Expected Demand

(1) Demand Interval (thousands)	(2) Interval Midpoint (thousands)	(3) Probability for Demands at or below Upper Limit (obtained from curve)	(4) Probability for Demand Interval	(5) Demand × Probability (2) × (4)
500–under 750	625	.02	.02	12.50
750–under 1,000	875	.08	.06	52.50
1,000–under 1,250	1,125	.25	.17	191.25
1,250–under 1,500	1,375	.50	.25	343.75
1,500–under 1,750	1,625	.68	.18	292.50
1,750–under 2,000	1,875	.80	.12	225.00
2,000–under 2,250	2,125	.89	.09	191.25
2,250–under 2,500	2,375	.95	.06	142.50
2,500–under 2,750	2,625	.98	.03	78.75
2,750–under 3,000	2,875	1.00	.02	57.50
			Approximate expected demand =	1,587.50

from a table that lists the possible variable values and their probabilities. To obtain such a table, it is necessary to approximate the cumulative probability curve by the method shown in Figure 20-5.

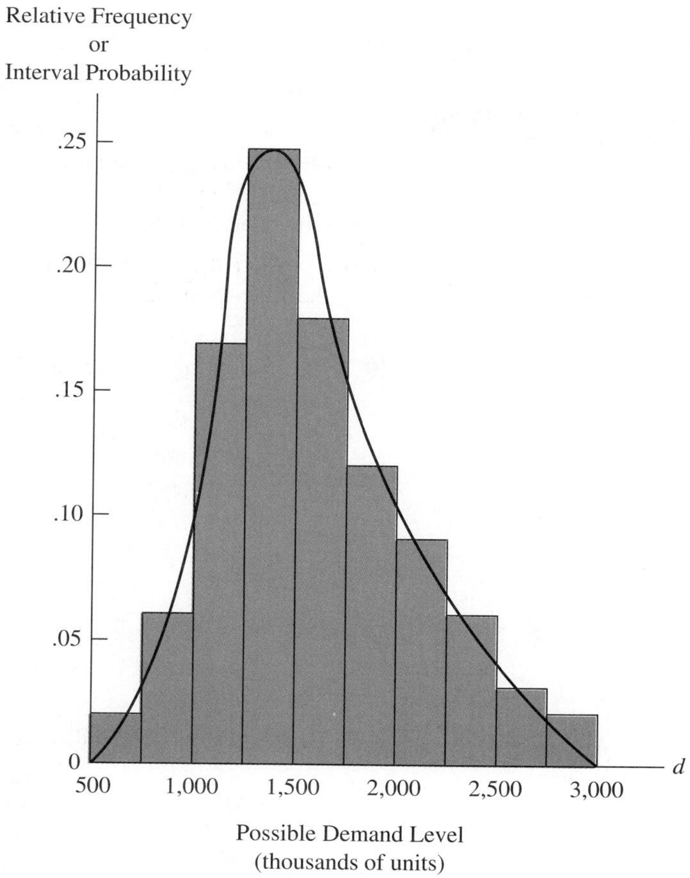

FIGURE 20-6 The frequency curve and the individual interval probabilities for snack food demand.

Each possible variable is represented by an interval. A fairly accurate approximation is obtained with 10 intervals of equal width. The probabilities for each interval are shown as the step sizes at the upper limit for the respective interval. The probabilities for individual intervals are determined by the difference between successive cumulative probability values. All values in an interval are represented by a typical value. For this purpose, the midpoint is used.

To see how this is done, suppose that the decision maker now wishes to establish subjective probabilities for intervals of demand from 500,000 to 3,000,000 units in increments of 250,000. Table 20-2 shows how these demand probabilities have been obtained by reading values from the cumulative probability curve in Figure 20-5. The resulting probability distribution may be used in further evaluations. From it, the approximate expected demand is computed to be 1,587,500 units.

The interval probabilities may be used to plot the histogram for demand shown in Figure 20-6. The height of .25 for the bar covering the interval from 1,250,000 to 1,500,000 units represents the probability that demand will fall somewhere between these amounts. Superimposed onto this histogram is a smoothed curve representing the judgmental frequency curve for demand. Note that the curve is positively skewed.

EXERCISES

20-5 Consider the cumulative probability distribution in Figure 20-7. Determine the following probabilities.

(a) $\Pr[D > 500]$ (c) $\Pr[D \geq 300]$
(b) $\Pr[D \leq 150]$ (d) $\Pr[200 \leq D \leq 800]$

20-6 Consider the cumulative probability distribution in Figure 20-7. Determine the following fractiles.

(a) .10 (b) .50 (c) .125 (d) .75 (e) .37

20-7 The following fractiles apply to the subjective probability distribution for the demand for a new product.

Fractile	Quantity
.0625	10,000
.125	25,000
.25	35,000
.50	40,000
.75	45,000
.875	55,000
.9375	75,000

Determine the probabilities that demand will fall within the following limits.

(a) 10,000 to 40,000 (c) 25,000 to 55,000
(b) 35,000 to 75,000 (d) 25,000 to 45,000

20-8 Willy B. Rich is a real estate investor who has established the following judgmental results regarding the rate of return on a proposed project. No value less than −20% or greater than 50% is possible.

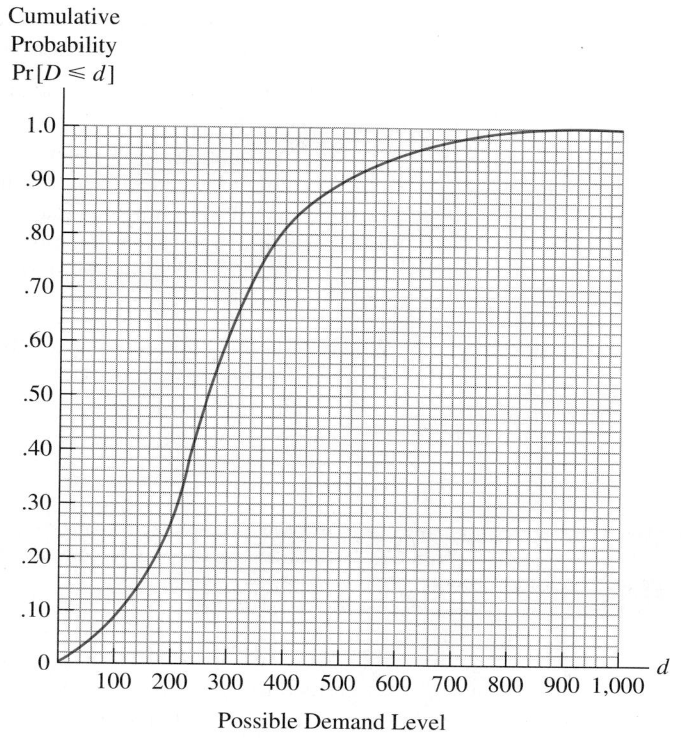

FIGURE 20-7

Rate of Return	50–50 point
all	15%
below 15%	7
above 15%	20
below 7%	3
above 20%	24
below 3%	−4
above 24%	28

(a) Complete the following table for Willy.

Fractile	Rate of Return
0	
.0625	
.125	
.25	
.50	
.75	
.875	
.9375	
1.000	

(b) Plot the cumulative probability distribution for Willy's rate of return.

(c) Using your graph, determine the investor's subjective probability that the rate of return is between 20% and 40%.

20-9 Envision your income during the first full calendar year after graduation. Establish your own subjective probability distribution for the adjusted gross income figure that you will report to the IRS. (If applicable, include your spouse's earnings, interest, dividends, and other income.) If your graph has an unusual shape, try to eliminate any inconsistencies or to identify the nonhomogeneous factors (such as pregnancy, unemployment, or divorce) that might explain the shape. Remember, you are the expert about yourself.

20-10 Use the cumulative probability distribution for demand in Figure 20-7. Construct the approximate probability distribution for demand, using five intervals in increments of 200. Select the midpoints of these intervals as representative values, and determine the approximate expected demand.

20-5 FINDING A PROBABILITY DISTRIBUTION FROM ACTUAL/FORECAST RATIOS

The interview method is most suitable for use on a one-time basis when uncertain circumstances are involved that may never be encountered again. When judgmental forecasts of a single value are made more often, they provide a history that can be used to determine the underlying probability distribution.

We will illustrate this procedure with an example involving weekly sales forecasts for Blitz Beer made by the company's sales manager. The relevant data over a 10-month period are provided in Table 20-3. We will assume that the forecasts have been made solely from judgment. The actual sales values are divided by the respective forecast sales figures to provide **actual/forecast ratios**.

Actual sales of Blitz Beer for the first week were 1,133 barrels. The manager had forecast 1,200 barrels. Thus,

$$\frac{\text{Actual sales}}{\text{Forecast sales}} = \frac{1{,}133}{1{,}200} = .94 \qquad \text{(actual/forecast ratio)}$$

TABLE 20-3 Judgment Forecasts and Actual/Forecast Ratios of Blitz Beer Weekly Sales (in barrels)

Actual	Forecast	Actual/Forecast
1,133	1,200	.94
1,422	1,150	1.24
1,288	1,300	.99
1,317	1,370	.96
1,080	1,410	.77
1,344	1,580	.85
1,506	1,650	.91
1,752	1,650	1.06
1,924	1,750	1.10
1,783	2,000	.89

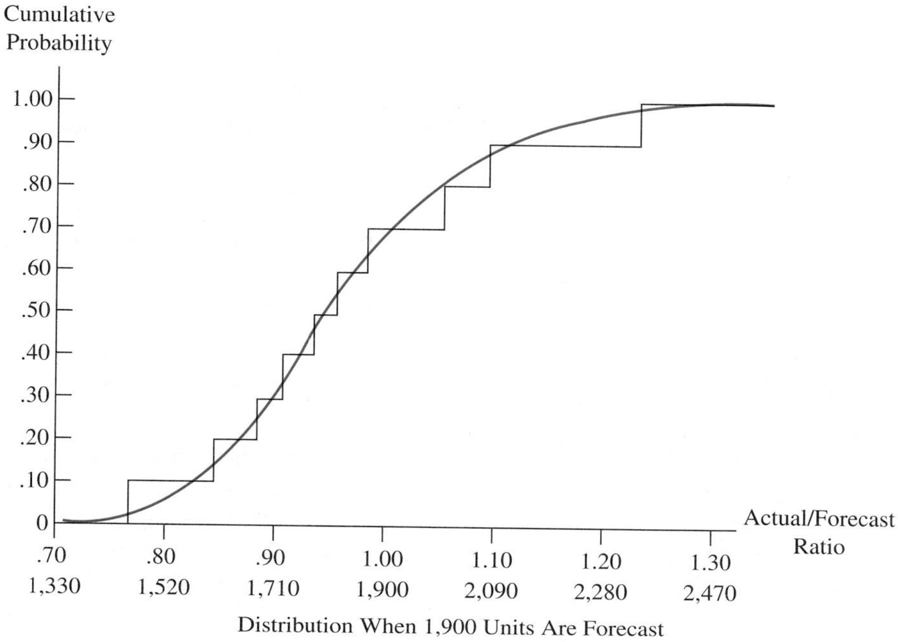

FIGURE 20-8 Subjective probability distribution for Blitz Beer sales based on actual/forecast ratios.

The sales manager's forecasting record is summarized in the cumulative probability graph in Figure 20-8. To plot this, the actual/forecast ratios are arranged in increasing value. There are 10 ratios, so each ratio is assigned a probability of 1/10. Thus, a .10 step in cumulative probability occurs at each value. A smoothed curve is then drawn freehand through the resulting cumulative probability stairway. This curve can be combined with the sales manager's next forecast to obtain the cumulative probability distribution for beer sales for that week. For instance, to find the probability distribution when the sales forecast is 1,900 barrels, the actual/forecast ratios on the horizontal axis are multiplied by 1,900.

EXERCISES

20-11 The following sales data apply to Deuce Hardware (in thousands of dollars).

Actual	Forecast
550	600
490	550
610	560
580	600
620	650

Actual	Forecast
650	700
700	690
680	700
780	750
800	850

(a) Compute the actual/forecast ratios. Plot the cumulative probability graph, and then sketch a smoothed curve through the stairway.

(b) Suppose that the sales forecast for next year is 1,000 dollars. Read from your curve the subjective probability that sales will fall at or below (1) 920; (2) 970; (3) 1,100.

20-12 A sports writer has forecast the Gotham City Hellcats' seasonal batting average for a 10-year period. The following values apply.

Actual	Forecast	Actual	Forecast
.273	.250	.350	.278
.332	.315	.364	.340
.366	.320	.359	.355
.307	.365	.331	.360
.318	.330	.388	.373

(a) Compute the actual/forecast ratios. Plot the cumulative probability graph, and then sketch a smoothed curve through the stairway.

(b) Suppose that the forecast batting average is .350 for the next baseball season. Read from your graph the subjective probability that the Hellcats' batting average will be (1) $\leq$ .300; (2) $\leq$ .360; (3) $\leq$ .375.

20-6 ADDITIONAL REMARKS

We have seen that probability values for decision making may sometimes be obtained from past history, but that past history is of limited use in business situations and may not exist at all for nonrepeatable circumstances. We have emphasized the direct assessment of a decision maker's judgment rather than traditional statistical techniques. But it should be noted that traditional techniques also rely heavily on judgmental inputs (usually of an indirect nature).

It is not necessary for a decision maker to obtain subjective probabilities personally. Such judgments can be delegated. For example, the chairman of General Motors might rely on various officers within the corporation to determine some or all of the probabilities to be used in analyzing a decision. After all, this is an area in which expert opinion should be relied on whenever possible. Exercising judgment to find subjective probabilities is similar to assessing attitudes toward decision outcomes. Chapter 29 shows how such attitudes may be summarized by a utility curve. It is dangerous for any decision maker to delegate the assessment of attitudes to others. Attitudes are highly personal and express unique tastes, whereas judgment can be shared. (The collective assessment of attitudes is prohibited by the axioms of utility theory. However, there is no reason why a committee cannot determine the subjective probabilities to be used.)

SUMMARY

1. **What is a subjective probability and the role of judgment in establishing its value?**

   A **subjective probability** expresses an individual's *strength of conviction* regarding the likelihood of an event occurring. Subjective probabilities are arrived at through *judgment* and may be applied to one-shot events for which frequency of occurrence has no meaning. Such judgment may be based on historical experience, although frequency of occurance need not be systematically applied—as would be the case with the objective probabilities discussed throughout the earlier portions of this book.

Under one interpretation, subjective probabilities serve as *betting odds*. Consider a decision maker who would be *indifferent* between the actual event fork and a hypothetical lottery having identical outcomes. The probabilities from the lottery may then serve as the subjective probability values for the actual events.

2. **How may we overcome the philosophical objections to using subjective probabilities?**
   Some statisticians object to using subjective probabilities at all. But since the probabilities in the hypothetical lottery would be generated by means of random selection, like a raffle, they are analogous to *long-run frequencies*. Those numbers are *objective* probabilities for the lottery, and at the same time *subjective* probabilities in the original event fork. If hypothetical lotteries are substituted for any event forks involving nonrepeatable random experiments, then all probabilities in the decision structure may be considered to be objective probabilities. As long as the decision maker would be indifferent between such a hypothetical structure and the original decision, with all hypothetical lotteries having identical outcomes with the original ones, those philosophical objections should not apply.

3. **How can we use 50–50 gambles to establish a subjective normal probability distribution?**
   Subjective probabilities may apply to discrete events, such as winning a contract. They may also apply to random variables. Such probabilities compose a **subjective probability distribution**. A common distribution involves a **subjective normal curve**, which is fully specified once its *mean* and *standard deviation* are determined. Both parameters may be arrived at through 50–50 gambles that are judgmentally selected for the particular random variable.

4. **What is the interview method for establishing a subjective cumulative probability distribution function?**
   A general subjective probability distribution, not necessarily a normal curve, may be arrived at through a judgmental assessment involving a series of 50–50 gambles. This is referred to as the *interview method* and it establishes a series of fractiles or percentiles, from which a cumulative probability distribution function may be fully specified graphically. A random variable with a unimodal, two-tailed density function will plot as an S-shape on the cumulative probability graph. A large class of distributions fall into that category.

5. **What is the actual/forecast ratio method for establishing a subjective cumulative probability distribution function?**
   When an expert has made predictions of a random variable over time, so that actual values and forecast values are both available from the past, those data may be used to establish a cumulative probability distribution *stairway*. The basic assumption is that all historical **actual/forecast values** are equally likely to prevail in the future, to that each successive step occurs at the next higher historical ratio. A future forecast then establishes the horizontal scale. A smoothed curve may then be fitted to the stairway to obtain the cumulative distribution function.

6. How can the graph for cumulative subjective probabilities be used to find a tabular representation of the probability distribution?
The cumulative distribution function may be approximated by a stairway involving a step for each class interval. The step sizes or interval probabilities may then be used as probabilities for the interval midpoints, levels of which serve as the events used to calculate expected values.

REVIEW EXERCISES

20-13 Use your judgment to assess probabilities for the following events.
(a) The New York Yankees will play in and win the next World Series.
(b) If you are presently single, you will marry within one year. If you are presently married, your spouse will change jobs within one year.
(c) You will replace one of your present automobiles in the coming year.

20-14 The dean of the Dover School of Business is assessing the probability distribution for next term's grade point average (GPA) for the entire school. It is "even money" that the GPA will fall at or below 2.75. The dean assigns a 50–50 probability that the low side will be at or below 2.70 and that the high side will be at or above 2.80. If the GPA is lower than 2.70, it is a coin-tossing proposition that it will fall at or below 2.60; similarly, the odds are even that the GPA will fall at or above 2.95, given that it lies above 2.80. Determine the subjective probability that the GPA will lie within the following limits.
(a) 2.60 and 2.95 (c) 2.60 and 2.75
(b) 2.70 and 2.80 (d) 2.75 and 2.95

20-15 The yield of an active ingredient from a chemical process is assumed to be normally distributed. The 50–50 point is 30 grams per liter. The interquartile range (middle 50%) spans 4 grams per liter.
(a) Calculate the mean and the standard deviation of the subjective probability distribution.
(b) Determine the probability that the yield falls (1) below 29 grams; (2) between 28.5 and 30.5 grams; (3) above 31.5 grams.

20-16 Consider the total size of the U.S. car market (passenger cars sold—both imported and domestic) from October of the current year to the following October. Establish your subjective probability distribution for this quantity, and plot the results on a cumulative probability graph.

CASE The Permian Plunge

Rod Shafter is a geologist who has formed a series of limited partnerships engaging in wildcat drilling for oil and gas. While evaluating a leasehold site in the Permian Basin of West Texas, Shafter employed Cal Crunch as a consultant. Crunch was to provide numbers useful for deciding whether the partnership should take the plunge and sink a wildcat shaft there.

The initial uncertainty pertains to whether a proper structural environment for fossil fuels exists beneath the site. Given the proper structure, there is some probability that the site will contain gas only, oil only, a combination of oil and gas, or neither. Shafter does not feel comfortable about arriving at the correct values for these probabilities. Crunch reassures him that satisfactory numbers may be "pulled out of thin air" using a box of marbles as a prop.

Even if there is oil or gas, Rod is uncertain about the recoverable quantities. Crunch plans to show him how to determine subjective probability distributions for each case. He plans to achieve this by conducting an interview that will "quantify Shafter's judgments."

QUESTIONS

1. With Cal's help, Rod arrives at the following probabilities.

$$\Pr[\text{structure}] = .40$$

$$\Pr[\text{oil only}|\text{structure}] = .10$$

$$\Pr[\text{gas only}|\text{structure}] = .05$$

$$\Pr[\text{oil } \textit{and} \text{ gas}|\text{structure}] = .20$$

$$\Pr[\text{neither}|\text{structure}] = .65$$

Determine the probability that the site contains the following. (Structure must be present in order for oil or gas to have formed.)
(a) oil only (b) gas only (c) oil and gas (d) neither

2. Gas is measured in units of thousand cubic feet (mcf). Rod estimates that given gas (with or without oil), there is a 50–50 chance that the field contains 100 million mcf of recoverable gas reserves. He judges that should the quantity be higher than 100 million mcf, there is an even chance that reserves will be at or below 150 million mcf; should it be lower than 100 million, there is a 50–50 chance that the field will yield at or below 75 million mcf. Above 150 million mcf, the median level is 250 million mcf, while below 75 million mcf the median is 60 million mcf. Should there be more than 250 million mcf, it is "even money" that the level of reserves will lie above or below 400 million mcf, and should there be less than 60 million mcf, it is even money again that reserves will be at or below 50 million mcf. Assuming some oil, it is virtually certain that the field will contain more than 25 million mcf and less than 750 million mcf.
(a) Construct a graph showing the cumulative probability distribution.
(b) Starting at 0 as the lower limit and using 8 intervals each at a width of 100 million mcf, construct a table approximating the cumulative probability distribution.
(c) Using your answer to (b), compute the expected level of gas reserves.

3. Oil is measured in barrels. Rod estimates that given oil (with or without gas), there is a 50–50 chance that the field contains 300,000 recoverable barrels of oil. He judges that should the quantity be higher than that level, there is an even chance that reserves are at or below 400,000 barrels; should it be lower than 300,000, there is a 50–50 chance that the field will yield at or below 250,000 barrels. Above 400,000 barrels the median level is 550,000 barrels, while below 250,000 the median is 220,000 barrels. Should there be more than 550,000 barrels, it is even money that the level of reserves will lie above or below 750,000 barrels, and should there be less than 220,000 barrels, it is even money again that reserves will be at or below 200,000 barrels. Assuming some oil, it is virtually certain that the field will contain more than 100,000 and less than 1,000,000 barrels of oil.

(a) Construct a graph showing the cumulative probability distribution.

(b) Starting at 50,000 barrels as the lower limit and using 10 intervals each at a width of 100,000 barrels, construct a table approximating the cumulative probability distribution.

(c) Using your answer to (b), compute the expected level of oil reserves.

CHAPTER 21

REVISING PROBABILITIES AND COUNTING POSSIBILITIES

BEFORE READING THIS CHAPTER, MAKE SURE YOU UNDERSTAND:

Basic concepts of probability (Chapter 5).

AFTER READING THIS CHAPTER, YOU WILL UNDERSTAND:

About the various kinds of probabilities encountered in using experiments.
About Bayes' theorem and its origin.
About the principle of multiplication underlying counting possibilities.
About permutations and combinations and how to count them.
About factorial products and what they represent.

This chapter describes two important probability topics. The first of these is crucial in decision analysis. The second is helpful in establishing a wide range of probability values.

In business decision making, probabilities are often needed at two different points in time. Such situations arise when the initial choices are whether or not to acquire *experimental information* that might prove helpful in making the basic decision, the outcomes of which are partly determined by two or more main events. *Prior probabilities* for the main events can be helpful in reaching the initial choice about experimenting. Should the experiment be performed, a revised set of *posterior probabilities* will apply for the main events. The levels of those posterior probabilities will depend on the particular experimental result achieved. *Bayes' theorem* allows us to find the revised main event probabilities by combining the prior probabilities with *conditional result probabilities* applicable to the specific experiment performed.

The process of converting prior probabilities into posterior probabilities often involves a mixture of *subjective* and *objective* probabilities. The hardest part can be establishing objective probabilities in the first place. In Chapter 5 we saw that sometimes these may be found through logical deduction using the *count-and-divide method*. But using that procedure requires first finding a numerator and a denominator. In this chapter we consider the various counting methods used to establish probabilities.

21-1 REVISING PROBABILITIES USING BAYES' THEOREM

You may find it valuable to apply the probability revision procedures originally proposed by the Reverend Thomas Bayes over 200 years ago. These involve changing an initial set of probability values in accordance with a particular experimental finding.

PRIOR PROBABILITIES

You often hear a weather forecast such as, "For tomorrow, there is a 50% chance of rain." You may even occasionally come up with your own chance percentage, or **prior probability**, for rain the next day. The adjective *prior* means that the probability value is temporary and might change, depending on what further information develops. There are two classes of prior probabilities

1. **Subjective probabilities:** The value 50% for rain is a subjective probability, since another forecaster might disagree, believing perhaps that there is instead a 40% chance of rain. This subjectivity exists because the underlying random experiment (tomorrow's weather, in this case) is strictly nonrepeatable. Similar uncertainties are common in business. Consider one-shot events such as a new product's reception in the marketplace, a company's sales, or the state of the economy.
2. **Objective probabilities:** A prior probability can be an objective value, reflecting the long-run frequency at which the event would occur in repeated random experiments. Such probabilities are encountered in sampling experiments when the population has known frequencies for various characteristics.

POSTERIOR PROBABILITIES

If you decide there is a .50 prior probability for rain, you might go to bed planning to dress "for the weather" when you arise. But in the morning you might first look outside at the cloud cover. If it is solid and black, you might revise your probability for rain upward to a value like .90; if the clouds are patchy, you might instead reduce that probability to a number like .20, choosing to leave your umbrella at home. Such a revised value is called a **posterior probability**.

Posterior probabilities are *conditional* probabilities of the form

$$\Pr[\text{event} \mid \text{result}]$$

The given event is the **result** of an experiment (in the preceding paragraph, looking at the sky) upon which the revised probability is based. Thomas Bayes proposed a formal mechanism for determining posterior probabilities by merging prior judgment with empirical results. In doing this, you encounter a third type of probability.

CONDITIONAL RESULT PROBABILITIES

Suppose that for an entire year you keep records of a weather forecaster's predictions and the actual next day's weather. Assume that this weatherperson makes one of two forecasts: (1) rain likely and (2) rain unlikely. You may consider your viewing of the 11 P.M. TV weather broadcast as an experiment having those two *results*. Suppose that 60% of the days when rain actually occurred were preceded by an 11 P.M. forecast in which rain was predicted "likely." Suppose further that 80% of the days when no rain fell were preceded by an "unlikely" forecast. Assuming that this pattern continues into the future, the conditional probability is .60 that the forecast will be "likely" given that rain follows and .80 that it will be "unlikely" given that no rain follows. These numbers are referred to as **conditional result probabilities**. They provide a measure of the *reliability* of predictive information.

BAYES' THEOREM

Using the concepts of prior and conditional result probabilities, Bayes arrived at a theorem for determining posterior probabilities.

BAYES' THEOREM: The posterior probability of event E for a particular result R of an empirical investigation can be found from

$$\Pr[E \mid R] = \frac{\Pr[E]\Pr[R \mid E]}{\Pr[E]\Pr[R \mid E] + \Pr[\text{not } E]\Pr[R \mid \text{not } E]}$$

Here E stands for "event" and R stands for "result." The prior probability for the main event of interest E is *specified in advance* as $\Pr[E]$, with $\Pr[\text{not } E] = 1 - \Pr[E]$. The conditional result probabilities must also be stipulated before making calculations.

You can apply Bayes' theorem to the weather illustration to find the posterior probability that it will rain (E) given a likely forecast (R). The prior probability is

$$\Pr[\text{rain}] = .50$$

and the conditional result probabilities are

$$\Pr[\text{likely}\,|\,\text{rain}] = .60$$
$$\Pr[\text{likely}\,|\,\text{no rain}] = 1 - \Pr[\text{unlikely}\,|\,\text{no rain}] = 1 - .80 = .20$$

Plugging these values into Bayes' theorem, you find

$$\Pr[\text{rain}\,|\,\text{likely}] = \frac{\Pr[\text{rain}] \times \Pr[\text{likely}\,|\,\text{rain}]}{\Pr[\text{rain}] \times \Pr[\text{likely}\,|\,\text{rain}] + \Pr[\text{no rain}] \times \Pr[\text{likely}\,|\,\text{no rain}]}$$
$$= \frac{.50(.60)}{.50(.60) + (1 - .50)(.20)} = \frac{.30}{.30 + .10} = .75$$

A similar calculation provides the posterior probability for rain (E) given an unlikely forecast (different R). The following conditional result probabilities apply.

$$\Pr[\text{unlikely}\,|\,\text{rain}] = 1 - .60 = .40$$
$$\Pr[\text{unlikely}\,|\,\text{no rain}] = .80$$

You find that

$$\Pr[\text{rain}\,|\,\text{unlikely}] = \frac{\Pr[\text{rain}] \times \Pr[\text{unlikely}\,|\,\text{rain}]}{\Pr[\text{rain}] \times \Pr[\text{unlikely}\,|\,\text{rain}] + \Pr[\text{no rain}] \times \Pr[\text{unlikely}\,|\,\text{no rain}]}$$
$$= \frac{.50(.40)}{.50(.40) + (1 - .50)(.80)} = \frac{.20}{.20 + .40} = .333$$

Notice how the posterior probability for rain *increases* to .75 from the prior level of .50 given a likely forecast. This is what we should expect with any reliable experimental result. Similarly the posterior probability for rain *decreases* from .50 to .33 given an unlikely forecast.

EXAMPLE: POSTERIOR PROBABILITIES FOR OIL WILDCATTING WITH A SEISMIC SURVEY

Based on 20 years of wildcatting experience, Lucky Luke assigns a prior probability of .20 for oil (O) beneath Crockpot Dome. Thus,

$$\Pr[O] = .20 \quad \text{and} \quad \Pr[\text{not } O] = 1 - .20 = .80$$

Luke has decided to order a seismic survey. A petroleum engineering consultant has rated this particular test as 90% reliable in confirming oil (C) when there is actually oil, but only 70% reliable in denying oil (D) when a site has no oil. These figures determine the conditional result probabilities.

$$\Pr[C|O] = .90 \quad \text{and} \quad \Pr[D|\text{not } O] = .70$$

Find the posterior probabilities for oil.

SOLUTION: Suppose that the seismic survey confirms the presence of oil. Luke's posterior probability for oil would then be

$$\begin{aligned}\Pr[O|C] &= \frac{\Pr[O] \times \Pr[C|O]}{\Pr[O] \times \Pr[C|O] + \Pr[\text{not } O] \times \Pr[C|\text{not } O]} \\ &= \frac{.20(.90)}{.20(.90) + .80(1 - .70)} = \frac{.18}{.18 + .24} \\ &= .429\end{aligned}$$

If you assume instead that the seismic survey denies any oil beneath Crockpot Dome, Luke's posterior probability for oil would be different.

$$\begin{aligned}\Pr[O|D] &= \frac{\Pr[O] \times \Pr[D|O]}{\Pr[O] \times \Pr[D|O] + \Pr[\text{not } O] \times \Pr[D|\text{not } O]} \\ &= \frac{.20(1 - .90)}{.20(1 - .90) + .80(.70)} = \frac{.02}{.02 + .56} \\ &= .034\end{aligned}$$

Notice how a positive experimental result raises the oil probability above its prior level, while a negative result lowers the oil probability below its initial value.

- Remember that a prior probability $\Pr[E]$ is a *given* value and is an *unconditional* probability.
- The posterior probability $\Pr[E|R]$ must be *computed.* This is a *conditional* probability.
- Don't confuse the posterior probability with the conditional result probabilities $\Pr[R|E]$ and $\Pr[R|\text{not } E]$. Here E and not E are the given events and are therefore listed last. Conditional result probabilties are *specified in advance.*

POSTERIOR PROBABILITIES COMPUTED FROM THE JOINT PROBABILITY TABLE

The fraction used in expressing Bayes' theorem is really nothing more than a detailed rephrasing of the conditional probability identity (page 173).

$$\Pr[E|R] = \frac{\Pr[E \text{ and } R]}{\Pr[R]}$$

At times, rather than use Bayes' theorem, you might find it easier to first construct a joint probability table and then apply the above identity to determine posterior probabilities.

To understand this, continue with the weather illustration. You can construct the following joint probability table using the data originally given.

	Result (forecast)		
Main Event	**Likely**	**Unlikely**	**Marginal Probability**
Rain	.30	.20	.50
No Rain	.10	.40	.50
Marginal Probability	.40	.60	1.00

The marginal probabilities for "rain" and "no rain" were given as the prior probability values. You determine the joint probability for "rain" and "likely" by using the general multiplication law (page 176).

$$\begin{aligned}\Pr[\text{rain } \textit{and} \text{ likely}] &= \Pr[\text{rain}] \times \Pr[\text{likely} \mid \text{rain}] \\ &= .50(.60) = .30\end{aligned}$$

Subtracting this value from the marginal probability for the first row (.50), you get the second joint probability of .20. You can likewise determine the joint probability for "no rain" and "unlikely."

$$\begin{aligned}\Pr[\text{no rain } \textit{and} \text{ unlikely}] &= \Pr[\text{no rain}] \times \Pr[\text{unlikely} \mid \text{no rain}] \\ &= .50(.80) = .40\end{aligned}$$

Now you determine the missing joint probability in the second row by subtracting .40 from the marginal probability for the row (.50). Finally, the marginal probabilities for the columns are determined by adding together the joint probabilities in each column.

To determine the posterior probability for rain given a likely weather forecast, you substitute the appropriate values into the identity directly from the joint probability table.

$$\Pr[\text{rain} \mid \text{likely}] = \frac{\Pr[\text{rain } \textit{and} \text{ likely}]}{\Pr[\text{likely}]} = \frac{.30}{.40} = .75$$

Likewise, the posterior probability for rain given an unlikely forecast is

$$\Pr[\text{rain} \mid \text{unlikely}] = \frac{\Pr[\text{rain } \textit{and} \text{ unlikely}]}{\Pr[\text{unlikely}]} = \frac{.20}{.60} = .333$$

EXERCISES

21-1 Felix Wild determines a prior probability for oil (O) of .2. A special rock sample survey will be made. Historically, a positive (P) survey result has been obtained on 70% of sites where oil was found, while negative (N)

survey results have occurred on 95% of the sites drilled and later found dry. Determine the posterior probability for oil given (a) a positive survey result, and (b) a negative survey result.

21-2 From a given response to a question, a marketing researcher wishes to determine whether a randomly selected person will choose BriDent when next purchasing toothpaste. The question is designed to reveal whether the selected person recalls the name BriDent—an event we will denote R. Previous testing has established that 99% of the people who bought BriDent previously recalled the name and that only 10% of the people who did not buy BriDent recalled this particular brand name. Since BriDent has cornered 30% of the toothpaste market, the researcher chooses .30 as the prior probability that the person selected will buy BriDent. Denoting this event B, we get the following probabilities.

$$\Pr[B] = .30 \qquad \Pr[R|B] = .99 \qquad \Pr[R|\text{not } B] = .10$$

(a) If the person who is selected remembers BriDent, what is the posterior probability that BriDent will be purchased next?
(b) If the person who is selected does *not* remember BriDent, what is the posterior probability that BriDent will be purchased next?

21-3 Nostra Damus is a local television weather reporter who makes a daily forecast indicating the probability that it will rain tomorrow. On one particular evening, she announces an 80% chance of rain (E) the next day. Prescient Pete manages the city golf courses. Pete will water the greens only if the probability for rain is less than 90%. Using the local TV forecast as his prior probability, Pete also relies on his mother-in-law's rheumatism. Historically, she gets a "rain pain" (R) on 90% of all days that are followed by rain, but she also gets a pain on 20% of the days that are not followed by rain. The following probabilities therefore apply.

$$\Pr[E] = .80 \qquad \Pr[R|E] = .90 \qquad \Pr[R|\text{not } E] = .20$$

(a) Assuming that Pete's mother-in-law is currently receiving pain signals, determine the posterior probability that it will rain tomorrow. Should Pete water the greens?
(b) If Pete's mother-in-law feels fine, what is the posterior probability for rain tomorrow?

21-4 An employment screening test is being evaluated by Kryptonite Corporation for possible inclusion in clerical services hiring decisions. Presently, only 50% of the persons hired for these positions perform satisfactorily. The test itself has been evaluated by outside consultants, who have given it an upside reliability of 90% (90% of all satisfactory employees will pass the test) and a downside reliability of only 80% (80% of all unsatisfactory employees will fail the test). One clerical applicant (acceptable in all other screening activities) is selected at random. Determine the following probabilities.
(a) The prior probability for satisfactory on-the-job performance if the applicant is hired.
(b) The posterior probability for satisfactory on-the-job performance if the applicant passes the screening test.

(c) The posterior probability for satisfactory on-the-job performance if the applicant is hired after failing the screening test.

21-5 A new movie "Star Struck" has a prior probability for success of .20. Ruth Grist is going to review the film. She has liked 70% of all the successful films and has disliked 80% of all the unsuccessful films she has reviewed. Determine the posterior probability that "Star Struck" will be a success if (a) Grist likes it; (b) Grist dislikes it.

21-2 COUNTING METHODS FOR DETERMINING PROBABILITIES

You can use the count-and-divide method even when there are so many possible elementary events that there wouldn't be enough sheets in a loose-leaf binder to completely list them. (For example, you will see later in this section that there are over 3 million different sequences in which the first 10 letters of the alphabet can be written.)

THE PRINCIPLE OF MULTIPLICATION

Rather than plod through such a listing, you can count large groups of elementary events by using the **principle of multiplication.**

1. **Break the problem into successive stages.** You may conveniently think of each stage as a branching point on a probability tree diagram.
2. **Multiply together the number of possibilities at each stage to obtain the total number of possibilities.** In this way, each path in your tree is counted.

The tree is simply a convenient conceptual prop. You can ordinarily apply the principle of multiplication without actually drawing a tree.

To illustrate, consider a student who must pick 1 of 5 mathematics courses and 1 of 10 social science offerings for her electives. Altogether she has

$$5 \times 10 = 50$$

possible pairs of elective courses from which to choose.

EXAMPLE: THE NUMBER OF DIFFERENT STEREO SYSTEMS

Vick Trolla is about to purchase his first stereo system from Speak-EZ Sounds. He has limited himself to one item from each of the following possible choices.

5 receivers	10 speakers
3 turntables	4 tape decks
2 cartridges	3 earphones

Figure 21-1 shows a probability tree diagram that conveniently summarizes the possibilities by incorporating a branching point for each choice. How many different stereo systems are there?

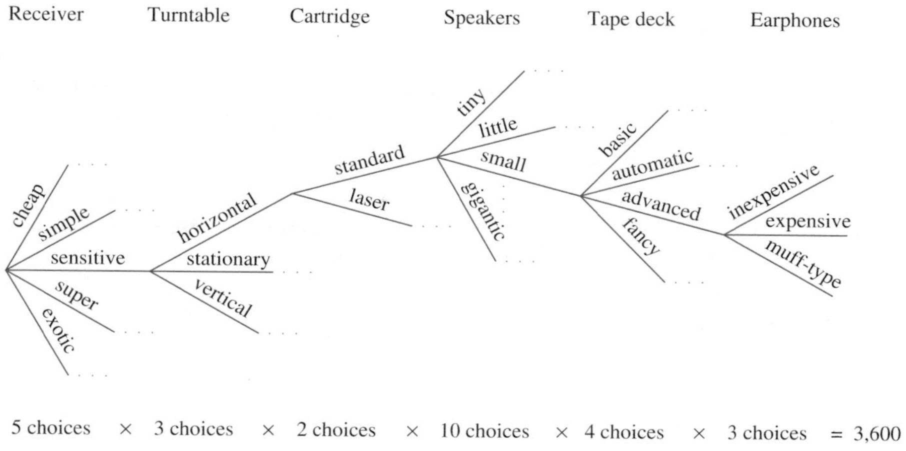

FIGURE 21-1 Probability tree for stereo system possibilities.

SOLUTION: By multiplying together the number of alternatives for each item, Vick finds the total number of different stereo systems he could buy.

$$5 \times 3 \times 2 \times 10 \times 4 \times 3 = 3{,}600$$

Each possible system would be represented on the tree by a different six-branch path. If all paths were included in Figure 21-1, the resulting tree would be over 300 feet tall!

NUMBER OF POSSIBILITIES RAISED TO A POWER

Chapter 6 discussed the sample space for a series of repeated experiments and gave an illustration of sampling with replacement. The selection of each sample item is referred to as a **trial**. An important class of random experiments involves a series of trials. We find the number of possible elementary events in the series' sample space by multiplying together the number of possible outcomes at each trial. For example, in 5 tosses of a coin, each of which involves just two possibilities (H or T), there are

$$2 \times 2 \times 2 \times 2 \times 2 = 32$$

possibilities for the entire series. Likewise, consider a quality control inspector who removes from a production line a sample of 6 items, each of which is classified into one of three categories: satisfactory, reworkable, or scrap. The number of possible sample outcomes is

$$3 \times 3 \times 3 \times 3 \times 3 \times 3 = 729$$

Notice that each product in these examples involves the same terms. Therefore, you may find it more convenient to express the two products in terms of powers.

$$2^5 = 32 \quad \text{and} \quad 3^6 = 729$$

In general, the number of possibilities from a series of n trials, each of which can result in the same k trial outcomes, is k raised to the power n. Consider the following table.

Trial Outcomes k	Number of Trials n	Number of Possibilities k^n
2	10	$2^{10} = 1{,}024$
5	2	$5^2 = 25$
2	5	$2^5 = 32$
10	3	$10^3 = 1{,}000$

THE NUMBER OF WAYS TO SEQUENCE ITEMS—THE FACTORIAL

For some experiments you must count the number of **sequences** in which items might be arranged. Consider the different sequences in which you can arrange the first 10 letters of the alphabet. The principle of multiplication indicates that the number of possibilities is

$$10 \times 9 \times 8 \times 7 \times 6 \times 5 \times 4 \times 3 \times 2 \times 1 = 3{,}628{,}800$$

The terms of this equation reflect the fact that one letter is being selected at a time in stages, with one less possibility for each successive stage. Think of each letter as a branching point in a tree, with the number of branches at each stage equal to the number of letters that remain to be selected for that particular sequence position.

Mathematicians refer to the product of all successive integers (whole numbers) ending at 1 as a **factorial**. A factorial product is expressed symbolically as a number followed by an exclamation point. Note the following examples.

$$5! = 5 \times 4 \times 3 \times 2 \times 1 = 120$$

$$6! = 6 \times 5 \times 4 \times 3 \times 2 \times 1 = 6 \times 5! = 720$$

$$7! = 7 \times 6 \times 5 \times 4 \times 3 \times 2 \times 1 = 7 \times 6! = 5{,}040$$

$$20! = \text{approximately 2.4 billion billion}$$

$$100! = \text{approximately 9 followed by 157 zeros}$$

In general, n factorial ($n!$) may be determined by the

FACTORIAL PRODUCT

$$n! = n \times (n - 1) \times (n - 2) \times \cdots \times 2 \times 1$$

STATISTICS AROUND US

Truth in Labeling

Have you ever wondered how a food processor can actually claim that the net contents of a can of corn is, say, 16 oz.? Even if any particular can is weighed with a very precise scale, it will be a little too heavy or too light. The processor's claim means that if the filling process is on target, exactly half the cans will be above the 16 oz. target (A) and the rest will be below (B).

Suppose a cannery inspector, to check the accuracy of the canning process, removes a sample of $n = 10$ cans and weighs their contents. Each can is classified in one of two ways ($k = 2$), and so altogether there are

$$2^{10} = 1{,}024$$

possible sample findings. The inspector's 10-can sample, with the cans listed in order of selection, might be

$$A\ B\ A\ B\ B\ A\ B\ B\ B\ A$$

Since any can is just as likely to be an A as a B, you can consider the listing to be an elementary event for the sampling experiment. Each elementary event is equally likely. Thus, you conclude

$$\Pr[A\ B\ A\ B\ B\ A\ B\ B\ B\ A] = \frac{1}{1{,}024}$$

We define

$$1! = 1$$
$$0! = 1$$

(There is only one way to sequence nothing.)

A SEQUENCE OF SOME OBJECTS—THE PERMUTATION

You may be interested in counting the number of possibilities when not all available objects are selected. Consider, again, various possible groupings of the first 10 letters of the alphabet.

ABC ABHIJ LADCJ LKJHICDAB A BK CDE EDCA

Each of these arrangements of letters is a permutation. A **permutation** is a collection of objects distinguished by which items are included and by their sequence. Thus, ABC and CBA are different permutations that happen to involve the same three letters. Although none of the groupings includes all 10 letters, a permutation *can* include all objects. No item can appear more than once in a single permutation.

THE NUMBER OF PERMUTATIONS

The number of possible permutations depends on the size of the original group and the number of items selected. It will be helpful to denote the number of permutations of size r from a group of n items ($r \leq n$) by the symbol P_r^n. You can find the number of possible permutations by using the following equation.

$$P_r^n = n \times (n-1) \times (n-2) \times \cdots \times (n-r+1)$$

Consider the following examples.

Group Size n	**Items Selected** r	**Number of Permutations** P_r^n
7	4	$7 \times 6 \times 5 \times 4 = 840$
10	2	$10 \times 9 = 90$
5	5	$5 \times 4 \times 3 \times 2 \times 1 = 120$
52	5	311,875,200

Factorials are helpful in computing the number of possible permutations. If you multiply the equation for the number of permutations by $(n - r)!$ and then divide by $(n - r)!$, the original value is preserved. However, this results in the following more concise expression.

NUMBER OF PERMUTATIONS: The number of possible permutations of r objects from a collection of size n, denoted by P_r^n, is

$$P_r^n = \frac{n \times (n-1) \times (n-2) \times \cdots \times (n-r+1) \times (n-r)!}{(n-r)!} = \frac{n!}{(n-r)!}$$

EXAMPLE: COUNTING NAME ARRANGEMENTS

Consider the following six names.

Ann Eve Fay Liz May Sue

How many four-name arrangements are possible?

SOLUTION: Picking names one at a time from this group and applying the principle of multiplication, you may establish the number of permutations of four names from the six.

Choices of first name		Choices of second name		Choices of third name		Choices of fourth name	
6	×	5	×	4	×	3	= 360

This result may also be found by working with factorials. Expressing the number of permutations for $n = 6$ names taken $r = 4$ at a time, you get

STATISTICS AROUND US

Five-Card Poker Hands

Imagine the various poker hands you can create by removing the top 5 cards from a deck of 52 playing cards. Listing the individual cards in order of their selection, each of the following hands may be viewed as a permutation.

♣K,	♣3,	♣J,	♣7,	♣10
♦2,	♠3,	♥4,	♥5,	♣6
♠5,	♥5,	♣7,	♥2,	♦2
♥A,	♥K,	♥Q,	♥J,	♥10

Notice that although the third hand involves two 5s and two 2s, each of these pairs is made up of two different cards. (The ♥2 cannot appear twice unless that particular card is replaced in the deck and reselected. A listing of any such outcome is not considered a permutation.) The top sequence is a club *flush*—all cards belonging to a common suit. The second hand is a *straight*—the cards can be arranged in a denominational sequence having no gaps. The last hand is a *royal flush* in hearts. The sequence in which a card gets selected is ordinarily unimportant in poker. If you consider just those cards in the heart royal flush, there are $5! = 120$ sequences in which they might be drawn.

$$P_4^6 = \frac{6!}{(6-4)!} = \frac{6!}{2!} = \frac{720}{2} = 360$$

Accounting for possibilities in terms of permutations may be more detailed than necessary. It is sometimes satisfactory to ignore the sequence of items.

THE COMBINATION

Any collection distinguishable only by which particular items are included (and not by their sequence) is a **combination**. A combination of the first 10 letters of the alphabet is the set of letters itself, ignoring their order of selection. All of the following sequences

ABC ACB BAC BCA CAB CBA

are counted as a single combination. But since there are different letter sets in the following

EFG JFK EIK ADJ BCL EDJ

each represents a different combination. It is often easier to count possibilities in terms of combinations.

THE NUMBER OF COMBINATIONS

As with permutations (where sequence counts), the number of combinations depends on the original group size and the number of items included. The expression C_r^n stands for the number of combinations of r items taken from n.

NUMBER OF COMBINATIONS: The number of combinations of r objects taken from n objects, denoted by C_r^n, may be determined from

$$C_r^n = \frac{n!}{r!(n-r)!}$$

Consider the following examples.

Group Size n	Items Selected r	Number of Combinations C_r^n
5	3	10
8	5	56
12	7	792
20	5	15,504
100	50	about 100,000 trillion trillion

As a further illustration, consider the number of combinations of $r = 4$ women's names taken from the $n = 6$ given in the preceding example.

$$C_4^6 = \frac{6!}{4!(6-4)!} = \frac{6!}{4!2!} = \frac{720}{24(2)} = 15$$

Each one of these 15 possible combinations is listed below, with names arranged alphabetically.

Ann Eve Fay Liz	Ann Eve May Sue	Eve Fay Liz May
Ann Eve Fay May	Ann Fay Liz May	Eve Fay Liz Sue
Ann Eve Fay Sue	Ann Fay Liz Sue	Eve Fay May Sue
Ann Eve Liz May	Ann Fay May Sue	Eve Liz May Sue
Ann Eve Liz Sue	Ann Liz May Sue	Fay Liz May Sue

Each of the 15 four-name combinations could be sequenced in $4! = 24$ different ways, giving rise to the $24 \times 15 = 360$ permutations found earlier.

More generally, the number of permutations may be obtained by multiplying the respective number of combinations by $r!$, while the number of combinations may be computed by dividing the corresponding number of permutations by $r!$.

STATISTICS AROUND US

Canned Corn Possibilities

Consider again the weight of the cans of corn. By counting combinations, you can establish various probabilities for the weight classifications of the 10 sample cans. To begin, represent each successive sample by a box.

1	2	3	4	5	6	7	8	9	10

Consider now the number of ways for getting exactly 3 cans that are above (A) 16 oz., with the rest below. This is the same as the number of ways to select 3 of the 10 boxes (which will then receive the letter A). One result is

1	2	3	4	5	6	7	8	9	10
A				A		A			

Another is

1	2	3	4	5	6	7	8	9	10
		A	A					A	

Altogether, there are

$$C_3^{10} = \frac{10!}{3!(10-3)!} = \frac{10!}{3!7!} = \frac{3{,}628{,}800}{6(5{,}040)} = 120$$

ways to place the As. Since you saw on page 892 that there are 1,024 possible elementary events, you can now use the count-and-divide method to determine the probability that there will be exactly 3 cans in the sample above 16 oz.

$$\Pr[\text{exactly 3 } A\text{s}] = \frac{120}{1{,}024} = .117$$

Thus,

$$P_r^n = r!C_r^n \quad \text{and} \quad C_r^n = \frac{P_r^n}{r!}$$

Because there are always a smaller number of combinations than of permutations, combinations usually form the basis for probability calculations using the count-and-divide method.

STATISTICS AROUND US

Poker Hand Probabilities

In most poker situations the *combination* of cards determines the winning hand. The number of combinations of $r = 5$ cards from $n = 52$ in the deck is

$$C_5^{52} = \frac{52!}{5!(52-5)!}$$

You can easily evaluate this fraction expressing the numerator and denominator as

$$\frac{52!}{5!47!} = \frac{52 \times 51 \times 50 \times 49 \times 48 \times 47!}{5!47!}$$

By canceling the 47! terms, expanding 5! into its product form, and canceling again, you can reduce the final computation.

$$\frac{52 \times 51 \times 50 \times 49 \times 48}{5 \times 4 \times 3 \times 2 \times 1} = 52 \times 51 \times 5 \times 49 \times 4 = 2{,}598{,}960$$

This is the number of possible combinations of poker hands. It may be treated as the number of elementary events in the sample space generated by dealing the top 5 cards from a shuffled deck.

Probability of a straight: The number of 2–3–4–5–6 straights is 4^5, since each of the 5 denominations may belong to any one of 4 suits. Altogether there are 9 denominational categories for straights—2 through 6, 3 through 7, and so on (treating ace as high). The number of possible straights then is

$$9 \times 4^5 = 9{,}216$$

It follows that

$$\Pr[\text{straight}] = \frac{9{,}216}{2{,}598{,}960} = .00355$$

Probability of a flush: The number of flushes (5 cards, all of the same suit) in any one suit is the number of combinations of $r = 5$ cards selected from the $n = 13$ cards in that suit. There are 4 suit possibilities in getting a flush, so that the number of possible flushes is

$$4 \times C_5^{13} = 4 \times \frac{13!}{5!(13-5)!} = 4 \times 1{,}287 = 5{,}148$$

Thus,

$$\Pr[\text{flush}] = \frac{5{,}148}{2{,}598{,}960} = .00198$$

Since the flush is rarer, it will beat a straight.

EXERCISES

21-6 Hoppy Scott is a traveling salesman who must visit ten cities in one trip. In how many sequences may he make his stops?

21-7 Freshmen at Old Ivy are required to take exactly one course from each of the following groupings.

Foreign Language	Communications	Social Science	Humanities
French	Speech	Economics	Art
German	English	Psychology	Philosophy
Italian		History	Music
Latin			Drama
Spanish			

How many different course combinations are possible in satisfying the requirement?

21-8 Consider all 5-card poker hands resulting in a 10-high straight consisting of black cards only. List all the combinations.

21-9 Cal Culator is purchasing a personal computer system. He will select one each of the following: computer (4 choices), disk drive (5 brands), monitor (3 colors), modem (5 makes), and printer (10 choices). How many distinct system possibilities does Cal have to choose from?

21-10 Determine the number of possible outcomes (distinguished by side obtained) for each of the following.
(a) a coin is tossed 7 times
(b) a die is rolled 5 times
(c) a 4-sided pyramid is flipped 4 times

21-11 Seven items are successively removed from a collection of 10 items. How many distinct possibilities are there for each of the following?
(a) the order of selection matters
(b) the order of selection doesn't matter
(c) once removed, an item is replaced and allowed to be selected later

21-12 A sample of 100 widgets is taken one at a time directly from production. Each item is classified as defective (D) or satisfactory (S). Answer the following, ignoring which particular items get selected.
(a) How many distinguishable quality outcomes are possible?
(b) Of the results counted in (a), how many involve exactly (1) 2 defectives; (2) 5 defectives; (3) 10 defectives?

21-13 Consider drawing the top 5 cards from a deck of 52 playing cards.
(a) How many possible hands are there that involve *exactly* one pair (excluding three- or four-of-a-kind)?
(b) Determine the probability for getting exactly one pair.

21-14 Consider poker hands involving 4-of-a-kind (same denomination).
(a) How many possible hands are there?
(b) Determine the probability for getting 4-of-a-kind.

21-15 A group contains 60 men and 40 women. Four names will be selected at random and without replacement for door prizes.
(a) How many different name combinations are possible?

(b) How many combinations of all female names are possible? What is the probability that women take all the door prizes?

21-16 Seating assignments are being made for the guests at an awards banquet. There are 20 guests (ten couples) to be seated along a table with ten chairs on each side. A name card is to appear at every place setting.
(a) In how many different ways is it possible to place the name cards?
(b) If no man is to sit beside or across from another man, how many arrangements are possible?
(c) If each couple is to sit side by side, how many arrangements are possible when (1) the sexes are alternated, and (2) members of the same sex may sit beside each other?

SUMMARY

1. What are the various probabilities encountered in using experimental results to revise probabilities for main events?

The process begins with probabilities for the *main events*, referred to as **prior probabilities**, since they apply prior to getting any experimental results. A second set of probabilities applies to the possible *results* of the experiment. These are called **conditional result probabilities**. These values must always be *known* and are like "batting averages" for how well the experiment has performed. They are usually established by the historical frequencies from previous applications of the experiment. When combined arithmetically with the prior probabilities, **posterior probabilities** may be found for the main events. These reflect how the prior probabilities would be revised should any particular result be experienced. Posterior probabilities are *conditional* probabilities of the form

$$\Pr[\text{main event}|\text{result}]$$

2. What is Bayes' theorem?

This is a procedure for computing a posterior probability. As the above expression shows, a posterior probability is a *conditional probability*. Bayes' theorem has a new twist and is really an expression of the conditional probability identity

$$\Pr[\text{main event}|\text{result}] = \frac{\Pr[\text{main event } \textit{and} \text{ result}]}{\Pr[\text{result}]}$$

or,

$$\Pr[E|R] = \frac{\Pr[E \textit{ and } R]}{\Pr[R]}$$

The numerator for the above is computed by applying the multiplication law, which expresses the joint probability as the product of the prior probability and the conditional result probability, both known values:

$$\Pr[E \textit{ and } R] = \Pr[E] \times \Pr[R|E]$$

The denominator reflects that the result can happen in two ways, jointly with the main event or jointly with its complement. The latter may be expressed as the following product:

$$\Pr[\text{not } E \textit{ and } R] = \Pr[\text{not } E] \times \Pr[R|\text{not } E]$$

By the addition law,

$$\begin{aligned}\Pr[R] &= \Pr[(E \textit{ and } R) \text{ or } (\text{not } E \textit{ and } R)] \\ &= \Pr[E \textit{ and } R] + \Pr[\text{not } E \textit{ and } R] \\ &= \Pr[E] \times \Pr[R|E] + \Pr[\text{not } E] \times \Pr[R|\text{not } E]\end{aligned}$$

Putting it all together, we have

$$\Pr[E|R] = \frac{\Pr[E] \times \Pr[R|E]}{\Pr[E] \times \Pr[R|E] + \Pr[\text{not } E] \times \Pr[R|\text{not } E]}$$

3. **What is the origin of Bayes' theorem?**
The Reverend Thomas Bayes proposed the above expression. He originally proposed using prior probabilities based on judgment, so that they would be *subjective* probabilities. The conditional result probabilities could be *objective* probabilities. Thus, the above expression mathematically combines two types of probabilities, one based on judgment and the other based on experience.

4. **What is the principle of multiplication that underlies counting methods used in probability?**
This principle is based on breaking the event-generating process into stages (actual or conceptual) and then multiplying together the number of possibilities in each stage. That product is the total number of possibilities. When each stage has the same number of possibilities, the total number of distinguishable outcomes is the number of possibilities raised to the power of the number of stages. For example, consider 10 tosses (stages) of a coin having 2 sides (possibilities). The number of overall results is 2^{10}.

5. **What are permutations and combinations and how do they differ?**
A **permutation** is a sequence that a group of objects may be arranged in. Not all objects need be included, and one permutation may differ from another both in terms of which objects are included and in terms of the order in which they are arranged. A **combination** is distinguished only by which objects are included, not by the sequence.

6. **What is a factorial product and what does it represent?**
We use **factorial** notation to express the number of possibilities. The quantity $n!$ is called "n-factorial." It is the number of ways of sequencing n objects. It is the product of the integers starting with the number n itself and including all successively smaller integers until reaching 1. For example,

$$5! = 5 \times 4 \times 3 \times 2 \times 1 = 120$$

The above expresses the number of possible ways to sequence 5 objects. If those objects are the first five letters of the alphabet, then 120 is the number of words that could be formed from those letters without repeating any letter. By definition, $1! = 1$ and $0! = 1$. (There is only one way to sequence one letter; there is also only one way to sequence no letters.)

7. **How do we count the number of permutations and combinations?**
The number of permutations of r objects taken from a group of n objects is found from

$$P_r^n = \frac{n!}{(n - r)!}$$

The above is $r!$ times as big as the number of combinations of r objects taken from a group of n objects, found from

$$C_r^n = \frac{n!}{r!(n - r)!}$$

8. When do we use the number of permutations instead of the number of combinations?
To compute probabilities, we ordinarily use the number of combinations, since for most sampling situations we are only interested in finding probabilities regarding which objects are selected, not in which sequence. But when sequence of selection matters, we would use the number of permutations to account for possibilities.

REVIEW EXERCISES

21-17 One student is selected at random from the sample space in Figure 5-3 (page 153).
(a) What is the prior probability that the student is a male (M)?
(b) Suppose that the student's major is known. What is the posterior probability that a male is selected given that the student is a finance major (Fi)?

21-18 Nancy Wheeler is ordering a car. She must specify her choices for the following: model (3 choices), engine (3 sizes), body style (4 types), color (7 shades), and option package (10 choices). How many different cars must Nancy choose from?

21-19 A phony card deck (P) contains 52 kings. This deck is placed into a sack with 4 standard decks (S) of 52 playing cards. One deck is selected at random.
(a) What is the prior probability that the phony deck is selected?
(b) A king is drawn at random from the selected deck. What is the posterior probability that the phony deck is selected?

21-20 Suppose that a group of 5 students is selected at random from those represented in Figure 5-3. No student is selected more than once, and their order of selection does not matter.
(a) How many distinct outcomes are possible?
(b) Suppose that the sample contains only graduate students.
(1) How many sample outcomes are possible?
(2) What is the probability that such a result will occur?

21-21 A *full house* in poker consists of 2 cards of one denomination and 3 cards of another. List each distinct combination of hands involving 3 aces and 2 kings.

21-22 Consider poker hands that involve a full house consisting of a pair and a triple of any two different denominations.

(a) How many possibilities are there?
(b) Determine the probability for getting a full house.

21-23 An admissions committee must select students for an MBA program. Past data show that 70% of all admitted students complete (C) the degree program. It is also known that 50% of the graduating students scored above 500 (A) on the Graduate Management Admissions Test (GMAT), while only 20% of the dropouts (D) scored that well. Consider a newly matriculated MBA student.

(a) What is the prior probability that she will complete the degree?
(b) Given that she scores 575 on the GMAT, what is the posterior probability that she will complete her MBA?
(c) Given that she scores 450 on the test, what is the posterior probability that she will graduate?

CASE Ourman Friday Temporaries

Ourman Friday Temporaries provides short-term support staff to local businesses. The employees are assigned to various pools. The following persons are in the financial support pool. All persons will be available for assignment next week.

	Specialty	Experience
Bob Browning	Accounting	High
Ted Chavez	Tax	Low
Myra Hansen	Programming	Low
Linda Isaacson	Accounting	Low
Biff Jones	Tax	Low
Jeffry Kennard	Accounting	High
Lisa Kincaid	Accounting	High
Todd Miller	Tax	Low
Yolanda Munro	Programming	High
Mildred Noonan	Programming	Low
Sandra Oynuchi	Tax	Low
Cesar Perez	Programming	High
Oliver Piscwizc	Programming	Low
Donald Quigly	Tax	High
Maureen Raatz	Programming	High
Morris Rabinowitz	Accounting	High
Syl Rutkowski	Accounting	Low
Billy Sol	Accounting	High
Midori Toguchi	Programming	Low
Chinh Tsien	Tax	Low
Ivan Tureg	Programming	Low
Doreen Zurn	Programming	High

The following clients have recently requested temporaries from the Ourman financial pool. The percentages represent the historical frequency at which the various skills have been requested.

	Accounting	Programming	Tax
(a) Ace Widgets	80%	15%	5%
(b) BugOff Chemical	20	10	70
(c) Comp-u-Com	0	100	0
(d) Dial-a-Pute	10	90	0
(e) Druid's Drayage	100	0	0
(f) Kryptonite Corp.	50	0	50
(g) VBM	10	80	10
(h) Woody Mills	70	10	20

It may be assumed that the above history applies in establishing probabilities for the requested specialty in any future request for Ourman temporaries.

QUESTIONS

1. One pool employee will be selected at random for the Ourman steering committee.
   (a) Determine the probability that he or she will be (1) an accountant, (2) a tax specialist, (3) a programmer.
   (b) Determine the probability that he or she will have (1) low experience, (2) high experience.

2. Suppose that the first two client requests are each for a tax-qualified person. Ourman will fill these assignments randomly.
   (a) List the employee initials for all possible choices.
   (b) What is the probability that one of the two persons has a high experience level?

3. Suppose that just 3 companies request people—all tax specialists. Construct a tree showing all the requesting company possibilities.

4. Although they are not equally likely, you can determine how many feasible assignments (person-request with matching skills) are possible. Do this for the first (1) accounting request, (2) tax request, (3) programming request.

5. It is equally likely that a request from any of the 8 listed clients will generate the first Ourman employee assignment. Consider the event that this assignment is made to the Kryptonite Corp.
   (a) What is the prior probability?
   (b) What is the posterior probability, given that the required specialty is: (1) accounting? (2) programming?

6. Consider the characteristics specialty versus experience level. One Ourman pool employee is selected at random.
   (a) Construct the joint probability table.
   (b) Find the conditional probabilities for each experience level given that the selected person's specialty is (1) accounting, (2) tax, and (3) programming.

(c) The following prior probabilities apply for the first request: .50—programmer, .30—accounting, .20—tax. Determine the posterior probabilities that each of these skills is actually requested when the selected person happens to have (1) low experience, (2) high experience.

7. All six Ourman tax specialists will be assigned next week as follows: two to BugOff Chemical, two to Kryptonite Corp., and one each to VBM and Woody Mills. How many distinct assignments of people to companies are possible?

8. During its busy season Ace Widgets gets exactly one Ourman accounting temporary each week. Assuming that a new random selection is made to fill that slot each week, how many distinct assignments are possible when Ace's busy season lasts (1) 2 weeks? (2) 4 weeks? (3) 6 weeks?

CHAPTER 22

IMPORTANT PROBABILITY DISTRIBUTIONS FOR BUSINESS DECISIONS

BEFORE READING THIS CHAPTER, MAKE SURE YOU UNDERSTAND:

Basic concepts of probability (Chapter 5).
Probability distributions (Chapter 6).
Normal distribution (Chapter 7).

AFTER READING THIS CHAPTER, YOU WILL UNDERSTAND:

About the hypergeometric distribution and how it is used.
About the Poisson distribution and how it is used.
About the uniform distribution and how it is used.
About the exponential distribution and how it is used.

There are several probability distributions of special importance in business decision making. Five of these have already been considered. This chapter describes four more, two discrete and two continuous.

Both of the discrete probability distributions to be described are similar to the binomial distribution but have different applications. The **hypergeometric distribution** is appropriate when sampling is done without replacement from a small qualitative population. The **Poisson distribution** provides probabilities for the number of events that will occur over a specified time interval or in some given space.

The two continuous distributions to be discussed are the uniform and the exponential. The **uniform distribution** applies to quantitative populations having frequency distributions shaped like a rectangle. It assumes that all possible values are equally likely, a common circumstance for many physical or random phenomena. The **exponential distribution**, which has the shape of a reversed *J*, is closely related to the Poisson and has similar applications.

These four distributions are tremendously important to sampling applications, and they also play important roles in some quantitative methods used in analyzing decisions. The Poisson, exponential, and uniform distributions are crucial in many models of waiting lines or queues. The uniform distribution also is fundamental to Monte Carlo simulation techniques.

22-1 THE HYPERGEOMETRIC DISTRIBUTION

As we have seen, the binomial distribution may be used to find the probabilities for the number of successes from a Bernoulli process. Thus, the binomial distribution may only be applied when sampling is done *with replacement* from small populations. Ordinarily, however, a sample is chosen from a population *without replacement*. For instance, when items are selected from a shipment of parts in order to determine the quality of the shipment, the items inspected are usually set aside and thus may not be chosen again. As we noted in Chapter 4, the sampling process itself may destroy the item, so that it is impossible to sample with replacement. The hypergeometric distribution allows us to overcome these difficulties and find the probabilities for the number of successes in samples taken without replacement from small populations.

FINDING PROBABILITIES WHEN SAMPLING WITHOUT REPLACEMENT

To illustrate the basic principles underlying the hypergeometric distribution, we will use a simple illustration involving the random selection of marbles from a box. Our initial view of sampling without replacement will be one where sample items are removed one at a time. Then we will develop the hypergeometric distribution by viewing the sample items as if they were withdrawn as a group. Identical probabilities will be obtained under either method.

A box contains 6 black and 4 white marbles. Four marbles are selected at random, one at a time, from the box. Once selected, a marble is set aside. We want to find the probability distribution for the number of black marbles obtained.

Figure 22-1 shows the probability tree diagram. At each stage the color composition of the marbles remaining in the box is provided inside the oval next to

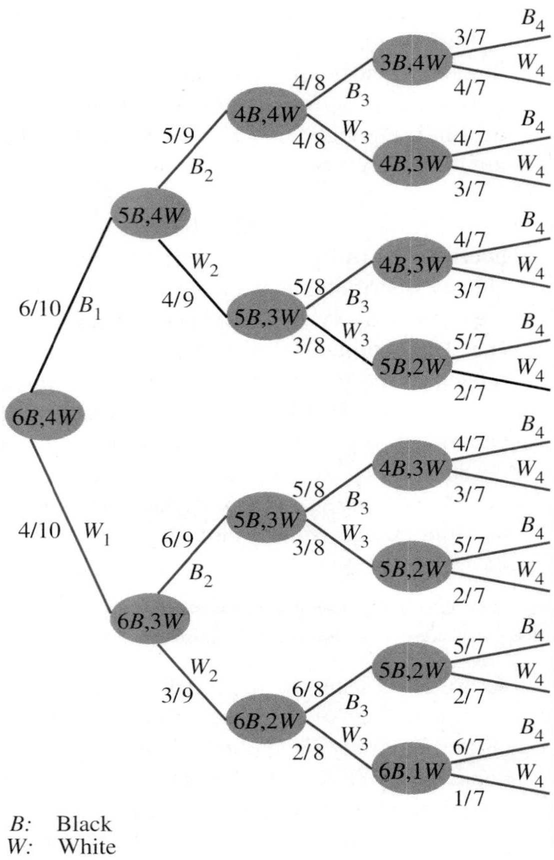

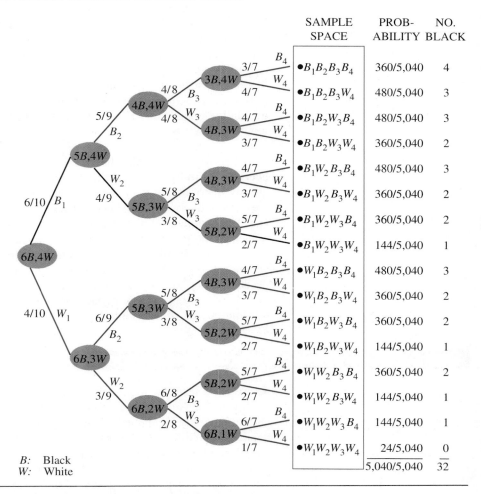

SAMPLE SPACE	PROBABILITY	NO. BLACK
• $B_1B_2B_3B_4$	360/5,040	4
• $B_1B_2B_3W_4$	480/5,040	3
• $B_1B_2W_3B_4$	480/5,040	3
• $B_1B_2W_3W_4$	360/5,040	2
• $B_1W_2B_3B_4$	480/5,040	3
• $B_1W_2B_3W_4$	360/5,040	2
• $B_1W_2W_3B_4$	360/5,040	2
• $B_1W_2W_3W_4$	144/5,040	1
• $W_1B_2B_3B_4$	480/5,040	3
• $W_1B_2B_3W_4$	360/5,040	2
• $W_1B_2W_3B_4$	360/5,040	2
• $W_1B_2W_3W_4$	144/5,040	1
• $W_1W_2B_3B_4$	360/5,040	2
• $W_1W_2B_3W_4$	144/5,040	1
• $W_1W_2W_3B_4$	144/5,040	1
• $W_1W_2W_3W_4$	24/5,040	0
	5,040/5,040	32

FIGURE 22-1 Probability tree diagram for sampling without replacement.

the branching point. The branches on the path leading to the end position $B_1W_2W_3W_4$ are shown as black lines. Initially there are 6 black and 4 white marbles. The probability that the first selection is black is therefore 6/10. If the first marble is black, 5 black and 4 white marbles remain for the second selection. The conditional probability that the second marble is white given that the first is black is 4/9. Continuing along this path we see that the conditional probabilities for white as the third selection, followed by white again as the fourth selection, are 3/8 and 2/7, respectively. Applying the multiplication law, we obtain

$$\Pr[B_1W_2W_3W_4] = \left(\frac{6}{10}\right)\left(\frac{4}{9}\right)\left(\frac{3}{8}\right)\left(\frac{2}{7}\right) = \frac{144}{5{,}040}$$

Note that there are four end positions of the probability tree diagram yielding exactly 1 black marble (which may be the first, second, third, or fourth marble selected); all have equal probabilities. The probability for exactly 1 black marble may be obtained by summing these, applying the addition law for mutually exclusive events. Alternatively, denoting by R the number of black marbles obtained, we may multiply the preceding result by 4 to calculate

$$\Pr[R = 1] = 4\left(\frac{144}{5{,}040}\right) = \frac{576}{5{,}040}$$

Figure 22-1 yields a sample space where the elementary events, such as $B_1W_2W_3W_4$, do not reflect which particular marbles were chosen. The same sampling procedure may be viewed in terms of a more complex sample space involving elementary events that do reflect which particular marbles are selected. The hypergeometric distribution involves such a combinatorial representation.

EXPRESSING THE HYPERGEOMETRIC DISTRIBUTION

The tree diagram approach in Figure 22-1 is too cumbersome to use when larger samples are involved. Instead, the hypergeometric distribution provides the desired probabilities by accounting for which marbles are selected. The total number of equally likely outcomes equals the number of combinations of 4 marbles out of 10:C_4^{10}. The number of outcomes yielding exactly 1 black marble is the number of ways to obtain 1 black out of 6, C_1^6, times the number of ways to select 3 white out of 4, C_3^4. Thus, we may also express the above probability as

$$\Pr[R = 1] = \frac{C_1^6 C_3^4}{C_4^{10}}$$

We verify that this ratio is identical in value to our previous result by expressing it in factorials as

$$\Pr[R = 1] = \frac{\left(\dfrac{6!}{1!5!}\right)\left(\dfrac{4!}{3!1!}\right)}{\dfrac{10!}{4!6!}}$$

which, by rearranging and canceling terms, equals

$$\begin{aligned}\frac{6 \times 4 \times 4! \times 6!}{10!} &= \frac{6 \times 4 \times 4!}{10 \times 9 \times 8 \times 7}\\ &= 4\left(\frac{6}{10}\right)\left(\frac{4}{9}\right)\left(\frac{3}{8}\right)\left(\frac{2}{7}\right)\\ &= \frac{576}{5{,}040}\end{aligned}$$

Thus, to find the probability for the number of successes, R, in a sample of size n taken *without replacement* from a population of size N, we use the

HYPERGEOMETRIC PROBABILITY DISTRIBUTION

$$\Pr[R = r] = \frac{C_r^S C_{n-r}^{N-S}}{C_n^N}$$

where $r = 0, 1, \ldots, n$ or S (whichever is smaller) and S = number of successes in the population.

In our example, $n = 4$, and $N = 10$. Since we consider drawing a black marble to be a successful event, $S = 6$. Using $r = 4$, so that $n - r = 4 - 4 = 0$, we find

$$\Pr[R = 4] = \frac{C_4^6 C_0^4}{C_4^{10}} = \frac{360}{5{,}040}$$

which is the same as $\Pr[B_1B_2B_3B_4]$ in Figure 22-1.

ILLUSTRATION: INSPECTING ELECTRONIC TEST EQUIPMENT

An inspector will examine a shipment of electronic test equipment. Due to time constraints only a sample of $n = 5$ units may be evaluated. Altogether the incoming lot contains $N = 40$ items.

The number of defective units is unknown. A good shipment would contain no more than 10% defectives ($S = 4$). If that is the case, then the following calculation provides the probability of getting exactly no defectives in the sample.

$$\Pr[R = 0] = \frac{C_0^4 C_{5-0}^{40-4}}{C_5^{40}} = \frac{\left(\frac{4!}{0!4!}\right)\left(\frac{36!}{5!31!}\right)}{\left(\frac{40!}{5!35!}\right)}$$

$$= 1\left(\frac{36!}{5!31!}\right)\left(\frac{5!35!}{40!}\right)$$

$$= \left(\frac{36}{40}\right)\left(\frac{35}{39}\right)\left(\frac{34}{38}\right)\left(\frac{33}{37}\right)\left(\frac{32}{36}\right)$$

$$= .5729$$

The probability for getting exactly one defective is

$$\Pr[R = 1] = \frac{C_1^4 C_{5-1}^{40-4}}{C_5^{40}} = \frac{\left(\frac{4!}{1!3!}\right)\left(\frac{36!}{4!32!}\right)}{\left(\frac{40!}{5!35!}\right)}$$

$$= 4\left(\frac{36!}{4!32!}\right)\left(\frac{5!35!}{40!}\right)$$

$$= 4\left(\frac{36}{40}\right)\left(\frac{35}{39}\right)\left(\frac{34}{38}\right)\left(\frac{33}{37}\right)\left(\frac{5}{36}\right)$$

$$= .3581$$

The inspector plans to accept the shipment if one or fewer defective units are found. Thus,

$$\begin{aligned}\Pr[\text{accept shipment}] &= \Pr[R = 0] + \Pr[R = 1] \\ &= .5729 + .3581 = .9310\end{aligned}$$

There is better than a 93% chance that a good shipment will pass the inspection.

A very bad shipment has at least 40% defectives. If the shipment were such, with $S = 16$, the following probabilities apply.

$$\Pr[R = 0] = \frac{C_0^{16} C_{5-0}^{40-16}}{C_5^{40}} = \frac{\left(\dfrac{16!}{0!16!}\right)\left(\dfrac{24!}{5!19!}\right)}{\left(\dfrac{40!}{5!35!}\right)}$$

$$= 1\left(\frac{24!}{5!19!}\right)\left(\frac{5!35!}{40!}\right)$$

$$= \left(\frac{24}{40}\right)\left(\frac{23}{39}\right)\left(\frac{22}{38}\right)\left(\frac{21}{37}\right)\left(\frac{20}{36}\right)$$

$$= .0646$$

and

$$\Pr[R = 1] = \frac{C_1^{16} C_{5-1}^{40-16}}{C_5^{40}} = \frac{\left(\dfrac{16!}{1!15!}\right)\left(\dfrac{24!}{4!20!}\right)}{\left(\dfrac{40!}{5!35!}\right)}$$

$$= 16\left(\frac{24!}{4!20!}\right)\left(\frac{5!35!}{40!}\right)$$

$$= 16\left(\frac{24}{40}\right)\left(\frac{23}{39}\right)\left(\frac{22}{38}\right)\left(\frac{21}{37}\right)\left(\frac{5}{36}\right)$$

$$= .2584$$

Unfortunately, the following probability applies for a very bad shipment.

$$\begin{aligned}\Pr[\text{accept shipment}] &= \Pr[R = 0] + \Pr[R = 1] \\ &= .0646 + .2584 = .3230\end{aligned}$$

HYPERGEOMETRIC DISTRIBUTION FOR THE PROPORTION OF SUCCESSES

As we noted in discussing the binomial distribution, we are usually more interested in the *proportion* of successes in the sample than in the number of successes. As before, π and P are the proportion of successes in the population and sample, respectively. Thus, since

$$P = \frac{R}{n} \quad \text{and} \quad \pi = \frac{S}{N}$$

we modify our earlier expression to provide the

HYPERGEOMETRIC PROBABILITY DISTRIBUTION FOR THE PROPORTION

$$\Pr\left[P = \frac{r}{n}\right] = \frac{C_r^{\pi N} C_{n-r}^{(1-\pi)N}}{C_n^N}$$

with $r = 0, 1, 2, \ldots, n$ or πN (whichever is smaller).

It may be established mathematically that the expected value and variance of P are

$$E(P) = \pi \quad \text{and} \quad \text{Var}(P) = \frac{\pi(1-\pi)}{n}\left(\frac{N-n}{N-1}\right)$$

Note that $E(P)$ is the same as for the binomial distribution, whereas $\text{Var}(P)$ differs from its binomial counterpart by the $(N-n)/(N-1)$ term. In Chapter 7, we saw that this factor plays an important role in analyzing samples taken from finite populations. As N gets very large, the term approaches 1. This suggests that for large N, the hypergeometric distribution probabilities will not differ much from those calculated using the binomial formula.

EXAMPLE: PROBABILITIES FOR FIREWORKS

Diablo Pyrotechnics, Ltd., is investigating a new compound to use in its Fantastic Spiroid rockets. It is supposed to produce a larger and brighter explosive pattern. Unfortunately, the new compound is highly unstable, so that some unknown proportion of the rockets will produce a loud pop instead of the intended dazzling display. The company sales manager wishes to know what the proportion of duds will be so that she can set prices to account for the uncertain results the customer must expect. She has decided to use a sample of rockets from the upcoming test shots in estimating this proportion.

Diablo has produced 100 Fantastic Spiroids for a variety of tests. A sample of 5 is selected at random. Supposing that 20% of the rockets produced will be duds, we may determine the probability that the proportion of duds in the sample will be between 0 and 40%.

SOLUTION: Using $n = 5$, $\pi = .20$, and $N = 100$, we calculate

$$\begin{aligned}
\Pr[0 \le P \le .40] &= \Pr[P = 0] + \Pr[P = .2] + \Pr[P = .4] \\
&= \Pr\left[P = \frac{0}{5}\right] + \Pr\left[P = \frac{1}{5}\right] + \Pr\left[P = \frac{2}{5}\right] \\
&= \frac{C_0^{20}C_5^{80}}{C_5^{100}} + \frac{C_1^{20}C_4^{80}}{C_5^{100}} + \frac{C_2^{20}C_3^{80}}{C_5^{100}} \\
&= \left(\frac{80}{100}\right)\left(\frac{79}{99}\right)\left(\frac{78}{98}\right)\left(\frac{77}{97}\right)\left(\frac{76}{96}\right) + 5\left(\frac{20}{100}\right)\left(\frac{80}{99}\right)\left(\frac{79}{98}\right)\left(\frac{78}{97}\right)\left(\frac{77}{96}\right) \\
&\quad + \frac{5 \times 4}{2}\left(\frac{20}{100}\right)\left(\frac{19}{99}\right)\left(\frac{80}{98}\right)\left(\frac{79}{97}\right)\left(\frac{78}{96}\right) \\
&= .3193 + .4201 + .2073 = .9467
\end{aligned}$$

We may compare this result to that obtainable from the binomial distribution (which would be *improper* to use here). Consider the second term in the above probability sum; this is the probability for getting exactly one dud in a sample of size 5. Using the binomial formula, we obtain

$$\frac{5!}{1!4!}(.2)^1(.8)^4 = .4096$$

which is close to the .4201 calculated above. Note that the binomial here understates the true probability; for some other values of r, it will overstate it.

EXERCISES

22-1 The WaySafe Market's personnel manager randomly selects $n = 3$ different names from a file of $N = 10$ job applicants, $S = 5$ of whom are experienced. Construct a probability tree diagram that has a separate stage for each person chosen, with forks containing branches for the events "experienced" and "inexperienced." Enter the appropriate probability values on each branch. Then, use the multiplication law to determine the probability for each end position. From your tree, determine the following probabilities.
(a) No selected persons are experienced.
(b) Only one selected person is experienced.
(c) Exactly two selected persons are experienced.
(d) All persons selected are experienced.

22-2 Professor Dull selects $n = 5$ names from her roster of $N = 30$ students. $S = 7$ are accounting majors. Determine the following probabilities.
(a) Exactly three of the students selected are accounting majors.
(b) Exactly four of the students selected are accounting majors.

22-3 A Make-Wave Corporation inspector accepts any shipment of 100 items whenever a sample of 4 units contains no defectives. Otherwise, he rejects

the shipment. Determine the probability for accepting a shipment when the following number of defectives apply.
(a) 5 (b) 10 (c) 20 (d) 25

22-4 Refer to the Diablo Pyrotechnics fireworks example. Assuming $\pi = .30$, determine the probability that the proportion of duds will fall between 0 and .40.

22-5 Kryptonite Corporation buys light bulbs by the gross (a dozen dozen, or 144). From each batch, $n = 5$ bulbs are selected and tested under excessive voltage (which destroys them for further use) in order to determine whether the entire batch of bulbs contains an excessive number of defectives. The company's rule for disposing of a batch states that when the sample contains no defectives, the batch is accepted; otherwise the batch is rejected and returned to the supplier for full credit, with no charges made for the destroyed bulbs.
(a) What is the probability that a "good" batch containing $S = 5$ defective bulbs will be rejected?
(b) What is the probability that a "poor" batch containing $S = 30$ defective bulbs will be accepted?
(c) Do you think that the rule provides protection against rejecting "good" batches and accepting "bad" batches? Explain.

22-6 Luxor Lamps, producer of the light bulbs in Exercise 22-5, occasionally takes a sample of $n = 50$ bulbs at random from the production line. Will the hypergeometric distribution help him to determine probabilities for the number of defectives to be found? Explain.

22-7 What is the probability for getting three or more kings when drawing five cards from a fully shuffled deck of cards? Using your answer, determine the probability for getting three or more cards of the same denomination.

22-2 THE POISSON DISTRIBUTION

Many practical statistical problems involve events occurring over time. One of the most notable of these problems is how to design a facility to service customers arriving at unpredictable times. Knowledge of the probability distribution for the number of arrivals may help the designer to achieve an optimal balance between the amount of time the facility is idle and the time spent by customers waiting in line. For example, the number of tellers hired for a bank's new branch office will be affected by the pattern of customer arrivals over a period of time. During 5 minutes, the number of newly arrived customers may be expected to vary from 0, 1, 2, or perhaps 20 or more up to the limit of space available in the bank. There will be times when all tellers are busy, so that lines will form. Because customers do not enjoy waiting and may switch their business to a competing bank if they feel unduly delayed, the bank may decide to have ten tellers when five would be sufficient to handle any day's transactions. Many familiar events, such as airplanes landing at an airport with limited capacity, persons arriving at a bank of elevators in a busy office building, or telephone calls arriving at a switchboard, require similar decisions.

Such decisions, which balance idle time against waiting time, are called waiting-line or **queuing** problems. In analyzing arrival patterns, we are concerned not with the nature of the event (an arrival) but rather with the number of event occurrences. Questions involving occurrences over time are also common in establishing inventory policies and in setting criteria for the reliability of a system. In some businesses, the distribution for customer orders over a period of time may be critical to finding the best inventory level. Enough stock must be available to fill orders, but too large an inventory could be quite costly. In designing systems to achieve a desired level of reliability, the pattern of failures over time is also an important consideration. For example, the probability distribution for the number of component malfunctions during the life of a communications satellite may be helpful in determining how much redundant capability ought to be provided. Likewise, a hospital would want a heart-lung machine to have a very small probability for malfunctioning during open-heart surgery.

THE POISSON PROCESS

There are many different patterns of unpredictable occurrences of events over time. A large class of situations in which events occur randomly may be characterized as a **Poisson process**, named after the eighteenth-century mathematician and physicist Siméon Poisson.

There are two very important probability distributions associated with a Poisson process. One, to be described here, provides probabilities for the *number* of events that occur in a time interval. This is the *discrete* Poisson distribution. The other, to be discussed in Section 22-4, is the *continuous* exponential distribution, used for determining the probabilities of *times between* the event occurrences.

The Poisson and Bernoulli processes are similar; however, it is important to note the differences between them. Recall that the binomial distribution provides probabilities for the number of events of a *particular kind* (successes) occurring in n independent trials of a random experiment. With a Poisson process, there is no fixed number of trials; the events occur randomly over time—which is continuous. There is only one kind of event, such as arrival of a customer or an equipment breakdown, instead of two complementary ones, success and failure, as in a Bernoulli process.

EXPRESSING THE POISSON DISTRIBUTION

The probabilities for the number of events X that occur in a Poisson process in a period of duration t may be obtained from the following expression for the

POISSON DISTRIBUTION

$$\Pr[X = x] = \frac{e^{-\lambda t}(\lambda t)^x}{x!}$$

where $x = 0, 1, 2, \ldots$. The constant e is the base of natural logarithms and is equal to 2.7183. The parameter λ (the lowercase Greek *lambda*) *represents the mean rate at which events occur during the process.* That is, on the average,

λ events per unit time will occur. Multiplying λ, a rate, by t, a duration of time, results in λt,* *the mean number of events occurring in a period of length t.* Note that we place no upper limit on the number of events that may occur; that is, X may assume any integral value from zero to infinity.

The Poisson distribution is completely defined by the process rate λ and the duration t. Its mean and variance are identical and are expressed as

$$E(X) = \lambda t \quad \text{and} \quad \text{Var}(X) = \lambda t$$

EXAMPLE: ARRIVALS AT A BARBERSHOP

Sammy Lee owns a one-man barbershop. A customer informs Sammy that during the lunchtime rush his customers arrive in a pattern that is approximately a Poisson process having a mean rate of 6 persons per hour. If Sammy spends 15 minutes (.25 hour) cutting one man's hair, what is the probability that exactly 2 new customers will arrive before he is finished?

SOLUTION: We have $\lambda = 6$ customers per hour and $t = .25$ hour. Therefore,

$$\lambda t = 6(.25) = 1.50 \text{ customers}$$

We obtain

$$\Pr[X = 2] = \frac{e^{-1.50}(1.50)^2}{2!}$$

From Appendix Table I, we find that $e^{-1.50} = .223130$, so that

$$\Pr[X = 2] = \frac{.223130(1.50)^2}{2!} = .2510$$

If the duration t is increased, the probabilities for large numbers of arrivals will become greater. This seems logical, since there is more time for events to occur. For example, if $t = .4$ hour, then $\lambda t = 6(.4) = 2.4$, so that

$$\Pr[X = 2] = \frac{e^{-2.4}(2.4)^2}{2!} = \frac{.090718(2.4)^2}{2!} = .2613$$

Analogously, the probabilties for few arrivals will be reduced when t is increased.

ASSUMPTIONS OF A POISSON PROCESS

As we have indicated, the events of a Poisson process occur randomly over time. Three additional assumptions are required to distinguish it from other types of occurrence patterns.

*In many books, $t = 1$, a standard unit of time, and λ represents the mean number of occurrences over a standard time period. There, $\lambda t = \lambda \times 1 = \lambda$.

1. A Poisson process has *no memory*. That is, the number of events occurring in one interval of time is *independent* of what happened in previous time periods.
2. The process rate λ *must remain constant* for the entire duration considered.
3. It is extremely *rare* for more than one event to occur during a short interval of time; the shorter the duration, the rarer the occurrence of two or more events becomes. The probability for exactly one event occurring in such an interval is approximately λ times its duration.

If we divide a duration into small time segments, letting each represent a trial with just two possible outcomes—(a) exactly one event occurring or (b) a non-occurrence—then the Poisson probabilities may be roughly represented by the binomial distribution. This is only approximately so, since more than one event may occur in each time segment (so that each "trial" actually has more than two possible outcomes, violating assumptions of the Bernoulli process). But our third assumption makes the probability of the occurrence of more than one event close to zero. When the time segments are very tiny, the approximation becomes quite close, and the Poisson distribution is obtained mathematically from the binomial formula.

PRACTICAL LIMITATIONS OF THE POISSON DISTRIBUTION

A very serious mistake to make when applying the Poisson distribution is to assume that the mean event occurrence rate λ holds over an extended duration when it does not. Many queuing situations, for example, involve random arrivals whose rate changes with the time of day, day of week, season, or other circumstances. The mean rate of vehicle arrivals at a metropolitan toll plaza will be different at 9 A.M. than at 3 A.M.; it will be different on Fridays than on Mondays; and it will be greater in the fall than in the summer, when many drivers are on vacation. It is still proper to treat such situations as a Poisson process, but care must be taken to keep short the durations considered and to apply the appropriate value of λ. Thus, a bank may keep only a third of its teller windows open at 10:30 A.M. on Tuesday, when λ is small, but it will probably keep them all open around 5 P.M. on a Friday that is also the first of the month, when transaction traffic proves heaviest.

A second difficulty is that the Poisson distribution sets no limit on the number of customers who may arrive. In Table 22-1, the probabilities for several possible values of X have been calculated for $\lambda t = 1.50$. Although $\Pr[9] = .0000$, this is a nonzero value that has been rounded off. There is a nonzero probability that 9 or 20 or even 100 customers may arrive at the barbershop in any 15-minute interval, but the probability is quite tiny. As discussed in connection with the normal distribution, even absurd outcomes have nonzero probabilities. For instance, there is a nonzero probability that 10,000 men would try to crowd into Sammy's barbershop during a 15-minute period.

Finally, a random variable is only approximated by a Poisson distribution. However, the approximation is often empirically well justified. For example, a statistician has shown that the number of U.S. Supreme Court seats vacated in a given year very closely fits a Poisson distribution. Some studies have shown that the deaths of Prussian army recruits kicked by horses and the very rare Lake

TABLE 22-1 Poisson Probabilities, When $\lambda t = 1.50$

x	Pr[X = x]
0	.2231
1	.3347
2	.2510
3	.1256
4	.0470
5	.0141
6	.0036
7	.0007
8	.0002
9	.0000

Zurich freezes are closely approximated by the Poisson process. Of far more practical significance is the fact that a vast number of waiting-line, reliability, and inventory situations are adequately characterized by the Poisson process.

USING POISSON PROBABILITY TABLES

Computing Poisson probabilities by hand may be an onerous chore. The cumulative values of the Poisson probabilities are computed in Appendix Table J for levels of λt ranging from 1 to 20.

The table provides values of $\Pr[X \leq x]$. For example, to find the cumulative probability values for the number of cars arriving at a toll booth during an interval of $t = 10$ minutes when the arrival rate is $\lambda = 2$ per minute, we consult Appendix Table J where $\lambda t = 2(10) = 20$. The probability that the number of arriving cars is ≤ 15 is

$$\Pr[X \leq 15] = .1565$$

whereas the probability that ≤ 20 cars will arrive during the 10-minute interval is

$$\Pr[X \leq 20] = .5591$$

Like the cumulative binomial tables discussed in Chapter 6, it is possible to obtain from Appendix Table J Poisson probability values for other cases (= , >, <, or ≥ some number, or the interval between two numbers). For example, the probability that exactly 15 cars will arrive in 10 minutes is

$$\Pr[X = 15] = \Pr[X \leq 15] - \Pr[X \leq 14] = .1565 - .1049 = .0516$$

Similarly, we may obtain the probability that the number of cars arriving lies between two values. Thus, the probability that between 16 and 20 cars will arrive in 10 minutes is

$$\Pr[16 \leq X \leq 20] = \Pr[X \leq 20] - \Pr[X \leq 15] = .5591 - .1565 = .4026$$

The probability that >20 cars will arrive is

$$\Pr[X > 20] = 1 - \Pr[X \leq 20] = 1 - .5591 = .4409$$

STATISTICS AROUND US

Searching for Tuna

The commodore of a fishing fleet is searching the Pacific Ocean for a school of tuna. His plane can search for a distance of 600 miles, and he can spot any school of fish within a lateral distance of ten miles to either side of the aircraft. Thus, the area searched in a day would be 2(10)600 = 12,000 square miles.

The location of schools of tuna in this area is completely random. We will assume that historically the mean density of large tuna schools in the area has been 1 per 100,000 square miles.

A storm is forecast to reach the fishing area in 6 days. The boats require at least one day to return to port. What is the probability that at least one school will be located no later than one day before the storm?

Since there is 1 school per 100,000 square miles, $\lambda = .00001$ school per square mile. The value of t (here representing area) is 5 days times the area searched in a day, or $5 \times 12{,}000 = 60{,}000$ square miles. Thus, $\lambda t = .00001(60{,}000) = .60$, which represents the mean number of schools to be encountered in 5 days of searching. The probability that at least one school is encountered is

$$\begin{aligned}\Pr[X \geq 1] &= 1 - \Pr[X = 0] \\ &= 1 - \frac{e^{-.60}(.60)^0}{0!} \\ &= 1 - e^{-.60} \\ &= 1 - .549 = .451\end{aligned}$$

Suppose that no tuna are found and that after docking for the storm, the search is resumed. We may find how many days must be committed to the search in order to ensure a probability of .95 that at least one school will be found. Since a Poisson process has no memory, we must start all over again. Otherwise the number of schools encountered in the first and second searches would be dependent events, violating the basic Poisson process assumptions. (The size of the remaining search area cannot even be reduced, since schools might enter the area previously scanned.) Thus, we want to find t such that

$$\begin{aligned}.95 = \Pr[X \geq 1] &= 1 - \Pr[X = 0] \\ &= 1 - \frac{e^{-\lambda t}(\lambda t)^0}{0!} \\ &= 1 - e^{-\lambda t}\end{aligned}$$

or

$$e^{-\lambda t} = 1 - .95 = .05$$

From Appendix Table I, we see that $e^{-y} = .05$ (rounded) when $y = 3.00$, so that using $\lambda t = 3.00$ we will have the smallest t for the above condition

STATISTICS AROUND US

to hold. Thus, dividing 3.00 by the number of schools encountered per square mile, $\lambda = .00001$, we obtain the total search area t required.

$$t = \frac{\lambda t}{\lambda} = \frac{3.00}{.00001} = 300{,}000 \text{ square miles}$$

Dividing this area by the area searched per day, we obtain the days required to yield a .95 probability of finding at least one school of tuna.

$$\frac{300{,}000 \text{ square miles}}{12{,}000 \text{ square miles per day}} = 25 \text{ days}$$

These 25 days are *in addition to the 5 days already spent searching.*

APPLICATIONS NOT INVOLVING TIME

Events occurring in space, as well as events occurring over time, may be characterized as Poisson processes. For instance, if finding objects spread randomly over a space (such as misspelled names in a telephone directory) is viewed as an event, then encountering objects while the space (in this case, pages of the directory) is searched may be viewed as a Poisson process. Application of the Poisson process to events occurring in space has proven fruitful in quality control and in such esoteric areas as developing search techniques for radar, establishing tactics for ships sailing through mine fields, and hunting for submarines. Here λ would represent the mean number of events per unit distance (such as an inch), area (a square mile), or space (a cubic centimeter). More generally, λ may be the mean number of particular events per observation made of the phenomena in question. Thus, λ may be 3 errors per page, or it may be 5 bad debts per 1,000 installment contracts. The "durations" would be analogous: the space searched, the number of pages scanned, the number of contracts written, and so on.

EXERCISES

22-8 Between 9 and 10 A.M. on Saturday, the peak business period, customers arrive at Sammy Lee's barbershop at a mean rate of $\lambda = 5$ per hour. During the Thursday slump, between 2 and 3 P.M., customers arrive at a rate of $\lambda = 1$ per hour. In either case, the arrivals may be represented as a Poisson process.

(a) Does this mean that there will always be more customers arriving during the peak than during the slump? Explain.

(b) Compare the probability of exactly two customers arriving during Sammy's slump to that of the same number arriving during his peak.

(c) If the mean rate of arrivals for the week as a whole is three customers per hour, can Sammy use the Poisson distribution with $\lambda = 3$ to determine the probability that next week's arrivals will be between 100 and 150? Explain.

22-9 Com Piler is a typesetter who makes on the average $\lambda = .5$ error per page. What is the probability that she will make no errors in the first $t = 10$ pages? What is the probability that she will make exactly 5 errors in the first 10 pages?

22-10 During the late Friday rush at Million Bank, an average of $\lambda = 5$ customers per minute arrive. What is the probability that no customers arrive during a specified 1-minute interval?

22-11 The Jekyl family receives an average of $\lambda = 2$ pieces of regular mail each delivery day. Assume that the Poisson distribution applies.
(a) What is the probability that they will get no mail on the next two consecutive days?
(b) What is the probability that, given two days without mail, they will get no mail for another two days?

22-12 Use Appendix Table J to determine the probabilities that the stated number of events occur in a Poisson process at a rate of $\lambda = 8$/hour when the following durations are considered.
(a) $t = 2$ hours; 10 or fewer events
(b) $t = 1.5$ hours; 6 or more events
(c) $t = 1$ hour; exactly 3 events
(d) $t = .5$ hour; between 1 and 5 events

22-13 A typist commits errors at the rate of .01 per word. Assuming that a Poisson process applies, use Appendix Table J to determine the probabilities for each of the following numbers of errors committed in a 500-word letter.
(a) exactly 5 (b) zero (c) more than 10 (d) between 3 and 7

22-14 A California Central Valley tomato grower wishes to protect his crop against destruction by aphids. Two alternatives are open to him: Spray with a powerful insecticide that may harm the local ecology or wait for ladybugs to eat the aphids. Each spring, massive flights of ladybugs are wafted by wind currents across the California valleys from their Sierra Nevada hibernating points. Unfortunately, where and when a flight of ladybugs lands is purely a matter of chance. Wherever there are plenty of aphids, they lay eggs that rapidly hatch. If at least one flight of ladybugs lands on part of the grower's crop within five days, they and their larvae will devour all the aphids. Otherwise he will spray, killing all aphids and the unfortunate late-coming aphid-eaters as well, for by that time irreparable crop damage will have been suffered. On any given day, 10% of the Central Valley is covered by ladybugs. Assume that the arrivals of ladybugs may be considered a Poisson process. (The size of the farm may be ignored.)
(a) Assuming that the mean arrival rate is $\lambda = .1$ flight of ladybugs per day, what is the probability that no flights arrive during $t = 5$ days?
(b) What is the probability that the farmer won't have to spray?

22-15 Two tourists are enjoying the view from San Francisco's Golden Gate Bridge. They have decided to spend a half hour waiting for ships to pass under the bridge. Suppose that ship arrivals at the Golden Gate (leaving or entering San Francisco Bay) are a Poisson process at the mean rate of $\lambda = .2$ per hour. Determine the probability that the tourists will see passing beneath them (a) no ships; (b) 1 ship; (c) 2 ships.

22-3 THE UNIFORM DISTRIBUTION

The uniform distribution provides probabilities for a random variable that has equal chances of assuming any value on a continuous scale. For example, it provides the probability that a wheel of fortune will stop so that its pointer lies within a particular segment. The uniform distribution has many interesting applications. One of the more notable is to generate random numbers, which are used for selecting a random sample.

The **uniform distribution** has the following probability density function.

$$f(x) = \begin{cases} \dfrac{1}{b-a} & \text{if} \quad a \le x \le b \\ 0 & \text{otherwise} \end{cases}$$

The top graphs in Figure 22-2 show the density functions for two different sets of values for a and b. Each function is a horizontal line segment of constant height $1/(b - a)$ over the interval from a to b. Outside the interval, $f(x) = 0$. This means that for a uniformly distributed random variable X, values below a or above b are impossible.

Recall from Chapter 6 that the probability that X will fall below a point is provided by the area under the density curve to the left of that point. The cumulative probability distribution function, $\Pr[X \le x]$, provides this area. The cumulative function for values of x between a and b is the area of the rectangle of height $1/(b - a)$ and base $x - a$, found by multiplying these two values together. To the left of a, the cumulative probabilities must be zero, whereas the probability that X lies below points beyond b must be 1. The following expression provides the

CUMULATIVE PROBABILITIES FOR THE UNIFORM DISTRIBUTION

$$\Pr[X \le x] = \begin{cases} 0 & \text{if} \quad x < a \\ \dfrac{x-a}{b-a} & \text{if} \quad a \le x \le b \\ 1 & \text{if} \quad x > b \end{cases}$$

The cumulative distribution functions for the two cases are shown in the bottom half of Figure 22-2.

EXAMPLE: PROBABILITY FOR BEING STUCK IN PEORIA

A traveling businesswoman must change planes in Peoria en route to New Haven. Her Peoria-bound plane is scheduled to arrive 20 minutes prior to the departure of the New Haven flight. If that flight is missed, she must spend 12 hours in Peoria waiting for the next plane. Assuming that her plane's arrival time is uniformly

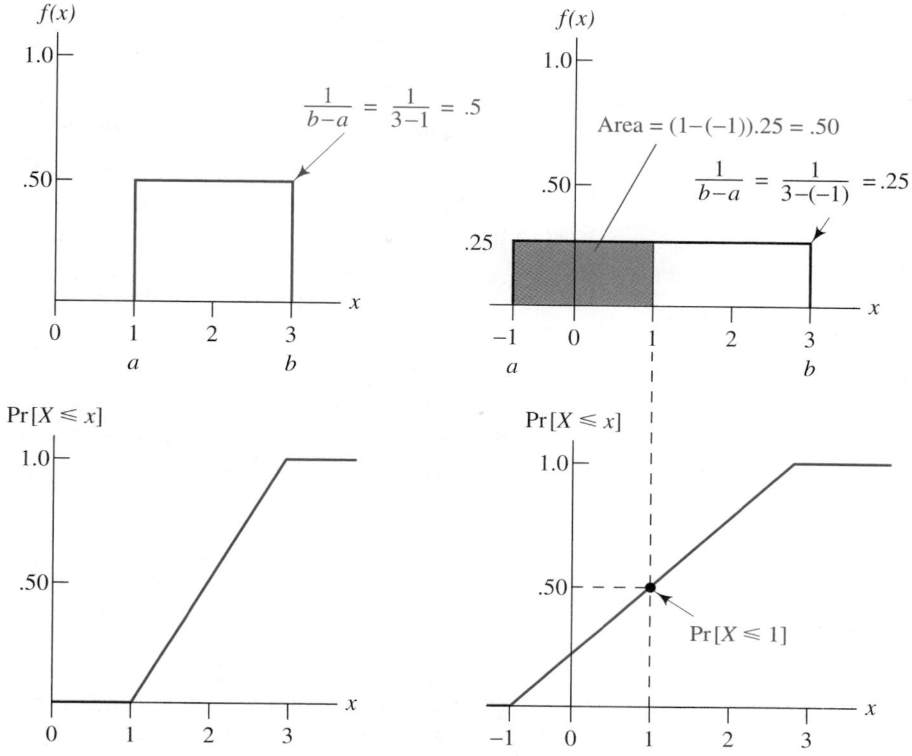

FIGURE 22-2 Two uniform probability distributions.

distributed over the interval from being 1 hour early to being 1 hour late, what is the probability that she will be stuck in Peoria (that is, that her Peoria-bound plane will be more than 20 minutes late)?

SOLUTION: Here, $a = -60$ minutes and $b = +60$ minutes. Letting X be the arrival time in Peoria, we have

$$\begin{aligned}\Pr[\text{stuck in Peoria}] &= \Pr[X > 20] \\ &= 1 - \Pr[X \leq 20] \\ &= 1 - \frac{20 - (-60)}{60 - (-60)} \\ &= 1 - \frac{80}{120} = \frac{40}{120} = \frac{1}{3}\end{aligned}$$

It is easy to obtain an expression for the expected value of a uniformly distributed random variable. The expected value of X is the long-run average result obtained from repeating the same random experiment. Since all values between

a and b have the same chance of occurring, the average of a and b is the long-run average of the individual outcomes, or

$$E(X) = \frac{a + b}{2}$$

The variance of a uniform random variable must be obtained mathematically. It is given by

$$\text{Var}(X) = \frac{(b - a)^2}{12}$$

Often it is necessary to determine the probability that a uniform random variable falls between two values. For instance, suppose that $a = 10$ and $b = 15$. The probability that X lies between 11 and 14 is equal to the rectangular area between 11 and 14. Therefore, we subtract the smaller probability (area) from the larger one to obtain

$$\begin{aligned} \Pr[11 \le X \le 14] &= \Pr[X \le 14] - \Pr[X \le 11] \\ &= \frac{14 - 10}{15 - 10} - \frac{11 - 10}{15 - 10} = \frac{3}{5} = .6 \end{aligned}$$

(Like the normal and any other continuous distribution, $P[X \le x] = P[X < x]$, so that the distinction between $\le$ and $<$ is unimportant.)

EXERCISES

22-16 The Red Mill cuts logs into planks 10 feet long. After cutting, the trimmed plank ends are apt to be any length smaller than 10 feet. What proportion of the trimmings have lengths between (a) 4 and 6 feet; (b) 3 and 7 feet; (c) 2.5 and 6.4 feet; (d) 5.52 and 8.52 feet?

22-17 The time taken by the Salem Daughters Construction Company to frame a house is uniformly distributed between 20 and 30 days. For each of the following time periods, determine the probability that the task will be completed.
(a) before the 26th day from starting
(b) in between 23.5 and 27.0 days
(c) within 29 days from starting

22-18 A pseudorandom number generator provides decimals uniformly distributed from 0 to 1. Determine probabilities for the following.
(a) A value is obtained below .30.
(b) The next two values are both less than .50.

22-19 A pilot is navigating her airplane by "dead reckoning" over the ocean. She does not know her precise speed and actual heading, since she has no way to gauge the effects of wind. She is flying at night and intends to home in on a light ship. The minimum distance at which the plane will pass the light ship is uniformly distributed from 0 miles to 50 miles. Assuming clear visibility, what is the probability that the pilot will see the light ship when flying at an altitude providing a line-of-sight range of (a) 50 miles; (b) 40 miles; (c) 30 miles; (d) 10 miles?

22-20 A farmer is scheduled to begin reaping his wheat at 6 A.M. on July 1, the date on which the combines belonging to his cooperative will be available. Harvesting must begin within 4 days after ripening or the crop will be lost. It cannot be reaped before it is ripe. If his wheat is not ready for reaping on the scheduled date or if it ripens too early, the farmer must pay for private equipment. Assuming that the crop will ripen at a time uniformly distributed from 6 A.M. on June 23 through 6 A.M. on July 3, what is the probability that the farmer will not be forced to rent his combines from outside? (June has 30 days.)

22-4 THE EXPONENTIAL DISTRIBUTION

We have seen that a Poisson process may be applied to events occurring randomly over time (or space). The Poisson distribution provides the probabilities that a particular number of events will occur. Of great importance in business applications is the time duration (or space encountered) *between* the events. To a person waiting in a bank line, the number of persons arriving before him is of little importance if his line moves quickly; his prime concern is the length of his wait. The commodore whose fleet has enough capacity to capture just one school of tuna cares only about how long it will take to locate the first one.

In this section we will present the exponential distribution, which, for a Poisson process, provides the probabilities for the time (or space traversed) between events or until the first event occurrence.

Illustration: Car Arrivals at a Toll Booth

Consider cars arriving at a toll booth. The cars are represented in Figure 22-3 by dots. The horizontal distance of each dot from the origin (at 9:00 A.M.) indicates when a car will arrive at the booth. Such a graph may be constructed from an aerial photograph taken at 9:00 A.M. of the two miles of highway leading to the station. Assuming that all cars are traveling at the speed limit, we may directly translate each car's distance from the booth into its arrival time. Note that the dots in Figure 22-3 are scattered with no apparent pattern, as if placed there randomly. This pattern is typical of a Poisson process.

FINDING INTEREVENT PROBABILITIES

The gaps between the dots in Figure 22-3 represent the **interarrival times**, or times between successive arrivals of cars. The exponential distribution is

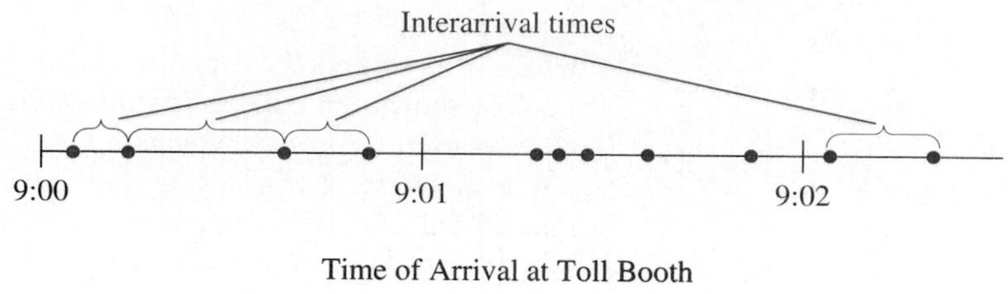

FIGURE 22-3 Times for random arrivals of cars at a toll booth.

concerned with the size of the gaps, measured in time units, separating successive cars. Although the dots are scattered randomly over time, the relative frequency of interarrival times of various sizes is predictable. Suppose that the cars arriving at the toll station are observed for several minutes, and that the time of each car's arrival is noted. Those data would provide a histogram similar to Figure 22-4(a). This approximates the shape of the underlying frequency curve in Figure 22-4(b), the height of which may be determined for any interarrival time t (or, generally, for the time or space between any two events in a Poisson process) from the expression

$$f(t) = \lambda e^{-\lambda t}$$

This is the probability density function for the exponential distribution.

The particular distribution applicable to a specific situation depends only on the level of λ. In our toll booth illustration, the mean arrival rate is $\lambda = 4$ cars per minute. Note that the frequency curve intersects the vertical axis at height λ. The mean and the standard deviation of the exponential distribution are identical and may be expressed in terms of λ as

$$E(T) = 1/\lambda \quad \text{and} \quad \text{SD}(T) = 1/\lambda$$

where our random variable is T, the uncertain time (or space) between any two successive events. (Unlike the Poisson distribution, the *standard deviation equals the mean*, whereas the variance equals the mean squared.)

The mean time between arrivals is the reciprocal of the mean rate of arrivals. Thus, if $\lambda = 4$ *cars per minute*, then the mean time between arrivals is $1/\lambda = 1/4 = .25$ *minute per car*. Another feature of the exponential distribution is that *shorter durations are more likely than longer ones*. The curve in Figure 22-4(b) decreases in height and the slope becomes less pronounced as t becomes larger. The tail of the exponential curve, like those of the normal curve, never touches the horizontal axis, indicating that there is no limit on how large the interarrival time t may be.

Probabilities for the exponential random variable may be found by determining the area under the frequency curve. The following expression provides the

CUMULATIVE PROBABILITY FOR THE EXPONENTIAL DISTRIBUTION

$$\Pr[T \le t] = 1 - e^{-\lambda t}$$

where T represents the time (or space) between any two successive events. Figure 22-4(c) shows the cumulative probability graph when $\lambda = 4$. Appendix Table I may be used to provide values for $e^{-\lambda t}$.

For example, using $\lambda = 4$ cars per minute, we find the probability that the interarrival time between any two cars is less than or equal to $t = .4$ minute.

$$\begin{aligned}\Pr[T \le .4] &= 1 - e^{-4(.4)} = 1 - e^{-1.6} \\ &= 1 - .201897 \\ &= .798 \text{ (rounded)}\end{aligned}$$

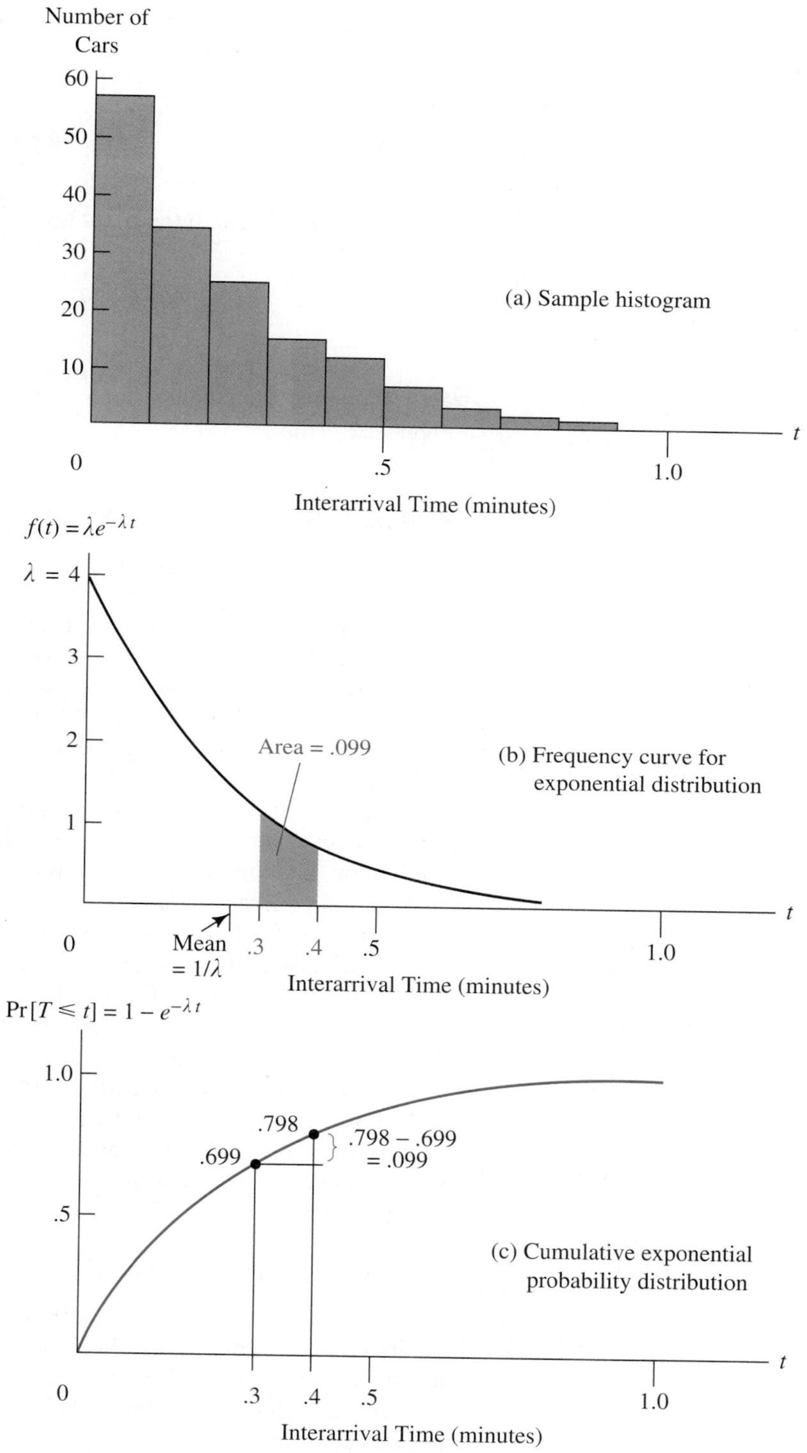

FIGURE 22-4 The exponential distribution for the interarrival times of cars.

The probability that the time is $t = .3$ minute or less is

$$\begin{aligned}\Pr[T \leq .3] &= 1 - e^{-4(.3)} = 1 - e^{-1.2} \\ &= 1 - .301194 \\ &= .699 \text{ (rounded)}\end{aligned}$$

The probability that an interarrival time between .3 and .4 minute will be achieved is

$$\begin{aligned}\Pr[.3 \leq T \leq .4] &= .798 - .699 \\ &= .099\end{aligned}$$

This value is the shaded area under the exponential frequency curve in Figure 22-4(b).

APPLICATIONS OF THE EXPONENTIAL DISTRIBUTION

Because a Poisson process has no memory, the exponential distribution applies to the time T between any two events—whether near the beginning of the process or near the end. The burning out of light bulbs in a new building, a process often characterized as a Poisson process, illustrates this point. The probability that the time from the 99th burnout to the 100th exceeds 50 hours would be the same as that for the period between the 78th and 79th or for the period of initial connection to the 1st burnout. A very common application of the exponential distribution is to intermittent processes. Thus, the time taken by a bank teller to service a customer may be an exponential random variable, so that the Poisson process ends when all customers have been processed. The teller is then "idle" (not making a transaction, although there may be other work to do during these occasions). The amount and pattern of idle time is a function of both the arrivals and the service. A new phase of a Poisson process begins with the arrival of the next customer.

One point should be made clear. There is no reason why the teller's service times must be exponentially distributed. Their historical frequency distribution may yield a histogram having a shape very different from that provided in Figure 22-4. In that case, the situation clearly would not fit the assumptions of a Poisson process. Whether the exponential distribution should be used is a matter of how closely it fits the situation. An exponential distribution, for instance, assigns low probabilities to long interevent times and high probabilities to short ones. But maybe both long and short are rare, which would make a normal distribution more appropriate.

Reliability Applications

The exponential distribution may be used to establish specifications for the reliability of equipment that will fail at some future time according to the probability pattern of this distribution. Operating requirements are often established in terms of mean time between failures (MTBF), which represents the mean number of failures per unit time: $1/\lambda$.

The MTBF figure itself may be established by a requirement that the equipment achieve some probability for lasting a minimum time before failing. For example, suppose that certain items must be designed so that 90% of them will last more than 100 hours. The requirements may be expressed in the following manner.

Choose λ so that

$$\begin{aligned} .90 = \Pr[T > 100] &= 1 - \Pr[T \leq 100] \\ &= 1 - (1 - e^{-\lambda(100)}) \\ &= e^{-\lambda(100)} \end{aligned}$$

From Appendix Table I, we find that the closest value is $e^{-y} = .905$ (rounded) when $y = .10$. Thus, setting $\lambda(100) = .10$, we obtain

$$\lambda = \frac{.10}{100} = .001 \text{ failure per hour}$$

and

$$\text{MTBF} = \frac{1}{\lambda} = \frac{1}{.001} = 1{,}000 \text{ hours}$$

We may determine the probability that a particular part built to these specifications will fail between 200 and 600 hours after operation by subtracting the probability that failure occurs by 200 hours from the probability that it occurs on or before 600 hours.

$$\begin{aligned} \Pr[200 \leq T \leq 600] &= \Pr[T \leq 600] - \Pr[T \leq 200] \\ &= (1 - e^{-.001(600)}) - (1 - e^{-.001(200)}) \\ &= e^{-.2} - e^{-.6} \\ &= .819 - .549 = .270 \end{aligned}$$

(As with the previously discussed continuous distributions, the distinction between $\leq$ and $<$ is unimportant.)

EXAMPLE: EMERGENCY HOSPITAL POWER

A hospital is reviewing its contingency plans for coping with power failures. Certain hospital functions, such as surgery, require a continuous power supply. The hospital has one emergency generator connected to auxiliary electrical circuits in critical locations. Since the auxiliary power could fail during a blackout while essential services are being rendered, funds for a back-up generator are being sought.

Assuming that the present generator has a mean time between failures ($1/\lambda$) rated as 100 hours, what is the probability that it will fail during the next 10-hour blackout?

SOLUTION: Here, $\lambda = .01$ failure per hour. Thus,

$$\begin{aligned} \Pr[T \leq 10] &= 1 - e^{-.01(10)} = 1 - e^{-.10} \\ &= 1 - .904837 = .095 \text{ (rounded)} \end{aligned}$$

The probability is .095 that a failure will occur and .905 that it will not. The chance of failure is rather high, considering the stakes involved. Suppose that there are $n = 5$ such blackouts in one year. The probability that the generator works through all of them may be determined from the binomial formula. Using $\pi = .905$ and $r = 5$, we calculate

$$\frac{5!}{5!0!}(.905)^5(.095)^0 = .61$$

an unsafe value, to be sure.

Consider how dramatically the probability changes with the purchase of a backup generator. We will assume that the generators operate independently and simultaneously. The probability that both of the generators fail in a 10-hour period would be $(.095)^2 = .0090$. Thus, the probability that at least one works throughout is

$$1 - .0090 = .9910$$

Considering five blackouts, the probability that at least one generator works during all the blackouts may be obtained from the binomial formula. Using $r = n = 5$ and $\pi = .991$, we find

$$C_5^5(.991)^5(.009)^0 = .956$$

If a third generator is purchased, the probability that all three fail in 10 hours becomes .00086, and the probability for no interruptions throughout five blackouts increases to .9957.

QUEUING APPLICATIONS

A very fruitful application of the exponential distribution has been its use in queuing problems. The Statistics Around Us box illustrates one such possible application.

STATISTICS AROUND US

Machine Shop Tool Cage

Miller Machine Works has a single, centralized tool cage where machinists obtain parts for their equipment. The plant superintendent wants to replace the present clerk with an experienced machinist whose direct costs are $10.00 per hour. This violates company policy, which dictates that the position should be filled by a clerk who is paid $5.00 per hour. The superintendent insists that the machinist, with his special knowledge, can provide service twice as quickly. And the superintendent has constructed an additional, very convincing argument.

He has assumed that the arrivals at the tool cage are a Poisson process with mean rate λ_A men per hour, and that the service time distribution for the clerk is exponential with mean rate λ_S men per hour (that is, counting just those times when someone is being serviced by the cage clerk). By a mathematical deduction, it may be established that the total time W that a

STATISTICS AROUND US

machinist must wait at the tool cage—both in line and while being serviced—has an exponential distribution with expected value

$$E(W) = \frac{1}{\lambda_S - \lambda_A}$$

Thus, if $\lambda_S = 10$ per hour and $\lambda_A = 5$ per hour, then

$$E(W) = \frac{1}{10 - 5} = .2 \text{ hour}$$

Since a machinist is unproductive while waiting in line or being serviced, which takes an average of $1/\lambda_S$ hours, his direct costs of $10.00 per hour are lost during these times. Thus, the total expected hourly cost of manning the tool cage with a clerk is the cost of the machinists' unproductive time plus the cost of the clerk. Since each machinist must be unproductive $E(W)$ hours, on the average, and there are λ_A arriving per hour, the total expected cost per hour is

$$\begin{aligned}\$\lambda_A[E(W)]10.00 + 5.00 &= \$5(.2)10.00 + 5.00 \\ &= \$15.00\end{aligned}$$

If an experienced machinist mans the cage, he can service at twice the clerk's rate, $\lambda_S = 2(10) = 20$ machinists per hour, so that

$$E(W) = \frac{1}{20 - 5} = \frac{1}{15} = .067 \text{ hour}$$

Thus, using a cost of $10.00 per hour for the man in the tool room, we obtain a total expected cost per hour of

$$\$5(.067)10.0 + 10.00 = \$13.35$$

By using an experienced machinist, an average of $1.65 per hour may be saved.

EXERCISES

22-21 On Tuesday mornings, customers arrive at the Central Valley National Bank at a rate of $\lambda = 1$ per minute. What is the probability that the time between the next two successive arrivals will be (a) shorter than 1 minute; (b) longer than 5 minutes; (c) between 2 and 5 minutes?

22-22 The final settlement claims filed by policyholders of Honest Abe's Insurance Company involving amounts of $100,000 or more are events from a Poisson process with a mean rate of $\lambda = 1$ per working day. Funds earmarked for large-claims settlement are invested in short-term government bonds at an interest rate of 5%, so that the timing of settlements affects company profits. What is the probability that the next large claim must be settled (a) within 5 days; (b) sometime after 2 days; (c) in between 2 and 5 days?

22-23 Admiral Motors wishes to determine the terminal mileage for the warranty coverage on the power train of its new compact car. A warranty is desired such that no more than 9.5% of the cars will have to use it. Assume that the time between power train failures is exponentially distributed for each car. How many miles should warranty coverage last when the power trains fail at a mean rate of once every 100,000 miles driven, so that $\lambda = .00001$ failure per mile?

22-24 The tuna fleet commodore in our earlier example (page 919) begins another air search for tuna. The airplane searches 20 square miles for every mile traveled. Schools of tuna are randomly distributed over the fishing area at a mean density of one school per 100,000 square miles.

(a) Find λ, the rate at which tuna schools are located per mile flown.

(b) What is the probability that the first school will be located before the search aircraft has flown 5,000 miles?

(c) How many miles must the airplane be capable of traveling in order to guarantee a 90% probability for spotting at least one school of tuna?

22-25 C. A. Gopher & Sons is excavating a site requiring the removal of 100,000 cubic yards of material. Mr. Gopher has leased 10 trucks at $20 per hour. He has the choice of using a scoop loader or a shovel crane to load the dirt into the trucks. A scoop loader costs $40 per hour, whereas the cost of a shovel crane is $60 per hour. Once work has been started, the trucks arrive according to a Poisson process with a mean rate of $\lambda_A = 7$ trucks per hour. The truck-filling times are exponentially distributed. A scoop loader can fill trucks at an average rate of $\lambda_S = 10$ per hour. The shovel crane is faster, filling on the average $\lambda_S = 15$ trucks per hour. (For simplicity, we assume the same truck arrival rate, regardless of equipment used.)

Since the number of truck arrivals required to excavate the site is fixed by the amount of dirt, the optimal choice of filling equipment will be one that will minimize the combined hourly costs of truck *unproductive time* plus the cost of the filling equipment. Adapting the procedures used in the machine shop tool cage example (page 930), determine the optimal equipment choice.

22-26 One of the fundamental principles of designing a system to be reliable is that it have redundant (that is, duplicate) critical subsystems. Suppose that two power supplies are to be used simultaneously on a communications satellite. Assuming the lifetime of each to be exponentially distributed, operating independently, determine the probability that the satellite will function for 1,000 hours before total power failure when the mean time between failures ($1/\lambda$) of each power supply is (a) 500 hours; (b) 1,000 hours; (c) 5,000 hours.

SUMMARY

1. What is the hypergeometric distribution and how is it used?

The discrete **hypergeometric distribution** for the number of successes R in a sample of size n is defined by

$$\Pr[R = r] = \frac{C_r^S C_{n-r}^{N-S}}{C_n^N}$$

where N is the population size and S is the number of population successes. The hypergeometric distribution has the advantage of properly accounting for probabilities when sampling is conducted without replacement when the proportion of items having a particular attribute is assumed to be π. That makes the distribution very important in evaluating acceptance sampling strategies involving shipments of small size N. In a variant form, the hypergeometric distribution also finds probabilities for the sample proportion P:

$$\Pr\left[P = \frac{r}{n}\right] = \frac{C_r^{\pi N} C_{n-r}^{(1-\pi)N}}{C_n^N}$$

Random variables associated with this distribution have the same expected value as their binomial counterparts, so that $E(P) = \pi$. The value of σ_P is $\sqrt{\pi(1-\pi)/n}$ times the *finite population correction factor* $\sqrt{(N-n)/(N-1)}$ introduced in earlier chapters. It is difficult to compute hypergeometric probabilities by hand. Computer programs are available to ease this task. Unfortunately, there are too many cases to be handled with published tables. To overcome these obstacles, the hypergeometric distribution is often approximated by the binomial or the normal distribution.

2. **What is the Poisson distribution and how is it used?**
The discrete **Poisson distribution** provides probabilities for the number of event occurrences X in a fixed time span t of time or space. The distribution does this for random variables generated by a **Poisson process**. We find that the Poisson distribution is common in waiting-line evaluations and in models used to optimize inventories.

Although similar to the familiar Bernoulli process that underlies the binomial distribution, a Poisson process considers only one type of event, such as a customer arrival or the receipt of an order. It is the *number* of these that is uncertain (versus fixed for the Bernoulli process). Among the assumptions of a Poisson process are a constant mean process rate λ, no memory of prior results, and negligible probabilities that more than one event will occur when t is of a short duration. Both the expected value and variance are identical.

$$E(X) = \lambda t \qquad \text{Var}(X) = \lambda t$$

Poisson probabilities may be computed from the following expression.

$$\Pr[X = x] = \frac{e^{-\lambda t}(\lambda t)^x}{x!}$$

Appendix Table J provides a list of cumulative Poisson probabilities for common levels of λ and t.

3. **What is the exponential distribution and how is it used?**
A Poisson process gives rise to a second important random variable, the *time or space* T between successive events. This is referred to as the continuous **exponential distribution**. It may be used in waiting-line evaluations, and is

widely used in life-testing and reliability evaluations. The expected value and standard deviation are both equal to the reciprocal of the mean process rate.

$$E(T) = 1/\lambda \qquad SD(T) = 1/\lambda$$

The probability density function $f(t) = \lambda e^{-\lambda t}$ is easy to apply, leading directly to the cumulative distribution function $1 - e^{-\lambda t}$.

4. **What is the uniform distribution and how is it used?**
Another important continuous probability distribution is the **uniform distribution**, which applies to any quantity X having equal likelihood for falling anywhere within a stipulated interval $[a, b]$. The distribution is useful for applications involving random numbers and is employed extensively in Monte Carlo simulation. The probability density function is $f(x) = 1/(b - a)$ over the interval $[a, b]$ and zero otherwise. The expected value and standard deviation are:

$$E(X) = \frac{a + b}{2} \qquad \text{Var}(X) = \frac{(b - a)^2}{12}$$

and cumulative probabilities are obtained from

$$\Pr[X \leq x] = \frac{x - a}{b - a}$$

when x lies in the interval $[a, b]$. The cumulative probability is 0 for $x < a$ and 1 for $x > b$.

REVIEW EXERCISES

22-27 A random sample of $n = 3$ persons is to be taken from a group of $N = 10$, $S = 4$ of whom are women. Determine the probabilities that the sample contains exactly two women, assuming that each of the following apply.
(a) the sampling is done with replacement
(b) the sampling is done without replacement

22-28 Suppose you deal yourself a poker hand consisting of 5 cards from a standard deck of playing cards. Determine the probability that you will draw three aces.

22-29 During noon hour on Fridays, customers arrive at a mean rate of 2 per minute to the tellers' windows of Chase-Haste Bank. The pattern of arrivals is considered to be purely random.
(a) Determine the probability that exactly 7 customers arrive between 12:15 P.M. and 12:17 P.M.
(b) What is the probability that the first customer arrives before 12:01 P.M.?

22-30 A computer program generates random decimal values in such a way that any value between 0 and 1 is equally likely to be obtained each time. Determine the probability that the next number is (a) less than .5; (b) between .25 and .35; (c) greater than .99; (d) greater than or equal to .05.

22-31 The Water Wheelies production process yields 10% defective items.

(a) Assuming that production is a Bernoulli process, determine the probability that in the next 100 items produced there will be at least 5 defectives.

(b) Assuming that production is a Poisson process, with defectives occurring at the mean rate of 10 per hour, determine the probability that at least 5 defectives will occur in any specific hour.

22-32 A communications satellite's power cells have an exponential time-to-failure distribution. The mean time between failures is 100 hours.

(a) What is the probability that any particular power cell will fail prior to 500 hours of operation?

(b) Suppose that there are four power cells altogether, that they operate independently, and that the satellite will function as long as there is at least one working cell. What is the probability that the satellite may still communicate at the end of 500 hours of operation?

22-33 A random number generator yields uniformly distributed random decimals between 0 and 1. Consider the sampling distribution for the mean $\bar{X}$ of 12 such decimals. $\bar{X}$ itself has an expected value (mean) of .5 and a standard deviation of 1/12.

(a) What probability distribution applies for $\bar{X}$?

(b) Determine the probability that $\bar{X}$ falls between .4 and .6.

CASE New Guernsey Toll Authority

The operations manager for the New Guernsey Toll Authority uses probability to make a variety of assessments. She is presently concerned with expanding the toll plaza of the Silver Slate Bridge.

Provision must be made for the nuisance of vehicles whose drivers left their money at home. These cars must be diverted to the central office while all cars are held at their respective toll stations until the way is clear, causing delays for commuters. Past records show that on the average 1 driver out of 500 has no money to pay the toll. A Bernoulli process approximates the toll-paying capabilities of successive vehicles.

Traffic intensity varies with time of day and day of week. The following situations are to be used in the manager's evaluations.

	(1) Weekday A.M. Rush	(2) Weekday P.M. Rush	(3) Saturday Afternoon	(4) Sunday Morning
Cars per minute	100	120	50	20

In each of the above cases, a Poisson process may be assumed.

One unusual feature uncovered in past studies is that the mean time to collect a toll and the corresponding standard deviation both decrease as the traffic becomes heavier. The following data apply.

	(1) Weekday A.M. Rush	(2) Weekday P.M. Rush	(3) Saturday Afternoon	(4) Sunday Morning
Mean (seconds)	12	10	15	16
Standard deviation	3	2	4	4

A normal distribution is assumed to apply for individual collection times.

QUESTIONS

1. Determine, for each of the major time periods, the probabilities that in any given six seconds (one-tenth of a minute) the following number of cars will arrive.
(a) 0 (b) 1 (c) 2 (d) 3 (e) 4 (f) 5 or more

2. Determine, for each of the major time periods, the probability that the time between the next two successive arriving cars will be
(a) $\leq$ 3 seconds (.05 minute).
(b) between 1.2 and 2.4 seconds (.02 and .04 minute).
(c) >1.8 seconds (.03 minute).

3. Determine, for each of the major time periods, the probability that the time to collect the toll for a particular car is
(a) less than 10 seconds.
(b) between 7 and 15 seconds.
(c) longer than 12 seconds.

4. New Guernsey rolls its coins using automatic devices. Its bank has a one dollar service charge for each roll whose contents are above or below the standard face amount.
(a) Assuming that quarter rolls are shipped in lots of 500 each, what is the expected error charge per lot when the proportion of miscounted rolls is (1) .10, (2) .05, (3) .01?
(b) It costs $20 per lot to weigh each roll of quarters after machine packing, but doing so eliminates errors. If it is equally likely that the proportion of bad rolls in a lot is either .02 or .03, should New Guernsey weigh rolls before they are shipped to the bank?
(c) Suppose that before shipping rolls to the bank, New Guernsey takes a random sample of 10 quarter rolls from each lot and determines the exact count for each. If the number of bad rolls is 1 or less, the lot is shipped to the bank without further weighing. Otherwise, all remaining rolls in the lot are weighed. Find the probability that a lot will be shipped unweighed (except for the sample items) when the proportion of bad rolls is (1) .01, (2) .02, (3) .05.

5. A bored New Guernsey toll taker likes to gamble with his colleagues about the kinds of license plates. In-state cars contain only a 3-digit license number. Assuming that all digits 0–9 are equally likely to appear in any position, a uniform distribution with a = 0 and b = 1,000 may be used to establish approximate probabilities for numbers falling into an interval.

(a) Find the probability that the next arriving car will have a number falling (1) at or below 150, (2) above 950, (3) between 200 and 450, inclusively.

(b) Find the exact probability that an in-state car will have a number that is (1) a straight (for example, 234, 789), (2) 3-of-a-kind (for example, 222, 444), and (3) a pair (for example, 112, 989). (*Hint:* use the count-and-divide method directly rather than the uniform distribution.)

(c) Compute the mean and standard deviation for the numerical value of an in-state license, assuming that the uniform distribution applies. These values would also be the mean and variance for the population of all license values.

(d) Suppose that the mean value is obtained from the licenses of the next 12 arriving in-state cars. Using your answer from (c) and the properties of the sampling distribution of the mean, (1) which distribution applies for finding the probabilities for this value? (2) What are the expected value and standard deviation for that distribution?

(e) Using your answers to (c) and (d), find the probability that the mean falls (1) below 500, (2) between 350 and 600, and (3) above 750.

CHAPTER 23

TESTING FOR GOODNESS OF FIT

BEFORE READING THIS CHAPTER, MAKE SURE YOU UNDERSTAND:

Basic concepts of probability (Chapter 5).
Probability distributions (Chapter 6).
Normal distribution (Chapter 7).
Hypothesis testing (Chapter 9).
Poisson, exponential, and uniform distributions (Chapter 22).

AFTER READING THIS CHAPTER, YOU WILL UNDERSTAND:

What a goodness-of-fit test is and why it is important.
How to use the chi-square distribution in testing for goodness of fit.
What restrictions apply in using the chi-square test.
About the Kolmogorov-Smirnov test for goodness of fit.

In this chapter we use a procedure called the **goodness-of-fit test** to make inferences regarding the type of distribution. The goodness-of-fit test determines whether or not sample data have been generated according to a particular probability distribution, such as the Poisson or exponential. It may also indicate whether or not the frequency distribution for the sampled population has a particular shape, such as the normal curve. It achieves this by comparing the sample frequency distribution (histogram) to the assumed theoretical frequency distribution (frequency curve).

23-1 IMPORTANCE OF KNOWING THE DISTRIBUTION

We have seen that many models used in statistical applications specify the probability distributions that must apply. For example, techniques developed for analyzing waiting lines in order to determine appropriate service facilities (such as the number of bank tellers) often assume that the number of arrivals has a Poisson distribution. Every rule developed in such queuing models depends on this assumption. (Other queuing models depend on other specified distributions.) As we have noted, the use of the Poisson distribution to characterize a random variable should be validated by collecting substantiating evidence. Recall that a Poisson process requires the following: (1) no memory (occurrences are independent over time); (2) constant mean occurrence rate; and (3) small likelihood that two or more events will occur during a short interval of time. The lack of any one of these requirements will make the Poisson distribution inappropriate. Only actual observation of the random process (or one believed to be identical in structure) may confirm that the above conditions are met.

When the Poisson distribution is wrongly used in place of the appropriate arrival distribution, the entire queuing solution is invalid. Consider, for example, the arrivals of baggage articles at the claims area of an airport. This may be a process with constant mean arrival rate and no memory, but it blatantly violates the requirement for rarity of simultaneous arrivals, as hundreds of pieces of luggage may arrive on a single flight. A facility designed to handle a fast-moving trickle of baggage (which is the case for Poisson arrivals) would be totally incapable of coping with an infrequent deluge of luggage.

Other statistical applications also rest on theoretical foundations that require particular population distributions. For example, the validity of the Student t distribution in making inferences about μ from small samples is limited to populations where the *normal curve* closely represents the underlying distribution. The random numbers list used in selecting the sample units is presumed to be *uniformly distributed* (that is, the number 21763 is just as likely to be the next number on a five-digit list as is any other value between 00000 and 99999). The *binomial distribution* provides probabilities for a variety of qualitative populations, but only if the underlying assumptions—constant π, independent and complementary trial outcomes—hold true.

There are practical reasons for wanting to know the population distribution rather than only the mean or variance. Many standardized tests used to measure aptitude and achievement are designed partly to provide scores that are normally distributed. This permits a common interpretation of resultant scores in terms of standard deviation units. Recall that *the distance of a person's score above or below the mean, in standard deviation units, can be directly translated into a percentile value if the normal curve applies to the population.* Thus, a personnel analyst or a dean of college admissions may readily resolve the conflicting scales on the various screening tests if their respective standard deviations are known. This is often done by converting data into *standard scores*, which are the same as normal deviates.

23-2 THE CHI-SQUARE TEST FOR GOODNESS OF FIT

In testing for goodness of fit, the following hypotheses apply.

H_0: The sample is from a population having a designated distribution (for example, Poisson, normal).

H_A: The sample is from a population having some other distribution.

We must formulate a decision rule that may be expressed in terms of a critical value for some test statistic. If the computed value for this test statistic lies to one side of the critical value, we will accept the null hypothesis; otherwise, we will reject it. Again, this procedure will contain two possible kinds of error: Type I, or rejecting a true null hypothesis, and Type II, or accepting a false null hypothesis.

In testing for goodness of fit, the Type II error probability β is not well defined. This is because there are so many ways in which the null hypothesis may be false. And if the sample does come from some other distribution, this must be specified in order to calculate β. In general, the larger the sample, the better the protection against Type II errors will be.

ILLUSTRATION: TESTING SAT SCORES FOR NORMALITY

To illustrate the procedure, the Scholastic Aptitude Test (SAT) has been designed to represent a population of high school seniors who receive a mean score of 500, with a standard deviation of 100. The population is assumed to be normally distributed. A university president has asserted that her students—all of whom took the SAT before matriculation—are representative of that population. Based on a random sample of 200 student SAT scores, a statistics professor at the university constructed the histogram in Figure 23-1 and then superimposed on it the normal curve assumed by the president. The professor disagrees with the president, since the histogram is positively skewed, with a lower mean and a greater variability than the supposed population frequency distribution indicates.

Not convinced by the graphical evidence, the president asks the statistician for a more conclusive argument. The professor begins by arranging the sample data from the frequency distribution in Table 23-1. (Note that the three lowest and the three highest class intervals from the histogram have been grouped into two broader categories; the reason for doing this will be explained later in this section.)

The professor wishes to determine whether these results are typical for the null hypothesis that the university's SAT scores are normally distributed with a mean of $\mu = 500$ and a standard deviation of $\sigma = 100$. To do this he must compare the scores with the results expected under the null hypothesis.

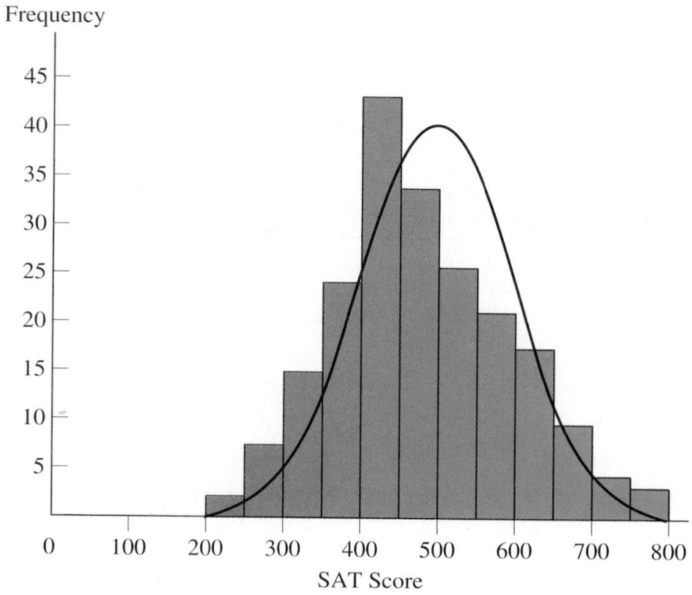

FIGURE 23-1 Sample histogram and assumed normal curve for SAT scores.

In sampling from any population, there is no reason why the frequency distribution for sample results must precisely resemble that for the population. Because of sampling error, a perfect match is extremely unlikely. But a drastically different shape for the frequency distribution is also unlikely. For testing purposes, we will compare the actual sample result to the frequency distribution for the sample results expected under the assumption of the null hypothesis. This is the distribution obtainable "on the average" from a large number of repeated sample selections from the population.

The numbers of occurrences in each class interval obtained under the null hypothesis are referred to as the **expected frequencies**. They are determined by

TABLE 23-1 Actual Sample Frequency Distribution for SAT Scores

SAT Score	Number of Students f_a
≤350	23
351–400	23
401–450	42
451–500	33
501–550	25
551–600	21
601–650	17
>650	16
	200

TABLE 23-2 Calculation of Expected Frequencies for SAT Scores

(1) SAT Score x = Upper Class Limit	(2) Normal Deviate $z = \frac{x - 500}{100}$	(3) Area to Left of x	(4) Area of Class Interval	(5) Expected Frequency f_e [(4) × 200]
350	−1.5	.0668	.0668	13.36
400	−1.0	.1587	.0919	18.38
450	−.5	.3085	.1498	29.96
500	0	.5000	.1915	38.30
550	.5	.6915	.1915	38.30
600	1.0	.8413	.1498	29.96
650	1.5	.9332	.0919	18.38
>650	∞	1.0000	.0668	13.36
			1.0000	200.00

multiplying the proportion of population values within each class interval by the sample size used. Here, a normal distribution is hypothesized for the population. Therefore, the expected frequency for SAT scores at or below 350 may be found by multiplying together (1) the area under the normal curve covering ≤ 350 and (2) the sample size $n = 200$.

To obtain the area, we calculate the normal deviate.

$$z = \frac{x - \mu}{\sigma} = \frac{350 - 500}{100} = -1.5$$

From Appendix Table D, this value corresponds to a lower tail area of $.5000 - .4332 = .0668$. Multiplying by the sample size, we obtain the expected frequency $.0668 \times 200 = 13.36$ students. The calculations for the remaining expected frequencies appear in Table 23-2.

THE CHI-SQUARE TEST STATISTIC

As the test statistic, we need a number that summarizes the amount of deviation between the frequencies of SAT scores actually obtained and the expected frequencies. The chi-square statistic serves this purpose.

We use the symbol f_e for the expected frequency of sample values in a particular class interval. Similarly, f_a represents the actual observed frequency of those values. We use the following expression to calculate the

CHI-SQUARE STATISTIC FOR THE GOODNESS-OF-FIT TEST

$$\chi^2 = \sum \frac{(f_a - f_e)^2}{f_e}$$

Table 23-3 provides the calculations for the SAT scores made using the actual and expected frequencies from Table 23-2. We find the computed value $\chi^2 = 21.614$ in Table 23-3.

The degrees of freedom in a chi-square test correspond to the number of f_e values that we are "free" to set. Because the number of f_e's must sum to the sample size n, all but one f_e are free to vary. Thus, in testing for goodness of fit, *the number of degrees of freedom is equal to the number of categories minus one.* As we will see, this rule must be modified slightly in some cases.

THE HYPOTHESIS-TESTING STEPS

STEP 1

Formulate the null hypothesis. We wish to determine whether the SAT scores come from a particular normal population. The following null hypothesis applies.

H_0: University SAT scores are normally distributed with $\mu = 500$ and $\sigma = 100$.

STEP 2

Select the test statistic and procedure. The chi-square serves as the test statistic.

STEP 3

Establish the significance level and identify the acceptance and rejection regions. The statistics professor desires an $\alpha = .01$ significance level, so that there is only a 1% chance of rejecting a true null hypothesis. From Appendix Table H, for $8 - 1 = 7$ degrees of freedom, we find the critical value $\chi^2_{.01} = 18.475$. Thus, if the university SAT score distribution is normal with a mean of 500 and a standard deviation of 100, there is a 1% chance that a sample will be obtained that yields a χ^2 value equal to or greater than 18.475. The acceptance and rejection regions are shown below.

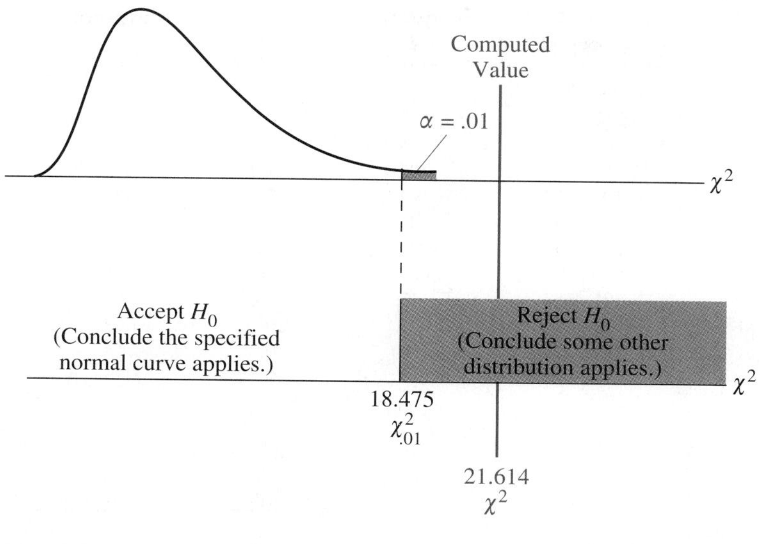

TABLE 23-3 Calculation of the χ^2 Test Statistic for SAT Scores

SAT Score	Actual Frequency f_a	Expected Frequency f_e	$f_a - f_e$	$(f_a - f_e)^2$	$\frac{(f_a - f_e)^2}{f_e}$
≤350	23	13.36	9.64	92.9296	6.956
351–400	23	18.38	4.62	21.3444	1.161
401–450	42	29.96	12.04	144.9616	4.839
451–500	33	38.30	− 5.30	28.0900	.733
501–550	25	38.30	−13.30	176.8900	4.619
551–600	21	29.96	− 8.96	80.2816	2.680
601–650	17	18.38	− 1.38	1.9044	.104
>650	16	13.36	2.64	6.9696	.522
	200	200.00	0.00		$\chi^2 = 21.614$

STEP 4

Collect the sample and compute the value of the test statistic. This step includes finding the values of f_a and f_e and computing χ^2. From Table 23-3, we find the computed value of the test statistic to be $\chi^2 = 21.614$.

STEP 5

Make the decision. Since the computed value of $\chi^2 = 21.614$ falls in the rejection region, the null hypothesis must be *rejected.* The professor must conclude that the university students' SAT scores are not normally distributed with the stated mean and standard deviation. The president now has some very convincing evidence that she is wrong.

TABLE 23-4 Calculation of the Sample Mean and Standard Deviation for SAT Scores

Class Interval	Frequency f	f/n	Midpoint X	$X(f/n)$	X^2	fX^2
201–250	2	.010	225	2.250	50,625	101,250
251–300	7	.035	275	9.625	75,625	529,375
301–350	14	.070	325	22.750	105,625	1,478,750
351–400	23	.115	375	43.125	140,625	3,234,375
401–450	42	.210	425	89.250	180,625	7,586,250
451–500	33	.165	475	78.375	225,625	7,445,625
501–550	25	.125	525	65.625	275,625	6,890,625
551–600	21	.105	575	60.375	330,625	6,943,125
601–650	17	.085	625	53.125	390,625	6,640,625
651–700	9	.045	675	30.375	455,625	4,100,625
701–750	4	.020	725	14.500	525,625	2,102,500
751–800	3	.015	775	11.625	600,625	1,801,875
	200			481.000		48,855,000

$$\bar{X} = \sum X(f/n) = 481.000$$

$$s = \sqrt{\frac{\sum fX^2 - n\bar{X}^2}{n-1}} = \sqrt{\frac{48,855,000 - 200(481)^2}{200 - 1}} = 113.93$$

TESTING USING UNKNOWN POPULATION PARAMETERS

In the testing procedure just described, the population mean and standard deviation were specified in advance. Most often, we are not only concerned with identifying the family (such as normal, uniform, exponential, or Poisson) to which the underlying distribution belongs, but we may also need to find the appropriate particular distribution for that family. For example, in addition to not knowing whether a sample comes from a normal distribution, we may also lack knowledge of μ and σ. The unknown population parameters may themselves have to be estimated from the sample data. As an additional feature, the goodness-of-fit test may provide these estimations.

To illustrate this, we will continue with the SAT score example. We caution that only one of these procedures should be used on the same data. We use both methods here only for ease of discussion and to compare the two methods.

In Table 23-4, the sample mean and the sample standard deviation for the SAT score data are computed to be $\bar{X} = 481$ and $s = 113.93$. Suppose that our statistician had instead chosen to use these values (rather than the 500 and 100 used before) as estimators of μ and σ. The following null hypothesis now applies.

H_0: SAT scores are normally distributed with $\mu = 481$ and $\sigma = 113.93$.

The alternative hypothesis includes all other possible distributions—even a normal distribution having other values for μ and σ. Remember that μ and σ have been estimated here from the sample observations.

The expected frequency calculations under the statistician's new hypothesis appear in Table 23-5, and the chi-square statistic is computed in Table 23-6. In Chapter 16 we indicated that when calculating χ^2, each expected frequency should round off to a value of at least 5. Thus, the first two categories are grouped, since the expected frequency 4.24 for ≤ 250 is smaller than 5. Likewise, the last two

TABLE 23-5 Calculation of Expected Frequencies When Parameters Are Estimated from Sample Data

(1) SAT Score x = Upper Class Limit	(2) Normal Deviate $z = \dfrac{x - 481}{113.93}$	(3) Area to Left of x	(4) Area of Class Interval	(5) Expected Frequency f_e [(4) × 200]
≤250	−2.03	.0212	.0212	4.24
300	−1.59	.0559	.0347	6.94
350	−1.15	.1251	.0692	13.84
400	−.71	.2388	.1137	22.74
450	−.27	.3936	.1548	30.96
500	.17	.5675	.1739	34.78
550	.61	.7291	.1616	32.32
600	1.04	.8508	.1217	24.34
650	1.48	.9306	.0798	15.96
700	1.92	.9726	.0420	8.40
750	2.36	.9909	.0183	3.66
>750	∞	1.0000	.0091	1.82
			1.0000	200.00

TABLE 23-6 Chi-Square Calculations When Parameters Are Estimated from Sample Data

SAT Score	Actual Frequency f_a		Expected Frequency f_e		$f_a - f_e$	$(f_a - f_e)^2$	$\frac{(f_a - f_e)^2}{f_e}$
≤250	2	9	4.24	11.18	−2.18	4.7524	.425
251–300	7		6.94				
301–350	14		13.84		.16	.0256	.002
351–400	23		22.74		.26	.0676	.003
401–450	42		30.96		11.04	121.8816	3.937
451–500	33		34.78		−1.78	3.1684	.091
501–550	25		32.32		−7.32	53.5824	1.658
551–600	21		24.34		−3.34	11.1556	.458
601–650	17		15.96		1.04	1.0816	.068
651–700	9		8.40		.60	.3600	.043
701–750	4	7	3.66	5.48	−1.52	2.3104	.422
>750	3		1.82				
	200		200.00		0.00		$\chi^2 = 7.107$

class intervals are grouped, yielding the expected frequency 5.48. These combinations reduce the number of final categories in Table 23-6 to ten.

When population parameters are estimated from the sample data, one additional degree of freedom is lost for each parameter. Thus, we have the

RULE FOR THE NUMBER OF DEGREES OF FREEDOM

$$\text{df} = \text{Number of categories} - \text{number of parameters estimated} - 1$$

In our illustration we have

$$\text{df} = 10 - 2 - 1 = 7$$

Suppose that the statistician uses the same significance level as before. Because the degrees of freedom are unchanged, we have the same critical value of $\chi^2_{.01} = 18.475$. Since the computed value of $\chi^2 = 7.107$ (from Table 23-6) is smaller than 18.475, H_0 must be *accepted.* This is the reverse of the conclusion that we reached using our previous null hypothesis. Although the data significantly refute a normally distributed population with a mean of $\mu = 500$ and a standard deviation of $\sigma = 100$ when these parameters are specified in advance, the results are quite consistent with the null hypothesis of normality when the parameters are estimated from the sample data.

TESTING FOR THE POISSON PROBABILITY DISTRIBUTION

As we noted at the outset, whether or not a particular probability distribution applies may be crucial when using probability concepts for decision making. The

TABLE 23-7 Frequency Distribution for the Number of Typesetters' Errors

Number of Errors per 100 Lines	Total Number of Errors in Category	Observed Frequency f_a
0	0	5
1	9	9
2	10	5
3	21	7
4	16	4
5	10	2
6	18	3
7	14	2
8	8	1
9	0	0
10	20	2
	126	40

$\bar{X} = 126/40 = 3.15$

following illustration shows how the goodness-of-fit test may be used to make a decision that depends on the data fitting the Poisson distribution.

Illustration: Number of Typesetters' Errors

From files containing galley proofs of all recently published books, a random sample of $n = 40$ segments of type 100 lines long and of comparable complexity is selected. Table 23-7 provides the sample frequency distribution for the number of errors per 100 lines. The mean number of errors for the sample is $\bar{X} = 3.15$. Thus, the mean error rate per line times the number of lines is

$$\lambda t = 3.15$$

STEP 1

Formulate the null hypothesis. The following null hypothesis applies.

H_0: The typesetters' errors have a Poisson distribution with $\lambda t = 3.15$.

The alternative hypothesis includes all other possible distributions—possibly even the Poisson distribution with λt at some other value. The value $\lambda t = 3.15$ has been estimated from the sample observations.

STEP 2

Select the test statistic and procedure. The chi-square serves as the test statistic.

STEP 3

Establish the significance level and identify the acceptance and rejection regions. The publisher selects a significance level of $\alpha = .05$. Only 5 category groupings are used, because some categories have been combined to achieve expected frequencies of 5 or more (see Table 23-8). The number of degrees of freedom is $5 - 1 - 1 = 3$, since only one parameter (the mean λt of the Poisson distribution)

TABLE 23-8 Chi-Square Calculations Using Typesetters' Errors

(1) Number of Errors x	(2) Actual Frequency f_a	(3) Poisson Probabilities	(4) Expected Frequency f_e	(5) $f_a - f_e$	(6) $(f_a - f_e)^2$	(7) $\frac{(f_a - f_e)^2}{f_e}$
0	5 } 14	.0428	1.71 } 7.11	6.89	47.472	6.68
1	9	.1350	5.40			
2	5	.2124	8.50	−3.50	12.250	1.44
3	7	.2233	8.93	−1.93	3.725	.42
4	4	.1759	7.04	−3.04	9.242	1.31
5	2	.1106	4.42			
6	3	.0581	2.32			
7	2	.0261	1.04			
8	1 } 10	.0106	.42 } 8.40	1.60	2.560	.31
9	0	.0036	.14			
10	2	.0011	.04			
11 or more	0	.0005	.02			
	40	1.0000	39.98*			10.16

$$f_e = 40\Pr[X = x] = 40\,\frac{e^{-3.15}(3.15)^x}{x!}$$

$$\chi^2 = \sum \frac{(f_a - f_e)^2}{f_e} = 10.16$$

*Total would be 40, except for rounding errors.

is estimated from the sample data. Appendix Table H provides the critical chi-square value of $\chi^2_{.05} = 7.815$. The acceptance and rejection regions are shown below.

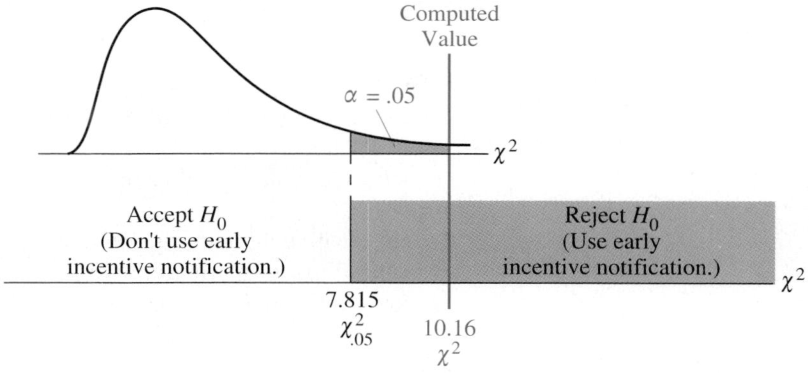

STEP 4

Collect the sample and compute the value of the test statistic. In Table 23-8, the expected frequencies for each error category are calculated in column (4) by multiplying the Poisson probabilities in column (3) by $n = 40$. The computed chi-square value is found to be 10.16.

STEP 5

Make the decision. Since the computed value of $\chi^2 = 10.16$ falls in the rejection region, the null hypothesis must be *rejected.*

EXERCISES

23-1 The personnel vice-president of Honest Abe's Insurance Company wishes to establish hiring policies for the company's clerical personnel. A key element of the company's screening procedures is a verbal aptitude test, which will be used to match applicants' capabilities to job requirements. Personnel planning requires that the percentages of the applicant population having test scores at various levels be determined. This will involve specification of the frequency distribution, which may only be inferred from a limited sample. It will be significantly simpler to generate plans if the population is normally distributed. Thus, the vice-president wishes to conduct a goodness-of-fit test for a normal null hypothesis. The psychologists who designed the test maintain that an ordinary cross section of persons have achieved a mean of 72 and a standard deviation of 10. The following results were obtained for a sample of 100 persons applying for positions at the company.

Score	Frequency
below 40	8
40–under 50	7
50–under 60	18
60–under 70	25
70–under 80	32
80–under 90	3
over 90	7
	100

(a) Construct the table of expected frequencies. (Use .4990 for the area between the mean and $z = 3.2$.)

(b) Calculate the χ^2 test statistic. (Remember to group the lower frequencies.)

(c) How many degrees of freedom are associated with this test statistic?

(d) Suppose that the vice-president wishes to protect herself at the .05 significance level against rejecting the null hypothesis when it is true. Determine the acceptance and rejection regions.

(e) Should the null hypothesis be accepted or rejected? What is the smallest significance level at which the hypothesis must be rejected?

23-2 Refer to the data in Exercise 23-1. Suppose that the vice-president does not believe that the psychologist's parameters are valid for her applicant population. Instead she wishes to use the sample results to estimate μ and σ. For the 100 test scores, assume the mean is 64.5 and the standard deviation is 16.8.

(a) Construct the table of expected frequencies. Then calculate the test statistic. At a significance level of .05, should the null hypothesis be accepted or rejected?

(b) Is the lowest probability at which the null hypothesis must be rejected lower or higher than in 23-1(e) above?

23-3 The Seven-High Bottling Company has been using a refillable bottle that has proven to be relatively safe from exploding. To modernize its image, a sleeker Seven-High bottle is being sought. Because of the obvious dangers posed by bottles that explode, tests are being conducted on a new bottle for which a special seal has been devised. The tests will be carried out on a special device in which bottles filled with Seven-High are heated and shaken. For the old bottle, it has been established that the number of bottles tested between explosions on this device is approximately exponentially distributed, with a mean of 3 bottles between explosions. It is hoped that the new bottle will have the same distribution. A sample of 1,000 new bottles is tested. The following frequency distributions were obtained.

Number of Bottles between Explosions	Class Interval	Actual Frequency	Expected Frequency
0	0–.999	97	86.75
1	1–1.999	54	65.25
2	2–2.999	58	49.50
3	3–3.999	25	28.00
4	4–4.999	27	21.00
5	5–5.999	15	15.80
6	6–6.999	10	12.70
7	7–7.999	5	9.30
8	8–8.999	11	6.20
9	9–9.999	2 }	3.10 }
10	10–10.999	0 }	3.10 }
11	11–11.999	2 }	3.10 }
12	12–12.999	1 }	3.10 }
13 or more	≥ 13	3 }	3.10 }
		310	310.00

The null hypothesis is that the distribution for the number of new bottles tested between explosions is identical to that for the old bottles. The alternative is that some other distribution applies.

(a) Calculate the χ^2 test statistic.

(b) How many degrees of freedom are associated with this test statistic?

(c) State, in a sentence, the Type I error; the Type II error.

(d) If a significance level of .05 is desired, determine the acceptance and rejection regions. What does this number mean? Formulate the decision rule. Should the null hypothesis be rejected?

(e) If the significance level is .02, how do your answers to (d) change?

23-4 Before random number tables were widely available, some statisticians used telephone digits. One concern is whether such numbers occur with the proper frequency. Assuming that the last four digits in the Manhattan telephone directory are used to generate decimal values between 0 and 1, a random sample of 100 successive numbers was obtained, and the following frequency distribution was determined. (A 0000 suffix is counted as 1.0000.)

Class Interval	Number of Values Obtained
.0001 – .1000	13
.1001 – .2000	12
.2001 – .3000	10
.3001 – .4000	9
.4001 – .5000	9
.5001 – .6000	11
.6001 – .7000	9
.7001 – .8000	11
.8001 – .9000	7
.9001 – 1.0000	9
	100

Use as your null hypothesis the assumption that the above numbers were obtained from a *uniformly distributed* population, so that all values between 0 and 1 are equally likely to occur.

(a) Construct a table of expected frequencies.

(b) Calculate the χ^2 test statistic.

(c) At an $\alpha = .10$ significance level, what conclusion should you make?

23-5 Admiral Motors wishes to determine the frequency distribution of warranty-financed repairs per car for its new minicar, the Colt. The number of such repairs per new automobile on its current line of cars has been established to have a Poisson distribution with parameter λ, the mean rate of repairs per car. The value of λ varies with the line of car. Management believes that the Colt will have nearly the same distribution for the number of repairs as the Pony, its next larger car. For the Pony, $\lambda = 3$ repairs per year. A random sample of 43 cars is selected for a year's study. Special records are kept on each car. The distribution for repairs per car is provided below.

Number of Repairs	Frequency
0	1
1	2
2	5
3	9
4	7
5	5
6	3
7	5
8 or more	6
	43

(a) Construct a table of expected frequencies, using Poisson probabilities with $\lambda t = 3$.

(b) Calculate the test statistic.

(c) Should the null hypothesis be accepted or rejected at a .05 significance level?

23-3 THE KOLMOGOROV-SMIRNOV ONE-SAMPLE TEST

AN ALTERNATIVE TO THE CHI-SQUARE TEST

In Section 23-2, the chi-square test was introduced as a procedure for inferring whether a sample is obtained from a population having a particular distribution. As a test for goodness of fit, the chi-square test has some serious limitations. The most significant of these is the requirement for a large sample. Recall that a rule for using the chi-square distribution is that each class interval must have an expected frequency of at least 5. Unless n is quite large, only the most frequent class intervals will retain their data; the less frequent class intervals must be combined before computing χ^2 and, in doing this, information is lost. When only a very tiny sample is available, the chi-square test cannot be used at all.

An alternative goodness-of-fit test is the **Kolmogorov-Smirnov one-sample test**, named after A. Kolmogorov and N. V. Smirnov, two Russian mathematicians who provided the theoretical foundations for this test. The test compares the observed cumulative frequency distribution for the sample to that expected for the population specified by the null hypothesis. The test statistic obtained is the maximum deviation between the observed and the expected distributions.

DESCRIPTION OF THE TEST: AIRCRAFT DELAY TIMES

We will describe the Kolmogorov-Smirnov test with the following illustration. Before deciding on a new scheduling policy, Ace Airlines must determine whether the takeoff delay times at El Paso are normally distributed. Only 1% of the biweekly El Paso departures have resulted in unpredictable delays. Thus, over a ten-year period, only 11 delays have occurred. The durations are provided in Table 23-9. From studies of other airports, Ace has judged that delays at El Paso should have a mean of 3 hours with a standard deviation of 1 hour. The null hypothesis is that the aircraft takeoff delays are normal with $\mu = 3$ hours and $\sigma = 1$ hour.

TABLE 23-9 Durations of Aircraft Takeoff Delays

Duration (hours) X	X^2
2.1	4.41
1.9	3.61
3.2	10.24
2.8	7.84
1.0	1.00
5.1	26.01
.9	.81
4.2	17.64
3.9	15.21
3.6	12.96
2.7	7.29
31.4	107.02

To find the value of the test statistic, we first establish the cumulative *relative* frequency distribution obtained for our sample results. This is shown in Table 23-10. Since the frequencies are relative, each sample value occurs with a frequency of 1/11 = .0909. The observations are not grouped in the usual manner. Instead, the durations obtained are listed in column (1) of Table 23-10 in increasing order of size. The cumulative frequencies in column (2) are obtained by adding the relative frequencies. Thus, .1818 is the frequency of durations of 1.0 hour or less (obtained by adding together the .0909 frequencies for .9 and 1.0 hours), and .6363 is the frequency of delays of 3.2 hours or less. We denote the actual frequency of values less than or equal to x by $F_a(x)$.

The expected frequencies under the null hypothesis, denoted by $F_e(x)$, must coincide with the normal curve for $\mu = 3$ and $\sigma = 1$. In column (3) of Table 23-10, the normal deviates z are calculated for each value of x. The cumulative frequencies in column (4) are obtained from Appendix Table D. For negative values of z, the lower tail areas corresponding to the cumulative frequencies may be obtained by subtracting the area in Appendix Table D from .5. Thus, when $x = 1.9$, $z = -1.1$, and Appendix Table D provides the area .3643, so that the expected frequency is

$$F_e(1.9) = .5 - .3643 = .1357$$

For positive z values, Appendix Table D provides areas between the mean and z standard deviations. These must be added to .5 to find the cumulative frequencies. Thus, when $x = 4.2$, $z = 1.2$, so Appendix Table D provides the area .3849. The cumulative frequency is

$$F_e(4.2) = .5 + .3849 = .8849$$

TABLE 23-10 Actual and Expected Cumulative Frequencies for Takeoff Delays, with Calculations of the Test Statistic

(1) Duration (hours) x	(2) Actual Cumulative Frequency $F_a(x)$	(3) $z = \frac{x-\mu}{\sigma}$	(4) Expected Cumulative Frequency $F_e(x)$	(5) Deviation $F_a(x) - F_e(x)$
.9	.0909	− 2.1	.0179	.0730
1.0	.1818	− 2.0	.0228	.1590
1.9	.2727	− 1.1	.1357	.1370
2.1	.3636	− .9	.1841	.1795
2.7	.4545	− .3	.3821	.0724
2.8	.5454	− .2	.4207	.1247
3.2	.6363	.2	.5793	.0570
3.6	.7272	.6	.7257	.0015
3.9	.8181	.9	.8159	.0022
4.2	.9090	1.2	.8849	.0241
5.1	.9999	2.1	.9821	.0178

$$D = \max|F_a(x) - F_e(x)| = .1795$$

TABLE 23-11 Calculation of the Test Statistic for Takeoff Delays

(1) Duration (hours) x	(2) $F_a(x)$	(3) $F_e(x)$	(4) $F_a(x) - F_e(x)$
.9	.0909	.0800	.0109
1.0	.1818	.1000	.0818
1.9	.2727	.2800	−.0073
2.1	.3636	.3200	.0436
2.7	.4545	.4400	.0145
2.8	.5454	.4600	.0854
3.2	.6363	.5400	.0963
3.6	.7272	.6200	.1072
3.9	.8181	.6800	.1381
4.2	.9090	.7400	.1690
5.1	.9999	.9200	−.0799

$D = \max|F_a(x) - F_e(x)| = .1690$

The deviation between the actual and the expected frequencies is calculated in column (5) of Table 23-10 for each duration. Large deviations indicate that the actual and the expected values have a poor fit. This type of comparison is illustrated in Figure 23-2, where the two cumulative frequency distributions are plotted on the same graph. The actual frequencies lie above the expected ones for all values of x obtained from the sample. The vertical distance between the two

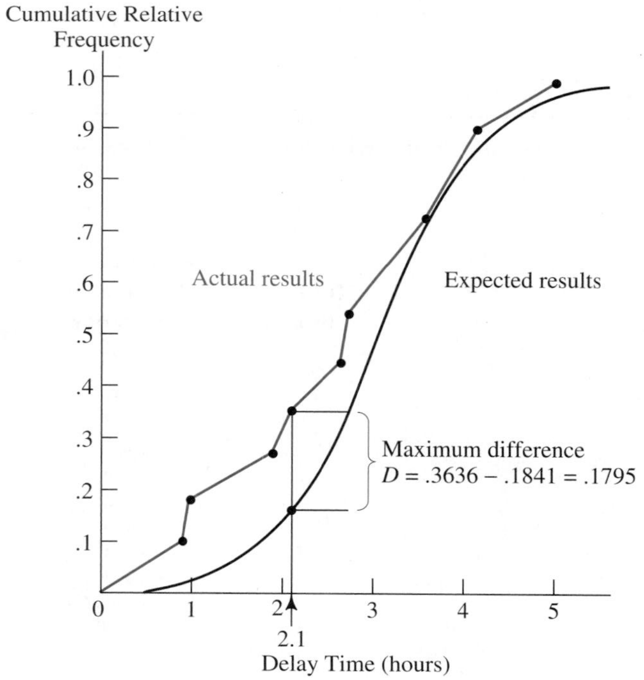

FIGURE 23-2 Actual and expected cumulative frequency distributions for takeoff delays.

curves indicates the magnitude of the deviations. The largest deviation occurs at $x = 2.1$, where

$$F_a(2.1) - F_e(2.1) = .1795$$

This will serve as our test statistic and be denoted by D. In general, the following expression provides the

KOLMOGOROV-SMIRNOV TEST STATISTIC

$$D = \max |F_a(x) - F_e(x)|$$

Note that we are interested only in absolute values; the sign of the difference is unimportant. Our test statistic, D, is the maximum frequency deviation.

FINDING THE DECISION RULE AND THE CRITICAL VALUE

Accept H_0 if $D \leq D_\alpha$ (Conclude that the normal distribution applies.)

Reject H_0 if $D > D_\alpha$ (Conclude that some other distribution applies.)

Large deviations tend to refute the null hypothesis. We will denote the critical value D_α, where α is the siginificance level at which a true null hypothesis will be rejected. To find the value of D_α, we must first find the sampling distribution of our test statistic D.

Because the sampling distribution of D is very complex and quite mathematical in nature, we will not describe its properties here. Instead, we will use Appendix Table L, which provides critical values D_α for several significance levels α and *sample sizes n*. (Unlike the chi-square test, these tabulated values depend on the entire sample size and not on the number of sample groups.) Thus, we can find D_α such that

$$\Pr[D \geq D_\alpha] = \alpha$$

For example, suppose that we wish to see whether the sample results are significant at $\alpha = .05$. We obtained $D = .1795$ in Table 23-10 with a sample size of $n = 11$. From Appendix Table L, for $n = 11$ and $\alpha = .05$, we obtain as our critical value $D_{.05} = .35242$. Since this value is greater than D, *the null hypothesis is accepted.* In fact, setting α as high as .10 leads to the same conclusion. The sample of takeoff delays appears to be quite consistent with the null hypothesis of normality.

INVESTIGATING THE TYPE II ERROR

It is interesting to note that in accepting the null hypothesis, there is a high likelihood of making a Type II error. Suppose that we choose instead a uniform distribution between .5 and 5.5 hours as our null hypothesis. Table 23-11 shows the calculation obtained from this distribution. The $F_e(x)$ values are obtained by calculating the proportion of the distance between .5 and 5.5 that is represented by the corresponding value for x.

Although here $D = .1690$, our sample may reasonably be expected to have come from a uniform distribution. We have no basis for choosing between the normal and the uniform distributions. All we may say is that *there is no significant evidence to reject either*. Using a larger sample size is the only recourse we have for avoiding the Type II error.

COMPARING THE KOLMOGOROV-SMIRNOV TEST AND THE CHI-SQUARE TEST

Comparisons have been made of the relative efficiencies of the χ^2 and Kolmogorov-Smirnov tests. The latter has been established to be more powerful for small samples; that is, for a fixed sample size, the Kolmogorov-Smirnov test provides a higher probability for rejecting a false null hypothesis.

A major disadvantage of the Kolmogorov-Smirnov test is that it does not allow us to estimate any of the population parameters from the sample data. *The population parameters must be specified in advance of testing*. Thus, in our example, we could not use $\bar{X}$ and s as estimates of μ and σ. (Had this been allowed, the fit would have been even closer.) The χ^2 test allows us to do this—at the price of a reduced number of degrees of freedom.

EXERCISES

23-6 A postmaster wishes to establish whether the Friday lunchtime arrivals at a new branch post office follow the Poisson distribution. From previous tests, he has estimated that the mean arrival rate is 2 customers per minute. A sample of the arrivals in 100 random one-minute time segments has been collected over a two-month period. The results obtained appear with the expected sample frequencies below.

Actual Observed Results			Expected Sample Results	
Number of Arrivals	Actual Frequency	Relative Frequency	Number of Arrivals	Relative Frequency
0	8	.08	0	.1353
1	19	.19	1	.2707
2	28	.28	2	.2707
3	24	.24	3	.1804
4	14	.14	4	.0902
5	2	.02	5	.0361
6	3	.03	6	.0120
7	1	.01	7	.0034
8	0	.00	8	.0009
9	1	.01	9	.0002
		1.00		.9999

(a) Determine the cumulative relative frequencies for the actual and the expected results.

(b) Calculate the maximum deviation D.

(c) What is the lowest significance level at which the null hypothesis of the Poisson distribution with $\lambda = 2$ must be rejected?

(d) Calculate the χ^2 test statistic. (Remember that χ^2 is based on whole frequencies instead of relative ones. Also recall that the low frequencies must be grouped.)

(e) What is the lowest significance level at which the null hypothesis must be rejected using the χ^2 test?

(f) In this example, which test do you believe is more discriminating—the χ^2 or the Kolmogorov-Smirnov? Explain.

23-7 Suppose that the postmaster in Exercise 23-6 estimated instead that 2.5 arrivals per minute apply. The following expected relative frequencies should be used.

Number of Arrivals	Relative Frequency
0	.0821
1	.2052
2	.2565
3	.2138
4	.1336
5	.0668
6	.0278
7	.0099
8	.0031
9	.0009
10	.0002
	.9999

(a) Determine the cumulative relative frequencies for the actual and the expected results.

(b) Calculate the maximum deviation D.

(c) At a significance level of $\alpha = .10$ should the postmaster reject the null hypothesis that the arrivals are a Poisson process?

23-8 Refer to the data in Exercise 23-1. Apply the Kolmogorov-Smirnov test at an $\alpha = .10$ significance level to determine whether or not the sample data are consistent with the indicated normal distribution.

23-9 Refer to the data in Exercise 23-3. Apply the Kolmogorov-Smirnov test at the $\alpha = .05$ significance level.

23-10 Refer to the data in Exercise 23-4. Apply the Kolmogorov-Smirnov test at the $\alpha = .10$ significance level.

23-11 Refer to the data in Exercise 23-5. Apply the Kolmogorov-Smirnov test at the $\alpha = .05$ significance level.

SUMMARY

1. **What is a goodness-of-fit test and why is it important?**
   Fit is a term that characterizes how well a set of data agree with what would be expected if the data were generated in accordance with an assumed underlying distribution. A **goodness-of-fit test** allows us to test hypotheses regarding that distribution. Such procedures are important because so much statistical theory assumes that a particular distribution applies. Knowing the form of the distribution can also be important in reaching a variety of business decisions.

2. **How may the chi-square distribution be used in testing for goodness of fit?**

The chi-square distribution allows us to systematically compare the actual sample frequencies f_a for a variate with what frequencies f_e would be expected if those values had been generated by a hypothetical distribution. The test statistic is computed from

$$\chi^2 = \sum \frac{(f_a - f_e)^2}{f_e}$$

which is used in an upper-tailed test of the null hypothesis to which a particular distribution applies. The procedure may be applied either when the population parameters are specified in advance or when those are estimated from the sample. The number of degrees of freedom is the number of frequency categories minus the number of parameters estimated, minus 1.

3. **What restrictions apply in using the chi-square test?**
The primary limitation of the chi-square test is that the categories must sometimes be grouped to achieve a minimum expected frequency of at least 5. That reduces the degrees of freedom and the efficacy of the procedure and requires large sample sizes.

4. **What is the Kolmogorov-Smirnov test for goodness of fit?**
As an alternative to the chi-square test, the **Kolmogorov-Smirnov one-sample test** may be used to test for goodness of fit. This procedure utilizes actual cumulative frequencies $F_a(x)$, comparing these to the counterpart expected cumulative frequencies $F_e(x)$ that would apply under the hypothesized distribution. The following test statistic is used:

$$D = \max|F_a(x) - F_e(x)|$$

Critical values for the above appear in Appendix Table L. This test may be used with small samples, but it does not allow us to estimate population parameters from the sample.

23-12 The actual frequency distribution for rush-hour automobile accidents reported in Gotham City for a 100-day period is given in the table below. Assuming that the data represent a random sample from a population where the number of daily accidents has the Poisson distribution at a mean rate of 5 per day, we obtain the expected frequencies in the last column.

Number of Accidents per Day	Actual Frequency	Expected Frequency
≤2	13	13
3	8	14
4	22	18
5	24	18
6	15	15
7	8	10
8	5	6
≥9	5	6
	100	100

Are the sample data consistent with the indicated Poisson distribution? Use the chi-square procedure with $\alpha = .05$.

23-13 The times between reported automobile accidents in Metropolis during rush hours have been obtained for a random sample of 200 accidents. Also obtained are the expected frequencies that would apply if the population were exponentially distributed with a mean accident rate of one every 20 minutes. The results are provided below.

Time between Accidents (minutes)	Actual Frequency	Expected Frequency
0–under 10	62	78.6
10–under 20	55	47.8
20–under 30	32	29.0
30–under 40	21	17.6
40–under 50	12	10.6
50–under 60	8	6.4
above 60	10	10.0
	200	200.0

Are the sample data consistent with the indicated exponential distribution? Use the chi-square procedure with $\alpha = .10$.

23-14 Repeat Exercise 23-12 using the Kolmogorov-Smirnov procedure.

23-15 Repeat Exercise 23-13 using the Kolmogorov-Smirnov procedure.

CASE University Consultants

University Consultants provides statistical advice to a variety of government agencies and companies. These include Simutronics, Ace Airlines, and the New Guernsey Toll Authority. These clients have different needs to determine whether a particular distribution applies. The firm has hired you as an intern to help with these evaluations.

QUESTIONS

1. Simutronics performs Monte Carlo simulations using pseudorandom numbers generated by computer. In one run the following values were supplied.

837	441	022	201	423
557	258	596	704	019
115	139	673	499	429
286	593	297	864	294
338	537	448	991	825
449	281	336	296	227
491	353	274	678	902
395	547	300	198	605
229	384	482	495	551
101	632	254	546	550

Use the chi-square procedure to test the null hypothesis that these were generated by a uniform distribution over the interval [0, 1,000]. At the $\alpha = .10$ level, what may you conclude?

2. Ace Airlines is investigating landing-gear failures. Industry experience is that these occur randomly at a mean rate of one every 10,000 landings. In its short life, Ace has experienced the following number of landings between landing gear failures:

7,246	13,846	2,937
22,928	31,297	9,002

Use the Kolmogorov-Smirnov procedure to test the null hypothesis that these were generated by an exponential distribution having the same mean rate as the industry. At the $\alpha = .10$ level, what may you conclude?

3. The New Guernsey Toll Authority has provided the following observed toll-collection times (seconds) obtained from a sample. Using $\alpha = .05$, test the null hypothesis that the normal distribution applies with parameters estimated from the data. Begin by constructing a frequency distribution with intervals of width 2 seconds, using 4.0—under 6.0 seconds as the first class interval.

10.4	9.0	8.0	8.3	7.4
11.2	9.3	8.2	10.1	10.4
12.1	17.6	5.4	11.3	9.5
10.3	10.2	11.5	15.0	8.9
7.0	7.7	8.7	8.6	9.4
9.2	9.5	10.6	10.1	8.0
11.0	12.2	13.3	10.2	9.4
7.2	8.3	8.5	9.6	9.1
10.2	9.4	10.0	8.0	7.3
8.1	7.9	9.0	9.3	8.5

4. From a sample, New Guernsey has obtained the following times (seconds) between successive arrivals during a one-hour time span. At an $\alpha = .05$ significance level, test the null hypothesis that the exponential distribution applies with the mean rate estimated from the data. In doing this, construct a frequency distribution with intervals of width .5 second, using 0–under .5 as the first class interval.

1.3	2.8	.5	.1	.2	.3	1.2	.5	.1	.1	0	.2	.2	.4	.6
.7	.8	.9	1.1	.9	1.2	1.5	.3	.4	.5	.7	1.2	1.0	.9	.8
2.1	2.0	1.0	1.0	.9	0	.1	.2	.2	1.5	2.7	4.8	.6	.9	.9
.5	.3	.2	.1	.4	.5	.3	.2	.1	.1	0	.1	.4	.5	.2

PART VI

DECISION ANALYSIS

CHAPTER 24

BASIC CONCEPTS OF DECISION MAKING

BEFORE READING THIS CHAPTER, MAKE SURE YOU UNDERSTAND:

Basic concepts of probability (Chapter 5).
Probability distributions and expected value (Chapter 6).
Subjective probability in decision making (Chapter 20).

AFTER READING THIS CHAPTER, YOU WILL UNDERSTAND:

About the basic elements of a decision under uncertainty.
Which two structural forms are commonly used in decision analysis.
How outcomes are ranked.
What inadmissible acts are and how identifying them can be useful.
About the Bayes decision rule and how it relates to expected payoffs.
About decision tree analysis.

Decision making under uncertainty has its roots in the area of study called **statistical decision theory**. Although most major developments in this field have occurred during the last 50 years, many contributions were made more than 200 years ago by the same pioneer mathematicians who formulated the theory of probability. In addition to probability, decision theory contains elements of statistics, economics, and psychology.

The central focus of this book is on the use of statistical procedures in decision making. This chapter considers the structure of decisions in general. We make a basic distinction between decision making under certainty, where no elements are left to chance, and decision making under uncertainty, where one or more random factors affect a choice's outcome.

We begin our discussion of decision theory by considering an underlying structural framework. This is followed by a presentation of the main decision-making criterion—the Bayes decision rule—which is based on expected values. In Chapter 25, our picture of decision theory will be enriched through consideration of several other criteria. In the remaining chapters we will consider special topics. Chapters 26–28 discuss how samples and other types of experimental information may be systematically incorporated into decision making. Chapter 29 concludes Part VI with a discussion of utility.

24-1 CERTAINTY AND UNCERTAINTY IN DECISION MAKING

The least complex applications of decision theory are encountered when we make decisions under certain conditions. Perhaps the simplest example of **decision making under certainty** is selecting what clothes to wear. Although the possibilities are numerous, we all manage to make this choice quickly and with little effort. But not all decisions are this easy to make. Remember how hard it was to choose from among an assortment of candy bars when you were a child? And not all decisions made under certainty are as trivial as choosing the day's apparel.

When the outcomes are only partly determined by choice, the decision-making process takes on an added complexity. So that we can see what is involved in structuring a decision under uncertainty, we will consider the choice of whether to carry an umbrella or some other rain protection. Here, we are faced with two alternatives: carrying an ungainly item that can, in the event of rain, help to defer a cleaning bill or a cough, or challenging the elements with hands free and hoping not to be caught in the rain. Because the weather prediction may be inaccurate, we are uncertain about whether it will rain. Yet faced with the needs of daily life, we must make a decision despite our uncertainty. This illustrates a common decision made under uncertainty: An action must be taken, even though its outcome is unknown and determined by chance.*

In this chapter, we will present a framework within which we can explain how and why particular choices are made. The decision that we must make in coping with the weather illustrates the essential features of making any decision under uncertainty. We choose to carry an umbrella when the chance of rain seems

*This class of decisions is often divided into two categories—decision making under *risk*, where outcome probabilities are known, and decision making under *uncertainty*, where outcome probabilities are unknown. We will make no distinction here, but will assume that probabilities may always be found somehow—either objectively, through long-run frequency, or subjectively.

uncomfortably high, and we choose not to carry it when rain seems unlikely. But two people will make two different choices occasionally. Is there always one correct decision? If so, how can two persons make different choices? We begin to answer these questions by identifying several key elements common to all decisions and then structuring them in a convenient form for analysis.

24-2 ELEMENTS OF DECISIONS

Every decision made under certainty exhibits two elements—**acts** and **outcomes**. The decision maker's choices are the acts. For example, when one must choose between three television programs in the 9 P.M. time slot, each program represents a potential act. The outcomes may be characterized in terms of the enjoyment we derive from each of the programs.

If the decision is made under uncertainty, a third element—**events**—exists. Continuing with our uncertainty about the rain, the acts are "carry an umbrella" and "leave the umbrella home." All decisions involve the selection of an act. But the outcomes resulting from each act are uncertain, because *an outcome is determined partly by choice and partly by chance.* For the act "carry an umbrella" there are two possible outcomes: (1) unnecessarily carting rain paraphernalia and (2) weathering a shower fully protected. For the other act, "leave the umbrella at home," the two outcomes are (1) getting wet unnecessarily and (2) remaining dry and unencumbered. Again, whether the first or second outcome occurs depends solely on the occurrence of rain. The outcome for any particular chosen act depends on which *event*, rain or no rain, occurs.

THE DECISION TABLE

To facilitate our analysis, we may summarize a decision problem by constructing a **decision table**, which indicates the relationship between pairs of decision elements. The decision table for the umbrella decision is provided in Table 24-1. Each row of the decision table corresponds to an event, and each column corresponds to an act. The outcomes appear as entries in the body of the table. There is a specific outcome for each act-event combination, reflecting the fact that the interplay between act and event determines the ultimate result.

Only the acts that the decision maker wishes to consider are included in this decision table. "Staying home" is another possible act, which we will exclude because it is not contemplated. The acts in Table 24-1 are mutually exclusive and collectively exhaustive, so that exactly one act will be chosen. The events in the table are also mutually exclusive and collectively exhaustive.

TABLE 24-1 Decision Table for the Umbrella Decision

	Act	
Event	**Carry Umbrella**	**Leave Umbrella Home**
Rain	Stay dry	Get wet
No Rain	Carry unnecessary burden	Be dry and free

THE DECISION TREE DIAGRAM

A decision problem may also be conveniently illustrated with a **decision tree diagram** like the one shown in Figure 24-1. It is especially convenient to portray decision problems in the form of decision trees when choices must be made at different times over an extended period of time. The decision tree diagram is similar to the probability tree diagrams we used in Chapter 5. The choice of acts is shown as a fork with a separate branch for each act. The events are represented by separate branches in other forks. We distinguish between these two types of branching points by using squares for act-fork nodes and circles for event-fork nodes. A basic guideline for constructing a decison tree diagram is that the flow should be chronological from left to right. The acts are shown on the initial fork, because the decision must be made *before* the actual event is known. The events are therefore shown as branches in the second-stage forks. The outcome resulting from each act-event combination is shown as the end position of the corresponding path from the base of the tree.

24-3 RANKING THE ALTERNATIVES AND THE PAYOFF TABLE

In this section, we will consider how the choice of an act should be determined. We all cope with rain and manage to make umbrella decisions. But if we analyze the decision-making process, we will be able to make better decisions about more

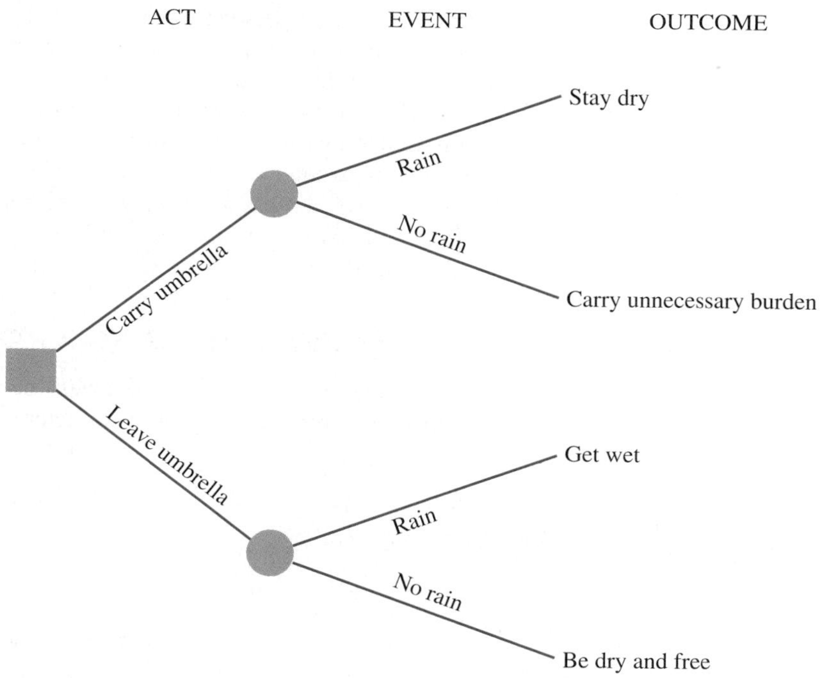

FIGURE 24-1 Decision tree diagram for the umbrella decision.

complex problems. Our analysis will focus on two measures: one for *uncertainty* and one for the *comparative worth* or **payoff** of the outcomes to the decision maker.

For now, we will consider examples with outcomes that have obvious payoffs, such as dollars. Every outcome—that is, every act-event combination—has a payoff value. Since the payoffs that the decision maker actually receives after choosing a particular act are conditional on whichever event occurs, these payoffs are sometimes referred to as **conditional values**. These values may be conveniently arranged in a **payoff table**, or a **conditional value table**, as shown in Table 24-2 for a gambling decision. The decision is to choose one of two acts: "gamble" or "don't gamble." Regardless of the choice made, a coin will be tossed, which will result in one of two possible events: "head" or "tail." The possible outcomes correspond to the four act-event combinations. A wager of $1 will be made if the decision maker chooses to gamble, and net winnings will be the payoff measure.

OBJECTIVES AND PAYOFF VALUES

In determining appropriate payoffs, we will assume that decision makers will choose to take actions that will bring them closest to their objectives. Each outcome must somehow be ranked in terms of how close it is to the decision maker's goal. The payoff table should provide a meaningful basis for comparison and enhance the decision maker's ability to make a good choice.

For example, if a business decision maker's goal is to achieve a high level of profits, then a natural payoff would be the profit for each outcome. Profit is a valid measure for a limited set of objectives, but it is by no means the top concern of all business managers. The goal of the founder of a successful corporation may be to maintain personal control, and the founder may consciously keep profits low so that the firm will not be attractive to other merger-minded entrepreneurs.

In general, decision making involves different kinds of goals, each requiring a distinct payoff measure. Decision makers with different goals may even select dissimilar measures for payoffs when considering the same set of alternatives. The Statistics Around Us box on page 967 illustrates this.

We conclude that a *payoff measure should be selected so that the payoff will rank outcomes by the degree to which they attain the decision maker's goals.* The goal dictates which payoff measures are valid.

ILLUSTRATION: CHOOSING A MOVEMENT FOR TIPPI-TOES

As a detailed example of a business decision made under uncertainty, we will consider a hypothetical toy manufacturer who must choose between four proto-

TABLE 24-2 Payoff Table for a Gambling Decision

	Act	
Event	**Gamble**	**Don't Gamble**
Head	$1	$0
Tail	–1	0

STATISTICS AROUND US

Finding the Way to San Jose

Charles Snyder, Herman Brown, and Sylvia Gold each wish to choose one of three routes from Los Angeles to San Jose: (1) Interstate 5, which is a freeway nearly all the way and has a high minimum speed limit; (2) State Highways 118 and 33, which are fairly direct and have no minimum speed limit; and (3) State Highway 1, which winds along the Pacific coast and is slow and long but very beautiful. Mr. Snyder is a salesman who travels to San Jose regularly; his goal is to reach his destination as quickly as possible. Mr. Brown is an economy "nut"; he wants to reach San Jose as cheaply as possible. Ms. Gold is on vacation and loves to drive on hilly, winding, scenic roads; she wishes to select the route that provides the greatest driving pleasure.

The payoffs that each person would assign to the three routes appear in Table 24-3.

Time savings is Mr. Snyder's payoff measure, so he chooses Interstate 5, which yields the greatest payoff of 4 hours. Mr. Brown likes to drive at a moderate speed to obtain maximum gasoline mileage, while taking the shortest route possible. His payoff measure is fuel savings (based on the amount of gasoline required on the most expensive route), so he chooses the back roads, State Highways 118 and 33, to save 7 gallons of gas. Ms. Gold has rated the routes in terms of points of interest, types of scenery, and number of hills and curves. This rating serves as her payoff measure, so her best route is scenic State Highway 1, which rates 10.

TABLE 24-3 Payoffs for the Alternative Routes Relevant to the Goals of Three Decision Makers

	Payoff Measure		
	Mr. Snyder	Mr. Brown	Ms. Gold
Alternative Route	Time Savings (hours)	Fuel Savings (gallons)	Enjoyment (subjective rating)
Interstate 5	4	3	1
Highways 118 & 33	3	7	3
Highway 1	0	0	10

type designs for Tippi-Toes, a dancing ballerina doll that does pirouettes and jetés. Each prototype represents a different technology for the moving parts, all powered by small, battery-operated motors. One prototype is a complete arrangement of gears and levers. The second is similar, with springs instead of levers. Another works on the principle of weights and pulleys. The movement of the fourth design is controlled pneumatically through a system of valves that open and close at the command of a small, solid-state computer housed in the head cavity. The dolls are identical in all functional aspects.

The choice of the movement design will be based solely on a comparison of the contributions to profits made by the four prototypes. The payoff table is provided in Table 24-4. The demand for Tippi-Toes is uncertain, but management feels that one of the following events will occur.

Light demand	(25,000 units)
Moderate demand	(100,000 units)
Heavy demand	(150,000 units)

The toy manufacturer in this example is considering only three possible events—here, levels of demand—which greatly simplifies our analysis. Demand does not have to be precisely 25,000 or 100,000 units, however. The problem could be analyzed at several hundred thousand possible levels of demand—say, from 0 to 500,000 dolls. The techniques we will develop here may be applied to a more detailed situation. Due to the computational requirements, the demand probability distribution could be approximated to the nearest 100, 1,000, or 10,000 units.

Similarly, our example has only four alternatives or acts. In the practical, business decision-making environment, the number of possible acts may be quite large. For instance, deciding what mix of toys to sell could easily involve trillions of alternatives. *The decision analysis should include only the alternatives that the decision maker wishes to consider.* When there is no compelling reason for choosing one of the alternatives, "doing nothing" should be an alternative. The search for attractive alternatives is essential to sound decision making. However, decision analysis cannot tell us what factors should and should not be considered, although it may be used to guide our selection.

EXERCISES

24-1 Willy B. Rich is deciding whether to spend his Christmas vacation skiing at a resort in Colorado or surfing in Hawaii. He must commit himself to one of these alternatives in the early fall, since reservations have to be made months in advance. He really enjoys skiing more than surfing. Unfortunately, he cannot be certain about December snow conditions, and his ski trip will be ruined if there is poor snow. The trip to Hawaii would be a sure bet. But if he must go there when the snow is good elsewhere, his trip will be somewhat spoiled by regrets that he did not make arrangements to spend his vacation skiing.

(a) Construct Willy's decision table.

(b) Construct his decision tree.

TABLE 24-4 Payoff Table for the Tippi-Toes Decision

Event (demand)	Act (choice of movement)			
	Gears and Levers	Spring Action	Weights and Pulleys	Pneumatic
Light	\$ 25,000	−\$ 10,000	−\$125,000	−\$300,000
Moderate	400,000	440,000	400,000	300,000
Heavy	650,000	740,000	750,000	700,000

24-2 Peggy Jones, the founder of a computer programming services firm, wishes to expand the firm's activities into the manufacture of peripheral equipment. Funds must be raised to build and operate the necessary facilities. Three financing alternatives are available: (1) issue additional common stock, (2) sell bonds, and (3) issue nonvoting preferred stock. A common stock issue will provide a strong financial base for future expansion through borrowing, but it will considerably reduce Jones' percentage of ownership and control from its current 100%. New common stock will also divide future earnings into smaller amounts per share to existing shareholders. Bonds will allow existing shareholders to accrue all of the benefits of new earnings, but they will also increase the risk of forced liquidation if the new venture proves unsuccessful. Preferred stock will give its holders no claims on the firm's assets, but it will drastically reduce the rate of earnings participation on the part of existing common stockholders. The following table summarizes the forecast financial status of the firm if the manufacturing venture is successful.

For each of the following goals, suggest an appropriate payoff measure. Then, use this measure to identify the best and the worst alternative choices for financing in terms of the degree to which each *single* goal is met. Indicate any ties.

(a) Maintain a high percentage of control by Jones.
(b) Maximize the earnings of Jones' shares.
(c) Maximize the availability of short-term credit.
(d) Maximize the potential for cash dividends to Jones.

Possible Payoff Measure	Financing Alternatives		
	Additional Common Stock	Bonds	Preferred Stock
1. Earnings after taxes and preferred dividends	$5,000,000	$3,500,000	$4,000,000
2. Common shares outstanding	1,000,000	500,000	500,000
3. Earnings per common share	$5.00	$7.00	$8.00
4. Jones' percentage of common ownership	50	100	100
5. Emergency line of credit	$1,000,000	$400,000	$500,000
6. Earnings available for common dividends	$5,000,000	$2,000,000	$4,000,000
7. Maximum possible dividends per share of common stock	$5.00	$4.00	$8.00

24-3 Shirley Smart has final examinations in accounting and finance on Monday and only 10 hours of study time left. The following anticipated grades apply, depending on the exam format.

Study Time (hours)	Multiple-choice Format		Case Format	
	Accounting	Finance	Accounting	Finance
0	C	B	B	C
5	C	B	A	B
10	B	A	A	A

Shirley plans to allocate her study time in one of the following ways.

Plan	Accounting	Finance
1	0 hours	10 hours
2	5	5
3	10	0

Although a single exam format will apply for any course, Shirley is uncertain which one each professor will pick, so any combination of multiple-choice and case formats is possible.

Using her combined accounting and finance grade point average (GPA) as her payoff measure (A = 4 points, B = 3 points, C = 2 points), construct Shirley's payoff table.

24-4 The Aero Spad plant manager must choose a method for assembling parts. The size of the production run will depend on the number of units ordered, which is an uncertain quantity. The following quantities are believed to be equally likely: 4,000, 6,000, 8,000, and 10,000. The parts will be sold for $200 each, regardless of quantity ordered.

The following data apply to the three methods of production.

	Method A	Method B	Method C
Set-up cost	$200,000	$160,000	$100,000
Unit material cost	20	30	40
Unit labor cost	20	20	30

(a) Using total profit from the parts as the payoff measure, construct the manager's payoff table.

(b) Determine the expected payoff for each act. Which method will maximize expected profit?

24-4 REDUCING THE NUMBER OF ALTERNATIVES: INADMISSIBLE ACTS

Regardless of the decision-making process that we ultimately employ to help us make a choice, an initial screening may be made to determine if there are any acts that will never be chosen. To illustrate this, consider the payoffs in Table 24-4. An interesting feature is exhibited by the payoffs of the acts "weights and pulleys" and "pneumatic": No matter which demand event occurs, the weights-and-pulleys act results in a greater payoff. If a light demand occurs, for instance, the payoff for weights and pulleys is −$125,000, which is more favorable than the −$300,000 payoff for the pneumatic movement. A similar finding results if we compare these two acts for the other possible demand events. Since the weights-and-pulleys movement will always be a superior choice to the pneumatic movement, we say that the first act **dominates** the second act. One act dominates another when it achieves a better or an equal payoff, no matter which events occur, and when it is strictly better for one or more events.

TABLE 24-5 Modified Payoff Table for the Tippi-Toes Decision

Event (demand)	Act (choice of movement)		
	Gears and Levers	Spring Action	Weights and Pulleys
Light	\$ 25,000	−\$ 10,000	−\$125,000
Moderate	400,000	440,000	400,000
Heavy	650,000	740,000	750,000

In general, whenever an act is dominated by another one, it is **inadmissible**. Thus, the pneumatic movement is an **inadmissible act**. The toy manufacturer's decision may be simplified by eliminating pneumatic movement from further consideration. Removing the pneumatic act leaves us with the modified payoff table in Table 24-5.

A simple way to determine if an act is inadmissible is to see if every entry in its column in the payoff table is less than or equal to the corresponding entry in some other column. It is easy to verify that this is not true for the entries in Table 24-5, so the remaining movement acts must be retained. The acts that remain are called **admissible acts**.

EXERCISES

24-5 Identify any inadmissible acts in the following payoff table.

Event	Act				
	A_1	A_2	A_3	A_4	A_5
E_1	3	4	4	5	1
E_2	6	2	1	4	2
E_3	1	8	8	7	3

24-5 MAXIMIZING EXPECTED PAYOFF: THE BAYES DECISION RULE

How does a decision maker choose an act? When there is no uncertainty, the answer is straightforward: Select the act that yields the highest payoff (although finding this particular optimal act may be very difficult when there are many alternatives). But when the events are uncertain, the act that yields the greatest payoff for one event may yield a lower payoff than a competing act for some other event.

Suppose that our toy manufacturer accepts the following probabilities for the demand for Tippi-Toes.

Light demand	.10
Moderate demand	.70
Heavy demand	.20
	1.00

TABLE 24-6 Calculation of Expected Payoffs for the Tippi-Toes Decision

Demand Event	Probability	Gear and Levers		Spring Action		Weights and Pulleys	
		Payoff	Payoff × Probability	Payoff	Payoff × Probability	Payoff	Payoff × Probability
Light	.10	$ 25,000	$ 2,500	−$ 10,000	−$ 1,000	−$125,000	−$ 12,500
Moderate	.70	400,000	280,000	440,000	308,000	400,000	280,000
Heavy	.20	650,000	130,000	740,000	148,000	750,000	150,000
Expected payoff			$412,500		$455,000		$417,500

We calculate the expected payoff for each act in Table 24-6 by multiplying each payoff by the respective event probability and summing the products from each column. We find that the spring-action movement results in the maximum expected payoff of $455,000. Thus, using maximum expected payoff as a decision-making criterion, our toy manufacturer would select the spring-action movement for the Tippi-Toes doll.

The criterion of selecting the act with the maximum expected payoff is sometimes referred to as the **Bayes decision rule**. This rule takes into account all the information about the chances for the various payoffs. But we will see that it is not a perfect device and can lead to a choice that is not actually the most desirable. However, we will also see that this criterion is a suitable basis for decision making under uncertainty when the payoff values are selected with great care.

EXERCISES

24-6 Consider the following payoff table.

Event	Probability	Act		
		A_1	A_2	A_3
E_1	.3	$10,000	$20,000	$ 5,000
E_2	.5	5,000	−10,000	10,000
E_3	.2	15,000	10,000	10,000

Compute the expected payoffs for each act. According to the Bayes decision rule, which act should be chosen?

24-7 Recompute the expected payoffs for the Tippi-Toes decision in Table 24-5, assuming that the following demand event probabilities now apply.

Light demand	.20
Moderate demand	.50
Heavy demand	.30

According to the Bayes decision rule, which act should the toy manufacturer choose?

24-8 A new product is to be evaluated. The main decision to be made is whether or not to market the product, in which case it will be a success (probability = .40) or a failure. The net payoff for a successful product is $10 million; a failure would result in a − $5 million payoff. Construct a payoff table for the decision, and then compute the expected payoffs. Should the product be marketed?

24-6 DECISION TREE ANALYSIS

The decisions under uncertainty encountered thus far may be portrayed in terms of a payoff table. But some problems are too complex to be presented in a table. Difficulties arise when the same events do not apply for all acts. For example, a contractor might have to choose between bidding on a construction job for a dam or on one for an airport, not having sufficient resources to bid on both. Regardless of the job chosen, there is some probability (which may differ for the two projects) that the contractor will win the job bid on. Separate sets of events and probabilities are required for each act.

Decisions must often be made at two or more points in time, with uncertain events occurring between decisions. Sometimes these problems may be analyzed in terms of a payoff table, but usually the earlier choice of the act will have a bearing on the type, quantity, and probabilities of later events. At best, this makes it cumbersome to attempt to force the decision into the limited confines of the rectangular arrangement of a payoff table.

The decision tree diagram described earlier allows us to meaningfully arrange the elements of a complex decision problem without the restrictions of a tabular format. A further advantage of the decision tree is that it serves as an excellent management communication tool, because the tree clearly delineates every potential course of action and all possible outcomes.

ILLUSTRATION: PONDEROSA'S MARKETING DECISION

The president of Ponderosa Record Company, a small independent recording studio, has just signed a contract with a four-person rock group called the Fluid Mechanics. A tape has been cut, and Ponderosa must decide whether or not to market the recording. If the record is to be test marketed, then a 5,000-record run will be made and promoted regionally; this may result in a later decision to distribute an additional 45,000 records nationally, for which a second pressing run will have to be made. If immediate national marketing is chosen, a pressing run of 50,000 records will be made. Regardless of the test market results, the president may decide to enter the national market or decide not to enter it.

A Ponderosa record is either a complete success or a failure in its market. A recording is successful if all records that are pressed are sold; the sales of a failure are practically nil. Success in a regional market does not guarantee success nationally, but it is a fairly reliable predictor.

THE DECISION TREE DIAGRAM

The structure of the Ponderosa decision problem is presented in the decision tree diagram in Figure 24-2. Decisions are to be made at two different points in time, or stages. The immediate choice is to select one of two acts: "test market" or "don't test market." These acts are shown as branches on the initial fork at node *a*. If test marketing is chosen, then the result to be achieved in the test marketplace

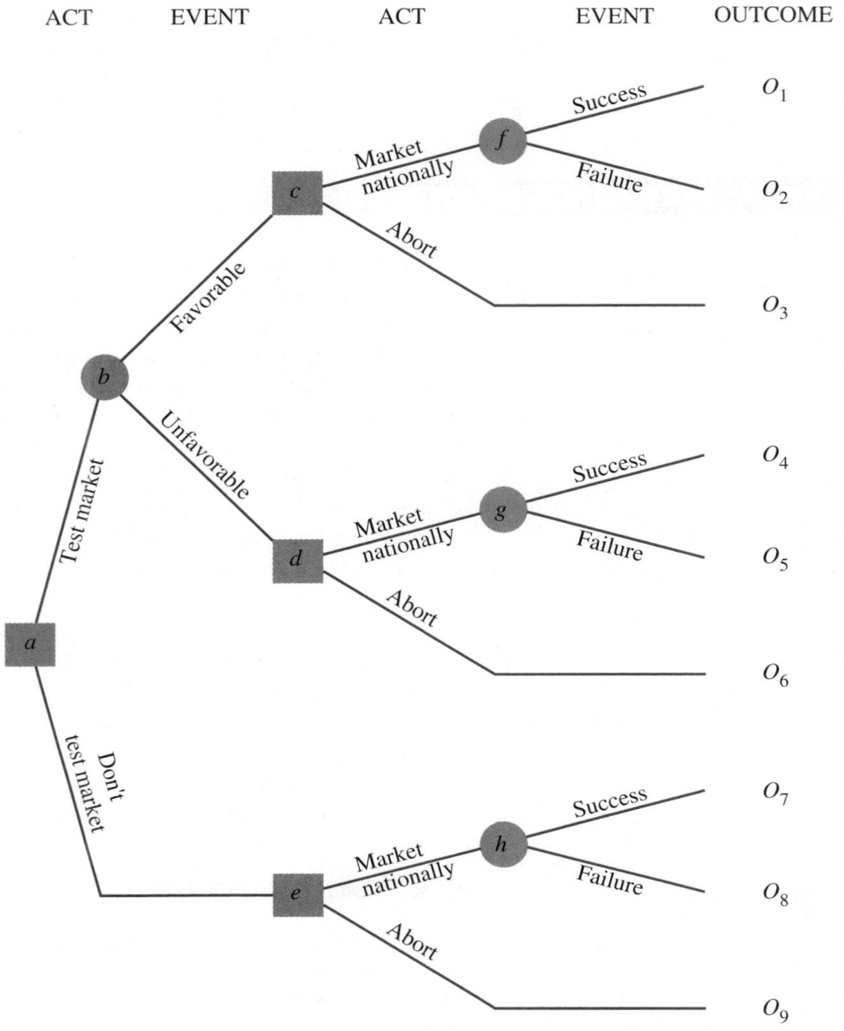

FIGURE 24-2 Decision tree diagram for the Ponderosa decision.

is uncertain. This is reflected by an event fork at node *b*, where the branches represent favorable and unfavorable outcomes. Regardless of which event occurs, a choice must be made between two new acts: "market nationally" or "abort." These acts occur at a later stage and are represented by a pair of act forks. Each fork corresponds to the two different conditions under which this decision may be made: at node *c*, when the test marketing is favorable, and at node *d*, when it is unfavorable. If national marketing is chosen at either node *c* or node *d*, the success or failure of the recording still remains unknown, and the possible events are reflected on the decision tree as branches on the terminal event forks at nodes *f* and *g*.

If the initial choice at decision point *a* is "don't test market," then a further choice must be made at the act fork represented by decision point *e*: "market nationally" or "abort." As before, node *h* reflects the two uncertain events that will arise from the choice to market nationally. The "abort" path leading from node *e* contains a "dummy" branch—a diagrammatical convenience that allows event and act forks of similar form to appear at the same stage of the problem and permits all paths to terminate at a common stage. Thus, all "abort" acts are followed by a dummy branch.

Every path from the base of the decision tree leads to a terminal position corresponding to a decision outcome. Each possible combination of acts and events, or each path, has a distinct outcome. For instance, O_1 represents the following sequence of events and acts: "test market," "favorable," "market nationally," "success."

The first step in analyzing the decision problem is to obtain a payoff for each outcome.

DETERMINING THE PAYOFFS

The contract with the Fluid Mechanics calls for a $5,000 payment to the group if records are produced. Ponderosa arranges with a record manufacturer to make its pressings. For each pressing run, there is a $5,000 fixed cost plus a $.75 fee for each record. Record jackets, handling, and distribution cost an additional $.25 per record. The total variable cost per record is therefore $1.00. Using these figures, we calculate the immediate cash effect of each act in the decision tree in Figure 24-2. Some of these cash effects, or **partial cash flows**, are computed in Table 24-7.

The negative cash flows indicate expenditures. The partial cash flows in Table 24-7 appear on the respective branches extending from decision points *a* and *e* of the decision tree in Figure 24-3. In a similar manner, we determine the partial cash flows for the acts at the forks at decision points *c* and *d*: − $50,000 to market nationally ($5,000 fixed pressing cost plus $1.00 each in variable costs for 45,000 records), and $0 to abort.

Ponderosa receives $2 for each record it sells through retail outlets. Since the events "favorable" and "unfavorable" or "success" and "failure" represent sales of all and no records, respectively, the partial cash flows may be obtained by multiplying the number of records sold by $2. The partial cash flows for the events at the fork at node *b* are therefore + $10,000 (for 5,000 records sold) and $0 (for no sales). The amounts for the events at nodes *f* and *g* are + $90,000 (for 45,000 records sold) and $0, whereas the amounts for the events at node *h* are + $100,000 and $0.

TABLE 24-7 Some Partial Cash Flows Used to Determine Ponderosa's Payoffs

Act		Partial Cash Flow	
Test market		−$ 5,000	(payment to group)
		−5,000	(fixed cost of pressing)
		−5,000	(variable costs of 5,000 records at $1.00)
	Total	−$15,000	
Don't test market		$0	
Market nationally (without test)		−$ 5,000	(payment to group)
		−5,000	(fixed cost of pressing)
		−50,000	(variable costs of 50,000 records at $1.00)
	Total	−$60,000	
Abort		$0	

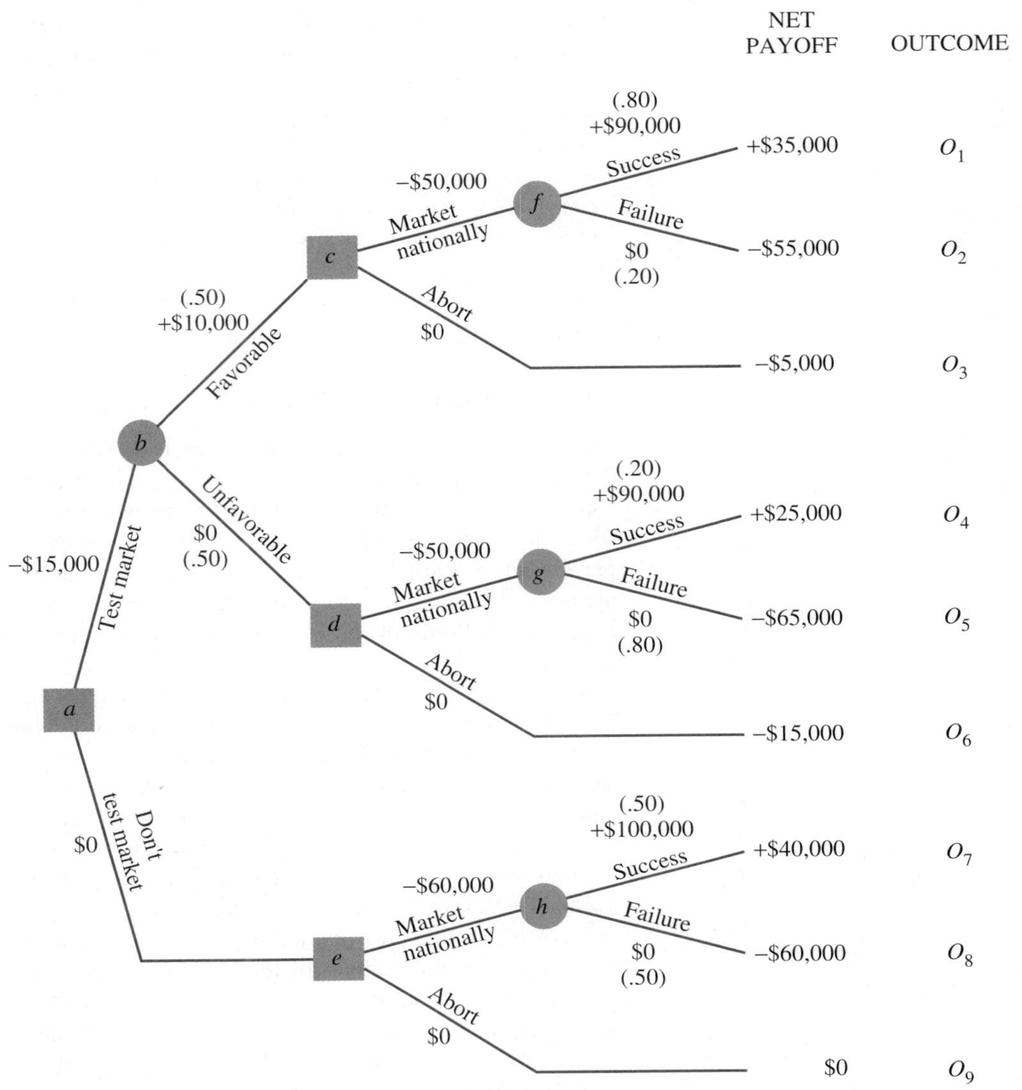

Note: Partial cash flows and probabilities are on the branches, with net cash-flow payoffs at the terminal positions.

FIGURE 24-3 The Ponderosa decision tree diagram.

The payoff for each outcome may be obtained by adding the partial cash flows on the branches of the path leading to its terminal position. Thus, for O_1, we add the partial cash flows − \$15,000, + \$10,000, − \$50,000, and + \$90,000. The payoff for O_1 is therefore + \$35,000. The payoffs calculated for each outcome are shown at the respective terminal positions of the decision tree in Figure 24-3.

ASSIGNING EVENT PROBABILITIES

Ponderosa's management wishes to choose the act that will yield the maximum expected payoff. But before this choice may be made, probability values must be assigned to the events in the decision structure. Suppose that Ponderosa's president believes that the chance of favorably test marketing the recording is .50. The probability of unfavorably test marketing the recording is also .50. These probability values are placed in parentheses along the branches at node b in Figure 24-3. In assigning probability values to the success and failure events for national marketing, our decision maker is faced with three distinctly different situations. With no test marketing, the chance of national success is judged to be .50. A favorable test marketing indicates that a record appeals to the regional segment of the market, so the chance of national success in this case is judged to be a much higher .80; this is a *conditional probability*. Similarly, unfavorable test marketing is a likely indication of national appeal, so the conditional probability for success is judged to be .20 in this case. The following probability values are placed on the branches for the events at the remaining forks in the decision tree diagram: .80 for success and .20 for failure at node f; .20 for success and .80 for failure at node g; and .50 for success and .50 for failure at node h. (It is just coincidental that the probability for national marketing success after unfavorable test marketing is .20, which is also the probability for national marketing failure after favorable test marketing. Our decision maker could have selected another value, such as .10.)

BACKWARD INDUCTION

We are now ready to analyze Ponderosa's decision. Our decision maker wishes to select an initial or immediate act at decision point a. The first act that we will evaluate is "test market." What is the expected payoff for this act? Referring to Figure 24-3, we see that six outcomes, O_1 through O_6, may result from this choice. How can we translate the corresponding payoffs into an expected value? We cannot do this until we specify the intervening acts that will be chosen at nodes c and d. In general, *it is impossible to evaluate an immediate act without first considering all later decisions that result from this choice.*

Thus, to find the expected payoff for the "test market" act, our decision maker must first decide whether to market nationally or to abort if (1) test marketing proves favorable or (2) test marketing proves unfavorable. This illustrates an essential feature of analyzing multistage decisions: *Evaluations must be made in reverse of their natural chronological sequence.* Before deciding whether to test market, our decision maker must decide what to do if the test marketing is favorable or if it is unfavorable. The procedure for making such evaluations is called **backward induction**.

We clarify this point by describing the procedure for our decision-making problem. For simplicity, the Ponderosa president's decision tree diagram is redrawn in Figure 24-4 without the partial cash flows.

Consider the act fork at decision point c. If the decision is to market nationally, then Ponderosa's president is faced with the event fork at node f. With a probability of .80 that marketing nationally will be a success, a net payoff of +\$35,000 will be achieved. The probability that marketing nationally will be a failure is .20, which leads to a net payoff of −\$55,000. The expected payoff for this event fork is calculated as

$$.80(+\$35{,}000) + .20(-\$55{,}000) = \$17{,}000$$

The amount + \$17,000 is entered on the decision tree at node f, since this is the expected payoff for the act to market nationally. For convenience, we place the expected payoff for a sequence of acts above the applicable node.

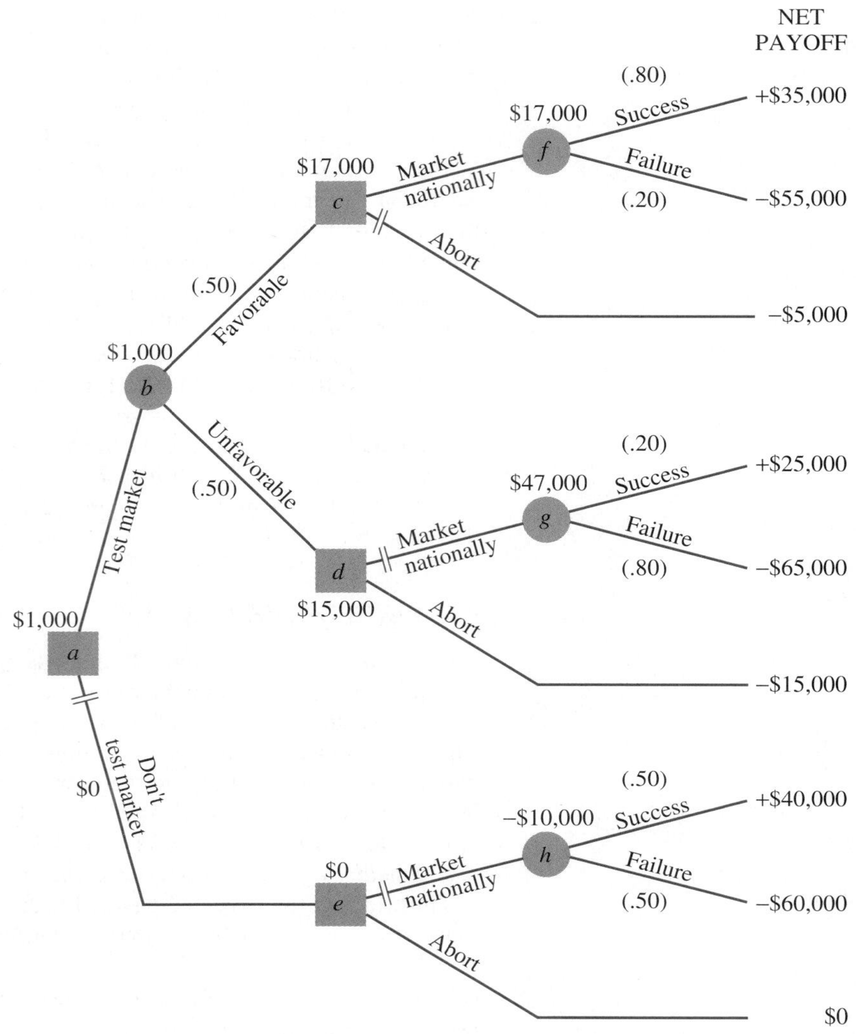

FIGURE 24-4 Ponderosa decision tree, showing backward induction analysis.

The act to abort at decision point *c* will lead to a certain payoff of −$5,000. Since the expected payoff for the act to market nationally (+$17,000) is larger than −$5,000, the choice to market nationally should be made over aborting. We may reflect on this future choice by *pruning* the branch from the tree that corresponds to the act "abort" at decision point *c*. This act merits no further consideration, since if decision point *c* is reached, the president will choose to market nationally. That is, if the decision maker initially decides to test market and the results turn out to be favorable, the president will choose to market nationally. Thus, +$17,000 is the expected payoff resulting from making the best choice at decision point *c*. We bring back the amount +$17,000 and enter it on the diagram above the node at *c*.

As a rule of thumb in performing backward induction, ultimately all but one act will be eliminated at each decision point (except in the case of ties), so that all branches except those leading to the greatest expected payoff will be pruned. Only the *best single payoff* from the later stage is brought backward to the preceding decision point (square). *Branch pruning takes place only in act forks—never in event forks.* Instead, event forks (circles) involve an expected value calculation, so that an average payoff is always computed from the later stage values.

The available choices when test marketing results are unfavorable may be handled in the same way. First, we calculate the expected payoff at node *g* that arises from the act "market nationally," or

$$.20(+\$25{,}000) + .80(-\$65{,}000) = -\$47{,}000$$

We place this figure on the decision tree diagram above node *g*. Since the act "abort" leads to a payoff of −$15,000, which is larger than −$47,000, the branch for the act to market nationally is pruned from the tree. The best choice when test marketing fails is to abort. We therefore bring back and enter the amount −$15,000 on the diagram at the node of decision point *d*.

In a similar fashion, the expected payoff of the event fork at node *h*, when the initial choice is to market nationally, is determined as follows.

$$.50(+\$40{,}000) + .50(-\$60{,}000) = -\$10{,}000$$

At decision point *e*, the act "abort" is superior to the act "market nationally," and the latter branch is pruned from the tree. Our decision maker must now compare the acts at decision point *a*. The expected payoff from the act "test market" is still to be determined. This is the expected payoff for the event fork at node *b*, which has two event branches. The branch corresponding to success leads to a portion of the tree with an expected payoff of +$17,000. The other branch leads to a choice with an expected payoff of −$15,000. We use these two amounts to calculate the expected payoff at node *b*.

$$.50(+\$17{,}000) + .50(-\$15{,}000) = +\$1{,}000$$

We enter the amount +$1,000 on the diagram above node *b*.

Ponderosa's president is now in a position to compare the two acts at decision point *a*: "test market" and "don't test market." Since the expected payoff for test marketing (+$1,000) is higher than the expected payoff for not testing ($0), our decision maker should choose to test market. The expected payoff of $1,000 is brought back and placed above node *a*. The branch corresponding to "don't test market" is pruned, and our backward induction is complete.

A decision is indicated. Ponderosa's president should choose to test market the Fluid Mechanics' record. If the test marketing is favorable, then the president should market nationally; if the test marketing is unfavorable, then the president should abort the recording. This result is illustrated in Figure 24-4 by the unpruned branches that remain on the decision tree.

ADDITIONAL REMARKS

Choices that are made in later stages are not irrevocable, and this analysis does not preclude the fact that the decision maker's mind may change over time. Before the future decision must be made at node *c*, new information may be received that would, for instance, indicate a need to revise the probability for national success downward. If there is bad publicity about one of the Fluid Mechanics, for example, the expected payoff for national marketing might be smaller than the expected payoff for aborting. Possible changes in conditions do not invalidate the original backward induction analysis. In our example, *the choice to test market is the best decision that may be made based on the currently available information.*

The decision tree structure is suitable for analyzing decisions that extend over a long time period. It indicates the best course of action for the *current* decision. As time progresses, however, some uncertainties may be reduced and new ones may arise. Acts previously identified as optimal may turn out to be obviously poor choices, and brand new candidates may be determined. The relevant portion of the decision tree may be updated and revised prior to each new immediate decision. But each such decision is analyzed in the same general manner, using the best information available at the time a choice must be made.

Although a decision tree is analyzed by moving backward in time, the analysis is really forward-looking because it indicates the optimal course of action to take when future decision points are reached. The dollar amount brought backward to each node represents the best payoff the decision maker may expect to achieve if that position is reached at a later time. Regardless of what events have occurred, the optimal course of action for future choices is still indicated by the original analysis.

EXERCISES

24-9 Suppose that the president of the Ponderosa Record Company uses the following probability values to analyze the decision about the Fluid Mechanics' recording.

$$\Pr[\text{national marketing success} \mid \text{favorable test marketing}] = .9$$

$$\Pr[\text{national marketing failure} \mid \text{unfavorable test marketing}] = .6$$

$$\Pr[\text{national marketing success}] = .7$$

$$\Pr[\text{test marketing success}] = .75$$

Repeat the Ponderosa decision tree analysis to determine the company's optimal marketing strategy. Assume that all payoffs remain unchanged.

24-10 The manager of Getting Oil's data processing operations personally interviews applicants for jobs as data-entry operators. Employees who are hired with no previous experience are placed in a one-month training program on a trial basis. Satisfactory employees are retained; all others are let go at the end of the month. Most of the people who have been let go in the past have been found to be lacking in aptitude. The manager is contemplating contracting the testing services of a personnel agency. For a fee the agency would administer a battery of aptitude tests. The manager has developed the decision tree in Figure 24-5 to help her in making her hiring decisions. Perform backward induction analysis to determine the strategy or course of action that will maximize the manager's expected payoff.

24-11 Spillsberry Foods must determine whether or not to market a new cake mix. Management must also decide whether to conduct a consumer test

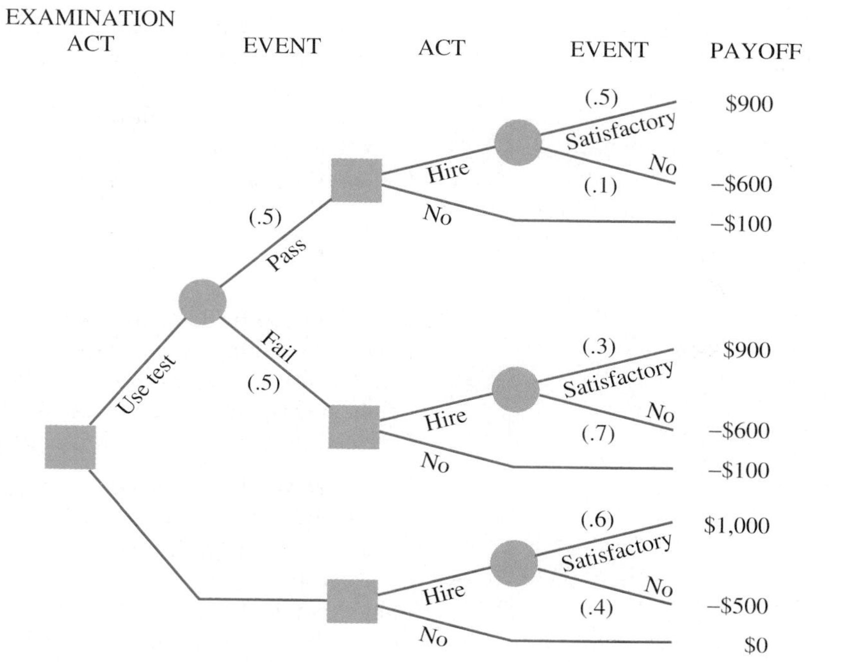

FIGURE 24-5

marketing program that would cost $25,000. If the mix is successful, Spillsberry's profits will increase by $1,000,000; if the mix fails, the company will lose $250,000. Not marketing the product will not affect profits. The cake mix is considered to have a 60% chance of success without testing. The assumed probability for a favorable test marketing result is 50%. Given a favorable test result, the chance of product success is judged to be 85%. However, if the test results are unfavorable, the probability for the product's success is judged to be only 35%.

Construct a decision tree diagram that may be used to determine the optimal course of action that will provide the greatest expected payoff. Include the choice of whether or not to use the test. Perfom backward induction analysis to determine which course of action maximizes the expected payoff.

24-12 Fiber Synthetics' manager must decide whether to process a chemical order or to contract it out at a cost of $20,000. The final product batch will be sold for $40,000. In-house processing involves direct costs for raw materials of $4,000. The first step is chlorosulfanation, for which there is an 80% chance of getting a satisfactory intermediate chemical base at a cost of $2,000. If the base is unsatisfactory, there will not be sufficient time to start a new batch, but there will still be a choice of turning down the order or contracting out the production. In the latter case, there is a 60% chance of being too late and having to dump the final product. The last stage of in-house processing may be a low-temperature one costing $10,000 or a high-temperature one costing $16,000. There is a 30% chance that the low-temperature process will fail, so that the resulting chemicals must be dumped; it would then be too late to go outside. The high-temperature procedure is certain to work.

(a) Using net cash flow (revenue minus costs) as the payoff measure, diagram the manager's decision tree.

(b) What action maximizes expected payoff?

SUMMARY

1. What are the basic elements of a decision under uncertainty?

An effective structure for analysis of decisions under uncertainty includes three components: (1) **acts** or choices, (2) **events**, and (3) **outcomes**. A distinct outcome corresponds to each combination of act and event. These may be arranged in two kinds of representations.

2. What are the two structural forms commonly used in decision analysis?

The **decision table** has a column for each act, a row for each event, and an outcome in each position in the body of the table. A **decision tree** represents each act and event as a branch on a tree. There are two types of branching points, **act forks** (or, decision points) and **event forks** (or, points of uncertainty). These are placed *chronologically*, so that earlier acts or events precede later ones. The branch for any act or event may be followed either by an act fork or by an event fork, depending on what sequence accurately reflects the underlying decision. In a decision tree diagram, each possible sequence of branches culminates in an outcome, so that there is a distinct outcome for every path from beginning to end.

3. How are outcomes ranked?

Decision analysis is concerned with the selection of acts. Unfortunately, the outcomes from any particular act are uncertain. The initial focus is placed on the *outcome*. A **payoff measure** needs to be chosen that will rank these in terms of how closely they satisfy the decision maker's goals. The choice of payoff measure is connected to the particular goal in question. Since there may be several goals, perhaps in competition with each other, more than one payoff measure might be needed.

There is often a single overriding objective, such as maximizing profit or cash flow. The common payoff measure in business decision making is *net cash flow*. When payoffs are assigned to each outcome and arranged in the same tabular format as a decision table, the resulting display is called the **payoff table**, with one column for each act. In evaluations involving a decision tree diagram, a final payoff for each outcome may be arrived at by accumulating **partial cash flows** assigned to each branch.

4. What are inadmissible acts and how can identifying them be useful?

Unfortunately, with uncertainty present there is usually no course of action that guarantees achieving the maximum payoff. There are occasional acts that may be eliminated because they are **inadmissible**, being dominated by some other single act that is under all circumstances as good or better. Without controversy, columns for inadmissible acts may be removed from the payoff table before the best act gets selected. But the final choice of act may involve serious pitfalls.

5. **What is the Bayes decision rule and how does it relate to expected payoffs?** Decision theory is concerned with the selection of an act, with the ultimate aim being to uncover the decision maker's preferred course of action. A favored approach is to make a choice so that the **expected payoff** is maximized. This decision criterion is referred to as the **Bayes decision rule.** Although the Bayes decision rule is very appealing, it sometimes indicates actions that are definitely not preferred. Chapter 25 explores some alternative decision criteria.

6. **What is decision tree analysis?** Decision trees are evaluated under the Bayes decision rule through a process called **backward induction**. This procedure begins at the futuremost branching points, with expected values computed for each event fork. Moving backwards in time, those branches leading to lower payoffs are pruned from the tree at act forks. The final pruned tree indicates the **strategy**, or course of action, that maximizes expected payoff.

REVIEW EXERCISES

24-13 Refer to the payoffs for the Tippi-Toes decision in Table 24-6. Suppose that the development cost of the spring-action movement is $40,000 higher than before (regardless of demand) and that revenues generated by the doll when demand is heavy are $50,000 lower than before (regardless of movement chosen).

(a) Construct a new payoff table reflecting these revisions.

(b) Using the payoff table, compute the expected payoff for each act. Which movement should be chosen under the Bayes decision rule?

24-14 Consider the following payoff table for a graphical design decision.

Texture Event	Probability	Color Theme Act				
		Brown	Orange	Red	Green	Yellow
Full-tone	.2	100	110	50	120	90
Half-tone	.5	80	70	80	60	100
Mixed	.3	100	90	90	90	110

(a) Identify any inadmissible color choices.

(b) Compute the expected payoff for each admissible act. Which color theme should be chosen?

24-15 A product manager for Sniff-n-Stuff wishes to determine whether or not to market a new deodorant. The manager may order a consumer testing program for $50,000. The present value of all future profits for a successful product is $1,000,000; the brand's failure would result in a net loss of $500,000. Not marketing the deodorant will not affect profits. The manager judges that the deodorant would have a 50–50 chance of success without testing. Customer testing will be either favorable (40% chance) or unfavorable. Given a favorable test result, the chance of product success is judged to be 80%. But for an unfavorable test result, the deodorant's success probability is judged to be only 30%.

Construct the product manager's decision tree diagram. Perform backward induction analysis to determine which course of action provides the greatest expected profit.

24-16 Using the new product in Exercise 24-8, the following two experiments have been proposed. (Both experiments cannot be used.)

Test market at a cost of $1 million. Results will be "favorable" (Probability = .48) or "unfavorable." Given a favorable result, the probability for product success is .75. Given an unfavorable result, the probability for product success is only .08.

Attitude survey at a cost of $.5 million. Results will be "warm" (Probability = .40) or "cold." Given a warm response, the probability for product success is .70. Given a cold response, the probability for success is only .20.

In addition to these choices, the main decision to market or not to market may be made without obtaining any further information.

Construct a decision tree diagram for this problem, indicating all of the probabilities and payoffs. Perform backward induction analysis to determine which course of action maximizes expected payoff. (Specify all choices that may then have to be made.)

CASE Gypsy Moth Eradication

A government official wishes to determine the most effective way to control tree damage from the gypsy moth. There are three methods for attacking the pest: (1) spray with DDT; (2) use a scent to lure and trap males, so that the remaining males must compete for mating with a much larger number of males that have been sterilized in a laboratory and then released; and (3) spray with a juvenile hormone that prevents the larvae from developing into adult moths.

The net improvement in current and future tree losses using DDT is lowest, because it is assumed that DDT will never completely eradicate the moth.

If the scent-lure program is instituted, the probability that it will leave a low number of native males is .5, with a .5 chance that it will leave a high number. Once the scent-lure results are known, a later choice must then be made either to spray with DDT or to release sterile males. The cost of the scent lures is $5 million and the cost of sterilization is an additional $5 million. But if this two-phase program is successful, the worth of present and future trees saved will be $30 million. If scent lures leave a small native male population, there is a 90% chance for success using sterile males; otherwise, there is only a 10% chance for success using sterile males. A failure results in no savings.

The juvenile hormone must be synthesized at a cost of $3 million. There is only a .20 probability that the resulting product will work. If it does, the worth of trees saved would be \$50 million, because the gypsy moth would become extinct. If the hormone does not work, savings would be zero.

Should one of the esoteric eradication procedures be chosen and then fail, the official's contingency plan is to spray with DDT. The savings from successful implementation of the sterile male or juvenile hormone procedures reflect the value of environmental damage and other costs avoided by not having to use DDT. To compare outcomes, the official proposes to use the net advantage (crop and environmental savings minus cost) relative to where she would be were she forced to spray with DDT.

QUESTIONS

1. Under the official's proposal, the selection of DDT without even trying the other procedures would lead to an outcome with zero payoff. Discuss the benefits of her proposed payoff measure.
2. Construct the official's decision tree diagram, using the proposed payoff measure.
3. What action will maximize the decision maker's expected payoff?

CHAPTER 25

ELEMENTS OF DECISION THEORY

BEFORE READING THIS CHAPTER, MAKE SURE YOU UNDERSTAND:

Basic concepts of probability (Chapter 5).
Subjective probability in decision making (Chapter 20).
Basic concepts of decision analysis (Chapter 24).

AFTER READING THIS CHAPTER, YOU WILL UNDERSTAND:

About criteria commonly employed in reaching a decision under uncertainty.
How the various criteria utilize available information.
About the Bayes decision rule and why it is a favored criterion.
About opportunity losses and how they relate to the Bayes decision rule.
About EVPI and its role in decision making.
About certainty equivalents and their relationship to decision making.

Modern analysis of decision making under uncertainty has its roots in the area of study called **statistical decision theory**. A primary focus of statistical decision theory is establishing systematic means for choosing an act, which is largely accomplished by using the payoff table introduced in Chapter 24. Various **decision-making criteria** may be employed in selecting the best act. The payoff measure itself is a key element in determining rules for decision making, and decision theory encompasses a variety of these measures.

We will begin our discussion of decision theory by examining some of the well-known criteria used in selecting a best act. Then, we will describe **opportunity loss**—a payoff measure that enables us to assess the worth of the *information* that is obtained about uncertain events. Indeed, we use the adjective *statistical* because sampling is a rich source of such information.

For various reasons, we will also see that the Bayes decision rule, which helps the decision maker select the act with the maximum expected payoff, is the favored criterion. The theoretical concepts of decision making largely expand on this rule, since this criterion makes use of all the information at the disposal of the decision maker. When the proper payoff measure is used, the Bayes decision rule always leads to the most desirable choice. The device that makes this possible is the **utility payoff**, which measures a decision maker's preference. **Utility theory** is a special field within the broader context of decision theory.

Although utility payoffs allow decision makers to make consistently optimal choices in the face of *risk*, they rest on a body of behavioral assumptions about which there is some disagreement. However, identical decisions may often be reached by another procedure described in this chapter which finds for each course of action a **certainty equivalent**. These quantities may be obtained by discounting the expected monetary payoff by a **risk premium**.

This chapter surveys decision theory. In later chapters, we will consider more specialized topics. Chapter 26 examines how experimental information may be systematically incorporated into decision making. Chapters 27 and 28 are more statistical in nature; there, specific probability distribution structures are melded with decision-making concepts. Chapter 29 describes utility theory and outlines the practical details of obtaining and using utility values.

25-1 DECISION CRITERIA

THE MAXIMIN PAYOFF CRITERION

No decision-making theory is complete until the decision maker has considered the various rules that may be used in selecting the most desirable act. We will begin with the simplest criterion, the **maximin payoff criterion**—a procedure that guarantees that the decision maker can do no worse than achieve the best of the poorest outcomes possible. As an illustration, we will use the payoff table given in Table 25-1, which represents the toy manufacturer's choices of movement for the Tippi-Toes doll.

Suppose that our toy manufacturer wishes to choose an act that will ensure a favorable outcome no matter what happens. This may be accomplished by taking a pessimistic viewpoint—that is, by determining the *worst* outcome for each act, regardless of the event. For the gears-and-levers movement, the lowest possible payoff is \$25,000 when light demand occurs. The lowest payoff for the spring-action movement is a negative amount, −\$10,000, also obtained when demand

TABLE 25-1 Payoff Table for the Tippi-Toes Decision

Event (demand)	Act (choice of movement)		
	Gears and Levers	Spring Action	Weights and Pulleys
Light	$ 25,000	−$ 10,000	−$125,000
Moderate	400,000	440,000	400,000
Heavy	650,000	740,000	750,000

is light. For the weights-and-pulleys movement, the lowest payoff is −$125,000, again when demand is light. By choosing the act that yields the largest lowest payoff, our decision maker can guarantee a minimum return that is the best of the poorest outcomes possible. In this case, a gears-and-levers movement for the doll will guarantee the toy manufacturer a payoff of at least $25,000.

The gears-and-levers movement is the act with the maximum of the minimum payoffs. A more concise statement would be to say that gears and levers is the **maximin payoff act**. To show how the maximin payoff can be determined in general, we reconstruct the payoff table for the Tippi-Toes decision in Table 25-2.

In most decision-making illustrations so far, we have used profit as the measure of payoff. As we noted in Chapter 24, a variety of measures may be used to rank outcomes. In business applications, *cost* is often used for this purpose when the goal is to minimize operational cost and when revenues are not subject to chance. We can apply the maximin payoff criterion to a situation involving costs by reversing our rule and selecting the act with the minimum of the maximum costs. The comparable terminology for this rule would be **minimax cost**. This criterion is identical to the maximin profit in the sense that cost can be viewed as negative profit, so that what is minimized and maximized must be reversed. Either criterion leads to choosing the best of the poorest outcomes. To avoid confusion, we will always use maximin and minimax as adjectives connected to a noun such as profit or cost.

The suitability of the maximin payoff criterion depends on the nature of the decision to be made. Consider the decision problem in Table 25-3. In this situation, the maximin decision maker chooses A_1 over A_2. A_2 may be a better choice

TABLE 25-2 Determining the Maximin Payoff Act

Event (demand)	Act (choice of movement)		
	Gears and Levers	Spring Action	Weights and Pulleys
Light	$ 25,000	−$ 10,000	−$125,000
Moderate	400,000	440,000	400,000
Heavy	650,000	740,000	750,000
Column minimums	$ 25,000	−$ 10,000	−$125,000

Maximum of column minimums = $25,000
Maximin payoff act = Gears and levers

TABLE 25-3 Determining the Maximin Payoff for Hypothetical Decision A

	Act	
Event	A_1	A_2
E_1	\$0	−\$1
E_2	1	10,000
Column minimum	\$0	−\$1

Maximum of column minimums = \$0
Maximin payoff act = A_1

if the probability of E_2 is high enough, but the maximin decision maker is giving up an opportunity to gain \$10,000 in order to avoid a possible loss of \$1. To avoid losing \$1, the decision maker chooses an act that will guarantee the maintenance of the status quo. We may, however, envision circumstances in which A_1 would be the better choice. If our decision maker had only \$1 and had to use it to pay a debt to a loan shark or lose his life, the payoffs would not realistically represent the true values that the decision maker assigned to them.

Consider the situation represented by the payoffs given in Table 25-4. Here, the maximin payoff act is B_1. This would be the better choice for a decision maker who could not tolerate a loss of \$10,000, no matter how unlikely it was. Few people would risk losing their businesses by choosing an act that could lead to bankruptcy unless the odds were extremely small. But an individual who could survive a loss of \$10,000 would find B_2 a superior choice if the probability of E_2 were substantially lower than E_1.

Our examples illustrate a key deficiency of the maximin payoff: It is an extremely conservative decision criterion and can lead to some very bad decisions. Any alternative with a slightly larger risk is rejected in favor of a comparatively risk-free alternative, which may be far less attractive. Taken to a ludicrous extreme, a maximin payoff policy would force any firm out of business. No inventories would be stocked, because there would always be a possibility of unsold items. No new products would be introduced, because management could never be certain of their success. No credit would be granted, because there would always be some customer who would not pay.

Another major deficiency of the maximin payoff criterion exists if the probabilities of the various events are known. The maximin payoff is primarily suited to decision problems with unknown probabilities that cannot be reasonably assessed. As our illustrations indicate, it is usually in the extreme cases—the

TABLE 25-4 Payoff Table for Hypothetical Decision B

	Act	
Event	B_1	B_2
E_1	\$1	\$10,000
E_2	−1	−10,000

person hounded by loan sharks or the business that could go bankrupt—that the maximin payoff criterion leads to the best decision.

THE MAXIMUM LIKELIHOOD CRITERION

Another rule that serves as a model for decision-making behavior is the **maximum likelihood criterion**, which focuses on the most likely event, to the exclusion of all others. Table 25-5 illustrates this criterion for the Tippi-Toes toy manufacturer's decision.

For this decision, we may see that the highest probability is .70 for a moderate demand. The maximum likelihood criterion tells us to ignore the light and heavy demand events completely—in effect, to assume that they will not occur. This rule then tells us to choose the best act assuming that a moderate demand will occur. In this example, the **maximum likelihood act** is to use the spring-action doll movement, which provides the greatest profit of $440,000 for a moderate demand.

How suitable is the maximum likelihood criterion for decision making? Using it in this example does not permit us to consider the range of outcomes for the spring-action movement, from a $10,000 loss if a light demand occurs to a $740,000 profit if demand is heavy. We also ignore most of the other possible outcomes, including the best (selecting weights and pulleys when demand is heavy, which yields a $750,000 profit) and the worst (selecting weights and pulleys when demand is light, which leads to a $125,000 loss). In a sense, the maximum likelihood criterion would have us "play ostrich," ignoring much that might happen. Then why is it discussed here?

ILLUSTRATION: EXPLAINING THE HOG CYCLE

We describe this criterion primarily because it seems to be so prevalent in the decision-making behavior of individuals and businesses. It may also be used to explain certain anomalies that would otherwise be hard to rationalize. These quirks are epitomized by the so-called "hog cycle" in the raising and marketing of pigs, which is related to the more or less predictable two-year-long pork price movement from higher to lower levels and back to higher levels again. Hog farmers have been blamed for this, since they expand their herds when prices are high, so that one year later the supply of mature hogs is excessive and prices are driven

TABLE 25-5 Determining the Maximum Likelihood Act

Event (demand)	Probability	Act (choice of movement)		
		Gears and Levers	Spring Action	Weights and Pulleys
Light	.10	$ 25,000	−$ 10,000	−$125,000
Moderate	.70	400,000	440,000	400,000
Heavy	.20	650,000	740,000	750,000

Most likely event = Moderate demand
Maximum row payoff = $440,000
Maximum likelihood act = Spring action

downward; then when prices are low, these same farmers reduce their herds, cutting the supply of marketable hogs, and next year's prices consequently rise.

Why don't the farmers break this cycle? It doesn't seem rational to be consistently wrong in timing hog production. One explanation is that the hog farmers use the maximum likelihood criterion. In their minds, the most likely future market price is the current one—and we know that this has proved to be a very poor judgment. Given such a premise, the maximum likelihood act is to increase herd sizes when current prices are high and to decrease them when prices are low.

THE CRITERION OF INSUFFICIENT REASON

Another criterion employed in decision-making problems is the **criterion of insufficient reason**. This criterion may be used when a decision maker has no information about the event probabilities. In this case, no event may be regarded as more likely than any other event, and all events are assigned equal probability values. Since the events are collectively exhaustive and mutually exclusive, the probability of each event must be

$$\frac{1}{\text{Number of events}}$$

Using these event probabilities, the act with the maximum expected payoff is chosen.

A major criticism of the criterion of insufficient reason is that, except in a few situations, some knowledge of the relative chances that events will occur is always available. When more realistic probabilities can be obtained, employing the Bayes decision rule will provide more valid results.

THE PREFERRED CRITERION: THE BAYES DECISION RULE

The three decision-making criteria just discussed have obvious inadequacies. *None of them incorporates all of the information available to the decision maker.* Maximin payoff totally ignores event probabilities. Although it is argued that this is a strength when probabilities cannot be easily determined, judgment may be used to arrive at acceptable probability values in all but a few circumstances.

The maximum likelihood criterion ignores all events but the most likely one, even if that event happens to be a lot less likely than the rest combined. (Out of 20 events, for instance, the most likely event may have a probability of .10, leaving a .90 probability that one of the other 19 events will occur.)

The criterion of insufficient reason essentially asks us to ignore judgments and "willy nilly" assume that all events are equally likely. According to this criterion, even such events as "war" and "peace," and "prosperity" and "depression," have equal probabilities.

The **Bayes decision rule** has become the central focus of statistical decision theory. This makes the greatest use of all available information and is the only criterion that allows us to extend decision theory to incorporate sampling or experimental information. The major deficiency of the Bayes decision rule occurs when alternatives involve different magnitudes of risk. To illustrate this point, we will consider the decision structure in Table 25-6. Acts C_1 and C_2 are equally attractive according to the maximum expected payoff criterion (Bayes decision

TABLE 25-6 Payoff Table for Hypothetical Decision C

Event	Probability	Act C_1		Act C_2	
		Payoff	Payoff × Probability	Payoff	Payoff × Probability
E_1	.5	−$1,000,000	−$ 500,000	$250,000	$125,000
E_2	.5	2,000,000	1,000,000	750,000	375,000
Expected payoff			$ 500,000		$500,000

rule). Yet most decision makers would clearly prefer C_2, because it avoids the rather large risk of a $1,000,000 loss.

EXERCISES

25-1 You have decided to participate in a gamble that offers the following monetary payoffs.

Event	Act	
	Choose Red	Choose Black
Red	$1	−$ 2
Black	−1	100

(a) Which act is the maximin payoff act?
(b) Supposing that the probability of red is .99, calculate the expected payoffs for each act. Which act is better according to the Bayes decision rule? Which act would you choose?
(c) Supposing that the probability of red is .5, calculate the expected payoffs for each act. Which act has the maximum expected payoff? Which act would you choose?
(d) In view of your answers to (b) and (c), what is your opinion of the maximin payoff decision criterion in this case?

25-2 A decision maker must choose one of three acts. The payoff table and the event probabilities are provided below.

Event	Probability	Act		
		A_1	A_2	A_3
E_1	.3	$10	$15	$20
E_2	.4	15	20	15
E_3	.3	25	15	15

(a) Which act is the maximin payoff act?
(b) Which act is the maximum likelihood act?
(c) Calculate the expected payoffs. According to the Bayes decision rule, which act should be chosen?

25-3 Rich Sod is a farmer who intends to sign a contract to provide a cannery with his entire crop. Rich must choose to produce one of the following five vegetables: corn, tomatoes, beets, asparagus, or cauliflower. Rich will plant his entire 1,000 acres with the selected crop. The yields of these vegetables will be affected by the weather to varying degrees. The following table indicates the approximate productivities for each vegetable in dry, moderate, and damp weather and also lists the price per bushel that the cannery has offered for each crop.

	Approximate Yield (bushels per acre)				
Weather	**Corn**	**Tomatoes**	**Beets**	**Asparagus**	**Cauliflower**
Dry	20	10	15	30	40
Moderate	35	20	20	25	40
Damp	40	10	30	20	40
Price per bushel	$1.00	$2.00	$1.50	$1.00	$.50

(a) Using as the payoff measure the approximate total cash receipts when the crop is sold, construct the payoff table for the farmer's decision.
(b) Identify any inadmissible acts and eliminate them from the payoff table.
(c) Which act is the maximin payoff act?
(d) Suppose that the following probabilities have been assigned to the types of weather. Calculate the expected payoff for each act; then identify the act that has the maximum expected payoff.

Weather	Probability
Dry	.3
Moderate	.5
Damp	.2

25-4 A newsdealer must decide how many copies of *Snappy Almanac* to stock in December. She will not stock less than the lowest possible demand or more than the highest possible demand. Each magazine costs her $.50 and sells for $1.00. At the end of the month the unsold magazines are thrown away. Three levels of monthly demand are equally likely: 10, 11, and 12. If demand exceeds stock, sales will equal stock.
(a) Using December profit as the payoff measure, construct the newsdealer's payoff table.
(b) According to the maximin criterion, how many copies should she stock?
(c) Which number of copies will provide the greatest expected payoff?

25-2 OPPORTUNITY LOSS AND THE EXPECTED VALUE OF PERFECT INFORMATION

Is it worthwhile to buy information that may help us choose the best act? Information is usually not free. Resources, for example, are required to take a sample or to administer a test. In this section, we will attempt to place a value on such information. To do this, we will introduce the concept of opportunity loss.

TABLE 25-7 Determining the Opportunity Losses for the Tippi-Toes Decision

Demand Event	Payoff			Row Maximum
	Gears and Levers	Spring Action	Weights and Pulleys	
Light	$ 25,000	−$ 10,000	−$125,000	$ 25,000
Moderate	400,000	440,000	400,000	440,000
Heavy	650,000	740,000	750,000	750,000
	Row maximum − Payoff = Opportunity loss (thousands of dollars)			
Light	25 − 25 = 0	25 − (−10) = 35	25 − (−125) = 150	
Moderate	440 − 400 = 40	440 − 440 = 0	440 − 400 = 40	
Heavy	750 − 650 = 100	750 − 740 = 10	750 − 750 = 0	

OPPORTUNITY LOSS

Suppose that we view each possible outcome in terms of a measure that expresses the difference between the payoff for the chosen act and the best payoff that could have been achieved.

DEFINITION: The **opportunity loss** for an outcome is the amount of payoff that is foregone by not selecting the act that has the greatest payoff for the event that actually occurs.

Table 25-7 shows how the opportunity losses are obtained for the payoffs for the toy manufacturer's decision. To calculate the opportunity losses, the maximum payoff for each row is determined. Each payoff is then subtracted from its respective row maximum.

The **opportunity loss table** for the Tippi-Toes decision appears in Table 25-8. All opportunity loss values are non-negative, since they measure how much worse off the decision maker is made by choosing some act other than the best act for the event that occurs. Let us consider the meaning of the opportunity loss values. For example, suppose that the gears-and-levers movement is chosen and that a light demand occurs. The opportunity loss is zero, because we see from Table 25-7 that no better payoff than $25,000 (the row maximum) could have been achieved if another act had been chosen. But if the gears-and-levers movement is chosen and a heavy demand occurs, the opportunity loss is $100,000, because the weights-and-pulleys movement has the greatest payoff for a heavy demand

TABLE 25-8 Opportunity Loss Table for the Tippi-Toes Decision

Event (demand)	Act (choice of movement)		
	Gears and Levers	Spring Action	Weights and Pulleys
Light	$ 0	$35,000	$150,000
Moderate	40,000	0	40,000
Heavy	100,000	10,000	0

($750,000). Since the gears-and-levers movement has a payoff of only $650,000, the payoff difference $750,000 − $650,000 = $100,000 represents the additional payoff foregone by not selecting the act with the greatest payoff. It should be emphasized that the $100,000 opportunity loss is not a loss in the accounting sense, because a net positive contribution of $650,000 to profits is obtained. Instead, the opportunity to achieve an additional $100,000 has been missed. We might say that should demand prove to be heavy, the decision maker would have $100,000 worth of *regret* by not choosing weights and pulleys instead of gears and levers.

THE BAYES DECISION RULE AND OPPORTUNITY LOSS

We can calculate the expected opportunity loss for each act and then select the act that has the minimum loss. This is done in Table 25-9 for the Tippi-Toes decision. The minimum expected opportunity loss is $5,500 for the spring-action movement, which is the *minimum expected opportunity loss act* in this example.

In Chapter 24, we saw that the spring-action movement was also the maximum expected payoff act and was therefore the best choice according to the Bayes decision rule. Our new criterion leads us to the same choice. It can be mathematically established that this will always be so. Since either criterion will always lead to the same choice, we can say that the *Bayes decision rule is to select the act that has the maximum expected payoff or the minimum expected opportunity loss.*

THE EXPECTED VALUE OF PERFECT INFORMATION

Up to this point, our toy manufacturer has selected an act without the benefit of any information except that acquired through experience with other toys. But it is possible to secure better information about next season's demand by test marketing, by taking opinion and attitude surveys, or by obtaining inside information concerning competitors' plans. How much should the decision maker be willing to pay for additional information?

It is helpful to know the payoff that may be expected from securing improved information about the events. We will consider the extreme case when the decision maker may acquire **perfect information**. Using the information, the decision maker may guarantee the selection of the act that yields the greatest payoff for whatever event actually occurs. Because we wish to investigate the worth of such

TABLE 25-9 Calculation of Expected Opportunity Losses for the Tippi-Toes Decision

		Gears and Levers		Spring Action		Weights and Pulleys	
Demand Event	Probability	Loss	Loss × Probability	Loss	Loss × Probability	Loss	Loss × Probability
Light	.10	$ 0	$ 0	$35,000	$3,500	$150,000	$15,000
Moderate	.70	40,000	28,000	0	0	40,000	28,000
Heavy	.20	100,000	20,000	10,000	2,000	0	0
Expected opportunity loss			$48,000		$5,500		$43,000

information *before* it is obtained, we will determine the **expected payoff with perfect information**.

To calculate the expected payoff with perfect information, we determine the highest payoff for each event. This is illustrated for the Tippi-Toes decision in Table 25-10. The maximum payoff for each demand level is determined by finding the largest payoff in each row. Thus, for a light demand, we find that choosing the gears-and-levers movement yields the largest payoff ($25,000). If perfect information indicated that light demand was certain to occur, our decision maker would choose this movement. Similarly $440,000 is the maximum payoff possible for moderate demand, and this amount may be achieved only if the spring-action movement is chosen. Likewise, $750,000 is the maximum possible payoff when a heavy demand occurs, and this amount corresponds to a choice of the weights-and-pulleys movement. The last column of Table 25-10 shows the products of the maximum payoffs and their respective event probabilities. Summing these, we obtain $460,500 as the expected payoff with perfect information. This figure represents the average payoff if the toy manufacturer were faced with the same situation repeatedly and always selected the act that yielded the best payoff for the event indicated by the perfect information. Keep in mind that the $460,500 represents the expected payoff viewed from some point in time *before* the information becomes available. *After* the information has been obtained, exactly one of the payoffs, $25,000, $440,000, or $750,000, is bound to occur. When the information is actually obtained, the payoff is a certainty.

We may now answer the question regarding the worth of perfect information to the decision maker. As we have seen, the Bayes decision rule leads to the choice of the particular act that maximizes the expected payoff without regard to any additional information. Since this is the best act that our decision maker may select without any new information, and since the expected payoff with perfect information is the average payoff that may be anticipated with the best possible information, the worth of perfect information to the decision maker is expressed by the difference between these two amounts. We call the resulting number the **expected value of perfect information**, which is conveniently represented by the abbreviation EVPI.

EXPECTED VALUE OF PERFECT INFORMATION

EVPI = Expected payoff with perfect information
− Maximum expected payoff (with no information)

For the toy manufacturer's decision, we obtain the EVPI by subtracting the maximum expected payoff of $455,000 (calculated in Table 24-6 on page 972) from the expected payoff with perfect information of $460,500.

$$\text{EVPI} = \$460{,}500 - \$455{,}000 = \$5{,}500$$

In this case, the EVPI represents the greatest amount of money that the decision maker would be willing to pay to obtain perfect information about what the

TABLE 25-10 Calculation of the Expected Payoff with Perfect Information for the Tippi-Toes Decision

		Act			With Perfect Information		
Event	**Probability**	**Gears and Levers**	**Spring Action**	**Weights and Pulleys**	**Maximum Payoff**	**Chosen Act**	**Payoff × Probability**
Light	.10	$ 25,000	−$ 10,000	−$125,000	$ 25,000	G&L	$ 2,500
Moderate	.70	400,000	440,000	400,000	440,000	SA	308,000
Heavy	.20	650,000	740,000	750,000	750,000	W&P	150,000
						Expected payoff with perfect information =	$460,500

demand will be. Stated differently, $5,500 is the increase in the decision maker's expected payoff that may be attributed to perfect knowledge of demand. Both $455,000 and $460,500 are meaningless values *after* the perfect information is obtained. Thus, the EVPI of $5,500 may be interpreted only *before* the perfect information has become known.

EVPI AND OPPORTUNITY LOSS

Note that $5,500 is the same amount as the minimum expected opportunity loss calculated in Table 25-9. Thus, we see that *the expected value of perfect information is equal to the expected opportunity loss for the optimal act.*

Therefore, we may calculate the expected value of perfect information by calculating the expected opportunity losses. The minimum loss is then the EVPI. Table 25-11 summarizes the relationship between expected payoff, expected opportunity loss, and expected value of perfect information for the toy manufacturer's decision. Note that for any act, the sum of the expected payoff and the expected opportunity loss is equal to the expected payoff with perfect information.

Since perfect information is nonexistent in most real-world decision making, why are we interested in the EVPI? Our answer is that it helps to establish a limit on the worth of less-than-perfect information. For example, if a marketing research study aimed at predicting demand costs $6,000, which exceeds the EVPI by $500, the study should not be conducted, regardless of its quality. We will investigate the concepts involved in decision making with experimental information further in Chapter 26.

TABLE 25-11 Relationships between EVPI, Expected Payoff, and Opportunity Loss

	Gears and Levers	**Spring Action**	**Weights and Pulleys**
Expected payoff	$412,500	$455,000	$417,500
Expected opportunity loss	48,000	5,500	43,000
Expected payoff with perfect information	$460,500	$460,500	$460,500
Expected value of perfect information (EVPI) = $5,500		↑ Optimal act	

EXERCISES

25-5 Use the payoff table below to construct an opportunity loss table.

		Act				
Event	**Probability**	A_1	A_2	A_3	A_4	A_5
E_1	.2	10	20	10	15	20
E_2	.2	−5	10	−5	10	−5
E_3	.6	15	5	10	10	10

Compute the expected opportunity loss for each act. Which act yields the lowest expected opportunity loss?

25-6 Answer the following questions based on the payoff table below.

		Act		
Event	**Probability**	A_1	A_2	A_3
E_1	.3	10	20	30
E_2	.5	40	−10	20
E_3	.2	20	50	20

(a) What is the maximum expected payoff? To which act does this payoff correspond?
(b) What is the expected payoff with perfect information?
(c) Using your answers to (a) and (b), calculate the expected value of perfect information.
(d) What is the minimum expected opportunity loss?
(e) What do you notice about your answers to (c) and (d)?

25-7 B. F. Retread, a tire manufacturer, wishes to select one of three feasible prototype designs for a new longer-wearing radial tire. The costs of making the tires are given below.

Tire	Fixed Cost	Variable Cost per Unit
A	\$ 60,000	\$30
B	90,000	20
C	120,000	15

There are three levels of unit sales: 4,000 units, 7,000 units, and 10,000 units; the respective probabilities are .30, .50, and .20. The selling price will be \$75 per tire.
(a) Construct the payoff table using total profit as the payoff measure.
(b) Determine the expected payoff for each act. According to the Bayes decision rule, which is the best act?
(c) Calculate the EVPI.
(d) Complete the opportunity loss table and compute the expected opportunity losses.

25-8 Rod Shafter is an oil wildcatter who must decide whether to drill on a candidate drilling site. His judgment leads him to conclude that there is a

50–50 chance of oil. If the wildcatter drills and strikes oil, his profit will be \$200,000. But if the well turns out to be dry, his net loss will be \$100,000.

(a) According to the Bayes decision rule, should Rod drill or abandon the site?

(b) What is Rod's EVPI?

(c) A seismologist offers to conduct a highly reliable seismic survey. The results could help the wildcatter make his decision. What is the most that Rod would consider paying for such seismic information?

25-3 ADVANTAGES AND LIMITATIONS OF THE BAYES DECISION RULE

Decision theory is useful because it shows how we might uncover that course of action which is truly preferred by the decision maker. There is no fail-safe system for achieving this goal. All decision criteria have imperfections.

Of the several criteria presented in this chapter, the **Bayes decision rule**—select that act having maximum expected payoff—appears to be most suitable. One advantage is that it makes use of more information than the others. As we have seen, a criterion based on expected values uses all the available probability data and assigns the proper weight to every outcome. The other decision-making criteria employ fewer structural elements from the decision. Expected values also provide us with a gauge for evaluating additional sources of information that may be used in decision making.

Consistently applied to routine day-to-day decisions, each of which involves little risk, the Bayes decision rule should lead to the best overall results. For example, envision a buyer for the magazine department in a high-volume bookstore. If the buyer always selects that order quantity for each magazine that maximizes its expected profit, then over the long haul the buyer will tend to experience higher average profits from the dozens of titles than what would be achievable using any other set of choices. (This conclusion may be reached only by assuming that demand probabilities used are correct values. There is no way to guarantee that, although in Chapter 20 we saw how the best available expertise may be employed to find workable probability values.)

Maximizing expected payoff has wide acceptance because it so often picks the course of action preferred by the decision maker. But this is not always the case. When applied to *monetary* payoffs, the Bayes decision rule often leads to a less preferred choice.

Perhaps the best example of this occurs in casualty insurance decisions, where the choices are to buy or not to buy a policy. Most drivers have liability insurance for their cars, and most carry greater coverage than the legal minimum. We know that the policyholder's annual insurance costs exceed the expected loss from an accident. (This is because insurance companies must charge more than what they expect to pay in claims just to meet overhead costs and expenses.) But according to the Bayes decision rule, the best decision would be not to insure, because no insurance would have a greater expected monetary payoff (that is, the expected cost of no insurance is less than the cost of insurance). This course of action contradicts the true preference of most people.

Similar breakdowns of the Bayes decision rule occur whenever a person prefers a less risky alternative to one that involves considerable risk but actually has a greater expected monetary payoff. Since other decision-making criteria have serious defects, too, how should we objectively analyze decisions that involve great risk?

Fortunately, *decision theory accounts for attitudes toward risk by permitting an adjustment in the payoff values themselves.* This is accomplished by establishing a true-worth index called a *utility value* for every outcome. Thus, a decision may be analyzed using utilities instead of dollars or some other standard payoff measure.

In Chapter 29, we will describe the theory of utility and its application in great detail. One very important principle will be established there: *When the Bayes decision rule is applied to a decision-making problem with utility payoffs, it always indicates the most preferred course of action.* This makes that rule the theoretically perfect criterion for decision making, no matter how complex the decision happens to be.

EXERCISES

25-9 You have been invited to participate in a lottery in which the payoff is determined by a coin toss. If a head is obtained, you receive \$10,000. Otherwise, you must forfeit \$5,000 (or sign a long-term note at the current interest rate).

(a) Would you be willing to participate?

(b) If your answer to (a) is *yes*, what is the least amount for which you would be willing to sell your rights to participate in the gamble? If your answer to (a) is *no*, and supposing that it is mandatory for you to participate, would you then pay \$100 for a release from that obligation? What is the most you would be willing to pay?

(c) What is the expected payoff from the gamble? In view of your response to (b), what can you conclude about blindly applying the Bayes decision rule?

25-10 Shirley Smart drives a 1979 Toyota Corolla with 147,234 miles and a few major dents. Although she has no comprehensive insurance, she is interested in buying a special theft policy that would give her \$1,000 (the replacement value) if her car were stolen. She judges that the probability of losing her car to theft in any given year to be 1/200.

(a) What would be Shirley Smart's expected theft loss by remaining uninsured?

(b) Shirley would be willing to pay \$10 per year for the insurance. According to the strictest interpretation of the Bayes decision rule, should she buy or not buy the insurance at that price?

(c) Clunkers Insurance Company will sell Shirley a policy for \$9 per year. Should she buy the insurance?

25-4 DECISION MAKING USING CERTAINTY EQUIVALENTS

The key issue in evaluating any decision under uncertainty is finding a summary number that clearly indicates for each choice its worth to the decision maker. A little introspection may be all that is required.

Suppose, for example, that you find a lottery ticket selected for a special drawing with a grand prize of $10,000. You may sell your ticket to a broker for cash now or you may wait for tomorrow's drawing; your chance of winning the prize has been judged to be only 1%, and you will get nothing if you lose. Think hard about your answer to this question: What is the minimum amount of money you would take now from the broker for your ticket? Write this amount on a piece of paper.

Of course, there is no "right" answer, since the amount depends upon your attitudes, needs, and preferences. Many people would sell for about $100, although some would want more and a few would settle for less. Your minimum selling price is your **certainty equivalent** for the act of keeping the lottery ticket. Once you have this number, it should be easy to decide what to do with the lottery ticket.

Suppose that the broker offers $75. Your choice would be easy. If your minimum selling price is greater than $75, you should keep the ticket and wait for the drawing; if your minimum selling price is smaller than $75, you should sell; and if your selected amount is exactly $75, you should be indifferent between selling and keeping the ticket.

This example illustrates how good decision making involves a fundamental valuation of uncertainties. In generalizing this concept, we will make the following

DEFINITION: The **certainty equivalent** is that payoff amount that the decision maker would be willing to receive in exchange for undergoing the actual uncertainty, with its rewards and risks.

A certainty equivalent may be positive or negative. For example, imagine a decision regarding whether or not to insure your luggage against total loss while you make a long airplane trip. You may be willing to pay $5 for complete protection; your certainty equivalent for the act *not* to insure would then be −$5. If such insurance could be bought for $2, you would get it; were the premium $10, you would forgo it.

The certainty equivalent is a personal valuation, and need not be tied to an actual exchange. There may be no broker willing to buy your lottery ticket at any price, and there may be no luggage insurance available. Nevertheless, your certainty equivalents still exist; they reflect the certain amount you would be willing to exchange, were such an opportunity to be made available.

DECISION RULE: CHOOSE THE GREATEST CERTAINTY EQUIVALENT

The hypothetical lottery ticket illustrates how we may evaluate a decision using certainty equivalents. Applied to a single-stage decision, with a structure summarized by a payoff table, the first step would be to find a certainty equivalent for each act (column). The optimal choice would be to select that act having the greatest certainty equivalent.

As we have seen, some decisions require a more complex structural representation. These are best represented by a decision tree diagram. To find the best course of action in such decisions, the tree must be pruned at each decision point. This may be accomplished by finding a certainty equivalent for each act in the fork, pruning all branches but the one leading to the greatest certainty equivalent.

The justification for such an approach is compelling. By selecting that act having the greatest certainty equivalent, you are simply picking the biggest certain amount available. This cannot be the wrong thing to do (in the sense of doing what you most prefer). Of course, decision makers will want to establish their certainty equivalents in a *consistent* manner. That is the hard part.

FINDING THE CERTAINTY EQUIVALENT

You were able to pull "from thin air" your certainty equivalent for keeping the lottery ticket. This may be considerably harder for you to do in deciding what amount you would accept in lieu of the right (or obligation) to participate in a different kind of gamble, one involving the same upside potential (+\$10,000, if you win) but with a downside (−\$1,000, if you lose). Your certainty equivalent should depend on the probabilities for winning or losing. At a 10% chance of winning, you would value the gamble differently than if the odds were more favorable.

The less clear-cut uncertainties involve a mixture of positive and negative payoffs and probabilities that may be hard to relate to. As we have seen, the expected payoff calculation integrates all available information in a neat package. For uncertain situations with a limited range of payoffs, many people will assign a certainty equivalent which turns out to be close to the expected payoff.

To see how this works, consider the following gambles. The payoff amounts represent your net monetary change, and the lottery probabilities are given in parentheses.

Lottery *A*		Lottery *B*		Coin Gamble *C*		Card Drawing *D*	
Win	+\$10(80%)	Win	+\$100(60%)	Head	+\$100	Face	+\$100
Lose	−\$10(20%)	Lose	− \$50(40%)	Tail	−\$100	Other	\$0

Write on a piece of paper your certainty equivalents for each gamble. Then, compute the respective expected payoffs.*

How do the two sets of amounts compare? You may want to revise some of your certainty equivalents. (Changing your mind is permissible in any evaluation involving these subjective values.)

Discrepancies between certainty equivalents and expected payoffs will ordinarily be substantial when the payoffs are large in magnitude or have great extremes. (To see this, just add a couple of zeroes to the payoffs in the above gambles, so that the outcomes involve thousands of dollars, and rethink your certainty equivalents.)

Experiments show that it is much easier for a person to arrive at a certainty equivalent for an act by first computing its expected payoff. That amount may then be adjusted up or down until the subject feels comfortable that the resulting figure is a satisfactory certainty equivalent. These experiments show that the most pronounced adjustments arise when there is a mixture of high-valued positive and negative payoffs, with the certainty equivalent for such risky acts ordinarily being smaller than the expected payoff.

*These are \$6 for *A*, \$40 for *B*, \$0 for *C*, and \$23.08 for *D*.

This should be no surprise. Consider the amount you are paying for collision and comprehensive insurance for your car. If you have a fairly new car, you undoubtedly have such coverage. Now consider what you may expect to collect in claims against your policy. Whatever that amount is, your insurance company has already figured it out and has priced your insurance accordingly. They must be charging more than they expect to pay in claims, perhaps double or more. (Otherwise, how could they meet operating expenses and earn a profit?) And yet, you still buy that "overpriced" coverage and may continue to buy it even if your rates were suddenly increased. The maximum premium you would be *willing to pay* is your certainty equivalent for that car risk.

Lots of people have no collision or comprehensive coverage. But they drive old cars, and have little to lose if their car is stolen and totaled by a wild teenager. But even they would buy insurance if it were cheap enough.

THE RISK PREMIUM

The difference between the expected payoff and the certainty equivalent for any act is the **risk premium** for that act. For example, consider again the lost luggage risk discussed earlier. Suppose that it would cost you \$300 to replace your baggage and contents, and that there is a 1% chance that you would lose everything. (For simplicity, we will ignore partial losses.) Your expected payoff from having no insurance would be

$$\text{Expected payoff} = (-\$300)(.01) + (\$0)(.99) = -\$3$$

Suppose that your certainty equivalent is − \$5. (That is, the maximum you would be willing to pay for complete replacement insurance is \$5.)

Your risk premium for the act of not insuring is computed as follows.

$$\begin{aligned}\text{Risk premium} &= \text{Expected payoff} - \text{Certainty equivalent}\\ &= -\$3 - (-\$5) = \$2\end{aligned}$$

The \$2 risk premium represents the amount you are willing to pay for insurance beyond what your expected loss would be. Generally, the more serious the risk, the greater would be the risk premium.

To further illustrate this concept, suppose you win as a door prize the privilege of engaging in a special lottery. If you participate, a fair coin will be tossed. Should a head appear, you will receive \$1,000; if a tail is obtained, you must forfeit \$500. (An easy-payment loan will be arranged if you do not have the \$500.) One of your friends wants to buy the right to gamble. What would be your asking price (certainty equivalent for gambling)?

The expected payoff from gambling is

$$\text{Expected payoff} = (\$1{,}000)(.5) + (-\$500)(.50) = \$250$$

Shirley Smart said she would sell for \$100, so that for her,

$$\text{Certainty equivalent} = \$100$$

and

$$\text{Risk premium} = \$250 - 100 = \$150 \quad \text{(Shirley Smart)}$$

This indicates that Shirley is considerably risk averse, willing to accept $150 less than her expected payoff to avoid the risk of gambling.

Willy B. Rich said he would take $200 for his rights. For him,

$$\text{Certainty equivalent} = \$200$$

and

$$\text{Risk premium} = \$250 - 200 = \$50 \quad \text{(Willy B. Rich)}$$

Willy has a higher certainty equivalent than Shirley does, and his risk premium is therefore smaller. He is less risk averse than she is.

As a positive quantity, the risk premium may be interpreted as the amount by which the subject would discount the expected payoff in arriving at his or her certainty equivalent. Sometimes a risk premium will turn out negative, which would be the case when a person is so attracted to the highest positive payoff that his certainty equivalent for the gamble exceeds the expected payoff. (The absolute value of a negative risk premium is the individual's "aspiration incentive"—that amount in excess of the expected payoff that must be received in exchange for the gamble.) Negative risk premiums are less common than positive values, and they are not ordinarily encountered in business decision making.

DISCOUNTING EXPECTED VALUES BY THE RISK PREMIUMS

For business decision making the direct approach is a clumsy way to arrive at certainty equivalents. A more workable alternative is to first compute, for each act, the expected value. The certainty equivalent for any act may be viewed as that act's *discounted* expected payoff, so that the certainty equivalent may be found by subtracting the appropriate risk premium from the expected payoff.

$$\text{Certainty equivalent} = \text{Expected payoff} - \text{Risk premium}$$

What makes this approach practical is that risk premiums are easily found. Since a single amount would be appropriate for a wide class of risks, a table of risk premiums may be established ahead of time. These may be applied as required to evaluate a series of decisions. The risk premium table may be periodically updated as circumstances change.

The selection of any act having uncertain payoff and possible loss involves risk. The seriousness of the risk may be gauged by two components: (1) the amount of loss (downside potential) and (2) the probability of loss. Experiments with people show that these two components are the primary determinants of the risk premium used in discounting expected payoff.

The entire adjustment is motivated by the loss and its likelihood. Subjects experiencing two gambles with the same downside will tend to have nearly the same risk premiums for both. For example, consider the following.

Coin Toss *A*		**Coin Toss *B***	
Head	$0	Head	+$1,000
Tail	−$500	Tail	−$500

One subject arrived at a risk premium of $100 each for gambles *A* and *B*, even though his certainty equivalents (discounted expected payoffs) of course differed.

	A	B
Expected payoff	−\$250	+\$250
Less risk premium	100	100
Certainty equivalent	−\$350	+\$150

Raising the loss probability in any gamble would increase the risk and should therefore result in a higher risk premium. Similarly, a greater downside potential, reflected in a more extreme negative payoff amount, would increase the risk and, thus, the risk premium.

Not all uncertain situations involve risk. Risk is not present unless there is a downside and some probability of ending there. For example, a coin toss where "heads you win \$100" and "tails you only win \$50" has no risk. For most persons, the risk premium would be zero for such an ideal gamble. They would not discount the expected payoff at all, so that it would equal their certainty equivalent.

ILLUSTRATION: PONDEROSA RECORD COMPANY

The Ponderosa Record Company decision in Chapter 24 illustrates how certainty equivalents, obtained by discounting expected payoffs, may be used in evaluating decisions. A consultant begins this process by obtaining a few risk premiums. These are found by interviewing the president, having him provide assessments for a few relevant risks.

Recording Equipment

Ponderosa's recording equipment has a replacement value of \$100,000. The president is asked what he would be willing to pay Lloyd's of London for full coverage against total loss of equipment due to flood, fire, or other natural disaster. To simplify this assessment, it is assumed that there is a 1% chance of such an occurrence in any given year. Because such a loss could wipe the company out, the president indicates a willingness to pay up to \$2,500 for such a policy. The consultant then computes the expected payoff from not having such insurance as

$$\text{Expected payoff} = (\$0)(.99) + (-\$100{,}000)(.01) = -\$1{,}000$$

The certainty equivalent is − \$2,500, and the difference between these amounts provides the

$$\text{Risk premium} = -\$1{,}000 - (-\$2{,}500) = \$1{,}500 \quad \text{(equipment)}$$

Earthquake Damage

The decision maker owns a home valued at \$200,000 that is fully insured against fire and flood, but not earthquake. The consultant brings up the idea of earthquake damage. He presents a scenario where a high-energy earthquake may cause such severe damage to his home and the neighborhood that its market value would be lost. The president is informed of one geologist who reported that an earthquake of that magnitude may be expected in his region once every thousand or so years. After some introspection, the president reluctantly agreed that he would feel comfortable with earthquake insurance and would pay up to \$500 for full coverage.

His certainty equivalent for that risk is − $500. Using a probability of .001 for total loss of his home value, the following

$$\text{Expected payoff} = \$0(.999) + (-\$200{,}000)(.001) = -\$200$$

would apply to not having insurance for the year. The difference in the two amounts gives for this risk the president's

$$\text{Risk premium} = -\ \$200 - (-\$500) = \$300 \quad \text{(earthquake)}$$

REAL ESTATE PARTNERSHIP

The president confesses to the consultant the details of a regretted investment involving $50,000 placed in a real estate limited partnership. The partnership has spent its entire capital on an option to buy for resale a piece of land. If the city council approves the buyer's building permit application, the partnership will receive enough proceeds to return the president a profit of $100,000. If the permit is refused, the option will be worthless and the entire investment will be lost. Both of the above monetary amounts are after-tax figures. There has been much anti-growth agitation lately, and there is only a 50–50 chance that the permit will be approved. (These odds are far worse than those which applied when he joined the partnership.)

The consultant suggests that another partner may offer to buy the president's partnership share now for the original stake plus a negotiated amount. The president decides that he would take no less than his investment plus an after-tax equivalent of $15,000, which becomes his certainty equivalent for staying in the partnership. That act has an expected payoff of

$$(-\$50{,}000)(.50) + (\$100{,}000)(.50) = \$25{,}000$$

and the difference provides his

$$\text{Risk premium} = \$25{,}000 - 15{,}000 = \$10{,}000 \quad \text{(partnership)}$$

TABLE OF RISK PREMIUMS

The amounts obtained above are highlighted in Table 25-12, which shows the risk premiums for a variety of losses and probabilities of loss. Since the seriousness of a risk increases as the loss magnitude rises, the risk premiums get larger as you move down each column. Likewise, the risk is higher as the probability for

TABLE 25-12 Risk Premiums for the President of Ponderosa Record Company

Nearest Possible Loss	Nearest Probability of Loss					
	.001	.01	.1	.20	.50	.75
$ 5,000	0	0	0	100	200	400
20,000	0	500	800	1,500	3,000	5,000
50,000	0	1,000	2,000	4,000	10,000	15,000
100,000	100	1,500	4,000	8,000	17,000	20,000
200,000	300	4,000	9,000	15,000	30,000	35,000

loss increases, so that in each row the risk premiums become progressively larger as you move from left to right.

Only the three "hard" numbers, highlighted in Table 25-12, were directly obtained from the subject. The remaining risk premiums are extrapolations that seem to fit into the president's risk premium "profile." After examining a rough draft of Table 25-12, the president changed only a few values from the consultant's original figures.

DECISION TREE ANALYSIS

The consultant reevaluated Ponderosa's decision tree, using certainty equivalents as the basis for selecting acts. Figure 25-1 shows the decision tree diagram. The

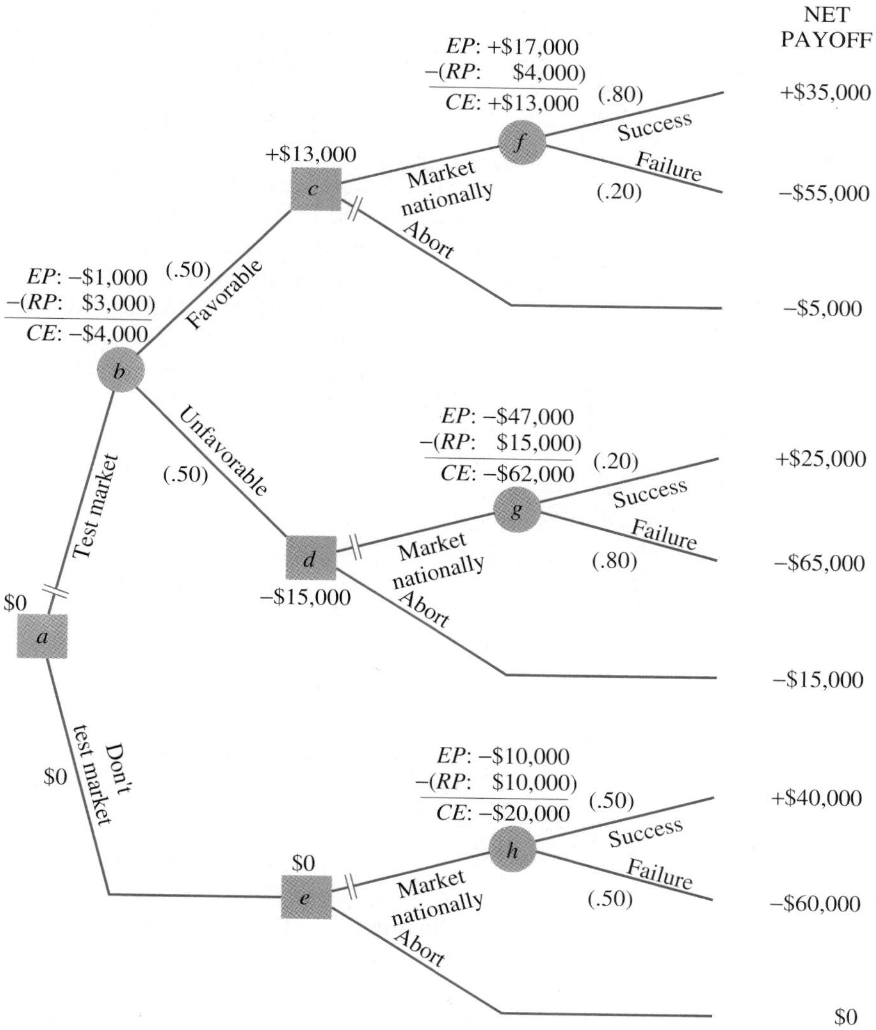

FIGURE 25-1 The Ponderosa decision tree diagram showing backward induction with certainty equivalents computed by discounting expected payoffs.

backward induction begins at nodes *f*, *g*, and *h*. First the expected payoffs (*EP*) are computed. Then, from Table 25-12 the respective risk premiums (*RP*) are read. For node *f* the loss value is \$55,000 (corresponding to the negative payoff amount); this figure is closest to \$50,000 in the table, and the entry in that row under the .20 probability column gives RP = \$4,000. Thus, at *f* the certainty equivalent is

$$CE = EP - RP = \$17{,}000 - 4{,}000 = \$13{,}000 \quad (\text{node } f)$$

The event fork at node *g* represents a huge risk, with the closest tabled risk premium occçurring in the \$50,000 loss row and the .75 probability column, RP = \$15,000. For that node, the certainty equivalent is

$$CE = -\$47{,}000 - 15{,}000 = -\$62{,}000 \quad (\text{node } g)$$

The event fork at node *h* represents a risk with an intensity lying between those of the above two nodes; from the \$50,000 loss row and the .50 probability column we find RP = \$10,000. The certainty equivalent is

$$CE = -\ \$10{,}000 - 10{,}000 = -\ \$20{,}000 \quad (\text{node } h)$$

The act fork at *c* leads to *f* (CE = \$13,000) if Ponderosa Records markets nationally and leads to a certain payoff of − \$5,000 if the recording is aborted. The latter branch is pruned, and the greater amount is brought back to node *c*. At that point, marketing nationally has a certainty equivalent to the president of \$13,000, and this figure is the best available valuation for that node. The tree is similarly pruned at node *d*, where abort is chosen for a certain payoff of −\$15,000 and at node *e*, where abort is also chosen for a certain payoff of \$0.

The valuation at node *b* requires first an expected value calculation, followed

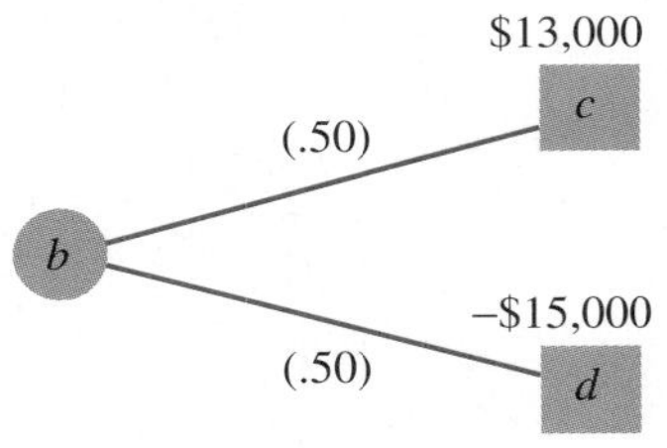

by a risk premium adjustment. In evaluating any event fork, *the evaluation is confined to the fork*. The values brought back are used to compute the expected payoff.

$$EP = \$13{,}000(.50) + (-\$15{,}000)(.50) = -\$1{,}000$$

In finding the risk premium from Table 25-12, the downside amount is \$15,000 (not \$65,000, which lies beyond the current fork). The nearest tabled loss is \$20,000, and the corresponding risk premium lies in that row in the .50 probability column, RP = \$3,000. Thus, the certainty equivalent at node *b* is

$$CE = -\$1{,}000 - 3{,}000 = -\$4{,}000 \quad (\text{node } b)$$

This amount, resulting from test marketing the recording, is worse than the $0 at node *e* from not testing and then aborting. The president should choose the latter.

This result differs from the conclusion reached in Chapter 24, where an evaluation based on undiscounted expected payoffs leads to the choice to test market, followed by a choice to market nationally only if that proves favorable. Although messier, the above analysis should indicate the action most preferred (which is the best that any decision analysis can possibly do).

EXERCISES

25-11 Refer to the risk premiums for the president of Ponderosa Record company in Table 25-12. For each of the following situations, determine (1) the expected payoff, (2) his risk premium, and (3) his certainty equivalent.

(a) Prob.	(a) Payoff	(b) Prob.	(b) Payoff	(c) Prob.	(c) Payoff	(d) Prob.	(d) Payoff
.90	+$50,000	.99	+$20,000	.50	+$10,000	.25	+$300,000
.10	−$100,000	.01	−$50,000	.50	−$5,000	.75	−$100,000

25-12 Refer to Exercise 25-9 and to your answers to that problem. Determine your personal levels of the following for the described hypothetical gamble.
(a) certainty equivalent (b) risk premium.

25-13 Refer to the Spillsberry Foods decision in Problem 24-11, page 980. Suppose that the following risk premiums apply.

Nearest Possible Loss	Nearest Probability of Loss .10	.40	.60
$ 25,000	$ 1,000	$ 3,000	$ 5,000
100,000	5,000	10,000	15,000
250,000	10,000	25,000	40,000

Construct the decision tree diagram and perform backward induction analysis using certainty equivalents obtained by discounting the expected payoffs.

25-14 Refer to Exercise 25-10 and to your answers to that problem. What are Shirley Smart's (a) certainty equivalent and (b) risk premium for remaining uninsured?

SUMMARY

1. **What are some of the key criteria employed in reaching a decision under uncertainty?**

   Uncertainty complicates decision analysis because the ultimate outcome from any particular choice cannot be known. Several **decision-making criteria** have been proposed for making the choice. This chapter describes four of these criteria in detail. The **maximin payoff** criterion selects that act having the best of the possible worst payoffs. The **maximum likelihood** criterion begins with the identification of the event most likely to occur; then—ignoring all other possibilities—the act having the highest payoff, supposing that event occurs, becomes the chosen one. A third criterion, **insufficient reason**, treats all events as equally likely; that act having greatest expected payoff is chosen.

2. **How well do the various criteria utilize available information?**
The above criteria all ignore essential information. Maximin payoff does not reflect probabilities for events, nor does it give any consideration to the ranges in payoffs available under each act. In a business environment, maximin is totally risk-avoiding; it would lead to inaction whenever there is the remotest possibility of loss, regardless of probability or size. The most likely event identified in exercising the maximum likelihood criterion may have a much lower probability than the union of the other events; and, this criterion ignores all payoffs from the remaining rows of the payoff table. The criterion of insufficient reason requires that we suspend any judgment regarding the events and always treat them as equally likely.

3. **What is the Bayes decision rule and why is it a favored criterion?**
The fourth criterion, the **Bayes decision rule**, selects that act leading to the greatest expected payoff. It makes better use of available information and is the favored decision criterion. But this criterion is not perfect, since it may indicate choices that are not most preferred. (For example, it will ordinarily indicate that casualty insurance not be bought.)

4. **What are opportunity losses and how do they relate to the Bayes decision rule?**
As an alternative framework to the payoff table, a table of **opportunity losses** may be employed. These numbers (always positive values) are found by subtracting the payoffs within each row from the best possible payoff under the respective event. These values express how much worse off the decision maker would be by choosing a particular act instead of picking the best act under the circumstances. Opportunity losses may therefore be considered measures of *regret*. (They are *not* analogous to accounting losses, and they may arise even when all outcomes have positive payoff.) One property of opportunity losses is that the minimum expected opportunity loss always occurs for the same act which has the maximum expected payoff. Thus, a corollary to the Bayes decision rule is to pick that act having minimum expected opportunity loss.

5. **What is the EVPI and what role does it play in decision making?**
A crucial concern in making decisions under uncertainty is making use of *predictive information*. A convenient gauge of such data's worth is the **expected value of perfect information** or **EVPI**. This number expresses the difference between the expected payoff that is achieved by having a perfect predictor and the maximum expected payoff when no information is available. The EVPI serves as the upper limit on the worth of any less-than-perfect information.

6. **What are certainty equivalents and how do they relate to making decisions?**

A **certainty equivalent** is the payoff that an individual would accept for certain rather than undergo the actual experience of letting the outcomes be determined by chance. If a decision maker can establish what values may be achieved under each act, the obvious choice would be to select that act yielding the greatest certainty equivalent. That way he or she will always select the preferred course of action.

7. **How can the shortcomings of the Bayes decision rule be overcome by using expected values as the starting point for establishing certainty equivalents?**
A certainty equivalent may ordinarily be thought of as a *discounted* expected payoff. The amount of the discount, or **risk premium**, varies from individual to individual and is ordinarily a function of (1) the potential downside loss and (2) the probability that such a loss will occur. It is analogous to the extra amount that people will pay—beyond the expected claim size—for casualty insurance. A situation's risk premium will generally increase either as the level of potential loss becomes greater or as the probability of loss increases. If a complete set of risk premiums is available, these can be used to transform expected payoffs into certainty equivalents.

REVIEW EXERCISES

25-15 Refer to the Tippi-Toes decision in Table 25-1. Suppose that reduction in the development cost of the gears-and-levers movement allows a $50,000 increase in all payoffs for that act. In addition, an upward revision of unit sales when demand is heavy results in a further $100,000 increase in all payoffs for that event. Finally, the following revised probabilities now apply to the demand levels: light, .50; moderate, .30; and heavy, .20.
(a) Construct the new Tippi-Toes payoff table.
(b) Determine the maximin payoff act.
(c) Determine the maximum likelihood act.
(d) Calculate the expected payoffs. According to the Bayes decision rule, which act should be chosen?

25-16 (*Continuation of Exercise 25-15*):
(a) Calculate the EVPI for the modified Tippi-Toes decision.
(b) Construct the opportunity loss table and compute the expected opportunity losses.

25-17 A product manager for Gimble and Proctor wishes to determine whether or not to market a new toothpaste. The present value of all future profits from a successful toothpaste is $1,000,000, whereas failure of the brand would result in a net loss of $500,000. Not marketing the toothpaste would not affect profits. The manager has judged that the toothpaste would have a 50–50 chance of success.
(a) Construct the payoff table for this decision.
(b) Which act will maximize the expected payoff?
(c) Compute the decision maker's EVPI. What is the minimum expected opportunity loss?

25-18 Refer to the Sniff-n-Stuff decision in Problem 24-15. Suppose that the following risk premiums apply.

Nearest Possible Loss	Nearest Probability of Loss				
	.20	.30	.50	.70	.80
$ 50,000	$ 100	$ 200	$ 1,000	$ 2,000	$ 3,000
100,000	500	3,000	10,000	20,000	25,000
500,000	3,000	10,000	25,000	40,000	50,000

Construct the decision tree diagram and perform backward induction analysis using certainty equivalents obtained by discounting the expected payoffs.

CASE SoftWhereHaus

Klaus DeBugger is the founder of SoftWhereHaus, a start-up software publishing company. The company's major product is the securities evaluation package, *Opt-a-Miser*. Version 1.0 of this program has been a moderate success. A variety of enhancements are contemplated for version 2.0, the release of which could be a vital boost to SoftWhereHaus' future.

Unfortunately, Exploiteers Inc. has developed a competing package called *Max-a-Myser*. DeBugger claims that this package has the "look and feel" of *Opt-a-Miser*, substantially violating SoftWhereHaus' copyright. He is contemplating retaliatory action.

DeBugger's immediate choices are (1) to negotiate with the help of a mediator (whose fee is $10,000), (2) to litigate (requiring a $20,000 nonrefundable attorney retainer), or (3) to ignore Exploiteers. Ultimately, SoftWhereHaus will either sell the program rights to GrossHaus for an amount dependent on what prior events transpire or keep the program and develop version 2.0 (at a cost of $20,000). Version 2.0 of *Opt-a-Miser* may be assumed to result in a success (culminating in enhanced profits having a present value of $200,000) or in a weak marketplace reception (yielding only $20,000).

Negotiation may bring about a favorable or unfavorable settlement. With a favorable outcome (50% chance), SoftWhereHaus may sell program ownership for $75,000; and, releasing instead version 2.0 will provide a 70% chance of success. An unfavorable negotiation result will drastically reduce the selling price to $20,000 and will lower the success probability of version 2.0 to .25.

Litigation may have three results: positive (40% chance), neutral (30% chance), or negative (30% chance). The following data apply in that case.

	Litigation Result		
	Positive	Neutral	Negative
V-2.0 success probability	.8	.5	.15
Proceeds from sale	$100,000	$50,000	$15,000

Ignoring Exploiteers will of course involve no unusual cash expenditure. In that case, there would be a 50–50 chance for version 2.0 success versus a weak reception, and GrossHaus will give DeBugger $50,000 to gain ownership of the unrevised *Opt-a-Miser*.

QUESTIONS

1. Construct Klaus DeBugger's decision tree diagram, placing all partial cash flows and probabilities alongside their respective branches. Then determine, for each outcome, the net cash flow.

2. Perform backward induction using the tree in Question 1. What course of action maximizes DeBugger's expected net cash flow?

3. Consider the *negotiation* case only.
   (a) Suppose that DeBugger chooses to keep *Opt-a-Miser* and makes version 2.0. From your decision tree analysis in Question 2, find the net expected payoff when the negotiation is (1) favorable and (2) unfavorable.
   (b) Using your answers from (a) as the payoff values for keeping the program, construct DeBugger's payoff table applicable under the negotiation case.
   (c) Determine the following.
      (1) Maximin act.
      (2) Maximum likelihood act.
      (3) Maximum expected payoff act.
   (d) Determine DeBugger's EVPI. How might this number help DeBugger in his evaluation? What kinds of predictive information might DeBugger find helpful in evaluating his negotiation choices?
   (e) Construct DeBugger's opportunity loss table. Which act minimizes expected opportunity loss?

4. Although less so than most people, Klaus DeBugger is nevertheless risk averse. This is evidenced by his willingness to buy casualty insurance at various amounts exceeding the expected claim size. The following table applies.

Greatest Possible Loss	Downside Risk Premium Component						
	Pr[Loss]						
	.15	.20	.25	.30	.50	.70	.85
$10,000	300	400	600	650	800	1,000	2,000
20,000	1,100	1,200	1,400	1,500	2,000	3,000	5,000

The above amounts must be subtracted from expected payoffs to arrive at Klaus' certainty equivalents.

But Klaus also expresses the need to make *upside* adjustments by *further* discounting. The following apply.

Greatest Possible Gain	Upside Risk Premium Component						
	Pr[Gain]						
	.15	.20	.25	.30	.50	.70	.85
$ 25,000	200	100	0	0	0	0	0
50,000	800	500	400	300	200	100	0
75,000	1,100	700	500	400	300	200	100
100,000	1,300	1,000	700	500	300	200	100
125,000	1,500	1,200	900	600	400	300	200
150,000	2,000	1,300	1,100	800	600	400	200
175,000	2,500	1,500	1,300	1,000	800	500	400
200,000	3,000	2,000	1,500	1,200	1,000	700	500

DeBugger's risk premium is the sum of the two components.

$$\text{Risk premium} = \text{Downside component} + \text{Upside component}$$

Using the nearest applicable tabled values, determine Klaus DeBugger's (1) expected payoff, (2) risk premium, and (3) certainty equivalent for each of the following gambles (probabilities in parentheses).

	(a)	(b)	(c)	(d)
Win	$100,000(.30)	$50,000(.50)	$200,000(.30)	$20,000(.90)
Lose	−$20,000(.70)	$20,000(.50)	−$20,000(.70)	−$20,000(.10)

5. Klaus DeBugger's certainty equivalents are determined by the rules in Question 4. Perform a second backward induction analysis of his decision tree to determine which course of action maximizes his certainty equivalent.

CHAPTER 26

BAYESIAN ANALYSIS OF DECISIONS USING EXPERIMENTAL INFORMATION

BEFORE READING THIS CHAPTER, MAKE SURE YOU UNDERSTAND:

Basic concepts of probability (Chapter 5).
Subjective probability in decision making (Chapter 20).
Basic concepts of decision analysis (Chapter 24).
Elements of decision theory (Chapter 25).

AFTER READING THIS CHAPTER, YOU WILL UNDERSTAND:

About the four stages of decision making with experimental information.
How to find and classify the various types of probabilities employed in a decision analysis.
About the two basic forms of posterior analysis.
About preposterior analysis and what summary measures are employed.

We usually associate the term *experiment* with a test or an investigation. All experiments have one feature in common: *They provide information.* This information may serve to realign uncertainty. Information obtained by observing a solar eclipse can support hypotheses regarding the effect of the sun's gravity on stellar light rays. The way in which a person responds to your questions can help you decide whether you want him or her for a friend. *An experiment helps us to make better decisions under uncertainty.*

However, most experiments are not conclusive. Any test may camouflage the truth. For instance, some potentially good employees will flunk well-designed employment screening tests, and some incompetents will pass them. Another good example is the seismic survey, which provides geological information about deep underground rock structures and is used to explore for oil deposits. Unfortunately, a seismic survey may deny the presence of oil in a field that is already producing oil and may confirm the presence of oil under a site that has already proved to be dry. Still, such imperfect experiments may be valuable. An unfavorable test result may increase the chance of rejecting a poor prospect—a job applicant or a drilling site—and a favorable test result may enhance the likelihood of selecting a good prospect.

In this chapter, we will incorporate experimentation into the framework of our decision-making analysis. The information we obtain will affect the probabilities of the events that determine the consequence of each act. We may revise the probabilities of these events upward or downward, depending on the evidence we obtain. Thus, a geologist will increase the subjective probability for oil if the seismic survey analysis is favorable and will lower this probability if the survey is unfavorable.

The seismic survey epitomizes the role of experimental information in decision making. In business situations, several other classic sources of such information are commonly employed. A marketing research study serves to realign uncertainty regarding the degree of success that a new product will achieve in the marketplace. An aptitude test is often used to help predict a job applicant's future success or failure if he or she is hired—a decision that involves considerable uncertainty. A sampling study is frequently employed to facilitate quality control decisions related to how satisfactorily items are produced or how many defective items are arriving from a supplier.

26-1 STAGES FOR ANALYZING DECISIONS USING EXPERIMENTS

Four stages are involved in analyzing decisions under uncertainty.

1. **Prior analysis.** In this evaluation stage, the decision maker identifies the decision structure, selects a payoff measure, and determines prior probabilities. The decision maker then computes the expected payoff for each act and the expected value of perfect information, or EVPI. If the latter is small, no further investigation is required, and the main decision should be made. Otherwise, the next stage commences.

2. **Preposterior analysis.** At this point in the evaluation, the decision maker looks for sources of information to predict the events in the decision structure. Only those sources that have low cost (in relation to the EVPI) and that have a history of reliable predictions need be evaluated. That evaluation

(to be described shortly) includes both probability and decision tree analyses.

3. **Posterior analysis.** When the source of experimental information has been chosen, the decision maker will revise probabilities, with one set of values coinciding with each result possible. The main decision is made after the experiment, according to how the actual result relates to the actions prescribed here.

4. **Future analysis.** It is common for one evaluation to raise further questions. Later decisions might have to be made that would involve some of the same uncertainties. In some cases, posterior probability values for events in the present investigation will serve as the prior probabilities for those or similar events in a future investigation. Data from ongoing evaluations should be collected in a data base to be used in future decisions. The following illustration expands on the four stages just described.

ILLUSTRATION: AN OIL WILDCATTER'S DRILLING DECISION

An oil wildcatter must decide whether or not to drill an oil well. His payoff table is provided in Table 26-1.

The subjective probabilities of .50 for oil and .50 for dry are the wildcatter's *prior probabilities* and are based on personal judgment formed during preliminary investigations. The payoffs result from the assumption that an oil-bearing leasehold will be sold for $250,000 and that the drilling will cost $100,000. The probability values are the culmination of the wildcatter's efforts in studying rock samples and correlating other evidence. Each bit of experimental information has refined the wildcatter's judgment. Dramatic shifts in probabilities may be expected to follow a high-reliability experiment, such as a seismic survey.

26-2 PRIOR ANALYSIS OF THE DECISION

Using the data in the payoff table, the wildcatter could make the main decision of whether to drill or to abandon—simply by applying the Bayes decision rule. The expected payoffs are

$$(\$150{,}000)(.50) + (-\$100{,}000)(.50) = \$25{,}000$$

for drill and $0 for abandon. If he wants to maximize expected payoff, he should choose to drill.

TABLE 26-1 Payoff Table for Wildcatting Decision

Event	Prior Probability	Act: Drill	Act: Abandon
Oil	.50	$150,000	$0
Dry	.50	−100,000	0

TABLE 26-2 Perfect Information Evaluation for Wildcatting Decision

		Act		With Perfect Information		
Event	Probability	Drill	Abandon	Maximum Payoff	Chosen Act	Payoff × Probability
Oil	.50	$150,000	$0	$150,000	Drill	$75,000
Dry	.50	−100,000	0	0	Abandon	0
						$75,000

Expected payoff with perfect information = $75,000

EVPI = Expected payoff with perfect information − Maximum expected payoff (with no information)
= $75,000 − $25,000 = $50,000

Another course of action would be to seek out some kind of experimental information, postponing the main decision until a result is achieved from that investigation.

THE ROLE OF EVPI

Before we look at any specific source of predictive data, consider the hypothetical case when perfect information is available. A perfect predictor will indicate, without error, either that there is oil or that the site is dry. Should the decision maker have that information, he would pick the better act for each case.

Table 26-2 shows the calculations for the oil wildcatter's expected value of perfect information. The practical significance of EVPI = $50,000 is what it implies regarding less-than-perfect information. Any imperfectly reliable predictor must have a worth to the decision maker of some amount less than the EVPI, which sets the threshold.

The EVPI may be a helpful screening device. If any information were to cost more than the EVPI, that source of data should be rejected out of hand regardless of its purported quality. For instance, if the wildcatter were offered a highly reliable seismic survey for a fee of $105,000, it could be turned down without a second thought.

The absolute level of the EVPI is itself a useful number. Imagine a decision where the computed value of EVPI is $50. It could hardly be worth the time and effort to consider further predictive information when the maximum benefit (in terms of expected payoff) is so small. The main decision under such circumstances should be made immediately on the basis of present knowledge alone. On the other hand, a large value, such as EVPI = $1,000,000, suggests that a great deal of effort should be devoted to the search for potential sources of predictive information.

EXERCISES

26-1 The exploration manager for Crockpot Domes must decide whether to drill on a parcel of leased land or to abandon the lease. She has judged the prior probability for oil to be .30. Drilling costs have been firmly established at $200,000. If oil is struck, Crockpot plans to sell the lease for $500,000.

(a) Construct the payoff table.

(b) If the drilling decision were to be made without further information, determine the expected payoffs. Which act maximizes expected payoff?

(c) Compute the EVPI. What is the most that Crockpot would be willing to pay for predictive information regarding the presence of oil?

26-2 The makers of Quicker Oats oatmeal have packaged this product in cylindrical containers for 50 years. Management believes that the cylindrical container is inseparable from the product's image. But consumer tastes change, and the new marketing vice president wonders if younger people will regard the round box as old fashioned and unappealing. The vice president wishes to analyze whether or not to package Quicker Oats in a rectangular box that will save significantly on transportation costs by eliminating dead space in the packing cartons. It is also believed that the change can actually expand Quicker Oats' market by modernizing the product's image. But previous study has shown that a small segment of the existing market buys the oatmeal primarily for the round box; these customers would be lost if the package were changed. The following payoff table has been established for the present net worth of retaining the old box versus using the new box.

National Market Response to New Box Events	Act	
	Retain Old Box	Use New Box
Weak (W)	\$0	−\$2,000,000
Moderate (M)	0	0
Strong (S)	0	3,000,000

As prior probabilities for the new box response events, the marketing vice president arrived at the following estimates: $\Pr[W] = .20$; $\Pr[M] = .30$; $\Pr[S] = .50$.

(a) If the packaging decision were to be made without further information, determine the expected payoffs. Would Quicker Oats change box shape?

(b) Compare the EVPI. Does it appear that management would find it attractive to defer the main decision until further testing is done of the marketplace?

26-3 Portentous Prospector must decide how to dispose of a particular gas lease, which may be sold now for \$20,000 or drilled on at a cost of \$100,000. The drilling events and their prior probabilities are dry (D) at .6, low-pressure gas (L) at .3, and high pressure gas (H) at .1. The lease will be abandoned for no receipts if D, it will be sold for \$300,000 if L, and it will be sold for \$500,000 if H.

(a) Which act—sell or drill—will maximize Prospector's expected profit?

(b) What is Prospector's EVPI?

26-3 PREPOSTERIOR AND POSTERIOR ANALYSIS

Let's continue to evaluate the oil wildcatter's decision. For a fee of \$30,000, a consulting firm will perform a complete seismic survey of the subterranean structure of the lease site. Two predictive results are assumed: favorable or unfavorable. Figure 26-1 shows the oil wildcatter's decision tree diagram, with an initial

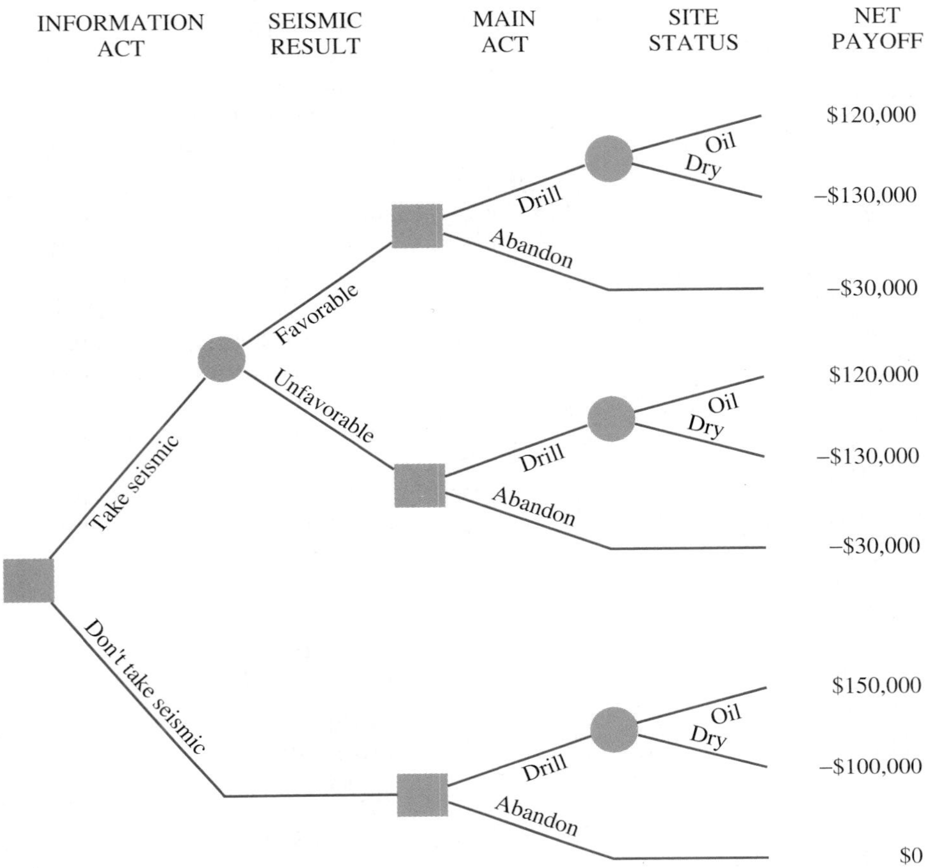

FIGURE 26-1 Decision tree diagram for the wildcatting decision (incomplete).

act fork for the decision to order the seismic survey or not. Notice that if the seismic survey is ordered the main decision will not be made until after its results have become known. The payoff values are the original ones, less the $30,000 cost of the survey for the applicable outcomes. Notice that there are no site status event forks following the abandon acts—reflecting the fact that oil and dry never become known unless drilling is done. (Although potentially misleading, it would not be improper to include those missing forks in the tree.)

Preposterior analysis is concerned largely with the decision about whether or not to take the seismic. Imbedded in that evaluation is the posterior analysis of what should actually be done for each possible finding, assuming that the seismic survey will be taken.

PROBABILITY EVALUATIONS

The decision maker usually makes some kind of judgment about the uncertain events, which may be expressed as a set of *prior probabilities* for the respective events. Occasionally, such a judgment must be quantified in terms of *subjective probabilities*, because the events in question frequently arise from nonrepeatable

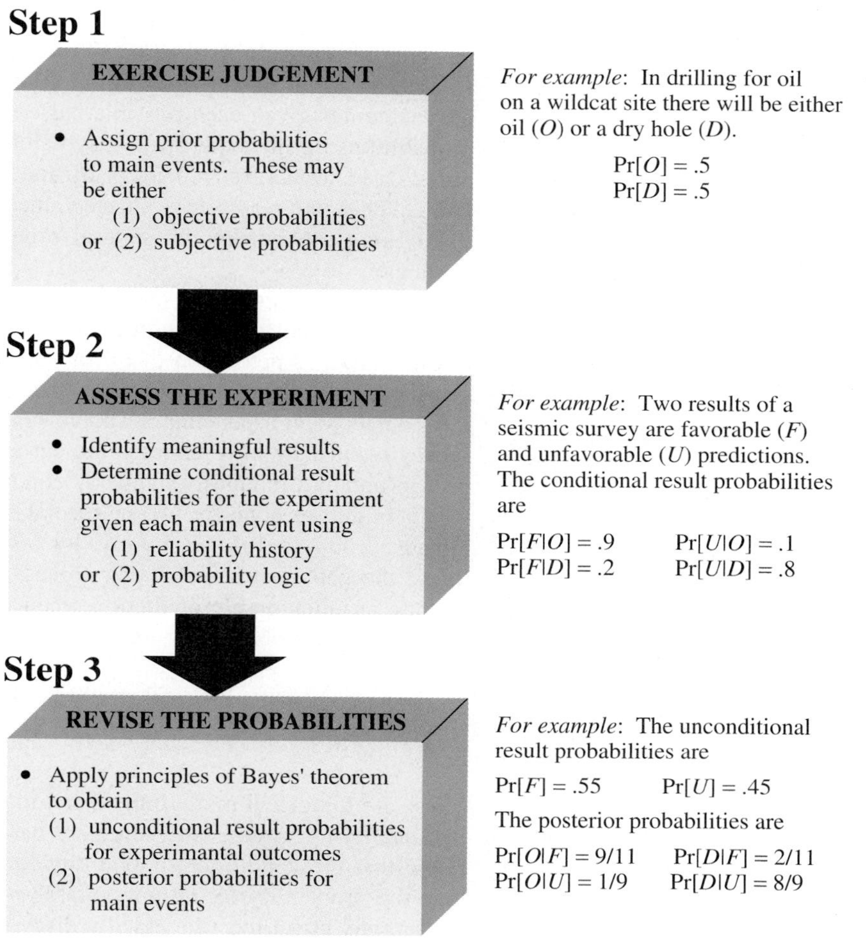
Step 1
EXERCISE JUDGEMENT
• Assign prior probabilities to main events. These may be either
(1) objective probabilities
or (2) subjective probabilities
For example: In drilling for oil on a wildcat site there will be either oil (O) or a dry hole (D).
Pr[O] = .5
Pr[D] = .5
Step 2
ASSESS THE EXPERIMENT
• Identify meaningful results
• Determine conditional result probabilities for the experiment given each main event using
(1) reliability history
or (2) probability logic
For example: Two results of a seismic survey are favorable (F) and unfavorable (U) predictions. The conditional result probabilities are
Pr[F|O] = .9 Pr[U|O] = .1
Pr[F|D] = .2 Pr[U|D] = .8
Step 3
REVISE THE PROBABILITIES
• Apply principles of Bayes' theorem to obtain
(1) unconditional result probabilities for experimantal outcomes
(2) posterior probabilities for main events
For example: The unconditional result probabilities are
Pr[F] = .55 Pr[U] = .45
The posterior probabilities are
Pr[O|F] = 9/11 Pr[D|F] = 2/11
Pr[O|U] = 1/9 Pr[D|U] = 8/9

FIGURE 26-2 Steps for performing the probability portion of the decision analysis using experimental information.

circumstances. At other times, the prior probabilities may be *objective* in nature. In accordance with the information obtained from the experiment, the event uncertainties are realigned to obtain **posterior probabilities**. Figure 26-2 presents the sequence of steps in this procedure—exactly the one originally proposed by Thomas Bayes. (Bayes' theorem was discussed in Chapter 21.)

As a first step, the wildcatter must *exercise judgment* regarding the likelihood of striking oil. Since no two unproved drilling sites are very similar, no historical frequency is available. The wildcatter has therefore established subjective probability values. Letting O represent oil and D represent a dry hole, the prior probabilities for the basic events are

$$\Pr[O] = .5 \qquad \Pr[D] = .5$$

The next step the wildcatter takes is to *assess the experiment*—the seismic survey, in this case. He begins by contemplating what results would be meaningful to him. Although the seismic output might be highly complex and varied, we will assume, for simplicity, that the geologist's analysis may lead to only two meaningful results: a favorable (F) prediction for oil or an unfavorable one (U). It is necessary to obtain **conditional result probabilities** for the respective seismic outcomes given each possible basic event. Ordinarily, the conditional result probabilities for the experiment may be obtained objectively, either by estimation based on historical frequencies or by application of the underlying logic of probability. Thus, we may refer to these values as "logical-historical" probabilities to distinguish them from the several other types of probabilities that we will encounter.

In our present example, the geologist has recorded the "batting average" for the procedure. Historical records show that on 90% of all fields known to produce oil, the survey's prediction of oil has been favorable; that is, 90% of all similar seismic survey data have provided favorable oil predictions when oil did exist. (Of course, such a percentage should not be biased by the fact that the seismic survey result may have affected the earlier decisions to drill on those sites. It is best to obtain a reliability figure by conducting a special test of the tester itself, which might be done by taking special seismic measurements on sites that are already producing oil.) Similarly, by taking simulated readings on known dry holes, the geologist has also determined that the survey is only 80% reliable in making an unfavorable prediction when no oil is present. The appropriate conditional result probabilities are

$$\Pr[F|O] = .90 \quad \text{and} \quad \Pr[U|O] = .10$$

$$\Pr[F|D] = .20 \quad \text{and} \quad \Pr[U|D] = .80$$

These are **historical probabilities** and may be regarded as statistical estimates of the underlying values, since they are based on limited samples of drilling sites. (Note that the conditional probability for a favorable result given oil is greater than the probability for an unfavorable prediction given a dry hole. There is no reason why a test must be equally discerning in both directions.)

In other situations conditional result probabilities for an informational experiment may be obtained more directly without relying on historical frequencies. This would be true, for example, in assessing a quality control sample. The precise probability distribution for the sample result may be determined through logical deduction, based only on the principles of probability and the type of events that characterize the sampled population. In Chapter 27, we will see how such **logical probabilities** may be determined using the binomial distribution.

The final step toward incorporating experimental information into the probability portion of decision analysis is to *revise the probabilities*. This revision ordinarily results in two kinds of probability values that are applicable at different stages of uncertainty: The *posterior probabilities* apply to the main events, and the **unconditional result probabilities** apply to the experimental outcomes themselves. Although the underlying concepts of Bayes' theorem are used to arrive at these values, there is a more streamlined procedure that proves more convenient when using probability tree diagrams to analyze a decision.

USING PROBABILITY TREES

The probability tree diagram in Figure 26-3(a) depicts the **actual chronology** of events in our illustration. The first fork represents the events for the site status: oil or dry. The second stage forks represent the seismic survey results. This

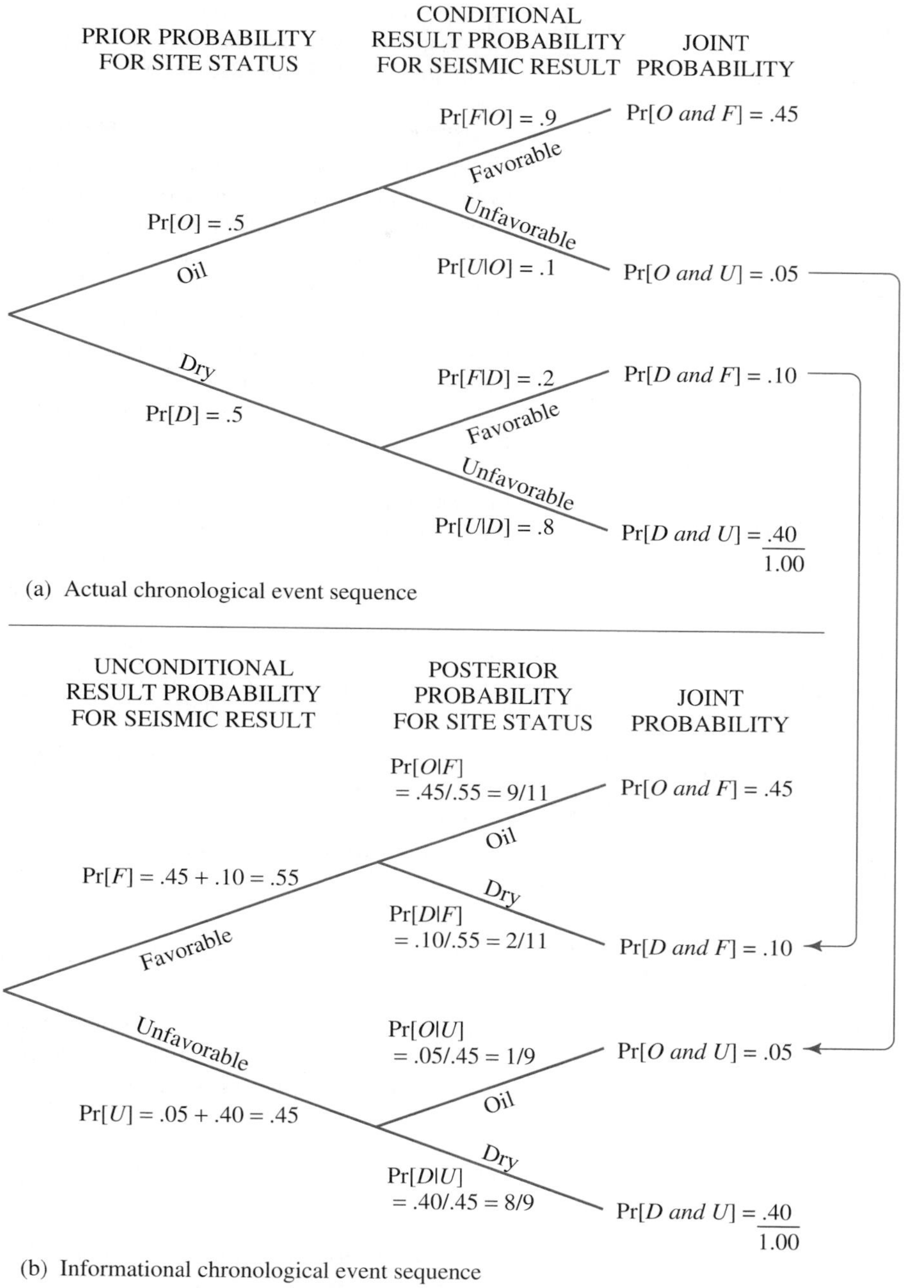

FIGURE 26-3 Probability tree diagrams for the wildcatter's event chronologies using a seismic survey.

particular arrangement follows the sequence in which the events actually occur: first, nature determined (several million years ago) whether this site would cover an oil field; second, our geologist conducts a seismic test today. The actual chronology also adheres to the manner in which the probability data were initially obtained. The wildcatter has directly assessed the probabilities for the site-status events, and the geologist has indicated the reliabilities for the survey. Thus, the values given earlier for the prior probabilities for oil and dry and the conditional result probabilities are placed on the corresponding branches in the probability tree in Figure 26-3(a).

The probability tree diagram in Figure 26-3(b) represents the **informational chronology**. This is the sequence in which the decision maker finds out what events occur. First, the wildcatter obtains the result for the seismic survey, which is portrayed by the initial event fork. Then, if he chooses to drill, he ultimately determines whether or not the site covers an oil field. This is the sequence of events as they would appear on a decision tree (which will be discussed later). But this particular chronology does not correspond directly to the initial probability data. Additional work is required to obtain the probability values shown on the tree diagram in Figure 26-3(b).

We begin by multiplying the branch probabilities together on each path in the tree diagram in Figure 26-3(a) to obtain the corresponding joint probability values. The same numbers apply regardless of the chronology, so the joint probabilities may be transferred to tree diagram (b). This must be done with care, since the in-between joint outcomes are not listed in the same order in (b) as they are in (a), because the analogous paths (event sequences) differ between the diagrams. For example, in diagram (a) we obtain the joint probability for oil and an unfavorable seismic result

$$\Pr[O \textit{ and } U] = \Pr[O] \times \Pr[U|O] = .5 \times .1 = .05$$

This is the second joint probability in diagram (a) and corresponds to the third end position in diagram (b).

Next, we work entirely in diagram (b). First, we compute the unconditional result probabilities at the first stage. Here, we use the addition law to obtain

$$\Pr[F] = \Pr[O \textit{ and } F] + \Pr[D \textit{ and } F] = .45 + .10 = .55$$
$$\Pr[U] = \Pr[O \textit{ and } U] + \Pr[D \textit{ and } U] = .05 + .40 = .45$$

These values are placed on the applicable branches at the first stage. Finally, the posterior probabilities for the second-stage events are computed using the basic property of conditional probability.

$$\Pr[A|B] = \frac{\Pr[A \textit{ and } B]}{\Pr[B]}$$

Thus, we determine the posterior probability for oil, given a favorable seismic survey result, to be

$$\Pr[O|F] = \frac{\Pr[O \textit{ and } F]}{\Pr[F]} = \frac{.45}{.55} = \frac{9}{11}$$

This value is placed on the second-stage branch for oil that is preceded by the earlier branch for a favorable result. Each of the other posterior probabilities shown in diagram (b) is found by dividing the respective end-position joint probability by the probability on the preceding branch.

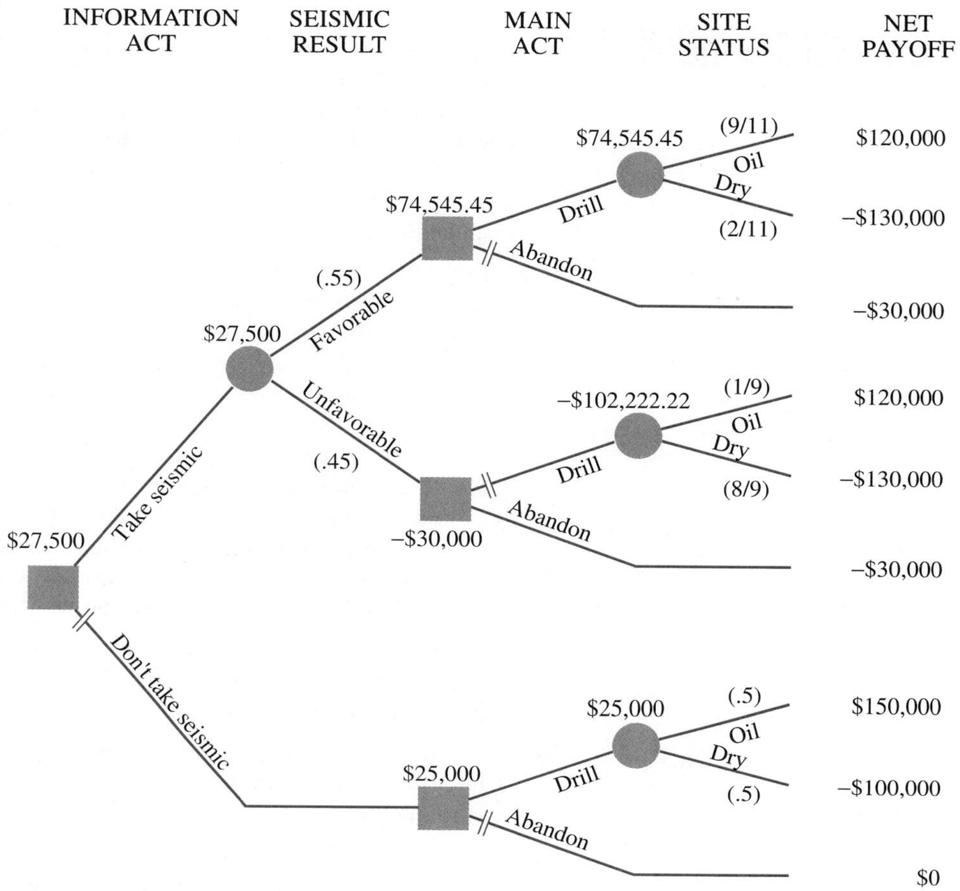

FIGURE 26-4 Complete decision tree diagram with backward induction for the wildcatting decision.

Probabilities must be revised in this manner whenever experimental information is used in decision making. This happens because we ordinarily obtain our probabilities in the reverse chronology from the chronology required to analyze the problem.

DECISION TREE ANALYSIS

The completed oil wildcatter's decision tree diagram is shown in Figure 26-4. Performing backward induction, we see that the decision maker would take the seismic. He should prune the abandon branch and drill if a favorable seismic result were obtained and would do the opposite in the case of an unfavorable prediction. Even though drilling will lead to identical payoffs for either seismic result, the posterior probabilities for oil and dry are different for the favorable and unfavorable predictions. The expected payoff from drilling is $74,545.45 for a favorable seismic result, but it is a negative value (−$102,222.22) for an unfavorable result. The wildcatter's expected payoff for the optimal strategy is $27,500.

EXERCISES

26-4 Oil wildcatter Rich Wells has assigned a .40 probability to striking oil on his property. He orders a seismic survey that has proved only 80% reliable in the past. Given oil, it predicts favorably 80% of the time; given no oil, it augurs unfavorably with a frequency of .8.

Construct probability trees for the actual and informational chronologies. Indicate the appropriate probability values for each branch and end position.

26-5 Inscrutable Smith places two coins in a box. The coins are identical in all respects, except that one is two-headed. Without looking, you select one coin from the box and lay it on the table.

(a) What is the prior probability that you will select the two-headed coin?

(b) As a source of predictive information about the selected coin, you may examine the showing face. Construct the probability tree diagram for the actual chronology of events.

(c) After you have examined the showing face of the coin, you may then turn it over to see what is on the other side. Construct the probability tree diagram for the informational chronology.

(d) If a head shows before you turn the coin over, what is the posterior probability that you selected the two-headed coin?

26-6 Solve the weather forecasting problem originally posed in Exercise 21-3 (page 889) by constructing probability trees for the actual and informational chronologies.

26-7 Solve the toothpaste-marketing problem posed in Exercise 21-2 (page 889) by constructing probability trees for the actual and informational chronologies.

26-8 Refer to the Crockpot Domes decision in Exercise 26-1. As an aid in making her drilling decision, the manager pays $30,000 for a seismic survey which will confirm or deny the presence of the anticlinal structure necessary for oil. For oil-producing fields of similar geology, her experience has shown that the chance of a confirming seismic is .9, but for dry holes with approximately the same characteristics, the probability that a seismic survey will deny oil has been established at only .7.

(a) Construct the manager's decision tree diagram, and determine the appropriate payoffs.

(b) Determine the revised probabilities for the informational chronology, and place these values on the corresponding branches of your decision tree diagram.

(c) Perform backward induction analysis to determine the course of action that will provide the maximum expected profit.

26-9 The makers of Quicker Oats oatmeal in Exercise 26-2 must decide whether to retain the old cylindrical container or to switch to a rectangular box. The new box is to be test marketed for six months in a "barometer" city. Three outcomes are possible: decreased sales (D), unchanged sales (U), and increased sales (I). Historical experience with other products has established the following conditional result probabilities.

$$\Pr[D|W] = .8 \qquad \Pr[D|M] = .2 \qquad \Pr[D|S] = 0$$
$$\Pr[U|W] = .2 \qquad \Pr[U|M] = .4 \qquad \Pr[U|S] = .1$$
$$\Pr[I|W] = 0 \qquad \Pr[I|M] = .4 \qquad \Pr[I|S] = .9$$

(a) Construct the probability tree diagrams for the actual and informational chronologies.
(b) Construct the Quicker Oats decision tree diagram, assuming that the new box will be test marketed.
(c) Perform backward induction. Then indicate the maximum expected payoff act for each test outcome. What is the optimal strategy?

26-10 The following payoff table of marketing choices for a new film has been determined by the management of a motion picture studio.

Box Office Result Events	Distribute as "A" Feature	Sell to TV Network	Distribute as "B" Feature
Success	\$5,000,000	\$1,000,000	\$3,000,000
Failure	−2,000,000	1,000,000	−1,000,000

The prior probability for a box office success has been judged to be .3. The studio plans a series of sneak previews. Historically, 70% of all the studio's successful films have received favorable previews, and 80% of all the studio's box office failures have received unfavorable previews.
(a) Construct the probability tree diagrams for the actual and informational chronologies.
(b) Construct a decision tree diagram for the studio, assuming that the film will definitely be previewed.
(c) Perform backward induction analysis. What is the optimal course of action?

26-11 Refer to the decision of Portentous Prospector in Exercise 26-3. For a cost of \$10,000, a 90% reliable seismic survey can predict gas favorably (F) with a probability of .90 if there is gas or unfavorably (U) with probability .90 if the site is dry, but it cannot measure pressure.
(a) Construct probability tree diagrams for the actual and informational chronologies, using the three gas events.
(b) Perform a decision tree analysis to determine what course of action will maximize Prospector's expected profit.

26-4 DECISION MAKING USING STRATEGIES

As we have seen, an important aspect of decision making is how to use experimental information. In establishing an employment policy based on a screening test, an applicant's score is the basis for hiring or rejecting that person. Regardless of the score achieved, a person who is hired will ultimately perform satisfactorily or not. When receiving components for assembly, manufacturers generally take a random sample to decide whether to accept or reject a shipment; the actual quality of the entire shipment will be known only after this decision has been made. As a further example, consider the choice between adding a new product to the line or abandoning it. This decision may be based on the results of a marketing research study; the success or failure of the new product will be known only after it has actually been marketed.

All of these situations are decisions with *two* points of uncertainty. The first uncertainty is the kind of information obtained—the screening test score, the number of defective sample items, or the results of the marketing research study.

The second uncertainty concerns the ultimate outcome—the new employee's performance, the quality of the shipment, the new product's performance. Between these points in time, a decision has to be made. The chosen act depends on which particular event has just occurred.

It is possible to determine the best acts to select for each informational event in advance. The resulting decision rule is called a **strategy**. The ultimate decision is what particular straiegy to select. We will show how this is done by means of a case illustration that involves sampling and inspection.

ILLUSTRATION: THE CANNERY INSPECTOR

A cannery inspector monitors tests for mercury contamination levels before authorizing shipments of canned tuna. The procedure is to randomly select two crates of canned fish from a shipment and determine the parts per million of mercury. The number of these crates R exceeding government contamination guidelines is determined. The inspector may then approve (A) or disapprove (D) the shipment. If approved, the shipment is sent to distributors who perform more detailed testing to determine whether the average mercury levels of the entire shipment are excessive (E) or tolerable (T). An excessively contaminated shipment is returned to the cannery. If the company inspector originally disapproves a shipment, the production batch is sent to the rendering department to be converted into pet food. At this time, it is determined whether the entire shipment actually contains excessive average levels of mercury.

The decision tree diagram for the cannery inspector's decision is provided in Figure 26-5. Eight strategies, S_1 through S_8, are identified in Table 26-3. A strategy must specify which act—"approve" or "disapprove"—should be chosen for each possible test result. From Table 26-3, we see that strategy S_1 is a decision rule specifying that the shipment must be approved no matter what the number of excessively contaminated crates R happens to be. Strategy S_2 specifies approval if $R = 0$ or $R = 1$, but disapproval if $R = 2$. Eight strategies are possible because there are 2 choices for each of the 3 events and therefore $2^3 = 8$ distinct decision rules.

As portrayed with the decision tree diagram, a strategy will be a particular pruned version of the tree. There are 8 distinct ways to prune the cannery inspector's tree, as shown in Figure 26-6. Only one of these versions will result from backward induction analysis.

A table may be constructed to indicate the payoff for each strategy-event combination. Such a payoff table, shown in Table 26-4, is identical in form to the payoff table for a single-stage decision, except that strategies are used in place

TABLE 26-3 Strategies for the Cannery Inspector's Decision

Test Result Event	Strategy							
	S_1	S_2	S_3	S_4	S_5	S_6	S_7	S_8
$R = 0$	A	A	A	D	A	D	D	D
$R = 1$	A	A	D	A	D	A	D	D
$R = 2$	A	D	A	A	D	D	A	D

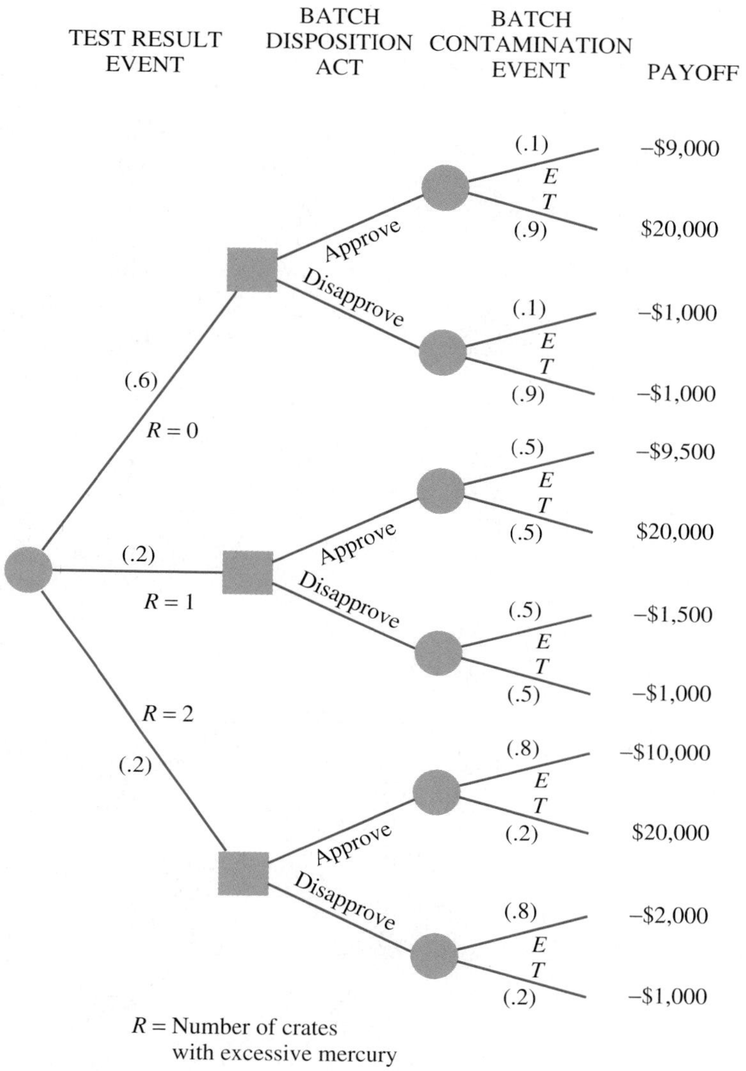

FIGURE 26-5 Decision tree diagram for the cannery inspector illustration.

of acts. Another difference is that there are uncertainties at two stages in the cannery decision: (1) how many excessively contaminated crates will be found in the sample and (2) whether the contamination level of the entire production batch will be found to be excessive or tolerable on the average. The six joint events are of the form $R = 0$ *and* E, $R = 2$ *and* T. The payoff values given in the table are the same as the payoff values on the decision tree in Figure 26-6 and correspond to the joint event that occurs for the specified strategy. Thus, if the joint event $R = 2$ *and* E occurs when S_1 is used, the payoff is -10 thousand dollars, since the inspector approves the shipment whenever $R = 2$, according to this particular strategy. If the inspector uses S_2, the same event indicates disapproval, and because the shipment contains excessive mercury, the payoff is -2 thousand dollars.

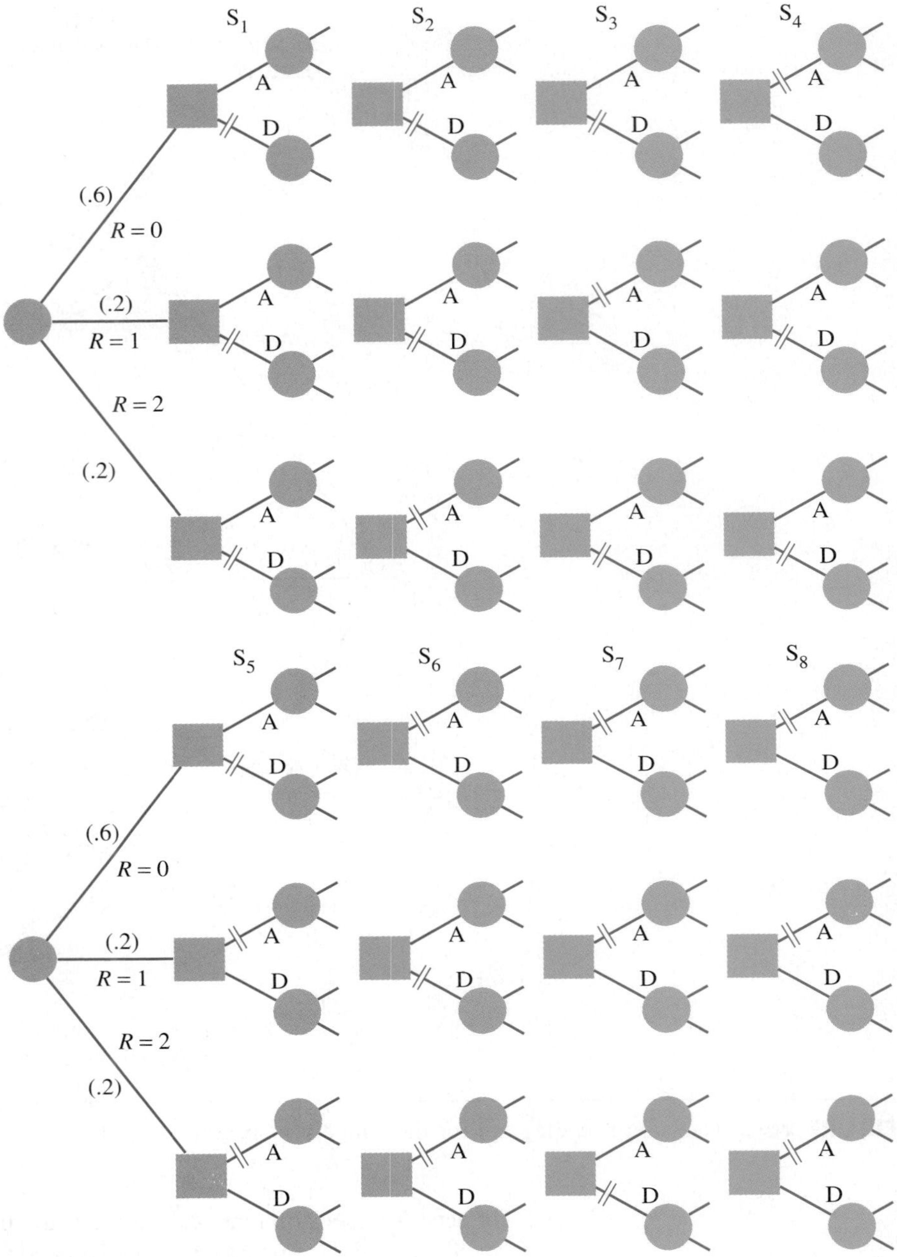

FIGURE 26-6 Pruned decision tree diagram illustrating the eight strategies for the cannery inspector's decision given in Table 26-3.

This strategy-selection decision may be analyzed by applying any of the various decision-making criteria we encountered earlier and then treating each strategy in the same way that an act is treated in a single-stage decision structure. However, we will continue to maximize expected payoff.

TABLE 26-4 Payoff Table for the Cannery Inspector's Decision Using Strategies (payoffs in thousands of dollars)

Joint Event	Strategy							
	S_1	S_2	S_3	S_4	S_5	S_6	S_7	S_8
$R = 0$ and E	−9	−9	−9	−1	−9	−1	−1	−1
$R = 0$ and T	20	20	20	−1	20	−1	−1	−1
$R = 1$ and E	−9.5	−9.5	−1.5	−9.5	−1.5	−9.5	−1.5	−1.5
$R = 1$ and T	20	20	−1	20	−1	20	−1	−1
$R = 2$ and E	−10	−2	−10	−10	−2	−2	−10	−2
$R = 2$ and T	20	−1	20	20	−1	−1	20	−1

EXTENSIVE AND NORMAL FORM ANALYSIS

The cannery strategy-selection decision may be analyzed using the Bayes decision rule and maximizing expected payoff either by (1) backward induction on the decision tree or (2) direct computation from the values given in the payoff table to determine the strategy with the maximum expected payoff. *The two approaches will provide identical results.* When a decision tree is used, the procedure is called an **extensive form analysis**. When the analysis is based on the payoff table, it is referred to as **normal form analysis**.

Figure 26-7 illustrates extensive form analysis. The probability value determined for each event is shown on the corresponding branch of the decision tree. Backward induction indicates that the best procedure is to approve the shipment when $R = 0$ or $R = 1$ and to disapprove the shipment when $R = 2$. Referring to Table 26-3, we see that this corresponds to strategy S_2.

The results of the normal form analysis for the cannery inspector's decision are shown in Table 26-5. Although similar calculations had to be made for each, there is room enough to illustrate only those for strategy S_2, which has the maximum

TABLE 26-5 Results of Normal Form Analysis for the Cannery Inspector's Decision Using Strategies, Showing the Expected Payoff Calculations for Strategy S_2 (payoffs in thousands of dollars)

(1) First-Stage Event Probability	(2) Second-Stage Event Probability	(3) Joint Probability (1) × (2)	(4) Payoff for S_2	(5) Payoff × Joint Probability (3) × (4)
$\Pr[R = 0] = .6$	$\Pr[E \mid R = 0] = .1$	.06	−9	−.54
$\Pr[R = 0] = .6$	$\Pr[T \mid R = 0] = .9$	.54	20	10.80
$\Pr[R = 1] = .2$	$\Pr[E \mid R = 1] = .5$	.10	−9.5	−.95
$\Pr[R = 1] = .2$	$\Pr[T \mid R = 1] = .5$	.10	20	2.00
$\Pr[R = 2] = .2$	$\Pr[E \mid R = 2] = .8$	.16	−2	−.32
$\Pr[R = 2] = .2$	$\Pr[T \mid R = 2] = .2$	.04	−1	−.04
			Expected payoff =	10.95

Strategy	S_1	S_2	S_3	S_4	S_5	S_6	S_7	S_8
Expected Payoff	10.51	10.95	9.21	−.35	9.65	.09	−1.65	−1.21

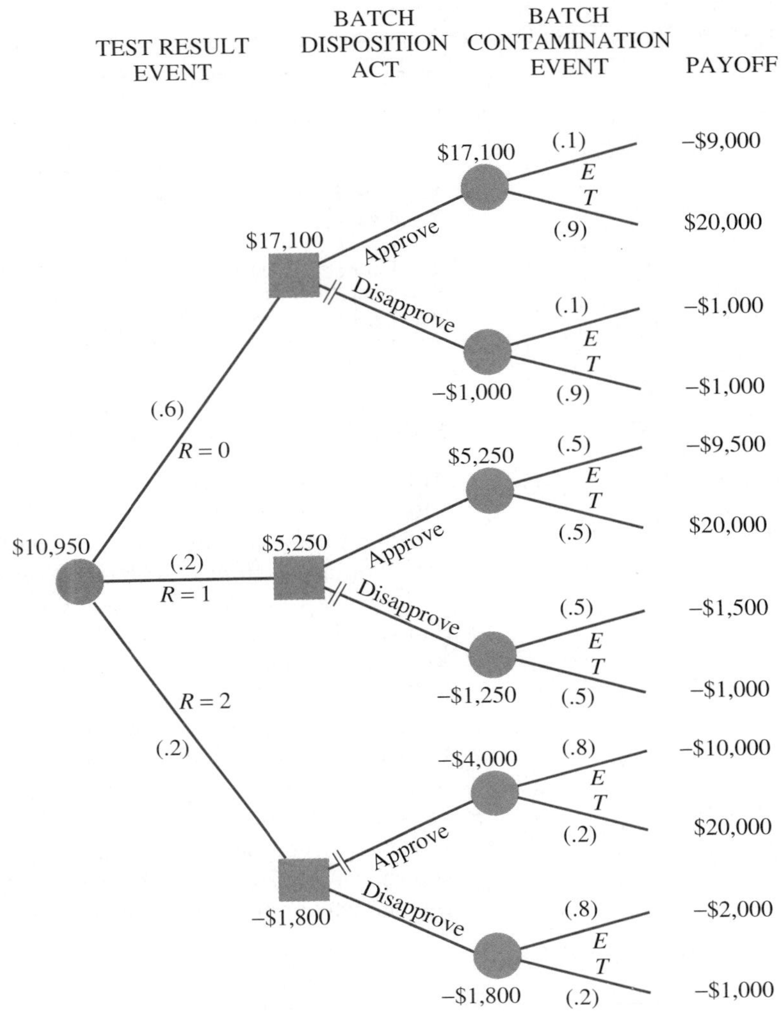

FIGURE 26-7 Extensive form analysis of the cannery inspector's decision using the decision tree diagram.

expected payoff of 10.95 thousand dollars. This is the same result we obtained in extensive form analysis ($10,950). Fortunately, extensive form analysis requires that we prune the tree for just one strategy. This makes decision tree analysis superior to payoff table analysis in terms of computational efficiency. In backward induction, only the maximum expected payoffs need to be brought back to the earlier branching point. It is not even necessary to catalog the various strategies.

Extensive form analysis using a decision tree is often the only possible approach, because the problem structure cannot be forced into the rectangular format of a payoff table. This is especially true of multistage problems that have two or more decision points, such as the Ponderosa Record Company problem diagrammed in Figure 24-2 (page 974). Only problems that result in a symmetrical decision tree like the one in Figure 26-5 may be analyzed either way in terms of expected payoff.

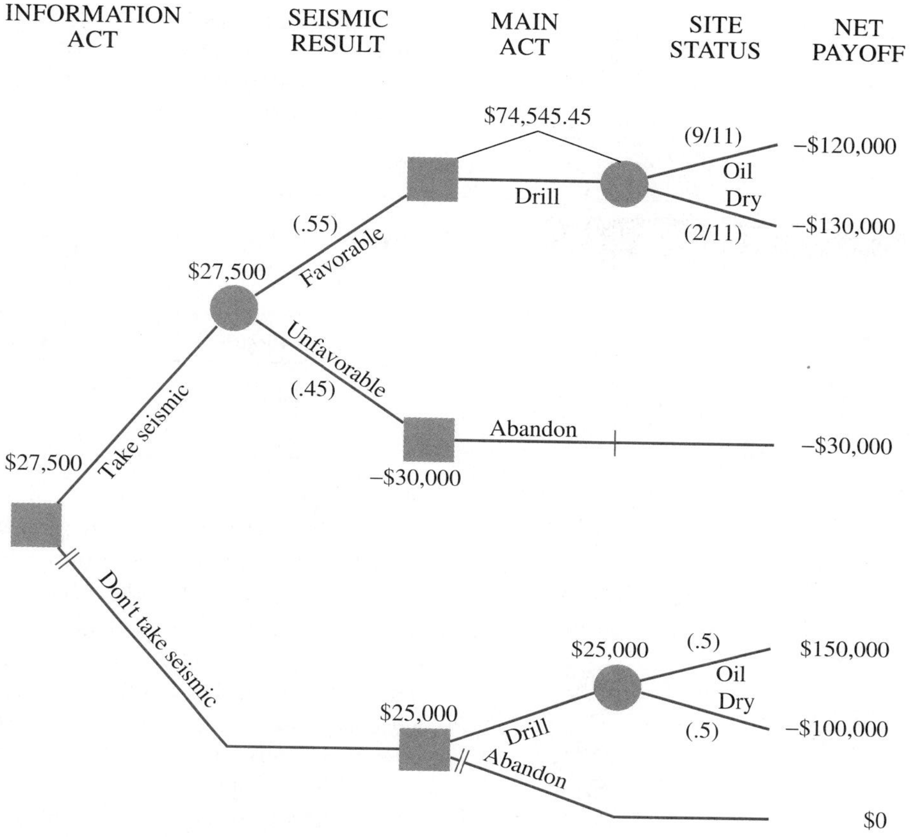

FIGURE 26-8 The simplified decision tree diagram for wildcatting decision with obviously nonoptimal strategies excluded.

OBVIOUSLY NONOPTIMAL STRATEGIES

In the simpler decision structures, it may be convenient to streamline the decision tree diagram. We conclude that the wildcatter discussed earlier in the chapter would prune the same branches in the seismic portion for almost any plausible payoffs that might apply. Since he is paying $30,000 for the seismic survey and this experiment provides fairly reliable predictions, the wildcatter should choose acts that are consistent with the information obtained. But the tree in Figure 26-4 allows for three other strategies: (1) drill regardless of the result (prune both abandon branches); (2) abandon in either case (prune the two drill branches); or (3) do the opposite of what is predicted (prune the drill branch if the seismic result is favorable, and prune the abandon branch if it is unfavorable). The last strategy is ridiculous and would never be considered. The other two strategies are inferior to two actions not shown on the present trees—drilling or abandoning without benefit of seismic results—since the $30,000 cost could be saved in either case by not even using the seismic. Such inferior strategies are *obviously nonoptimal strategies.*

Figure 26-8 illustrates how the wildcatter's decision tree diagram could have been drawn to exclude the obviously nonoptimal strategies. This representation may help to simplify an otherwise complex decision tree. However, for expository convenience we will always use the complete decision tree diagram. When more than two acts or experimental results are involved, it is not easy to determine which strategies are obviously nonoptimal.

EXERCISES

26-12 Suppose that the following probabilities apply to the cannery illustration in Section 26-4.

Test Result	Probability	Conditional Probabilities
$R = 0$	.4	.2(*E*) .8(*T*)
$R = 1$	.3	.6(*E*) .4(*T*)
$R = 2$	.3	.9(*E*) .1(*T*)

(a) Conduct a new extensive form analysis (using a corrected decision tree) to determine the strategy that maximizes expected payoff.

(b) Conduct a new normal form analysis (using corrected joint probabilities) to select the strategy that maximizes expected payoff.

26-13 A dispatcher classifies each truckload of apricots purchased by Yellow Giant under contract from local orchards as underripe, ripe, or overripe. She must then decide whether a particular truckload will be used for dried apricots (*D*) or for apricot preserves (*P*). A truckload of apricots used for preserves yields a profit of $6,000 if the fruit has a high sugar content, but only $4,000 if the sugar content is low (because costly extra sugar must be added). Regardless of sugar content, a truckload of dried apricots yields a profit of $5,000. In either case, the actual sugar content can be determined only during final processing.

The probabilities are .3 for an underripe truckload, .5 for a ripe one, and .2 for an overripe one. The following probabilities for sugar content have been established for given levels of ripeness.

Sugar Content	Underripe	Ripe	Overripe
Low	.9	.4	.2
High	.1	.6	.8
	1.0	1.0	1.0

(a) Construct the dispatcher's decision tree diagram and perform an extensive form analysis to determine the maximum expected payoff strategy for disposing of a truckload of apricots.

(b) List the possible strategies for disposing of a truckload of apricots. Perform a normal form analysis to select the strategy that yields the greatest expected profit.

26-14 Suppose that the manager in Exercise 25-17, page 1011, wishes to implement a consumer testing program at a cost of $50,000. Consumer testing will be either favorable (a 40% chance) or unfavorable. Given a favorable test result, the chance of product success is judged to be 80%. For an unfavorable test result, the toothpaste's success probability is judged to be only 30%.

(a) Assuming that testing is used, construct a decision tree diagram. Then, perform backward induction analysis to determine the optimal strategy to employ in using the test results.

(b) Identify the basic strategies involving the use of the results of the consumer testing program. Construct a payoff table with these strategies as the choices and the joint market outcomes and test results as the events. Then, conduct a normal form analysis to determine which strategy maximizes expected payoff.

26-5 PREPOSTERIOR ANALYSIS: VALUING AND DECIDING ABOUT EXPERIMENTAL INFORMATION

We have seen that the EVPI may be useful as a filter to eliminate very expensive sources of predictive information. And, when the EVPI is large, it signals that an improved decision may be achieved if the main decision is deferred until potential sources of experimental information have been examined. At the other extreme, EVPI may be so obviously tiny that little would be gained from such an evaluation, and the main decision should be made without delay.

Candidate sources of predictive information may be measured in an analogous fashion to the theoretically perfect (but almost never actually available) forecast. To illustrate how less-than-perfect information may be so valued, we will examine the oil wildcatter's decision using an alternative approach.

We begin with a fresh decision tree analysis of just the seismic survey portion, shown in Figure 26-9. (For simplicity, the obviously nonoptimal strategies, abandoning no matter what, and so on, have been prepruned from the tree.) Under this alternative analysis, the outcomes are quantified in terms of *gross* payoffs that do not reflect the cost of the experimental information. The \$30,000 survey cost has therefore been added back into the payoff column. (That amount will be accounted for at a later stage of the evaluation.)

THE EXPECTED VALUE OF EXPERIMENTAL INFORMATION: EVEI

Backward induction prunes the new smaller tree exactly as before, with an ultimate expected payoff of \$57,500. This quantity is referred to as the **expected payoff with experimental information**. The expected payoff advantage of having that information may be found by subtracting the maximum expected payoff (with no information), found earlier to be \$25,000 (from drilling) for the oil wildcatter. This difference is the **expected value of experimental information**, or EVEI.

$$\text{EVEI} = \text{Expected payoff with experimental information (from tree)} - \text{Maximum expected payoff (with no information)}$$

For the oil wildcatter's seismic survey, we compute

$$\text{EVEI(seismic)} = \$57{,}500 - \$25{,}000 = \$32{,}500$$

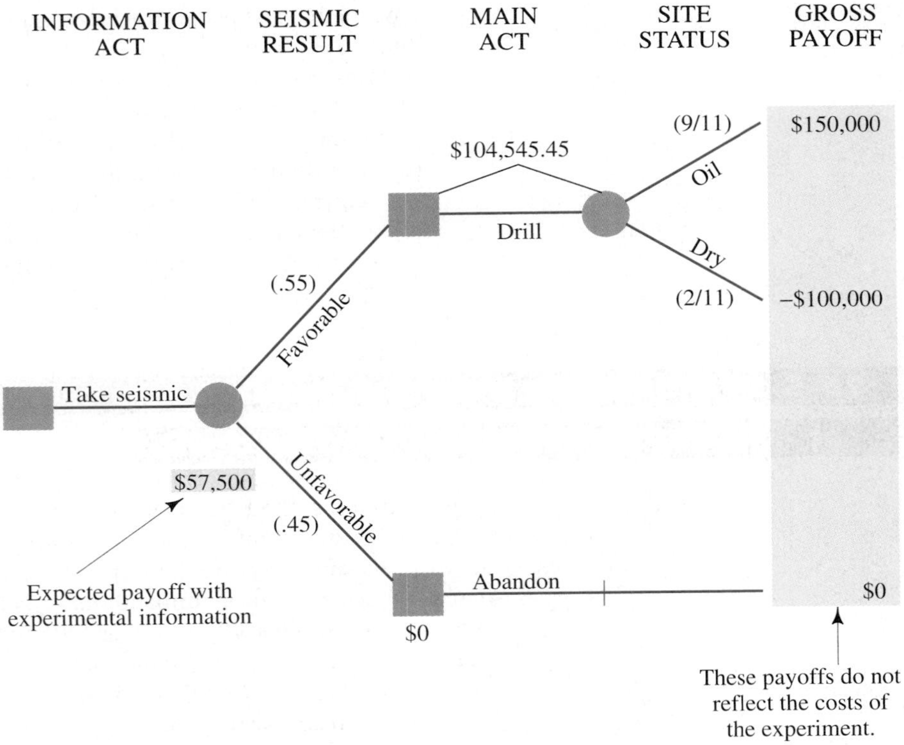

FIGURE 26-9 The alternative decision tree analysis for wildcatting decision using seismic survey.

The above quantity indicates that the decision maker would experience a $32,500 advantage in expected payoff by first taking a seismic survey, followed by the indicated choices, over deciding (drilling) without benefit of that experimental information. This amount is totally analogous to the earlier EVPI figure of $50,000. The EVEI must be smaller than the EVPI, however, because an actual experiment is not 100% reliable (as a perfect predictor would be).

THE EXPECTED NET GAIN OF EXPERIMENTING: ENGE

Although the EVEI is analogous to EVPI, it cannot be used as the final yardstick because it does not incorporate the *cost* of the experiment. (And, we have never bothered to consider a cost for perfect information, which is strictly hypothetical.) The net advantage from predictive information must reflect its cost. Subtracting the cost from EVEI, we obtain the **expected net gain of experimenting**, or ENGE.

$$\text{ENGE} = \text{EVEI} - \text{Cost}$$

The seismic survey will cost $30,000, and thus has an expected net gain of

$$\text{ENGE(seismic)} = \$32{,}500 - \$30{,}000 = \$2{,}500$$

This amount conveys the net expected payoff advantage from using a seismic survey—and then taking the best action indicated for the results achieved—over choosing the best main act without that information.

USING ENGE TO CHOOSE ALTERNATIVE EXPERIMENTS

A decision maker may have several candidate experiments helpful in predicting the main events. The ENGE may be determined for each, resulting in a value that reflects the respective experiment's reliability and cost. Since the ENGEs will summarize, in a consistent manner, the worth of each source of information, those values may be used in choosing among the possible experiments.

This may be demonstrated by continuing with our oil wildcatter's decision. Suppose that a second experiment may be employed as an alternative to the seismic survey. This involves an aerial mapping of the lease site with a magnetic anomaly detector, a procedure that has proven successful in helping to pinpoint promising drilling locations.

For simplicity, we assume that just three outcomes are possible: generally positive readings, neutral findings, and an overall negative result. Previous experience with this procedure has shown that it will give a positive result with .70 probability in similar fields known to have oil; for those same sites it will give a neutral result 20% of the time and a negative one 10% of the time. Also, in regions known to have no oil it predicts negative 60% of the time, neutral 30%, and positive 10%. Using the same prior probabilities as before, Figure 26-10 provides the probability trees for the actual and informational chronologies.

The probabilities for the informational chronology with the magnetic anomaly detection are entered onto the decision tree in Figure 26-11. (Since there are three experimental results, the nonoptimality of some strategies is not clear-cut, and all act forks are portrayed in complete form.) As with the last tree, gross payoffs are used, and the cost of the procedure is not reflected. A backward induction analysis indicates that the wildcatter should drill if a positive reading is achieved, will achieve tying expected payoffs if it is neutral, and should abandon the lease site if the results are negative. Magnetic anomaly detection provides an expected payoff with experimental information of \$47,500, the amount brought back to the initial event node.

Subtracting the maximum expected payoff when no information is used, we have

$$\text{EVEI(magnetic)} = \$47{,}500 - \$25{,}000 = \$22{,}500$$

This amount is smaller than the counterpart found for the seismic, reflecting the lower reliability of magnetic anomaly detection. But the complete analysis must consider cost as well. The surveyor will do the job for \$22,000—quite a bit less than the cost of the seismic survey. But that is not low enough to justify the procedure, since we compute the expected net gain to be

$$\text{ENGE(magnetic)} = \$22{,}500 - \$22{,}000 = \$500$$

which is worse than what may be achieved using the original seismic survey. The oil wildcatter will maximize expected payoff by using the seismic survey in preference to magnetic anomaly detection.

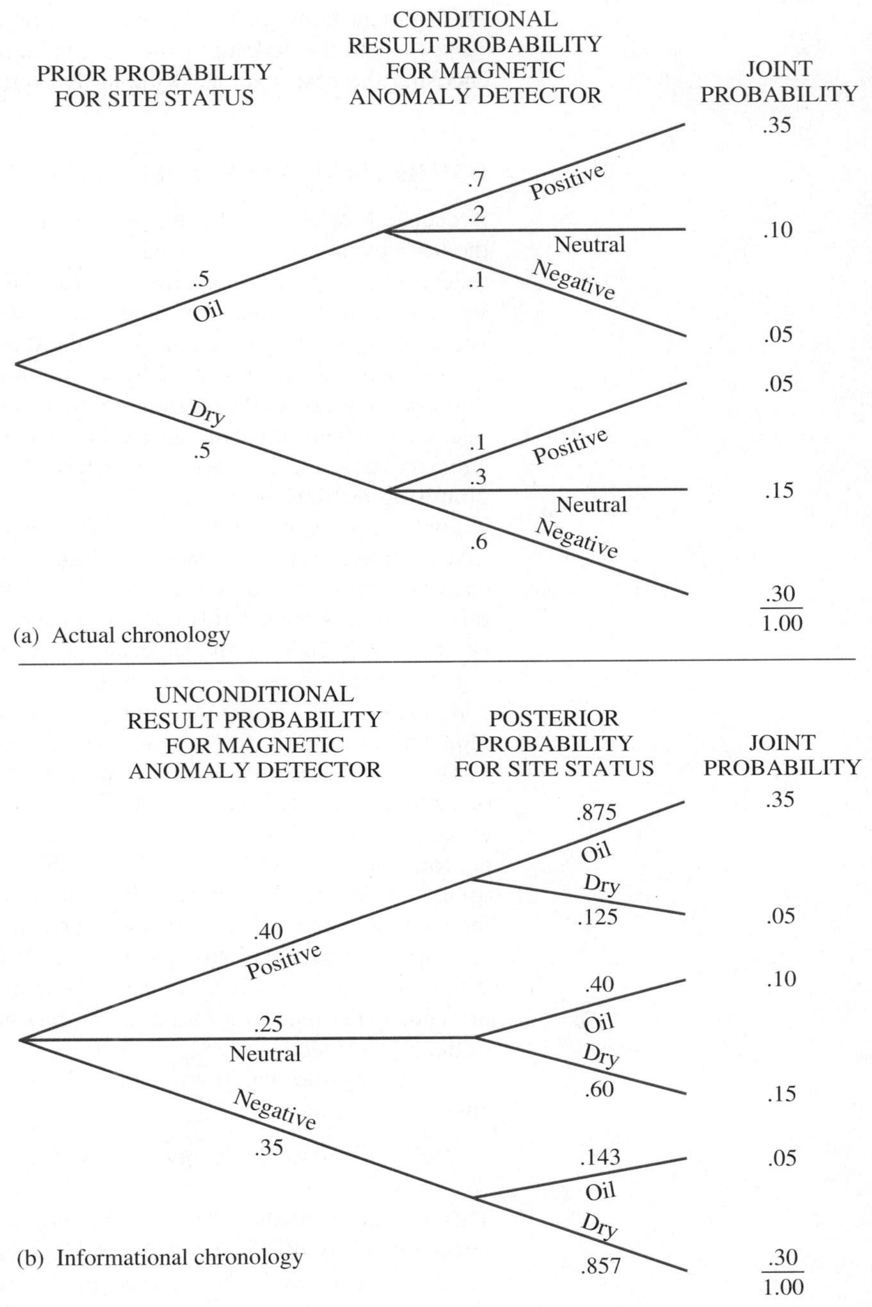

FIGURE 26-10 Probability tree diagrams for the wildcatter's event chronologies using a magnetic anomaly detector.

FINDING EVEI USING A STRATEGY TABLE

In the preceding section we saw that for many decisions the course of action maximizing expected payoff can sometimes be determined through normal form analysis, using a payoff table with strategies as the acts. As an alternative to using

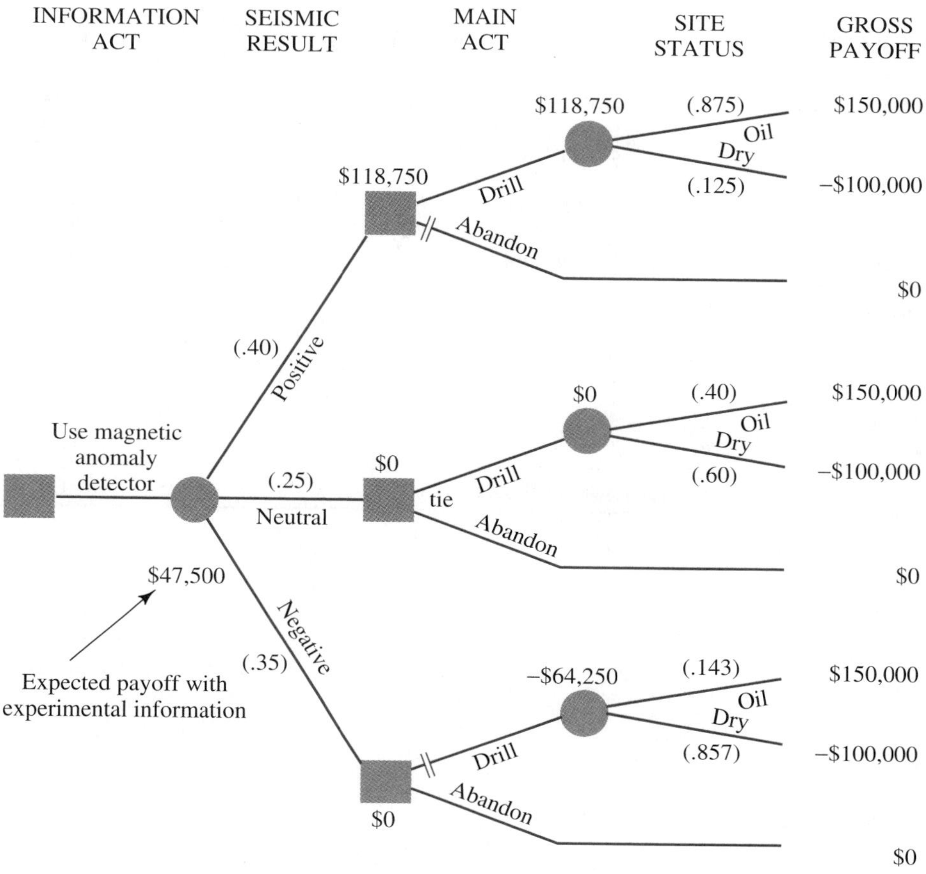

FIGURE 26-11 The alternative decision tree analysis for wildcatting decision using a magnetic anomaly detector.

a decision tree, that approach can sometimes be used to establish EVEI. Table 26-6 shows the normal form counterpart analysis to that done with the tree in Figure 26-11. Expected payoff is maximized by selecting either strategy S_2 (drill only if positive or neutral) or strategy S_5 (drill only if positive). The same result was found through backward induction in Figure 26-11. The expected payoff with experimental information is the maximum expected payoff found for each of these strategies, $47,500, and is also identical to the amount established in the decision tree analysis. As before, an identical EVEI may be achieved by subtracting from this the maximum expected payoff with no information, $25,000.

EXERCISES

26-15 Consider, again, the oil wildcatter in Section 26-5. Suppose that, for an additional $10,000, a special computer run can enhance the magnetic

TABLE 26-6 Normal Form Analysis Using a Strategy Table to Evaluate the Oil Wildcatter's Magnetic Anomaly Detector

			Strategy							
			S_1	S_2	S_3	S_4	S_5	S_6	S_7	S_8
		If Positive:	D	D	D	A	D	A	A	A
Joint Event	Joint Probability	If Neutral:	D	D	A	D	A	D	A	A
		If Negative:	D	A	D	D	A	A	D	A
Pos. & Oil	.35		150	150	150	0	150	0	0	0
Pos. & Dry	.05		−100	−100	−100	0	−100	0	0	0
Neu. & Oil	.10		150	150	0	150	0	150	0	0
Neu. & Dry	.15		−100	−100	0	−100	0	−100	0	0
Neg. & Oil	.05		150	0	150	150	0	0	150	0
Neg. & Dry	.30		−100	0	−100	−100	0	0	−100	0
		Expected Payoff ($1,000):	25	47.5	25	−15	47.5	0	−22.5	0

anomaly detection results. The new procedure will provide the following conditional result probabilities.

Result	Given Oil	Given No Oil
Positive	.90	.05
Neutral	.07	.20
Negative	.03	.75

(a) Construct the new probability trees for the informational and actual chronologies.
(b) Compute the new EVEI and ENGE for enhanced magnetic anomaly detection.
(c) In terms of the expected payoff advantage, is the enhancement worth the added cost? Of the two original ones and the new one, which source of experimental information would now be best for the oil wildcatter to use?

26-16 Refer to Exercises 26-2 and 26-9 and to your answers.
(a) Using the given prior probabilities for the national response, determine the expected payoff for retaining the old box and for using the new box. Which act maximizes expected payoff?
(b) Determine Quicker Oats' EVPI.
(c) Compute the EVEI for the test marketing.
(d) Suppose that the test marketing costs $100,000. Compute the ENGE. Does Quicker Oats actually maximize expected net payoff by using test marketing?

26-17 Refer to Exercise 26-10 and to your answers. Suppose that a special version of the film must be used in the sneak preview.
(a) Assuming that the same probabilities apply as before, compute the EVEI.
(b) If the new film costs $100,000 to make, compute the ENGE.
(c) For an additional $100,000, a special statistical analysis may be done following the sneak preview results. That analysis will result in an

overall favorable or unfavorable rating. But each of the percentages given in Exercise 26-10 will be 15 points higher. Construct the new probability trees for the actual and informational chronologies.

(d) Determine the expected payoff with the enhanced experiment in (c).

(e) Compute the EVEI and ENGE for the enhanced experiment in (c). Would the extra $100,000 be justified?

26-18 Refer to the decision in Exercises 26-3 and 26-11 and to your answers.

(a) Construct the Prospector's decision tree diagram assuming that the seismic is used. (Eliminate obviously non-optimal strategies.) Then, using gross payoffs, determine the expected payoff with experimental information.

(b) Compute the EVEI and ENGE. Does using the seismic have an expected payoff advantage over making the main decision with no experimental information?

26-6 FUTURE ANALYSIS

The future analysis stage may or may not come into play. In the context of the wildcatter's decision, a future analysis may only be made once the seismic result is known. Should it turn out favorably, the wildcatter might want to defer the main decision whether or not to drill until after considering a second test, for example, based on finding magnetic anomalies. The posterior probabilities of 9/11 for oil and 2/11 for dry would serve as the prior probabilities in such an evaluation.

SUMMARY

1. **What are the four stages of decision making with experimental information?**

Decision making using experimental information is concerned with subsidiary decisions about what type of information, if any, to get and what actions to take when a particular experimental result is obtained. Decisions using experiments may be broken into four stages. **Prior analysis** involves selecting a payoff measure and determining prior probabilities for the events. Expected payoffs are then computed, along with the EVPI.

Should the EVPI be large enough to suggest potential improvements in expected payoffs by deferring the main decision until after an experiment, a **preposterior analysis** may be performed. This provides an overall expected payoff for each experiment contemplated. Preposterior analysis includes for each source of information a **posterior analysis** that indicates what action would be optimal under the various possible results. A **future analysis** considers issues beyond the present main decision.

2. **How do we find and classify the various types of probabilities employed in a decision analysis with experimental information?**

Although Bayes' theorem may be used to determine the necessary posterior probabilities, it may be easier to work with two sets of probability trees. One involves an event sequence portraying the **actual chronology**. All events are originally generated in this sequence. This tree exhibits the **prior probabilities** for the main events, followed by **conditional result probabilities** for the experimental results. The prior probabilities are often subjective in nature, while the conditional result probabilities may be obtained historically and express the underlying reliability of the experiment in predicting the main events. Each path in the tree corresponds to a joint event, and the multiplication law is used to establish the respective **joint probabilities**.

The second probability tree reverses the sequence and shows the **informational chronology**. The decision structure itself represents events in this sequence, reflecting that we usually find things out backwards from the sequence in which they happen. The initial stage involves an event fork for the experimental results, which have **unconditional result probabilities**. The second stage gives the **posterior probabilities** for the main events. Both sets of probability values are computed using the respective joint probabilities transferred from the first tree.

3. **What are the two basic forms of posterior analysis?**
Posterior analysis may be performed with decision trees. That requires first constructing the probability trees for the actual and informational chronologies. That procedure is sometimes called an **extensive form analysis**. Backward induction on the decision tree provides the course of action maximizing expected payoff. An alternative tabular procedure treats as acts all strategies or decision rules for utilizing the experimental results. A payoff table is then constructed using joint events composed from the main events and the possible experimental results. The same course of action maximizes expected payoff under this approach, which is called **normal form analysis**.

4. **What is preposterior analysis and which summary measures are employed?**
Preposterior analysis is concerned with selecting among various possible experiments. For each of these a summary measure, the **EVEI** (expected value of experimental information) may be found. That quantity expresses the advantage, in terms of expected payoff, of having that *experimental* information. It is analogous to EVPI (for *perfect* information), and is computed from the difference.

$$\text{EVEI} = \text{Expected payoff with experimental information} \\ - \text{Maximum expected payoff (with no information)}$$

The above is always smaller than EVPI, and like EVPI it does not account for any cost of getting the information. The first term, the expected payoff with experimental information, may be found either through a backward induction with a decision *tree* or by finding the maximum expected payoff among the strategies comprising a payoff *table*. The second term is the maximum expected payoff computed during prior analysis. When the cost of the experiment is subtracted from EVEI, the **ENGE** (expected net gain of experimenting) is obtained. The best experiment is generally the one that maximizes ENGE.

REVIEW EXERCISES

26-19 The decision tree diagram in Figure 26-12 has been constructed by a marketing manager who wishes to determine how to introduce a new product. The manager judges that the prior probability for marketing success is .40.

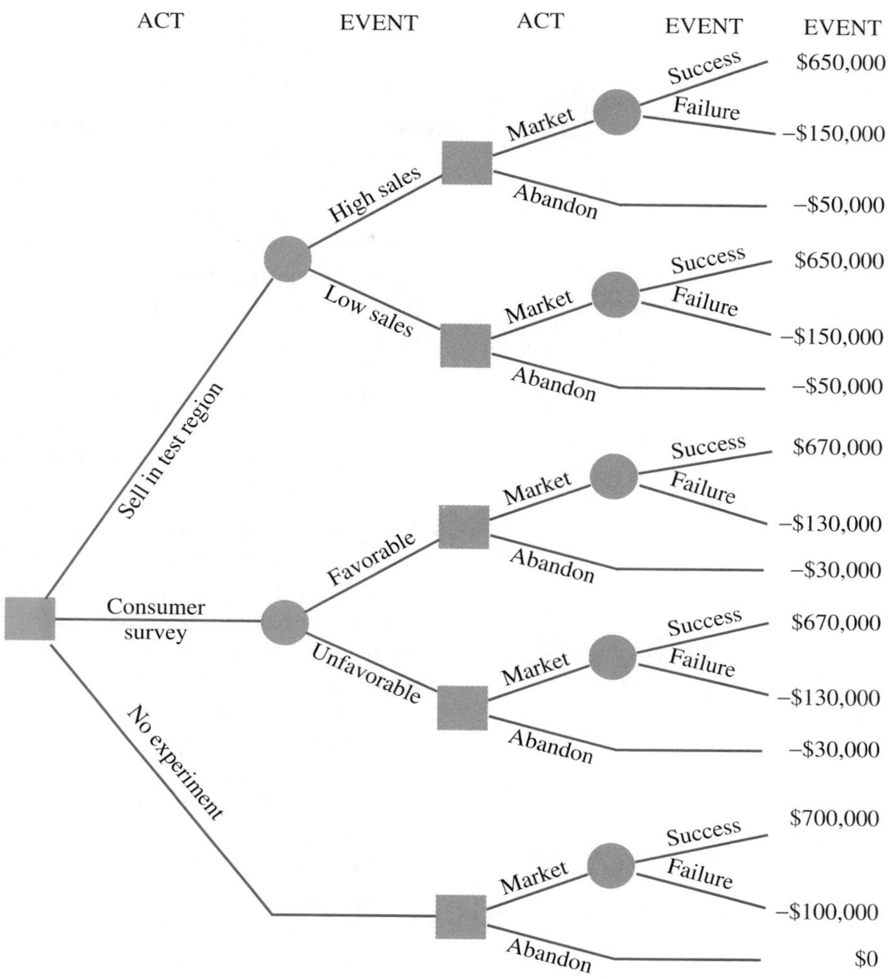

FIGURE 26-12

(a) From a consumer survey costing $30,000, the manager obtains an 80% reliable indication of the product's impact in the marketplace. Thus, the probability for a favorable survey result given market success is .80, and the probability for an unfavorable result given market failure is .80. Determine the posterior probabilities for the market events and the unconditional result probabilities for the survey events.

(b) A sales program costing $50,000 might be conducted in a test region. The results are judged to be 95% reliable. Determine the posterior and unconditional result probabilities.

(c) Using the information given in the problem statement and your answers to (a) and (b), perform backward induction to find the manager's optimal course of action. (The payoffs in Figure 26-12 include the cost of experimenting.)

26-20 Solve the movie reviewer's prediction problem originally posed in Exercise 21-5 (page 890) by constructing the probability trees for the actual and informational chronologies.

26-21 Solve the employment screening test problem originally posed in Exercise 21-4 (page 889) by constructing the probability trees for the actual and informational chronologies.

26-22 A box contains two pairs of dice. One pair is a fair one. The other pair consists of one die cube with a three on every side and one die cube with a four on every side. A pair is to be selected at random and tossed. You will only be able to see the top showing faces and not the sides. The main events of interest pertain to the crookedness or fairness of the tossed dice. (Both dice in the tossed pair will fall into the same category.) In each of the following cases, construct probability trees for the actual and informational chronologies.

(a) The experimental result is determining whether or not a seven-sum (three and four, two and five, one and six) occurs.

(b) The experimental result is determining whether or not a three-four combination occurs, which has a greater predictive worth than the result in (a).

26-23 Lucky Jones must decide whether to participate in a card game offered by Inscrutable Smith. For the price of \$5, Jones will draw a card from an ordinary deck of playing cards. If the card is a king, Smith is to pay Jones \$60 (so that Jones wins \$55). But if the card is not a king, Jones will receive nothing for the \$5. Smith, eager for action, offers Jones an additional enticement. For \$3, Jones can draw a card without looking at it. Smith will then tell Jones whether or not the card is a face card. If Jones wishes to continue, an additional payment of \$5 must be made for the game to proceed.

(a) Construct a decision tree diagram showing the structure of Jones' decision.

(b) Determine the probabilities for the events and the total profit for the end positions.

(c) What course of action will provide Jones with the greatest expected payoff?

26-24 Suppose that the manager in Exercise 25-17 wishes to implement a consumer testing program at a cost of \$50,000. Consumer testing will be either favorable (a 40% chance) or unfavorable. Given a favorable test result, the chance of product success is judged to be 80%. For an unfavorable test result, the toothpaste's success probability is judged to be only 30%. Assuming that testing is used, construct a decision tree diagram. Then perform backward induction analysis to determine the optimal strategy to employ in using the test results.

26-25 Refer to the decision in Problem 26-8 and to your answers.

(a) Construct the manager's prepruned decision tree diagram assuming that the seismic is used. Then, using gross payoffs, determine the expected payoff with experimental information.

(b) Compute the EVEI and ENGE. Does using the seismic have an expected payoff advantage over making the main decision with no experimental information?

CASE Comp-u-Com

Comp-u-Com is a telecommunications equipment manufacturing company specializing in computer-telephone interfacing. Management is deciding what items to introduce in the company product mix in the coming season. One possibility is a high-speed modem intended for home use. If successful, the new product is expected to increase Comp-u-Com's profits by $200,000. If unsuccessful, the modem's introduction cost of $100,000 will be lost.

On a trial basis, the company has in the past employed an outside panel of experts to screen new products. In evaluating that arrangement for a six-month trial period, Comp-u-Com found that the panel approved 7 out of 11 products that later proved to be successful. The panel disapproved 5 out of 7 products that had been introduced anyway and eventually failed.

A high-tech marketing research firm proposes, instead, to give a market prognostication. For similar products, the firm's batting average has been 90% in making favorable forecasts for items that later prove to be successful and 95% in making unfavorable predictions for devices that later fail in the marketplace.

Management judges the new modem very positively, assigning a 40% chance that it will be a successful new product.

QUESTIONS

1. The decision has not yet been made to employ the panel.
   (a) If the main modem decision were to be made now, which act would maximize expected payoff?
   (b) What is the upper limit on what management would pay for highly reliable information predicting the success or failure of the modem?
2. For the modem events and the panel results, construct the probability trees for the actual and informational chronologies.
3. The panel cost is $10,000. Using gross payoffs, construct a decision tree diagram for this experiment and perform a backward induction analysis to determine the expected payoff using this information. Compute the EVEI and ENGE.
4. Suppose that we use the marketing researcher's prognostication. As an alternative to employing a decision tree, a normal form analysis can be performed to establish the value of using the prognostication.
   (a) List Comp-u-Com's possible strategies from using the prognostication.
   (b) Ignoring any cost of experimenting, construct Comp-u-Com's payoff table, using as acts the strategies in (a) and the various joint events for prognostications and market outcomes.
   (c) Which panel strategy maximizes Comp-u-Com's expected gross payoff with this experimental information?
   (d) The marketing researcher will charge $20,000. Determine the EVEI and ENGE.
5. What should Comp-u-Com do to maximize expected payoff?

CHAPTER 27

BAYESIAN ANALYSIS OF DECISIONS USING SAMPLE INFORMATION

BEFORE READING THIS CHAPTER, MAKE SURE YOU UNDERSTAND:

Basic concepts of probability (Chapter 5).
Probability distributions and expected value (Chapter 6).
Normal distribution (Chapter 7).
Subjective probability in decision making (Chapter 20).
Basic concepts of decision analysis (Chapter 24).
Elements of decision theory (Chapter 25).
Bayesian analysis of decisions using experimental information (Chapter 26).

AFTER READING THIS CHAPTER, YOU WILL UNDERSTAND:

About the fundamental features of Bayesian analysis with samples.
About the probability elements in a posterior analysis with the proportion.
How to establish decision rules.
About the elements of preposterior analysis using sample information.
About Bayesian sampling with the mean.
About the differences and relative advantages of Bayesian statistics and traditional hypothesis testing.

In Chapter 26, we considered the general problem of using experimental information in decision making. We will now consider a decision, commonly encountered in business situations, that involves just *two acts*. The experiment is taking a **random sample** from a population whose characteristics will affect the ultimate payoffs. The decision maker's choice depends on the particular sample result obtained.

Two types of populations are encountered in these sampling experiments. The **qualitative population** is composed of units that may be classified into categories. Examples are persons who may be categorized by occupation (blue-collar, professional), sex (male, female), or preference (preferring a product, disliking a product); and production items that may be classified in terms of quality (satisfactory, unsatisfactory), weight (below the limit, above the limit), or color (light, medium, dark). The **quantitative population** associates a numerical value with each unit. For example, people may be measured in terms of income levels, aptitude test scores, or years of experience; and items may be assigned numerical values to indicate weight, volume, or quantity of an ingredient.

A sample from a qualitative population tells us how many sample units fall into a particular category, and this number reflects the prevalence of that attribute in the population, which in turn affects the payoff associated with the incidence of the attribute. For example, in deciding how to dispose of a supplier's shipment, a receiving inspector may discover that 12 of the items out of a random sample of 100 are defective, indicating that there is a high probability that the entire shipment is bad and that returning it might maximize expected payoff. The payoffs in such a problem are often expressed in terms of the proportion π of the population having the key attribute (for example, the proportion of defective items in the entire shipment). As in most decision making using experiments, the value of π itself and the number of defectives that will turn up in the sample are both uncertain. Probabilities for the number of defectives may be determined by using the binomial distribution.

A sample taken from a quantitative population provides a similar basis for action, such as accepting or rejecting a machine setting in a chemical process. Here, the mean quantity of a particular ingredient in each gallon may be the determining factor in establishing the payoff. The population mean μ measures the central quantity of the ingredient in all gallons made under that setting. The true value of μ is uncertain. A second area of uncertainty involves the quantities in the sample itself; here, the sample mean $\bar{X}$ may serve as the basis for decision making.

In this chapter, we will consider how to integrate sample information into the basic decision-making structure. As in Chapter 26, the procedure involves prior probabilities for π or μ, which must be revised to coincide with possible sample results to provide posterior probabilities for these population parameters. Backward induction with revised probabilities then provides the optimal decision rule, based on the sample statistic that is obtained. The analysis may be expanded to consider how many sample observations must be made.

27-1 DECISION MAKING WITH THE PROPORTION

We begin our discussion of Bayesian sampling with procedures based on the proportion. There are surprising features. First, good decision making might be reached without sampling at all; that is because sampling may be very expensive in relation to the value of perfect information. Second, a great deal of information may be gleaned from very small sample sizes.

APPLICATION TO ACCEPTANCE SAMPLING: DISK DRIVE QUALITY

A quality assurance manager for a computer OEM (original equipment manufacturer) wishes to establish a procedure for determining whether to accept or reject shipments of hard disk drives. Each drive unit in an accepted shipment will be directly installed, untested, in computer housings. Should an installed unit later prove to be defective, the computer must be disassembled and a new disk drive installed, at great expense. This expense may be avoided if the manager instead rejects the shipment and then routes all disk drive units to an inspection facility to be tested prior to assembly.

The manager is primarily concerned with the proportion π of defective units in each shipment. Should π be small, then it may be cheaper to accept the shipment and install untested disk drives. But for a large π it may be considerably less expensive to reject the shipment and test all incoming drives before installation. Of course, the value of π for any given shipment is an uncertain quantity.

The payoff measure for this decision is based on \$50 value added to the final product per installed disk drive, which establishes a basic value of \$50,000 for a 1,000-unit shipment. The net payoff is found by subtracting any relevant costs. Replacing a defective drive already installed in a computer costs \$100, so that for the entire shipment the cost of accepting is $\$100\pi(1{,}000) = \$100{,}000\pi$. The cost of 100% testing of the disk drives (in rejected shipments) is \$20 per unit. Because the supplier gives full credit for returned units, the total cost of rejecting a shipment is $\$20(1{,}000) = \$20{,}000$, so that the net payoff is $\$50{,}000 - \$20{,}000 = \$30{,}000$.

The manager's payoffs may be expressed algebraically as

$$\text{Payoff} = \begin{cases} \$50{,}000 - \$100{,}000\pi & \text{for accept} \\ \$30{,}000 & \text{for reject} \end{cases}$$

Using the above, the payoff table is constructed in Table 27-1 applicable to each shipment containing 1,000 disk drives. Five possible levels are provided for π, with subjective prior probabilities based on previous experience with the supplier and the manager's judgment. The analysis is simplified by considering π

TABLE 27-1 Payoff Table for Disk Drive Decision

Proportion Defective Event	Probability	Act: Accept	Act: Reject	Payoff with Perfect Information
$\pi = .05$	.10	\$45,000	\$30,000	\$45,000
$\pi = .10$	.15	40,000	30,000	40,000
$\pi = .15$	.20	35,000	30,000	35,000
$\pi = .20$	.25	30,000	30,000	30,000
$\pi = .25$	.30	25,000	30,000	30,000
	Expected payoff	\$32,500	\$30,000	\$34,000

to the nearest whole 5%. (The same procedures would apply if we considered $\pi = .01, .02, \ldots .27$.)

PRIOR ANALYSIS OF THE DECISION

The expected payoff for accept is $32,500, which is greater than the $30,000 payoff achieved by reject. This indicates that without pursuing any further experimental information the manager should accept each shipment, replacing only those disk drives that are found to be defective after they are installed.

However, the expected value of perfect information is

$$\text{EVPI} = \$34{,}000 - \$32{,}500 = \$1{,}500$$

which indicates that considerable potential savings may be achieved by sampling each incoming shipment and testing randomly selected disk drives.

POSTERIOR ANALYSIS USING SAMPLE INFORMATION

If a sample is used, the manager will not decide what to do with a shipment until after obtaining the sample results. If the sample contains a high number of defectives, the manager should reject the shipment. The shipment should be accepted if the sample contains a low number of defectives.

The choice of sample size, and the question of whether to sample at all, will be considered shortly. For now, suppose that the manager will use a sample of $n = 2$ items. The decision tree diagram in Figure 27-1 applies. Notice that there are three possible levels for the number of defectives R found in the sample. In each case, an act fork follows with accept and reject as the choices. The event forks in the final stage each have five branches, one for each π event. The final payoffs were determined from the above expression. For brevity, there is no event fork following reject, because the payoffs will be the same regardless of the level for π. The probability values are found using the same basic procedure as in Chapter 26.

The conditional result probabilities are obtained using the following binomial formula.*

$$\Pr[R = r] = \frac{n!}{r!(n - r)!}\pi^r(1 - \pi)^{n - r}$$

The result probabilities follow logically from the given n and the assumed level for π. Table 27-2 shows the calculations using the above to determine the conditional result probabilities for the number of sample defectives R. The values obtained appear on the second-stage branches in the probability tree for the actual chronology in Figure 27-2.

Each level of π corresponds to a *different population* and therefore requires a separate set of binomial probabilities. In calculating these values, *it is important not to confuse the level of π with its prior probability*. For example, in calculating the conditional result probabilities for the number of defectives in the sample

*The binomial serves only as an approximation when sampling from a finite population. The true sampling distribution for R in those cases is the hypergeometric, which should be used instead when the population size N is small.

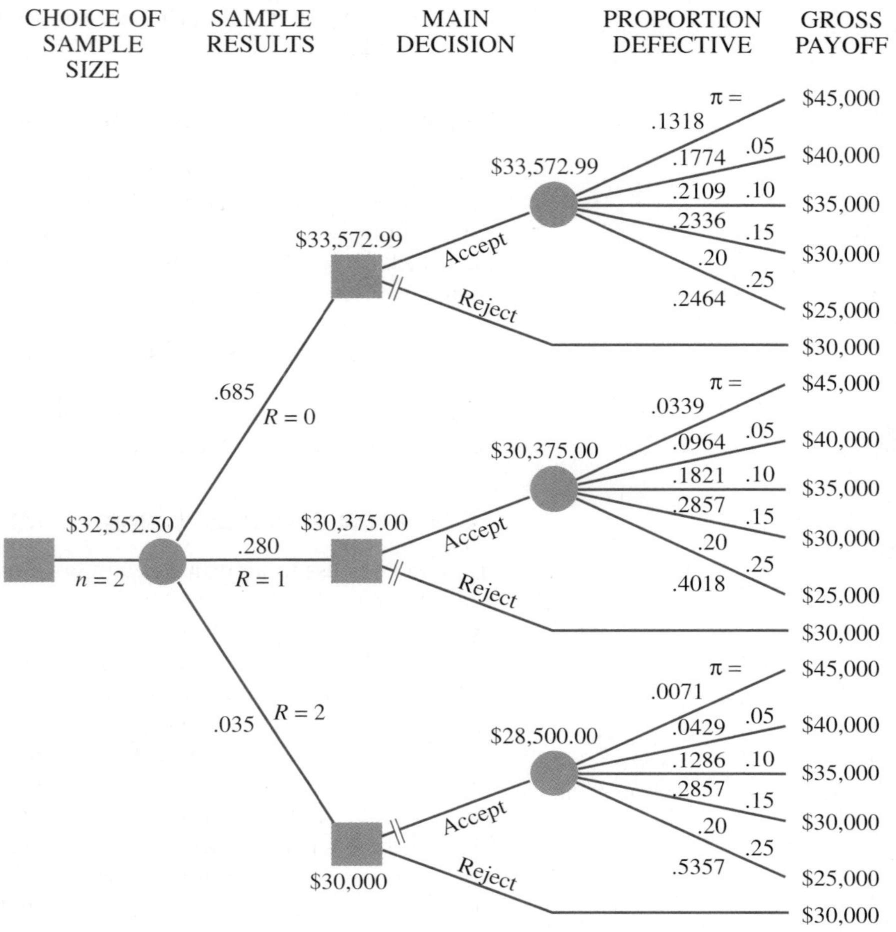

FIGURE 27-1 One of several decision trees for acceptance sampling of disk drives.

when $\pi = .05$, we use .05 as the trial success probability π; we do not use .10, which is the prior probability of the event and is applied in a later step of the analysis.

The joint probabilities are then computed, as in Chapter 26, by multiplying the probabilities on the respective branches. These are transferred to their proper location in the probability tree for the informational chronology in Figure 27-3. In making the computations, *the events should not be confused with their probabilities*. Remember that $\pi = .05$ and $\pi = .10$ are the *events* and represent possible levels for the number of defectives in the population. (Because these equations are events, it makes no sense to combine the values of π arithmetically. Since they should not be added together, they certainly do not have to add up to 1.) The prior probabilities .10, .15, . . . are the multipliers. Thus, the top joint probability in Figure 27-2 is

$$\Pr[\pi = .05 \textit{ and } R = 0] = .10 \times .9025 = .09025$$

and the other joint probabilities are calculated in the same way.

TABLE 27-2 Binomial Conditional Result Probabilities for the Number of Defective Disk Drives ($n = 2$)

π	r	$Pr[R = r] = \frac{n!}{r!(n-r)!}\pi^r(1-\pi)^{n-r}$
.05	0	$1(.05)^0(.95)^2 =$ .9025
.05	1	$2(.05)^1(.95)^1 =$ .0950
.05	2	$1(.05)^2(.95)^0 =$ .0025
		1.0000
.10	0	$1(.10)^0(.90)^2 =$ .8100
.10	1	$2(.10)^1(.90)^1 =$ .1800
.10	2	$1(.10)^2(.90)^0 =$ .0100
		1.0000
.15	0	$1(.15)^0(.85)^2 =$ .7225
.15	1	$2(.15)^1(.85)^1 =$ .2550
.15	2	$1(.15)^2(.85)^0 =$ .0225
		1.0000
.20	0	$1(.20)^0(.80)^2 =$ .6400
.20	1	$2(.20)^1(.80)^1 =$ .3200
.20	2	$1(.20)^2(.80)^0 =$ .0400
		1.0000
.25	0	$1(.25)^0(.75)^2 =$ .5625
.25	1	$2(.25)^1(.75)^1 =$ .3750
.25	2	$1(.25)^2(.75)^0 =$ .0625
		1.0000

Figure 27-3 shows the probability tree for the informational chronology. Shown there are the unconditional result probabilities found for R and the posterior probabilities established for π for each given level of R. These are the probabilities that were transferred to the manager's original decision tree diagram in Figure 27-1.

Backward induction with the decision tree (page 1050) indicates that when $n = 2$, the maximum expected payoff for $R = 0$ is \$33,572.99. The result corresponds to choosing the act *accept*. When $R = 1$, the same act provides a maximum expected payoff of \$30,375.00. For $R = 2$, the payoff \$30,000 for reject is greater than the expected payoff for accept, so that reject is the selected act.

THE DECISION RULE AND CRITICAL VALUE

The result of the backward induction may be summarized in terms of the following **decision rule**.

Act 1 (accept) if $R \leq 1$

Act 2 (reject) if $R > 1$

Since we may use the Bayesian procedure for a variety of situations besides acceptance sampling, the decision involves the more general choice between Act 1 and Act 2. The greatest level for R at which Act 1 (here, accept) is the better choice is called the **critical value**, which we denote by C. In quality assurance applications, this is ordinarily called the **acceptance number**. In the present evaluation $C = 1$. Here, C represents the maximum number of sample defectives for which accepting a shipment is the act maximizing expected payoff.

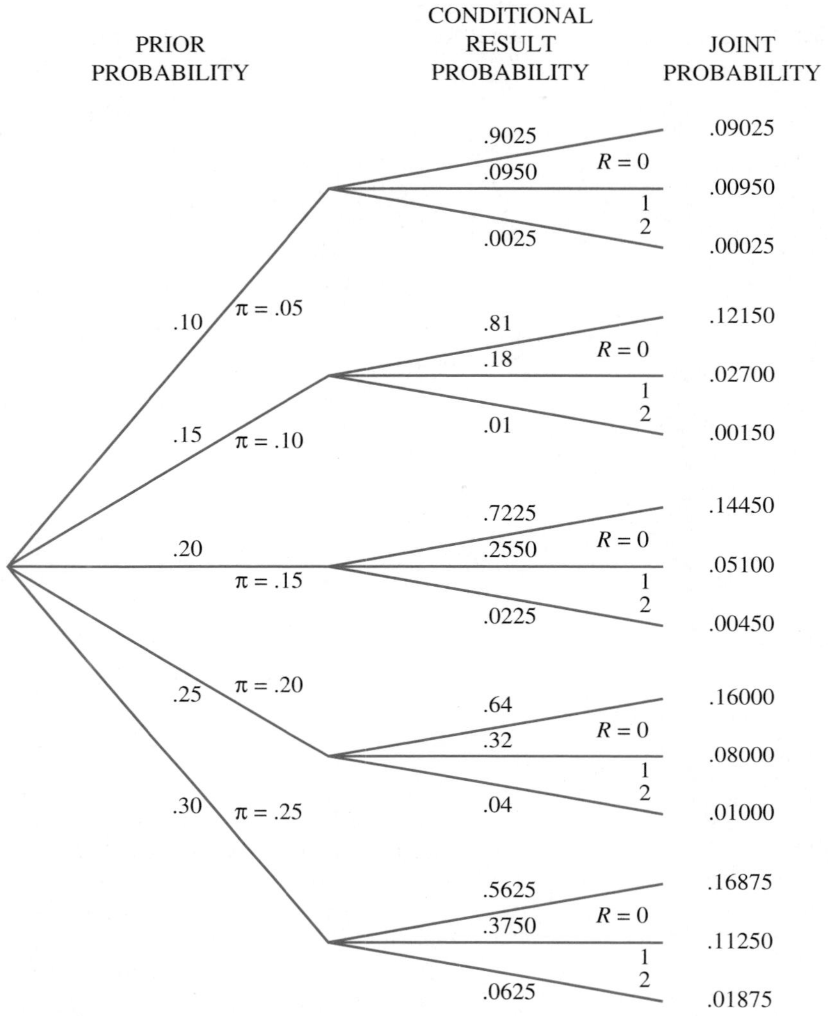

FIGURE 27-2 Probability tree for actual chronology in disk drive acceptance sampling.

The expected payoff in using a sample of $n = 2$ disk drives is \$32,552.50. That amount is greater than the expected payoff of \$32,500 found in Table 27-1 for accept. This suggests that sampling shipments first may be better than accepting them without inspection. Should the cost be low enough, sampling would be superior. But, by itself, the decision tree analysis cannot settle this issue, since the cost of sampling was not reflected. We next consider a systematic evaluation of the sampling issue.

EXERCISES

27-1 High Crock, the brewmaster and part owner of High & Higher Distilleries, has discovered a new fermentation process for malt ale that reclaims corn mash from whiskey vats to begin fermentation. Get, the marketing manager and joint owner of High & Higher, is excited about the revolutionary ale and has assigned the prior probabilities of $\Pr[\pi = .10] = .20$,

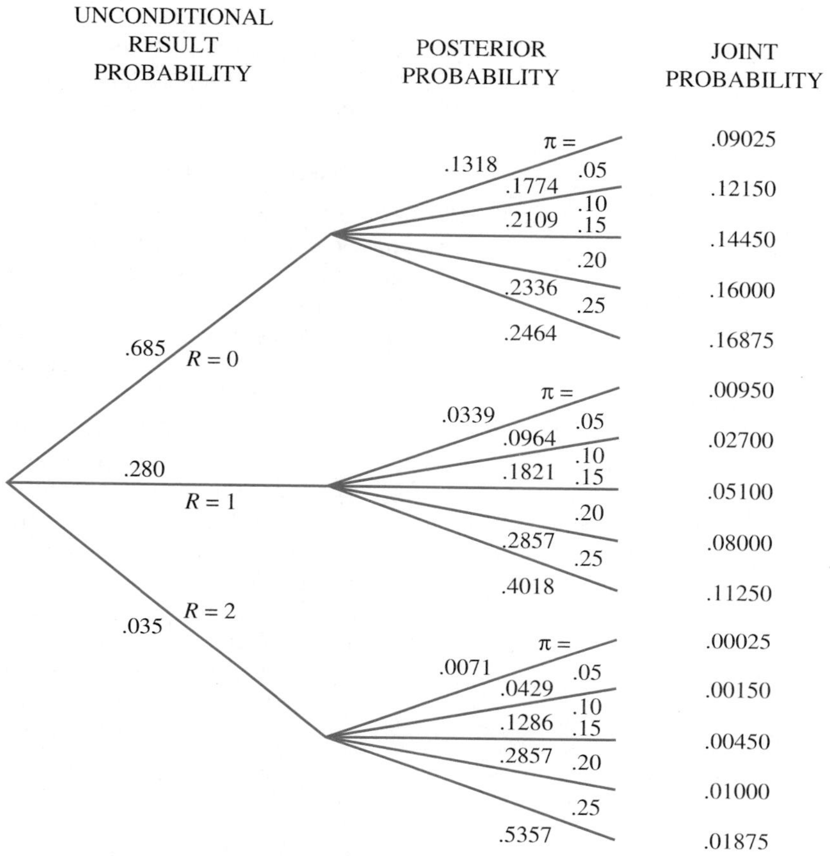

FIGURE 27-3 Probability tree for informational chronology in disk drive acceptance sampling.

$\Pr[\pi = .20] = .50$, and $\Pr[\pi = .30] = .30$ to the proportion π of the market segment he feels will buy the new beer. Get must decide whether to market the new ale or to abandon it. A 10% market share will result in losses of $500,000, 20% is the breakeven level, and 30% will bring $500,000 in present value of future profits.

(a) Perform the prior analysis to determine which act maximizes expected payoff.

(b) Determine the EVPI.

27-2 The president of Admiral Mills believes that the proportion of children π who will like Crunchy Munchy has the following probability distribution.

Possible Proportion π	Probability
1/4	1/3
1/2	1/3
3/4	1/3
	1

The president must decide whether to market Crunchy Munchy now or to abandon the product. If the cereal is marketed, there will be a \$50,000 loss if $\pi = 1/4$, a \$100,000 gain if $\pi = 1/2$ and a \$200,000 profit if $\pi = 3/4$.

(a) Perform the prior analysis to determine which act maximizes expected payoff.

(b) Determine the EVPI.

27-3 (*Continuation of Exercise 27-2*): The president wishes to conduct a preposterior analysis. A portion of this evaluation considers a sample of three children who have been chosen at random, given Crunchy Munchy, and then asked if they like it.

(a) (1) Construct the actual chronological probability tree diagram for the outcomes. Let the values of π represent the events of the branches in the first-stage fork and let the number of children found to like Crunchy Munchy represent the events of the second-stage branches. Use the binomial distribution.

(2) Enter the above probabilities for the possible π values on the appropriate branches. Then, use the binomial formula to determine the probabilities for the branches in the remaining forks, and enter them on your diagram.

(3) Determine the joint probabilities for each end position.

(4) Construct the probability tree diagram for the informational chronology, reversing the event sequences so that the branches of the first fork represent the number of children who like Crunchy Munchy, followed by forks for the values of π. Determine the probabilities for the events represented by each branch.

(5) If all three children like Crunchy Munchy, what are the posterior probabilities for π?

(b) Construct the president's decision tree diagram using gross payoffs to obtain the expected payoff with sample information. What is the critical value at or below which it is best to abandon the product?

27-4 (*Continuation of Exercise 27-1*): Get wishes to conduct a preposterior analysis. A portion of this evaluation considers a sample of $n = 3$ connoisseurs who will be chosen at random to test the new ale. For each person, it will be determined whether or not they would buy the new ale.

(a) Construct the actual chronological probability tree diagram, using the prior probabilities assigned by the marketing manager and the applicable binomial, conditional result probabilities obtained from Appendix Table C.

(b) Using the probabilities generated in the actual chronology, construct the probability tree diagram for the informational chronology. Indicate the unconditional result, posterior, and joint probabilities.

(c) Construct Get's decision tree diagram using gross payoffs to obtain the expected payoff with sample information. What is the critical value at or below which it is best to abandon the new ale?

27-5 Consider the disk drive acceptance sampling illustration in the chapter. For a sample size of $n = 4$, answer the following.

(a) Construct the probability tree diagrams for the actual and informational chronologies. (Use the binomial distribution.)

(b) Construct the decision tree diagram for this sample size. What is the acceptance number?

27-6 A presidential campaign manager asks two politicians what they believe to be the true proportion π of voters favoring their party's candidate. The respective replies are .40 and .50. The manager's judgment leads her to assign equal chances that either politician is correct. A random sample of $n = 100$ registered voters has been selected, and the number R preferring the candidate is to be found. Consider the following possible sample results:

$$R < 40 \qquad 40 \leq R \leq 50 \qquad R > 50$$

(a) Construct the actual chronological probability tree diagram, using the sample results in the second stage. (Appendix Table C provides the conditional result probabilities.)
(b) Construct the probability tree diagram for the informational chronology.
(c) Determine the posterior probability that $\pi = .40$, given each of the following results.
(1) $R < 40$ (2) $40 \leq R \leq 50$ (3) $R > 50$

27-2 VALUING SAMPLE INFORMATION

We are now ready to quantify sample information itself in terms of expected payoff. The decision tree analysis in Figure 27-1 for the disk drive acceptance sampling illustration provides a maximum expected payoff of $32,552.50 when the sample size is $n = 2$. We refer to this quantity as the expected payoff with sample information. It is based on gross payoffs, and does not reflect the cost of sampling. Of course, sampling costs must ultimately be considered. Thus far, our analysis may be classified as *posterior* (oriented toward actions after sampling). We still have to consider the more basic decision of whether or not to sample in the first place, and, if we sample, how large a sample to take. To answer these questions, we must move into the area of *preposterior* analysis (where the vantage is before sampling).

THE EXPECTED VALUE OF SAMPLE INFORMATION

Recall that the EVPI establishes the worth of perfect information and represents the expected payoff advantage that perfect information would have over making the best choice with no information at all. It is computed from the following difference.

$$\begin{aligned}\text{EVPI} = &\text{ Expected payoff with perfect information (under certainty)}\\ &- \text{Maximum expected payoff (with no information)}\end{aligned}$$

Earlier, we computed the quality assurance manager's EVPI to be

$$\text{EVPI} = \$34{,}000 - \$32{,}500 = \$1{,}500$$

The following measure is similar to the EVPI, but it expresses the worth of the information contained in the sample. The expected value of sample information is calculated as

$$\text{EVSI} = \text{Expected payoff with sample information} - \text{Maximum expected payoff (with no information)}$$

This is analogous to EVEI introduced in Chapter 26, with S (for sample) replacing E (for experimental). (Indeed, a sample is just a special type of experiment that results in predictive information.) The EVSI expresses the net advantage, in terms of gross expected payoff, of having sample results over having no information at all.

To illustrate, we continue with the disk drive acceptance sampling illustration. From the decision tree in Figure 27-1, we read the expected payoff of $32,552.50 from using a sample of size $n = 2$ and accepting only those shipments having $C = 1$ defective or fewer. That amount is the manager's expected payoff with imperfect sample information. (The $32,552.50 plays the same role in establishing EVSI that the $34,000 does in obtaining EVPI.) Subtracting the maximum expected payoff (with no information) found earlier, we have

$$\text{EVSI} = \$32{,}552.50 - \$32{,}500 = \$52.50$$

This amount represents how much better off the quality assurance manager would be on the average if he had the $n = 2$ sample result instead of no information at all. The EVSI is totally analogous to the EVPI, but it applies to less reliable information gleaned from the sample. Like the EVPI, the EVSI establishes an upper limit on the amount a decision maker should pay to obtain the sample results.

THE EXPECTED NET GAIN OF SAMPLING

Preposterior analysis often begins (as in this illustration) with *gross* payoffs rather than net payoffs, and sampling costs must therefore be integrated at a later stage. (One reason for waiting to include the sampling costs is that it is sometimes easier to minimize expected opportunity loss than it is to maximize expected payoff. It is more convenient to include sampling costs at the end when such an approach is used.)

In terms of gross annual savings, the manager is better off by the EVSI of $52.50 if he obtains the sample results and then applies the optimal decision rule with $C = 1$. Thus, the manager should be willing to pay up to $52.50 for the sample but should not sample at a higher cost. *As long as the cost of sampling is less than the EVSI, the decision maker is better off with the sample than without it.*

How large should n be? This question is ordinarily a matter of economics. We could compute EVSI for several levels of n, subtracting the sampling costs in each case. Each resulting value would then represent the **expected net gain of sampling** or ENGS. Treating n as a variable, the expected net gain of sampling is expressed as

$$\text{ENGS}(n) = \text{EVSI}(n) - \text{Cost}(n)$$

(The above is analogous to ENGE found in Chapter 26.) Continuing with our illustration, when $n = 2$,

$$\text{ENGS}(2) = \text{EVSI}(2) - \text{Cost}(2)$$

Using a cost per inspected item of \$20, we have

$$\text{ENGS}(2) = \$52.50 - 2(\$20) = \$12.50$$

Comparable figures could be obtained for other sizes of n, and the **optimal sample size** would be the one with the greatest expected net gain.

Depending on the payoffs and on the prior probability distribution for π, the Bayesian procedure may indicate that no sample should be used. In some cases the optimal n is no larger than 5 or 10 observations. Such small sample sizes are unheard of in traditional statistics.

PREPOSTERIOR ANALYSIS OF SAMPLE INFORMATION

Since in the present illustration it is better to sample than not, the analysis may be continued into the preposterior stage. There, an optimal sample size is established. To find that n, the preceding analysis must be duplicated for each candidate n. In each case, a new set of probability trees and probability values must be found (as in Figures 27-2 and 27-3) and then a fresh backward induction analysis must be performed (as in Figure 27-1) to compute the expected payoff and to find the applicable acceptance number.

The ensuing computational task may be formidable, and is a chore gladly relegated to a computer. Figure 27-4 shows a portion of the *QuickQuant Plus* report when $n = 3$ and binomial probabilities are again used. There, Act 1 represents accept and Act 2 signifies reject. (As an exercise, you may sketch the two probability trees and the decision tree diagram, placing numbers from the printout onto the respective branches.)

Table 27-3 shows a partial listing of computer results for the disk drive acceptance sampling illustration. (These data appear in a modified format from the actual computer report, a more detailed example of which is provided later.) Notice that the sample sizes $n = 2$ through $n = 7$ all provide the same acceptance number, $C = 1$. The best sample size in that group is $n = 6$, having the highest ENGS(n). The second grouping includes $n = 8$ through $n = 13$, all with $C = 2$ as the acceptance number. In this second group, $n = 11$ provides the greatest expected net gain. The boldface rows in the remainder of Table 27-3 list the payoff information for the best sample size in each successive C-level group.

Since each shipment involves $N = 1{,}000$ units and sampling is done without replacement, the *hypergeometric* distribution represents the true probabilities for R. Using these, Figure 27-5 was constructed. The graph in Figure 27-5(a) plots EVSI(n) against sample size for all n's from 1 to 100. Notice the cusping effect for those n's that share a common acceptance number C. Notice also that EVSI(n) gets steadily higher as n becomes greater, approaching a threshold level of \$1,500 (the EVPI). (Indeed, as n becomes arbitrarily large, sample data become perfect information, so that in the limiting case EVSI(n) converges to EVPI.) But the best choice for n lies at a much lower level. Reflecting the cost of sampling, ENGS(n) is used to find the best n.

Figure 27-5(b) plots ENGS(n) against sample size. That graph shows that each cusp achieves a local maximum for the n's within each group. The global maximum is \$258.79, occurring at $n = 22$. The greatest expected payoff overall is achieved when ENGS(n) is maximized, so that $n = 22$ is the *optimal sample size*.

DECISION MAKING WITH PROPORTION--ACTUAL PROBABILITY CHRONOLOGY

Sample Size	Level for Proportion	Prior Probability	Sample Result	Cond. Result Probability	Joint Probability
n=3	P=.050	0.100000	R=0	0.857375	0.085738
			R=1	0.135375	0.013538
			R=2	0.007125	0.000712
			R=3	0.000125	0.000012
n=3	P=.100	0.150000	R=0	0.729000	0.109350
			R=1	0.243000	0.036450
			R=2	0.027000	0.004050
			R=3	0.001000	0.000150
n=3	P=.150	0.200000	R=0	0.614125	0.122825
			R=1	0.325125	0.065025
			R=2	0.057375	0.011475
			R=3	0.003375	0.000675
n=3	P=.200	0.250000	R=0	0.512000	0.128000
			R=1	0.384000	0.096000
			R=2	0.096000	0.024000
			R=3	0.008000	0.002000
n=3	P=.250	0.300000	R=0	0.421875	0.126562
			R=1	0.421875	0.126562
			R=2	0.140625	0.042188
			R=3	0.015625	0.004688

DECISION MAKING WITH PROPORTION--INFORMATIONAL PROBABILITY CHRONOLOGY

Sample Size	Sample Result	Unconditional Probability	Level of Proportion	Posterior Probability
n=3	R=0	0.572475	P=.050	0.149766
			P=.100	0.191013
			P=.150	0.214551
			P=.200	0.223591
			P=.250	0.221080
n=3	R=1	0.337575	P=.050	0.040102
			P=.100	0.107976
			P=.150	0.192624
			P=.200	0.284381
			P=.250	0.374917
n=3	R=2	0.082425	P=.050	0.008644
			P=.100	0.049136
			P=.150	0.139218
			P=.200	0.291174
			P=.250	0.511829
n=3	R=3	0.007525	P=.050	0.001661
			P=.100	0.019934
			P=.150	0.089701
			P=.200	0.265781
			P=.250	0.622924

DECISION MAKING WITH PROPORTION--DECISION TREE SUMMARY

Sample Size	Critical Value	Expected Payoff	Sample Result	EXPECTED PAYOFFS Act 1	Act 2	Best Act
n=3	C=1	$32539.93	R=0	$34048.98	$29485.00	Act 1
			R=1	$30794.83	$29485.00	Act 1
			R=2	$28882.96	$29485.00	Act 2
			R=3	$27783.14	$29485.00	Act 2

FIGURE 27-4 Portion of a *QuickQuant Plus* report showing actual and informational binomial probabilities and decision tree analysis results for disk drive acceptance sampling when $n = 3$.

TABLE 27-3 Partial Summary of Sample Size Evaluations for Disk Drive Acceptance Sampling

Sample Size	Using Binomial Probabilities For R				Using Hypergeometric Probabilities For R			
n	EVSI(n)	Cost(n)	ENGS(n)	c	EVSI(n)	Cost(n)	ENGS(n)	c
1	$32,500.00	$ 20.00	$ −20.00	0	$32,500.00	$ 20.00	$ −20.00	0
2	32,552.50	40.00	12.50	1	32,552.55	40.00	12.55	1
3	32,620.75	60.00	60.75	1	32,621.11	60.00	61.11	1
4	32,683.58	80.00	103.58	1	32,684.48	80.00	104.48	1
5	32,729.91	100.00	129.91	1	32,731.46	100.00	131.46	1
6	32,755.02	120.00	135.02	1	32,757.20	120.00	137.20	1
7	32,758.05	140.00	118.05	1	32,760.74	140.00	120.74	1
8	32,811.15	160.00	151.15	2	32,812.85	160.00	152.85	2
9	32,866.14	180.00	186.14	2	32,868.76	180.00	188.76	2
10	32,909.27	200.00	209.27	2	32,912.85	200.00	212.85	2
11	32,938.82	220.00	218.82	2	32,943.29	220.00	223.29	2
12	32,954.15	240.00	214.14	2	32,959.39	240.00	219.39	2
13	32,955.47	260.00	195.47	2	32,961.32	260.00	201.32	2
16	33,069.30	320.00	249.30	3	33,075.83	320.00	255.83	3
17	33,088.93	340.00	248.93	3	33,096.36	340.00	256.36	3
22*	33,189.39	440.00	249.39	4	33,198.80	440.00	258.80	4
27	33,268.55	540.00	228.55	5	33,279.79	540.00	239.79	5
32	33,333.37	640.00	193.37	6	33,346.37	640.00	206.37	6
37	33,387.93	740.00	147.93	7	33,402.61	740.00	162.61	7
42	33,434.82	840.00	94.82	8	33,451.08	840.00	111.08	8
47	33,475.69	940.00	35.69	9	33,493.49	940.00	53.49	9
53	33,526.12	1,060.00	−33.88	10	33,546.11	1,060.00	−13.89	10
58	33,557.81	1,160.00	−102.19	11	33,579.19	1,160.00	−80.81	11
63	33,586.23	1,260.00	−173.77	12	33,608.91	1,260.00	−151.09	12
68	33,611.93	1,360.00	−248.07	13	33,635.86	1,360.00	−224.14	13
74	33,645.07	1,480.00	−334.93	14	33,670.57	1,480.00	−309.43	14
79	33,666.09	1,580.00	−413.91	15	33,692.68	1,580.00	−387.32	15
84	33,685.39	1,680.00	−494.61	16	33,713.02	1,680.00	−466.98	16
89	33,703.13	1,780.00	−576.88	17	33,731.73	1,780.00	−548.27	17
94	33,720.33	1,880.00	−659.67	17	33,749.10	1,880.00	−630.90	18
95	33,726.22	1,900.00	−673.78	18	33,755.85	1,900.00	−644.15	18
100	33,741.17	2,000.00	−758.83	19	33,771.72	2,000.00	−728.28	19

PAYOFF FUNCTIONS IN DECISION MAKING

Decision making with sample information ordinarily involves *two acts*. This reflects the general thrust of statistical decision making, where there are two actions.

Accept the null hypothesis

Reject the null hypothesis

(Hypothesis testing is briefly reviewed in Section 27-4.) The payoffs for the two acts may be characterized as *functions* of π.

Figure 27-6 shows the commonly encountered situations and how the statistical decision rule fits in. Figure 27-6(a) portrays the payoff functions as lines. For low levels of π, Act 1 provides greater payoffs. Act 2 is the better choice for high π levels. That payoff ranking is reflected in the statistical decision rule, which

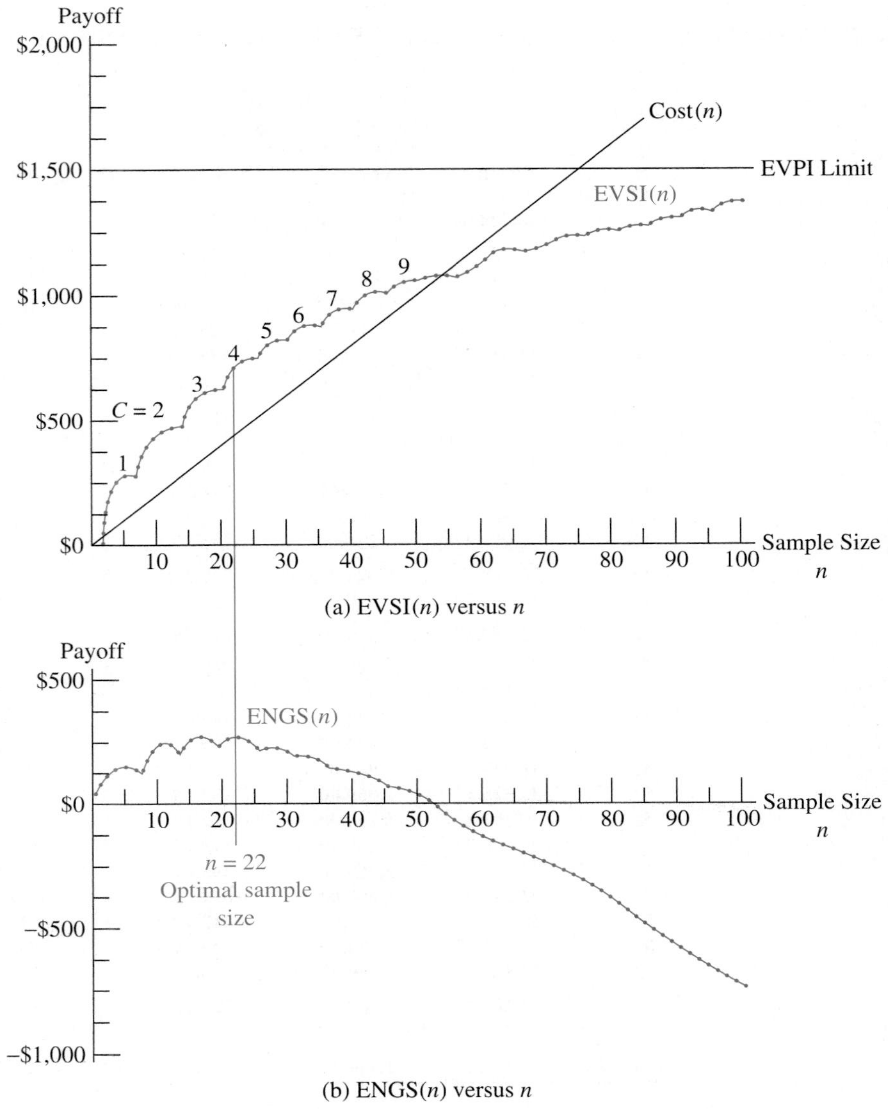

FIGURE 27-5 Graphs for disk drive acceptance sampling showing how EVSI(n) and ENGS(n) relate to sample size, sampling cost and EVPI (based on hypergeometric probabilities).

requires choosing Act 1 when the number of sample successes R is $\leq$ the critical value C and Act 2 when $R > C$.

Figure 27-6(b) graphs the linear payoff functions when Act 1 dominates Act 2. In such a case, EVPI $= 0$ and there is no advantage from sampling. (Why?) Figure 27-6(c) illustrates the case when payoff functions are nonlinear. This case ordinarily results in the same type of decision rule as those found with linear payoffs. Decisions involving linear payoff functions may be analyzed using the simple geometry of lines to achieve computational advantages. Nonlinear payoff functions may be more cumbersome and will ordinarily require evaluation in terms of payoff tables.

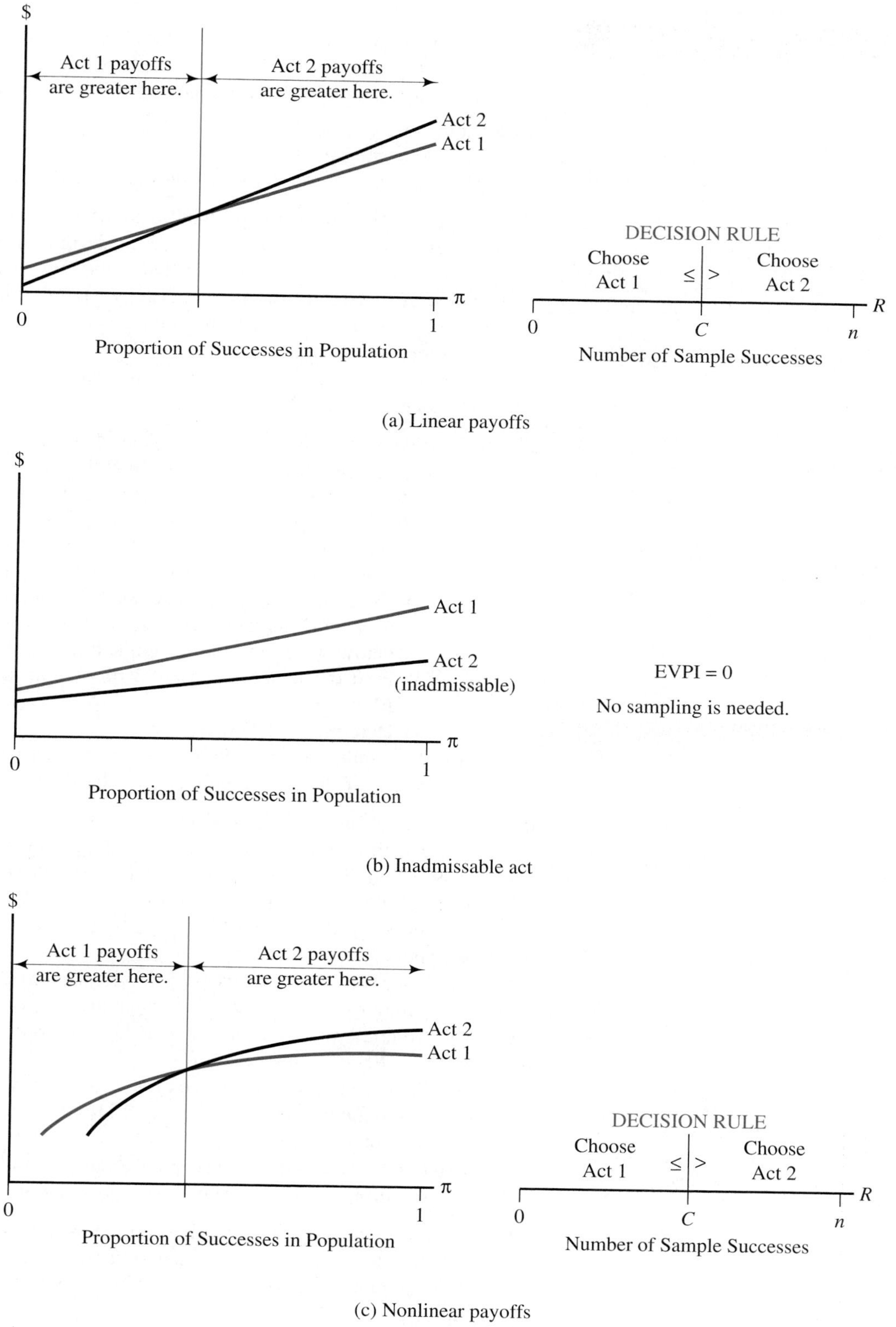

FIGURE 27-6 Payoff functions encountered in decision making with proportion.

EXERCISES

27-7 Refer to Exercises 27-1 and 27-4 and to your answers.
(a) Determine EVSI (3).
(b) Each sample observation costs \$100. Determine ENGS (3).

27-8 Refer to Exercises 27-2 and 27-3 and to your answers.
(a) Determine EVSI (3).
(b) Each sample observation costs \$100. Determine ENGS (3).

27-9 Suppose that the prior probabilities for the proportion π of CornChox buyers favoring a new package design are $\Pr[\pi = .4] = .5$ and $\Pr[\pi = .6] = .5$. Also suppose that if the new design is used, the present value of future profits will decrease by \$10,000 when $\pi = .4$ and increase by \$10,000 when $\pi = .6$. It must be decided whether to use the new design or keep the old one.
(a) Compute the expected payoffs for each act. Which one is best?
(b) Determine the EVPI.

27-10 (*Continuation of Exercise 27-9*): A company marketing researcher wishes to conduct a preposterior analysis. Sampling is very costly, \$500 an observation to determine for a test subject whether or not he or she likes the new product design. For (a) $n = 1$ and (b) $n = 2$, answer the following.
(1) Using the binomial distribution, construct the probability tree diagrams for the actual and informational chronologies.
(2) Using gross payoffs, construct the decision tree. Then, perform backward induction analysis to determine the critical value at or below which the old design should be retained.
(3) Find the expected payoff with sample information and compute EVSI(n).
(4) Determine ENGS(n).
(c) Does sampling provide a greater expected payoff than not sampling? Which of the two sample sizes is best?

27-11 The quality control manager for the computer manufacturer in the text is faced with a similar evaluation regarding a second supplier for the same disk drives. That supplier has a better reputation than the first, with prior probabilities for the proportion of defectives in a 1,000-unit shipment of .20 for $\pi = .10$ and .80 for $\pi = .20$. The payoffs are the same for both suppliers.
(a) Compute the expected payoffs for accepting and rejecting shipments without sampling. Which act maximizes expected payoff?
(b) Compute the manager's EVPI. Does it appear that sampling might be beneficial in this case?
(c) Suppose that a sample size of $n = 10$ is used. Construct the probability tree diagrams for the actual and informational chronologies. (Use the binomial distribution.)
(d) For $n = 10$, find the acceptance number and expected payoff. Would the inspector be better off using $n = 10$ or no sample at all?

27-12 Comp-u-Quick must select the optimal sample size to use in determining whether to accept or reject incoming shipments of black boxes. The following payoffs apply to the various assumed levels of the proportion defective.

Proportion Defective	Prior Probability	Act	
		Accept	Reject
$\pi = .05$	.3	\$100	−\$100
$\pi = .10$	.4	0	0
$\pi = .20$	.3	−100	100

The following expected payoffs with sample information (ignoring the cost of sampling) have been obtained.

Sample Size	Expected Payoff
$n = 1$	\$ 9.00
$n = 2$	15.70
$n = 3$	20.50
$n = 4$	24.22

(a) Calculate the expected payoff using sample information when $n = 5$. What acceptance number applies to the number of sample defectives R? (Use the binomial distribution.)
(b) Assuming that each sample observation costs \$3, determine ENGS(n) for $n = 1$ through $n = 5$. What is the optimal sample size?

27-3 DECISION MAKING WITH THE SAMPLE MEAN

A procedure completely analogous to decision making using binomial probabilities applies when samples are taken from quantitative populations.

ILLUSTRATION: A COMPUTER MEMORY DEVICE DECISION

To illustrate decision making based on the sample mean, we will consider the decision of a computer center manager regarding the kind of peripheral memory storage device to use in the computer system. The two proposed units are based on laser technology, and both units will operate more efficiently than the current memory storage device. One alternative is based on photographic principles and requires special film for storing the data. The other alternative employs holography—a process in which a three-dimensional image is retrieved from a special wafer. A photographic memory unit costs less to lease than a holographic unit, but it is slower and therefore more costly to operate. The storage capacities and reliabilities of the two units are identical.

The annual savings from using either alternative unit depends on the daily volume of peripheral memory access. Although the actual number of bits stored or retrieved varies daily, the mean daily access level may be used to establish an average annual access savings for each alternative. When this savings is added to the fixed lease cost, the resulting mean total annual savings serves as the payoff measure for this decision. This payoff depends on the mean daily gigabits (billion bits) accessed μ, which represents the average volume over all days.

The computer center manager is uncertain about the value of μ, since historical data on the density of peripheral memory traffic are incomplete.

PRIOR ANALYSIS

Figure 27-7 presents the manager's decision structure when no sample information is available. Notice that different payoff values for mean annual savings are obtained for each type of unit and μ combination. Using prior probabilities of .5 for $\mu = 2$ and .5 for $\mu = 3$, we find that the holographic memory unit provides the greatest expected payoff of $750,000 in mean annual savings.

The attractiveness of deferring the main decision until after experimentation through sampling is roughly gauged by the EVPI. With a perfect predictor, the chosen payoffs would be $715,000 (for photographic) when $\mu = 2$ and $810,000 (for holographic) when $\mu = 3$. The expected payoff with perfect information is thus,

$$\$715{,}000(.50) + \$810{,}000(.50) = \$762{,}500$$

Subtracting the $750,000 maximum expected payoff with no information found earlier, we have

$$\text{EVPI} = \$762{,}500 - \$750{,}000 = \$12{,}500$$

This amount is big enough to justify further analysis of sample information, from which a considerable expected payoff advantage may be achieved.

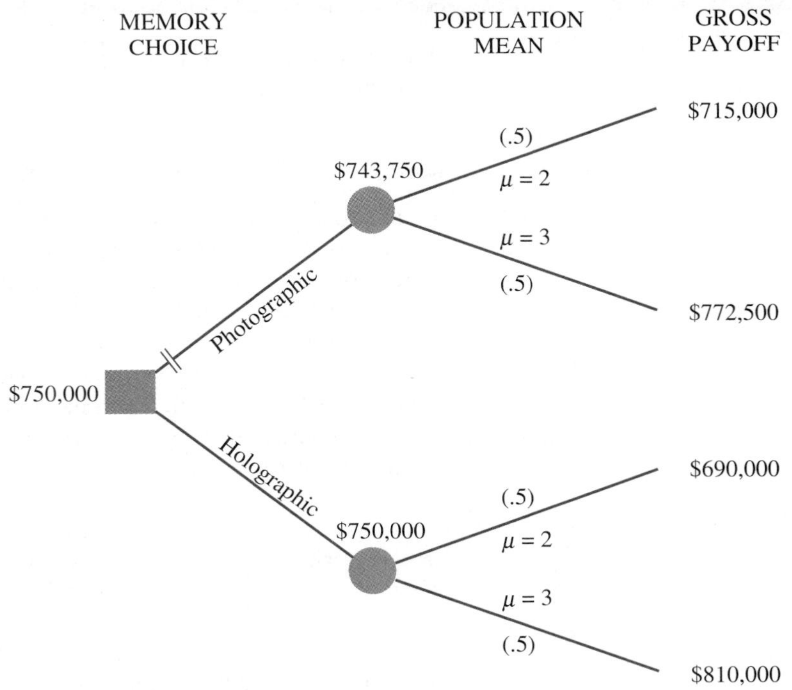

FIGURE 27-7 The computer center manager's decision structure when no sample is used.

POSTERIOR ANALYSIS

We will now consider the manager's analysis using sample data. The manager believes that for an extra few hundred dollars per day she can determine the precise level of peripheral memory access on sample days by adding a special accounting program to the software system. Any sampling cost arises from the slower processing that will result. Suppose that a sample of $n = 9$ days is to be used.

Since the sample data will be used to predict mean daily access levels, it is appropriate to summarize the sampling results in terms of the sample mean memory access level, which is computed from

$$\bar{X} = \frac{X_1 + X_2 + \ldots + X_n}{n}$$

where $X_1, X_2, \ldots, X_n$ are the observed levels for individual sample days. A large $\bar{X}$ will lend credence to the greater population mean value of $\mu = 3$ gigabits per day, and a small $\bar{X}$ will support $\mu = 2$. But since the sample results are not yet known, the actual value of $\bar{X}$ is uncertain. In Chapter 7, we investigated the properties of the sample mean. For large n, the sample mean is approximately normally distributed (under appropriate conditions that are assumed to apply here) with a mean of μ.

There will be a separate normal curve for $\bar{X}$ for each level of μ, as shown in Figure 27-8. Recall, from Chapter 7, that the standard deviation for the $\bar{X}$ normal curve is related to the population standard deviation σ_I (where the subscript

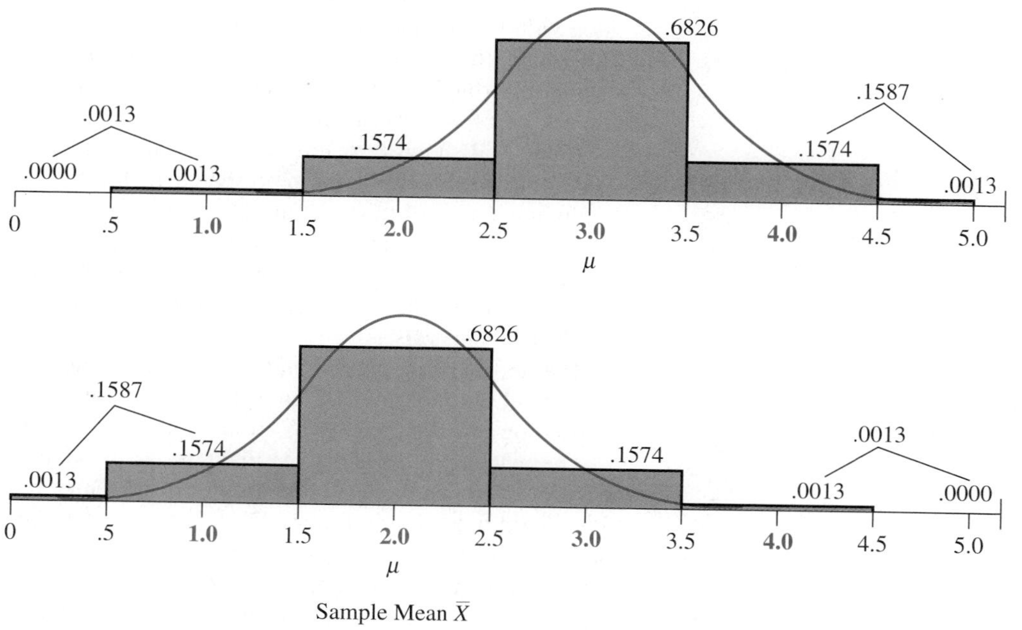

FIGURE 27-8 Normal distribution for $\bar{X}$ used in establishing approximate conditional result probabilities.

TABLE 27-4 Interval Probabilities for Sample Mean in Computer Memory Device Decision

	$\mu = 2.0$			$\mu = 3.0$		
Interval for $\bar{X}$	**Normal Deviate z**	**Cumulative Probability**	**Interval Probability**	**Normal Deviate z**	**Cumulative Probability**	**Interval Probability**
<.5	−3.00	.5 − .4987 = .0013	.0013 }	−5.00	.0000	.0000 }
.5–1.5	−1.00	.5 − .3413 = .1587	.1574 }	−3.00	.0013	.0013 }
1.5–2.5	1.00	.5 + .3413 = .8413	.6826	−1.00	.1587	.1574
2.5–3.5	3.00	.5 + .4987 = .9987	.1574	1.00	.8413	.6826
3.5–4.5	5.00	1.0000	.0013 }	3.00	.9987	.1574 }
>4.5	∞	1.0000	.0000 }	∞	1.0000	.0013 }

emphasizes that the measure summarizes *individual* differences) by the following transformation.

$$\sigma_{\bar{X}} = \frac{\sigma_I}{\sqrt{n}}$$

In the present illustration, it is assumed that $\sigma_I = 1.5$ gigabit per day, so that when $n = 9$,

$$\sigma_{\bar{X}} = \frac{1.5}{\sqrt{9}} = .5 \text{ gigabit per day}$$

The procedure for evaluating a decision with the mean parallels that for a decision with the proportion. Conditional result probabilities for $\bar{X}$ must be found for the actual chronology. These must be obtained from the respective normal distribution through an approximation procedure that begins with dividing the possible levels for $\bar{X}$ into intervals.

Table 27-4 shows how this is done using six intervals for each case. Each nonzero interval probability is represented in Figure 27-8 by a rectangle. Interval midpoints are used to represent all possible $\bar{X}$'s falling in the respective interval. To simplify the ensuing tree evaluations, the extreme cases for each normal curve tail are grouped into one category. This leaves four representative levels for $\bar{X}$ in each case. (Of course, the accuracy of the procedure will improve with a greater number of intervals.)

The approximate conditional result probabilities for $\bar{X}$ are used in the tree for the actual chronology in Figure 27-9(a). The probabilities for the informational chronology in Figure 27-9(b) are obtained in the usual manner.

The manager's decision tree diagram using sample information is provided in Figure 27-10. The revised probabilities used there are obtained from Figure 27-9. Backward induction in Figure 27-10 indicates that the maximum expected annual savings will be achieved by selecting the photographic memory unit for $\bar{X} = 1$ or $\bar{X} = 2$ and the holographic peripheral storage unit for $\bar{X} = 3$ or $\bar{X} = 4$. We express this result in terms of the decision rule

$$\text{Select photographic unit} \quad \text{if } \bar{X} \leq C$$

$$\text{Select holographic unit} \quad \text{if } \bar{X} > C$$

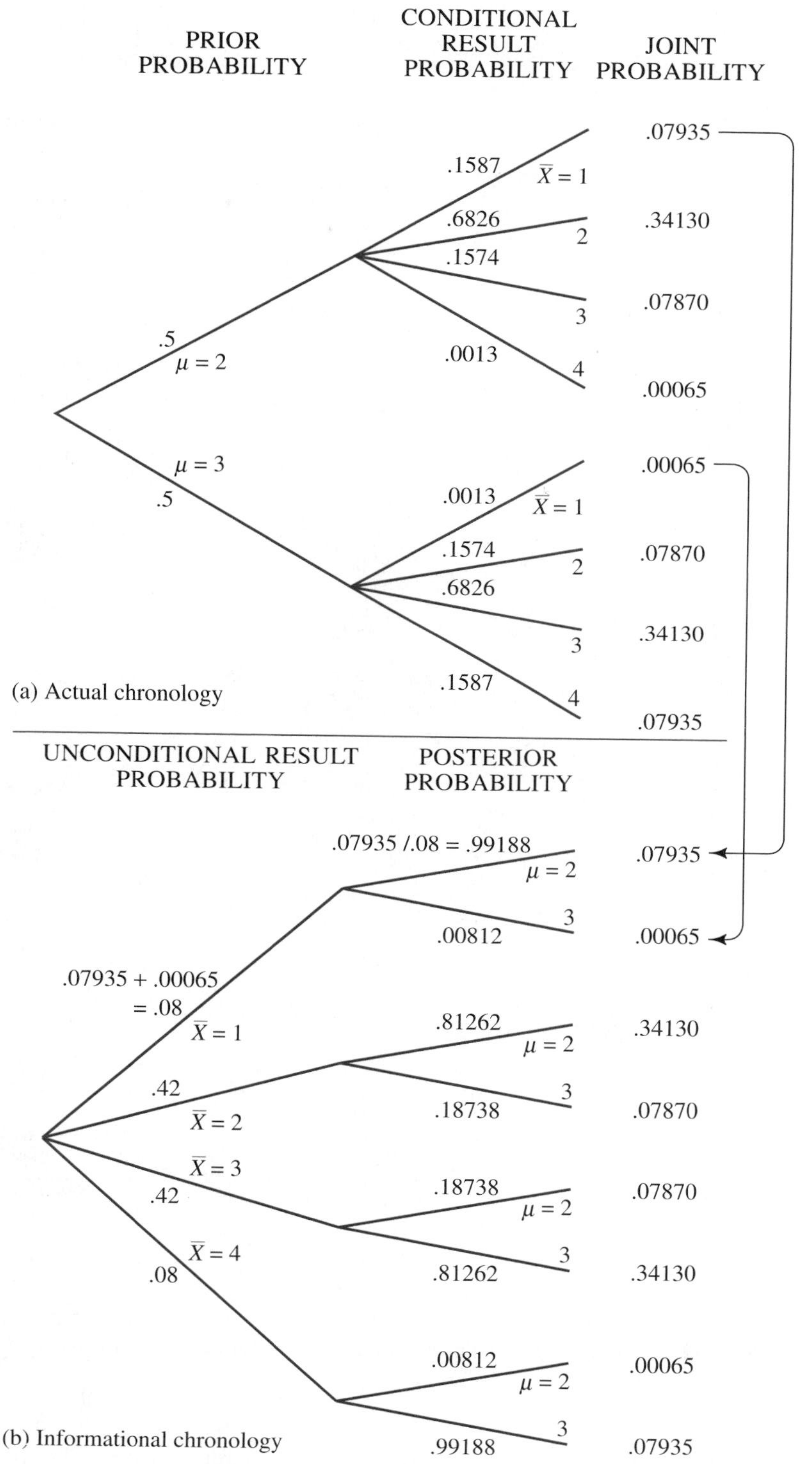

FIGURE 27-9 Revised probability trees for the computer center manager's decision.

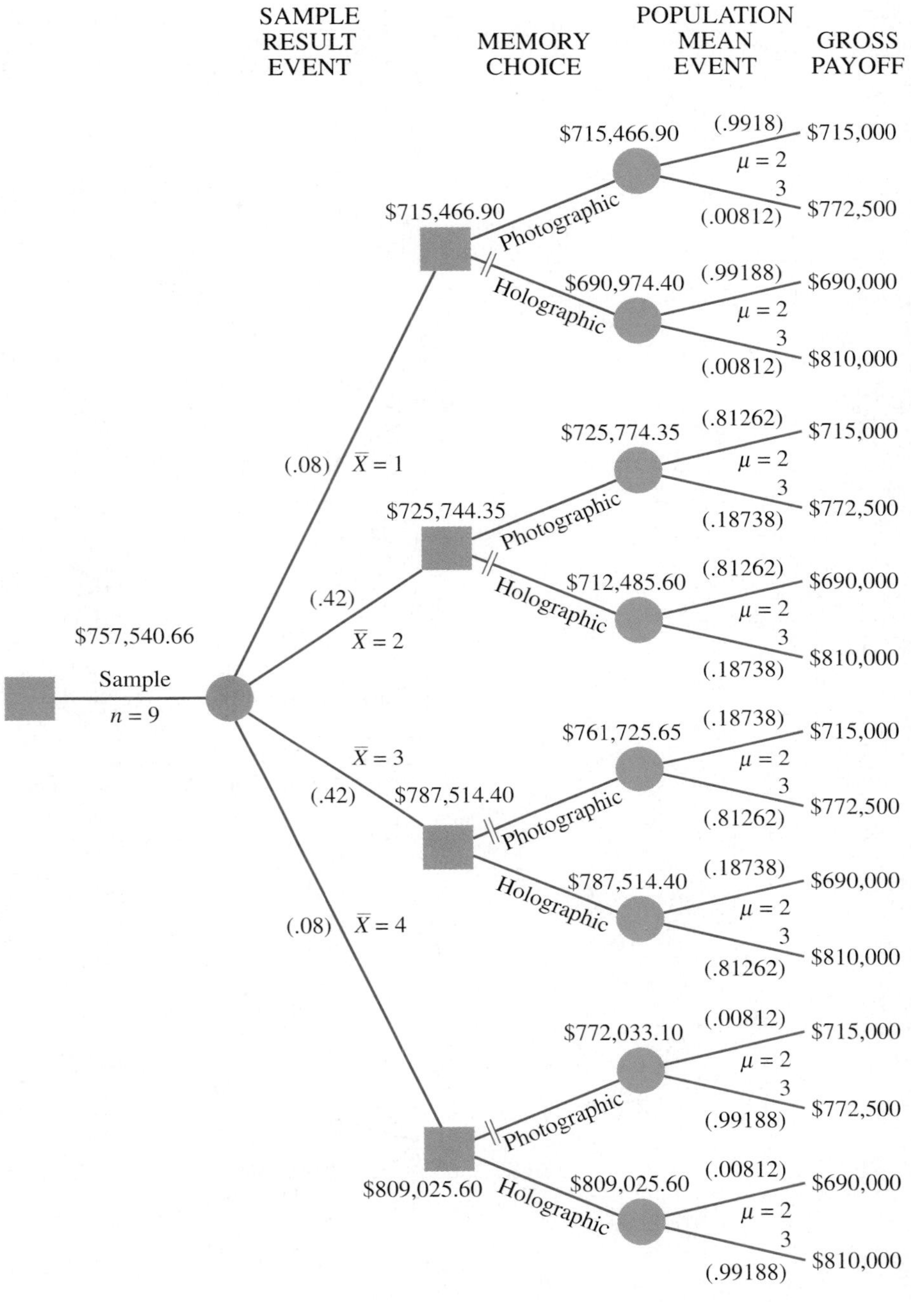

FIGURE 27-10 The computer center manager's decision structure using a sample of size $n = 9$.

where $C = 2$ gigabits per day. The manager would thus select the photographic unit if $\bar{X} = 1.53$ or 1.95 and the holographic unit if $\bar{X} = 3.13$ or 2.04.

The amount $757,540.66 is the expected payoff with sample information. Subtracting from this the maximum expected payoff of $750,000 found earlier for using a holographic memory without getting sample information, we obtain

$$\text{EVSI}(9) = \$757{,}540.66 - \$750{,}000 = \$7{,}540.66$$

The extra software required to monitor memory during testing will slow down the computer, resulting in extra daily costs of \$100. The cost of sampling for nine days would then be \$900. The expected net gain of sampling is thus,

$$\text{ENGS}(9) = \text{EVSI}(9) - \text{Cost}(9) = \$7{,}540.66 - \$900 = \$6{,}640.66$$

PREPOSTERIOR ANALYSIS

The sample size used above may not provide a maximum level for ENGS(n). A complete preposterior analysis would consider other levels for n, some of which may be considerably better. Each n will involve its own set of conditional result probabilities for $\bar{X}$. Finding those probabilities would be a formidable task, since for each n, distinct normal curves apply, the standard deviations of which become smaller as n becomes larger. All of these must be approximated by a few representative values of $\bar{X}$, and the respective probability trees for the actual chronology must have a branch for each $\bar{X}$ in every fork that follows a μ branch.

This job defies human patience and is best done with computer assistance. Even computers will get bogged down when there are many levels of μ and when a large number of intervals are involved. An alternative procedure, described in Chapter 28, is ordinarily used in those cases.

EXERCISES

27-13 Consider a slight modification in the computer-memory device decision discussed in this chapter. Suppose that the following prior probabilities for the mean memory access levels apply.

$\mu = 2$ gigabits per day: .6

$\mu = 3$ gigabits per day: .4

Determine the new probabilities for the actual and informational chronologies in Figure 27-9 (page 1067), assuming that the same conditional result probabilities apply.

27-14 The marketing manager of Blitz Beer must determine whether or not to sponsor Blitz Day with the Gotham City Hellcats. She is uncertain what the effect of the promotion will be in terms of the mean increase in daily sales volume that would result during the 100-day baseball season. The cost of sponsorship is \$10,000, and each can of Blitz has a marginal cost of \$.20 and sells for \$.40. Two levels are judged equally likely for the mean increase in sales for the season: $\mu = 490$ and $\mu = 530$ cans per day.

(a) Construct the manager's payoff table.

(b) If the manager wishes to maximize expected payoff, what action should she take?

(c) Further experimental information may be desired before making a final decision. Calculate the EVPI. Would a sample from the underlying population—assuming it is cheap enough—be helpful in reaching this decision? Explain.

27-15 Sonic Phonics is considering modifying the components in a quadraphonic speaker system to boost its effective power. The ultimate result depends on the mean signal-to-noise ratio μ, an unknown quantity for which the following subjective probability distribution applies.

Mean Signal-to-Noise Ratio	Probability
$\mu = 90$	.20
$\mu = 100$	.40
$\mu = 110$	.40

Unfortunately, the modified system may result in a poorer overall performance rating than the system's current 30 points, rising or dropping .25 point for each unit that μ falls above or below 100.

The following approximate probabilities apply for the level of the sample mean $\bar{X}$ when $n = 5$.

Possible Sample Mean	Given Level of Population Mean		
	$\mu = 90$	$\mu = 100$	$\mu = 110$
$\bar{X} = 85$	.40	.10	.10
$\bar{X} = 95$	.30	.40	.20
$\bar{X} = 105$	.20	.40	.30
$\bar{X} = 115$	.10	.10	.40
	1.00	1.00	1.00

(a) Assuming that no sample is used, construct Sonic Phonics' payoff table. In order to maximize expected final system rating points, should the system be modified?

(b) Construct the probability trees for the actual and informational chronologies.

(c) Ignoring the cost of collecting the sample, construct Sonic Phonics' decision tree diagram when the sample is used. Find the level of the acceptance number C, representing the largest level for the sample mean at which the present system will provide the greatest expected rating payoff.

27-16 In evaluating a new electronic scanning cash register, the facilities planner for WaySafe Markets judges that the mean \$30-purchase customer checkout time with the new device is equally likely to be either (1) $\mu = 3.0$ or (2) $\mu = 4.0$ minutes. In either case, individual checkout times have a standard deviation of $\sigma_I = 2$ minutes. A sample of $n = 25$ customers will be monitored.

(a) The sampling distribution for $\bar{X}$ is normally distributed, with mean μ and standard deviation $\sigma_{\bar{X}} = \sigma_I/\sqrt{n}$. Determine, for each μ, the following conditional result probabilities for $\bar{X}$.

Class Interval $\bar{X}$	Normal Deviate at Upper Limit	Approximate Cumulative Probability	Interval Midpoint $\bar{X}$	Interval Probability
.75–under 1.25				
1.25–under 1.75				
1.75–under 2.25				
2.25–under 2.75				
2.75–under 3.25				
3.25–under 3.75				
3.75–under 4.25				
4.25–under 4.75				
4.75–under 5.25				
5.25–under 5.75				
5.75–under 6.25				

(b) Construct the probability tree diagrams for the actual and informational chronologies, using $\bar{X}$ branches for each interval midpoint.

27-17 Suppose that the peripheral memory device decision problem in this chapter is modified so that the following prior probabilities for the mean memory access levels apply.

$\mu = 2$ gigabits per day: .3

$\mu = 3$ gigabits per day: .7

The decision tree diagram in Figure 27-11 now applies.

(a) Perform backward induction.

(b) What is the value of C that will maximize expected payoff? Formulate the optimal decision rule.

(c) Calculate the EVSI.

(d) Determine the expected net gain of sampling for a sample costing $900.

27-4 COMPUTER EVALUATIONS OF DECISION MAKING WITH THE PROPORTION

QuickQuant Plus may be used to evaluate decision situations having either linear or nonlinear payoffs. The program allows data entry in two modes, a *tabular* or a *functional* form. When the data are nonlinear the tabular form must be used.

TABULAR DATA INPUT

The simplest data input mode is the tabular one, which is based on the payoff table. The method is illustrated next with a decision involving product design.

Illustration: A Product Design Decision

A soft drink manufacturer is evaluating a potential restoration of a historical design for its bottles. The choices are the standard cylindrical container and a revived "aerodynamic" shape. The key parameter is the proportion π of persons

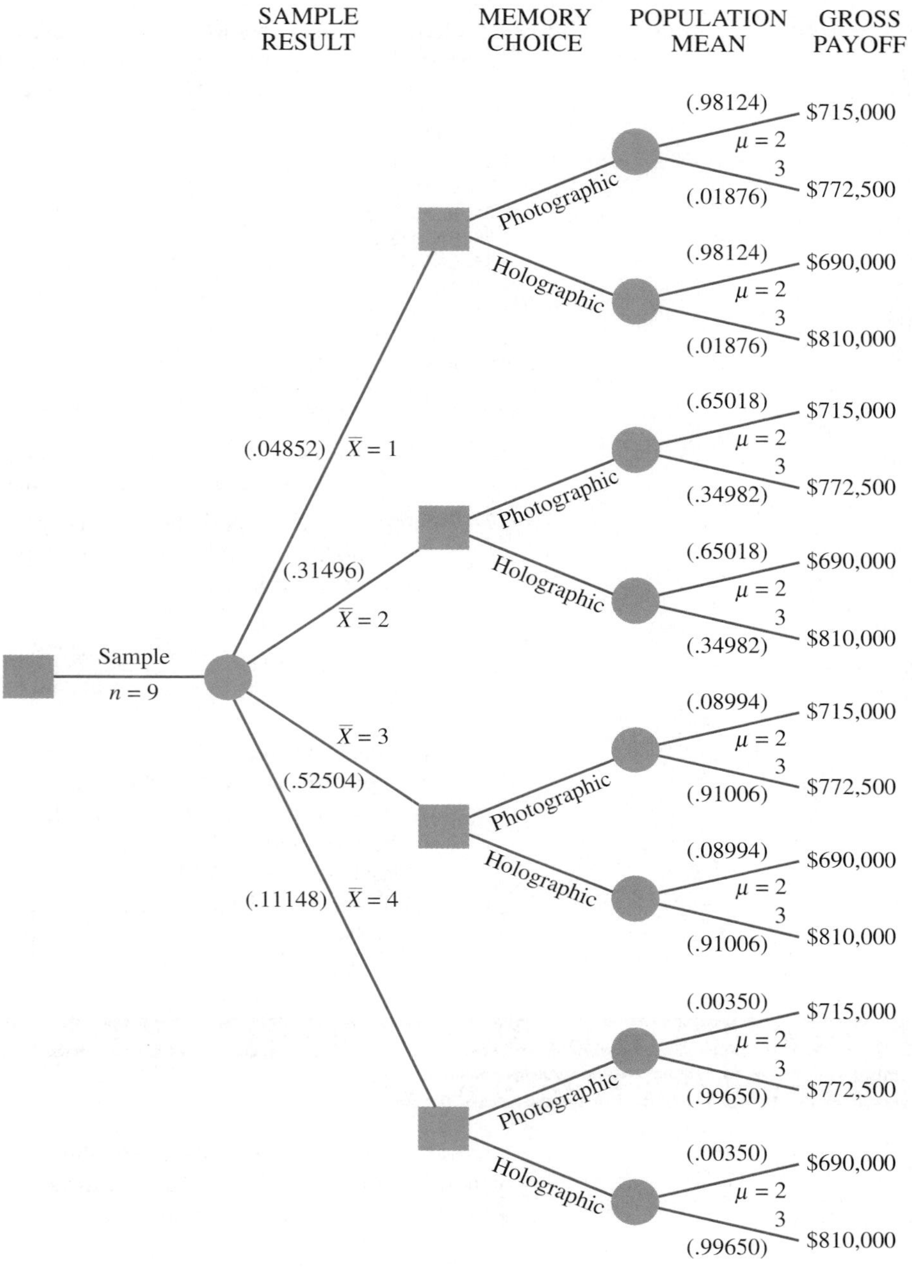

FIGURE 27-11

in the target market who prefer the aerodynamic bottle. Based on a complicated formula involving production costs and on potential market share during follow-on test marketing, the payoffs in Table 27-5 apply.

A *QuickQuant Plus* run begins with prior analysis, in which the expected payoffs are computed for each act and the EVPI determined. Upon examining these values, the user may request preposterior analysis. In the present example this

TABLE 27-5 Payoff Table for Bottle Design Decision

Proportion Preferring Aerodynamic Shape	Prior Probability	Act 1 Cylindrical	Act 2 Aerodynamic
$\pi = .4$	.10	\$50,000	\$−15,000
$\pi = .5$	.23	42,000	28,000
$\pi = .6$	.38	35,000	41,000
$\pi = .7$	.29	30,000	50,000

will involve an evaluation of sample size and the determination of critical values for R. Here, R is the number of sample persons who prefer the aerodynamic design. The program requires that Act 1 always be the choice which yields the greater payoff when π is small. In the present illustration, Act 1 is to choose the cylindrical design, while Act 2 is to select the aerodynamic design.

Figure 27-12 shows the first portion of the *QuickQuant Plus* report. The greatest expected payoff is achieved with Act 1 (cylindrical design). The EVPI is \$8,080, which suggests that further experimental information might be valuable. This may be true even though sampling is expensive, with a \$100 cost per sample observation. (That cost was entered into the computer with the payoff data.) *QuickQuant Plus* was requested to perform the preposterior analysis.

Using a beginning sample size of $n = 1$ and a maximum of $n = 30$, the *QuickQuant Plus* run continues. The binomial distribution was selected, since the population size is well into the millions. Figure 27-13 shows the report generated. There, we see that the optimal sample size is $n = 17$ with $C = 9$, which provides the maximum ENGS of \$3,343.33. The following decision rule will be used.

Choose cylindrical (Act 1) if $R \leq 9$

Choose aerodynamic (Act 2) if $R > 9$

FUNCTIONAL INPUT FOR LINEAR PAYOFFS

The earlier disk drive quality decision was kept simple to convey essential concepts. But there are several unrealistic elements. First, the original analysis (pages 1048–1061) presupposes that defective units found in the sample will be reinspected when a shipment is rejected (in which case, a 100% inspection will be made). To avoid wasted effort, a good quality assurance plan would mandate that already-inspected items instead be set aside; the resulting cost savings were not reflected in the original evaluation. Second, those items found defective in a sample will not be installed, as suggested earlier. Not installing known defectives should provide considerable downstream savings of costs that would otherwise arise when those computers with defective components must eventually be rebuilt. Third, the variable cost of inspecting with a thousand items (in a rejected lot) should be lower than with a handful of sample items. There may be differences in fixed inspection costs as well.

QuickQuant Plus can accommodate an analysis with a general linear payoff function involving, for each act, a constant term and coefficients for π, n, and R. Some or all of these may differ between Act 1 (accept) and Act 2 (reject). To illustrate, suppose that the variable cost of inspection is \$25 when done on a sampling basis, but only \$20 in high volumes (the case with rejected shipments).

```
              PROBLEM PARAMETERS FOR DECISION WITH PROPORTION

                  Maximum n =  30   Beginning n =  1
                  Maximum number of P levels =  4
                  Population size =  1E+20
                  Cost per Sample Observation =  100

                     PRIOR PROBABILITY DISTRIBUTION

                           P Level    Probability
                          ------------------------
                           .400         0.1000
                           .500         0.2300
                           .600         0.3800
                           .700         0.2900

                               PAYOFF TABLE

                     P Level         Act 1              Act 2
                  --------------------------------------------
                       .400         50000.00         -15000.00
                       .500         42000.00          28000.00
                       .600         35000.00          41000.00
                       .700         30000.00          50000.00

              DECISION MAKING WITH PROPORTION--PRIOR ANALYSIS

                           Act 1              Act 2
  Expected Payoffs:      $36660.00          $35020.00
  Best Act = Act 1
  Expected Value of Perfect Information =        $8080.00
```

FIGURE 27-12 *QuickQuant Plus* report for prior analysis of bottle shape decision.

Furthermore, there is a set-up expense (fixed cost) of \$500 for inspecting rejected shipments, regardless of size. There are cost savings for early detection of defective disk drives of \$100 (avoided rebuilding expenses). The revised payoff function is thus,

$$\text{Payoff} = \begin{cases} \$50{,}000 - \$100{,}000\pi + \$100R - \$25n & \text{if accept (Act 1)} \\ \$50{,}000 - \$20(1{,}000) - \$500 - \$5n & \\ \text{or} & \\ \$29{,}500 + 0\pi + 0R - \$5n & \text{if reject (Act 2)} \end{cases}$$

The \$50,000 constant term (called the intercept) for accept (Act 1) is the same as before. The counterpart for reject (Act 2) is now \$29,500, reflecting both the fixed and variable costs of 100% inspection for the rejected shipments. The coefficients for π are $-\$100{,}000$ and 0, as in the original evaluation. Reflecting the savings from early detection of bad disk drives, the coefficients of R apply only to those defectives found in the sample. For reject (Act 2), that coefficient is 0,

DECISION MAKING WITH PROPORTION--SUMMARY ANALYSIS

Sample Size n	EVSI(n)	Cost(n)	ENGS(n)	Critical Value C
1	$1,218.00	$100.00	$1,118.00	0
3	$2,126.64	$300.00	$1,826.64	1
4	$2,692.26	$400.00	$2,292.26	2
6	$3,286.37	$600.00	$2,686.37	3
8	$3,730.08	$800.00	$2,930.08	4
10	$4,077.57	$1,000.00	$3,077.57	5
11	$4,265.54	$1,100.00	$3,165.54	6
13	$4,579.96	$1,300.00	$3,279.96	7
15	$4,834.27	$1,500.00	$3,334.27	8
17	**$5,043.30**	**$1,700.00**	**$3,343.30**	**9**
18	$5,120.09	$1,800.00	$3,320.09	10
20	$5,322.66	$2,000.00	$3,322.66	11
22	$5,491.27	$2,200.00	$3,291.27	12
24	$5,632.82	$2,400.00	$3,232.82	13
25	$5,661.54	$2,500.00	$3,161.54	14
27	$5,803.34	$2,700.00	$3,103.34	15
29	$5,923.48	$2,900.00	$3,023.48	16

FIGURE 27-13 Abbreviated *QuickQuant Plus* report for the preposterior analysis of bottle shape decision.

reflecting that any defective disk drives would have been removed anyway, so that early detection would yield no savings. But, for accept (Act 1), the coefficient of R is $+\$100$. Finally, the coefficients for n are $-\$25$ for accept (Act 1) and $-\$5$ for reject (Act 2). The latter applies because there would then only be a $5 net cost per sample unit, reflecting the small-scale inspection cost of $25 per item, less the $20 saved by not reinspecting each sample item during the follow-on large-scale 100% inspection.

A second computer run was performed using the modified payoffs. The printout in Figure 27-14 shows the *QuickQuant Plus* report. There, we see that the optimal sample size for the modified evaluation is $n = 42$ with $C = 8$. When sampling costs differ between Acts 1 and 2, the computer performs backward induction using *net* payoffs, so that the report in Figure 27-14 lists values for the *net* payoffs with sample information, rather than EVSI, which is not very useful when sampling costs differ between acts. In those cases, the computer finds the expected net gain of sampling from the following difference.

$$\text{ENGS}(n) = \text{Expected } net \text{ payoff with sample information} \\ - \text{Maximum expected payoff (with no information)}$$

For example, by subtracting the original $32,500 maximum expected payoff for accepting disk drives without sampling from the expected net payoff with sample information of $32,841.28 when $n = 42$, we have

$$\text{ENGS}(42) = \$32{,}841.28 - \$32{,}500 = \$341.28$$

```
PROBLEM PARAMETERS FOR DECISION WITH PROPORTION

Maximum n =  100   Beginning n =  1
Maximum number of P levels =  5
Population size =  1000

Coefficients of Accept Line:
    Intercept =  50000
    Coefficient of P = -100000
    Coefficient of R =  100
    Coefficient of n = -25

Coefficients of Reject Line:
    Intercept =  29500
    Coefficient of P =  0
    Coefficient of R =  0
    Coefficient of n = -5
```

PRIOR PROBABILITY DISTRIBUTION

P Level	Probability
.050	0.1000
.100	0.1500
.150	0.2000
.200	0.2500
.250	0.3000

```
DECISION MAKING WITH PROPORTION--PRIOR ANALYSIS

                      Act 1          Act 2
Expected Payoffs:   $32500.00      $29500.00
Best Act = Act 1
Expected Value of Perfect Information =     $1350.00
```

DECISION MAKING WITH PROPORTION--SUMMARY ANALYSIS

Sample Size n	Net Expected Payoff with Sample Information	ENGS(n)	Critical Value C
4	$32,555.99	$55.99	1
10	$32,660.64	$160.64	2
16	$32,732.99	$232.99	3
21	$32,782.20	$282.20	4
26	$32,812.88	$312.88	5
31	$32,830.73	$330.73	6
37	$32,839.80	$339.80	7
42	**$32,841.32**	**$341.32**	**8**
47	$32,836.97	$336.97	9
52	$32,827.94	$327.94	10
57	$32,815.04	$315.04	11
62	$32,799.00	$299.00	12
66	$32,780.59	$280.59	13
71	$32,759.92	$259.92	14
76	$32,737.27	$237.27	15
81	$32,712.90	$212.90	16
87	$32,685.00	$185.00	17
92	$32,657.32	$157.32	18
97	$32,628.41	$128.41	19

FIGURE 27-14 Abbreviated QuickQuant printout for the modified disk drive acceptance sampling illustration, using hypergeometric probabilities for *R*.

The following decision rule applies to this modified decision.

Accept the lot (Act 1) if $R \leq 8$

Reject the lot (Act 2) if $R > 8$

EXERCISES

27-18 *Computer exercise.* Refer to Exercises 27-1 and 27-4. Find the optimal sample size.

27-19 *Computer exercise.* Refer to Exercises 27-2 and 27-3. Find the optimal sample size.

27-20 *Computer exercise.* Suppose that the OEM illustrated in the chapter also receives *hard* disk drives in shipments of 500 units each. The installed components add \$200 in value to the final product.

Replacement of installed defective drives costs \$400, and the cost of prior inspection and testing is \$35. Accepted shipments will be untested and installed directly, while rejected ones will receive 100% testing prior to installation, at a cost of \$10 each. Other costs for rejecting a shipment of hard disk drives are \$11,500.

(a) Express the payoff function for accepting and rejecting in terms of the proportion of defectives π in the shipment.

(b) The following subjective prior probability distribution applies for one supplier.

Proportion Defective	Probability
$\pi = .03$	.08
$\pi = .06$	.37
$\pi = .09$	.41
$\pi = .12$	.14

Find the optimal sample size and decision rule for disposing of incoming shipments. Use *binomial* conditional result probabilities.

27-21 *Computer exercise.* Repeat Exercise 27-20 using *hypergeometric* conditional result probabilities.

27-22 *Computer exercise.* NewScents has just been introduced. Its proportional present market share is uncertain. The following probabilities apply.

Share	Probability
.20	.05
.25	.13
.30	.17
.35	.27
.40	.16
.45	.13
.50	.09

The choices are whether or not to conduct a special promotion. The profit gain from the promotion declines with market share of the millions of potential buyers. Starting at $40,000, it drops $1,000 for each percentage point that market share falls above 0%.

A sample will have a fixed cost of $100 and a variable cost of $10 per observation. Only if the promotion is used, follow-on testing will be worth $20 for every potential buyer identified in the sample, while non-buyers found will yield nothing.

(a) Assuming that no sample is used, determine the expected payoffs, identify the best act, and calculate the EVPI.

(b) Assuming that sampling will be used, find the optimal sample size and critical value.

27-23 *Computer exercise.* An advertising agency must decide between a feminine slanted commercial for BriDent toothpaste and another with a masculine orientation. The ultimate payoff from the spot will depend on the proportion of female buyers, not presently known. The following payoffs and probabilities are assumed to apply.

Female Proportion	Probability	Masculine	Feminine
$\pi = .47$	.05	$180,000	$ 50,000
$\pi = .48$	.10	140,000	80,000
$\pi = .49$	.17	130,000	120,000
$\pi = .50$	.29	125,000	150,000
$\pi = .51$	.14	122,500	190,000
$\pi = .52$	.11	120,000	230,000
$\pi = .53$	.09	119,000	240,000
$\pi = .54$	.05	118,000	260,000

(a) Determine the expected payoffs, identify the best act, and calculate the EVPI.

(b) A sample of buyers may be selected and the person's sex established. The cost of sampling is $1 per observation. Find, for each n from 1 to 100, EVSI(n), Cost(n), ENGS(n), and C.

(c) What do you notice that is unusual about this problem?

27-5 BAYESIAN AND TRADITIONAL STATISTICS

To complete our discussion of decision making using sample information, a few comments should be made about the procedure presented here and the traditional statistical approach. In the above disk drive evaluation, the critical value is $C = 8$. Traditional statistics also finds a critical value, but the process is totally different.

HYPOTHESIS-TESTING CONCEPTS REVIEWED

In traditional statistics, the basic uncertainty is couched in special terminology. The main events are expressed as *hypotheses*. Each decision has two kinds of hypotheses. One is referred to as the **null hypothesis** (originally used to represent "no change"), and the other is the complementary **alternative hypothesis**. In the language of classical statistics, the following hypotheses would apply to disk drive acceptance sampling.

TABLE 27-6 Decision Table for the Traditional Statistical Decision

	Act	
Event	**Accept Null Hypothesis** (Accept the lot.)	**Reject Null Hypothesis** (Reject the lot.)
Null Hypothesis True (Lot is good.)	**Correct Decision**	**Type I Error** Probability $= \alpha$ (Reject a good lot.)
Null Hypothesis False (Lot is poor.)	**Type II Error** Probability $= \beta$ (Accept a poor lot.)	**Correct Decision**

Null hypothesis: $\pi = .10$ (The lot is good.)

Alternative hypothesis: $\pi > .10$ (The lot is poor.)

The decision rule we formulated earlier may be expressed in terms of these hypotheses. For disk drive acceptance sampling, they take the form

Accept the null hypothesis if $R \leq C$

Reject the null hypothesis if $R > C$

Traditional statistics focuses on the worst outcomes of the decision. These are called *errors* and are of two types. The **Type I error** occurs when the null hypothesis is rejected when it is actually true; the **Type II error** occurs when the null hypothesis is accepted when it is actually false. For the disk drive acceptance sampling inspection problem, these errors are

Type I error: Reject the lot when it is good.

Type II error: Accept the lot when it is poor.

The decision structure for traditional statistical analysis is presented in Table 27-6. The main events themselves are not assigned probabilities. Rather, the controlling factors in establishing the decision rule (the value of C) are the probabilities for the two kinds of errors.

$$\alpha = \text{Pr[Type I error]} = \text{Pr[Reject the null hypothesis when it is true.]}$$

$$\beta = \text{Pr[Type II error]} = \text{Pr[Accept the null hypothesis when it is false.]}$$

These probabilities are usually established in advance of sampling and are actually conditional probabilities (for which the status of the null hypothesis—true or false—is the given event). Conventionally, the Greek letters α (alpha) and β (beta) are used to represent the error probabilities. In the disk drive acceptance sampling, α represents the probability for rejecting a good lot, which is sometimes referred to as the **producer's risk**, and β is the probability for accepting a poor lot, or the **consumer's risk**.

Parameters: n = 42 P = .1 N = 1000

Number of Successes r	Probability Pr[R=r]	Cumulative Probability Pr[R<=r]
0	0.010849	0.010849
1	0.053044	0.063893
2	0.125179	0.189072
3	0.189973	0.379045
4	0.208430	0.587475
5	0.176212	0.763687
6	0.119480	0.883167
7	0.066775	0.949942
8	0.031373	0.981315
9	0.012576	0.993891
10	0.004351	0.998242

Source: *QuickQuant Plus.*

FIGURE 27-15 Hypergeometric probabilities for disk drive quality decision.

Both types of errors are undesirable, but obviously neither error may be avoided entirely. Traditional statistics is concerned with selecting the sample size n and the decision rule (the value of C) that will achieve an acceptable balance between α and β. If n is fixed, one error probability may be reduced only by increasing the probability for the other error. Because the sample size itself is often dictated by economic or other considerations, it is usually possible to control only one error completely.

Generally, the null and alternative hypotheses are formulated in such a way that the Type I error is more serious. The tolerable probability for this error is specified at a level such as $\alpha = .001$, $\alpha = .05$, or $\alpha = .10$. A value of C is then chosen that guarantees that this level of α is not exceeded.

To illustrate, we will return to the disk drive acceptance sampling problem. Suppose that $\alpha = .01$, so that C must be the smallest value such that

$$\text{Pr[Rejecting the null hypothesis when it is true.]} \leq \alpha$$

or

$$\Pr[R > C \mid \pi = .10] \leq .01$$

To find C, the binomial (or hypergeometric) probabilities must be determined. These may be computed directly, found from tables, approximated, or determined with computer assistance. Using the same sample size $n = 42$ as in the preceding illustration, exact hypergeometric probabilities in Figure 27-15 were obtained with computer assistance. The critical value will be that possible level for R having a cumulative probability closest to, but not falling below, $1 - \alpha = .99$. The number fitting the bill is $R = 9$, for which

$$\Pr[R \leq 9 \mid \pi = .10] = .99389$$

Parameters: n = 42 P = .15 N = 1000

Number of Successes r	Probability Pr[R=r]	Cumulative Probability Pr[R<=r]
0	0.000928	0.000928
1	0.007227	0.008155
2	0.027252	0.035407
3	0.066310	0.101717
4	0.117043	0.218760
5	0.159742	0.378502
6	0.175474	0.553976
7	0.159449	0.713425
8	0.122249	0.835674
9	0.080269	0.915943
10	0.045659	0.961602

Source: *QuickQuant Plus.*

FIGURE 27-16 Second set of hypergeometric probabilities for disk drive quality decision.

so that

$$\Pr[R > 9] = 1 - .99389 = .00611$$

The traditional hypothesis testing approach provides $C = 9$, a slightly different value than found earlier. The achieved Type I error probability is thus,

$$\Pr[\text{Reject } H_0 | H_0 \text{ true}] = \Pr[R > 9 | \pi = .10] = .00611$$

How good is the decision rule with $C = 9$? As we have seen, traditional statistics is also concerned with the Type II error. A second computer run using $\pi = .15$ provides the report in Figure 27-16. There, we see that there is a considerable chance that such a poor quality lot will be accepted.

$$\beta = \Pr[R \leq 9 | \pi = .15] = .915943$$

A β probability may be found for any specified level for π. An examination of these might be helpful in making a final choice of C.

Traditional statistics will often provide different decision rules than those found using the Bayesian approach, even when the sample sizes are the same, which will not usually be the case.

CONTRASTING THE TWO APPROACHES

Why do Bayesian and traditional statistical analysis lead to different decision rules? This is because of the differences between these two procedures.

1. The decision-theory procedure considers the payoffs from every possible outcome. Payoffs are not explicitly considered in hypothesis testing, although they may influence the choice of α.

2. Prior probabilities are applied directly in the decision-theory approach. Like payoffs, prior probabilities ought to play some role in establishing α.

3. Hypothesis testing proceeds directly from the prescribed α to the decision rule. Decision-theory analysis arrives at the optimal decision rule by means of the Bayes decision rule, using the appropriate posterior probabilities and the payoffs for each outcome. The resulting decision maximizes expected payoff.

Which procedure is preferable? Bayesian analysis is plagued by subjective prior probabilities, which are considered by many to be the weakest link in its analytical chain. Many statisticians deny the existence of subjective probabilities, thereby relegating much of statistical decision theory to the ash heap. A major feature that makes traditional hypothesis testing procedures more universally accepted is that no prior probabilities are required at all. *But the uncertainties regarding the population parameter still exist*, and traditional statistical procedures must also involve some sort of subjective assessment of these uncertainties when desired error probabilities are being established. In hypothesis testing, everything hinges on the prescribed significance level α (and also on β when there is the freedom or the capability to prescribe β). Unless α is carefully determined, inferior decisions are bound to occur. Decision theory permits the consistent and systematic treatment of chance and payoffs as well as attitude toward risk. In addition, decision theory does not burden the decision maker by requiring him or her to do everything at once by choosing a single number—"an α for all seasons."

When the outcomes do not have a natural numerical payoff measure or when the decision maker is risk-seeking or risk-averse, then the strengths of decision-theory analysis rest on a foundation of utility values. As we will see in Chapter 29, obtaining utilities requires a set of assumptions about attitudes, which are obtained by means of an elaborate procedure. Although any difficulties involved in employing utilities may be avoided by traditional statistics, α embodies everything, so that even more care must be exercised in choosing the appropriate target value.

The final and perhaps the most significant advantage of Bayesian analysis is that *it considers whether or not a sample should even be used.* We have seen that a greater expected payoff may be achieved by deciding what to do immediately, without incurring the expense of a sample. Traditional statistics never satisfactorily copes with this question. In addition, the choice of proper sample size is too often an *ad hoc* process in traditional statistics. (A sample size of 30 may be used, for example, because the Student t table stops at 30 degrees of freedom.) Decision theory explicitly considers the costs of the various sample sizes.

At this point you might wonder why classical hypothesis testing is used at all. Although classical hypothesis testing has roots in biological and medical studies, its use has been expanded into all areas of science. Traditional statistics permeates our society—used in the social sciences, in education, in government, and even in business.

Traditional statistics prevails in public arena decision making, where there is little room for anything subjective. Indeed, science epitomizes objectivity. Therefore, any use of subjective prior probabilities is unacceptable; they only create controversy and destroy credibility. Also, public decision making involves societal issues and human lives. In such a decision-making environment the very notion of a payoff value may be at best controversial, perhaps even irrelevant.

The Bayesian statistics of this chapter coexist side-by-side with classical hypothesis testing. Factors that determine the appropriate procedure to use include the type of application, who is making the decision, and who will see the analysis. The Bayesian approach is best suited to private decision making, where the decision maker alone is held accountable for the outcome and no controversy need ever arise from using subjective probabilities and the selection of payoffs. The classical approach works best in public.

A pharmaceutical house may use both types of statistics. Experiments done with new drugs in order to gain government approvals involve public issues and must be strictly based on classical hypothesis testing. But decisions regarding what types of new drugs to develop and market may be made in private, where Bayesian statistics should be more beneficial.

EXERCISES

27-24 Refer to the disk drive quality discussion on pages 1080–1081. Suppose that α is changed to .05. Determine the new critical value.

27-25 Refer, again, to the disk drive quality discussion.

(a) Suppose that $n = 20$ is used instead and that $\alpha = .05$. Using binomial probabilities as an approximation to the true ones, determine the critical value.

(b) Determine the Type II error probabilities applicable to your answer to (a) when (1) $\pi = .20$ and (2) $\pi = .30$.

27-26 A market researcher wishes to determine whether to accept the null hypothesis regarding the proportion π of Appleton smokers who will switch to a new mentholated version, Mapleton. Her null hypothesis is that $\pi = .1$. She takes a random sample of 100 current Appleton smokers, who will be contacted in six months to see if they have switched. The researcher wishes to protect against the Type I error with a probability of $\alpha = .005$. Using Appendix Table C, determine the smallest acceptance number C such that the probability that the number of switchers will exceed this number is less than or equal to the desired α. Then, formulate the researcher's decision rule.

27-27 Referring to Exercise 27-26, suppose that the following prior probabilities are obtained for π.

π	**Probability**
.05	1/3
.10	1/3
.15	1/3
	1

The following conditional result probabilities for the number of switchers R apply.

	$\pi = .05$	$\pi = .10$	$\pi = .15$
$R \leq 17$	1.0000	.9900	.7633
$R = 18$	0	.0054	.0739
$R \geq 19$	0	.0046	.1628

The decision maker's payoffs, including the cost of sampling, are

	Accept Null Hypothesis	Reject Null Hypothesis
$\pi = .05$	$10,000	−$2,000
$\pi = .10$	5,000	0
$\pi = .15$	−2,000	4,000

(a) Determine the posterior probability distribution for π, given each of the sample result events above. Then, find the unconditional result probabilities.

(b) Construct the market researcher's decision tree diagram. Enter the probabilities that you found in (a) on the appropriate branches, and place the payoffs along the respective end positions.

(c) Should the decision maker accept or reject the null hypothesis if $R = 18$? Compare this result with your result in Exercise 27-26.

27-6 ADDITIONAL REMARKS

In this chapter, we have learned to analyze decision making using sampling. By employing the procedures described here, we exercise judgment about the population characteristics by assigning prior probabilities to the possible values of the decision parameter π or μ. The benefits and costs of sampling may be systematically evaluated in a way that explicitly accounts for the payoffs for every outcome. This makes it possible even to consider the question of whether or not to sample in the first place. The principles of decision theory permit a more thorough analysis to be made than traditional statistics provides.

The procedures presented in this chapter have drawbacks. The main difficulties arise from the nature of decision tree analysis itself. Because the possible number of sample results and population parameters may be huge, many problems are too large to fit conveniently on a tree. Some problems require such a large amount of computational effort that a computer is needed to evaluate them.

But decision tree analysis presents a more fundamental problem. It is an inherently *discrete* procedure, since each event must be represented by a separate branch. Many problems involve *continuous* random variables. For example, π and μ may range over a continuous spectrum of possible values. Also, the sample mean $\bar{X}$ is often a continuous variable that is generally represented by the normal distribution. In Chapter 29, we will consider the case in which the normal curve serves as the prior distribution for μ. Nevertheless, it is still possible to apply decision tree analysis to these problem situations by approximating the continuous distributions. Methods for doing this with a few typical values representing the entire range of the continuous variable were described in Chapter 20.

SUMMARY

1. **What are the fundamental features of Bayesian analysis with samples?**
Sample data may be treated like special experimental information that may be useful in a wide class of two-action decision situations. Bayesian analysis begins with a prior analysis to determine which of the two acts, conveniently summarized as accept and reject, provides the greater expected payoff. Structures are evaluated that have *population parameter* levels as the main events. Thus, for a qualitative population there are several possible levels of π, with each level having a separate payoff under the two acts. And, a quantitative population involves several μ events and is treated analogously. A **prior probability distribution** is assumed to apply for either π or μ.
Should the prior analysis yield a sufficiently high EVPI, a preposterior analysis may be conducted to determine which sample size—if sampling is to be used—is the best to obtain before a main decision is made. As with the more general Bayesian analysis in Chapter 26, the preposterior analysis includes a posterior analysis with each contemplated sample size.

2. **What are the probability elements in a posterior analysis with the proportion?**
Consider a decision where levels of the population proportion π are the main events. A posterior analysis begins with probability trees for the actual and informational chronologies. The actual tree utilizes the prior probability distribution for π in the first stage. Each π level branch leads to a separate event fork for the sample results. There will be one branch in each of those event forks corresponding to a possible number R of successes. A different set of **conditional result probabilities** will apply in each fork, with the parameters n and π determining those values. Should the underlying population be large, R is a random variable having a *binomial distribution*.
Once the actual chronological probability tree has been constructed and all probabilities obtained, the joint probabilities are computed for each path. These numbers are transferred onto the informational chronological probability tree, where the R events for the sample results appear in the first stage and the π events in the second. The **unconditional result probabilities** for R and the several **posterior probabilities** for π are computed. The values from this second probability tree are then transferred to a decision tree diagram, and a backward induction analysis is performed.

3. **How is the decision rule established?**
The pruned tree indicates, for each level of R, whether the greater expected payoff is achieved by accepting or by rejecting. The designations of *accept* and *reject* are made so that accept is the better act when R is small. In those cases, the largest level of R at which the pruned tree leads to a choice to accept is called the **acceptance number** C. The pruned decision tree may be summarized in terms of a *decision rule*.

4. **What are the elements of preposterior analysis using sample information?**
The final expected payoff computed for the π event fork is the **expected payoff with sample information**. Should the original payoffs not include any sampling costs, then when the maximum expected payoff found in the prior analysis is subtracted, the resulting quantity is the **expected value of sample information** or **EVSI**. A separate EVSI and C will be obtained for each sam-

ple size, with a separate posterior analysis conducted for each candidate n. Subtracting the cost of sampling, the **expected net gain of sampling** or **ENGS** is obtained. Preposterior analysis includes a comparison of the ENGS(n) to determine which n is the best.

5. **What are the elements of Bayesian sampling with the mean?**
The procedure for decision making with the mean is analogous. The sample results are summarized in terms of the sample mean $\bar{X}$. Instead of binomial conditional result probabilities, an appropriate *normal distribution* is used. Each normal curve must be approximated by an event fork involving a few discrete levels of $\bar{X}$. The acceptance numbers C signify the greatest level of $\bar{X}$ at which accept is the best act. The optimal sample size provides the maximum ENGS.

6. **What are the differences and relative advantages of Bayesian statistics and traditional hypothesis testing?**
The Bayesian approach may be compared to classical hypothesis testing, first introduced in Chapter 9. Both procedures lead to a decision rule. The Bayesian approach utilizes the decision maker's payoffs and has the advantage of systematically incorporating prior probabilities for μ or π. The classical approach merely controls the incidence of the Type I and Type II errors. Implementation of Bayesian decision making is limited, however, to the private arena where payoffs are easily determined and where judgment may be used to establish *subjective* prior probabilities. Neither apply to decisions in the public arena, however, where traditional hypothesis testing is the only acceptable procedure.

REVIEW EXERCISES

27-28 The decision tree diagram in Figure 27-17 has been constructed to determine whether to accept shipments from a particular supplier.
(a) Perform backward induction. What action—not to sample, to sample with $n = 1$, or to sample with $n = 2$—should be taken?
(b) What is the optimal value of the acceptance number C if $n = 1$ is used? If $n = 2$ is used?

27-29 Let π be the proportion of dogs that will like a new dog food, SuperPooch. Suppose that the prior probabilities established for π are $\Pr[\pi = .20] = .1$ and $\Pr[\pi = .30] = .9$. A random sample of the responses of $n = 2$ dogs is obtained.
(a) Construct the actual chronological probability tree diagram.
(b) Construct the informational chronological probability tree diagram.
(c) Determine the posterior probability that $\pi = .20$ if the following situations apply.
(1) no dogs are found to like the food
(2) exactly one dog likes it
(3) both dogs like it

27-30 The chemical processing for Anomaly perfume yields a mean of μ grams of active ingredient for every liter of gland extract processed. Due to variations in the raw material and in the control settings, the true population mean for any particular batch is unknown until processing is complete. From past history, the plant superintendent judges that the following prior probabilities for μ apply.

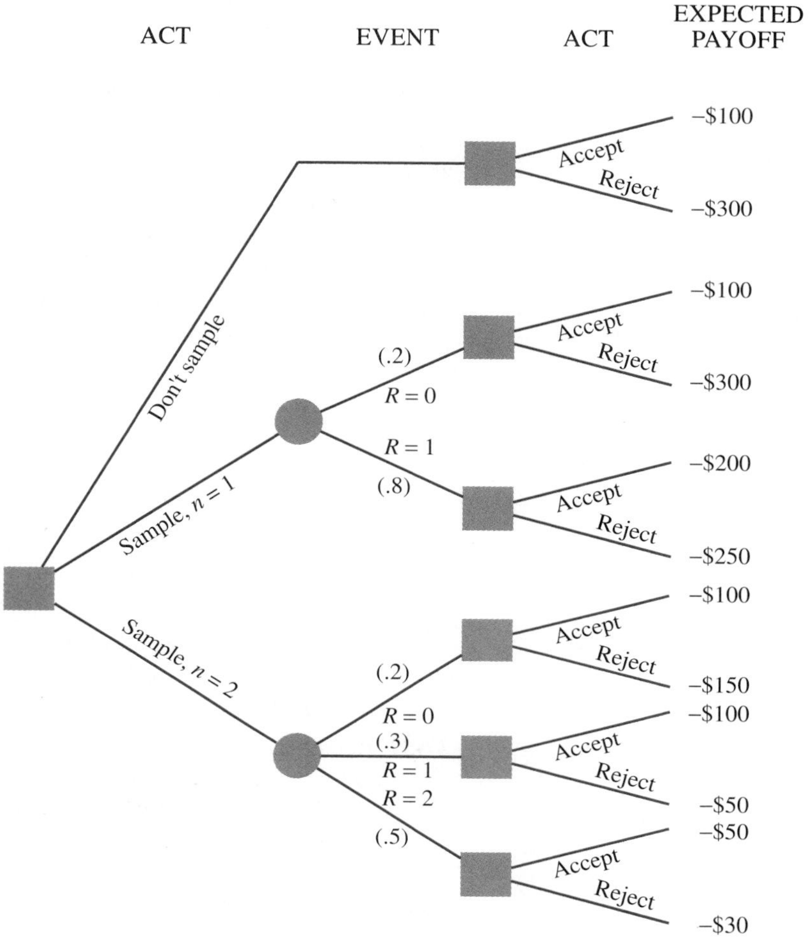

FIGURE 27-17

Possible Mean μ	**Probability**
25 g	.3
30	.4
35	.3

The plant superintendent must decide whether to adjust the control settings in processing a batch of Anomaly. Suppose that the following payoff table applies.

Population Mean	**Act**	
μ	**Adjust**	**Leave Alone**
25 g	$ 500	−$500
30	0	0
35	−1,000	500

(a) Assuming that no sample is taken, what course of action will maximize the expected payoff?
(b) Calculate the plant superintendent's EVPI. Would he use a sample to facilitate his decision if it cost \$400? (Answer yes, no, or maybe.) If it cost \$200? Explain.

27-31 Refer to Exercise 27-30. Suppose that the plant superintendent will base the decision for control settings on a sample. The sample will consist of $n = 3$ liters of gland extract, for each of which the precise amount of resulting active gland ingredient will be determined after processing. The sample mean will then be calculated from these readings. Suppose that the following approximate conditional result probabilities apply.

	Probabilities for $\bar{X}$		
$\bar{X}$	$\mu = 25$ g	$\mu = 30$ g	$\mu = 35$ g
25 g	.7	.2	.2
30	.2	.6	.3
35	.1	.2	.5

(a) Construct the probability tree diagram for the actual chronology.
(b) Using the probabilities that you found in (a), construct the probability tree diagram for the informational chronology and to compute the unconditional result and posterior probabilities for μ.

27-32 Refer to Exercises 27-30 and 27-31 and to your answers.
(a) Construct the plant superintendent's decision tree diagram, assuming that he is committed to taking a sample. Use gross payoff figures.
(b) Perform backward induction to determine the value of C (for accepting the need for adjustment) that will maximize expected gross payoff. Formulate the optimal decision rule.
(c) Calculate the EVSI.
(d) Suppose that a sample of $n = 3$ liters costs \$50. Calculate the superintendent's expected net gain of sampling.

CASE Charismatic Chimeras

Three-dimensional puzzles are the specialty products of Charismatic Chimeras. The company must decide whether or not to introduce the Snuggler Puzzler as the replacement for its Cozy Cubit. But there is some uncertainty about the proportion π of the market that will actually prefer the new product. The marketing vice-president assumes that π is normally distributed, believing it to be a 50–50 proposition that π will lie at or above .70. She also feels that it is equally as likely for π to fall in the limits .65 to .75 as outside that range. She knows that the payoff for introducing the Snuggler Puzzler is $-$\$100,000, plus or minus \$20,000 for each percentage point by which π exceeds .60. At a cost of \$100 per observation, it is possible to tell whether or not a Cozy Cubit fan prefers the Snuggler Puzzler.

A related decision must be made by the operations vice-president whether to manufacture the Snuggler Puzzlers in-house or to have them made under contract. The major uncertainty pertains to the mean unit direct cost of production μ. The breakeven level is \$10 per unit. The vice-president believes that there is a 50–50 chance that μ will lie at or below \$9 per unit, with an even proposition that μ lies between \$7.50 and \$10.50 rather than higher or lower. As with π, a normal curve applies.

QUESTIONS

1. Determine the expected value and standard deviation of the subjective prior probability distribution for π. Using the following intervals, determine the applicable probabilities.

Class Interval
below .55
.55–.65
.65–.75
.75–.85
above .85

2. Using $\pi = .50$, $\pi = .60$, $\pi = .70$, $\pi = .80$, and $\pi = .90$ as the main events, construct a payoff table for the marketing vice-president's product decision. Using your interval probabilities from Question 1 as the respective main event probabilities, determine the expected payoff for each act.

3. Using your answer to Question 2, compute the EVPI. Does a cost of \$100 per sample observation seem reasonable?

4. Determine the expected net gain of sampling when $n = 3$.

5. Determine the expected value and standard deviation for the subjective prior probability distribution for the mean unit direct cost of production μ. Then, using the following intervals, determine the applicable probabilities.

Class Interval
below \$6
\$6–\$8
\$8–\$10
\$10–\$12
above \$12

6. A production run of 20,000 Snuggler Puzzlers will be made. A contractor will do them for \$12 each. The fixed cost of in-house manufacturing is \$40,000. Each unit will provide a net revenue of \$20. Use $\mu = \$5$,

μ = \$7, μ = \$9, μ = \$11, and μ = \$13 as the main events and construct a payoff table for the operations vice-president's production decision. Using the respective interval probabilities from Question 5 for the event probabilities, determine the expected payoff for each act.

7. Determine the EVPI for the production decision. Do you think sample information would even be appropriate here?

CHAPTER 28

BAYESIAN ANALYSIS USING THE NORMAL DISTRIBUTION

BEFORE READING THIS CHAPTER, MAKE SURE YOU UNDERSTAND:

Basic concepts of probability (Chapter 5).
Probability distributions and expected value (Chapter 6).
Normal distribution (Chapter 7).
Subjective probability in decision making (Chapter 20).
Basic concepts of decision analysis (Chapter 24).
Elements of decision theory (Chapter 25).
Bayesian analysis of decisions using experimental information (Chapter 26).
Bayesian analysis with sample information (Chapter 27).

AFTER READING THIS CHAPTER, YOU WILL UNDERSTAND:

About the basic structure of Bayesian analysis using the normal distribution.
About the four stages of a Bayesian analysis with the normal distribution.
Which symbols are employed and how they relate to the four stages.
About the common pitfalls in performing a Bayesian analysis with the normal distribution.

In Chapter 27, we saw how sampling may be used to obtain experimental information to facilitate decision making. There, we applied sampling to situations involving two acts with payoffs determined by the value of an uncertain population parameter, such as the mean μ or the proportion π. Our earlier discussion of decision making using the mean considered only discrete probability distributions, which apply when the number of possible values for the population mean or the sample mean is limited. But in most situations, both μ and $\bar{X}$ may be any point in a continuous range of values. In such cases, it is more realistic to analyze the decision in terms of continuous probability distributions.

In describing the procedures for doing this, we will expand the computer center manager's decision described in Chapter 27. Recall that a choice must be made between two peripheral memory storage units based on laser technology. One alternative is photographic in nature; the other employs the principles of holographic imagery. Our earlier analysis was based on only two values of the population mean of memory access levels μ, expressed in gigabits per day. There, we used prior probabilities of .5 for $\mu = 2$ and .5 for $\mu = 3$. We will now treat the unknown μ as a random variable with a *continuous* **prior probability distribution**, reflecting the possibility that μ may assume many other levels. For any given level of μ, we will also assume that there is a *continuous conditional probability distribution* for the possible values of $\bar{X}$, instead of the four whole numbers used earlier.

In both cases, the particular distributions are members of the *normal distribution* family. Although a variety of other prior distributions might be used for μ, we know from the central limit theorem (discussed in Chapter 7) that $\bar{X}$ tends to be normally distributed and that this is the only appropriate distribution to use.*

28-1 STRUCTURE OF DECISION MAKING WITH THE NORMAL DISTRIBUTION

In this chapter, we will assume that μ is a random variable having prior probabilities obtainable from the normal curve. Recall, from Chapter 7, that any particular normal curve may be specified entirely by its mean and standard deviation (or variance). These parameters are denoted by μ_0 and σ_0, where the subscript zeros indicate that these are the initial, prior values and are not based on sampling information. Here, μ_0 is the expected value of the unknown population mean. This is the central value, and we will refer to μ_0 as the **prior expected mean**. The **prior standard deviation** σ_0 summarizes the variability in possible levels of μ.

The values of μ_0 and σ_0 must be based largely on judgment, when no historical data are directly related to μ. Or, μ_0 and σ_0 might be obtained from previous experience. For example, μ might represent the mean ingredient yield in several successive batches of a raw material used in chemical processing, and records might have been kept of the mean yield that each batch achieved. Chapter 20 describes how subjective prior probability distributions may be obtained.

We will illustrate the structure of decision making with the normal curve using the computer memory device decision first encountered in Chapter 27.

*The necessary conditions are that the population variance be finite and known and that the samples be large and independently selected.

COMPUTER MEMORY DEVICE DECISION

Recall, from Chapter 27, the decision by the computer center manager regarding which peripheral memory device to lease, the photographic one or the holographic one. The evaluation is based on the annual cost savings over the existing system. The photographic memory will save $600,000 in base costs, while the holographic will save $450,000. Additionally, there will be further operating cost savings, depending on the overall mean daily level of memory access. For the photographic memory, the additional savings amount to $57,500 for each gigabit (billion bits), while the holographic memory yields $120,000 in further cost reductions.

Of course, the daily memory traffic is anticipated to fluctuate considerably, with individual daily figures such as 2,245,000,000 or 5,907,550,000 bits conceivable. The level of memory access could be as low as .5 gigabit (500,000,000 bits) or as high as 20 gigabits (20,000,000,000 bits). The center manager is uncertain about the mean value μ of this population of individual daily memory access levels.

The manager assumes that μ is normally distributed. Using the procedures in Chapter 20, he selected 2.50 gigabits per day as the 50–50 point for mean daily memory access level. Thus, the center of the prior normal curve for μ is $\mu_0 = 2.50$. He also found it to be "even money" that μ would fall inside the interval 2.40–2.60 versus outside. From this he arrived at the standard deviation $\sigma_0 = .15$ for the prior subjective probability distribution for μ.

28-2 DECISION MAKING USING OPPORTUNITY LOSSES

In Chapter 27, we saw how we might evaluate this decision using the payoff table in Table 28-1. As events, representative levels for μ are listed.

TABLE 28-1 Payoff Table for Computer Memory Device Decision

Mean Daily Memory Access Levels	Memory Device Choices	
μ	Photographic	Holographic
1.90	$709,250	$678,000
2.00	715,000	690,000
2.10	720,750	702,000
2.20	726,500	714,000
2.30	732,250	726,000
2.40	738,000	738,000
2.50	743,750	750,000
2.60	749,500	762,000
2.70	755,250	774,000
2.80	761,000	786,000
2.90	766,750	798,000
3.00	772,500	810,000
3.10	778,250	822,000

LINEAR PAYOFF FUNCTIONS AND THE BREAKEVEN MEAN

The population mean is a continuous variable, so that the payoffs may be computed for an infinite number of levels for μ. In such cases, it is ordinarily more convenient to express the payoffs as *linear functions of* μ.

Figure 28-1 shows the essential relationship between payoff and opportunity loss for the computer memory device decision. The gross payoffs for the two memory units may be expressed in terms of the unknown mean daily access level as

$$\text{Gross payoff} = \begin{cases} \$600{,}000 + \$\ 57{,}500\mu & \text{for photographic} \\ \$450{,}000 + \$120{,}000\mu & \text{for holographic} \end{cases}$$

These payoffs are plotted as two lines in the graph in Figure 28-1. The height of the respective lines at any level μ may be determined from the preceding equations. The slope of the photographic-unit payoff line is \$57,500, and the slope of the steeper holographic-unit payoff line is \$120,000. The two lines cross at that value of μ where the gross payoff is identical under each act. This value is referred to as the **breakeven mean** and is denoted as μ_b. The breakeven mean is found by setting the two payoff expressions equal to each other and solving for μ_b. In this case,

$$\$600{,}000 + \$57{,}500\mu_b = \$450{,}000 + \$120{,}000\mu_b$$

so that

$$(\$120{,}000 - \$57{,}500)\mu_b = \$600{,}000 - \$450{,}000$$
$$\$62{,}500\mu_b = \$150{,}000$$

and

$$\mu_b = \$150{,}000/\$62{,}500 = 2.4 \text{ gigabits per day}$$

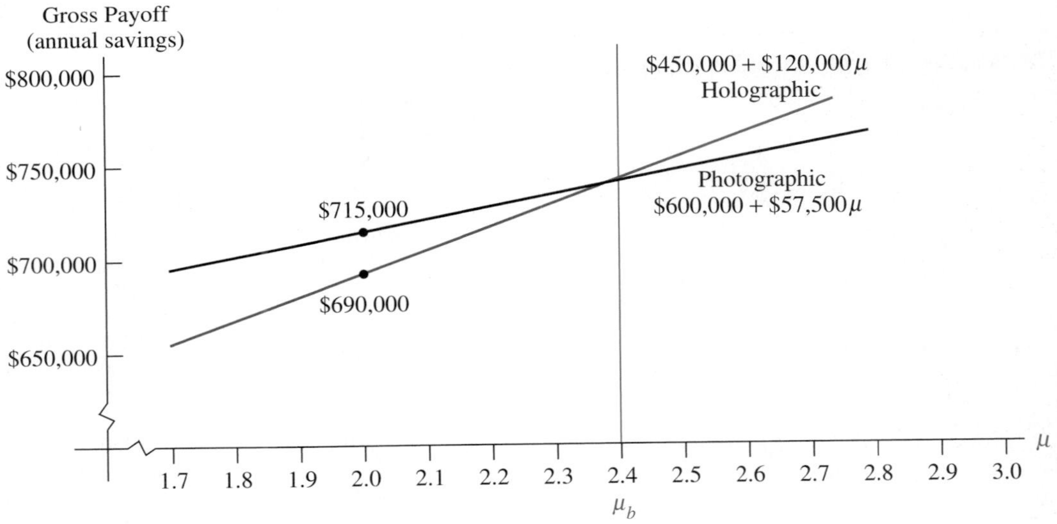

FIGURE 28-1 Linear payoff functions for memory device decision.

For values of μ less than $\mu_b = 2.4$, the photographic memory yields the greatest annual savings; for means greater than μ_b, the holographic unit is preferable. At $\mu = \mu_b$, the annual savings is \$738,000 using either alternative.

FINDING OPPORTUNITY LOSSES

Until this point, we have been able to analyze decisions by maximizing expected payoff—a procedure sometimes referred to as the *Bayes decision rule.* We have established that an equivalent criterion is to minimize expected opportunity loss. For two-action problems involving continuous probability distributions, it is more convenient to focus on opportunity losses as a basis for decision making.

The opportunity losses may be found for any row in Table 28-1 by first identifying the maximum payoff with the event for that row and subtracting every payoff of the row from that amount. The opportunity loss for picking the photographic memory when $\mu = 2.00$ is zero, since that act provides the maximum payoff in the $\mu = 2.00$ row. The opportunity loss for picking the holographic memory when $\mu = 2.00$ is the following difference in payoffs from that same row.

$$\$715{,}000 - 690{,}000 = \$25{,}000$$

Duplicating this for each row of the payoff table, the complete listing of opportunity losses for the computer memory device decision were found, as shown in Table 28-2.

The opportunity losses may also be plotted as a graph, shown in Figure 28-2. We see that the photographic unit is the better choice when the true population mean lies below the breakeven level μ_b. Thus, whenever $\mu \leq \mu_b$, choosing the photographic unit will result in zero opportunity loss, which is represented by the horizontal line segment to the left of μ_b. If the true mean exceeds the breakeven level, the opportunity losses for the photographic unit rise, as represented by the upward-sloping line segment beginning at μ_b. The reverse holds for the holo-

TABLE 28-2 Opportunity Loss Table for Computer Memory Device Decision

Mean Daily Memory Access Levels μ	Memory Device Choices: Photographic	Memory Device Choices: Holographic
1.90	\$ 0	\$31,250
2.00	0	25,000
2.10	0	18,750
2.20	0	12,500
2.30	0	6,250
2.40	0	0
2.50	6,250	0
2.60	12,500	0
2.70	18,750	0
2.80	25,000	0
2.90	31,250	0
3.00	37,500	0
3.10	43,750	0

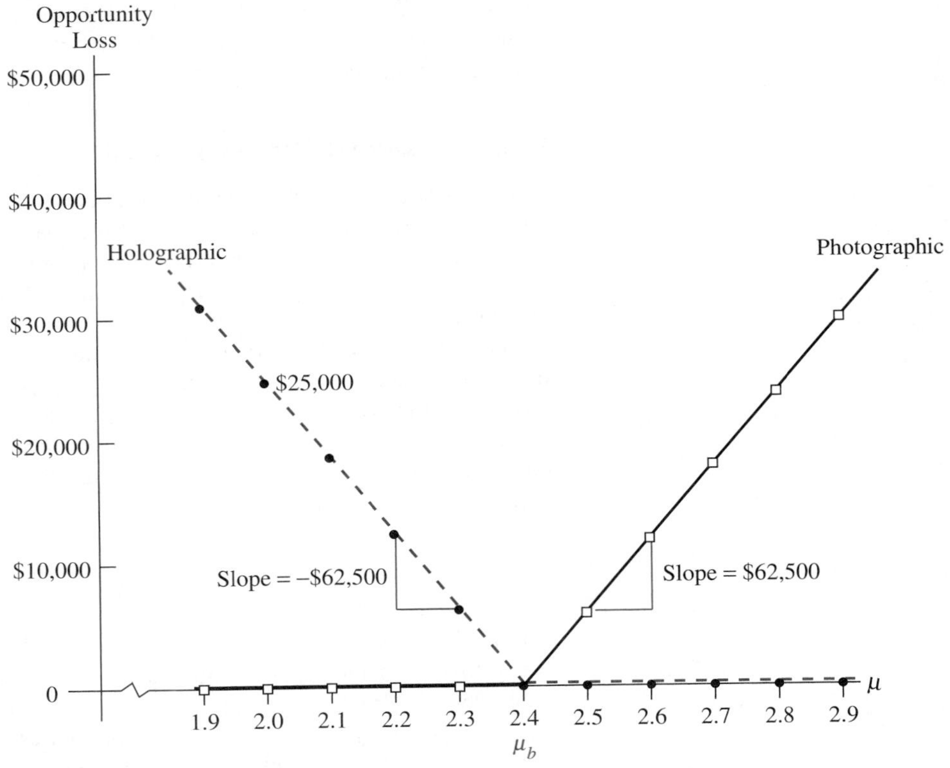

FIGURE 28-2 Opportunity loss functions for memory device decision.

graphic unit. For true population means above μ_b, the holographic alternative is better and its opportunity losses must be zero, as represented by the dashed horizontal line segment to the right of μ_b. To the left of μ_b, the opportunity losses for the holographic unit are represented by the downward-sloping dashed line segment falling toward μ_b. The heights of points lying on the V-shaped portion represent the difference in savings between the best and worst acts at each level of μ. The V is symmetrical, and the two rising line segments have identical slopes (with opposite signs) of a magnitude equal to the difference between the slopes of the two payoff lines: \$120,000 − \$57,500 = \$62,500.

APPROXIMATING PROBABILITIES FOR THE NORMAL CURVE

Since μ is a continuous random variable, the events could be listed to any detail, and since the normal distribution applies, there would be no theoretical beginning or end to the list of μ events. The probabilities for the listed events are found in Table 28-3, where each listed μ is actually at the midpoint of a class interval of width .10. The normal deviates z for each interval upper limit μ were computed using the relationship

$$z = \frac{\mu - \mu_0}{\sigma_0}$$

These probabilities may be used to compute expected values.

TABLE 28-3 Prior Probabilities for μ Intervals in Memory Device Decision

(1) Interval for μ	(2) Normal Deviate z	(3) Cumulative Probability	(4) Midpoint μ	(5) Interval Probability
1.85–under 1.95	−3.67	.0001	1.90	.0001
1.95–under 2.05	−3.00	.0013	2.00	.0012
2.05–under 2.15	−2.33	.0099	2.10	.0086
2.15–under 2.25	−1.67	.0475	2.20	.0376
2.25–under 2.35	−1.00	.1587	2.30	.1112
2.35–under 2.45	−.33	.3707	2.40	.2120
2.45–under 2.55	.33	.6293	2.50	.2586
2.55–under 2.65	1.00	.8413	2.60	.2120
2.65–under 2.75	1.67	.9525	2.70	.1112
2.75–under 2.85	2.33	.9901	2.80	.0376
2.85–under 2.95	3.00	.9987	2.90	.0086
2.95–under 3.05	3.67	.9999	3.00	.0012
3.05–under 3.15	4.33	1.0000	3.10	.0001

FINDING EXPECTED OPPORTUNITY LOSSES

The expected opportunity loss for each act may be computed by multiplying each value in the respective loss column of Table 28-2 by the probability values in column (5) of Table 28-3.

Figure 28-3 shows the relationship between these values when the prior normal curve for μ is superimposed on the loss function for the holographic-unit choice. That act provides the following *approximate* value.

$$\text{Expected opportunity loss} = \$1{,}360 \quad \text{(holographic)}$$

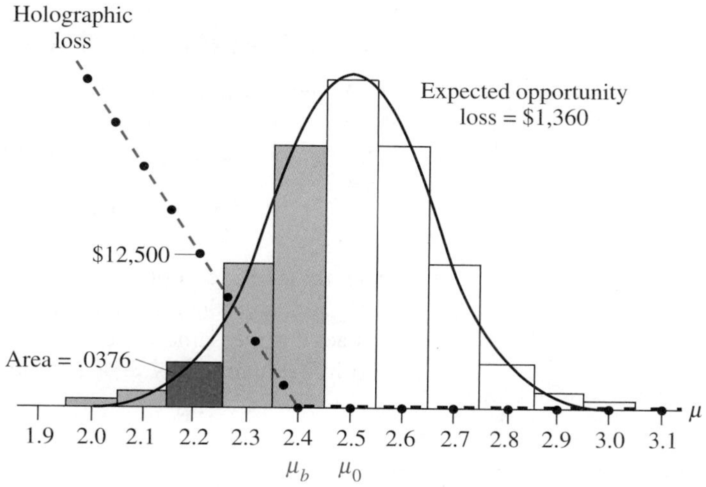

FIGURE 28-3 Illustration of how expected opportunity loss may be computed using loss function and prior normal curve for μ.

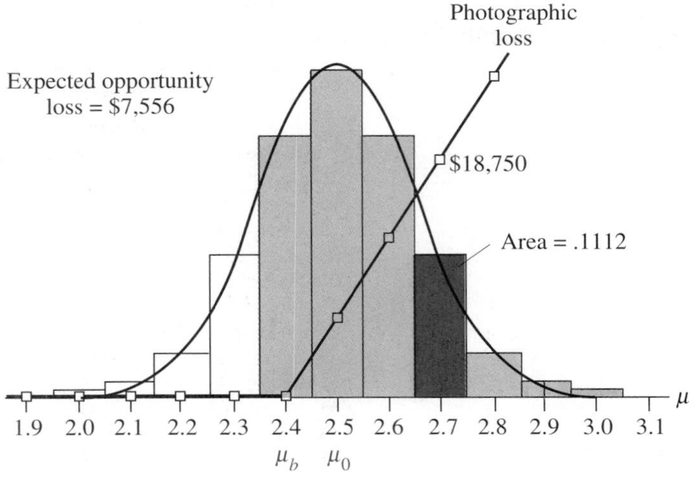

FIGURE 28-4 Illustration of how expected opportunity loss may be computed using loss function and prior normal curve for μ

The analogous interrelationship is shown in Figure 28-4 for the photographic-unit choice. That act provides

$$\text{Expected opportunity loss} = \$7{,}556 \quad \text{(photographic)}$$

The main decision might be made right now. The Bayes decision rule indicates that the holographic memory device should be chosen. This act not only minimizes expected opportunity loss, but it must also maximize expected payoff. Rather than commit himself to the main decision, the computer center manager wanted to explore the possibility of using *sample information.* The decision maker needs to determine if it might be worthwhile to pursue such information.

EVPI: MINIMUM EXPECTED OPPORTUNITY LOSS

The expected value of perfect information is useful in gauging the potential worth of less-than-perfect sample information. We should compute the EVPI before deciding about a sample. Recall, from Chapter 25, that the following applies.

$$\text{EVPI} = \text{Expected opportunity loss for best act}$$

Thus, the expected opportunity loss for the best act equals the needed value.

We next introduce a streamlined procedure that the manager could have used in reaching the same conclusion. The following procedure would ordinarily be used in evaluating any decision having a structure similar to his.

EXERCISES

28-1 Suppose that the computer center manager modifies the subjective normal curve for the mean daily access level, so that the expected level is 2.6 gigabits per day with a standard deviation of .20. Also, the payoff function coefficient for μ is increased for the photographic memory from 57,500 to 60,000.

(a) Using tabled areas under the normal curve, complete the following table.

Class Interval	Midpoint	Interval Probability
1.80–2.00	1.9	________
2.00–2.20	2.1	________
2.20–2.40	2.3	________
2.40–2.60	2.5	________
2.60–2.80	2.7	________
2.80–3.00	2.9	________
3.00–3.20	3.1	________
3.20–3.40	3.3	________

(b) Construct the payoff table for the decision using interval midpoints as the events.

(c) Construct the opportunity loss table and compute the expected opportunity losses using the probabilities found in (a). Which act minimizes expected opportunity loss?

(d) Find the expected value of perfect information.

28-3 STREAMLINED PRIOR ANALYSIS WITHOUT SAMPLE INFORMATION

The streamlined procedure begins with some preliminaries. First is the definition of the population for which the mean μ is unknown and pivotal in establishing payoffs. The next step is to identify the linear payoff function for each act. From these the breakeven level μ_b is obtained. Figure 28-5 shows the general situation. Note that μ_b divides the range for μ into one segment where Act 1 has greater payoffs and one where Act 2 is better. The final preliminary step is to establish the expected value μ_0 and standard deviation σ_0 for the prior normal distribution for μ.

IDENTIFYING THE ACT HAVING MINIMUM EXPECTED OPPORTUNITY LOSS

Figure 28-6 relates the opportunity losses to the probabilities for μ by superimposing the normal curve for μ onto the respective opportunity loss graphs for the two acts involved. Figure 28-6(a) shows the possible arrangements when the expected mean μ_0 lies below the breakeven level. If $\mu_0 < \mu_b$, it is easy to see that the expected opportunity loss for Act 1 will be smaller than the expected opportunity loss for Act 2, since most of the area under the normal curve is concentrated in the range of μ where Act 1 has zero opportunity loss. (Remember that the *area* under the normal curve provides the probability.) The positive opportunity losses for Act 1, represented by the rising solid line segment, occur for unlikely levels of μ that are covered by the upper tail of the normal curve. On the other hand, the falling portion of the line for Act 2 occurs over the most likely range of μ values, so the expected opportunity loss is greater for that act.

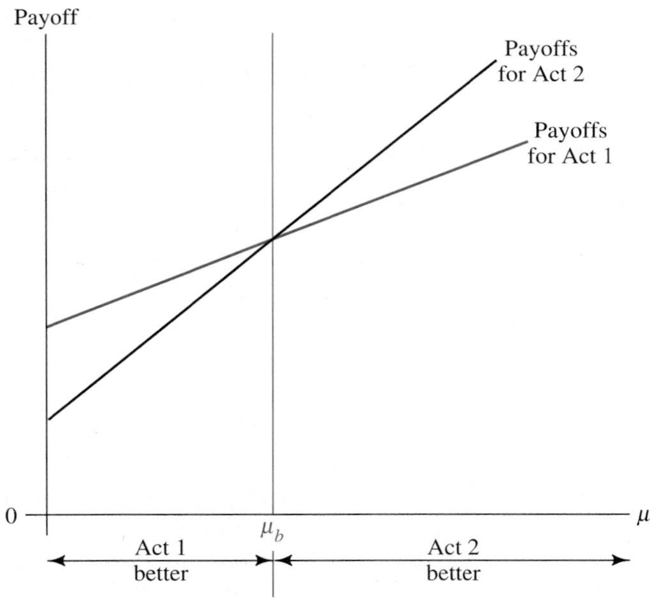

FIGURE 28-5 Identifying better acts.

The reverse situation is shown in Figure 28-6(b), where $\mu_0 > \mu_b$ and the expected opportunity loss for Act 2 is smaller.

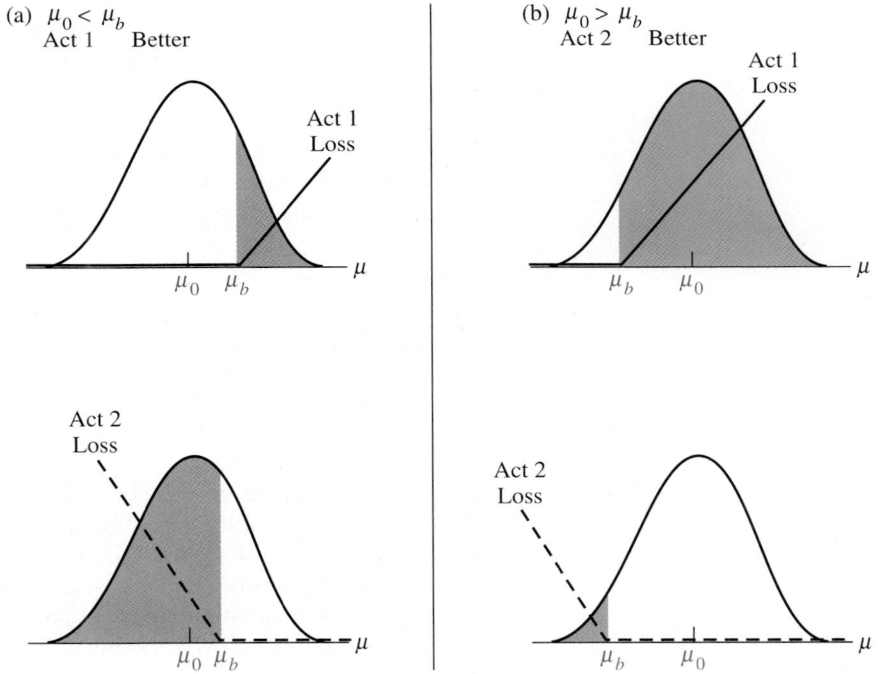

FIGURE 28-6 Prior normal curves for μ with loss functions superimposed.

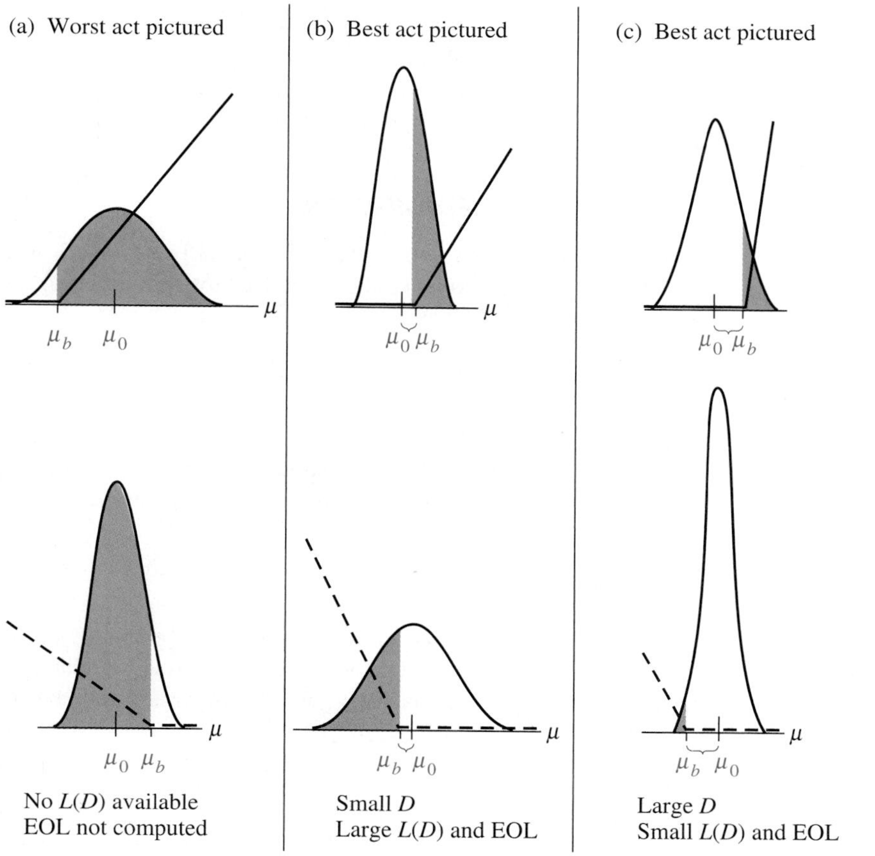

FIGURE 28-7 Various cases encountered in decision making using the normal distribution.

From these graphs, we conclude that the *optimal act having the minimum expected opportunity loss is the one with zero opportunity losses that lie on the same side of the breakeven level as the expected mean.* In our present example, Act 1 is optimal when $\mu_0 < \mu_b$, whereas Act 2 is optimal when $\mu_0 > \mu_b$. *If the expected mean coincides with the breakeven level, then the two alternatives are equally attractive.*

THE NORMAL LOSS FUNCTION

It is unnecessary to go to the trouble of first approximating the normal curve by intervals and then multiplying by opportunity losses calculated in a table. Those calculations have largely been done when the loss lines have slope one and the prior normal curve has unit standard deviation. The resulting values describe the **normal loss function** $L(D)$ tabled in Appendix Table N. There $L(D)$ is given for any standard deviation distance D separating μ_0 and μ_b.

Figure 28-7 shows some cases from six different decision problems. The losses are only tabled for the best act (with μ_0 lying on its good side of breakeven). The expected opportunity losses and $L(D)$ get smaller as D becomes greater. (That is reflected by a smaller tail area under the normal curve covering μ's that involve nonzero opportunity loss.)

The $L(D)$ values from Appendix Table N equal the respective opportunity loss when the loss function has unit slope and the normal curve for μ has unit standard deviation. To compute an expected value, we must ordinarily adjust the tabled value to account for other levels in slope and standard deviation.

FINDING THE EVPI

As noted, it is not actually necessary to compute the expected opportunity loss to make the main decision, but rather to establish the worth of perfect information, since

$$\text{EVPI} = \text{Expected opportunity loss for best act}$$

Thus, the expected opportunity loss for the best act equals the needed value.

Under the streamlined procedure, the expected opportunity loss for the best act is the EVPI, which may be computed from

$$\text{EVPI} = |\text{slope}|\sigma_0 L(D_0)$$

Three constants must be specified: (1) the absolute value of the **slope** of the opportunity loss line; (2) the standard deviation of the prior probability distribution for μ; and (3) the **standardized distance**

$$D_0 = \frac{|\mu_b - \mu_0|}{\sigma_0}$$

which expresses the separation between μ_b and μ_0 in units of standard deviation. (The numerator must always be positive, so absolute values are used.)

Returning to the computer memory device decision, we may use this streamlined procedure to find the EVPI. We have already seen that the holographic memory unit would be the better choice. Referring to Figure 28-2, we see that the holographic loss line has a slope of $-\$62{,}500$, so that $|\text{slope}| = \$62{,}500$. Using the same values as before, $\mu_0 = 2.5$, $\sigma_0 = .15$, and $\mu_b = 2.4$, the standardized distance separating the expected mean from the breakeven level is

$$D_0 = \frac{|\mu_b - \mu_0|}{\sigma_0} = \frac{|2.4 - 2.5|}{.15} = .67$$

Referring to Appendix Table N, we find that for $D_0 = .67$

$$L(D_0) = L(.67) = .1503$$

and the expected value of perfect information is

$$\begin{aligned}\text{EVPI} &= \$62{,}500(.15)L(.67) \\ &= \$62{,}500(.15)(.1503) \\ &= \$1{,}409\end{aligned}$$

The above amount is also the expected opportunity loss for the holographic-unit choice. This is a more precise value than the approximate one obtained earlier. The greater accuracy is due to the L table (which was constructed with many more, narrower μ intervals).

This tells us that a perfect prediction for μ is worth only \$1,409. This is the upper limit on the amount the decision maker might be willing to pay for less-than-perfect sample information. (This value differs from the EVPI of \$12,500 calculated in Chapter 27. The discrepancy is due to the change in the prior probability distribution; our earlier example involved only two levels of μ, each with a probability of .5.)

ILLUSTRATION: ATM TRANSACTION TIMES

The Million Bank has successfully reduced its personnel by using automated teller machines (ATMs). An engineering firm is deciding whether or not to contract with the bank to develop a second-generation machine. Although nobody knows what the mean cash-withdrawal time μ will be for the new machine, the engineers will receive an incentive of \$100,000 for each second that μ falls below the current overall ATM average of 20 seconds, but must forfeit from a performance bond the same amount for each second that μ goes beyond that time. All of the firm's direct costs will be reimbursed by the Million Bank.

The firm's payoff function for taking the contract is

$$\begin{aligned}\text{Payoff} &= 100{,}000(20 - \mu)\\ &= \$2{,}000{,}000 - 100{,}000\mu \quad \text{(accept contract)}\end{aligned}$$

The above plots on the graph in Figure 28-8 as a downward-slanting line with intercept \$2,000,000 and slope = −\$100,000. The alternative is to refuse the contract, which involves the following neutral payoff function.

$$\text{Payoff} = \$0 \quad \text{(refuse contract)}$$

This appears on the same graph in Figure 28-8 as a horizontal line lying directly on the μ axis. As with the computer memory device decision, the breakeven level for the mean is that level for μ where the two payoff lines cross, here $\mu_b = 20$ seconds.

The owner feels that a normal distribution would be appropriate for generating probabilities for the unknown μ. He also believes that the state-of-the-art for the needed mechanisms has advanced to the point where it is "even money" that his firm will create a design which will yield a mean time at or below 15 seconds. Thus, the center of his prior normal curve is $\mu_0 = 15$. His judgment also leads to a standard deviation of $\sigma_0 = 2$ seconds for the subjective normal curve.

If the main decision were to be made without getting any further information, the owner would maximize his firm's expected profit (and minimize the expected opportunity loss) by accepting the contract. This is because μ_0 falls on that side of breakeven where accepting the contract yields greater payoffs.

However, it may be advantageous to do some further investigating before making the main decision. The potential worth of such information may be gauged by reference to the EVPI.

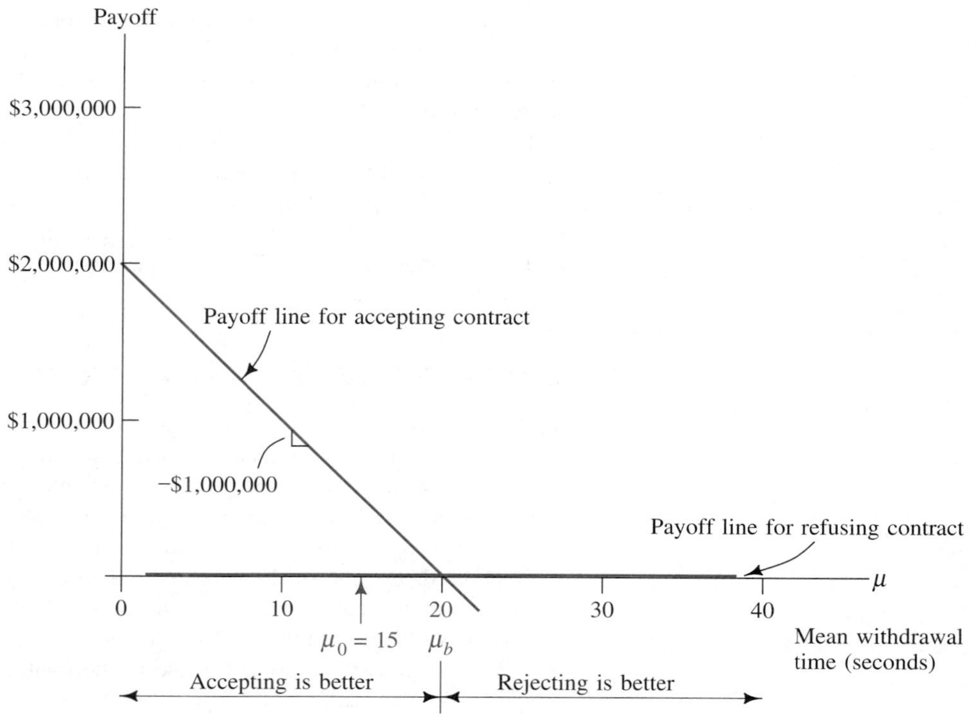

FIGURE 28-8 Payoff lines for ATM decision.

Accepting the contract, the better act, has an opportunity loss function with a rising line segment above μ_b. The slope of this portion is found by subtracting the slope $0 of the payoff line for refusing the contract from the slope −$100,000 of the payoff line for accepting the contract. The absolute value of this difference is the constant needed in computing EVPI, so that

$$|\text{slope}| = |-\$100{,}000 - 0| = \$100{,}000$$

The standardized distance separating the breakeven level of μ from its expected value is

$$D_0 = \frac{|20 - 15|}{2} = 2.50$$

so that from Appendix Table N, $L(2.50) = .002004$ and

$$\text{EVPI} = \$100{,}000(2)(.002004) = \$400.80$$

This amount is so relatively small that the owner decided that there would be little benefit from any further investigation. He signed the contract.

EXERCISES

28-2 Use the unit normal loss function to recompute the computer center manager's EVPI when the situation is revised as in Exercise 28-1.

28-3 In each of the following situations, the prior probability distribution for the population mean is represented by the normal curve.

	(a)	(b)	(c)	(d)
Mean	50	100	60	40
Standard deviation	10	10	20	10
Breakeven level	55	90	62	38
Slope	$1,000	$5,000	$5,000	$10,000

Below the breakeven level for the mean, Act 1 is more profitable; beyond the breakeven level, Act 2 is better. In each case, (1) indicate which act is better and (2) calculate the EVPI.

28-4 Sonic Phonics specializes in stereo headphones. It is considering adding a new stereo helmet receiver for motorcyclists, but the owner is uncertain about the mean annual sales volume per outlet in the retail chain it supplies. He believes that the mean is normally distributed, with a mean of 60 and a standard deviation of 10 helmets per store. Altogether, 100 stores are involved. The helmet will have a product life of about one year, after which it is believed that the novelty will wear off. Production set-up costs will be $50,000. Each helmet will have a variable cost of $30 and will sell for a retail price of $40.

(a) Assume that the total increase in profits is to be maximized. In terms of the mean number of helmets sold per store, determine an expression for the payoff for making the helmet and for not making the helmet. What is the breakeven level?

(b) Should Sonic Phonics make the helmet?

(c) Calculate the EVPI.

28-5 The marketing manager of Blitz Beer must determine whether or not to sponsor Blitz Day with the Gotham City Hellcats. She is uncertain what the effect of the promotion will be in terms of the mean increase in daily sales volume that would result during the 100-day baseball season. The cost of sponsorship is $10,000, and each can of Blitz has a marginal cost of $.20 and sells for $.40.

(a) Assuming that change in profit is to be maximized, express the payoff function for the two alternatives in terms of the mean daily increase in cans sold.

(b) Suppose that Blitz Day will result in a mean increase that is judged to be normally distributed with a mean of 600 and a standard deviation of 50 cans per day. Should the brewer sponsor the event?

(c) What is the EVPI? Do you think it is worthwhile to obtain further information? Can a sample from the underlying population even be helpful in making this decision? Explain.

28-6 Lett's Party provides accounting services for its franchises. The home office is going to establish a policy for contacting delinquent accounts receivable. The payoff from the new policy will depend on the mean amount of the late receivables. The two alternatives are (1) to make personal telephone calls to late payers at an annual fixed cost of \$50,000 with a savings of \$100 per dollar in mean amount delinquent and (2) to send computer generated messages for which the fixed costs and savings are both double. The prior probability distribution for the mean has expected value of \$600 and standard deviation of \$100.

(a) Lett's Party wants to maximize expected net savings. What is the break-even level for the mean amount delinquent?

(b) If the decision were to be made without sampling, which alternative should be selected?

(c) Calculate the EVPI.

28-4 DECISION STRUCTURE WHEN SAMPLING IS CONSIDERED

The structure for the computer memory device decision using sample information is provided by the decision tree diagram in Figure 28-9. Here, the initial choice of whether or not to use sample information is made. If no sample is taken, the prior probability distribution for μ applies. If sampling is chosen, the sample size must be selected, the sample data collected, and the sample mean calculated. Based on the value achieved for $\bar{X}$, either the photographic or the holographic memory unit is chosen. With sampling, the posterior probability distribution applies to the population mean μ. The event forks for the values of $\bar{X}$ and μ have many branches, since each variable is continuous. In each case, probability values may be obtained only by finding the appropriate areas under the respective normal curves.

The probability distributions provided in the upper portion of the decision tree represent the informational chronology. This event sequence is the reverse of the order in which probability information is generally presented.

Since our probability distributions are continuous, it is not easy to obtain the revised versions needed to construct the decision tree. The backward induction required to determine the optimal decision rule, which specifies the action to take for each possible sample result, is also complicated. We therefore depart from decision tree analysis and revert to *normal form analysis*, which itself must now be dressed in unfamiliar clothing.

28-5 DECISIONS REGARDING THE SAMPLE: PREPOSTERIOR ANALYSIS

We are now ready to consider the decision of whether or not to take a sample from the population of individual values. This will also involve choice of the sample size n. Once that has been decided, the sample observations will be made and from these the sample mean $\bar{X}$ then computed.

Designating as Act 1 that choice that is better when $\mu_0 < \mu_b$ and Act 2 as the better one for $\mu_0 > \mu_b$, a decision rule of the following form will be used in making the final choice.

$$\text{Choose Act 1} \quad \leq \quad \underset{C}{|} \quad > \quad \text{Choose Act 2} \quad \bar{X}$$

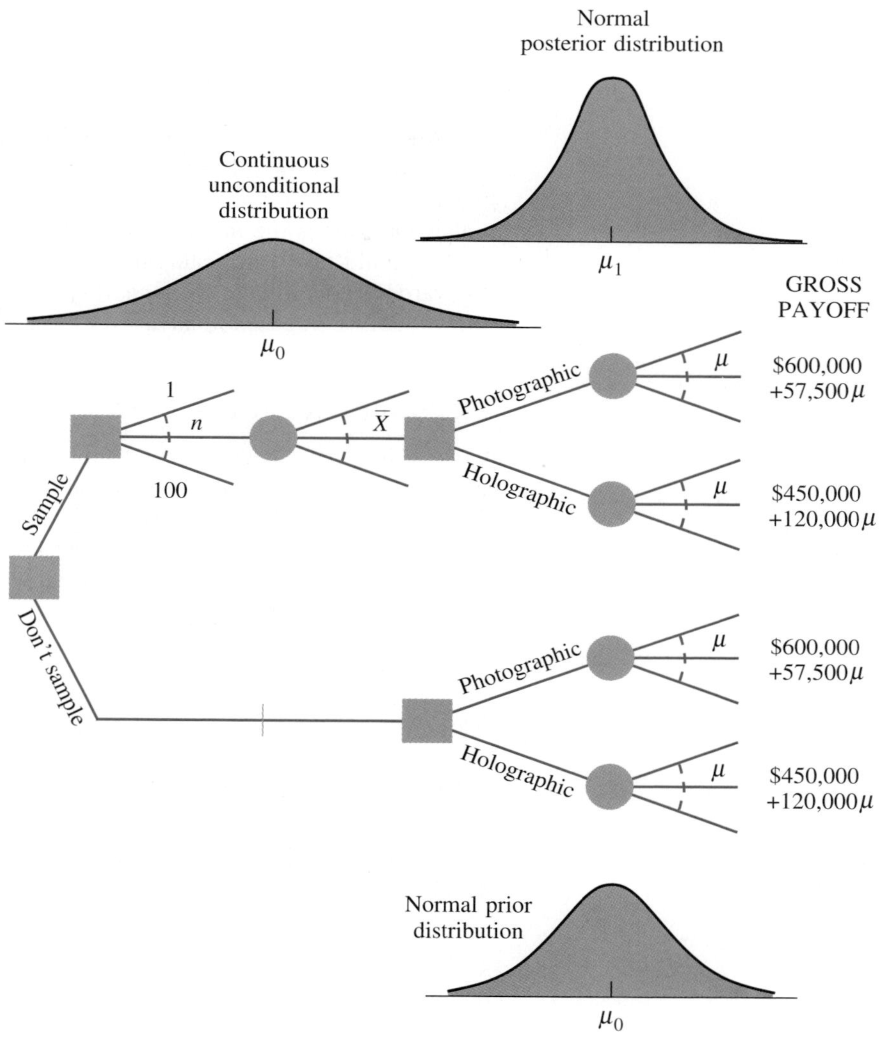

FIGURE 28-9 The structure of the computer memory device decision when a prior normal probability distribution applies to the population mean.

The rationale is that a low value for $\bar{X}$ is evidence favoring a smaller level for μ, in which case Act 1 would be the better choice. And, a high value for $\bar{X}$ favors a greater μ, the case when Act 2 is better. In Section 28-6, we will see how to find the point of demarcation C. But first, we must determine how large the sample size n must be.

THE POPULATION FREQUENCY DISTRIBUTION

In all decisions having the applicable structure, the sample is drawn from the population of individual values, the mean μ of which is uncertain. It is not necessary to know anything regarding the form of the frequency distribution, and its frequency curve may have a shape that is non-normal. A good guess must be made of the value for the population standard deviation, denoted as σ_I (where I reminds us that the distribution applies to *individual* population values).

In the computer memory device decision, the manager examined past data and compared his operation to similar systems. He established an educated guess for the population standard deviation of $\sigma_I = .5$ gigabit per day. (This is smaller than the value used in Chapter 27.) Of course, the mean μ of that population remains unknown. This is the major uncertainty.

We should take extra caution not to confuse σ_I, really an index summarizing the variability in *individual population values*, with σ_0, a parameter summarizing the variability in *possible means* μ of that population.

PROBABILITIES FOR $\bar{X}$

Once values have been assumed for the parameters μ and σ_I of the underlying population, probabilities may be found for the possible levels of the sample mean. These will reflect the chosen sample size n. The central limit theorem tells us $\bar{X}$ has a probability distribution (sometimes referred to as the sampling distribution) closely approximated by a normal curve when n is large. This curve is centered on μ and has a standard deviation of

$$\sigma_{\bar{X}} = \frac{\sigma_I}{\sqrt{n}}$$

(The above quantity is sometimes referred to as the standard error of $\bar{X}$.)

Continuing with the memory device decision, if the manager were to use a sample of size $n = 25$, then

$$\sigma_{\bar{X}} = \frac{.5}{\sqrt{25}} = .1$$

A different value would be achieved for each possible n.

The sampling distribution for $\bar{X}$ is represented by a *second* normal curve, distinct from the prior normal curve for μ discussed earlier in the chapter. The $\bar{X}$ curve is centered on μ (which is unknown). Its standard deviation depends both on σ_I and on the sample size n that will be used. Since n is not fixed and may be chosen by the decision maker, the particular normal curve for $\bar{X}$ is not set until the final choice is made for the sample size.

Figure 28-10 illustrates how the possible normal curves for $\bar{X}$ become more compact as n gets larger. The sample mean in a taller, thinner curve (achieved by increasing the level for n) will tend to be closer in value to μ. Thus, as n is raised it will become more likely that a value will be computed for $\bar{X}$ that falls close to its μ target.

In effect, large sample sizes provide greater informational content, which should be reflected in the value of that information. As in Chapter 27, we may quantify a sample's potential worth in terms of the **expected value of sample information**, EVSI.

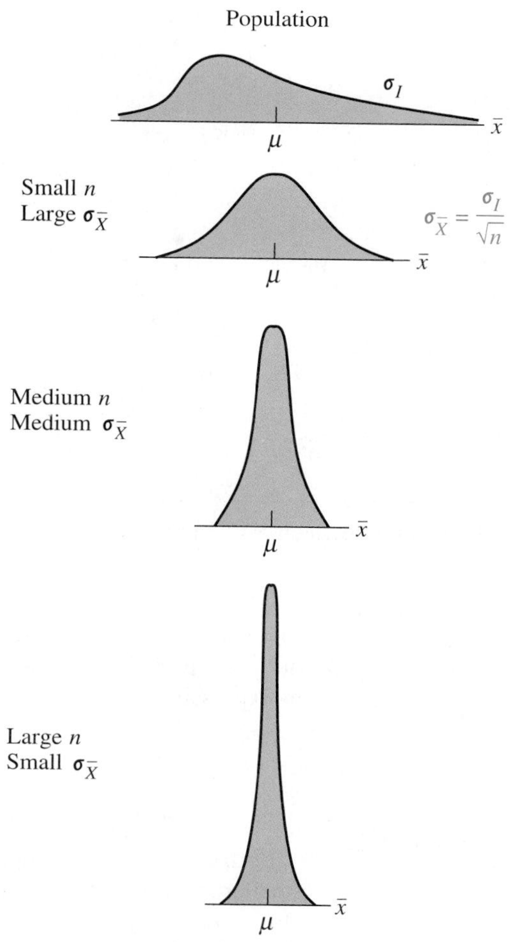

FIGURE 28-10 Sampling distributions (normal curves) for $\bar{X}$ at various sample sizes.

THE EXPECTED VALUE OF SAMPLE INFORMATION

Recall, from Chapter 27, that EVSI should approach EVPI as greater reliability is achieved from increasing the sample size. This is illustrated in Figure 28-11.

The unit normal loss function may be used in an analogous fashion in computing EVSI. The following expression applies.

$$\text{EVSI}(n) = |\text{slope}|\sqrt{v_n}\,\sigma_0 L(D_n)$$

The above is similar to the expression for EVPI. New is the added term involving v_n and a modified distance D_n. A different value for EVSI is achieved for each possible level for n. The new term is the **variance fraction**.

$$v_n = \frac{\sigma_0^2}{\sigma_0^2 + \sigma_{\bar{X}}^2} = \frac{\sigma_0^2}{\sigma_0^2 + \sigma_I^2/n}$$

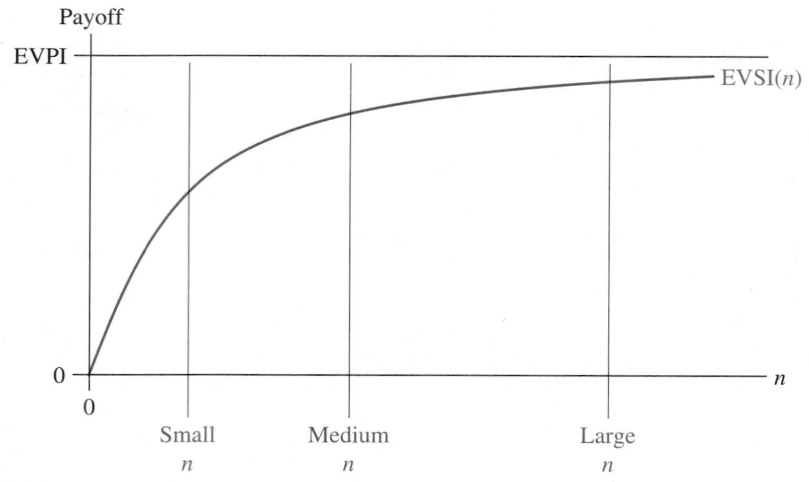

FIGURE 28-11 Relationship between EVSI (n) and sample size.

The above fraction provides a modified variance $v_n\sigma_0^2$ that is smaller than that of the prior probability distribution for μ. The modified standard deviation is used in expressing the distance between μ_b and μ_0.

$$D_n = \frac{|\mu_b - \mu_0|}{\sqrt{v_n}\sigma_0}$$

Both v_n and D_n will change as n is changed. As n becomes larger, $\sigma_{\bar{X}}$ gets smaller; this makes the denominator for v_n shrink, and the v_n fraction becomes closer to 1 in value. That, in turn, gives a value for D_n which approaches D_0. Thus, EVSI(n) must approach the level of EVPI as n increases. (In the theoretical case when the sample size is so great it is in effect a *census*, sample information would be perfect information.)

For the computer memory device decision, $\mu_b = 2.4$, $\mu_0 = 2.5$, $\sigma_0 = .15$, $|\text{slope}| = \$62{,}500$, and $\sigma_{\bar{X}} = .1$ when $n = 25$. The variance fraction is

$$v_n = \frac{(.15)^2}{(.15)^2 + (.1)^2} = .692$$

and the standardized distance is

$$D_n = \frac{|2.4 - 2.5|}{\sqrt{.692}(.15)} = .80$$

so that, from Appendix Table N

$$L(D_n) = L(.80) = .1202$$

and

$$\text{EVSI}(25) = \$62{,}500\sqrt{.692}(.15)(.1202) = \$938$$

The above indicates that \$938 is the true worth of a sample of $n = 25$ to the decision maker. As long as the sampling cost is less than this amount, the computer center manager will be better off with the sample information than without it.

THE DECISION TO SAMPLE AND FINDING THE OPTIMAL *n*

Now suppose that the computer center manager has established the cost of sampling at \$10 per day. With $n = 25$, the sampling cost would be \$250. Since this amount is smaller than EVSI(25), *the manager should definitely make a decision based on a sample of some size* rather than choose an act without any information at all. The question remaining is: How large should n be?

We answer this question by finding the **expected net gain from sampling** for various sample sizes, which is computed

$$\text{ENGS}(n) = \text{EVSI}(n) - \text{Cost}(n)$$

The optimal sample size is the one with the greatest ENGS(n) value. By trial and error, trying various values of n, we determine the appropriate sample size. Table 28-4 provides the ENGS(n) values for a few sample sizes. Notice that the expected net gain increases until $n = 29$, after which it decreases. Thus, $n = 29$, for which ENGS(29) = \$702, is the optimal sample size.

EXERCISES

28-7 Refer to the Lett's Party decision for how to handle delinquent accounts described in Exercise 28-6 and to your answers. The size of a randomly selected delinquent account may be established at a cost of \$.50. The population standard deviation for individual amounts overdue is assumed to be \$250. Determine the expected net gain from sampling for the following sample sizes.

(a) 9 (b) 25

(c) 100 (d) Which one of the above sample sizes is best?

28-8 Reconsider the illustration in the chapter of choosing between photographic and holographic peripheral memory storage units. Suppose that the

TABLE 28-4 The Expected Net Gain of Sampling Computed for Several Sample Sizes

n	$\sigma_{\bar{X}} = \sigma_I/\sqrt{n}$	v_n	D_n	$L(D_n)$	EVSI(n)	Cost(n)	ENGS(n)
10	.1581	.4737	.97	.08819	\$ 569	\$100	\$469
15	.1291	.5745	.88	.1042	740	150	590
20	.1118	.6429	.83	.1140	857	200	657
25	.1000	.6923	.80	.1202	938	250	688
28	.0945	.7159	.79	.1223	970	280	690
29	.0928	.7230	.78	.1245	992	290	702
30	.0913	.7297	.78	.1245	997	300	697
40	.0791	.7826	.75	.1312	1,088	400	688
50	.0707	.8182	.74	.1334	1,131	500	631
60	.0645	.8438	.73	.1358	1,169	600	569

following annual savings payoff function applies, where the access portion depends on the unknown mean access level of μ gigabits per day.

$$\text{Payoff} = \begin{cases} \$500{,}000 + \$\ 65{,}000\mu & \text{for photographic} \\ \$330{,}000 + \$150{,}000\mu & \text{for holographic} \end{cases}$$

The prior probability distribution for the population mean access level has an expected value of 2.3 gigabits per day and a standard deviation of .75 and the population of individual daily access levels has a standard deviation of 3.5 gigabits per day.

(a) Find the breakeven level for the population mean.
(b) Which unit maximizes annual savings when the prior expected mean is $\mu_0 = 2.5$ gigabits per day?
(c) Calculate the EVPI.

28-9 (*Continuation of Exercise 28-8*): The sample size has not been chosen, but the cost of each daily observation is now \$500. Use the constants provided earlier to calculate the expected net gain from sampling for the indicated sample sizes.

(a) 4 (c) 100
(b) 9 (d) Which one of the above sample sizes is best?

28-10 Two configurations are possible for rigging test equipment to monitor a chemical process. The payoff depends on the mean batch pressure μ (in pounds per square inch). The following applies.

$$\text{Payoff} = \begin{cases} -\ \$10{,}000 + 50\mu & \text{for configuration } A \\ -\ \$20{,}000 + 60\mu & \text{for configuration } B \end{cases}$$

The level of μ is uncertain, and this quantity is judged to be normally distributed with prior expected mean 1,010 psi and standard deviation 25 psi. Individual batch pressures have standard deviation assumed to be 50 psi.

(a) If the main decision were to be made now, which configuration would maximize expected payoff?
(b) Compute the EVPI.
(c) Sample observations cost \$.50 per test batch. Compute the ENGS(n) for each of the following sample sizes.
(1) $n = 5$ (2) $n = 10$ (3) $n = 15$ (4) $n = 20$ (5) $n = 25$
(d) Which of the above sample sizes comes closest to being optimal?
(e) Plot ENGS(n) against n. Sketch a curve through the data points.
(f) Your curve should be concave (from below). This means that successive levels for ENGS(n) will steadily increase until reaching the maximum, after which they will drop steadily in value. Over which range do you know for certain that the optimal sample size lies?

28-6 POSTERIOR ANALYSIS FOR A GIVEN SAMPLE SIZE

Once the sample size has been determined, the next step is to collect the sample data. The computed value for $\bar{X}$ will then be compared to the critical value C and the act selected for which $\bar{X}$ lies on the best side. The sample information also provides the basis for revising the prior probability distribution for μ.

Although the mathematical justifications are beyond the scope of this book, the concepts of Bayes' theorem may be extended to continuous normal curves in establishing the **posterior probability distribution for** μ. Like the prior probability distribution, a normal curve applies. We use the subscript 1 to distinguish the parameters of the posterior probability distribution. The center of the normal curve is denoted by μ_1 and its standard deviation by σ_1.

Figure 28-12 helps to explain this process. The non-normal population of individual daily access levels is provided at the top of the figure. Although the stan-

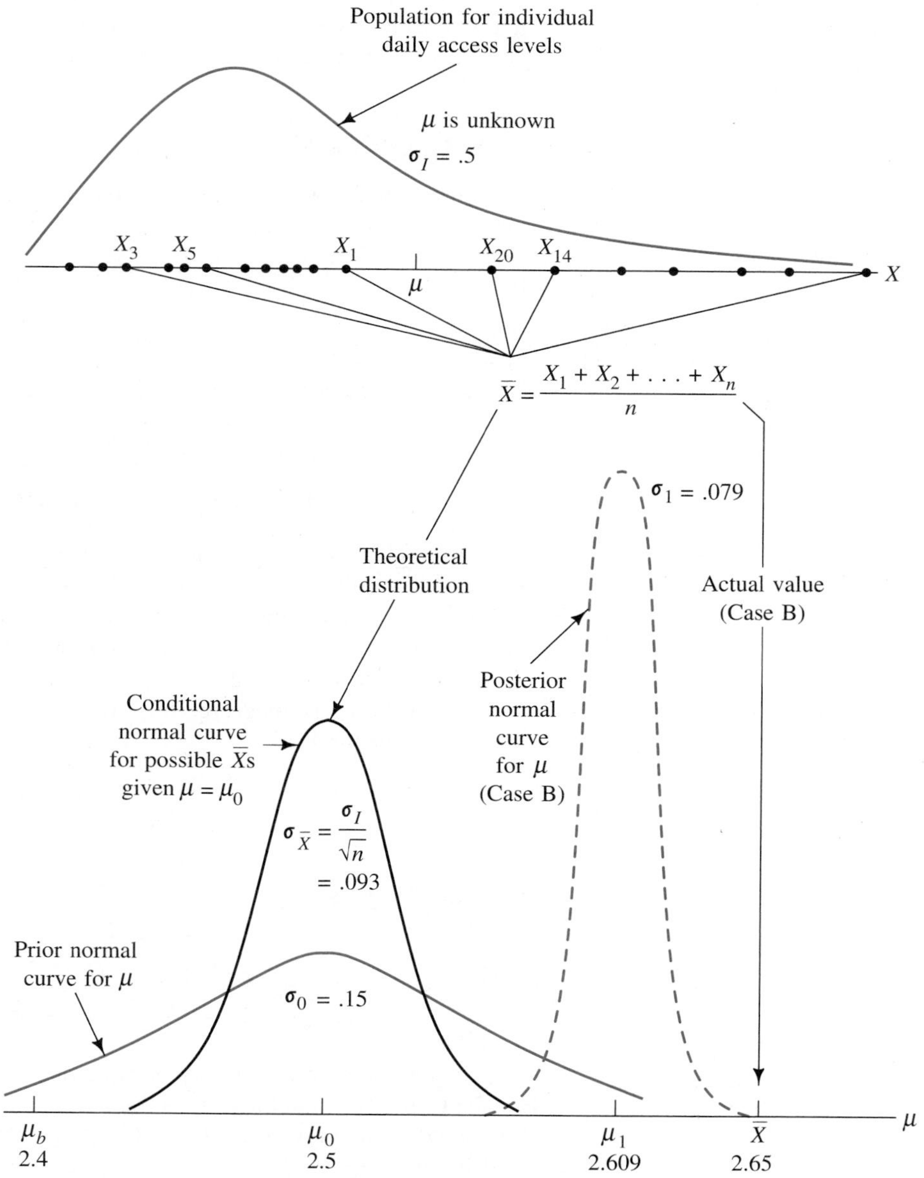

FIGURE 28-12 Distributions involved in posterior analysis with sampling (not drawn to scale).

dard deviation of individual daily access levels is presumed to be $\sigma_I = .5$, the population center is unknown. This unknown mean μ is the entire focus of our analysis. The sample mean of n random daily observations $\bar{X}$ is to be computed. Since its value is presently unknown, statistical theory tells us that the tall, solid normal curve in the lower portion of Figure 28-12 provides the probabilities for $\bar{X}$. This is a conditional curve, since it is presumed to be centered on the prior expected mean μ_0. The flatter, solid normal curve represents the prior probabilities for the value of the unknown μ and is also centered on μ_0.

When it is actually computed, the sample mean value may fall anywhere in the vicinity of μ_0. Depending on the location of the sample mean, the appropriate posterior normal curve for μ (represented here by the dashed curve centered on μ_1) is obtained. The center of the posterior normal curve will always lie between μ_0 and the computed $\bar{X}$.

POSTERIOR EXPECTED VALUE OF μ

The **posterior expected mean** μ_1 of the posterior probability distribution is computed by taking a *weighted average* of μ_0 and $\bar{X}$.

$$\mu_1 = \frac{I_0\mu_0 + I_S\bar{X}}{I_0 + I_S}$$

The weights are the following indexes.

Index for prior information: $I_0 = 1/\sigma_0^2$

Index for sample information: $I_0 = 1/\sigma_{\bar{X}}^2$

In averaging μ_0 and $\bar{X}$, proportional weight is given to prior judgment and to the sample results. The indexes are the reciprocals of the respective variances.

Returning to the computer memory device decision, where $\mu_0 = 2.5$ gigabits per day and $\sigma_0 = .15$, suppose that the optimal sample size is used. Thus, $n =$ 29 days will be monitored by a special program and the individual daily access levels will be determined precisely for each. Using $\sigma_I = .5$ gigabit per day, the standard error for $\bar{X}$ is

$$\sigma_{\bar{X}} = \frac{.5}{\sqrt{29}} = .093$$

The above values give

$$I_0 = 1/\sigma_0^2 = 1/(.15)^2 = 44.44$$
$$I_S = 1/\sigma_{\bar{X}}^2 = 1/(.093)^2 = 115.62$$

We cannot compute μ_1 until the sample data have been collected.

The resulting value for μ_1 must lie *between* the prior value of $\mu_0 = 2.5$ and the *computed value* for $\bar{X}$. Since $I_S = 115.62$ is greater than $I_0 = 44.44$, greater weight will be given to $\bar{X}$, and μ_1 must lie closer to that computed value. Consider the following possibilities.

Case *A*	**Case *B***
$\bar{X} = 2.2$	$\bar{X} = 2.65$
$\mu_1 = \dfrac{44.44(2.5) + 115.62(2.2)}{44.44 + 115.62}$	$\mu_1 = \dfrac{44.44(2.5) + 115.62(2.65)}{44.44 + 115.62}$
$= 2.283$	$= 2.608$
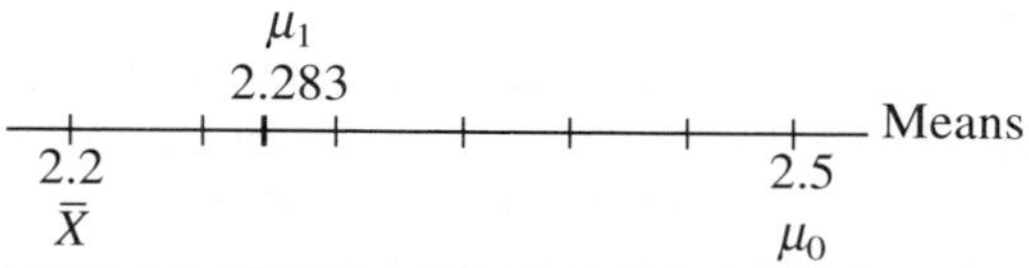	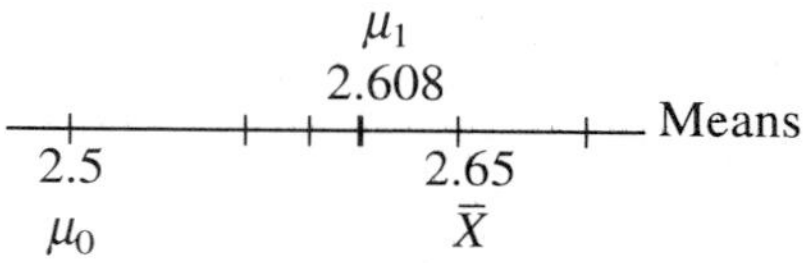

THE DECISION RULE AND CRITICAL VALUE FOR THE SAMPLE MEAN

We now consider the problem of finding the appropriate decision rule to apply to the posterior analysis. This involves selecting the critical value of C that minimizes the expected opportunity loss according to the decision rule

$$\text{Select Act 1} \quad \text{if } \bar{X} \leq C$$

$$\text{Select Act 2} \quad \text{if } \bar{X} > C$$

where, as before, Act 1 is the better choice when μ_0 falls below μ_b and Act 2 is the better choice when μ_0 exceeds μ_b.

The value of C is the point of demarcation between those levels of $\bar{X}$ where Act 1 is the better choice and those levels of $\bar{X}$ where Act 2 is better. This is the level of $\bar{X}$ where the expected opportunity losses are identical under either act. Both acts are equally attractive when the expected mean is equal to the breakeven level. After sampling, the posterior expected mean applies, so that the point of demarcation must be the value of $\bar{X}$ that provides a posterior expected mean where

$$\mu_1 = \mu_b$$

Thus, we substitute C for $\bar{X}$ in the earlier expression for μ_1 and set this expression equal to μ_b.

Solving algebraically for C, an expression may be derived. The following equation is obtained and may be used in computing the critical value.

$$C = \frac{(I_0 + I_S)\mu_b - I_0\mu_0}{I_S}$$

The above expression may be used to compute the critical value for any problem where μ_0, μ_b, and the informational indexes are given.

Consider once more the computer memory device decision. Substituting $\mu_b = 2.4$, $\mu_0 = 2.5$, $I_0 = 44.44$, and $I_S = 115.62$ into the above expression, we obtain

$$C = \frac{(44.44 + 115.62)(2.4) - 44.44(2.5)}{115.62} = 2.36$$

The decision rule for a sample of size $n = 29$ is therefore

Select photographic unit if $\bar{X} \leq 2.36$

Select holographic unit if $\bar{X} > 2.36$

Thus, if the manager decides to sample with $n = 29$ and $\bar{X}$ turns out to be larger than $C = 2.36$ (say, $\bar{X} = 2.65$), then the holographic memory unit should be chosen. But, if a smaller mean is found (say, $\bar{X} = 2.2$), then the photographic unit would instead be chosen.

It may seem perplexing that $C = 2.36$ is a value smaller than $\mu_b = 2.4$. But C represents that level for $\bar{X}$ below which the sample result is extreme enough to force the main decision the other way from that suggested during prior analysis. C will therefore always lie on the opposite side of μ_b from μ_0.

POSTERIOR VARIANCE AND STANDARD DEVIATION FOR μ

The **posterior variance** (standard deviation) for the posterior probability distribution for μ may be computed from

$$\sigma_1^2 = \left(\frac{\sigma_{\bar{X}}^2}{\sigma_0^2 + \sigma_{\bar{X}}^2}\right)\sigma_0^2$$

The above states that σ_1^2 must be a fraction of σ_0^2, with the fraction becoming smaller as n gets larger ($\sigma_{\bar{X}}$ gets smaller). Also, if we rearrange terms, the following expression may be obtained from the above.

$$\sigma_1^2 = \left(\frac{\sigma_0^2}{\sigma_0^2 + \sigma_{\bar{X}}^2}\right)\sigma_{\bar{X}}^2$$

You see that σ_1^2 is also just a fraction of $\sigma_{\bar{X}}^2$. Thus, σ_1 must be smaller than either σ_0 or $\sigma_{\bar{X}}$.

Continuing with the computer memory device decision, the following results are obtained.

$$\sigma_1^2 = \left(\frac{(.093)^2}{(.15)^2 + (.093)^2}\right)(.15)^2 = .0062$$

$$\sigma_1 = \sqrt{.0062} = .079$$

Notice that the posterior standard deviation for μ is smaller than both $\sigma_0 = .15$ and $\sigma_{\bar{X}} = .093$. This illustrates an essential feature of *information theory.*

CONCEPTS FROM INFORMATION THEORY

As I_0 and I_S are defined, a smaller variance (standard deviation) gives a larger index value, reflecting greater informational content. Thus, a larger n gives a more reliable sample having a smaller $\sigma_{\bar{X}}$ and a bigger I_S. Likewise, an expert with greater knowledge about μ should provide a subjective prior probability distribution having a smaller σ_0 and a greater I_0.

Information theory postulates that the informational content indexes are additive, so that

$$\text{Posterior information} = \text{Prior information} + \text{Sample information}$$

$$I_1 = I_0 + I_S$$

where I_1 denotes the index of the content of information posterior to (after) sampling. In fact, it may be established mathematically that

$$1/\sigma_1^2 = 1/\sigma_0^2 + 1/\sigma_{\bar{X}}^2$$

so that the index for the information available posterior to sampling is

$$I_1 = 1/\sigma_1^2$$

For the computer memory device decision the index for posterior information is

$$I_1 = 1/\sigma_1^2 = 1/.0062 = 160$$

or, equivalently,

$$I_1 = I_0 + I_S = 44.44 + 115.62 = 160$$

which exceeds both original informational indexes. Altogether, more is known regarding μ after the sampling experiment than before, but the earlier judgment still has an effect too.

EXERCISES

28-11 Refer to Exercise 28-8 and to your answers.

(a) If a random sample of $n = 16$ days is chosen, find the optimal value of C that will maximize expected annual savings.

(b) Suppose that the sample mean turns out to be 1.75 gigabits per day. Determine the mean and the standard deviation of the posterior probability distribution for μ. Which memory unit will be chosen?

(c) Use your results from (b) to find the probability that the mean daily access level lies above the breakeven level.

28-12 Refer to Exercise 28-10 and to your answers.

(a) Suppose that a sample of size $n = 16$ is used. Find the critical value and decision rule for deciding which configuration to use.

(b) Suppose that $\bar{X} = 987.5$.

(1) Applying your answer to (a), what configuration should be selected in order to maximize expected payoff?

(2) Determine the parameters of the posterior normal distribution for μ.

(3) Determine the probability that μ falls below the original breakeven level.

28-13 A facilities planner for Waysafe Market is evaluating a new electronic scanning cash register. The planner is uncertain about the mean time μ that the new equipment will take to check out a typical customer with 2 sacks of groceries. Experience with present automatic registers yields a standard deviation for individual checkout times of $\sigma_I = 1$ minute, and this value is assumed to apply to the new system. It is the planner's judgment that μ has a prior normal probability distribution with a mean of $\mu_0 = 3$ minutes and a standard deviation of $\sigma_0 = .20$ minute.

(a) Determine the probability that (1) $\mu \geq 3.5$ and (2) $\mu \leq 2.75$.

A random sample of new system checkout times is to be obtained for further study.

(b) Assuming that $n = 100$ typical customers' checkout times will be obtained, calculate $\sigma_{\bar{X}}$ and determine the following conditional result probabilties.

(1) $\bar{X} \leq 2.75$ minutes, given $\mu = 2.90$

(2) $\bar{X} > 3.25$ minutes, given $\mu = 3.10$

(3) $\bar{X}$ lies between 2.85 and 3.15 minutes, given $\mu = 3.00$

(c) Calculate the standard deviation σ_1 of the posterior probability distribution for μ. This should be smaller than its prior probability distribution counterpart.

(d) Suppose that the sample results yield a computed value of $\bar{X} = 3.20$ minutes. Compute the expected value μ_1 of the posterior probability distribution for μ. In revising the probability distribution for μ, which source of information—prior judgment or the sample results—has been given the greater weight?

(e) According to the prior probability distribution for μ, there is a .50 probability that the true population mean checkout time will be $\mu \leq 3.00$ minutes. For future study, the posterior probability distribution will apply. Determine the new probability that μ will fall at or below 3 minutes.

28-14 Yokum University's president knows that the population standard deviation in height of his male students is 2.5 in. He is uncertain about the mean height, which he characterizes as having a prior normal probability distribution with a mean of 69.5 in. and a standard deviation of .25 in. He wishes to decide whether or not to gamble with the president of Near Miss, whose men are known to be an average of 69 in. tall. The terms are that Yokum will get (give up) 100,000 druthers or fraction for each inch or fraction that the mean height of Yokum men exceeds (lies below) the Near Miss mean.

(a) Calculate the EVSI when a sample of $n = 100$ Yokum men are measured.

(b) Suppose that $n = 25$ Yokum men are measured in the sample. Find the level of $\bar{X}(C)$ that would make Yokum's president indifferent between gambling and not gambling.

(c) A sample of $n = 25$ Yokum men has a mean of $\bar{X} = 69.2$ in. Find the mean and the standard deviation of the posterior probability distribution for the mean height of Yokum men. Then, determine the probability that Yokum men are actually shorter than Near Miss men on the average.

28-7 ADDITIONAL REMARKS

The special difficulties encountered when dealing with several different normal curves have forced us to depart from our usual decision tree analysis. If we approximated the various continuous probability distributions by discrete tables (using typical values for μ and $\bar{X}$), then we could apply the methods presented in Chapter 27 to reach nearly identical conclusions to those we achieved using the procedures discussed in this chapter. But it is more convenient to focus on opportunity losses and to use normal form analysis when the prior probability distribution for μ may be represented by the normal curve and the sample observations themselves range over a continuous scale (so that the probabilities for $\bar{X}$ are represented by another normal curve).

But what do we do if the prior probability distribution for μ is not a normal curve? An amazing fact, established by Robert Schlaifer, who originally proposed the procedures examined in this chapter,* is that *for practically any other type of prior probability distribution, the posterior probability distribution for μ will still very closely approximate a normal curve.* Thus, what form applies to the prior distribution for μ really makes very little difference.

Another nice feature of the present approach to decision making using sample information is that it is simpler than applying decision tree analysis with approximate probability distributions, which involves a tremendous number of computations that are unnecessary here. The present procedure entirely avoids the problem of finding the unconditional result probabilities for $\bar{X}$. The nature of the opportunity loss lines permits us to evaluate the two-action problem through a breakeven analysis that considers only the central value of μ and the nature of its prior probability distribution.

There are limitations to the procedures presented here, however. For instance, they cannot be used when the payoffs cannot be graphed as straight lines or when more than two basic actions are contemplated. We have presented a special-purpose tool that applies only to limited situations. Fortunately, many practical business decision-making applications fall into this category.

SUMMARY

1. **What is the basic structure of Bayesian analysis using the normal distribution?**
   Figure 28-13 shows the steps of Bayesian analysis with the normal distribution. The same four stages apply that were introduced in earlier chapters.

2. **What are the four stages of a Bayesian analysis with the normal distribution?**
   The process begins with **prior analysis**, during which the prior distribution for the unknown μ is obtained, generally through judgment. During this stage, payoffs are determined as linear functions of μ, leading directly to a breakeven analysis. The main decision might be made in this stage by comparing the

*Much of the material in Schlaifer's books, *Probability and Statistics for Business Decisions* (New York: McGraw-Hill, 1959; reprint, Melbourne, Fla.: Kreiger, 1983) and *Introduction to Statistics for Business Decisions* (New York: McGraw-Hill, 1961; reprint, Melbourne, Fla.: Kreiger, 1982), carefully develops the concepts discussed in this chapter.

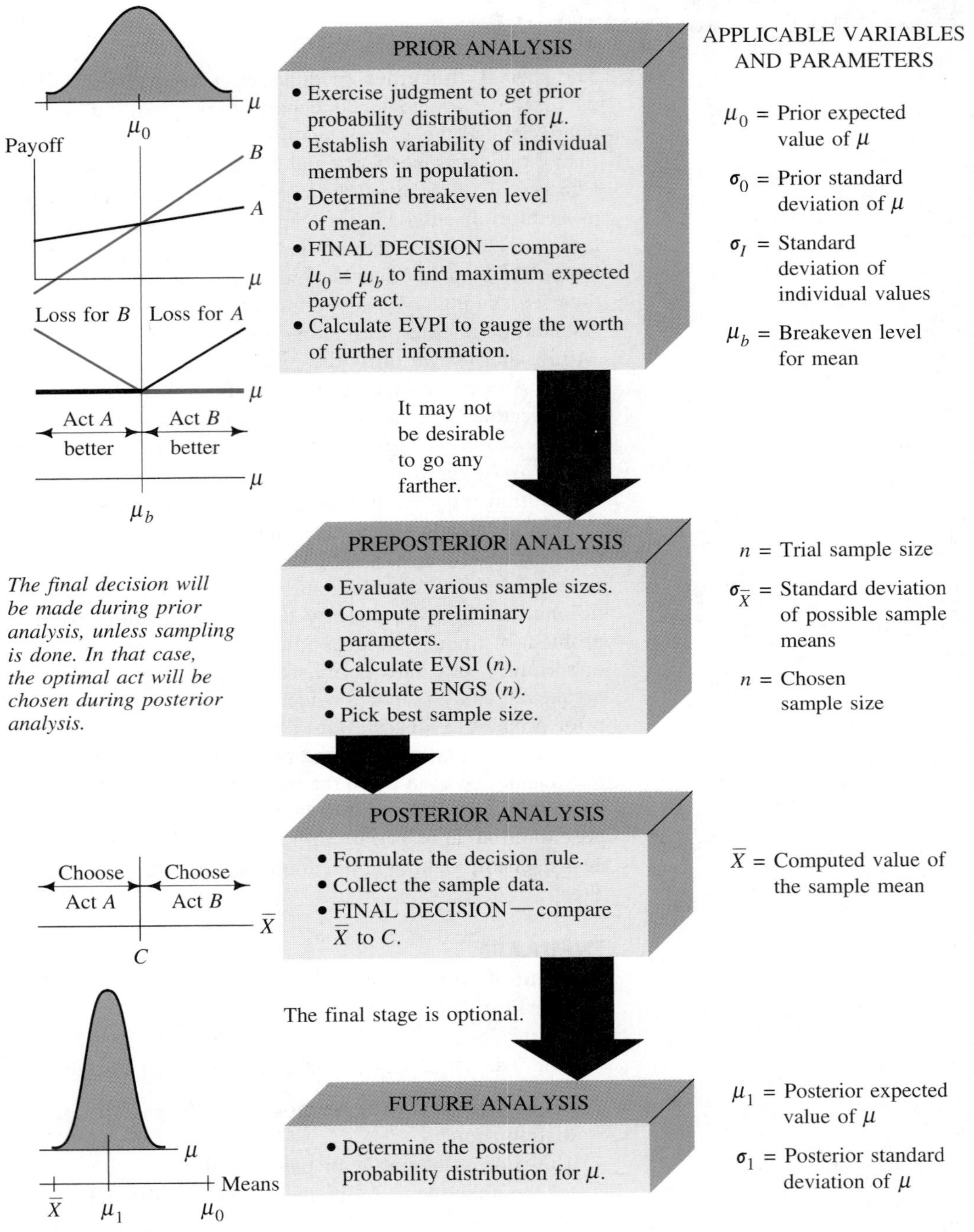

FIGURE 28-13 A summary of the relationship between the concepts and procedures for decision making using the normal distribution.

mean μ_0 of the prior distribution to the breakeven level μ_b. Whether or not we stop at this stage depends on how worthwhile any further information about μ happens to be. This is roughly gauged by the EVPI, and further investigation is warranted only if the EVPI is great enough to justify the extra bother of evaluating the sample information. (Clearly, an EVPI of only \$10 would not justify any further analysis; even an EVPI of \$100 is apt to be smaller than the cost of a modest sampling study.)

If it might be worthwhile to obtain further information, then **preposterior analysis** follows. Here, the question is primarily whether or not to sample, and if sampling is chosen, what sample size n to take. The evaluation is computationally lengthy, involving calculations of various EVSI's and sampling costs for several values of n, so that the size with the greatest expected net gain from sampling may be determined.

The next stage involves **posterior analysis**. Here, the decision rule is established, the sample is collected, and the actual sample mean $\bar{X}$ is calculated. Depending on the value obtained for $\bar{X}$, the choice of the act for the main decision is indicated.

An *optional* fourth stage completes the procedure. Here, **future analysis** is concerned with the posterior probability distribution for μ. *This distribution is not required to make the main decision*, although it may serve as the starting point for future decisions involving μ.

3. **What are the various symbols employed and how do they relate to the four stages?**

Most students of this material suffer from a mild form of "symbol shock"—and for good reason! We have introduced four different standard deviations and five means. Moreover, $\bar{X}$ appears as a subscript to another symbol. Unfortunately, this Greek "alphabet soup" is unavoidable. Table 28-5 provides a glossary to help you keep track of these symbols. It may also help to mention a few of the pitfalls commonly encountered in applying the various analyses. It will also be helpful to refer to Figure 28-13, which puts the symbols in their stage context. Only a portion of the symbols need be juggled at any step of an evaluation.

4. **What are some of the common pitfalls in performing a Bayesian analysis with the normal distribution?**

The following reminders should be helpful.

- **Remember that some expressions involve the standard deviation σ and that others involve the variance σ^2.** Be sure to take the square root of the variance to obtain the corresponding standard deviation when it is needed, and to square the standard deviation to obtain the variance.

- **Prior analysis compares μ_b and μ_0, whereas posterior analysis compares $\bar{X}$ and C. Only one of these comparisons is ultimately used in making the main decision.**

- **Do not confuse σ_0 with σ_I.** The former expresses variability in μ itself and gauges how close to μ_0 we judge that μ lies. The standard deviation σ_I pertains to individual population values. Ordinarily, σ_0 and σ_I are not equal. (In a decision involving human heights, σ_0 might be $\frac{1}{4}$ inch, reflecting our lack of precision in predicting the population mean, and σ_I might be $2\frac{1}{2}$ inches, expressing variability from person to person.)

TABLE 28-5 Glossary of Statistical Symbols for Decision Making Using the Normal Distribution

Symbol	Means
μ	*The mean of the underlying population.* The value of μ is the main uncertainty. Payoffs depend on the level of μ. Although probabilities for μ may be revised, we will never know the true value of μ.
μ_b	*The breakeven level for μ.* This is a known value, representing the level of μ where the payoff lines cross.
μ_0	*The expected or central value of the prior normal probability distribution for μ.* Largely a *matter of judgment*, this quantity is the decision analyst's 50–50 point for where μ might fall.
μ_1	*The expected or central value of the posterior normal probability distribution for μ.* This quantity is a weighted average of μ_0 and the computed sample mean $\bar{X}$, and it may be calculated only after obtaining sample results. This quantity provides the decision analyst with a revised 50–50 point for μ.
$\bar{X}$	*The sample mean.* The computed value of $\bar{X}$ determines which act will be chosen.
	Standard Deviations
σ_0	*The standard deviation of the prior normal probability distribution for μ.* Largely *judgmental*, this value summarizes (or indexes) the magnitude of the decision analyst's uncertainty about the value of μ.
σ_1	*The standard deviation of the posterior normal probability distribution for μ.* Based on both earlier judgment and actual sample results, this value also expresses the magnitude of uncertainty about the value of μ (but after revision in accordance with sample results).
σ_I	*The standard deviation of the population of individual values.* This is an index of the extent of individual differences. Like μ itself, σ_I is ordinarily unknown, and we must make an "educated guess" or use a "ballpark figure" for its value.
$\sigma_{\bar{X}}$	*The standard error (deviation) of $\bar{X}$.* This tells us how tightly $\bar{X}$ values will cluster about μ. It is computed by dividing the population standard deviation σ_I by $\sqrt{n}$.

- **Keep in mind that μ remains unknown.** There will be no population census, and the value of μ will be uncertain throughout the entire analysis. On the other hand, μ_0 and μ_1 are the expected values of μ at the beginning and the end of the analysis, respectively. The value of μ_0 is known throughout, but μ_1 is uncertain throughout most of the analysis and may only be calculated last. The value of $\bar{X}$ is also uncertain until after the sample has been collected.

REVIEW EXERCISES

28-15 Sonic Phonics is considering modifying the components in its quadraphonic speaker system to boost its effective power. The ultimate result depends upon the mean signal-to-noise ratio μ. The latter index is unknown, although its prior probability distribution has been judged to be normally distributed with a mean of 100 and a standard deviation of 10. Unfortunately, the modified system may result in a poorer overall performance rating than the current system's 30 points, rising or dropping .25 points for each unit that μ lies above or below 90.

(a) Assuming that system performance rating is to be maximized, what is the breakeven level for the mean signal-to-noise ratio?

(b) Should Sonic Phonics modify its quadraphonic speakers?
(c) Calculate the EVPI.

28-16 The first stage of a chemical process yields a mean of μ grams of active ingredient for every liter of raw material processed. Due to variations in the raw material and in the control settings, the true population mean for any particular batch is unknown until processing is complete. The plant superintendent believes that μ is normally distributed with a mean of 30g and a standard deviation of 2g. The amount of variation in individual liters within a batch is summarized by a standard deviation of 6g.

The plant superintendent will use the active ingredient in either a high-pressure or a low-pressure final-stage process. Each process provides an identical final product. The ultimate profit from each alternative is partly determined by μ. The following payoff function applies.

$$\text{Payoff} = \begin{cases} \$10{,}000 + \$300\mu & \text{for high-pressure process} \\ \$13{,}100 + \$200\mu & \text{for low-pressure process} \end{cases}$$

(a) Determine the breakeven level of μ. Will the high-pressure or the low-pressure process yield the greater expected profit?
(b) Calculate the value of the slope of the opportunity loss lines and the superintendent's EVPI.

28-17 (*Continuation of Exercise 28-16*): For a cost of \$1 per liter, the superintendent determines the actual yield of active ingredient per liter.
(a) Calculate the EVSI for (1) $n = 4$; (2) $n = 9$; (3) $n = 16$.
(b) Calculate ENGS(n) for each of the sample sizes in (a). Which sample size is the best?
(c) Determine the optimal decision rule for the optimal sample size you found in (b). Which process should be used if (1) $\bar{X} = 30$g? (2) $\bar{X} = 32$g? (3) $\bar{X} = 33$g?

28-18 A decision must be made between two procedures. The following function expresses the payoff in terms of an unknown population mean.

$$\text{Payoff} = \begin{cases} -\$500 + \$10\mu & \text{for } A \\ \$1000 - \$5\mu & \text{for } B \end{cases}$$

The normal prior distribution for the mean has expected value of 110 with a standard deviation of 10. Individual observations may be made of the underlying population, which has a standard deviation of 30.
(a) Determine the breakeven level for the mean. Based on the prior distribution only, which alternative maximizes expected payoff?
(b) Calculate the EVPI.
(c) A sample of size $n = 9$ will be used in helping to make the decision. What are the EVSI and ENGS if each observation costs \$.10?
(d) Find the decision rule involving the sample mean $\bar{X}$.
(e) Suppose that a sample mean of $\bar{X} = 96$ is obtained. What procedure should be chosen?
(f) For a sample result of $\bar{X} = 96$, determine the applicable mean and standard deviation for the posterior normal distribution for μ. Then, find the applicable probability that μ exceeds its breakeven level.

CASE Pickwick Pipe Shoppes

Rod Tamper is the marketing director for Pickwick Pipe Shoppes, a chain of franchises specializing in tobacco products. Rod is evaluating the second-phase expansion of the Gentrytown Mall as a possible site for a new store. The proposed site lies on the main concourse, just beyond a barricade that will be removed in a few months. The major uncertainty is the amount of foot traffic that will pass the store front. Although historically mall traffic varies by time of day and day of week, peaking on Saturday afternoons, and by seasonal fluctuations as well, the sales potential of a new store may be gauged closely by the mean number of customers passing the store front in the Saturday afternoon rush during non-Christmas selling periods.

Rod acknowledges uncertainty regarding the mean level, judging it just as likely to lie at or below 1,000 per hour as above that level. He furthermore thinks that it is just as likely for the mean to fall between 900 and1,100 per hour as outside that interval.

Another major uncertain quantity is the percentage of the traffic flow that will stop in the store and eventually make a purchase. Previous experience with other malls leads Rod to conclude that the following probabilities apply: .23 for .5%; .28 for .6%; .17 for .7%; .15 for .8%; .11 for .9%; and .06 for 1.0%. Also uncertain is the average transaction amount, which he judges equally likely to be \$5 or \$6. Annual sales for stores in Rod's franchises are expected to be about 3,000 times hourly sales during non-Christmas Saturday afternoons.

The annual operating costs for the proposed store are \$30,000 plus 50% of sales for cost of goods. Additionally, Rod expects new stores to make a \$20,000 operating profit in the first year.

To help in his evaluation, Rod hires students to count customers passing specific spots in the open portion of the mall. The cost for this service is \$10 per hour.

QUESTIONS

1. Determine the expected value and standard deviation for the subjective prior probability distribution for the mean level μ of Saturday afternoon foot traffic.

2. Compute the expected percentage of passing persons who will stop at the new store.

3. The following levels for μ are possible: (a) $\mu = 800$, (b) $\mu = 1{,}100$, and (c) $\mu = 1{,}200$. In each case, answer the following.
   (1) Compute the expected annual revenue for the new store.
   (2) Find the expected annual profit.
   (3) Would Rod find the new store to meet his profit goal?

4. Treating μ as an unknown variable, express Rod's expected payoff as a function of μ. Find the breakeven level for μ that yields an expected profit of exactly \$20,000. Assuming that Rod wishes to maximize expected payoff, would he build the proposed store?

5. Determine the EVPI. Does there seem to be the potential for improvement in expected payoff by deferring the main decision until after collecting sample information?

6. Individual hourly traffic levels in Rod's other mall stores on Saturday afternoons have a standard deviation of 650 persons. Assuming that this value applies for the new store site, answer the following.
   (a) Compute the expected net gain from sampling when (1) $n = 25$ and (2) $n = 100$.
   (b) Which of the two sample sizes provides the greater expected payoff?

7. Suppose a sample of $n = 25$ hourly foot traffic counts will be obtained. Express Rod's decision rule.

CHAPTER 29

DECISION MAKING WITH UTILITY

BEFORE READING THIS CHAPTER, MAKE SURE YOU UNDERSTAND:

Basic concepts of decision analysis (Chapter 24).
Elements of decision theory (Chapter 25).

AFTER READING THIS CHAPTER, YOU WILL UNDERSTAND:

What a utility is.
What theoretical assumptions underlie utility.
How utility values are found.
How utility payoffs make the Bayes decision rule an ideal criterion.
About the basic attitudes toward risk characterized by the shape of the utility curve.
How utilities relate to certainty equivalents.

The goal of this chapter is to broaden the scope of decision theory through the introduction of a new payoff measure. We have seen that a good payoff measure should rank all possible outcomes in terms of how well they meet the decision maker's goals. This is often an easy task when there is no uncertainty. But the presence of uncertainty may severely complicate the issue when the possible outcomes from a decision are extreme. Such decisions contain elements of *risk*. Because people usually have different attitudes toward risk, two persons faced with an identical decision may actually prefer different courses of action.

The crucial role that attitude plays in any decision is illustrated by the divergent behavior of different persons faced with the same decision. The *umbrella situation* nicely demonstrates this point. *How can we explain why everyone does not carry an umbrella when we do?* To a certain extent, we say that all individuals are not equally adept at selecting and exercising appropriate decision criteria. But this is only one possible explanation. With much justification, however, we conclude that the difference in behavior may also be explained by differing attitudes toward the consequences. Some people may enjoy getting wet, but others may view it as an invitation to pneumonia and possibly the first step to a premature grave. Some people think it is chic to carry rain paraphernalia when it's not raining; others would rather lug around a ball and chain. Even if we find two persons who have identical attitudes toward the decision consequences, they may still make opposite decisions because they may not have made identical *judgments* regarding the chance of rain.

In this chapter, we will discuss utility as an alternative expression of payoff that reflects a person's attitudes. We will begin by examining the rationale for buying insurance. A brief historical discussion of utility and the underlying assumptions of a theory of utility will then be presented. Finally, a procedure will be introduced that may be used to determine utility values. The utility function so obtained provides a basis for our discussion of some basic attitudes toward risk.

29-1 ATTITUDES, PREFERENCES, AND UTILITY

In Chapter 25, we examined several procedures and criteria that help decision makers to make choices in the presence of uncertainty. In all cases, the payoff value of each outcome is required to analyze the decision. As we have seen, not all outcomes have an obvious numerical payoff. In this section, we will see how payoffs may be determined in such cases. Later in the chapter, we will develop methods of quantifying such consequences as reduced share of the market, loss of corporate control, and antitrust suits. Even when numerical payoffs may be naturally determined, we have seen that it may be unrealistic to select the act with the maximum expected payoff. In some cases, an extremely risky act fares better under the Bayes decision rule than an obviously preferred act. As noted in Chapter 25, this difficulty is not the fault of the Bayes criterion, but is caused by payoff values that do not reflect their true worth to the decision maker.

THE DECISION TO BUY INSURANCE

The inadequacy of using such obvious measures as dollar cost or profit to indicate payoffs may be vividly illustrated by evaluating an individual's decision of whether or not to buy fire insurance. Spiro Pyrophobis wishes to decide whether

TABLE 29-1 Payoff Table for the Decision to Buy Fire Insurance

		Act			
		Buy Insurance		Don't Buy Insurance	
Event	**Probability**	**Payoff**	**Payoff × Probability**	**Payoff**	**Payoff × Probability**
Fire	.002	−$100	−$ .20	−$40,000	−$80.00
No fire	.998	−100	−99.80	0	0
	Expected payoff		−$100.00		−$80.00

to buy a fire insurance policy for his home. Our decision maker's payoffs will be expressed in terms of his out-of-pocket costs, which we will represent by negative numbers. Our question is: Will the Bayes decision rule lead to the choice of the act that is actually preferred?

In answering this question, we will use the hypothetical payoff table provided in Table 29-1. Here, we have greatly simplified the decision. The acts are to buy or not to buy an annual policy with a $100 premium charge. If there is a fire, we will assume that Spiro's home and all its contents, valued at $40,000, will be completely destroyed.

Insurance actuaries have established that historically 2 out of every 1,000 homes in the category of Spiro's home burn down each year. The probability that Spiro's home will burn down is therefore set at 2/1,000 = .002. Thus, the complementary event—no fire—has a probability of 1 − .002 = .998. We use these probability values to calculate the expected payoffs for each act in Table 26-1. The maximum expected payoff is −$80, which corresponds to the act "don't buy insurance" and is larger than the −$100 payoff from buying fire insurance.

In this example, the *Bayes decision rule indicates that it is optimal to buy no insurance.* Insurance policy premiums are higher than the expected claim size, which is equivalent to the policyholder's expected dollar loss, so that the insurance company can pay wages and achieve profits. Thus, buying insurance may be considered an unfair gamble, where the payoff is not in the buyer's favor. Individuals can expect to pay more in insurance premiums than they will collect in claims,* and they feel fortunate if they never have to file a claim. Yet most persons faced with this decision choose to buy fire insurance. Loss of a home, which composes the major portion of a lifetime's savings for many people, is a dreadful prospect. The expenditure of an annual premium, although not exactly appealing, buys a feeling of security that seems to outweigh the difference between the expected payoffs.

The Bayes decision rule selects the *less preferred act*. Does this mean that it is an invalid criterion? Rather than answer no immediately, let us consider the payoffs used. The true worth of the outcomes is not reflected by the dollar payoffs. A policyholder is willing to pay more than the expected dollar loss to achieve "peace of mind." We say that the policyholder derives greater **utility** from having insurance. If dollar losses are valued on a scale of true worth or utility, then each additional dollar loss will make our decision maker feel disproportionately worse off. Thus, a 10% reduction in wealth may be more than twice

*This is not true of life insurance, which is ordinarily a form of savings.

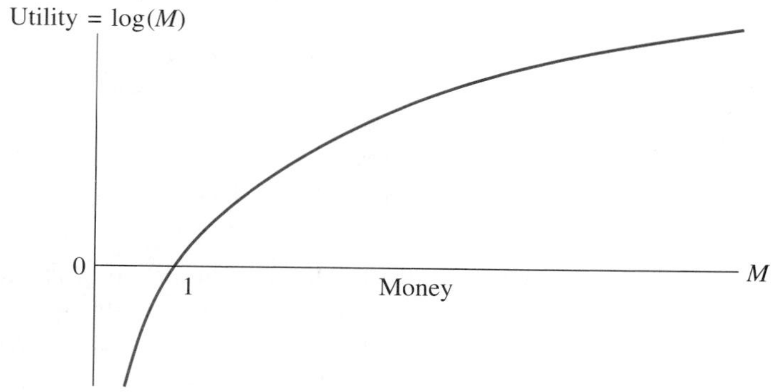

FIGURE 29-1 Bernoulli's utility function for money.

as bad as a 5% reduction. The same is usually true for gains in dollar wealth; the second increase may not increase the decision maker's sense of well being as much as the first. In the parlance of economics, *the policyholder's marginal utility for money is decreasing*. Each successive dollar gain buys a smaller increase in utility; each additional dollar loss reduces utility by a greater amount than before.

Thus, we may question the validity of using dollars as our payoff measure. Instead, it might be preferable to measure the payoff of an outcome in terms of its worth or utility.

29-2 NUMERICAL UTILITY VALUES

We wish to obtain *numerical utility values* that express the true worth of the payoffs that correspond to decision outcomes. We refer to such numbers as **utilities**. Much investigation has been made of the true worth of monetary payoffs. The early eighteenth-century mathematician Daniel Bernoulli—a pioneer in developing a measure of utility—proposed that *the true worth of an individual's wealth is the logarithm of the amount of money possessed*. Thus, a graphical relationship between utility and money would have the basic shape of the curve in Figure 29-1. Note that although the slope of this curve is always positive, it decreases as the amount of money increases, reflecting the assumption of decreasing marginal utility for money.

THE SAINT PETERSBURG PARADOX

A gambling game called the **Saint Petersburg Paradox** led Bernoulli to his conclusion. In the game, a balanced coin is fairly tossed until the first head appears. The gambler's winnings are based on the number of tosses that are made before the game ends. If a head appears on the first toss, the player wins \$2. If not, the "kitty" is doubled to \$4—the reward if a head appears on the second toss. If a tail occurs on the second toss, the kitty is doubled again. The pot is doubled after every coin toss that results in a tail. The winnings are \$2 raised to the power of the number of tosses until and including the first head. This procedure will be more interesting if you pause to think about what amount you would be willing to pay for the privilege of playing this game.

The probability that $n + 1$ tosses will occur before payment is the probability that there is a run of n tails and that the $(n + 1)$st toss is a head, or $(1/2)^{n+1}$. The payoff for $n + 1$ tosses is 2^{n+1}. We calculate the player's expected receipts from the sum

$$\$2(1/2) + \$2^2(1/2)^2 + \$2^3(1/2)^3 + \cdots = \$1 + \$1 + \$1 + \cdots = \$\infty$$

Since the number of \$1's in this sum is unlimited, the *expected receipts from a play of this game are infinite*! Whatever amount you were willing to pay to play must have been a finite amount and therefore less than the expected receipts. Thus, the expected payoff for this gamble is also infinite, no matter what price is paid to play.

Few people are willing to pay more than \$10 to play this game, and even at this price, a player would win only 1 out of 8 games on the average. A player paying \$500 would show a profit in only 1 out of every 256 gambles on the average. The natural reticence of players to pay very much for this gamble led Bernoulli to his conclusion about the utility for money. In general, we say that a person who prefers not to participate in a gamble in which the expected receipts exceed the price to play has a **decreasing marginal utility** for money.

THE VALIDITY OF LOGARITHMIC VALUES

Via different paths of reasoning, other early mathematicians arrived at conclusions similar to Bernoulli's—that the marginal utility for money is decreasing—and proposed other utility curves with the same basic shape. A major fault of these early works is that they do not account for individual differences in the assignment of worth. A more modern treatment of utility in the abstract sense was advanced by John von Neumann and Oskar Morgenstern in 1947 in their book *Theory of Games and Economic Behavior*. There, they proposed that a utility curve may be tailored for any individual, provided certain assumptions about the individual's preferences hold. These assumptions provide several valid, basic shapes for the utility curve, including curves similar to Bernoulli's. We will investigate some of these utility curves later in the chapter.

OUTCOMES WITHOUT A NATURAL PAYOFF MEASURE

Until now, the outcomes of our examples have had a *natural* numerical payoff measure, such as dollar profits, gallons of gasoline, or time saved. But we have noted that some decisions have no numerical outcomes. As decision makers, we should be able to assess the relative worth of such an outcome.

In the case of most decisions, it is possible to determine preferences, although this is not always an easy task. Indeed, value judgments may be the most difficult step in analyzing a decision. Consider the student selecting a school from several top universities, the child choosing a candy bar, the single person contemplating getting married and forgoing the carefree life, the tired corporate founder pondering merger and retirement versus retaining control and delegating operating responsibility, or the innocent person choosing between pleading guilty to manslaughter or facing trial for murder. If we assume that we have the capability of ranking the consequences in order of preference, we extend the notion of utility so that numerical payoffs may be made for the most intangible outcomes.

EXERCISES

29-1 Suppose that you are offered a gamble by Ms. I. M. Honest, a representative of a foundation studying human behavior. A fair coin is to be tossed. If a head occurs, you will receive \$10,000 from Ms. Honest. But if a tail results, you must pay her foundation \$5,000. If you do *not* have \$5,000, a loan will be arranged, which must be repaid over a five-year period at \$150 per month but may be deferred until you have graduated from school.

(a) Calculate your expected profit from participating in this gamble.

(b) Would you be willing to accept Ms. Honest's offer? Does your answer indicate that your marginal utility for money is decreasing?

29-2 Mr. Smith has offered you a gamble similar to that of Ms. Honest in Exercise 29-1. If a head occurs, he will hand you \$1.00. But if a tail results you must pay Mr. Smith \$.50.

(a) Calculate your expected profit from participating in this gamble.

(b) Would you be willing to accept Mr. Smith's offer?

29-3 A homeowner whose house is valued at \$40,000 is offered tornado insurance at an annual premium of \$500. Suppose that there are just two mutually exclusive outcomes—complete damage or no damage from a tornado—and that the probability of damage from a tornado is .0001.

(a) Construct the homeowner's payoff table for the decision of whether or not to buy tornado insurance.

(b) Calculate the decision maker's expected monetary payoff for each act. Which act has the maximum expected payoff?

(c) Suppose that the homeowner decides not to buy tornado insurance. Does this contradict the decreasing marginal utility for money? Explain.

29-3 THE ASSUMPTIONS OF UTILITY THEORY

The fundamental proposition of the modern treatment of utility is that it is possible to obtain a numerical expression for an individual's preferences. We rank a set of outcomes by preference and then assign utility values that convey these preferences. The largest utility number is assigned to the most preferred outcome, the next largest number is assigned to the second most preferred outcome, and so forth. Suppose, for instance, that you are contemplating a menu. If you prefer New York steak to baked halibut and you wish to assign utility values to the entrees in accordance with your preferences, the utility for steak will be 5, or $u(\text{steak}) = 5$, and $u(\text{halibut})$ will be some number smaller than 5.

Before we describe how specific utility numbers may be obtained, we will discuss some of the assumptions underlying the theory of utility. Various assumptions have been made about the determination of utilities.* All of them have one feature in common—that the values obtained pertain only to a *single individual* who behaves *consistently* in accordance with his or her own tastes.

Preference Ranking

The first assumption of utility theory is that a person can determine for any pair of outcomes O_1 and O_2 whether he or she prefers O_1 to O_2, prefers O_2 to O_1, or

*The assumptions discussed in this book are simplifications of the original axioms postulated by von Neumann and Morgenstern.

regards them equally. This assumption is particularly advantageous when we consider monetary values, because then we assume that more money is always better than less. But we have seen that it may be very difficult to rank preferences when qualitative alternatives are considered. Can a person always determine a preference for or establish an indifference toward outcomes? If not, then utilities cannot be found for these outcomes.

Transitivity of Preference

The second assumption of utility theory is that if A is preferred to B and B is preferred to C, then A must be preferred to C. This property is called **transitivity of preference** and reflects an individual's consistency. Again, when we are dealing with monetary outcomes, we usually assume transitivity.

The Assumption of Continuity

The third assumption of utility theory is that of **continuity**, which tells us that the individual considers some *gamble* having the best and worst outcomes as rewards to be equally preferable to some middle or in-between outcome. To illustrate continuity, we will consider the following example.

Homer Briant owns a small hardware store in a deteriorating neighborhood and is contemplating a move. Because Homer is still young and has no special skills, he will not consider leaving the hardware business. A move cannot be guaranteed to be successful, since relocating will involve the maximum extension of his credit and there will be no time for a gradual buildup of business. Therefore, moving will either improve Homer's present business or be disastrous. Thus, Homer is faced with one of the following outcomes.

Most preferred O_3	Increasing sales (if move is a success)
O_2	Decreasing sales (if Homer stays)
Least preferred O_1	Imminent bankruptcy (if the move is a failure)

Whether a move will be a success depends largely on luck or chance. Our assumption of continuity presumes that there is some probability value for a successful move that will make Homer indifferent between staying and moving. Figure 29-2 presents the decision tree diagram for this decision. The fork at node b represents

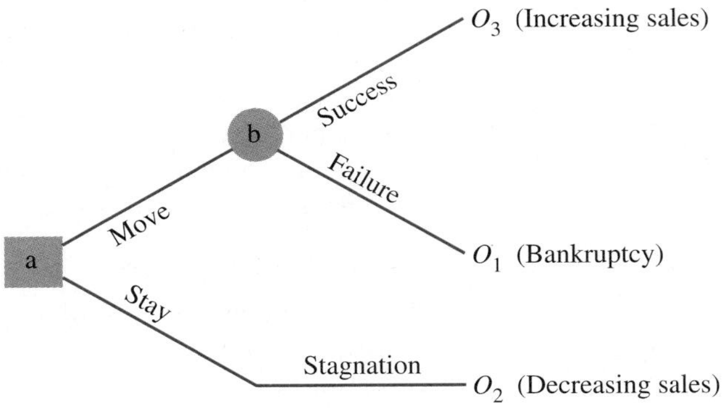

FIGURE 29-2 Decision tree diagram for Homer Briant's decision.

a gamble between O_3 and O_1 resulting from the act "move." Continuity may be justified by observing that if the value of Pr[success] is close to 1, so that a move will almost certainly be a success, Homer will prefer the gamble of moving to staying. But if Pr[success] is close to 0, making bankruptcy a near certainty, Homer will prefer to stay in his present location. Thus, there must be a success probability somewhere between 0 and 1 beyond which Homer's preference will pass from O_2 to the gamble. This value for Pr[success] makes the gamble as equally attractive as O_2.

Continuity is a crucial assumption of utility theory, but it may be hard to accept, especially if the outcomes include the ultimate one—death. Suppose that you are allowed to participate in a lottery that offers you \$100 if you win and death if you lose. Is there any probability for winning that would make you indifferent between the status quo and playing? A natural response is that this is not a very meaningful gamble, so we will recast the situation. Suppose that you are informed by a reliable source that you can drive your car one mile down the road and someone will be passing out \$100 bills, one to a person. There are no gimmicks, and you will not be inconvenienced by a mob of people. Would you go? If you answer yes, then consider your chances of getting killed in an automobile accident on your journey. For the past several years, approximately 50,000 persons have been killed in such accidents in the United States annually. So although it is quite small, the probability that your rather untimely death will occur while you are collecting your \$100 is not zero. Going to get your \$100 is a gamble having death as a possible outcome, and you prefer the gamble to the status quo. Now suppose that we increase the chance of death. To reach your benefactor, you must cross a condemned bridge. Would you still go? Probably not, because the chance of death would be significantly higher. Somewhere in between these two extremes lies a probability for safely getting your \$100 and a complementary probability for death that would make you indifferent between the status quo and the gamble.

The Assumption of Substitutability

A fourth assumption of utility theory allows us to revise a gamble by *substituting* one outcome for another outcome that is equally well regarded. The premise is that the individual will be indifferent between the original and the revised gambles. The **substitutability** assumption may be illustrated by means of an example.

A husband and wife cannot agree on how to spend Saturday night. In desperation, they decide to gamble by tossing a coin to determine the kind of entertainment they will select. If a head occurs, they will spend the evening at the opera (her preference), and if a tail occurs, they will go to a basketball game. Suppose that the wife changes her mind and wants to go to a dance instead. The husband dislikes dancing just as much as the opera, so he would be indifferent between tossing for the opera or basketball and a revised gamble between dancing and basketball. This will hold regardless of the odds, providing that the chance of going to the basketball game remains the same for the orginal and the revised gambles.

The principle of substitutability also holds if we treat a gamble as an outcome. For any outcome, we substitute an *equivalent gamble* with two other outcomes as rewards that is equally as well regarded as the outcome the gamble replaces. For example, suppose that the wife insists on a movie instead. She wants to see a romance story, but he feels that as compensation for being dragged to a movie, they should see an adventure film. Suppose that the husband is indifferent between an opera or a coin toss to determine which of the two movies to see.

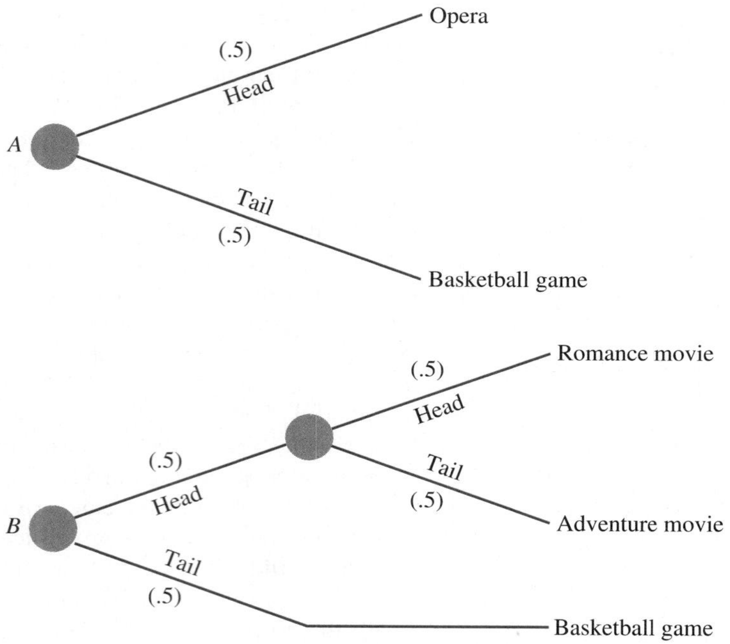

FIGURE 29-3 An illustration of the assumption of substitutability. The single-stage gamble at *A* and the two-stage gamble at *B* are equally well regarded.

The second coin toss is an equivalent gamble to the opera outcome. Thus, the husband should be indifferent between the single- and the two-stage gambles in Figure 29-3.

The Assumption of Increasing Preference

The final assumption of utility theory concerns any pair of gambles with identical outcomes. The gamble that has the greater probability for the more desirable outcome must be preferred. Thus, the preference for gambles between the same two outcomes *increases* as the probability for attaining the better outcome increases. The plausibility of **increasing preference** should be apparent. Suppose that when a coin is tossed, you are paid $100 if a head occurs and nothing if a tail occurs. The probability for winning $100 is 1/2. It should be obvious that this gamble would be decidedly inferior to a gamble with the same outcomes and a probability for winning greater than 1/2.

29-4 ASSIGNING UTILITY VALUES

Utility numbers must be assigned to outcomes in such a way that the outcome for which a person has a greater preference receives the greater value. The resulting values gauge that person's relative preferences. Any numbers satisfying these requirements will be suitable as utilities, and their absolute magnitudes may be arbitrarily set.

To lay the foundation for the methodology used in finding utility values, we again view the uncertain situation as a gamble.

GAMBLES AND EXPECTED UTILITY

We are presently concerned with making choices under uncertainty. Thus, the payoffs for decision acts are unknown, and each act may be viewed as a gamble with uncertain rewards. To evaluate such decisions, we must extend the concept of utility to gambles.

Recall that the Bayes decision rule involves comparisons between the expected payoffs of acts or strategies, so that the "optimal" choice has the maximum expected payoff. But the major difficulty with this criterion, as we have seen, is that the indicated course of action may be less attractive than some other action. For example, the Bayes decision rule tells us not to buy fire insurance when most people feel that insurance is desirable. We wish to overcome this obstacle by using utilities in place of dollar payoffs. We therefore require that the expected utility payoffs provide a valid means of comparing actions so that the action having the greatest expected utility is actually preferred to the alternative actions. Thus, buying fire insurance should have greater expected utility than not buying it.

But we can go one step further. Suppose that the most preferred action has the greatest expected utility, the next most preferred action has the next greatest utility, and so forth. Then expected utility would express preference ranking, and the *expected utility values would themselves be utilities.* Each utility value would express the worth of a *gamble* between outcomes obtained by averaging the utility values of the outcomes, using their respective probabilities as weights. This may be stated more precisely as a utility theory

PROPERTY: In any gamble between outcome A and outcome B, with probabilities of q for A and $1-q$ for B

$$u(\text{gamble}) = qu(A) + (1-q)u(B)$$

Thus, the utility for a gamble between two outcomes is equal to the expected utility for the gamble. When acts having uncertain outcomes are viewed as gambles, the utility for an act is equal to the expected utility for its outcomes. *When payoffs are measured in terms of utilities, the Bayes decision rule will indicate that the act having the maximum expected utility is optimal*, so that this criterion may always be used to select the most preferred act or strategy.

We are now ready to assign utility values to outcomes. Figure 29-4 outlines this procedure. The numbers are obtained from a series of gambles between a pair of outcomes.

THE REFERENCE LOTTERY

The process begins with a preference ranking of all the outcomes to be considered. The most preferred and the least preferred outcomes are determined, and a gamble between these outcomes establishes the individual's utilities. We call this a **reference lottery**. It has two events: "win," which corresponds to achieving the best outcome, and "lose," which corresponds to attaining the worst outcome. Such a gamble is purely *hypothetical* and only provides a framework for assessing utility. The events "win" and "lose" do not relate to any events in the actual decision structure and are used to divorce the reference lottery from actual similar gambles. The *probability for winning the hypothetical reference lottery is a variable*, denoted by q, which changes according to the attitudes of the decision maker.

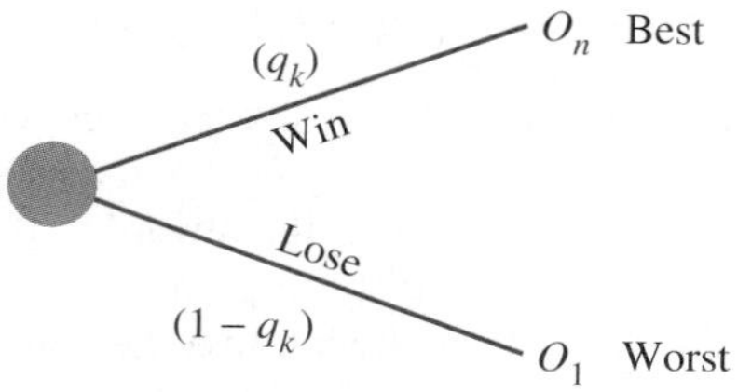

FIGURE 29-4 The procedure for assigning values to a set of outcomes.

The initial assignment of utility values to the best and worst outcomes is *completely arbitrary*. It does not matter what values are chosen; assigning different values to these arbitrary utilities will result in different utility scales. This is similar to temperature measurement, in which two different and quite arbitrary values are used to define the Fahrenheit and Celsius scales. The choices of 32° Fahrenheit and 0° Celsius for the freezing point of water and of 212°F and 100°C for its boiling point, result in quite different values on these two scales for any particular temperature.

OBTAINING UTILITY VALUES

Once the extreme utility values are determined, the decision maker may use the reference lottery to obtain utilities for the intermediate outcomes. This is accomplished by varying the "win" probability q until the decision maker establishes a value of q that serves as a *point of indifference* between achieving that outcome for certain and letting the reward be determined by the reference lottery. That particular value of q makes the reference lottery a gamble that is equivalent to the intermediate outcome so evaluated. We have seen that the assumption of continuity makes this possible.

Again, we add meaning to this procedure by considering its similarities to temperature measurement.

The decision maker's subjective evaluation is analogous to designing a thermometer. A thermometer is designed by determining a core diameter that will permit a substance such as mercury to rise to various levels within its tubular cavity. For each level of heat, there is a corresponding height to which the mercury must rise. On the Celsius scale, the 100° mark corresponds to the mercury's height when the thermometer is placed in boiling water. Various levels of heat between the freezing and boiling points of water correspond to marks at prescribed heights above the zero mark, allowing heat to be measured in relative degrees. Similarly, the values of q established to make the decision maker indifferent between respective intermediate outcomes and the reference lottery serve to measure his or her relative preferences. The indifference values of q are like the markings on a thermometer, and the different outcome preferences are analogous to different levels of heat. These values of q are established through introspection and have no more to do with the actual chance of winning than the design of a thermometer is related to tomorrow's temperature.

Once an indifference value of q has been established for an outcome, its utility value may be determined by calculating the expected value of the reference lottery

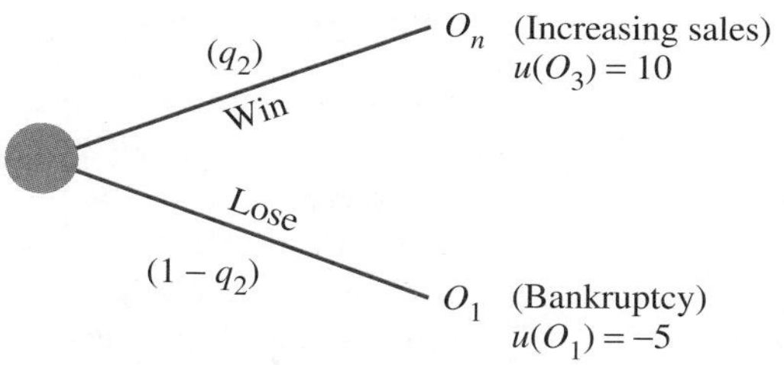

FIGURE 29-5 The reference lottery for Homer Briant's decision.

using that value of q. Letting O_1 and O_n represent the least and the most preferred outcomes, we then find the utility of an outcome O_k of intermediate preference from

$$u(O_k) = q_k u(O_n) + (1 - q_k)u(O_1)$$

Here, q_k is the value of q that makes the decision maker *indifferent* between the certain achievement of O_k and taking a chance with the reference lottery. The utility value $u(O_k)$ is analogous to a numerical degree value beside a marking on a thermometer.

To illustrate, we will continue with Homer Briant's contemplated business relocation. Homer has ranked his preferences for the outcomes of increasing sales (O_3), decreasing sales (O_2), and bankruptcy (O_1), and the reference lottery is shown in Figure 29-5. Suppose that the utility values of the extreme outcomes are arbitrarily set at 10 and − 5, so that

$$u(O_3) = 10 \qquad u(O_1) = -5$$

Now assume that Homer contemplates the reference lottery in terms of 100 marbles in a box, some labeled W for "win" and the rest labeled L for "lose." A marble is to be selected at random. If it is a W, then Homer will be guaranteed outcome O_3 (increasing sales), but if it is an L, he will go bankrupt for certain, achieving outcome O_1. Homer is then asked what number of W marbles would make him indifferent between facing declining sales (outcome O_2) or taking his chances with the lottery. After considerable thought, Homer replies that 75 W marbles would make him regard O_2 and the reference lottery equally well. This establishes a reference lottery win probability of q_2 that makes it an equivalent gamble to outcome O_2.

$$q_2 = 75/100 = .75$$

This probability may then be used to calculate the utility of declining sales.

$$\begin{aligned} u(O_2) &= q_2 u(O_3) + (1 - q_2)u(O_1) \\ &= .75(10) + .25(-5) \\ &= 6.25 \end{aligned}$$

ATTITUDE VERSUS JUDGMENT

It must be emphasized that the value $q_2 = .75$ is merely a device used to establish indifference. *The selected probability for winning the lottery has nothing to do with the chance that the most favorable outcome will occur.* In setting $q_2 = .75$, the decision maker is expressing an *attitude* toward one outcome in terms of the rewards of a hypothetical gamble. This value was obtained through introspection in an attempt to balance tastes and aspirations between remaining in a declining business or gambling to improve it. Homer is assumed to be capable of switching from introspection to dispassionate *judgment* when asked later what he thinks the actual chance is that moving his business will be a success. To arrive at the probability of success, our decision maker must use his experience and knowledge of such factors as the history of failures by relocated businesses, prevailing economic conditions, and possible competitor reactions.

Suppose that Homer judges his chance of success after moving to be 1/2. We now analyze his decision problem by applying the Bayes decision rule, using utilities as payoff values. The decision tree diagram is shown in Figure 29-6. The expected utility payoff for the event fork at b is 2.5, which is the utility achieved by moving. Since this value is smaller than the 6.25 utility achieved by remaining in his present location, Homer Briant should not move. Thus, we prune the branch corresponding to the act "move" and bring the 6.25 utility payoff back to node a.

UTILITY AND THE BAYES DECISION RULE

This example illustrates why the Bayes decision rule is valid when utility payoffs are used. The utility for a gamble is the expected value of the utilities assigned to its rewards. Since any act with uncertain outcomes may be viewed as a gamble, the act that provides the greatest utility—and therefore the one that must be preferred—is the act with the maximum expected utility payoff. The Bayes decision rule may therefore be viewed as an extension of utility theory, and the criterion serves only to translate the decision maker's preferences into a choice of act. Homer Briant decides to stay because this act provides the greater utility—which

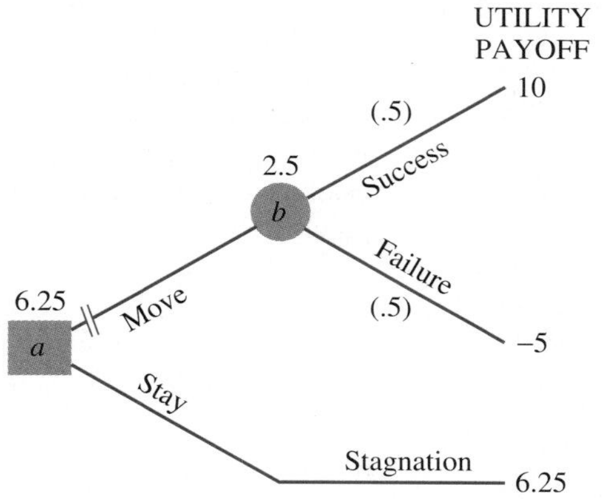

FIGURE 29-6 Homer Briant's decision tree diagram showing backward induction analysis with utility payoffs.

may only be the case, our theory states, if remaining in the present location is the preferred act. *In arriving at a choice, both the decision maker's attitudes toward the consequences and judgment regarding the chances of the events are considered and integrated.* The choice indicated by the Bayes criterion is optimal because it is preferred above all others.

If some other success probability (say, .90), had been determined, Homer would relocate, because doing so would have the higher utility: $.9(10) + .1(-5) = 8.5$. This might be the case, for example, if Homer learned that his major would-be competitor had just been taken over by his incompetent son. Changing event probabilities reflects only the decision maker's judgment regarding the factors that influence their occurrence. Only the *expected* utilities of uncertain *acts* may be affected by the revision of event probabilities. Regardless of the chance of the success of the relocation, the decision maker's utilities for the ultimate *outcomes* must remain unchanged. Only a change of taste or attitude, which might be caused by a death in the family or by a change in personal finances, can justify revising the ultimate outcome utilities.

EXERCISES

29-4 Actor Nathan Summers enjoys wearing costumes in front of audiences. Nathan likes dressing up like a little old lady the most and hates to dress up like an animal. Somewhere in between lies his preference for wearing a cowboy outfit. Assigning a utility of 10 to being a lady and a utility of -5 to being an animal, what is Nathan's utility for playing a cowboy if he is indifferent between this outcome and a coin toss determining which of the other two roles he will play?

29-5 Ty Kune, a potential entrepreneur, is faced with the following outcomes.

O_3 Successfully established in his own business
O_2 Maintaining present employee status
O_1 Personal bankruptcy

Ty would be indifferent between remaining on his present job and opening a restaurant when the probability is q_2 for success and $1 - q_2$ forbankruptcy.

(a) At age 22, Ty finds that $q_2 = .50$ makes him indifferent. If he arbitrarily sets $u(O_3) = 200$ and $u(O_1) = -100$, calculate Ty's utility value for keeping his present job (and not going into business for himself).
(b) At age 30 Ty's outlook has changed drastically, and $q_2 = .90$ now applies. Find $u(O_2)$ again when $u(O_3) = 200$ and $u(O_1) = -100$.
(c) Undergoing a midlife crisis at age 40, Ty revises his indifference probability to .20. Preferring big numbers, he arbitrarily establishes $u(O_3) = 10{,}000$ and $u(O_1) = 0$. Calculate Ty's utility for remaining on somebody else's payroll.

29-6 You may achieve the following outcomes (no rights are transferable).

- 100 new record albums of your choice
- A grade of *C* on the next examination covering utility
- A year's assignment to Timbuktu, Mali
- Confinement to an airport during a three-day storm
- A month of free telephone calls to anywhere

(a) Rank these outcomes in descending order of preference, designating them O_5, O_4, O_3, O_2, and O_1.
(b) Let the utilities be $u(O_5) = 100$ for the best outcome and $u(O_1) = 0$ for the worst outcome. Consider a box containing 1,000 marbles, some of which are labeled "win" and the remaining of which are labeled "lose." If a "win" marble is selected at random from the box, you will achieve O_5. If a "lose" marble is chosen, you will attain O_1. Determine how many marbles of each type would make you indifferent between gambling or achieving O_2. Determine the same for O_3 and O_4.
(c) The corresponding probabilities for winning q_k may be determined by dividing the respective number of "win" marbles by 1,000. Use these probabilities to calculate $u(O_4)$, $u(O_3)$, and $u(O_2)$.

29-5 THE UTILITY FOR MONEY

APPLYING THE UTILITY FUNCTION IN DECISION ANALYSIS

The reference lottery may be used to construct a **utility function** for money. To do this, the best outcome is selected so that it is no smaller than the greatest possible payoff, and the worst outcome is selected so that it is no larger than the lowest possible payoff. Monetary outcomes offer some special advantages. A monetary amount may be measured on a continuous scale, so that the utility function itself will be continuous. This suggests that it may be determined by finding an appropriate smoothed curve relating money values to their utilities. To do this, only a few key dollar amounts and some knowledge of the curve's general shape are required. The curve obtained by connecting the points can then serve as an approximation of the utility function.

Such a curve is shown in Figure 29-7 for the Ponderosa Record Company decision in Chapter 24. This utility curve has been derived according to the

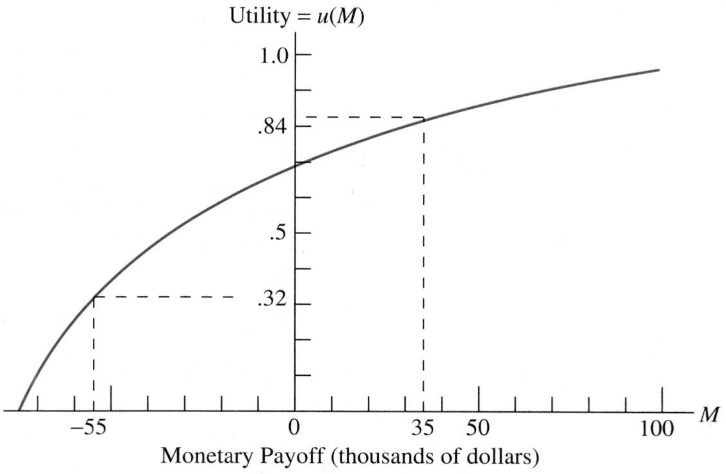

FIGURE 29-7 The utility function for the president of the Ponderosa Record Company.

procedures just described by applying a reference lottery and using a few key monetary amounts as the outcomes. The reference lottery that is used ranges from +\$100,000 (win) to −\$75,000 (lose), which, for ease of evaluation, are more extreme than any possible payoff. Arbitrary utility values of $u(+\$100{,}000) = 1$ and $u(-\$75{,}000) = 0$ have been set for simplicity.

In practice, a utility function is found empirically by personally interviewing the decision maker. Ordinarily, the function will be described graphically by reading the utilities directly from the curve rather than by using a mathematical equation.

We use the utility curve in Figure 29-7 to analyze the Ponderosa president's decision problem. The original decision tree diagram is reconstructed in Figure 29-8. The utilities corresponding to each monetary payoff have been obtained from the utility curve and added to the tree. For instance, the utilities for the monetary payoffs \$35,000 and −\$55,000 are .84 and .32, respectively.

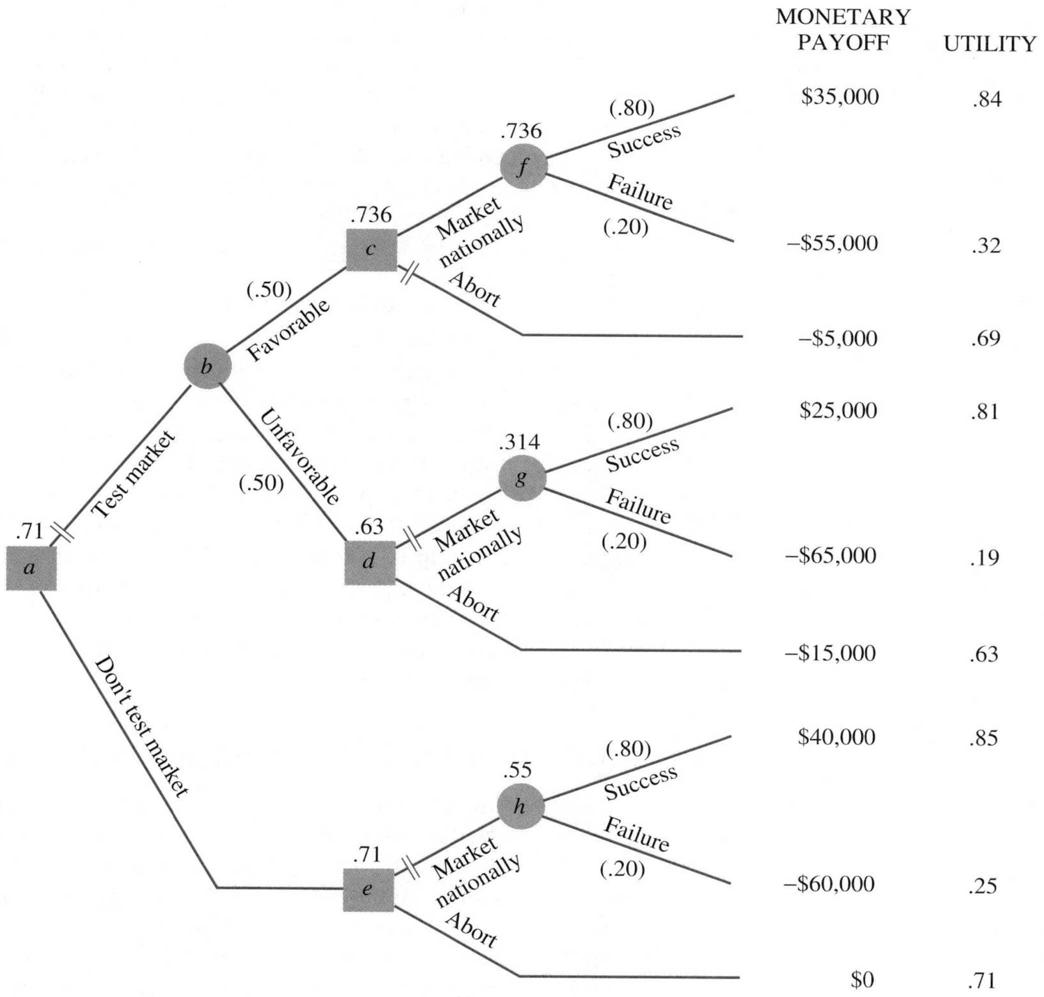

FIGURE 29-8 The Ponderosa decision tree diagram showing backward induction analysis with utility payoffs.

Backward induction is then performed using utilities instead of dollars. Here, we find that the optimal choice is "don't test market" and "abort." The two alternatives that involve marketing the record are too risky. Recall that we reached a different conclusion in Chapter 24 when expected monetary values were used. But since utility values express the true worth of monetary outcomes, our latest solution is the valid one.

CERTAINTY EQUIVALENTS AND UTILITIES

In Chapter 25, we encountered **certainty equivalents**, payoff amounts that the decision maker would be willing to accept in lieu of undergoing the uncertainty. There, a cumbersome procedure is described for finding certainty equivalents. That involves discounting expected payoffs by the risk premium amount, a method requiring tabulation of risk premiums. These are not only hard to find, but only a few amounts may be listed from the infinite number of possibilities.

A backward induction using utility payoffs is more streamlined and consistent than one using certainty equivalents. And working with expected utilities will accomplish precisely the same thing. This is because any utility amount has a matching dollar amount, found by reading the utility graph in reverse order.

Consider the Ponderosa decision tree in Figure 29-8. Take the utility value of .736 at node *f* and read the corresponding *M* from the utility curve in Figure 29-7. This corresponds to about +$11,000 on the monetary scale; that amount may be interpreted as the decision maker's certainty equivalent for node *f*. Each utility value above the nodes in the decision tree may be converted into a unique certainty equivalent by reading the corresponding monetary value from the utility function graph.

Doing this will provide nearly the same values found in Chapter 25 for the Ponderosa decision in Figure 25-1 (page 1007). The utility-generated certainty equivalents differ slightly from those, because of the approximations taken in establishing the risk premiums used in Chapter 25.

The backward induction itself in Figure 29-8 was conducted wholly with utility values, the expected values computed directly, without any adjustments in the values obtained. Certainty equivalents would not be used in pruning the tree, and are not needed at all to complete the decision analysis. The role of the certainty equivalent is to help in communicating the results. (Ponderosa's president would relate to $11,000 more easily than to .736, the utility of that amount.) The decision analyst might prevent some unnecessary controversy by converting all expected utilities to their certainty equivalent amounts before showing the pruned tree to the decision maker.

UTILITY AND THE DECISION TO BUY INSURANCE

Earlier, we showed how the Bayes decision rule will ordinarily indicate that the greatest expected *monetary* payoff is achieved by not buying casualty insurance. But when *utility* payoffs are employed, that same procedure reaches the opposite conclusion: *Utility is maximized by buying the insurance.* This confirms the choices most of us have made in determining our own insurance needs.

To illustrate, we will return to our first insurance example. Suppose that Spiro Pyrophobis values the dollar changes in his assets according to the utility function in Figure 29-9. There we read the following values.

$$u(-\$40{,}000) = -200$$
$$u(\$0) = 0$$
$$u(-\$100) = -.25$$

Each act is a gamble. Buying insurance is a gamble having two identical outcomes in terms of dollar expenditure of $-\$100$, since the same amount applies whether or not there is a fire. Buying no insurance is a gamble having cash outcomes of $-\$40{,}000$ if there is a fire and $0 if there is no fire. The utilities for the respective acts are therefore the expected utilities for the corresponding gambles. We see from Table 29-2 that the expected utilities are $-.25$ for buying insurance and $-.40$ for not buying insurance. Since buying insurance has the higher utility, it must be preferred by the decision maker. Stated differently, the act "buy insurance" has the maximum expected utility payoff, so the Bayes decision rule indicates that this act is the optimal choice.

Thus, when we use utilities as payoff values, the Bayes decision rule indicates the "proper" result. However, this does not permit us to conclude that whenever utilities are used as payoffs, this criterion will lead to a decision to buy insurance.

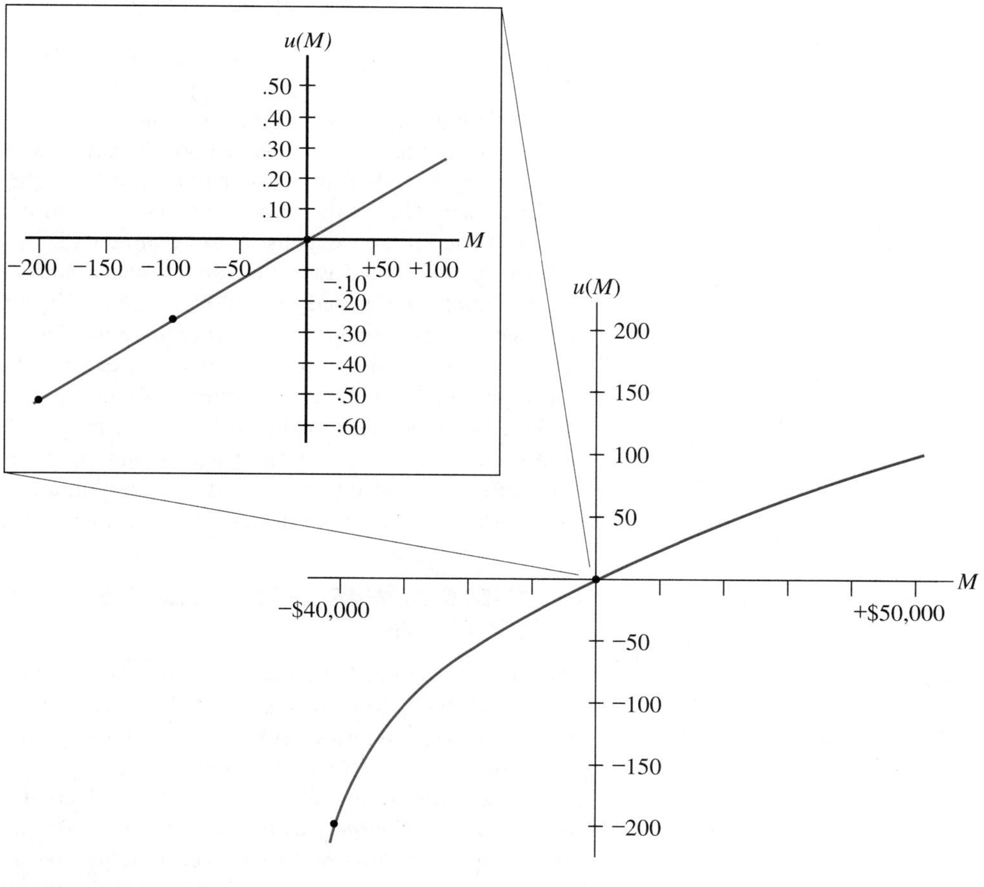

FIGURE 29-9 Utility function for Spiro Pyrophobis.

TABLE 29-2 Determination of Utilities for Outcomes of the Fire Insurance Decision and Calculation of Expected Utilities

(1) Event	(2) Probability	(3) Cash Change M	(4) Utility	(5) Utility × Probability
		Buy Insurance		
Fire	.002	−$100	−.25	−.0005
No fire	.998	−100	−.25	−.2495
			Expected utility =	−.2500
		Don't Buy Insurance		
Fire	.002	−$40,000	−200	−.40
No fire	.998	0	0	0
			Expected utility =	−.40

The choice depends on the relationship between the chance of fire and the price of the insurance policy. Suppose, for example, that the price of Spiro's policy is raised to $200, so that Figure 29-9 provides

$$u(-\$200) = -.50$$

The expected utility for buying insurance must therefore be −.50, so that if the probability for fire remains the same, the act "don't buy insurance" will have a utility of −.40, which is greater than −.50, making "don't buy insurance" the preferred act. This is the opposite outcome from our earlier decision. The insurance has become too expensive to be attractive.

Many people faced with the same circumstances would buy insurance even if the premium were raised to $1,000 or more. *Their tastes would be different and this would be reflected by the different utility values that they would assign to each outcome.* Premium prices may partly explain the prevalence of fire insurance coverage and the paucity of protection against natural disasters, such as earthquakes, tornados, and floods. One reason why people do not generally buy insurance policies to cover natural disasters is the high premium required by insurance companies for such coverage (if it is offered at all) in relation to the probabilities for occurrence (which are difficult to obtain actuarially for such rare phenomena).

ATTITUDES TOWARD RISK AND THE SHAPE OF THE UTILITY CURVE

The utility function for money may be used as the basis for describing an individual's attitudes toward risk. Three basic attitudes have been characterized. The polar cases are the **risk averter**, who will accept only favorable gambles, and the **risk seeker**, who will pay a premium for the privilege of participating in a gamble. Between these two extremes lies the **risk-neutral individual**, who considers the face value of money to be its true worth. The utility functions for each basic attitude appear in Figure 29-10. Each function has a particular shape, corresponding to the decision maker's fundamental outlook. All three utility functions show that utility increases with monetary gains. This reflects the underlying assumption of utility theory that utility increases with preference, which is combined with the

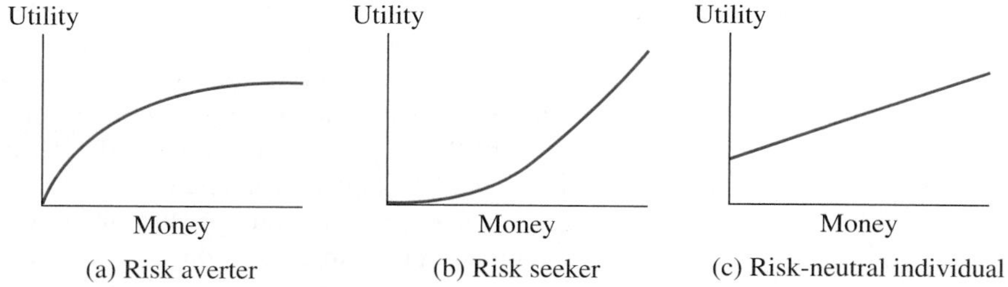

FIGURE 29-10 Utility functions for basic attitudes toward risk.

additional assumption that more money will always increase an individual's well-being, so that the outcomes with greater payoffs are preferred. (This assumption may not be strictly true, but with the exception of eccentrics, most people behave in a manner that supports it.)

THE RISK AVERTER

Throughout most of their lives, people are typically risk averters. These individuals buy plenty of casualty insurance. They avoid actions that involve high risks (chances of large monetary losses). Only gambles with high expected payoffs will be attractive to them. A risk averter's utility drops more and more severely as losses become larger, and the utilities for positive amounts do not grow as fast with monetary gains. The risk averter's marginal utility for money diminishes as the rewards increase, so that the risk averter's utility curve, shown in Figure 29-10(a), exhibits a decreasing positive slope as the level of monetary payoff becomes larger. Such a curve is *concave* when viewed from below.

THE RISK SEEKER

The risk seeker's behavior is the opposite of the risk averter's behavior. Many of us are risk seekers at some stage of our lives. This attitude is epitomized by the "high roller," who may behave recklessly and who is motivated by the possibility of achieving the maximum reward in any gamble. The risk seeker will prefer *some* gambles with negative expected monetary payoffs to maintaining the status quo. The greater the maximum reward, the more the risk seeker's behavior will diverge from the risk averter's behavior. The risk seeker is typically self-insured, believing that the risk is superior to forgoing money spent on premiums. The risk seeker's marginal utility for money is increasing: Each additional dollar provides a disproportionately greater sense of well-being. The loss of one more dollar is felt only slightly more severely for large absolute levels of loss than for small ones. Thus, the slope of the risk seeker's utility curve, shown in Figure 29-10(b), increases as the monetary change improves. This curve is *convex* when viewed from below.

THE RISK-NEUTRAL INDIVIDUAL

Our third characterization of attitude toward risk is the risk-neutral individual, who prizes money at its face value. The utility function for such an individual is a straight line, as shown in Figure 29-10(c). His or her utility for a gamble is equal to the utility for the expected monetary payoff. Risk-neutral individuals buy no casualty insurance, since the premium charge is greater than the expected loss. Risk-neutral behavior is epitomized by individuals who are enormously wealthy. The decisions of large corporations are often based on the Bayes decision rule applied directly to monetary payoffs, reflecting that increments in dollar assets are valued at their face amount.

In general, risk neutrality holds only over a limited range of money values. For example, many large firms do not carry casualty insurance, but almost all giant corporations will insure against extremely large losses—airlines buy hijacking insurance, for example. The same holds for individuals. Many risk-averse persons are risk-neutral when the stakes are small. The player in the World Series office pool falls into this category; losses are hardly noticeable, and winnings permit the individual to indulge in some luxury. (Small gambles may add spice to a person's life—they are a form of entertainment. Thus, a person might play poker with more skillful players, where the expected payoff would be negative, just for the fun of it.) That people are risk-neutral for small risks is illustrated by their car insurance purchases. Many generally risk-averse people carry deductible comprehensive coverage when they first purchase an automobile, and they usually keep only the liability coverage when their car gets old. Again, this reflects risk neutrality over a limited range of monetary outcomes. This behavior does not contradict the curve shapes in Figure 29-10(a) and (b), because each curve can be approximated by a straight line segment throughout a narrow monetary interval.

COMPOSITE ATTITUDES TOWARD RISK

Many people may be both risk averters and risk seekers, depending on the range of monetary values being considered. To an entrepreneur founding a business, the risks are very high—a lifetime's savings, plenty of hard work, burned career bridges, a heavy burden of debt, and a significant chance of bankruptcy. Those who embark on the hard road of self-employment may often be viewed as risk seekers. They are motivated primarily by the rewards—monetary and otherwise—of being their own boss. Once entrepreneurs become established and are viewed by peers as future pillars of the community, their attitudes toward risk will have evolved to a point where they may be characterized as risk averters. They are much more conservative (now that there is something to conserve), and probably no venture imaginable could persuade them to risk everything they own to further their wealth.

We conceive of an individual's attitudes varying between risk seeking and risk aversion over time. Usually a risk seeker has some definite goal or **aspiration level**, which may be achieved by obtaining a specific amount of money. A young sports enthusiast might be willing to participate in an unfair gamble if winning would provide sufficient cash for a down payment on a first motorcycle. The young professional may speculate in volatile stocks to try to earn enough money for a down payment on a fashionable home. To these risk seekers, losing is not much worse than maintaining the status quo. But once the goal is achieved, the risk seeker's outlook changes, and with a sated appetite, the risk seeker becomes a risk averter until some new goal enters the horizon.

A hybrid-shaped utility function might also occur for persons having few assets. For them, losing $5,000 may not be materially worse than losing a couple of thousand. Shirley Smart's utility function in Figure 29-11 illustrates this

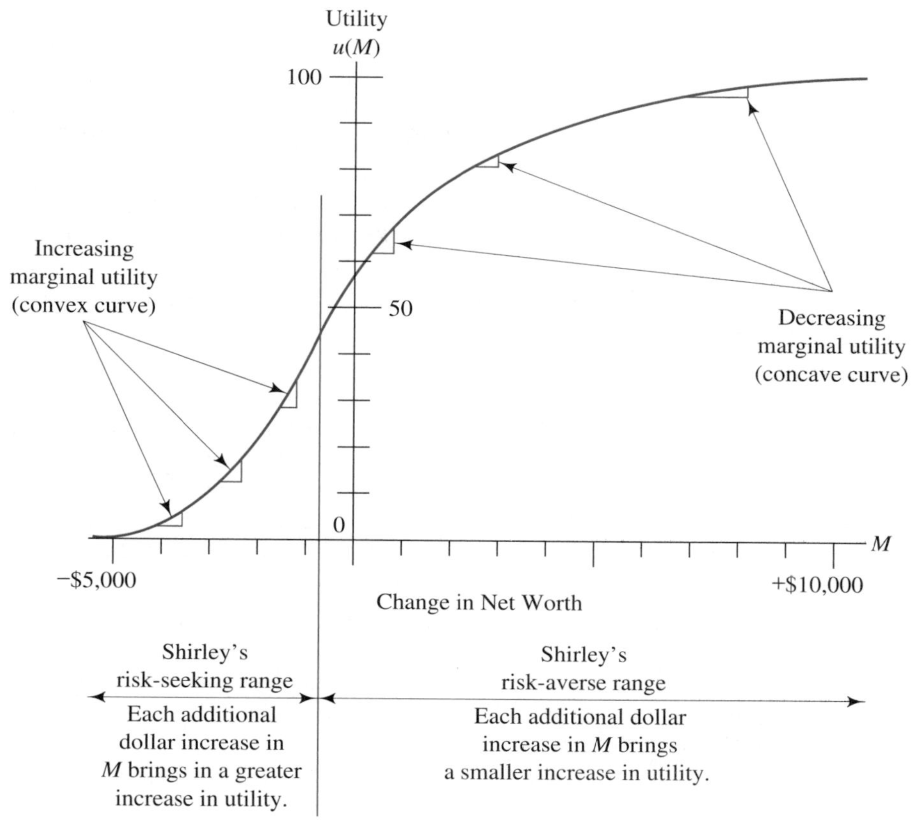

FIGURE 29-11 Shirley Smart's utility function illustrating simultaneous risk-seeking and risk-averse attitudes, depending on ranges of monetary outcomes.

commonly encountered shape. (In Section 29-6 we will see how this utility curve was constructed.) Somewhere around −$1,000, her utility function goes from convex to concave, and she moves from a risk-seeking posture to one of risk aversion for possible changes in her net worth above that level.

Regardless of the shape of a person's utility function, he or she will always find his or her preferred course of action by maximizing expected utility.

EXERCISES

29-7 A contractor must determine whether to buy or rent the equipment required to do a job up for bid. Because of lead-time requirements, he must decide whether to obtain the equipment before he knows if he has been awarded the contract. If he buys the equipment, the contract will result in $120,000 net profit after equipment resale returns, but if he loses the job, then the equipment will have to be sold at a $40,000 loss. By renting, his profit from the contract (if he wins it) will be only $50,000, but there will be no loss of money if the job is not won. The contractor's chances of winning are 50–50, and his utility function is $u(M) = \sqrt{M + 40{,}000}$.

(a) Construct the contractor's payoff table using profit as the payoff measure.
(b) Calculate the expected profit for each act. According to the Bayes decision rule, what act should the contractor select?
(c) Construct the contractor's payoff table using utilities as the payoff measure.
(d) Calculate the expected utility payoff for each act. Which act provides the maximum expected utility?
(e) Which act should the decision maker choose? Explain.

29-8 Suppose that the Ponderosa Record Company's utility function for money is $u(M) = [(M + 65{,}000)/10{,}000]^2$.
(a) Redraw Figure 29-8 (page 1141), and calculate the utility for each end position.
(b) Perform backward induction analysis using the new utilities you have calculated. What strategy is optimal?
(c) On a piece of graph paper, plot the utilities you calculated in (a) as a function of monetary payoffs M. Sketch a curve through the points. Of what attitude toward risk is the shape of your curve indicative?

29-9 Willy B. Rich wants his utility curve constructed for the change M in his net worth over the range from −\$10,000 to +\$20,000. He arbitrarily sets the respective utilities at 0 and 100. In response to queries regarding hypothetical gambles involving these amounts, Willy establishes the following equivalences.

Equivalent Amount	Probability for Winning \$20,000
−\$5,000	.60
0	.80
+10,000	.95

(a) Calculate his utilities for the above monetary amounts.
(b) On graph paper, sketch Willy's utility function.
(c) From your curve read Willy's utilities for the following changes in net worth.
(1) −\$2,000 (2) +\$2,000 (3) +\$5,000

29-10 Suppose that Alvin Black's attitude toward risk is generally averse. For each of the following 50–50 gambling propositions, indicate whether Alvin (1) would be willing, (2) might desire, or (3) would be unwilling to participate. Explain.
(a) \$10,000 versus \$0
(b) \$10,000 versus −\$1,000
(c) \$15,000 versus −\$10,000
(d) \$500 versus −\$600
(e) \$20,000 versus \$10,000

29-11 Lucille Brown is risk-neutral. Would she buy comprehensive coverage for her automobile if she agreed with company actuaries regarding the probability distribution for future claim sizes? Explain.

29-12 Victor White is a risk seeker. Does this necessarily imply that he will never buy casualty insurance? Explain.

29-6 CONSTRUCTING THE UTILITY FUNCTION

A person's utility function is easily constructed from the information gleaned in a short interview. The following example, involving two MBA students, illustrates how this may be done.

THE INTERVIEW METHOD

Guy Sharpe asks a few questions of Shirley Smart. Each involves a series of hypothetical win-lose gambles, with various dollar rewards; each time Shirley is asked to establish a win probability that would make her indifferent between the choices of gambling or accepting an intermediate amount. A range of monetary outcomes is used that Shirley, still a student, can relate to; the highest amount is +$10,000, with −$5,000 as the lowest. These two amounts serve as the outcomes of the initial reference lottery.

The interview proceeds as follows.

Guy Suppose that you are offered a gamble in which you will receive +$10,000 if you win and must forfeit $5,000 if you lose, so that losing results in a change in your net worth of −$5,000. For simplicity, let's keep this discussion on an "after-tax" basis.

Shirley That part is easy. I'm presently in the zero tax bracket. But where will I get the $5,000 if I lose?

Guy A special student loan will be arranged, and you can pay it back for five years after graduation. Interest will be prime plus 2%. Let's begin. You have signed a contract obligating you to participate in the gamble and to take the consequences.

Shirley Boy, am I glad this is not for real.

Guy You'll change your mind fast. *You get to pick the win probability*! Before we begin, I want to define the starting utility values. One utility value is arbitrarily given to each outcome of the gamble (reference lottery). These will define your utility scale. Under this scale, a change in your net worth of + $10,000 will have a utility of 100, and your utility for −$5,000 will be 0.

$$u(+\$10{,}000) = 100 \qquad u(-\$5{,}000) = 0$$

Shirley Why don't you use a negative value for the utility of 0?

Guy We could. But I make mistakes mixing positives and negatives. It really makes no difference. I also like the Fahrenheit temperature scale, which rarely goes negative in our city. It's hard to relate to the Celsius scale, with negatives throughout most of the winter. Our utility scale is totally arbitrary and has nothing to do with how you feel about risk, any more than our comfort is affected by where the marks are printed on our thermometer. I will be happy to change the utility benchmarks if you want.

Shirley I like your temperature scale analogy. I'm ready. Let's proceed.

Guy I'm going to plot the two values defining the "Shirley scale" as two points on a graph (see Figure 29-12). These points will lie on a curve that represents

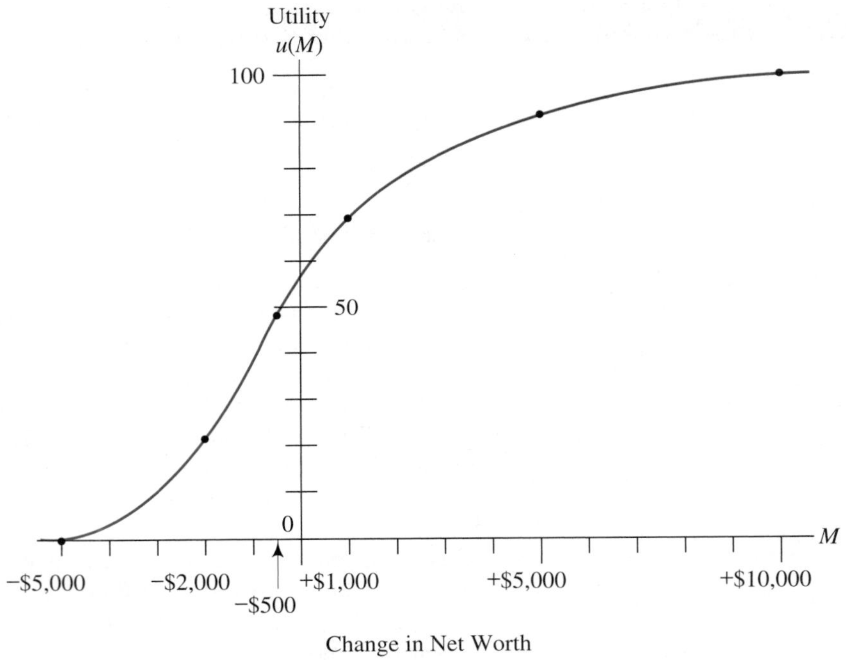

FIGURE 29-12 Shirley Smart's utilty function.

your utility function. We need only a few points to provide a detailed graphical description of your utility function. To help us keep track of things, I am going to designate our first reference lottery as gamble *A* (where you get +\$10,000 if you win and −\$5,000 if you lose).

Shirley I think I'm going to enjoy this.

Guy Now, suppose that you may exchange your contract for + \$1,000. If the gamble *A* probabilities were 50–50, would you do it?

Shirley Of course I would take the thousand. What have I got to lose by doing that?

Guy A crack at the \$10,000 gain. Let's adjust the odds a bit. Suppose that the probabilities are now .90 for winning and .10 for losing. Would you still take the + \$1,000, or would you keep the gamble contract?

Shirley Oh, I see. Golly, I think I would gamble. My expected payoff would be huge, and if I lose, I'll only have to pay \$100 a month for a few years. I'd definitely gamble.

Guy I hate to shatter the illusion, but I want to change the probabilities. I'm trying to find your point of indifference. Suppose that we reduce the win probability to .60 (increasing the lose probability to .40). How do you feel about the gamble now?

Shirley Awful! I'll take the thousand dollars and run.

Guy All right, let's raise the odds a bit. Suppose that the win probability is now .70. Would you gamble or take the thousand?

Shirley Wow, this is tough! I really would like the thousand, but the gamble is terribly appealing. I really don't know which I would take.

Guy Good. We have established your indifference win probability at $q = .70$. We now have a new point for your utility function graph. Your utility for the latest gamble is its expected utility.

$$\begin{aligned} u(\text{gamble } A \mid q = .70) &= .70u(+\$10{,}000) + .30u(-\$5{,}000) \\ &= .70(100) + .30(0) = 70 \end{aligned}$$

And, since you are indifferent between + \$1,000 and the gamble, they must have the same utility. Thus,

$$u(+\$1{,}000) = u(\text{gamble } A \mid q = .70) = 70$$

Shirley Amazing.

Guy Although we could stay with gamble *A* for the remainder of our interview, things would get a little stale. It will also be easier on you if we narrow the payoff range a little bit. Let's change the gamble to a new reference lottery involving +\$10,000 if you win and +\$1,000 if you lose. This is gamble *B*.

Shirley I'll take it. But who's dumb enough to offer me such a deal?

Guy You're jumping the gun. First of all, I have not told you the probability for winning. Secondly, you must remember that we are playing "let's pretend." We won't worry about whether or not the gamble will ever take place. If you prefer, think of me as emcee Monty Hall and imagine yourself as a contestant on "Let's Make a Deal."

Shirley As a kid, that was one of my favorite programs. I hope I don't win a goat. Fire away, Monty.

Guy Now, suppose that you may trade your rights to gamble *B* for a certain +\$5,000. The outcome will be determined by the toss of a coin.

Shirley I'll take the five thousand. Although the ten thousand looks mighty appealing, I wouldn't feel that much more comfortable with that than I would with five thousand.

Guy All right, now let's improve the gamble. The win probability is now .70. Do you still prefer not to gamble?

Shirley Yes, but we're close. Raise the win probability to .75 and I'll gamble.

Guy Your indifference win probability here is $q = .75$. We have another data point for your utility function. Using the utility value of 70 established earlier for +\$1,000, and using your latest indifference probability of .75, the following applies.

$$\begin{aligned} u(+\$5{,}000) = u(\text{gamble } B \mid q = .75) &= .75u(+\$10{,}000) + .25u(+\$1{,}000) \\ &= .75(100) + .25(70) \\ &= 92.5 \end{aligned}$$

Shirley I guess I said that.

Guy Now, Shirley, I'm sure you would prefer a goat to the following reference lottery, which we will label gamble *C*. If you lose, you end up with −\$5,000. If you win, you only get +\$1,000 this time. Suppose that you have to pay to get out of this one, and the price for doing so is \$500, so that you are looking at a change in your net worth of −\$500 if you don't gamble. Furthermore, the outcome will be determined by a coin toss.

Shirley I'll pay to get out of that one.

Guy Let's raise the odds a bit. Suppose that there is a 60 percent chance of winning. What would you do?

Shirley I would still pay.

Guy Okay, let me raise the win probability to .65.

Shirley I would be indifferent if the probability for winning were .70.

Guy Using $q = .70$, we now add one more point to our graph. Your utility for −\$500 is calculated as follows.

$$\begin{aligned} u(-\$500) = u(\text{gamble } C \mid q = .70) &= .70u(+\$1{,}000) + .30u(-\$5{,}000) \\ &= .70(70) + .30(0) \\ &= 49 \end{aligned}$$

We need one more point to completely specify your utility function. Consider gamble C one more time, but in comparison to being \$2,000 in the hole.

Shirley We've gone from bad to worse. I cannot even fathom such a situation.

Guy Well, you have a well-used car, which I guess would cost you about \$2,000 to replace.

Shirley That's right.

Guy Okay. Imagine that you will lose your car if you don't take gamble C.

Shirley I can't imagine how *I* could ever get into such a situation.

Guy Well, you signed a contract to participate in gamble C, and now the ante has been raised.

Shirley This is awful. All right, proceed.

Guy You've already indicated indifference between gamble C and − \$500 with a win probability of .70. Suppose that the odds are lowered to 50–50. Would you give up your car or gamble?

Shirley Being five thousand down is not much worse than being without a car. I would gamble, hoping to get out of the mess and be a thousand ahead.

Guy What if the win probability were only .10?

Shirley I would give up my car. The chance of getting out of hock would be too low. I think if you split the difference, giving me a win probability half way between those values, I might be indifferent. But I feel emotionally drained by all of this introspection. I don't think I can do another one of these gambles.

Guy Relax. We're finished playing "Let's Make a Deal." Using an indifference win probability of $q = .30$, you have established the following utility for −\$2,000.

$$\begin{aligned} u(-\$2{,}000) = u(\text{gamble } C \mid q = .30) &= .30u(+\$1{,}000) + .70u(-\$5{,}000) \\ &= .30(70) + .70(0) \\ &= 21 \end{aligned}$$

IMPLEMENTING THE UTILITY FUNCTION

Guy Sharpe completed Shirley Smart's utility graph, as shown in Figure 29-12. Shirley can use this curve in any personal decision analysis in which the payoffs fall between −$5,000 and +$10,000. A fresh utility function would be required for evaluating a decision with more extreme payoffs or if Shirley's attitudes change because of a new job or lifestyle change. Utility functions must be revised over time.

Utility functions are totally empirical. Only a few well spread out graphed points (three or four, plus the main reference lottery values) are required. As the above interview shows, it can be exasperating to get these points. The interviewer needs some skill, and the subjects must have patience and a willingness to let their minds be probed.

The intimacy of the interview process can inhibit implementation of utility functions in decision analysis, especially in organizations. A junior decision analyst should not expect to use this method on senior executives. An outside consultant would be in a stronger position to interview those decision makers.

This could be the major reason why there is not an extensive history of utility being applied in business decision making. Nevertheless, utility theory has compelling advantages. And, as we shall see, the theory is useful in generally qualifying decision analysis.

EXERCISES

29-13 J. P. Tidewasser has just undergone the first traumatic phase of determining his utility function for a range of money values. By his response to a series of gambles, it has been established that he is indifferent between making the 50–50 gambles on the left and receiving the certain amounts of money shown on the right.

Rewards of Gamble		Equivalent Amount
+ $30,000	− $10,000	$ 0
+ 30,000	0	+ 10,000
0	− 10,000	− 7,000
+ 10,000	− 7,000	1,000

(a) If J. P. sets $u(\$30{,}000) = 1$ and $u(-\$10{,}000) = 0$, determine his utility for $0.

(b) Calculate J. P.'s utilities for +$10,000 and − $7,000.

(c) Calculate J. P.'s utility for +1,000. What, if any, inconsistencies do you notice between this and your previous answers?

29-14 Conduct an interview with another person and construct a graph for the individual's utility function. Use changes in net worth ranging from a low of −$5,000 to a high of +$10,000. You may use any arbitrary utility scale. Ignore any tax implications.

29-15 Refer to the Spillsberry decision in Exercise 24-11 (page 980). The decision maker wants to maximize his expected utility. He arbitrarily assigns utilities of 100 to +$1,000,000 and −100 to −$300,000. Using these as the outcomes from his reference lottery, an interviewer found the following indifference probabilities for in-between amounts.

Amount	Indifference Probabililty
+\$500,000	.90
−\$100,000	.50
+\$200,000	.80

(a) Sketch the manager's utility function.
(b) Construct the manager's decision tree diagram. Then determine the monetary payoff for each end position.
(c) Determine the utility value for each end position. Then perform backward induction analysis to determine which course of action maximizes expected utility.

29-7 ATTITUDES TOWARD RISK AND VALUATION IN DECISION MAKING

The shape of a person's utility function fundamentally affects the relationships between utilities, expected payoffs, certainty equivalents, and risk premiums. We are ready to explore in detail those relationships, which are distinctly different, depending on the individual's underlying attitude toward risk.

THE RISK AVERTER

When all possible monetary outcomes fall in the decision maker's range of risk aversion, the following properties hold.

1. Expected payoffs (EP) are greater than their counterpart certainty equivalents (CE).
2. Expected utilities will be less than the utility of the respective expected monetary payoff.
3. Risk premiums ($RP = EP - CE$) are *positive.*

Figure 29-13 illustrates the above for Shirley Smart when evaluating gamble A for which there is a 50–50 chance for experiencing a change in her net worth by −\$500 or +\$2,000. Shirley's expected payoff for this gamble is

$$EP = .50(-\$500) + .50(\$2{,}000) = \$750 \quad (\text{gamble } A)$$

Her utility curve provides respective utilities of 49 and 78 for the gamble payoffs. Her expected utility for the gamble is thus,

$$\begin{aligned}\text{Expected utility} &= .50u(-\$500) + .50u(\$2{,}000)\\ &= .50(49) + .50(78)\\ &= 63.5 \quad (\text{gamble } A)\end{aligned}$$

The certainty equivalent for any gamble is that monetary amount such that

$$u(CE) = \text{Expected utility}$$

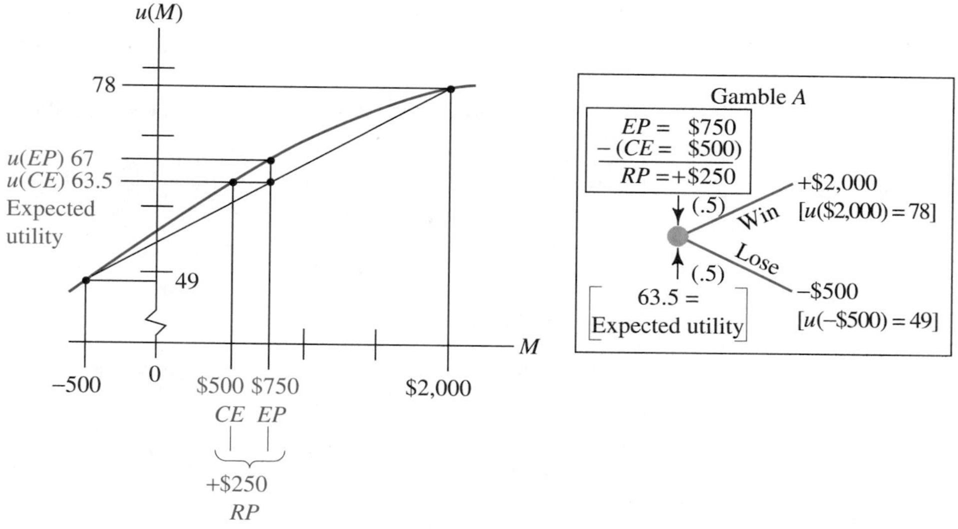

FIGURE 29-13 Illustration of the relationship between expected payoff, expected utility, certainty equivalent, and risk premium when Shirley Smart is risk averse.

Shirley Smart's utility curve achieves a height of 63.5 at M = $500, so that

$$u(\$500) = 63.5$$

This establishes her certainty equivalent for the gamble.

$$CE = \$500 \quad \text{(gamble } A\text{)}$$

Shirley's risk premium for the gamble is found by subtracting the certainty equivalent from the expected payoff.

$$RP = EP - CE = \$750 - \$500 = \$250$$

We may view Shirley's certainty equivalent valuation of the gamble as the discounted expected payoff,

$$CE = EP - RP = \$750 - \$250 = \$500$$

A similar result would apply to any gamble having outcomes falling in her risk-averse range.

Although the utility curve directly provides *CE*'s, these amounts will always equal that amount reached by discounting an individual's expected payoff by the amount of the risk premium (which will vary with the magnitude of the risk). As long as all monetary payoffs lie within the risk averse range, the above procedure should provide *positive RP*'s—even when all possibilities involve positive monetary payoffs.

To illustrate, consider gamble *B*, involving a coin toss that determines which of two positive payoffs will occur. A head provides Shirley with $5,000 [$u(\$5{,}000) = 92.5$] and a tail yields her only $1,000 [$u(\$1{,}000) = 70$]. Her expected utility is 81.25, which corresponds to a certainty equivalent of about \$2,500. The expected payoff is \$3,000, and Shirley's risk premium is

$$RP = EP - CE = \$3{,}000 - \$2{,}500 = \$500 \quad (\text{gamble } B)$$

Even though we would not ordinarily consider such a win-win situation as having risk, Shirley would still be willing to accept a discounted certain amount in lieu of gambling.

THE RISK SEEKER

When all possible monetary outcomes fall in the decision maker's risk-seeking range, the following properties hold.

1. Expected payoffs (EP) are less than their counterpart certainty equivalents (CE).
2. Expected utilities will be greater than the utility of the respective expected monetary payoff.
3. Risk premiums ($RP = EP - CE$) are *negative.*

Figure 29-14 illustrates the above for Shirley Smart when evaluating gamble C for which there is a 50–50 chance for experiencing a change in her net worth by $-\$4{,}000$ or $-\$1{,}000$. Shirley's expected payoff for this gamble is

$$EP = .50(-\$4{,}000) + .50(-\$1{,}000) = -\$2{,}500 \quad (\text{gamble } C)$$

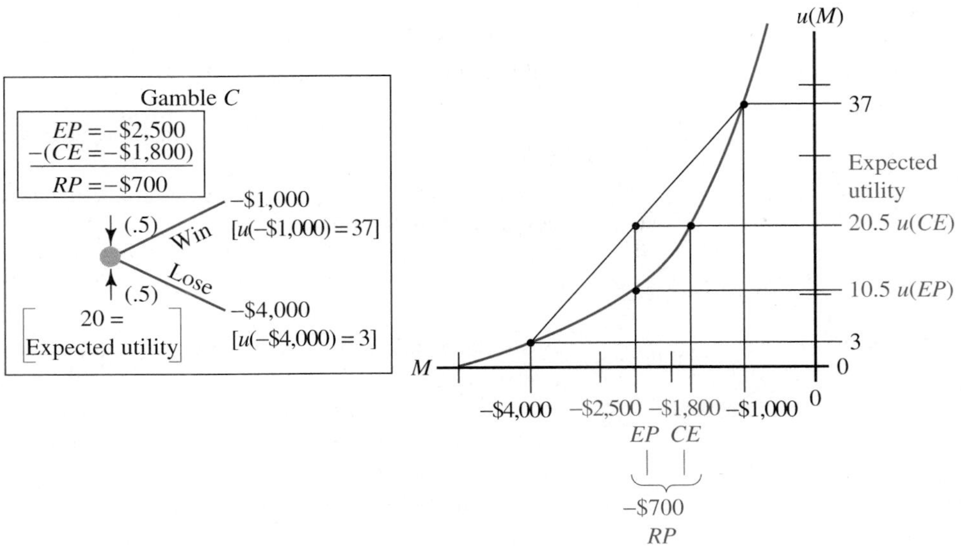

FIGURE 29-14 Illustration of the relationship between expected payoff, expected utiltiy, certainty equivalent, and risk premium when Shirley Smart is risk seeking.

Her utility curve provides respective utilities of 3 and 37 for the gamble payoffs. Her expected utility for the gamble is thus,

$$\begin{aligned}\text{Expected utility} &= .50u(-\$4{,}000) + .50u(-\$1{,}000)\\ &= .50(3) + .50(37)\\ &= 20 \quad (\text{gamble } C)\end{aligned}$$

Shirley's utility curve achieves a height of 20 at about $M = -\$1{,}800$, so that her certainty equivalent for the gamble is

$$CE = -\$1{,}800 \quad (\text{gamble } C)$$

Shirley's risk premium for the gamble is

$$RP = EP - CE = -\$2{,}500 - (-\$1{,}800) = -\$700$$

Here, Shirley's certainty equivalent valuation of the gamble implies that she would be indifferent between gambling and paying $1,800 to relieve herself of the obligation to do so. In effect, her *CE* may be reached by *adding* +$700 to the expected payoff.

$$CE = EP - RP = -\$2{,}500 - (-\$700) = -\$2{,}500 + \$700 = -\$1{,}800$$

Any gamble having monetary payoffs in Shirley's risk-seeking range will involve a similar negative risk premium.

This of course does not mean that Shirley likes gamble *C*. She would be willing to pay up to $1,800 not to have to undergo it. But that amount is $700 greater than the −$2,500 payoff she would expect by remaining with the gamble. In effect, her *valuation* of terrible gamble *C* is skewed in the opposite direction (vis-a-vis the expected payoff) to that which applies to favorable gambles *A* and *B*.

THE RISK-NEUTRAL INDIVIDUAL

The Ponderosa Record Company example shows how the decision maker's course of action can differ tremendously if he maximizes expected monetary payoff (as in Chapter 24) from what he would do by maximizing his expected utility. This is true when the decision maker is risk seeking or risk averse. That is not the case, however, for the risk-neutral person, whose payoff function graphs as a straight line. Such an individual will have an expected utility equal to the utility of the expected payoff. Risk-neutral persons will have certainty equivalents equal to their expected payoffs. In effect, their utility functions become superfluous.

DECISION MAKING WITH A NARROW PAYOFF RANGE

Paradoxically, regardless of shape, all utility functions are best approximated by a line segment over a narrow range of monetary outcomes. To see that this is so, look at Figure 29-12 and consider the shape of Shirley Smart's utility function from −$2,500 to −$2,000, from +$500 to +$1,000, or from +$8,000 to +$9,000. She would, in effect, be almost risk neutral over any of these intervals.

To verify this, let's compute her expected utility for a coin-toss gamble with payoffs of +\$500 and +\$1,000. Reading her curve in Figure 29-12, we have $u(+\$500) = 65$ and $u\ (+\$1{,}000) = 70$. Thus,

$$u(\text{coin toss}) = .50(65) + .50(70) = 67.5$$

Next, we find Shirley's expected monetary payoff from the gamble to be

$$.50(+\$500) + .50(+\$1{,}000) = \$750$$

Shirley's curve provides a utility value very close to 67.5 for getting \$750. In effect, the utility of the gamble is nearly equal to the utility of the gamble's expected monetary payoff. She is almost risk neutral over the gamble's range of monetary outcomes.

Since Shirley is nearly risk neutral over the narrow range of payoffs, her utility function would not really be needed to identify her most preferred course of action. This would be true of any decision where the possible payoffs are all close together. The original Bayes decision rule, maximize monetary payoff directly, would nicely find for her what action to take in those cases.

But how narrow must the monetary range be before the discrepancies between maximizing expected utility and maximizing expected monetary payoff matter? That depends on the individual and the particular utility function shape. And this partly depends on the individual's overall level of assets.

A teenager might feel comfortable with any gambling situation of ±\$5, while a college student's utility function might be linear over ±\$100. A young professional person might have a linear utility function over any change in net worth of ±\$1,000, while for a small business entrepreneur this might be ±\$2,000, and for an established professional, perhaps ±\$5,000 might be appropriate. For a corporate officer, we might find that linearity could be assumed over any range of bottom-line impact within ±\$10,000. For a chief executive, maybe ±\$1 million would work.

Utility theory is important because it permits us to do a better job at decision analysis, by explicitly incorporating risk attitude, but it implies much more than that.

RATIFYING THE BAYES DECISION RULE AND THE DELEGATION OF AUTHORITY

Utility theory implies that an individual always does the preferred thing when he or she maximizes utility. That will be achieved in any decision under uncertainty when *expected* utility is maximized. If we somehow do that, we will end up with a perfect tool for decision making.

Thus, *utility theory ratifies the original Bayes decision rule*, as long as the payoffs are limited to a *narrow range*. We need to know nothing about its shape; it will always be a straight line over a narrow monetary range. Maximizing expected monetary payoff in effect maximizes expected utility. And, since doing that maximizes utility itself, it will also indicate the preferred action. Using Bayes decision rule would, in those cases with original monetary payoffs, always lead to the best choice.

This allows managers to delegate routine decisions (ones having narrow monetary consequences) to others, with the prescription that expected payoff always be maximized. Only the decisions having extreme outcomes need to be evaluated with special care regarding attitude toward risk. Utility theory provides the rationale for delegation of decision-making authority.

EXERCISES

29-16 Refer to Shirley Smart's utility function in Figure 29-12 (page 1150). Shirley is faced with the following gambles.

(1) Gamble *V*		(2) Gamble *W*		(3) Gamble *Y*		(4) Gamble *Z*	
Prob.	**Payoff**	**Prob.**	**Payoff**	**Prob.**	**Payoff**	**Prob.**	**Payoff**
.90	+$5,000	.50	+$1,000	.75	+$4,000	.20	+$10,000
.10	−$5,000	.50	−$1,000	.25	−$1,000	.80	−$ 2,000

(a) Calculate Shirley's expected utilities for each gamble.
(b) Find Shirley's certainty equivalent for each gamble.
(c) Compute Shirley's expected monetary payoff for each gamble.
(d) For each gamble, subtract your answer to (b) from that for (c), to find Shirley's risk premium.

29-17 Refer to Exercise 29-15 and to your answers. Copy a fresh decision tree. Indicate for each node the expected monetary payoff, the certainty equivalent, and the risk premium. Prune your tree to maximize certainty equivalent.

SUMMARY

1. What is utility?
A **utility value** is a number that for any outcome conveys its worth to a particular individual. As such, it is the ultimate payoff measure, since by maximizing one's utility the most preferred choice will always be made. When the outcomes are monetary values, the utility values establish a **utility function**.

2. What is a typical characteristic of a utility function?
The St. Petersburg paradox establishes for most people that they have **decreasing marginal utility** for money. When plotted on a graph, their utility functions $u(M)$ will be steadily increasing as the levels for a change in their monetary net worth M become greater. That implies that additional wealth brings progressively less of an increase in one's sense of well-being, while reductions are felt severely.

3. What theoretical assumptions underlie utility?
A few assumptions establish an axiomatic theory of utility. Key among these is **preference ranking**, which is assumed possible for any collection of outcomes. Further axioms are **transitivity of preference, continuity, substitutability,** and **increasing preference.** These axioms allow us to find utility

values, using a **reference lottery** in which the best outcome would be achieved by winning and the worst outcome by losing.

4. **How are utility values found?**
According to the theory, a reference lottery win probability q can be selected for any outcome in such a way that an individual is indifferent between that outcome for certain and taking the lottery instead. In effect, the lottery is analogous to a thermometer that, instead of measuring temperature, gives a reading of how relatively well regarded an outcome is. That is done by computing the expected utility for the reference lottery, which establishes the utility value for the outcome being evaluated. The utility values so obtained will lie on a scale that is analogous to a temperature scale. The extreme outcome utilities are arbitrarily set at some level, just as the 0 and 100 degrees in Celsius arbitrarily represent freezing and boiling points of water. Utilities will vary from person to person due to (1) different reference lotteries and (2) different levels for the indifference probabilities.

5. **How do utility payoffs make the Bayes decision rule an ideal criterion?**
An ideal decision criterion is one that always picks the course of action preferred by the decision maker. When utility values serve as payoffs, the utility of an act is always equal to its expected utility. Thus, by applying the Bayes decision rule to such payoffs, maximizing expected payoff will always maximize utility. The preferred choices will always be made when that rule is employed.

6. **What basic attitudes toward risk are characterized by the shape of the utility curve?**
The utility function is monotonically increasing, which follows from the fact that more money is always better than less. But the rate of increase may vary. A **risk averter** will have a concave utility curve with decreasing slope (marginal utility) as the level of change in monetary net worth becomes larger. Such an individual will sometimes prefer a lesser certain amount to gambling, even though the gamble has greater expected monetary payoff, especially if the gamble could result in a loss. Risk averters are heavy buyers of casualty insurance. The **risk seeker** will have a slope that increases with the monetary amount and will often prefer unfavorable gambles to certain amounts exceeding the expected monetary payoff. He or she will often not buy casualty insurance. A **risk-neutral** individual will have a linear utility function; exactly the same acts will be chosen whether that person maximizes expected monetary payoff or, instead, maximizes expected utility. The shape of the utility function will depend on the particular range of monetary outcomes, and the same person can be a risk seeker over one range and a risk averter over another. When the range is very narrow, a straight line may be assumed for any individual's utility function.

7. **How do utilities relate to certainty equivalents?**
When the utility curve is read in reverse, the monetary amount corresponding to any expected utility is the **certainty equivalent**. It may be more meaningful to present the results of a decision analysis in terms of certainty equivalents rather than expected utilities. One gauge of risk at an event fork is the **risk premium**, which may be found by subtracting the certainty equivalent from the expected monetary payoff. The risk premium for a risk averter will be

positive, while it will be negative for a risk seeker and zero for a risk-neutral individual.

REVIEW EXERCISES

29-18 An insurance policy would cost Hermie Hawks $1,000 per year to protect his home from tornado damage. Assume that any actual tornado damage to Hermie's house, valued at $100,000, would be totally destructive and that the probability that a tornado will hit his house during the year is .0025.

(a) If Hermie is risk neutral, what would his optimal decision be regarding buying tornado insurance? Show your computations.

(b) How much above its expected claim size is the insurance company charging Hermie for its combined overhead and profit on the proposed policy?

(c) Hermie's utility function for any change in his monetary position for any amount M is

$$u(M) = 10{,}000 - (M/1{,}000)^2$$

What action should Hermie take to maximize his expected utility?

(d) What annual insurance premium charge would make Hermie indifferent between buying or not buying tornado insurance?

29-19 Hoopla Hoops is a retail boutique catering to current crazes. The owner must decide whether or not to stock a batch of Water Wheelies. Each item costs $2 and sells for $4. Unsold items cannot be returned to the supplier, who sells them in batches of 500. The following probability distribution is assumed to apply for the anticipated demand for Water Wheelies.

Demand	Probability
100	.05
200	.10
300	.15
400	.20
500	.20
600	.15
700	.10
800	.05
	1.00

Consider demand to mean the potential for sales. No more than what is demanded may be sold; but if demand exceeds on-hand inventory, then not all of the demand may be fulfilled.

(a) Calculate the expected demand. If you assume that the expected demand will actually occur, what profit corresponds to this amount? Use the utility curve shown in Figure 29-15 to determine the corresponding utility value.

(b) Calculate the expected profit from stocking 500 Water Wheelies. Does this differ from the amount you found in (a)? Explain this. Determine the utility for the expected profit.

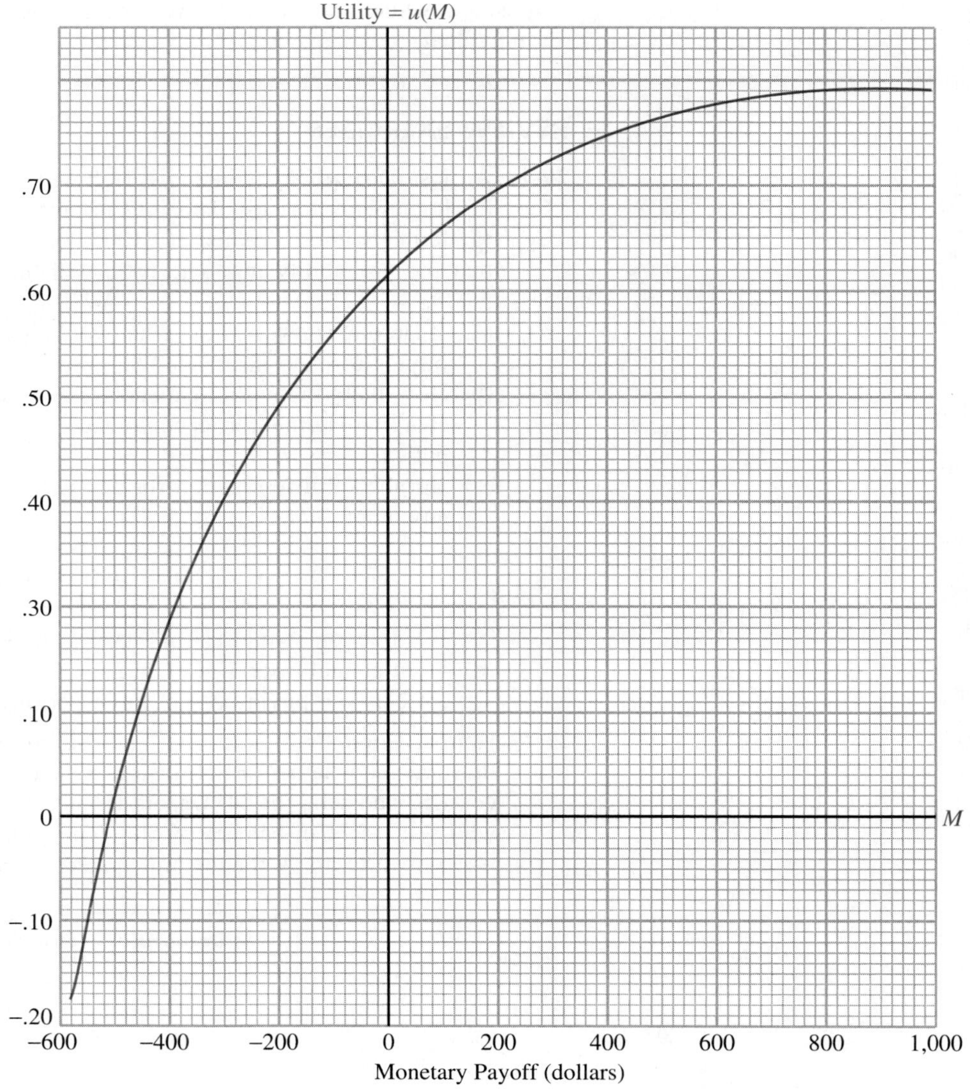

FIGURE 29-15 Utility function for Exercises 29-19 and 29-20.

(c) Calculate the expected utility for stocking 500 Water Wheelies. (First, calculate the profit for each level of possible demand; then, find the utility for each level; finally, apply the probability weights.) Which act—stocking or not stocking Water Wheelies—provides the greatest expected utility?

29-20 Consider the plight of the decision maker in Problem 24-10 (page 980). She must interview dozens of candidates annually for data entry jobs. Losses of her recoverable training expenses may therefore be significant. Suppose that she has constructed the utility function shown in Figure 29-15.

(a) Redraw Figure 24-5 (page 981).
(b) For the monetary payoff value for each end position, determine the decision maker's approximate utility value from the curve in Figure 29-15.
(c) Perform backward induction analysis using utilities as payoffs. Which strategy is optimal?

CASE Wendy Storm's Career Plans

Wendy Storm is a senior marketing major who must decide whether to go to graduate school for an MBA or to accept a full-time traveling sales position. Her major uncertainty about the MBA is whether she will successfully complete the program; she judges her chances of completion at .70. If she finishes the MBA, Wendy will apply for a consulting position, which she believes she will then get with a probability of .80; otherwise, she will take a position in corporate sales. Should Wendy not complete the MBA, she will have no recourse but to assume a traveling sales position—a year later than if she had gone to work immediately after graduation. Wendy believes there is a 50–50 chance she can move from a traveling job to corporate sales within one year after starting.

Listed in decreasing order of preference, the following outcomes apply to Wendy's decision.

MBA plus consulting
MBA plus corporate sales
Corporate sales, no graduate school
Corporate sales, unfinished MBA
Traveling sales position, early start
Traveling sales position, late start

Wendy arbitrarily assigns a utility value of 1,000 to the outcome "MBA plus consulting" and a utility value of 100 to "traveling sales position, late start." She would be indifferent between "MBA plus corporate sales" and a 50–50 gamble yielding those two outcomes. Using this same reference lottery, she would be indifferent between it and "corporate sales, no graduate school" if the probability for achieving the best outcome were .40. The stigma of failure would so taint the outcome, "corporate sales, unfinished MBA," that she would reduce her indifference probability to .20 for winning the reference lottery in exchange. Finally, she would be indifferent between the gamble and "traveling sales position, early start" if the probability of the best outcome were only .10.

QUESTIONS

1. Find Wendy's utility for the listed outcomes.
2. Construct Wendy's decision tree diagram, using utility payoffs.

3. What should Wendy do?
4. Interview a colleague who plays the role of Wendy Storm. Establish her utility function over the range of net change in her net worth from −\$5,000 to +\$10,000. Plot the results on a graph.
5. Determine from your graph "Wendy Storm's" (1) expected utility and (2) certainty equivalent for each of the following situations.
   (a) Fair coin toss: −\$500 if tails and +\$1,000 if heads.
   (b) Lottery: +\$5,000 if won (probability .10) and \$0 if lost.
   (c) Investment: +\$10,000 if success (probability .20) and −\$2,000 if failure.

SELECTED REFERENCES

The Role of Statistics

Careers in Statistics. The American Statistical Association (no date available).

Huff, Darrell. *How to Lie with Statistics.* New York: W. W. Norton, 1954.

Moroney, M. J. *Facts from Figures.* Baltimore: Penguin Books, 1952.

Reichmann, W. J. *Use and Abuse of Statistics.* New York: Oxford University Press, 1962.

Wallis, W. A. and H. V. Roberts. *The Nature of Statistics.* New York: The Free Press, 1965.

Probability

Feller, William. *An Introduction to Probability Theory and Its Applications,* Vol. 1, 3rd. ed. New York: John Wiley & Sons, 1968.

Hodges, J. L., Jr., and E. L. Lehmann. *Elements of Finite Probability.* San Francisco: Holden-Day, 1965.

Laplace, Pierre Simon, Marquis de. *A Philosophical Essay on Probabilities.* New York: Dover Publications, 1951.

Mosteller, F., R. Rourke, and G. Thomas, Jr. *Probability and Statistics.* Reading, Mass.: Addison-Wesley, 1961.

Parzen, Emanuel. *Modern Probability Theory and Its Applications.* New York: John Wiley & Sons, 1960.

Regression and Correlation Analysis

Ezekiel, Mordecai, and Karl A. Fox. *Methods of Correlation and Regression Analysis,* 3rd ed. New York: John Wiley & Sons, 1959.

Johnston, John. *Econometric Methods,* 2nd ed. New York: McGraw-Hill, 1971.

Neter, John, and William Wasserman. *Applied Linear Statistical Models,* 3rd ed. Homewood, Ill.: Richard D. Irwin, 1990.

Williams, E.J. *Regression Analysis.* New York: John Wiley & Sons, 1959.

Wonnacott, Ronald J., and Thomas H. Wonnacott, *Econometrics,* 2nd ed. New York: John Wiley & Sons, 1979.

Time Series Analysis and Index Numbers

Brown, Robert G. *Smoothing, Forecasting and Prediction of Discrete Time Series,* Englewood Cliffs, N.J.: Prentice-Hall, 1963.

Makridakis, S., and S. C. Wheelright. *Forecasting: Methods and Applications,* 2nd ed. New York: John Wiley & Sons, 1983.

———. *Interactive Forecasting: Univariate and Multivariate Methods,* 2nd ed. San Francisco: Holden-Day, 1978.

McKinley, David H., Murray G. Lee, and Helene Duffy. *Forecasting Business Conditions.* The American Bankers Association, 1965.

Mudgett, Bruce D. *Index Numbers,* New York: John Wiley & Sons, 1951.

Spencer, Milton H., Colin G. Clark, and Peter W. Hoguet. *Business and Economic Forecasting: An Econometric Approach.* Homewood, Ill.: Richard D. Irwin, 1965.

Analysis of Variance and Design of Experiments

Cochran, William G., and Gertrude M. Cox. *Experimental Designs,* 2nd ed. New York: John Wiley & Sons, 1957.

Cox, David R. *Planning of Experiments.* New York: John Wiley & Sons, 1958.

Guenther, W. C. *Analysis of Variance.* Englewood Cliffs, N.J.: Prentice-Hall, 1964.

Mendenhall, William. *An Introduction to Linear Models and the Design and Analysis of Experiments.* Belmont, Calif.: Wadsworth, 1968.

Neter, John, and William Wasserman. *Applied Linear Statistical Models,* 3rd ed. Homewood, Ill.: Richard D. Irwin, 1990.

Scheffé, Henry. *The Analysis of Variance.* New York: John Wiley & Sons, 1959.

Nonparametric Statistics

Bradley, James V. *Distribution-Free Statistical Tests.* Englewood Cliffs, N.J.: Prentice-Hall, 1968.

Conover, W. J. *Practical Nonparametric Statistics,* 2nd ed. New York: John Wiley & Sons, 1980.

Gibbons, Jean D. *Nonparametric Statistical Inference.* New York: McGraw-Hill, 1970.

Hájek, Jaroslav, *Nonparametric Statistics.* San Francisco: Holden-Day, 1969.

Kraft, Charles H., and Constance van Eeden. *A Nonparametric Introduction to Statistics.* New York: Macmillan, 1968.

Noether, Gottfried E. *Introduction to Statistics: A Nonparametric Approach,* 2nd ed. Boston: Houghton Mifflin, 1976.

Siegel, Sidney. *Nonparametric Statistics for the Behavioral Sciences.* New York: McGraw-Hill, 1956.

Statistical Quality Control

Deming, W. E. *Some Theory of Sampling.* New York: Dover, 1984.

Dodge, H. F., and H. G. Romig. *Sampling Inspection Tables—Single and Double Sampling,* 2nd ed. New York: John Wiley & Sons, 1959.

Enrick, N. L. *Quality Control and Reliability,* 5th ed. New York: The Industrial Press, 1966.

Grant, Eugene L., and Richard S. Leavenworth. *Statistical Quality Control,* 5th ed. New York: McGraw-Hill, 1979.

Juran, J. M. (ed.). *Quality Control Handbook,* 4th ed. New York: McGraw-Hill, 1988.

Wadsworth, Harrison M., Kenneth S. Stephens, and B. Blanton Godfrey. *Modern Methods for Quality Control and Improvement.* New York: John Wiley & Sons, 1986.

Decision Theory and Utility

Chernoff, Herman, and L. E. Moses. *Elementary Decision Theory.* New York: Dover, 1986.

Jones, J. Morgan. *Introduction to Decision Theory.* Homewood, Ill.: Richard D. Irwin, 1977.

Luce, R.D., and H. Raiffa. *Games and Decisions.* New York: John Wiley & Sons, 1957.

Miller, David W., and M. K. Starr. *Executive Decisions and Operations Research,* 2nd ed. Englewood Cliffs, N.J.: Prentice-Hall, 1969.

Morris, W. T. *Management Science: A Bayesian Introduction.* Englewood Cliffs, N.J.: Prentice-Hall, 1968.

Pratt, J. W., H. Raiffa, annd R. Schlaifer. *Introduction to Statistical Decision Theory.* New York: McGraw-Hill, 1965.

Raiffa, H. *Decision Analysis: Introductory Lectures on Choices Under Uncertainty.* New York: Random House, 1986.

Schlaifer, R. *Analysis of Decisions Under Uncertainty.* New York: McGraw-Hill, 1969.

———. *Introduction to Statistics for Business Decisions.* Melbourne, Florida: Robert E. Krieger Publishing Co., Inc., 1982.

Statistical Tables

Beyer, William H. (ed.). *Handbook of Tables for Probability and Statistics,* 2nd ed. Cleveland, Ohio: The Chemical Rubber Co., 1968.

Burington, Richard S., and Donald C. May. *Handbook of Probability and Statistics with Tables,* 2nd ed. New York: McGraw-Hill, 1970.

Fisher, Ronald A., and F. Yates. *Statistical Tables for Biological, Agricultural and Medical Research,* 6th ed. London: Longman Group, 1978.

National Bureau of Standards. *Tables of the Binomial Distribution.* Washington, D.C.: U.S. Government Printing Office, 1950.

Owen, D. B. *Handbook of Statistical Tables.* Reading, Mass.: Addison-Wesley, 1962.

Pearson, E. S., and H. O. Hartley, eds. *Biometrika Tables for Statisticians,* 3rd ed. Monticello, N.Y.: Lubrecht & Cramer, 1976.

The Rand Corporation. *A Million Random Digits with* 100,000 *Normal Deviates.* New York: The Free Press, 1955.

APPENDIX

TABLE A Four-Place Common Logarithms

											Proportional Parts								
N	**0**	**1**	**2**	**3**	**4**	**5**	**6**	**7**	**8**	**9**	**1**	**2**	**3**	**4**	**5**	**6**	**7**	**8**	**9**
10	0000	0043	0086	0128	0170	0212	0253	0294	0334	0374	4	8	12	17	21	25	29	33	37
11	0414	0453	0492	0531	0569	0607	0645	0682	0719	0755	4	8	11	15	19	23	26	30	34
12	0792	0828	0864	0899	0934	0969	1004	1038	1072	1106	3	7	10	14	17	21	24	28	31
13	1139	1173	1206	1239	1271	1303	1335	1367	1399	1430	3	6	10	13	16	19	23	26	29
14	1461	1492	1523	1553	1584	1614	1644	1673	1703	1732	3	6	9	12	15	18	21	24	27
15	1761	1790	1818	1847	1875	1903	1931	1959	1987	2014	3	6	8	11	14	17	20	22	25
16	2041	2068	2095	2122	2148	2175	2201	2227	2253	2279	3	5	8	11	13	16	18	21	24
17	2304	2330	2355	2380	2405	2430	2455	2480	2504	2529	2	5	7	10	12	15	17	20	22
18	2553	2577	2601	2625	2648	2672	2695	2718	2742	2765	2	5	7	9	12	14	16	19	21
19	2788	2810	2833	2856	2878	2900	2923	2945	2967	2989	2	4	7	9	11	13	16	18	20
20	3010	3032	3054	3075	3096	3118	3139	3160	3181	3201	2	4	6	8	11	13	15	17	19
21	3222	3243	3263	3284	3304	3324	3345	3365	3385	3404	2	4	6	8	10	12	14	16	18
22	3424	3444	3464	3483	3502	3522	3541	3560	3579	3598	2	4	6	8	10	12	14	15	17
23	3617	3636	3655	3674	3692	3711	3729	3747	3766	3784	2	4	6	7	9	11	13	15	17
24	3802	3820	3838	3856	3874	3892	3909	3927	3945	3962	2	4	5	7	9	11	12	14	16
25	3979	3997	4014	4031	4048	4065	4082	4099	4116	4133	2	3	5	7	9	10	12	14	15
26	4150	4166	4183	4200	4216	4232	4249	4265	4281	4298	2	3	5	7	8	10	11	13	15
27	4314	4330	4346	4362	4378	4393	4409	4425	4440	4456	2	3	5	6	8	9	11	13	14
28	4472	4487	4502	4518	4533	4548	4564	4579	4594	4609	2	3	5	6	8	9	11	12	14
29	4624	4639	4654	4669	4683	4698	4713	4728	4742	4757	1	3	4	6	7	9	10	12	13
30	4771	4786	4800	4814	4829	4843	4857	4871	4886	4900	1	3	4	6	7	9	10	11	13
31	4914	4928	4942	4955	4969	4983	4997	5011	5024	5038	1	3	4	6	7	8	10	11	12
32	5051	5065	5079	5092	5105	5119	5132	5145	5159	5172	1	3	4	5	7	8	9	11	12
33	5185	5198	5211	5224	5237	5250	5263	5276	5289	5302	1	3	4	5	6	8	9	10	12
34	5315	5328	5340	5353	5366	5378	5391	5403	5416	5428	1	3	4	5	6	8	9	10	11
35	5441	5453	5465	5478	5490	5502	5514	5527	5539	5551	1	2	4	5	6	7	9	10	11
36	5563	5575	5587	5599	5611	5623	5635	5647	5658	5670	1	2	4	5	6	7	8	10	11
37	5682	5694	5705	5717	5729	5740	5752	5763	5775	5786	1	2	3	5	6	7	8	9	10
38	5798	5809	5821	5832	5843	5855	5866	5877	5888	5899	1	2	3	5	6	7	8	9	10
39	5911	5922	5933	5944	5955	5966	5977	5988	5999	6010	1	2	3	4	5	7	8	9	10
40	6021	6031	6042	6053	6064	6075	6085	6096	6107	6117	1	2	3	4	5	6	8	9	10
41	6128	6138	6149	6160	6170	6180	6191	6201	6212	6222	1	2	3	4	5	6	7	8	9
42	6232	6243	6253	6263	6274	6284	6294	6304	6314	6325	1	2	3	4	5	6	7	8	9
43	6335	6345	6355	6365	6375	6385	6395	6405	6415	6425	1	2	3	4	5	6	7	8	9
44	6435	6444	6454	6464	6474	6484	6493	6503	6513	6522	1	2	3	4	5	6	7	8	9
45	6532	6542	6551	6561	6571	6580	6590	6599	6609	6618	1	2	3	4	5	6	7	8	9
46	6628	6637	6646	6656	6665	6675	6684	6693	6702	6712	1	2	3	4	5	6	7	7	8
47	6721	6730	6739	6749	6758	6767	6776	6785	6794	6803	1	2	3	4	5	5	6	7	8
48	6812	6821	6830	6839	6848	6857	6866	6875	6884	6893	1	2	3	4	4	5	6	7	8
49	6902	6911	6920	6928	6937	6946	6955	6964	6972	6981	1	2	3	4	4	5	6	7	8
50	6990	6998	7007	7016	7024	7033	7042	7050	7059	7067	1	2	3	3	4	5	6	7	8
51	7076	7084	7093	7101	7110	7118	7126	7135	7143	7152	1	2	3	3	4	5	6	7	8
52	7160	7168	7177	7185	7193	7202	7210	7218	7226	7235	1	2	2	3	4	5	6	7	7
53	7243	7251	7259	7267	7275	7284	7292	7300	7308	7316	1	2	2	3	4	5	6	6	7
54	7324	7332	7340	7348	7356	7364	7372	7380	7388	7396	1	2	2	3	4	5	6	6	7
N	**0**	**1**	**2**	**3**	**4**	**5**	**6**	**7**	**8**	**9**	**1**	**2**	**3**	**4**	**5**	**6**	**7**	**8**	**9**

TABLE A ***(continued)***

											Proportional Parts								
N	**0**	**1**	**2**	**3**	**4**	**5**	**6**	**7**	**8**	**9**	**1**	**2**	**3**	**4**	**5**	**6**	**7**	**8**	**9**
55	7404	7412	7419	7427	7435	7443	7451	7459	7466	7474	1	2	2	3	4	5	5	6	7
56	7482	7490	7497	7505	7513	7520	7528	7536	7543	7551	1	2	2	3	4	5	5	6	7
57	7559	7566	7574	7582	7589	7597	7604	7612	7619	7627	1	2	2	3	4	5	5	6	7
58	7634	7642	7649	7657	7664	7672	7679	7686	7694	7701	1	1	2	3	4	4	5	6	7
59	7709	7716	7723	7731	7738	7745	7752	7760	7767	7774	1	1	2	3	4	4	5	6	7
60	7782	7789	7796	7803	7810	7818	7825	7832	7839	7846	1	1	2	3	4	4	5	6	6
61	7853	7860	7868	7875	7882	7889	7896	7903	7910	7917	1	1	2	3	4	4	5	6	6
62	7924	7931	7938	7945	7952	7959	7966	7973	7980	7987	1	1	2	3	3	4	5	6	6
63	7993	8000	8007	8014	8021	8028	8035	8041	8048	8055	1	1	2	3	3	4	5	5	6
64	8062	8069	8075	8082	8089	8096	8102	8109	8116	8122	1	1	2	3	3	4	5	5	6
65	8129	8136	8142	8149	8156	8162	8169	8176	8182	8189	1	1	2	3	3	4	5	5	6
66	8195	8202	8209	8215	8222	8228	8235	8241	8248	8254	1	1	2	3	3	4	5	5	6
67	8261	8267	8274	8280	8287	8293	8299	8306	8312	8319	1	1	2	3	3	4	5	5	6
68	8325	8331	8338	8344	8351	8357	8363	8370	8376	8382	1	1	2	3	3	4	4	5	6
69	8388	8395	8401	8407	8414	8420	8426	8432	8439	8445	1	1	2	2	3	4	4	5	6
70	8451	8457	8463	8470	8476	8482	8488	8494	8500	8506	1	1	2	2	3	4	4	5	6
71	8513	8519	8525	8531	8537	8543	8549	8555	8561	8567	1	1	2	2	3	4	4	5	5
72	8573	8579	8585	8591	8597	8603	8609	8615	8621	8627	1	1	2	2	3	4	4	5	5
73	8633	8639	8645	8651	8657	8663	8669	8675	8681	8686	1	1	2	2	3	4	4	5	5
74	8692	8698	8704	8710	8716	8722	8727	8733	8739	8745	1	1	2	2	3	4	4	5	5
75	8751	8756	8762	8768	8774	8779	8785	8791	8797	8802	1	1	2	2	3	3	4	5	5
76	8808	8814	8820	8825	8831	8837	8842	8848	8854	8859	1	1	2	2	3	3	4	5	5
77	8865	8871	8876	8882	8887	8893	8899	8904	8910	8915	1	1	2	2	3	3	4	4	5
78	8921	8927	8932	8938	8943	8949	8954	8960	8965	8971	1	1	2	2	3	3	4	4	5
79	8976	8982	8987	8993	8998	9004	9009	9015	9020	9025	1	1	2	2	3	3	4	4	5
80	9031	9036	9042	9047	9053	9058	9063	9069	9074	9079	1	1	2	2	3	3	4	4	5
81	9085	9090	9096	9101	9106	9112	9117	9122	9128	9133	1	1	2	2	3	3	4	4	5
82	9138	9143	9149	9154	9159	9165	9170	9175	9180	9186	1	1	2	2	3	3	4	4	5
83	9191	9196	9201	9206	9212	9217	9222	9227	9232	9238	1	1	2	2	3	3	4	4	5
84	9243	9248	9253	9258	9263	9269	9274	9279	9284	9289	1	1	2	2	3	3	4	4	5
85	9294	9299	9304	9309	9315	9320	9325	9330	9335	9340	1	1	2	2	3	3	4	4	5
86	9345	9350	9355	9360	9365	9370	9375	9380	9385	9390	1	1	2	2	3	3	4	4	5
87	9395	9400	9405	9410	9415	9420	9425	9430	9435	9440	0	1	1	2	2	3	3	4	4
88	9445	9450	9455	9460	9465	9469	9474	9479	9484	9489	0	1	1	2	2	3	3	4	4
89	9494	9499	9504	9509	9513	9518	9523	9528	9533	9538	0	1	1	2	2	3	3	4	4
90	9542	9547	9552	9557	9562	9566	9571	9576	9581	9586	0	1	1	2	2	3	3	4	4
91	9590	9595	9600	9605	9609	9614	9619	9624	9628	9633	0	1	1	2	2	3	3	4	4
92	9638	9643	9647	9652	9657	9661	9666	9671	9675	9680	0	1	1	2	2	3	3	4	4
93	9685	9689	9694	9699	9703	9708	9713	9717	9722	9727	0	1	1	2	2	3	3	4	4
94	9731	9736	9741	9745	9750	9754	9759	9763	9768	9773	0	1	1	2	2	3	3	4	4
95	9777	9782	9786	9791	9795	9800	9805	9809	9814	9818	0	1	1	2	2	3	3	4	4
96	9823	9827	9832	9836	9841	9845	9850	9854	9859	9863	0	1	1	2	2	3	3	4	4
97	9868	9872	9877	9881	9886	9890	9894	9899	9903	9908	0	1	1	2	2	3	3	4	4
98	9912	9917	9921	9926	9930	9934	9939	9943	9948	9952	0	1	1	2	2	3	3	4	4
99	9956	9961	9965	9969	9974	9978	9983	9987	9991	9996	0	1	1	2	2	3	3	3	4
N	**0**	**1**	**2**	**3**	**4**	**5**	**6**	**7**	**8**	**9**	**1**	**2**	**3**	**4**	**5**	**6**	**7**	**8**	**9**

TABLE B
Random Numbers

12651	61646	11769	75109	86996	97669	25757	32535	07122	76763
81769	74436	02630	72310	45049	18029	07469	42341	98173	79260
36737	98863	77240	76251	00654	64688	09343	70278	67331	98729
82861	54371	76610	94934	72748	44124	05610	53750	95938	01485
21325	15732	24127	37431	09723	63529	73977	95218	96074	42138
74146	47887	62463	23045	41490	07954	22597	60012	98866	90959
90759	64410	54179	66075	61051	75385	51378	08360	95946	95547
55683	98078	02238	91540	21219	17720	87817	41705	95785	12563
79686	17969	76061	83748	55920	83612	41540	86492	06447	60568
70333	00201	86201	69716	78185	62154	77930	67663	29529	75116
14042	53536	07779	04157	41172	36473	42123	43929	50533	33437
59911	08256	06596	48416	69770	68797	56080	14223	59199	30162
62368	62623	62742	14891	39247	52242	98832	69533	91174	57979
57529	97751	54976	48957	74599	08759	78494	52785	68526	64618
15469	90574	78033	66885	13936	42117	71831	22961	94225	31816
18625	23674	53850	32827	81647	80820	00420	63555	74489	80141
74626	68394	88562	70745	23701	45630	65891	58220	35442	60414
11119	16519	27384	90199	79210	76965	99546	30323	31664	22845
41101	17336	48951	53674	17880	45260	08575	49321	36191	17095
32123	91576	84221	78902	82010	30847	62329	63898	23268	74283
26091	68409	69704	82267	14751	13151	93115	01437	56945	89661
67680	79790	48462	59278	44185	29616	76531	19589	83139	28454
15184	19260	14073	07026	25264	08388	27182	22557	61501	67481
58010	45039	57181	10238	36874	28546	37444	80824	63981	39942
56425	53996	86245	32623	78858	08143	60377	42925	42815	11159
82630	84066	13592	60642	17904	99718	63432	88642	37858	25431
14927	40909	23900	48761	44860	92467	31742	87142	03607	32059
23740	22505	07489	85986	74420	21744	97711	36648	35620	97949
32990	97446	03711	63824	07953	85965	87089	11687	92414	67257
05310	24058	91946	78437	34365	82469	12430	84754	19354	72745
21839	39937	27534	88913	49055	19218	47712	67677	51889	70926
08833	42549	93981	94051	28382	83725	72643	64233	97252	17133
58336	11139	47479	00931	91560	95372	97642	33856	54825	55680
62032	91144	75478	47431	52726	30289	42411	91886	51818	78292
45171	30557	53116	04118	58301	24375	65609	85810	18620	49198
91611	62656	60128	35609	63698	78356	50682	22505	01692	36291
55472	63819	86314	49174	93582	73604	78614	78849	23096	72825
18573	09729	74091	53994	10970	86557	65661	41854	26037	53296
60866	02955	90288	82136	83644	94455	(6560	78029	98768	71296
45043	55608	82767	60890	74646	79485	13619	98868	40857	19415
17831	09737	79473	75945	28394	79334	70577	38048	03607	06932
40137	03981	07585	18128	11178	32601	27994	05641	22600	86064
77776	31343	14576	97706	16039	47517	43300	59080	80392	63189
69605	44104	40103	95635	05635	81673	68657	09559	23510	95875
19916	52934	26499	09821	87331	80993	61299	36979	73599	35055
02606	58552	07678	56619	65325	30705	99582	53390	46357	13244
65183	73160	87131	35530	47946	09854	18080	02321	05809	04898
10740	98914	44916	11322	89717	88189	30143	52687	19420	60061
98642	89822	71691	51573	83666	61642	46683	33761	47542	23551
60139	25601	93663	25547	02654	94829	48672	28736	84994	13071

SOURCE: The Rand Corporation. *A Million Random Digits with 100,000 Normal Deviates.* New York: The Free Press, 1955. Reproduced with permission of The Rand Corporation.

TABLE C
Cumulative Values for the Binomial Probability Distribution

Pr[R ≤ *r*]

n = 1

r	*r/n*	π .01	.05	.10	.20	.30	.40	.50
0	.00	0.9900	0.9500	0.9000	0.8000	0.7000	0.6000	0.5000
1	1.00	1.0000	1.0000	1.0000	1.0000	1.0000	1.0000	1.0000

n = 2

r	*r/n*	π .01	.05	.10	.20	.30	.40	.50
0	.00	0.9801	0.9025	0.8100	0.6400	0.4900	0.3600	0.2500
1	.50	0.9999	0.9975	0.9900	0.9600	0.9100	0.8400	0.7500
2	1.00	1.0000	1.0000	1.0000	1.0000	1.0000	1.0000	1.0000

n = 3

r	*r/n*	π .01	.05	.10	.20	.30	.40	.50
0	.00	0.9703	0.8574	0.7290	0.5120	0.3430	0.2160	0.1250
1	.33	0.9997	0.9927	0.9720	0.8960	0.7840	0.6480	0.5000
2	.67	1.0000	0.9999	0.9990	0.9920	0.9730	0.9360	0.8750
3	1.00	1.0000	1.0000	1.0000	1.0000	1.0000	1.0000	1.0000

n = 4

r	*r/n*	π .01	.05	.10	.20	.30	.40	.50
0	.00	0.9606	0.8145	0.6561	0.4096	0.2401	0.1296	0.0625
1	.25	0.9994	0.9860	0.9477	0.8192	0.6517	0.4752	0.3125
2	.50	1.0000	0.9995	0.9963	0.9728	0.9163	0.8208	0.6875
3	.75	1.0000	1.0000	0.9999	0.9984	0.9919	0.9744	0.9375
4	1.00	1.0000	1.0000	1.0000	1.0000	1.0000	1.0000	1.0000

n = 5

r	*r/n*	π .01	.05	.10	.20	.30	.40	.50
0	.00	0.9510	0.7738	0.5905	0.3277	0.1681	0.0778	0.0313
1	.20	0.9990	0.9774	0.9185	0.7373	0.5282	0.3370	0.1875
2	.40	1.0000	0.9988	0.9914	0.9421	0.8369	0.6826	0.5000
3	.60	1.0000	1.0000	0.9995	0.9933	0.9692	0.9130	0.8125
4	.80	1.0000	1.0000	1.0000	0.9997	0.9976	0.9898	0.9688
5	1.00				1.0000	1.0000	1.0000	1.0000

TABLE C (continued)

		n = 10						
r	r/n	π .01	.05	.10	.20	.30	.40	.50
0	.00	0.9044	0.5987	0.3487	0.1074	0.0282	0.0060	0.0010
1	.10	0.9957	0.9139	0.7361	0.3758	0.1493	0.0464	0.0107
2	.20	0.9999	0.9885	0.9298	0.6778	0.3828	0.1673	0.0547
3	.30	1.0000	0.9990	0.9872	0.8791	0.6496	0.3823	0.1719
4	.40	1.0000	0.9999	0.9984	0.9672	0.8497	0.6331	0.3770
5	.50	1.0000	1.0000	0.9999	0.9936	0.9526	0.8338	0.6230
6	.60	1.0000	1.0000	1.0000	0.9991	0.9894	0.9452	0.8281
7	.70				0.9999	0.9984	0.9877	0.9453
8	.80				1.0000	1.0000	0.9983	0.9893
9	.90						0.9999	0.9990
10	1.00						1.0000	1.0000

		n = 20						
r	r/n	π .01	.05	.10	.20	.30	.40	.50
0	.00	0.8179	0.3585	0.1216	0.0115	0.0008	0.0000	0.0000
1	.05	0.9831	0.7358	0.3917	0.0692	0.0076	0.0005	0.0000
2	.10	0.9990	0.9245	0.6769	0.2061	0.0355	0.0036	0.0002
3	.15	1.0000	0.9841	0.8670	0.4114	0.1071	0.0160	0.0013
4	.20	1.0000	0.9974	0.9568	0.6296	0.2375	0.0510	0.0059
5	.25	1.0000	0.9997	0.9887	0.8042	0.4164	0.1256	0.0207
6	.30	1.0000	1.0000	0.9976	0.9133	0.6080	0.2500	0.0577
7	.35	1.0000	1.0000	0.9996	0.9679	0.7723	0.4159	0.1316
8	.40	1.0000	1.0000	0.9999	0.9900	0.8867	0.5956	0.2517
9	.45	1.0000	1.0000	1.0000	0.9974	0.9520	0.7553	0.4119
10	.50				0.9994	0.9829	0.8725	0.5881
11	.55				0.9999	0.9949	0.9435	0.7483
12	.60				1.0000	0.9987	0.9790	0.8684
13	.65					0.9997	0.9935	0.9423
14	.70					1.0000	0.9984	0.9793
15	.75						0.9997	0.9941
16	.80						1.0000	0.9987
17	.85							0.9998
18	.90							1.0000

TABLE C
(continued)

		n = 50						
r	r/n	π .01	.05	.10	.20	.30	.40	.50
0	.00	0.6050	0.0769	0.0052	0.0000	0.0000	0.0000	0.0000
1	.02	0.9106	0.2794	0.0338	0.0002	0.0000	0.0000	0.0000
2	.04	0.9862	0.5405	0.1117	0.0013	0.0000	0.0000	0.0000
3	.06	0.9984	0.7604	0.2503	0.0057	0.0000	0.0000	0.0000
4	.08	0.9999	0.8964	0.4312	0.0185	0.0002	0.0000	0.0000
5	.10	1.0000	0.9622	0.6161	0.0480	0.0007	0.0000	0.0000
6	.12	1.0000	0.9882	0.7702	0.1034	0.0025	0.0000	0.0000
7	.14	1.0000	0.9968	0.8779	0.1904	0.0073	0.0001	0.0000
8	.16	1.0000	0.9992	0.9421	0.3073	0.0183	0.0002	0.0000
9	.18	1.0000	0.9998	0.9755	0.4437	0.0402	0.0008	0.0000
10	.20	1.0000	1.0000	0.9906	0.5836	0.0789	0.0022	0.0000
11	.22	1.0000	1.0000	0.9968	0.7107	0.1390	0.0057	0.0000
12	.24	1.0000	1.0000	0.9990	0.8139	0.2229	0.0133	0.0002
13	.26	1.0000	1.0000	0.9997	0.8894	0.3279	0.0280	0.0005
14	.28	1.0000	1.0000	0.9999	0.9393	0.4468	0.0540	0.0013
15	.30	1.0000	1.0000	1.0000	0.9692	0.5692	0.0955	0.0033
16	.32				0.9856	0.6839	0.1561	0.0077
17	.34				0.9937	0.7822	0.2369	0.0164
18	.36				0.9975	0.8594	0.3356	0.0325
19	.38				0.9991	0.9152	0.4465	0.0595
20	.40				0.9997	0.9522	0.5610	0.1013
21	.42				0.9999	0.9749	0.6701	0.1611
22	.44				1.0000	0.9877	0.7660	0.2399
23	.46					0.9944	0.8438	0.3359
24	.48					0.9976	0.9022	0.4439
25	.50					0.9991	0.9427	0.5561
26	.52					0.9997	0.9686	0.6641
27	.54					0.9999	0.9840	0.7601
28	.56					1.0000	0.9924	0.8389
29	.58						0.9966	0.8987
30	.60						0.9986	0.9405
31	.62						0.9995	0.9675
32	.64						0.9998	0.9836
33	.66						0.9999	0.9923
34	.68						1.0000	0.9967
35	.70							0.9987
36	.72							0.9995
37	.74							0.9998
38	.76							1.0000

TABLE C
(continued)

		n = 100						
r	r/n	π .01	.05	.10	.20	.30	.40	.50
0	.00	0.3660	0.0059	0.0000	0.0000	0.0000	0.0000	0.0000
1	.01	0.7358	0.0371	0.0003	0.0000	0.0000	0.0000	0.0000
2	.02	0.9206	0.1183	0.0019	0.0000	0.0000	0.0000	0.0000
3	.03	0.9816	0.2578	0.0078	0.0000	0.0000	0.0000	0.0000
4	.04	0.9966	0.4360	0.0237	0.0000	0.0000	0.0000	0.0000
5	.05	0.9995	0.6160	0.0576	0.0000	0.0000	0.0000	0.0000
6	.06	0.9999	0.7660	0.1172	0.0001	0.0000	0.0000	0.0000
7	.07	1.0000	0.8720	0.2061	0.0003	0.0000	0.0000	0.0000
8	.08	1.0000	0.9369	0.3209	0.0009	0.0000	0.0000	0.0000
9	.09	1.0000	0.9718	0.4513	0.0023	0.0000	0.0000	0.0000
10	.10	1.0000	0.9885	0.5832	0.0057	0.0000	0.0000	0.0000
11	.11	1.0000	0.9957	0.7030	0.0126	0.0000	0.0000	0.0000
12	.12	1.0000	0.9985	0.8018	0.0253	0.0000	0.0000	0.0000
13	.13	1.0000	0.9995	0.8761	0.0469	0.0001	0.0000	0.0000
14	.14	1.0000	0.9999	0.9274	0.0804	0.0002	0.0000	0.0000
15	.15	1.0000	1.0000	0.9601	0.1285	0.0004	0.0000	0.0000
16	.16	1.0000	1.0000	0.9794	0.1923	0.0010	0.0000	0.0000
17	.17	1.0000	1.0000	0.9900	0.2712	0.0022	0.0000	0.0000
18	.18	1.0000	1.0000	0.9954	0.3621	0.0045	0.0000	0.0000
19	.19	1.0000	1.0000	0.9980	0.4602	0.0089	0.0000	0.0000
20	.20	1.0000	1.0000	0.9992	0.5595	0.0165	0.0000	0.0000
21	.21	1.0000	1.0000	0.9997	0.6540	0.0288	0.0000	0.0000
22	.22	1.0000	1.0000	0.9999	0.7389	0.0479	0.0001	0.0000
23	.23	1.0000	1.0000	1.0000	0.8109	0.0755	0.0003	0.0000
24	.24				0.8686	0.1136	0.0006	0.0000
25	.25				0.9125	0.1631	0.0012	0.0000
26	.26				0.9442	0.2244	0.0024	0.0000
27	.27				0.9658	0.2964	0.0046	0.0000
28	.28				0.9800	0.3768	0.0084	0.0000
29	.29				0.9888	0.4623	0.0148	0.0000
30	.30				0.9939	0.5491	0.0248	0.0000
31	.31				0.9969	0.6331	0.0398	0.0001
32	.32				0.9984	0.7107	0.0615	0.0002
33	.33				0.9993	0.7793	0.0913	0.0004
34	.34				0.9997	0.8371	0.1303	0.0009
35	.35				0.9999	0.8839	0.1795	0.0018

TABLE C
(*continued*)

		n = 100						
r	r/n	π .01	.05	.10	.20	.30	.40	.50
36	.36				0.9999	0.9201	0.2386	0.0033
37	.37				1.0000	0.9470	0.3068	0.0060
38	.38					0.9660	0.3822	0.0105
39	.39					0.9790	0.4621	0.0176
40	.40					0.9875	0.5433	0.0284
41	.41					0.9928	0.6225	0.0443
42	.42					0.9960	0.6967	0.0666
43	.43					0.9979	0.7635	0.0967
44	.44					0.9989	0.8211	0.1356
45	.45					0.9995	0.8689	0.1841
46	.46					0.9997	0.9070	0.2421
47	.47					0.9999	0.9362	0.3086
48	.48					0.9999	0.9577	0.3822
49	.49					1.0000	0.9729	0.4602
50	.50						0.9832	0.5398
51	.51						0.9900	0.6178
52	.52						0.9942	0.6914
53	.53						0.9968	0.7579
54	.54						0.9983	0.8159
55	.55						0.9991	0.8644
56	.56						0.9996	0.9033
57	.57						0.9998	0.9334
58	.58						0.9999	0.9557
59	.59						1.0000	0.9716
60	.60							0.9824
61	.61							0.9895
62	.62							0.9940
63	.63							0.9967
64	.64							0.9982
65	.65							0.9991
66	.66							0.9996
67	.67							0.9998
68	.68							0.9999
69	.69							1.0000

SOURCE: From *Management Science for Business Decisions* by Lawrence L. Lapin, copyright © 1980 by Harcourt Brace Jovanovich, Inc. Reproduced by permission of the publisher.

TABLE D
Areas Under the Standard Normal Curve

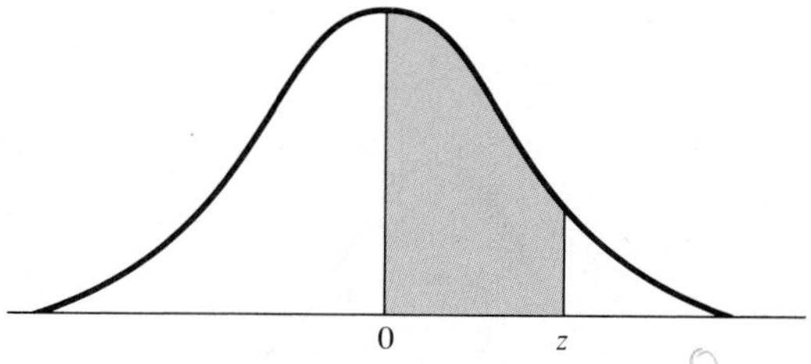

The following table provides the area between the mean and normal deviate value *z*.

Normal Deviate z	.00	.01	.02	.03	.04	.05	.06	.07	.08	.09
0.0	.0000	.0040	.0080	.0120	.0160	.0199	.0239	.0279	.0319	.0359
0.1	.0398	.0438	.0478	.0517	.0557	.0596	.0636	.0675	.0714	.0753
0.2	.0793	.0832	.0871	.0910	.0948	.0987	.1026	.1064	.1103	.1141
0.3	.1179	.1217	.1255	.1293	.1331	.1368	.1406	.1443	.1480	.1517
0.4	.1554	.1591	.1628	.1664	.1700	.1736	.1772	.1808	.1844	.1879
0.5	.1915	.1950	.1985	.2019	.2054	.2088	.2123	.2157	.2190	.2224
0.6	.2257	.2291	.2324	.2357	.2389	.2422	.2454	.2486	.2518	.2549
0.7	.2580	.2612	.2642	.2673	.2704	.2734	.2764	.2794	.2823	.2852
0.8	.2881	.2910	.2939	.2967	.2995	.3023	.3051	.3078	.3106	.3133
0.9	.3159	.3186	.3212	.3238	.3264	.3289	.3315	.3340	.3365	.3389
1.0	.3413	.3438	.3461	.3485	.3508	.3531	.3554	.3577	.3599	.3621
1.1	.3643	.3665	.3686	.3708	.3729	.3749	.3770	.3790	.3810	.3830
1.2	.3849	.3869	.3888	.3907	.3925	.3944	.3962	.3980	.3997	.4015
1.3	.4032	.4049	.4066	.4082	.4099	.4115	.4131	.4147	.4162	.4177
1.4	.4192	.4207	.4222	.4236	.4251	.4265	.4279	.4292	.4306	.4319
1.5	.4332	.4345	.4357	.4370	.4382	.4394	.4406	.4418	.4429	.4441
1.6	.4452	.4463	.4474	.4484	.4495	.4505	.4515	.4525	.4535	.4545
1.7	.4554	.4564	.4573	.4582	.4591	.4599	.4608	.4616	.4625	.4633
1.8	.4641	.4649	.4656	.4664	.4671	.4678	.4686	.4693	.4699	.4706
1.9	.4713	.4719	.4726	.4732	.4738	.4744	.4750	.4756	.4761	.4767
2.0	.4772	.4778	.4783	.4788	.4793	.4798	.4803	.4808	.4812	.4817
2.1	.4821	.4826	.4830	.4834	.4838	.4842	.4846	.4850	.4854	.4857
2.2	.4861	.4864	.4868	.4871	.4875	.4878	.4881	.4884	.4887	.4890
2.3	.4893	.4896	.4898	.4901	.4904	.4906	.4909	.4911	.4913	.4916
2.4	.4918	.4920	.4922	.4925	.4927	.4929	.4931	.4932	.4934	.4936
2.5	.4938	.4940	.4941	.4943	.4945	.4946	.4948	.4949	.4951	.4952
2.6	.4953	.4955	.4956	.4957	.4959	.4960	.4961	.4962	.4963	.4964
2.7	.4965	.4966	.4967	.4968	.4969	.4970	.4971	.4972	.4973	.4974
2.8	.4974	.4975	.4976	.4977	.4977	.4978	.4979	.4979	.4980	.4981
2.9	.4981	.4982	.4982	.4983	.4984	.4984	.4985	.4985	.4986	.4986
3.0	.49865	.4987	.4987	.4988	.4988	.4989	.4989	.4989	.4990	.4990
4.0	.49997									

z = 3.09 [=] .4990
z = 4. [=] .49997
↑ If between, go to which ever is closest.

If z exceeds 4, area is .5

TABLE E
Normal Deviate Values

Normal Deviates for Statistical Estimation

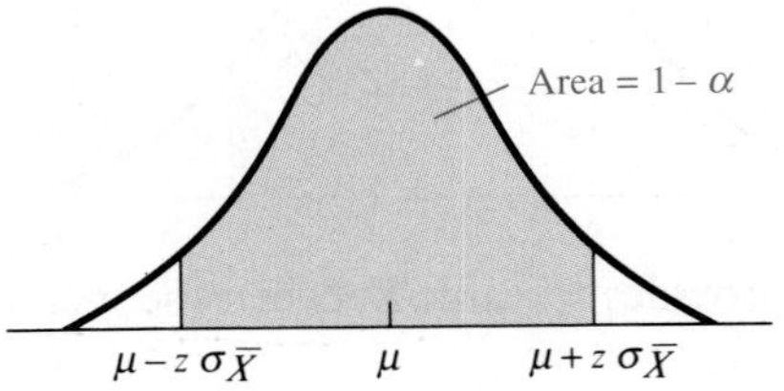

Reliability or Confidence Level $1-\alpha$	Normal Deviate $z_{\alpha/2}$
.80	1.28
.90	1.64
.95	1.96
.98	2.33
.99	2.57
.998	3.08
.999	3.27

Critical Normal Deviates for Hypothesis Testing

One-Sided Tests

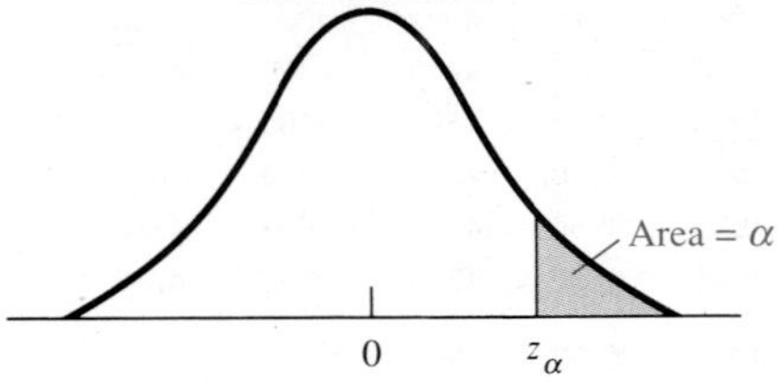

Two-Sided Tests

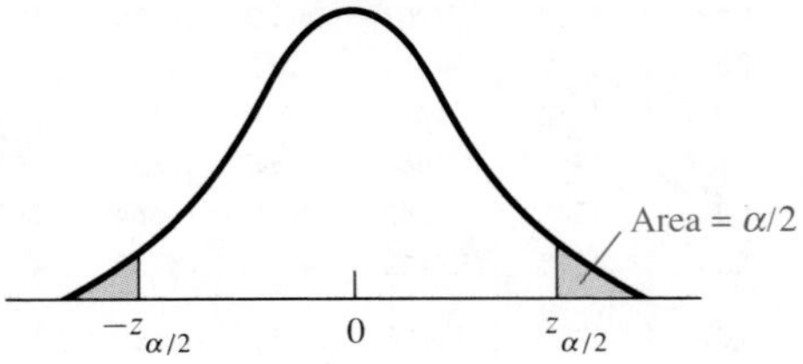

Significance Level α	Normal Deviate z_{α}
.10	1.28
.05	1.64
.025	1.96
.01	2.33
.005	2.57
.001	3.08

Significance Level α	Normal Deviate $z_{\alpha/2}$
.10	1.64
.05	1.96
.025	2.24
.01	2.57
.005	2.81
.001	3.27

TABLE F
Student t Distribution

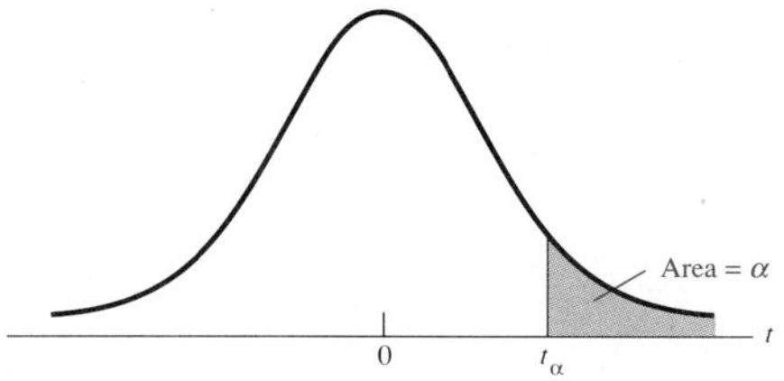

The following table provides the values of t_α that correspond to a given upper tail area α and a specified number of degrees of freedom.

Degrees of Freedom	Upper Tail Area α									
	.4	.25	.1	.05	.025	.01	.005	.0025	.001	.0005
1	0.325	1.000	3.078	6.314	12.706	31.821	63.657	127.32	318.31	636.62
2	.289	.816	1.886	2.920	4.303	6.965	9.925	14.089	22.327	31.598
3	.277	.765	1.638	2.353	3.182	4.541	5.841	7.453	10.214	12.924
4	.271	.741	1.533	2.132	2.776	3.747	4.604	5.598	7.173	8.610
5	0.267	0.727	1.476	2.015	2.571	3.365	4.032	4.773	5.893	6.869
6	.265	.718	1.440	1.943	2.447	3.143	3.707	4.317	5.208	5.959
7	.263	.711	1.415	1.895	2.365	2.998	3.499	4.029	4.785	5.408
8	.262	.706	1.397	1.860	2.306	2.896	3.355	3.833	4.501	5.041
9	.261	.703	1.383	1.833	2.262	2.821	3.250	3.690	4.297	4.781
10	0.260	0.700	1.372	1.812	2.228	2.764	3.169	3.581	4.144	4.587
11	.260	.697	1.363	1.796	2.201	2.718	3.106	3.497	4.025	4.437
12	.259	.695	1.356	1.782	2.179	2.681	3.055	3.428	3.930	4.318
13	.259	.694	1.350	1.771	2.160	2.650	3.012	3.372	3.852	4.221
14	.258	.692	1.345	1.761	2.145	2.624	2.977	3.326	3.787	4.140
15	0.258	0.691	1.341	1.753	2.131	2.602	2.947	3.286	3.733	4.073
16	.258	.690	1.337	1.746	2.120	2.583	2.921	3.252	3.686	4.015
17	.257	.689	1.333	1.740	2.110	2.567	2.898	3.222	3.646	3.965
18	.257	.688	1.330	1.734	2.101	2.552	2.878	3.197	3.610	3.922
19	.257	.688	1.328	1.729	2.093	2.539	2.861	3.174	3.579	3.883
20	0.257	0.687	1.325	1.725	2.086	2.528	2.845	3.153	3.552	3.850
21	.257	.686	1.323	1.721	2.080	2.518	2.831	3.135	3.527	3.819
22	.256	.686	1.321	1.717	2.074	2.508	2.819	3.119	3.505	3.792
23	.256	.685	1.319	1.714	2.069	2.500	2.807	3.104	3.485	3.767
24	.256	685	1.318	1.711	2.064	2.492	2.797	3.091	3.467	3.745
25	0.256	0.684	1.316	1.708	2.060	2.485	2.787	3.078	3.450	3.725
26	.256	.684	1.315	1.706	2.056	2.479	2.779	3.067	3.435	3.707
27	.256	.684	1.314	1.703	2.052	2.473	2.771	3.057	3.421	3.690
28	.256	.683	1.313	1.701	2.048	2.467	2.763	3.047	3.408	3.674
29	.256	.683	1.311	1.699	2.045	2.462	2.756	3.038	3.396	3.659
30	0.256	0.683	1.310	1.697	2.042	2.457	2.750	3.030	3.385	3.646
40	.255	.681	1.303	1.684	2.021	2.423	2.704	2.971	3.307	3.551
60	.254	.679	1.296	1.671	2.000	2.390	2.660	2.915	3.232	3.460
120	.254	.677	1.289	1.658	1.980	2.358	2.617	2.860	3.160	3.373
∞	.253	.674	1.282	1.645	1.960	2.326	2.576	2.807	3.090	3.291

SOURCE: E. S. Pearson and H. O. Hartley, *Biometrika Tables for Statisticians*, Vol. I. London: Cambridge University Press, 1966. Partly derived from Table III of Fisher and Yates, *Statistical Tables for Biological, Agricultural and Medical Research*, published by Longman Group Ltd., London (previously published by Oliver & Boyd, Edinburgh, 1963). Reproduced with permission of the authors and publishers.

TABLE G
F Distribution

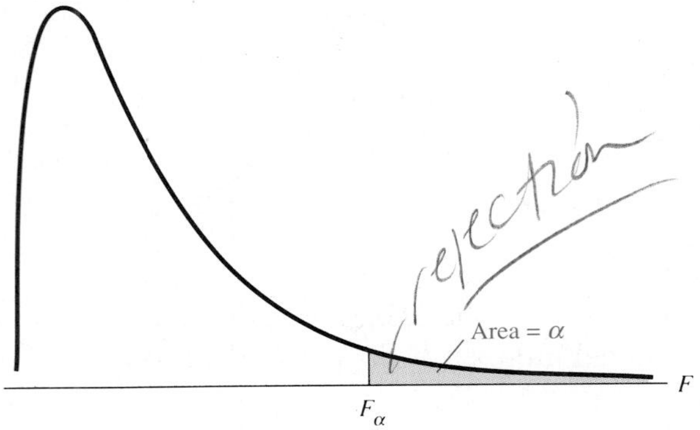

The following table provides the values of F_α that correspond to a given upper tail area α and a specified degrees of freedom pair. The values of $F_{.05}$ are in lightface type, while those for $F_{.01}$ are given in boldface type. The number of degrees of freedom for the *numerator* mean square is indicated at the head of each *column*, while the number of degrees of freedom for the *denominator* mean square determines which *row* is applicable.

Degrees of Freedom for Denominator	Degrees of Freedom for Numerator											
	1	2	3	4	5	6	7	8	9	10	11	12
1	161	200	216	225	230	234	237	239	241	242	243	244
	4,052	**4,999**	**5,403**	**5,625**	**5,764**	**5,859**	**5,928**	**5,981**	**6,022**	**6,056**	**6,082**	**6,106**
2	18.51	19.00	19.16	19.25	19.30	19.33	19.36	19.37	19.38	19.39	19.40	19.41
	98.49	**99.01**	**99.17**	**99.25**	**99.30**	**99.33**	**99.34**	**99.36**	**99.38**	**99.40**	**99.41**	**99.42**
3	10.13	9.55	9.28	9.12	9.01	8.94	8.88	8.84	8.81	8.78	8.76	8.74
	34.12	**30.81**	**29.46**	**28.71**	**28.24**	**27.91**	**27.67**	**27.49**	**27.34**	**27.23**	**27.13**	**27.05**
4	7.71	6.94	6.59	6.39	6.26	6.16	6.09	6.04	6.00	5.96	5.93	5.91
	21.20	**18.00**	**16.69**	**15.98**	**15.52**	**15.21**	**14.98**	**14.80**	**14.66**	**14.54**	**14.45**	**14.37**
5	6.61	5.79	5.41	5.19	5.05	4.95	4.88	4.82	4.78	4.74	4.70	4.68
	16.26	**13.27**	**12.06**	**11.39**	**10.97**	**10.67**	**10.45**	**10.27**	**10.15**	**10.05**	**9.96**	**9.89**
6	5.99	5.14	4.76	4.53	4.39	4.28	4.21	4.15	4.10	4.06	4.03	4.00
	13.74	**10.92**	**9.78**	**9.15**	**8.75**	**8.47**	**8.26**	**8.10**	**7.98**	**7.87**	**7.79**	**7.72**
7	5.59	4.74	4.35	4.12	3.97	3.87	3.79	3.73	3.68	3.63	3.60	3.57
	12.25	**9.55**	**8.45**	**7.85**	**7.46**	**7.19**	**7.00**	**6.84**	**6.71**	**6.62**	**6.54**	**6.47**
8	5.32	4.46	4.07	3.84	3.69	3.58	3.50	3.44	3.39	3.34	3.31	3.28
	11.26	**8.65**	**7.59**	**7.01**	**6.63**	**6.37**	**6.19**	**6.03**	**5.91**	**5.82**	**5.74**	**5.67**
9	5.12	4.26	3.86	3.63	3.48	3.37	3.29	3.23	3.18	3.13	3.10	3.07
	10.56	**8.02**	**6.99**	**6.42**	**6.06**	**5.80**	**5.62**	**5.47**	**5.35**	**5.26**	**5.18**	**5.11**
10	4.96	4.10	3.71	3.48	3.33	3.22	3.14	3.07	3.02	2.97	2.94	2.91
	10.04	**7.56**	**6.55**	**5.99**	**5.64**	**5.39**	**5.21**	**5.06**	**4.95**	**4.85**	**4.78**	**4.71**
11	4.84	3.98	3.59	3.36	3.20	3.09	3.01	2.95	2.90	2.86	2.82	2.79
	9.65	**7.20**	**6.22**	**5.67**	**5.32**	**5.07**	**4.88**	**4.74**	**4.63**	**4.54**	**4.46**	**4.40**
12	4.75	3.89	3.49	3.26	3.11	3.00	2.92	2.85	2.80	2.76	2.72	2.69
	9.33	**6.93**	**5.95**	**5.41**	**5.06**	**4.82**	**4.65**	**4.50**	**4.39**	**4.30**	**4.22**	**4.16**
13	4.67	3.80	3.41	3.18	3.02	2.92	2.84	2.77	2.72	2.67	2.63	2.60
	9.07	**6.70**	**5.74**	**5.20**	**4.86**	**4.62**	**4.44**	**4.30**	**4.19**	**4.10**	**4.02**	**3.96**
14	4.60	3.74	3.34	3.11	2.96	2.85	2.77	2.70	2.65	2.60	2.56	2.53
	8.86	**6.51**	**5.56**	**5.03**	**4.69**	**4.46**	**4.28**	**4.14**	**4.03**	**3.94**	**3.86**	**3.80**

TABLE G
(continued)

Degrees of Freedom for Denominator	Degrees of Freedom for Numerator											
	14	16	20	24	30	40	50	75	100	200	500	∞
1	245	246	248	249	250	251	252	253	253	254	254	254
	6,142	**6,169**	**6,208**	**6,234**	**6,258**	**6,286**	**6,302**	**6,323**	**6,334**	**6,352**	**6,361**	**6,366**
2	19.42	19.43	19.44	19.45	19.46	19.47	19.47	19.48	19.49	19.49	19.50	19.50
	99.43	**99.44**	**99.45**	**99.46**	**99.47**	**99.48**	**99.48**	**99.49**	**99.49**	**99.49**	**99.50**	**99.50**
3	8.71	8.69	8.66	8.64	8.62	8.60	8.58	8.57	8.56	8.54	8.54	8.53
	26.92	**26.83**	**26.69**	**26.60**	**26.50**	**26.41**	**26.30**	**26.27**	**26.23**	**26.18**	**26.14**	**26.12**
4	5.87	5.84	5.80	5.77	5.74	5.71	5.70	5.68	5.66	5.65	5.64	5.63
	14.24	**14.15**	**14.02**	**13.93**	**13.83**	**13.74**	**13.69**	**13.61**	**13.57**	**13.52**	**13.48**	**13.46**
5	4.64	4.60	4.56	4.53	4.50	4.46	4.44	4.42	4.40	4.38	4.37	4.36
	9.77	**9.68**	**9.55**	**9.47**	**9.38**	**9.29**	**9.24**	**9.17**	**9.13**	**9.07**	**9.04**	**9.02**
6	3.96	3.92	3.87	3.84	3.81	3.77	3.75	3.72	3.71	3.69	3.68	3.67
	7.60	**7.52**	**7.39**	**7.31**	**7.23**	**7.14**	**7.09**	**7.02**	**6.99**	**6.94**	**6.90**	**6.88**
7	3.52	3.49	3.44	3.41	3.38	3.34	3.32	3.29	3.28	3.25	3.24	3.23
	6.35	**6.27**	**6.15**	**6.07**	**5.98**	**5.90**	**5.85**	**5.78**	**5.75**	**5.70**	**5.67**	**5.65**
8	3.23	3.20	3.15	3.12	3.08	3.05	3.03	3.00	2.98	2.96	2.94	2.93
	5.56	**5.48**	**5.36**	**5.28**	**5.20**	**5.11**	**5.06**	**5.00**	**4.96**	**4.91**	**4.88**	**4.86**
9	3.02	2.98	2.93	2.90	2.86	2.82	2.80	2.77	2.76	2.73	2.72	2.71
	5.00	**4.92**	**4.80**	**4.73**	**4.64**	**4.56**	**4.51**	**4.45**	**4.41**	**4.36**	**4.33**	**4.31**
10	2.86	2.82	2.77	2.74	2.70	2.67	2.64	2.61	2.59	2.56	2.55	2.54
	4.60	**4.52**	**4.41**	**4.33**	**4.25**	**4.17**	**4.12**	**4.05**	**4.01**	**3.96**	**3.93**	**3.91**
11	2.74	2.70	2.65	2.61	2.57	2.53	2.50	2.47	2.45	2.42	2.41	2.40
	4.29	**4.21**	**4.10**	**4.02**	**3.94**	**3.86**	**3.80**	**3.74**	**3.70**	**3.66**	**3.62**	**3.60**
12	2.64	2.60	2.54	2.50	2.46	2.42	2.40	2.36	2.35	2.32	2.31	2.30
	4.05	**3.98**	**3.86**	**3.78**	**3.70**	**3.61**	**3.56**	**3.49**	**3.46**	**3.41**	**3.38**	**3.36**
13	2.55	2.51	2.46	2.42	2.38	2.34	2.32	2.28	2.26	2.24	2.22	2.21
	3.85	**3.78**	**3.67**	**3.59**	**3.51**	**3.42**	**3.37**	**3.30**	**3.27**	**3.21**	**3.18**	**3.16**
14	2.48	2.44	2.39	2.35	2.31	2.27	2.24	2.21	2.19	2.16	2.14	2.13
	3.70	**3.62**	**3.51**	**3.43**	**3.34**	**3.26**	**3.21**	**3.14**	**3.11**	**3.06**	**3.02**	**3.00**

TABLE G
(continued)

Degrees of Freedom for Denominator	Degrees of Freedom for Numerator											
	1	2	3	4	5	6	7	8	9	10	11	12
15	4.54	3.68	3.29	3.06	2.90	2.79	2.70	2.64	2.59	2.55	2.51	2.48
	8.68	**6.36**	**5.42**	**4.89**	**4.56**	**4.32**	**4.14**	**4.00**	**3.89**	**3.80**	**3.73**	**3.67**
16	4.49	3.63	3.24	3.01	2.85	2.74	2.66	2.59	2.54	2.49	2.45	2.42
	8.53	**6.23**	**5.29**	**4.77**	**4.44**	**4.20**	**4.03**	**3.89**	**3.78**	**3.69**	**3.61**	**3.55**
17	4.45	3.59	3.20	2.96	2.81	2.70	2.62	2.55	2.50	2.45	2.41	2.38
	8.40	**6.11**	**5.18**	**4.67**	**4.34**	**4.10**	**3.93**	**3.79**	**3.68**	**3.59**	**3.52**	**3.45**
18	4.41	3.55	3.16	2.93	2.77	2.66	2.58	2.51	2.46	2.41	2.37	2.34
	8.28	**6.01**	**5.09**	**4.58**	**4.25**	**4.01**	**3.85**	**3.71**	**3.60**	**3.51**	**3.44**	**3.37**
19	4.38	3.52	3.13	2.90	2.74	2.63	2.55	2.48	2.43	2.38	2.34	2.31
	8.18	**5.93**	**5.01**	**4.50**	**4.17**	**3.94**	**3.77**	**3.63**	**3.52**	**3.43**	**3.36**	**3.30**
20	4.35	3.49	3.10	2.87	2.71	2.60	2.52	2.45	2.40	2.35	2.31	2.28
	8.10	**5.85**	**4.94**	**4.43**	**4.10**	**3.87**	**3.71**	**3.56**	**3.45**	**3.37**	**3.30**	**3.23**
21	4.32	3.47	3.07	2.84	2.68	2.57	2.49	2.42	2.37	2.32	2.28	2.25
	8.02	**5.78**	**4.87**	**4.37**	**4.04**	**3.81**	**3.65**	**3.51**	**3.40**	**3.31**	**3.24**	**3.17**
22	4.30	3.44	3.05	2.82	2.66	2.55	2.47	2.40	2.35	2.30	2.26	2.23
	7.94	**5.72**	**4.82**	**4.41**	**3.99**	**3.76**	**3.59**	**3.45**	**3.35**	**3.26**	**3.18**	**3.12**
23	4.28	3.42	3.03	2.80	2.64	2.53	2.45	2.38	2.32	2.28	2.24	2.20
	7.88	**5.66**	**4.76**	**4.26**	**3.94**	**3.71**	**3.54**	**3.41**	**3.30**	**3.21**	**3.14**	**3.07**
24	4.26	3.40	3.01	2.78	2.62	2.51	2.43	2.36	2.30	2.26	2.22	2.18
	7.82	**5.61**	**4.72**	**4.22**	**3.90**	**3.67**	**3.50**	**3.36**	**3.25**	**3.17**	**3.09**	**3.03**
25	4.24	3.38	2.99	2.76	2.60	2.49	2.41	2.34	2.28	2.24	2.20	2.16
	7.77	**5.57**	**4.68**	**4.18**	**3.86**	**3.63**	**3.46**	**3.32**	**3.21**	**3.13**	**3.05**	**2.99**
26	4.22	3.37	2.89	2.74	2.59	2.47	2.39	2.32	2.27	2.22	2.18	2.15
	7.72	**5.53**	**4.64**	**4.14**	**3.82**	**3.59**	**3.42**	**3.29**	**3.17**	**3.09**	**3.02**	**2.96**
27	4.21	3.35	2.96	2.73	2.57	2.46	2.37	2.30	2.25	2.20	2.16	2.13
	7.68	**5.49**	**4.60**	**4.11**	**3.79**	**3.56**	**3.39**	**3.26**	**3.14**	**3.06**	**2.98**	**2.93**
28	4.20	3.34	2.95	2.71	2.56	2.44	2.36	2.29	2.24	2.19	2.15	2.12
	7.64	**5.45**	**4.57**	**4.07**	**3.76**	**3.53**	**3.36**	**3.23**	**3.11**	**3.03**	**2.95**	**2.90**
29	4.18	3.33	2.93	2.70	2.54	2.43	2.35	2.28	2.22	2.18	2.14	2.10
	7.60	**5.52**	**4.54**	**4.04**	**3.73**	**3.50**	**3.33**	**3.20**	**3.08**	**3.00**	**2.92**	**2.87**
30	4.17	3.32	2.92	2.69	2.53	2.43	2.34	2.27	2.21	2.16	2.12	2.09
	7.56	**5.39**	**4.51**	**4.02**	**3.70**	**3.47**	**3.30**	**3.17**	**3.06**	**2.98**	**2.90**	**2.84**
32	4.15	3.30	2.90	2.67	2.51	2.40	2.32	2.25	2.19	2.14	2.10	2.07
	7.50	**5.34**	**4.46**	**3.97**	**3.66**	**3.42**	**3.25**	**3.12**	**3.01**	**2.94**	**2.86**	**2.80**
34	4.13	3.28	2.88	2.65	2.49	2.38	2.30	2.23	2.17	2.12	2.08	2.05
	7.44	**5.29**	**4.42**	**3.93**	**3.61**	**3.38**	**3.21**	**3.08**	**2.97**	**2.89**	**2.82**	**2.76**
36	4.11	3.26	2.86	2.63	2.48	2.36	2.28	2.21	2.15	2.10	2.06	2.03
	7.39	**5.25**	**4.38**	**3.89**	**3.58**	**3.35**	**3.18**	**3.04**	**2.94**	**2.86**	**2.78**	**2.72**
38	4.10	3.25	2.85	2.62	2.46	2.35	2.26	2.19	2.14	2.09	2.05	2.02
	7.35	**5.21**	**4.34**	**3.86**	**3.54**	**3.32**	**3.15**	**3.02**	**2.91**	**2.82**	**2.75**	**2.69**

TABLE G
(continued)

Degrees of Freedom for Denominator	Degrees of Freedom for Numerator											
	14	16	20	24	30	40	50	75	100	200	500	∞
15	2.43	2.39	2.33	2.29	2.25	2.21	2.18	2.15	2.12	2.10	2.08	2.07
	3.56	**3.48**	**3.36**	**3.29**	**3.20**	**3.12**	**3.07**	**3.00**	**2.97**	**2.92**	**2.89**	**2.87**
16	2.37	2.33	2.28	2.24	2.20	2.16	2.13	2.09	2.07	2.04	2.02	2.01
	3.45	**3.37**	**3.25**	**3.18**	**3.10**	**3.01**	**2.96**	**2.89**	**2.86**	**2.80**	**2.77**	**2.75**
17	2.33	2.29	2.23	2.19	2.15	2.11	2.08	2.04	2.02	1.99	1.97	1.96
	3.35	**3.27**	**3.16**	**3.08**	**3.00**	**2.92**	**2.86**	**2.79**	**2.76**	**2.70**	**2.67**	**2.65**
18	2.29	2.25	2.19	2.15	2.11	2.07	2.04	2.00	1.98	1.95	1.93	1.92
	3.27	**3.19**	**3.07**	**3.00**	**2.91**	**2.83**	**2.78**	**2.71**	**2.68**	**2.62**	**2.59**	**2.57**
19	2.26	2.21	2.15	2.11	2.07	2.02	2.00	1.96	1.94	1.91	1.90	1.88
	3.19	**3.12**	**3.00**	**2.92**	**2.84**	**2.76**	**2.70**	**2.63**	**2.60**	**2.54**	**2.51**	**2.49**
20	2.23	2.18	2.12	2.08	2.04	1.99	1.96	1.92	1.90	1.87	1.85	1.84
	3.13	**3.05**	**2.94**	**2.86**	**2.77**	**2.69**	**2.63**	**2.56**	**2.53**	**2.47**	**2.44**	**2.42**
21	2.20	2.15	2.09	2.05	2.00	1.96	1.93	1.89	1.87	1.84	1.82	1.81
	3.07	**2.99**	**2.88**	**2.80**	**2.72**	**2.63**	**2.58**	**2.51**	**2.47**	**2.42**	**2.38**	**2.36**
22	2.18	2.13	2.07	2.03	1.98	1.93	1.91	1.87	1.84	1.81	1.80	1.78
	3.02	**2.94**	**2.83**	**2.75**	**2.67**	**2.58**	**2.53**	**2.46**	**2.42**	**2.37**	**2.33**	**2.31**
23	2.14	2.10	2.04	2.00	1.96	1.91	1.88	1.84	1.82	1.79	1.77	1.76
	2.97	**2.89**	**2.78**	**2.70**	**2.62**	**2.53**	**2.48**	**2.41**	**2.37**	**2.32**	**2.28**	**2.26**
24	2.13	2.09	2.02	1.98	1.94	1.89	1.86	1.82	1.80	1.76	1.74	1.73
	2.93	**2.85**	**2.74**	**2.66**	**2.58**	**2.49**	**2.44**	**2.36**	**2.33**	**2.27**	**2.23**	**2.21**
25	2.11	2.06	2.00	1.96	1.92	1.87	1.84	1.80	1.77	1.74	1.72	1.71
	2.89	**2.81**	**2.70**	**2.62**	**2.54**	**2.45**	**2.40**	**2.32**	**2.29**	**2.23**	**2.19**	**2.17**
26	2.10	2.05	1.99	1.95	1.90	1.85	1.82	1.78	1.76	1.72	1.70	1.69
	2.86	**2.77**	**2.66**	**2.58**	**2.50**	**2.41**	**2.36**	**2.28**	**2.25**	**2.19**	**2.15**	**2.13**
27	2.08	2.03	1.97	1.93	1.88	1.84	1.80	1.76	1.74	1.71	1.68	1.67
	2.83	**2.74**	**2.63**	**2.55**	**2.47**	**2.38**	**2.33**	**2.25**	**2.21**	**2.16**	**2.12**	**2.10**
28	2.06	2.02	1.96	1.91	1.87	1.81	1.78	1.75	1.72	1.69	1.67	1.65
	2.80	**2.71**	**2.60**	**2.52**	**2.44**	**2.35**	**2.30**	**2.22**	**2.18**	**2.13**	**2.09**	**2.06**
29	2.05	2.00	1.94	1.90	1.85	1.80	1.77	1.73	1.71	1.68	1.65	1.64
	2.77	**2.68**	**2.57**	**2.49**	**2.41**	**2.32**	**2.27**	**2.19**	**2.15**	**2.10**	**2.06**	**2.03**
30	2.04	1.99	1.93	1.89	1.84	1.79	1.76	1.72	1.69	1.66	1.64	1.62
	2.74	**2.66**	**2.55**	**2.47**	**2.38**	**2.29**	**2.24**	**2.16**	**2.13**	**2.07**	**2.03**	**2.01**
32	2.02	1.97	1.91	1.86	1.82	1.76	1.74	1.69	1.67	1.64	1.61	1.59
	2.70	**2.62**	**2.51**	**2.42**	**2.34**	**2.25**	**2.20**	**2.12**	**2.08**	**2.02**	**1.98**	**1.96**
34	2.00	1.95	1.89	1.84	1.80	1.74	1.71	1.67	1.64	1.61	1.59	1.57
	2.66	**2.58**	**2.47**	**2.38**	**2.30**	**2.21**	**2.15**	**2.08**	**2.04**	**1.98**	**1.94**	**1.91**
36	1.98	1.93	1.87	1.82	1.78	1.72	1.69	1.65	1.62	1.59	1.56	1.55
	2.62	**2.54**	**2.43**	**2.35**	**2.26**	**2.17**	**2.12**	**2.04**	**2.00**	**1.94**	**1.90**	**1.87**
38	1.96	1.92	1.85	1.80	1.76	1.71	1.67	1.63	1.60	1.57	1.54	1.53
	2.59	**2.51**	**2.40**	**2.32**	**2.22**	**2.14**	**2.08**	**2.00**	**1.97**	**1.90**	**1.86**	**1.84**

TABLE G
(continued)

Degrees of Freedom for Denominator	*Degrees of Freedom for Numerator*											
	1	**2**	**3**	**4**	**5**	**6**	**7**	**8**	**9**	**10**	**11**	**12**
40	4.08	3.23	2.84	2.61	2.45	2.34	2.25	2.18	2.12	2.08	2.04	2.00
	7.31	**5.18**	**4.31**	**3.83**	**3.51**	**3.29**	**3.12**	**2.99**	**2.88**	**2.80**	**2.73**	**2.66**
42	4.07	3.22	2.83	2.59	2.44	2.32	2.24	2.17	2.11	2.06	2.02	1.99
	7.27	**5.15**	**4.29**	**3.80**	**3.49**	**3.26**	**3.10**	**2.96**	**2.86**	**2.77**	**2.70**	**2.64**
44	4.06	3.21	2.82	2.58	2.43	2.31	2.23	2.16	2.10	2.05	2.01	1.98
	7.24	**5.12**	**4.26**	**3.78**	**3.46**	**3.24**	**3.07**	**2.94**	**2.84**	**2.75**	**2.68**	**2.62**
46	4.05	3.20	2.81	2.57	2.42	2.30	2.22	2.14	2.09	2.04	2.00	1.97
	7.21	**5.10**	**4.24**	**3.76**	**3.44**	**3.22**	**3.05**	**2.92**	**2.82**	**2.73**	**2.66**	**2.60**
48	4.04	3.19	2.80	2.56	2.41	2.30	2.21	2.14	2.08	2.03	1.99	1.96
	7.19	**5.08**	**4.22**	**3.74**	**3.42**	**3.20**	**3.04**	**2.90**	**2.80**	**2.71**	**2.64**	**2.58**
50	4.03	3.18	2.79	2.56	2.40	2.29	2.20	2.13	2.07	2.02	1.98	1.95
	7.17	**5.06**	**4.20**	**3.72**	**3.41**	**3.18**	**3.02**	**2.88**	**2.78**	**2.70**	**2.62**	**2.56**
55	4.02	3.17	2.78	2.54	2.38	2.27	2.18	2.11	2.05	2.00	1.97	1.93
	7.12	**5.01**	**4.16**	**3.68**	**3.37**	**3.15**	**2.98**	**2.85**	**2.75**	**2.66**	**2.59**	**2.53**
60	4.00	3.15	2.76	2.52	2.37	2.25	2.17	2.10	2.04	1.99	1.95	1.92
	7.08	**4.98**	**4.13**	**3.65**	**3.34**	**3.12**	**2.95**	**2.82**	**2.72**	**2.63**	**2.56**	**2.50**
65	3.99	3.14	2.75	2.51	2.36	2.24	2.15	2.08	2.02	1.98	1.94	1.90
	7.04	**4.95**	**4.10**	**3.62**	**3.31**	**3.09**	**2.93**	**2.79**	**2.70**	**2.61**	**2.54**	**2.47**
70	3.98	3.13	2.74	2.50	2.35	2.32	2.14	2.07	2.01	1.97	1.93	1.80
	7.01	**4.92**	**4.08**	**3.60**	**3.29**	**3.07**	**2.91**	**2.77**	**2.67**	**2.59**	**2.51**	**2.45**
80	3.96	3.11	2.72	2.48	2.33	2.21	2.12	2.05	1.99	1.95	1.91	1.88
	6.95	**4.88**	**4.04**	**3.56**	**3.25**	**3.04**	**2.87**	**2.74**	**2.64**	**2.55**	**2.48**	**2.41**
100	3.94	3.09	2.70	2.46	2.30	2.19	2.10	2.03	1.97	1.92	1.88	1.85
	6.90	**4.82**	**3.98**	**3.51**	**3.20**	**2.99**	**2.82**	**2.69**	**2.59**	**2.51**	**2.43**	**2.36**
125	3.92	3.07	2.68	2.44	2.29	2.17	2.08	2.01	1.95	1.90	1.86	1.83
	6.84	**4.78**	**3.94**	**3.47**	**3.17**	**2.95**	**2.79**	**2.65**	**2.56**	**2.47**	**2.40**	**2.33**
150	3.91	3.06	2.67	2.43	2.27	2.16	2.07	2.00	1.94	1.89	1.85	1.82
	6.81	**4.75**	**3.91**	**3.44**	**3.13**	**2.92**	**2.76**	**2.62**	**2.53**	**2.44**	**2.37**	**2.30**
200	3.89	3.04	2.65	2.41	2.26	2.14	2.05	1.98	1.92	1.87	1.83	1.80
	6.76	**4.71**	**3.88**	**3.41**	**3.11**	**2.90**	**2.73**	**2.60**	**2.50**	**2.41**	**2.34**	**2.28**
400	3.86	3.02	2.62	2.39	2.23	2.12	2.03	1.96	1.90	1.85	1.81	1.78
	6.70	**4.66**	**3.83**	**3.36**	**3.06**	**2.85**	**2.69**	**2.55**	**2.46**	**2.37**	**2.29**	**2.23**
1,000	3.85	3.00	2.61	2.38	2.22	2.10	2.02	1.95	1.89	1.84	1.80	1.76
	6.66	**4.62**	**3.80**	**3.34**	**3.04**	**2.82**	**2.66**	**2.53**	**2.43**	**2.34**	**2.26**	**2.20**
∞	3.84	2.99	2.60	2.37	2.21	2.09	2.01	1.94	1.88	1.83	1.79	1.75
	6.64	**4.60**	**3.78**	**3.32**	**3.02**	**2.80**	**2.64**	**2.51**	**2.41**	**2.32**	**2.24**	**2.18**

TABLE G (continued)

Degrees of Freedom for Denominator	Degrees of Freedom for Numerator											
	14	16	20	24	30	40	50	75	100	200	500	∞
40	1.95	1.90	1.84	1.79	1.74	1.69	1.66	1.61	1.59	1.55	1.53	1.51
	2.56	**2.49**	**2.37**	**2.29**	**2.20**	**2.11**	**2.05**	**1.97**	**1.94**	**1.88**	**1.84**	**1.81**
42	1.94	1.89	1.82	1.78	1.73	1.68	1.64	1.60	1.57	1.54	1.51	1.49
	2.54	**2.46**	**2.35**	**2.26**	**2.17**	**2.08**	**2.02**	**1.94**	**1.91**	**1.85**	**1.80**	**1.78**
44	1.92	1.88	1.81	1.76	1.72	1.66	1.63	1.58	1.56	1.52	1.50	1.48
	2.52	**2.44**	**2.32**	**2.24**	**2.15**	**2.06**	**2.00**	**1.92**	**1.88**	**1.82**	**1.78**	**1.75**
46	1.91	1.87	1.80	1.75	1.71	1.65	1.62	1.57	1.54	1.51	1.48	1.46
	2.50	**2.42**	**2.30**	**2.22**	**2.13**	**2.04**	**1.98**	**1.90**	**1.86**	**1.80**	**1.76**	**1.72**
48	1.90	1.86	1.79	1.74	1.70	1.64	1.61	1.56	1.53	1.50	1.47	1.45
	2.43	**2.40**	**2.28**	**2.20**	**2.11**	**2.02**	**1.96**	**1.88**	**1.84**	**1.78**	**1.73**	**1.70**
50	1.90	1.85	1.78	1.74	1.69	1.63	1.60	1.55	1.52	1.48	1.46	1.44
	2.46	**2.39**	**2.26**	**2.18**	**2.10**	**2.00**	**1.94**	**1.86**	**1.82**	**1.76**	**1.71**	**1.68**
55	1.88	1.83	1.76	1.72	1.67	1.61	1.58	1.52	1.50	1.46	1.43	1.41
	2.43	**2.35**	**2.23**	**2.15**	**2.06**	**1.96**	**1.90**	**1.82**	**1.78**	**1.71**	**1.66**	**1.64**
60	1.86	1.81	1.75	1.70	1.65	1.59	1.56	1.50	1.48	1.44	1.41	1.39
	2.40	**2.32**	**2.20**	**2.12**	**2.03**	**1.93**	**1.87**	**1.79**	**1.74**	**1.68**	**1.63**	**1.60**
65	1.85	1.80	1.73	1.68	1.63	1.57	1.54	1.49	1.46	1.42	1.39	1.37
	2.37	**2.30**	**2.18**	**2.09**	**2.00**	**1.90**	**1.84**	**1.76**	**1.71**	**1.64**	**1.60**	**1.56**
70	1.84	1.79	1.72	1.67	1.62	1.56	1.53	1.47	1.45	1.40	1.37	1.35
	2.35	**2.28**	**2.15**	**2.07**	**1.98**	**1.88**	**1.82**	**1.74**	**1.69**	**1.63**	**1.56**	**1.53**
80	1.82	1.77	1.70	1.65	1.60	1.54	1.51	1.45	1.42	1.38	1.35	1.32
	2.32	**2.24**	**2.11**	**2.03**	**1.94**	**1.84**	**1.78**	**1.70**	**1.65**	**1.57**	**1.52**	**1.49**
100	1.79	1.75	1.68	1.63	1.57	1.51	1.48	1.42	1.39	1.34	1.30	1.28
	2.26	**2.19**	**2.06**	**1.98**	**1.89**	**1.79**	**1.73**	**1.64**	**1.59**	**1.51**	**1.46**	**1.43**
125	1.77	1.72	1.65	1.60	1.55	1.49	1.45	1.39	1.36	1.31	1.27	1.25
	2.23	**2.15**	**2.03**	**1.94**	**1.85**	**1.75**	**1.68**	**1.59**	**1.54**	**1.46**	**1.40**	**1.37**
150	1.76	1.71	1.64	1.59	1.54	1.47	1.44	1.37	1.34	1.29	1.25	1.22
	2.20	**2.12**	**2.00**	**1.91**	**1.83**	**1.72**	**1.66**	**1.56**	**1.51**	**1.43**	**1.37**	**1.33**
200	1.74	1.69	1.62	1.57	1.52	1.45	1.42	1.35	1.32	1.26	1.22	1.19
	2.17	**2.09**	**1.97**	**1.88**	**1.79**	**1.69**	**1.62**	**1.53**	**1.48**	**1.39**	**1.33**	**1.28**
400	1.72	1.67	1.60	1.54	1.49	1.42	1.38	1.32	1.28	1.22	1.16	1.13
	2.12	**2.04**	**1.92**	**1.84**	**1.74**	**1.64**	**1.57**	**1.47**	**1.42**	**1.32**	**1.24**	**1.19**
1,000	1.70	1.65	1.58	1.53	1.47	1.41	1.36	1.30	1.26	1.19	1.13	1.08
	2.09	**2.01**	**1.89**	**1.81**	**1.71**	**1.61**	**1.54**	**1.44**	**1.38**	**1.28**	**1.19**	**1.11**
∞	1.69	1.64	1.57	1.52	1.46	1.40	1.35	1.28	1.24	1.17	1.11	1.00
	2.07	**1.99**	**1.87**	**1.79**	**1.69**	**1.59**	**1.52**	**1.41**	**1.36**	**1.25**	**1.15**	**1.00**

SOURCE: Reprinted by permission from *Statistical Methods* by George W. Snedecor and William G. Cochran, 7th ed. © 1980 by Iowa State University Press, Ames, Iowa 50010.

TABLE H
Chi-Square Distribution

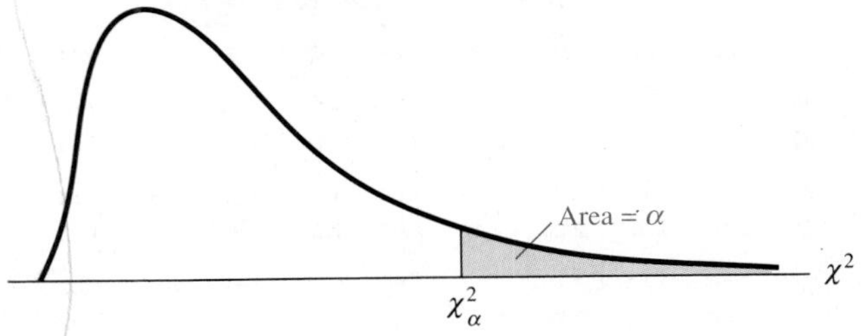

The following table provides the values of χ^2_α that correspond to a given upper tail area α and a specified number of degrees of freedom.

Degrees of Freedom	Upper Tail Area α						
	.99	.98	.95	.90	.80	.70	.50
1	$.0^3157$	$.0^3628$	.00393	.0158	.0642	.148	.455
2	.0201	.0404	.103	.211	.446	.713	1.386
3	.115	.185	.352	.584	1.005	1.424	2.366
4	.297	.429	.711	1.064	1.649	2.195	3.357
5	.554	.752	1.145	1.610	2.343	3.000	4.351
6	.872	1.134	1.635	2.204	3.070	3.828	5.348
7	1.239	1.564	2.167	2.833	3.822	4.671	6.346
8	1.646	2.032	2.733	3.490	4.594	5.527	7.344
9	2.088	2.532	3.325	4.168	5.380	6.393	8.343
10	2.558	3.059	3.940	4.865	6.179	7.267	9.342
11	3.053	3.609	4.575	5.578	6.989	8.148	10.341
12	3.571	4.178	5.226	6.304	7.807	9.034	11.340
13	4.107	4.765	5.892	7.042	8.634	9.926	12.340
14	4.660	5.368	6.571	7.790	9.467	10.821	13.339
15	5.229	5.985	7.261	8.547	10.307	11.721	14.339
16	5.812	6.614	7.962	9.312	11.152	12.624	15.338
17	6.408	7.255	8.672	10.085	12.002	13.531	16.338
18	7.015	7.906	9.390	10.865	12.857	14.440	17.338
19	7.633	8.567	10.117	11.651	13.716	15.352	18.338
20	8.260	9.237	10.851	12.443	14.578	16.266	19.337
21	8.897	9.915	11.591	13.240	15.445	17.182	20.337
22	9.542	10.600	12.338	14.041	16.314	18.101	21.337
23	10.196	11.293	13.091	14.848	17.187	19.021	22.337
24	10.856	11.992	13.848	15.659	18.062	19.943	23.337
25	11.524	12.697	14.611	16.473	18.940	20.867	24.337
26	12.198	13.409	15.379	17.292	19.820	21.792	25.336
27	12.879	14.125	16.151	18.114	20.703	22.719	26.336
28	13.565	14.847	16.928	18.939	21.588	23.647	27.336
29	14.256	15.574	17.708	19.768	22.475	24.577	28.336
30	14.953	16.306	18.493	20.599	23.364	25.508	29.336

TABLE H
(continued)

Degrees of Freedom	Upper Tail Area α						
	.30	.20	.10	.05	.02	.01	.001
1	1.074	1.642	2.706	3.841	5.412	6.635	10.827
2	2.408	3.219	4.605	5.991	7.824	9.210	13.815
3	3.665	4.642	6.251	7.815	9.837	11.345	16.268
4	4.878	5.989	7.779	9.488	11.668	13.277	18.465
5	6.064	7.289	9.236	11.070	13.388	15.086	20.517
6	7.231	8.558	10.645	12.592	15.033	16.812	22.457
7	8.383	9.803	12.017	14.067	16.622	18.475	24.322
8	9.524	11.030	13.362	15.507	18.168	20.090	26.125
9	10.656	12.242	14.684	16.919	19.679	21.666	27.877
10	11.781	13.442	15.987	18.307	21.161	23.209	29.588
11	12.899	14.631	17.275	19.675	22.618	24.725	31.264
12	14.011	15.812	18.549	21.026	24.054	26.217	32.909
13	15.119	16.985	19.812	22.362	25.472	27.688	34.528
14	16.222	18.151	21.064	23.685	26.873	29.141	36.123
15	17.322	19.311	22.307	24.996	28.259	30.578	37.697
16	18.418	20.465	23.542	26.296	29.633	32.000	39.252
17	19.511	21.615	24.769	27.587	30.995	33.409	40.790
18	20.601	22.760	25.989	28.869	32.346	34.805	42.312
19	21.689	23.900	27.204	30.144	33.687	36.191	43.820
20	22.775	25.038	28.412	31.410	35.020	37.566	45.315
21	23.858	26.171	29.615	32.671	36.343	38.932	46.797
22	24.939	27.301	30.813	33.924	37.659	40.289	48.268
23	26.018	28.429	32.007	35.172	38.968	41.638	49.728
24	27.096	29.553	33.196	36.415	40.270	42.980	51.179
25	28.172	30.675	34.382	37.652	41.566	44.314	52.620
26	29.246	31.795	35.563	38.885	42.856	45.642	54.052
27	30.319	32.912	36.741	40.113	44.140	46.963	55.476
28	31.391	34.027	37.916	41.337	45.419	48.278	56.893
29	32.461	35.139	39.087	42.557	46.693	49.588	58.302
30	33.530	36.250	40.256	43.773	47.962	50.892	59.703

SOURCE: From Table IV of Fisher and Yates, *Statistical Tables for Biological, Agricultural and Medical Research*, published by Longman Group Ltd., London (previously published by Oliver & Boyd, Edinburgh, 1963). Reproduced with permission of the authors and publishers.

TABLE I
Exponential Functions

y	e^y	e^{-y}	y	e^y	e^{-y}
0.00	1.0000	1.000000	3.00	20.086	.049787
0.10	1.1052	.904837	3.10	22.198	.045049
0.20	1.2214	.818731	3.20	24.533	.040762
0.30	1.3499	.740818	3.30	27.113	.036883
0.40	1.4918	.670320	3.40	29.964	.033373
0.50	1.6487	.606531	3.50	33.115	.030197
0.60	1.8221	.548812	3.60	36.598	.027324
0.70	2.0138	.496585	3.70	40.447	.024724
0.80	2.2255	.449329	3.80	44.701	.022371
0.90	2.4596	.406570	3.90	49.402	.020242
1.00	2.7183	.367879	4.00	54.598	.018316
1.10	3.0042	.332871	4.10	60.340	.016573
1.20	3.3201	.301194	4.20	66.686	.014996
1.30	3.6693	.272532	4.30	73.700	.013569
1.40	4.0552	.246597	4.40	81.451	.012277
1.50	4.4817	.223130	4.50	90.017	.011109
1.60	4.9530	.201897	4.60	99.484	.010052
1.70	5.4739	.182684	4.70	109.95	.009095
1.80	6.0496	.165299	4.80	121.51	.008230
1.90	6.6859	.149569	4.90	134.29	.007447
2.00	7.3891	.135335	5.00	148.41	.006738
2.10	8.1662	.122456	5.10	164.02	.006097
2.20	9.0250	.110803	5.20	181.27	.005517
2.30	9.9742	.100259	5.30	200.34	.004992
2.40	11.023	.090718	5.40	221.41	.004517
2.50	12.182	.082085	5.50	244.69	.004087
2.60	13.464	.074274	5.60	270.43	.003698
2.70	14.880	.067206	5.70	298.87	.003346
2.80	16.445	.060810	5.80	330.30	.003028
2.90	18.174	.055023	5.90	365.04	.002739
3.00	20.086	.049787	6.00	403.43	.002479

TABLE J
Cumulative Probability Values for the Poisson Distribution

λt	Pr[X ≤ x]									
	1.0	2.0	3.0	4.0	5.0	6.0	7.0	8.0	9.0	10.0
x										
0	0.3679	0.1353	0.0498	0.0183	0.0067	0.0025	0.0009	0.0003	0.0001	0.0000
1	0.7358	0.4060	0.1991	0.0916	0.0404	0.0174	0.0073	0.0030	0.0012	0.0005
2	0.9197	0.6767	0.4232	0.2381	0.1247	0.0620	0.0296	0.0138	0.0062	0.0028
3	0.9810	0.8571	0.6472	0.4335	0.2650	0.1512	0.0818	0.0424	0.0212	0.0103
4	0.9963	0.9473	0.8153	0.6288	0.4405	0.2851	0.1730	0.0996	0.0550	0.0293
5	0.9994	0.9834	0.9161	0.7851	0.6160	0.4457	0.3007	0.1912	0.1157	0.0671
6	0.9999	0.9955	0.9665	0.8893	0.7622	0.6063	0.4497	0.3134	0.2068	0.1301
7	1.0000	0.9989	0.9881	0.9489	0.8666	0.7440	0.5987	0.4530	0.3239	0.2202
8		0.9998	0.9962	0.9786	0.9319	0.8472	0.7291	0.5926	0.4557	0.3328
9		1.0000	0.9989	0.9919	0.9682	0.9161	0.8305	0.7166	0.5874	0.4579
10			0.9997	0.9972	0.9863	0.9574	0.9015	0.8159	0.7060	0.5830
11			0.9999	0.9991	0.9945	0.9799	0.9466	0.8881	0.8030	0.6968
12			1.0000	0.9997	0.9980	0.9912	0.9730	0.9362	0.8758	0.7916
13				0.9999	0.9993	0.9964	0.9872	0.9658	0.9262	0.8645
14				1.0000	0.9998	0.9986	0.9943	0.9827	0.9585	0.9165
15					0.9999	0.9995	0.9976	0.9918	0.9780	0.9513
16					1.0000	0.9998	0.9990	0.9963	0.9889	0.9730
17						0.9999	0.9996	0.9984	0.9947	0.9857
18						1.0000	0.9999	0.9993	0.9976	0.9928
19							0.9999	0.9997	0.9989	0.9965
20							1.0000	0.9999	0.9996	0.9984
21								1.0000	0.9998	0.9993
22									0.9999	0.9997
23									1.0000	0.9999
24										0.9999
25										1.0000

TABLE J
(continued)

λt	Pr[X ≤ x]									
	11.0	12.0	13.0	14.0	15.0	16.0	17.0	18.0	19.0	20.0
x										
0	0.0000	0.0000	0.0000	0.0000	0.0000	0.0000	0.0	0.0	0.0	0.0
1	0.0002	0.0001	0.0000	0.0000	0.0000	0.0000	0.0000	0.0000	0.0000	0.0
2	0.0012	0.0005	0.0002	0.0001	0.0000	0.0000	0.0000	0.0000	0.0000	0.0000
3	0.0049	0.0023	0.0011	0.0005	0.0002	0.0001	0.0000	0.0000	0.0000	0.0000
4	0.0151	0.0076	0.0037	0.0018	0.0009	0.0004	0.0002	0.0001	0.0000	0.0000
5	0.0375	0.0203	0.0107	0.0055	0.0028	0.0014	0.0007	0.0003	0.0002	0.0001
6	0.0786	0.0458	0.0259	0.0142	0.0076	0.0040	0.0021	0.0010	0.0005	0.0003
7	0.1432	0.0895	0.0540	0.0316	0.0180	0.0100	0.0054	0.0029	0.0015	0.0008
8	0.2320	0.1550	0.0998	0.0621	0.0374	0.0220	0.0126	0.0071	0.0039	0.0021
9	0.3405	0.2424	0.1658	0.1094	0.0699	0.0433	0.0261	0.0154	0.0089	0.0050
10	0.4599	0.3472	0.2517	0.1757	0.1185	0.0774	0.0491	0.0304	0.0183	0.0108
11	0.5793	0.4616	0.3532	0.2600	0.1847	0.1270	0.0847	0.0549	0.0347	0.0214
12	0.6887	0.5760	0.4631	0.3585	0.2676	0.1931	0.1350	0.0917	0.0606	0.0390
13	0.7813	0.6815	0.5730	0.4644	0.3632	0.2745	0.2009	0.1426	0.0984	0.0661
14	0.8540	0.7720	0.6751	0.5704	0.4656	0.3675	0.2808	0.2081	0.1497	0.1049
15	0.9074	0.8444	0.7636	0.6694	0.5681	0.4667	0.3714	0.2866	0.2148	0.1565
16	0.9441	0.8987	0.8355	0.7559	0.6641	0.5660	0.4677	0.3750	0.2920	0.2211
17	0.9678	0.9370	0.8905	0.8272	0.7489	0.6593	0.5640	0.4686	0.3784	0.2970
18	0.9823	0.9626	0.9302	0.8826	0.8195	0.7423	0.6549	0.5622	0.4695	0.3814
19	0.9907	0.9787	0.9573	0.9235	0.8752	0.8122	0.7363	0.6509	0.5606	0.4703
20	0.9953	0.9884	0.9750	0.9521	0.9170	0.8682	0.8055	0.7307	0.6472	0.5591
21	0.9977	0.9939	0.9859	0.9711	0.9469	0.9108	0.8615	0.7991	0.7255	0.6437
22	0.9989	0.9969	0.9924	0.9833	0.9672	0.9418	0.9047	0.8551	0.7931	0.7206
23	0.9995	0.9985	0.9960	0.9907	0.9805	0.9633	0.9367	0.8989	0.8490	0.7875
24	0.9998	0.9993	0.9980	0.9950	0.9888	0.9777	0.9593	0.9317	0.8933	0.8432
25	0.9999	0.9997	0.9990	0.9974	0.9938	0.9869	0.9747	0.9554	0.9269	0.8878
26	1.0000	0.9999	0.9995	0.9987	0.9967	0.9925	0.9848	0.9718	0.9514	0.9221
27		0.9999	0.9998	0.9994	0.9983	0.9959	0.9912	0.9827	0.9687	0.9475
28		1.0000	0.9999	0.9997	0.9991	0.9978	0.9950	0.9897	0.9805	0.9657
29			1.0000	0.9999	0.9996	0.9989	0.9973	0.9940	0.9981	0.9782
30				0.9999	0.9998	0.9994	0.9985	0.9967	0.9930	0.9865
31				1.0000	0.9999	0.9997	0.9992	0.9982	0.9960	0.9919
32					0.9999	0.9999	0.9996	0.9990	0.9978	0.9953
33					1.0000	0.9999	0.9998	0.9995	0.9988	0.9973
34						1.0000	0.9999	0.9997	0.9994	0.9985
35							0.9999	0.9999	0.9997	0.9992
36							1.0000	0.9999	0.9998	0.9996
37								1.0000	0.9999	0.9998
38									1.0000	0.9999
39										0.9999
40										1.0000

SOURCE: From *Management Science for Business Decisions* by Lawrence L. Lapin, copyright © 1980 by Harcourt Brace Jovanovich, Inc. Reproduced by permission of the publisher.

TABLE K
Critical Values for Studentized Range

Parameter for Denominator	$q_{.90}$ Parameter for Numerator								
	2	3	4	5	6	7	8	9	10
1	8.93	13.4	16.4	18.5	20.2	21.5	22.6	23.6	24.5
2	4.13	5.73	6.77	7.54	8.14	8.63	9.05	9.41	9.72
3	3.33	4.47	5.20	5.74	6.16	6.51	6.81	7.06	7.29
4	3.01	3.98	4.59	5.03	5.39	5.68	5.93	6.14	6.33
5	2.85	3.72	4.26	4.66	4.98	5.24	5.46	5.65	5.82
6	2.75	3.56	4.07	4.44	4.73	4.97	5.17	5.34	5.50
7	2.68	3.45	3.93	4.28	4.55	4.78	4.97	5.14	5.28
8	2.63	3.37	3.83	4.17	4.43	4.65	4.83	4.99	5.13
9	2.59	3.32	3.76	4.08	4.34	4.54	4.72	4.87	5.01
10	2.56	3.27	3.70	4.02	4.26	4.47	4.64	4.78	4.91
11	2.54	3.23	3.66	3.96	4.20	4.40	4.57	4.71	4.84
12	2.52	3.20	3.62	3.92	4.16	4.35	4.51	4.65	4.78
13	2.50	3.18	3.59	3.88	4.12	4.30	4.46	4.60	4.72
14	2.49	3.16	3.56	3.85	4.08	4.27	4.42	4.56	4.68
15	2.48	3.14	3.54	3.83	4.05	4.23	4.39	4.52	4.64
16	2.47	3.12	3.52	3.80	4.03	4.21	4.36	4.49	4.61
17	2.46	3.11	3.50	3.78	4.00	4.18	4.33	4.46	4.58
18	2.45	3.10	3.49	3.77	3.98	4.16	4.31	4.44	4.55
19	2.45	3.09	3.47	3.75	3.97	4.14	4.29	4.42	4.53
20	2.44	3.08	3.46	3.74	3.95	4.12	4.27	4.40	4.51
24	2.42	3.05	3.42	3.69	3.90	4.07	4.21	4.34	4.44
30	2.40	3.02	3.39	3.65	3.85	4.02	4.16	4.28	4.38
40	2.38	2.99	3.35	3.60	3.80	3.96	4.10	4.21	4.32
60	2.36	2.96	3.31	3.56	3.75	3.91	4.04	4.16	4.25
120	2.34	2.93	3.28	3.52	3.71	3.86	3.99	4.10	4.19
∞	2.33	2.90	3.24	3.48	3.66	3.81	3.93	4.04	4.13

TABLE K (*continued*)

Parameter for Denominator	$q_{.95}$ *Parameter for Numerator*								
	2	**3**	**4**	**5**	**6**	**7**	**8**	**9**	**10**
1	18.0	27.0	32.8	37.1	40.4	43.1	45.4	47.4	49.1
2	6.08	8.33	9.80	10.9	11.7	12.4	13.0	13.5	14.0
3	4.50	5.91	6.82	7.50	8.04	8.48	8.85	9.18	9.46
4	3.93	5.04	5.76	6.29	6.71	7.05	7.35	7.60	7.83
5	3.64	4.60	5.22	5.67	6.03	6.33	6.58	6.80	6.99
6	3.46	4.34	4.90	5.30	5.63	5.90	6.12	6.32	6.49
7	3.34	4.16	4.68	5.06	5.36	5.61	5.82	6.00	6.16
8	3.26	4.04	4.53	4.89	5.17	5.40	5.60	5.77	5.92
9	3.20	3.95	4.41	4.76	5.02	5.24	5.43	5.59	5.74
10	3.15	3.88	4.33	4.65	4.91	5.12	5.30	5.46	5.60
11	3.11	3.82	4.26	4.57	4.82	5.03	5.20	5.35	5.49
12	3.08	3.77	4.20	4.51	4.75	4.95	5.12	5.27	5.39
13	3.06	3.73	4.15	4.45	4.69	4.88	5.05	5.19	5.32
14	3.03	3.70	4.11	4.41	4.64	4.83	4.99	5.13	5.25
15	3.01	3.67	4.08	4.37	4.59	4.78	4.94	5.08	5.20
16	3.00	3.65	4.05	4.33	4.56	4.74	4.90	5.03	5.15
17	2.98	3.63	4.02	4.30	4.52	4.70	4.86	4.99	5.11
18	2.97	3.61	4.00	4.28	4.49	4.67	4.82	4.96	5.07
19	2.96	3.59	3.98	4.25	4.47	4.65	4.79	4.92	5.04
20	2.95	3.58	3.96	4.23	4.45	4.62	4.77	4.90	5.01
24	2.92	3.53	3.90	4.17	4.37	4.54	4.68	4.81	4.92
30	2.89	3.49	3.85	4.10	4.30	4.46	4.60	4.72	4.82
40	2.86	3.44	3.79	4.04	4.23	4.39	4.52	4.63	4.73
60	2.83	3.40	3.74	3.98	4.16	4.31	4.44	4.55	4.65
120	2.80	3.36	3.68	3.92	4.10	4.24	4.36	4.47	4.56
∞	2.77	3.31	3.63	3.86	4.03	4.17	4.29	4.39	4.47

TABLE K (continued)

Parameter for Denominator	$q_{.90}$ Parameter for Numerator									
	11	12	13	14	15	16	17	18	19	20
1	25.2	25.9	26.5	27.1	27.6	28.1	28.5	29.0	29.3	29.7
2	10.0	10.3	10.5	10.7	10.9	11.1	11.2	11.4	11.5	11.7
3	7.49	7.67	7.83	7.98	8.12	8.25	8.37	8.48	8.58	8.68
4	6.49	6.65	6.78	6.91	7.02	7.13	7.23	7.33	7.41	7.50
5	5.97	6.10	6.22	6.34	6.44	6.54	6.63	6.71	6.79	6.86
6	5.64	5.76	5.87	5.98	6.07	6.16	6.25	6.32	6.40	6.47
7	5.41	5.53	5.64	5.74	5.83	5.91	5.99	6.06	6.13	6.19
8	5.25	5.36	5.46	5.56	5.64	5.72	5.80	5.87	5.93	6.00
9	5.13	5.23	5.33	5.42	5.51	5.58	5.66	5.72	5.79	5.85
10	5.03	5.13	5.23	5.32	5.40	5.47	5.54	5.61	5.67	5.73
11	4.95	5.05	5.15	5.23	5.31	5.38	5.45	5.51	5.57	5.63
12	4.89	4.99	5.08	5.16	5.24	5.31	5.37	5.44	5.49	5.55
13	4.83	4.93	5.02	5.10	5.18	5.25	5.31	5.37	5.43	5.48
14	4.79	4.88	4.97	5.05	5.12	5.19	5.26	5.32	5.37	5.43
15	4.75	4.84	4.93	5.01	5.08	5.15	5.21	5.27	5.32	5.38
16	4.71	4.81	4.89	4.97	5.04	5.11	5.17	5.23	5.28	5.33
17	4.68	4.77	4.86	4.93	5.01	5.07	5.13	5.19	5.24	5.30
18	4.65	4.75	4.83	4.90	4.98	5.04	5.10	5.16	5.21	5.26
19	4.63	4.72	4.80	4.88	4.95	5.01	5.07	5.13	5.18	5.23
20	4.61	4.70	4.78	4.85	4.92	4.99	5.05	5.10	5.16	5.20
24	4.54	4.63	4.71	4.78	4.85	4.91	4.97	5.02	5.07	5.12
30	4.47	4.56	4.64	4.71	4.77	4.83	4.89	4.94	4.99	5.03
40	4.41	4.49	4.56	4.63	4.69	4.75	4.81	4.86	4.90	4.95
60	4.34	4.42	4.49	4.56	4.62	4.67	4.73	4.78	4.82	4.86
120	4.28	4.35	4.42	4.48	4.54	4.60	4.65	4.69	4.74	4.78
∞	4.21	4.28	4.35	4.41	4.47	4.52	4.57	4.61	4.65	4.69

TABLE K
(continued)

Parameter for Denominator	$q_{.95}$ *Parameter for Numerator*									
	11	**12**	**13**	**14**	**15**	**16**	**17**	**18**	**19**	**20**
1	50.6	52.0	53.2	54.3	55.4	56.3	57.2	58.0	58.8	59.6
2	14.4	14.7	15.1	15.4	15.7	15.9	16.1	16.4	16.6	16.8
3	9.72	9.95	10.2	10.3	10.5	10.7	10.8	11.0	11.1	11.2
4	8.03	8.21	8.37	8.52	8.66	8.79	8.91	9.03	9.13	9.23
5	7.17	7.32	7.47	7.60	7.72	7.83	7.93	8.03	8.12	8.21
6	6.65	6.79	6.92	7.03	7.14	7.24	7.34	7.43	7.51	7.59
7	6.30	6.43	6.55	6.66	6.76	6.85	6.94	7.02	7.10	7.17
8	6.05	6.18	6.29	6.39	6.48	6.57	6.65	6.73	6.80	6.87
9	5.87	5.98	6.09	6.19	6.28	6.36	6.44	6.51	6.58	6.64
10	5.72	5.83	5.93	6.03	6.11	6.19	6.27	6.34	6.40	6.47
11	5.61	5.71	5.81	5.90	5.98	6.06	6.13	6.20	6.27	6.33
12	5.51	5.61	5.71	5.80	5.88	5.95	6.02	6.09	6.15	6.21
13	5.43	5.53	5.63	5.71	5.79	5.86	5.93	5.99	6.05	6.11
14	5.36	5.46	5.55	5.64	5.71	5.79	5.85	5.91	5.97	6.03
15	5.31	5.40	5.49	5.57	5.65	5.72	5.78	5.85	5.90	5.96
16	5.26	5.35	5.44	5.52	5.59	5.66	5.73	5.79	5.84	5.90
17	5.21	5.31	5.39	5.47	5.54	5.61	5.67	5.73	5.79	5.84
18	5.17	5.27	5.35	5.43	5.50	5.57	5.63	5.69	5.74	5.79
19	5.14	5.23	5.31	5.39	5.46	5.53	5.59	5.65	5.70	5.75
20	5.11	5.20	5.28	5.36	5.43	5.49	5.55	5.61	5.66	5.71
24	5.01	5.10	5.18	5.25	5.32	5.38	5.44	5.49	5.55	5.59
30	4.92	5.00	5.08	5.15	5.21	5.27	5.33	5.38	5.43	5.47
40	4.82	4.90	4.98	5.04	5.11	5.16	5.22	5.27	5.31	5.36
60	4.73	4.81	4.88	4.94	5.00	5.06	5.11	5.15	5.20	5.24
120	4.64	4.71	4.78	4.84	4.90	4.95	5.00	5.04	5.09	5.13
∞	4.55	4.62	4.68	4.74	4.80	4.85	4.89	4.93	4.97	5.01

TABLE K (continued)

Parameter for Denominator	$q_{.99}$ Parameter for Numerator								
	2	3	4	5	6	7	8	9	10
1	90.0	135	164	186	202	216	227	237	246
2	14.0	19.0	22.3	24.7	26.6	28.2	29.5	30.7	31.7
3	8.26	10.6	12.2	13.3	14.2	15.0	15.6	16.2	16.7
4	6.51	8.12	9.17	9.96	10.6	11.1	11.5	11.9	12.3
5	5.70	6.97	7.80	8.42	8.91	9.32	9.67	9.97	10.2
6	5.24	6.33	7.03	7.56	7.97	8.32	8.61	8.87	9.10
7	4.95	5.92	6.54	7.01	7.37	7.68	7.94	8.17	8.37
8	4.74	5.63	6.20	6.63	6.96	7.24	7.47	7.68	7.87
9	4.60	5.43	5.96	6.35	6.66	6.91	7.13	7.32	7.49
10	4.48	5.27	5.77	6.14	6.43	6.67	6.87	7.05	7.21
11	4.39	5.14	5.62	5.97	6.25	6.48	6.67	6.84	6.99
12	4.32	5.04	5.50	5.84	6.10	6.32	6.51	6.67	6.81
13	4.26	4.96	5.40	5.73	5.98	6.19	6.37	6.53	6.67
14	4.21	4.89	5.32	5.63	5.88	6.08	6.26	6.41	6.54
15	4.17	4.83	5.25	5.56	5.80	5.99	6.16	6.31	6.44
16	4.13	4.78	5.19	5.49	5.72	5.92	6.08	6.22	6.35
17	4.10	4.74	5.14	5.43	5.66	5.85	6.01	6.15	6.27
18	4.07	4.70	5.09	5.38	5.60	5.79	5.94	6.08	6.20
19	4.05	4.67	5.05	5.33	5.55	5.73	5.89	6.02	6.14
20	4.02	4.64	5.02	5.29	5.51	5.69	5.84	5.97	6.09
24	3.96	4.54	4.91	5.17	5.37	5.54	5.69	5.81	5.92
30	3.89	4.45	4.80	5.05	5.24	5.40	5.54	5.65	5.76
40	3.82	4.37	4.70	4.93	5.11	5.27	5.39	5.50	5.60
60	3.76	4.28	4.60	4.82	4.99	5.13	5.25	5.36	5.45
120	3.70	4.20	4.50	4.71	4.87	5.01	5.12	5.21	5.30
∞	3.64	4.12	4.40	4.60	4.76	4.88	4.99	5.08	5.16

TABLE K (continued)

Parameter for Denominator	$q_{.99}$ Parameter for Numerator									
	11	12	13	14	15	16	17	18	19	20
1	253	260	266	272	277	282	286	290	294	298
2	32.6	33.4	34.1	34.8	35.4	36.0	36.5	37.0	37.5	37.9
3	17.1	17.5	17.9	18.2	18.5	18.8	19.1	19.3	19.5	19.8
4	12.6	12.8	13.1	13.3	13.5	13.7	13.9	14.1	14.2	14.4
5	10.5	10.7	10.9	11.1	11.2	11.4	11.6	11.7	11.8	11.9
6	9.30	9.49	9.65	9.81	9.95	10.1	10.2	10.3	10.4	10.5
7	8.55	8.71	8.86	9.00	9.12	9.24	9.35	9.46	9.55	9.65
8	8.03	8.18	8.31	8.44	8.55	8.66	8.76	8.85	8.94	9.03
9	7.65	7.78	7.91	8.03	8.13	8.23	8.32	8.41	8.49	8.57
10	7.36	7.48	7.60	7.71	7.81	7.91	7.99	8.07	8.15	8.22
11	7.13	7.25	7.36	7.46	7.56	7.65	7.73	7.81	7.88	7.95
12	6.94	7.06	7.17	7.26	7.36	7.44	7.52	7.59	7.66	7.73
13	6.79	6.90	7.01	7.10	7.19	7.27	7.34	7.42	7.48	7.55
14	6.66	6.77	6.87	6.96	7.05	7.12	7.20	7.27	7.33	7.39
15	6.55	6.66	6.76	6.84	6.93	7.00	7.07	7.14	7.20	7.26
16	6.46	6.56	6.66	6.74	6.82	6.90	6.97	7.03	7.09	7.15
17	6.38	6.48	6.57	6.66	6.73	6.80	6.87	6.94	7.00	7.05
18	6.31	6.41	6.50	6.58	6.65	6.72	6.79	6.85	6.91	6.96
19	6.25	6.34	6.43	6.51	6.58	6.65	6.72	6.78	6.84	6.89
20	6.19	6.29	6.37	6.45	6.52	6.59	6.65	6.71	6.76	6.82
24	6.02	6.11	6.19	6.26	6.33	6.39	6.45	6.51	6.56	6.61
30	5.85	5.93	6.01	6.08	6.14	6.20	6.26	6.31	6.36	6.41
40	5.69	5.77	5.84	5.90	5.96	6.02	6.07	6.12	6.17	6.21
60	5.53	5.60	5.67	5.73	5.79	5.84	5.89	5.93	5.98	6.02
120	5.38	5.44	5.51	5.56	5.61	5.66	5.71	5.75	5.79	5.83
∞	5.23	5.29	5.35	5.40	5.45	5.49	5.54	5.57	5.61	5.65

SOURCE: E. S. Pearson and H. O. Hartley, *Biometrika Tables for Statisticians*, Vol. I. London: Cambridge University Press, 1966. Partly derived from J. Pachares. Reproduced with permission of the authors and publishers.

TABLE L
Critical Values of D for Kilmogorov-Smirnov Goodness-of-Fit Test

The following table provides the critical values D_α corresponding to an upper tail probability α of the test statistic D. The following relationship holds

$$\alpha = \Pr[D \geq D_\alpha]$$

n	$\alpha = .10$	$\alpha = .05$	$\alpha = .025$	$\alpha = .01$	$\alpha = .005$
1	.90000	.95000	.97500	.99000	.99500
2	.68377	.77639	.84189	.90000	.92929
3	.56481	.63604	.70760	.78456	.82900
4	.49265	.56522	.62394	.68887	.73424
5	.44698	.50945	.56328	.62718	.66853
6	.41037	.46799	.51926	.57741	.61661
7	.38148	.43607	.48342	.53844	.57581
8	.35831	.40962	.45427	.50654	.54179
9	.33910	.38746	.43001	.47960	.51332
10	.32260	.36866	.40925	.45662	.48893
11	.30829	.35242	.39122	.43670	.46770
12	.29577	.33815	.37543	.41918	.44905
13	.28470	.32549	.36143	.40362	.43247
14	.27481	.31417	.34890	.38970	.41762
15	.26588	.30397	.33760	.37713	.40420
16	.25778	.29472	.32733	.36571	.39201
17	.25039	.28627	.31796	.35528	.38086
18	.24360	.27851	.30936	.34569	.37062
19	.23735	.27136	.30143	.33685	.36117
20	.23156	.26473	.29408	.32866	.35241
21	.22617	.25858	.28724	.32104	.34427
22	.22115	.25283	.28087	.31394	.33666
23	.21645	.24746	.27490	.30728	.32954
24	.21205	.24242	.26931	.30104	.32286
25	.20790	.23768	.26404	.29516	.31657
26	.20399	.23320	.25907	.28962	.31064
27	.20030	.22898	.25438	.28438	.30502
28	.19680	.22497	.24993	.27942	.29971
29	.19348	.22117	.24571	.27471	.29466
30	.19032	.21756	.24170	.27023	.28987
31	.18732	.21412	.23788	.26596	.28530
32	.18445	.21085	.23424	.26189	.28094
33	.18171	.20771	.23076	.25801	.27677
34	.17909	.20472	.22743	.25429	.27279
35	.17659	.20185	.22425	.25073	.26897
36	.17418	.19910	.22119	.24732	.26532
37	.17188	.19646	.21826	.24404	.26180
38	.16966	.19392	.21544	.24089	.25843
39	.16753	.19148	.21273	.23786	.25518
40	.16547	.18913	.21012	.23494	.25205

TABLE L (*continued*)

n	$\alpha = .10$	$\alpha = .05$	$\alpha = .025$	$\alpha = .01$	$\alpha = .005$
41	.16349	.18687	.20760	.23213	.24904
42	.16158	.18468	.20517	.22941	.24613
43	.15974	.18257	.20283	.22679	.24332
44	.15796	.18053	.20056	.22426	.24060
45	.15623	.17856	.19837	.22181	.23798
46	.15457	.17665	.19625	.21944	.23544
47	.15295	.17481	.19420	.21715	.23298
48	.15139	.17302	.19221	.21493	.23059
49	.14987	.17128	.19028	.21277	.22828
50	.14840	.16959	.18841	.21068	.22604
51	.14697	.16796	.18659	.20864	.22386
52	.14558	.16637	.18482	.20667	.22174
53	.14423	.16483	.18311	.20475	.21968
54	.14292	.16332	.18144	.20289	.21768
55	.14164	.16186	.17981	.20107	.21574
56	.14040	.16044	.17823	.19930	.21384
57	.13919	.15906	.17669	.19758	.21199
58	.13801	.15771	.17519	.19590	.21019
59	.13686	.15639	.17373	.19427	.20844
60	.13573	.15511	.17231	.19267	.20673
61	.13464	.15385	.17091	.19112	.20506
62	.13357	.15263	.16956	.18960	.20343
63	.13253	.15144	.16823	.18812	.20184
64	.13151	.15027	.16693	.18667	.20029
65	.13052	.14913	.16567	.18525	.19877
66	.12954	.14802	.16443	.18387	.19729
67	.12859	.14693	.16322	.18252	.19584
68	.12766	.14587	.16204	.18119	.19442
69	.12675	.14483	.16088	.17990	.19303
70	.12586	.14381	.15975	.17863	.19167
71	.12499	.14281	.15864	.17739	.19034
72	.12413	.14183	.15755	.17618	.18903
73	.12329	.14087	.15649	.17498	.18776
74	.12247	.13993	.15544	.17382	.18650
75	.12167	.13901	.15442	.17268	.18528
76	.12088	.13811	.15342	.17155	.18408
77	.12011	.13723	.15244	.17045	.18290
78	.11935	.13636	.15147	.16938	.18174
79	.11860	.13551	.15052	.16832	.18060
80	.11787	.13467	.14960	.16728	.17949

TABLE L (continued)

n	α = .10	α = .05	α = .025	α = .01	α = .005
81	.11716	.13385	.14868	.16626	.17840
82	.11645	.13305	.14779	.16526	.17732
83	.11576	.13226	.14691	.16428	.17627
84	.11508	.13148	.14605	.16331	.17523
85	.11442	.13072	.14520	.16236	.17421
86	.11376	.12997	.14437	.16143	.17321
87	.11311	.12923	.14355	.16051	.17223
88	.11248	.12850	.14274	.15961	.17126
89	.11186	.12779	.14195	.15873	.17031
90	.11125	.12709	.14117	.15786	.16938
91	.11064	.12640	.14040	.15700	.16846
92	.11005	.12572	.13965	.15616	.16755
93	.10947	.12506	.13891	.15533	.16666
94	.10889	.12440	.13818	.15451	.16579
95	.10833	.12375	.13746	.15371	.16493
96	.10777	.12312	.13675	.15291	.16408
97	.10722	.12249	.13606	.15214	.16324
98	.10668	.12187	.13537	.15137	.16242
99	.10615	.12126	.13469	.15061	.16161
100	.10563	.12067	.13403	.14987	.16081

SOURCE: Reprinted by permission from L. H. Miller, "Table of Percentage Points of Kolmogorov Statistics," *Journal of the American Statistical Association*, 51 (1956), pages 111–121.

TABLE M
Constants for Computing Control Chart Limits

Sample Size n	Conversion Constant for Range d_R	Standard Deviation Ratio σ_w
2	1.128	.8525
3	1.693	.8884
4	2.059	.8798
5	2.326	.8641
6	2.534	.8480
7	2.704	.8332
8	2.847	.8198
9	2.970	.8078
10	3.078	.7971
11	3.173	.7873
12	3.258	.7785

SOURCE: Values for d_R were obtained from American Society of Testing Materials, *A.S.T.M. Manual on Quality Control of Materials*, Philadelphia, 1951. Values for σ_w were obtained from E. S. Pearson and H. O. Hartley, *Biometrika Tables for Statisticians*, Vol. I, Cambridge University Press, 1966. Reproduced with permission of the authors and publishers.

TABLE N
Loss Function for Decision Making with the Normal Curve

	L(D)				
D	.00	.01	.02	.03	.04
.0	.3989	.3940	.3890	.3841	.3793
.1	.3509	.3464	.3418	.3373	.3328
.2	.3069	.3027	.2986	.2944	.2904
.3	.2668	.2630	.2592	.2555	.2518
.4	.2304	.2270	.2236	.2203	.2169
.5	.1978	.1947	.1917	.1887	.1857
.6	.1687	.1659	.1633	.1606	.1580
.7	.1429	.1405	.1381	.1358	.1334
.8	.1202	.1181	.1160	.1140	.1120
.9	.1004	.09860	.09680	.09503	.09328
1.0	.08332	.08174	.08019	.07866	.07716
1.1	.06862	.06727	.06595	.06465	.06336
1.2	.05610	.05496	.05384	.05274	.05165
1.3	.04553	.04457	.04363	.04270	.04179
1.4	.03667	.03587	.03508	.03431	.03356
1.5	.02931	.02865	.02800	.02736	.02674
1.6	.02324	.02270	.02217	.02165	.02114
1.7	.01829	.01785	.01742	.01699	.01658
1.8	.01428	.01392	.01357	.01323	.01290
1.9	.01105	.01077	.01049	.01022	$.0^{2}9957$
2.0	$.0^{2}8491$	$.0^{2}8266$	$.0^{2}8046$	$.0^{2}7832$	$.0^{2}7623$
2.1	$.0^{2}6468$	$.0^{2}6292$	$.0^{2}6120$	$.0^{2}5952$	$.0^{2}5788$
2.2	$.0^{2}4887$	$.0^{2}4750$	$.0^{2}4616$	$.0^{2}4486$	$.0^{2}4358$
2.3	$.0^{2}3662$	$.0^{2}3556$	$.0^{2}3453$	$.0^{2}3352$	$.0^{2}3255$
2.4	$.0^{2}2720$	$.0^{2}2640$	$.0^{2}2561$	$.0^{2}2484$	$.0^{2}2410$
2.5	$.0^{2}2004$	$.0^{2}1943$	$.0^{2}1883$	$.0^{2}1826$	$.0^{2}1769$
2.6	$.0^{2}1464$	$.0^{2}1418$	$.0^{2}1373$	$.0^{2}1330$	$.0^{2}1288$
2.7	$.0^{2}1060$	$.0^{2}1026$	$.0^{3}9928$	$.0^{3}9607$	$.0^{3}9295$
2.8	$.0^{3}7611$	$.0^{3}7359$	$.0^{3}7115$	$.0^{3}6879$	$.0^{3}6650$
2.9	$.0^{3}5417$	$.0^{3}5233$	$.0^{3}5055$	$.0^{3}4883$	$.0^{3}4716$
3.0	$.0^{3}3822$	$.0^{3}3689$	$.0^{3}3560$	$.0^{3}3436$	$.0^{3}3316$
3.1	$.0^{3}2673$	$.0^{3}2577$	$.0^{3}2485$	$.0^{3}2396$	$.0^{3}2311$
3.2	$.0^{3}1852$	$.0^{3}1785$	$.0^{3}1720$	$.0^{3}1657$	$.0^{3}1596$
3.3	$.0^{3}1273$	$.0^{3}1225$	$.0^{3}1179$	$.0^{3}1135$	$.0^{3}1093$
3.4	$.0^{4}8666$	$.0^{4}8335$	$.0^{4}8016$	$.0^{4}7709$	$.0^{4}7413$
3.5	$.0^{4}5848$	$.0^{4}5620$	$.0^{4}5400$	$.0^{4}5188$	$.0^{4}4984$
3.6	$.0^{4}3911$	$.0^{4}3755$	$.0^{4}3605$	$.0^{4}3460$	$.0^{4}3321$
3.7	$.0^{4}2592$	$.0^{4}2486$	$.0^{4}2385$	$.0^{4}2287$	$.0^{4}2193$
3.8	$.0^{4}1702$	$.0^{4}1632$	$.0^{4}1563$	$.0^{4}1498$	$.0^{4}1435$
3.9	$.0^{4}1108$	$.0^{4}1061$	$.0^{4}1016$	$.0^{5}9723$	$.0^{5}9307$
4.0	$.0^{5}7145$	$.0^{5}6835$	$.0^{5}6538$	$.0^{5}6253$	$.0^{5}5980$
4.1	$.0^{5}4566$	$.0^{5}4364$	$.0^{5}4170$	$.0^{5}3985$	$.0^{5}3807$
4.2	$.0^{5}2891$	$.0^{5}2760$	$.0^{5}2635$	$.0^{5}2516$	$.0^{5}2402$
4.3	$.0^{5}1814$	$.0^{5}1730$	$.0^{5}1650$	$.0^{5}1574$	$.0^{5}1501$
4.4	$.0^{5}1127$	$.0^{5}1074$	$.0^{5}1024$	$.0^{6}9756$	$.0^{6}9296$
4.5	$.0^{6}6942$	$.0^{6}6610$	$.0^{6}6294$	$.0^{6}5992$	$.0^{6}5704$
4.6	$.0^{6}4236$	$.0^{6}4029$	$.0^{6}3833$	$.0^{6}3645$	$.0^{6}3467$
4.7	$.0^{6}2560$	$.0^{6}2433$	$.0^{6}2313$	$.0^{6}2197$	$.0^{6}2088$
4.8	$.0^{6}1533$	$.0^{6}1456$	$.0^{6}1382$	$.0^{6}1312$	$.0^{6}1246$
4.9	$.0^{7}9096$	$.0^{7}8629$	$.0^{7}8185$	$.0^{7}7763$	$.0^{7}7362$

SOURCE: From Robert O. Schlaifer, *Introduction to Statistics for Business Decisions.* New York: McGraw-Hill Book Co., 1961. Reproduced by permission of the copyright holder, the President and Fellows of Harvard College.

TABLE N
(continued)

L(D)				
.05	**.06**	**.07**	**.08**	**.09**
.3744	.3697	.3649	.3602	.3556
.3284	.3240	.3197	.3154	.3111
.2863	.2824	.2784	.2745	.2706
.2481	.2445	.2409	.2374	.2339
.2137	.2104	.2072	.2040	.2009
.1828	.1799	.1771	.1742	.1714
.1554	.1528	.1503	.1478	.1453
.1312	.1289	.1267	.1245	.1223
.1100	.1080	.1061	.1042	.1023
.09156	.08986	.08819	.08654	.08491
.07568	.07422	.07279	.07138	.06999
.06210	.06086	.05964	.05844	.05726
.05059	.04954	.04851	.04750	.04650
.04090	.04002	.03916	.03831	.03748
.03281	.03208	.03137	.03067	.02998
.02612	.02552	.02494	.02436	.02380
.02064	.02015	.01967	.01920	.01874
.01617	.01578	.01539	.01501	.01464
.01257	.01226	.01195	.01164	.01134
$.0^{2}9698$	$.0^{2}9445$	$.0^{2}9198$	$.0^{2}8957$	$.0^{2}8721$
$.0^{2}7418$	$.0^{2}7219$	$.0^{2}7024$	$.0^{2}6835$	$.0^{2}6649$
$.0^{2}5628$	$.0^{2}5472$	$.0^{2}5320$	$.0^{2}5172$	$.0^{2}5028$
$.0^{2}4235$	$.0^{2}4114$	$.0^{2}3996$	$.0^{2}3882$	$.0^{2}3770$
$.0^{2}3159$	$.0^{2}3067$	$.0^{2}2977$	$.0^{2}2889$	$.0^{2}2804$
$.0^{2}2337$	$.0^{2}2267$	$.0^{2}2199$	$.0^{2}2132$	$.0^{2}2067$
$.0^{2}1715$	$.0^{2}1662$	$.0^{2}1610$	$.0^{2}1560$	$.0^{2}1511$
$.0^{2}1247$	$.0^{2}1207$	$.0^{2}1169$	$.0^{2}1132$	$.0^{2}1095$
$.0^{3}8992$	$.0^{3}8699$	$.0^{3}8414$	$.0^{3}8138$	$.0^{3}7870$
$.0^{3}6428$	$.0^{3}6213$	$.0^{3}6004$	$.0^{3}5802$	$.0^{3}5606$
$.0^{3}4555$	$.0^{3}4398$	$.0^{3}4247$	$.0^{3}4101$	$.0^{3}3959$
$.0^{3}3199$	$.0^{3}3087$	$.0^{3}2978$	$.0^{3}2873$	$.0^{3}2771$
$.0^{3}2227$	$.0^{3}2147$	$.0^{3}2070$	$.0^{3}1995$	$.0^{3}1922$
$.0^{3}1537$	$.0^{3}1480$	$.0^{3}1426$	$.0^{3}1373$	$.0^{3}1322$
$.0^{3}1051$	$.0^{3}1012$	$.0^{4}9734$	$.0^{4}9365$	$.0^{4}9009$
$.0^{4}7127$	$.0^{4}6852$	$.0^{4}6587$	$.0^{4}6331$	$.0^{4}6085$
$.0^{4}4788$	$.0^{4}4599$	$.0^{4}4417$	$.0^{4}4242$	$.0^{4}4073$
$.0^{4}3188$	$.0^{4}3059$	$.0^{4}2935$	$.0^{4}2816$	$.0^{4}2702$
$.0^{4}2103$	$.0^{4}2016$	$.0^{4}1933$	$.0^{4}1853$	$.0^{4}1776$
$.0^{4}1375$	$.0^{4}1317$	$.0^{4}1262$	$.0^{4}1208$	$.0^{4}1157$
$.0^{5}8908$	$.0^{5}8525$	$.0^{5}8158$	$.0^{5}7806$	$.0^{5}7469$
$.0^{5}5718$	$.0^{5}5468$	$.0^{5}5227$	$.0^{5}4997$	$.0^{5}4777$
$.0^{5}3637$	$.0^{5}3475$	$.0^{5}3319$	$.0^{5}3170$	$.0^{5}3027$
$.0^{5}2292$	$.0^{5}2188$	$.0^{5}2088$	$.0^{5}1992$	$.0^{5}1901$
$.0^{5}1431$	$.0^{5}1365$	$.0^{5}1301$	$.0^{5}1241$	$.0^{5}1183$
$.0^{6}8857$	$.0^{6}8437$	$.0^{6}8037$	$.0^{6}7655$	$.0^{6}7290$
$.0^{6}5429$	$.0^{6}5167$	$.0^{6}4917$	$.0^{6}4679$	$.0^{6}4452$
$.0^{6}3297$	$.0^{6}3135$	$.0^{6}2981$	$.0^{6}2834$	$.0^{6}2694$
$.0^{6}1984$	$.0^{6}1884$	$.0^{6}1790$	$.0^{6}1700$	$.0^{6}1615$
$.0^{6}1182$	$.0^{6}1122$	$.0^{6}1065$	$.0^{6}1011$	$.0^{7}9588$
$.0^{7}6982$	$.0^{7}6620$	$.0^{7}6276$	$.0^{7}5950$	$.0^{7}5640$

ANSWERS TO EVEN-NUMBERED EXERCISES

1-2 Answers will vary.

1-4 Answers will vary.

1-6 (a) ordinal (b) nominal (c) interval (d) ratio (e) interval

1-8 Answers will vary.

1-10 (a)

slipper, hat	hat, dog	dog, thimble
slipper, dog	hat, thimble	dog, car
slipper, thimble	hat, car	thimble, car
slipper, car		

(b)

slipper, hat, dog	slipper, thimble, car
slipper, hat, thimble	hat, dog, thimble
slipper, hat, car	hat, dog, car
slipper, dog, thimble	hat, thimble, car
slipper, dog, car	dog, thimble, car

1-12 Answers will vary.

1-14 (a) deductive (c) deductive
(b) inductive (d) inductive

1-16 Answers will vary.

1-18 Answers will vary.

1-20 Answers will vary.

2-2 (a)

0.	4 7 3 7 6 3 5 8
1.	6 2 8 8 2 0 5 2 5 1 8
2.	9 8 6 6 2 9 6 0 9 7 2 1 9 9 9 3 9 0 9 2 7 4 4
3.	8 1 4 7 0 7 3 4 6 2 2 6 7 3 9 6 1 4 6 8 5 3 9 6 6 2 3 1 4
4.	4 0 2 0 1 0 8 5 0 0
5.	0 9 4 8 4

(b)

Class Interval (inches)	Frequency
0.0–under 1.0	8
1.0–under 2.0	11
2.0–under 3.0	23
3.0–under 4.0	29
4.0–under 5.0	10
5.0–under 6.0	5
	86

2-4 (a)

Class Interval	Frequency	Class Interval	Frequency
\$ 3,000–under 5,000	4	\$15,000–under 17,000	2
5,000–under 7,000	6	17,000–under 19,000	1
7,000–under 9,000	13	19,000–under 21,000	0
9,000–under 11,000	13	21,000–under 23,000	1
11,000–under 13,000	7	23,000–under 25,000	1
13,000–under 15,000	1	25,000–under 27,000	1
			50

2-6 (a)

Class Interval (inches)	Frequency
58–under 59	2
59–under 60	2
60–under 61	4
61–under 62	7
62–under 63	7
63–under 64	12
64–under 65	9
65–under 66	4
66–under 67	2
67–under 68	1
	50

2-8

Letter	Frequency	Letter	Frequency	Letter	Frequency
a	20	j	0	s	7
b	2	k	0	t	22
c	7	l	5	u	4
d	8	m	1	v	3
e	26	n	20	w	5
f	3	o	17	x	0
g	6	p	2	y	2
h	9	q	1	z	0
i	14	r	16		200

2-10 (a) ambiguous designations (c) some values not included
(b) overlapping intervals

2-14

Class Interval (mpg)	(a) Relative Frequency	(b) Cumulative Frequency
14.0–under 16.0	.09	9
16.0–under 18.0	.13	22
18.0–under 20.0	.24	46
20.0–under 22.0	.38	84
22.0–under 24.0	.16	100

2-16

Consecutive Days Absent	(a) Relative Frequency	(b) Cumulative Relative Frequency
0–under 5	.620	.620
5–under 10	.162	.782
10–under 15	.102	.884
15–under 20	.064	.948
20–under 25	.024	.972
25–under 30	.006	.978
30–under 60	.022	1.000
	1.000	

2-18

Number of Shares (thousands)	Cumulative Relative Frequency	(a) Relative Frequency	(b) Frequency [(a) × 1,000)]	(c) Cumulative Frequency
0–under 5	.36	.36	360	360
5–under 10	.63	.63 − .36 = .27	270	630
10–under 15	.81	.81 − .63 = .18	180	810
15–under 20	.90	.90 − .81 = .09	90	900
20–under 25	.97	.97 − .90 = .07	70	970
25–under 30	1.00	1.00 − .97 = .03	30	1,000
		1.00	1,000	

2-20 Answers will vary.

2-22

Major	Marital Status: Single	Marital Status: Married	Total
Electrical	10	19	29
Mechanical	27	28	55
Civil	6	10	16
Total	43	57	100

There is a lower tendency for mechanical engineers to be married than with other majors.

2-28 Out of control days are 3, 4, 5, 6, and 9.

2-30 (b) A peak in average fuel consumption was reached in 1970. It remained steady until 1978, when it declined dramatically.

2-32

	Sex		
Major	**Male**	**Female**	**Total**
Electrical	19	10	29
Mechanical	35	20	55
Civil	14	2	16
Total	68	32	100

2-34

	(a)	(c)	(d)
Class Interval (inches)	**Frequency**	**Relative Frequency**	**Cumulative Relative Frequency**
61.5–under 62.5	1	.02	.02
62.5–under 63.5	1	.02	.04
63.5–under 64.5	1	.02	.06
64.5–under 65.5	2	.04	.10
65.5–under 66.5	3	.06	.16
66.5–under 67.5	2	.04	.20
67.5–under 68.5	5	.10	.30
68.5–under 69.5	5	.10	.40
69.5–under 70.5	7	.14	.54
70.5–under 71.5	7	.14	.68
71.5–under 72.5	6	.12	.80
72.5–under 73.5	3	.06	.86
73.5–under 74.5	3	.06	.92
74.5–under 75.5	2	.04	.96
75.5–under 76.5	1	.02	.98
76.5–under 77.5	1	.02	1.00
	50	1.00	

(f) (1) .54 (2) .96 (3) .16

2-36 (a)

Sex	**Frequency**
male	220
female	130
	350

(c)

Occupation	**Frequency**
blue collar	155
white collar	173
professional	22
	350

(b)

Marital Status	**Frequency**
married	171
single	179
	350

2-38 (a)

Sex	Marital Status		Total
	Single	Married	
Male	96	124	220
Female	83	47	130
Total	179	171	350

(b)

Marital Status	Occupation			Total
	Blue Collar	White Collar	Professional	
Single	67	104	8	179
Married	88	69	14	171
Total	155	173	22	350

(c)

Sex	Occupation			Total
	Blue Collar	White Collar	Professional	
Male	130	75	15	220
Female	25	98	7	130
Total	155	173	22	350

2-40 Answers will vary.

2-42 (b)

1991			2100		
Country	Relative Frequency	Cumulative Relative Frequency	Country	Relative Frequency	Cumulative Relative Frequency
1. China	.298	.298	1. India	.233	.233
2. India	.222	.520	2. China	.224	.457
3. U.S.	.065	.585	3. Nigeria	.072	.529
4. Indonesia	.047	.632	4. Indonesia	.051	.580
5. Brazil	.040	.672	5. Pakistan	.045	.625
6. Russia	.038	.710	6. U.S.	.044	.669
7. Japan	.032	.742	7. Bangladesh	.042	.711
8. Nigeria	.032	.774	8. Brazil	.042	.753
9. Pakistan	.030	.804	9. Mexico	.028	.781
10. Bangladesh	.030	.834	10. Russia	.026	.807
11. Mexico	.022	.856	11. Ethiopia	.025	.832
12. Germany	.021	.877	12. VietNam	.024	.856
13. VietNam	.017	.894	13. Iran	.023	.879
14. Philippines	.016	.910	14. Zaire	.020	.899
15. Thailand	.015	.925	15. Japan	.018	.917
16. Iran	.015	.940	16. Philippines	.018	.935
17. Turkey	.015	.955	17. Tanzania	.017	.952
18. Italy	.015	.970	18. Kenya	.017	.969
19. U.K.	.015	.985	19. Burma	.016	.985
20. France	.015	1.000	20. Egypt	.016	1.001

(c)

	1991		2100	
Continent	Population	Relative Frequency	Population	Cumulative Relative Frequency
Asia/Europe	3,254,400,000	.841	5,049,400,000	.720
N. America	338,500,000	.087	504,200,000	.072
S. America	153,300,000	.040	293,200,000	.042
Africa	122,500,000	.032	1,167,500,000	.166
	3,868,700,000	1.000	7,014,300,000	1.000

3-2 Choose CompuQuick.

3-4 $\overline{X} = 26.18$ hours

3-6 (a)

A	B	C	D	E
30.2%	17.4%	13.5%	32.5%	22.8%

(b) 23.28% (c) B, C, and E

3-8 (b) $\overline{X} = 24.0\%$ (c) $\overline{X} = 23.28\%$, above by .72%

3-10 2.893 inches

3-12 (a) 2.75 (b) 2 (c) 2

3-14 $2,129

3-16 Answers will vary.

3-18 3.050 inches

3-20 (a) .1 (b) 1.25 (c) 2.50 (d) 6.50 (e) 8

3-22 (a)

0.	3 3 4 5 6 7 7 8
1.	0 1 2 2 2 5 5 6 8 8 8
2.	0 0 1 2 2 2 3 4 4 6 6 6 7 7 8 9 9 9 9 9 9 9
3.	0 1 1 1 2 2 2 3 3 3 3 4 4 4 4 5 6 6 6 6 6 6 7 7 7 8 8 9 9
4.	0 0 0 0 0 1 2 4 5 8
5.	0 4 4 8 9

(b) (1) .94 (2) 2.075 (3) 3.050 (4) 3.7 (5) 4.26

3-24 (a) 10 (b) 4 (c) 3 (d) 7 (e) 5

3-26 (a) $Q_{.25} = 415$ $Q_{.50} = 485$ $Q_{.75} = 555$

3-28 (a) 184.30 (b) 13.58

3-30 Answers will vary.

3-32 (a) 1,643 (b) 111,480.1 (c) 333.9

3-34 140

3-36 (a) (1) 5.6 (2) 1.625

3-38 (a) 2.75 (b) .63

3-40 Population is normally distributed.

3-42 (a) 1.615 (b) 1.271

3-44 (a) .30 (b) .35 (c) .575 (d) .875

3-46 Answers will vary.

3-48 (a) .10 (b) .04 (c) .03 (d) .07 (e) .04 (f) .05

3-50 (a) 450 (b) 573 (c) 165

3-52 (a) 126.2 (b) 124.86 (c) 385.41 (d) 19.63

3-54 (a) $\bar{X} = 77.615$; $s^2 = 208.55$ (b) $\bar{X} = 78.077$; $s^2 = 176.30$
(c) $-.461$

3-56 (c) (1) 77.62 (2) 14.44
(d) (1) 57.40 (2) 73.50 (3) 89.00
(e) 78.50
(f) (1) 66 (2) 15.50

3-58 Answers will vary.

3-60 Answers will vary.

3-62 $\bar{X} = 551.3$ $s = 202.9$ 74%

4-2 Answers will vary.

4-4 Answers will vary.

4-6 Answers will vary.

4-8 Answers will vary.

4-10 (a) convenience (c) random
(b) judgment (d) judgment or convenience

4-12 Answers will vary.

4-14 A judgment-convenience sample applies.

4-16 Solti, Maag, Abbado, Rowicki, Bloomfield, Krips, Prêtre, Frühbeck de Burgos, Newman, Schippers

4-18 Beecham, Dragon, Golschmann, Karajan, Krips, Pedrotti, Rignold, Scherchen, Stein, Svetlanov

4-20 Answers will vary.

4-22 Answers will vary.

5-2 1/38

5-4 (a) 1/20 (b) 1/10

5-6 (a) .140 (b) .400 (c) .260 (d) .200

5-8 (a) 24/72 (b) 5/72 (c) 11/72 (d) 6/72 (e) 7/72

5-10

Occupation	Family Income			Marginal Probability
	Low	Medium	High	
Homemaker	.04	.13	.03	.20
Blue-collar	.08	.20	.07	.35
White-collar	.03	.31	.06	.40
Professional	0	.01	.04	.05
Marginal Probability	.15	.65	.20	1.00

5-12

Sex	Major				Marginal Probability
	Accounting	Finance	Marketing	Management	
Male	10/72	14/72	10/72	6/72	40/72
Female	6/72	10/72	10/72	6/72	32/72
Marginal Probability	16/72	24/72	20/72	12/72	1

5-14 (a)

Sex	Marital Status		Marginal Probability
	Married	Unmarried	
Male	3/35	17/35	20/35
Female	5/35	10/35	15/35
Marginal Probability	8/35	27/35	1

(b) (1) 3/35 (2) 5/35 (3) 10/35 (4) 17/35

5-16 (a) equally likely outcomes
(b) .03125 for each

5-18 (a)

Sex	Marital Status: Married	Marital Status: Unmarried	Marginal Probability
Man	.35	.15	.50
Woman	.35	.15	.50
Marginal Probability	.70	.30	1.00

(b)

Sex	Marital Status: Married	Marital Status: Unmarried	Marginal Probability
Man	.30	.20	.50
Woman	.40	.10	.50
Marginal Probability	.70	.30	1.00

5-20 (a) 31/42 (b) 41/42 (c) 41/42 (d) 11/42 (e) 41/42 (f) 1

5-22 (a) .97 (b) .83 (c) .27 (d) .02

5-24 (a) $.90 \times (1 - .95) = .045$

(b)

Action	Quality: Good (G)	Quality: Bad (B)	Marginal Probability
Accept (A)	.895	.005	.900
Reject (R)	.055	.045	.100
Marginal Probability	.950	.050	1.00

(c) (1) 5.5% (2) 89.5% (3) .5%
(d) Pr[incorrect] = .005 + .055 = .060

5-28 Pr[good] = .90

(a)

Shipment Quality	Inspector Action: Accept	Inspector Action: Reject	Marginal Probability
Good	.855	.045	.900
Bad	.010	.090	.100
Marginal Probability	..865	.135	1.000

(b) .055

5-30 (a) .288 (b) .200 (c) .0625 (d) .0714

5-32 (a) (1) .40 (2) .80 (3) .32
(b) (1) .60 (2) .90 (3) .54

5-34 (a) 13/26 (b) 12/20 (c) 13/26 (d) 4/12 (e) 20/40 (f) 16/28

5-36 (a) (1) .60 (2) .40
(b) (1) .360 (2) .320

(c)

Result	Direction L	Direction R	Marginal Probability
H	.216	.128	.344
O	.384	.272	.656
Marginal Probability	.600	.400	1.000

Pr[H *and* L] = .60 × .36 = .216
Pr[H *and* R] = .40 × .32 = .128

(d) (1) .372 (2) .628

5-38 (a) (1) 1/52 (2) 0
(b) (1) (2) 0

5-42 (a) (1) 3/52 (2) 22/52
(b) (1) 2/52 (2) 28/52
(c) (1) 4/52 (2) 12/52
(d) (1) 5/52 (2) 28/52

5-44 (a) .48 (b) .51 (c) .36 (d) .50

5-46 (a) (1) .299 (2) .205 (3) .266

5-48 (a)

Highest Degree	Academic Assignment: Teaching	Research	Admin.	Marginal Probability
Doctorate	14/64	11/64	8/64	33/64
Master	5/64	8/64	18/64	31/64
Marginal Probability	19/64	19/64	26/64	1

(b) not independent
(c) (1) .161 (2) .258 (3) .581
(d) (1) .579 (2) .421

5-50 (a) .729 (b) .2916 (c) .40951

5-52 (a) 1/4 (b) 1/2 (c) 3/10 (d) 1/5 (e) 9/20 (f) 3/10

5-54 (a) (1) 11/20 (2) 3/4 (3) 4/5
(b) (1) 3/5 (2) 9/20 (3) 3/5

5-56

Discipline	Employment Status: Full-time	Part-time	Marginal Probability
Accounting	7/71	7/71	14/71
Finance	8/71	6/71	14/71
Management	10/71	8/71	18/71
Marketing	14/71	11/71	25/71
Marginal Probability	39/71	32/71	1

5-58 (a) (1) .05 (2) .01 (3) .90

(b)

Quality	Inspector Action: Accept	Reject	Marginal Probability
Good	.891	.009	.900
Bad	.005	.095	.100
Marginal Probability	.896	.104	1.000

(c) .014

5-60 (a)

Marital Status	Sex: Male	Female	Marginal Probability
Single	2/10	1/10	3/10
Married	3/10	1/10	4/10
Divorced	1/10	1/10	2/10
Widowed	0	1/10	1/10
Marginal Probability	6/10	4/10	1

(b) (1) 3/10 (2) 5/10 (3) 7/10 (4) 7/10

5-62 (b) .467

5-64 (a) (1) .729 (2) .243 (3) .027 (4) .001
(b) (1) .028 (2) .999 (3) .271

5-68 Answers will vary.

5-70 (a)

Country	Medal: Gold	Silver	Bronze	Marginal Probability
Germany	10/171	10/171	6/171	26/171
Unified Team	9/171	6/171	8/171	23/171
Austria	6/171	7/171	8/171	21/171
Norway	9/171	6/171	5/171	20/171
Italy	4/171	6/171	4/171	14/171
U.S.	5/171	4/171	2/171	11/171
Others	14/171	19/171	23/171	56/171
Marginal Probability	57/171	58/171	56/171	1

(b) 10/57
(c) 5/11

5-72 (a)

Mileage	Car Type: Two Seater	Minicompact	Marginal Probability
10–under 20	4/36	3/36	7/36
20–under 30	15/36	7/36	22/36
30–under 40	5/36	1/36	6/36
40 and above	1/36	0	1/36
Marginal Probability	25/36	11/36	1

Pr[minicompact *or* 30–under 40] = 16/36
Pr[10–under 20 *and* two-seater] = 1/9
Pr[two-seater|40 and above] = 1

(b) Pr[mileage $<$ 20] = 7/36
Pr[mileage $>$ 26] = 11/36
Pr[18 $\leq$ mileage $\leq$ 27] = 26/36
Pr[mileage $>$ 25|two seater] = 8/25
Pr[two seater|mileage $<$ 30] = 19/29
Pr[mileage $\geq$ 30|minicompact] = 1/11

6-2

Cost	Probability
\$2,200	.09
2,400	.15
2,600	.06
2,700	.21
2,900	.35
3,100	.14
	1.00

6-4 (b) (1) .729 (3) .027 (5) .271
(2) .243 (4) .001 (6) .999

6-6 (b) (1) .72398 (3) .02295 (5) .27600
(2) .25254 (4) .00051 (6) .99947

6-8 (a)

w	$Pr[W = w]$
−\$1	20/36
1	14/36
2	1/36
3	1/36
	1

6-10 (a) .99 (b) .969900 (c) .985

6-12 (a) 2.1 (b) 1.2690 (c) 1.136

6-14 (a) \$155.25 for High-Volatility Engineering
\$103.50 for Stability Power

6-16 (a) (1) 2.52 (2) 2.25 (3) 1.50

(b)

x	$Pr[X = x]$
0	.08
1	.16
2	.32
3	.20
4	.12
5	.08
6	.04

(c) (1) 2.52 (2) 2.2496 (3) 1.50

6-18

Possible Mean $\bar{x}$	Corresponding Possibilities	$Pr[\bar{X} = \bar{x}]$
950	(R,P)(R,A)	2/10
1,000	(A,P)	1/10
1,050	(R,D)(R,J)	2/10
1,100	(A,D)(A,J)(P,D)(P,J)	4/10
1,200	(D,J)	1/10
		1

6-20 (a)

$\bar{x}$	$Pr[\bar{X} = \bar{x}]$
900	1/25
950	4/25
1,000	4/25
1,050	4/25
1,100	8/25
1,200	4/25
	1

(b) (1) 1.060 (2) 7,200 (3) 84.85

6-22 (a) 24 (b) 720 (c) 5,040 (d) 40,320

6-24 (a) (1) .1642 (2) .2734 (3) .0078 (4) .2734
(b) same answers as in (a)

6-26 (a) .16807 (b) .00243 (c) .3087

6-28 .05

6-30 (a) .1390 (c) .7822 (e) .0009
(b) .1224 (d) .0848 (f) .3105

6-32

$r/5$	$Pr[P = r/5]$	$Pr[P \leq r/5]$
.0	.00243	.00243
.2	.02835	.03078
.4	.13230	.16308
.6	.30870	.47178
.8	.36015	.83193
1.0	.16807	1.00000
	1.00000	

6-34 0.0000 (rounded)

6-36 (a) .0565 (c) .8744 (e) .25000
(b) .0710 (d) .5956 (f) .8534

6-38 (a) .63396 (b) .86738 (c) .95245 (d) .99408

6-40

Cost	Probability
$2,400	.09
2,900	.15 + .21 = .36
3,100	.06
3,400	.35
3,600	.14
	1.00

6-42 (a) .03125 (b) .03125 (c) .31250

6-44 (a) .4096 (b) .1536 (c) .9586 (d) .0588

6-46 (a)

Possible Mean Age $\bar{x}$	Corresponding Possibilities	$Pr[\bar{X} = \bar{x}]$
19.5	(H,M)	1/10
20.0	(H,J)	1/10
20.5	(J,M)	1/10
21.0	(H,T)	1/10
21.5	(C,H)(M,T)	2/10
22.0	(C,M)(J,T)	2/10
22.5	(C,J)	1/10
23.5	(C,T)	1/10
		1

(b) (1) 21.40 (2) 1.29 (3) 1.14
(c) 1.85 (d) 1.31

6-48 (a)

Proportion	Applicable Combinations	Probability
0	(Bob, Don)(Bob, Eve)(Don, Eve)	3/10
.5	(Ann, Bob)(Ann, Don)(Ann, Eve) (Bob, Cal)(Cal, Don)(Cal, Eve)	6/10
1.0	(Ann, Cal)	1/10
		1

(b)

Range	Applicable Combinations	Probability
0	(Ann, Cal)(Bob, Eve)	2/10
1	(Ann, Bob)(Ann, Don)(Ann, Eve) (Bob, Cal)(Cal, Don)(Cal, Eve)	6/10
2	(Bob, Don)(Don, Eve)	2/10
		1

6-50 (a) (1) 15/100 (2) 85/100 (3) 14/99 (4) 15/99 (5) 85/99 (6) 84/99
(b) (1) 13/98 (2) 14/98 (3) 14/98 (4) 15/98 (5) 85/98 (6) 84/98 (7) 84/98 (8) 83/98

6-52 Answers will vary.

6-54 Answers will vary.

7-2 (a) .4332 (b) .1915 (c) .2420 (d) .0062 (e) .0968 (f) .9861 (g) .97585 (h) .0606

7-4 (a) .2734 (b) .4772 (c) .0668 (d) .0668 (e) .3085 (f) .9772 (g) .0928 (h) .1026

7-6 86.92 inches

7-8 (a) .01 (b) .10 (c) .50 (d) 2.00 (e) 10.00

7-10 (a) (1) 1.60 (2) .4714
(b) (1) .80 (2) .7888
(c) (1) .566 (2) .9232
(d) (1) .358 (2) .9948

7-12 (a) (1) .0749 (2) .2242 (3) .1631 (4) .0668
(b) (1) 6.698″ (2) 7.055″ (3) 7.925″ (4) 8.282″

7-14 (a) .9876 (b) .7888 (c) .4714 (d) .2434

7-16 (a) .0456 (b) .83995 (c) .16005

7-18 .1814

7-20 (a) .0490
(b) .0207
(c) (1) .0495 (2) .0043

7-22 (a) .0027 (b) .0011

7-24 (a) .9050 (b) .7888 (c) .6826

7-26 (a) .0207 (b) .0036

7-28 (a) .0062 (b) .1587

7-30 .00135

7-32 (a) .4525 (c) 0 (approximately) (e) .9734
(b) .0475 (d) 0 (approximately)

7-34 (a) .0228 (b) .0062

7-36 Anwers will vary.

7-38 Anwers will vary.

7-40 (a) .4545 (b) .0170 (c) .0055 (d) .8810

7-42 (a) .9742 for Chilean (b) .9566 for Chilean (c) No
.4746 for Bolivian .9556 for Bolivian
.9652 for Arizonian .9556 for Arizonian

8-2 (a) $14,800 (b) $11,708 (c) .6 (d) .1

8-4 (a) 5 (b) 1.94 (c) No

8-6 15.9 ± .10 ounces

8-8 Ratings constitute the population.

8-10 (16.71, 27.13)

8-12 (a) 1.812 (b) 2.650 (c) 2.080 (d) 2.358

8-14 (a) \$8.00 ± 4.12
(b) \$15.03 ± .40 minutes
(c) 27.30 ± 1.43 pounds

8-16 \$73,249 ± 14,817

8-18 (a) $t_{.005} = 2.704$; $\mu = 52{,}346 \pm 1{,}113$ miles

8-20 (a) 3 ± 1.43 (b) negligible

8-22 (.20640, .23627)

8-24 (a) .2 ± .025 (b) .04 ± .0086 (c) .01 ± .0087

8-26 (a) .5 ± .013 (b) .4 ± .10

8-28 (a) .04 ± .038 (b) .0013

8-30 (a) 661 (b) 385
(c) 166; it is one-fourth as large.
(d) 2,642; it increases by a factor of 4.

8-32 (a) 4^{11} (b) \$30,000 (c) 40% (d) .01

8-34 (a) .8414 (b) 1.39

8-36 (a) 385 (b) 350; 35

8-38 1,246 + 22.7

8-40 5.4 ± .08 gallons

8-42 (a) \$43,150 (b) 135,113,880 (c) .5

8-44 (a) 83.7 ± 14.43 (b) 83.7 ± 9.92 (c) 83.7 ± 8.00
(d) 83.7 ± 16.48

8-46 3.5 ± .02

8-48 76,400 ± 1,040

8-50 Answers will vary.

8-52 Answers will vary.

9-2 (a) (1) correct (2) Type II error (3) correct (4) Type I error
(b) (1) Type II error (2) correct (3) Type I error (4) correct
(c) (1) Type I error (2) correct (3) correct (4) Type II error

9-4 (a) Type I error: Adopt the new process when it is no improvement.
Type II error: Don't adopt the new process when it is an improvement.
(b) Type I error: Sign the contract when output will not increase.
Type II error: Don't sign the contract when output will increase.
(c) Type I error: Lobby for the new law when it does not meet greater approval.
Type II error: Don't lobby for the new law when it does meet greater approval.

9-6 $\alpha = .0918$ $\beta = .0228$

9-8 $\alpha = .0294$ $\beta = .0023$
Both α and β decrease (are smaller).

9-10 $t_{.05} = 1.711$ $t = 1.67$ *Accept* H_0

9-12 (a) (1) $H_0{:}\mu = 16$ ounces $H_A{:}\mu \neq 16$ ounces
(2) $\bar{X}$ or z *(recurring decision)*
(3) Accept H_0 if $15.88 \leq \bar{X} \leq 16.12$ $(-19.6 \leq z \leq 1.96)$
Reject H_0 otherwise.
(b) (1) *Accept* H_0 (Take no action.)
(2) *Reject* H_0 (Take remedial action.)

9-14 $z_{.005} = 2.57$ $z = 3.5$ *Reject* H_0.

9-16 *Reject* H_0 (adjust).

9-18 (a) $t_{.01} = 2.423$
Accept H_0 if $t \geq -2.423$.
Reject H_0 if $t < -2.423$.
(b) $t = -3.12$ *Reject* H_0.

9-20 (a) $H_0{:}\mu = 1''$
(b) $\bar{X}$ or z
(c) *Accept* H_0 if $.9974'' \leq \bar{X} \leq 1.0026''$ $(-2.57 \leq z \leq 2.57)$
Reject H_0 otherwise.
(d) (1) *Reject* H_0 (2) *Accept* H_0.

9-22 (a) $H_0{:}\mu \geq 2$ days
Accept H_0 if $t \geq -1.711$.
Reject H_0 if $t < -1.711$.
(b) $t = -5.00$
Reject H_0 and use new formulation.

9-24 (a) $H_0{:}\mu \leq \$5.00$ $H_A{:}\mu > \$5.00$
(b) \$5.12
Accept H_0 if $\bar{X} \leq \$5.12$.
Reject H_0 if $\bar{X} > \$5.12$.
(c) (1) *Reject* H_0 (2) *Accept* H_0 (3) *Accept* H_0 (4) *Reject* H_0

9-26 (a) (1) ship (2) render
(b) $\alpha = .01$
Accept H_0 if $\bar{X} \geq 513.35$ $(z \geq -2.33)$.
Reject H_0 otherwise.
(c) (1) *Accept* H_0 (2) *Accept* H_0 (3) *Accept* H_0 (4) *Reject* H_0

9-28 (a) $z = 5.79$ 0.0000
(b) rejected

9-30 (a) $\bar{X} = 53.87$ $s = 7.76$
(b) accept

9-32 (a) Upper-tailed
(b) (1) accepted (2) accepted (3) rejected

9-34 rejected

9-36 accepted

9-38 (a) *Reject* H_0 (b) *Reject* H_0 (c) *Reject* H_0

9-40 (a) $H_0{:}\mu \leq 10$ minutes
$H_A{:}\mu > 10$ minutes
(b) *Accept* H_0 if $\bar{X} \leq 10.47$ minutes $(z \leq 2.33)$
Reject H_0 if $\bar{X} > 10.47$ minutes $(z > 2.33)$
(c) (1) *Reject* H_0 (2) *Accept* H_0 (3) *Accept* H_0

9-42 (a) $H_0{:}\mu = .5''$
(b) t
(c) *Accept* H_0 if $-2.617 \leq t \leq 2.617$.
Reject H_0 if $t < -2.617$.
or if $t > 2.617$.
(d) (1) *Reject* H_0 and correct for undersizing.
(2) *Reject* H_0 and correct for oversizing.

9-44 Change design.

9-46 *Accept* H_0 and don't take corrective action.

9-48 (a) $H_0{:}\mu \leq 86$
Accept H_0 if $t \leq 1.711$.
Reject H_0 if $t > 1.711$.
(b) *Accept* H_0 and keep present procedure.

9-50 Answers will vary.

9-52 Answers will vary.

10-2 (a) \$258 billion (b) \$446 billion (c) \$634 billion

10-4

Dependent Variable	Independent Variable
(a) Time deposits	Employee income
(b) Income	Stock purchases
(c) Savings	Wages

10-6 .791

10-8 (a) correlation (b) regression (c) regression (d) both

10-10 (b) $\hat{Y}(X) = 22.405 + 3.619X$

10-12 (a) $\hat{Y}(X) = 20.03 + .412X$
(c) (1) 102.4 (2) 164.2 (3) 184.8

10-14 (a) $\hat{Y}(X) = 1{,}980 + .4062X$ (b) $\hat{Y}(X) = 15.07 + .06053X$

10-16 (b) $\hat{Y}(X) = 31.0 + 1.42X$
(c) (1) 8.50 (2) 5.484

10-18 (b) $\hat{Y}(X) = 30.4 + 5.64X$

10-20 (a)

(1) Number of Components X	(2) Simulated Actual Time Y	(3) Theoretical Time $\mu_{Y.X}$	(4) Estimated Time $\hat{Y}(X)$	(5) Error Term $\epsilon = Y - \mu_{Y.X}$	(6) Residual $Y - \hat{Y}(X)$
5	49.2	60.5	58.6	−11.3	−9.4
7	81.6	70.7	69.9	10.9	11.7
10	83.0	86.0	86.8	−3.0	−3.8
12	86.7	96.2	98.1	−9.5	−11.4
13	122.7	101.3	103.7	21.4	19.0
15	114.0	111.5	115.0	2.5	−1.0
16	121.3	116.6	120.6	4.7	.7
20	136.2	137.0	143.2	−.8	−7.0
22	152.5	147.2	154.5	5.3	−2.0
25	174.7	162.5	171.4	12.2	3.3

(b) No (c) No

10-22 (a) 1,600 ± 41.38 and ± 211.00
(b) 2,275 ± 139.82 and ± 249.71
(c) 2,950 ± 270.29 and ± 340.39

10-24 (a) \$44.12 ± 20.16 (b) \$54.98 ± 42.61

10-26 (a) (1) (34.95, 46.88) (2) (40.79, 49.54) (3) (47.45, 57.05)
(b) (1) (26.93, 54.90) (2) (31.78, 58.55) (3) (38.72, 65.78)

10-28 (a) $\hat{Y}(X) = 16.83 + 8.769X$ (b) positive (d) .998

10-30 (a) 99.8% (b) .999

10-32 (a)

Observation i	Distance X	Charge Y	Predicted $\hat{Y}(X)$	Residual $Y - \hat{Y}(X)$
1	14	68	73.0714	−5.0714
2	23	105	105.6429	−0.6429
3	9	40	54.9762	−14.9762
4	17	79	83.9286	−4.9286
5	10	81	58.5952	22.4048
6	22	95	102.0238	−7.0238
7	5	31	40.9500	−9.5000
8	12	72	65.8333	6.1667
9	6	45	44.1190	0.8810
10	16	93	80.3095	12.6905

10-34 (a) (1) .972 (2) +.986

10-38 .761

10-40 (a) $42.0 billion (b) $54.0 billion (c) $66.0 billion

10-42 (a) 60 ± 1.170 (b) 60 ± 4.300

10-44 Answers will vary.

10-46 Answers will vary.

10-48 (a) 27 ± 7.25
(b) rejected
(c) $t = 10.457$ *rejected*

11-2 $a = -8.17$ $b_1 = 4.250$ $b_2 = -3.417$

11-4 (a) 3.189 (b) 3.254 (c) 2.975 (d) 3.708

11-6 (a) $\hat{Y} = -26 + 4X_1 + 6X_2$

11-8 (a) $\hat{Y}(X_1) = 4 + X_1$ (b) $s_{Y \cdot X1} = 9.325$ $S_{Y \cdot 12} = 3.02$

11-10 (a) $\hat{Y} = 4.2 + .7668X_1 + 192.9X_2 - .634X_3$ (b) 422.7 (c) yes

11-12 (a) $\hat{Y} = 36.6584 - .0670X_1 - 1.6525X_2 - 1.6013X_3$
(b) 1.79 (c) yes

11-14 $\hat{Y} = 1.5045 + .030X_1 + .250X_2 + .444X_3 - .038X_4$

11-16 (a) (1) ($7,299, 8,321) (2) ($6,656, 8,964)
(b) (1) $.767 \pm .350$ (2) 192.9 ± 514.9 (3) $-.634 \pm 1.980$

11-18 (a) (1) (5.186, 6.392) (2) (4.216, 7.362)
(b) (1) $.0297 \pm .0145$ (2) $.2504 \pm .5664$
(3) $.4436 \pm .2469$ (4) $-.03802 \pm .7527$

11-20 (a) $S_{Y\cdot12} = 1.759$ $R^2_{Y\cdot12} = .786$ 78.6%
(b) 96.4% (c) Yes (d) $r^2_{Y3\cdot12} = .465$

11-22 (a) .646 (b) .055 (c) .566 (d) 56.6%

11-24 (a) $S_{Y\cdot12} = 4.714$ $R^2_{Y\cdot12} = .893$ 89.3% (b) 96.4%
(c) .664 66.4%

11-26 (a) (1) $\hat{Y}(X_1) = 1{,}667 + .6333\,X_1$
$r^2_{Y1} = .8595$
(2) $\hat{Y}(X_2) = 7{,}538.4 + 115.4\,X_1$
$r^2_{Y2} = .0124$
(3) $\hat{Y}(X_3) = 7{,}099 + 1.287X_3$
$r^2_{Y3} = .202$
(b) X_1
(c) (1) $\hat{Y} = -58.82 + .6765X_1 + 323.5X_2$
$r^2_{Y2\cdot1} = .665$
(2) $\hat{Y} = 444.84 + .8410X1 - 1.2218X3$
$r^2_{Y3\cdot1} = .637$

11-28 (a) $\hat{Y} = -9.082 - .09552X_2 + .020944\,X_6 + .06411X_8$
$S_{Y\cdot568} = 4.584$

Player	Card Pr. Y	Games X_5	At Bats X_6	RBI X_8	Predicted	Residual $Y-\hat{Y}$
8	3.0	761	2,717	426	2.4408	0.5592
18	15.0	1,024	3,941	646	17.0578	−2.0578
19	20.0	1,773	6,109	1,060	17.4589	2.5411
20	5.0	736	2,700	447	5.8192	−0.8192
29	12.0	830	3,032	518	8.3452	3.6548
40	0.7	810	2,703	427	−2.4689	3.1689
49	3.5	740	2,707	400	2.5705	0.9295
56	10.0	1,378	4,819	812	12.2736	−2.2736
64	6.0	1,299	4,670	803	16.1223	−10.1223
67	0.8	703	2,657	422	6.4681	−5.6681
75	30.0	1,117	4,416	759	25.3669	4.6331
79	1.0	578	1,944	305	−4.0254	5.0254
80	3.0	623	2,173	429	4.4218	−1.4218
86	45.0	2,135	7,997	1,373	42.4881	2.5119
88	0.7	1,209	4,271	569	1.3611	−0.6611

(c) $\hat{Y} = -9.14 - .0905X_5 + .0183X_6 + .0729\,X_8$
$S_{Y\cdot568} = 3.405$

11-30 (b) $\hat{Y} = -4.443 + 1.1609X_1 + 2.5804X_2$
(d) $\hat{Y}(X_1) = -.686 + .8477X_1$

11-32 (a) $\overline{X} = 8.5$ (men) $\overline{X} = 6.08$ (women)
$\overline{Y} = 5.42$ $\overline{Y} = 5.2$
(b) Men have higher test scores and productivity.

11-34 (b) $\hat{Y} = 138.8 + .277X_1 + 138.6X_2 + .075X_1X_2$

11-36 (a) $\hat{Y} = -.412 + .631X_1 + .00223X_2$
(b) (1) 2.96 (2) 2.25 (3) 3.06 (4) 2.93

11-38 $\hat{Y} = -.386 + .637X_1 + .002X_2 - .007X_3$

11-40 (a) $\hat{Y} = -16.563 + 1.518X_1 + .1554X_2 + .6847X_3$
(b) Yes

11-42 (a) No (b) X_8, X_{11}, X_5

11-44 (a) $\hat{Y} = -17.5 - .0899X_5 + .426X_8 - .706X_{11} - 9.4X_4$
(b) .850
(c) .045 4.5% reduction

11-46 (a) $\hat{Y} = 253 + 308X_4 + 1.49X_{10} + .07487X_{12}$
(b) .841
(c) Drop fielding.

11-48 Answers will vary.

11-50 (a) X_1 = distance X_2 = gender (male = 0, female = 1)
$\hat{Y} = 10.8 + 1.37X_1 - 5.20X_2$
(b) $s_Y = 11.434$ $S_{Y \cdot 12} = 5.872$
(c) $R^2_{Y \cdot 12} = .771$ $r^2_{Y1} = .734$ $r^2_{Y2} = .105$
$r^2_{Y1 \cdot 2} = .771$ $r^2_{Y2 \cdot 1} = .139$
(d) 21.99

11-52 (b) parabola
(c) $\hat{Y} = 20.4 + 8.26X - .185X^2$ (parabola)
$\hat{Y} = -407 + 67.2X - 2.58X^2 + .0294X^3$ (3rd degree polynomial)
(e) 22.5″ for parabola
22″ for 3rd degree polynomial
(f) 101.3 with parabola
81 with 3rd degree polynomial

11-54 (b) 3rd degree polynomial
(c) $\hat{Y} = 18.7 + 4.11X - 1.76X^2 + .116X^3$
(f) 18.3

12-2

Fall 19X1	$1,000,000.00
Winter 19X2	1,090,000.00
Spring	1,188,100.00
Summer	1,295,029.00
Fall	1,411,581.61

12-4 Winter: 2,016
Spring: 99
Summer: 120
Fall: 95

12-6 (b) $\hat{Y}(X) = 200.67 + 9.673X$ $(X = 0 \text{ in } 1982)$ (c) 374.78

12-8 (a) (1) $\hat{Y}(X) = 945{,}000 + 10{,}000X$ (2) $\hat{Y}(X) = 955{,}000 + 30{,}000X$
(b) (1) $\hat{Y}(X) = 8{,}525 + 50X$ (2) $\hat{Y}(X) = 8{,}575 + 150X$

12-10

Quarter	Forecast
Winter 1992	5,000
Spring	21,600
Summer	14,500
Fall	3,100
Winter 1993	6,600
Spring	28,000
Summer	18,500
Fall	3,900

12-12 (a)

	Four-Quarter Moving Average	Centered Moving Average	Original Data as Percentage of Moving Average
1988 Winter			
Spring	104.25		
Summer	108.25	106.250	101.647
Fall	107.75	108.000	117.593
1989 Winter	110.50	109.125	129.210
Spring	116.00	113.250	48.565
Summer	117.25	116.625	102.036
Fall	118.25	117.750	126.539
1990 Winter	119.00	118.625	123.077
Spring	122.00	120.500	48.963
Summer	123.00	122.500	99.592
Fall	123.75	123.375	130.496
1991 Winter	124.50	124.125	120.846
Spring	123.75	124.125	49.950
Summer	125.50	124.625	100.301
Fall	126.75	126.125	125.273
1992 Winter	128.75	127.750	122.896
Spring	134.25	131.500	50.951
Summer			
Fall			

(b)

Winter	123.2
Spring	49.5
Summer	101.1
Fall	126.1

12-14 (a) (b)

	Seasonal Index	Cash Required
J	43.0	$ 430,000
F	99.4	994,000
M	138.2	1,382,000
A	59.9	599,000
M	106.3	1,063,000
J	94.4	944,000
J	87.0	870,000
A	122.3	1,223,000
S	183.3	1,833,000
O	145.4	1,454,000
N	75.0	750,000
D	45.8	458,000
	1,200.0	

12-16 (a)

Period t	Forecast Sales F_t ($\alpha = .40$)
1	
2	4,890
3	4,898.0
4	4,926.8
5	4,960.1
6	5,000.0
7	5,040.0
8	5,044.0
9	5,094.4
10	5,128.6
11	5,173.2
12	5,191.9
13	5,227.1
14	5,268.3
15	5,313.0
16	5,363.8
17	5,402.3
18	5,449.4
19	5,465.6
20	5,499.4

(b) 8,386.6

12-18 (a)

Period t	Forecast Sales F_t ($\alpha = .50$)
1	
2	4,890
3	4,900.0
4	4,935.0
5	4,972.5
6	5,016.3
7	5,058.1
8	5,054.1
9	5,112.0
10	5,146.0
11	5,193.0
12	5,206.5
13	5,243.3
14	5,286.6
15	5,333.3
16	5,386.7
17	5,423.3
18	5,471.7
19	5,480.8
20	5,515.4

(b) 5,963.8

12-20 (a)

Period t	Forecast F_t
1	—
2	—
3	4,910
4	4,951.6
5	4,996.2
6	5,046.3
7	5,096.6
8	5,113.9
9	5,165.5
10	5,205.4
11	5,253.5
12	5,279.1
13	5,315.1
14	5,356.2
15	5,401.4
16	5,453.3
17	5,496.1
18	5,545.4
19	5,567.7
20	5,600.2

(b) 1,560.4
(c) Winter 15.93
Spring 21.10
Summer 13.76
Fall 21.79

12-24 (e) set (c).

12-26 Winter: 110
Spring: 105
Summer: $326,700
Fall: 105

12-28 (a) $\hat{Y}(X) = 297.95 + 25.945X$ $(X = 0$ at $1983)$
(b) (1) 583.35 (2) 713.07 (3) 842.80

12-30 (a) $\hat{Y}(X) = 142.4 + 64.0X$ $(X = 0$ in $1988)$
(b) 398.4 thousand

12-32

Quarter	Deseasonalized Data	Trend
1988 W	35.0	35
S	35.0	38
S	33.3	41
F	30.0	44
1989 W	58.3	47
S	45.0	50
S	50.6	53
F	35.0	56
1990 W	65.0	59
S	68.3	62
S	65.0	65
F	95.0	68
1991 W	130.0	71
S	121.7	74
S	75.6	77
F	75.0	80
1992 W	90.0	83
S	95.0	86
S	88.9	89
F	72.5	92

12-34

	(a)			(b)	(c)
	Four-Quarter Moving Average	Centered Moving Average	Sales as Percentage of Moving Average	Seasonal Index S_t	Deseasonalized Data
1988 Winter				90.4	9.4
Spring				113.2	9.2
	9.550				
Summer		9.675	77.52	78.7	9.5
	9.800				
Fall		10.025	117.71	117.6	10.0
	10.250				
1989 Winter		10.413	91.23	90.4	10.5
	10.575				
Spring		10.800	112.96	113.2	10.8
	11.025				
Summer		11.138	79.01	78.7	11.2
	11.250				
Fall		11.413	119.16	117.6	11.6
	11.575				
1990 Winter		11.688	88.98	90.4	11.5
	11.800				
Spring		11.738	115.01	113.2	11.9
	11.675				
Summer		11.563	83.89	78.7	12.3
	11.450				
Fall		11.225	116.70	117.6	11.1
	11.000				
1991 Winter		10.838	87.65	90.4	10.5
	10.675				
Spring		10.650	109.86	113.2	10.3
	10.625				
Summer		10.800	77.78	78.7	10.7
	10.975				
Fall		11.225	114.92	117.6	11.0
	11.475				
1992 Winter		11.688	93.26	90.4	12.1
	11.900				
Spring		12.163	112.64	113.2	12.1
	12.425				
Summer				78.7	12.8
Fall				117.6	12.8

(d) $\hat{Y}(X) = 9.750 + .1384X$ ($X = 0$ for Winter 1988)

12-36 (a) Sales: $\hat{Y}(X) = 2{,}529{,}918 + 311{,}383X$ ($X = 0$ at 1979)
Net Income: $\hat{Y}(X) = 77{,}524 + 36{,}441X$ ($X = 0$ at 1979)
Net Income per Share: $\hat{Y}(X) = 0.478 + .113X$ ($X = 0$ at 1979)

(c)

Sales	Net Income	Net Income/Share
(1) $ 6,889,280	$ 587,698	$2.06
(2) 8,757,578	806,334	2.74
(3) 10,625,876	1,024,990	3.42

12-38 (a) Sales: $\hat{Y}(X) = 283{,}681 + 30.029X$ ($X = 0$ at 1980)
Net Income: $\hat{Y}(X) = 10{,}139 + 3{,}644X$ ($X = 0$ at 1980)
Net Income per Share: $\hat{Y}(X) = 0.421 + .124X$ ($X = 0$ at 1980)

(c)

Sales	Net Income	Net Income/Share
(1) $674,058	$57,511	$2.03
(2) 764,145	68,443	2.41
(3) 914,290	86,663	3.03

12-40 Answers will vary.

12-42 Answers will vary.

13-2 (a) LCL = .046 UCL = .094
(b) 6/21 and 6/28
(c) LCL = .041 UCL = .087
(d) (1) in control (2) out (3) in (4) out (5) in

13-4 LCL = .0526 UCL = .0846
out of control on 10/01, 4, 6, 7, 9, 12, 14, 15, 19, 22, 23, 24, 28

13-6 (a) .2177 (b) .7823 (c) .9292 (d) .9798

13-8 (a,b)

Sample	$\bar{X}$	R
1	16.034	.36 in control
2	16.028	1.25 out of control (R)
3	16.512	.47 out of control ($\bar{X}$)
4	15.694	.39 in control
5	16.036	.47 in control

13-10 (a)

Sample	$\bar{X}$	R
1	4.96	.2
2	5.00	.5
3	4.94	.2
4	4.84	.5
5	4.88	.7
6	4.94	.7
7	5.04	.6
8	4.98	.5
9	5.10	.4
10	5.04	.1
11	4.86	.5
12	5.36	.1
13	5.32	.3

Sample	$\bar{X}$	R
14	5.02	.5
15	4.94	.5
16	5.02	.3
17	4.90	.2
18	4.96	1.0
19	4.98	.4
20	5.00	.4
21	5.12	.4
22	4.98	.2
23	4.86	.5
24	5.00	.2
25	4.84	.3

$\bar{\bar{X}} = 5.00 \quad \bar{R} = .42$

(b) LCL = 4.76 UCL = 5.24
12 and 13 are out of control
(c) LCL = 0 ULC = .89
18 is out of control
(d) $\bar{\bar{X}} = 4.97$ $\bar{R} = .41$
(1) LCL = 4.73 UCL = 5.21
(2) LCL = 0 UCL = .87

13-12 (a) 10 (b) 9 (c) 8

13-14 (a) 7 (b) 5 (c) 5

13-16 (a) 4 (b) (1) accepted (2) accepted (3) accepted

13-18 (a) $n = 10$ reject (c) n = 20 accept
(b) n = 30 accept (d) n = 10 accept

13-20

	$\bar{X}$	R
(a)	1.93	.6 (1)
(b)	1.98	.8 (1)
(c)	1.98	1.4 (3)
(d)	1.58	1.2 (4)

13-22 (a) 10 (b) accepted for (1)–(4)

14-2 7.4%

14-4 (a) $I = 101.3$, a 1.3% increase. (b) $I = 98.7$, a 1.3% increase from 1988 to 1989.

14-6 1986 100.0
1987 106.6
1988 130.4
1989 142.2
42.2%

14-8 (a) $I = 108.41$ 8.41% (b) $I = 92.24$ 8.41%

14-10

Year	CPI (1982–84 = 100)	Shifted Index (1946 = 100)
1946	19.5	100.0 = (19.5/19.5) × 100
1947	22.3	114.4 = (22.3/19.5) × 100
1948	24.1	123.6
1949	23.8	122.1
1950	24.1	123.6
1951	26.0	133.3
1952	26.5	135.9
1953	26.7	136.9
1954	26.9	137.9
1955	26.8	137.4
1956	27.2	139.5
1957	28.1	144.1
1958	28.9	148.2
1959	29.1	149.2
1960	29.6	151.8
1961	29.9	153.3
1962	30.2	154.9
1963	30.6	156.9
1964	31.0	159.0
1965	31.5	161.5
1966	32.4	166.2
1967	33.4	171.3
1968	34.8	178.5
1969	36.7	188.2
1970	38.8	199.0
1971	39.5	202.6
1972	41.8	214.4
1973	44.4	227.7
1974	49.3	252.8
1975	53.8	275.9
1976	56.9	291.8
1977	60.6	310.8
1978	65.2	334.4
1979	72.6	372.3
1980	82.4	422.6
1981	90.9	466.2
1982	96.5	494.9
1983	99.6	510.8
1984	103.9	532.8
1985	107.6	551.8
1986	109.6	562.1
1987	113.6	582.6
1988	118.3	606.7
1989	124.0	635.9
1990	130.7	670.3

14-12

Year	Deflated Value
1985	$ 795,000
1986	915,556
1987	1,043,243
1988	1,224,242
1989	1,283,422

14-14 (a) 4.4% increase (b) 3.6% increase (c) 22.8% increase (d) 87.5% increase

14-16

Year	Shifted Series (1970 = 100)
1970	100.0
1	107.3
2	107.3
3	110.9
4	121.8
5	129.1
6	140.0
7	150.9
8	156.4
9	169.1
1980	181.8
1	209.1
2	218.2
3	223.6
4	236.4
5	245.5
6	240.0
7	247.3
8	254.5
9	261.8

14-18 1988: 4,111.8 1989: 4,194.2 1990: 4,181.4

14-20 $35.68 million

15-2 1.5 ± 1.41 mph

15-4 $1.12 \pm .69$ sec

15-6 $.128 \pm .045$

15-8 $2 \pm .40$ mpg

15-10 $t = 1.152$ *Accept* H_0.

15-12 $t = 4.20$ *Reject* H_0.

15-14 $t = 5.81$ *Reject* H_0.

15-16 rejected

15-18 $t = 3.0$ *Reject* H_0.

15-20 $z = -.56$ *Reject* H_0.

15-22 $z = -.60$ *Accept* H_0.

15-24 (a) $\overline{X}_A = 157.7$ $\overline{X}_B = 163.1$
$s_A^2 = 67.57$ $s_B^2 = 137.88$
(b) $t = -1.191$ *Accept* H_0.

15-26 (a) $\overline{d} = -5.4$ pounds $s_{d\text{-paired}} = 6.096$ pounds (b) *Reject* H_0.

15-28 *Reject* H_0 and use new system.

15-30 (a) $\mu_A - \mu_B = 2{,}000 \pm 1{,}430.6$ miles (b) *Reject* H_0.

15-32 (a) $\mu_A - \mu_B = .2 \pm .79$ (b) *Accept* H_0.

15-34 (a) $\mu_A - \mu_B = .2 \pm .055$ mpg (b) *Reject* H_0.

15-36 Answers will vary.

15-38 Answers will vary.

16-2 (a) rejected (b) rejected (c) rejected (d) accepted

16-4 (a) (1) df = 1 (2) $\chi^2_{.01} = 6.635$

(b) (1)

Preference	Marital Status (1) Single	Marital Status (2) Married	Total
(1) *A*	20 / 12	10 / 18	30
(2) *B*	20 / 28	50 / 42	70
Total	40	60	100

(2) 12,699

(c) *Reject* H_0.

16-6 (a)

Degree of Acceptance	Region (1) East	(2) Middle	(3) South	(4) West	Total
(1) Poor	26.28	21.47	6.02	8.23	62.00
(2) Moderate	72.50	59.21	16.60	22.69	171.00
(3) Strong	32.22	26.32	7.38	10.08	76.00
Total	131.00	107.00	30.00	41.00	309.00

(b) 57.412 (c) 6 (d) *Reject* H_0.

16-8 $\chi^2 = 11.546$ *Reject* H_0.

16-10 $\chi^2 = 11.782$ *Reject* H_0.

16-12 $\chi^2 = 5.364$ *Accept* H_0.

16-14 $\chi^2 = 1.407$ Yes

16-16 *Accept* H_0 and conclude identical proportions.

16-18 $\chi^2 = 10.788$ *Reject* H_0.

16-20 Answers will vary.

16-22 $\chi^2 = 6.136$. *Reject* independence when $\alpha = .05$ and *accept* when $\alpha = .01$

16-24

	(a)	(b)	(c)	(d)
(1)	lower	upper	lower	upper
(2)	13.848	21.666	10.865	26.296
(3)	28.5	9.45	16.594	26.492
	accept	accept	accept	reject

16-26 (a) $56.20 \leq \sigma^2 \leq 83.68$ (b) *Accept* H_0.

16-28 (a) $2{,}929{,}800 \leq \sigma^2 \leq 6{,}302{,}000$ (b) No

17-2 (a) 3.88 (b) *Reject* H_0. (c) *Reject* H_0. (d) *Accept* H_0.

17-4 (a) (1) Numerator df $= 3 - 1 = 2$ (2) $F_{.05} = 3.89$
Denominator df $= (5 - 1)3 = 12$
(b) (1) $\bar{X}_1 = 87.8$ $\bar{X}_2 = 64.2$ (2) $SSTR = 1{,}392.4$
$\bar{X}_3 = 64.2$ $\bar{\bar{X}}_1 = 76.0$ $SSE = 2{,}001.6$
$SSTO = 3{,}394.0$

(3)

Variation	Degrees of Freedom	Sum of Squares	Mean Square	F
Explained by treatments	2	1,392.4	696.2	4.17
Error or unexplained	12	2,001.6	166.8	
Total	14	3,394.0		

(c) *Reject* H_0.

17-6 *Reject* H_0 and conclude that level of impurities affects mean dissolving time.

17-8 (a) 84
(b) $B_1 = -4$ $B_2 = 3$ $B_3 = 1$

(c)

i	ϵ_{i1}	ϵ_{i2}	ϵ_{i3}
1	−3	−4	−5
2	−1	4	−3
3	7	7	1
4	5	1	0
5	−2	−2	−5

17-10 (a) 9 ± 2.77 (b) 7 ± 3.92 (c) Yes

17-12 significantly different

17-14 (a) (1) $\mu_1 - \mu_2 = 23.6 \pm 21.90$
(2) $\mu_1 - \mu_3 = 11.8 \pm 21.90$
(3) $\mu_3 - \mu_2 = 11.8 \pm 21.90$
(b) The only significant difference occurs with pair (1), where the pyramid has a significantly greater mean than the rectangle.

17-16 (a) (1) $\mu_1 - \mu_2 = 23.6 \pm 21.77$
(2) $\mu_1 - \mu_3 = 11.8 \pm 21.77$
(3) $\mu_3 - \mu_2 = 11.8 \pm 21.77$
(b) The only significant difference occurs with pair (1), where the pyramid has a significantly greater mean than the rectangle.

17-18 (a) $\mu_1 = 11.000 \pm 2.492$
$\mu_2 = 14.514 \pm 2.492$
$\mu_3 = 11.343 \pm 2.492$
$\mu_4 = 16.757 \pm 2.492$
(b, c) $\mu_1 - \mu_2 = -3.514 \pm 3.144$ (significant)
$\mu_1 - \mu_3 = -.343 \pm 3.144$ (not significant)
$\mu_1 - \mu_4 = -5.757 \pm 3.144$ (significant)
$\mu_2 - \mu_3 = -3.171 \pm 3.144$ (significant)
$\mu_2 - \mu_4 = -2.243 \pm 3.144$ (not significant)
$\mu_3 - \mu_4 = -5.414 \pm 3.144$ (significant)
(d) 93%
(e) eliminated 2 and 4

17-20 Answers may vary.

17-22 (a)

Variation	Degrees of Freedom	Sum of Squares	Mean Square	F
Treatments	5	78	15.60	3.57
Error	24	105	4.375	
Total	29	183		

(b) $F_{.01} = 3.90$ *Accept* H_0.

17-24 (a)

Variation	Degrees of Freedom	Sum of Squares	Mean Square	F
Treatments	3	33.34	11.11	14.24
Error	28	21.88	.78	
Total	31	52.22		

(b) $F_{.01} = 4.57$ *Reject* H_0.

17-26 (a) (1) 2.75 ± 1.20 (3) $.625 \pm 1.20$ (5) -2.175 ± 1.20
(2) 1.25 ± 1.20 (4) -1.50 ± 1.20 (6) $-.625 \pm 1.20$

(b) (1) 2 over 1 (3) neither (5) 2 over 4
(2) 3 over 1 (4) 2 over 3 (6) neither

(c) 2

17-28 (a)

Variation	Degrees of Freedom	Sum of Squares	Mean Square	F
Treatments	4	280.40	70.10	39.38
Error	20	35.60	1.78	
Total	24	316.00		

(b) $F_{.01} = 4.43$ (c) *Reject* H_0.

18-2 (a)

Display Density A	Lighting Brightness B				Factor A Sample Mean
	(1) Dim	(2) Low	(3) Medium	(4) High	
(1) Loose	245	200	240	220	226.25
(2) Tight	210	225	245	262	235.50
Factor B Sample Mean	227.5	212.5	242.5	241	230.875

Variation	Degrees of Freedom	Sum of Squares	Mean Square	F
Factor *A*	1	684.5	684.5	93.38
Factor *B*	3	4,693.5	1,564.5	213.44
Interactions	3	6,593.5	2,197.83	299.84
Error	24	176	7.33	
Total	31	12.147.5		

(b) (1) reject
(2) reject
(3) reject

(c) 3

18-4 (a)

Primary Computer A	Major B (1) IRM	(2) Management Science	(3) Accounting	(4) Finance	Sample Mean B
(1) PC at Home	92.25	85.00	90.00	75.00	85.5625
(2) Lab	81.25	78.00	71.00	68.00	74.5625
Sample Mean B	86.75	81.50	80.50	71.50	80.0625

Variation	Degrees of Freedom	Sum of Squares	Mean Square	F
Factor A	1	968.000	968.000	10.430
Factor B	3	962.375	320.792	3.456
Interactions	3	192.000	64.000	.690
Error	24	2,227.500	92.813	
Total	31	4,349.875		

(b) (1) accept (2) reject (3) reject
(c) 1 and 2 only

18-6 (a)

Experience A	Major B (1) Business	(2) Technical	(3) Nontechnical	Sample Mean A
(1) Sales	602	594	556	584
(2) Staff	640	696	557	631
(3) Management	574	594	584	584
(4) Nonbusiness	592	640	583	605
Sample Mean B	602	631	570	601

Variation	Degrees of Freedom	Sum of Squares	Mean Square	F
Factor A	3	22,140	7,380	47.61
Factor B	2	37,240	18,620	120.13
Interactions	6	28,100	4,683	30.21
Error	48	7,440	155	
Total	59	94,920		

(b) (1) reject (2) reject (3) reject
(c) 3

18-8 (a)

Variation	Degrees of Freedom	Sum of Squares	Mean Square	F
Education	4	800,000	200,000	2.5
Error	15	1,200,000	80,000	
Total	19	2,000,000		

No

(b)

Variation	Degrees of Freedom	Sum of Squares	Mean Square	F
Occupation	3	900,000	300,000	4.36
Error	16	1,100,000	68,750	
Total	19	2,000,000		

Yes

(c)

Variation	Degrees of Freedom	Sum of Squares	Mean Square	F
Factor *A*:				
Education	4	800,000	200,00	8.0
Factor *B*:				
Occupation	3	900,000	300,000	12.0
Error	12	300,000	25,000	
Total	19	2,000,000		

Reject both null hypotheses.

18-10 Computer at home (1) yields a significantly higher mean test score than lab (2). Also, IRM majors (1) have higher mean scores than finance only; no other major pairs yield significant differences.

18-12 Low chlorine concentration (1) provides a significantly greater mean drop in alkalinity than either medium (2) or (3) high concentrations; the latter do not differ. Also, pH = 7.2 (1) and pH = 7.4 (2) each provide significantly greater mean drops than pH = 7.8 (4); no other pH pairings provide significant differences.

18-14 (b) $\mu_{21} - \mu_{11} = -35 \pm 9.5$ (significant)

(c) There are 24 out of 28 pairings of cell means having significant differences.

(d) (1) $L_1 = -21.75 \pm 4.74$ (significant)

(2) $L_2 = -9.25 \pm 4.74$ (significant)

18-16 (a) $\bar{X}_{1.} = 86.33$ $\quad \bar{X}_{2.} = 77.00$ $\quad \bar{X}_{3.} = 69.33$ $\quad \bar{X}_{4.} = 72.33$

$\bar{X}_{5.} = 75.00$ $\quad SSBL = 500.00$

(b)

Variation	Degrees of Freedom	Sum of Squares	Mean Square	*F*
Treatments	2	1,392.4	696.2	3.71
Blocks	4	500.0	125.0	
Error	8	1,501.6	187.7	
Total	14	3,394.0		

(c) It is reduced by 500.00. (d) accepted

18-18 (a) (1) 7.0 ± 3.5 (2) 5.6 ± 3.5 (3) 1.4 ± 3.5
(b) (1) half dosage (2) (2) half dosage (2) (3) neither
(c) Use half dosage (2).

18-20 (a) (1) 1.0 ± 1.93 (2) 4.83 ± 1.93 (3) 3.83 ± 1.93
(b) (1) neither (2) mixed (3) mixed

18-22

Variation	Degrees of Freedom	Sum of Squares	Mean Square	*F*
Treatments	3	97	32.33	5.11
Columns	3	53	17.67	
Rows	3	48	16.00	
Error	6	38	6.33	
Total	15	236		

Reject H_0 and conclude means differ.

18-24

Variation	Degrees of Freedom	Sum of Squares	Mean Square	*F*
Treatments:				
Material	4	42.64	10.66	66.63
Columns:				
Vibrations	4	77.44	19.36	
Rows:				
Stress	4	105.04	26.26	
Error	12	1.92	.16	
Total	24	227.04		

Reject H_0 and conclude that the means differ.

18-26 (a)

Variation	Degrees of Freedom	Sum of Squares	Mean Square	*F*
Explained by factor A	2	2,328	1,164	91.29
Explained by factor B	3	2,934	1,467	115.06
Explained by interactions	6	1,176	196	15.37
Error or unexplained	24	306	12.75	
Total	35	6,744		

(b) No (c) No (d) No

18-28 (b) $\mu_{21} - \mu_{11} = 10 \pm 13.7$
(c) About half of the 66 possible cell mean pairs involve significant differences.
(d) $L = -14.0 \pm 5.6$

18-30

Variation	Degrees of Freedom	Sum of Squares	Mean Square	F
Treatments:				
Program	3	12.75	4.25	2.04
Columns:				
Job type	3	520.25	173.42	
Rows:				
Complexity	3	70.25	23.42	
Error	6	12.50	2.08	
Total	15	615.75		

Accept H_0 and conclude that means are identical.

19-2 Yes

19-4 $W = 93.5$ *Accept* H_0.

19-6 (a) rejected (b) accepted (c) rejected (d) accepted

19-8 gasohol

19-10 (b) *Reject* H_0 and conclude that the new supplement is more effective.

19-12 (a) accepted (b) accepted (c) rejected (d) rejected

19-14 $V = 93$ *Accept* H_0 and conclude that method A scores are at least as great as B scores.

19-16 (a) *Reject* H_0 if $z < -1.96$ or if $z > 1.96$. *Accept* otherwise.
(b) $V = 346$ $z = 2.33$ *Reject* H_0 and conclude that new book's scores are higher.

19-18 $V = 103.5$ *Reject* H_0 and use gasohol.

19-20 (a) $R_a = 5$ *Accept* H_0. (c) $R_a = 7$ *Reject* H_0.
(b) $R_a = 2$ *Reject* H_0. (d) $R_a = 4$ *Accept* H_0.

19-22 Answers will vary.

19-24 Answers will vary.

19-26 .78

19-28 .503 **19-30** $R = 5.18$ *Accept* H_0.

19-32 (a) $d = 6.00$ $s_{d\text{-paired}} = 6.505$ $\mu_A - \mu_B = 6.00 \pm 4.16$
(b) *Reject* H_0.

19-34 *Reject* H_0. **19-36** $R_a = 18$ $z = 2.80$ *Reject* H_0.

19-38 (a) $-.037 \pm .432$ (b) *Accept* H_0. (c) $W = 68$ *Accept* H_0.

19-40 .88 **20-2** Answer will be subjective.

20-4 Answer will be subjective.

20-6 (a) 110 (b) 260 (c) 130 (d) 360 (3) 230

20-8 (a)

Fractile	Rate of Return
0	−20%
.0625	−4
.125	3
.25	7
.5	15
.75	20
.875	24
.9375	28
1.000	40

(c) .25

20-10

Demand	Probability
100	.26
300	.54
500	.14
700	.05
900	.01

expected demand = 302

20-12 (a)

Actual	Forecast	Actual/Forecast
.273	.250	1.09
.332	.315	1.05
.366	.320	1.14
.307	.365	.84
.318	.330	.96
.350	.278	1.26
.364	.340	1.07
.359	.355	1.01
.331	.360	.92
.388	.373	1.04

(b) Answers will vary: (1) .06 (2) .50 (3) .68

20-14 (a) .750 (b) .500 (c) .375 (d) .375

20-16 Answers will vary.

21-2 (a) .809 (b) .005

21-4 (a) .50 (b) .82 (c) .11 **21-6** 10!

21-8

6	7	8	9	10
C	C	C	C	C
C	C	C	C	S
C	C	C	S	C
C	C	S	C	C
C	S	C	C	C
S	C	C	C	C
C	C	C	S	S
C	C	S	C	S
C	S	C	C	S
S	C	C	C	S
C	C	S	S	C
C	S	C	S	C
S	C	C	S	C
C	S	S	C	C
S	C	S	C	C
S	S	C	C	C

6	7	8	9	1
S	S	S	S	S
S	S	S	S	C
S	S	S	C	S
S	S	C	S	S
S	C	S	S	S
C	S	S	S	S
S	S	S	C	C
S	S	C	S	C
S	C	S	S	C
C	S	S	S	C
S	S	C	C	S
S	C	S	C	S
C	S	S	C	S
S	C	C	S	S
C	S	C	S	S
C	C	S	S	S

21-10 (a) 128 (b) 7,776 (c) 256

21-12 (a) 2^{100} (b) (1) 4,950 (2) 75,287,520
(3) 17,310,308,000,000

21-14 (a) 624 (b) .00024

21-16 (a) 20! (b) $2 \times 10! \times 10!$ (c) (1) $2 \times 10!$ (2) $10!\,(2^{10})$

21-18 2,520

21-20 (a) 13,991,544 (b) (1) 142,506 (2) .01

21-22 (a) 3,744 (b) .00144

22-2 (a) .062 (b) .006 **22-4** .8425 **22-6** No

22-8 (a) No (b) .183930 for slump .084225 for peak (c) No

22-10 .006738

22-12 (a) .0774 (b) .9797 (c) .0286 (d) .7668

22-14 (a) .606531 (b) .393469

22-16 (a) .20 (b) .40 (c) .39 (d) .30

22-18 (a) .30 (b) .25

22-20 .40

22-22 (a) .993 (b) .135 (c) .128

22-24 (a) .0002 school per mile (b) .632 (c) 11,500 miles

22-26 (a) .2524 (b) .6004 (c) .9671

22-28 .00174

22-30 (a) .5 (b) .010 (c) .01 (d) .95

22-32 (a) .993262 (b) .0267

23-2 (a)

Score	f_e
under 40	7.21
40–under 50	12.28
50–under 60	19.87
60–under 70	23.57
70–under 80	19.19
80–under 90	11.45
above 90	6.43

(b) between .01 and .001

$\chi^2 = 17.47$; rejected

23-4 (a) $\chi^2 = 2.8$ (c) *Accept* H_0.

23-6 (a) D = .1360
(b) $\alpha = .025$
(d) $\chi^2 = 10.56$ $\alpha = .10$
(f) Kolmogorov-Smirnov

23-8 D = .2149 rejected

23-10 D = .10 accepted

23-12 $\chi^2 = 6.194$ accepted

23-14 D = .0578 accepted

24-2

	Payoff Measure	Best Act	Worst Act
(a)	4	(tie) bonds, preferred	common stock
(b)	3	preferred stock	common stock
(c)	5	common stock	bonds
(d)	7	preferred stock	bonds

24-4

Size	Probability	Method A	Method B	Method C
4,000	.25	$ 440,000	$ 440,000	$ 420,000
6,000	.25	760,000	740,000	680,000
8,000	.25	1,080,000	1,040,000	940,000
10,000	.25	1,400,000	1,340,000	1,200,000
	Expected payoff:	$ 920,000	$ 890,000	$ 810,000

24-6 \$8,500 for A_1
\$3,000 for A_2
\$8,500 for A_3
Choose A_1 for A_3.

24-8

Event	Probability	Act	
		Market	Don't Market
Success	.40	\$10 million	\$0
Failure	.60	−5 million	0
	Expected payoff:	\$ 1 million	0

Yes

24-10 Use no test and hire each applicant.

24-12 (b) The manager should contract the job.

24-14 (a) Red is inadmissible.
(b)

Color:	Brown	Orange	Green	Yellow
Expected Payoff:	90	84	81	101

Choose yellow.

24-16 Test market. Then, market if favorable and don't market if unfavorable.

25-2 (a) A_2 and A_3 (tie) (b) A_2 (c) Choose A_2.

25-4 (a)

Event	Act		
	Stock 10	Stock 11	Stock 12
Demand 10	\$5.00	\$4.50	\$4.00
Demand 11	5.00	5.50	5.00
Demand 12	5.00	5.50	6.00

(b) 10 (c) 11

25-6 (a) 27 for A_1 (b) 39 (c) 12 (d) 12 (e) same

25-8 (a) drill (b) \$50,000 (c) \$50,000

25-10 (a) −\$5 (b) not buying (c) buy

25-12 Answers will vary.

25-14 (a) −$10 (b) $5

25-16 (a) $10,000

(b)

Demand Event	Probability	Act: Gears and Levers	Spring Action	Weights and Pulleys
Light	.50	$ 0	$85,000	$200,000
Moderate	.30	0	10,000	50,000
Heavy	.20	50,000	10,000	0
Expected Opportunity Loss:		$10,000	$47,500	$115,000

25-18 Test and then market if favorable and don't market otherwise.

26-2 (a) $0 for old box (b) $400,000
$1,100,000 for new box
Change to new box

26-6 (a) .947, don't water (b) .333

26-8 (c) Take seismic; then drill if it confirms and abandon if it denies.

26-10 (c) Distribute the film as an "A" feature if the sneak preview results are favorable, but sell to TV otherwise.

26-12 (b)

Joint Event	Joint Probability	Strategy: S_1	S_2	S_3	S_4	S_5	S_6	S_7	S_8
$R = 0$ and E	.08	−9	−9	−9	−1	−9	−1	−1	−1
$R = 0$ and T	.32	20	20	20	−1	20	−1	−1	−1
$R = 1$ and E	.18	−9.5	−9.5	−1.5	−9.5	−1.5	−9.5	−1.5	−1.5
$R = 1$ and T	.12	20	20	−1	20	−1	20	−1	−1
$R = 2$ and E	.27	−10	−2	−10	−10	−2	−2	−10	−2
$R = 2$ and T	.03	20	−1	20	20	−1	−1	20	−1
Expected payoff:		4.27	5.80	3.19	−1.81	4.72	−.28	−2.89	−1.36

S_2 maximizes expected payoff.

26-14 (a) Market if the test is favorable and don't market if it is unfavorable.

(b)

Joint Event	Probability	Strategy: S_1	S_2	S_3	S_4
Fav. and successful	.32	$950,000	$950,000	−$ 50,000	−$50,000
Fav. and failure	.08	− 550,000	− 550,000	− 50,000	− 50,000
Unfav. and successful	.18	950,000	− 50,000	950,000	− 50,000
Unfav. and failure	.42	− 550,000	− 50,000	− 500,000	− 50,000
Expected payoff:		$200,000	$230,000	−$ 59,000	−$50,000

The strategies are:

Test Result	S_1	S_2	S_3	S_4
Favorable	Market	Market	Don't	Don't
Unfavorable	Market	Don't	Market	Don't

S_2 maximizes expected payoff, the same result as in (a).

26-16 (a) $0 for old; $1,100,000 for new
(b) $400,000 (c) $320,000 (d) $220,000; yes

26-18 (a) $95,558 (b) EVEI = $45,558 ENGE = $35,558

26-20 (a) Pr[S/L] = .467 (b) Pr[S/D] = .086

26-24 (a) Market if the test is favorable and don't market if it is unfavorable.

27-2 (a) $50,000 from marketing
(b) $16,666.67

27-4 (c) c = 0

27-6 (c) (1) .9633 (2) .4995 (3) .0352

27-8 (a) $1,822.07 (b) $1,522.07

27-10 (a) (3) $1,000 (4) $500
(b) (2) 1 (3) $1,000 (4) $0
(c) Yes. $n = 1$.

27-12 (a) $c = 0$ $26.77 for $n = 5$
(b) $n = 4$ is optimal

27-14 (a)

Mean Daily Sales	Probability	Act: Sponsor	Act: Don't sponsor
$\mu = 490$	.5	−$200	$0
$\mu = 530$	.5	600	0
	Expected payoff:	$200	$0

(b) sponsor (c) $100 No

27-16 (a)

(1) $\mu = 3.0$

Class Interval $\bar{X}$	Interval Probability
.75–1.25	0
1.25–1.75	.0009
1.75–2.25	.0292
2.25–2.75	.2342
2.75–3.25	.4714
3.25–3.75	.2342
3.75–4.25	.0292
4.25–4.75	.0009
4.75–5.25	.0000
5.25–5.75	.0000
5.75–6.25	.0000

(2) $\mu = 4.0$

Class Interval $\bar{X}$	Interval Probability
.75–1.25	0
1.25–1.75	0
1.75–2.25	0
2.25–2.75	.0009
2.75–3.25	.0292
3.25–3.75	.2342
3.75–4.25	.4714
4.25–4.75	.2342
4.75–5.25	.0292
5.25–5.75	.0009
5.75–6.25	.0000

27-18 $c = 8$

27-20 $c = 18$

27-22 $n = 79$

27-24 (a)

$$\text{Payoff} = \begin{cases} \$100{,}000 - 200{,}000\,\pi + 400R - 35n \text{ for Accept} \\ 85{,}000 - 25n \text{ for Reject} \end{cases}$$

(b) $n = 11$ with $c = 1$

27-26 (a) Promotion is best. EVPI = \$1,550
(b) $n = 72 \quad c = 30$

27-28 (a) Sample with $n = 2$.
(b) (1) $c = 1$ (2) $c = 0$

27-30 (a)

Population Mean	Prior Probability	Payoff × Probability: Adjust	Leave Alone	Row Maximum
μ = 25g	.3	\$150	−\$150	\$150
μ = 30g	.4	0	0	0
μ = 35g	.3	− 300	150	150
	Expected Payoff:	−\$150	\$ 0	\$300

Leave alone is the act maximizing expected payoff at \$0.

(b) EVPI = \$300 − \$0 = \$300 Don't sample if cost > \$300; maybe otherwise. Leave alone maximizes expected payoff.
(b) EVPI = \$300. No if cost is \$400. May if cost is \$200.

27-32 (b) $c = 25$ g for adjust.
(c) \$120.23
(d) \$70.23

28-2 \$2,373.60

28-4 (a)

$$\text{Payoff} = \begin{cases} -\$50{,}000 + 1{,}000\mu \text{ for helmet} \\ \$0 \text{ for no helmet} \end{cases}$$

$\mu_b = 50$ helmets/store
(b) make
(c) \$833.20

28-6 (a) μ = mean amount of late receivables

$$\text{Payoff} = \begin{cases} -\$50{,}000 + 100\mu \text{ for telephone} \\ -\$100{,}000 + 200\mu \text{ for computer} \end{cases}$$

$\mu_b = \$500$
(b) computer
(c) \$833.20

28-8 (a)

$$\text{Gross payoff} = \begin{cases} \$500{,}000 + 65{,}000\mu \text{ for photographic} \\ \$330{,}000 + 150{,}000\mu \text{ for holographic} \end{cases}$$

$\mu_b = 2$ gigabits/day

28-10 (a) 1,000 (b) 57.6 (d) $n = 15$
(f) between 10 and 20

28-12 (a) $c = 997.50$ (b) (1) A (2) $\mu_1 = 992.0$ $\sigma_1 = 11.1803$
(c) .7642

28-14 (a) \$12.16 (b) 67.0″
(c) $\mu_1 = 69.44''$ $\sigma_1 = .224''$ $\Pr[\mu < 69''] = .0250$

28-16 (a) 90 (b) Yes (c) .208

28-18 (a) $\mu_b = 100$ A (b) \$12.50
(c) ENGS(9) = \$2.90
(d) $c = 90$ (e) A
(f) $\mu_1 = 103$ $\sigma_1 = 7.071$ $\Pr[\mu > \mu_b] = .6628$

29-2 (a) \$.25 (b) Answers will vary.

29-4 (a) u (lady) = 10 u (animal) = −5
u (cowboy) = 2.5

29-6 Answers will vary.

29-8 (a) Don't test and market.
(c) Risk seeking

29-10 (a) willing (b) might be willing
(c) might be willing (d) unwilling
(e) willing

29-12 No

29-14 Answers will vary.

29-16 (a) (1) 83.25 (2) 53.50 (3) 76 (4) 36.80
(b) (1) \$3,200 (2) −\$250 (3) \$1,800 (4) −\$1,100
(c) (1) \$4,000 (2) \$0 (3) \$2,750 (4) \$400
(d) (1) \$800 (2) \$250 (3) \$950 (4) \$1,500

29-18 (a) not insure, −\$250 (b) \$750
(c) insure u (insurance) = 9,999
u (no insurance) = 9,975

29-20 Use the test and hire only if the candidate passes.

CREDITS

The author is indebted to the following for permission to reprint from copyrighted material.

Page 19 Shelter Intake Form. Copyright © 1991 and reprinted by permission of Emergency Housing Consortium, San Jose, California.

Page 67 Table from, *The World Almanac and Book of Facts,* 1988 edition, copyright © Pharos Books and reprinted with permission.

Page 111 Material from, *The Universal Almanac,* copyright © 1992. Reprinted by permission of Universal Press Syndicate.

Page 920–21 Table from, *Introduction to Statistics for Business Decisions.* Published by McGraw-Hill Book Company: New York, 1961. Reproduced by permission of the copyright holder, the President and Fellows of Harvard College.

Page 951 Table from, *Statistical Analysis for Decision Making,* 2nd ed. by Morris Hamburg. Copyright © 1977 by Harcourt Brace Jovanovich, Inc. Reprinted with permission.

Page 954–59 Table from, *Statistical Methods* by George W. Snedecor and William G. Cochran, 7th ed. Copyright © 1980 by Iowa State University Press, Ames, Iowa 50010. Reprinted with permission.

Page 960–61 Table from, *Statistical Tables for Biological, Agricultural and Medical Research* 6th ed. Copyright © 1974 by Fisher and Yates. Reprinted by permission of Longman Group UK and the authors.

Pages 972–74 Table from, "Table of Percentage Points of Kolmogorov Statistics," *Journal of American Statistical Association,* 51 (1956). Reprinted with permission from the *Journal of the American Statistical Association.* Copyright © 1956 by the American Statistical Association. All rights reserved.

INDEX

SYMBOL	DESCRIPTION
π_A, π_B	Proportions of populations A and B that are compared in hypothesis tests
Q_d	Percentile value below which $100 \times d\%$ of observations lie
$q_{1-\alpha}$	Critical value of studentized range. Used to construct Tukey intervals
q_k	Indifference probability established for winning reference lottery or achieving outcome O_k for certain
q_n, q_0	Quantities of an item in year n and in base period 0; used to find index numbers
R	(1) A random variable denoting the number of successes obtained from several trials of a Bernoulli process (2) The test statistic for the matched-pairs sign test; R is the number of positive sign differences for the paired difference between observations
R_a	Number of runs of type a obtained in a sample; used as the test statistic for the number-of-runs test
$R_{Y \cdot 12}$, $R_{Y \cdot 123}$	Sample multiple correlation coefficient
$R^2_{Y \cdot 12}$, $R^2_{Y \cdot 123}$	Sample coefficient of multiple determination; represents the proportion of variation in Y that can be explained by the multiple regression equation
$\bar{R}$	Overall mean range used in quality control
r	(1) One of several possible values of the random variable R (2) The sample correlation coefficient; expresses the strength and direction of the relationship between X and Y (3) Number of rows in an analysis-of-variance layout
r^2	Sample coefficient of determination; represents the proportion of the variation in Y that can be explained by linear regression on X
r_s	Spearman rank correlation coefficient
r^2_{Y1}	Sample coefficient of determination for regression of Y on X_1; used in multiple correlation analysis
$r^2_{Y1 \cdot 2}$, $r^2_{Y3 \cdot 12}$	Coefficients of partial determination for multiple regression of Y on the independent variables X_1, X_2 (and X_3); measures the proportional reduction in previously unexplained variation in Y by adding X_2 or X_3 to the multiple regression analysis
ρ (rho)	Population correlation coefficient; estimated by r
ρ^2	Population coefficient of determination; estimated by r^2
S	Number of successes in a population; used in conjunction with the hypergeometric distribution
S_t	Seasonal component in time series
$S_{Y \cdot 12}$, $S_{Y \cdot 123}$	Standard error of the estimate about the multiple regression plane

SYMBOL	DESCRIPTION
SD(X)	Standard deviation of the random variable
SSA	Sum of squares between rows for a two-factor analysis of variance
$SSAB$	Interactions sum of squares; used in two-factor analysis of variance
SSB	Sum of squares between columns for a two-factor analysis of variance
$SSBL$	Sum of squares between blocks; used in analysis of variance
$SSCOL$	Sum of squares between columns for a Latin-square design in a three-factor analysis of variance
SSE	Error sum of squares: (1) (within columns) for a one-factor analysis of variance (2) (residual) for a two-factor or a three-factor analysis of variance
SSR	Regression sum of squares
$SSROW$	Sum of squares between rows for a Latin-square design in a three-factor analysis of variance
$SSTO$	Total sum of squares in analysis of variance
$SSTR$	Sum of squares: (1) (between columns) for the treatments in a one-factor analysis of variance (2) (between letters) in an analysis of variance with Latin square
s	(1) Sample standard deviation (2) Number of contrasts used in a multiple comparison
s^2	Sample variance
s^2_A, s^2_B	Variances of sample from populations A and B; used in two-sample hypothesis tests
s_X	Sample standard deviation of the independent variable X; used in correlation analysis
s_Y	Sample standard deviation of the dependent variable Y; usued in correlation analysis
$s_{Y \cdot X}$	Standard error of the estimate about the regression line; $s^2_{Y \cdot X}$ is an unbiased estimator of $\sigma^2_{Y \cdot X}$
s_{b_k}	Standard error of partial regression coefficient
s_d	The estimator of the standard error σ_d for the difference between: (1) two sample means (2) two sample proportions
$s_{d\text{-paired}}$	Sample standard deviation of matched-pairs differences
$s_{d\text{-small}}$	Sample standard deviation of the difference in means of independent samples
slope	Slope of loss function
$\sum$	Summation sign
σ (sigma)	Population standard deviation
σ_0, σ_1	Prior and posterior standard deviations for mean
σ^2	Population variance